EARLY AMERICAN
PROVERBS
AND
PROVERBIAL PHRASES

EARLY AMERICAN
PROVERBS

AND

PROVERBIAL PHRASES

BARTLETT JERE WHITING

THE BELKNAP PRESS

of HARVARD UNIVERSITY PRESS

Cambridge, Massachusetts
and
London, England
1977

Library of Congress Cataloging in Publication Data

Whiting, Bartlett Jere, 1904-
    Early American proverbs and proverbial phrases.
    Bibliography: p.
    Includes index.
    1. English language in the United States.
2. English language—Terms and phrases. 3. English
language—Dictionaries. 4. Proverbs, American.
I. Title.
PE2839.W5   398.9'21   77-2139
ISBN 0-674-21981-3

For
Jedediah
Jacob   *Jesse*
Jobyna
Jonas

PREFACE

After Archer Taylor and I had completed *A Dictionary of American Proverbs and Proverbial Phrases, 1820-1880* (1958), my attention for a decade was largely devoted to proverbs in Old and Middle English writings. Even the heady experience of reading and rereading the monuments of earlier English literature left some interstices of precious time to be occupied in such a fashion as to keep Satan from filling idle hands. It occurred to me to go through a few American books from before 1820 and perhaps make a small collection of sayings recorded anterior to those which Taylor and I had compiled. Like salted nuts, one book led to another until I had combed, in my fashion, the volumes listed on pp. xxxiii-lxiv. The central period of the years with which Taylor and I dealt has been referred to as the American Renaissance. Since few things are more alluring than schematization, it might be said that here I have sampled the American Classical Period (the seventeenth century), and the American Middle Ages (the eighteenth century). Not every Americanist will care to divide our literature in this fashion, but *de gustibus* begins an ancient saying, and Horace's *Dulce est desipere in loco* may excuse jests which the unco guid, be their interests religion or literary history, hold in abhorrence.

Among the many persons who assisted me and to whom I owe thanks I must mention particularly W. J. Bate and D. M. Staines, one time my students, some time my colleagues, and long time my friends. My wife, who did not live to see the appearance of this book, aided me almost throughout, and I was encouraged and supported by the staff of the Harvard University Press, especially my exemplary former student Maud Wilcox and that lynx-eyed (see L261 below) editrix Natalie Frohock, the flour, to adapt Chaucer, of hem that edit in Cambridge.

Included in the many things that I owe to my father, Manasseh Barzilla Whiting (1858-1939) is an interest in the early history and literature of this country without which some of the writings quoted below might have seemed more arid than they did. For his pleasure as well as mine this book is dedicated to his great-grandchildren, in whose names he would recognize, sympathetically perhaps, the tradition which gave him his own.

Northport   B. J. W.
Waldo County
Maine

CONTENTS

INTRODUCTION

When Archer Taylor and I named our volume *A Dictionary of American Proverbs and Proverbial Phrases, 1820-1880* (1958) (hereafter referred to as TW), the dates were so precise that we soon found ourselves forced to confess that some of our sources were before 1820 and some after 1880. In the title of my *Proverbs, Sentences, and Proverbial Phrases from English Writings Mainly before 1500* (1968) (hereafter referred to as Whiting) the weasel word "mainly" left me free to wander beyond 1500. The title of the present book, *Early American Proverbs and Proverbial Phrases* (hereafter referred to as W) has the merit of brevity, but it has the accompanying defect that it requires some explanation. For W. W. Skeat's *Early English Proverbs* (1910), "early" ranged from Anglo-Saxon times to the century after Chaucer. Here it extends from the first decades of the seventeenth century to 1820, save, of course, that some works are drawn on that were written after 1820. These last documents are mainly by persons who had been writing before 1820, but a few are books which we would have utilized for TW had we come upon them in time. In any case, TW may fairly be said to cover a period of sixty years, whereas W stretches over at least two centuries.

Since TW and W are allied in more ways than one, some comparisons between the two seem inevitable, perhaps even necessary. In both cases the authors drawn upon were largely from what may be called, without prejudice, British stock; but although those quoted in TW were almost all born in North America, many of those in W were born in Britain, usually England, and, indeed, a considerable number were birds of passage in that they spent only parts of their lives in the English colonies in North America. The American experience justifies their inclusion, especially when one remembers that our American proverbial lore is basically British and for most of the entries in W basically English, as distinguished from Scots and Irish. Sayings of demonstrably American origin fall for the greater part into what are called proverbial phrases (see below p. xxi), and these are much more common after 1820 than before. It is not to oversimplify to say that the contents of this book are English proverbs used by writers who happened to be in North America at the time. The great majority of our authors lived, wrote, and died in what is now the

United States, but enough Canadian writings are included to require the saving phrase "North America."

The major difference between TW and W does not lie in the fact that the former is chronologically later than the latter, but rather in the nature of the documents upon which the two volumes draw. The following statement occurs in the Preface to TW: "The years [1820-1880] with which we concerned ourselves saw the emergence and flowering in the United States of regional literature, extravagant, brash, exaggerated, humorous sketches, tales and novels whose purpose was to depict the life and language of non-urban areas in New England (Down East), the South, and the Old Southwest. Description and dialogue are couched in local dialects, sometimes faithfully reproduced, sometimes heightened, and are studded with proverbs and proverbial phrases. There is no exaggeration in the statement that at no other time have so many American writers made proverbs so obvious an ingredient in their style" (pp. vii-viii). Thus the richest, though not the only sources for TW, were in the various fields of creative literature, in which proverbial material was used to characterize an individual, a type, or a locality, usually for the amusement of an audience which, to use a jargon word of modern criticism, "distanced" itself smugly from the persons being depicted. There was nothing new in the comic use of proverbs, as a glance through Tilley and *Oxford,* to say nothing or little of my *Proverbs in the Earlier English Drama* (1938), will show. For this book the situation is altogether different. Whatever its virtues, American writing of the Colonial and Early National periods was not overly concerned with creative, perhaps fanciful is a better word, composition. There were, to be sure, satiric and comic efforts in both prose and verse, and, toward the end, a certain number of plays and novels in some of which proverbs were introduced for stylistic effect. The plays were unreal and the novels, except for H. H. Brackenridge's long unfolding *Modern Chivalry* (1792-1815), were too stodgy to include the lively dialogue which invites proverbs. Brackenridge's fondness for proverbs was doubtless due to Cervantes, but as for Charles Brockden Brown, one may slightly vary Dr. Johnson's quip about Richardson. "Why, Sir, if you were to read him for the proverbs, your impatience would be so much fretted that you would hang yourself."

The main sources for the present volume are utilitarian or, if one likes, workaday writings: histories, letters, diaries, memoirs, biographies, books of travel, sermons, polemical papers (religious, political, or economic), and the like, in which style as such played a minor role. In works of this kind proverbs appear for their innate worth or their argumentative value rather than by the contrived introduction which gives them their place in more imaginative literature. In other words, the users believed in the validity of the sayings they employed.

In the preparation of collections such as these, the matter of selection becomes a problem. Unless one attempts to be inclusive, as I did in dealing with English writings before 1500, one must decide what to read. In the case of

TW, Archer Taylor and I had both been excerpting in a desultory way from American authors before we discovered our common activity and decided to join and make a book. We read with regard to our own tastes and the resources of our two university libraries. I wish that for this book I could claim some "scientific" and rigorous rules for inclusion, but that is far from the truth. To say that the collection just "growed" like Topsy would come closer to fitting the fact. To begin with, certain authors were inevitable, from, let us say, William Bradford to the first seven presidents of the United States. After that one turned to the bibliographies and notes of modern histories and editions, to such invaluable special bibliographies as William Matthews' *American Diaries* (1945) and *Canadian Diaries and Autobiographies* (1950), to the published series of societies such as the Massachusetts Historical, Colonial Society of Massachusetts, New-York Historical, and the various quarterlies and annuals which reproduce documents of one kind or another. The proverb says that One rat brings another (R24), and just so, one well-edited diary or collection of letters brings others from their holes. Literary histories are of scant use, since their authors, more concerned with greater themes, rarely mention proverbs. The proverb industry will pick up its crumbs (C361) when some scholar in search of an article discovers that a Proverb can be claimed as a Symbol or as a verbal Talisman. The prospect, it must be admitted, is not completely attractive to the confirmed lover of old said saws.

However arrived at, my list of books seems reasonably representative and has met with the general approval of a number of eminent Americanists who have been kind enough to look it over. Candor suggests that I mention some of the materials which I have not touched, or have touched but gently. I made no attempt whatever to use manuscripts. Sermons may well be food for the soul, but the American pulpit of our period apparently harbored no pious and witty proverbmonger such as the English Puritan Thomas Adams (c1583-c1655), and once the soul had been fed, I found it possible to shun them. It must be said that clerical authors, who loom large in our list, when away from the pulpit or lectern made free use of proverbs in their writings, especially those of a polemical nature. They were, to be sure, particularly fond of sayings of Biblical origin, which accounts for the much larger proportion of those here than in TW. One or two reviewers of TW chided us for the omission of periodical literature, and out of a sense of guilt I have tried, as the bibliography shows, to make some reparation. The fact, painful at times, is that magazines afforded little grain for the chaff sifted, although there are some things which one is happy not to have missed: for example, the "Thoughts on Proverbs" of S. P. L., which I reprint in Appendix A. Perhaps some scholar, a blend of Argus and Methuselah with eyes enough and time, will excerpt the newspapers of the period, but I did not venture beyond the few that have been reproduced in readable form or in such sectional anthologies as *Newspaper Extracts*. Further, perhaps unwisely, I have neglected schoolbooks and copybooks, though childhood memories remind me that they are rich in improving axioms. In general I have preferred to include proverbs worked into a context rather than those brought together in a heap. At one time I even thought of omitting Franklin's *Poor Richard* and *Way to Wealth* (a "connected discourse," as he called it, taken in the main from *Poor Richard*),[1] but caution warned me that to do so would be like offering *Hamlet* without the Prince of Denmark (*Oxford* 345-6). Later almanacs have been slighted, but enough are included to show that most of their makers depended mainly on *Poor Richard* or more often *Way to Wealth* for their proverbial page fillers.

One aspect of this book that distinguishes it from TW, and indeed from most similar collections, is the wide range of individuals from which its sayings come. The educational and cultural spectrum is almost complete. Our authors run from the most highly educated and best-read people of their time to those who can barely write and who probably have never read a book. At one end we have divines as learned as any in the English-speaking world, educators, scientists, generals, historians, the bright products of Harvard, Yale, Princeton, and the College of William and Mary, governors of British colonies, presidents of the United States, lawyers, politicians, some of whom came to be regarded as statesmen and others who did not, journalists, wealthy merchants—the list could be extended. At the other end are farmers, foot soldiers, sailors, artisans, country storekeepers, hunters and trappers, Indians, slaves, and many others who lived near what are called the grass-roots.

With so broad-based a constituency spread over two centuries it is not feasible to establish patterns of usage, but two things of a general nature emerge. Among the barely educated there seems to have been little change: some people like to employ proverbs, some do not, and those who do not can find no place in a collection of proverbs. In the group of the educated and, if the word is not invidious, cultured, there appears to be a change, though not one that can be called universal. Most of the writers of the seventeenth and early eighteenth centuries, from the first Winthrops to Cotton Mather, used proverbs as did their equivalents among British authors of the same period.

By the middle of the eighteenth century there seems to emerge a feeling in the mother country as well as in America, that proverbs, at least taken seriously, have little place in elevated literature. Lord Chesterfield may be said to sum up the new attitude when he wrote to his son on July 25, 1741 (first printed 1774):

> There is, likewise, an awkwardness of expression and words, most carefully to be avoided; such as false English, bad pronounciation, old sayings, and common proverbs; which are so many proofs of having kept bad and low company. For example: if, instead of saying that tastes are different, and that every man has his own peculiar one, you should let off a proverb, and say, That what is one man's

---

1. For an excellent study, see Stuart A. Gallacher, "Franklin's *Way to Wealth*," JEGP 48 (1949), 229-51.

meat is another man's poison; or else, Every one as they like, as the good man said when he kissed his cow; everybody would be persuaded that you had never kept company with anybody above footmen and housemaids.[2]

As Dr. Johnson's antipathy toward Chesterfield was stronger than his love of proverbs,[3] this may not be one of the passages which led him to say that the *Letters* "teach the morals of a whore, and the manners of a dancing master," but all right thinkers will agree with the Doctor's summation. A few years before Chesterfield's letter, Jonathan Swift had ridiculed the use, or at least the improper use, of proverbs in his *Complete Collection of Genteel and Ingenious Conversation* (1738), which achieves its purpose by example rather than precept. This diverting performance could have set off Chesterfield, if only because he may have suspected that he was one of the "persons of quality" for whom Swift's Simon Wagstaff intended his instructive work. A modern parallel, perhaps only coincidental, to Swift's dialogues is in Frank Sullivan's papers starring Mr. Arbuthnot (is the name a hint of sorts?), the expert on clichés. A shorter and more specialized attack, which was to have an American echo,[4] is "A New Song of New Similes" (1727), sometimes hesitantly ascribed to John Gay.

Although other eighteenth-century English adverse comments on proverbs could easily be cited, it is more fitting to call attention to the relatively few appropriate American passages. In his *Itinerarium* (1744) the earlier and more engaging Alexander Hamilton gives a number of lively vignettes. Of one man he writes, "Most of his knowledge was pedantry, being made up of common place sentences and trite proverbs" (169). Earlier he had been more kindly but still grudging: "He dealt much in proverbs and made use of one which I thought pretty significant when well applied" (83). A character in Robert Munford's play *Candidates* (1770), who has scented an insult, says "Let's have no more of your algebra, nor proverbs here" (28), and a little later, "Don't preach your damn'd proverbs here." Since there had been no proverbs, nor algebra either, this may represent instinct rather than conviction. In 1782 Simeon Baldwin wrote, "[I] had a very good dinner; but a great many disagreeable Lattin proverbs" (*Life and Letters* 97), and in a slightly

---

2. *The Letters of Philip Dormer Stanhope, 4th Earl of Chesterfield*, ed. Bonamy Dobrée, 6 vols. (London, 1932), 2.461. The original printing is in *Letters written by the late right honourable Philip Dormer Stanhope, Earl of Chesterfield, to his son Philip Stanhope Esq.*, 2 vols. (London, 1774), 1.147, Cf. B177, quote 1801.

3. In fact, Dr. Johnson, for all his other virtues, had no love of proverbs. He rarely quoted them in his own right and seldom introduced them into the remarks of his fictitious characters. In *Rambler* 197 (Feb. 4, 1752), Captator's mother uses proverbs to teach him self-interest, and in *Idler* 57 (May 19, 1759), we find Sophron creeping along with proverbs on his lips. We are not, however, to admire Captator or Sophron. There were no vulgar proverbs in the Happy Valley. Dr. Johnson might have liked proverbs better had they not been such little fishes beside the moral whales of Juvenal and Seneca.

4. See Appendix B.

later letter, "Dom. had not so many Lattin proverbs as usual" (103). Here it is hard to know if Baldwin's objection is to proverbs or to Latin, clearly a language not dear to Baldwin's orthography. An anonymous play, *The Politician Out-witted* (1788), contains a simple fellow named Humphrey who uses many proverbs and who himself attaches "as the old saying is" to things unproverbial as well as proverbial. Of him another character says, "He is a mere son of nature, every thing he says is express'd in such a Gothic, uncouth, Anti-Chesterfieldian stile" (47). In William H. Brown's *Power of Sympathy* (1789) there is a group of silly young men who affect to follow Lord Chesterfield's system and "They are on the rack if an old man should let fall a proverb" (2.6). Whatever we may deduce from the description of Humphrey, Brown is surely anti-Chesterfieldian. In 1807 *Salmagundi* printed a drama review in verse, "With flimsy farce, a comedy miscall'd, Garnished with vulgar cant, and proverbs bald" (160).

Not to end on a sour note, let me introduce Noah Webster for the defense. In 1785 he wrote somewhat testily:

> The correspondent [unidentified] seems to mistake my views in mentioning two or three vulgar proverbs. I wanted to prove the ill consequences resulting from a neglect of our own language. The examples I brought as proofs were laughable, perhaps, but this was a matter of no consequence, when the conclusion drawn from my state of facts was a serious one and very important, *viz.* that corruptions in orthography and pronunciation often turn very expressive phrases into nonsense. I question whether your correspondent ever understood the force of the two proverbs I mentioned, before last Thursday evening.
>
> (*Letters* 48)

The praise of proverbs here is muted, but that cannot be said of what he wrote in 1841, his eighty-third year:

> It is this brevity which constitutes the great value of *proverbs* and *maxims,* of which Solomon has given a sublime example. The same may be said of our popular proverbs, many of which contain important truth in a nutshell. These being short and easily committed to memory are learned and repeated by our yeomanry from generation to generation. But the sentiments or truths which they contain in continuous discourse would never be learned and repeated at all. It is surprising that men who superintend instruction should make such mistakes in estimating the powers of the human mind.
>
> (*Letters* 519-20)

It is a pleasing coincidence that exactly a century had passed between the letter of Lord Chesterfield and that of Lexicographer Webster.

Among eminent American writers of the second half of the eighteenth century, Chesterfield's view would seem to prevail, especially when they were writing for public consumption. The more formal the composition the less likely are we to find proverbs. Jefferson, who was an elegant stylist, used relatively few proverbs, and the same is true of the less elegant Hamilton, Madison, and Monroe. The name of Washington appears often in our entries, but not in proportion to the documents which have survived under his name. Much that he signed was composed by his secretaries and consultants, among them Jefferson and Hamilton, and here we find a paucity of proverbs and none of the colloquialism to which proverbial phrases are native. The bulk of his contributions to this volume are from the letters which his editor has marked with an asterisk as being in Washington's own hand. Even here we find Washington employing proverbs most frequently in the last years of his life when he was writing easily to friends, relatives, and subordinates, where he not only quotes proverbs but emphasizes his faith in their validity, sometimes in an attractively simplistic way.

Washington may well have had a larger role in the field of proverbs than has been recognized hitherto. One of his favorite sayings is "Many mickles make a muckle" (M154). He identifies it as an old Scotch adage and is almost ecstatic in praise of its truth. Although it has close parallels (see *Oxford* 508; Whiting L402), Washington's form is used, so far as the evidence goes, only by Washington. Despite its balance, rhythm, and alliteration, all characteristics of a memorable saying, it has also the almost fatal flaw of failure to make sense. Washington's application is that many smalls make a great, which requires a contrast between mickle (small) and muckle (great). In fact, mickle means a large amount and muckle is only a dialect variant, with no change of meaning, of mickle. Thus Washington's adage means that Many greats make a great, which is not what he had in mind. If Washington invented the proverb, it shows him to have had a feeling for an elegant proverbial pattern and a better ear for how Scots sounds than a knowledge of Scots vocabulary. Of course, he may have heard it used by someone equally unaware of the mickle-muckle muddle, or it may have been foisted off on him by a trickster willing to pull the President's proverbial leg. Could it have been Hamilton? He was, as John Adams reminds us in his kindly way, of Scottish paternity, and he was sly enough to deceive his Chief. What removes Hamilton from consideration is that he had no discernible sense of humor, and for a jape like this slyness is not enough. We probably must conclude that Washington was not only our first President, but also our first and last President to coin a proverb. That the coin turns out to be a counterfeit does not detract from the accomplishment. Washington had a mind which set store by generalizations, none the worse for being cast in proverbial form. If Mrs. Washington had not destroyed their personal letters we would probably have a larger number of his proverbial locutions. Apparently it was not Lady Washington alone who deprived us of the great man's correspondence *en pantoufles*. There is a horrid story, fairly well authenticated, that a notable collector, perhaps the elder Morgan, burned a batch of Washington's letters because they contained anecdotes and language which the collector thought improper to preserve among the writings of the Man first in the hearts of his countrymen. If the tradition is based on fact it bears out the truth of the later saying, It takes one to know one.

Of the Founding Father—and *now* we must include a Mother—John Adams, amply seconded by his redoubtable Abigail, bears away the bell (B139) as a user of proverbs. It is no accident that the Harvard College Library possesses a copy of John Ray's *Collection of English Proverbs* (1670)[5] with John Adams' autograph scrawled on the title page. Because his is not the only contemporary signature, it seems likely that it indicates no more than temporary possession of a book from the College Library. What in 1754 or so must have been considered defacement is now reason to be immured in a special collection. Whatever bent the twig, Adams' tree was inclined (TW 387[1]) to a generous employment of proverbs, and he married a wife who kept him company in that as in other respects. Their son John Quincy followed them to some degree, but he lacked his parents' enthusiasm for colorful sayings. His sister Abigail, who became a Smith by marriage, seems not to have shared the family predilection, since we find a letter to her from John Q., in which he writes, "You have given me such a rap on the knuckles with respect to proverbs and wise sayings, that I must take care how I show my gravity. . . . But as to proverbs and wise sayings, I am not ambitious of producing any. I will endeavor henceforth to change my style, and follow your examples in employing satirical irony, and leave you to your own reflections" (Smith *Journal and Correspondence* 2[1] 112-3). John Q. was Harvard's first Boylston Professor of Rhetoric and Oratory and like many another professor he published in 1810 the only set of lectures which he delivered during his short and interrupted tenure of that chair. The lectures were rarely read during his lifetime, except by himself, or thereafter, perhaps because he made only one reference to proverbs, and that one calculated to please sister Abigail, "And under this name [of witnesses] are included authorities from eminent writers, common proverbs, and oracles from the ancients, instead of which we substitute the sacred scriptures" (*Lectures* 1.244).

Since we have discussed or dismissed our first six presidents, it is only equitable to mention the seventh. Andrew Jackson was described by his Federalist/Whig enemies as semiliterate, coarse, vulgar in speech and manners—a characterization that is not altogether extinct. His surviving writings, most of which appear to be of his own composition, regrettably fail to bear out the picture. He wrote rather ordinary standard English, not as finished as Jefferson's but as good as Washington's, and although he used a fair number of proverbs, there are almost none of the coarse colloquialisms which his opponents would lead us to expect.

We justly grieve over the destruction of Washington's letters and of many

5. Ray (1628-1705) is, after John Heywood (1497-c1580), the best-known of English proverbialists, yet outside the sacred circle Ray is famous only as a great natural scientist who in some ways anticipated Linnaeus. The parallel with Franklin is clear, though it must be admitted that Ray led a less active public and private life.

similar collections which are known to have perished either wilfully or through ignorance, accident, or carelessness. Perhaps more provoking to the honest and diligent collector of proverbs are the editorial practices of some of those who produced the books on which we draw. Again and again the editors of letters, journals, and memoirs complain that the mass of the material before them prohibits complete publication and that they are omitting all that does not deal directly with public events. Thus the very passages most likely to contain colloquial and proverbial language have remained in manuscript if, indeed, the manuscripts themselves survive. To a sober historian, if such there be, accounts of battles, conventions, treaties, economic problems, and the like are of paramount importance. For him the easy give-and-take of family and friendly correspondence is so much wasteland to be passed over rapidly in search of facts and figures. *Suum cuique pulcrum* (E1) is a proverb of sorts and Every one to his taste (or research) is another (E89). An equally pernicious trick of editors is to make silent omissions or alterations in the documents they do print, distortions brought to light only by later and more conscientious editors. Here, it is possible, may be an explanation of the almost complete absence in our collection of sayings that are what used to be called indelicate in language or purport. Though there is comfort in the thought of ancestral purity, a virtue not always transmitted, it does seem odd that from the large and heterogeneous group of citizens represented there should be so seldom even a whiff of coarseness. Expurgation may be part of the answer. To be sure, the monumental editions of the Papers of Great Americans print everything, and annotate it too, but, as we have seen, most of them did not write in an easy and unbuttoned style. To alter Ovid (and Robert Herrick) a trifle, if their lives were ever jocund their writings were almost ever chaste.

To describe the sources of this book is easier than to describe its contents. What is a proverb? The question has been often asked, frequently by those dissatisfied with definitions previously given. Of such queries there is no end. What is truth? asked jesting Pilate, but, jester or not, Pilate, wise in his generation, would not stay for an answer. If Pilate has access to modern collections he can find many proverbs about Truth[6], but no one will furnish him with an answer. Some, indeed, may confuse him. What, for example, does he make of Truth lies at the bottom of a well (T268) beside Truth seeks no corners (T272) or of Truth is not to be spoken at all times (T267) beside Tell truth and shame the Devil (T264) and Truth ought to be spoken (T271)?

There are proverbs about proverbs,[7] but most of them are more diverting than defining, though they are shorter and easier to understand than those put forward in the name of scholarship. They may not satisfy, but they rarely offend or invite refutation and replacement. It is the somewhat disconcerting experience of one who, through the years (since, to be definite, 1932), has

6. *Oxford* 843-5; Tilley T560-94; TW 383-4; Whiting T495-515, and, if he will stay, W T263-74.
7. Champion 3-7.

made several attempts at formulating a definition, that those who do stay for an answer are rarely pleased with what they receive.[8] One might, in effect, as well answer Why is a mouse when it spins?

From Aristotle (and to some degree from Plato) on there has been a stream of definitions, and the flow has certainly not reached its end.[9] Perhaps it will be better to use the word "describe" rather than "define," since the former may be less likely to raise the hackles of the Anthropophagi and men whose heads Do grow beneath their shoulders. I shall then attempt to describe W's contents which, like all similar collections since Erasmus', are an olla podrida, to use the phrase at a little distance from its etymology.

First we have proverbs, and here a distinction must be made. There are popular proverbs and learned proverbs, the latter frequently called sentences or sententious remarks. A popular proverb is one which has no known or presumed particular point of origin, and which circulated orally among the unlettered both before and after it was written down. An excellent descriptive phrase for a popular proverb is "an old said saw"[10] since it indicates antiquity and oral currency. It must be admitted that "saw" was used in the sense of "proverb" centuries before More, but even so, the etymology suggests something oral rather than written. That "said saw" is a tautological combination may easily escape attention. A favorite quotation about proverbs, usually given as "The wisdom of many, the wit of one," has been termed by one enthusiast as a "beautiful definition" and is listed by Champion (p. 4) among proverbs about proverbs. The form indeed fits a proverbial pattern, but it brings to mind the learned rather than the popular variety. The quotation is frequently attributed to Lord John Russell (1792-1878), an attribution which seems as good as such things are likely to be. In the autumn of 1823 Sir James Mackintosh (1765-1832), a man famous for his many intellectual and social activities, spent three months in Wales. While there an anonymous admirer recorded some examples of his table talk which later fell into the hands of Mackintosh's son and were incorporated in his life of his father. For October 6 we have the following: "Among other witty sayings, M. cited, as at once witty, and conveying a lesson of much practical value, Lord Halifax's, that *'caution is the lower story of prudence,'* and a definition of a proverb which Lord John Russell gave one morning at breakfast, at Mardocks — *'one man's wit, and all men's wisdom.'* "[11] Most

8. Dr. Johnson, always a likely source for an apt quotation, begins *Rambler* 125 (May 28, 1751) thus: "It is one of the maxims of the civil law, that *definitions are hazardous.*"

9. Recently we find two ambitious and elaborate attempts by social scientists, the second of which finds much to disagree with in the first; see *Proverbium* 14 (1969), 379-83, 25 (1975), 961-73. Both authors have in common a distaste for earlier definitions, or their lack.

10. The earliest occurrence known to me is in Sir Thomas More's *Dialogue Concerning Tyndale*, ed. W. E. Campbell and A. W. Reed (London, 1927), p. l. It was common later and found its way into phrase-books and dictionaries as the English equivalent of Latin *adagium* and *proverbium*, and French *proverbe*.

11. *Memoirs of the Life of the Right Honourable Sir James Mackintosh,* edited by his Son Robert James Mackintosh, Esq., 2 vols. (London, 1835), 2.472.

of us are not in the habit of throwing off good things at breakfast or, even if we do, of having them remembered. That breakfast at Mardocks may well have been as literary an affair as the celebrated ones given by Samuel Rogers, where the only beverage unavailable was probably orange juice, where all the guests tried to be as witty and caustic as their host, and where there was sure to be a chiel's amang them takin' notes. Since Mackintosh undoubtedly got Lord Halifax's witticism otherwise than from Halifax's mouth, there is no absolute proof that he was present at Mardocks, but it has been found in print nowhere before the *Memoirs* and it would appear to owe its currency to that volume. Its next use known to me is by George C. Lewis in 1849, where it "is attributed to a living statesman."[12] Here we have an instance of an apparently casual remark, written down by someone other than the speaker, put in print by a third person, altered in phraseology by subsequent users, and finally come to be called a proverb.

Examples of popular proverbs are All is well that ends well (A76), While the grass grows the horse (steed) starves (G152), A short horse is soon curried (H314), Dead men tell no tales (M23), When the steed is stolen, shut the stable-door (S419), Winter never rots in the sky (W232). When we call a proverb "popular" we must not forget that our proverbs, like those in all the standard collections, are not the product of more or less skilled gatherings from word of mouth, but were written down by individuals and then put into print by them or others. Another addendum is that collecting proverbs from informants is a tricky business and often requires more nudging than is true of ballads or even riddles.[13]

A learned proverb (sententious remark, sentence) is usually distinguishable by its heavier diction and often by the fact that we, if not all of its users, are aware of its source in literature, either domestic or foreign. Diction is no sure guide. One swallow makes no summer (S534) seems as native to America as to England, and yet it is of demonstrably classical origin.[14] A few additional examples follow: Honesty is the best policy (H264), The mountain was in labor and brought forth a mouse (M269), Self-preservation is the first law of nature (S99),[15] To take time (occasion) by the forelock (T147), The voice of the people is the voice of God (V31), A word to the wise is enough (W329).

What are called proverbial phrases fall into two groups, one fairly fixed in formulation, the other little more than a convenient catchall. Comparisons and similes are easy to identify, though some are learned or literary rather

---

12. For this and other early occurrences, see Whiting, "The Nature of the Proverb," *Harvard Studies and Notes in Philology and Literature* 14 (1932), 300, n. 1.

13. See Whiting in Brown *Collection* 1.347ff.

14. See Whiting xv, n. 19, S924, and especially *Oxford* 791.

15. Many learned proverbs have their popular equivalents. In this case, Every man for himself (E81), to which some add "and the Devil take the hindmost" (D130), or the more pious "and God for us all" (E82).

than popular.[16] The following may be regarded as popular: As busy as a bee (B106), As sick as a dog (D229), As thick as hasty pudding (H95), As black as a (my) hat (H96), As black as a sloe (S252), As quick as a wink (W228); To be like April skies (A112), To live like fighting-cocks (F95), To avoid like a (the) pest (P90), To run like sheep (S135), To change like the wind (W197). Others are more clearly out of the inkpot: As white as alabaster (A62), As drunk as Bacchus (B5), As blooming as a blossom in May (B219), As red as a comet (C266), As wealthy as Croesus (C348), As mad as a Turk (T288), As unstable as the wind (W180), Like babes in the wood (B3), Like a dog in a dancing school (D248), Like stars on a frosty night (S411), To stand like a statue (S418), To wallow like swine (S543), To be tossed like a tennis-ball (T33), To run on like a Salem witch (W250), To scold like Xantippe (X1).

There are no common formulas for the miscellaneous, and the most that one can say is that some seem more popular than others. In the first group we may instance In Aunt Gowen's day (A139), To bear (wear) the bell (B139), The bird has flown (B171), To be in the wrong box (B296), To wear the breeches (B319), Safe and sound (S9), Sink or swim (S224). The second group can be illustrated by To sell one's birthright (B191), Crocodile tears (C347), First catch a dolphin (D275), To put on the fox's skin (F286), To dine with St. Anthony (S24), Between Scylla and Charybdis (S78).

Those who put together volumes such as this rarely read with a set of definitions in their minds; rather, they depend on three responses.[17] First the author of their source may use the designations "proverb," "adage," "saying," or words to that effect. He may, to be sure, be mistaken or misleading,[18] but he cannot be ignored. Second, the compiler is almost obligated to include what those who preceded him have included in similar collections: if something is found in Erasmus or *Oxford* or Tilley the knowledgeable user may well ask, Why is it not here? Finally, and perhaps most important if least tangible, the compiler depends on his own judgment. Just as Humpty Dumpty said that "a word . . . means just what I choose it to mean, neither more nor less," so the editor comes to believe that something is proverbial because he feels that it is just that. Such assurance may be ill-founded, but there is comfort in the thought that while what is included may be questioned, what is omitted cannot be assessed.

Paroemiologists, to allow us one of our more erudite designations, have often amused themselves, and occasionally others, by attempts "to identify national or local traits in proverbs and to use them in describing and defining national or racial temperament." The quotation is from Archer Taylor,[19] who

16. The best discussion of comparisons and similes is in Taylor *Comparisons* 1ff.; see also Whiting xvi.

17. For a longer discussion, see Whiting xii-xiv.

18. See Appendix C for examples from our texts of other than generally accepted uses of "proverb," "proverbial," and "proverbially."

19. *The Proverb* (Cambridge, Mass., 1931), p. 164.

goes on to demonstrate that such efforts are futile, at least in the light of our present knowledge of the diffusion of proverbs.[20] Some inferences might, of course, be drawn from the proverb store of a small isolated community, say a remote and seldom visited island, but even here the tendency of proverbs to contradict themselves[21] puts hedgehogs, if not lions, in the way (L160), and the analyst can be expected to pick and choose in order to exemplify preconceived judgments. Even if we accept all this, there is still a temptation to draw inferences, and I have succumbed to the temptation. Surely something can be learned from examining the sayings which appear most frequently in a given body of writings. The authors represented in W are a relatively homogeneous group from a relatively limited area who lived and wrote over a period of approximately two centuries. For the reader's delectation, if not improvement, there follow the sayings (sixty-four in all), which, save for the exclusion of a few neutral proverbial phrases, turn up most often. The sayings are presented in decreasing order of occurrence and, to avoid any guarantee of absolute accuracy of count, I do not give precise figures, except to say here that thirteen occur between 100 and 50 times, forty-five between 48 and 20 times, and six between 18 and 14 times. In a few cases, as will be indicated, closely related sayings have been joined and "editorial" comments of a sort are usually provided. To give some standards of comparison I refer, wherever possible, to Middle English occurrences (Whiting) and to American appearances after 1820 (TW). The yardsticks, to be sure, are parochial, but Whiting and TW lead the way to the principal collections. These citations appear at the end of the entries and are accompanied by indications of relative frequency: very frequent, frequent, seldom, very seldom. I suspect that the somewhat surprising paucity, or even lack, of examples in TW is because Taylor and Whiting were more chary of including learned proverbs than was Whiting alone in later years. Sententiousness grows with age.

1. **T134** Time is precious (precious time). It is appropriate that the most common of our sayings is the one that best exemplifies the Puritan work ethic, the cornerstone of the American way of life. It must not slake our pleasure that the references are almost always to the *loss* of precious time. We rarely hear of the beneficial employment of precious time. Apparently time is

---

20. For a bag of mixed opinions, see the introductions to the various collections in Champion (pp. xxxv-cviii), whose very title, *Racial Proverbs* is suggestive of a certain bias. It must be said that most of Champion's specialists are diffident. The curious may like to consult Lt. Colonel V. S. M. de Guinzbourg's *Wit and Wisdom of the United Nations*, subtitled *Proverbs and Apothegms on Diplomacy*, privately printed, United Nations, N.Y., 1961. Part One of this large and handsome volume consists of statements by the official representatives of the countries then members of the United Nations. In 1961 Lt. Colonel de Guinzbourg was Permanent Secretary of the Paroemiological Society, of which he had been the founder.

21. For a classic demonstration of this trait, see Nicholas Breton, *Crossing of Proverbs* (1616).

one of those entities, perhaps like virginity, made precious by its loss. Whiting T322: frequent; TW 374: very seldom.

2. **R149, 150** Sub rosa, Under the rose. The Latin form is more than half as frequent as the English and, along with the next item, is our writers' most common evidence of classical learning. The urgent desire for secrecy and discretion is too obvious to require emphasis. The phrase seems to be neither classical nor medieval. TW 312: seldom.

3. **W329** A word to the wise is enough. More than half the examples are in Latin, often variously curtailed. Here is a hedging saying by means of which the writer does not altogether commit himself and thus leaves the onus of interpretation upon the reader. The frequent use of Latin, especially bluntly abbreviated, is not without an added slyness. Whiting W588: frequent: TW 412(3): very seldom.

4. **E102** Of two evils choose the least. The advice is sound, but observe that the choice is always between evils. Nowhere in W do we find anything like Of two goods choose the better, although that saying does occur in Middle English (Whiting G357). Whiting E193: very frequent; TW 122: seldom.

5. **D174** The die is cast. If we add To pass the Rubicon (R158), a phrase commonly linked to it by the best authority, the combination would exceed by far Precious time. The phrases rarely have an optimistic connotation, but rather suggest, "Well, friends, we have taken the fatal step and are probably in for it." TW 102(3): very seldom, 313: seldom.

6. **O25** The olive branch (of peace). The disconcerting aspect of the phrase, more or less of Biblical origin, is that the bearer is all too often said also to carry the sword of war. In other words, accept the branch or feel the sword. Whiting O32: frequent; TW 270: very seldom.

7. **L2-4** To have one's labor for his pains, To have one's labor (to labor) in vain, To lose one's labor. These allied sayings, which supplement the loss of precious time (no. 1 above), indicate a basic and pathetic sense of inevitable frustration. That they are sparsely represented in TW may suggest that the nineteenth century nurtured an ill-founded spirit of optimism. Whiting L11, T442, V1: very frequent; TW 212, 391: very seldom.

8. **N20-3** Necessity became a law, Necessity has compulsion, Necessity has (knows) no law, Necessity is the mother of invention. Except for the last, which has an element of hope, these sayings encourage self-interest to rise above all else. If we add To make a virtue of necessity (no. 31 below), a singularly face-saving aphorism, the group outnumbers most other sayings. To them is allied Self-preservation is the first law of nature (no. 14 below). Whiting N51: very frequent; TW 258-9: frequent.

9. **S457** To leave no stone unturned. Here we have a sound guide for energetic investigation, unless we are experienced enough to remember the rather unappealing things likely to be found under stones. TW 356(14): very seldom.

10. **C56** To build castles in the air. Here is another expression of the

temporary triumph of hope over experience. Rather oddly we do not have the companion phrase To build castles in Spain, though it is found in Whiting (C77) and TW (57[2]). TW 57(1): very common.

11. **S499** To be a (stumbling-) block in one's way. There is always trouble, probably unavoidable, ahead. Whiting B355: very seldom.

12. **D88** To pay the debt of (to) nature. No comment seems necessary, except to note the sense of obligation, since the inevitability of death, if not exhilarating, is common in and out of sententious lore. Whiting D116: very frequent; TW 96: seldom.

13. **M269** The mountain was in labor and brought forth a mouse. No matter how extensive and noisy our plans, the result will be minimal. Whiting H388: very seldom.

14. **S99** Self-preservation is the first law of nature. One of the most selfish of all sayings and one which encourages us to take any action, no matter how violent and excessive, so that we may have and hold. TW 322: seldom.

15. **F269, 273** Fortune and her wheel, Fortune is fickle. The first of these occurs twice as often as the second. In theory the wheel of Fortune is impartial: if one is down he goes up and if he is up he goes down, as Pandarus puts the case with his customary persuasiveness in Chaucer's *Troilus* i 841-54. Almost every reference, however, makes it clear that the wheel is rigged and that the direction is fatally down. In W as elsewhere the changes of Fortune are for the worse. Whiting F502ff.: *very* frequent; TW 144(1) wheel: seldom.

16. **H264** Honesty is the best policy. We observe that honesty is not stated to be a virtue in itself, but as a policy, a means to an end. Of our nearly fifty examples, only a very few questioned its validity, and of these only Jefferson recognized its cynicism. It was, perhaps significantly, one of Washington's favorite proverbs. This saying can be used to illustrate the contamination of proverbs. On April 7, 1916, Miss Helen Wescott, a pupil in the Belfast (Me.) Grammar School, wrote an essay entitled "Honesty is its Own Reward." Her paper was based on the Aesopic fable of Mercury and the Workmen (Thompson *Motif-Index* Q 3.1). In this case contamination was allied to combination, because within a year Miss Wescott met someone who was to be her collaborator in proverbial and other matters for nearly sixty years. TW 186-7: very common.

17. **S78** Between Scylla and Charybdis. Here there is not so much as a choice of evils. If we manage to escape one disaster it is only to encounter another equally destructive. Whiting S101: seldom; TW 320-1: seldom.

18. **R137** Rope(s) of sand. Another gloomy phrase: nothing in which we might have confidence will hold. The earliest occurrence seems to be in the *Adagia* of Erasmus. TW 311(1): very seldom.

19. **W264** A wolf in sheep's clothing. To put it even more succinctly: Trust nobody, and remember that Little Red Riding Hood is in a fairy tale. The saying derives from Matt. 7:15. Whiting W474: very frequent; TW 407(1): frequent.

20. **W25** War's chance (fortune, *etc.*) is uncertain. Ancient and universal as this realistic truism has been, it is usually forgotten between wars. Our own examples, it will be seen, are heavily concentrated between 1773 and 1783. Whiting W39: very frequent; TW 144(4): very seldom.

21. **H289** The horns of cuckoldry. That a deceived husband, less often a deceived wife, wears horns no less tangible for being invisible is a commonplace from the Middle Ages on and a fruitful source of vicarious merriment. It is, in a way, gratifying that it was not the twentieth century that first saw the American marriage bed defiled. Whiting H483: very frequent; TW 188(2): very seldom.

22. **S111** To catch at the shadow and lose the substance. How prone is man (and dog) to self-deception, how ready to be beguiled by empty show! The saying, derived from an Aesopic fable (Thompson *Motif-Index* J 1791.4) has not been recorded in English before 1548. [*Oxford* 110; Tilley S951.]

23. **C51** The case is altered. The original meaning of the phrase was that an impartial judgment will be reversed if the judge finds his own interest involved. In most of our examples, however, it merely suggests that a situation has changed, usually for the worse. Whiting C67: very seldom; TW 57(4): very seldom.

24. **B253** A bone of contention. There is always a cause for strife, and no counterbalancing saying refers to a bone at which two can gnaw in peace. Jack Sprat and his wife are in rhyme not life, and even then the cat got the picked bone. TW 36(1): very seldom.

25. **M191, N51, P182, S281, T222** One's mischief returns on his head, To be caught in one's own net, To fall into the pit one digs for another, To fall into one's own snare, To be caught in one's own trap. Whatever the phrasing, the moral is clear and the implication melancholy. The only deterrent to our natural instinct to deceive and betray others is the thought that our tricks are likely to backfire. Whiting P232 pit, S427 snare: both very frequent; TW 381(1) trap: seldom.

26. **R116** To kiss the rod. A relic from nonpermissive school days, the general application is that obsequiousness may perhaps ingratiate us with those who have, and enforce, power over us. TW 309(1): very seldom.

27. **L239** The love of money is the root of all evil. From 1 Tim. 6:10. A distinction has been made, sometimes casuistically, between an excessive love of money, that is, covetousness, avarice, and money itself. The examples deserve attention, as does the nest of proverbs about money (M206ff.). Whiting C491: *very* frequent; TW 230(13): frequent.

28. **T65, 66** A thorn in the flesh (side). Almost anything or anyone, especially those who are near and should be dear, can be a cause of pain. TW 370: seldom.

29. **V31** The voice of the people is the voice of God. Almost all of our examples are given in Latin (Vox populi [est] vox Dei) and several have only the last two words. The sentiment is admirably democratic, although a num-

ber of instances indicate that the users apply the proverb in a highly ironic sense. Whiting V54: seldom; TW 392: seldom.

30. **G99** Whom God (Jupiter) would destroy he first makes mad. The application of this comforting classical saying is that those who oppose us are demented and headed for a divinely arranged extermination. Our foes can unscrupulously misapply the proverb: Gott mit uns! [*Oxford* 313; Tilley G257.]

31. **V27** To make a virtue of necessity. This phrase, which should be compared with the Necessity sayings (no. 8 above), is a touching admonition to save face and gain credit when we find ourselves against the wall. Relax and enjoy it. The Church Fathers knew it, who better, and Chaucer employed it three times. Whiting V43: frequent; TW 392(1): seldom.

32. **C120** Charity begins at home. Earlier examples imply that charity, in its broadest sense, should begin in and extend from the individual, but it later became an excuse to do as little as possible for others. Whiting C153: seldom; TW 65(2): seldom.

33. **C97** To be (made) a cat's paw. Based on a variously expressed fable, best known from La Fontaine's version, we learn from the phrase that someone is always ready to take advantage of someone else. TW 66(3): very seldom.

34. **C239** Let the cobbler stick to his last. Most of our examples are in Latin (Ne sutor ultra crepidam), sometimes with an English translation. Leave things to the expert, but the application is often the undemocratic one of subordination. Whiting D190: very seldom; TW 75: seldom.

35. **B177** Birds of a feather flock together. There are good birds and bad birds, but the birds that flock together are always bad birds. TW 28(16): very frequent.

36. **S209** Silence gives consent. If you ask a man if he will give you his purse and at the same time choke him, you will understand the validity of the proverb. In a different situation you can save argument if you merely look wise when confronted with an unsavory proposition. The first application is criminal, the second political. Silence cannot be taped. Whiting S733: frequent; TW 333: seldom

37. **S275** The snake in the grass. Everywhere there is danger, especially in the grass or among flowers. Even in a desert one is warned against sand vipers. Stay in the house and keep your feet on a hassock. Even there you must beware of garter snakes. Whiting S153: very frequent; TW 341(1): seldom.

38. **R53** The remedy (cure) is worse than the disease. As a comment on medical and surgical practice the saying is not without a grisly truth, but the broader application is sheer pessimism and frequently used as an argument against any new law or regulation. Price and wage controls indeed! [*Oxford* 671; Tilley R68.]

39. **S255** Slow and (but) sure. Sound though the sense may be, it too often serves to explain why expected progress is not being made. TW 339: very seldom.

40. **P298** To promise and not perform. The sad and realistic contrast

between what is said and what is done is universal in proverbial lore. Whiting P409: very seldom, cf. W642: *very* frequent.

41. **B324** To make bricks without straw. Exod. 5:7 has long furnished an excuse, often as valid as Biblical, for not getting on with an assigned task. The saying, as can be seen below, was frequently in the minds of Washington and other leaders of the Revolutionary forces. TW 357(6): very seldom.

42. **R6** The race is not to the swift nor the battle to the strong. By authority as Biblical (Eccles. 9:11) as the preceding saying, we are encouraged to persevere against odds. A charming echo of the proverb is found in Alice Cary's poem which begins "Three little bugs in a basket." Whiting R240: very seldom; TW 301: frequent.

43. **S540** By the sweat of our brow shall we eat our bread. God's doom (Gen. 3:19) has been passed on from generation to generation by this saying. That bread is now proclaimed to be neither touched nor sliced by human hands, or that the word has acquired a new meaning, does not detract from the basic glumness of the saying. Whiting S940: frequent.

44. **T226** Travellers may lie by authority. The healthy skepticism of the stay-at-home about tales brought from far-away is found in nearly all ages and peoples. Its scarcity in TW is doubtless due to an increase in both travel and credulity. An admirable commentary for our period is in Percy G. Adams. *Travellers and Travel Liars, 1660-1800*, Berkeley, Cal., 1962. Whiting J27: very seldom, P18: frequent, S251: very seldom; TW 381(2): very seldom.

45. **A103** Appearances are deceiving. Don't believe what you see. It may look like a sheep and be a wolf (no. 19 above). Even if you look closer you are apt to be wrong. In other and foreign words, *En garde!* TW 7(2): seldom.

46. **G64** To strain at a gnat and swallow a camel. Originally (Matt. 23:24) an attack on hypocrisy and outward show, it later became also a warning against a foolish, or self-interested, discrimination in belief. Whiting G178: frequent; TW 153-4: seldom.

47. **P270** To practise what one preaches. The precept is admirable but the application is usually in the negative. The Aesopic fable of the crab and its mother (Whiting C514) is a moving exemplum. Whiting P358-60: seldom; TW 295: seldom.

48. **W41** To fish in troubled waters. We have the authority of Izaak Walton (*Compleat Angler,* Fourth Day) that troubled waters are best for the use of artificial flies. The proverb, however, never is applied to the gentle breed of angler, but rather to rascals from Satan down who trouble the waters that they may deceive the innocent. TW 395(14): very seldom.

49. **R61** Republics are ungrateful. As one might guess, our earliest example is from 1776, and to read the entries is more illuminating than any comment could be. By whom the exact wording was first coined is obscure, but Middle English offers sour remarks on the unreliability of the common people. TW 306: seldom; cf. Whiting P134.

50. **M26** A drowning man will catch at a straw, S483 To catch at

straws. This is one of the "despair" proverbs and lacks the cheerfulness of the less frequent Any port in a storm (P238), which I once heard used as a more or less jocose excuse for miscegenation. Whiting M137: very seldom; TW 233(1): frequent.

51. **L192** Loaves and fishes. The account of Jesus as a miraculous caterer (John 6:9-29) is in our examples blasphemously applied to the spoils of political office. Whiting L414: very seldom.

52. **B159** To make the best of a bad market (bargain). The market is always bad, and thus the saying can be compared to Of two evils choose the least (no. 4 above). TW 26(4): very seldom.

53. **R47** To be a broken reed. The phrase is Biblical (see the references in Whiting) and more often than not states that the reed will not only break and let us fall, but that its broken ends will pierce us as we fall. Trust not lest you be betrayed. Whiting R70: seldom.

54. **D55** Speak well of the dead. The saying, often given in its Latin form (De mortuis nil nisi bonum) is occasionally joined to De vivis nil nisi verum. We are rarely, if ever, admonished to speak *well* of the living. In fairness one must note that Abigail Smith Adams told her husband John (Adams *D and A* 2.72) that her father "never inculcated any Maxim of Behaviour upon his Children, so often as this — never to speak ill of any Body. To say all the handsome Things she could of Persons but no Evil. . . . He was always remarkable for observing these rules in his own Conversation." She went on, however, to add that "Her Grandfather Quincy was remarkable for never praising any Body, He did not often speak evil, but he seldom spoke well." There is, one recognizes, more Quincy than Smith in the New England character, not excluding Abigail and John Adams. TW 94(3): very seldom.

55. **M194** Misfortunes seldom come alone. If we could find a saying to the effect that Good fortunes fall over each other's heels, one might comment on the contrast, but we do not. Whiting H139: frequent; TW 246(1): very seldom.

56. **V29** Virtue is its own reward. How do we take this saying? Spenser expanded it to "immortall praise and glory wyde," while Sir Thomas Browne called it "but a cold principle" (for both, see *Oxford* 861). The learned Doctor seems closer to the general application: To do good may make one feel better, but will not get him many thanks. TW 392(2): frequent.

57. **R145** No rose without a thorn. Beauty may be in the eye of the beholder, but it seems sure to be painful in the hands of the holder. Whiting R204, 206: *very* frequent.

58. **A28** Actions speak louder than words. Although the precise wording is late, the contrast between what is said and what is done is almost universal. In our own day it is manifest in the cynicism which greets the planks of party platforms and the "position papers" of candidates for office. TW 3(2): seldom; cf. Whiting W642.

59. **B127** Set a beggar on horseback and he will ride (to the Devil). In

the longer form the proverb means that a poor man given power will destroy himself; in the shorter, that he will injure those who give him a mount. Either way the message is clear: Subordination is the first law of upper-class nature. TW 24(2): seldom; cf. Whiting B186, C271.

60. **T241**   New England (New York, Connecticut, Jersey, Yankee) trick. Of these more than half specify Yankee. In almost every case the tribute is offered from outside the region named. We may not trust our own people too much, but we do expect to be defrauded by those from away. In this derogatory sense Yorkshire would seem to have been the New England of Old England. A striking parallel may be seen in the various geographical appelations given to venereal disease. TW 416 (from DA): seldom; cf. *Oxford* 926-7.

61. **V24**   A viper (*etc.*) in one's bosom. This saying, derived from an Aesopic fable, warns us against giving assistance to those whose instinct will be to harm a benefactor. Since we cannot judge instinct, the implied lesson is to take no chances. Misanthropy is safer than philanthropy. Whiting A42: seldom.

62. **S250**   There's many a slip twixt the cup and the lip. That is, Don't count your chickens before they are hatched, a saying slightly less common in our collection (C138). The Slip proverb seems to come from the *Adagia*, and the Chickens from a medieval folk tale (Thompson *Motif-Index* J2061.1.2). TW 339(2) slip: frequent, 67(3) chickens: frequent.

63. **T176**   Never put off to tomorrow what may be done today. The saying would have little force if we were accustomed to do things promptly. Procrastination is the thief of time (P294, with due credit to Edward Young). Perhaps it is worth noting that half of our examples come from Franklin, Washington, and Jefferson. Whiting T348: frequent; TW 377-8: seldom.

64. **P240**   Possession is eleven (*etc.*) points of the law. A principle much abhorred by landowners, but sancrosanct to squatters. It is used today, however, against the claims of American Indians to the hunting grounds of their ancestors. TW 292: frequent; cf. Whiting P311.

If words may be said to speak at least as loudly as actions, the composite picture to be drawn from our most commonly used sayings is not an inspiring one, nor is it likely to gratify the Society of Mayflower Descendants or the Daughters of the American Revolution. Hardly a redeeming quality emerges. Those who tamed the howling wilderness and founded the Republic would seem to be characterized by varying degrees of cynicism, cunning, distrust, expediency, suspicion, self-interest, misanthropy, despair, frustration, pessimism, secrecy, caution, elitism, ingratitude, regional prejudice, and furtiveness. If some of the categories overlap, so do the sayings. In a word which our sources could not know, and would not have liked, here we have most of the classic features of paranoia. The best defense is perhaps in the protest of a depressed and now defunct critic: "But even a paranoid can have enemies." Our ancestors did have obstacles to surmount. There were at first Indians, wolves, mosquitoes, and Quakers; later, stamp officers, redcoats, loyalists, insurgents, and, depending on the point of view, Federalists and Democrats. Their souls were certainly tried at times, but even this does not altogether lighten the gloomy prospect painted by their favorite sayings.

Explanations may be sought in our sources, and in the nature of proverbs themselves. First, no more than a fifth of the sayings can be called popular, nearly half are learned, and the remainder, all miscellaneous proverbial phrases, are mainly literary rather than popular. Almost all the authors responsible for the sayings belong to the group which I earlier called learned and cultured. For example, nearly a third of the sixty-four sayings are borrowed from the Bible, Latin (classical or later), and Aesopic fables. No other group of sixty-four taken at random or consecutively would show such an emphasis on book learning. Those who doubt that scholars are more melancholy than the average run of mankind need only reread Robert Burton. There is also, one fears, a tinge of cynicism in the scholarly mind which comes in part from introspection and in part from association with other scholars and their writings. If the last sentence be taken as cynical, the chips will have to fall (Whiting C235 and the late Roscoe Conkling).

The easiest way to absolve our ancestors, or at the very least to make them appear less unpleasant, is to admit that proverbs tend to be pessimistic and misanthropic, even misogynistic. Proverbs take a dim view of humanity and in them the seamy side prevails over the good, though this aspect may be a trifle more evident in learned sayings than in popular. I remember a student as he read for the first, and perhaps for the last, time the *Proverbs of Alfred* (c1250), which, as we know, owes much to the *Disticha Catonis*, shaking his head in doleful wonder that the poem should be so full of mistrust for man- and womankind. The student is older now and a teacher and may have become disillusioned. Nearly any comprehensive and inclusive collection, certainly Whiting, could provide a chamber of moral horrors such as ours. To cut a long story short (S468) and to make the best of a bad bargain (B159), our forefathers were probably not much less charitable than other proverbial moralists.

The entry forms in this volume follow those in Whiting, which were generally similar to those in Tilley.[22] There is for each entry a lemma, or standard form, which ordinarily gives the usual wording of common sayings. Authors, however, reworded sayings so frequently that the lemma, even with important variations included in parentheses, cannot always reproduce the modifications presented in the quotations. In such cases the notation (*varied*) follows the lemma to remind the reader to check the quotations against the lemma.

The alphabetical arrangement is based on a key word in each saying. Usually the word chosen is the first important noun but, where there is no suitable noun, the first important verb serves, and in the rare cases where there is

22. The ensuing paragraphs owe as much as possible, including direct but unmarked quotations, to Whiting xviii-xix.

neither noun nor verb of importance, some other significant part of speech is used. Parasyntactic forms follow the full form—thus Snow-white comes after As white as snow—and share the same number (S293). All sayings which come under a single key word are grouped by the first words of the lemma, except that articles are ignored. I could wish, as did some of the reviewers of Whiting, that there were fewer sayings under such neutral words as "man" and "thing," and the reader cannot be expected to realize the efforts which have been taken to limit these categories.

Each lemma has a number which consists of the appropriate letter of the alphabet followed by a numeral. Thus, we have A1 to A144, and then B1 and so on. All quotations are dated, although some of the dates are indicated as conjectural, and are arranged in chronological order.

With twenty-five exceptions, all occurrences that I have noted have been entered. Those represented by a selection only include one proverb of the learned variety (W329), one proverbial comparison (S293), and twenty-three miscellaneous proverbial phrases (C44, D174, E6, 63, F266, H231, L258, O25, R149, 150, S328, 457, 499, T3, 22, 38, 134, 305, W45, 245, 264, 322, Y7). The selections have been made to give chronological spread, to illustrate variations of phrasing, and to cite illustrious writers such as Roger Williams, Cotton Mather, and presidents of the United States. None of the underprivileged phrases are of especial interest or indicative value, they are rarely varied, and it is hoped that no reader will be like Oliver Twist and ask for more.

After the quotations, references are given, wherever possible, to works in which other examples of the sayings can be found. The books usually cited are *Oxford*, Tilley, TW, and Whiting. The somewhat more extensive references in TW and Whiting are ordinarily not repeated. It should be noted that since TW and Whiting there has been a third edition of *Oxford*, so that the page references to *Oxford* in the two earlier volumes no longer apply. Further, the latest *Oxford* draws generously upon Tilley and also gives the pertinent numbers of that work. Finally, I give cross-references to more or less parallel sayings within the collection itself. References of this kind are easy to multiply and I have made no attempt to compete with the Index.

BIBLIOGRAPHICAL REFERENCES

The entries below constitute a short-title finding list for this volume; the list has, unlike some bibliographies, no independent value. Only enough detail is given to enable the user to locate the source. It has seemed pointless to indicate whether a book has been read from an original or from microfilm, but published facsimiles are identified. Works quoted only two or three times are not entered; for these, adequate references are supplied in the text.

Short titles that contain the words "Letters" or "Papers" are given in italics when the collection is miscellaneous, of the sort now often called an archive; when a proper name identifies the author of the bulk of the material, only "Letters" or "Papers" is italicized. Thus Asbury *Letters* and *Cary Letters* and Austin *Literary Papers* and *Belknap Papers*.

Adams *Correspondence*: *Correspondence of the Late President [John] Adams, originally published in the Boston Patriot,* Boston, 1809(-10).

Adams *D and A*: *Diary and Autobiography of John Adams,* ed. L. H. Butterfield et al., 4 vols., Cambridge, Mass., 1961.

Adams *Diary*: "Diary of John Quincy Adams, 1787-1789," Massachusetts Historical Society, *Proceedings*, November. 1902, 295-464.

Adams *Earliest Diary*: *The Earliest Diary of John Adams,* ed. L. H. Butterfield et. al., Cambridge, Mass., 1966.

Adams FC: *Adams Family Correspondence,* ed. L. H. Butterfield et al., Cambridge, Mass., I, II (1963), III, IV (1973). (Abigail Adams is cited as AA, and John Adams as JA.)

Adams *Lectures*: John Quincy Adams, *Lectures on Rhetoric and Oratory*, 2 vols., Cambridge, Mass., 1810, with a new Introduction by J. J. Auer and J. L. Banninga, New York, 1962.

Adams *Legal Papers*: *Legal Papers of John Adams,* ed. L. K. Wroth and H. B. Zobel, 3 vols., Cambridge, Mass., 1965.

Adams(A) *Letters*: *Letters of Mrs. [Abigail] Adams,* ed. Charles F. Adams, 4th ed., Boston, 1848.

Adams(TB) *Letters:* "Letters of Thomas Boylston Adams to William Smith Shaw, 1799-1823," ed. C. G. Washburn, American Antiquarian Society, *Proceedings*, N.S. 27 (1917), 83-176.

Adams *Letters on Silesia:* John Quincy Adams, *Letters on Silesia, Written During A Tour Through that Country in the Years 1800, 1801,* London, 1804.

Bibliographical References

Adams *Memoirs: Memoirs of John Quincy Adams,* ed. Charles F. Adams, 12 vols., Philadelphia, 1874-7. (Not used beyond vol. VI.)

Adams *New Letters: New Letters of Abigail Adams, 1788-1801,* ed. Stewart Mitchell, Boston, 1947.

Adams *Works: The Works of John Adams,* ed. Charles F. Adams, 10 vols., Boston, 1850-6.

Adams *Writings: Writings of John Quincy Adams,* ed. Worthington C. Ford, 7 vols., New York, 1913-7.

Adams(S) *Writings: The Writings of Samuel Adams,* ed. Harry A. Cushing, 4 vols., New York, 1904-8.

Adams-Cunningham Letters: Correspondence Between the Hon. John Adams . . . and . . . Wm. Cunningham, Esq., Boston, 1823.

Adams-Jefferson Letters: The Adams-Jefferson Letters, ed. Lester J. Cappon, 2 vols., Chapel Hill, N.C., 1959.

Adams-Warren Correspondence: "Correspondence Between John Adams and Mercy Warren," Massachusetts Historical Society, *Collections,* 5th ser. 4 (1878), 321-511.

Adams-Waterhouse Correspondence: Statesman and Friend, Correspondence of John Adams with Benjamin Waterhouse, 1784-1822, ed. Worthington C. Ford, Boston, 1927.

Alden *Epitaphs:* Timothy Alden, *A Collection of American Epitaphs and Inscriptions,* 5 vols., New York, 1814. (A majority of the quotations from Alden are not from epitaphs.)

Allen *Extracts: Extracts from Chief Justice William Allen's Letter Book,* ed. Lewis B. Walker, Pottsville, Pa., 1897.

Allen *Narrative: A Narrative of Colonel Ethan Allen's Captivity* (1779), New York, 1930.

Allen *Vermont:* Ira Allen, *The Natural and Political History of the State of Vermont* (London, 1798), Vermont Historical Society, *Collections* 1 (1870), 331-486.

Alsop *Maryland:* George Alsop, *A Character of the Province of Maryland* (1666), ed. Newton D. Mereness, Cleveland, 1902.

American Museum: The American Museum, or, Repository of Ancient and Modern Fugitive Pieces, Philadelphia, I (1787)-. (Not used after vol. V.)

American Wanderer: The American Wanderer Through Various Parts of Europe . . . By a Virginian, London, 1783.

Ames *Almanacs: The Essays, Humor, and Poems of Nathaniel Ames, Father and Son . . . from their Almanacks, 1726-1775,* ed. Sam. Briggs, Cleveland, 1891.

Ames *Diary: Jacobin and Junto, or Early American Politics as Viewed in the Diary of Dr. Nathaniel Ames, 1758-1822,* by Charles Warren, Cambridge, Mass., 1931.

Ames *Letters: Works of Fisher Ames, with a Selection from his Speeches and Correspondence,* ed. Seth Ames, 2 vols., Boston, 1854.

Ames *Mariner's:* (Nathaniel Ames), *A Mariner's Sketches,* Providence, 1830. (Of a voyage taken in 1815.)

Ames *Nautical:* (Nathaniel Ames), *Nautical Reminiscences,* Providence, 1832.

Anarchiad: (David Humphreys et al.), *The Anarchiad* (1786-7), reproduced from the ed. of 1861 by William K. Bottorff, Scholars' Facsimiles and Reprints, Gainesville, Fla., 1967.

Anburey *Travels:* Thomas Anburey, *Travels through the Interior Parts of America* (1789), ed. William H. Carter, 2 vols., Boston, 1923.

Anderson *Diary: The Diary and Journal of Richard Clough Anderson, Jr., 1814-1826,* ed. A. Tischendorf and E. T. Parks, Durham, N.C., 1964.

Andrews *Letters: Letters of John Andrews, Esq., of Boston, 1772-1776,* ed. Winthrop Sargent, Massachusetts Historical Society, *Proceedings* 8 (1864-5), 322-412.

Andrews *Prisoners' Memoirs*: Charles Andrews, *The Prisoners' Memoirs, or Dartmoor Prison,* New York,1815.

Andros Tracts: The Andros Tracts, ed. W. H. Whitmore, 3 vols., Publications of the Prince Society 5-7, Boston, 1868-74.

Angell *Diary: Diary of Colonel Israel Angell, 1778-1781,* ed. Edward Field, Providence, R.I., 1899.

Apperson: G. L. Apperson, *English Proverbs and Proverbial Phrases: A Historical Dictionary,* London, 1929.

Asbury *Journal: The Journal and Letters of Francis Asbury,* ed. J. M. Potts et al., 3 vols., London, 1958.

Asbury *Letters:* as above.

Aspinwall Papers: The Aspinwall Papers, 2 vols., Massachusetts Historical Society, *Collections,* 4th ser. 9, 10 (1871).

Audubon *1826 Journal: The 1826 Journal of J. J. Audubon,* ed. Alice Ford, Norman, Okla., 1967.

Austin *Constitutional:* Benjamin Austin, Jr., *Constitutional Republicanism, In Opposition to Fallacious Federalism,* Boston, 1803.

Austin *Literary Papers: Literary Papers of William Austin,* ed. J. W. Austin, Boston, 1890.

Austin Papers: The Austin Papers, ed. E. C. Barker, Annual Report of the American Historical Society, 1919, 2, parts 1, 2, Washington, D.C.,1924.

Bache *Notes:* (Richard Bache), *Notes on Columbia, Taken in the Years 1822-3,* Philadelphia, 1827.

Bailey *Journal: The Frontier Missionary . . . the Rev. Jacob Bailey,* by William S. Bartlett, Boston, 1853.

Baily *Journal:* Francis Baily, *Journal of a Tour in Unsettled Parts of North America in 1796 & 1797,* London, 1856.

Bailyn *Pamphlets:* Bernard Bailyn, ed., *Pamphlets of the American Revolution,* I, Cambridge, Mass., 1965.

Baldwin *Diary: Diary of Christopher Columbus Baldwin, 1829-35,* Worcester, Mass., 1901.

Baldwin *Journal: The Revolutionary Journal of Col. Jeduthan Baldwin, 1775-78,* ed. T. W. Baldwin, Bangor, Me., 1906.

Baldwin *Letters: Reliquiae Baldwinianae: Selections from the Correspondence of . . . William Baldwin,* compiled by William Darlington (1843), with an Introduction by Joseph Ewan, New York, 1969.

Baldwin *Life and Letters: Life and Letters of Simeon Baldwin,* ed. Simeon E. Baldwin, New Haven, 1919.

Banks *Maine:* Ronald F. Banks, *Maine Becomes a State,* Middletown, Conn., 1970.

Barbary Wars: Naval Documents Relating to the United States Wars with the Barbary Powers, 6 vols., Washington, D.C., 1939-44.

Bibliographical References

Barbour: Frances M. Barbour, *Proverbs and Proverbial Phrases of Illinois*, Carbondale, Ill., 1965.

Barker *How to Try a Lover*: (James Barker), *How to Try a Lover*, New York, 1817.

Barker *Tears: James N. Barker, 1784-1858, with a Reprint of his Comedy Tears and Smiles (1808)*, by Paul H. Musser, Philadelphia, 1929.

Barlow *Letters: Life and Letters of Joel Barlow*, by Charles B. Todd, New York, 1886.

Barlow *Works: The Works of Joel Barlow*, ed. W. K. Bottorff and A. L. Ford, 2 vols., Scholars' Facsimiles and Reprints, Gainesville, Fla., 1970.

Barney *Memoir: A Biographical Memoir of the Late Commodore Joshua Barney: from Autographical Notes and Journals*, by Mary Barney, Boston, 1832.

Barton *Disappointment:* Andrew Barton, *The Disappointment; or, The Force of Credulity*, 2d ed., revised and corrected, with large additions by the Author, Philadelphia, 1796.

Bartram *Diary:* John Bartram, *Diary, 1765-1766*, ed. Francis Harper, American Philosophical Society, *Transactions*, N.S. 33.1 (1942), 1-55.

Bartram *Report:* William Bartram, *Travels in Georgia and Florida, 1773-74, A Report to Dr. John Fothergill*, American Philosophical Society, *Transactions*, N.S. 33.2 (1943), 123-71.

Bartram *Travels:* William Bartram, *Travels through North and South Carolina, Georgia, East and West Florida* (1791), ed. Francis Harper, New Haven, 1958.

Bates *Papers: The Life and Papers of Frederick Bates*, ed. Thomas M. Marshall, 2 vols., St. Louis, 1926.

Battle of Brooklyn: The Battle of Brooklyn, A Farce . . . Performed at Long-Island (1776), Edinburgh, 1777.

Baxter Manuscripts: Documentary History of the State of Maine Containing The Baxter Manuscripts, ed. James P. Baxter, 24 vols., Portland, 1869-1916. (Baxter's editorship began with vol. 4 [1889].)

Bayard *Journal: The Journal of Martha P. Bayard, London, 1794-1797*, ed. S. Bayard Dod, New York, 1894.

Bayard *Letters: Letters of James A. Bayard*, Historical Society of Delaware, *Papers* 31 (1901).

Bayard *Papers: Papers of James A. Bayard, 1796-1815*, ed. Elizabeth Donnan, Annual Report of the American Historical Association, 1913, 2, Washington, D.C., 1915.

Beauties of Brother Bull-us: The Beauties of Brother Bull-us, by His Loving Sister Bull-a, New York, 1812.

Beecher *Autobiography: Autobiography, Correspondence, etc. of Lyman Beecher*, ed. Charles Beecher, 2 vols., New York, 1864.

Beekman Papers: The Beekman Mercantile Papers, 1746-1799, ed. Philip L. White, 3 vols., New York, 1956.

Beete *Man:* Mr. Beete, *The Man of the Times . . . A Farce*, Charleston, 1797.

Belcher *Papers: The Jonathan Belcher Papers*, Massachusetts Historical Society, *Collections*, 6th ser. 6, 7, (1893-4).

Belknap *Foresters:* (Jeremy Belknap), *The Foresters*, Boston, 1792.

Belknap *History:* Jeremy Belknap, *The History of New Hampshire* (1791-2), 2d ed., 3 vols., Boston, 1813.

Belknap Papers: The [*Jeremy*] *Belknap Papers,* Massachusetts Historical Society, *Collections,* 5th ser. 2, 3 (1877), 6th ser. 4 (1891).

Bentley *Diary: The Diary of William Bentley,* 4 vols., Salem, Mass., 1905-14.

Bernard *Retrospections:* John Bernard, *Retrospections of America, 1797-1811,* ed. Mrs. Bayle Bernard, New York, 1887.

Berrey: Lester V. Berrey and Melvin Van den Bark, *The American Thesaurus of Slang,* New York, 1947.

Beverley *History:* Robert Beverley, *The History and Present State of Virginia* (1705), ed. Louis B. Wright, Chapel Hill, N.C., 1947.

Biddle *Autobiography: Autobiography of Charles Biddle,* ed. J. S. Biddle, Philadelphia, 1883.

Bierce *Travels: Travels in the Southland 1822-1823: The Journal of Lucius Verus Bierce,* ed. G. W. Knepper, Columbus, O., 1966.

Bingham's Maine: William Bingham's Maine Lands, 1790-1820, ed. Frederick S. Allis, Jr., Colonial Society of Massachusetts, *Publications* 36, 37 (1954).

Black *Journal: Journal of William Black* [*1744*], in *PM* 1 (1877), 177-32, 233-49, 404-19, 2 (1878), 40-9.

Blane *Excursion:* (William N. Blane), *An Excursion through the United States and Canada during the Years 1822-23,* London, 1824.

Blockheads: The Blockheads: or, The Affrighted Officers, A Farce, Boston 1776.

Blount Papers: The John Gray Blount Papers, ed. Alice B. Keith and W. H. Masterson, 3 vols., Raleigh, N.C., 1952-65.

Bobin *Letters: Letters of Isaac Bobin, 1718-1730,* New York Colonial Tracts 4, Albany, 1872.

Boucher *Autobiography:* Jonathan Boucher, *Reminiscences of an American Loyalist, 1738-1789,* ed. J. Boucher, Boston, 1925.

Boucher *View:* Jonathan Boucher, *A View of the Causes and Consequences of the American Revolution; in Thirteen Discourses Preached in North America Between the Years 1763 and 1775,* London, 1797.

Boudinot *Journey:* Elias Boudinot, *Journey to Boston in 1809,* ed. M. H. Thomas, Princeton, 1955.

Bowdoin Papers: The Bowdoin and Temple Papers, Massachusetts Historical Society, *Collections,* 6th ser. 9 (1897), 7th ser. 6 (1907).

Bowen *Journals: The Journals of Ashley Bowen* (*1728-1813*) *of Marblehead,* ed. Philip C. F. Smith, Colonial Society of Massachusetts, *Publications* 44, 45 (1973). (Two volumes, paged continuously.)

Bowne *Letters: A Girl's Life Eighty Years Ago; Selections from the Letters of Eliza Southgate Bowne,* ed. Clarence Cook, New York, 1887.

Boyd *Eighteenth Century Tracts: Some Eighteenth Century Tracts Concerning North Carolina,* ed. William K. Boyd, North Carolina Historical Commission, *Publications,* Raleigh, 1927.

Brackenridge *Gazette:* H. H. Brackenridge, *Gazette Publications,* Carlisle, Pa., 1806.

Brackenridge *Journal:* H. M. Brackenridge, *Journal of a Voyage up the River Missouri; Performed in Eighteen Hundred and Eleven,* 2d ed., Baltimore, 1815.

Brackenridge *Modern*: H. H. Brackenridge *Modern Chivalry* (1792-1815), ed. Claude M. Newlin, New York, 1937.

Bibliographical References

Brackenridge *South America:* H. M. Brackenridge, *Voyage to South America . . . in the Years 1817 and 1818,* 2 vols., Baltimore, 1819.

Brackenridge *Views*: H. M. Brackenridge, *Views of Louisiana,* Pittsburgh, 1814.

Bradford *Dialogue:* William Bradford, *A Dialogue or Third Conference* (1652), ed. Charles Deane, Boston, 1870.

Bradford *History*: William Bradford, *History of Plymouth Plantation, 1620-1647* (al656), ed. Worthington C. Ford, 2 vols., Boston, 1912.

Bradstreet *Works: The Works of Anne Bradstreet in Prose and Verse,* ed. John H. Ellis (1867), New York, 1932.

Brainerd *Memoirs:* Jonathan Edwards, *Memoirs of the Rev. David Brainerd,* ed. S. E. Dwight, New Haven, 1822.

Brooke *Emily:* Frances Brooke, *The History of Emily Montague* (1769), ed. Carl F. Klinck, New Canadian Library, 1961.

Brown *Better:* (William H. Brown), *The Better Sort,* Boston, 1789.

Brown *Collection: The Frank C. Brown Collection of North Carolina Folklore,* ed. Newman I. White and Paull F. Baum, 7 vols., Durham, N.C., 1952-64.

Brown *Power*: William H. Brown, *The Power of Sympathy* (1789), ed. Milton Ellis, 2 vols., Facsimile Text Society, New York, 1937.

Buckingham *Specimens:* Joseph T. Buckingham, *Specimens of Newspaper Literature,* 2 vols., Boston, 1850.

Bulger Papers: *The Bulger Papers,* ed. R. G. Thwaites, Wisconsin Historical Collections 13, Madison, 1895.

Bulkeley *People's Right*: Gershom Bulkeley, *The People's Right to Election* (1689) in Connecticut Historical Society, *Collections* 1 (1860), 57-81.

Bulkeley *Will*: Gershom Bulkeley, *Will and Doom* (1692), ed. Charles J. Hoadly, Connecticut Historical Society, *Collections* 3 (1895), 79-269.

Burd *Letters*: *Selections from Letters Written by Edward Burd, 1763-1828,* ed. Lewis B. Walker, Pottsville, Pa., 1899.

Burnett *Letters*: Edmund C. Burnett, ed., *Letters of Members of the Continental Congress,* I, Washington, D.C., 1921.

Burr *Correspondence: Correspondence of Aaron Burr and his Daughter Theodosia,* ed. Mark Van Doren, New York, 1929.

Burr *Journal: The Private Journal of Aaron Burr,* ?ed. W. K. Bixby, 2 vols., Rochester, N.Y., 1903.

Burr *Memoirs*: Matthew L. Davis, *Memoirs of Aaron Burr,* 2 vols., New York, 1836, 1837. (D. was B.'s literary executor and boasts that he destroyed all letters to or from Burr which could harm any lady's reputation—which apparently included nearly all the many letters from ladies which B. had preserved.)

Burroughs *Memoirs: Memoirs of the Notorious Stephen Burroughs of New Hampshire* (1811), with a Preface by Robert Frost, London, 1924.

Byrd *Another Secret Diary: Another Secret Diary of William Byrd of Westover, 1739-1741, with Letters and Literary Exercises, 1696-1726,* ed. Maude H. Woodfin, Richmond, Va., 1942.

Byrd *Dividing Line*: William Byrd, *Histories of the Dividing Line Betwixt Virginia and North Carolina,* ed. W. K. Boyd, Raleigh, N.C., 1929.

Byrd *Journey:* William Byrd, *A Journey to the Land of Eden* (1733) *and Other Papers,* ed. Mark Van Doren, New York, 1928.

Byrd *London Diary:* William Byrd, *The London Diary (1717-1721) and Other Writings*, ed. Louis B. Wright and Marion Tinling, New York, 1958.

Byrd *Progress:* W. Byrd, *A Progress to the Mines* (1732), in *Journey* 314-67.

Byrd *Secret Diary: The Secret Diary of William Byrd of Westover, 1709-1712*, ed. Louis B. Wright and Marion Tinling, Richmond, Va., 1941.

Cabot Family: L. Vernon Briggs, *History and Genealogy of the Cabot Family, 1475-1927*, 2 vols., Boston, 1927.

Cabot *Letters:* Henry Cabot Lodge, *Life and Letters of George Cabot*, Boston, 1877.

Calef *More Wonders:* Robert Calef, *More Wonders of the Invisible World* (1700), Salem, Mass., 1823.

Callender *Annual Register 1796:* (James T. Callender), *The American Annual Register, or, Historical Memoirs of the United States for the Year 1796*, Philadelphia, 1797.

Callender *Political Register:* James T. Callender, *The Political Register; or, Proceedings in the Session of Congress, Commencing November 3d, 1794, and Ending March 3d, 1795*, Philadelphia, 1795.

Campbell *Travels:* Patrick Campbell, *Travels in the Interior Inhabited Parts of North America in the Years 1791 and 1792* (1793), ed. H. H. Langton, Champlain Society, *Publications* 23, Toronto, 1937.

Carey *Plumb:* Matthew Carey, *A Plumb Pudding for . . . Peter Porcupine*, Philadelphia, 1799.

Carey *Porcupiniad:* Matthew Carey, *The Porcupiniad*, 2d ed., Philadelphia, 1799. (Canto I has separate pagination.)

Carroll *Copy-Book:* "A Lost Copy-Book of Charles Carroll of Carrolton," ed. J. G. D. Paul, in *MHM* 32(1937), 193-225.

Carroll *Correspondence:* Kate M. Rowland, *The Life of Charles Carroll of Carrolton . . . with his Correspondence and Public Papers*, 2 vols., New York, 1898.

Carter *Diary: The Diary of Colonel Landon Carter of Sabine Hall, 1752-1778*, ed. Jack P. Greene, 2 vols., Charlottesville, Va., 1965.

Carter *Letters: Letters of Robert Carter, 1720-1727*, ed. Louis B. Wright, San Marino, Cal., 1940.

Carver *Travels:* Jonathan Carver, *Travels Through the Interior Parts of North America in the Years 1766, 1767, and 1768*, London, 1778.

Cary Letters: The Cary Letters, ed. Caroline Gardiner Curtis, Cambridge, Mass., 1891.

Case *Poems:* (Wheeler Case), *Poems*, New Haven, 1778.

Cathcart *Journal:* "The Diplomatic Journal and Letter Book of James Leander Cathcart, 1788-1796," American Antiquarian Society, *Proceedings*, N.S. 64 (1954), 304-436.

Chalkley: *A Collection of the Works of that Ancient, Faithful Servant of Jesus Christ, Thomas Chalkley*, 4th ed., London, 1766. (All references to Chalkley's various works are to this volume. The dates for *Journal* entries are suspect, as C. seems to have revised and rewritten them.)

Champion: Selwyn G. Champion, *Racial Proverbs: A Selection of the World's Proverbs Arranged Linguistically*, New York, 1938.

Chandler *Friendly Address:* (Thomas B. Chandler), *A Friendly Address to All Reasonable Americans*, New York, 1774.

Bibliographical References

Chester *Federalism*: (Leonard Chester), *Federalism Triumphant in the Steady Habits of Connecticut Alone . . . A Comic Opera or, Political Farce*, New York, 1802.

Chester *Papers:* Mrs. Dunbar Rowland, *Peter Chester*, Mississippi Historical Society, *Publications* 5 (1925), 17-183.

Chipman *Writings*: Daniel Chipman, *The Life of the Hon. Nathaniel Chipman*, Boston, 1846.

Church *History*: Benjamin Church, *The History of King Philip's War* (1716), ed. H. M. Dexter, 2 vols., Boston, 1865-7.

Churchman *Account: An Account of the Gospel Labours . . . of . . . John Churchman* (died 1775), Philadelphia, 1780.

Claiborne *Letter Books: Official Letter Books of W. C. C. Claiborne, 1801-1816*, ed. Dunbar Rowland, 6 vols., Jackson, Miss., 1917.

Clark *Letters: The Letters of Willis Gaylord Clark and Lewis Gaylord Clark*, ed. Leslie W. Dunlap, New York, 1940.

Clay *Letters: Letters of Joseph Clay, Merchant of Savannah, 1776-1793*, Georgia Historical Society, *Collections* 8 (1913).

Clay *Papers: The Papers of Henry Clay*, ed. James F. Hopkins, 1 (1959)-, Lexington, Ky.

Claypoole *Letter Book: James Claypoole's Letter Book, London and Philadelphia, 1681-1684*, ed. Marion Balderston, San Marino, Cal., 1967.

Clayton *Writings: The Reverend John Clayton . . . His Scientific Writings and Other Related Papers*, ed. Edmund and D. S. Berkeley, Charlottesville, Va., 1965.

Cleveland *Letters: Voyages of a Merchant Navigator . . . Compiled from the Journals and Letters of . . . Richard J. Cleveland*, ed. H. W. S. Cleveland, New York, 1886.

Clifford *Letters*: Philip G. Clifford, *Nathan Clifford, Democrat (1803-1881)*, New York, 1922.

Clinton Papers: Public Papers of George Clinton, First Governor of New York, 1777-1795, 1801-1804, ed. Hugh Hastings, 9 vols., New York and Albany, 1899-1911.

Clubb *Journal:* Stephen Clubb, *A Journal Containing an Account of the Wrongs . . . Experienced by Americans in France* (Boston, 1809), *Magazine of History*, Extra Number 51, 1916.

Cobbett *Letters: Letters from William Cobbett to Edward Thornton*, ed. G. D. H. Cole, London, 1937.

Cobbett *Porcupine*: William Cobbett, *Porcupine's Works*, 12 vols., London, 1801.

Cobbett *Year's*: William Cobbett, *A Year's Residence in the United States of America* (1819), Carbondale, Ill., 1964.

Codman Letters: An Appendix to the Exposition of the Pretended Claims of William Vans on the Estate of John Codman, Boston, 1837.

Coffin *Memoir*: Cyrus Woodman, *The Memoir and Journals of Rev. Paul Coffin, D.D.*, Portland, Maine, 1855.

Coke *Journals: Extracts of the Journals of the Rev. Dr. [Thomas] Coke's Five Visits to America*, London, 1793.

Colby *Life: The Life, Experience, and Travels, of John Colby, Preacher of the Gospel, Written by Himself* (1817), Lowell, Mass., 1838.

Colcord: Joanna C. Colcord, *Sea Language Comes Ashore*, New York, 1945.

Colden Letters: The Letters and Papers of Cadwallader Colden, 9 vols., New-York Historical Society, *Collections* 50-68 (1917-37).

Colonial Currency: Colonial Currency Reprints, 1682-1751, ed. Andrew M. Davis, 4 vols., Publications of the Prince Society 32-35, Boston, 1910-11.

Columbia: Voyages of the "Columbia" to the Northwest Coast, 1787-1790 and 1790-1793, ed. Frederic W. Howay, Massachusetts Historical Society, *Collections* 79 (1941).

Columbian Magazine: The Columbian Magazine I (1786)-IV (1790) — thereafter called *The Universal Asylum and Columbian Magazine.*

Commerce of Rhode Island: Commerce of Rhode Island, 1726-1800, Massachusetts Historical Society, *Collections*, 7th ser. 9, 10 (1914-5).

Connecticut Historical Collections: Collections of the Connecticut Historical Society, 1 (1860).

Connecticut Vindicated: Their Majesties Colony of Connecticut Vindicated (Boston, 1694), in *Connecticut Historical Collections* 83-130.

Cook *Bacon:* Ebenezer Cook, *The History of Colonel Nathaniel Bacon's Rebellion* in "The Maryland Muse of Ebenezer Cooke," by Lawrence C. Wroth, American Antiquarian Society, *Proceedings* N.S. 44 (1934), 309-26.

Cook *Sot-Weed*: Ebenezer Cook, *The Sot-Weed Factor*, London, 1708 (reprinted ?New York, 1865).

Cooper *Letters: The Letters and Journals of James Fenimore Cooper,* ed. James F. Beard, 6 vols., Cambridge, Mass., 1960-8.

Copley *Letters: Letters and Papers of John Singleton Copley and Henry Pelham, 1739-1776*, Massachusetts Historical Society, *Collections* 71 (1914).

Cotgrave: Randle Cotgrave, *A Dictionarie of the French and English Tongues* (London, 1611), ed. William S. Woods, Columbia, S.C., 1950.

Cottle *Life*: "The Life of Elder Jabez Cottle (1747-1820): A Spiritual Autobiography in Verse," ed. W. G. McLoughlin, *New England Quarterly* 38 (1965), 375-86.

Cresswell *Journal*: *The Journal of Nicholas Cresswell, 1774-1777*, New York, 1924.

Croswell *New World:* Joseph Croswell, *A New World Planted . . . An Historical Drama*, Boston, 1802.

Cuming *Sketches*: Fortescue Cuming, *Sketches of a Tour to the Western Country (1807-09)* (1810), ed. Reuben G. Thwaites, Cleveland, 1904.

Curwen *Journal: The Journal of Samuel Curwen, Loyalist*, ed. Andrew Oliver, 2 vols., Cambridge, Mass., 1972.

Curwen *Journal and Letters: Journal and Letters of the Late Samuel Curwen*, ed. G. A. Ward, 2d ed., London, 1844.

Custis *Letters*: "The Correspondence of Peter Collinson and John Custis," ed. E. G. Swam, American Antiquarian Society, *Proceedings*, N.S. 58 (1948), 37-108.

Cutler *Life: Life, Journals and Correspondence of Rev. Manasseh Cutler, LL.D.*, by W. P. Cutler and J. P. Cutler, 2 vols., Cincinnati, 1888.

DA: *A Dictionary of Americanisms*, ed. Mitford M. Mathews, 2 vols., Chicago, 1951.

Dalton *Travels*: Wm. Dalton, *Travels in the United States of America and Parts of Upper Canada* (1819-20), Appleby, 1821.

Danforth *Poems*: "The Poetry of John Danforth" (1660-1730), by Thomas A. Ryan, American Antiquarian Society, *Proceedings*, N.S. 78 (1969), 129-93.

Davenport *Letters: Letters of John Davenport,* ed. Isabel M. Calder, New Haven, 1937.

David *Letters: A Rhode Island Chaplain in the Revolution, Letters of Ebenezer David,* ed. J. D. Black and W. G. Roelker, Providence, 1949.

Bibliographical References

Davis *Colonial Virginia Satirist:* Richard B. Davis, ed., *The Colonial Virginia Satirist,* American Philosophical Society, *Transactions,* N.S. 57 (part 1), 1967.

Davis *Travels:* John Davis, *Travels of Four Years and a Half in the United States of America; During 1798, 1799, 1800, 1801, and 1802,* London, 1803.

Deane Brothers Papers: The Deane Papers: Correspondence Between Silas Deane, His Brothers, and Their Business and Political Associates, 1771-1795, Connecticut Historical Society, *Collections* 23 (1930).

Deane Correspondence: Correspondence of Silas Deane, Delegate to the First and Second Congress at Philadelphia, 1774-1776, Connecticut Historical Society, *Collections* 2 (1870).

Deane *Papers: The Deane Papers, 1774-1790,* 5 vols., New-York Historical Society, *Collections* (1886-91).

De Brahm *Report:* De Brahm's *Report,* ed. Louis De Vorsey, Jr., Columbia, S.C., 1971.

Delano *Narrative:* Amasa Delano, *A Narrative of Voyages and Travels in the Northern and Southern Hemispheres,* Boston, 1817.

Dennie *Lay Preacher:* Joseph Dennie, *The Lay Preacher* (1795-1801), ed. Milton Ellis, Scholars' Facsimiles and Reprints, New York, 1943.

Dennie *Letters: The Letters of Joseph Dennie, 1768-1812,* ed. Laura G. Pedder, University of Maine Studies, 2d ser. 36, Orono, Me., 1936.

Denny *Journal: Military Journal of Major Ebenezer Denny,* Historical Society of Pennsylvania, *Memoirs* 7 (1860), 237-477.

DHR: The Dedham Historical Register, Dedham, Mass., 1 (1890)-14(1903).

Dickinson *Journal:* Jonathan Dickinson, *Journal of God's Protecting Providence* (1697), ed. E. W. and Charles M. Andrews, New Haven, 1945.

Dickinson *Letters:* (John Dickinson), *Letters from a Farmer in Pennsylvania,* Philadelphia, 1768.

Dickinson *Writings: The Writings of John Dickinson, vol 1: Political Writings, 1764-1777,* ed. Paul L. Ford, Historical Society of Pennsylvania, *Memoirs* 14 (1895). (No more published.)

Digges *Adventures:* (Thomas A. Digges), *Adventures of Alonzo,* 2 vols., London, 1775, Scholars' Facsimiles and Reprints, New York, 1943.

Doddridge *Logan:* Joseph Doddridge, *Logan* (1823) . . . [and] *The Dialogue of the Backwoodsman and the Dandy* (1821), Cincinnati, 1868.

Doddridge *Notes:* Joseph Doddridge, *Notes on the Settlement and Indian Wars of the Western Parts of Virginia and Pennsylvania from 1763 to 1783* (1824), ed. J. S. Ritenour and W. T. Lindsey, Pittsburgh, 1912.

Dorr *Letters:* "Letters of Sullivan Dorr," ed. Howard Corning, Massachusetts Historical Society, *Proceedings* 67 (1841-4), 178-364.

Dow *Journal:* Lorenzo Dow, *History of Cosmopolite, or The Four Volumes of Lorenzo Dow's Journal,* 5th ed., Wheeling, W. Va., 1848.

Drake *Works: The Life and Works of Joseph Rodman Drake,* ed. Frank L. Pleadwell, Boston, 1935.

Drinker *Journal: Extracts from the Journal of Elizabeth Drinker, from 1759-1807,* ed. Henry D. Biddle, Philadelphia, 1889.

Drinker *Not So Long Ago:* Cecil K. Drinker, *Not So Long Ago,* New York, 1967.

(Based on selections from Elizabeth Drinker's journal [see above] and family letters.)

Duane *Colombia:* Wm. Duane, *A Visit to Colombia in the Years 1822 and 1823,* Philadelphia, 1826.

Dunlap *Darby's Return:* William Dunlap, *Darby's Return* (1789), in Meserve and Reardon, 107-13.

Dunlap *Diary: Diary of William Dunlap* (*1766-1839*), ed. Dorothy C. Barck, 3 vols., New-York Historical Society, *Collections* 62-4 (1930).

Dunlap *Father:* William Dunlap, *The Father or American Shandyism* (1789), ed. T. J. McKee, New York, 1887.

Dunton *Letters*: John Dunton, *Letters from New-England*, Publications of the Prince Society 4, Boston, 1867.

Dunwoody: H. H. C. Dunwoody, *Weather Proverbs*, Washington, D.C., 1883.

Durand *Life*: James Durand, *An Able Seaman of 1812* (1820), ed. G. S. Brooks, New Haven, 1926.

Durang *Memoir: The Memoir of John Durang, American Actor, 1785-1816*, ed. Alan S. Downer, Pittsburgh, 1966.

Dwight *Journey*: Margaret Van Horn Dwight (Bell), *A Journey to Ohio in 1810,* ed. Max Farrand, New Haven, 1913.

Eaton *Life*: (Charles Prentiss), *The Life of the Late Gen. William Eaton*, Brookfield, Mass., 1813.

Echo: The Echo, with Other Poems, New York, 1807.

Eddis *Letters:* William Eddis, *Letters from America*, ed. Aubrey C. Land, Cambridge, Mass., 1969.

Eliot *Essays:* Jared Eliot, *Essays upon Field Husbandry in New England, and Other Papers, 1748-1762,* ed. H. J. Carman and R. G. Tugwell, New York, 1934.

Eliot *Letters: Letters from Andrew Eliot to Thomas Hollis,* Massachusetts Historical Society, *Collections*, 4th ser. 4 (1858), 398-461.

Ellicott *Journal: The Journal of Andrew Ellicott* (1803), Chicago, 1962.

Emerald: The Emerald, 1, 2 and N.S. 1, Boston 1806-08. (Earlier *The Boston Magazine*.)

Emigrant's Guide: The Emigrant's Guide; or, a Picture of America . . . by an Old Scene Painter, London, 1816.

Evans *Pedestrious:* Estwick Evans, *A Pedestrious Tour of Four Thousand Miles . . . During the Winter and Spring of 1818* (1819), ed. Reuben G. Thwaites, Cleveland, 1904.

Evans *Poems*: Nathaniel Evans, *Poems on Several Occasions* (1772), ed. Lewis Leary, New York, 1970.

Fairservice *Plain Dealing:* James Fairservice, *Plain Dealing: Or, The Proud Main fairly dealt with* (Boston, 1750), in *Magazine of History*, Extra Number 66 (1919).

Fanning *Narrative: Fanning's Narrative, Being the Memoirs of Nathaniel Fanning, An Officer of the Revolutionary Navy, 1778-1784* (1806), ed. John S. Barnes, Naval History Society, *Publications* 2 (1912). (Apparently abridged and expurgated.)

Farmers' Museum: The Spirit of the Farmers' Museum and Lay Preacher's Gazette, Walpole, N.H., 1801.

Bibliographical References

Faux *Memorable Days:* W. Faux, *Memorable Days in America* (1818-20), ed. Reuben G. Thwaites, 2 vols., Cleveland, 1905.

Fearon *Sketches*: Henry B. Fearon, *Sketches of America*, London, 1818.

Fessenden *Ladies Monitor*: Thomas G. Fessenden, *The Ladies Monitor,* Bellows Falls, Vt., 1818.

Fessenden *Modern Philosopher*: (Thomas G. Fessenden), *The Modern Philosopher: or Terrible Tractoration . . . by Christopher Caustick*, 2d American ed., Philadelphia, 1806.

Fessenden *Pills*: (T. G. Fessenden), *Pills, Poetical, Political and Philosophical . . . By Peter Pepper-Box*, Philadelphia, 1809.

Fidfaddy *Adventures*: Frederick Augustus Fidfaddy (pseud.), *The Adventures of Uncle Sam in Search after his Lost Honor*, Middletown, Conn., 1816.

Fitch *New-York Diary:* The *New-York Diary of Lieutenant Jabez Fitch* (1776-7), ed. W. H. W. Sabine, New York, 1954.

Fitch Papers: The Fitch Papers: Correspondence and Documents During Thomas Fitch's Governorship of the Colony of Connecticut, 1754-1766, Connecticut Historical Society, *Collections* 17, 18 (1918, 1920).

Fithian *Journal:* Philip Vickers Fithian, *Journal, 1775-1776*, ed. R. G. Albion and L. Dodson, Princeton, 1934.

Fithian *Journal and Letters: Journal and Letters of Philip Vickers Fithian, 1733-1774*, ed. H. D. Farish, Williamsburg, Va., 1945.

Fitzhugh *Letters: William Fitzhugh and His Chesapeake World, 1676-1701*, ed. Richard B. Davis, Virginia Historical Society, *Documents* 3, Chapel Hill, 1963.

Fletcher *Letters: The Letters of Elijah Fletcher*, ed. Martha von Briesen, Charlottesville, Va., 1965.

Fletcher *Narrative: The Narrative of Ebenezer Fletcher* (1813), 4th ed., New Ipswich, N.H., 1827 (reprinted 1866, 1970).

Flint *Letters*: James Flint, *Letters from America* (1818-20), ed. Reuben G. Thwaites, Cleveland, 1904.

Flint *Recollections:* Timothy Flint, *Recollections of the Last Ten Years*, Boston, 1826.

Floy *Diary: The Diary of Michael Floy, Jr. . . . 1833-1837*, ed. Richard A. E. Brooks, New Haven, 1941.

Force *Tracts:* Peter Force, *Tracts . . . Relating to the . . . Colonies in North America*, 4 vols., Washington, D.C., 1836-46.

Foster *Coquette*: Hannah W. Foster, *The Coquette* (1797), ed. Herbert R. Brown, New York, 1939.

Foster *Jeffersonian America*: Augustus J. Foster, *Jeffersonian America: Notes on the United States of America Collected in the Years 1805-6-7 and 11-12*, ed. R. B. Davis, San Marino, Cal., 1954.

Franklin *Drinkers: Drinkers Dictionary*, in *Papers* (below), 2.173-7.

Franklin *Papers: The Papers of Benjamin Franklin*, ed. Leonard W. Labaree et al., New Haven 1(1959)-.

Franklin *PR*: Franklin *Poor Richard*, in *Papers* as above.

Franklin *Writings: The Writings of Benjamin Franklin*, ed. Albert H. Smyth, 10 vols., New York, 1905-7.

Franklin *WW: The Way to Wealth or Poor Richard Improved* (1758), in *Papers* 7.340-50.

Franklin-Mecom: The Letters of Benjamin Franklin and Jane Mecom, ed. Carl Van Doren, American Philosophical Society, *Memoirs* 27 (1950).

Fraser *Letters and Journals: The Letters and Journals of Simon Fraser, 1806-1808*, ed. W. Kaye Lamb, Toronto, 1960.

Freneau *Last Poems: The Last Poems of Philip Freneau*, ed. Lewis Leary, New Brunswick, N.J., 1945.

Freneau *Poems: The Poems of Philip Freneau*, ed. Fred L. Pattee, 3 vols., Princeton, 1902-7.

Freneau *Poems(1786): The Poems of Philip Freneau*, Philadelphia, 1786.

Freneau *Poems(1795): Poems . . . by Philip Freneau*, Monmouth, N.J., 1795.

Freneau *Poems(1809)*: Philip Freneau, *Poems*, 2 vols., Philadelphia, 1809.

Freneau *Poems(1815): A Collection of Poems . . . by Philip Freneau*, 2 vols., New York, 1815.

Freneau *Prose: The Prose of Philip Freneau*, ed. Philip M. Marsh, New Brunswick, N.J., 1955.

Fudge Family: The Fudge Family in Washington, edited by Harry Nimrod, Baltimore, 1820.

G. C. *Little Looking Glass*: G. C., *A Little Looking-Glass for the Times* (1764), in *Magazine of History*, Extra Number 6 (1913), 22, 69-93.

Gadsden *Writings: The Writings of Christopher Gadsden, 1764-1805*, ed, Richard Walsh, Columbia, S.C., 1966.

Gallacher *Franklin's Way to Wealth*: Stuart A. Gallacher, "Franklin's *Way to Wealth*: A Florilegium of Proverbs and Wise Sayings," *Journal of English and Germanic Philology* 48(1949), 229-51.

Gallatin *Diary: The Diary of James Gallatin (1813-1827)*, ed. Count Gallatin, new ed., New York, 1916.

Galloway *Diary*: Grace G. Galloway, *Diary*, PM 55(1931), 36-94, 58(1934), 152-89.

Gass *Journal*: Patrick Gass, *Journal of the Lewis and Clark Expeditions* (1807), Chicago, 1904.

Gates *Five Fur Traders*: Charles M. Gates, ed., *Five Fur Traders of the Northwest*, Minneapolis, 1933.

Georgia Records: The Colonial Records of the State of Georgia, ed. Allen D. Candler et. al., *Original Papers, 1735-1752*, 21-6 (1910-16).

Gerry *Diary: The Diary of Elbridge Gerry, Jr.* (1803), ed. Claude G. Bowers, New York, 1927.

Gerry *Letters*: James T. Austin, *The Life of Elbridge Gerry*, 2 vols., Boston, 1828-9.

Gibbes: Robert W. Gibbes, *Documentary History of the American Revolution*, 3 vols. (though not so numbered), Columbia, S.C. (1852), New York (1855, 1857).

Gibbs *Memoirs*: George Gibbs, *Memoirs of the Administration of Washington and John Adams, ed. from the Papers of Oliver Wolcott*, 2 vols., New York, 1846.

Gordon *Letters*: "Letters of the Reverend William Gordon, Historian of the American Revolution," Massachusetts Historical Society, *Proceedings* 63 (1929-30), 303-613.

Graham *Vermont*: J. A. Graham, *A Descriptive Sketch of the Present State of Vermont*, London, 1797.

Grant *Memoirs*: Anne Grant, *Memoirs of an American Lady* (1808), ed. J. G. Wilson, New York, 1909.

Bibliographical References

Graydon *Memoirs:* (Alexander Graydon), *Memoirs of a Life, Chiefly Passed in Pennsylvania, within the Last Sixty Years* (1811), Edinburgh, 1822.

Griffith *Journal: The Journal of the Life, Travels, and Labours . . . of John Griffith,* London, 1779.

Gyles *Memoirs: Memoirs of Odd Adventures . . . In the Captivity of John Gyles, Esq., . . . Written by Himself,* Boston, 1736.

Habersham *Letters: The Letters of Hon. James Habersham,* Georgia Historical Society, *Collections* 6 (1904).

Hall *Travels:* Francis Hall, *Travels in Canada and the United States in 1816 and 1817,* Boston, 1818.

Hamilton *Itinerarium: Gentleman's Progress: The Itinerarium of Dr. Alexander Hamilton, 1744,* ed. Carl Breidenbaugh, Chapel Hill, N.C., 1948.

Hamilton *Law Practice: The Law Practice of Alexander Hamilton,* ed. Julius Goebel, Jr., 2 vols., New York, 1964, 1969.

Hamilton *Papers: The Papers of Alexander Hamilton,* ed. Harold C. Syrett and J. E. Cooke, New York, 1 (1961)-.

Hamilton *Works: The Works of Alexander Hamilton,* ed. Henry Cabot Lodge, 12 vols., New York, 1904.

Hammond *Leah:* John Hammond, *Leah and Rachel,* London, 1656.

Harmon *Sixteen Years: Sixteen Years in the Indian Country; The Journal of Daniel W. Harmon, 1800-1816,* ed. W. Kaye Lamb, Toronto, 1957.

Harris *Letter: A Rhode Islander Reports on King Philip's War; The Second William Harris Letter of August, 1676,* ed. Douglas E. Leach, Providence, 1963.

Harrower *Journal: The Journal of John Harrower, An Indentured Servant in the Colony of Virginia, 1773-1776,* ed. Edward M. Riley, Williamsburg, 1963.

Harvard College Rebellion: "The Great Rebellion in Harvard College," by Samuel E. Morison, Colonial Society of Massachusetts, *Transactions* 27 (1927-30), 54-112.

Hawkins *Letters: Letters of Benjamin Hawkins, 1796-1806,* Georgia Historical Society, *Collections* 9 (1916).

Hearne *Journey:* Samuel Hearne, *A Journey from Prince of Wales's Fort in Hudson's Bay to the Northern Ocean, in the Years 1769, 1770, 1771, and 1772* (1795), ed. J. B. Tyrrell, Champlain Society, Toronto, 1911.

Heath *Memoirs: Memoirs of Major-General (William) Heath . . . Written by Himself,* Boston, 1798.

Heath Papers: The Heath Papers, 3 vols., Massachusetts Historical Society, *Collections,* 5th ser. 4, 7th ser. 4, 5 (1878-1904).

Hempstead *Diary: Diary of Joshua Hempstead of New London, Connecticut, 1711-1758,* New London Historical Society, *Collections* 1 (1901).

Henry *Account:* John J. Henry, *An Accurate and Interesting Account of the . . . Campaign Against Quebec in 1775,* Lancaster, Pa., 1812.

Henry *Life: Patrick Henry: Life, Correspondence and Speeches,* by William W. Henry, 3 vols., New York, 1891.

Henry *Travels:* Alexander Henry, *Travels and Adventures in Canada and the Indian Territories Between the Years 1760 and 1776* (1809), ed. James Bain, Boston, 1901.

Hinckley Papers: The Hinckley Papers, Massachusetts Historical Society, *Collections,* 4th ser. 5 (1861).

Hislop: Alexander Hislop, *The Proverbs of Scotland,* Edinburgh, 1868.

Hitchcock *Poetical Dictionary:* David Hitchcock, *A Poetical Dictionary; or Popular Terms Illustrated in Rhyme,* Lenox, Mass., 1808.

Hitchcock *Social*: David Hitchcock, *The Social Monitor* (1812), 2d ed., New York, 1814.

Hitchcock *Works*: David Hitchcock, *Poetical Works,* Boston, 1806.

Hodgkins *Letters*: Herbert T. Wade and R. A. Lively, *This Glorious Cause . . . The Adventures of Two Company Officers in Washington's Army,* Princeton, 1958, 167-245.

Hodgson *Letters*: Adam Hodgson, *Letters from North America*, 2 vols., London, 1824.

Holcombe *First Fruits:* Henry Holcombe, *The First Fruits, In a Series of Letters*, Philadelphia, 1812.

Hone *Diary:* *The Diary of Philip Hone, 1828-1851,* ed. Allan Nevins, 2 vols., New York, 1927.

Honyman *Journal: Colonial Panorama 1775: Dr. Robert Honyman's Journal,* ed. Philip Padelford, San Marino, Cal., 1939.

Hopkinson *Miscellaneous Essays*: Francis Hopkinson, *The Miscellaneous Essays and Occasional Writings,* 3 vols., Philadelphia, 1792.

Howison *Sketches*: John Howison, *Sketches of Upper Canada,* Edinburgh, 1921 (reprinted 1965).

Hubbard *Indian*: William Hubbard, *The History of the Indian Wars in New England* (1677), ed. Samuel G. Drake, 2 vols., Roxbury, Mass., 1865.

Hubbard *New England:* William Hubbard, *A General History of New England from the Discovery to MDCLXXX,* 2d ed., Boston, 1848 (1878).

Hull *Diary: Diary of John Hull* in *Archæologia Americana*, American Antiquarian Society, *Transactions and Collections* 3 (1857), 141-250.

Humphreys *Works: The Miscellaneous Works of David Humphreys* (1804), ed. William K. Bottorff, Scholars' Facsimiles and Reprints, Gainesville, Fla., 1968.

Humphreys *Yankey*: (David Humphreys), *The Yankey in England,* n.p. (?Boston, 1815).

Hunter *Androboros*: Robert Hunter, *Androboros* (1714), in Meserve and Reardon, 5-39.

Hunter *Quebec: Quebec to Carolina in 1785-1786, Being the Travel Diary . . . of Robert Hunter, Jr., a Young Merchant of London,* ed. Louis B. Wright and Marion Tinling, San Marino, Cal., 1943.

Huntington *Papers: Huntington Papers. Correspondence of the Brothers Joshua and Jedediah Huntington During the Period of the American Revolution,* Connecticut Historical Society, *Collections* 20 (1923).

Hutchinson *Diary: The Diary and Letters of . . . Thomas Hutchinson, Esq.,* compiled by Peter O. Hutchinson, 2 vols., London, 1883, 1886.

Hutchinson *History*: Thomas Hutchinson, *The History of the Colony and Province of Massachusetts Bay,* ed. Lawrence S. Mayo, 3 vols., Cambridge, Mass., 1936.

Hutchinson *Papers: The Thomas Hutchinson Papers,* Publications of the Prince Society 1, 2, Albany, 1865 (reprinted 1967).

Hyamson: Albert M. Hyamson, *A Dictionary of English Phrases,* London, 1922.

Independent Reflector: The Independent Reflector . . . by William Livingston and

Others, ed. Milton M. Klein, Cambridge, Mass., 1963.

Ingles *Reply:* Mungo Ingles, *A Modest Reply to Mr. Commissary Blair's Answer* (1705), *VHM* 9(1901), 18-29, 152-62.

Ingraham *Journal:* John Ingraham, *Journal of the Brigantine Hope on a Voyage to the Northwest Coast of North America, 1790-92* (1793), ed. Mark D. Kaplanoff, Barre, Mass., 1971.

Innes (James) and his Brothers: Jane Carson, *James Innes and his Brothers of the F.H.C.,* Charlottesville, Va., 1965.

Iredell *Correspondence:* Life and Correspondence of James Iredell, by Griffith J. McRee, 2 vols., New York, 1857-8.

Irving *Corrector:* Washington Irving, *Contributions to The Corrector* (1804), ed. Martin Roth, Minneapolis, 1968.

Irving *History:* Washington Irving, *A History of New York . . . by Diedrich Knickerbocker* (1809), 3d ed., 2 vols., Philadelphia, 1819.

Irving *Jonathan:* Washington Irving, *Letters of Jonathan Oldstyle,* ed. Stanley T. Williams, New York, 1941.

Irving *Journals:* Washington Irving, *Journals and Notebooks I* (1803-1806), ed. Nathalia Wright, Madison, Wis., 1969.

Irving *Journals (Trent):* The Journals of Washington Irving, 1815-1842, ed. W. P. Trent and G. S. Hellman, 3 vols., Boston, 1919.

Irving(P) *Journals: Peter Irving's Journals,* ed. L. B. Beach et al., New York, 1943.

Irving *Sketch Book:* Washington Irving, *The Sketch Book of Geoffrey Crayon, Gent.* (1819-20), rev. ed., 1848, *Works,* Knickerbocker Edition, 16.

Izard *Correspondence: Correspondence of Mr. Ralph Izard of South Carolina,* New York, 1844. (Vol. 1 only appeared.)

J. W. *Letter:* J. W., *Letter from New England* (1682), in *Boston in 1682 and 1699,* reprinted by G. P. Winship, Providence, 1905.

Jackson *Correspondence: Correspondence of Andrew Jackson,* ed. John S. Bassett, 6 vols., Washington, D.C., 1926-33.

Jackson *Papers: The Papers of James Jackson, 1781-1798,* ed. Lilla M. Hawes, Georgia Historical Society, *Collections* 11 (1955).

Jacksons and Lees: The Jacksons and the Lees, Two Generations of Massachusetts Merchants, 1765-1844, ed. Kenneth W. Porter, 2 vols., Cambridge, Mass., 1937.

James *Three Visitors:* Sydney V. James, Jr., *Three Visitors to Early Plymouth,* Plimoth Plantation, Mass., 1963.

Janson *Stranger:* Charles W. Janson, *The Stranger in America,* London, 1807.

Jantz: Harold S. Jantz, *The First Century of American Verse,* New York, 1962. (Orig. publ. in American Antiquarian Society, *Proceedings,* N.S. 53 [1943], 219-508.)

Jay *Correspondence: The Correspondence and Public Papers of John Jay,* ed. H. P. Johnston, 4 vols., New York, 1890-3.

Jefferson *Family Letters: The Family Letters of Thomas Jefferson,* ed. Edwin M. Betts and J. A. Bear, Jr., Columbia, Mo., 1966.

Jefferson *Notes:* Thomas Jefferson, *Notes on the State of Virginia* (1781-2), ed. William Peden, Chapel Hill, N.C., 1955.

Jefferson *Papers: The Papers of Thomas Jefferson,* ed. Julian P. Boyd et al., 1 (1950)-, Princeton.

Jefferson *Writings: The Writings of Thomas Jefferson,* ed. Albert E. Bergh, 20 vols., Washington, 1907.

Johnson Papers: The Papers of Sir William Johnson, ed. James Sullivan et al., 14 vols., Albany, N.Y., 1921-65.

Johnson *Wonder-Working:* Edward Johnson, *Wonder-Working Providence of Sions Saviour in New England* (1654), ed. W. F. Poole, Andover, Mass., 1867.

Johnson *Writings: Samuel Johnson, President of King's College: His Career and Writings,* ed. Herbert and C. Schneider, 4 vols., New York, 1929.

Johnston *Papers: Carolina Chronicle, The Papers of Commissary Gideon Johnston, 1707-1716,* ed. Frank J. Klingbery, Berkeley, Cal., 1946.

Jones: Hugh P. Jones, ed., *Dictionary of Foreign Phrases and Classical Quotations,* Edinburgh, 1923.

Jones *History*: Thomas Jones, *History of New York During the Revolutionary War,* ed. Edward F. De Lancey, 2 vols., New York, 1879.

Jones *Journal*: David Jones, *A Journal of Two Visits Made to Some Nations of Indians . . . In the Years 1772 and 1773,* Burlington, N.J., 1774 (Sabin Reprints 2, New York, 1865).

Jones *Letters: Letters of Joseph Jones of Virginia, 1773-1787,* ed. Worthington C. Ford, Washington, D.C., 1889.

Jones *Sketches:* George Jones, *Sketches of Naval Life,* 2 vols., New Haven, 1829.

Jones *Virginia:* Hugh Jones, *The Present State of Virginia* (1724), ed. Richard L. Morton, Chapel Hill, N.C., 1956.

Joslin *Journal: Journal of Joseph Joslin, Jr.* (1777-8), Connecticut Historical Society, *Collections* 7 (1899), 299-369.

Josselyn *Account*: Joseph Josselyn, *An Account of Two Voyages to New-England,* London, 1674.

Josselyn *New-Englands Rarities:* John Josselyn, *New-Englands Rarities Discovered* (1672), ed. Edward Tuckerman, Boston, 1865.

Journal of Two Cruises: Journal of Two Cruises Aboard the American Privateer Yankee, ed. E. M. Eller, New York, 1967.

Keayne *Apologia: The Apologia of Robert Keayne,* ed. Bernard Bailyn, New York, 1965.

Kemble *Papers: The Kemble Papers,* 2 vols., New-York Historical Society, *Collections* (1884).

Kendall *Travels:* Edward A. Kendall, *Travels Through the Northern Parts of the United States in the Years 1807 and 1808,* 3 vols., New York, 1809.

Kennon Letters: "Kennon Letters," *VHM* 31-40(1923-32). (One or more selections are printed in each volume.)

Ker *Travels:* Henry Ker, *Travels Through the Western Interior of the United States from the Year 1803 up to the Year 1816,* Elizabethtown, N.J., 1816.

Kerr *Barclay:* Jacob Kerr, *The Several Trials of the Reverend David Barclay,* Elizabethtown, N.J., 1814.

Kimball: Gertrude S. Kimball, ed., *The Correspondence of the Colonial Governors of Rhode Island, 1723-1775,* 2 vols., Boston, 1902, 1903.

King *Life: The Life and Correspondence of Rufus King,* ed. Charles R. King, 6 vols., New York, 1894-1900.

Kingston: Kingston Before the War of 1812, A Collection of Documents, ed. Richard A. Preston, Champlain Society, Toronto, 1959.

Kinloch *Letters:* (Francis Kinloch), *Letters from Geneva and France,* 2 vols., Boston, 1819.

Bibliographical References

Kirkland *Letters:* Frederic R. Kirkland, *Letters on the American Revolution in the Library at "Karolfred",* 2 vols., Philadelphia, New York, 1941, 1952.

Knight *Journal: The Journal of Madame Knight,* ed. G. P. Winship, New York, 1935.

Knight *Poems:* Henry C. Knight, *Poems,* 2 vols, 2d ed., Boston, 1821.

Knopf *War of 1812*: Richard C. Knopf, ed., *Document Transcriptions of the War of 1812 in the Northwest,* 6 vols., Columbus, O. 1957-9.

Ladd *Remains: The Literary Remains of Joseph B. Ladd* (died 1786), New York, 1832.

Lambert *Travels:* John Lambert, *Travels Through Canada and the United States of North America, In the Years 1806, 1807, & 1808,* 2 vols., 3d ed., London, 1816.

Latrobe *Journal: The Journal of* [*Benjamin H.*] *Latrobe . . . from 1796 to 1820,* ed. J. H. B. Latrobe, New York, 1905.

Laurens *Papers: The Papers of Henry Laurens,* ed. Philip M. Hamer et al., Columbia, S.C., 1(1968)-.

Law Papers: The Law Papers: Correspondence and Documents During Jonathan Law's Governorship of the Colony of Connecticut, 1741-1750, 3 vols., Connecticut Historical Society, *Collections* 11, 13, 15 (1907-14).

Lawson *Voyage:* John Lawson, *A New Voyage to Carolina* (1709), ed. H. T. Lefler, Chapel Hill, N.C., 1967.

Leake *Lamb:* Isaac Q. Leake, *Memoir of the Life and Times of General John Lamb,* Albany, N.Y., 1857.

Lean: Vincent S. Lean, *Lean's Collectanea,* 4 vols. in 5, Bristol, Eng., 1902-4.

Ledyard *Journal of Cook's Last Voyage:* John Ledyard, *Journal of Captain Cook's Last Voyage,* ed. James K. Munford, Corvallis, Ore., 1963.

Ledyard *Russian Journal*: John Ledyard, *Journal Through Russia and Siberia, 1787-1788,* ed. Stephen D. Watrous, Madison, Wis., 1966.

Lee *Diary and Letters: A Yankee Jeffersonian, Selections from the Diary and Letters of William Lee of Massachusetts, Written from 1796 to 1840,* ed. Mary Lee Mann, Cambridge, Mass., 1958.

Lee *Letters: The Letters of Richard Henry Lee,* ed. James C. Ballagh, 2 vols., New York, 1911, 1914.

Lee(W) *Letters: Letters of William Lee, 1766-1783,* ed. Worthington C. Ford, 3 vols., Brooklyn, 1891.

Lee *Memoirs:* Henry Lee, *Memoirs of the War in the Southern Department of the United States,* 2 vols., Philadelphia, 1812.

Lee *Papers: The Lee Papers,* 4 vols., New-York Historical Society, *Collections* (1871-4).

Letters from Hudson Bay: Letters from Hudson Bay, 1703-40, ed. K. G. Davies, Hudson's Bay Record Society 25, London, 1965.

Letters to Washington: Letters to Washington and Accompanying Papers, ed. Stanislaus M. Hamilton, 5 vols., Boston, 1898-1902.

Lewis and Clark Expedition: Letters of the Lewis and Clark Expedition, ed. Donald Jackson, Urbana, Ill., 1962.

Lincoln Papers: The Papers of Captain Rufus Lincoln, compiled by James M. Lincoln, privately printed, Cambridge, Mass., 1904.

Lindsley *Love:* A. B. Lindsley, *Love and Friendship; or, Yankee Notions: A Comedy,* New York, 1809.

Littell *Festoons:* William Littell, *Festoons of Fancy* (1814), ed. Thomas D. Clark, Lexington, Ky., 1940.

Livingston *Democracy:* (Brockholst Livingston), *Democracy: An Epic Poem,* New York, 1794.

Lloyd *Papers: Papers of the Lloyd Family of . . . Lloyd's Neck, Long Island, New York,* ed. Dorothy C. Barck, 2 vols., New-York Historical Society, *Collections* 69, 70 (1926-7).

Long *Voyages:* John Long, *Voyages and Travels of an Indian Interpreter and Trader,* London, 1791.

Longfellow *Letters: The Letters of Henry Wadsworth Longfellow,* ed. Andrew Hilen, I, Cambridge, Mass., 1966.

Louisbourg Journals: Louisbourg Journals, 1745, ed. Louis E. de Forest, New York, 1932.

Luttig *Journal:* John C. Luttig, *Journal of a Fur-Trading Expedition on the Upper Missouri, 1812-1813,* ed. Stella M. Drumm, Missouri Historical Society, St. Louis, 1920.

Lynde *Diaries: The Diaries of Benjamin Lynde and of Benjamin Lynde, Jr.,* ed. Fitch E. Oliver, privately printed, Boston, 1880.

McClure *Diary: Diary of David McClure, Doctor of Divinity, 1748-1820,* ed. F. D. Dexter, New York, 1899.

McDowell *Documents:* William L. McDowell, Jr., ed., *Documents Relating to Indian Affairs,* 2 vols., Colonial Records of South Carolina, Columbia, S.C., 1958, 1970.

McGillivray *Letters:* John W. Caughey, *McGillivray of the Creeks,* Norman, Okla., 1938.

McHenry *Letters: The Life and Correspondence of James McHenry,* by Bernard C. Steiner, Cleveland, 1907.

Mackay *Letters: The Letters of Robert Mackay to his Wife,* ed. Walter C. Hartridge, Athens, Ga., 1949.

Mackenzie *Diary: Diary of Frederick Mackenzie . . . An Officer of the Regiment of the Royal Welch Fusiliers During the Years 1775-1781,* 2 vols., Cambridge, Mass., 1930.

Maclay *Journal: The Journal of William Maclay,* ed. Charles A. Beard, New York, 1927.

Maclay(S) *Journal: Journal of Samuel Maclay . . . In 1790,* Williamsport, Pa., 1887.

M'Nemar *Kentucky:* Richard M'Nemar, *The Kentucky Revival,* Cincinnati, 1808.

Madison *Papers: The Papers of James Madison,* ed. William T. Hutchinson and W. M. E. Rachal, Chicago, 1(1962)-.

Makemie *Writings: The Life and Writings of Francis Makemie,* ed. B. S. Schlenther, Philadelphia, 1971.

Mann *Female:* (Herman Mann), *The Female Review: Life of Debora Sampson* (1797), ed. J. A. Vinton, Boston, 1866.

Manning *Key:* William Manning, *The Key of Libberty* (1798), ed. Samuel E. Morison, Billerica, Mass., 1922.

Marshall *Diary: Extracts from the Diary of Christopher Marshall . . . 1774-1781,* ed. William Duane, Albany, 1877.

Marshall *Kentucky*: Humphrey Marshall, *The History of Kentucky,* 2d ed., 2 vols., Frankfort, Ky., 1824.

Bibliographical References

Mason *Memoir: Memoir and Correspondence of Jeremiah Mason* [by G. S. Hillard], Cambridge, Mass., 1873.

Mason *Papers: The Papers of George Mason, 1725-1792,* ed. Robert A. Rutland, 3 vols., Chapel Hill, N.C., 1970.

Mather *Bonifacius:* (Cotton Mather), *Bonifacius: An Essay upon the Good,* Boston, 1710, Scholars' Facsimiles and Reprints, Gainesville, Fla., 1967.

Mather *Diary: Diary of Cotton Mather,* ed. W. C. Ford, 2 vols., Massachusetts Historical Society, *Collections,* 7th ser. 7-8 (1911, 1912).

Mather *Letters: Selected Letters of Cotton Mather,* ed. Kenneth Silverman, Baton Rouge, La., 1971.

Mather *Magnalia:* Cotton Mather, *Magnalia Christi Americana* (1702), 2 vols., Hartford, 1853-5.

Mather Papers: The Mather Papers, Massachusetts Historical Society, *Collections,* 4th ser. 8 (1868).

Mather *Wonders:* Cotton Mather, *The Wonders of the Invisible World* (1692), London, 1862.

Maxwell *Mysterious:* William B. Maxwell, *The Mysterious Father, A Tragedy in Five Acts* (1807), ed. Gerald Kahan, Athens, Ga., 1965.

Maxwell *Poems:* William Maxwell, *Poems,* Philadelphia, 1812.

May *Journal: Journal and Letters of Col. John May of Boston . . . Relative to Two Journeys to the Ohio Country in 1788 and '89,* ed. R. S. Edes, Cincinnati, 1873.

Melish *Travels:* John Melish, *Travels Through the United States of America in the Years 1806 & 1807, and 1809, 1810 & 1811,* London, 1818 (reprint 1970).

Meserve and Reardon: Walter J. Meserve and W. R. Reardon, eds., *Satiric Comedies,* America's Lost Plays 21, Bloomington, Ind., 1969.

MHM: Maryland Historical Magazine, Baltimore, 1(1906)-.

Milledge *Correspondence: Correspondence of John Milledge,* ed. Harriet M. Salley, Columbia, S.C., 1949.

Monroe *Writings: The Writings of James Monroe,* ed. Stanislaus M. Hamilton, 7 vols., New York, 1898-1903.

Monthly Anthology: The Monthly Anthology and Boston Review, 1 (1804)- 4(1807).

Montresor *Journals: Journals of John Montresor,* ed. G. D. Scull, New-York Historical Society, *Collections* 14 (1881).

Moore *Diary*: Frank Moore, *Diary of the American Revolution from Newspapers and Original Documents,* 2 vols., New York, 1859.

Moose Fort Journals: Moose Fort Journals, 1783-85, ed. E. E. Rich, Hudson's Bay Record Society 17, London, 1954.

Morgan *Journal: The Journal of Dr. John Morgan of Philadelphia,* ed. Julia M. Harding, Philadelphia, 1907.

Morison *Journal:* George Morison, *An Interesting Journal of Occurrences During the Expedition to Quebec* (Hagerstown, 1803), reprinted in *The Magazine of History,* Extra Number 13, no. 52 (1916).

Morris *Diary:* Gouverneur Morris, *A Diary of the French Revolution,* ed. Beatrix C. Davenport, 2 vols., Boston, 1939.

Morris *Diary and Letters: The Diary and Letters of Gouverneur Morris,* ed. Anne C. Morris, 2 vols., New York, 1888.

Morton *New-Englands Memoriall:* Nathaniel Morton, *New-Englands Memoriall* (1669), ed. Arthur Lord, Boston, 1903.

Morton *New English Canaan: The New English Canaan of Thomas Morton* (1637), ed. C. F. Adams, Jr., Publications of the Prince Society 14, Boston, 1883.

Moultrie *Memoirs:* William Moultrie, *Memoirs of the American Revolution,* 2 vols., New York, 1802.

Mourt's Relation: Mourt's Relation or Journal of the Plantation at Plymouth (1622), ed. Henry M. Dexter, Boston, 1870. (Usually ascribed to William Bradford and Edward Winslow.)

Munford *Candidates:* Robert Munford, *The Candidates* (1770), ed. Jay B. Hubbell and Douglass Adair, *W&MCQ,* 3d. ser. 5 (1948), 217-57.

Munford *Patriots:* Robert Munford, *The Patriots* (1777), ed. C. Canby, *W&MCQ,* 3d ser. 6 (1949), 448-503.

Murdock *Politicians*: (John Murdock), *The Politicians; or, A State of Things,* Philadelphia, 1798.

Murdock *Triumphs*: (John Murdock), *The Triumphs of Love . . . A Comedy,* Philadelphia, 1795.

Murphey *Papers: The Papers of Archibald D. Murphey,* ed. William H. Hoyt, 2 vols., Raleigh, N.C., 1914.

Murray *Letters: Letters of James Murray, Loyalist,* ed. N. M. Tiffany and S. I. Lesley, Boston, 1901.

Musings: Musings at An Evening Club in Boston, Boston, 1819.

Naval Documents: Naval Documents of the American Revolution, ed. William B. Clark et al., Washington, D.C., 1(1964)-.

Neal *American Writers:* John Neal, *American Writers: A Series of Papers Contributed to Blackwood's Magazine (1824-1825),* ed. Fred L. Pattee, Durham, N.C., 1937.

NED: *A New English Dictionary on Historical Principles,* 13 vols. (*with Supplement*), Oxford, 1844-1933.

New-England Courant: The New-England Courant. A Selection of Certain Issues Containing Writings of Benjamin Franklin, or Published by Him During his Brother's Imprisonment, with an Introduction by Perry Miller, Boston, 1956.

New England Merchants: New England Merchants in Africa, ed. Norman R. Bennett and G. E. Brooks, Jr., Boston, 1965.

Newspaper Extracts(I): Extracts from American Newspapers, Relating to New Jersey, ed. William Nelson and A. Van Doren Honeyman, 11 vols., Archives of the State of New Jersey, 1st ser., 1894-1923.

Newspaper Extracts (II): Extracts from American Newspapers Relating to New Jersey, ed. William S. Stryker et al., 5 vols., Archives of the State of New Jersey, 2d ser., 1901-17.

Nichols *Jefferson*: J. H. Nichols, *Jefferson and Liberty . . . A Patriotic Tragedy,* n.p., 1801 (reissue 1965).

Noah *Travels:* Mordecai M. Noah, *Travels in England, France, Spain, and the Barbary States In the Years 1813-14 and 15,* New York, 1819.

Norton Papers: John Norton & Sons, Merchants of London and Virginia, Being the Papers from their Counting House for the Years 1750 to 1795, ed. Frances N. Mason, Richmond, Va., 1937.

Olden Time: The Olden Time Series: Gleanings Chiefly from Old Newspapers of Boston and Salem, Massachusetts, ed. Henry M. Brooks, 6 vols., Boston, 1886.

Oliver *Origin:* Peter Oliver, *Origin and Progress of the American Rebellion* (1781), ed. Douglass Adair and J. A. Schutz, San Marino, Cal., 1961.

Bibliographical References

Ordway *Journal: The Journals of Captain Meriwether Lewis and Sergeant John Ordway*, ed. M. M. Quaiffe, State Historical Society of Wisconsin, *Publications* 22 (1916).

Otis *Letters: The Life and Letters of Harrison Gray Otis, Federalist, 1765-1848*, by Samuel E. Morison, 2 vols, Boston, 1913.

Oxford: The Oxford Dictionary of English Proverbs, 3d ed., rev. by F. P. Wilson, Oxford, 1970 (with occasional references to the 2d ed., rev. by Paul Harvey, 1948).

Paine: *The Complete Writings of Thomas Paine*, ed. Philip S. Foner, 2 vols., New York, 1945, (All citations of Paine's individual writings are to this edition.)

Paine *Works:* Robert Treat Paine, Jr., *Works in Verse and Prose*, Boston, 1812.

Palmer *Diary: The Diary of Benjamin F. Palmer, Privateersman* (1813-5), The Acorn Club, *Publications* 11 (1914).

Parkinson *Tour:* Richard Parkinson, *A Tour in America in 1798, 1799, and 1800*, London, 1805.

Parkman *Diary:* "The Diary of Ebenezer Parkman," ed. Francis G. Wallett, American Antiquarian Society, *Proceedings*, N.S. 71 (1961) 95-227, 362-448; 72 (1962) 32-233, 330-481; 73 (1963) 46-120, 386-464; 74 (1964) 38-203; 75 (1965) 49-199; 76 (1966) 73-201.

Parsons *Life: Life and Letters of Samuel Holden Parsons*, by Charles S. Hall, Binghamton, N.Y., 1905.

Partridge: Eric Partridge, *A Dictionary of Slang and Unconventional English*, 5th ed., London, 1961.

Paterson *Glimpses: Glimpses of Colonial Society and the Life at Princeton College, 1766-1773, by One [William Paterson] of the Class of 1763*, ed. W. Jay Mills, Philadelphia, 1903.

Patten *Diary: The Diary of Matthew Patten of Bedford, N.H.*, Published by the Town, Concord, N.H., 1903.

Paulding *Lay:* (James K. Paulding), *The Lay of the Scottish Fiddle*, New York, 1813.

Paulding *Letters(I)*: (James K. Paulding), *Letters from the South, Written During an Excursion in the Summer of 1816*, 2 vols., New York, 1817.

Paulding *Letters(II): The Letters of James Kirke Paulding*, ed. Ralph M. Aderman, Madison, Wis., 1962.

Paxton Papers: The Paxton Papers, ed. John R. Dunbar, The Hague, 1957.

Pearse *Narrative: A Narrative of the Life of James Pearse* (1825), reissue, Chicago, 1962.

Peirce *Rebelliad*: (Augustus Peirce), *Rebelliad* (1819), Boston, 1842.

Pemberton *Life: The Life and Travels of John Pemberton*, London, 1844.

Penn-Logan Correspondence: Correspondence Between William Penn and James Logan . . . and Others, 1700-1750, ed. Edward Armstrong, 2 vols., Historical Society of Pennsylvania, *Memoirs* 9, 10 (1870, 1872).

Pepperrell Papers: The Pepperrell Papers, Massachusetts Historical Society, *Collections*, 6th ser. 10 (1899).

Perkins *Diary: The Diary of Simeon Perkins* (1766-), ed. H. A. Innis et al., 4 vols., Champlain Society, *Publications* 29, 36, 39, 43 (1948-67). (There should be one more volume.)

Peters *Connecticut:* (Samuel Peters), *A General History of Connecticut* (London, 1781), New Haven, 1829.

Pickering *Life: The Life of Timothy Pickering,* by Octavius Pickering, 4 vols., Boston, 1867-73.

Pickering *Review: A Review of the Correspondence Between the Hon. John Adams . . . and . . . Wm. Cunningham, Esq.,* Salem, Mass., 1824.

Pickman *Letters: The Diary and Letters of Benjamin Pickman (1740-1819),* ed. George F. Dow, Newport, R.I., 1928.

Pike *Travels:* Zebulon M. Pike, *Exploratory Travels Through the Western Territories* (1811), Denver, 1889.

Pinkney *Travels:* Ninian Pinkney, *Travels Through the South of France,* London, 1809.

Pinkney *Works: The Life and Works of Edward C. Pinkney,* ed. T. O. Mabbott and F. L. Pleadwell, New York, 1926.

Pintard *Letters: Letters from John Pintard to his Daughter, . . . 1816-1833,* 4 vols., New-York Historical Society, *Collections* 70-73 (1940-1).

Plumer *Memorandum: William Plumer's Memorandum of Proceedings in the United States Senate, 1803-1807,* ed. Everett S. Brown, New York, 1923.

Plumstead: A. W. Plumstead, ed., *The Wall and the Garden: Selected Massachusetts Election Sermons, 1670-1775,* Minneapolis, 1968.

PM: The Pennsylvania Magazine of History and Biography 1 (1877)-.

Politician: The Politician Out-witted, A Comedy . . . Written in the Year 1788. By an American, New York, 1789.

Pope *Tour:* John Pope, *A Tour Through the Southern and Western Territories of the United States of North America,* Richmond, 1792 (reprinted, New York, 1888).

Porter *Journal:* David Porter, *Journal of a Cruise Made to the Pacific Ocean . . . in the Years 1812, 1813, and 1814,* 2 vols., Philadelphia, 1815.

Porter *Negro Writing:* Dorothy Porter, ed. *Early Negro Writing, 1760-1837,* Boston, 1971.

Port Folio: The Port Folio, Philadelphia, 1 (1801)-.

Pote *Journal: The Journal of Captain William Pote, Jr., During his Captivity in the French and Indian War from May 1745, to August 1747,* New York, 1896.

Preble *Genealogical Sketch:* Geo. H. Preble, *Genealogical Sketch of the First Three Generations of Prebles in America,* Boston, 1868.

Prince *Journals: Journals of Hezekiah Prince, Jr., 1822-1828,* ed. Arthur Spear, New York, 1965.

Putnam *Memoirs: The Memoirs of Rufus Putnam* (c1812) *and Certain Official Papers and Correspondence,* ed. Rowena Buell, Boston, 1903.

Pynchon *Diary: The Diary of William Pynchon of Salem,* ed. F. E. Oliver, Boston, 1890.

Quincy *JQuincy:* Edmund Quincy, *Life of Josiah Quincy,* Boston, 1867.

Quincy *London Journal: Journal of Josiah Quincy, Jr., 1774-1775,* Massachusetts Historical Society, *Proceedings* 50 (1917), 433-96.

Quincy *Memoir:* Josiah Quincy, *Memoir of the Life of Josiah Quincy, Jr.,* 3d ed., Boston, 1875.

Radisson *Voyages: Voyages of Peter Esprit Radisson* (c1680), ed. Gideon D. Scull, Publications of the Prince Society 16, Boston, 1885 (reissue 1967).

Randall *Miser:* Samuel Randall, *The Miser, A Comedy,* Warren, R.I., 1812.

Randolph *Letters:* Edward Randolph, *His Letters and Official Papers from the New*

Bibliographical References

England, Middle, and Southern Colonies . . . 1676-1703, 7 vols., ed. R. N. Toppan and A. T. S. Goodrick, Publications of the Prince Society 25-31, Boston, 1898-1909 (reprinted 1967).

Randolph (J) *Letters: Letters of John Randolph to a Young Relative* (Theodore Dudley), Philadelphia, 1834.

Randolph *Virginia:* Edmund Randolph, *History of Virginia* (c1810), ed. Arthur H. Shaffer, Charlottesville, Va., 1970.

Read *Correspondence: Life and Correspondence of George Read,* by William T. Read, Philadelphia, 1870.

Reed *Life: Life and Correspondence of Joseph Reed,* by William B. Reed, 2 vols., Philadelphia, 1847.

Remarks on the Jacobiniad: Remarks on the Jacobiniad, parts 1, 2, Boston, 1795, 1798.

Reviewers: The Reviewers Reviewed, or British Falsehoods Detected by American Truths, New York, 1815.

Robertson *Letters:* Colin Robertson, *Correspondence Book, September 1817 to September 1822,* ed. E. E. Rich, Champlain Society, Toronto, 1939.

Rodney *Letters: Letters to and from Caesar Rodney, 1756-1784,* ed. George H. Ryden, Philadelphia, 1933.

Rowe *Diary: Letters and Diary of John Rowe, 1759-62, 1764-79,* ed. Anne Rowe Cunningham, Boston, 1903.

Rowson *Charlotte:* Susanna H. Rowson, *Charlotte Temple* (1794), ed. F. W. Halsey, 2 vols. in 1, New York, 1905.

Royall *Letters:* Anne N. Royall, *Letters from Alabama, 1817-1822,* ed. Lucille Griffith, University, Alabama, 1969.

Royall *Sketches:* (Anne Royall), *Sketches of History, Life, and Manners in the United States, by a Traveller,* New Haven, 1826.

Ruffin Papers: The Papers of Thomas Ruffin, ed. J. G. de Roulhac Hamilton, 4 vols., Raleigh, N.C., 1918-20.

Rush *Autobiography: The Autobiography of Benjamin Rush,* ed. G. W. Corner, Princeton, 1948.

Rush *Letters:* Benjamin Rush, *Letters,* ed. L. H. Butterfield, 2 vols., Princeton, 1951.

Saffin *His Book:* John Saffin, *His Book* (1665-1708), ed. Caroline Hazard, New York, 1928.

St. Clair Papers: The St. Clair Papers: The Life and Public Services of Arthur St. Clair, ed. William H. Smith, 2 vols., Cincinnati, 1882.

Salmagundi: Salmagundi, by William Irving, J. K. Paulding, and W. Irving (1807-8), Knickerbocker Edition of Washington Irving's Works 15, Philadelphia, 1873.

Saltonstall Papers: The Saltonstall Papers, 1607-1815, ed. Robert E. Moody, Massachusetts Historical Society, *Collections* 80, 1 (1972)-.

Sans Souci: Sans Souci, Alias Free and Easy, Boston, 1785.

Sargent *Loyalist:* (Winthrop Sargent), *The Loyalist Poetry of the Revolution,* Philadelphia, 1857.

Savery *Journal: A Journal of the Life . . . of William Savery,* compiled by Jonathan Evans, London, 1844.

Scattergood *Journal: Journal of the Life and Religious Labors of Thomas Scattergood,* Philadelphia, 1874.

Schaw *Journal:* (Janet Schaw), *Journal of a Lady of Quality . . . 1774 to 1776,* ed. E. W. and C. M. Andrews, New Haven, 1934.

Schultz *Travels:* Christian Schultz, *Travels on an Inland Voyage,* 2 vols., New York, 1810 (reproduced, Ridgewood, N.J., 1968).

Scott *Blue Lights:* Jonathan M. Scott, *Blue Lights, or the Convention,* New York, 1817.

Scott *Journal:* Job Scott, *Journal of the Life, Travels, and Gospel Labours of Job Scott,* New York, 1815.

Scottow *Narrative:* (Joshua Scottow), *A Narrative of the Planting of the Massachusetts Colony* (Boston, 1694), Massachusetts Historical Society, *Collections,* 4th ser. 4 (1858), 281-330.

Seabury *Letters:* Samuel Seabury, *Letters of a Westchester Farmer (1774-1775),* ed. C. H. Vance, Westchester County Historical Society, *Publications* 8 (1930).

Serle *Journal: The American Journal of Ambrose Serle . . . 1776-1778,* ed. E. H. Tatum, Jr., San Marino, Cal., 1940.

Sewall *Diary: Diary of Samuel Sewall, 1674-1729,* 3 vols., Massachusetts Historical Society, *Collections,* 5th ser. 5-7 (1878-82).

Sewall *Letter-Book: Letter-Book of Samuel Sewall,* 2 vols., Massachusetts Historical Society, *Collections,* 6th ser. 1, 2 (1886, 1888).

Sewall *Parody:* J. M. Sewall, *A Parody on . . . "A Letter to a Federalist,"* by Vernon H. Quincey, Portsmouth, N.H., 1805.

Sewall *Poems:* J. M. Sewall, *Miscellaneous Poems,* Portsmouth, N.H., 1801.

Shaw *Journals: The Journals of Major Samuel Shaw,* ed. Josiah Quincy, Boston, 1847.

Shaw *Letter Book:* "The Mercantile Letter Book of Nathaniel Shaw, Jr.," in *Connecticut's Naval Office at New London,* ed. Ernest E. Rogers, New London County Historical Society, *Collections* 2 (1933), 169-337.

Shepard *Autobiography: The Autobiography of Thomas Shepard,* Colonial Society of Massachusetts, *Publications* 27, *Transactions,* 1927-30, 352-400.

Shepard *Hints:* A. M. Davis, "Hints of Contemporary Life in the Writings of Thomas Shepard," Colonial Society of Massachusetts, *Publications* 12 (1908), 136-62.

Sherman *Almanacs:* "The Almanacs of Roger Sherman, 1750-1761," by Victor H. Paltsits, American Antiquarian Society, *Proceedings,* N.S. 18 (1907), 213-58.

Shippen *Journal: Nancy Shippen Her Journal Book,* ed. Ethel Armes, Philadelphia, 1935.

Short *Letters:* "To Practice Law . . . The Short-Ridgely Correspondence," ed. George G. Shackelford, *MHM* 64(1969), 342-95.

Silliman *Travels:* Benjamin Silliman, *A Journal of Travels in England, Holland, and Scotland . . . in the Years 1805 and 1806,* 2d ed., 2 vols., Boston, 1812.

Silverman: Kenneth Silverman, ed., *Colonial American Poetry,* New York, 1968.

Simpson: Claude M. Simpson, *The British Broadside Ballad and Its Music,* New Brunswick, N.J., 1966.

Simpson *Journal:* George Simpson, *Journal of Occurrences in the Athabasca Department, 1820 and 1821, and Report,* ed. E. E. Rich, Champlain Society, *Publications,* Hudson's Bay Company Series 1 (1938).

Smith *American Poems:* Elihu H. Smith, ed., *American Poems* (1793), Scholars' Facsimiles and Reprints, Gainesville, Fla., 1966.

Smith *Diary: The Diary and Selected Papers of Chief Justice William Smith (1784-*

1793), ed. L. F. S. Upton, 2 vols., Champlain Society, *Publications* 41, 42 (1963, 1965).

Smith(EH) *Diary: The Diary of Elihu Hubbard Smith (1771-1798)*, ed. James E. Cronin, American Philosophical Society, Philadelphia, 1973.

Smith(John) *Diary*: in *Hannah Logan's Courtship*, ed. Albert C. Myers, Philadelphia, 1904.

Smith *Journal: Journals of the Rev. Thomas Smith and the Rev. Samuel Deane*, ed. Wm. Willis, Portland, Me., 1849.

Smith *Journal and Correspondence*: *Journal and Correspondence of Miss Adams, Daughter of John Adams*, edited by her Daughter [Caroline De Wirt], 2 vols., Boston, 1841, 1842. (The second volume, *Correspondence of Miss Adams*, is in two parts, paged separately.)

Smith *Letters: Forty Years of Washington Society, Portrayed by the Family Letters of Mrs. Samuel Harrison Smith*, ed. Gaillard Hunt, London, 1906.

Smith *Life: The Life, Conversion, Preaching, Travels and Sufferings of Elias Smith, Written by Himself*, Portsmouth, N.H., 1816. (This is called vol. I, but no further volume appeared.)

Smith *Life and Correspondence: The Life and Correspondence of the Rev. William Smith*, by Horace W. Smith, 2 vols., Philadelphia, 1879-80.

Smith *Memoirs(I): Historical Memoirs from 16 March 1763 to 9 July 1776 of William Smith*, ed. William H. W. Sabine, New York, 1956.

Smith *Memoirs(II): Historical Memoirs from 12 July 1776 to 25 July 1778 of William Smith*, ed. W. H. W. Sabine, New York, 1958.

Smith Papers: John Cotton Smith Papers, 7 vols., Connecticut Historical Society, *Collections* 25-31 (1948-67).

Smith *Works: The Works of William Smith, D.D.*, 2 vols., Philadelphia, 1803. (Vol. 1 is in two parts, paged separately.)

Smyth *Tour*: J. F. D. Smyth, *A Tour in the United States of America*, 2 vols., London, 1784.

South Carolina Gazette: Henning Cohen, *The South Carolina Gazette, 1732-1775*, Columbia, S.C., 1953.

Sparks *Correspondence*: Jared Sparks, ed., *Correspondence of the American Revolution, being Letters of Eminent Men to George Washington*, 4 vols., Boston, 1853.

S.P.L. *Thoughts*: S.P.L., "Thoughts on Proverbs," *Universal Asylum* 7 (1791), 76-8, 166-8.

Stansbury *Pedestrian*: P. Stansbury, *A Pedestrian Tour of Two Thousand Three Hundred Miles, in North America*, New York, 1822.

Stark *Memoir*: Caleb Stark, *Memoir and Official Correspondence of Gen. John Stark*, Concord, N.H., 1860.

Stebbins *Journal: The Journal of William Stebbins . . . In 1810*, ed. L. W. Labaree, Acorn Club 31 (1968).

Steele Papers: The Papers of John Steele, ed. H. M. Wagstaff, 2 vols., Raleigh, N.C., 1924.

Steere *Daniel*: Richard Steere, *The Daniel Catcher* (1682) [and other poems], Boston, 1713.

Stephens *Journal(I)*: William Stephens, *Journal of the Proceedings in Georgia Beginning October 20, 1737*, 2 vols., *Georgia Records* 4 (1906), Suppl. to 4 (1908).

Stephens *Journal(II)*: *The Journal of William Stephens, 1741-45*, ed. E. M. Coulter, 2 vols., Athens, Ga., 1958-9.

Stiles *Diary: The Literary Diary of Ezra Stiles*, ed. Franklin B. Dexter, 3 vols., New York, 1901.

Stiles *Itineraries: Extracts from the Itineraries and other Miscellanies of Ezra Stiles . . . with a Selection from his Correspondence*, ed. Franklin B. Dexter, New Haven, 1916.

Stiles *Letters: Letters and Papers of Ezra Stiles,* ed. Isabel M. Calder, New Haven, 1933.

Stiles *Three Judges*: Ezra Stiles, *A History of Three of the Judges of King Charles I,* Hartford, 1794.

Stith *History*: William Stith, *The History of the First Discovery and Settlement of Virginia,* Williamsburg, Va., 1747 (reprint, Spartanburg, S.C., 1965).

Stoddard *Sketches:* Amos Stoddard, *Sketches, Historical and Descriptive, of Louisiana,* Philadelphia, 1812.

Story *Shop*: (Isaac Story), *A Parnassian Shop, Opened in the Pindaric Stile; by Peter Quince, Esq.*, Boston, 1801.

Strachey *Historie*: William Strachey, *The Historie of Travell into Virginia Britania* (1612), ed. L. B. Wright and V. Freund, Hakluyt Society, 2d ser. 103, London, 1953.

Sullivan *Journals: Journals of the Military Expedition of Major General John Sullivan . . . in 1779,* ed. Frederick Cook, Albany, 1887.

Sullivan *Letters: Letters and Papers of Major-General John Sullivan, Continental Army*, ed. Otis G. Hammond, 3 vols., New Hampshire Historical Society, *Collections* 13-5 (1930-9).

Sumter *Letters: Fifteen Letters of Nathalie Sumter*, ed. Mary V. S. White, Columbia, S.C., 1942.

Svartengren: T. Hilding Svartengren, *Intensifying Similes in English*, Lund, 1918.

Symmes *Utile*: Thomas Symmes, *Utile Dulci. Or, A Joco-Serious Dialogue Concerning Regular Singing*, Boston, 1723.

Tablet: The Tablet, May 19-August 11, Boston, 1795.

Taggart *Letters:* "Letters of Samuel Taggart, Representative in Congress, 1803-1814," ed. George H. Haynes, American Antiquarian Society, *Proceedings,* N.S. 33 (1923), 113-226, 297-438. (Probably not by Taggart, but rather supplied to him by a professional writer of circular letters.)

Talbot *Letters*: Edgar L. Pennington, *Apostle of New Jersey, John Talbot, 1645-1727,* Philadelphia, 1938.

Talcott *Papers: The Talcott Papers: Correspondence and Documents During Joseph Talcott's Governorship of the Colony of Connecticut, 1724-41,* ed. Mary K. Talcott, 2 vols., Connecticut Historical Society, *Collections* 4, 5 (1892-1896).

Tales: Tales of an American Landlord; Containing Sketches of Life South of the Potomac, 2 vols., New York, 1824.

Tatham *Tobacco*: William Tatham, *An Historical and Practical Essay on the Culture and Commerce of Tobacco* (London, 1800), facsimile, ed. G. M. Herndon, Coral Gables, Fla., 1969.

Taylor *Christographia*: Edward Taylor, *Christographia*, ed. Norman S. Grabo, New Haven, 1962.

Taylor *Comparisons*: Archer Taylor, *Proverbial Comparisons and Similes from Cali-*

fornia, Folklore Studies 3, Berkeley, Cal., 1954.

Taylor *Poems: The Poems of Edward Taylor*, ed. Donald E. Stanford, New Haven, 1960.

Thacher *Journal*: James Thacher, *A Military Journal During the American Revolutionary War, From 1775 to 1783*, Boston, 1823. (Clearly revised years after the events.)

Thomas *Travels*: David Thomas, *Travels Through the Western Country in the Summer of 1816*, Auburn, N.Y., 1819.

Thompson *Motif-Index*: Stith Thompson, *Motif-Index of Folk-Literature*, rev. ed., 6 vols., Bloomington, Ind., 1955-8.

Thomson Papers: The Papers of Charles Thomson, Secretary of the Continental Congress, New-York Historical Society, *Collections* 11 (1879).

Thornton *Glossary*: Richard H. Thornton, *An American Glossary*, 2 vols., Philadelphia, 1912.

Thornton *Pulpit*: John W. Thornton, *The Pulpit of the American Revolution*, Boston, 1860.

Tilghman *Letters:* "Letters of Molly and Hetty Tilghman," ed. J. H. Pleasants, *MHM* 21(1926) 20-39, 123-49, 219-41.

Tilghman *Memoir: Memoir of Lieut. Col. Tench Tilghman . . . Together with . . . Revolutionary Journals and Letters*, Albany, 1876.

Tilley: Morris P. Tilley, *A Dictionary of the Proverbs in England in the Sixteenth and Seventeenth Centuries*, Ann Arbor, Mich., 1950.

Timberlake *Memoirs*: Henry Timberlake, *Memoirs, 1756-1765*, ed. S. C. Williams, Johnson City, Tenn., 1927.

Tompson *Poems*: Benjamin Tompson, *His Poems*, ed. Howard J. Hall, Boston, 1924.

Trelawny Papers: Documentary History of the State of Maine (vol. 3) *Containing the Trelawny Papers,* ed. J. P. Baxter, Portland, 1884.

Trial of Atticus: The Trial of Atticus Before Justice Beau, for a Rape (Boston, 1771), in Meserve and Reardon 43-78.

Trumbull *Autobiography: The Autobiography of Colonel John Trumbull*, ed. Theodore Sizer, New Haven, 1953.

Trumbull Papers: The Trumbull Papers, 4 vols., Massachusetts Historical Society, *Collections*, 5th ser. 9, 10, 7th ser. 2, 3 (1885-1902).

Trumbull *Satiric Poems: The Satiric Poems of John Trumbull: The Progress of Dulness and M'Fingal*, ed. Edwin T. Bowden, Austin, Tex., 1962.

Trumbull *Season: A Season in New York 1801: Letters of Harriet and Maria Trumbull,* ed. Helen M. Morgan, Pittsburgh, 1969.

Tucker *Essays*: (George Tucker), *Essays on Various Subjects . . . By a Citizen of Virginia*, Georgetown, D.C., 1822.

Tudor *Letters*: (William Tudor), *Letters on the Eastern States*, New York, 1820.

TW: Archer Taylor and B. J. Whiting, *Dictionary of American Proverbs and Proverbial Phrases, 1820-1880*, Cambridge, Mass., 1958.

Tyler *Algerine:* (Royall Tyler), *The Algerine Captive; or, The Life and Adventures of Doctor Updike Underhill*, 2 vols., Walpole, N.H., 1797.

Tyler *Chestnut:* Royall Tyler, *The Chestnut Tree* (1824) [North Montpelier, Vt.], 1931.

Tyler *Contrast:* Royall Tyler, *The Contrast, A Comedy* (1787), ed. J. B. Wilbur, Boston, 1920.

Tyler *Island*: Royall Tyler, *The Island of Barrataria* (c1800) in Royall Tyler, *Four Plays*, ed. A. W. Peach and G. F. Newbrough, Princeton, 1941.

Tyler Letters: Leon G. Tyler, *The Letters and Times of the Tylers*, 3 vols., Richmond, 1884-96 (reprint, New York, 1970).

Tyler *Prose: The Prose of Royall Tyler*, ed. Marius B. Péladeau, Montpelier, Vt., 1972.

Tyler *Verse: The Verse of Royall Tyler*, ed. Marius B. Péladeau, Colonial Society of Massachusetts, *Transactions* 44 (1968).

Tyler *Yankey*: (Royall Tyler), *The Yankey in London,* New York, 1809. (This is called vol. I, but no further volume seems to have appeared.)

Universal Asylum: See *Columbian Magazine.*

Valpey *Journal: Journal of Joseph Valpey, Jr., of Salem, November 1813 to April 1815*, Michigan Society of Colonial Wars, 1922.

Vanderpoel *Chronicles*: Emily N. Vanderpoel, *Chronicles of a Pioneer School from 1792 to 1833*, Cambridge, Mass., 1903.

Vanderpoel *More Chronicles:* Emily N. Vanderpoel, *More Chronicles of a Pioneer School from 1792 to 1833*, New York, 1927.

Van Schaack *Letters*: Henry C. Van Schaack, *The Life of Peter Van Schaack, LL.D., Embracing Selections from his Correspondence*, New York, 1842.

Verplanck *State*: (G. C. Verplanck), *The State Triumvirate*, New York, 1819.

VHM: The Virginia Magazine of History and Biography 1(1893-4)-.

W&MCQ: The William and Mary (College) Quarterly 1(1892)-.

Waln *Hermit*: (Robert Waln, Jr.), *The Hermit in America, on a Visit to Philadelphia*, Philadelphia, 1819.

Walter *Choice Dialogue*: (Thomas Walter), *A Choice Dialogue Between John Faustus, A Conjurer, and Jack Tory his Friend*, Boston, 1720.

Wansey *Journal*: Henry Wansey, *The Journal of an Excursion to the United States of North America in the Summer of 1794*, Salisbury, Eng., 1796 (reissue, New York, 1969).

Ward *Correspondence: Correspondence of Governor Samuel Ward, May 1775-March 1776*, ed. Bernhard Knollenberg, Providence, 1952.

Ward *Simple Cobler:* Nathaniel Ward, *The Simple Cobler of Aggawam in America* (1647), ed. L. C. Wroth, New York, 1937.

Ward *Trip:* (Edward Ward), *A Trip to New England* (1699), in G. P. Winship, *Boston in 1682 and 1699*, Providence, 1905.

Warren-Adams Letters: Warren-Adams Letters: Being Chiefly a Correspondence among John Adams, Samuel Adams, and James Warren, 2 vols., Massachusetts Historical Society, *Collections* 72, 73 (1917, 1925).

Warren-Gerry Correspondence: A Study in Dissent: The Warren-Gerry Correspondence, 1776-1792, ed. C. Harvey Gardiner, Carbondale, Ill., 1968.

Washington *Diaries: The Diaries of George Washington*, ed. John C. Fitzpatrick, 4 vols., Boston, 1925.

Washington *Writings: The Writings of George Washington*, ed. John C. Fitzpatrick, 39 vols., Washington, D.C., 1931-44. (Entries marked with an asterisk are from documents stated to be in Washington's handwriting.)

Waterhouse *Journal*: (?Benjamin Waterhouse), *A Journal of a Young Man of Massachusetts* (Boston, 1816) in *The Magazine of History* 5, Extra Number 18 (1911). (If the author is Benjamin Waterhouse, he has taken liberties with his own chronology.)

Watterston *Letters*: (George Watterston), *Letters from Washington, On the Constitution and Laws*, Washington, D.C., 1818.

Watterston *Wanderer*: (George Watterston), *Wanderer in Washington*, Washington, D.C., 1827.

Watterston *Winter*: (George Watterston), *The L. . . . Family at Washington; or, A Winter In the Metropolis*, Washington, D.C., 1822.

Watts *Letter Book*: *Letter Book of John Watts, 1762-1765*, New-York Historical Society, *Collections* 61 (1928).

Wayne *Correspondence*: *Anthony Wayne . . . The Wayne-Knox-Pickering-McHenry Correspondence*, ed. Richard C. Knopf, Pittsburgh, 1960.

Webb *Correspondence*: *Correspondence and Journals of Samuel B. Webb*, ed. W. C. Ford, 3 vols., New York, 1893.

Webster *Letters*: *Letters of Noah Webster*, ed. Harry R. Warfel, New York, 1953.

Weekly: *The Weekly Inspector*, ed. Thomas G. Fessenden, 2 vols., New York, 1806-7.

Weems *Adultery*: Mason L. Weems, *God's Revenge Against Adultery* (1815) in Weems, *Three Discourses*, 145-89.

Weems *Drunkard*: M. L. Weems, *The Drunkard's Looking Glass* (1813) in Weems, *Three Discourses*, 59-136.

Weems *Franklin*: M. L. Weems, *The Life of Benjamin Franklin*, Philadelphia, 1817.

Weems *Gambling*: M. L. Weems, *God's Revenge Against Gambling* (1811), 2d ed., Philadelphia, 1812.

Weems *Hymen*: M. L. Weems, *Hymen's Recruiting Sargeant* (1805) in Weems, *Three Discourses*, 19-48.

Weems *Letters*: *Mason Locke Weems: His Works and Ways*, ed. Emily E. F. Skeel, 3 vols., New York, 1929. (The letters [1794-1825] are in vols. 2 and 3.)

Weems *Marion*: M. L. Weems (and P. Horry), *The Life of Gen. Francis Marion* (1809), 3d ed., Baltimore, 1815. (Horry's only share in the work was to give some information to Weems.)

Weems *Murder*: M. L. Weems, *God's Revenge Against Murder* (1807), 4th ed., Philadelphia, 1808.

Weems *Penn*: M. L. Weems, *The Life of William Penn* (1822), Philadelphia, 1836.

Weems *Philanthropist*: M. L. Weems, *The Philanthropist*, Dumfries, Va., 1799.

Weems *Three Discourses*: M. L. Weems, *Three Discourses*, ed. Emily E. F. Skeel, New York, 1929.

Weems *Washington*: M. L. Weems, *The Life of Washington* (1809), ed. Marcus Cunliffe, Cambridge, Mass., 1962.

Welby *Visit*: Adlard Welby, *A Visit to North America and the English Settlements in Illinois* (1821), ed. Reuben G. Thwaites, Cleveland, 1905.

Wendell *Letters*: "A Gentlewoman of Boston [Catherine Wendell Davis]," by Barrett Wendell, American Antiquarian Society, *Proceedings*, N.S. 29 (1919), 242-93.

Wentworth: Harold Wentworth and Stuart B. Flexner, *Dictionary of American Slang*, New York, 1960.

Wheatley *Poems*: *The Poems of Phillis Wheatley*, ed. Julian D. Mason, Jr., Chapel Hill, N.C., 1966.

Wheelock's Indians: Letters from Eleazar Wheelock's Indians, ed. James D. McCallum, Hanover, N.H., 1932.

Wheelwright *Writings*: John Wheelwright, *His Writings, Including his Fast-Day Sermon, 1637, and His Mercurius Americanus, 1645*, ed. Charles H. Bell, Publications of the Prince Society 9, Boston, 1876.

Whiting: B. J. Whiting, *Proverbs, Sentences, and Proverbial Phrases from English Writings Mainly before 1500*, Cambridge, Mass., 1968.

Whiting *Ballad*: "Proverbial Material in the Popular Ballad," *Journal of American Folklore* 47(1934), 22-44.

Whiting *Devil*: "The Devil and Hell in Current English Literary Idiom," *Harvard Studies and Notes in Philology and Literature* 20(1938), 201-47.

Whiting *Drama: Proverbs in the Earlier English Drama*, Harvard Studies in Comparative Literature 14, Cambridge, Mass., 1938.

Whiting *NC*: "Proverbs and Proverbial Sayings," in Brown *Collection* 1.331-501.

Whiting *Scots* 1, 2: "Proverbs and Proverbial Sayings from Scottish Writings before 1600," *Mediaeval Studies* 11(1949), 123-205; 13(1951), 87-164.

Wigglesworth *Diary: The Diary of Michael Wigglesworth, 1653-1657*, ed. Edmund S. Morgan, New York, 1965.

Willard *Letters*: Margaret W. Willard, *Letters on the American Revolution, 1774-1776*, Boston, 1925.

Willard *Ne Sutor*: Samuel Willard, *Ne Sutor ultra Crepidam, or Brief Animadversions Upon the New-England Anabaptists*, Boston, 1681.

Williams *Penrose*: William Williams, *Mr. Penrose, The Journal of Penrose, Seaman* (1783), ed. David H. Dickason, Bloomington, Ind., 1969.

Williams *Writings: The Complete Writings of Roger Williams*, 7 vols., New York, 1963.

Wilson *Letters*: George Ord, *Sketch of the Life of Alexander Wilson*, Philadelphia, 1828.

Wingate *Letters: Paine Wingate's Letters to his Children*, ed. C. E. L. Wingate, Medford, Mass., 1934.

Winslow *Broadside:* Ola Elizabeth Winslow, *American Broadside Verse,* New Haven, 1930.

Winslow *Diary: Diary of Anna Green Winslow, A Boston School Girl of 1771*, ed. Alice M. Earle, Boston, 1894.

Winslow *Hypocrisie*: Edward Winslow, *Hypocrisie Unmasked* (1646), ed. H. M. Chapin, Providence, 1916.

Winslow Papers: Winslow Papers, A.D., 1776-1826, ed. W. O. Raymond, St. John, N.B., 1901.

Winthrop *Journal*: [*John*] *Winthrop's Journal History of New England, 1630-1649*, ed. James K. Hosmer, 2 vols., New York, 1908.

Winthrop Papers(A): Winthrop Papers, 1498-1649, 5 vols., Massachusetts Historical Society, 1929-47.

Winthrop Papers(B): The Winthrop Papers, 6 vols., Massachusetts Historical Society, *Collections*, 4th ser. 6, 5th ser. 1, 8, 6th ser. 3, 5, 1863-92.

Wirt *Bachelor*: (William Wirt), *The Old Bachelor*, Richmond, Va., 1814.

Bibliographical References

Wirt *British Spy:* William Wirt, *The Letters of the British Spy* (1803), 10th ed., New York, 1832.

Wirt *Letters: Memoirs of the Life of William Wirt*, by John P. Kennedy, 2 vols., Philadelphia, 1849.

Wise *Churches*: John Wise, *The Churches Quarrel Espoused* (New York, 1713), ed. George A. Cook, Scholars' Facsimiles and Reprints, Gainesville, Fla., 1966.

Wise *Vindication:* John Wise, *A Vindication of the Government of New-England Churches,* Boston, 1717.

Wise *Word:* (John Wise), *A Word of Comfort to a Melancholy Country,* Boston, 1721. (Also in *Colonial Currency* 2.162-223.)

Wister *Journal: Sally Wister's Journal*, ed. Albert C. Myers, Philadelphia, 1902.

Witherspoon *Works*: John Witherspoon, *Works*, 2d ed., 4 vols., Philadelphia, 1802.

Wolcott *Papers: The Wolcott Papers: Correspondence and Documents During Roger Wolcott's Governorship of the Colony of Connecticut, 1750-1754*, Connecticut Historical Society, *Collections* 16 (1916).

Wolcott *Poetical Meditations:* Roger Wolcott, *Poetical Meditations*, New London, 1725. (Club of Odd Volumes: Early American Poetry 5 [1898].)

Wood *New-England*: William Wood, *New-England's Prospect* (1634), Publications of the Prince Society 5, Boston, 1865.

Woodmason *Journal: The Carolina Backcountry on the Eve of the Revolution: The Journal and Other Writings of Charles Woodmason, Anglican Itinerant*, ed. R. J. Hooker, Chapel Hill, N.C., 1953.

Woodworth *Beasts*: Samuel Woodworth, *Beasts at Law*, New York, 1811.

Woodworth *Melodies*: Samuel Woodworth, *Melodies, Duets, Trios, Songs, and Ballads,* New York, 1826.

Woodworth *Poems*: Samuel Woodworth, *Poems, Odes, Songs, and other Metrical Effusions*, New York, 1818.

Wright *Views*: Frances Wright, *Views of Society and Manners in America* (1821), ed. Paul R. Baker, Cambridge, Mass., 1963.

Wyllys Papers: The Wyllys Papers: Correspondence and Documents, Chiefly of Descendants of Gov. George Wyllys of Connecticut, 1590-1796, Connecticut Historical Society, *Collections* 21 (1924).

Yankee: The Yankee (later *The Yankee and Boston Literary Gazette*), ed. John Neal, Portland, Me., 1828-9.

Yankee Phrases: "Yankee Phrases," *Port Folio* 3 (1803), 87. ("A poem, by a Yankee bard, who thus jeers the woeful insipidity of the simple style.")

Young *Life*: Peter Young, *A Brief Account of the Life and Experience . . . of Peter Young*, Portsmouth N.H., 1817.

EARLY AMERICAN
PROVERBS
AND
PROVERBIAL PHRASES

A

A1   From A to Z

1809 Fessenden *Pills* 97: From A to Z below presented. TW 1(2). See **B2.**

A2   To be all Aback

1783 EWinslow in *Winslow Papers* 157: On this subject I am literally as the sailors say all aback. Colcord 19; NED Aback 3.

A3   A,B,C

1652 Williams *Writings* 7.215: In the A.B.C. and *Horn-book* of Judaism, **1676** 5.177: *The Beginning,* or A.B.C. of the *Christian Religion.* **1778** Paine *American Crisis* 1.132: You have the A,B,C stratagem yet to learn. **1786** Baldwin *Life and Letters* 239: He did not appear to know scarcely the A B C of the languages. Whiting A2.

A4   As clear as the A,B,C

1784 Washington *Writings* 27.306: This is as clear to me as the A,B,C.

A5   As easy as one's A,B,C

1797 Cobbett *Porcupine* 5.234: Lord! 'tis as easy as one's A B C. **1813** Morris *Diary and Letters* 2.553: The future conduct of the war is comparatively an A B C business. TW 1(2).

A6   As familiar as A,B,C

1809 EHall in *Port Folio* 2NS 2.424: 'Tis as familiar as my A,B,C.

A7   As plain as A,B,C

1776 Paine *American Crisis* 1.56: In language as plain as A. B. C. **1813** Weems *Drunkard* 122: The reason of all this is as plain as A, B, C. TW 1(4). See **O26.**

A8   In Abraham's bosom

1676 Williams *Writings* 5.34: In *Abrahams Bosome.* **1702** Mather *Magnalia* 1.398: A "true child of Abraham," now safely lodged in the *Sinu-Abraha.* **1703** FNicholson in *W&MCQ* 2S 22(1942) 394: My meeting of you in Abraham's bosom. **1759** Adams *D and A* 1.77: You are going . . . to Abrahams Bosom. **1775** Freneau *Poems* 1.180: Where Abrah'm's bosom may be had for all. **1776** *Battle of Brooklyn* 24: "Where are the rest of the guard?" "In Sarah's bosom, I hope." "In Abraham's bosom, he means." **1777** Asbury *Journal* 1.249, **1785** 1.492. **1788** Wendell *Letters* 274: Your Uncle Quincy is gone to Father Abram's bosom. **1793** Asbury *Journal* 1.758. **1801** Weems *Letters* 2.216. **1812** Alden *Epitaphs* 5.233. **a1814** Dow *Journal* 415. **1814** Alden *Epitaphs* 2.268. **1830** Ames *Mariner's* 111: Abraham's bosom is, as one of the fathers of the church has declared, "a place containing about ninety acres." *Oxford* 1; Whiting A15.

A9   To sham Abraham

1781 Witherspoon *Works* 4.473: Low methods of shamming *Abraham* [W. explains as a seaman's phrase for feigning illness]. **1826** Pintard *Letters* 2.322: This I infer to be *sham Abram,* for they are delighted with their visit. **1830** Ames *Mariner's* 193: Many of them as well as officers "shammed Abraham" or "sogerd" as it was called, to get out of the weather. NED Sham 6; Partridge 2.

A10   As handsome as Absolon

1809 Weems *Marion* 32: As handsome as

Absolom or the blooming Adonis. Whiting A18.

A11 **Absence** increases affection (*varied*)

1755 CRay in Franklin *Papers* 6.96: For Absence rather increases than lesens my affections. **1775** MWard in Ward *Correspondence* 50: How absenc endears a beloved object to us. **1783** Mrs. TBurr in Burr *Memoirs* 1.244: Some think absense tends to increase affection; the greater part that it wears it away. **1797** Foster *Coquette* 149: I think you formerly remarked that absence served but to height real love. *Oxford* 1; TW 2.

A12 **Absence** is a cure for love (*varied*)

1709 *Wyllys Papers* 360: Distance and Absense may cure a passion that may be greatly detrimental to My wife's onely Son. **1781** Baldwin *Life and Letters* 56: Tho absence they say is a general cure for love. Cf. *Oxford* 1; Whiting A16, 17.

A13 To speak ill of the **Absent** (*varied*)

1763 Ames *Almanacs* 338: Some take a Liberty to speak ill of the Absent. **1801** Morris *Diary and Letters* 2.407: The maxim "Les absents ont toujours tort," is never more true than in the societies of Paris. *Oxford* 1; Whiting Q10.

A14 An **Abundance** of tenderness and an abundance of discretion

c1705 Byrd *Another Secret Diary* 216: But I have one expedient . . . which is to conclude even against the authority of an old saying, that you have at the same time abundance of tenderness & abundance of discretion. Cf. *Oxford* 2; Tilley A12.

A15 Of the **Abundance** of the heart the mouth speaks

c1645 JCotton in Williams *Writings* 2.182: The mouth is most full of the aboundance of the heart. **1699** Chalkley *Fruits* 351: Out of the Abundance of the Heart the Mouth speaketh. **1747** Brainerd *Memoirs* His mouth spake out of the abundance of his heart. **1764** AA in *Adams FC* 1.25. **1807** *Emerald* 2.277. **1812** AAdams in Smith *Journal and Correspondence* 1.224. **1812** Melish *Travels* 271. **1814** Kerr *Barclay* 385.

1814 Wirt *Bachelor* 105. **1820** Pintard *Letters* 1.328-9. **1824** Pickering *Review* 57. Whiting A22.

A16 **Accidents** will happen

1769 *Commerce of Rhode Island* 1.269: These are Accidents unforeseen and frequently happen. **1802** Ames *Diary* 315: Tim Gay's hogs this dark stormy day let out into my corn—a pretended accident, and she says accidents will happen, but I say they sha'nt! **1810** Adams *Memoirs* 2.113: The girls and boys are kept very carefully separate, and although marriages between them are encouraged, yet Mr Grootten says not a single *accident* has happened. **1831** Longfellow *Letters* 1.361: Accidents will happen. TW 2(1).

A17 **Accidents** will happen in the best (regulated) families

1815 Humphreys *Yankey* 63: It [getting drunk] is what happens in the best of families sometimes. **1819** Waln *Hermit* 29: Accidents will happen in the best regulated families. *Oxford* 2; TW 2(2).

A18 There is no **Accounting** for tastes (*varied*)

1808 Barker *Tears* 162: There's no accounting for men's tastes. **1810** Mackay *Letters* 113: There is no accounting for a woman's whims. **1812** *Kennon Letters* 33.274: You know there is no accounting for the whims and caprices of young creatures like me. *Oxford* 2; TW 2. See **D201, E89.**

A19 To cast up one's **Accounts**

1737 Franklin *Drinker's* 2.173: He's casting up his Accounts. **1803** Davis *Travels* 419: You must leave off casting up your accounts [vomiting]. Partridge 3.

A20 Not to abate an **Ace**

1759 TPownall in *Baxter Manuscripts* 13.153: I woud not have you abate one Ace of Your Steadiness. **1775** TLynch in Sparks *Correspondence* 1.84: Do not bate them an ace, my dear General. **1782** Trumbull *Satiric Poems* 110: Would rather ruin all her race, Than 'bate Supremacy an ace. NED Ace 3. Cf. *Oxford* 32; Tilley A20.

A21 To be within an **Ace**

1777 *Pennsylvania Evening Post* in *Newspaper Extracts* (*II*) 1.410: I was within an ace of taking the whole. **1780** Franklin *Writings* 8.106: They were . . . within an Ace of destroying the Bank. **1792** Brackenridge *Modern* 36: In the course of my experience at the bar, I have had one hung, and several others within an ace of it, who were innocent. TW 3(3).

A22 To differ an **Ace**

1741 Johnson *Writings* 3.147: To differ an ace from you. NED Ace 3. Cf. Whiting A26, 27.

A23 **Achilles** heel

1702 Mather *Magnalia* 2.567: They discovered a "vulnerable heel." **1774** Izard *Correspondence* 30: Even the heel of our Achilles is perfectly covered. **1774** JWentworth in *Belknap Papers* 3.66: Achilles had a tender heel. **1776** Lee *Letters* 1.196: We should endeavor . . . to be more invulnerable than Achilles, not exposing even the heel, where the stake is so immense. **1782** Trumbull *Satiric Poems* 185: Her foes have found her mortal part. As famed Achilles, dipt by Thetis In Styx, as sung in antient ditties, Grew all caseharden'd o'er like steel, Invulnerable, save his heel. **1791** NHazard in Hamilton *Papers* 9.535: Every Man had his Tendo Achilles. **1845** Paulding *Letters*(*II*) 400: It is a better shield than the Invulnerability of Achilles, for it covers the very heel. NED Tendon, Suppl. Heel le; *Oxford* 366.

A24 **Achilles'** (Telephus') spear

1768 Dickinson *Letters* 67: Like the spear of *Telephus*, it will cure as well as wound. **1816** *Port Folio* 4NS 1.451: Perhaps they, like Achilles' spear, May heal the wound they give. **a1820** Tucker *Essays* 233: A further emission of paper . . . is not likely to prove the spear of Achilles, and heal the wound it has made. *Oxford* 762-3; Whiting A30.

A25 Sudden **Acquaintance** brings repentance

1774 Ames *Almanacs* 449: Sudden Acquaintance brings Repentance. *Oxford* 727; Tilley A23.

A26 An **Act** of God shall prejudice no man

1748 Wolcott *Papers* 479: There is this Maxim in the English in Your Favour, viz that the act of god Shall prejudice no man. NED Act 4.

A27 **Action** is rest

1817 Pintard *Letters* 1.48: *In labore quies.* Action is Rest is one of my maxims.

A28 **Actions** speak louder than words (*varied*)

1692 Bulkeley *Will* 212: Actions are more sufficient than words. **1699** Makemie *Writings* 120: Actions with vulgar People, are more demonstrative, than Words. **1713** Sewall *Letter-Book* 2.20: Actions are Stronger than Words. **1721** Wise *Friendly Check* in *Colonial Currency* 2.249: Actions will better shew a Mans design than his Words. **1736** *Melancholy State* in *Colonial Currency* 3.137: Actions speak louder than Words. **1766** PSyng in Franklin *Papers* 13.190: Actions . . . speak louder than Words. **1768** *Commerce of Rhode Island* 1.230: I . . . hope my Actions will express that plainer then my words. **a1770** Mecom in *Franklin-Mecom:* But obligeing Actions are more substantial than words. **1770** Carter *Diary* 1.392: I know him so disposed to lying that I cannot help imagining he that pays no regard to his word will never regard his actions. **1774** Hutchinson *Diary* 1.186. **1775** JBelton in *Naval Documents* 2.15: Experiments will speak plainer than words. **1784** Adams(A) *Letters* 202: Actions, to quote an old phrase, speak louder than words. **1791** Maclay *Journal* 385: But actions are louder than words. **1797** Foster *Coquette* 80: But then, according to the vulgar proverb *that actions speak louder than words*, I have no reason to complain. **1816** Fidfaddy *Adventures* 79: But as the proverb says, "words speak in a whisper, and actions through a trumpet." **1816** CChester in Vanderpoel *More Chronicles* 192. **1825** Fletcher *Letters* 285: It is an old maxim, and not less true than old. **1836** Floy *Diary* 230: My action showed my sincerity; and "you know," say I, "they often speak louder than words." **1843** Jackson *Correspondence* 6.201: It is a just maxim that acts speaks louder than words. *Oxford* 3; TW 3(2).

A29 Adam's ale

1708 Cook *Sot-Weed* 2: And was in fact but *Adam's Ale*. **1728** Byrd *Dividing Line* 178: We had no other Drink but what Adam drank in Paradise, 187. **1792** Freneau *Poems* 3.67: Such virtue lies in—Adam's Ale! **1795** 3.126: Or, in its stead [drenched] with Adam's ale. TW 3(1).

A30 Not to know one from Adam

1787 WSSmith in Smith *Journal and Correspondence* 1.140: In a country where I am not known from Adam—without the *s*—*alias* the husband of Eve. **1801** Trumbull *Season* 93: They to be sure did not know me from Adam. *Oxford* 435; TW 3(3).

A31 The old Adam

c1645 JCotton in Williams *Writings* 2.28: That which is left of the old *Adam* in them. **1654** JHull in *Winthrop Papers*(B) 2.534: Wee have soe much of the old man in vs, that will make such lessons to be harder learnt. **1805** Sewall *Parody* 22: And felt old Adam rising in your throat. **1848** Cooper *Letters* 5.290: Old Adams is buried, and a good deal of old Adam with him, notwithstanding all their eulogies. *Oxford* 3; Whiting A35.

A32 When Adam delved and Eve span, *etc.*

1764 OThacher *Sentiments* in Bailyn *Pamphlets* 1.496-7: They must then adopt Jack Straw's verses, *When Adam delved, and Eve span, Who was then the gentleman?* **1765** Ames *Almanacs* 366: When *Adam* dalve and *Eve* span, who was then the Gentleman? A. B. Friedman in *The Learned and the Lewed*, ed. Larry D. Benson (Cambridge, Mass., 1974) 213-230: *Oxford* 3; Whiting A38.

A33 As firm as Adamant

1777 Munford *Patriots* 498: Firm as adamant. TW 4(1).

A34 As hard as Adamant

1754 Smith *Works* 1[1].7: Harder than adamant. Whiting A40.

A35 As deaf as an Adder

1770 Adams *Legal Papers* 3.270: Deaf as an adder. **1777** JBurgoyne in Moore *Diary* 1.363. **1789** Brown *Better* 41. **1811** Graydon *Memoirs* 357: They were every where deaf as adders to the claims of a general interest. **1848** Cooper *Letters* 5.310: Poor old Mrs. DeLancey, who was deaf as an adder. Barbour 4; *Oxford* 172; Tilley A32.

A36 To feed upon Adders

1811 Adams *Writings* 4.258: He will have according to a French proverbial expression *to feed upon adders*.

A37 Much Ado about nothing

1781 Hopkinson *Miscellaneous Essays* 1.163: *The march to the Valley Forge; or much ado about nothing.* **1811** JAdams in *Adams-Jefferson Letters* 2.286: Why do you make so much ado about nothing? **1817** Wirt *Letters* 1.416: Much ado about nothing—it sounds to me very much like nonsense. [**1830**] Cooper *Letters* 1.405: One remembers the condensed, matter of fact biographies of Johnson, in reading so much ado about nothing. *Oxford* 549; Tilley A38.

A38 Adultery is no sin

1702 Mather *Magnalia* 2.545: To teach them that fornication and adultery is no sin, 550: He would plead, "that there was no sin in adultery." Whiting L167.

A39 Old Adventures are as disagreeable as old women

1764 Watts *Letter Book* 252: Old Adventures, especially small Ones, are as disagreeable as old Women. Cf. *Oxford* 324: Good small beer. See **W268.**

A40 Adversity is the touchstone of friendship

1775 Cresswell *Journal* 123: Experience teaches me adversity is the touchstone of friendship. Cf. *Oxford* 650-1; Whiting A56.

A41 Adversity makes a man wise

1739 Ames *Almanacs* 129: Adversity makes Men Wise. *Oxford* 4; Tilley A42.

A42 We may give **Advice,** but we cannot give conduct

1751 Franklin *PR* 4.88, **1758** *WW* 349: We may give Advice, but we cannot give Conduct. *Oxford* 4.

A43 **Afflictions** are good promotions

1701 Sewall *Diary* 2.43: I had read in the morn, Mr. Dod's saying; Sanctified Afflictions are good Promotions. Cf. *Oxford* 5; Tilley A53.

A44 More **Afraid** than hurt

a1700 Hubbard *New England* 161: As it proved in the sequel, they were more afraid than hurt. **1724** Johnson *Writings* 3.219: They are more sacred [*for* scared] than hurt. **1728** Parkman *Diary* 71.210: Lydia fell from the horse but more surpriz'd than dammag'd. **1739** Stephens *Journal(I)* 1.364: So that the old Adage of being more afraid than hurt, was literally verified. **1755** AStephen in *Letters to Washington* 1.122: The Inhabitants of Pennsylvania are more scared than hurt. **1765** Bartram *Diary* 20: I frequently heard yᵉ women talk how fearfull thay was if A thunder gust arose . . . which I looked upon as A feminin weakness or as yᵉ common Saying, more afraid than hurt. **1807** Janson *Stranger* 18: He had been more terrified than hurt by the disgusting animal. **1822** Watterston *Winter* 148: We found him more frightened than hurt. **1825** Jones *Sketches* 1.25: More frightened . . . than hurt. *Oxford* 543; Whiting A64.

A45 Mr. **After** and Mr. By-and-by

1777 Carter *Diary* 2.1138: But now I resolve that Mr. After and Mr. By and By shall never be again suffered on my plantation. Cf. *Oxford* 849; Tilley A249.

A46 Beware of an **Afterclap** (*varied*)

1642 Bradstreet *Works* 336: This is forerunner of my Afterclap. **1654** Johnson *Wonder-Working* 139: Let *N.England* beware of an after-clap. **1743** Stephens *Journal(II)* 1.166: It was to be wished that it might not forbode an after Clap severe upon our Mulberries and Vines, **1744** 2.63: We were in fear of an after Clap and to guard against it . . . we found it most advisable yet to forbear cutting our Vines. **1781** Franklin *Writings* 8.326: I . . . was obliged to go with this After-Clap to the Ministers. **1787** TBlount in *Blount Papers* 1.244: Best to do it myself—then there can be no afterclaps. **1788** *Washington *Writings* 30.128: I would give no credit, or have any after claps to negotiate. **1797** Cobbett *Porcupine* 7.114: I do not like these *after-claps.* **1798** Washington *Writings* 36.254: To guard against these *after claps.* **1816** Jefferson *Writings* 14.411: That you may not be surprised with afterclaps of expense, not counted on before hand. **1821** Simpson *Journal* 244: I am anxious to expunge these after claps. *Oxford* 58; Whiting A67.

A47 **After-wit** is of no use (*varied*)

1779 Gordon *Letters* 416: Americans are not eminent for foresight but for after-wisdom, alias post-sight. **1803** Davis *Travels* 380: After-wit is of no use. **1803** Morris *Diary and Letters* 2.446: Observations which might now be called *after-wit. Oxford* 6; Tilley A58-60.

A48 **Age** listens to the voice of experience

1783 RMorris in *Clinton Papers* 8.98: It is common for age to listen more to the voice of Experience than youth is inclined to. Cf. Tilley A62.

A49 **Age** must have allowance

1690 BGedney in *Baxter Manuscripts* 5.109: Lin is much out of Breath Since this time twelve: month: but age must have allowance.

A50 Old **Age** has no cure

1803 Rush *Letters* 2.870: Old age has no cure. Cf. *Oxford* 587; Tilley A72, 73. See **H198, R54.**

A51 **Agreement** makes kingdoms flourish

1703 Sewall *Letter-Book* 1.278: I have sent you another Motto; *Florent Concordia Regna;* Agreement makes Kingdoms flourish. Cf. Whiting C404. See **C275.**

A52 As common as the **Air**

1818 Fessenden *Ladies Monitor* 65: Whose boasted charms are common as the air, 127. Barbour 4.

A53   As free as Air

1753 *Independent Reflector* 282: Let your Choice be free as Air. **1769** Brooke *Emily* 110: My Emily is now as free as air. **1774** Adams *Works* 4.29: As free for their use as the air. **1779** *Washington *Writings* 16.66: To give it [money] a circulation as free as the air we breathe in. **1783** *American Wanderer* 372: The fairest work of his hand which he [God] created "free and gay as air." **1783** Pickman *Letters* 135. **1785** *Washington *Writings* 28.35: As free and independent as the air, 28.93: As independent as the Air. **1788** Dunlap *Diary* 1.27. **1792** *Echo* 45. **1794** Tyler *Verse* 33. **1795** Murdock *Triumphs* 34. **1802** Chester *Federalism* 30. **1804** Brackenridge *Modern* 339: As free as the air that we breathe. **1804** *Echo* 302. **1806** Austin *Papers* 1.112: My ideas . . . shall always flow free as air. **1811** Burroughs *Memoirs* 104: And yet walked at liberty, free as the air in which he breathed. **1816** Ker *Travels* 328: Religion . . . is . . . as free as the air we breathe. **1818** Fearon *Sketches* 441. **1818** *The Missouri Expedition, 1818-1820*, ed. Roger L. Nichols (Norman, Okla., 1969) 39: Free as the air which they breathe. **1822** Gallatin *Diary* 205: I feel now as free as the air. *Oxford* 286; TW 4(1).

A54   As liberal as Air

1781 Barlow *Works* 2.35: Liberal as air and unconfin'd as day.

A55   As light as Air

1760 Adams *D and A* 1.171: Trifles light as Air. **1769** Winslow *Broadside* 133: Light as empty air. **1775** Freneau *Poems* 1.164: Light as air, as free as winds I stray'd. **1777** Washington *Writings* 7.240: Trifle. **1778** SAdams in *Warren-Adams Letters* 2.57: Trifles. **1785** Adams(A) *Letters* 234. **1796** Dennie *Lay Preacher* 87: Trifles. **1805** Asbury *Journal* 2.487. **1807** Adams *Writings* 3.172: Trifle. **1809** Weems *Washington* 102: Like an uncaged bird, and light as the air he breathes. **1816** Adams *Writings* 6.40. **1818** Fearon *Sketches* 196. Taylor *Comparisons* 53; Shakespeare *Othello* III iii 322; Tilley A90.

A56   As weak as Air

1650 JWoodbridge in Bradstreet *Works* 86: Your works are solid, others weak as Air.

A57   To be in one's Airs

1737 Franklin *Drinkers* 2.173: He's in his Airs.

A58   To beat (fight) the Air

1620 RCushman in Bradford *History* 1.117: Let them beat the eair. **1637** EHowes in *Winthrop Papers(A)* 4.22: If I speake in an vnknowne tongue, I doe but beat the Aire. **1643** Hutchinson Papers 1.137: You do but beate the ayre, and strive for that which . . . you cannot reach. **1669** Gorton *Letter* in Force *Tracts* 4.7.10: Which is but a beating of the aire. **1694** *Connecticut Vindicated* 119: He intends not to beat Air. **1770** HHusband in Boyd *Eighteenth Century Tracts* 280: And leave the Governor to fight the Air. **1805** Paine *Correspondence* 2.1468: It was fighting the air to take any notice of them. *Oxford* 36. See **W203**.

A59   To put on Airs

1742 Belcher *Papers* 2.441: I was truly surpriz'd to see you put on so many grave airs. **1775** WShirriff in *Baxter Manuscripts* 14.262: They gave themselves Airs. **1793** *Belknap Papers* 2.326: Come, come, citizen pricklouse, do not give yourself such airs as these! **1806** JCoffee in Jackson *Correspondence* 1.130: If Mr. Swann put on airs with him, he could cane him. ?**1814** Freneau *Poems* 3.371: Not Perry, when he said, "they're mine!" Put on such airs. TW 5.

A60   To vanish into thin Air

1832 Barney *Memoir* 84: All, all was gone: vanished into thin air! Hyamson 9; NED Vanish 2c. See **M197, S262**.

A61   As empty as an Air-balloon

1818 Fessenden *Ladies Monitor* 33: With head as empty as an air-balloon.

A62   As white as Alabaster

1827 Watterston *Wanderer* 136: Her teeth were white as alabaster. TW 5.

A63   Albany beef

1779 Thacher *Journal* 199: This fish [sturgeon] is a favorite with the Dutch, at Albany, and is on that account by some called Albany beef. **1791** Long *Voyages* 118: This fish is very common in Albany, and is sold at 1d. per lb. York currency. The flesh is called Albany beef. DA Albany 3. See **B18, G7.**

A64 To know no more than the pump at **Aldgate**
1783 Lee(W) *Letters* 3.921: Adventurers, that knew no more of Geography or the proper Limits of Canada then the Pump at Aldgate. Cf. Lean 1.136; NED Pump *sb.*[1] lb; TW 298(1).

A65 As welcome as sour **Ale** in summer
1686 Dunton *Letters* 77: I am satisfy'd that I'm as welcome to 'em as Sowr Ale in Summer.

A66 To (a)mend like sour **Ale** in summer
1721 *Boston News-Letter* in Buckingham *Specimens* 1.8: The said Jack promises to amend like soure Ale in Summer. **1721** *Letter* in *Colonial Currency* 2.259: I fear our Circumstances will mend, like Sowre Ale in Summer. *Oxford* 526; Whiting A80.

A67 An **Alibi** is the last refuge of a felon
1810 Adams *Lectures* 1.307: To set up an alibi is proverbial among those, who are conversant in the practice of our criminal courts, as the last desperate refuge of an all but convicted felon.

A68 As sure (true) as one is **Alive**
1714 Hunter *Androboros* 34: I am Dead, as sure as I'm Alive. **1757** *Johnson Papers* 9.681: As sure as you are alive, **1762** 3.635: I have seen Mr. Banyar who as he is alive declares that he has wrote to you since you to him. **1774** PHutchinson in Hutchinson *Diary* 1.274: Why, the King and Queen, as you are alive. **1799** Freneau *Prose* 423: Reality — 'tis every word as true as you are alive. TW 5(5). See **L186.**

A69 After **All** is said and done
1792 JRumsey in *W&MCQ* 25(1916) 27: After all is Said and done. NED Suppl. Say *v.*[1] 1.

A70 **All** I had and much more, like the widow's mite
1796 DAllison in *Blount Papers* 3.44: As I have forwarded you a small supply, like the widow's mite all I had and much more. NED Widow *sb*[1] 5.

A71 **All** in good time
1776 Huntington *Papers* 270: All in good Time is a vulgar Saying and often a true one.

A72 **All** is fair in trade
1815 *Reviewers* 20: One of John Bull's favorite axioms is, "all is fair in trade." Cf. TW 5(3).

A73 **All** is not lost which is deferred
1692 Bulkeley *Will* 233: *Quod differtur non aufertur*, delay upon just and weighty cause is no injustice to any. **1820** Jefferson *Writings* 15.243: I . . . console myself with the French proverb that "all is not lost which is deferred," 18.310: But "tout ce qui est différé n'est pas perdu," says the French proverb, **1821** 19.277. Lean 3.413. Cf. Whiting T538.

A74 **All** is not lost which is in danger
1795 Murdock *Triumphs* 67: Remember the old saying: all is not lost which is in danger. *Oxford* 487; Whiting A96.

A75 **All** is vanity
1653 Wigglesworth *Diary* 52: Vanity of vanities all is vanity and vexation of spirit. **1754** Plumstead 319: All that cometh is vanity (Eccles. 11.8). **1766** JOtis in *Warren-Adams Letters* 1.1: I am . . . convinced of the vanity of things under the sun. **1786** Adams(A) *Letters* 286: Vanity of vanities, all is vanity. **1796** Perkins *Diary* 3.403: Vanity of Vanitys! **1798** Adams *New Letters* 135: All is vanity and vexation of spirit. **1807** Rush *Letters* 2.941: Vanity of vanities, all is vanity. Whiting A92.

A76 **All** is well that ends well
1705 *Penn-Logan Correspondence* 1.354: All's well that ends well. **1764** Watts *Letter Book* 239: It might have been worse, all is well that ends well, 277, **1765** 335. **1771** *Franklin-Mecom* 126. **1775** Bowen *Journals*

2.443. **1779** Huntington *Papers* 109: And in the End [we] hope all things will End well. **1780** Adams *Works* 7.167. **1789** EHazard in *Belknap Papers* 2.135. **1797** Jefferson *Writings* 9.360: I claim absolution under the proverb, that "all is well that ends well." **1806** Dow *Journal* 303: And all is well that ends well, is the proverb. **1814** *Kennon Letters* 36.368. *Oxford* 879; Whiting E83.

A77 As cruel to spare **All** as to spare none

1762 Ames *Almanacs* 327: 'Tis as cruel to spare all, as to spare none.

A78 Grasp **All** lose all

1738 Franklin *PR* 2.195: Thou'lt end in nothing, if thou grasps at all. **1774** Seabury *Letters* 126: If we grasp at too much, we shall lose every thing. **1774** Van Schaack *Letters* 23: By grasping at more, they will probably lose all. **1786** *Columbian Magazine* 1.173: Let us take care, lest by grasping at too much, we lose all. *Oxford* 331; Whiting M774. See **M242, 294.**

A79 To know **All** one must see all

1789 Morris *Diary* 1.63: But to know all one must see all.

A80 When **All** comes to all

1756 LCarter in *Letters to Washington* 1.235: And when all comes to all as the saying [is] who believes it Perhaps one man in a hundred.

A81 **Almost** and hard-by save many a lie

1800 Cobbett *Porcupine* 11.254: When I was a boy, we used to say, that *almost* and *hard-by* saved many a *lie*. *Oxford* 12; Tilley A221.

A82 **Alpha** and Omega

1782 Adams *D and A* 3.91: The Alpha and Omega of British Policy. **1782** Alden *Epitaphs* 1.116: Christ hath been the Alpha and Omega to him. **1803** Austin *Constitutional* 134: Federalism was the Alpha and Omega, 137: Economy . . . is the alpha and omega of a republican government. **1806** Plumer *Memorandum* 386: It was the Alpha & omega of our former negociation. NED Alpha 2.

A83 From **Alpha** to Omega

1776 Jefferson *Papers* 15.577: In time to attack it in the house from Alpha to Omega. **1802** Weems *Letters* 2.236: And all the Engravers between Alpha & Omega give you Gipies [sic] Bantlings for Angels. **1815** Jefferson *Writings* 14.340: Nicholas . . . combatted the answer from *alpha* to *omega*. TW 6.

A84 An **American** will go to hell for a bag of coffee

1809 *Port Folio* 2NS 2.108: Dessalines has been heard to say, that "If a bag of coffee was to be placed on the brink of Hell, an American would be the first man to go for it." **1830** Ames *Mariner's* 113: It was truly said during the "forced trade" with the West Indies, "that if there was a bag of coffee hanging over the middle of hell, there was not a merchant in New-England that would not sell his soul to the devil to get it."

A85 To run (A)**muck**

1779 TMifflin in *Thomson Papers* 441: Payne . . . was determined to run the *muck* — he sallied forth, stab'd three or four slightly. **1792** Delano *Narrative* 167: A Malay will not voluntarily use this plant in order to run mad, or *run the muck*, as it is termed. **1796** Morris *Diary and Letters* 2.241: He is running amuck at popularity. **1797** Beete *Man* 28: I'll chew opium, and run muck, like a Indian. **1807** *Salmagundi* 47: I would not have any of my courteous and gentle readers suppose that I am running a *muck*, full tilt, cut and slash, upon all foreigners indiscriminately. **1830** JRandolph in Jackson *Correspondence* 4.176: Has he taken opium and does he mean like a Malay to "run a muck?" None of these except that he *will* "run a muck" not drunk with opium or wine. *Oxford* 688; TW 6.

A86 To cast an **Anchor** to windward

1774 Smith *Memoirs(I)* 179: It is not worth a Trip to this Place to cast this Anchor to windward of the next Admn. **1783** Williams *Penrose* 248: I have fairly laid my Anchor to the Windward of you. **1786** WGordon in *Bowdoin Papers* 2.88: I might lay an anchor to windward against the blasts of ill nature

& prejudice. **1787** *Columbian Magazine* 1.515: Frog had laid an anchor to windward of him. **1787** Cutler *Life* 1.303: I am to go on to Connecticut and Rhode Island . . . and to lay an anchor to the windward with them. **1799** *Washington *Writings* 37.452: Which makes me desirous of laying (to use a Sea term) an anchor to windward for something else. **1812** Woodworth *Beasts* 17: We've some anchor thrown to windward. **1821** Robertson *Letters* cxi: Here is an anchor to windward for myself. **1824** Neal *American Writers* 75: Thus Cowper . . . laid an anchor to windward. Colcord 23; NED Windward Ab.

A87   To cast Anchor

1735 Belcher *Papers* 2.198: And there, Jonathan, we must cast anchor if we intend to ride out safe. **1802** Asbury *Journal* 2.365: I cast anchor, with a determination to give up Georgia and go . . . to Camden. Tilley A241.

A88   As beautiful as an Angel

1773 Paterson *Glimpses* 103: You were . . . beautiful as an Angel. **1824** Lee *Diary and Letters* 220. TW 6(1). Cf. Whiting A125.

A89   As handsome as an Angel

1719 Byrd *London Diary* 309: Then went and drank tea with . . . Mrs. Polhill, who is as handsome as an angel. **1815** Brackenridge *Modern* 795. TW 6(3).

A90   As happy as an Angel

1717 Byrd *Another Secret Diary* 305: For I cant wish her as happy as an Angel.

A91   As honest as an Angel

1777 JA in *Adams FC* 2.176: As honest as an Angell.

A92   As innocent as an Angel

1717 Byrd *Another Secret Diary* 305: At the same time as innocent as an Angel. Taylor *Comparisons* 51.

A93   As pretty as an Angel

1719 Byrd *London Diary* 309: As pretty as an angel. TW 6(4).

A94   Enough to make an Angel swear

1802 Chester *Federalism* 6: 'Tis enough . . . to make an angel swear. See **D52, J39, M28, 181, Q3, S72.**

A95   Anger is a short madness

1652 Williams *Writings* 4.387: What is this Anger but Fury, *Ira furor brevis est*? **1770** Adams *Legal Papers* 3.264: Anger, which is a short fit of madness. **1781** Van Schaack *Letters* 202: Remember, *ira brevis furor est.* **1804** *Port Folio* 4.157: Ira furor brevis est. **1829** PWinston in *Ruffin Papers* 1.469-70: They all concurred in thinking that these unfavourable impressions, rather I should say *anger (Ira brevis furor) might* pass away before the next session of the legislature. *Oxford* 13-4; Whiting W705.

A96   To get one's Ankles scratched

a**1814** Dow *Journal* 418: Hence many get the *ankles* scratched, if no more! [of young girls, almost seduced]. Cf. Partridge 13.

A97   A soft Answer turns away wrath (*varied*)

1642 RJordan in *Trelawny Papers* 320: Soft words pacifie wrath; but subtle soothings blind the wise. **1692** Bulkeley *Will* 135: A soft answer turns away wrath, but grievous words stir up anger. *Prov.* 15.1. **1692** Mather *Wonders* 90: If we would use to one another none but the *soft Answers, which turn away wrath*. **1702** Mather *Magnalia* 1.123-4: Were it not for . . . the . . . skill of this wise man, *at giving soft answers*, one would not chuse to relate those instances of wrath which he had sometimes to encounter with. **1768** Habersham *Letters* 71: A soft answer turneth away Wrath. **1770** Carter *Diary* 1.375: However it is Solomon's advice, a soft answer yet awhile will be best. **1777** Asbury *Journal* 1.231. **1791** EHazard in *Belknap Papers* 2.269. **1814** Adams *Memoirs* 3.50. *Oxford* 750; Whiting A132, W615.

A98   To be on the Anvil

1703 *Penn-Logan Correspondence* 1.245: If such a constitution . . . could be brought on the anvil. **1724** Mather *Diary* 2.744: I have some works upon the Anvil. **1733** Belcher *Papers* 1.500, **1734** 2.39. **1740** WDouglass *Discourse* in *Colonial Currency* 3.308: The many Schemes at present upon the Anvil in Boston. **1745** *Georgia Records*

24.378. **1756** Johnson *Writings* 2.338. **1756** RNicholas in *Letters to Washington* 1.337. **1764** Franklin *Papers* 11.327. **1782** EHazard in *Belknap Papers* 1.115, 130. **1783** Madison *Papers* 6.482: The system for foreign affairs . . . will be long on the anvil. **1784** ERandolph in Jefferson *Papers* 7.117: Mr . . . Smith has on the anvil, I am told, a tract. **1788** Smith *Diary* 2.244. **1792** EHazard in *Belknap Papers* 2.280. **1792** Jefferson *Papers* 8.379. **1796** Hamilton *Works* 10.152. **1807** *Port Folio* NS 4.414: In the future, instead of asking what is on the *tapis*, we must inquire, what is on the *anvil*. [Five U.S. Senators were named Smith.] **1821** King *Life* 6.374. **1831** WBrockenbrough in *Ruffin Papers* 2.30: Our whole Judiciary system is now under the Anvil in the House of Delegates—whether they will beat it out into anything valuable I know not. NED Anvil 2.

A99 When you are an **Anvil** hold you still, *etc.*

1758 Franklin *PR* 7.351: When you're an Anvil, hold you still; When you're a Hammer, strike your Fill. *Oxford* 15; Tilley A261.

A100 The **Ape** loves the cat to death

1723 *New-England Courant* 95[1.1]: If he does love Truth, 'tis not as the Ape loves the Cat, *viz.* so as to *hug her to death.* Cf. Tilley A264.

A101 To scramble like **Apes** for nuts

1777 JA in *Adams FC* 2.245: Scrambling for Rank and Pay like Apes for Nutts. *Oxford* 583; Tilley N363.

A102 He that **Appears** not perishes

1702 Mather *Magnalia* 2.581: The Spanish proverb, *Quien no parece perece;* i.e. "He that apears not, perishes;" he that shows not himself to the world is undone.

A103 **Appearances** are deceiving (*varied*)

1759 Franklin *Papers* 8.308: But there is no Dependance on Appearances. **1759** THutchinson in *Saltonstall Papers* 1.429: And what is more Fronti nulla Fides. **1777** Smith *Memoirs(II)* 150: How false the Reasoning from Appearances & yet the best History is often founded upon such Virisimilitudes. **1777** *Washington *Writings* 8.157: But appearances are deceiving. **1778** Curwen *Journal* 1.510: Frequent disappointments teach me not to depend on appearances. **1779** Adams *D and A* 2.400: Appearances are often deceitful. **1779** Bailey *Journal* 146: Appearances often change in this various world, 151: Nothing can be more uncertain and delusive than appearances at sea. **1779** JSullivan in Washington *Writings* 17.267: Appearances may Deceive even an Angel. **1780** Curwen *Journal* 2.702: Appearances are fair for enjoyment here, experience here has taught me not to rely on them. **1781** Hopkinson *Miscellaneous Essays* 1.172: They judge from appearances only, and appearances are generally delusive. **1784** *Belknap Papers* 2.186: The appearances in those mountainous regions are extremely deceptive. **1785** JQAdams in Smith *Journal and Correspondence* 2[1] 34: The first rule a person . . . should adopt, should be never to judge from appearances. **1785** HCruger in Van Schaack *Letters* 408: *Nulla fides fronti.* **?1786** MCosway in Jefferson *Papers* 10.393: You dont always judge by appearances. **1789** *Columbian Magazine* 3.426: As little judging of one as the other by appearances; *fronti nulla fides,* 600: First appearances deceive us. **1794** Drinker *Journal* 254: Appearances . . . are often fallacious. **1794** Jay *Correspondence* 4.29: But appearances merit only a certain degree of circumspect reliance, in King *Life* 1.568: You know appearances are often fallacious. **1795** Murdock *Triumphs* 27: The world is sometimes deceived by appearances. **1803** Austin *Literary Papers* 263: You must not judge by appearances. **1804** GCabot in King *Life* 4.370: I insist that our appearance is deceptive. **1807** Maxwell *Mysterious* 5.13: Trust not appearance. **1808** SWest in Alden *Epitaphs* 3.202: Never to judge a person's character by external appearance. **1809** *Port Folio* 2NS 1.198: If appearances deceive me not. **1813** Gerry *Diary* 87: I advised them not to rely too much on appearances. **1817** Anderson *Diary* 70: If I had not been long enough in the world to know that appearances are deceiving. **1826** Austin *Literary Papers* 22:

Nothing in this world is so deceitful as appearances. *Oxford* 415; TW 7(1, 2, 4, 5).

A104 The **Apple** of discord

1778 CRamsey in Sullivan *Letters* 2.4: The Same Purpose, for which the goddess of Discord Sent down from heaven the golden Apple. **1794** King *Life* 1.479: I opposed the project . . . on the ground that it was throwing the Apple of Discord into Congress. **1798** Adams *Writings* 2.284: Throwing out such a new apple of discord. **1810** JMason in King *Life* 5.203: The projected scheme will only prove upon trial an apple of discord. **?1813** AAdams in Smith *Journal and Correspondence* 1.225: I perceive the apple of discord is thrown out in Congress. **1829** Pintard *Letters* 3.111: The president has thrown an apple of discord into our monied market. *Oxford* 17; TW 8(7). See **B33, 253.**

A105 The **Apple** of one's eye

1631 JHumfrey in *Winthrop Papers(A)* 3.52: But that he should . . . tender us as the apple of his eye. **1637** JUnderhill in *Winthrop Papers(A)* 3.461: Yow are as deare to god as the Aple of his eye. **1644** Williams *Writings* 3.298: The Apple of the Eye, **1652** 4.55: The Apple of his eye, 4.302. **1703** Mather *Diary* 1.471, 486, 487, **1705** 1.511. **1714** Plumstead 154: The son of God's right hand, whom he loves as dearly as a man doth his right hand or the apple of his eye. **1722** Mather *Diary* 2.671: But, my opportunities to do good, which have been to me as the Apple of my Eye, have been strangely struck, **1724** 2.752, 754. **1755** Johnson *Writings* 1.227: God . . . keep him as the apple of an eye. **1765** Watts *Letter Book* 406. **1771** Asbury *Journal* 1.7. **1786** Adams *Works* 8.417. **1797** Cobbett *Porcupine* 7.407: Preserve it as you would a golden casket, the apple of your eye. **1800** *Echo* 281. **1809** Kendall *Travels* 1.169. **1809** *Kennon Letters* 31.302. **1820** GCutler in Vanderpoel *Chronicles* 200: There is a sweet little letter from her that is dearer than the apple of my eye. Whiting A156. See **E136.**

A106 How we **Apples** swim! (*varied*)

1761 Adams *D and A* 1.197: And if we say this we must run off to avoid the Reply, of a Pigs turd to a Pine Apple. **1780** *New Jersey Gazette* in *Newspaper Extracts(II)* 5.95: The author's assuming so respectable a character, put me in mind of the story of the apples and horse-turd (pardon the expression) when floating down stream they happened to drift near to each other. The latter, you know, assumed an air of equality, and he accosted the former by calling out "we apples." **1799** Carey *Porcupiniad* 2.11: How WE apples swim! **1802** Adams (TB) *Letters* 166: Thus you "see how we pippins swim." **1812** Rush *Letters* 2.1158: The fellow has not profited by the line in the fable, "See! how we apples swim." **1838** Hone *Diary* 1.306: I made them all pledge themselves to make one of us three President of the United States. How we apples swim! *Oxford* 17; TW 8(8).

A107 A rotten **Apple** spoils its companion

1736 Franklin *PR* 2.140: The rotten Apple spoils his Companion. *Oxford* 684; Whiting A167. See **S127.**

A108 To overset the **Apple-cart**

1788 *Belknap Papers* 2.17: S. Adams had almost overset the apple-cart by intruding an amendment of his own fabrication. **1795** *Remarks on the Jacobinaid* 1.31-2: Lest wee over-sett our apple-cart, and so stick our foot in it. **1805** Sewall *Parody* 47: Babylon is fallen! . . . Ah, hapless Babylon! Oh ill-fated apple-cart! *Oxford* 17; TW 8.

A109 He who takes the **Application** makes it

1814 Wirt *Bachelor* 93: The maxim will be remembered—"*qui capit, ille facit*"—he who takes the application to himself, makes it. Cf. TW 55(1): Cap. See **C29.**

A110 **April** borrows three days from March

1824 Doddridge *Notes* 55: It was a common saying that we must not expect spring until the *borrowed days*, that is, the three first days of April were over. Dunwoody 96; *Oxford* 511: March; Tilley A307.

A111 **April** showers bring May flowers (*varied*)

1671 DRussell in Silverman 117; The Proverb's well verifi'd, that April Showers On Maia's Fields do rain down glittering Flowers. **1756** Sherman *Almanacs* 254: Now *April* showers, Impregnate the Flowers. **1758** Carter *Diary* 1.213: That which used to be called April Showers in order to produce the flowers in May are now nothing but cold scudds of Snow. Barbour 163; *Oxford* 17; Tilley S411; Whiting *NC* 362(1). Cf. Whiting A173.

A112 To be like **April** skies

c1800 Dennie *Lay Preacher* 109: Like April skies, life is coquettish, capricious, and changeable. *Oxford* 18; TW 8-9(1); Whiting A172.

A113 To be tied to **Apron-strings** *(varied)*

1647 Ward *Simple Cobler* 63: Apron-string *tenure* is very weak . . . It stands not with our Queens honour to weare an Apron, much lesse her Husband, in the strings. **1776** Moore *Diary* 1.204: Great lounging infants tied to mama's apron at two-and-twenty. **1777** TDavis in *Innes (James) and His Brothers* 37: Spin out a childish Existence at your Mother's Apron Strings. **1787** Tyler *Contrast* 36: But when she had once looked down on her apron strings, as all modest young women us'd to do. **1799** Barlow *Works* 1.380: Tie himself to the apron-strings of the same Juno. **1802** *Port Folio* 2.380: She . . . Kept Kitty near her apron string. **1818** Fessenden *Ladies Monitor* 59: Fasten'd in triumph to their apron strings. **1819** Wirt *Letters* 2.101: I take it for granted that you visit us this winter (without being tied to Holmes' apron-string). **1851** *Ruffin Papers* 2.314: I suppose, from what Katy said in her letter to her Mother, that you, too, are at the apron-string by this time. **1858** Paulding *Letters(II)* 582: They are tied to the Apron Strings of the government. *Oxford* 18; TW 9. See **L72.**

A114 **Argus** and his eyes

1634 Wood *New-England* 36: That seeke fresh water brookes with Argus eyes. **1676** Winslow *Broadside* 9: *Briarius* hands to set his virtues forth, And *Argus* Eyes to weep his golden worth. **1702** Mather *Magnalia* 1.32: If I had . . . as many eyes as an Argos, 2.682: It seems the hands of Briareus, and the eyes of Argus, will not prevent them [errata]. **1774** JWentworth in *Belknap Papers* 3.66: Argus's thousand eyes were put to sleep. **1775** RRichardson in Gibbes 2.220: A man must have the eyes of Argus, and as many ears as eyes. **1781** Hopkinson *Miscellaneous Essays* 1.171: By this I have gained their confidence and blinded the Argus eyes of power. **a1788** Jones *History* 1.87: Who had in matters of this kind as many eyes as Argus. **1789** Washington *Writings* 30.366: The eyes of Argus are upon me. **1794** SHigginson in Hamilton *Papers* 16.594: It requires the Eyes of Argus to watch & discover the movements & pursuits of that party. **1794** Stiles *Three Judges* 181: He was an insidious spy upon New-England, with Argos eyes. **1807** *Port Folio* NS 4.207: The hundred eyes of Argus. **1807** *Salmagundi* 225: Having, however, looked about me with the Argus eyes of a traveller. **1821** Simpson *Journal* 288: We have got to the blind side of these Argus eyed Gentlemen. *Oxford* 236; Whiting A180.

A115 As long as my **Arm**

1767 JDevotion in Stiles *Itineraries* 462: An Epistle as long as my Arm. **1778** *Washington *Writings* 13.36. **1787** *Columbian Magazine* 1.315. **1795** Cobbett *Porcupine* 2.58, **1797** 6.295. **1802** Irving *Jonathan* 14. **1817** Robertson *Letters* 24. TW 9. See **L97.**

A116 To be up in **Arms**

1774 AA in *Adams FC* 1.176: Come and dine with me, you will find me a little up in arms as they say but very glad to see you. TW 9.

A117 As straight as an **Arrow**

1709 Lawson *Voyage* 40: Limbs as straight as an Arrow. **1769** Adams *Legal Papers* 2.91. **1777** JA in *Adams FC* 2.247. **1795** Iredell *Correspondence* 2.446. **1809** Lee *Diary and Letters* 102: All the little girls of your age in Paris are straight as arrows. Barbour 6(1); TW 9(2).

A118 As swift as an **Arrow**

1634 Wood *New-England* 30: As swift as arrow from Tartarian Bow. **1639** Winthrop *Journal* 1.294: It ran as swift as an arrow toward Cherlton. **1705** Knight *Journal* 70: Wee come to the other side as swiftly passing as an arrow shott out of the Bow by a strong arm. **1783** Williams *Penrose* 88. **1791** Bartram *Travels* 80. Barbour 6(2); *Oxford* 794; Whiting A186.

A119 A good **Arrow** cannot be made of a sow's tail

1742 Franklin *PR* 2.335: Ne'er was good Arrow made of a Sow's Tail. See **P60, 323.**

A120 To have but one **Arrow** in his quiver

1809 Weems *Letters* 2.397: It w^d be immensely wrong to have but one arrow in your quiver when you cou'd have two equally feather'd & sure. See **S495.**

A121 **Arsy-versy**

1797 Brackenridge *Modern* 267: Everything seems to be *arsa-versa* here, the wrong side uppermost. NED Arsy-versy; *Oxford* 424; Tilley A328.

A122 **Art** is long and life is short

1713 Wise *Churches* 88: Theology, as well as Art, is a long study, and Life is very short. **1778** Franklin *Writings* 7.208: Alas! art is long, and life is short! **1787** Adams *Diary* 347: Ars longa, vita brevis, is a maxim the truth of which I am experiencing. **1804** *Port Folio* 4.193. **1810** Adams *Lectures* 1.362. **1833** Wirt *Letters* 2.413: *Vita brevis, ars longa.* Barbour 6; *Oxford* 19; Whiting L245. See **L122.**

A123 As dry as **Ashes**

1796 Ames *Letters* 1.197: Our gardens are as dry as ashes. TW 10(1).

A124 As pale as **Ashes**

1774 Adams *D and A* 2.117: Pale as ashes. **1794** Rowson *Charlotte* 1.102: She turned pale as ashes, 2.42. **1802** *Port Folio* 2.381. **1806** Fessenden *Modern Philosopher* 136, 215. **1811** *Port Folio* 2NS 5.191: He sunk pale as ashes, and lifeless as marble. *Oxford* 608; Whiting A205.

A125 As white as **Ashes**

1800 Hamilton *Law Practice* 1.729: He appeared as white as ashes. TW 10(3).

A126 To spit in one's own **Ashes**

1768 *Johnson Papers* 6.523: A . . . place that I could with propperty call my Home where I could . . . Spitt in My Owne Asshes. Cf. Whiting B505.

A127 **Ask** and have

1755 Franklin *PR* 5.471: Ask and have, is sometimes dear buying. *Oxford* 20; Tilley A343.

A128 To quake (shake, tremble) like an **Aspen** (leaf).

c1700 Taylor *Poems* 388: Whose single Frown will make the Heavens shake Like an aspen leafe the Winde makes quake. **1775** EHazard in *Deane Correspondence* 193: The former . . . trembles like an aspen leaf. **1777** Wister *Journal* 67: And my hand shook like an aspen leaf. **1809** Weems *Marion* 50: Both trembled like aspen leaves, *Washington* 210: Tembling like an aspen. **1811** Dunlap *Diary* 2.416: He trembled like an aspen leaf. **1814** Palmer *Diary* 40: Run aft singing out murder . . . and trembling like an aspen leaf. **1819** Noah *Travels* 305: Curadi . . . trembled like an aspen leaf. **1827** Watterston *Wanderer* 110: He shook, like an aspen. **1832** Smith *Letters* 338: As tremulous as an aspen. *Oxford* 21; Whiting A216. See **L75, 76.**

A129 As stupid as **Asses**

1809 Weems *Marion* 159: Others looked as stupid as asses. Svartengren 50. Cf. Whiting A218, 220.

A130 An **Ass** between two bundles of hay

1847 Paulding *Letters(II)* 456: We are thus left between fire and water, like a certain animal between two bundles of Hay. *Oxford* 199; TW 10(1).

A131 An **Ass** in a lion's skin (*varied*)

1637 Morton *New English Canaan* 327: The asses eares will peepe through the lyons hide. **c1700** Byrd *Another Secret Diary* 259: The asses Ears thrust themselves always above the Lions skin. **1768** *New-York Gazette* in *Newspaper Extracts(I)* 7.113: I may . . . divest the ass of his lion's skin. **1807** *Salmagundi* 17: The ass's head may rise up in judgment against him. *Oxford* 21; Whiting A224.

A132 An **Ass** will bray

1745 *Johnson Papers* 1.25: I am in no Shape at the Least apprehensive, but an A — s will bray.

A133 As firm as **Atlas**

1775 DCobb in *Bingham's Maine* 1.402: The Doctor is as firm as Atlas. **1781** *Washington Writings* 22.481: As unshaken as Mount Atlas. **1794** Stiles *Three Judges* 95: He, like Mount Atlas, stood firm.

A134 As high as **Atlas**

1797 Bentley *Diary* 2.245: He piles bug bears higher than Atlas.

A135 To dance **Attendance**

1794 RBlackledge in *Blount Papers* 2.431: I went to Rawleigh . . . and have been dancing Attendance untill the 7ᵗʰ. *Oxford* 165-6; Whiting A235.

A136 **Attic** salt

1783 *American Wanderer* 199: They would not lavish their Attic salt, 312: His discourse was so powdered with Attic salt that it excited thirst. **1785** Tilghman *Letters* 132: They have both so large a portion of the attic Salt that they might be flint and steel to each other. **1789** *Columbian Magazine* 3.182: They taste the truly *Attic* salt therein contained. **1799** Adams *Works* 8.649: Seasoned with no more than was useful and agreeable of Attic salt. **1802** CARodney in Burr *Memoirs* 2.191: Your tea-sippers and salts-men (not Attic). **1809** *Port Folio* 2NS 1.94: There was no lack of attic salt. NED Attic 2.

A137 To cleanse (clean) the **Augean** stable

1765 Woodmason *Journal* 81: When will this *Augean* Stable be cleans'd? **1769** 290: He was too feeble a *Hercules* to cleanse the *Augean* Stable. **1775** PSchuyler in Sparks *Correspondence* 1.4: I shall have an Augean stable to clean there. **1778** Lee(W) *Letters* 2.480: Congress will nearly have an Augean stable to cleanse. **1779** WGlasscock in *McIntosh Papers* 80: An Herculean task we have almost cleansed the stable. **1789** Morris *Diary* 1.154: Kersan tells me that the Augean Stable of Versailles is now quite cleaned. **1806** WChipman in *Winslow Pa-pers* 556: Here is an Augean stable to be cleaned. NED Augean, Stable *sb.*¹ 1b.

A138 **August** and December

1788 *Politician* 5: What a blessed union there will be between August and December. See **D89, J16.**

A139 In **Aunt** Gowen's day

1804 Bentley *Diary* 3.75: In Aunt Gowen's day, is a phrase to ridicule the claims of antiquity among seamen. In the Becket family they tell me she has been dead about thirty years. In the winter the phrase is Molly Becket's shining free. . . . I have noticed these common phrases before, but I do not recollect readily in what place, & common conversation obliges me to notice them, **1814** 4.245: Aunt Cowen, who has given occasion to the proverb, "It was not so in Aunt C's day."

A140 **Avarice** never grows old (*varied*)

1757 Franklin *PR* 7.89: When other Sins grow old by Time, Then Avarice is in its prime. **1772** Smith *Works* 1¹.201: Now one fault, which too often creeps on with old age, to render it despicable, is extreme Avarice and Penuriousness. **1775** Madison *Papers* 1.152: We all know age is no stranger to avarice. **1816** Smith *Life* 205: Young men are commonly liberal, and it is the most common thing to see old men covetous. *Oxford* 727; Whiting C490.

A141 **Avoidance** is better than repentance

1761 *Boston Gazette* in *Olden Time* 2.30: Avoidance is better than late repentance. See **R57.**

A142 A lean **Award** is better than a fat judgment

1753 Franklin *PR* 4.406: A lean Award is better than a fat Judgment. **1789** Morris *Diary* 1.143: I am about to conclude an indirect Agreement . . . because *un mauvais Accomodement vaut mieux qu'un bon Procés. Oxford* 397; Tilley A78.

A143 To have an **Ax** to grind

1810 *American Republic* in DA Ax 2: He evidently has an axe to grind. *Oxford* 24; TW 10-1.

A144 To lay the **Ax** to the root of the tree **1637** Wheelwright *Writings* 171: He layeth the axe to the roote of the tree. **1643** SGorton in Winslow *Hypocrisie* 35: Now the axe is laid to the root of the tree. **1689** Bulkeley *People's Right* 71: The Ax is laid to our own Root. **1691** *News* in *Baxter Manuscripts* 5.189: God is now come forth ag[t] us wth an ax, a French Ax, accompanied wth Indian Hatchetts our very roote is like to receiue y[e] Stroake. **a1700** Hubbard *New England* 166. **1702** Taylor *Christographia* 290.95-6. **1707** Makemie *Writings* 175: So must the Sinner lay the Ax of Repentance to the Root of his old Sins. **1718** Chalkley *Observations* 426, 451. **1765** Dickinson *Writings* 201, **1768** 364. **1769** Woodmason *Journal* 120: The Ax is laid to the Root of Licentiousness. **1770** Adams *Legal Papers* 3.163. **1779** *New Jersey Journal* in *Newspaper Extracts(II)* 3.256. **1780** Adams *Works* 7.164. **1781** Deane *Papers* 4.416: It laid the axe to the root of our commerce. **1785** Sullivan *Letters* 3.396. **1787** *Anarchiad* 36: At power's deep root to lay the patriot ax. **1791** Paine *Address* 2.534, *Rights of Man* 1.266. **1791** Scott *Journal* 289. **1792** Barlow *Works* 1.182. **1794** WGrove in *Steele Papers* 1.112: They premeditated the putting the ax to the root. **1794** Paine *Age of Reason* 1.476-7: The axe goes at once to the root. **1802** Chester *Federalism* 29: That bill is an ax . . . at the very root of the tree of liberty. **1807** JAdams in *Adams-Warren Correspondence* 344. **1807** *Weekly* 2.17. **1813** Jefferson in *Adams-Jefferson Letters* 2.389: These laws . . . laid the axe to the root of Pseudo-aristocracy. **1816** Paulding *Letters* (*I*) 2.102. **1832** Ames *Nautical* 158: They have certainly laid the axe at the wrong end of the tree, 179. **1832** Barney *Memoir* 137. Whiting A253.

B

B1 Not to know a **B** from a bull's foot

1792 Brackenridge *Modern* 24: For there were persons there who scarcely knew a B from a bull's foot, **1804** 419. **1812** DCWallace in Knopf *War of 1812* 2.207: Their is not an officer belonging to it that knows a Bee from a Bulls foot. Barbour 7; *Oxford* 437; Whiting B1.

B2 From **B** to Z

1811 Graydon *Memoirs* 344: "She hated them all from B to Z," the saying, I presume, must be taken inclusively. See **A1**.

B3 **Babes** in the wood

1704: Knight *Journal* 12: I must either Venture my fate of drowning, or be left like y[e] Children in the wood. **1808** Barker *Tears* 195: Two babes in the wood. **1809** Paulding *Letters (II)* 28: Poor Brevoort & unfortunate I—are left disconsolate and alone, like the dear little Babes in the wood. **1813** Gerry *Diary* 173: I however, like the babes in the woods, made a fine feast on blackberries. **1821** Knight *Poems* 1.115: And *Ellen* as simple as child in the wood. Barbour 7; TW 12.

B4 No more harm than a sucking **Babe**

1770 Munford *Candidates* 26: Mr. Wou'dbe has no more harm about him, than a sucking babe. TW 12(3).

B5 As drunk as **Bacchus**

1813 Palmer *Diary* 5: The ships company last night were all as Drunk as Bachus, **1815** 202. Svartengren 195.

B6 **Bachelors** are but half of a pair of scissors

1781 EPartridge in [W. Duane] *Letters to Benjamin Franklin from his Family and Friends* (New York, 1859) 121: Brother Tuthill lives single yet and I believe will die the half of the scissors. **1783** Franklin *Writings* 9.14: Single and separate, they are not the compleat human Being; they are like the odd Halves of Scissors, **1787** 583: A bachelor . . . is like the odd half of a pair of scissors, which has not yet found its fellow, and therefore is not even half so useful as they might be together.

B7 **Bachelors** seldom get rich

1788 *American Museum* 3.51: Hence the vulgar remark that bachelors seldom get rich. Cf. *Oxford* 24.

B8 **Bachelors'** wives and old maids' children

1790 *Belknap Papers* 2.232: Bachelors' wives and old maids' children, you know, are always the best educated and best behaved of any in the world. *Oxford* 24-5; Whiting B3.

B9 To keep **Bachelor's** Hall

1746 *Johnson Papers* 1.44: I shall . . . keep Biahalors Hall one year Longer. **1763** *Franklin-Mecom* 76: I have half a mind to keep House, that is, Bachelor's Hall, in that which was Sister Douse's. **1783** POliver in Hutchinson *Diary* 2.396: Daniel and Louisa keep a true bachelor's and maiden hall, **1784** 2.399: With maids' wives' and batchelors' Hall compliments. **1783** *Washington

Writings 27.209: In a Batchelors Hall. **1795** JDavis in *Belknap Papers* 3.603: I frequently visit him at his Bachelor's Hall. **1800** JAlston in American Antiquarian Society *Proceedings* NS 29(1919) 102. **1806** *Port Folio* NS 2.96: 'Twas bachelor's therefore, 'twas liberty hall. **1809** ADKelly in *W&MCQ* 17 (1908) 28. **1810** Mackay *Letters* 210, 213, 216, 228. **1814** Adams *Writings* 5.89. **1830** Beecher *Autobiography* 2.225. DA bachelor 2(5); NED Bachelor 6.

B10 The **Back** is equal to its burden (*varied*)

1792 JRumsey in *W&MCQ* 25(1916) 25-6: My back is always equal to the burthen that I have to bear! **1810** Cuming *Sketches* 312: The truth of the old adage, that *custom is second nature*, and always fits the back to the burden. **1814** Smith *Letters* 116: The back is fitted to the burden. *Oxford* 312; TW 13(1).

B11 Fall **Back** fall edge

1740 Belcher *Papers* 2.304: But fall back fall edge, I have nothing to do in that matter, yet the Devil will be busy. **1754** GCadogan in McDowell *Documents* 1.500: [He] is very anxious to ride hard; fall back fall edge as he says. **1757** Davis *Colonial Virginia Satirist* 20: "How ere that turns, to good or ill, the people here alledge, Somebody will, his pocket fill, let that fall back or edge." *Oxford* 242; Tilley B12.

B12 To give the **Back** of one's hand

1806 Pike *Travels* 124: They made motions to exchange them for liquor, to which I returned the back of my hand. **1816** Wirt *Letters* 1.402: I mean his solemn style, to which, in Irish phrase, I give the back of my hand, **1817** 2.12: Or do you put aside a silly opinion . . . with a contemptuous back of your hand, (as the Scotch Irish say). Cf. Partridge 23-4.

B13 To have one's **Back** up

1783 Williams *Penrose* 370: Otherwise their backs had Certainly been up on account of his disdainful Speech. TW 13(3).

B14 To stroke one's **Back**

1782 WSSmith in Webb *Correspondence* 2.441: I have expressed a wish to the Gen'l to be relieved, but he strokes my back with the idea of command &c. *Oxford* 125; Whiting B5.

B15 **Backwards** and forwards

1788 *Politician* 7: There's such a monstrous sight of people a scrouging backards and forards, as the old saying is. NED Backward 5b.

B16 To take the **Back** track

1802 *Balance* in Thornton *Glossary* 1.29: I must have been taking the course which hunters would call the *Back Track*. TW 14.

B17 As black as **Bacon**

1764 JAdams in *Adams FC* 1.33: He is . . . as black as bacon.

B18 Small-boned **Bacon**

1809 Weems *Washington* 194: This *small-boned bacon*, as they call it [salted herring]. See **A63, G7.**

B19 To save one's **Bacon**

1666 Alsop *Maryland* 20: To save my Bacon. **1707** *Winthrop Papers*(B) 5.392: A false story to save their own bacon. a**1731** Cook *Bacon* 320: For tho' they could not save their Bacon. **1746** *Georgia Records* 25.67. **1747** *New York Weekly Post Boy* in *Newspaper Extracts*(I) 2.406: To safe yure bacon and secure yure Interest. **1755** AStephen in *Letters to Washington* 1.104. **1764** *Paxton Papers* 220. **1774** *Pennsylvania Journal* in *Newspaper Extracts*(I) 10.348. **1776** "Tory Poetry" in *PM* 8(1884) 432. **1779** Hopkinson *Miscellaneous Essays* 3 (part 2) 183. **1780** HGates in Reed *Life* 2.194. **1780** Sargent *Loyalist* 120. **1781** Rawdon in Moore *Diary* 2.432. **1782** Freneau *Poems* 2.127, 154. **1782** Sargent *Loyalist* 144. **1789** Boucher *Autobiography* 116. **1792** *Echo* 28. **1797** Cobbett *Porcupine* 6.289. **1803** Weems *Letters* 2.267. **1804** *Echo* 298. **1804** Irving *Corrector* 68. **1805** Weems *Hymen* 19. **1806** Hitchcock *Works* 157, **1808** *Poetical Dictionary* 16. **1808** *Port Folio* NS 5.157. **1809** Asbury *Letters* 3.415. **1809** Fessenden *Pills* 112. **1809** Weems *Marion* 221. **1810** *Port Folio* 2NS 3.170: "Afraid of his bacon," from foes so galvanic, The mouse beat retreat." **1813** Weems *Drunkard* 98. **1815**

Bad

Freneau *Poems* (*1815*) 2.139. **1826** WBiglow in Buckingham *Specimens* 2.292. *Oxford* 700; TW 14(2). See **C340.**

B20   Bad is the best

1767 Johnson *Writings* 1.402: Bad is the best country in the world. **1772** Stiles *Diary* 1.271: Dudly behaves in Office as well as any of them: but bad is the best. **1775** MWard in Ward *Correspondence* 51: We try to Make out as well as we Can with the farm, tho bad will be the best I Fear. **1800** Ames *Letters* 1.286. *Oxford* 26; Tilley B316.

B21   To make Bad worse

1777 Hopkinson *Miscellaneous Essays* 3 (part 2) 166: Bad measures often end in worse. **1785** Smith *Diary* 2.34: He went to Brooks's to retrieve his Fortunes by Gambling and made bad much worse. **1793** Ingraham *Journal* 185: [It] would only be making bad worse. Tilley B27.

B22   As grey as a Badger

1767 *Norton Papers* 26: 'Tis as grey as a Badger. c**1775** Hopkinson *Miscellaneous Essays* 3 (part 2) 160: Tho' grey as a badger, and old as a weazel. **1809** Weems *Marion* 138. **1815** Freneau *Poems* (*1815*) 2.138. *Oxford* 337; Svartengren 236.

B23   As helpless as a Bag

1809 Weems *Marion* 160: He . . . fell off, and came to the ground, as helpless as a miller's bag, **1813** *Drunkard* 76: He was tumbled over sprawling and helpless as a cotton bag.

B24   Bag and baggage

1728 Byrd *Dividing Line* 40: The Landlord was lately removed, Bag and Baggage, from Maryland. a**1731** Cook *Bacon* 318: So, Bag and Baggage, they by Night To Acomack again took Flight. **1736** Gyles *Memoirs* 8, 15. **1755** *Johnson Papers* 13.75. **1762** Drinker *Journal* 19. **1775** EInman in Murray *Letters* 201. **1775** *Virginia Gazette* in *Naval Documents* 1.885. **1777** Moore *Diary* 1.427. **1778** *New Jersey Gazette* in *Newspaper Extracts* (*II*) 2.102. **1779** CCuthbert in Lee *Papers* 3.355. **1783** JDickinson in Read *Correspondence* 383. **1783** AMacaulay in *W&MCQ* 11(1902) 182. **1784** TBarclay in *Winslow*

Papers 199. **1784** WPynchon in Curwen *Journal and Letters* 398: Alcock *evasit et abdicavit* with bag and baggage. **1789** JHarmar in Denny *Journal* 445. **1801** ANMcLeod in Gates *Five Fur Traders* 180. **1803** HWadsworth in *Barbary Wars* 2.416: The First set having decamped bag and baggage. **1805** Irving *Journals* 1.170. **1810** Mackay *Letters* 109. TW 14(2). See **P3, S2.**

B25   An empty Bag (sack) cannot stand upright

1740 Franklin *PR* 2.248: An empty Bag cannot stand upright, **1750** 3.446: An empty Sack can hardly stand upright; but if it does, 'tis a stout one! **1758** *WW* 348: 'Tis hard for an empty Bag to stand upright, **1786** *Writings* 9.496: The truth of those proverbs which teach us . . . that It is hard for an empty sack to stand upright. *Oxford* 220; Tilley B30; TW 14(3).

B26   Put them in a Bag and shake them

1769 JParker in Franklin *Papers* 16.141: I have such a Conception of them and their Chicanery that were you too shake them all in a Bag together, the first that comes out would be as good as any other. **1813** JAdams in *Adams-Jefferson Letters* 2.347: If I were summoned . . . to say upon Oath, which Party had excited . . . the most terror . . . and which had really felt the most, I could not give a more sincere Answer, than in the vulgar Style "Put them in a bagg and shake them, and then see which one comes out first." *Oxford* 655; Tilley M957.

B27   To give one the Bag

1666 Alsop *Maryland* 92: The best way to give them the bag, is to go out of the World and leave them. **1768** *Commerce of Rhode Island* 1.222: I have met with some that would as willingly leave me the bagg as he did you. **1783** Baldwin *Life and Letters* 168: Electric fire which . . . is sure to give *the bag* to all Bodies not equally charged. **1798** TGFessenden in Buckingham *Specimens* 2.218: Should you give me the bag . . . I'll hang my "nown self" with a bridle. c**1800** Tyler *Island* 27: On his promise to marry me I gave all my other sweethearts the bag. **1828** *Yankee* 288: I never was courted but once in my life, and then I gave the bag. *Oxford* 26-7; TW 14(5).

B28 To give one the **Bag** to hold
1760 Montresor *Journals* 236: The Enemy once fixed here would be, the English term it, given us the Bag to hold. **1787** Tyler *Contrast* 55: Since General Shea has sneaked off and given us the bag to hold. **1791** Washington *Writings* 31.392: He will leave you the bag to hold. **1793** Jefferson *Writings* 9.145: She will leave Spain the bag to hold. **1813** Paulding *Lay* 94: Flouted his suit with scorn so cold, And gave him oft the bag to hold, 225 [note to above]: If on the contrary side [a girl being courted] remains in the room with her parents, he is said, I know not for what special reason, "to get the bag to hold." *Oxford* 27; TW 14(6).

B29 As one **Bakes** so he must brew
1839 Hone *Diary* 1.404: As he has baked, so he must brew. *Oxford* 27; Tilley B52; Whiting B529.

B30 A **Baker's** dozen
1732 Byrd *Progress* 337: This famous town consists of . . . and a baker's dozen of ruinous tenements. **1778** *New Jersey Gazette* in *Newspaper Extracts (II)* 2.195: Here is what is called a baker's dozen. **1789** *Columbian Magazine* 3.102: A baker's dozen of squalling brats. **1800** Weems *Letters* 2.127: Promising to take one for each of her children (a bakers dozen). Barbour 8; TW 15(2).

B31 Be not a **Baker** if your head be of butter
1722 *New-England Courant* in Buckingham *Specimens* 1.61: The old proverb, Be not a baker, if your head be made of butter. *Oxford* 27; Tilley B53.

B32 As round as a **Ball**
1744 Hamilton *Itinerarium* 108: This man was round as a ball. **1830** Fletcher *Letters* 117: Your little Poney is as round as a ball. *Oxford* 685; Whiting B24.

B33 A **Ball** of contention
a1700 Hubbard *New England* 602: The late Synod was . . . to become a ball of conten-

tion among the churches of the Massachusetts. See **A104, B253.**

B34 To have the **Ball** at one's foot
1721 WKeith in *Colden Letters* 1.138: But even when a Man has the Ball at his foot it is not always best to strike with ones whole force. **1773** ALeslie in Montresor *Journals* 531: The Tea Consignees have the Ball at their foot; a little exertion now would show them in their true colours. **1775** Smith *Memoirs(I)* 224: You have the Ball at your Feet. **1777** Murray *Letters* 264: That house . . . has the ball at foot; the present gale is in their favour. **1782** Franklin *Writings* 8.524: Our Enemies may now do what they please with us; *they have the Ball* at their Foot. **1784**: JTemple in *Bowdoin Papers* 2.38: France . . . has the ball very much before her. **1802** Morris *Diary and Letters* 2.419: The ball was at their feet; they had got over all difficulty. **1805** WChipman in *Winslow Papers* 539: He then thought the ball under his feet. **1814** Morris *Diary and Letters* 2.571: These instructions place the ball at the foot of our enemy, who will . . . kick it in the manner most agreable to him. *Oxford* 28; Tilley B63; Whiting B28.

B35 To keep the **Ball** rolling
1770 *Johnson Papers* 7.524: And so the Ball is to be kept rolling. TW 15(3).

B36 **Balm** in Gilead
1647 in Stiles *Itineraries* 357: Is there no Balm in Gilead? **1652** Williams *Writings* 4.223: Is there no *Balme* in *Gilead*? **1653** Wigglesworth *Diary* 18: Is there no baulm in Gilead for these sores, **1653** 42. **1692** Bulkeley *Will* 258: There is that balm in Gilead that will soon heal us if it be applied. **1761** Smith *Works* 2.377-8: A good man will be apt to cry out — "Is there no balm in Gilead?" **1783** EStiles in Thornton *Pulpit* 515: But is there no balm in Gilead to heal the wound? **1812** CANorton in Knopf *War of 1812* 3.38: There is no Valur in Gilead! *Oxford* 28; Whiting NC 365.

B37 **Baltimore reports**
1781 JLovell in *Adams FC* 4.213: I will not

give you *Baltimore Reports,* which are become proverbial, for Falsities.

B38 Nice as (out of) a **Band-box**

1787 *American Museum* 2.412: Nice, as a band-box were his dwelling place. **1800** Trumbull *Season* 61: He is a strange man as ever I saw—I should think he had just this minute come out of a band box. TW 15-6.

B39 As good (honest) as the **Bank**

1759 PDemere in McDowell *Documents* 2.485: I imagined they were as good as the Bank. **1801** Weems *Letters* 2.189: The Gentleman is rich & honest as the bank, **1802** 243: McClenachan is as good as the bank, **1806** 353: as good as the Bank. *Oxford* 691; TW 16(1).

B40 **Banyan Day**

1777 Fitch *New-York Diary* 247: We had a curious dinner on Oatmeal; this being what is call'd by Seamen, Banyan day & no meat deliver'd us, 248. Colcord 29; NED Banian 4.

B41 He's been at **Barbadoes**

1737 Franklin *Drinkers* 2.174: He's been at Barbadoes.

B42 A **Bargain** is a bargain

1705 Sewall *Diary* 2.125: I said Gov*r* Dudley's saying was, A bargain's a Bargain and must be made good. **1714** JKnight in *Letters from Hudson Bay* 38: A bargain is a bargain. **1722** *New-England Courant* in Buckingham *Specimens* 1.76. **1752** *Beekman Papers* 1.154: A Bargain is a bargin and I will stand to it. **1802** Dow *Journal* 156. *Oxford* 30; TW 16(1).

B43 As close as the **Bark** to the tree

1692 Mather *Wonders* 155: She would stick as close to Abbot as the Bark stuck to the tree. TW 16(1).

B44 Hard to meddle between the **Bark** and the tree

1629 TFones in *Winthrop Papers(A)* 2.79: Tis hard medling betweene the barke and the tree. *Oxford* 30; Whiting H79.

B45 One's **Bark** is worse than his bite

1841 Cooper *Letters* 4.207: With best re-

gards to Mrs. Shubrick, and a hint that her bark is worse than her bite. *Oxford* 30; TW 17.

B46 He that **Barks** may well bite

a1700 Hubbard *New England* 445: For those who now began to bark, might ere long be as ready to bite. *Oxford* 196:Dog; Whiting D309.

B47 Not a **Barley-corn's** odds

1733 Belcher *Papers* 1.373: 'Tis not a barly corn's odds. Cf. NED Barley-corn 3.

B48 To burn a **Barn** to kill the rats

1807 *Weekly* 2.383: The conduct of the man who burned his barn to destroy the rats it sheltered. **1809** Fessenden *Pills* 22-3: A certain hind, it has been said . . . Burn'd down his barn to kill the rats. *Oxford* 91; Whiting B49. See **H340.**

B49 Never a **Barrel** better herring

1685 Dunton *Letters* 12: Nor was he at all singular, for in the whole Town, there was never a Barrel better Herring. **1723** Symmes *Utile* 42: There's ne'er a Barrel the Better Herring. **1767** Paterson *Glimpses* 30: But never a barrel better herring: both letters were equally short, and alike deficient in news. **1796** Barton *Disappointment* 33: The devil a barrel the better shad. *Oxford* 31; Whiting B54.

B50 As leaky as a **Basket**

a1820 Biddle *Autobiography* 68: She was a miserable old vessel, as leaky as a basket.

B51 To pin (up) the **Basket**

1637 Morton *New English Canaan* 344: Though when hee came in Company of basket makers, hee would doe his indevoure to make them pinne the basket, if he could, as I have seene him. **1692** Bulkeley *Will* 254: And now we hope they have pin'd the basket and set to their seal that all we said before is true. **1740** Belcher *Papers* 2.357: This is my 34th Grant, & I must pin up the basket, **1741** 410: The journals . . . pin up the basket with your old friend. **1769** Johnson *Writings* 1.455: [This] is one of the best wrote pieces of controversy I ever saw, and I think must pin up the basket, as they say. NED Basket ld.

B52 To smile like a **Basket** of chips

1803 *Yankee Phrases* 87: She smil'd like a basket of chips. NED Suppl. Basket 2; TW 17-8.

B53 **Basket-making**

1797 JJackson in Milledge *Correspondence* 49: The old trade of Basket making goes on, let the world be as it may. Partridge 36.

B54 As blind as a **Bat**

1787 *American Museum* 2.596: North blind as a bat. **1788** *Politician* 3. **1804** Brackenridge *Modern* 388, **1805** 569. **1809** Fessenden *Pills* 31: Spiteful as vipers, blind as bats. **1833** Floy *Diary* 41. *Oxford* 66; TW 18(1).

B55 To the **Bat's** end

1754 Wolcott *Papers* 423: Drive it to the batts End that none may Escape. **1820** MVan Buren in King *Life* 6.254: They will support Tompkins to the bat's end if you refuse or he should not decline. NED Bat *sb.*² 2.

B56 To get over the **Bay**

1787 Adams *Diary* 331: Two or three gentlemen got rather over the bay [drunk]. TW 18.

B57 As bold as (blind) **Bayard**

1676 Williams *Writings* 5.79: Some have been such bold *Bayards* as to say they are Christ and God, 285: As boldly as Blind Bayard. *Oxford* 72; Whiting B71.

B58 **Bayard** on ten toes

1686 Dunton *Letters* 249: I rambled to Salem all alone . . . and upon Bayard on Ten Toes, too, like a meer Coriat. *Oxford* 33; Tilley B110.

B59 To flourish like a green **Bay** tree (ass)

1699 Ward *Trip* 56: There live and flourish, as the *Righteous,* like a Bay-Tree under the Noses of their Enemies. **1776** Curwen *Journal* 1.172: May the righteous flourish as the palm tree, and may the wicked wither and their root consume away. **1809** Weems *Letters* 2.415: Your enterprize in a year or two's time will spread abroad like a green bay tree by the courses of water, *Washington* 195:

The town of Alexandria which now flourishes like a green bay tree. **1817** Scott *Blue Lights* 70: Like the green bay their party grew. **1819** Peirce *Rebelliad* 49: And flourish, like a green bay ass, High fed upon his native grass. Ps. 37.35.

B60 What has **Been** may be again

1723 SCranston in Kimball 1.9: But as the Proverb is what hath been may be againe. Cf. *Oxford* 504: Whatever man; Whiting T146.

B61 To kick the **Beam**

1807 *Salmagundi* 57: There is no judging which will "kick the beam," 274: Fine fellows—both of a weight, can't tell which will kick the beam. *Oxford* 422.

B62 To be on one's **Beam-ends**

1801 Weems *Letters* 2.193: But here I am on my beam ends. **1815** Brackenridge *Modern* 650: And hit the tup a stroke, that, in the sailor's phrase, brought him on his beam ends. **1831** JOverton in Jackson *Correspondence* 4.237: Crawford has now Calhoun pretty well on his beams end. Colcord 31; NED Beam *sb.*¹ 18.

B63 A **Bean** with freedom, *etc.*

1767 Ames *Almanacs* 387: A bean with freedom is better than a sugar plumb in prison. *Oxford* 33; Tilley B114.

B64 Every **Bean** has its black

1767 Ames *Almanacs* 387: Every bean has its black. *Oxford* 34; Tilley B115.

B65 Three blue **Beans,** *etc.*

1789 *American Museum* 5.298: [They] are as clear proofs of it, as that three blue beans are equal in number to three white ones. **1816** *Port Folio* 4NS 1.155: The old saying of three blue beans in one blue bladder. *Oxford* 816; Tilley B124.

B66 Are you there with your **Bears**?

1714 Hunter *Androboros* 36: Are you there with your Bears? *Oxford* 18; Tilley B133.

B67 As cross as a **Bear**

1835 Floy *Diary* 145: Earned my shilling, but came home as cross as a bear. Barbour 12(3); *Oxford* 35; TW 19(5).

B68 As fat as a **Bear**

1815 *Port Folio* 3NS 5.431: The true origin of the expression, as fat as a bear. **1830** Pintard *Letters* 3.151: The Judge is fat as a bear. TW 19(7).

B69 As rough as a **Bear**

1780 Sargent *Loyalist* 4: Rough as a bear. Barbour 12(10); TW 20(16).

B70 As sour as a **Bear**

1813 Weems *Drunkard* 115: Sitting . . . sour and sullen as a bear. Cf. TW 20(23).

B71 **Bears** lick their cubs into shape (*varied*)

1728 Byrd *Dividing Line* 175: As soon as dinner was over the Protesters return'd to their Drudgery to lick their Cubb into shape. **1736** WByrd in *VHM* 36(1928) 355: The Bashfull Bears hide their Cubb, till they have lickt them into shape. **1809** Kendall *Travels* 1.229: They [bear foetuses] did not require to be licked into shape, as old tradition has pretended. *Oxford* 458; Tilley S284.

B72 **Bears** suck their paws in winter (*varied*)

1708 Cook *Sot-Weed* 13: Or could with well contented Maws Quarter like Bears upon their Paws. **1728** Byrd *Dividing Line* 196: Nor can they [bears] live very long upon licking their Paws, as Sr John Mandevil and some Travellers tell us, 223: But Astrolabe I was in less pain for, because he had more Patience & cou'd subsist longer upon licking his Paws, 224. **1752** Joseph Robson, *An Account of Six Years Residence in Hudson's Bay* (London, 1752) 47: The black bear generally lies in his den as long as he finds any moisture in his paws to subsist on, but when that is gone he is forced abroad again. **1757** HBacon in McDowell *Documents* 2.431: They have . . . but five Months' Provision in the Fort, and when it is consumed they may suck their Fingers. **1767** Ames *Almanacs* 387: He that now neglects his hoe, must in winter suck his paw. **1780** *Washington Writings* 20.459: It would be well for the Troops, if . . . they could . . . like the Bear, suck their paws for sustenance. **1792** WHeth in Hamilton *Papers* 12.554: The throng in that way, will be presently over when, like the bears, I may suck my paws all winter. **1797** Baily *Journal* 208: Bears . . . sit there

. . . till spring, without any other sustenance than what they procure from *sucking their paws*. **1815** Palmer *Diary* 168: They may now return like the Bear to their homes & suck their Claws & pay their Taxes as they can. Lean 2.798; NED Suck 10, quote 1774.

B73 Like a **Bear** bereaved (robbed) of its whelps

1702 Mather *Magnalia* 2.556: The enemy came up . . . like "bears bereaved of their whelps." **1725** Wolcott *Poetical Meditations* 65: Foes . . . This mighty Man on every side Engag'd Like Bears bereav'd of their Whelps enrag'd. **1768** *New-York Gazette* in *Newspaper Extracts(I)* 7.110: Thwart them in the least, and they are like so many bears robbed of their whelps. **1799** Eaton *Life* 103: Tunis is robbed of her prey; and is as restless as a bear robbed of her whelps. Whiting B103.

B74 Like a **Bear** to the stake

1640 TGostlin in *Winthrop Papers(A)* 4.213: But never was Beare draune to stake with more vnwillingness than I to wrighting of letters. **1739** Belcher *Papers* 2.261: They have been persecuted by the petitioners & drag'd as a bear to the stake to make report. *Oxford* 34; Tilley B127; Whiting B102.

B75 Like a **Bear** with a sore head

1803 Davis *Travels* 448: He grumbles and growls like a bear with a sore head. TW 19-20(5, 9, 24, 31). Cf. *Oxford* 35.

B76 Like young **Bears** whose misfortunes are to come

1789 Anburey *Travels* 2.140: He could only compare their situation to that of so many *young bears*, whose misfortunes were all to come. *Oxford* 927; TW 20(28).

B77 To eat like a **Bear**

c1680 Radisson *Voyages* 35: I began to eat like a bear. Barbour 12(4). Cf. TW 19(11).

B78 To escape the **Bear** and fall to the lion

1631 JHumfrey in *Winthrop Papers(A)* 3.52: What is it to scape the beare and to fall in to the paws of the lion? Cf. Whiting S101.

B79 To see the **Bears**
1737 Franklin *Drinkers* 2.174: He sees the Bears.

B80 **Bear** and forbear
1637 Morton *New English Canaan* 312: Mine Host . . . knew not what hee should doe in this extremity but bear and forbeare, as Epictetus says: it was bootelesse to exclaime. 1818 Watterston *Letters* 29: The maxim of Zeno—bear and forbear. 1823 JLowell in Otis *Letters* 2.253: We must bear and forbear. *Oxford* 34; Tilley B135; TW 20(1).

B81 To sell the **Bearskin** before the bear is caught (*varied*)
1748 Lloyd *Papers* 1.399: I wish it may not be selling the Bear Skin before it be caught. 1750 *Massachusetts* in *Colonial Currency* 4.441: They divided the Skin before they had caught the Beast. 1776 Deane *Papers* 1.383: You may smile, and recollect the sale of the bearskin in the fable. 1781 4.413: They acted the parts of the hunters who quarrelled about the bearskin. 1782 Gadsden *Writings* 195: I . . . reminded them of the proverb not to sell the bear-skin before they had catched the bear. 1795 Adams *Writings* 1.453: Whether . . . these exulters have not purchased the skin before the chase was killed. 1797 Bentley *Diary* 2.213: That pride which had nearly sold the bear before he was caught. *Oxford* 713; Tilley B132. See **C138.**

B82 If **Beards** made policy, he-goats could be ambassadors
1713 Wise *Churches* 87: It is a story in the History of Persia . . . [that] . . . the young Grecians very smartly Answered, *That if state Policy did consist in Beards, then He-Goats would do for Embassadors, as well or better than Men.* 1721 *New-England Courant* 1[1.1]: Barba non facit Philospham. *Oxford* 35; TW 21; Tilley G169.

B83 To be at one's **Beard**
1779 AMcDougall in *Clinton Papers* 4.746: The Law of the State . . . give no aid to the public Service, but when the Enemy is at our Beards. Whiting B117.

B84 As drunk as a **Beast**
1756 *Johnson Papers* 2.564: They were all as Drunk as Beasts. 1806 Fanning *Narrative* 113: He was . . . as drunk as a beast, 222. TW 21(1).

B85 As stupid as **Beasts**
1776 David *Letters* 27: As stupid as the beasts that pearish.

B86 Ill to fight a **Beast** in its own den
1677 Hubbard *Indian* 1.87: It is ill fighting with a wild Beast in his own Den. Cf. Whiting C350.

B87 **Beauty** and folly are old companions
1734 Franklin *PR* 1.353: Beauty and folly are old companions. Tilley B164; Whiting B151.

B88 **Beauty** cannot compensate for want of heart
1819 Waln *Hermit* 170: You are now testing the truth of a favorite maxim of mine, that no *Beauty* can compensate for the want of a Heart. Cf. *Oxford* 38; Whiting B152.

B89 **Beauty** is but skin-deep
1710 JDummer in *W&MCQ* 3S 24(1967) 409: I consider beauty is extremely Superficial, but Skin deep. 1834 Floy *Diary* 99: They say beauty is only skin deep. *Oxford* 38; Tilley B170. See **V28.**

B90 As brisk as a **Beaver**
1821 Knight *Poems* 1.168: Brisk as a beaver, we must fence the flocks in. Cf. TW 21(1).

B91 As industrious as a **Beaver**
1816 Paulding *Letters* (*I*) 1.68: As industrious as a beaver. Cf. TW 21(1).

B92 As mad as a **Beaver**
1809 *Massachusetts Spy* in Thornton *Glossary* 2.568: He is naturally as mad as a beaver, and will scold like a termagant. Svartengren 92.

B93 To love as the **Beaver** does the willow
1674 Josselyn *Account* 92-3: There is an old proverbial saying, *sic me jubes quotidie, ut fiber solicem;* you love me as the *Beaver* does the willow; who eateth the Bark and killeth the Tree.

B94 To work like a **Beaver**

1771 Copley *Letters* 160: When I must work like a Beaver. **1788** *American Museum* 4.65: With the industry of the beaver, we support our rights [Hatters' motto]. **1809** Henry *Travels* 136: We toiled like beaver. **1812** Ames *Diary* 259: Worked like beavers. **1821** Pintard *Letters* 2.42: I have had to work like a beaver. **1849** Paulding *Letters(II)* 500. TW 21(6).

B95 It is so **Because** it is so

1804 Dow *Journal* 354: This "five linked chain" hath two hooks and a swivel — Flattery and Despair — it is so because it is so. *Oxford* 38; Tilley B179.

B96 A **Bed** of roses

1780 JDuane in Sparks *Correspondence* 3.173: Our enemies . . . do not repose on a bed of roses. **1783** JAdams in *Warren-Adams Letters* 2.206: A man does not sleep on a Bed of Roses. **1786** Jay *Correspondence* 3.216: Though patriots seldom rest on beds of roses. **1789** WGrayson in Henry *Life* 3.393: The federalists are not altogether on a bed of roses. **1792** CGore in King *Life* 1.406: I fear he will not find a bed of roses or crown of roses in this new sphere. **1801** Adams *Writings* 2.527, n.1: The contested place is not a bed of roses. **1810** *Tyler Letters* 1.246: Lay me down softly on a bed of *roses in my latter days;* for I have been on thorns long enough. **1811** Adams *Writings* 4.64, **1812** *Memoirs* 2.276. **1812** WSSmith in Smith *Journal and Correspondence* 1.115. Adams *Works* 10.148: I had not trod upon feathers and slept upon beds of roses, **1819** *Writings* 6.546. Barbour 13(1); NED Bed 6b.

B97 A **Bed** of thorns

1785 Jefferson *Papers* 6.604: A reserve for subsistence independent of the usual one which spreads our couch with thorns. **1795** Monroe *Writings* 2.353: I have rested on a bed of thorns. **1829** Otis *Letters* 2.255: He is on a bed of thorns. See **T67.**

B98 Early to **Bed** and early to rise, *etc.* (*varied*)

a1700 Saffin *His Book* 187: He that to much loved his bed Will surely scratch a poor man's head But he that Early doth arise: Is in a way to win the prise. **1735** Franklin *PR* 2.9: Early to bed and early to rise, makes a man healthy wealthy and wise, **1758** *WW* 342, **1779** *Writings* 7.382: *Early to bed and early to rise, will make a man healthy, wealthy and wise.* **1782** Curwen *Journal* 2.804: Early to bed, early to rise, moderate exercise. *Oxford* 211; TW 21(1); Whiting R143.

B99 Rather go to **Bed** supperless than rise in debt

1739 Franklin *PR* 2.221: Rather go to bed supperless, than run in debt for a Breakfast, **1757** 7.89: Sleep without Supping, and you'll rise without owing for it, **1758** *WW* 349: than rise in debt. **1767** Ames *Almanacs* 388: Rather go to bed supperless than rise in debt, **1770** 413: Rather go to bed supperless than rise in debt. *Oxford* 53, 742; Tilley B183, S1006.

B100 To get out of **Bed** wrong end foremost

c1725 Byrd *Another Secret Diary* 464: Who . . . is so wise as to get out of bed with the wrong-end foremost. Cf. *Oxford* 678-9; TW 21(2); Whiting S303.

B101 To make a hard **Bed**

1774 Carter *Diary* 2.815: Indeed this fine girl has made a hard bed, such has been her deception, 875: And endeavor to keep her clean, warm, and alive if I can, to feel the hard bed she had been advised to make. *Oxford* 502; Tilley B189.

B102 As mad as **Bedlam**

1804 Plumer *Memorandum* 176: If judge Pickering was now here as mad as Bedlam it would make no difference. Svartengren 410. Cf. Tilley B199.

B103 Between you and I and the **Bed-post**

1821 Royall *Letters* 218: Between you and I, and the bed post, I begin to think it [religion] is all a plot of the priests. *Oxford* 57; TW 22.

B104 As airy as a **Bee**

1773 Paterson *Glimpses* 101: A Smile makes you as airy as a Bee.

B105 As brisk as a **Bee**

1787 Tyler *Contrast* 36: She was as brisk and as merry as a bee. **1844** Hone *Diary* 2.690: "Brisk as a bee and loquacious as a whip-poor-will." TW 22(1).

B106 As busy as **Bees**

1756 Franklin *PR* 6.326: The busy Nation flies from Flow'r to Flow'r, And hoards, in curious Cells, the golden Store. **1758** Winslow *Broadside* 127: Busy as Bees. **1772** McHenry *Letters* 3: Others, busy as the bees. **1795** HKnox in *Bingham's Maine* 1.550: I hope to be there but as busy as a bee. **1804** Baldwin *Life and Letters* 347. **1815** Andrews *Prisoners' Memoirs* 112. **1815** Humphreys *Yankey* 48-9: Bissy as bees, when they ring a brass kettle to hive 'em. **1821** Cary *Letters* 288. **1827** Wirt *Letters* 2.238. *Oxford* 93; Whiting B165.

B107 As busy as a **Bee** in a tar-barrel

1783 Williams *Penrose* 300: We became as busy as Bees in a Barrel of Tar. **1789** Brackenridge *Gazette* 89: He is as busy as a bee in a tar barrel, **1805** *Modern* 577: The Methodost . . . is as busy as a bee in a tar-barrel. **1822** Wirt *Letters* 2.147: Did you ever see a bee in a tar-barrel? Or, if you never did, did you ever hear tell of one, &c., &c., according to Sterne's case of the white bear? **1823** Lee *Diary and Letters* 213. **1836** Clark *Letters* 91: And in truth, mother, busy as a bee is said to be in a tar-barrel. TW 22(3). See **B110, T95.**

B108 As diligent as **Bees**

1777 CTufts in *Adams FC* 2.345: Our People are as diligent as Bees.

B109 As industrious as a **Bee**

1779 Rodney *Letters* 324: As industrious as Bees. **1812** EGLutwyche in *Winslow Papers* 674: He is as industrious as a bee. TW 22(6).

B110 As nimble as a **Bee** in a tar-barrel

1731 Franklin *Papers* 1.219: He sprung out again right briskly, verifying the common Saying, *As nimble as a Bee in a Tarbarrel.* See **B107.**

B111 As nimble as **Bees**

c1680 Radisson *Voyages* 145: Here we are stiring about in our boats as nimble as bees. Tilley B203, quote 1610.

B112 As thick as **Bees**

1765 Bartram *Diary* 23: Y^e musketos being as thick as bees in A swarm. **1775** JAdams in *Warren-Adams Letters* 1.51: Uniforms and Regimentals are as thick as Bees. **1779** Rodney *Letters* 324: Those termed Speculators are as thick and as industrious as Bees. **1791** Delano *Narrative* 96. **1804** Weems *Letters* 2.298, **1813** *Drunkard* 75. ?**1814** Freneau *Poems* 3.370. **1814** Palmer *Diary* 100: We stowd down in the lower hole, as thick as Bees in a Hive. Whiting B167.

B113 **Bees** gather honey from every flower, *etc.*

1720 *Letter* in *Colonial Currency* 2.230: The Bee gathers Honey from every Flower; 'tis the Beetle that delights in Horse dung. *Oxford* 40; Tilley B221.

B114 The **Bee** in May has recourse to all sorts of flowers

1685 JStanton in *Trumbull Papers* 1.141: The bee in the month of May hath recourse to all sorts of flowers. Cf. Tilley B205.

B115 The **Bee** sucks honey from the mire (mud)

1812 Jackson *Correspondence* 1.234: When you recollect the adage that the bee sucks honey from the mire, **1817** 2.272: Under a recollection of the old adage, that the Bee may suck honey from the mire, **1837** 5.490: As the adage of old says, the bee sucks honey from the mud. Cf. *Oxford* 39; Tilley B205.

B116 To flock like **Bees** unhived

1814 Palmer *Diary* 236: The men flock, round like bees unhived. TW 23(9).

B117 To gather like **Bees** round a hive

1813 Colby *Life* 1.169: The young converts and mourning sinners . . . gathered up round me like bees round a hive. TW 23(10).

B118 To swarm forth like **Bees**

1782 Trumbull *Satiric Poems* 187: And ev'ry Yanky full of mettle, Swarm forth, like bees at sound of kettle. Whiting B177.

B119 To work like **Bees**

1783 Gordon *Letters* 488: We may go on working and swarming like bees. **1795** *Washington *Writings* 34.264: The latter are always working, like bees, to distill their poison. TW 23(16).

B120 Where there are **Bees** there is honey

1748 *Word* in *Colonial Currency* 4.358: There always *will be Honey where there are Bees.* Oxford 39; Tilley B213; Whiting *NC* 368(9).

B121 To be small **Beer**

1706 FJWinthrop in *Winthrop Papers(B)* 5.343: 'Tis a small-beere country, and I doubt there's little to comfort a hard jorney. **1790** Morris *Diary* 1.383: If the reigning Prince were not the small beer character that he is. NED Beer 1b, Small beer 2; *Oxford* 744; TW 23(2).

B122 As blind as a **Beetle**

1756 EHubbart in Franklin *Papers* 7.69: Has been for many years as Blind as a Beetle. **1796** Tyler *Verse* 48: One blundering mare, than beetle blinder, **1825** 233: Blind as a beetle, *Prose* 157. *Oxford* 66-7; Whiting B180.

B122a **Beetle-blind**

1812 Adams *Writings* 4.304: Beetle-blind idiotism. Whiting B180a.

B123 As dull as a **Beetle**

1777 JA in *Adams FC* 2.170: The remainder are chiefly Quakers as dull as Beetles. **1787** *Columbian Magazine* 1.558: On coxcombs dear will fix her eyes, As beetles dull, and light as flies. *Oxford* 208; Whiting B181.

B124 As drunk as a **Beggar**

1737 Franklin *Drinkers* 2.174: He's as Drunk as a Beggar. *Oxford* 205; Tilley B225.

B125 **Beggar's** benison

1766 *Johnson Papers* 5.84: [   ] the Beggars Bennizon as I [   ] [context destroyed by fire]. **1780** EErskine in Webb *Correspondence* 2.255: I most sincerely wish you the Beggars benison of a Guinea always in your pocket. Partridge 44.

B126 **Beggars** must not be choosers

1719 Byrd *Another Secret Diary* 366: In matters of happiness we men are no more than Beggars, and they we are told must not be chusers. **1748** *Law Papers* 3.277: A decision here will be of no significancy till Beggars may be Choosers. **1783** JWarren in *Warren-Gerry Correspondence* 171: Beggars must not Choose. **1793** EHazard in *Belknap Papers* 2.340. Oxford 42; Whiting B185.

B127 Set a **Beggar** on horseback, *etc.*

1684 ERandolph in *Mather Papers* 525: Mr. Mather . . . has at last attained his end in setting his fools a horseback. If they do not mend their manners, some of them may ride to the divill, **1689** *Letters* 5.27: His partners make true the proverb, sett beggars on horseback and they will ride to yᵉ Divell. **?1689** ?Mather *Vindication* in *Andros Tracts* 2.56: [It] had Erected *Horse Blocks* for those *Beggers* to mount and ride that poor people even to Death. **1699** Ward *Trip* 39: Which, I think, plainly proves Two old Adages true, *viz* . . . and, *set a Beggar on Horse-back he'll Ride to the Devil.* **c1700** Taylor *Poems* 394: For set a Beggar upon horseback, see He'll ride as if no man so good as hee. **1702** Mather *Magnalia* 2.629: No sooner was this "beggar set on horseback" . . . but the mettlesome horse furiously and presently ran with him out of sight. Neither *horse* nor *man* were ever seen any more. . . . A few days after, they found one of his legs [and that was all]. **1741** Stephens *Journal (I)* 2.218: On his Master's Death he found Means to get into the Saddle in his Stead, fitly qualified to verify the old Proverb of a Beggar on Horseback. **1786** *Anarchiad* 109: As beggars set on horseback, ride. **1797** Cobbett *Porcupine* 4.343: They have fully verified the old maxim: "Set a beggar on horseback, and he'll ride to the devil." **1799** Carey *Porcupiniad* 2.36: You've a proverb heard, Pronounc'd with solemn stroke of beard, A beggar place upon a horse, And he will drive a headlong course. With utmost speed will wing his way, Unto the devil without delay. **1800** *Echo* 272: Says the proverb. **1809** Bentley

Diary 3.413: Such are beggars on horseback. Men who would be something & are nothing. **1809** Irving *History* 1.44: It is an old and vulgar saying about a "beggar on horseback." **1811** Adams *Writings* 4.127: They only verified the old proverb about setting a beggar on horseback. **1815** Humphreys *Yankey* 50: Set a beggar a horseback, and —. **1816** Paulding *Letters(I)* 2.152: The present fashionable banking Plutus, which has set so many splendid paupers on horseback, 188: Beggars can get on horse-back, and ride to the d——l, if they please. **1830** Ames *Mariner's* 71: The old proverb, "set a beggar on horseback, &." **1847** Paulding *Letters(II)* 2.462: He scorns . . . all sorts of ultraisms, on the backs of which Parsons, politicians, and Philanthropists, now a days mount like Beggars and ride to the Devil. *Oxford* 41; TW 24(2). Cf. Whiting B186.

B128 Sue a **Beggar** and catch a louse

1769 Woodmason *Journal* 158: Sue a Beggar and Catch a Louse. **1786** Washington *Writings* 29.100: Keeping the old proverb in view, not to "sue a beggar and catch a louse." *Oxford* 784; Tilley B240.

B129 All **Beginnings** are difficult

1758 Carroll *Correspondence* 1.35: All beginnings are difficult. *Oxford* 42; Whiting B198.

B130 A bad **Beginning** may end well

1755 *Washington *Writings* 1.117: If an old proverb can claim my belief I am certainly [words obliterated] share of success; for surely no man ever made a worse beginning than I have, **1776** 4.383: We have the proverb on our side, however, that "a bad beginning will end well." **1796** Barton *Disappointment* 19: A bad beginning sometimes makes a good ending. *Oxford* 317; Whiting B205.

B131 A good **Beginning** makes a good ending

1624 *Winthrop Papers* (A) 1.311: God sende a good ende to these happie beginninges. **1772** *Norton Papers* 229: A proper beginning often Terminates in a happy Issue. **1786** JEliot in *Belknap Papers* 3.304: A good

beginning! Well, may it never have a bad ending. **1833** Cooper *Letters* 2.400: I never knew as good a beginning make a good ending. *Oxford* 317; Whiting B204. See **B375**.

B132 A rash **Beginning** makes a foolish ending

1761 *Boston Gazette* in *Olden Time* 2.31: A rash Beginning makes a foolish Ending. *Oxford* 397; Whiting B199.

B133 A small **Beginning** produces great things

a**1656** Bradford *History* 2.117: Thus out of smalle beginings greater things have been produced. *Oxford* 42; Tilley B264. See **C99**.

B134 One **Believes** what one wishes to believe (*varied*)

1753 Sherman *Almanacs* 254: Men are slow to believe what dont suit their intent, 258: What suits mens Wishes is forwardly believed. **1763** JBoucher in *MHM* 7(1912) 164: I trust the report was not true—Quod volumas facile credimus. **1795** TBlount in *Blount Papers* 2.495: If I have an opinion . . . it is that Macon has won the race; for what we wish, we are always most inclined to believe. **1798** Cobbett *Porcupine* 8.143: What men *wish to be true* they generally *believe*. *Oxford* 43; TW 235(22); Tilley B269; Whiting M75.

B135 To **Believe** when one sees (*varied*)

1732 Belcher *Papers* 1.165: I took it as a compliment, and shall believe it when I see it. **1743** Stephens *Journal(II)* 1.181: Which I shall believe when I see. **1786** Hunter *Quebec* 241: Seeing, they say, is believing. **1825** Smith *Letters* 172: But I wish people wold not like Thomas be so incredulous, and would believe without seeing. **1846** Paulding *Letters(II)* 440: It might possibly rain, but I wont believe it till I see it. *Oxford* 710; TW 321-2(1); Whiting B220.

B136 As clear as a **Bell**

1851 Cooper *Letters* 6.278: My head is as clear as a bell. Barbour 14(2); TW 24(1).

B137 **Bell,** book and candle

1764 *Paxton Papers* 175: And curse with Bell, Book and Candle. **1796** Cobbett *Por-*

cupine 4.220: Instead of bell, book and candle, they would have cursed us with all the gods of heathenish calendar. **1808** *Port Folio* NS 6.265: His flagitious page should be condemned by bell, book, and candle. **1811** Taggart *Letters* 364: They went on to curse the British by bill, book and candle. **1812** Dow *Journal* 434: And cursed to eternal misery, with *"bell* book and *candle* light." *Oxford* 44; Whiting B456.

B138 The **Bell** calls others but never minds the sermon

1754 Franklin *PR* 5.184: The Bell calls others to Church, but itself never minds the Sermon. *Oxford* 44; Tilley B278.

B139 To bear (wear) the **Bell**

1666 Alsop *Maryland* 34: That have borne the Bell away, 51: The only Opinion that bears the Bell away. **1686** Dunton *Letters* 159: The Pilgrim's Progress bears away the Bell. **1698** Taylor *Poems* 133: Man then bore the Bell, **1704** 194: It therefore bears the bell away from all, **1718** 339: All Queens and Concubines that bear the bell, **1722** 371: Faith . . . hath . . . born away the bell. **c1739** Franklin *Writings* 7.434: Friends and a bottle still bear the bell. **1775** JAllen in *PM* 9(1885) 185: Miss Sally Robinson bore the belle. **1780** JLovell in Lee *Papers* 3.405. **1806** Wirt *Letters* 1.143: Sally . . . seemed to bear off the bell. **1814** Dow *Journal* 477: This is intended . . . to gain a fanciful preeminence and wear the bell, as first in fashion. **1819** *Musings* 12: In all intrigues, admit they wear the bell. *Oxford* 44; Whiting B230.

B140 To be **Bell-wether**

1793 SHigginson in Hamilton *Papers* 15.128: Dr. Jarvis, the Bell Wether of the flock. NED Bell-wether; *Oxford* 269; Whiting B616.

B141 The **Belly** and the members

1775 Adams *D and A* 2.206: Is it not realizing the Quarrell of the Belly and the Members. SThompson *Motif-Index* A1391, J461.1.

B142 The **Belly** has no ears

a1700 Hubbard *New England* 145: And being pinched with hunger (for "venter non habet aures") broke into an English house in sermon time to get victuals. **1720** SSewall in *Wyllys Papers* 392: And you know, the belly has no ears. **c1800** Tyler *Island* 26: A hungry belly has no ears. *Oxford* 45; Tilley B286. See **H359.**

B143 A full **Belly** is the mother of evil

1744 Franklin *PR* 2.399: A full Belly is the Mother of all Evil, **1755** 5.473: A full Belly brings forth every Evil. *Oxford* 45; Whiting B243.

B144 My **Belly** cries cupboard

c1800 Tyler *Island* 10: How shall I listen to the calls of Justice when my belly is crying cupboard all the time? 26: My soul races through my bowells crying — cupboard. *Oxford* 44-5; Tilley B301.

B145 To rob the **Belly** to adorn the back

1789 *Columbian Magazine* 3.100: While thousands "rob the belly to adorn the back."

B146 Were it not for the **Belly** the back might wear gold

1750 Franklin *PR* 3.442: If it were not for the Belly, the Back might wear Gold. *Oxford* 45; Tilley B288.

B147 To have a **Bellyful**

?1689 ?Mather *Vindication* in *Andros Tracts* 2.35: Let them have their belly full, 67: To wish their belly-full of such Joy. **1720** JColman *Distressed State* in *Colonial Currency* 1.401: Every body's Belly is full of the Publick Bank. **1738** *Georgia Records* 22[1]. 76: Our Neighbours . . . have their Belly-full of 'em. **1785** Pynchon *Diary* 212. **1787** Tyler *Contrast* 104: And I'll laugh your belly full, where the old creature's a-dying. **1813** Paulding *Lay* 185: But to use a homely phrase, "got his belly full" of something else. *Oxford* 46; Whiting B245.

B148 **Bend** or break

1865 DSwain in *Ruffin Papers* 4.42: He must either bend or break. *Oxford* 52; TW 25. Cf. Whiting B484.

B149 He who feels the **Benefit** should feel the burden

1768 Dickinson *Writings* 364: *Qui sentit*

commodum, sentire debet et onus. They who feel the benefit, ought to feel the burden. Jones 101.

B150 A **Benjamin's** portion (mess)

1716 TMcCliesh in *Letters from Hudson Bay* 55: We shall have a Benjamin's portion. **1754** Eliot *Essays* 114: If you give *Benjamin's* Mess, five Times more than he can eat. TW 25.

B151 The **Bent** of one's bow

c1700 Taylor *Poems* 439: Satan beguiles thee so Thou judgst the bend of the back side of the bow Dost press thyselfe too hard. *Oxford* 46; Whiting B252.

B152 Not give a **Bermingham** groat

1718 Byrd *Another Secret Diary* 318: And for his part he wou'd not give a Bermingham groat for it. Partridge s.v. Brummagem. Cf. *Oxford* 339; Whiting G474.

B153 If **Bermuda** lets you pass, then beware of Hatteras

1830 Ames *Mariner's* 83: The old sea adage, "If Bermuda lets you pass, Then beware of Cape Hatteras." *Oxford* 46; TW 25.

B154 **Bernard** saw not all

1702 Mather *Magnalia* 1.429: And afterwards Bernard, who yet (no more than his name's sake) "saw not all things." *Oxford* 47; Whiting B255.

B155 To watch as old **Bess** watched her daughter

1739 Franklin *PR* 2.217: The stars are watch'd as narrowly as old Bess watch'd her Daughter.

B156 **Best** is best cheap

1637 Morton *New English Canaan* 303: And this the best; yea, and the best cheap too, for, no good done, the man would nothing take. **c1816** Durang *Memoir* 83: Here we meet with the best house on the road and of course the dearest—and cheapest in the long run. **1817** Bentley *Diary* 4.450: They lived . . . & generally on the best as cheapest. **1826** Duane *Columbia* 116: The best is always the cheapest, 117: And, I repeat the best kind are the cheapest. *Oxford* 48; Whiting B266. See **B398**.

B157 Hope for the **Best,** and prepare for the worst

1813 Jay *Correspondence* 4.367: To hope for the best and prepare for the worst, is a trite but a good maxim. Barbour 15(2); *Oxford* 384; Tilley B328.

B158 To come off second **Best**

1779 Hutchinson *Diary* 2.280: The latter came off, as the vulgar saying is, second best. **1781** ISmith in *Adams FC* 4.126: Yet as the Old saying is he came off second best as the battle ruined him haveing 700 killed, taken &c. TW 26(5).

B159 To make the **Best** of a bad market (bargain) (*varied*)

1703 *Penn-Logan Correspondence* 1.183: I . . . hope to make the best of a bad market. **a1731** Cook *Bacon* 320: Yet *Bacon's* Friends (I say't in Jest) Of their bad Market made the best. **1740** Belcher *Papers* 2.308: When it is as you fear, it will be time enough to make the best of a bad market. **1766** JParker in Franklin *Papers* 13.326. **1770** *Commerce of Rhode Island* 1.312. **1775** JCollet in *Naval Documents* 1.845: I'll make the most of a bad game. **1778** Lee *Papers* 3.146: To make the best of a bad bargain. **1779** PBrown in *Baxter Manuscripts* 17.289-90: I saw that every Vessel was making the Best of a bad Bargain. **1786** Hunter *Quebec* 230-1: We . . . endeavored to make the best of a bad thing. **1792** Belknap *Foresters* 21. **1793** Ingraham *Journal* 126: We were obliged to make the best of a bad bargain, 183. **1795** TBlount in *Blount Papers* 2.514: [I] quit him, convinced that it is the best that can be made of a bad bargain. **1795** Cobbett *Porcupine* 2.26: This was making the best of a bad market with a vengeance! **1797** Mann *Female* 127: She must . . . make the best of what might prove a bad choice. **1799** Eaton *Life* 110: We have now only to make the best of a bad bargain. **1807** *Emerald* NS 1.88: He *"made the best of a bad bargain."* **1809** Irving *History* 2.48: But knowing, like a wise man, that all he had to do was to make the best out of a bad bargain. **1810** Schultz *Travels* 1.111: I . . . endeavoured to make the best of so bad a bargain. **1811** Asbury *Letters* 3.459: I want to live to make

the best of a poor day's work. **1812** NEd-
wards in Knopf *War of 1812* 6(2) 122: I will
. . . make the best of a bad situation. **1817**
Weems *Franklin* 126: To make the best of a
bad bargain. Barbour 15(3); *Oxford* 48;
TW 26(4).

B160   To make the **Best** of a Bargain
1777 Kemble *Papers* 1.141: But we must
make the best of the bargain. **1808** Fraser
Letters and Journals 82: We shall endeavor
to make the best of it. **1816** Freneau *Last
Poems* 5: He made of his bargain the best.
Oxford 48; TW 26(4); Tilley B326. See
M79.

B161   To be no **Better** than one should be
1769 Brooke *Emily* 302: So the maiden
aunts . . . think Miss Williams no better
than she should be. **1787** Adams *Works*
4.409: They are constrained to believe human nature no better than it should be.
1789 Brown *Power* 1.54: Most women, with
her, are no better than they should be. **1806**
Drinker *Journal* 403: Our Peter . . . was
married . . . to a girl . . . who is not free,
and by all accounts not as good as she ought
to be. **1807** Morris *Diary and Letters* 2.492.
1807 *Salmagundi* 402. **1808** Barker *Tears*
163. **1809** Irving *History* 2.33: And has so
often near being made "no better than she
should be," **1820** *Sketch Book* 49. **1824**
Longfellow *Letters* 1.93: I have been
cheated to that amount by taking a Wiscas-
set bill, which it seems is no better than it
should be, — that is to say — good for nothing. **1827** Watterston *Wanderer* 200. **1831**
Cooper *Letters* 2.78. **1832** Ames *Nautical*
198. **1837** Paulding *Letters (II)* 200. *Oxford*
568; TW 26(1).

B162   One's **Better** half
1774 TMumford in *Deane Correspondence*
139: Mrs. Mumford joins me in love to your
Better Half. **1790** Lloyd *Papers* 2.836. **1796**
Smith(EH) *Diary* 179. **1820** RMWelman in
Drake *Works* 88. *Oxford* 53; Tilley H49.

B163   To kiss black **Betty**
1737 Franklin *Drinkers* 2.174: He's kiss'd
black Betty. DA black *a* 4 (1).

B164   To give one **Betty** Martin
1815 "A Trip" in Otis *Letters* 2. opp.168:
We'll give 'em "Betty Martin." TW 26. Cf.
Oxford 10.

B165   To be out of **Bias**
1782 Perkins *Diary* 2.146: I am So Ill it puts
me a Little out of my Byas to be so Alarmed.
Oxford 58; Tilley B339.

B166   One's best **Bib** and tucker
1809 *Kennon Letters* 32.161: You all must
put on your best bibs and tuckers. **1809**
Weems *Marion* 42. **1814** Palmer *Diary* 74:
You see all hands putting on their best bib
and Tucker — it being Sunday. **1828** Smith
Letters 248: The ladies of the Cabinet in
their best bibs and tuckers. Barbour 15; TW
26.

B167   **Billingsgate** language (*varied*)
1676 Williams *Writings* 5.134: Was there
ever fouler Language given by any poor
Oister-woman at *Billingsgate*? **1699** Randolph *Letters* 7.576: He treated me with
worse than Billingsgate Language. **1737**
Georgia Records 21.459-60: I have had a
great deal of Billingsgate Language from
M[r] Wilson & his Wife, **1742** 23.219: The
many abuses, with Billingsgate Language,
that he has . . . been casting at me. **1750**
Johnson Papers 1.302. **1774** Hopkinson *Miscellaneous Essays* 1.85: And raved and
stormed like a Billingsgate. **1775** Willard
Letters 81: This nest of filth and Billingsgate. **1779** Brackenridge *Gazette* 149. **1779**
GMorris in Deane *Papers* 3.387: This is certain: that Billingsgate language marks at
most a Billingsgate education. **1805** Jefferson *Writings* 11.73: These heroes of Billingsgate. **1807** IChauncey in *Barbary Wars*
6.532: Insulted with Language better suit-
ing a *Billingsgate fish woman* then a person
wearing the Livery of his country. **1814**
Morris *Diary and Letters* 2.573: The bitter-
est vulgarity of Billingsgate. **1816** Paulding
Letters (I) 2.132: An obscure, contemptible
kind of a Billingsgate production. *Oxford*
59; Tilley B350. See **F160.**

B168   Fast (safe) **Bind** fast (safe) find
1761 *Boston Gazette* in *Olden Time* 2.30:
Fast bind fast find. **1796** Barton *Disappoint-*

ment 39: Safe bind safe find. *Oxford* 246; Whiting B287.

B169   As blithe as a Bird

1791 Bartram *Travels* 134: They [Indians] appear as blithe and free as the birds of the air. 1798 Adams *New Letters* 135: Gay and blithe as a bird. *Oxford* 286; Whiting B289-30, 295.

B170   As gay as a Bird

1756 Franklin *Papers* 6.429: I have been well ever since . . . and as gay as a bird. 1798 [see above]. Whiting *NC* 370(9).

B171   The Bird has flown

1637 Morton *New English Canaan* 285: Theire grande leader . . . tore his clothes for anger, to see the empty nest, and their bird gone. 1708 Cook *Sot-Weed* 23: I found the Bird was newly flown, a1731 *Bacon* 318: The Birds being fled. 1742 *Georgia Records* 23.384. 1744 Stephens *Journal(II)* 2.138. 1770 Mason *Papers* 1.118: The Nest was there, but the Birds were flown. 1775 Lord Dunmore in *Naval Documents* 2.1210. 1775 Moore *Diary* 1.30: Told Cæsar ·that the *"geese were flown,"* 1776 344. 1776 *Pennsylvania Journal* in *Newspaper Extracts(II)* 1.232. 1777 Mackenzie *Diary* 154: *The bird had fled.* 1777 JMcKesson in *Clinton Papers* 2.169. 1779 JFogg in Sullivan *Journals* 101: The nests are destroyed, but the birds are still on the wing. 1802 Asbury *Journal* 2.327. 1806 Fanning *Narrative* 203. 1808 Barker *Tears* 152: Finding the bird flown, and the empty cage. a1811 Henry *Account* 331. 1815 Asbury *Journal* 2.792: He has flown away like a bird. 1820 Irving *Sketch Book* 224: The window was open, and the bird had flown. 1824 Longfellow *Letters* 1.81. 1826 Audubon *1826 Journal* 52: The bird . . . had flown; and I looked on the empty nest. *Oxford* 61; Whiting B303, N18.

B172   A Bird in a cage will fly away

1818 Flint *Letters* 40: But put bird in cage, give him plenty to eat, still he fly away. Whiting B300.

B173   A Bird in a gilded cage

1769 Brooke *Emily* 110: A sweet little bird escaped from the gilded cage. Bartlett *Familiar Quotations* (14th ed., 1968) 903a: first quote 1900. See **B182.**

B174   A Bird in the hand is worth two in the bush

c1700 Taylor *Poems* 423: A Bird in hand doth far Transcend the Quires that in the Hedges are. 1781 Shippen *Journal* 101: A Bird in hand is worth 2 in a bush. 1788 Jefferson *Papers* 14.387: The old proverb is not always true "that a bird in the hand is worth two in the bush," 1789 15.522: I think you and I calculate alike . . . that a bird in the hand is worth two in the bush. 1791 Bentley *Diary* 1.301: With a sign of a "Bird in the Hand is worth two in the Bush." 1795 Murdock *Triumphs* 44: One bird in the bush is better than two out of the hand. 1796 Barton *Disappointment* 82: It's an old saying and a true one, aye, I have it! "One bird in hand is better far than two that's in the bush"—no, no, "than two that in bushes are." 1829 Beecher *Autobiography* 2.210. 1837 Clark *Letters* 39: Should that bird in the bush be so certain as to be equal in value to the one you have in hand. *Oxford* 59; Whiting B301.

B175   A Bird of passage

1777 Curwen *Journal and Letters* 105: I shall take my flight northwards, as birds of passage you know do, on the approach of spring. 1778 AA in *Adams FC* 3.81: I wish I had a Bird of passage. 1780 MTucker in *Norton Papers* 438. 1784 Gadsden *Writings* 222, 235, 237. 1785 Franklin *Writings* 9.470: I hope your Princes and Princesses . . . are not birds of passage. 1789 JHarmer in Denny *Journal* 445. 1818 Woodworth *Poems* 253. 1820 Hodgson *Letters* 1.324: They had migrated, like birds of passage, to a colder clime. 1820 Simpson *Journal* 39, 1821 291. NED Passage le.

B176   A Bird that can sing, etc.

1796 Cobbett *Porcupine* 4.61: They have adopted the bird-catcher's maxim: "a bird that can sing, and won't sing, ought to be made sing." *Oxford* 469; Tilley B366; Whiting *NC* 370(3).

B177   Birds of a feather flock together

1674 Josselyn *Account* 213: Birds of a

feather will rally together. **1691** *Revolution* in *Andros Tracts* 1.114-5: *Randolph,* a Bird of the same Feather with themselves. **1701** Taylor *Christographia* 34.27-8: Birds of a kinde imitate one another. Beasts of the Same kinde do follow one another. **1702** Mather *Magnalia* 2.589: Ned Randolph, a bird of their own feather. **1709** Lawson *Voyage* 244: The remainder . . . will prove themselves Birds of the same Feather. **1782** Freneau *Poems* 2.153: This famous man, and two birds of his feather. **1788** Dunlap *Diary* 1.17: Yet all birds of a feather, 27: All birds of one black feather, 30: One flock, one feather, genus, stamp & kind, 31: Than moving with the birds of my own feather. **1789** *Massachusetts Centinel* in Buckingham *Specimens* 2.55. **1790** Ames *Letters* 1.91: I now lodge with Gerry, Aste, Sevier, and Parker. Birds of a feather. **1791** S.P.L. *Thoughts* 77: Birds of a feather flock together. **1792** Pope *Tour* 12: Evincing well, that Birds of a Feather, Always chirp and flock together. **1793** *Echo* 98: When e'er they're found, like birds of equal feather, I'll lay my ears you'll find them both together. **1796** Barton *Disappointment* 38: Burds of a fedder flock togedder. **1796** Cobbett *Porcupine* 4.16. **1797** Callender *Annual Register 1796* 200: says the proverb. **1798** Cobbett *Porcupine* 9.216, **1799** 10.170: the old adage. **1800** *Echo* 274: Where birds of every name and feather, Flock, and at times *get drunk* together, **1801** 284: But birds of every note and feather, And snakes, and toads should flock together. **1801** *Port Folio* 1.50: However impolite or unclassical the use of a vulgar proverb may be pronounced, upon the authority of lord Chesterfield, a village writer ventures to observe, that *birds of a feather* naturally assemble in the same grove or meadow. **1805** Paine *Another Callender* 2.984. **1806** EClarke in *Ruffin Papers* 1.102: The old proverb that *birds of a feather always flock together.* **1815** Humphreys *Yankey* 87: Birds of a feather have all flocked together. **1816** Paulding *Letters(I)* 2.186. **1819** Faux *Memorable Days* 1.70: Who . . . had all there met as gay proud birds of a feather. **1822** Watterston *Winter* 141: Wha on earth wad hae thought noo that sa many birds o' the same feather would

hae forgethered thegither. **1824** *Tales* 2.36: "Birds of a feather"—you understand. **1829** Smith *Letters* 253: the old adage. **1831** Jackson *Correspondence* 4.316, 384. **1839** Hone *Diary* 1.380: Who would of course appoint a majority of birds of his own feather, **1842** 2.585: The two latter birds of a feather overruled the judge. *Oxford* 60; TW 28(16); Tilley B393.

B178 Far **Birds** have fair feathers
1794 *Philadelphia Gazette* in Callender *Annual Register 1796* 44: A proverb says, that birds which have flown far have fair feathers. *Oxford* 244; Tilley F625; Whiting F565.

B179 If you want a **Bird** and a cage, buy the cage first
1807 *Salmagundi* 264: They began at the wrong end—maxim—If you want a bird and a cage, always buy the cage first.

B180 An ill **Bird** that befouls its own nest (*varied*)
1666 Alsop *Maryland* 24: For its an ill Bird *will befoule her own Nest.* **?1689** ?Mather *Vindication* in *Andros Tracts* 2.72: This Youth is an Unfledged Bird who thus defiles the Neast in which he was Hatcht. **1786** Rush *Letters* 1.393: It is a sorry bird that betrays its own nest. **1793** Gadsden *Writings* 258: It is like a bad bird betraying his own nest. **1815** *Port Folio* 3NS 6.508: An expression I once heard a Scotchman apply to one of his countrymen . . . "it is an ill bird which befouls her own nest." **1834** JRuffin in *Ruffin Papers* 2.112: It is a foul bird that bewrays [*for* berays] its own nest. *Oxford* 397-8; Whiting B306.

B181 A little **Bird** told me
1815 Brackenridge *Modern* 699: Hence the language of mothers to their children . . . "a little bird told me of it." **1821** Robertson *Letters* 158: Without the aid of a little bird to whisper them in my ear. **1822** Adams *Memoirs* 5.471: A bird had told him that it would be advisable. *Oxford* 60; Whiting B304.

B182 To be a **Bird** in a cage
1640 JLuxford in *Winthrop Papers(A)*

4.175: The cage doth soome burds good, beinge therein better to have, and by restraynt of liberty are brought and taught a better note. **1822** Gallatin *Diary* 216: He is like a bird in a cage when at home. **1845** Jackson *Correspondence* 6.362: Have the bird secure in the cage. Whiting B307. See **B173.**

B183 To be too old a **Bird** to learn a new tune

1820 Pintard *Letters* 1.319: [I] am too old a Bird to learn to whistle a new tune. See **D272.**

B184 To breed up **Birds** to pick out one's eyes

1742 *Georgia Records* 23.344: I find her shewing the same Aversion to bring up Children in the Art of winding Silk, which she thinks (with the English Proverb) is breeding up young Birds to pick out her Eyes. *Oxford* 60; Tilley B372.

B185 To hit the **Bird** in the eye

1784 JTemple in *Bowdoin Papers* 2.35: That young statesman has hit the bird in the eye! Tilley B387. See **N9.**

B186 To kill two **Birds** with one stone

1692 Mather *Wonders* 186-7: He is for, *Killing many Birds with one stone.* **1710** Mather *Bonifacius* 111: This may do two Executions *with one Stone.* **1763** Gadsden *Writings* 49: They can kill 2 birds with one stone. **1767** Franklin *Papers* 14.94: It is said to be clever to kill two Birds with one Stone: you may make three or four more alive by one little Visit at the same time. **1787** Cutler *Life* 1.235. **1789** Maclay *Journal* 99. **1810** Kennon *Letters* 32.276. **1815** Smith *Letters* 124. **1821** Weems *Letters* 3.321: My idea is as it ever has been that, *two birds may be kill*^{d} *at a throw.* **1828** *Yankee* 254. *Oxford* 423; TW 29(21).

B187 To save the **Bird** in one's bosom

1675 Williams *Writings* 6.378: Let us make sure to save the bird in our bosom, and to enter in that straight door and narrow way. NED Bird 5; *Oxford* 59; Tilley B386.

B188 You cannot catch old **Birds** with chaff

1755 Davis *Colonial Virginia Satirist* 25: Chaff will catch, some sort of Birds. **1776** JA in *Adams FC* 2.103: But he cannot catch old Birds. They are aware of the snare. **1776** *Battle of Brooklyn* 21: Don't you think . . . to catch old birds with chaff. **1777** AA in *Adams FC* 2.172: But Experienced Birds are not to be caught with chaff. **1778** Gordon *Letters* 400: As young as the Americans are they are too old to be caught by such chaff. **1785** Curwen *Journal* 2.1039: I often thought of the proverb — Old birds are not caught [with chaff]. **1788** *American Museum* 3.525: Don't think to catch old birds with chaff. **1789** EHazard in *Belknap Papers* 2.93: But old birds want a more substantial temptation than chaff. **1803** Davis *Travels* 359: Old birds is not to be catched with chaff. **1812** Randall *Miser* 37: It is hard to . . . catch birds with chaff. **1815** Humphreys *Yankey* 21: I'm tu old a bird to be ketch'd with chaff. **1827** Beecher *Autobiography* 2.101. *Oxford* 110; Whiting B308.

B189 To cling (stick) like **Bird-lime**

1739 Belcher *Papers* 2.240: Depend I'll cling like birdlime & part with no thing but according to the great Savoyard, **1740** 259: But will stick to it like bird-lime, 262: For I will stick like bird-lime to what affects my interest or honor.

B190 A **Bird's-eye** view

1799 Dennie *Letters* 167: They have not a bird's eye view of your politics. NED Bird's-eye 3.

B191 To sell one's **Birthright**

a**1700** Hubbard *New England* 667: Thereby, as it were, proffering them a mess of pottage instead of the birthright of the land. **1702** HAshurst in *Winthrop Papers*(B) 6.110: That successors shuld sel thar birthright for a mess of pottage. **1713** Wise *Churches* 144: They are . . . in *Esau's* straits, who thought he might Sell his Birthright for a mess of Pottage. **1753** *Independent Reflector* 281: But sell my Birthright for a Song. **1763** Gadsden *Writings* 25: Such fools, like Esau of old, to sell their birthright for a mess of pottage. **1770** *New-York Gazette* in *Newspaper Extracts*(I) 8.225: May this be the Fate of every Wretch who would sell his Country for a Mess of Pottage.

1775 Committee of Deer Island [Maine] in *Naval Documents* 1.910: They were such sons of Esau; as to sell their birth rights for a mess of Pottage. 1777 Paine *American Crisis* 1.69: He that would sell his birthright for a little *salt,* is as worthless as he who sold it for pottage without salt. 1807 *Weekly* 2.159: The freedom of America is a birth-right which ought not to be sold for a mess of pottage. 1817 Weems *Franklin* 86: Who will ever *sell his birth right* of a honest vote, for an electioneering dinner. *Oxford* 713; Whiting H364, R130.

B192   No Bishop no king
1647 Ward *Simple Cobler* 56: Is no Bishop no King, such an oraculous Truth, that you will pawne your Crowne and life upon it? 1703 Talbot *Letters* 96: I count, No Bishop no Church, as true as No Bishop No King. 1771 Boucher *View* 102: King James's maxim—"No bishop, no king!" *Oxford* 568; Tilley B408.

B193   To get the Bit in one's teeth (mouth)
1637 Williams *Writings* 6.21: To get the bits into their mouths. 1820 Tudor *Letters* 294: If the courser chooses to take the bit between his teeth, and run aside, there is no curb to prevent him. 1863 FRuffin in *Ruffin Papers* 3.340: Meanwhile labour shews signs of taking the bit in its teeth. *Oxford* 800; TW 30(1).

B194   The hasty Bitch brings forth blind puppies
1755 Franklin *PR* 5.471: The hasty Bitch brings forth blind Puppies. *Oxford* 356; Tilley B425.

B195   To make two Bites of a cherry
1843 Paulding *Letters(II)* 325: I would not compass my subject in a smaller space and did not wish to make two bites of a cherry. *Oxford* 849; TW 30.

B196   The Biter bit
1780 Sargent *Loyalist* 112: 'Twas, *who should bite the biter.* 1809 Fessenden *Pills* 25: The biter being sorest bitten. 1809 *Port Folio* 2NS 2.421: A new comedy called "Nolens Volens," or "The Biter Bit", written

by Everard Hall, a gentleman of North Carolina. *Oxford* 62; TW 30.

B197   To take the Bitter with the sweet
1778 *Washington *Writings* 11.414: Those Officers who take the bitter with the Sweet. Whiting B324. See S541.

B198   As opposite as Black and white
1720 Carter *Letters* 8: These areas much reverse to my nature as white is to black. 1781 *New Jersey Gazette* in *Newspaper Extracts (II)* 5.172: As evident as that white is not black. 1814 Kerr *Barclay* 239: As opposite as black was to white. *Oxford* 64; Whiting B331.

B199   In Black and white
1637 Morton *New English Canaan* 307: The wages might be paid out of the cleare proffit, which there in black and white was plainely put downe. 1722 *New-England Courant* in Buckingham *Specimens* 1.69: A Painter, who, in black and white, Would every roguish face discover. 1733 Belcher *Papers* 1.496: For I can't put into black & white what I wou'd show you & what I wou'd say. 1739 Franklin *PR* 2.225. 1742 Belcher *Papers* 2.421. 1763 Jefferson *Papers* 1.12: I retire . . . to converse in black and white with an absent friend, 1766 21. 1774 Franklin *Writings* 6.196: Asham'd of it, when in black and white. 1775 Fithian *Journal* 55. 1777 Munford *Patriots* 465. 1779 Gordon *Letters* 415: Material . . . that I chuse not to clothe in black and white, 424, 1782 477: She was assuring you in black and white. 1786 Jefferson *Papers* 10.600. 1796 Weems *Letters* 2.34, 1806 352. 1806 *Weekly* 1.112. 1807 *Port Folio* NS 4.37: So overjoyed was I withal to see myself in black and white. 1808 *Emerald* NS 1.314: Caroline is advised not to put herself in black and white. 1813 Paulding *Lay* 51. 1825 Neal *American Writers* 204: But how are we to speak of one, who has been guilty of such an outrage, in black and white, upon our noble system of speech? 1833 Cooper *Letters* 6.322. 1838 Hone *Diary* 1.351: The least said, particularly in *black and white,* the soonest mended. *Oxford* 63; Whiting B328.

B200   To make **Black** (white) white (black)
1734 *New-York Weekly Journal* in *Newspaper Extracts* (*I*) 1.404: Envy . . . delights in making *White* appear *Black*. **1744** Stephens *Journal*(*II*) 2.123: For that he would swear White was Black. **1746** *Georgia Records* 25.65: Not be so over nice and scrupulous as to deny that White was Black, or Black was White. **1774** Hamilton *Papers* 1.67: They may as well tell you, that black is white. **1776** Baldwin *Journal* 69: Faithless bloody minded men who assert that Black is white & White is Black. **1779** *New Jersey Gazette* in *Newspaper Extracts* (*II*) 3.175: It would operate against him to say in direct terms that black is white, and white is black. **1780** Freneau *Poems* 2.46: He could . . . Persuade you black was white or white was black. **1783** Williams *Penrose* 185: Swear Black was White or the contrary. **1788** Freneau *Prose* 130: If she says *black* is *white,* it is not for men . . . to contradict her. **1791** Rush *Letters* 1.604: To persuade men that white is *black,* or black *white,* it is necessary sometimes to make them believe that they are *gray.* **1794** *Echo* 122: Prov'd white is black, and then prov'd black is white. **1824** *Tales* 2.184: He'll make you b'lieve black is white, and white black. *Oxford* 64, 884; Whiting B330.

B201   To mar **Black**
1796 NAmes in *DHR* 7(1896) 34: Dr. Bullard . . . determined to mar black & bewray all I could say. Cf. *Oxford* 65; Whiting B327.

B202   As plenty as **Blackberries**
1797 Callender *Annual Register 1796* 205: To take a simile from Falstaff, Catos, Phocions, and Polybiuses, are "as plenty as blackberries." **1832** Ames *Nautical* 83: As plenty as blackberries. **1832** Barney *Memoir* 161: Excuses . . . were always, like Falstaff's reasons, "as plenty as blackberries." **1843** Cooper *Letters* 4.416. *Oxford* 634; TW 31(1).

B203   **Blanket** Bay
1775 Harrower *Journal* 106: Upon which I steered my course for Blanket Bay within School Cape, 129: I found the Anthony . . .

and the Lucy Friggat both Moor'd head & stern along side of each other in Blanket Bay within school cape. Partridge 61; TW 32.

B204   Can **Blessing** and cursing come from the same mouth?
1720 Walter *Choice Dialogue* xxi: Can Blessing and Cursing proceed from the same Mouth? See **B225.**

B205   The **Blind** leading the Blind (*varied*)
1654 Johnson *Wonder-Working* 132: The depthlesse ditches that blinde guides lead into. **1676** Tompson *Poems* 66: Whome the blind follow while the blind man leads. **1692** Bulkeley *Will* 255: Whither will these blind guides lead us, if we follow them, but into the ditch of rebellion. **1733** Johnson *Writings* 3.27: While the blind lead the blind, they both fall into the ditch, **1734** 39. **1744** Carter *Diary* 2.896: Thus does the blind lead the blind. **1778** PPayson in Thornton *Pulpit* 335: The fate of blind guides and their followers. **1793** Scott *Journal* 350: The blind leaders of the blind, 354. **1803** Davis *Travels* 36: *When the blind leads the blind, they shall both of them fall. Oxford* 67; Whiting B350.

B206   None so **Blind** as those who will not see
1713 Chalkley *Forcing* 401: Which puts me in mind of a Proverb, *Who is so blind as those as will not see?* **1745** WBorden in Boyd *Eighteenth Century Tracts* 97. **1798** *Washington *Writings* 36.209: None are more dull than those who will not perceive. **1819** Murphey *Papers* 1.138. *Oxford* 67; TW 32(1); Whiting D75. See **D56.**

B207   Earthly **Bliss** is unstable
1805 Sewall *Parody* 47: Away with all old saws and proverbs on the instability and transitory nature of earthly bliss — Corporal Trim's stick and all. Whiting W671. (L. Sterne *T. Shandy* bk.5, c.7.)

B208   To stick as fast as a **Blister**
1790 Lee *Letters* 2.514: The plaguey Influenza Cough sticks faster than a blister. Cf. TW 33(1).

B209 As stupid as a (barber's) **Block**

1806 Fessenden *Modern Philosopher* 4: Thus one Miss Sibyll remained stupid as a barber's block. **1812** Hitchcock *Social* 71: Their hearts were stupid as a block. *Oxford* 68; Svartengren 48; Tilley B453.

B210 As well talk to a **Block**

1724 Jones *Virginia* 62: You may as well talk reason . . . to a block, as to them. See **W215.**

B211 To batter **Blocks** with a razor

1819 Drake *Works* 285: He'd not be battering his razor upon blocks. *Oxford* 163: To cut blocks.

B212 All **Blood** is alike ancient

1745 Franklin *PR* 3.5: All blood is alike ancient. *Oxford* 69.

B213 As red as **Blood**

1672 Josselyn *New-England Rarities* 105: Flowers red as blood, 131, **1674** *Account* 100. **1709** Lawson *Voyage* 45. **1768** *Johnson Papers* 12.611. **1771** Hearne *Journey* 182. **1777** JAllen in *PM* 9(1885) 428. *Oxford* 668; Whiting B358.

B213a **Blood-red**

1683 Taylor *Poems* 12: The Blood Red Pretious Syrup of this Rose. **1688** Sewall *Diary* 1.241: His Coat and Breeches of blood-red silk. **1688** Taylor *Poems* 46: Oh! fill my Pipkin with thy Blood red Wine, **1707** 223. **1758** AGarden in *Colder Letters* 5.229. **1765** Timberlake *Memoirs* 63. **1789** Washington *Diaries* 4.45. **1807** Janson *Stranger* 229. **1813** Paulding *Lay* 52, 58. **1817** Drake *Works* 154. Whiting B358a.

B214 **Blood** is thicker than water

1821 Simpson *Journal* 278: Blood is thicker than water. **1848** Cooper *Letters* 5.289: There is no saying more true than that. *Oxford* 69; TW 33(3).

B215 The **Blood** of the Martyrs is the seed of the church

1747 Stith *History* 233-4: The Blood of these People would be the Seed of the Plantation. **1778** Paine *American Crisis* 1.121: As the blood of the martyrs has been the seed of the Christian church. **1781** Baldwin *Life and Letters* 68: To increase from the Blood of every Martyr. **1781** Oliver *Origin* 15: For as the Blood of Martyrs is usually termed, the Seed of the Church; so those Severities served but as the Implements of Husbandry, to convert the New England Wilderness into a fruitfull Field. **1796** Savery *Journal* 130. *Oxford* 69; TW 33-4.

B216 **Blood** requires blood

1764 *Paxton Papers* 116: And 'tis a common Saying, BLOOD REQUIRES BLOOD. *Oxford* 69; Whiting B361.

B217 True **Blood** never lies

1801 *Port Folio* 1.260: True blood . . . never lies. Whiting B368.

B218 You cannot get **Blood** from a flint (turnip)

1800 Cobbett *Letters* 94: You cannot have blood of a flint stone. a**1834** Wirt *Letters* 2.440: Blood from a turnip, sir, was ne'er extracted. TW 34(12). Cf. Whiting B365.

B219 As blooming as a **Blossom** in May

1821 Knight *Poems* 2.164: So blooming you look, as a blossom in May. Cf. Whiting B374-80. See **F194.**

B220 As charming as **Blossoms** in May

1789 *Columbian Magazine* 3.437: Eloquence . . . charming as blossoms in May. Cf. Whiting B374-80.

B221 When the **Blossoms** fall, *etc.*

1782 Adams *D and A* 3.73: We have a saying in Boston that when the Blossoms fall the Haddock begin to crawl, i.e. to move out into deep Water, so that in Summer you must go out some distance to fish.

B222 A **Blot** in (on) the escutcheon

1737 *Pennsylvania Gazette* in *Newspaper Extracts(I)* 1.505: A perfect Blot in that Escutcheon of Reason. **1756** *Johnson Papers* 2.450: We apprehend it has been no small Blott in Mr. Shirleys Escutcheon, **1768** 6.405: Submission would blot the Escutcheon of their Illustrious . . . Attchievments. **1787** WSSmith in Smith *Journal and Correspondence* 1.147: Henry . . . bears a blot on his escutcheon. **1795** Morris *Diary and Letters* 2.94: **1819** Bentley *Diary* 4.629. Tilley B470.

B223   A **Blot** is not a blot till it's hit

1742 Belcher *Papers* 2.447: A blot's no blot 'till it's hit. 1768 Franklin *Papers* 15.235: But, say we, a blot is never a blot till it is hit. *Oxford* 69; Tilley B471.

B224   The first **Blow** is half the battle

1763 FBernard in *Baxter Manuscripts* 13.318-9: They always give the first blow, which with them is the best part of the Battle. 1776 Washington *Writings* 4.454: The old proverb, of the first blow being half the battle. 1781 DSwart in *Clinton Papers* 7.613-4: A General should not let his Enemy know when he intended to strike, but give the Blow and think afterwards. 1835 Jackson *Correspondence* 5.365: The first blow is half the battle. *Oxford* 261; Tilley B472.

B225   To **Blow** hot and cold

1736 Lynde *Diaries* 94: Mr Ba——d . . . blew hot and cold. 1754 Eliot *Essays* 108: This blowing Hot and Cold out of the same Mouth. 1764 Franklin *Papers* 11.296: There are Mouths that blow hot as well as cold. 1780 Van Schaack *Letters* 249. 1784 Gadsden *Writings* 210. 1795 Cobbett *Porcupine* 2.28: Prudence would prevent the employment of one whose only talent is *blowing hot and cold with the same mouth,* 1797 6.100: Mr. Drayton can . . . blow hot and cold with the same breath. 1802 MCarey in Weems *Letters* 2.220. 1814 Kerr *Barclay* 322: The same constitution cannot blow hot, and cold, with the same breath. 1816 Fidfaddy *Adventures* 140: He . . . can always serve all occassions, sail in all winds, and blow hot and cold, wet and dry through the same whistle. 1820 Pintard *Letters* 1.336. 1824 Adams *Memoirs* 6.308: This . . . was in Forsyth blowing hot and cold with the same breath. 1827 Watterston *Wanderer* 156: You blow hot and cold with the same mouth. *Oxford* 70; TW 193(2). See **B204.**

B226   Till all is **Blue**

1806 *Port Folio* NS 2.123: Therefore we'll fight *till all is blue.* Colcord 36; TW 34(1).

B227   To be true **Blue**

1767 JBoucher in *MHM* 7(1912) 340: Rigid true-blue Presbyterians. 1768 Adams(S)

Writings 1.209: A true blue *protestant* town. 1768 *Pennsylvania Gazette* in *Newspaper Extracts* (I) 7.324: Some stanch *True Blue* in the City of *New-York.* 1771 Paterson *Glimpses* 88: You hardly have sufficient Caledonian blood, to call you true blue. 1774 Adams *Works* 4.66: True blue Calvinists. 1775 Fithian *Journal* 107: One *Covenanter* resides here, a stiff, true blue, warm, obstinate Precisian. 1783 Freneau *Poems* 2.238: And he'll turn a true Blue-Skin, or just what you will. 1787 *American Museum* 2.596. 1787 Tyler *Contrast* 54: But I am a true blue son of liberty, for all that, 56. 1792 Ames *Letters* 1.126: It is important to have all the Massachusetts members true blue, 1795 178. 1797 Callender *Annual Register 1796* 173: No true-blue democrat will entertain a doubt of it. 1797 WVMurray in McHenry *Letters* 248. 1807 JAdams in *Adams-Warren Correspondence* 393: Every true blue Jacobin. 1816 Paulding *Letters* (I) 1.177: He is an Irishman, honey, true blue, pluck, liver and lights, midriff, and all. 1817 Scott *Blue Lights* 137: Some true-blue seaman. 1832 Ames *Nautical* 151: A true blue smuggler. *Oxford* 841; Whiting B384.

B228   To look **Blue**

1650 Bradstreet *Works* 125: Nay milksops at such brunts you look but blue. TW 35(5).

B229   True **Blue** will never stain

1802 Irving *Jonathan* 16: True blue will never stain! *Oxford* 841; Tilley T543.

B230   **Blue Flujin** where fire freezes

1830 Ames *Mariner's* 130: That part of the world generally known to sailors by the name of "Blue Flujin" where it is said fire freezes. TW 35.

B231   The **Blue Hen's** chickens

1818 Royall *Letters* 146: He told one of our party, he was "one of the blue hen's chickens." DA blue hen; NED Suppl. Blue Hen.

B232   To have the **Blues**

1770 *Johnson Papers* 7.411: Gamble has been long indisposed with the Blues. 1813 Gerry *Diary* 177: The loss of my friends gave me the blues. 1816 PRobertson in *W&MCQ* 2S 11(1931) 62: A little touched with the

Blues, 65. **1818** Royall *Letters* 118: Have you got the blues again, or blacks, 179: If this does not cure you of the *blues,* nothing that I can give you will. TW 35. See **D118, W119.**

B233   At (the) first **Blush**

1644 Williams *Writings* 3.161: At the very first blush. **1744** Johnson *Writings* 3.459: At first blush. **1775** JAdams in *Warren-Adams Letters* 1.132: At first blush. **1775** WHDrayton in Gibbes 2.57. **1775** NGreene in Ward *Correspondence* 110: At first blush. **1780** *New Jersey Gazette* in *Newspaper Extracts (II)* 5.78. **1781** Oliver *Origin* 101. **1781** Reed *Life* 2.374. **1787** Jefferson *Papers* 12.24. **1787** HKnox in *Warren-Adams Letters* 2.299. **1789** Morris *Diary* 1.46, **1793** 2.595. **1794** TBlount in *Blount Papers* 2.418. **1796** Morris *Diary and Letters* 2.151, 154. **1798** Adams *Works* 8.575. **1822** Mason *Memoir* 263. Whiting B385.

B234   As hard as a **Board**

1772 Hearne *Journey* 342: It soon freezes as hard as a board. Whiting B409.

B235   As level as a **Board**

1820 Hodgson *Letters* 2.398: You will be told to keep such a road, as it is as level as a board. Barbour 19(1): flat; Taylor *Comparisons* 41: flat.

B236   As smooth as a **Board**

c1680 Radisson *Voyages* 118: The country smooth like a board, 191.

B237   The greatest **Boasters** are worst soldiers

1756 TGage in *Letters to Washington* 1.254: The ridiculous Gasconades of the New Englanders, who I believe to be the greatest Boasters & werst Soldiers on the Continent. Cf. Whiting B415, *etc.*

B238   Little **Boats** must keep near shore

1751 Franklin *PR* 4.97: Great Estates may venture more; Little Boats must keep near Shore, **1758** *WW* 347. Barbour 19(2); Tilley S352; Whiting *NC* 373.

B239   To row one's own **Boat**

1829 TTurner in *Ruffin Papers* 1.524: And

left him, in seaman's phrase to "row his own Boat." TW 35(2). See **C27.**

B240   To be a **Bob** to the kite

1819 WStorer in Banks *Maine* 138: We shall still remain a bob to the kite during this generation. Cf. NED Bob *sb.*[1] 6.

B241   To kick up **Bobbery**

1800 Dorr *Letters* 209: The Russians having kicked a baubery with the Chineese, 216: They will . . . pull hair and kick up too much baubery. NED Bobbery.

B242   Great **Bodies** move slow

1775 Lee *Letters* 1.152: Great bodies, you know, move slow. *Oxford* 333; Tilley B503.

B243   To keep **Body** and soul together

1784 Adams(A) *Letters* 165: To keep body and soul together. **1786** WWhiting in American Antiquarian Society, *Proceedings* NS 66(1956) 143: The Small Pittance . . . was but barely Sufficient to keep Soul and Body together. **1787** Adams(A) *Letters* 331. **1788** Freneau *Prose* 184. **1800** Adams *Letters on Silesia* 15. **1821** Simpson *Journal* 271. NED Body 1b.

B244   What is a **Body** without a head?

1649 EElmer in *Winthrop Papers(A)* 5.361: What is a body without a head what is a people without a guide. Cf. Whiting H254.

B245   As brag and brisk as a **Body-louse**

1692 Bulkeley *Will* 150: And who afterwards was . . . as brag and brisk as a body-louse. Tilley B504. Cf. *Oxford* 581.

B246   As dull as the **Bœotians**

1776 Adams *D and A* 3.439: The Bœotians were remarkable, even to a proverb, for their dullness. NED Bœotia, Bœtian.

B247   As sore as a **Boil**

1765 JWatts in *Aspinwall Papers* 2.568: The times are sore as a bile. **1802** *Port Folio* 2.152: My heart was sorer than a bile. Barbour 19; TW 36.

B248   **Boils** are wholesome but not toothsome

1776 Hodgkins *Letters* 200: People say thay [boils] are holsome But not Toothsome, 203: Sorry to hear you are trobled with boyles . . .

but as you Say they are counted holsom. Cf. NED Toothsome 1.

B249 Bolt upright

1666 Alsop *Maryland* 86: Women stand bolt upright. **1816** Paulding *Letters(I)* 1.91: Cocking his stump-tail bolt upright. **1824** *Tales* 1.68: He sat . . . bolt upright. Whiting B432a.

B250 To shoot one's **Bolt** (in the dark)

1703 Taylor *Christographia* 345.13-5: This is a good way to Stop all mouths from Shooting their bolts out against Such proceedings. **1744** Smith *Memoirs(I)* 186: That the best Step was to call a Congress, & shoot no Bolt, because it would expose our weakness. **1744** Stephens *Journal(II)* 2.154: Wherefor I was cautious in shooting my bolt in the dark. **1747** Franklin *Papers* 3.152: At present I shoot my Bolt pretty much in the Dark. **1786** Smith *Diary* 2.65: I did not care to shoot the Bolt of asking an Introduction to Mr. Pitt. **1808** Grant *Memoirs* 2.87: I sat silent when my bolt was shot. *Oxford* 728; Whiting B434. See **F226.**

B251 Bongre malgre

1769 *Beekman Papers* 2.694: So that Bon gre Mal gré, it must be used in my family as Common Tea. **1785** JQAdams in Smith *Journal and Correspondence* 2.(1) 50: *bon-grés malgré*, as the French say. **1805** GDavis in *Barbary Wars* 6.7: Bon gre, Malgre qu'Il en ait. Whiting B453.

B252 Before one can say **Bone**

c1800 Tyler *Island* 15: Who cast away his old wife and got a young one in less time than you could say Bone. See **J12, 44, P42.**

B253 A **Bone** of contention

a1700 Hubbard *New England* 177: Which . . . proved a bone of contention between them. **1721** Carter *Letters* 106: So that matter will be no longer a bone of contention. **1722** *New-England Courant* 25(3.2). **1754** Carter *Diary* 1.114. **1766** Adams *D and A* 1.293. **1768** Franklin *Papers* 15.36. **1770** *Colden Letters* 9.231. **1771** ISmith in *Adams FC* 1.72. **1775** AInnes in *Naval Documents* 1.347. **1776** Gordon *Letters* 320. **1778** Burd *Letters* 101. **1778** Montresor *Journals* 119.

1779 *Washington *Writings* 17.51. **1781** Peters *Connecticut* 87-8. **1782** *Belknap Papers* 3.350: I am very loth to be a burden or a bone of contention to you. **1783** Curwen *Journal and Letters* 372. **1783** Van Schaack *Letters* 349. **1785** Adams(A) *Letters* 268. **1787** Jefferson *Papers* 12.173. **1788** Bowen *Journals* 2.565. **1790** FSkipwith in Jefferson *Papers* 17.510: The formation of this body seems to breed the chief and weighty bone of contention. **1792** Morris *Diary and Letters* 1.597, **1796**, 2.224. **1797** Baily *Journal* 275, 437. **1798** Jefferson *Writings* 1.423. **1799** JCathcart in *Barbary Wars* 1.309. **1804** Irving *Corrector* 100. **1807** *Weekly* 1.224: Contention's bone to snarl about. **1809** WCunningham in *Adams-Cunningham Letters* 77. **1810** King *Life* 5.199. a**1811** Henry *Account* 117: Here it was that the most serious contention took place: this became the bone of strife. **1812** Hitchcock *Social* 14. **1813** Harmon *Sixteen Years* 157. **1816** Fidfaddy *Adventures* 45. **1816** Paulding *Letters(I)* 1.91. **1820** Robertson *Letters* 116. **1821** Simpson *Journal* 356: Beaver is the grand bone of contention. **1831** Baldwin *Diary* 96: Became a bone of strife. **1844** FBlair in Jackson *Correspondence* 6.300: They want Texas only as a bone of contention. *Oxford* 73; TW 36(1). See **A104, B33.**

B254 A **Bone** to pick (chaw, gnaw) on (with)

1764 Watts *Letter Book* 298: But there he will have a tougher Bone to pick. **1776** JA in *Adams FC* 2.68: You love to pick a political Bone. **1776** Adams *Works* 9.397: I have one bone to pick with your colony. **1777** JA in *Adams FC* 2.178: There is a Bone for you to pick. **1779** Adams *Works* 9.484. **1782** JAdams in *Warren-Adams Letters* 2.1777: Canada, Nova Scotia, Boundaries, Tories, Fisheries, are Bones to pick. **1783** *Belknap Papers* 1.228: Glad of an opportunity to put into their hands so clever a *bone to pick*. **1789** Maclay *Journal* 132: I answered . . . in a way that gave him a bone to chaw. **1806** *Port Folio* NS 2.64: So pick that bone, my Dick. **1809** Irving *History* 1.250: But fortune, who seems always careful . . . to throw a bone for hope to gnaw upon. **1811** Burroughs *Memoirs* 46. *Oxford* 73-4; TW 37(7); Tilley B522; Whiting B447. See **C355.**

B255 The nearer the **Bone** the sweeter the meat

1778 SCooper in Franklin *Writings* 8.258: We all agree the nearer the bone the sweeter the meat. **1787** *Franklin-Mecom* 300. **1796** Hamilton *Papers* 20.236: She had not the proverb in her favour *"The nearer the bone &c."* But I dare say she is sweet enough. **1834** Hone *Diary* 1.132: The cattle . . . had sharp biting lately—little too sweet. The last expression was a joke, which I understand is sometimes applied to scant pasturage; "the nigher the bone the sweeter the meat." *Oxford* 557: Whiting B444.

B256 Not to make old **Bones**

1833 Pintard *Letters* 4.139: It was often predicted . . . that I sh^d never live to make old bones. *Oxford* 588; Whiting *NC* 373(3).

B257 To come off with whole **Bones**

1766 *Johnson Papers* 12.43: I was Very much Obliged to them to Come of with whole Bones. **1781** EStevens in Jefferson *Papers* 4.562: Their greatest Study is to Rub through their Tower of Duty with whole Bones. Cf. NED Whole lc. See **S235.**

B258 To feel in one's **Bones**

1789 EHazard in *Belknap Papers* 2.102: As I apprehended he "feels in his bones," as Mrs. H. says. *Oxford* 253; TW 37(7).

B259 To have no **Bone** in one's throat

1783 Williams *Penrose* 191: I have no bone in my throat. I think I speak clere enough. *Oxford* 73; Tilley B517.

B260 To make no **Bones** of

1634 Wood *New-England* 26: One of them made no bones to runne away with a Pigge, than a Dogge to runne away with a Marrow bone. **1710** Sewall *Diary* 2.289: They made no bones of voting against them in Council. **1722** *New-England Courant* 25 (3.2): Who is it that . . . makes no Bones of calling the Town a MOB? **1728** Byrd *Dividing Line* 174: They had made no Bones of Staying from prayers. **1736** WByrd in *VHM* 36 (1928) 213: The Plague of Workmen who make no Bones of abusing the honest Landlord. **1770** HHusband in Boyd *Eighteenth Century Tracts* 326. **1815** *Journal from Bos-*

ton . . . to New Orleans by William Richson, 1815-1816 (New York, privately printed, 1940) 4: I made no bones in telling him my mind. **1819** JWalker in *Ruffin Papers* 1.225. **1829** Wirt *Letters* 2.266. *Oxford* 74; TW 36(4).

B261 To plunder to the **Bone**

1783 *Clinton Papers* 8.244: And he said he would plunder some people to the bone. Whiting B449, 451.

B262 What is bred in the **Bone** will not out of the flesh (*varied*)

1637 Morton *New English Canaan* 326: It has bin an old saying, and a true, what is bred in the bone will not out of the flesh. **1764** AA in *Adams FC* 1.32: What is bred in the bone will never be out of the flesh (as Lord M would have said). **1764** *Paxton Papers* 262: But alass whats bred in the Bone will never come out of the Flesh. **1765** Watts *Letter Book* 400: His hands have been so full, owing to his own impolitick Conduct, which is bred in the Bone. **1775** JEliot in *Belknap Papers* 2.78: What was bred in the bone would creep out in the flesh. **1790** Adams *Works* 9.571: Politics are bred in the bones of both of you. **1791** WSeton in Hamilton *Papers* 8.4: What is bred in the bone will appear in the flesh. **1806** Ames *Letters* 1.376: Experience will yet whip out of our flesh what folly has bred in our bone. *Oxford* 83; Whiting F273.

B263 A **Book's** a friend

1807 *Salmagundi* 120: A book's a friend.

B264 To be in one's black **Book**

1829 Otis *Letters* 2.255: In his black book. **1830** Jackson *Correspondence* 4.206: *I keep no black books for my friends.* *Oxford* 64. Cf. Whiting B458. See **L173.**

B265 To speak without **Book**

1786 Smith *Diary* 2.114: He suspected Mr. Nepean spoke without Book on 1st Sep^r. **1787** *Washington *Writings* 29.153: But I may be speaking without book. *Oxford* 762; Tilley B532.

B266 To talk like a **Book**

1807 *Salmagundi* 226: They are . . . kind of

people who . . . talk like a book. *Oxford* 803; TW 38(8).

B267 The **Boot** is on the other (wrong) leg
1815 Palmer *Diary* 153: I think the boot is on the other leg. **1823** Weems *Letters* 3.353: *'Pon my shoul now honey, but the boot was on the wrong leg.* *Oxford* 74; TW 38(5).

B268 Burn his **Boots!**
1777 Joslin *Journal* 312: And then I Came back 3 mild [miles] to one boyds, a very Deer place, burn his boots.

B269 He does not always ride who puts his **Boots** on
1807 Mackay *Letters* 71: He does not always ride when he puts his Boots on, **1810** 97-8. *Oxford* 75; Tilley B538.

B270 To get through without **Boots**
1832 Ames *Nautical* 159: Our beloved country has, to use a sea expression, "got through it without boots."

B271 To play **Bopeep**
1748 Johnson *Writings* 3.213: A perpetual course of quibbling and dodging and playing boo-peep on both sides of a contradiction. **1758** *Pennsylvania Journal* in *Newspaper Extracts(I)* 4.302: Monsieur Chateleau, who seems to be playing Bow-peep with our Cruizers. *Oxford* 75; Tilley B540. Cf. Whiting B576.

B272 As naked as one was **Born**
1697 Dickinson *Journal* 44: All stripped as naked as we were born, 112: Stripped . . . as naked as when we came into the world. **1702** Mather *Magnalia* 2.527: Women . . . stark naked as ever they were born. **1734** *Colden Letters* 8.217: As through yᵉ Streets they run forlorn Naked and bare as they were born. **1764** Hutchinson *History* 1.174: Naked as she came into the world. **1774** Harrower *Journal* 74. **1774** Schaw *Journal* 78. **1775** TRoberts in *Naval Documents* 2.74: They got a shore as they came in the world — not the Least thing Sav'd out of her. **1781** JMazaret in Jefferson *Papers* 4.694. **1782** EHuntington in Webb *Correspondence* 2.388: As naked as when they came into the world. **a1800** Bowen *Journals* 1.25. **1813**

Weems *Drunkard* 65. *Oxford* 553-4; Whiting B466. See **S507**.

B273 As sure as one was **Born**
1809 Weems *Marion* 184: As sure as ever they were born. **1812** Woodworth *Beasts* 22: As sure as I was born. **1813** Weems *Drunkard* 78: As sure as ever you were born. Barbour 20; TW 38(2).

B274 Better never **Born** than ill-bred
1687 Fitzhugh *Letters* 203: Better be never born than ill bred. *Oxford* 56-7; Whiting C200.

B275 Better to be **Born** fortunate than rich
1778 Lee(W) *Letters* 2.370: 'Tis certainly better to be born fortunate than rich. Cf. Whiting H104, 106.

B276 He that is **Born** to be hanged will never be drowned (*varied*)
a1731 Cook *Bacon* 320: Who's born for Hanging (Proverb says) Ne'er needs fear Drowning in the Seas. **1775** Moore *Diary* 1.136: According to the old saying. **1776** POliver in Hutchinson *Diary* 2.52-3: Happy for him if the old proverb — He that is born to be hanged will never be drowned — is not his protection. **1779** Freneau *Poems* 2.8: Who are born to be hang'd, will never be shot. **1784** Shaw *Journals* 135: Never go in an old ship when he can get a new one, unless he knows he is born to be hanged. **1799** *Echo* 249: "Men," says the ancient proverb sound, "Born to be hang'd will ne'er be drown'd." **1804** Irving *Corrector* 91: An old and well known proverb — "he that's born to be hang'd," etc. **1817** Scott *Blue Lights* 121: The old proverb "that he who was born to be hanged could never be drowned." *Oxford* 75-6; TW 39(3); Whiting D419.

B277 We are not **Born** for ourselves alone
1713 Wise *Churches* 32: The Received maxim, *Non soli nobis nati sumus.* **1720** *Letter* in *Colonial Currency* 2.238: That Noble Maxim, *Man was not born for himself.* **1815** Brackenridge *Modern* 696: There is a Latin maxim, "non nobis metipsis, nascimur;" we are not born for ourselves alone. *Oxford* 75; Tilley B141.

B278 The **Borrower** is a slave to the lender

1757 Franklin *PR* 7.86: The *Borrower* is a Slave to the Lender; the Security to both, 1758 *WW* 348: The Borrower is a Slave to the Lender, and the Debtor to the Creditor. Lean 4.112; Prov. 22.7.

B279 He that goes a **Borrowing** goes a sorrowing

1743 Franklin *PR* 2.370: Borgen macht sorgen, 1758 *WW* 347: He that goes a borrowing goes a sorrowing. 1770 Carter *Diary* 1.374: He may oblige the poor planter to make good the proverb that whenever he goes a borrowing he goes a sorrowing. *Oxford* 314; Tilley B545. Cf. Whiting B467, S625.

B280 **Boston** folks are full of notions

1788 *Maryland Journal* in Thornton *Glossary* 2.616: The Boston folks are deucid lads, And always full of notions. 1793 *Massachusetts Spy* in Thornton *Glossary* 2.616: Boston folks are full of notions. 1807 *Emerald* 2.230: The proverb says. 1815 Humphreys *Yankey* 42-3: They are . . . pritty much like the Boston folkes, "full of notions," as the saying is. 1832 Ames *Nautical* 71. DA Boston 5(6).

B281 **Boston** is Lost-town

1694 Scottow *Narrative* 306-7: O poor *New-England*, especially *Boston*, in the Day of it, poor to a proverb, of being the lost Town in our first Founding. 1702 Mather *Magnalia* 1.91: For a while Boston was proverbially called *Lost-town*, for the mean and sad circumstances of it.

B282 As light as a **Bottle**

1756 Laurens *Papers* 2.327: The Vessel went out as light as a Bottle, and we hope by this she is well advanc'd on her way.

B283 As smooth as a **Bottle**

c1800 PPond in Gates *Five Fur Traders* 49: They soon had his head as smooth as a Bottle. Cf. TW 39(2).

B284 **Bottle-green**

1805 Weems *Letters* 2.316: This. . . and that a bottle green. TW 39(1).

B285 To venture (all) in one **Bottom**

1690 SSewall in *Baxter Manuscripts* 5.64: We mind the same thing & venture on the same Bottom. a1700 Hubbard *New England* 103: Yet had he this consideration, as not venture all his own stock . . . in one single bottom. *Oxford* 859; Tilley A209.

B286 As crooked as a **Bow**

1821 Freneau *Last Poems* 35: Were you as crooked as a bow. Svartengren 277. Cf. Whiting B479.

B287 A **Bow** long bent loses its spring (*varied*)

1770 Paterson *Glimpses* 78: A bow long bent loses its spring. 1818 Fessenden *Ladies Monitor* 104: The bow is weakened that is ever bent. 1826 Audubon *1826 Journal* 177: To relax the bent bow of his morning's abstracted business. *Oxford* 78-9; Whiting B478.

B288 The **Bow** of Ulysses

1796 Morris *Diary and Letters* 2.169: It is not given to every man to bend the bow of Ulysses. *Oxford* 79; Tilley B562.

B289 To draw a **Bow** at a venture

1722 *New-England Courant* 27(2.1): Beware how they draw the Bow upon bare *Surmise*, or doubtful *Report*. 1727 Danforth *Poems* 176.114: Their Bow they seldom at Adventure drew. 1765 Adams(S) *Writings* 1.38: This News Writer shoots his Bow at a Venture. 1781 Sullivan *Letters* 3.272: My Letter . . . was Like Drawing a Bow at a venture, 1785 415. 1811 Colby *Life* 1.100, 1812 145, 156: The bow was drawn at a venture, but God directed the arrow. NED Draw 9, Venture 1c.

B290 To draw (shoot with) a long **Bow**

1784 RNelson in *MHM* 55(1960) 350: Smyth had always a trick of Shooting with a long bow. 1801 *Port Folio* 1.101: Mr. Duane begins to draw his long bow. 1832 Ames *Nautical* 96: It is said that travellers that are somewhat inclined to Major Longbowism [come to believe their own stories]. *Oxford* 479; TW 39-40; Tilley B570.

B291 To out-shoot one in his own **Bow**

1647 Ward *Simple Cobler* 17: Rather then the devill will lose his game, he will out-shoot Christ in his own bow. **1669** Gorton's *Letter* in Force *Tracts* 4.7.11: Overshooting them in their owne bow. **1669** Morton *New-Englands Memoriall* 12: But God out-shoots Satan oftentimes in his own Bow. **1692** Mather *Wonders* 107: Now that the Devil may be thus outshot in his own Bow. *Oxford* 602; Tilley B563.

B292 As level as a **Bowling-green**

a**1811** Henry *Account* 27: Firm ground, level as a bowling green. NED Bowling-green; Svartengren 272.

B293 (Keep) a taut **Bowstring**

1815 Waterhouse *Journal* 173: *"A taut bowstring"* was always my motto.

B294 To be in a bad **Box**

1761 *Johnson Papers* 3.578: He would certainly be in a bad Box. **1766** JParker in Franklin *Papers* 13.413: I see vastly many in worse Boxes. **1778** *Beekman Papers* 3.1306: Thay Will all be Now in a fine Box at New York [ironic], **1779** 1340: So I am In a Bad Box. **1784** EWinslow in *Winslow Papers* 228: Should we be disappointed we shall be in a terrible Box. **1800** TBlount in *Blount Papers* 3.405. a**1800** Bowen *Journals* 1.23: So [I] was in a fine box [ironic]. **1809** Weems *Marion* 110, 155, **1813** *Drunkard* 5, 61, **1823** *Letters* 3.355. TW 40(1). Cf. *Oxford* 924.

B295 To be in a **Box**

1728 Talcott *Papers* 2.48: If . . . his Majesty should put us into the same box. **1784** Adams(A) *Letters* 156: He is in a certain box without knowing it. TW 40(2).

B296 To be in the wrong **Box**

1698 JUsher in *W&MCQ* 3S 7(1950) 106: Judge my selfe then in the wrong box. **1744** Hamilton *Itinerarium* 144. **1769** *Norton Papers* 97. **1812** Melish *Travels* 307. *Oxford* 924; Whiting B492.

B297 His **Brains** cannot fill his belly

1735 Franklin *PR* 2.6: There's many witty men whose brains can't fill their bellies.

B298 As litigious as **Braintree**

1760 Adams *D and A* 1.137: I have absolutely heard it used as a Proverb in several Parts of the Province, "as litigious as Braintree."

B299 To sift and bolt to the **Bran**

1787 *New-York Journal* in Hamilton *Papers* 4.281, n.3: Being sifted and bolted to the brann. Whiting B499.

B300 The **Brave** can pity and excuse, *etc.*

1752 Franklin *PR* 4.252: The Brave and the Wise can both pity and excuse; when Cowards and Fools shew no Mercy. **1776** Heath *Memoirs* 87: The truly brave are always humane. *Oxford* 151: Cowards; Whiting C509. See **C330, S307.**

B301 **Bread** is the staff of life

c**1687** ?JCotton in Alden *Epitaphs* 3.271: The staff of bread, and water eke the stay. **1768** Franklin *Papers* 15.65: Your farmers [are] charged . . . as cruelly withholding the staff of life. **1779** EFreeman in *Baxter Manuscripts* 16.151. **1779** *New Jersey Gazette* in *Newspaper Extracts(II)* 3.84: We . . . are threatened with a great scarcity of the staff of life. **1779** Thacher *Journal* 216: The whole army has been . . . entirely destitute of the staff of life. **1782** Smith *Life and Correspondence* 2.66. **1784** Smyth *Tour* 1.292: Indian corn is the great staff of life in America. **1790** JSwanwick in Jefferson *Papers* 18.157: They expected a great want of the first staff of life. **1791** Bartram *Travels* lii. **1798** Allen *Vermont* 483: Bread, figuratively speaking, is called the staff of life. **1804** Adams *Writings* 2.98. **1806** Cabot *Letters* 354: It is maintained that a country which sells provisions (the staff of life) . . . possesses such a decided advantage. **1812** AAdams in Smith *Journal and Correspondence* 1.222. **1815** Waterhouse *Journal* 97: We found, in all our sufferings, that bread was literally the staff of life. **1816** Adams *Writings* 6.78: This struggle to give scarcity to the staff of life. **1819** Faux *Memorable Days* 1.199. **1821** Pintard *Letters* 2.8: And what a kind Providence intended as the staff of life sh^d be converted into liquid poison. **1823** Bierce *Travels* 88: Here we purchased some of the staff of life. *Oxford* 81; Tilley B613.

B302 To ask for **Bread**
1813 Weems *Letters* 3.96: Some men asking for bread have been complimented with a brick bat. *Oxford* 20; Whiting B516.

B303 To bake better **Bread** than can be made of wheat
1816 Paulding *Letters* (*I*) 1.249: By attempting to bake better bread than can be made of wheat. *Oxford* 52; Whiting B515.

B304 To be in good **Bread**
1763 TPickering in *Essex Institute Historical Collections* 49 (1913) 139: He is now in good bread, and seems loth to affront his people. 1777 AA in *Adams FC* 2.340: He is not in so good Bread as he was at Philadelphia, he cannot procure any Material to work up. NED Suppl. Bread 5b.

B305 To be no **Bread** and butter of mine
1791 S.P.L. *Thoughts* 167: It is no bread and butter of mine. NED Bread-and-butter 3; Partridge 90.

B306 To butter one's **Bread**
1692 Bulkeley *Will* 196: And others to fall in with and support it because they see they can butter their bread by it. Cf. NED Butter 1c.

B307 To butter one's **Bread** on both sides
1738 Stephens *Journal* (*I*) 1.64: I understood he intended to butter his Bread on both Sides (meaning his Design of taking Lands in both Provinces). *Oxford* 81; TW 41(6).

B308 To carry the **Bread** and cheese to the knife, *etc.*
1744 Stephens *Journal*(*II*) 2.89: And put in practice the Old saying of carrying the Bread and Cheese to the Knife, where the Knife can't be carried to the Bread and Cheese. Cf. TW 252: Mountain (1).

B309 To eat the **Bread** out of one's mouth
1705 Makemie *Writings* 149: Strangers eat the Bread out of our Mouths, as the common saying is. *Oxford* 800: take; Tilley B629.

B310 To mind one's **Bread** and butter
1791 S.P.L. *Thoughts* 167: To advance the public good . . . by moderately *minding their bread and butter.*

B311 To quarrel with one's **Bread** and butter
1739 Stephens *Journal*(*I*) 1.265: Thinking it the wisest Way not to quarrel with the Bread and Butter they got, though perhaps not spread to their Liking. 1741 *Georgia Records* 23.182: [They] were not so weak to fall out with their own Bread & Butter. 1770 Franklin *Papers* 17.267: Like froward Children that quarrel with their Bread and Butter. 1782 Curwen *Journal* 2.811. 1785 EHazard in *Belknap Papers* 1.418: But we must stick to our bread and butter. 1807 *Emerald* NS 1.88. 1812 Jefferson *Writings* 13.163: The Anglomen will consent to make peace with their bread and butter. 1818 Short *Letters* 372: This is . . . like a silly child who quarrels or gets disgusted with his bread & butter. 1820 Jefferson *Writings* 15.281. 1832 Cooper *Letters* 2.267, 1850 6.206. *Oxford* 658; TW 41(3).

B312 Where **Bread** is wanting all is to be sold
1733 Franklin *PR* 1.317: Where bread is wanting, all's to be sold. Tilley B631.

B313 To be but a **Breakfast** for one
1776 JArmstrong in Lee *Papers* 2.11: The perverse Soldiery . . . to whom 39 lashes wou'd prove but a light breakfast. 1777 Munford *Patriots* 476: Thirty thousand of them will be but a breakfast for us. 1799 JIngraham in *Barbary Wars* 1.315: The whole marine . . . would not furnish a breakfast to such force. 1811 Graydon *Memoirs* 310: Why not rather turn out *en masse*, surround, and make a breakfast of Mr. Howe and his mercenaries. Whiting B253. See **D182**.

B314 Keep one's **Breath** to cool one's pottage
1783 Williams *Penrose* 298: I know how to keep my breath to cool my pottage. *Oxford* 418-9; TW 42(2).

B315 Spend not your **Breath** against a man of wind

1721 *Boston News-letter* in Buckingham *Specimens* 1.10: *Contra verbosus, noli contendere verbis*. Against a man of wind spend not thy Breath. Whiting S91.

B316 Better **Bred** than taught

1686 Dunton *Letters* 113: It is a Proverbial Phrase, of ill People, that they have been better bred than taught. *Oxford* 52: fed; Tilley F174; Whiting F107.

B317 His **Breech** makes buttons

1772 Carroll *Copy-Book* 217: I have heard that his Majesty is a great adept at making buttons [a pun of sorts]. 1775 FLLee in *Naval Documents* 2.1086: I am glad that amidst all the breeches button making in Virga . . . you keep up your spirits. *Oxford* 84; Tilley A381.

B318 To have one's sitting **Breeches** on

1801 Trumbull *Season* 148-9: He had indeed his sitting breeches on and I did not know as he ever would have gone.

B319 To wear the **Breeches**

1666 Alsop *Maryland* 85: I never observed . . . that ever the Women wore the Breeches. 1723 *New-England Courant* 112(1.2): They [husbands] dare as well die as wear the Breeches. 1766 Ames *Almanacs* 376: Others strive who shall wear the breeches. 1775 Creswell *Journal* 102: My Landlady, who wears the breeches. 1777 Moore *Diary* 1.528: I have only to observe that the generality of the women in that county, having for above a century *worn the breeches*, it is highly reasonable that the men should now, and especially upon so important an occasion, make booty of the petticoats. 1782 EHazard in *Belknap Papers* 1.163: I should suspect that she sometimes *claims the breeches* as her right. 1797 Tyler *Prose* 219: The married lady discards the . . . skirt, for the immemorial insignia of the man. 1801 *Port Folio* 1.278: My aunt Peg . . . often exchanges the petticoats for the breeches. 1805 Irving *Journals* 1.385: It is fortunate that the women have not assumed the breeches also. 1806 Hitchcock *Works* 134:

She never wears my pantaloons or breeches. 1810 Fletcher *Letters* 20: Another peculiarity among the Virginians is, according to the vulgar New-England expression, "the women wear the breeches." 1819 Peirce *Rebelliad* 62: Thus Logic fairly lost his breeches [to his wife]. *Oxford* 874; TW 42(2); Whiting M406. See **P94, S389.**

B320 To beat (blow) up a **Breeze**

1772 Adams(S) *Writings* 2.344: The Tories give out . . . that they expect what they call a Breese before long, 1775 3.206: They would take that Occasion to beat up a Breeze. 1778 Stiles *Diary* 2.262: A Faction in the Army . . . endeavoring to blow up a breeze & get Gen. Wash. superseded by G. Gates. TW 42(2).

B321 **Brevity** is the soul of eloquence

1804 Brackenridge *Modern* 365: Brevity is the soul of eloquence, and amplification the usual fault. *Oxford* 84-5; TW 42.

B322 As hard as a **Brick**

1786 JMadison in Jefferson *Papers* 9.661: The earth is as dry and as hard as a brick. 1803 *Yankee Phrases* 87: Her heart is as hard as a brick. 1819 Cobbett *Year's* 81. Svartengren 260; TW 42(1).

B323 As red and solid as a **Brick**

1801 Story *Shop* 18: Their cheeks too, red and solid as a brick. Svartengren 247: red; Whiting *NC* 375(3): solid. Cf. NED Brick-red.

B324 To make **Bricks** without straw

a1700 Saffin *His Book* 99: Bricks without Straw, is stricktly now Requir'd. 1720 JColman *Distressed State* in *Colonial Currency* 1.401: Their Tale of Brick was Exacted, without supplying them with Straw. c1725 Chalkley *Personal Election* 533: Forcing them to make Brick without Straw. 1737 *Proposal* in *Colonial Currency* 3.170: They can't make Brick without Straw. 1755 Franklin *Papers* 6.265: This is demanding *Brick without Straw*. 1762 Ames *Almanacs* 328. 1770 Adams *Legal Papers* 1.217. 1770 Franklin *Papers* 17.54: You shall make the full Tale of Bricks whether you can find Straw or not. 1771 WBollan in *Bowdoin*

Papers 1.275: It wou'd be easier to make bricks without straw than it is to prosecute the Province service . . . without admissable authority from it. **1771** Woodmason *Journal* 249. **1774** Boucher *View* 291: To imitate the tyranny of the Egyptians in demanding bricks where no straw had been given. **1775** Adams *D and A* 2.214. **1776** *Clinton Papers* 1.459: I have not yet learned the art of making Brick without straw. **1777** JWarren in *Warren-Adams Letters* 1.372. **1778** AMcDougall in *Clinton Papers* 4.387. **1779** JLangdon in Deane *Papers* 3.348: At the Time you went to France, when everything was new, and Bricks to be made without Straw. **1780** EBulkley in Webb *Correspondence* 2.259. **1780** NGreene in Sparks *Correspondence* 3.192. **1781** *Washington Writings* 21.342: Bricks are not to be made without straw, 379: To expect bricks without straw is idle, 22.178: To require Brick without straw was the complaint of old time. **1782** JRicker in *Baxter Manuscripts* 19.479. **1783** Pynchon *Diary* 147: He tells them that he can't make bricks without straw: they answer that he can as well as any man. **1783** Washington *Writings* 27.128: As cruel as the Edict of Pharoah which compelled the Children of Israel to Manufacture Bricks without the necessary Ingredients. **1788** Rush *Letters* 1.495. **1790** Morris *Diary and Letters* 1.342. **1793** *Bingham's Maine* 1.262, **1797** 2.879. **1803** Austin *Constitutional* 151. *Oxford* 85; Tilley B660.

B325 Make a silver **Bridge** for a flying enemy

1809 *Port Folio* 2NS 2.431: Make a silver bridge for a flying enemy. *Oxford* 316; Tilley B665.

B326 Praise the **Bridge** one goes over

1769 Montresor *Journals* 236: It is natural for me to praise the Bridge I go over. **1797** Baily *Journal* 279: But let every one speak well of the bridge which carries him safe over. *Oxford* 644; TW 43(3); Tilley M210.

B327 To bite upon the **Bridle**

1768 *Johnson Papers* 6.457: He has bit sufficient upon the Bridle which it's to be hoped will reclaim Him. *Oxford* 62; Whiting B533.

B328 To leave in (keep out of) the **Briers**

a1656 Bradford *History* 2.132: Having brought them into the briers, he leaves them to gett out as they can. **1758** Adams *D and A* 1.55: Pursue the Gain of it [law] enough to keep out of the Briars. *Oxford* 452; Whiting B544.

B329 The **Brink** of the grave (pit)

1638 Williams *Writings* 6.87: Canonicus, lately recovered from the pit's brink, 94: Your return from the brink of the pit of rottenness. **1724** *Correspondence of James Logan and T. Story*, ed. N. Penney (Philadelphia, 1927) 17: Brought me . . . to the brink of yᵉ grave. **1725** Sewall *Letter-Book* 2.190. **1742** RRichardson in *Colden Letters* 8.287. **1747** *Boston Gazette* in *Newspaper Extracts(I)* 2.145. **1755** Indian Trader in McDowell *Documents* 2.57: [He is] upon the Brink of the Grave, ready to step into it. **1757** EBurr in Burr *Memoirs* 1.23. **1768** Smith *Works* 2.208: A man is tottering on the brink of the grave. **1799** Adams *Works* 8.646. **1806** TLear in *Barbary Wars* 6.488. Alden *Epitaphs* 2.244-5. **1812** Baldwin *Letters* 65: For years have I been struggling on the brink of the grave. **a1820** Biddle *Autobiography* 168. **1831** Austin *Literary Papers* 49: An old man tottering on the brink of the grave. *Oxford* 217; Tilley E57; Whiting P231. See **F253, G25.**

B330 To have one's **Bristles** up

1782 RHopkins in MHM 23(1928) 280: Professor Kuhn has his Bristles up about it. NED Bristle 4.

B331 **Bristol** is remarkable only for women and geese

1750 James Birket *Some Cursory Remarks* (New Haven, 1916) 26: It is a proverb here that Bristol [Rhode Island] is Only remarkable for its plenty of women and Geese.

B332 As **Broad** as it is long

1748 *Word* in *Colonial Currency* 4.370: It has been as broad as it is long. *Oxford* 87; Tilley B677.

B333 He's pissed in the **Brook**

1737 Franklin *Drinkers* 174: He's Piss'd in the Brook.

B334 New **Brooms** sweep clean (*varied*)

1752 GClinton in *Colden Letters* 9.121: What I propose saying . . . in answer as I look upon this, as only their being new brooms for you see they are General. **1768** JParker in Franklin *Papers* 15.27: New Brooms sweep clean. **1800** *Echo* 277: Old *Broomes* sweep clean, and creak old *Gates* [puns on personal names]. **1819** Bentley *Diary* 4.581: We are at this moment trying the new brooms. **1845** Cooper *Letters* 5.43: He appears in the parish next week, when we hope that the new broom will begin its work. *Oxford* 564; Whiting B563.

B335 To jump over the **Broom**

1783 Williams *Penrose* 145: This done, I bade Harry fetch me one of our brooms and I caused them both to jump over it, 176-7, 245, 251, 276 [an informal marriage ceremony]. Barbour 24(3); *Oxford* 88; TW 44.

B336 To love one as a **Brother**

1757 WPeachey in *Letters to Washington* 2.235: In poor Spotswood I lost a man I loved as a brother. **c1800** Rush *Autobiography* 129: He loved you like a brother, **1809** *Letters* 2.1014: The young man . . . was as dear to him as a brother. Whiting B569.

B337 To stick closer than a **Brother**

1830 Ames *Mariner's* 54: The prickly heat "sticketh closer than a brother." TW 44(2). See **F298.**

B338 To be tarred with the same **Brush**

1820 Faux *Memorable Days* 2.93: All are tarred with the same brush. *Oxford* 805; TW 353: stick (5).

B339 As brisk as a **Buck**

1824 *Tales* 1.14: As brisk as a buck, ate as hearty a dinner of fish as man could desire. TW 45(1).

B340 As fast as **Bucks**

1744 Hamilton *Itinerarium* 90: Running over the plain as fast as wild bucks upon the mountains.

B341 As fresh and strong as a **Buck**

1809 Weems *Washington* 15: He . . . jumps up fresh and strong as a little buck. TW 45(3): fresh; Whiting *NC* 376: strong.

B342 As hearty as a **Buck**

1776 David *Letters* 7: Our men . . . all as hearty as Bucks. **1780** Franklin *Writings* 8.138: I . . . continue as hearty as a buck. **1799** TPierce in Vanderpoel *Chronicles* 376. **1810** EGLutwyche in *Winslow Papers* 644: Royal is 88 and as hearty as a Buck. **1815** Humphreys *Yankey* 78: Harty as a buck: but I can't jump so high. **1817** Wirt *Letters* 2.23 TW 45(5).

B343 As wild as a **Buck**

1719 Byrd *Another Secret Diary* 408: P——lly, wanton, gay and airy, Wild as Buck, or Midnight Fairy. **1775** Honyman *Journal* 33: Hazard, the Princeton student . . . as wild as a buck. Barbour 24; *Oxford* 889; Whiting B573.

B344 A **Buck** of the first head

1822 DMcKenzie in Robertson *Letters* 196: He figures as a buck of the first head . . . some tapering Brule would cause him to moult his horns. *Oxford* 88; Tilley B693.

B345 To kick the **Bucket**

1789 JSmith in *The Columbian Muse* (New York, 1794) 111: And ev'ry mother's son soon *kick the bucket*. **1793** *Echo* 107: And kick life's bucket to the shades of death. **1808** Hitchcock *Poetical Dictionary* 11. **1823** GHowland in *New England Merchants* 130. **1825** Prince *Journals* 211: [The cow] has been sick for some time and last night she kicked the bucket. **1827** Watterston *Wanderer* 102, 113. **1830** Ames *Mariner's* 54. **1835** Longfellow *Letters* 1.508. Barbour 24; *Oxford* 422; TW 45.

B346 To keep **Buckle** and thong together

1773 Carter *Diary* 2.763: The Pernicious company he Keeps, Gamesters and Spendthrifts; who by taking no care, are reducing themselves, whilst I am keeping as well as I can, my buckle and thong together. *Oxford* 89; TW 45; Whiting B577.

B347 As stiff as **Buckram**

1793 Ingraham *Journal* 98: Apologies are . . . stiff as buckram. Svartengren 262. Cf. NED Buckram 4b.

B348 To nip in the **Bud**

1656 Hammond *Leah* 3: The bud of this growing happinesse was again nipt. **1683** ECranfield in JSJenness *Transcripts of Original Documents* (New York, 1876) 144: The not nipping them in the budd may prove of great inconveniences. a**1700** Hubbard *New England* 37, 524. **1702** Mather *Magnalia* 1.82: The . . . Pequots had like to have nipt the plantation in the bud, **1713** *Diary* 2.207: To nip the Impiety of their Language in the Bud. **1713** Wise *Churches* 106. **1724** Jones *Virginia* 65. **1735** *Georgia Records* 21.17, **1738** 22¹.76: Sorry I am to see so desirable a Work nipt, as it were in the Bud. **1741** Chalkley *Journal* 1: That light Spirit . . . they were careful to nip in the Bud. **1756** Laurens *Papers* 2.264. **1757** EAtkin in *Letters to Washington* 2.105: You will check it in the Bud. **1762** *Johnson Papers* 10.465: Any Schemes . . . may be crushed in the Bud. **1764** *Paxton Papers* 120. **1764** Watts *Letter Book* 291: It certainly would be wise to Nip these freedoms in the Bud. **1766** WFranklin in Franklin *Papers* 13.256. **1774** Adams *Works* 4.43: Nip the shoots of arbitrary power in the bud. **1774** Boucher *View* 383. **1775** NGreene in Ward *Correspondence* 155: Such buding mischiefs cannot be to early Nipt. **1776** SJohnston in *Naval Documents* 5.223. **1776** Washington *Writings* 5.277. **1780** JSewall in Curwen *Journal and Letters* 267: Nip her in the bud. **1781** BJoel in Jefferson *Papers* 4.569: Why not stop it in the Bud? **1782** Heath *Memoirs* 343. **1787** *American Museum* 1.366: To behold the fruits of his labour nipt in the bud, **1788** 4.121. **1789** Brown *Power* 1.38: A habitual vacancy nips it in the bud. **1812** Lee *Memoirs* 2.290. **1818** Adams *Works* 10.281. **1823** RDunlap in Jackson *Correspondence* 3.200: It ought in my opinion to be *checked in the bud*. **1832** Pintard *Letters* 4.22: It wᵈ have been stifled in the bud. *Oxford* 567; TW 45(3). See **D192.**

B349 As strong as a **Buffalo**

1809 Weems *Marion* 77: Strong as a buffalo.

B350 As snug as a **Bug** in a rug

1772 Franklin *Writings* 5.439: Here Skugg

Lies snug, As a bug In a rug. **1776** Curwen *Journal* 1.212: I . . . to use a very homely comparison lay as snug as a bug in a rug. **1802** *Port Folio* 2.72: The sleek black bug, (So fond of rug) Which lies so snug In glassy case. *Oxford* 749; TW 45(3). See **F171, 173.**

B351 To go to the **Bugs**

1828 *Yankee* 288: But no matter about the affair, let it all go to the bugs. TW 46(6). See **D259.**

B352 The highest **Building** is in most danger of falling

1789 Brown *Power* 1.54: The highest building is in the most danger of falling. Whiting H606, T434, W344.

B353 As savage as a **Bull**

1796 Cathcart *Journal* 372: The Dey . . . is as savage as a mad Bull. Cf. Whiting B585.

B354 As surly as **Bulls**

1813 Fletcher *Narrative* 39: They . . . looked as surly as bulls. Svartengren 101.

B355 To bellow like a **Bull** (of Bashan)

1773 Stiles *Diary* 1.381: We . . . can bear . . . the Bellowings &c of those Bulls of Bashan the Patriots and Sons of Liberty in England and America. **1807** JEarly in *VHM* 34(1926) 244: He started bellowing like a bull. TW 17(2), 46(9). Cf. *Oxford* 44; Whiting B588.

B356 To have no more chance than a stump-tail **Bull** in fly-time

1819 *Ky. Alman.* in DA fly time: (He) has no more chance for the worth of his dollar than a stump tail bull in fly time. TW 46(7).

B357 To roar like a **Bull**

1772 Asbury *Journal* 1.32: He roared like a bull in a net. **1774** Carter *Diary* 2.845: He roared like a bull. a**1820** Biddle *Autobiography* 144. *Oxford* 680; Whiting B590.

B358 To take the **Bull** by the horns

1768 TBChandler in Johnson *Writings* 1.434: I have advised Inglis to begin the attack—to take this rough bull by the horns. **1768** Woodmason *Journal* 290: He took a Bull by the Horns, that gor'd Him to Death. **1776** Willard *Letters* 307: They took the wrong bull by the horn. **1779** TPaine in Deane *Papers* 3.318. a1778 Jones *History* 1.51, 52, 53. **1795** Gordon *Letters* 578. **1797** Callender *Annual Register 1796* 230. **1816** Fidfaddy *Adventures* 43. **1816** Paulding *Letters(I)* 2.211: We are the true liberty boys, and will take the bull by the horns at once. **1821** Beecher *Autobiography* 1.439: The time has . . . come to take hold of the Unitarian controversy by the horns. **1833** Pintard *Letters* 4.120. **1848** Cooper *Letters* 5.326. *Oxford* 800; TW 47(11).

B359   As big as **Bull-beef**

1769 Woodmason *Journal* 153: By carrying Matters very high, and looking as big as Bull Beef. NED Bull *sb.*[1] 11; Svartengren 288.

B360   To fight like **Bulldogs**

1818 WLewis in Jackson *Correspondence* 6.463: The Kentuckians . . . faught like bull dogs. Cf. TW 47.

B361   Two **Bullets** never go in one place

1779 Thacher *Journal* 214: Massa, you never know two bullets go in one place. Cf. TW 221: Lightning (11). See **S185.**

B362   To strut like a **Bullfrog**

1756 AStephen in *Letters to Washington* 1.206: He . . . Struts like a Bull Frog. Cf. TW 47.

B363   A **Bundle** of arrows (sticks, rods, twigs)

1677 Hubbard *Indian* 2.85: Like his Arrows, that being bound up in one Bundle, could not be broken by a ordinary Force; but being loose, were easily snapt *asunder,* by a single Hand. **1757** *Johnson Papers* 9.710: As I formerly told you the Six Nations when heartily united are like a Bundle of Sticks which cannot be broken when tied together, but if untied a Child may break Stick upon Stick. **1765** JHughes in Franklin *Papers* 12.265: In order to unite, and become, as they express it, *like a Bundle of Rods,* alluding to the Fable of the Old Man and his Sons. **1768** Smith *Works* 2.199: You have heard of the bundle of twigs which the dying father gave his sons to break. While the twigs were tied together, the strength of all the sons could make no impression on

them. When disunited, they were easily broken, one by one, with the strength of a single son. **1781** *Washington *Writings* 21.374: The Fable of the bunch of Rods or sticks might well be applied to us. **1787** *American Museum* 2.201. **1797** Graham *Vermont* 3: To America, Great Britain, and Ireland, the allegory of the *Bundle of Twigs* may with strictest propriety be applied. Thompson *Motif-Index* J1021; Whiting H90. Cf. *Oxford* 854. See **U4.**

B364   To stick like a **Bur**

1728 Byrd *Dividing Line* 113: Where we had the grief to part with that sweet temper'd Gentleman, & the Burr that stuck with him Orion. **1796** Cobbett *Porcupine* 4.271: They will stick to us like a bur. *Oxford* 126; Whiting B597.

B365   The **Burden** of the song

1682 Plumstead 99: This may be the burden of the song. **1705** Ingles *Reply* 27: He Repeats ye Burden of his Song. **1775** Hamilton *Papers* 1.135: This was the burthen of the song. **1777** Smith *Memoirs* 2.214: A Militia Law & Taxes the Burden of the Song. **1778** JSewell in *Winslow Papers* 36. **1779** JDavenport in Huntington *Papers* 108: Money is the burden of my song. **1787** Adams *Works* 9.552. **1791** Ames *Letters* 104. **1799** DCobb in *Bingham's Maine* 2.951: This subject . . . has ever been with me the burthen of the song. NED Burden 11.

B366   Beat a country **Bush** and out starts a calf

1787 *American Museum* 2.597: For do but beat a *country bush,* And lo! out starts a calf. Cf. Tilley B739.

B367   One beats the **Bush,** another gets the bird (*varied*)

1773 Quincy *Memoir* 81: American fools, thirsting for honors and riches, beat the bush; British harpies seize the poor bird. **1774** JLovell in Quincy *London Journal* 484: He must be an Idiot indeed to desire to beat the Bush for some future General's Profit and Glory. **1781** DMerit in *Baxter Manuscripts* 19.191: Neither do we Desire to be so Sneeking as Leave our Friends at the Westerd to Beat the Bush & we to catchh the

Hare. **1784** EWinslow in *Winslow Papers* 237: In this as in former instances I have beat the Bush for others. **1807** Bowen *Journals* 2.616: He having beat the bush Saunders hath caught the bird. *Oxford* 37; Whiting B604. See **S353.**

B368   To beat about the **Bush**

1762 Watts *Letter Book* 30: I beat about the Bush, but found it entirely useless. **1767** Patten *Diary* 206: The Presby after a considerable beating round the bush adjourned. **1783** Williams *Penrose* 247: For this purpose I began about the bush, as is said. **1802** *Port Folio* 2.105: This is only beating about the bush. **1818** Adams *Memoirs* 4.37. **1839** Paulding *Letters(II)* 247: I have delayed replying to your long and interesting Letter, untill I could beat about the bush. *Oxford* 36; Whiting B608.

B369   To beat the **Bush**

1743 Stephens *Journal(II)* 1.154: In beating the bush where nothing that we sought for was to be found. **1769** Smith *Memoirs* 1.59: And so it was recommended . . . to beat the Bush for him. **1776** JRead in Webb *Correspondence* 1.216: After beating the Bush upon the Subject we had first in View, we found it must originate with the General or there would be no Prospect of success. **1777** SHParsons in Webb *Correspondence* 1.373: I hope to take a comfortable napp to-morrow night, or beat the Bush in which dwell some of the fairest Birds. NED Bush *sb.*[1] 1b.

B370   To carry too much **Bush**

1816 Smith *Life* 231: I here leave a word to young preachers, and *old* ones in particular, which is, *"that they do not carry too much bush,"* 205: The cause of all these things is, they carry too much bush. [Perhaps, to act in worldly ways.]

B371   It takes a **Bushel** of corn to fatten a pig's tail

1819 Thomas *Travels* 104-5: The quaint adage in our country, that "it takes a bushel of corn to fatten a pig's tail."

B372   To hide (one's candle, light, etc.) under a **Bushel**

1652 Williams *Writings* 7.152: *Not to hide my Candle under a* Bed *of* Ease *and* Pleasure, *or a* Bushel *of* Gain *and* Profit. **1681** Willard *Ne Sutor* 16: Their light was put under a bushel. **1686** Dunton *Letters* 170: And yet wou'd bring Scripture to Apologize for his Impertinence, telling us that a Candle shou'd not be hid under a Bushel. **1694** Scottow *Narrative* 302: Which Light hath not been hid in a Bushel. **1702** Mather *Magnalia* 2.533: Their light was put under a bushel. **1763** Watts *Letter Book* 129: Such a Transaction could not be hid under a Bushell. **1778** *Washington *Writings* 13.23: If you have any News worth communicating, do not put it under a bushel. **1786** WCarmichael in Jefferson *Papers* 10.429: Their Light is not to be hid under a Bushel. **1792** Barlow *Works* 1.181: Every moral light has been smothered under the bushel of perpetual imposition. **1797** Cobbett *Porcupine* 7.51: The candle is now lighted and . . . it shall not be kept under a bushel. **1797** Smith (EH) *Diary* 30: It is enjoined on us not to put our light under a bushel. **1803** Wirt *British Spy* 236: They have not hid their light under a bushel. Their city is built on a high place. **1806** Baldwin *Life and Letters* 452: And my knowledge is not hid under a Bushel. **1810** *Port Folio* 2NS 4.293: Do not hide your light under a bushel, **1815** 3NS 5.101: The "Candle" . . . shall not lie concealed under a bushel. **1817** Weems *Franklin* 125: God . . . has lighted up this candle for our use, it must not be hid under a bushel. **1819** Brackenridge *South America* 2.6: She . . . was shrewd and intelligent, and far from being inclined to hide her light under a bushel. **1819** Wirt *Letters* 2.95: His friend ought to hang upon him . . . 'till he places, on a candlestick and on a hill, that candle which God never lighted to be put under a bushel. **1838** Cooper *Letters* 3.363: Try to improve in your hand-writing, without which all your learning will be hid under a bushel. Barbour 28(1), 109(1); *Oxford* 371; TW 48, 55(6); Tilley L275; Whiting L73. See **T17.**

B373   To go like a **Bush-fire**

1756 AGSpangenberg in Franklin *Papers* 6.423: But hath stopp'd our cruel Enemy from going on like a Bush-Fire in his wicked ways. See **F133, 162, W159.**

B374 **Business** before pleasure

1767 Hutchinson *Diary* 1.243: Pleasure should always give way to business. **1816** Wirt *Letters* 1.415: Business first, and then pleasure, is my motto. **1834** Clifford *Letters* 70: Business before parties is my motto. *Oxford* 93; TW 48(1).

B375 A **Business** well begun is hopeful

1636 EHowes in *Winthrop Papers(A)* 3.292: A business wel begun is plesant and hopefull. Cf. Whiting B204. See **B131**.

B376 Drive thy **Business** or it will drive thee

1738 Franklin *PR* 2.197: Drive thy business, let not that drive thee, **1744** 399: Drive thy Business, or it will drive thee, **1758** *WW* 342: as **1738**. *Oxford* 204.

B377 Everybody's **Business** is nobody's business

?**1629** Hutchinson *Papers* 1.33: That which is common to all is proper to none. **1735** *South Carolina Gazette* 215-6: We have . . . set up for Reformers, (that is of ourselves) or Meddlers of Nobody's business, or to speak plainer, of every body's: For we have set that refin'd Maxim of *Nobody's* means *Every* body. **1755** *Johnson Papers* 1.588. **1757** Washington *Writings* 2.43: With us it is every body's business, and no one's, to supply. **1762** FBrinley in *Saltonstall Papers* 1.437: What was Every mans business, was no body's, soe there it rested. **1789** *Belknap Papers* 3.453: What is every body's, you know, is no body's, &c. **1791** S.P.L. *Thoughts* 167. **1797** NAmes in *DHR* 8(1897) 54. **1806** Jotham Waterman *Two Better Than One* (Boston, 1806) 5. **1810** Dwight *Journey* 9. **1828** *Yankee* 38. *Oxford* 231; TW 49(5). See **E78**.

B378 If one would have his **Business** well done, he must do it himself (*varied*)

1706 FJWinthrop in *Winthrop Papers(B)* 5.358: I have heard one say, if a man would have his business done, he must get one to doe it, but if he would have it *well* done, he must doe it himself. **1763** *Johnson Papers* 4.34: A man cannot have his business (completely done, but by Himself). **1809** *Port Folio* 2NS 2.549: He who would have a thing done quickly and well, must do it himself. **1825** Anderson *Diary* 220: I tell you again my son never to get your friends to do what can be done by yourself. Barbour 50: Do(3); *Oxford* 865; TW 369(5); Tilley M195. See **S106**.

B379 If you would have your **Business** done, go; if not, send

1743 Franklin *PR* 2.372: If you'd have it done, Go: If not, send, **1758** *WW* 344: your Business. TW 369(5).

B380 Mind your (own) **Business**

1793 *Connecticut Courant* in *W&MCQ* 3S 7(1951) 420: The motto, "mind your business." **1801** *Farmer's Museum* 183: The old paper money adage, "mind your own business." **1817** Adams *Writings* 6.279: The good old maxim "Mind your business." *Oxford* 533; TW 49(3); Tilley B752.

B381 Much **Business** must have much pardon

1750 Franklin *Papers* 4.70: And desire you would remember in my favour the old Saying, *They who have much Business must have much Pardon.*

B382 To do one's **Business**

1803 Harmon *Sixteen Years* 69: There is little doubt but they would have done our business for us — as they look upon us as there enemies also. NED Business 12d.

B383 Better pay the **Butcher** than the doctor

1811 *Port Folio* 2NS 5.374: It is better to pay the butcher than the doctor. Lean 1.504.

B384 As fat as **Butter**

1782 Adams *D and A* 3.35: Carps large and fat as butter. **1801** Mackay *Letters* 31. **1805** Sewall *Parody* 31: Sweet children, fat as butter. **1847** Cooper *Letters* 5.248: Lucy, he says, is as fat as butter and as sweet. *Oxford* 247; TW 49(1).

B385 As soft as **Butter**

1801 *Farmer's Museum* 77: Mine [a lass] is softer than butter or whey. TW 49(2).

51

B386 No **Butter** will stick to their bread
1702 Mather *Magnalia* 2.399: But have we not seen afterwards, that after this, (as we say) "no butter would ever stick upon their bread." *Oxford* 95; Whiting B620.

B387 To melt like **Butter**
1767 Franklin *Papers* 14.194: It will melt away like Butter in the Sunshine. *Oxford* 94; Tilley B780.

B388 To break a **Butterfly** on the wheel
1789 Brown *Power* 2.9: These ladies wisely consider them as the butterflies of a day, and therefore generally scorn *to break them on a wheel! Oxford* 82; TW 50(3).

B389 To scold like two **Butter-women**
1765 JWatts in *Aspinwall Papers* 2.568: He & the old man scold like two Butter Women. *Oxford* 704; Tilley B781.

B390 As bright as a **Button**
1803 *Yankee Phrases* 87: As bright as a button her eyes. TW 50(1).

B391 Not to care a **Button**
1792 Mason *Papers* 3.1256: He cares not a button. **1806** Fessenden *Modern Philosopher* 183: That none would care a single button. **1807** *Salmagundi* 178: The only rules of right and wrong he cared a button for, were the rules of multiplication and addition. **1830** Cooper *Letters* 1.435. *Oxford* 102; TW 50(3).

B392 Not to give a **Button**
1770 *Washington *Writings* 3.1: I would hardly give any Officer a button for his Right. **1788** *Politician* 9: I wou'dn't give a leather button for the choice, as the old proverb goes. Whiting B630.

B393 Not to see further than one's **Buttons**
1649 Shepard *Hints* 158-9: [He] can see no further than his own buttons. See **I26.**

B394 Not to value a **Button**
1702 Mather *Magnalia* 2.390: That monster, pulling off a button on the good man's coat, said, *he did not value what he preached any more than that.* Whiting B633.

B395 Not worth a **Button**
1765 JOtis *Vindication* in Bailyn *Pamphlets* 1.575: The only filial pen worth a button. **1771** TSDrage in Franklin *Papers* 18.48. **1797** RMorris in *PM* 6(1882) 112: And that is not worth Doctr. Logan's apple-tree buttons. **1832** Cooper *Letters* 2.238: His opinion was not worth a button. *Oxford* 95; Whiting B635.

B396 To shine like glass **Buttons**
1798 TGFessenden in Buckingham *Specimens* 2.217: My dearest has two pretty eyes, Glass buttons shine never so bright. TW 50(6).

B397 To **Buy** and sell (be bought and sold)
1652 Williams *Writings* 7.206: Such as *buy* and *sell* Christ Jesus. **1743** Belcher *Papers* 2.446: The *wild cat* I am afraid will be bought & sold by Sancho. **1782** Paine *American Crisis* 1.215: We are neither to be bought nor sold. **1804** Asbury *Letters* 3.275: Never be bought or sold. **1812** JWilled in Knopf *War of 1812* 2.52: In all his seling & buying of the army. **1814** Morris *Diary and Letters* 2.559: We . . . are not to be bought and sold like silly sheep. *Oxford* 77-8; Whiting B637.

B398 What one **Buys** cheap is the dearest
1809 *Port Folio* 2NS 2.430: That which is bought cheap is the dearest. Whiting C166, 167. See **B156.**

B399 **Buyer,** look to!
1758 Eliot *Essays* 138: Makes the old Proverb truly availing. *Buyer look to. Oxford* 96; Tilley B788.

B400 Good **Buyers** but poor payers
1634 JWinter in *Trelawny Papers* 46: The most parte of the dwellers heare ar good buyers but bad payers.

B401 Let **Bygones** be bygones
1710 Mather *Letters* 94: There is a Scotch proverb that you must keep to: *Bygones be Bygones, and fair play for the time to come.* **1849** Hone *Diary* 2.864: I begged him to "let by-gones be by-gones." *Oxford* 96; TW 51.

C

C1 To come in at the **Cabin** window

1794 *Federal Orrery* in Buckingham *Specimens* 2.234: But if your bar 'gainst cabin windows, Your would-be captain's progress hinders, Put me, if you would raise me fast, In federal ships before the mast. **1832** Ames *Nautical* 26: No better can be expected from one who came in at the cabin window. **a1841** Trumbull *Autobiography* 14: I had entered [Harvard] in an unusual way, (a sailor would say that I got in at the cabin windows). Colcord 46; TW 405. Cf. *Oxford* 134-5; Whiting W349. See **C286.**

C2 As big as **Caesar**

1814 Palmer *Diary* 67: Rear Adm. Griffis, who was walking along the Strand as Big as pomy Ceazer.

C3 As brave as (Julius) **Caesar**

1806 NMcNairy in Jackson *Correspondence* 1.140: But give him an advantage and he is as brave as Julius Caesar. **1821** Pintard *Letters* 2.55: He is as brave as Caesar, & pretty heady. TW 52(2).

C4 **Caesar's** wife must be above suspicion (*varied*)

1778 *New Jersey Gazette* in *Newspaper Extracts* (*II*) 2.46: Caesar's wife was not only to be virtuous, but she was to be free from all suspicion, 501. **1779** AA in *Adams FC* 3.148: Caesars wife ought not to be suspected. **1789** Hamilton *Papers* 6.1: You remember the saying with regard to Caesar's Wife . . . *Suspicion* is ever eagle eyed. **1801** Jackson *Correspondence* 1.58: In politics, like Caesar's

wife, not only chaste but unsuspected. **1802** JTaylor in *Steele Papers* 1.272: [He] stood, as Caesar said his wife should. **1804** JDarby in *Barbary Wars* 4.492: For as Caesar says by his wife a man shou'd not only be honest but unsu[s]pectedly so. **1804** *Monthly Anthology* 1.213: Like Cesar's wife, they must be free not only from guilt, but even from suspicion. **1808** JAdams in *Adams-Cunningham Letters* 38: Caesar's wife must not be suspected, was all the reason he gave for repudiating her. **1827** Watterston *Wanderer* 127: I wish them to be like Caesar's wife, not only guiltless, but free from suspicion of guilt. *Oxford* 97; TW 52(4).

C5 Give **Caesar** his due

1680 Randolph *Letters* 3.62: Shee would have Caesar have his due. Barbour 27; *Oxford* 671; Whiting C1.

C6 As good as ever was since **Cain**

1777 Joslin *Journal* 339: It is as good Carting Sledding or Slaying as Ever was Since Cain.

C7 As sweet as a **Cake**

1801 Story *Shop* 27: My love is as sweet as a cake. Cf Whiting *NC* 379(1): good.

C8 One cannot have his **Cake** and eat it too

1742 *Georgia Records* 23.306: Would you (like the Child) cry to have your Cake, that you had eaten. **1781** Oliver *Origin* 76: There was another Set of Men . . . who having ate their Cake & being turned away, cried to have their Cake again. **1812** BFStickney in Knopf *War of 1812* 6(1) 204: We cannot have our cake and eat it too. **1816** Paulding

Letters(*I*) 2.223: Brother Jonathan is one of those people who are for eating their cake and having their cake. Barbour 28(2); *Oxford* 215; Whiting C5.

C9 The **Calf** died in the cow's belly

1724 Mather *Letters* 380: You know whose maxim it was, and whose it will be, that when the cow was dead, the calf died in the belly of it. **1764** Hutchinson *History* 1.305: The charter being vacated, the people was told that their titles to their estates were of no value. The expression in vogue was that "the calf died in the cow's belly."

C10 Make the **Calf** blare and the cow will come

1740 *Boston Weekly News-Letters* in *Newspaper Extracts*(*I*) 2.18: They ("Irish all") had tortur'd it [a child] in order to find the Mother, saying, Make the Calf Blair, and the Cow will come. Cf. F. J. Child, *The English and Scottish Popular Ballads* 93 *Lamkin* A 11-7, K 5-7.

C11 To eat the **Calf** in the cow's belly

1712 Johnston *Papers* 114: All they did for me was to advance *Six* Months Sallary before hand. This is Eating the Calf in the Cowes Belly. **1767** JParker in Franklin *Papers* 14.146: I shall eat part of the Calf in the Cow's Belly. **1792** Belknap *Foresters* 162: Lord Strut . . . generally anticipated his revenues, (or as the vulgar phrase is, ate the calf in the cow's belly). *Oxford* 216; Tilley C18.

C12 To groan like a dying **Calf**

1813 Weems *Drunkard* 99: And miserably groaning, like a dying calf. Whiting *NC* 379(5). Cf. TW 53(4, 5).

C13 To kill the fatted **Calf**

1770 CCarroll in *MHM* 13(1918) 65: I shall then kill a fatted Calf but not for a Prodigall son. *Oxford* 422; Whiting C11.

C14 The **Calm** before the storm (*varied*)

1754 Smith *Works* 1¹.6: A flattering calm portends a gathering storm. **1763** *Washington Writings* 2.402: At this Instant a calm is taking place, which forbodes some mischief. **1775** ALee in Izard *Correspondence* 69:

There is a silence in the New-England provinces, which argues an approaching storm. **1782** Freneau *Prose* 61: As at the present there is something like a calm, though not improbably of that delusory kind which are observed in the indian ocean to be the prelude of a more violent tempest. **1796** Ames *Letters* 1.202: All is calm at present; and because it is calm, we ought to expect a storm. **1796** UTracy in Gibbes 1.298: The stillness . . . which in the natural world precedes a storm. **1797** OWalcott, Jr., in Hamilton *Papers* 20.573: It is a calm which forbodes a hurricane. **1797** *Washington Writings* 36.105: I hope the calm . . . will not be succeeded by a storm. **1805** Adams *Writings* 3.106: We are here in a state of momentary calm, which perhaps may be the presage of a violent storm. Barbour 28; *Oxford* 6; Whiting C12.

C15 The **Camel** and the needle's eye

1776 Asbury *Journal* 1.180: With as much apparent difficulty as the passage of a camel through the eye of a needle. **1782** Trumbull *Satiric Poems* 120: Run thro' the land as easily As camel thro' a needle's eye. **1783** Freneau *Prose* 306: It is as easy for a first rate ship's cable to pass thro' the eye of a needle, as for a man of large property to be a good patriot. Barbour 28; *Oxford* 559; Whiting C13.

C16 The more the (**Camomile**) is trodden on the more it flourishes

1762 JBoucher in *MHM* 7(1912) 151: An injured Innocence, w'c, like some creeping Plants ye more they are trampled upon, ye more vigorous do they rise & flourish. *Oxford* 100; Tilley C34.

C17 **Camp** news

1779 Leake *Lamb* 221-2: This I believe to be no more than camp news, and (as is but too common) the lie of the day. Cf. Partridge 471: latrine; Wentworth 313. See **G8, M168**.

C18 In **Canada** it requires great interest to hang a man

1816 Lambert *Travels* 1.171: It has occasioned a singular proverbial saying among the people, that "*it requires great interest for a man to be hung in Canada.*"

C19 One **Candle** will light a (ten) thousand
1643 Williams *Writings* 1.20: *One Candle will light ten thousand.* a1656 Bradford *History* 2.117: And as one small candle may light a thousand, so the light here kindled hath shone to many. Whiting C24.

C20 To be unworthy (unable) to hold a **Candle** to
1643 Williams *Writings* 1.386: I acknowledge my self unworthy to hold the candle to them, **1652** 7.153: *I . . . acknowledge my unworthiness to hold a* Candle *or* Book *unto them.* **1775** JLovell in *Essex Institute Historical Collections* 13(1875) 201: The Savages . . . are . . . unworthy to hold a Candle to these scientific Barbarians from Oxford. **1789** Brown *Better* 24-5: You can't hold a candle to me for telling a story. **1809** Weems *Washington* 2: A swindler to whom not *Arnold's self* could hold a candle. **1811** *Port Folio* 2NS 5.85: Dan Æsop's fox to him in wit Was not to hold a candle fit. Barbour 29(3); *Oxford* 377; TW 54-5; Tilley C44.

C21 To burn one's **Candle** at both ends
1798 *Codman Letters* 76: It appears to me like a candle burning out at both ends. **1819** Gallatin *Diary* 148: The life of a young man is a very gay one, burning the candle at both ends, 153: I have been literally burning the candle at both ends. Barbour 29; *Oxford* 91-2; Tilley C48; Whiting *NC* 379(3).

C22 To hold a **Candle** to the Devil
1733 Belcher *Papers* 1.324: Because I know he can't well avoid holding a candle to the Devil. **1776** *Battle of Brooklyn* 4: I must hold a candle to this Devil. **1779** HGriffith in *Aspinwall Papers* 2.792: Others . . . [are] obliged to stand the brunt and hold a Candle to the Devil. **1787** Smith *Diary* 2.174: Haldimand had held the Candle to the French to get Credit at Home, 179: I hold Candles to his Vanity by holding him in Respect for his Blood. **1797** Cobbett *Porcupine* 6.376: He really holds a candle to the Devil with the best grace of any man I ever saw. **1818** Jefferson *Writings* 1.273: To this [game] I was most ignorantly and innocently made to hold the candle. **1828** Pintard *Letters* 3.2-3: The Doctor must do as other courtiers, *hold the Candle to the Devil,* for in my guess, J. will be Prest, 3: I always make it a rule "to hold the Candle to the Devil." *Oxford* 377; Whiting C25.

C23 To hold a **Candle** to the sun
1643 Williams *Writings* 1.369: To prove this were to bring forth a Candle to the bright shining of the Sun at noon day. **1645** TPeters in *Winthrop Papers(A)* 5.26: But I hold a wax candle before heaven's lamp. **1734** *New-York Weekly Journal* in *Newspaper Extracts(I)* 1.384: Any Thing I can say . . . will be like *holding a Candle to the Sun.* **1780** *New Jersey Gazette* in *Newspaper Extracts (II)* 4.243: To prove what he undertakes *is like holding a candle to the sun.* **1781** FShaw in *Baxter Manuscripts* 19.245: To repeat that we are Friendly to the Cause of the United States wou'd be like Burning Tapers at Noon day to Assist the Sun in inlightning the world. **1794** RRutherford in Callender *Political Register* 1.102: To praise him was like holding up a rush candle to let us see the sun. *Oxford* 788; Tilley S988. See **S525.**

C24 To play or hold the **Candle**
1795 Cobbett *Porcupine* 2.56: If a man does not know how to play at cards, it is kind of him to hold the candle. Cf. *Oxford* 931; Whiting C23, *NC* 379(4).

C25 **Candlemas** Day (February 2)
1778 Smith *Memoirs(II)* 309: And the Frost severe agreable to the old Monkish Observation the Sun shining on Candlemas Day very bright. Dunwoody 101-2; *Oxford* 100; Whiting C30.

C26 Not to care a **Candlewick**
1809 Fessenden *Pills* 99: And care not a candlewick for a cold.

C27 To paddle one's own **Canoe**
1802 Dow *Journal* 129: I leave every man to paddle his own canoe. **1803** WGrove in *Steele Papers* 1.387: I have partly resolved to adopt the Indian plan, of "letting every man paddle his own Canoe." **1832** Pintard *Letters* 4.35. Barbour 29(1); *Oxford* 606; TW 55.

C28 A **Canterbury** story (tale)

1723 *New-England Courant* 84 (1.2): You may then expect, one will to you direct A Canterbury Story. **1728** Byrd *Dividing Line* 64: He told us a Canterbury Tale of a North Briton, whose Curiosity Spurr'd him a long way into this great Desart, as he call't it, near 20 years ago. **1787** *American Museum* 2.vi: If I told them such a Canterbury tale, I need not *expect* any more of them. **1787** WSSmith in Smith *Journal and Correspondence* 1.125: I must insist . . . that you do not receive it as a Canterbury story. **1792** Ames *Letters* 1.109: The public will be made to see that the charges of violence and oppression on the part of the United States . . . are Canterbury tales. *Oxford* 101; Partridge 125; Tilley C59. See **C42.**

C29 If the **Cap** (coat) fits, put it on

1738 Stephens *Journal(I)* 1.131: And not let the World see that the Cap fitted their Heads, by putting it on themselves. **1747** *New-York Evening Post* in *Newspaper Extracts(I)* 2.379: If there be any that find the Coat does fit them they are welcome to wear it. **1753** *Independent Reflector* 346: The Cap was not there 'till the Buffoon clap'd it on. **a1767** Evans *Poems* 152: You take the cap ne'er made to fit. **1769** Woodmason *Journal* 137: Why should You fit on a Cap upon Your Head, that no one cut out for You? **1770** Munford *Candidates* 15: That every fool will wear the cap that fits. **1776** Carter *Diary* 2.1006: Indeed he must be a curious Capmaker who fits on his own cap, though he takes pains to shew it don't fit him, 1064: A cap for him who pleases to put it on. **1777** Sullivan *Letters* 1.566: So far as you are conscious the Garment suits I have no objection to your wearing it; that part which does not fit, you need not meddle with. **1793** WBiglow in Buckingham *Specimens* 2.281: "Where a coat fits," the say is, "there let it be worn." **1793** Paine *Works* 144: The cap receive again, 'tis thine alone. **1795** Murdock *Triumphs* 29: Why — will you put the cap on, Trifle? **1798** *Washington Writings* 36.211: If the Cap did not fit, why put it on? **1799** Carey *Plumb* 21: I took the cap, tried it, thought it did not fit, and

threw it among the rest of the Irish booksellers. **1806** Jackson *Correspondence* 1.126: If I thought proper to trim or pare my head to fit the cap, he could not help it. **1815** Brackenridge *Modern* 699: If any thinks the cap will fit him, let him put it on. *Oxford* 101; TW 55(1). See **S164.**

C30 To pull **Caps**

1787 Tyler *Contrast* 42: Half the belles in the city will be pulling caps for him. *NED* Cap *sb.*[1] 9.

C31 To set one's **Cap** at (for) someone

1774 PHutchinson in Hutchinson *Diary* 1.275-6: I should be tempted to set my cap at him. **1781** Mrs. MBland in *VHM* 43(1935) 245: All setting Caps for the best places and pushing each other down for a little Air. **1784** EWinslow in *Winslow Papers* 227: You have literally set your Cap at no creature on earth but me. **1789** *Belknap Papers* 2.98: The girls who had been setting their caps for him are chagrined. **1795** Freneau *Poems* (*1795*) 360: Ladies, no more for salmon set your caps. **1801** Smith *Letters* 27: What think you . . . of setting your cap for him? **1803** Tyler *Verse* 122. **1807** *Kennon Letters* 31.193. **1808** *Port Folio* NS 5.127: She could now *set her cap* at the men without reproach. **1809** *Kennon Letters* 32.161, **1810** 272: for him. **1810** Mackay *Letters* 91: The Widow Oliver is setting her cap at *Old Massa.* **1816** Fidfaddy *Adventures* 51: Uncle Sam's wife began to set her cap for the government of a new territory. Barbour 29; *Oxford* 716; TW 55(2).

C32 To take off (put on) one's considering **Cap**

1737 Franklin *Drinkers* 2.174: Sir Richard has taken off his considering Cap. **1741** Belcher *Papers* 2.386: If my letters by Skinner, and what I now say, don't bring you to your considering cap. **1793** JAdams in Smith *Journal and Correspondence* 2(2).126: If he does not keep his considering cap always on his head. **1800** Gadsden *Writings* 287: Put on your considering cap. *Oxford* 656-7; Tilley C613.

C33 To cut **Capers**

1737 Franklin *Drinkers* 2.174: He cuts his

Capers. **1753** *Independent Reflector* 114: The French are not more remarkable for . . . the cutting of Capers. **1777** *Philadelphia Evening Post* in *Newspaper Extracts(II)* 1.314: The Hessians . . . cut a few capers. **1782** Freneau *Poems* 2.144. **1783** Baldwin *Life and Letters* 245. **1792** *Echo* 36: Where squaws cut capers o'er the desart ground. **1792** Freneau *Poems* 3.78: Since first on this world's stage you cut your caper. **1806** Fessenden *Modern Philosopher* 129: For he ('tis told in publick papers) Can make dead people cut droll capers. **1806** *Weekly* 1.113. **1808** Hitchcock *Poetical Dictionary* 9: To cut electioneering capers. **1809** Fessenden *Pills* 34. **1809** Lindsley *Love* 101. **1809** JBrace in Vanderpoel *More Chronicles* 135. **1810** *Port Folio* 2NS 4.188. **1812** Luttig *Journal* 80. **1819** Peirce *Rebelliad* 32, 33, 76. **1820** Durand *Life* 24: He thought to cut as many capers. **1823** Prince *Journals* 108. **1830** Ames *Mariner's* 100. **1832** Cooper *Letters* 2.258: And if you cut capers with the book, I wash my hands of it. Barbour 29; TW 56.

C34 Like **Captain** like soldiers
1745 RRutherford in *Baxter Manuscripts* 11.307: The scripture Aphorism, like priest like people, is Equally true if thus Apply'd, Like Capt like soldiers. *Oxford* 102; Whiting C34. See **M109, O13.**

C35 Once a **Captain** always a captain
1792 Brackenridge *Modern* 6: For the rule is, once a captain, and always a captain. **1807** Janson *Stranger* 442: They rigidly adhere to the vulgar adage, "once a captain always a captain." Cf. *Oxford* 594.

C36 Where the **Carcass** is there will the eagles (*etc.*) be gathered
1654 Johnson *Wonder-Working* 48: Where the dead carkass is, thither will the Eagles resort. **1734** Franklin *PR* 1.352: Where carcasses are, eagles will gather, And where good laws are, much people flock thither. **1778** JAdams in *Warren-Adams Letters* 2.73: Where the Carcas is, there the Crows will assemble. **1786** *Massachusetts Centinel* in Buckingham *Specimens* 2.43: Where carrion lies, the hungry crows abound. **1790**

Maclay *Journal* 332: Wherever the carcass of commerce is thither will the eagles of traffic be gathered. **1809** Weems *Marion* 188: British princes, and nobles . . . shall swarm over your devoted country, as thick as eagles over a new-fallen carcase. **1810** Bentley *Diary* 3.499: As soon as they hear of the sick, there the eagles and crows are gathered together. **1810** *Tyler Letters* 1.260: The ravens follow the carcass. **1824** Flint *Recollections* 337. **1831** HStith in *Ruffin Papers* 2.32: Where the carcass is, there buzzards will be gathered together. Barbour 29; *Oxford* 102; Whiting B430, *NC* 380.

C37 (Lucky in **Cards,** unlucky in love)
1801 Trumbull *Season* 93: He said that good luck in cards denoted much worse success in matters of *far greater* importance. Barbour 29(1); *Oxford* 496.

C38 To be in the **Cards**
1815 Brackenridge *Modern* 673: It is in the cards, to use a phrase taken from the gamblers. Partridge 127.

C39 To manage one's **Cards** badly
1758 *Beekman Papers* 1.323: Some have managed their Cards very badly this season. NED Card *sb.*^2 2d.

C40 To play one's **Cards**
1764 *Johnson Papers* 11.342: The latter has play'd his Cards so well as to carry all before him. **1775** Digges *Adventures* 1.97-8: I played my cards so well, that Donna Mariana chose to spend her retired hours in my company. **1777** Lee *Letters* 1.313-4: But I am also inclined to think that if our Cards are well plaid, it may prove his ruin. **1777** TNelson in Jefferson *Papers* 2.4: As indeed he might, had he play'd his Cards well. **1778** Lee *Letters* 1.396: Great Britain has now two Cards to play, but which she will choose we cannot tell. **1797** Weems *Letters* 2.77, 79-80. **1811** Graydon *Memoirs* 230: She played her cards with much address. *Oxford* 631; TW 56(1).

C41 **Care** killed a cat
1824 *Tales* 1.16: Care killed a cat. *Oxford* 103; Tilley C84; Whiting *NC* 380(3).

C42 Carolina story

1779 Shaw *Journals* 62: Take the following as an indisputable fact; — it is no Carolina story. See **C28**.

C43 To fish for **Carps**

1702 Mather *Magnalia* 2.581: The readers, who every where "fish for nothing but carps" . . . may find fault enough with it [perhaps a pun only]. NED Carp *sb.*[2]

C44 To be on the **Carpet** [The following is a selection from 95 occurrences of the phrase]

1740 *Letter* in *Colonial Currency* 4.28: In bringing it on the Carpet. **1741** Stephens *Journal(I)* 2.179: What Event so many things have found, that have been so long on the Carpet. **1744** Hamilton *Itinerarium* 151: I was surprised to find that no matters of philosophy were brought upon the carpet. **1769** Adams(S) *Writings* 1.294: Before I bring this gentleman on the carpet at B——— n. **1777** Jefferson *Papers* 2.18. **1779** Hamilton *Papers* 2.174. **1782** Paine *American Crisis* 1.213. **1785** Washington *Writings* 28.254: Tell me what is on the carpet. **1788** Adams *Diary* 373: Singing soon came on to the carpet. **1792** Brackenridge *Modern* 15: The Captain coming up, and finding what was on the carpet, was greatly chagrined. **1802** Adams *D and A* 3.272. **1802** Dow *Journal* 124: And soon drinking, cursing, swearing, and taking God's name in vain, appeared on the carpet. **1809** Lee *Diary and Letters* 88: Tell Susan I have another letter for her on the carpet. **1818** Jefferson *Writings* 1.273: Another [game] was on the carpet. NED Carpet 1b; Tilley C97. See **T22**.

C45 Carpet knight

1814 Wirt *Bachelor* 36: I speak not of honest dolts, of "carpet knights" or men of dubious integrity. *Oxford* 103; Tilley C98.

C46 He who rides in his **Carriage,** *etc.*

1824 Lee *Diary and Letters* 218: This passion for carriages here always puts me in mind of the Italian proverb: that "he who rides in his carriage and has a bad dinner at home, draws his coach with his teeth."

C47 As bare as a scraped **Carrot**

1772 Adams *D and A* 2.72: Makes them poor, as bare as a scraped Carrot. Cf. *Oxford* 258: Fine.

C48 To put the **Cart** before the Horse

1676 Randolph *Letters* 2.213: This is ὕστερον πρότερον and denotes some deviation from his Ma[ties] methods. **1766** Adams *D and A* 1.330: The Cart may as well be put before the Horse, as the Horse before the Cart. **1773** Franklin *Writings* 6.103: Some People always ride before the Horse's Head. **1774** Adams *Works* 4.24: He put the cart before the horse. **1774** WBradford in Madison *Papers* 1.109: He put the Cart before the horse: he was a father before he was a husband. **1788** Henry *Life* 3.482. **1793** *Washington *Writings* 32.499-500: Would not the granting a Patent then . . . have too much the appearance of placing the Cart before the horse? **1802** *Port Folio* 2.268. **1804** Dow *Journal* 350. **1804** Paine *Remarks* 2.961. **1807** *Salmagundi* 226, 247: After showing me . . . his new invented cart which was to go before the horse . . . he was pleased to return home to dinner. **1809** Irving *History* 1.249: He was much given to mechanical inventions . . . carts that went before the horses. **1811** Weems *Letters* 3.40. Barbour 30; *Oxford* 104-5; Whiting C60.

C49 A **Cart-wheel** is a cart-wheel

1718 JUsher in *Saltonstall Papers* 1.323: I am fully resolved to send my Son where he may know and learn good manners. In a word your Grand fathers Saying a Cart wheel is a Cart wheel. [The grandfather was John Leverett (1616-1679).]

C50 To be one's own **Carver**

c1608 Wingfield *Discourse* in *Transactions and Collections of the American Antiquarian Society* 4(1860) 87: Others would saie . . . that, unless I would amend their allowance, they would be their owne Carvers. **1756** Laurens *Papers* 2.295: At a time when Every One is looking Out for Bills we cant be Our Own Carvers. **1762** Watts *Letter Book* 39: I leave it to you to settle the freight as I would by no means be my own Carver, 41. **1778** Smith *Memoirs(II)* 344: I told him that I would not be my own Carver in the Matter with Mr. Grant. *Oxford* 105; Tilley C110.

C51 The **Case** is altered

1644 Williams *Writings* 3.378: Otherwise the case is altred. **1690** WDean in *Hinckley Papers* 237: But now the case is altered. **1704** Talbot *Letters* 107: Now the case is strangly alter'd. **1709** Lawson *Voyage* 185. **1713** Johnston *Papers* 134: The Case being now quite altered. **1730** *New-York Gazette* in *Newspaper Extracts(I)* 1.225: The Case is altered, but the Men the same. **1734** Johnson *Writings* 3.67. **1743** Franklin *PR* 2.374: Then this Accident *alters the Case.* **1758** Smith *Works* 1². 131. **1760** Franklin *Papers* 9.89: The case is greatly alter'd now. **1760** Smith *Works* 2.325: But now the case is much altered. **a1761** NScull in Silverman 373. **1764** *Paxton Papers* 116, 175: But now the Case is alter'd quite. **1775** JMartin in *Naval Documents* 1.150: The case . . . is now altered, 2.186. **1775** *New York Journal* in *Newspaper Extracts(I)* 11.33: But now the case is altered. **1776** Adams *D and A* 3.445. **1776** Paine *Common Sense* 1.34. **1777** BArnold in Sparks *Correspondence* 1.354. **1778** *Beekman Papers* 3.1312. **1779** Hamilton *Papers* 2.24: The case will be altered. **1780** *New Jersey Gazette* in *Newspaper Extracts(II)* 4.336: The case is now greatly altered. **1780** *New-York Gazette* in *Newspaper Extracts(II)* 5.106: But their still keeping near, quite alter'd the case. **1780** Paine *Correspondence* 2.1186. **1781** Freneau *Poems* 2.84, **1782** *Prose* 52. **1786** JJay in Sparks *Correspondence* 4.135. **1792** Hamilton *Papers* 12.107. **1793** Clay *Letters* 257. **1794** Rowson *Charlotte* 1.127. **1794** Stiles *Three Judges* 91. **1797** Cobbett *Porcupine* 5.378. **1809** JAdams in *Adams-Cunningham Letters* 105: But Napoleon came in and altered the case a little. **1811** Graydon *Memoirs* 273. **1812** *Kennon Letters* 33.270. **1813** Valpey *Journal* 9. **1816** Paulding *Letters(I)* 1.182. **1818** Baldwin *Letters* 267: *Now the case is quite altered.* **1819** Royall *Letters* 199: This is beautifully illustrated by the judge who reversed his own judgment, in the case of the ox. **1830** Ames

Mariner's 271: The case is now somewhat altered. *Oxford* 105; Tilley C111; Whiting C67. See **C188.**

C52 In doubtful **Cases** the negative is safer

1714 *Letter* in *Colonial Currency* 1.277: The old Maxim . . . that in doubtful Cases the negative is the safer. Cf. *Oxford* 200: Doubt.

C53 To be out of **Case**

1765 Patten *Diary* 159: My wife was Very much out of Case, **1766** 180. NED Case *sb.*¹ 5b.

C54 An empty **Cask** (makes the greatest sound)

1676 Williams *Writings* 5.493: This *Empty Cask,* this loud Boaster and Censurer is one of them. *Oxford* 220; Whiting V25. See **V12.**

C55 A musty **Cask** mars wine

c1700 Taylor *Poems* 431: A Musty Cask doth marre rich Malmsy Wine. Cf. Lean 4.112.

C56 To build **Castles** in the air

1634 Wood *New-England* 60: Building of Castles in the Aire. **a1656** Bradford *History* 1.325-6: They proved castels in the aire. **1691** *Revolution* in *Andros Tracts* 1.117: To Build Cities and Castles (in the Air if he could). **1713** Wise *Churches* 136: It is held in opinion that Castles in the Air and Immaterial Substances do not occupy space. **1721** *Second Part* in *Colonial Currency* 2.324. **1733** Byrd *Journey* 275: We did not build castles only, but also cities in the air. **1741** ?WDouglas *Second Letter* in *Colonial Currency* 4.121. **1759** Ames *Almanacs* 295. **1766** JBoucher in *MHM* 7(1912), 301: It is there . . . I generally build my Castles. **1769** Brooke *Emily* 209: It destroys my air-built scheme of happiness. **1769** Davis *Colonial Virginia Satirist* 59. **1769** Hamilton *Papers* 1.4. **1773** *Norton Papers* 311. **1775** Paine *Useful Hints* 2.1022. **1775** Sewall *Poems* 74: Howe'er we soon this castle-builder find Dropt from his summit. **1776** Lee *Papers* 2.177. **1777** Cresswell *Journal* 187. **1778** Barney *Memoir* 72: Converted your "castle in the air" into a *floating* castle. **1778** Galloway *Diary* 63. **1779** Barlow *Letters* 23:

We built castles much higher than the hills. **1779** Galloway *Diary* 163. **1780** AA in *Adams FC* 3.355, 425. **1781** *New Jersey Gazette* in *Newspaper Extracts(II)* 5.182: The tow'ring castles fancy rais'd, As quick as lightning disappears. **1782** AA in *Adams FC* 4.296. **1782** Freneau *Poems* 2.136. **1784** EWinslow in *Winslow Papers* 194: They do not arise from reveries or a propensity to castle-building, 237. **1785** Coke *Journals* 27: All my castles which I had built in the air. **1789** *Columbian Magazine* 3.195: The clouds build castles in the air. **1789** THutchinson in Hutchinson *Diary* 2.432. **1790** Dennie *Letters* 38, 50: Even you with all your care can not avoid laying at least the first stone of an air castle. **1792** Ames *Letters* 1.111: Sober people are justly scared and disgusted to see the wild castle-builders at work. **1794** Paine *From the Castle in the Air* 2.1096. **1795** *Tablet* 16. **1797** Mann *Female* 111: She planned many schemes and fabricated many castles. **1799** Carey *Porcupiniad* 2.36: His airy castles quick decay. **1800** Cleveland *Letters* 59: Building airy castles and persuing them nearly round the globe till they vanish. **1801** *Port Folio* 1.30: My imagination was . . . busy castle-building, 348: A choice of castles, "roughly rushing to the skies," 388: There are innumerable air-castles scattered all over this district. **1802** Paulding *Letters(II)* 15. **1803** JAllen in *W&MCQ* 2S 6(1926) 82: If this castle should turn out to be an airy one. **1803** Davis *Travels* 221. **1803** Harmon *Sixteen Years* 68. **1803** *Port Folio* 3.355. **1804** Wilson *Letters* xxxiv: I have been so long accustomed to the building of airy castles and brain windmills. **1805** *Port Folio* 5.105: Fragments of Bonaparte's air castles. **1806** Hitchcock *Works* 88. **1806** Weems *Letters* 2.349: You talk of my castle building & ordering books in which you have no interest. **1807** *Port Folio* NS 4.98. **1807** Rush *Letters* 2.938. **1807** *Salmagundi* 300, 323. **1808** TBurr in Burr *Correspondence* 271: My plans in that respect were built in air. **1809** Irving *History* 1.45, 209, 211, 212. **1809** Lindsley *Love* 5: My ærial plans of happiness generally miscarry. **1811** Burroughs *Memoirs* 106. **1811** Graydon *Memoirs* 80: My imagination went to castle-building in the remote prospect of a trip to England. **1811** Wirt *Letters* 1.315: The airy castles tower! **1812** Hitchcock *Social* 34. **1812** *Port Folio* 2NS 7.583. **1813** *Kennon Letters* 35.156: Like many other air built castles, this has tumbled to the ground. **1814** Wirt *Letters* 1.366. **1816** *Port Folio* 4NS 1.29: He may erect castles in the air. **1818** Fessenden *Ladies Monitor* 45-6: Has built . . . A thousand stately palaces in air. **1818** Wirt *Letters* 2.82: And it will remain a castle in the air till the end of time. **1820** Irving *Sketch Book* 443: While I lay on the grass and built castles in a bright pile of clouds. **1821** Howison *Sketches* 87. **1821** Knight *Poems* 2.113: And builds his walls — not castles in the air. **1823** Adams *Memoirs* 6.199: Mr. Gallatin still builds castles in the air. **1838** Hone *Diary* 2.347: Our air-built castles began to totter. **1845** Jackson *Correspondence* 6.363: What a splendid castle in the air. Barbour 30; *Oxford* 107; TW 57(1).

C57 All **Cats** are grey in the dark

1745 Franklin *Papers* 3.31: And as in the dark all Cats are grey. **1791** S.P.L. *Thoughts* 78: All cats are grey in the dark. *Oxford* 111; Whiting C27. See **D15, J34.**

C58 As dull as a **Cat**

1790 Freneau *Poems* 3.44: As dull as a cat.

C59 As ignorant as a **Cat**

1806 Weems *Letters* 2.335: He seem'd as ignorant as a Cat.

C60 As kindly as a **Cat** learns to lap milk

1779 Galloway *Diary* 168: [He] learnt his lesson from him as kindly as a Cat learns to lap Milk. Cf. *Oxford* 108; Tilley C167.

C61 As melancholy as a **Cat**

1818 CBeecher in Vanderpoel *Chronicles* 187: Down in her chair, sad Betsey sat, As melancholy as any cat. *Oxford* 524; TW 59(15).

C62 As quick as a **Cat**

a**1855** Beecher *Autobiography* 2.72: Lambert was . . . quick as a cat to see. TW 59(17).

C63 As speechless as **Cats** in cloudy weather

1781 Pynchon *Diary* 85: When met (the waggs say) we sit looking at one another speechless as the cats in cloudy weather.

C64 As spry as a **Cat**

1801 Story *Shop* 27: He can . . . spring as sprigh as a cat. **1803** *Yankee Phrases* 87: And playful and spry as a cat. TW 59(24).

C65 As weak as a **Cat**

1819 Cobbett *Year's* 162: He is pot-bellied, and weak as a cat. **1835** Floy *Diary* 201: And when I think about them I feel as weak as a Cat. Barbour 31(44); TW 59(29).

C66 Better have **Cats'** good will than their ill will

1809 *Kennon Letters* 32.85: The old saying: "It is better to have the good will of cats, than their ill will."

C67 Can the **Cat** help it, if the maid be a fool

1810 *Port Folio* 2NS 3.314: How can the cat help it, if the maid be a fool. *Oxford* 108; Tilley C151.

C68 **Cat** after kind

1791 S.P.L. *Thoughts* 77: Cat after kind. *Oxford* 107; Tilley C135; Whiting C89.

C69 The **Cat** can yield but her skin

1764 Franklin *Papers* 11.181: The Cat can yield but her skin. **1786** WWhiting in American Antiquarian Society, *Proceedings* NS 66(1956) 143: Who found they could get no more of a Cat than her Skin. *Oxford* 572; Tilley M1167. Cf. Whiting F600.

C70 A **Cat** falls on its legs (feet)

1716 Church *History* 2.160: [He] generally had Cat luck, falling on his feet. **1765** Watts *Letter Book* 379: Mr. G. falls on his Legs, perhaps some others. **1797** Cobbett *Porcupine* 6.296: There I fell on my feet, let me tell you, and you may guess if I did not profit by my good fortune. **1831** Cooper *Letters* 2.166: Truth is like a cat, and always comes down on its feet, jerk it as high as you please. NED Leg 2c(c); *Oxford* 107-8; Whiting C86. Cf. TW 142(1).

C71 A **Cat** has nine lives

1709 Lawson *Voyage* 125: If a Cat has nine Lives, this Creature [opossum] surely has nineteen. **1755** Davis *Colonial Virginia Satirist* 24: Z——ds have I nine lives like a Cat. **1773** Trumbull *Satiric Poems* 89: No cat hath half so many lives. **1785** Tilghman *Letters* 36: Some of them have as many lives as a Cat. **1795** *Tablet* 32: And thy nine lives but poorly pay, For his lamented one. **1803** JJackson in Milledge *Correspondence* 90: I begin to think I am somewhat beyond the cats nine lives. **1806** Fessenden *Modern Philosopher* 133: Give rogues the *nine* lives of a cat. **1806** *Port Folio* NS 1.320: *Nine Lives:* To all the *Tabby* kind alone Fate has a partial kindness shown; Their thread thrice three lengths is run, *etc.,* 2.81: Without even the nine struggles of a cat. **1813** JAdams in *Adams-Jefferson Letters* 2.346: It would require as many lives as those of a Cat. **1822** Lee *Diary and Letters* 205: They swear that, like their own cats, he has nine lives. **1830** Ames *Mariner's* 235: Puss was . . . killed by a cask of beef rolling upon him, which extinguished all nine of his lamps of life at once. *Oxford* 108; TW 58(4); Whiting W510.

C72 A **Cat** in a sack

1786 Drinker *Journal* 171: Little Dan came this morning with a load on his back, Not a Pig in a poke, but a cat in a sack. Whiting C102. See **P121.**

C73 The **Cat** in gloves catches no mice

1754 Franklin *PR* 5.184: The Cat in Gloves catches no Mice, **1758** *WW* 343. **1770** Ames *Almanacs* 412: The Cat in Gloves catches no mice. Barbour 31(34); *Oxford* 108; Tilley C145, 147.

C74 A **Cat** may look at a king

1788 Barlow *Letters* 81: A cat may look upon a king: by the same ascending scale a king may look upon me. *Oxford* 109; Whiting C88.

C75 **Cat** will not eat cat

1818 Royall *Letters* 170: Cat will not eat cat. See **D235.**

C76 Like a **Cat** in a strange garret

1823 Bierce *Travels* 98: I got inside a good bed in a decent house where I felt like a cat in a strange garret. TW 59(31).

C77 Like **Cats** in a bag

1802 Irving *Jonathan* 30: *Like Cats in a bag.* TW 59(28).

C78 Like pulling a **Cat** by the tail

1778 WButler in *Clinton Papers* 3.596: It would be like pulling a Cat by the Tail to get out the Militia at this time. **1778** JStark in Sullivan *Letters* 2.87: We have no troops but Militia &c they turn out like drawing a Cat by the tail.

C79 Not room to swing a **Cat**

1747 Pote *Journal* 125-6: We had not Room to Swing a Cat Round by yᵉ Tail, without Danger of Dashing her Brains out. **c1770** Tyler *Verse* 4: And thought his Shop a room of State When you co'd'nt swing a Cat. **1801** *Farmers' Museum* 182: A small room, not large enough to swing a cat. **1844** Beecher *Autobiography* 2.509: He couldn't pray unless he had a room big enough to swing a cat in by the tail. *Oxford* 683; TW 59(35); Tilley C603a.

C80 A scalded **Cat** fears cold water

c1680 Radisson *Voyages* 244: But wee answered them that a scalded cat fears yᵉ water though it be cold. *Oxford* 703; Tilley C163. Cf. Whiting W87.

C81 To be (like) a singed **Cat**

1752 Carter *Diary* 1.81: [He] set forth the Poverty of the People and shewed himself to be a singed Cat. **1816** Paulding *Letters(I)*. 1.138-9: He is like a singed cat, and very often takes as much pains to appear worse than he is, as some people among us do to appear better. *Oxford* 736; Whiting C99. Cf. TW 60(36).

C82 To bell the **Cat**

1797 Cobbett *Porcupine* 5.244: They are like the mice in council, who, by an unanimous vote, determined that the cat should be hanged. **1844** Cooper *Letters* 4.476: No one will bell the cat. *Oxford* 44; Whiting B232.

C83 To know (see) how the **Cat** jumps

1811 PTJackson in *Jacksons and Lees* 1.711: This will enable you to look round to know how the cat is jumping. **1833** Pintard *Letters* 4.152: On the subject of Dʳ Hawks make no comment, untill we see how the cat jumps next autumn. *Oxford* 108; TW 60(47).

C84 To know no more than a **Cat** in a wallet

1827 Watterston *Wanderer* 161: I didn't know . . . whereabouts I was going, any more than a cat in a wallet. Cf. TW 60(45, 46).

C85 To let the **Cat** out of the bag

1769 Adams(S) *Writings* 1.296: The cat will be let out of the bag. **1769** Woodmason *Journal* 139: I would let the Cat out of the Bag. **1773** *Norton Papers* 313. **1776** JA in *Adams FC* 2.53. **1779** Burd *Letters* 105: The cat is not yet let out of the bag. **1779** Shaw *Journals* 70. **1782** JEliot in *Belknap Papers* 3.236. **1784** Pynchon *Diary* 180: The cats get out of the bag, and are tossed backward & forward from bench to bar. **1787** *American Museum* 2.595. **a1788** Jones *History* 1.15: The cat was fairly out of the bag. **1789** EHazard in *Belknap Papers* 2.94. **1792** *Washington *Writings* 32.152: The Cat is let out. **1795** Cobbett *Porcupine* 2.219. **1797** Callender *Annual Register 1796* 11: Randall instantly turned out the cat. **1807** Taggart *Letters* 224. **1809** Weems *Marion* 30. **1810** TPickering in King *Life* 5.193. **1811** Wirt *Letters* 1.321: The cat is out of the bag, — and what odds does it make how she came in it. **1814** Kerr *Barclay* 296. **1815** JAdams in *Adams-Jefferson Letters* 2.445. **1850** Cooper *Letters* 6.191. Barbour 31(37); *Oxford* 457; TW 61(48). See **P123.**

C86 To play as a **Cat** does with a mouse

1780 Lee(W) *Letters* 3.787: To play with as a cat does with a dead mouse. **1821** Gallatin *Diary* 192: Father . . . likes playing the latter as a cat does a mouse. Whiting C80.

C87 To quarrel (*etc.*) like **Cat** and dog

1777 JA in *Adams FC* 2.245: They Quarrell like Cats and Dogs. **1804** Dow *Journal* 210: It is as much impossible for them to live agreeably and happy together, as for the cat and dog to agree. **1805** Weems *Hymen* 22: Making, between them, a fine cat-and-dog concert of it for life. **1810** *Port Folio* 2NS 4.80: And even dogs and cats agree, Before he'll come to love her, **1815** 3NS 6.624: Strephon and his Molly Now fight like cat and dog. Barbour 30(13); TW 61(58).

C88 To rain **Cats** and dogs

1816 Weems *Letters* 3.169: If it were raining cats & dogs there w^d be some comfort. **1850** Cooper *Letters* 6.116: It rained cats and dogs. Barbour 30(19); *Oxford* 662; TW 62(60).

C89 To set the **Cat** to watch the cream pot

1798 Manning *Key* 30: But that appears to me like seting the Cat to watch the Creem pot. Cf. *Oxford* 108; Tilley C139; Whiting C109.

C90 To turn **Cat** in pan

1720 TLechmere in *Winthrop Papers*(B) 6.392: They say yor Doct^r is turned catt in pann with Mr Thatcher. **1720** *Letter in Colonial Currency* 2.237: As to turn *Cat-in-pan* on every occasion. **1748** GClinton in *Colden Letters* 4.33: Which plainly demonstrats y^t he has plaid Cat in pan with me. **1779** Sargent *Loyalist* 97: I turn'd the cat in pan once more, And so became a Whig, Sir. **1809** WCunningham in *Adams-Cunningham Letters* 77: Mr. Pinckney, in the game of cat-in-pan, is making himself contemptible. *Oxford* 847; Whiting C107.

C91 To watch as a **Cat** watches a mouse

1734 Belcher *Papers* 2.461: I'll watch him as a starv'd cat watches a mouse. **1799** Beecher *Autobiography* 1.103: The people continue to watch me as narrowly as a mouse is watched by a cat. **1807** *Monthly Anthology* 4.80: Absorbed . . . like an assiduous old tabby at the entrance of a mouse-hole. *Oxford* 869; TW 61(57).

C92 To whip the **Cat**

1816 Paulding *Letters*(I) 2.172: There was a terrible "whipping of the cat," as it is called, on the day the notes became due. This whipping the cat is nothing more than a parcel of traders puffing at one another's heels . . . to borrow money. **1850** Cooper *Letters* 6.152: He kept school within six miles of Cooperstown . . . whipping the cat, just as young Munro did! TW 62(61). Cf. *Oxford* 883.

C93 When the **Cat** is away the mice will play

1802 *Port Folio* 2.323: It is an old saying, that "When the cat is away, the mice will play." Barbour 31(45); *Oxford* 109-10; Whiting M736.

C94 To lie upon the **Catch**

1747 Stith *History* 235: [They] were rather profuse in their Expenses for the Good of the Colony, than lying upon the Catch for little Advantages and mean Gains. *Oxford* 459; Tilley C188.

C95 **Catch** as catch can

1721 Wise *Word* 222: Catch it who can catch. **1734** Plumstead 241: While the royal ball is thus tossed about, and catch who can, the state will become giddy. **1792** Brackenridge *Modern* 137: Things must take their course; and the rule be, catch, catch can. **1813** *Port Folio* 3NS 1.515: 'Tis catch as catch can. Barbour 31; *Oxford* 111; Whiting C112.

C96 **Catching** is before hanging

1818 Royall *Letters* 183: Yes, says Marchant, but catching's before hanging—the villain's cleared out. Whiting *NC* 382. Cf. TW 62.

C97 To be (made) a **Cat's paw**

1690 Palmer *Account* in *Andros Tracts* 1.28: As the Monkey did the Cats Foot, to pluck the Chestnut out of the Fire. **1707** INorris in *Penn-Logan Correspondence* 2.239: I know not who will be the cat's-paw. **1733** Belcher *Papers* 1.301: To be made one of the cat's paws, tools & f—ls of the party. **1741** Stephens *Journal*(I) 2.105: Yet it would be hard to persuade me into a Belief, that he can be so silly, to be made a Cat's Paw still. **1747** CCarroll in *MHM* 22(1927) 288. **1747** GClinton in *Law Papers* 3.37. **1763** Laurens *Papers* 3.253: 'Tis to support the Honour of the Family I suppose that they have suffer'd their paws to be thrust into hot Ashes. **1772** Habersham *Letters* 168. **1773** *Norton Papers* 337. **1775**

HCruger in Van Schaack *Letters* 36. **1775** Smith *Memoirs(I)* 220. **1775** Willard *Letters* 245. **1777** Gordon *Letters* 339: Suffering himself to be made a paw of by the Hows. **1778** Lee(W) *Letters* 2.419. **1778** MWilson in *PM* 8(1884) 52. **1779** Allen *Narrative* 106. **1779** Lee *Letters* 2.69: Have you rescued the fishery from the paws that are used to pull the chestnuts out of the fire. **1780** Gordon *Letters* 431: Whether Lowell was the cat's-paw he missed his aim and lost the chesnuts. **a1778** Jones *History* 1.10. **1789** Brown *Better* 34. **1791** Morris *Diary* 2.270: Mirabeau and others endeavored to make him the Cat's paw that in Case of Need he might be converted into the Scape Goat. **1794** JAdams in Smith *Journal and Correspondence* 2(2) 129. **1796** Cobbett *Porcupine* 4.131: The father has served the silly son, as the monkey served the cat, when he took her paw to rake the chestnuts out of the fire with. **1797** RMorris in *PM* 6(1882) 112. **1800** Cobbett *Porcupine* 11.249. **1800** Jefferson *Writings* 10.157: It is truly the fable of the pulling the nuts out of the fire with the cat's paw. **1803** Cary *Letters* 173. **1805** Silliman *Travels* 2.130. **1810** *Port Folio* 2NS 4.188: But monkeys have been observed to roast the chestnuts they have stolen, and the origin of "cats paw," is much in their favour. **1818** Hall *Travels* 6. **1818** WLewis in Jackson *Correspondence* 6.463. **1822** EKing in King *Life* 6.487. *Oxford* 110, 118: chestnuts; TW 66(3), 277.

C98 He that is angry without a **Cause**, *etc.*
1734 Belcher *Papers* 2.23: He that is angry without a cause is commonly oblig'd to be pleas'd without amends. *Oxford* 14; Whiting C120.

C99 Little **Causes** produce great effects
1784 CThomson in Jefferson *Papers* 7.272: Little causes often produce great effects. **1791** JHoskins in *Columbia* 192: As well in civilized, so in savage governments, from small causes, great evils spring. See **B133, C189, E77, F128, I29, S97, 361, T52.**

C100 Similar **Causes** produce similar effects (*varied*)
1689 JNelson in *Baxter Manuscripts* 5.26:

Naturally the cawse hath some Proportion to the Effect. **1744** *Letter* in *Colonial Currency* 4.234: The Effect ever following the Cause. **1771** Carroll *Copy-Book* 204: Similar causes produce similar events. TW 63(2). See **S496.**

C101 Take away the **Cause** and the effect ceases
1718 Chalkley *Observations* 425: The Cause being taken away, the Effect of course ceaseth. **1748** *Word* in *Colonial Currency* 4.365: Remove the wicked Cause, and then see if the Effect ceaseth not. **1749** *Brief Account* in *Colonial Currency* 4.388: Remove the Cause and the Effect will cease. **1802** Humphreys *Works* 102.190: Take but the cause, we take th'effect away. *Oxford* 112; Whiting C121. See **F316.**

C102 To make the worse appear the better **Cause**
1788 King *Life* 1.317: For that reason they appear to be able to make the worse appear the better cause. *Oxford* 920.

C103 Not care a **Cent**
1807 Ames *Letters* 1.393: Nobody here seems to care a cent about Burr's plan. **1815** Humphreys *Yankey* 70: I don't care a cent. **1816** Freneau *Last Poems* 5: She cared not a cent what he writ. **1818** Royall *Letters* 124. TW 63(1).

C104 To save a **Cent** by wasting an eagle
1806 Adams *Memoirs* 1.432: This is economy—saving a cent by wasting an eagle. Cf. TW 280: Penny (5). See **P79.**

C105 **Ceres** and Bacchus walk hand in hand
a1700 Hubbard *New England* 35: As used to be said of old, "Sine Baccho et Cerere friget Venus," i.e. ebriety and gluttony produces venery. **1783** *American Wanderer* 307: Ceres and Bacchus walk hand in hand. *Oxford* 112; Whiting C125.

C106 As common as **Chaff**
1766 Ames *Almanacs* 377: Acquaintance are common as chaff. Svartengren 397.

C107 **Chaff** and grain (wheat)
c1700 Taylor *Poems* 444: To Chaff away the

Chaff and Choose the grain. **1746** Brainerd *Memoirs* 288: Some corrupt mixture, some *chaff* as well as *wheat*. **1773** Asbury *Journal* 1.84: But what is the chaff to the wheat? **1777** WLivingston in *Newspaper Extracts (II)* 1.301: It has winnowed the chaff from the grain. **1786** *Washington *Writings* 29.50: If there are any grains among them Colo. H. can easily separate them from the chaff. **1790** Asbury *Journal* 1.624: I find a little wheat and a great deal of chaff. **1798** Jefferson *Writings* 10.5: It has winnowed the grain from the chaff. **1798** *Washington *Writings* 36.374: Hands that may be able to seperate the grain from the chaff. **1803** Davis *Travels* 138: This ode may be likened to *the grain in the bushel of chaff*. **1810** Asbury *Letters* 3.433: We must or shall have some chaff among the wheat. **1811** Adams *Memoirs* 2.323: Winnowing the chaff from the wheat, **1815** *Writings* 5.376: It was winnowing the grain from the chaff. **1815** Jefferson *Writings* 14.363: In sifting the grain from its chaff, **1819** 15.221: Winnowing the grain from the chaff, **1820** 259: To winnow the grain from the chaff. **1820** Weems *Letters* 3.285: There is a world of chaff among the good wheat in this self same Atlas. TW 399(3, 4); Whiting C428, W205.

C108   Like **Chaff** before the wind

1785 Washington *Writings* 28.350: Their obligation to surrender them is no more than chaff before the wind when opposed by the scale of possession. **1812** Taggart *Letters* 393: He . . . is driven by them like chaff before the wind. **1831** Murphey *Papers* 1.394: As things of this kind fly like chaff before the wind. Whiting C129. See **F63**.

C109   **Chains** of gold

1779 Hamilton *Papers* 2.167: Commerce . . . has [fitted] their inhabitants for the chain, and that the only condition they sincerely desire is that it may be a golden one. **1787** Lee *Letters* 2.445: Chains being still chains, whether made of gold or iron. *Oxford* 495: Fetters; Tilley M338, cf. C214; Whiting M237.

C110   To brighten the **Chain**

1754 Massachusetts Historical Society *Col-* *lections* 3 Ser. 5.41: Brightening the covenant chain. **1790** Pickering *Life* 2.465: The chain of friendship is made bright. **1794** Jay *Correspondence* 4.35: It would have given me pleasure to have called upon you, and (to use an Indian expression) have *brightened the chain*. DA chain 4(2), 4b.(1).

C111   Golden **Chalices** and wooden priests

1713 Sewall *Diary* 2.382: Seeing the former decay'd Building is consum'd, and a better built in the room, Let us pray, May that Proverb, "Golden Chalices and Wooden Priests," never be transfer'd to the Civil order. NED Chalice 2γ, quote 1528.

C112   As white as **Chalk**

1707 Sewall *Diary* 2.203: All are as white as chalk. **1748** Eliot *Essays* 45. **1774** Batram *Report* 137. **1807** Gass *Journal* 92. Barbour 32; Whiting C133.

C113   **Chalk** and cheese

1750 AHamilton in *MHM* 59(1964) 212: The one gentleman, as the proverb goes, talked of chalk and the other of cheese. **1801** *Farmers' Museum* 102: To know the odds 'twixt cheese and chalk. **1811** Wirt *Letters* 1.322: There is no more doubt of your confirmation than — chalk's like cheese. *Oxford* 113; Whiting C134.

C114   The **Chameleon** lives on air

1680 Randolph *Letters* 3.63: You must, Camelion-like, live on the aire. **1731** Belcher *Papers* 1.15: For I think it cannot be judged just . . . that I must live on air. **1780** HKnox in *Heath Papers* 3.40-1: They think . . . that we have the properties of the camelion, and can subsist on air. **1780** *Washington *Writings* 20.459: It would be well for the Troops, if like Chameleons, they could live upon Air. **1822** Freneau *Last Poems* 94: He had been doom'd at *Beaurepaire* Camelion-like to feed on air. **1822** Wirt *Letters* 2.146: I must address a prayer to Jupiter to change my family into chameleons. **1827** Jones *Sketches* 2.185: The fact that they will live a long time without nourishment, has given rise to the story that "they eat the air for food." *Oxford* 474; Tilley M226; Whiting C135. See **W205**.

C115 To change like a **Chameleon**

1643 FWilliams in *Winthrop Papers(A)* 4.376: If I should camelion licke, change my selfe to every object, I might well be censured for A timorist. **1652** Bradford *Dialogue* 42: Comonly, camelion-like, they chang their hue with the nearest object. **1773** Trumbull *Satiric Poems* 81: Chamaeleons thus, whose colours airy As often as Coquettes can vary. **1779** Chipman *Writings* 30: The color changeable like a chameleon, but not like them stuffed with air. **1806** *Emerald* 1.193: He can live by mere *taste of air*. A Cameleon, that would change color, but from want of shame. **1806** Hitchcock *Works* 131: Chameleon-like, their size and colour changes, **1812** *Social* 151: The Camelion is an animal proverbial for the quality of changing its colour. **1816** Paulding *Letters(I)* 1.34: The changes which succeed each other, in this camelion country. *Oxford* 114; Whiting C135, 137.

C116 **Change** of Devils is blithesome

1779 Hutchinson *Diary* 2.252: The Scotch proverb, change of Devils is blithesome. [H. says that Franklin uses this of Morris and Denny in "the History of Pennyslyvania."] Hislop 71: Change o' deils is lightsome.

C117 **Character** (reputation) is dearer than life

1709 JBridger in *Baxter Manuscripts* 9.270: Reputation is Eaquall wth life. **1777** ESayer in *Baxter Manuscripts* 15.24: His Character (which to a man of the least Sensibility is dearer than Life). **1779** PRevere in *Baxter Manuscripts* 17.215: What is more dearer to me than life; my character. Cf. *Oxford* 52; Tilley H576.

C118 As black as **Charcoal**

1773 *New York Journal* in *Newspaper Extracts(I)* 9.529: Black as charcoal. **1814** Palmer *Diary* 238: And beat your hides as black as charcoal. **1822** Watterston *Winter* 56. See **C218.**

C119 As cold as **Charity**

1612 Strachey *Historie* 20: A charity more cold. **1692** TFootman in *Baxter Manuscripts* 5.381: Charritye also grone Cold. **1737**

Ames *Almanacs* 112: As Cold as Charity. **1768** CChauncy in Stiles *Itineraries* 446: His charity as cold as death. **1774** SDeane in Webb *Correspondence* 1.31: The hand of charity was seldom very warm. **1774** Fithian *Journal and Letters* 84: Mr. Smith gave us a Sermon 14 Minutes long on Charite—But poor Fellow he seem'd Cold as his Subject. **1776** Curwen *Journal and Letters* 59: [They] will find to their cost the hand of charity very cold. **1781** EHazard in *Belknap Papers* 1.113: The cold hand of charity will be their principal dependence. **1803** Wirt *Letters* 1.96: My death would throw my wife and children on the charity of a cold and selfish world. *Oxford* 115; Whiting C152.

C120 **Charity** begins at home

1628 THawes in *Winthrop Papers(A)* 1.379: Your self [JWinthrop] sayth we must follow the old, and good Rule Charity must begin at home. **1693** CRodes in *VHM* 34.363: Charity begins at whome. **1697** Chalkley *God's Great Love* 345: One that is covetous may say, that Charity begins at Home. **1710** Mather *Bonifacius* 43: The *Charity* we are upon, why should it not *Begin at Home?* **1712** *Wyllys Papers* 373. **1732** Byrd *Progress* 350. **1776** Carter *Diary* 2.991. **1780** JBrown in *W&MCQ* 9(1900) 77: I am afraid that Charity will begin at home. **1788** *Politician* 24. **1789** Bentley *Diary* 1.134. **1794** *Echo* 121. **1794** Rowson *Charlotte* 2.91. **1796** Barton *Disappointment* 82. **1796** Cobbett *Porcupine* 3.298: says the old proverb. **1803** Davis *Travels* 37. **1803** *Port Folio* 3.92. **1805** Brackenridge *Modern* 474. **1806** Fraser *Letters and Journal* 238: Charity ought to begin at home. **1806** Hitchcock *Works* 114: Employ their charity at home. **1808** *Emerald* NS 1.433: Charity should begin at home. **1809** Weems *Letters* 2.397: Why not let some of your Charity begin at home? *Marion* 96. **1811** Adams *Writings* 4.137: But it is not like their charity. It never begins at home. **1811** Murphey *Papers* 1.51: As charity ought to begin at home, so ought benevolence. **1812** Dow *Journal* 419: One seeks to take care of himself only, as charity is said to begin at home. **1812** CANorton in Knopf *War of 1812* 3.38: I have the charity to believe, that he is governed by a patriotic principle, which begins at home. **1813** Paulding *Lay* 20-1: Which lovely charity derides, Save, that which vulgar bosoms wins, That which at home with self begins. **1816** Adams *Writings* 6.125: By bringing motives of charity closer home. **1816** *Port Folio* 4NS 1.297: "Charity" is seen not only "beginning," but too often ending at "home." **1818** Royall *Letters* 161. **1819** Adams *Memoirs* 4.330: Some [motives] highly honorable and generous, others more partaking of those virtues that begin at home. **1822** Austin *Papers* 1.477. Barbour 32; *Oxford* 115; Whiting C153.

C121 **Charity** covers a multitude of sins

c1645 JCotton in Williams *Writings* 2.24: Love covereth a multitude of offences, **1654** 6.265: Love covereth a multitude of sins. **c1705** Byrd *Another Secret Diary* 211: This covers more failings than charity. **1723** *New-England Courant* 78(1.1): Charity covers a multitude of Sins. **1744** Franklin *PR* 2.401: While Money, like Charity, covers all Crimes. **1754** Parkman *Diary* 76, 121. **1767** JArmstrong in *Letters to Washington* 3.305: It [dress] cover'd a multitude of Sins. **1771** Adams(S) *Writings* 2.305: His foibles are now "buried under the mantle of charity." **1777** Cresswell *Journal* 249: O! Matrimony . . . thou coverest more female frailities than charity does sins. **1777** Munford *Patriots* 486: hides. **1783** AMacaulay in *W&MCQ* 11(1903) 188. **1786** JQAdams in Smith *Journal and Correspondence* 2(1) 105: £20,000 sterling will cover almost as great a number of faults as charity. **1789** *Massachusetts Centinel* in Buckingham *Specimens* 2.52: Though *charity* cover a sin, now and then. **1789** Morris *Diary* 1.159: To be an *Étranger* (like charity) covers a Multitude of Sins. **1794** Adams *Writings* 1.191: *Faction* covers at least as great a multitude of sins as *charity*. **1803** Austin *Constitutional* 76, 306: hides. **1810** Adams *Lectures* 1.247. **1811** *Port Folio* 2NS 5.53. **1814** Alden *Epitaphs* 3.30. **1816** *Port Folio* 4NS 2.32. **1818** Bentley *Diary* 4.525: Thus ended this humble experiment of pride under the Mask of charity. **1826** Duane *Colombia* 221. *Oxford* 115; TW 230: Love (5); Whiting C155.

C122 Between **Charlestown** and hell is one thin sheet of paper

1777 EHazard in *VHM* 62(1954) 423: The Chevalier de la Roche lodged with us at Sumner's. He described the *Heat* of Charlestown by saying, "between Sharlestown & Hell is no more as one Sheet Papier, & dat very tin too." Whiting *Devil* 229(53).

C123 **Charley** on the spot

1805 *Massachusetts Spy* in Thornton *Glossary* 1.162, 3.68: And I will be upon the spot, As punctual as "Charley." TW 65. Cf. DA Johnny 7(8).

C124 To act (*etc.*) like a **Charm**

1787 *American Museum* 1.34: It acted like a charm. **1803** *Port Folio* 3.141: They operated like a charm. **1812** Stoddard *Sketches* 84: They operate like a charm. **1817** Randolph(J) *Letters* 199. **1819** Baldwin *Letters* 318. **1820** Simpson *Journal* 89: A little rum . . . operates like a charm among the Crees. **1839**: Hone *Diary* 1.444: The nomination of Gen. Harrison works like a charm among the Whigs. **1851** Cooper *Letters* 6.271: The tonic . . . works like a charm. TW 65(1).

C125 To behave (acquit) to a **Charm**

1781 EPendleton in Madison *Papers* 2.307: It is said that . . . the Militia behaved to a Charm. **1787** Shippen *Journal* 249: Nancy . . . acquitted herself to a charm. TW 65(2).

C126 To love the **Chase,** but scorn the prey

1773 Trumbull *Satiric Poems* 90: She lov'd the chace, but scorn'd the prey, And fish'd for hearts to throw away.

C127 A wild-goose **Chase**

1647 Ward *Simple Cobler* 14: It is a most toylsome task to runne the wild-goose chase after a well breath'd opinionist. **a1731** Cook *Bacon* 314: Oblig'd the Wild-Goose Chase to quit. **1764** CCarroll in *MHM* 12(1917) 169. **1769** *Johnson Papers* 6.784: It was a foolish wild goose scheme. **1770** Carter *Diary* 1.462. **1775** Harrower *Journal* 97: I was informed you intended to send me on a wild Goose hunting by giving me a Draught on another. **1776** *Blockheads* 16. **1777** Huntington *Papers* 74: We have Don nothing but ben on the Goos Chase all this Summer. **1777** *St. Clair Papers* 1.382. **1778** ABillings in *Clinton Papers* 2.677. **1779** JBeatty in Webb *Correspondence* 2.209. **1780** Gordon *Letters* 444. **a1788** Jones *History* 1.351: Instead of his wild-goose expedition to the head of the Elk. **1789** *Columbian Magazine* 3.425. **1793** Ingraham *Journal* 242-3. **1794** DAllison in *Blount Papers* 2.399. **1799** SJohnston in Iredell *Correspondence* 2.544: Buonaparte's wild-goose expedition. **1801** *Farmers' Museum* 64. **1809** Irving *History* 1.57: It was doubtless some philosophical wild goose chase. **1810** Taggart *Letters* 346, **1812** 382. **1822** Robertson *Letters* 190. **1822** Watterston *Winter* 24, 159. **1832** Ames *Nautical* 133: A wild goose chase through a dozen volumes of the Spectator. *Oxford* 889; TW 65(2).

C128   Great Cheats will flourish, *etc.*

1797 Tyler *Prose* 303: It is said in a pair of verses I read when I was a boy . . . A little knavery is a dangerous thing, Great Cheats will flourish, while the small ones swing. *Oxford* 335: Thieves; Tilley T119; Whiting T68, 71. See **R102.**

C129   Two Cheats make an even bargain

1748 *Word* in *Colonial Currency* 4.370: That *unjust* Proverb, "Two Cheats is an even Bargain." **1795** *Tablet* 21: Two cheats make an even bargain. **1801** *Port Folio* 1.325: Two cheats make an even bargain.

C130   Cheating never thrives

1805 Parkinson *Tour* 506: It is a common saying in England, that "Cheating never thrives:" but, in America, with honest trading you cannot succeed. Barbour 33: Cheater; Lean 2.38.

C131   Cheek by jowl

1654 Johnson *Wonder-Working* 119*: Whose first foundation was laid cheke by joule with the most glorious . . . truth. **1676** Williams *Writings* 5.226: He may be (and the Quakers are) cheek by joll with him, 261. **1694** *Connecticut Vindicated* 118: Why thus Cheek by Jole with the Soveraign power? **1740** Belcher *Papers* 2.336: The Assemblies will set jig by jole, at Salisbury & Hampton. **1770** Habersham *Letters* 88: Till

you meet Tete a Tete or if you like English better, Check by Jowl. **1776** Curwen *Journal* 1.253. **1780** *Royal Gazette* in *Newspaper Extracts(II)* 5.104: They were found in the night, horizontal, Cheek by Jowl. **1782** Trumbull *Satiric Poems* 174. **c1790** Brackenridge *Gazette* 106. **1798** Cobbett *Porcupine* 8.166. **1807** *Weekly* 1.209. **1824** *Tales* 2.26. **1825** Neal *American Writers* 149: Don't . . . put . . . all your qualifications, cheek by jowl, into the same period. **1830** Ames *Mariner's* 98: Cheek by jowl with a horse on one side and a church steeple on the other, **1832** *Nautical* 199: A sleigh load of turkies cheek by jowl. NED Cheek 5; *Oxford* 117; Whiting C171.

C132   As plenty as Cherries

1827 Cooper *Letters* 1.202: Ducs were as plenty as cherries in June. Cf. Whiting C182.

C133   As red as a Cherry

1714 Taylor *Poems* 303: Thy Cherry Cheeks sende Charms out to Loves Coast. **1773** Trumbull *Satiric Poems* 79: With lips of rose and cheeks of cherry. **1805** *Port Folio* 5.336: Her cheeks . . . are as red as a cherry. Barbour 33(1); *Oxford* 667-8; Whiting C180.

C134   Not to care a Chew of tobacco

1804 Irving *Journals* 1.151: You can only take my life & that I don't care a chew of tobacco for.

C135   As loving as two Chicks

1801 Nichols *Jefferson* 4: I seed them go arm in arm, as loving as two chicks. Cf. *Oxford* 491; Tilley C286.

C136   To have neither Chick nor child

1705 Ingles *Reply* 155: He has neither chick nor child. **1734** Belcher *Papers* 2.169: Mr Pemberton has neither chick nor child in the world. **1766** JBoucher in *MHM* 7(1912) 301. **1801** Story *Shop* 85. TW 67.

C137   To be no Chicken

1790 Morris *Diary* 1.366: His Father being 71 and his Mother no chicken. **1802** Ames *Letters* 1.301: You are no chicken, and ought not to calculate on a very long period of drudgery at the bar. Barbour 33(5); *Oxford* 118(b).

C138 To count one's **Chickens** before they are hatched

1764 *Paxton Papers* 113: I'm afraid you count your Chickens before they are hatch'd. **1770** Carter *Diary* 1.390: To be sure these Chickens were reckoned before they hatched. **1775** DCobb in *Bingham's Maine* 1.403. **1777** Curwen *Journal* 1.292: [They] are, in our country language, reckoning their chickens before they are hatched. **1801** Jefferson *Family Letters* 191. **1805** Sewall *Parody* 47: Even the chicken reckoning damsel, with her basket of eggs pregnant with her future fortune, so renowned, and proverbial for ages, shrinks in thy presence. **1809** Weems *Marion* 98. **1811** EDillard in *Ruffin Papers* 1.132: It may be well not to "count the chickens before the eggs are hatched." **1818** Cobbett *Year's* 303. **1821** Royall *Letters* 220. **1830** Paulding *Letters* (*II*) 110. **1834** Baldwin *Diary* 255: He had been counting his chickens too soon. **1856** Paulding *Letters*(*II*) 569: And giving vitality to the chicken before it is hatched. Barbour 33(2); *Oxford* 147; TW 67(3). See **B81.**

C139 When **Chickens** are pecking at one another, *etc.*

1690 *Further Quaeries* in *Andros Tracts* 1.208: Whether when Chickens are pecking at one another, the *Kite* will not see it then a time to carry them both away.

C140 As feeble as a **Child**

1817 Pintard *Letters* 1.59: He is as feeble as a child. Cf. TW 67(9).

C141 As helpless as a **Child,** *etc.*

1733 JAdams in *Letters from Hudson Bay* 181: As helpless as a child. **1741** Hempstead *Diary* 372: He was as a new born Babe, **1744** 429: Lying in ye bed helpless as a new born Babe. **1769** Lloyd *Papers* 2.719: Almost the whole time as Helpless as an Infant. TW 12(4), 67(5), 199(2).

C142 As innocent (*etc.*) as a Child (*etc.*) unborn

1664 *Wyllys Papers* 151: I am as Innocent as

the childe unborn. **1683** JWhiting in *Mather Papers* 471: As faultles therein as the child unborne. **1771** Adams *Legal Papers* 1.151: He was innocent . . . as the Child in the Womb. **1777** Washington *Writings* 9.95: I know no more than the Child unborn. **1781** Parsons *Life* 322: I know no more than a child yet unborn. **1792** Brackenridge *Modern* 33: I am innocent as the child unborn, 144. **1792** WHeth in Hamilton *Papers* 13.161: [They] were as innocent as children of the transaction. **1801** Weems *Letters* 2.197: I am just as innocent of all this as the Babe of Bethlehem. **1804** Brackenridge *Modern* 419: I am innocent of letters as the child unborn. **1807** LMartin in American Antiquarian Society *Proceedings* NS 29 (1919) 123: Burr is as innocent . . . as the child unborn. **1822** Watterston *Winter* 138: I had na mair intention till do it than the bairn unborn. **1831** Jackson *Correspondence* 4.337: Van Buren . . . is as innocent as a babe, 349, **1833** 5.17: As innocent as a child. *Oxford* 404; TW 12(5), 67(6).

C143 As sober as a new born **Child**

1744 *Georgia Records* 24.341: Parker was as sober as a New Born Child.

C144 Better die a **Child** at four, *etc.*

1777 AHutchinson in *Collections of the Vermont Historical Society* 1 (1870) 79: Better die a child at four, Than live and die so at four score.

C145 A burnt **Child** dreads the fire

1755 *Johnson Papers* 1.812: A Burnt child dreads the Fire. **1775** Adams *Works* 9.367, 396. **1775** Seabury *Letters* 160: It may do them good: it may make them dread the fire hereafter; for, like children, they seem incapable of learning from *any* experience but *their own*. **1775** CWebb in *Naval Documents* 1.922. **1777** Carter *Diary* 2.1106. **1781** Burr *Memoirs* 1.234: If you have fears about *brat* [a child], I have none. He will never burn himself but once [in part, at least, literal]. **1787** Adams(A) *Letters* 343: In the general flames which threaten Europe, I hope and pray our own country may have wisdom sufficient to keep herself out of the fire. I am sure she has been a sufficiently burnt child. **1787** Washington *Writings* 29.165. **1815** STaggart in Cutler *Life* 2.334. **1815** Waterhouse *Journal* 63. **1816** JAdams in *Adams-Jefferson Letters* 2.461. **1817** Adams *Memoirs* 3.486. **1844** AKendall in Jackson *Correspondence* 6.316. Barbour 33(1); *Oxford* 92; Whiting C201.

C146 A **Child** must first creep and then go (*varied*)

1733 Belcher *Papers* 1.517: You must first creep, then go, & then run. **1788** Burroughs *Memoirs* 185: You are sensible "you must creep" again "before you can go." **1819** *Musings* 48: Teach but the child to creep, he soon will go. *Oxford* 120: Children; Whiting C202.

C147 A **Child** must not play with a razor

1795 Cobbett *Porcupine* 2.75: When I see you flourishing with a metaphor, I feel as much anxiety as I do when I see a child playing with a razor. *Oxford* 120, 796; Tilley S1050. See **F234.**

C148 Happy is the **Child** whose father goes to the Devil

1738 WDouglass *Essay* in *Colonial Currency* 3.234: *Happy is the Child whose Father goes to the Devil. Oxford* 352; Tilley C305.

C149 It is a wise **Child** that knows his own father

1723 *New-England Courant* 94(1.2): He is always counted *a wise child that knows his own Father;* But in this Case he is *a wise Father that knows his own child.* **1783** AMacaulay in *W&MCQ* 11(1902) 182: "He is my Father," says a Man who handed me the Grog; "You are a wise child." **1788** *Politician* 23: It's a wise son knows his own father, as the old saying is. **1795** Murdock *Triumphs* 65: "What do mine eyes behold? Art thou my son Jacob?" "I am not quite wise enough . . . to answer that question." Barbour 34(6); *Oxford* 899; TW 68(15).

C150 Late **Children,** early orphans

1742 Franklin *PR* 2.334: Late Children, early Orphans, **1768** *Papers* 15.184: *Late Children,* says the Spanish Proverb, *are early Orphans. Oxford* 443; Tilley C310.

C151 To be **Child's** (boy's) play

1766 JParker in Franklin *Papers* 13.491: But as Children's Play to that which for some Time afflicts me. **1779** JBeatty in *Clinton Papers* 5.349: It will . . . appear . . . like children's play in the Eyes of the Enemy. **1804** SDecatur in *Barbary Wars* 4.346: I find hand to hand is not childs play, 'tis kill or be killed. a**1811** Henry *Account* 88: This victory in huzzaing . . . was boy's play. **1813** TBenton in Jackson *Correspondence* 1.318: It was our intention, if driven to our arms, to have no childsplay. **1816** Adams *Writings* 6.118: All is children's play. Whiting C200, 221.

C152 To be twice a **Child** (second childhood, *etc.*)

1650 Bradstreet *Works* 161: But now *Bis pueri senes,* is too true. **1694** Scottow *Narrative* 282: The Delyrious dotage of Bis Puerile and Superannuated Brains. **1702** Mather *Magnalia* 1.365: At those years wherein men use to be *twice children,* 454: He never became "twice a child." **1754** Smith *Works* 1¹. 10: Our old age . . . is a second childhood, **1768** 2.212: Old Age . . . the weak Drivelings of a second Childhood. **1774** Wendell *Letters* 256: Once a man and twice a child. **1776** CLee in Sparks *Correspondence* 1.160: They are in their second childhood. **1787** Freneau *Prose* 88: The world would never think the worse of him for having lived to be only "once a man, not twice a child." **1790** Asbury *Letters* 3.82: They betray nothing of second childhood. **1795** Bentley *Diary* 2.169: Her rational faculties . . . had sunk into a second childhood. **1799** Adams *New Letters* 215: I have heard of once a Man & twice a child, and the Ladies caps are an exact coppy of the Baby caps. **1807** Bentley *Diary* 3.324: His gross food & diminished exercise was attended with a second childhood. **1807** Janson *Stranger* 51: Whalley was then in a state of second childhood. **1808** Bentley *Diary* 3.391: A man in his second childhood. **1809** Boudinot *Journey* 7: Reduced to a second Childhood. **1810** Asbury *Journal* 2.629: Sunk to second childhood. **1813** *Letters* 3.470: If the thought of visiting Europe is thought to be in the birth of a second childhood. **1813** Rush *Letters* 2.1188: The babblings of a second childhood. **1816** Paulding *Letters(I)* 1.7: Do not all nations relapse into a sort of second childhood? *Oxford* 591; TW 68; Whiting M117.

C153 To cry like a **Child**

1769 *Johnson Papers* 6.566: Tho' strictly Sober he Cryed like a Child. TW 68(20).

C154 **Children** are riches

1750 RTilghman in *MHM* 33(1938) 167: If Children are riches you see I shall be very wealthy. *Oxford* 120; Tilley C331.

C155 The **Children** of good men are as bad as others

a1794 Witherspoon *Works* 4.27: I know not a common saying either more false or pernicious, than "that the children of good men are as bad as others." Cf. *Oxford* 900; TW 94; Tilley M421, 611; Whiting C230.

C156 **Children** should be seen and not heard

1788 Adams *Diary* 425: The daughters sat like just so many young misses whose mamma had told them that little girls must be seen and not heard, **1820** *Memoirs* 5.165: My dear mother's constant lesson in childhood, that children in company should be seen and not heard. Barbour 33(3); *Oxford* 120; Whiting M11.

C157 **Children** tell the truth

1785 Gordon *Letters* 511: We know from the proverb that children speak *true*, not being versed in the arts of deceit. **1788** Wingate *Letters* 14: If the old saying is true that children tell the truth, some of the truth is quite news to me. Barbour 33(2); *Oxford* 119; Whiting C229. See **F224.**

C158 As black as a (Pluto's) **Chimney**

1705 Ingles *Reply* 24: They make us as black as Pluto's Chimney. **1756** RDemere in McDowell *Documents* 2.267: As black as the Chimney. Whiting *NC* 384(1).

C159 As useless as a **Chimney** in summer

1758 Franklin *Papers* 8.197: And render improper, for the future, the old saying, *as useless as a chimney in summer.*

C160 It is easier to build two **Chimneys,** *etc.*

1758 Franklin *PR* 7.78: 'Tis easier to build two Chimneys, than maintain one in Fuel, **1758** *WW* 349. **1770** Ames *Almanacs* 413: Tis easier to build two chimnies than to keep one in fewel. *Oxford* 89; Tilley C347.

C161 A little **Chimney** is soon fired

a1700 Hubbard *New England* 111: A little chimney is soon fired, so was the Plymouth captain. Cf. TW 293(2); Whiting P321.

C162 To cock up one's **Chin**

1718 TLechmere in *Winthrop Papers(B)* 6.388: Doct^r Noyes has cocked up his chinn since y^e departure of his wife. Cf. NED Cock $v^1$3.

C163 To hold up by the **Chin**

1687 Randolph *Letters* 6.228: Every man can swim when held up by the head. **1689** *Appeal* in *Andros Tracts* 3.196: Who clapt these Knaves on the Back and held them by the Chin in these Rogueries? Who went Snips with them? NED Chin 1d; *Oxford* 794-5; Whiting C232.

C164 As dry as a **Chip**

1705 Taylor *Poems* 195: But I, as dry, as is a Chip. Barbour 34(2); TW 68(1).

C165 A **Chip** of the old block

1682 J. W. *Letter* 5: There was one H——n L——tt, a true Chip of the old Block. **1764** *Johnson Papers* 11.473: He is now Sending a Son of his . . . (a *Chip* of the old Block). **1782** *Belknap Papers* 1.123. **1795** Cobbett *Porcupine* 2.12: A right chip of the Old "Block," as *Poor Richard* says. **1799** Adams *Writings* 2.402: The late decree about the *rôle d'équipage* is a chip of the same block. **1801** Story *Shop* 94: Since Time's but a chip from Eternity's block. **1806** *Weekly* 1.85: A *genuine* chip of a *genuine* block. **1808** WCunningham in *Adams-Cunningham Letters* 59: In the old block I may see the nature of the chip. **1814** Wirt *Bachelor* 173. **1832** Ames *Nautical* 168: Good for nothing chips of the old block. **1845** Paulding *Letters(II)* 398. **1848** Cooper *Letters* 5.292. Barbour 34(1); *Oxford* 121; TW 69(2).

C166 Like a **Chip** in wort, *etc.*

1697 Calef *More Wonders* 279: At these trials some of the jury made inquiry of the court, what account they ought to make of the spectre evidence; and received for answer, *As much as of chips in wort.* **1746** *Georgia Records* 25.45: Mr Spencer was Mr Spencer still, as a chip in Broth. **1785** Washington *Writings* 28.372-3: Precedents . . . are dangerous things . . .: they may indeed assume the garb of plausibility and moderation, and are generally spoken of by the movers as a *chip in the porridge* (to avoid giving alarm). **1802** Chester *Federalism* 9: You have been chips in porridge, neither hot nor cold, 18: My defence of *John Adams* will be chips and porridges. *Oxford* 121; Tilley C353.

C167 To knock the **Chip** off one's shoulder

1816 Paulding *Letters(I)* 2.250: The boyish custom of knocking a chip off the shoulder. Barbour 34(5); TW 69(4).

C168 To value no more than **Chips**

1811 Fletcher *Letters* 37: I value the dollars no more than chips. NED Chip *sb.*[1] 5, 8. Cf. Whiting C237.

C169 A **Choke-pear**

1763 Laurens *Papers* 3.295: This . . . prov'd to him . . . a real "Choak Pear" almost to suffocation. NED Choke-pear 2; Whiting C242: plum.

C170 Of the first **Chop**

1810 Dwight *Journey* 49: He thinks himself a gentlemen of the *first chop*. **1811** Bentley *Diary* 4.54: [He] has since become a fanatic of the first chop. **1816** Paulding *Letters(I)* 2.199: Who was to use a mercantile phrase, *first chop* in our city. She went to England, expecting to be first chop there too. TW 69(1).

C171 To **Chop** and change

1742 Belcher *Papers* 2.434: It cannot be consistent with the King's honour . . . to chop & change so quick. **1769** CCarroll in *MHM* 12(1917) 285: They . . . occassion many chops & changes. **1781** JLovell in *Adams FC* 4.83: If you wish to chip and change. **1800** Cobbett *Porcupine* 11.252:

Who . . . had chopped and changed from science to science. *Oxford* 122; Whiting C242.

C172 As obstinate as a **Christian**

1652 Williams *Writings* 4.90: Hence came that hellish *Proverb*, That nothing was more *obstinate* then a *Christian*.

C173 It takes six **Christians** to cheat a Jew, *etc.*

1804 Irving *Journals* 1.143: It is a saying in Italy that "It takes six Christians to cheat a Jew and six Jews to cheat a genoese but a genoese Jew is a match for the d——l himself." Cf. Lean 1.309.

C174 As cold as **Christmas**

1766 Bowen *Journals* 1.149: Cold as Christmas, **1779** 2.547 [both entries are for December 25]. Lean 1.816; Svartengren 315.

C175 **Christmas** is coming

1803 Davis *Travels* 399: Coming! you *Jonas!* So is Christmas coming. Barbour 34-5; *Oxford* 136; Whiting *NC* 384(2).

C176 A green **Christmas** makes a fat churchyard

1794 Drinker *Journal* 254: A green Christmas it is but I trust it does not follow that we shall have fat churchyards. Barbour 34(1); *Oxford* 337; TW 69(3).

C177 Till **Christmas**

1781 Pickering *Life* 1.305: They might fire till Christmas without materially lessening the enemy's force.

C178 As steady as a **Church**

1820 *Port Folio* 4NS 9.515: *She* fuit steady as a Church. Svartengren 60. Cf. TW 70(3).

C179 As stiff as a **Church**

1789 Jefferson *Papers* 15.560: Our vessel was . . . stiff as a church. **1803** Davis *Travels* 410: She [a ship] was . . . stiff as a church.

C180 The nearer the **Church**, the farther from God

1803 Davis *Travels* 158: The proverb, that *the nearer the church, the further from heaven.* Barbour 35; *Oxford* 557; Whiting C251.

C181 As poor as a **Church** mouse

1692 Randolph *Letters* 7.434: Plymouth as poore as a Church mouse. **1722** Franklin *Papers* 1.17: Many of them . . . liv'd as poor as Church Mice. **1731** Winslow *Broadside* 163: Thus Father Abbey left his Spouse, As rich as Church or College Mouse. **1775** SWard in Ward *Correspondence* 128. **1792** Brackenridge *Modern* 148: But be poor as a church mouse, or a rat. **1793** Freneau *Prose* 306: Time has been when ye were nearly allied to church-mice, **?1798** *Poems* 3.212: Turned out as poor as Christ-church rat. **c1800** Dennie *Lay Preacher* 147: As lank and lean as my old tabby cat, who has had nothing to eat but church-mice for a year. **1801** Jefferson *Family Letters* 202: Mrs. Madison left us two days ago to commence house keeping, so that Capt. Lewis and myself are like two mice in a church. **1822** Watterston *Winter* 21. Barbour 125(3); *Oxford* 638; TW 70. See **R21**.

C182 As big as a **Church** steeple

1804 Brackenridge *Modern* 354: Deir foutres and parbleus, would make a book, as big as a church steeple.

C183 As slow as **Church-work**

1777 Gordon *Letters* 232: The repairs go on as slow as tho' it was church work. NED Church-work; *Oxford* 123; Tilley C383. See **P22**.

C184 Claw a **Churl** by the breech and he will shit in your fist

1674 Josselyn *Account* 122-3: Claw a churl by the britch and he will shit in your fist. Tilley C386; Whiting C264. See **J15**.

C185 He that drinks his **Cider** alone, *etc.*

1744 Franklin *PR* 2.395: He that drinks his Cyder alone, let him catch his Horse alone.

C186 Never praise your **Cider**, horse or bedfellow

1736 Franklin *PR* 2.138: Never praise your Cyder, Horse or Bedfellow. *Oxford* 127; Tilley W345.

C187 To be a **Cipher** (*varied*)

1677 Hubbard *Indian* 2.248: Cyphers standing alone and not joyned with others, as some have said, do not increase the Number. **1692** NSaltonstall in *Saltonstall Papers* 1.207-8: If in any Case there wants a Cypher to be added to your number (as soon as I can) you shall have me. **1714** WWinthrop in *Winthrop Papers*(B) 6.282: As I desired no place . . . which would put me to charg to stand as a cipher. **1739** *Georgia Records* 22².5: Most of 'em are no better than Cyphers. **1755** WLithgow in *Baxter Manuscripts* 12.373: [They] has not been of any [more] Service sence I have been Conserned at yᵉ above Fort then four siphores. **1756** Franklin *Papers* 6.389: But how would it surprize you.to know that they are no better than Cyphers. **1759** INorris in Franklin *Papers* 8.228: He appears among us as A Cypher of no Importance. **1775** Willard *Letters* 245: The Governor . . . is a mere cypher. **1803** Ellicott *Journal* 162: He was determined not to be made a cypher of, and would rule the district with a rod of iron. **1807** Janson *Stranger* 20-1: Her husband was a mere cypher in the house. **a1814** Dow *Journal* 412: And sets him aside as a mere cypher. *Oxford* 124; Whiting C273.

C188 **Circumstances** alter cases

1776 Heath *Memoirs* 92: Our General reflected for a moment, that as circumstances alter cases. **1777** JA in *Adams FC* 2.228: But Circumstances since may have altered Cases. **1780** Baldwin *Life and Letters* 60: It is a well known Maxim. **1783** Pickman *Letters* 130. **1784** *Deane Brothers Papers* 202: Men and manners are always changing with the times & circumstances. **1785** *Beekman Papers* 3.1001. **1791** Rush *Letters* 1.601: Circumstances I know should alter cases. **1800** Gadsden *Writings* 295: *In different circumstances a different conduct is necessary.* **1815** Humphreys *Yankey* 45: Circumstances alter manners. Barbour 35; *Oxford* 124; TW 70(1). See **C51**.

C189 Small **Circumstances** produce great events

1774 JWentworth in *Belknap Papers* 3.57: Small circumstances often produce great events, or lead to them. **1805** WTatham in *W&MCQ* 2S 16(1926) 178: Trivial circumstances sometimes produce great ends. See **C99, E77, F128.**

C190   A **City** on a hill cannot be hid

1689 Bulkeley *People's Right* 66: *A Citty set on a Hill cannot be hid,* and these things cannot *be done* in a Corner. **1782** Alden *Epitaphs* 1.116: *A city that is set upon a hill cannot be hid,* **1814** 3.140, 4.49. Whiting C275.

C191   As cold as **Clay**

1791 Maclay *Journal* 368: When we, cold as clay. **1801** *Farmers' Museum* 77: Their lasses are colder than clay. *Oxford* 132; Whiting C281.

C191a   **Clay-cold**

1769 JBoucher in *MHM* 8(1913) 43: His Clay-cold Hand. **1769** Wheatley *Poems* 65: Behold him in his Clay-cold bed. **1770** Winslow *Broadside* 47: He kissed her Clay Lips so sweet, When they were almost cold with Death. **1782** Freneau *Poems* 2.178: Peace to your verse!—we do not rob the dead, The clay-cold offspring of a brazen head. a**1786** Ladd *Remains* 106: Clay-cold dust. **1789** Brown *Power* 1.10: Thy clay cold carcase. **1791** Maclay *Journal* 397: And clay-cold was the conduct of the President. **1801** *Farmers' Museum* 231: I mark each *clay-cold obit* down. **1803** Davis *Travels* 29: The clay-cold ground. **1809** Paine *Works* 417: The clay-cold cemetery of her honours. NED Clay-cold; Whiting *Ballads* 26-7.

C192   To wet one's **Clay**

1808 *Port Folio* NS 5.112: And when he thus has wet his clay. **1819** Peirce *Rebelliad* 61: Let's take a glass of Holland Gin, By way of moistening our clay. TW 71(2). See **E139, W134.**

C193   **Cleanliness** is allied to godliness

1806 *Monthly Anthology* 3.578: A gentleman once told me, that cleanliness was nearly allied to godliness. This is rather bold. Barbour 35; *Oxford* 125; TW 71. See **D332.**

C194   A **Clew** through a labyrinth

1786 PVan Schaack in Hamilton *Papers* 3.692: You will hit upon a clue to lead us

through the Labyrinth. NED Clew *sb.*[1] 3; *Oxford* 439; Tilley L14.

C195   From **Clew** to earing

1783 Williams *Penrose* 268: He had . . . been shewn large Hills and Clifts split from clew to Earing by them [earthquakes] as we sailors term it. Colcord 54; NED Clew *sb.*[1] 7.

C196   To kiss the **Clink**

1652 Shepard *Hints* 161: Kiss the clinke. *Oxford* 429; Tilley C416.

C197   Let the **Cloak** go after the coat

1639 *Winthrop Papers*(A) 4.100: We have rules to walk by: one is that we should let the Cloke goe after the Coat. a**1700** Hubbard *New England* 111: He . . . had forgot his first lessons . . . to part with the cloak rather than needlessly contend for the coat, though taken away without order.

C198   To make a **Cloak** for something

1689 SDavis in *Baxter Manuscripts* 9.41: Thay to make a Cloke for thaire Removing Doe say thay did wante Amonition. *Oxford* 127; Tilley C419.

C199   As calm as a **Clock**

1770 Adams *Legal Papers* 3.133: He had no stick and was as calm as a Clock. TW 72(1).

C200   As quiet as a **Clock**

1829 Dr. Porter in Beecher *Autobiography* 2.165: Connecticut was quiet as a clock. Lean 2.865; Svartengren 61, 383.

C201   As regular as a **Clock**

1811 Graydon *Memoirs* 11: In his latter days he became a perfect clock in regularity. TW 72(4). See **T149.**

C202   As still as a **Clock**

1783 Williams *Penrose* 57: The day came on as still as a clock.

C203   As true as a **Clock**

1783 Freneau *Poems* 2.197: That, as true as a clock, both early and late. Lean 2.885. Cf. TW 72(4).

C204   To put the **Clock** back

1741 Belcher *Papers* 2.367: This folly of yours has put the clock back with me & with you more than your young head can imagine. *Oxford* 656; TW 72(7).

C205 To move (go) like **Clock-work**

1776 *Washington *Writings* 6.115: An Army formed of good Officers moves like Clock-Work, **1779** 17.255: Troops . . . *ought* and *may* move like clock work, **1799** 37.460: Every thing would move like *clock work.* **1804** Weems *Letters* 2.305: A Gentleman who has everything to go on like Clockwork. **1811** Adams *Writings* 4.34: Everything moves like a piece of clockwork. TW 72(3).

C206 As cold as **Clods**

1771 Adams *D and A* 2.37: Her Hands were as cold as clods. Lean 2.817.

C207 As dull as a **Clod**

1814 JRandolph in Quincy *JQuincy* 350: The Virginia landholder who is not duller than the clod beneath his feet.

C208 To be made out of whole **Cloth**

1771 Adams *D and A* 2.50: He made it . . . out of the whole Cloth. It never existed out of his imagination. TW 72(4).

C209 Fine **Clothes** make fine men

1783 *Washington *Writings* 26.40: Do not conceive that fine Clothes make fine Men any more than fine feathers make fine Birds. Whiting C313. See **C232, F61.**

C210 As dark as a **Cloud**

1784 Freneau *Poems* 2.271: On Sundays their faces were dark as a cloud.

C211 Not every **Cloud** brings rain

1796 Ames *Letters* 1.207: Yet it is not every cloud that brings rain. *Oxford* 128; Tilley C443.

C212 To be in the **Clouds**

a1656 Bradford *History* 2.110: Foulded up in obscuritie, and kepte in the clouds. TBurr in Burr *Correspondence* 268: Little B. is still in the clouds about his books. NED Cloud 9b. Cf. Barbour 36(2); TW 177(16).

C213 To be under a **Cloud**

1720 JGyles in *Baxter Manuscripts* 9.456:

The inhabitants will be Vndar a Darke Cloude. *Oxford* 128; Whiting C318.

C214 As soft as **Clover**

1798 Bentley *Diary* 2.257: The bed to man soft as clover, Father likes it best with mother.

C215 To live (*etc.*) in **Clover**

a1731 Cook *Bacon* 322: Will (who with Friends did live in Clover). **1775** Fithian *Journal* 15: As the Song says, I "live in Clover." **1777** Moore *Diary* 1.430. **1782** Gadsden *Writings* 188. **1791** Ames *Letters* 1.99: You have been sleeping in clover—I do not mean in the barn, neither. **1801** *Farmers' Museum* 109: And in clover you'll wallow, you Dog, till you die. **1806** Weems *Letters* 2.347: And in a few years you may be in clover. **1811** Asbury *Journal* 2.666: The clover of Baltimore circuit. **1812** Bayard *Letters* 24. **1815** Waterhouse *Journal* 60: We now lived in clover compared with our former hard fare and cruel treatment. *Oxford* 129; TW 73. See **P125.**

C216 **Club-law**

1802 Dorr *Letters* 326: Crocker . . . regulated the conduct of his men and Officers by what is called Club Law. **a1820** Biddle *Autobiography* 17: There being no law but club-law, the strongest always took the wood. *Oxford* 129.

C217 An old **Coachman** loves to hear the smack of the whip

1741 Custis *Letters* 92: I . . . am like an old coachman tho I cannot drive love to hear the smack of the whip. Lean 4.133: The old coachman loves the crack of the whip.

C218 As black as a **Coal**

1692 Mather *Wonders* 144: Black Puppy . . . as Black as a Cole. **a1700** Hubbard *New England* 656: They made their faces black as a coal. **1709** Lawson *Voyage* 32. **1723** *New-England Courant* 76(1.1). **1764** Hutchinson *History* 1.174. **1770** Washington *Diaries* 1.409. **1795** *Remarks on the Jacobiniad* 1.32. **1801** Story *Shop* 30. **1803** Harmon *Sixteen Years* 66. **1807** Gass *Journal* 92. **1830** Ames *Mariner's* 144. Barbour 36(1); Whiting C324. See **C118.**

C218a Coal-black

1687 Taylor *Poems* 40: My Coal-black doth thy Milke white hand avoide. **1705** Beverley *History* 159: Hair. **1744** Black *Journal* 1.416: Hair. **1779** Freneau *Poems* 1.237: chariot. **1783** Williams *Penrose* 251: hair. **1794** Tyler *Verse* 29: shoe, **1801**, 112: Than Romeo—coal black Romeo. **1809** Weems *Marion:* hair. **1810** *Port Folio* 2NS 3.87: hair. **1821** Knight *Poems* 2.159: ghosts. **1830** Ames *Mariner's* 107: hair. Whiting C324a.

C219 As hot as a Coal

1801 *Port Folio* 1.264: My heart waxed hot as a coal. *Oxford* 388; Whiting C327.

C220 As red as Coals

1791 Bartram *Travels* 167: His eyes red as burning coals. **1809** Weems *Marion* 108: Cheeks red as fire coals. Whiting C329.

C221 Let him that needs blow the Coal

1750 *Law Papers* 3.423: The old Saying dropps to yᵉ Ground Let him that needs blow yᵉ Coal. *Oxford* 132; Whiting C334.

C222 Punch Coal, cut candle, *etc.*

1745 Franklin *PR* 3.7: Punch-coal, cut candle, and set brand on end, Is neither good house-wife, nor good house-wife's friend. *Oxford* 654; Tilley C461.

C223 To blow (up) the Coals

1742 Stephens *Journal(II)* 2.19: Unless a certain person whom I left with her, thinks himself well employ'd in Blowing up the Coals. **1760** AGarden in *Colden Letters* 5.362: They were spirited on by many . . . who would rather have help'd to blow up the Coals & irritate them to fresh barbarities. **1767** Franklin *Papers* 14.244: That . . . nation would like . . . to . . . blow up the coals between Britain and her colonies. **1771** Chester *Papers* 50: It would be but proper gently to blow the Coals. **1776** Cresswell *Journal* 165: Serve to blow the cole of discord. **1777** WCarmichael in *MHM* 44 (1949) 8: Mutual ill will . . . blow the coals of dissension. **1778** *Heath Papers* 2.267: It may be that those who wish to make a scism at this time may be blowing the coal. **1783** Jones *Letters* 100: [They] are determined to blow the coals of discord. **1822** Adams *Memoirs* 6.49: The main object of the . . . instigation in this affair is to blow the coals. NED Blow 17b, Coal 11. Cf. Whiting C334.

C224 To burn like Coals of fire

1809 Weems *Marion* 212: His eye-balls burning like coals of fire. Whiting C335.

C225 To carry Coals to Newcastle

1679 Fitzhugh *Letters* 67: But relating farther to you would be carrying Coals to new Castle. **1768** Habersham *Letters* 68: [He] asked, if I wanted to carry Coals to New Castle. **1776** JAdams in *Naval Documents* 5.437: It may be Sending Coals to New Castle. **1785** Tilghman *Letters* 13: It was really sending from New Castle for Coals. c**1790** Brackenridge *Gazette* 112, **1792** *Modern* 42: The inventing more, would be like bringing timber to a wood, or coals to Newcastle. **1796** Wayne *Correspondence* 536: trite adage. **1798** *Echo* 160. **1799** *Port Folio* 2NS 7 (1812) 339: To take produce to a glutted market is "like carrying coals to Newcastle." **1805** Brackenridge *Modern* 491: Why carry coal to New-Castle, or timber to the wood? **1813** JAdams in *Adams-Jefferson Letters* 2.378: It would be sending Coal to Newcastle, **1815** 444. **1816** Fidfaddy *Adventures* 64. **1819** *Port Folio* 4NS 8.8: *Ne in sylvam ligna feris*, or, to speak English, we carry no coals to Newcastle. **1823** Jefferson *Writings* 15.439: I am sinning against the adage of carrying coals to Newcastle. **1829** FNash in *Ruffin Papers* 1.472: And it is carrying coals to Newmarket to tell news to a Raleighan. **1830** Ames *Mariner's* 114. Barbour 36(3); *Oxford* 104; TW 74(3). See O52.

C226 To cover (old) Coals

1764 Franklin *Papers* 11.150: And the sudden Flame in which they broke out again, showing that the old Coals were only covered. **1785** AAdams in Jefferson *Papers* 8.179: Whilst the Coals are cover'd the blaize will not burst. Whiting F185.

C227 To haul over the Coals

1776 Lee *Letters* 1.226: If the Tories do not mend their manners, they will shortly be haled over the coals in such a manner as will make this country too hot to hold them. **1788** *Belknap Papers* 2.55: His coadjutors here will be hawled over the coals. **1800** Dorr *Letters* 210. **1806** Fessenden *Modern Philosopher* 121: For which we had him o'er the coals. **1838** Paulding *Letters(II)* 235: I gave a general sanction to have the Navy hauled over the coals. *Oxford* 358; TW 74(2).

C228 To heap **Coals** of fire on the head

1649 Williams *Writings* 6.167: Heap coals of fire on Captain Mason's head. **a1700** Hubbard *New England* 437: And thereby heaped coals on their enemies' heads. **1726** Chalkley *Journal* 194. **1734** Belcher *Papers* 2.146. **1741** Stephens *Journal(I)* 2.216: I condescended to let him have a Cask of Rice . . . thinking therein I heap'd coals of Fire on his head. **1775** AA in *Adams FC* 1.263. **1775** Hopkinson *Miscellaneous Essays* 1.44. **1781** EEdwards in Lee *Papers* 3.463: Wretches always disposed to heap coals on the head of the injured. **1786** JEliot in *Belknap Papers* 3.308. **1790** Morris *Diary* 1.498. **1794** Jefferson *Writings* 9.288. **1795** Gordon *Letters* 579: By heaping coals of kindness upon his head. **1798** Jefferson *Writings* 10.10. **1801** Ames *Letters* 1.292. **1807** Jefferson *Writings* 11.366. **c1810** Randolph *Virginia* 231. **1817** JAdams in *Adams-Jefferson Letters* 2.508: Enemies who mean to heap coals of fire on my head. **1821** Jackson *Correspondence* 3.101: I at least possess magnanimity by which I will heap coals upon his head. **1822** Wirt *Letters* 2.145. **1824** *Tales* 2.251: This is heaping coals of fire on my head with a vengeance! **1830** Jackson *Correspondence* 4.168. Barbour 37(4); *Oxford* 129; Whiting C337.

C229 To stand upon **Coals**

1676 Williams *Writings* 5.308: They stood here upon *Coals*.

C230 To stir **Coals**

1637 Williams *Writings* 6.58: I dare not stir coals. NED Coal 11.

C231 The **Coast** is clear

1672 RSaltonstall in *Saltonstall Papers* 1.159: That the Coast may be clier. **1677**

Hubbard *Indian* 1.128: The Coast was pretty clear of them, 200. **1711** WWinthrop in *Winthrop Papers(B)* 6.238, 243. **1716** Church *History* 1.165: To see if the Coast were clear. **1776** NBiddle in *Naval Documents* 5.29. **1776** JCadwalader in Reed *Life* 1.280-1. **1776** Lee *Papers* 1.277. **1776** Washington *Writings* 4.435. **1777** JAllan in *Baxter Manuscripts* 14.427. **1777** Moore *Diary* 1.452. **1779** HDearborn in Sullivan *Journals* 74. **1788** Freneau *Prose* 114. **1789** *Columbian Magazine* 3.434. **1791** Long *Voyages* 66. **1796** Barton *Disappointment* 49. **1797** Graham *Vermont* 112. **1809** Woodworth *Poems* 235: He'll rob a dwelling while the coast is clear. **1812** Jefferson *Writings* 18.22. **1812** Luttig *Journal* 66. **c1825** Tyler *Prose* 130: When, in the Yankee phrase the coast was clear. **1841** Paulding *Letters(II)* 313. *Oxford* 129; Whiting C339.

C232 The **Coat** does not make the man

1815 *Port Folio* 3NS 5.258: The coat, as we say at home, does not make the man. Cf. TW 72(1): Clothes. See **C209, F61.**

C233 Not to be in one's **Coat**

1809 Weems *Marion* 110: I would not be in your coat . . . your jacket, though it was stiff with gold. Tilley C473; Whiting C341. See **S168.**

C234 To turn one's **Coat**

1689 SPike in *Baxter Manuscripts* 6.482: Corenell Tinge can terne his coate when he please. **1755** *Johnson Papers* 1.612: I will make them turn their Coats, **1769** 6.594: To be . . . a turn Coat. **1775** Moore *Diary* 1.134: It makes the patriot turn his coat. **1777** Bowen *Journals* 2.522: Yet not so fixed on this head, But I can turn my coat for bread. **1800** RTroup in King *Life* 3.289: He has long worn his political coat wrong side out. *Oxford* 847; TW 74(2); Whiting T2.

C235 To cut one's **Coat** according to his cloth

1720 Carter *Letters* 11: I must cut my coat according to my cloth. **1761** *Boston Gazette* in *Olden Time* 2.30-1. **1775** Murray *Letters* 224. **1778** *Washington *Writings* 13.79: [He must] yield to necessity; that is, to use a vulgar Phraze, shape his Coat according to his

Cloth. **1783** WQuynn in *MHM* 31(1936) 194. **1786** JMecom in *Franklin-Mecom* 284: But as the old saying is. **1800** Adams *New Letters* 259. **1805** Brackenridge *Modern* 469. *Oxford* 164; Whiting C342.

C236 To stretch one's **Coat-tail**

1799 BHoward in *VHM* 30(1922) 249: Taylor is driving away stretching his coat tail and that he will do well I think *no man will deny.* Cf. TW 75.

C237 **Coaxing** is better than driving

1814 Palmer *Diary* 111: Coaxing does better than driving. See **L71.**

C238 **Cobblers** have the best wives

1813 *Port Folio* 3NS 2.487: For example, who have, proverbially, better wives than the whole race of *cobblers*? Cf. Barbour 163: Shoemaker.

C239 Let the **Cobbler** stick to his last (*varied*)

1647 Ward *Simple Cobler* Title page: This is no time to feare *Apelles gramm: Ne sutor quidem ultra crepidam.* **1650** Bradstreet *Works* 321: This my presumption some now to requite, *Ne sutor ultra crepidam* may write. **1681** IMather in *Mather Papers* 98: The Narrator . . . is *sutor ultra crepidam.* **1681** Samuel Willard, *Ne Sutor ultra Crepidam* (Boston, 1681). a**1700** Hubbard *New England* 624: Surely he was not well aware of the old adage, *ne sutor ultra crepidam,* or else he would not have made such botching work. **1701** Charles Wolley, *A Two Years Journal* (London, 1701), ed. E. B. O'Callaghan (New York, 1860) 44: *Miles equis, piscator aquis,* an hammer for the Smith, an Homer for the School, let the Shooe-maker mind his Boot, and the Fisherman his Boat, the Divine his Sermon, and the Doctor his Salmon. **1702** Mather *Magnalia* 2.535: Latin only. **1723** Symmes *Utile* 46: *Ne sutor ultra Crepidam,* Let not the Shoemaker go beyond his last. **1727** WDouglass in *Colden Letters* 1.238: Latin only. **1738** *Georgia Records* 22.163: The old Adage: Latin only. **1744** *Colden Letters* 3.87: Latin only. **1768** *Pennsylvania Chronicle* in *Newspaper Extracts(I)* 7.115: A Cobbler should stick to his last. **1775** Sullivan *Letters* 1.58: I shall con-

clude with reminding him, "that a Shoe Maker never ought to go beyond his Last." **1783** Madison *Papers* 6.254: Latin only. **1788** *American Museum* 3.528: *Ne sutor ultra crepidam.—Cobler, stick to your last.* **1789** Brackenridge *Gazette* 316: The saying . . . "Let every cobler stick t'his trade. **1792** Brackenridge *Modern* 11: But after all, it comes to the old proverb at last, *Ne sutor ultra crepidam,* Let the cobler stick to his last. **1795** *Remarks on the Jacobiniad* 1.17: The old adage; *"ne sutor ultra crepidam"* . . . *let not the cobbler go beyond his last.* **1797** Cobbett *Porcupine* 7.195: Latin and English. **1799** Freneau *Prose* 395: I much fear you'll find the truth of the old Latin proverb: Latin and English. **1801** *Port Folio* 1.38: Latin and English. **1804** *Monthly Anthology* 1.501: *Ne sutor ultra crepidam,* is an old proverb. The text is in *Horace.* **1806** Fessenden *Modern Philosopher* 67: To "stick, good cobbler, to your last." **1807** *Port Folio* NS 4.39: *Ne sutor ultra crepitam* . . . a cobbling proverbial phrase of Pliny. **1809** WCunningham in *Adams-Cunningham Letters* 89: Latin only. **1813** Bentley *Diary* 4.224: This man who was as skillful a Shoemaker as Friar Blas, but beyond his last. **1815** *Port Folio* 3NS 4.101: Latin and English, 5.64: No literary cobler has ever yet transgressed in the least degree *ultra crepidam.* **1822** Watterston *Winter* 70: Stick to his last. **1827** Carroll *Correspondence* 2.355: Latin only. **1827** Watterston *Wanderer* 138: Let them stick to their last. **1854** RMason in *Ruffin Papers* 2.419: I must remember the adage *"Ne sortor ultra crepidam."* *Oxford* 130; TW 75, 329.

C240 To bind one with **Cobwebs**

1756 *Johnson Papers* 2.493-4: A Certain Gentle[n] has done all in his power to bind him with Cobwebs and make the world believe they were bell Ropes.

C241 As the old **Cock** crows the young one learns

1809 WCunningham in *Adams-Cunningham Letters* 183: We have "cockerels that crow as they have heard the old one." **1846** Paulding *Letters(II)* 423: But as the Old

Cock Crows the young one learns. *Oxford* 588-9; Whiting C347.

C242   A Cock-and-bull story

1780 UHay in *Clinton Papers* 5.892: In which he tells a Cock & a bulls story of six ships having been detached from the rest. **1788** *Politician* 45: A fine story of a cock and a bull. **1792** Bentley *Diary* 1.388: And after his "cock and bull story" pressed . . . homewards. **1792** Mason *Papers* 3.1270. **1796** Barton *Disappointment* 25. **1806** *Weekly* 1.75. **1809** Irving *History* 1.113. **1817** Scott *Blue Lights* ix. **1827** Cooper *Letters* 1.222: A cock-and-bull sort of a fellow has sent me a bundle of Pamphlets for you. **1830** Ames *Mariner's* 195. *Oxford* 130; TW 75; Tilley S910.

C243   A Cock on its own dunghill (*varied*)

1634   Wood *New-England* 86: These heartlesse *Indians* were so cowed with so slender an onset on their own dunghill. **1702** Mather *Magnalia* 1.188: Soldiers who were *Galli in suo sterquilinio*, or "cocks crowing on their own dunghill." **1796** Cobbett *Porcupine* 4.131: It is the blustering noise of a poor timid trembling cock, crowing upon his own dunghill, **1797** 7.269: The publication of it at the time was a sort of dunghill cock triumph over Great Britain, **1798** 9.31: I do not fear to fight such a cock on his own dunghill. **1805** Parkinson *Tour* 480: The truth of the old adage . . . "A cock fights best on his own dunghill." *Oxford* 130-1; Whiting C350.

C244   Cocks make free with the horse's corn

1797 Callender *Annual Register 1796* 48: *Cocks make free with the horse's corn*, says a proverb.

C245   Cock of the walk (*varied*)

1785 Tilghman *Letters* 36: You . . . are the Cock of the Company, (to use an Expression of Sally Chews). **1790** Maclay *Journal* 335: So much does he long to be the cock of the school that he seems actually to court the company of children. **1805** Irving *Journals* 1.164: The present "cock of the walk" appears to be an old rich Greek. **1846** Paulding *Letters(II)* 421: It would be quite laughable to behold this little Bantam cock

of the walk. Barbour 37(1); *Oxford* 131; Whiting *NC* 385(1).

C246   To be Cock-a-hoop

1795 Adams *Memoirs* 1.140-1: The democrats were quite cock-a-whoop — talked very high of impeaching the President. **1809** Irving *History* 1.203: They possessed that ingenuous habit of mind which . . . rides cock-a-hoop on the tongue. *Oxford* 130; TW 75; Whiting C356.

C247   Cockneys are born within sound of Bow bells

1805 Silliman *Travels* 1.306: There is a church in Cheapside, called Bow Church, and it is a common remark in London, that all born within the sound of its bells are *cockneys*. *Oxford* 76; Tilley S671. See **S341**.

C248   To be Cock-sure

1691 *Humble Defence* in *Andros Tracts* 2.248: The *Publicans* thought themselves cock-sure. **1701** INorris in *Penn-Logan Correspondence* 1.57: They are now . . . cock-sure. **1741** Custis *Letters* 91: [He] is cock sure of getting the court in England. **1760** RPeters in *Aspinwall Papers* 1.325. **1765** *Johnson Papers* 11.842. Whiting C358.

C249   As black as a Coffin

1783 Williams *Penrose* 304: [A fish] appeared as Black as a Coffin.

C250   To pay one in his own Coin

1637 JWhite in *Winthrop Papers(A)* 3.337: But seing he takes pleasure in suits I believe we shall ere long paye him home in his own Coyne. **1684** Randolph *Letters* 6.156: Whom I hope in a little tyme to pay in her own Coine. **1694** Makemie *Writings* 94: He payes them home again in the same Coine. **1702** Mather *Magnalia* 2.638: March repaid 'em in their own *leaden coin*. **1705** Beverley *History* 54. **1762** Watts *Letter Book* 19: To pay you in your own friendly Coin. **1769** Davis *Colonial Virginia Satirist* 63: The votary of Bacchus repays him in his own coin. **1779** Galloway *Diary* 68. **1789** Wingate *Letters* 16: This sort of criminality seldom fails of being repaid in its own coin. **1790** Morris *Diary* 2.4. **1790** RSpaight in *Blount Papers* 2.156: I shall certainly return it in better coin. **1798** Freneau *Poems* 3.215: Will pay, in the coin that was paid. **1800** Cobbett *Porcupine* 11.236. **1800** CJohnson in *VHM* 29(1921) 268. **1812** *Kennon Letters* 33.271: You must pay me in my own coin. **1816** Paulding *Letters(I)* 1.191. **1819** Wirt *Letters* 2.93: I am indebted to you for three or four *Popiana,* which I wish it was in my power to pay in like *coin.* a1824 Marshall *Kentucky* 1.19. *Oxford* 614; TW 76(2). See **K15.**

C251 As opposite as **Cold** to heat

1746 *Georgia Records* 25.71: And the other half to act as opposite as cold is to heat.

C252 As black as a **Collier**

1793 Campbell *Travels* 44: As black as a collier. Cf. Whiting C371.

C253 No one can be called a **Colonel,** *etc.*

1744 Hamilton *Itinerarium* 77: It is a common saying here that a man has no title to that dignity (A colonel's commission) until he has killed a rattlesnake. DA rattlesnake 2(2).

C254 Once a **Colony** always a colony

1819 Brackenridge *South America* 2.358: The maxim of Spain, once a colony always a colony, is one she must settle with the colonies as well as she can.

C255 As bitter as **Coloquintida**

1692 Bulkeley *Will* 212: He must yield obedience, and that is a pill as bitter as coloquintida. Lean 2.807; Svartengren 303. Cf. *Oxford* 133.

C256 To come off with flying **Colors**

1700 INorris in *Penn-Logan Correspondence* 1.4: They would seem to come off with flying colors. **1766** WFranklin in Franklin *Papers* 13.334: I have come off with Flying Colours. **1816** JDavenport in *Smith Papers* 6.211. **1824** Lee *Diary and Letters* 225. **1829** Pintard *Letters* 3.95. NED Colour 7d.

C257 As ragged as a **Colt**

1797 Cobbett *Porcupine* 9.352: It is not at all uncommon to see a *'Squire* as ragged as a colt. *Oxford* 661; TW 77(2).

C258 As wild as **Colts**

1728 Byrd *Dividing Line* 69: We saw several pretty Girls here as wild as Colts, tho' not so ragged. TW 77(4).

C259 To have a **Colt's** tooth

c1800 Tyler *Island* 22: Got a colt's tooth in his head. **1810** *Port Folio* 2NS 4.73: Your two *wise teeth* soon took their flight; Now one alone, a *colt's,* is left you. *Oxford* 134; Whiting C377.

C260 To shoe **Colts**

1765 Rowe *Diary* 83: Went in the eve'ng at Blodgets with a Number of the General Court where they were Shoeing Colts—that is, the New Members that are chosen treat the Council & House of Representatives, **1766,** 98: Spent part of the afternoon with the House of Representatives in Shoeing Colts. Cf. Partridge 171: colt *vb.*

C261 Wild **Colts** often make good horses

a1776 HFlynt in CELWingate *Life and Letters of Paine Wingate* (Medford, Mass., 1930) 1.64: Wild colts often make good horses. *Oxford* 662; Whiting C376.

C262 To cut one's **Comb**

1741 Winslow *Broadside* 117: Resolv'd to cut the *Spaniards* Comb. **1770** Carter *Diary* 1.458: I wish he would send down a cargoe of it that I might cut Mr. Ritchie's comb a little. *Oxford* 164; TW 77.

C263 Easy **Come** easy go (*varied*)

1650 Bradstreet *Works* 259: For that which easily comes, as freely goes. **1656** Hammond *Leah* 4: Wealth, which they rather profusely spent (as gotten with ease) then providently husbanded. **1797** Washington *Writings* 35.498: [Money] comes easy and is spent freely. **1811** Weems *Gambling* 7: "*Light come light go,*" was the order of the day. **1814** Brackenridge *Views* 149: What is easily earned is carelessly spent. **1819** Welby *Visit* 173: That is probably according to the old adage "lightly come lightly go." Barbour 57(1); *Oxford* 213; Whiting C384. See **S364.**

C264 First **Come** first served (speed)

1630 Hutchinson *Papers* 1.52: Those that come first speed best here. **1736** Stephens

Journal(II) 1.242: But whether so or not, first come first served is a rule here. **1785** Hopkinson *Miscellaneous Essays* 2.80-1: It seems to be a general scramble now—first come first served. **1787** Ledyard *Russian Journey* 192: It is remarkable that he was the *first* served & the *best* served on every occasion. **1793** Campbell *Travels* 185. Barbour 65(2); *Oxford* 262; Whiting C382.

C265   What is to **Come** will come

1809 Weems *Washington* 33: "Well, what is to come, will come," said poor Paddy, when going to the gallows.

C266   As red as a **Comet**

1809 Weems *Marion* 163: A face as red as a comet.

C267   Cold **Comfort**

a1656 Bradford *History* 1.258: All this was but could comfort to fill their hungrie bellies. **1744** Hamilton *Itinerarium* 117: This is but cold comfort. **1755** *Johnson Papers* 9.330: But whats that to us—youl Say . . . sorry Comfort. **1758** REastburn *Faithful Narrative* in Ashbel Green, *Memoirs of the Rev. Joseph Eastburn* (Philadelphia, 1828) 188: Which was cold comfort to one almost frozen. **1777** AA in *Adams FC* 2.212: That is a consolation to me, tho a cold comfort in a winters night. **1777** JAdams in Sullivan *Letters* 1.367. **1778** Galloway *Diary* 47. **1791** Paine *Rights of Man* 1.319. **1796** Barton *Disappointment* 90. **1815** Adams *Works* 10.138. **1823** GHowland in *New England Merchants* 130. **1826** Jones *Sketches* 1.191: It was cold comfort, but the doctor came with something warmer. *Oxford* 132; Whiting(C387.

C268   Little **Comfort** little care

1760 Murray *Letters* 111: My Motto may be now little Comfort little Care. Cf. Whiting C386.

C269   To wet one's **Commission**

1739 Stephens *Journal(I)* 1.439: Taking the Hint, I willingly agreed to what they termed wetting my Commission; and took a cheerful Glass with them. **1746** Hempstead *Diary* 468: Danll Starr Wet his Commission.

Treated both Companys with Cakes & Drink Enough. NED Wet 8.

C270   Evil **Communications** corrupt good manners

1649 *Connecticut Historical Collections* 26: Evil words corrupt good manners. I Cor. 15:33. **1691** *Humble Address* in *Andros Tracts* 2.256: Evil Communications . . . by which men corrupt one another. **1730** Chalkley *Youth* 556: Evil Communication corrupts good Manners. **1746** *Diaries of Rev. Timothy Walker*, ed JBWalker (Concord, N.H., 1889) 21: Evil communications corrupt good manners. **1758** CCarroll in *MHM* 10 (1915) 226. AA in *Adams FC* 1.21. **1764** Watts *Letter Book* 314. **1766** *New-York Gazette* in *Newspaper Extracts(I)* 6.87. **1774** Seabury *Letters* 108. **1779** Hutchinson *Diary* 2.289. **1780** AA in *Adams FC* 4.29. **a1793** Scott *Journal* 16: I put myself in the way of much evil communication; and it mournfully corrupted good manners. **1794** DJarratt in *W&MCQ* 3S 9(1952) 376. **1797** Dunlap *Diary* 1.172. **1804** SRuffin in *Ruffin Papers* 1.50, **1805** 1.69. **1811** Graydon *Memoirs* 105: Perhaps I approached her under unfavourable auspices, those of a young man debauched by evil communications. **1815** Adams *Writings* 5.354. **1815** Waterhouse *Journal* 120. **1819** Verplanck *State* 73: The common adage. **1831** Jackson *Correspondence* 4.316: If ever he was a man of truth . . . his evil communications has corrupted his morales, 384: The old adage appear to be realised, "that evil communications corrupt good principles." *Oxford* 232; Whiting S602.

C271   One is known by his **Company**

1737 Stephens *Journal(I)* 1.42: *Noscitur ex Sociis* was the common By-word. **1777** ALawrence in *Clinton Papers* 2.545: A man is known by his Company. **1809** WCunningham in *Adams-Cunningham Letters* 96: *Noscitur ex sociis.* **1817** Royall *Letters* 102: Every one is known by their company. **1821** Randolph(J) *Letters* 217: There is one of your good shots . . . with whom I hope you do not associate. "Tell me your company," &c, **1822** 234: Noscitur è sorio. "Tell me your company, and I will tell you what you are." 1848 Paulding *Letters(II)* 484: According to the old saying, the world judges a man by the Company he keeps. Barbour 115 (5); *Oxford* 138; Whiting C395. See **M45.**

C272 **Comparisons** are odious (invidious)
1652 Bradford *Dialogue* 45: Comparisons are odious. 1694 Calef *More Wonders* 176: This comparison is indeed very odious. 1702 Mather *Magnalia* 1.239: Without *any odious comparisons*, 2.119: I will now make no odious comparisons between Harvard-Colledge and other Universities. 1740 HVance *Inquiry* in *Colonial Currency* 3.442: To run a Comparison between these *Coins* and our *Bills* would be odious and detestable. 1769 Brooke *Emily* 313: I allow Rivers all his merit; but comparisons, my dear —. 1776 Shaw *Journals* 23. 1777 JWarren in *Warren-Gerry Correspondence* 79: But I forbear to make Comparisons. 1789 Ames *Letters* 1.74: they say. 1792 Bentley *Diary* 1.387: After some odious comparisons . . . we parted. 1792 Freneau *Prose* 276: Comparisons are sometimes odious, but they are often useful. 1797 Cobbett *Porcupine* 4.365: you know, 5.238: Let not this comparison be called invidious. 1798 HKnox in Washington *Writings* 36.348. 1806 *Port Folio* NS 2.33: He has no desire of provoking an *invidious* comparison, 218: Comparison, which, according to the proverb, *is odi-* 1807 HLee in *Jacksons and Lees* 2.821: The Comparison . . . (which I am sorry appears so odious to you). 1814 Wirt *Bachelor* 51: Comparisons are *odorous* (odious, you mean, Deborah). 1815 Brackenridge *Modern* 758: That would . . . induce comparison which, according to the proverb, *is odious.* 1819 Wright *Views* 38: I intend no invidious comparison. 1825 Jones *Sketches* 1.74: I am not fond of comparisons: they are invidious. *Oxford* 138-9; Whiting C400.

C273 To box the **Compass**
1797 Cobbett *Porcupine* 5.103: This, Mr. Editor, is called boxing the compass. 1837 Jackson *Correspondence* 5.516: [Calhoun] had boxed the political compass all round. NED Box *v*[1] 12.

C274 To **Complain** before one is hurt
1647 WBradford in *Winthrop Papers(A)* 5.139: They complaine before they were hurte. 1723 Symmes *Utile* 24-5: It's time enô for People to complain, when they'r hurt. 1834 *Adventures of CHawkins*, ed. Charles I. Bushnell (New York, 1864) 26: I see you will not bawl before you are hurt. *Oxford* 158; Tilley C874.

C275 **Concord** makes small things grow
1643 Williams *Writings* 1.123: By concord little things grow great, by discord the greatest come to nothing. *Concordia parvae res crescunt, Discordia magnae dilabuntur.* 1686 Dunton *Letters* 274: [Latin only] as in 1643. 1768 Dickinson *Writings* 312: Concordia res parvæ crescunt. Small things grow great by concord. 1775 Izard *Correspondence* 103: The Dutch motto, "*Concordia parva res crescunt,*" is a wise observation. The provinces of America must, if firmly united, prove irrestible. 1779 Brackenridge *Gazette* 135: Latin only. 1787 Adams *Works* 6.200: The smallest things increase by concord. *Oxford* 854; Whiting C404. See **A51.**

C276 What avails **Confession** without amendment?
1761 Franklin *Papers* 9.374: But what avails Confession without Amendment. Tilley C588.

C277 **Confidence** is a plant of slow growth
1794 Lee *Letters* 2.564: And perhaps it may be owing to this love of my Country . . . together with that period of life when *Confidence is a plant of slow growth. Oxford* 139.

C278 **Connecticut** trick: see **T241.**

C279 A guilty **Conscience** needs no accuser
1755 Bailey *Journal* 30: Guilty persons seldom need any accuser but their own conscience, or witnesses beside themselves to declare their crimes. 1770 HBarnes in Murray *Letters* 174: As a Guilty Conscience needs no accuser so conscious Innocence fears none. 1797 Cobbett *Porcupine* 6.187: An old saying. 1812 *Kennon Letters* 33. 271: A poor servant of mine used to say, a guilty conscience needs no "excusial." 1814 Kerr

Barclay 388. **1816** Jackson *Correspondence* 2.230. *Oxford* 340-1; Whiting G492. See **S533, W144.**

C280 An ignorant **Consent** is no consent
1709 Sewall *Diary* 2.267: An ignorant Consent is no Consent.

C281 **Contentment** is better than riches (*varied*)
1753 GHume in *VHM* 20(1912) 409: Contentment with a small living must certainly be better than great riches with discontent. **1783** Pickering *Life* 1.448: Contentment will make a poor man rich. *Oxford* 873; Tilley C629, W194.

C282 No **Conveniency** without an inconveniency
1733 Franklin *Papers* 1.325: 'Tis an old Saying and a true one, that *there is no Conveniency without an Inconveniency.* **1797** Smith(EH) *Diary* 284: There is never a convenience, without an inconvenience, as the old saying is. **1801** *Cary Letters* 164: All conveniences, they say, are attended with difficulties. *Oxford* 228: Every commodity; Tilley C555. See **I30.**

C283 (Chief) **Cook** and bottle washer
1809 Lindsley *Love* 40: I acts cook, steward, cabin boy, sailor, mate, and bottle washer. **1844** Hone *Diary* 2.705: Gen. Jackson's chief cook and bottle washer, Col. Polk. NED Bottle *sb.*[2] 5.

C284 It is a sorry **Cook** that cannot lick his own fingers
1692 Bulkeley *Will* 126: It is a sorry cook that cannot lick his own fingers. **1798** Cobbett *Porcupine* 8.51: For cooks, by report, though greasy the trick, In turning the roast, always get the first lick. *Oxford* 143; Whiting C418. See **S174.**

C285 Too many **Cooks** spoil the broth
a1700 Hubbard *New England* 525: But many times, according to the old proverb, the more cooks the worse broth, and the more masters the worse mariners. **1723** *New-England Courant* 94(1.1): The old Proverb is verify'd, *The more Cooks the worse Broth.* **1778** Curwen *Journal and*

Letters 177: 'Tis therefore, I fancy, equally indifferent who are or shall be our political cooks; the pottage, I fear, will be spoiled. **1779** *New Jersey Gazette* in *Newspaper Extracts(II)* 3.712: It is often as true in politics as in cookery, that too many cooks spoil the broth. **1786** Smith *Diary* 2.200. **1801** Asbury *Letters* 3.232: We have so many cooks, and some very unskilful. **1820** Adams *Memoirs* 5.163: There were too many makers of that treaty, and it was a very bad one. Barbour 39(3); *Oxford* 831; TW 79(1). See **O33.**

C286 To come in at the **Cook-room-door**
1715 Mather *Letters* 169: Some very good commanders . . . think it is not absolutely necessary, nor perhaps convenient, that I should enter at the cook-room door. Cf. TW 405. See **C1.**

C287 As crazy as a **Coot**(?)
1783 JChester in Webb *Correspondence* 3.248: He was for some time Crazy as a Cont [?*for* Coot]. Cf. Svartengren 42; TW 80; Whiting C421.

C288 Not a **Copper** before a beggar
1788 *Politician* 7: There an't one of 'um that's a single copper before a beggar, as the old saying is.

C289 Not give a **Copper**
1769 Adams *Legal Papers* 2.89: Would not give a Copper for an Iron Hole. **1770** *Johnson Papers* 7.334: I would not give one Copper to decide it. **1793** Jefferson *Writings* 1.344: He would not give a copper for it. TW 80(1, 3, 4).

C290 Not worth a **Copper**
1777 JBurgoyne in Moore *Diary* 1.462: Nor deems the contest worth a copper. **1805** Brackenridge *Modern* 569: The word of their mouth is a bubble, And not worth a copper indeed. TW 80(3, 4).

C291 To cool one's **Coppers**
1750 *Johnson Papers* 1.271: We . . . turnd down a couple of Quarts of Home brew [MS torn] Cooling our Coppers which had been made so warm. NED Copper *sb.*[1] 8; Partridge 178.

C292 A **Cord** stretched too much may break

1765 Watts *Letter Book* 379: These Folks I am afraid stretch the Cord too much, it may chance to break. Whiting C425.

C293 As light as (a) **Cork**

1710 Sewall *Letter-Book* 1.406: As, light as Cork (as one may say). **1755** *Beekman Papers* 1.267: Its as light as a Cork. **c1792** Paine *Works* 97: Though light as cork, your passions reign. **1803** *Yankee Phrases* 87: My heart being lighter than cork. **1821** Knight *Poems* 2.185: And light as cork thy fickle heart. TW 80(2).

C294 To float like a **Cork**

1792 Mason *Papers* 3.1270: The Cypress Scantlin wou'd float like a Cork. *Oxford* 794: Swim; Whiting *NC* 387.

C295 To eat like a **Cormorant**

1728 Byrd *Dividing Line* 195: Our Chaplain . . . began to eat like a Cormorant. NED Cormorant 2b.

C296 To feed on soft **Corn**

1814 TPickering in Cabot *Letters* 541: We have fed this nation too long with *soft* corn, sir. TW 81(2).

C297 To measure another's **Corn** by one's bushel

1676 Williams *Writings* 5.314: W. Edm. charged me that I had a false heart . . . and would measure others by my bushel, 315: We will measure him with his own Bushel. **1744** *Georgia Records* 24.350: As knowing no Shadow of reason that Mr. Watson had to Mete my Corn by his measure. **1808** Clubb *Journal* 11: I measured his corn by my bushel, but was mistaken. Barbour 39 (1); *Oxford* 521; TW 81(3).

C298 To have **Corns** in one's head

1737 Franklin *Drinkers* 2.174: Has got Corns in his Head. Apperson 114; Partridge: Corns.

C299 To tread on another's **Corns**

1810 Wirt *Letters* 1.292: He spoke his mind, on all occasions, without reserve, and was constantly treading on somebody's corns. NED Corn *sb.*² 2.

C300 In a **Corner**

1654 Johnson *Wonder-Working* 106*: They have done nothing in holes and corners, but their workes are obvious to all the World. **a1656** Bradford *History* 1.401: If things had bene done in a corner. **1692** Mather *Wonders* 191: He would have us trie the Justice of God; but how? By venturing upon Sin in a *Corner* with an Imagination that God will never bring us out. **1699** Ward *Trip* 40-1: But the good humor'd Lasses to make you amends, will Kiss the kinder in a Corner. **1705** Makemie *Writings* 146: Carry on Fraud against Strangers, by trading in a corner, 152: Carry on . . . cheating Tricks in a Corner or secret Trade. **1762** *Johnson Papers* 3.775: Business shou'd not be done in a Corner, **1767** 5.484: The thing was not done in a Corner. **1826** Longfellow *Letters* 1.193: A kind of "Q in the corner affair." NED Corner *sb.*¹ 6; Whiting C442.

C301 A **Cornish** hug

1681 Randolph *Letters* 3.114: They will easily give you a Cornish Hugg. NED Hug 2; *Oxford* 144; Tilley H804.

C302 **Corporations** have no souls

1812 *Port Folio* 2NS 7.416: There is an ancient doctrine of the common law, that corporations have no souls; to which common opinion has added as a corollary, that they have no consciences. **1822** JMay in *Ruffin Papers* 1.267: It is a pity that corporations should have all the bad passions and feelings incident to human beings; without a Soul to answer for, if not to correct and control them. *Oxford* 145.

C303 As cold as a **Corpse**

1803 Dow *Journal* 176: Her body was cold as a corpse, **1804** 207: We are in perspiration, whilst they are as cold as corpses. Whiting *NC* 387(1).

C304 As pale as a **Corpse**

1815 Weems *Adultery* 160: Poor Mrs. Wilson, pale as a corpse, sunk . . . to the floor, 183: Pale as a corpse . . . she confessed all. Barbour 40(1); Svartengren 234. Cf. TW 81(1).

C305 High up to picking **Cotton**

1813 Weems *Drunkard* 60: High up to picking cotton [Georgia: drunk]. DA cotton 7.

C306 A church-yard **Cough**

1816 Colby *Life* 2.5: Yes, replies another, that's a church-yard cough. TW 81.

C307 Every **Council** brings forth war

1652 Bradford *Dialogue* 46: Mr. Bullinger, speaking of councells, affirms that in old time it grue into a proverbe; how that every counsell brings forth warre.

C308 To give **Counsel** uncalled

1633 EDowning in *Winthrop Papers(A)* 3.129: But here in I must check my selfe in that I give councell and advice before I am called thereto. *Oxford* 125; Whiting C447.

C309 He that won't be **Counselled,** can't be helped

1747 Franklin *PR* 3.104: He that won't be counsell'd, can't be help'd, 1758 *WW* 349. *Oxford* 147; Tilley C702.

C310 He that is his own **Counsellor** has a fool for a client

1809 *Port Folio* 2NS 2.132: He who is always his own counseller will often have a fool for his client. *Oxford* 146; TW 234(7). See **S105.**

C311 The **Country** pays for all

1692 Bulkeley *Will* 214: It is their maxim, *The country pays for all,* 216: It is growing into a proverb, *Drink lustick boys, the country pays for all,* 241: But it is no matter for that, they knew who pays for all.

C312 Every **Country** has its peculiar manners

1783 *American Wanderer* 35: But *chaque pays, chaque façon.* 1814 Wirt *Bachelor* 18: Every country and every age has its peculiar manners. 1815 *Port Folio* 3NS 5.52: Every country has its peculiarities. *Oxford* 147; TW 82(1); Tilley C711; Whiting T63.

C313 It is pleasant to die for one's **Country**

1797 Callender *Annual Register 1796* 117: It is pleasant, says the proverb, to die for your country. Horace *Odes* I 11 13. See **G84.**

C314 **Country** pay

1685 Mather *Letters* 17: I send you a few almanacs, for which you shall pay me in country-pay, I mean, with acceptance and love, 1702 *Magnalia* 2.580-1: The most ungrateful treats imaginable (which are too well known by the name of "country-pay"). DA Country pay.

C315 The **Course** of true love, *etc.*

1833 Wirt *Letters* 2.393: "The course of true love never did run smooth," nor the course of any thing else that belongs to man. *Oxford* 148; TW 82.

C316 Far from **Court,** far from care

1767 Ames *Almanacs* 387: Far from court, far from care. *Oxford* 244; Tilley C722.

C317 He that would rise at **Court** must begin by creeping

1757 Franklin *PR* 7.76: He that would rise at Court, must begin by Creeping. Cf. *Oxford* 210; Tilley C724.

C318 Full of **Courtesy,** full of craft

1735 Franklin *PR* 2.5: Full of courtesie, full of craft. Barbour 49(3); *Oxford* 293; Tilley C732.

C319 To send one to (put one in) **Coventry**

1774 Andrews *Letters* 350: To send him to Coventry. 1787 *American Museum* 1.472: A bad husband ought to be put in Coventry by all good ones. 1790 Maclay *Journal* 249: The amount of it was to put that state in a kind of commercial coventry. 1797 Freneau *Prose* 392: The whole hive are instantly in arms against him: he is put in coventry—he is killed or maimed. 1802 Chester *Federalism* 3. 1804 WEaton in *Barbary Wars* 5.224: Both got black eyes, in consequence of which they have kept themselves in Coventry. 1804 Jefferson *Family Letters* 255: It is likely to end in those two families putting themselves into Coventry. 1805 AMurray in *Barbary Wars* 5.400: Eaton . . . is in Coventry. 1821 Robertson *Letters* 164. 1831 Jackson *Correspondence* 4.273: My friends were . . . put into coventry by my family. *Oxford* 149; TW 82, 149. See **S450.**

C320 No **Cover** is large enough to hide itself

1802 Paine *To the Citizens* 2.924: The Spanish proverb says, *"there never was a cover large enough to hide itself,"* **1805** 949: "No cover is large enough to hide itself," says the Spanish proverb.

C321 **Covetousness** brings nothing home

a1656 Bradford *History* 2.73: Covetousnes never brings ought home, as the proverb is. *Oxford* 150; Tilley C745.

C322 A **Cow** in a cage

1637 Morton *New English Canaan* 268: Bubble . . . paddels out like a Cow in a cage. *Oxford* 135; Whiting C499; Whiting *NC* 387(4).

C323 Curst **Cows** have short horns

1733 Belcher *Papers* 1.369: And yet the old proverb holds good, Curst cows have short horns, **1741** 2.363: But curst cows, brother, they say, have short horns. **1781** Peters *Connecticut* 89. **1815** Humphreys *Yankey* 70: 'Tis well that cussed keows have short horns, as the proverb says. *Oxford* 162; TW 82(3); Whiting G234.

C324 A good **Cow** may have a bad calf

1816 Cooper *Letters* 1.33: Juvenal says that a Good Cow may have a Bad Calf [note p. 35 cfs. Juvenal *Satire* viii 56-67]. *Oxford* 318; Whiting C502.

C325 Like a **Cow** chasing a hare

1830 Ames *Mariner's* 227: The U.S. schooner Dolphin went in chase of her next day, but it was "a cow chasing a hare." *Oxford* 151; Tilley C763. See **S482.**

C326 To fling a **Cow** by the tail

1788 *Politician* 48: I wou'dn't trust such a friend as far as I cou'd fling a cow by the tail. Cf. *Oxford* 842; Tilley T556.

C327 To grow downward like a **Cow's** tail

1816 Paulding *Letters(I)* 2.32: O — then the world grew downwards, like a cow's tail, 75: Every thing in this country has been, for two centuries at least, growing downwards, like unto a cow's tail. *Oxford* 340; Tilley C770; Whiting *NC* 388(10).

C328 To know no more than a **Cow,** *etc.*

1789 *Columbian Magazine* 3.403: These town's folks know no more how to behave to girls than a *cow does to churn buttermilk.* **1792** Brackenridge *Modern* 56: It knows no more of Indians than a cow does of Greek. Cf. TW 82(4).

C329 To swallow the **Cow** and stick on the tail

1746 *Colden Letters* 3.269: But I must not swallow the Cow and stick on the Tail. Apperson 480: Ox(10); *Oxford* 791. See **G64.**

C330 **Cowards** are cruel (*varied*)

1775 GBenson in *Naval Documents* 2.376: Cowardice & Cruelty are Inseparable Companions. **1776** Carroll *Correspondence* 1.395: His behaviour justifies the old observation, that cowards are generally cruel. **1809** Weems *Washington* 71: That's exactly up to our old English proverb — "*the greater the coward, the crueller the devil!*" *Oxford* 151; Tilley C778; Whiting C509.

C331 **Cowards** are most often in danger

1802 Drinker *Journal* 376: Cowards are oftenest in danger. Cf. *Oxford* 151; Tilley C774.

C332 **Cowards** provoked will do wonders

1771 JTemple in *Bowdoin Papers* 1.283-4: 'Tis said, cowards provoked will do wonders. *Oxford* 151; Tilley C777, D216, N62. See **D11.**

C333 It is not the **Cowl** that makes the monk

1831 Cooper *Letters* 2.87: "But who is this person," his mother asked — "was it a gentleman?" "Mais peutêtre, Maman — il en avait l'air — *ma non e l'abito che fa il monaco,*" giving as you see, an Italian proverb by way of expressing his doubts. The proverb means, "it is not the cowl that makes the Monk." *Oxford* 152; Whiting H2.

C334 As crabbed as a **Crab-tree**

1758 Patten *Diary* 56: They were both as Crabid as a Crab tree. Cf. TW 83.

C335 All the **Craft** is in the catching

1675 JEliot in *Winthrop Papers(B)* 3.425: We w^r too ready to think y^t we could easyly supp^rsse y^t flea; but now we find y^t all the craft is in the catching of them. *Oxford* 153; Tilley C796.

C336 **Craft** must be at charge for clothes, *etc.*

1747 Franklin *PR* 3.104: *Craft* must be at charge for clothes, but *Truth* can go naked. *Oxford* 153.

C337 To be cut in the **Craw**

1813 Weems *Drunkard* 60: Cut in the craw [drunk].

C338 As rich as **Cream**

1820 Weems *Letters* 3.289: All Tobacco Planters & all rich as cream, 292, 294. TW 84(2).

C339 The **Cream** of the jest (joke)

1789 Brown *Better* 33: The cream of the jest. 1802 Irving *Jonathan* 16: Then came the cream of the joke. 1806 *Port Folio* NS 1.73: joke. 1807 *Weekly* 2.198: jest. *Oxford* 154; Tilley C811.

C340 To save one's **Credit** and bacon too

1775 AA in *Adams FC* 1.323: Some folks have saved their credit, and their Bacon too (as the phraze is). 1785 Eugenio in Smith *Journal and Correspondence* 2.(2) 40-1: For now, to use a common expression, I save my credit and bacon too. 1816 Fidfaddy *Adventures* 141: Save Our credit and our *bacon.* See **B19.**

C341 **Creditors** have better memories than debtors

1736 Franklin *PR* 2.141: Creditors have better memories than debtors, 1758 *WW* 348. 1822 Weems *Letters* 3.342: As creditors generally have good memories. Barbour 42; *Oxford* 154; Tilley C818.

C342 **Cretans** are liars

1731 *Trade* in *Colonial Currency* 2.381: People might become like the *Cretians,* always liars. 1774 Jones *Journal* 72: It is said of the Cretians, that they were "always liars, evil beasts, slow bellies." Tilley C822.

C343 As gay as a **Cricket**

1801 Story *Shop* 76: A making of the wretched gay as crickets. TW 84(1).

C344 As lively as a **Cricket**

1834 Floy *Diary* 86: Took tea there and was as lively as a cricket. TW 84(4).

C345 As merry as a **Cricket**

1777 JWebb in Webb *Correspondence* 1.322: Little Sally is as merry as a Cricket. 1788 *Politician* 70: I am as merry as a cricket. 1789 *American Museum* 5.297. 1799 Weems *Philanthropist* 20: Merry as crickets. 1803 Davis *Travels* 395. 1804 Irving *Journals* 1.79. 1804 Weems *Letters* 2.298. 1817 Pintard *Letters* 1.46. 1820 *Fudge Family* 62: As merry as so many crickets. 1822 Watterston *Winter* 27. 1837 Austin *Literary Papers* 69: She was as merry as a cricket in autumn. 1854 Paulding *Letters(II)* 550: Ellen . . . dances about as merry as a cricket. *Oxford* 527; Whiting C550.

C346 Enough to make a **Cripple** dance

1738 *Georgia Records* 22.119: Such joyfull news as were almost sufficient to make a Cripple dance.

C347 **Crocodile** tears

1634 Wood *New-England* 83: The *Crocodiles* teares may sooner deceive them, than the *Hienas* smiles. 1692 Randolph *Letters* 7.405: The Crocadiles Tears Appeased the Rabble. 1775 [MWarren] *The Group* (Boston, 1775) 10: And with a phiz of Crocodilian stamp, Can weep. 1781 AA in *Adams FC* 4.178: [He] is now in the most specious manner crocodile like whining over the prey he means to devour. 1796 Dennie *Lay Preacher* 13: His was a . . . crocodile grief, that though he wept, he could wound. 1814 Kerr *Barclay* 132: The crocodile tears of Mr Barclay. 1814 Morris *Diary and Letters* 2.573. Barbour 43; *Oxford* 155; Whiting C555.

C348 As wealthy as **Croesus**

1808 Hitchcock *Poetical Dictionary* 28: Our citizens soon will be wealthy as Croesus. Barbour 43; *Oxford* 674; Whiting C556.

C349 To stick in one's **Crop** (throat)

1767 DFowler in *Wheelock's Indians* 108: This soon stuck in my Crop. 1775 *Deane Brothers Papers* 2: There is one or two things that stick in my Crop. 1792 Belknap *Foresters* 40: This was a matter which stuck in

John's throat a great while. **1802** Chester *Federalism* 28. TW 85. Cf. Tilley T266. See **G51, L190, S450.**

C350 **Cross** and pile
1781 Jefferson *Writings* 2.179: It is better to toss up cross and pile in a cause, than to refer it to a judge whose mind is warped, **1784** *Papers* 6.569: You must learn to bear these things by always calculating on the possibility of a cross as well as pyle, **1798** *Writings* 10.17: The question of war and peace depends now on a toss of cross and pile. **1817** Royall *Letters* 110: I knew from her looks, it would be a cross and pile chance whether she would condescend to set a part of it on the table for me till she saw her own time, **1821** 205: And here they lay cross and pile, heads and points, yelling and screaming like wild beasts of the forest. *Oxford* 155; Whiting C560.

C351 The heavier the **Cross** the brighter the crown
1809 Weems *Marion* 217: *"The heavier the cross the brighter the crown."* Cf. *Oxford* 568; Tilley C839. See **D12.**

C352 As black as (a) **Crow**
1797 Tyler *Prose* 227: A fine crow black [coat]. **1799** Carey *Porcupiniad* 2.31: As black as crow. Barbour 43(1); *Oxford* 63; Whiting C565.

C353 A **Crow** thinks her own bird fairest
1639 EHowes in *Winthrop Papers(A)* 4.115: Yet a Crow thinkes her owne bird the fairest. **1719** Mather *Letters* 294: I gave a madwoman . . . a splendid shilling for this: that having a little daughter of my own in my hand, and asking her whether this were not a very pretty and comely creature, she wisely and with a very instructive satire turned upon me, *The crow thinks so, Sir,* **1724** 391: It is proper for me to give Your Honor some account of him, tho' how to do it without incurring the censure of *the crow thinks so,* is not very easy. Barbour 43(3); *Oxford* 156; Whiting C568.

C354 Not fit for a **Crow**
1776 GClinton in *Naval Documents* 5.1188: His Share of the Plunder was a Handker-

chief full of Salt & a Pigg so very Poor that a Crow would scarcely deign to eat it. **1799** DRoss in *Bingham's Maine* 2.960: My carcase is hardly fit for the crows to pick. Cf. TW 85(1).

C355 To have a **Crow** to pluck (pick)
1797 Callender *Annual Register 1796* 87: It is needless to be reserved in plucking a crow with this editor. **1811** *Port Folio* 2NS 5.223: With Atticus I have a crow to pick. Barbour 43(8); *Oxford* 157; Whiting C572. See **B254.**

C356 To hazard one's **Crows**
1777 Carter *Diary* 2.1096: But o! he'd hazard his crows, but he would subdue.

C357 To strut like **Crows** in a gutter
1776 Lee *Papers* 2.96: Old Jennifer and little Nourse strutted like Crows in a gutter. *Oxford* 156; Tilley C852.

C358 As stiff as a **Crowbar**
1787 WSSmith in Smith *Journal and Correspondence* 1.167: I used to see him stand as stiff . . . as if he had swallowed a crowbar. **1814** Palmer *Diary* 54: Miller—Stiff as a crow bar. TW 86(2).

C359 **Crow** claws
1808 *Port Folio* NS 5.126: The crow claws which are visible in the corners of her eyes. NED Crow's foot, quote 1579; Whiting C578.

C360 That **Crown** is well spent that saves ten
1809 *Port Folio* 2NS 2.549: That crown is well spent which saves you ten. Cf. *Oxford* 619; Tilley P210; Whiting P123.

C361 To pick up one's **Crumbs**
1654 Johnson *Wonder-Working* 207: The owners may pick up their crums again. **1777** Hodgkins *Letters* 232: And lost most all my flesh But I hope soon to Pick up my Crumes again. *Oxford* 623; Whiting C581.

C362 Great **Cry** and little wool (*varied*)
1686 Dunton *Letters* 30: This Noise about the Sally-man, it was like the Devil's Sheering Hogs. **1691** ?CMather *Bills of Credit* in *Colonial Currency* 1.192: A great cry of

Hog-sheering, where there is no Wool. **1720** Carter *Letters* 54: I wish for the sake of his remain, at the winding up of his cotton, the cry did not exceed the wool. **a1731** Cook *Bacon* 324: A mighty Cry, but little Wool. **1744** Hamilton *Itinerarium* 83: I back'd it [an adage] with *great cry and little wool, said the devil when he shore his hogs,* applicable enough to the ostentation and clutter he made with his learning. **1763** Smith *Memoirs(I)* 19: He said "Great cry & little wool!" **1774** Franklin *Writings* 6.301: They were not worth shearing & at best that we sh^d raise a cursed outcry & get but little wool. **1799** Carey *Plumb* 25: As . . . Belzebub is reported to have declared, when he caught a hog, and sheared him, that there had been "great cry and little wool." **1818** Weems *Letters* 3.238: My complaints . . . like pig-sh[e]aring—all cry & no wool. *Oxford* 333; Whiting C585.

C363 As clear as **Crystal**

1623 JPory in James *Three Visitors* 9: The water being as clear as crystal. **c1680** Radisson *Voyages* 144: Fishes, wch are seene in the water so cleare as christiall. **1728** Byrd *Dividing Line* 239: A stream as clear as liquid chrystal, **1733** *Journey* 290. **1743** JBartram in *Colden Letters* 3.5: A fine Stone as Clear as Cristal. **c1775** *Connecticut Journal* in Buckingham *Specimens* 1.314: His head clear as crystal. **1776** Curwen *Journal* 1.230. **1785** Hunter *Quebec* 84, 166. **1794** Adams *Memoirs* 1.52. **1797** Baily *Journal* 222: A rivulet as clear as the purest crystal. **1798** Latrobe *Journal* 94, 236. **1800** Adams *Letters on Silesia* 192. **1805** Ordway *Journal* 238. **1812** Melish *Travels* 489. **c1813** Dow *Journal* 309. **1816** UBrown in *MHM* 11(1916) 358. **1816** Ker *Travels* 59. **1819** Wright *Views* 124. **1821** Beecher *Autobiography* 1.459. **1825** Jones *Sketches* 1.70. Barbour 44; Whiting C589. See **G53.**

C364 As limpid as **Crystal**

1791 Jefferson *Family Letters* 89: Its waters limpid as chrystal.

C365 As pure as **Crystal**

1822 GHowland in *New England Merchants* 124: Water as pure as cristal.

C366 As transparent as **Crystal**

1819 Adams *Memoirs* 4.391: Attempts . . . as transparent as crystal. TW 86(3). See **G56.**

C367 **Cuckolds** go to heaven

1686 Dunton *Letters* 145: If he can but make a shift to scuffle thro' this World, if I ben't mis-inform'd, his Wife has taken care for his well-doing in the next, unless the Proverb fails. *Oxford* 159; Tilley R12.

C368 The **Cuckoo** has but one note (song)

1676 Williams *Writings* 5.78: G. Fox Answers (still like the *Cuckow* in one silly Note), 136: When their *Cuckoes note* and *song* was over. **1797** Cobbett *Porcupine* 6.43: They have but one answer to all kinds of arguments on the subject; but one unvarying cuckoo-song, 143: Protect us . . . from repetition more irksome than the monotonous song of the cuckoo. Barbour 44; *Oxford* 84; Whiting C600.

C369 To hedge in the **Cuckoo**

1702 Mather *Magnalia* 2.588: This was but a project to "hedge in the cuckow." **1744** *Letter* in *Colonial Currency* 4.234: All such Attempts being as fruitless as to enclose the *Cuckow* by a Wall. **1802** Moultrie *Memoirs* 1.96: We may as well build a wall round a Cuckoo to keep him in. [A footnote to "cuckoo" reads "owl."] *Oxford* 899; Tilley M636. See **G132.**

C370 As cold as a **Cucumber**

1787 Tilghman *Letters* 142: Arnold was as cold as a Cucumber. Barbour 44(2); *Oxford* 143; Tilley C895; Whiting *NC* 389(1).

C371 As cool as a **Cucumber**

1809 Lindsley *Love* 10: Cool as a keowcumber. **1834** Longfellow *Letters* 1.456: I think it [a review] rather in the *cucumber* style— quite cool. **1835** Floy *Diary* 144: I was cool as a cucumber. Barbour 44(3); *Oxford* 143; TW 86-7.

C372 To chew the **Cud**

1733 Lynde *Diaries* 45: It is, as it were, chewing the cud of the creatures—a holy ruminating. **1783** Freneau *Poems* 2.203: And cursing and swearing, and chewing their cuds. **1794** Brackenridge *Gazette* 244: I maun . . . gae chew my cud. **1818** Pintard *Letters* 1.131: But England may pause & chew the cud of reflection. **1825** Wirt *Letters* 1.35: Leaving me sitting alone in the boat to chew the cud of disappointment and neglect as well as I could. *Oxford* 118; Whiting C604.

C373 To lay down (take up) the Cudgels
1690 SSewall in *Baxter Manuscripts* 5.63-4: 'Tis of absolute necessity That Albany lay down the Cudgels, and submit to York. **1699** Makemie *Writings* 133: To hear of a Presbyterian taking up the Cudgels, against a . . . Minister of the English Church. *Oxford* 801; Tilley C897, 898.

C374 As grand as Cuffy
1815 Humphreys *Yankey* 88: And you are as grand as Cuffy. TW 87.

C375 As white as a Curd
1821 Knight *Poems* 2.181: You're white as a curd. Lean 2.891; TW B7(1).

C376 What can't be Cured must be endured
1698 Sewall *Diary* 1.476: He at first said, *That which can't be cur'd must be endur'd.* **1755** Laurens *Papers* 1.263: What can't be cur'd must be submitted to. **1770** SHood in *Bowdoin Papers* 1.210: But as the old saying is. **1777** AA in *Adams FC* 2.212: What can't be help'd must be endured. **1797** JWTomlin in *VHM* 30(1922) 226. **1798** RTroup in King *Life* 2.429: We endeavor to fortify each other with philosophy to bear the ills we cannot cure. **c1800** Tyler *Island* 11. **1810** *Kennon Letters* 32.170, **1811** 345: The evils we cannot cure, we must try to bear, 349, **1813** 35.16. **1832** Barney *Memoir* 245: The wisdom of the old proverb. **1833** Jackson *Correspondence* 5.28: the old adage. **1847** Paulding *Letters(II)* 460: they say. *Oxford* 161; TW 87(2); Tilley C922.

C377 Curses light on one's own head
a1656 Bradford *History* 1.149: Thus his curses light on his owne head. *Oxford* 162; TW 88(6). Cf. Whiting C640. See F214, M191, N51, P182, S281.

C378 Not care a Curse
1777 Moore *Diary* 1.452: But they kept their position, and car'd not a curse. TW 88(2).

C379 Not give a Curse
1763 Jefferson *Papers* 1.7: I do not conceive that any thing can happen in my world which you would give a curse to know. NED Curse 2.

C380 Not worth a Curse
1795 Cobbett *Porcupine* 2.84: That genius is not worth a curse, **1796** 3.191. **1798** Adams *New Letters* 183. **1825** Neal *American Writers* 166: My other essays . . . were not worth a curse. *Oxford* 154, 162; TW 88(4). Cf. Whiting C549.

C381 Curtain lecture
c1725 Byrd *Another Secret Diary* 452: Nor can Furistante well avoid being a vixen and a Termagant, yea and exceeding loud in her Curtain lectures, **1728** *Dividing Line* 288: No more rest all night than a poor Husband subject to Curtain Lectures. **1744** Stephens *Journal(II)* 2.176: But that all she did was thro his advice behind the Curtain. **1770** Adams *D and A* 1.349: She gave him such Curtain Lectures. **1778** Gordon *Letters* 371. **1791** *Columbian Centinel* in *Olden Time* 6.71. **1791** *Universal Asylum* 7.102: The nocturnal disease, called by the inhabitants, *a Curtain Lecture.* **1792** Belknap *Foresters* 149: She . . . held a *curtain* conference with Mr. Bell, 167. **1797** Cobbett *Porcupine* 5.418: She . . . awakens him by night to the refreshing eloquence of a curtain lecture. **1797** Tyler *Prose* 219. **1801** *Farmers' Museum* 304. **1809** Irving *History* 2.139: The ox-eyed Juno, who had gained a pair of black eyes over night, in one of her curtain lectures with old Jupiter. **1817** Scott *Blue Lights* 119: [Jupiter] having missed the customary lecture of his spouse Juno. **1832** Ames *Nautical* 198. *Oxford* 162; TW 88.

C382 To miss the Cushion
1645 Wheelwright *Writings* 224: He mist not the *cushion.* NED Cushion 10a; *Oxford* 536; Whiting C641.

C383 To set beside the Cushion
1721 *Wyllys Papers* 398: You have sate be-

sides Cushion in y^t one word. NED Cushion 10b, c. Cf. *Oxford* 47; Whiting C642.

C384 A bad **Custom** is better broken than kept

1765 Adams *Legal Papers* 1.95: Vulgar Custom refuted by a vulgar Proverb. A bad Custom better broke than kept. *Oxford* 25; Tilley C931.

C385 A bad **Custom** is easier introduced than removed

1753 *Georgia Records* 26.429: [It is] well known y^t a bad Custom is easier introduced than remov'd. Whiting C652. See **H4**.

C386 **Custom** makes law

1713 Wise *Churches* 86: Custom, when full of days, and of Noble Examples, becomes the *Common Law* of a Nation. **1800** Dorr *Letters* 208: Custom is law with 'em. Whiting C647.

C387 **Custom** reconciles most evils (*varied*)

1643 Williams *Writings* 1.146: *O what a Tyrant's Custome long, How doe men make a tush, At what's in use, though ne're so fowle: Without once shame or blush?* **1728** Byrd *Dividing Line* 95: But Custome that reconciles most Evils, made him bear it with Christian Patience. **1807** Janson *Stranger* 58: Custom will, however, reconcile man to all things. a**1820** Biddle *Autobiography* 184: Custom reconciles most things. Cf. TW 88; Tilley C934. See **H3, U14.**

C388 **Custom-House** oath

1753 *Independent Reflector* 267: So flagrant are the instances of their foreswearing themselves, that a *Custom-House* Oath is grown into a Proverb, 267: A Master of a Vessel . . . who, yet, could not help saying, *God forbid that a Custom-House Oath should be a Sin.* NED Custom-house 2.

C389 **Cut** and come again

1779 Sargent *Loyalist* 38: But solid victuals, cut and come again. **1789** Hopkinson *Miscellaneous Essays* 3^2 .202: For noses lost — and cut and come again. **1795** Freneau *Poems* (*1795*) 352: 'Twas fish on fish — and cut — and come again. **1828** Wirt *Letters* 2.242: I find myself generally ready "to cut and come again," 438. *Oxford* 162-3; TW 89(2).

C390 **Cut** and run (go)

1788 EWinslow in *Winslow Papers* 503: I was among the first who were obliged to cut and run. **1810** Asbury *Journal* 2.631: We went, cut and go, through the bleak weather. **1815** Brackenridge *Modern* 772: The alternative was to go to jail, or, as the phrase is, to *cut and run.* Berrey 58.6: go; TW 89(3).

C391 The **Cut** of one's jib

1796 Latrobe *Journal* 38: By the cut of your jib. Colcord 108; TW 89(1).

C392 To be **Cut** and dried

1765 Franklin *Papers* 12.365: It was all cut and dry'd. **1776** Freneau *Poems* 1.243: Prayers, cut and dry, by ancient prelates made. **1777** CCushing in *Baxter Manuscripts* 10.143. **1779** JLovell in Adams *Works* 9.488: A cut-and-dried commission. **1794** SHodgdon in Hamilton *Papers* 16.1794. **1801** Cutler *Life* 2.46: The principal business of Congress is already cut and dried. **1803** *Port Folio* 3.120: Your ghost, with a *message* from hell cut and dried. **1804** *The Centinel* in Otis *Letters* 1.286. **1805** CWPeale in *PM* 9(1885) 122. **1807** *Weekly* 1.208. **1810** Taggart *Letters* 338. **1812** Hitchcock *Social* 51. **1815** Waterhouse *Journal* 112. **1817** Robertson *Letters* 12: A pocket full of mock warrants "cut and dry," 21: Pick up these sentiments "cut and dry." **1819** *Musings* 53. **1821** Beecher *Autobiography* 1.449: Some society's committee will be cut and dried, ready to call in a Cambridge student. **1825** Wirt *Letters* 2.197: If Cicero had had all this he could not have kept his *exordia* cut and dry, as he is said to have done. TW 89(1).

D

D1 To be at **Daggers** drawn

1777 Hopkinson *Miscellaneous Essays* 1.109: These nations are now at daggers drawn. **1779** Lee *Papers* 3.319: Men with whom you . . . are at daggers drawn. **1792** Morris *Diary* 2.573: Fifteen or twenty who are at Daggers' Drawing. **1802** RTroup in King *Life* 4.121: The Clintonians and the Burrites are at dagger's points. *Oxford* 165; TW 90(1). See **S545.**

D2 Who **Dainties** love shall beggars prove

1749 Franklin *PR* 3.340: Who dainties love, shall Beggars prove, **1758** *WW* 345. **1770** Ames *Almanacs* 413: Who dainties love shall beggars prove. *Oxford* 165; Tilley D13.

D3 Not care a **Damn**

1775 SMoylan in *Naval Documents* 2.590: A person who did not Care a damn for them. **1797** Hawkins *Letters* 125. **1805** *Port Folio* 5.4. **1806** Fessenden *Modern Philosopher* 249: You need not care a single damn. **1812** Burr *Journal* 2.328. **1816** Lambert *Travels* 1.480. a**1820** Biddle *Autobiography* 96. **1820** Robertson *Letters* 277. NED Damn 2.

D4 Not give a **Damn**

1827 Watterston *Wanderer* 60-1: I would not give *A-dam,* for the whole of them.

D5 Not worth a **Damn**

1807 JAdams in *Adams-Warren Correspondence* 327: No government was worth a damn. NED Damn 2.

D6 From **Dan** to Beersheba

1633 EHowes in *Winthrop Papers(A)* 3.134: They flock to you even from Dan to Bersheba, from Plymouth to Barwick. **1748** Eliot *Essays* 31: The Holy Land from Dan to *Beer-sheba.* **1759** CWhittelsey in Stiles *Itineraries* 582. **1764** Watts *Letter Book* 293: All well from Dan to Beersheba. **1774** Boucher *View* 427. **1774** Seabury *Letters* 87-8: They go begging from Dan to Beersheba . . . from Nova Scotia to Georgia. **1783** *American Wanderer* 202: In search of happiness from Dan to Beersheba. **1783** Freneau *Poems* (*1786*) 384: Drove them from Beersheba to Dan. **1791** Hamilton *Papers* 9.34: I do not publish it in Dan & Bersheba. **1796** Dennie *Lay Preacher* 98, 178. **1800** MCarey in Weems *Letters* 2.140: I could not have supposed it possible that you would travel from Dan to Bersheba & receive only ten or twelve dollars in two or three days. **1801** *Farmers' Museum* 162: Yet like Smollet, I never travel from Dan to Beersheba, and cry, "it is all barren." **1801** *Port Folio* 1.364: These long journies, from Dan to Beersheba, **1804** 4.125: Sauntering along . . . *from Dan to Beersheba.* **1806** Fessenden *Modern Philosopher* 31. **1807** Bates *Papers* 1.167. **1807** *Salmagundi* 115. **1808** Barker *Tears* 143: Curse the way, From Dan to Beersheba, and back to Dan. **1809** Weems *Marion* 232: The hardy mountaineers rise up as one man from Dan to Beersheba. **1811** *Port Folio* 2NS 5.402. **1814** *Cary Letters* 201: Those who according to Sterne, travel from Dan to Beersheba, 228. **1814** Freneau

Poems 3.344: And rove from Beersheba to Dan. **1815** Brackenridge *Modern* 762. **1815** Kerr *Barclay* 192: It is likely to go from Dan to Bersheba, 314. **1817** Weems *Letters* 3.215: I dashing, like one mad, from Dan to Beersheba to meet the Sub[s]. **1836** Floy *Diary* 238: They have been so weak as to have it circulated from Dan to Beersheba that he intended running away with their daughter. *Oxford* (2nd ed.) 128; Whiting D7. See **G35, J45.**

D7 Publish it not in **Dan** or Beersheba

1791 Jefferson *Writings* 1.284: I do not publish it in Dan or Bersheba. See **D6**(1791), **G26.**

D8 To lead someone a **Dance**

1771 *Johnson Papers* 8.129: We are determined to Lead them Another Dance. **1777** *Washington *Writings* 8.315: They have it much in their power to lead us a very disagreeable dance. **1795** Cobbett *Porcupine* 2.73: For you had led us a confounded jack-in-a-lanthorn dance. Whiting D12.

D9 To lead the **Dance**

1738 Stephens *Journal*(*I*) 1.240: If it proved true, that Darien led up the Dance, there were not wanting others . . . ready to fall in with them, **1742** (*II*) 1.59: One of our first Runaways who led the Dance . . . now entreated that he might be admitted.

D10 To pay for one's **Dancing**

1810 Sumter *Letters* 66: And now as Mr. S. says *Now we are in we must pay for our Dancing. Oxford* 615: Pay the piper, quote 1638. See **F84, P147.**

D11 **Danger** makes men bold

1775 AA in *Adams FC* 1.225: Danger you [know] sometimes makes timid men bold, 239: Danger they say makes people valiant. See **C332.**

D12 No **Danger** no glory

1792 Brackenridge *Modern* 49: For where there is no danger, there is no glory. Lean 4.125; *Oxford* 641; Tilley D35; Whiting P147. See **C351.**

D13 **Darby** and Joan

1779 Webb *Correspondence* 2.175: Jog'd slowly on like Darby and Jone, saying nothing, but much thinking. **1781** JLovell in *Adams FC* 4.227: Take the Song of Darby and Joan in Hand. **1788** Ledyard *Russian Journey* 219: Their Carnival is at hand & I could wish to see it as among their Joan & Darby Nobless one might recontre at least with something Buxom. **1795** Freneau *Poems* (*1795*) 102: Darby and Joan their growing loves approv'd. **1803** Davis *Travels* 128: An old negro-man and negro-woman huddle together, like *Darby* and *Joan.* **1810** Cuming *Sketches* 149: Marion and . . . his old wife, reminded me of Baucis and Philemon, or of Darby and Joan. **1811** *Kennon Letters* 32.349: When like Darby and Joan she and the lord of her affection are together. a**1815** Freneau *Poems* 3.305: Poor Darby, and without a Joan. **1821** Hodgson *Letters* 2.137: I . . . met more Darbys and Joans jogging away on their farm horses. *Oxford* 167; TW 91.

D14 To be in the **Dark**

1692 Mather *Letters* 37: To determine a matter so much in the dark as to know the guilty employers of the devils in this work of darkness. **1777** WBedlow in *Clinton Papers* 2.276: Mr. Comfort Sands writes me he is in the dark respecting my appointment. TW 91.

D15 To pass in the **Dark**

1815 Palmer *Diary* 140: Had he not those failings he might pass in the Dark. Cf. Partridge: Crowd. See **C57, J34.**

D16 To whistle in the **Dark** (burying-yard)

1815 Humphreys *Yankey* 77: I'll du as the boys du, when they go by the berrying-yard alone, in a dark light, and see a ghost in the form of a white hoss; and an Indian in every black stump. [Whistles.] **1818** Wirt *Letters* 2.70: For I am really laughing to keep myself from crying, as cowards whistle in the dark.

D17 **Darts** foreseen are better warded off

1754 Parkman *Diary* 76.82: But Darts foreseen may be better warded off. Cf. Whiting A183, W49.

D18 To cut a **Dash**

1799 Carey *Porcupiniad* 2.37: In Britain's court to "cut a dash" When here he'd made so "grand a splash." **1819** *Musings* 18: Proud of the hopeful child, that *cuts a dash*. TW 91(1).

D19 The **Daughters** of the horse-leech

1664 Bradstreet *Works* 61: It . . . like the daughters of the horsleach, crys give, give! **1755** Davis *Colonial Virginia Satirist* 23: So cry the twins of the horse Leech! **1796** Dennie *Lay Preacher* 85: Why do you cry . . . "Give! Give!" like the daughters of the horse-leach. **1803** Austin *Constitutional* 152: They are the political horse-leaches, crying, give, give. **1830** Ames *Mariner's* 45: The "daughters of the house-leech" whose cry is still "give, give," **1832** *Nautical* 62: I thought of the horse-leech and her two daughters. *Oxford* 168; Whiting W91.

D20 Marry your **Daughter** and eat fresh fish betimes

1736 Franklin *PR* 2.143: Marry your Daughter and eat fresh Fish betimes. *Oxford* 168; Tilley D45. See **S318.**

D21 As drunk as **David's** sow

1737 Franklin *Drinkers* 2.177: As Drunk as David's Sow. **1795** Murdock *Triumphs* 64: They are . . . both as drunk as David's sow. **1806** *Port Folio* NS 1.108: Drunk as old David's sow is he. **1812** *Journal of Two Cruises* 134: After King Antonio and his nobility had got as drunk as David's son [*for* sow]. **1815** Humphreys *Yankey* 63: You are as drunk as David's — I won't say *what* — for that isn't a pretty name. **1830** Ames *Mariner's* 278. *Oxford* 206; Tilley S1042.

D22 **Davy** Jones's locker

1774 Cresswell *Journal* 12: "They are gone to Davy Jones's Locker." This is a common saying when anything goes over board. **1774** Schaw *Journal* 51: We would certainly have thought it was Davy Jones the terror of all sailors, come to fetch us away, 52: And every thing else gone to Davy Jones' locker, that is to the Devil. **1776** Barney *Memoir* 49:

We are all to go to old *Davy Jones's* locker. **1783** Williams *Penrose* 185: Stow a poor unfortunate man in Davy Jones's locker. **1790** AThomas in *Blount Papers* 2.72: I began to be apprehensive he had made a visit to David Jones. **1792** *Belknap Papers* 2.303: I know nothing of the man . . . nor whether he is gone to Davy Jones's locker, as the sailors say. **1796** Weems *Letters* 2.37: But for her crew and cargo I w^d not weep were she at moorings in Davy Jones's locker. **1802** JTaylor in *Steele Papers* 1.265: The probability is that they are gone to David Jones. **1802** Wilson *Letters* xxvii: Rowan has gone to Davie's Locker at last: he died in the West Indies. **1803** Davis *Travels* 423: The deepest receptacle of *Davy Jones'* Locker. **1806** Fessenden *Modern Philosopher* 249: Give a quick passport to old Davy. **1806** *Weekly* 1.48: And you deserve for that alone, *The dry dock of Old Davy*. **1807** *New-England Palladium* in Buckingham *Specimens* 2.169: His . . . navy, Which thousands of Frenchmen has sent to old Davy. **1809** Fessenden *Pills* 83: Our commerce cleared out for old Davy. **1809** Lindsley *Love* 38, 41. **1813** *Port Folio* 3NS 2.581: All sent broken-ribbed to old Davy, 584: There's many a noble Briton's soul Must weigh for grim old Davy, **1814** 3.200: I fancy we'll all meet at Davy's again As jovial as e'er we met here. **a1815** Freneau *Poems* 3.311, 326: Is gone to Davy Jones's chest. **1815** Palmer *Diary* 213: If I did not feel very anxious to get home I would see them to old Davy before I would stand for them. **a1820** Biddle *Autobiography* 158. **1823** GHowland in *New England Merchants* 130: It is all day with him — he will soon be in "Davy Jones locker." **1846** Paulding *Letters(II)* 446. Colcord 63; *Oxford* 169; TW 91-2.

D23 A **Daw** (jackdaw) in borrowed plumage (*varied*)

1696 Taylor *Poems* 108: Like to the Daugh all glorious made when drest In feathers borrowed of other birds Must need be King of birds. **1769** JDevotion in Stiles *Letters* 17: Is it not best for every Bird to wear his own Feathers, and Feed his own Flock? **1781** Reed *Life* 2.359: If I should live to finish what I have begun, I shall certainly strip

every Jack Daw of his borrowed plumage.
1786 Adams(A) *Letters* 291: The designing
jackdaw will sometimes borrow the plumes
of the jay, and pass himself off to those who
judge only by appearances. **1788** Dunlap
Diary 1.31: Or else be mark'd & shun'd like
Esops daw. **1796** Washington *Writings*
35.282: The last would . . . expose you to
the reproach of the daw in borrowed feathers. **1803** Davis *Travels* 209: Nay, *Franklin*
is a downright plagiarist. Let him retain
only his own feathers; let those he has stolen
be restored to their lawful possessors, and,
Franklin, who now struts about expanding
the gayest plumage, will be without a single
feather to cover his rump. **1807** *Weekly*
2.239: [He] so thoroughly stripped the jackdaw of his borrowed plumage, that we fancy
he will not ape the eagle in the future.
a1814 Dow *Journal* 412: Some young gentleman . . . offers his hand to one of these
"*jackdaws* dressed in peacock feathers."
1825 *Austin Papers* 2.1215: Groce may Borrow what plumage he will, yet he will be
Groce still. **1827** Jackson *Correspondence*
3.335: I will unrobe his hypocrisy and strip
him of much of his borrowed plumage. *Oxford* 60; TW 203; Tilley B375.

D24 No wiser than a **Daw**

1708 Cook *Sot-Weed* 24: No wiser than a
Daw in Steeple. Whiting D27.

D25 As mild as **Dawn**

1773 Paterson *Glimpses* 103: You were . . .
mild as the Dawn of a Summer Day.

D26 After three **Days** men grow weary of a
wench, *etc.*

1733 Franklin *PR* 1.314: After 3 days men
grow weary, of a wench, a guest, and
weather rainy. Cf. *Oxford* 287; Tilley F310.
See **F144.**

D27 As clear as **Day**

1728 Byrd *Dividing Line* 127: We made it as
clear as Noon Day. **1756** RBland in *Letters
to Washington* 1.387: I pretend to shew
you, as clear as the Day. **1759** Tossitee in
McDowell *Documents* 2.494: The Chain . . .
be kept clear and bright as the Day. **1778**
Lee *Papers* 3.264: A truth, simple and clear
as the day. **1798** Adams *Writings* 2.330:

The fact will appear clear as day. **1820**
Fudge Family 79. *Oxford* 125; Whiting
D34.

D28 As certain as **Day**

1806 *Monthly Anthology* 3.73: As certain as
day. Cf. TW 92(15).

D29 As happy as the **Day** is long

1736 *Georgia Records* 21.257: We live as
happy as y[e] day is long. **1755** Washington
Writings 1.138: Make me happier than the
Day is long. **1788** Adams *Diary* 394. **1795**
Cobbett *Porcupine* 2.145. **1811** Weems
Gambling 39. **1816** Paulding *Letters(I)*
2.26. **1817** Wirt *Letters* 2.33. **1825** Longfellow *Letters* 1.138. **1833** Pintard *Letters*
4.153: She said that M[rs] D's family . . . was
as happy & merry as the day was long.
Barbour 45(4); *Oxford* 527; TW 92(8).

D30 As honest as the **Day**

1849 Cooper *Letters* 6.34: He is honest as
the day. TW 92(9).

D31 As many as **Days** in the year

1809 Kendall *Travels* 3.149: It does not
occur to them, that the specification of this
number is only a periphrasis of the proverbial expression—*as many as there are days
in the year.*

D32 As plain as **Day**

1802 *Port Folio* 2.152: 'Tis every bit as plain
as day. **1820** *Fudge Family* 71: The law is
plain as day. TW 92(14).

D33 The better **Day** the better deed

1677 Hubbard *Indian* 1.190: The Lords-day
also (no doubt the betterness of the Day will
increase the badness' of their Deed attempted thereon). **1791** S.P.L. *Thoughts*
77: The better day, the better deed. **1803**
Paine *To Mr. Jefferson* 2.1101: For with the
learned world it is agreed, The better day
the better deed. **1830** Paulding *Letters(II)*
111. Barbour 46(16); *Oxford* 52; TW
93(26).

D34 A cold **Day** or two does not make
winter

1755 *Johnson Papers* 2.156: A cold day or
two or a little Ice does not make Winter. See
S531.

D35 A **Day** after the fair

1788 AAdams in Smith *Journal and Correspondence* 2(2) 65: Col. Trumbull brought . . . the two letters of recall, the day after the fare [*for* fair], to be sure. **1793** Ingraham *Journal* 103: We were the day after the fair. **1808** HWWilkinson in *Kingston* 352. **1809** Weems *Letters* 2.394. **1855** Paulding *Letters(II)* 560. *Oxford* 169; Whiting D60.

D36 He that rises late must trot all **Day**

1742 Franklin *PR* 2.337: He that riseth late, must trot all day, and shall scarce overtake his business at night, **1758** *WW* 341-2. **1770** Ames *Almanacs* 412. Barbour 45(6); *Oxford* 679.

D37 Many lose more in a **Day** than others gain in a year

1748 Ames *Almanacs* 215: Many lose more in a Day, than others gain in a Year. Cf. *Oxford* 113; Whiting D56.

D38 Not to know if it is **Day** or night

1757 RDemere in McDowell *Documents* 2.320: By the Pains I have taken . . . I scarce know when it is Day or Night. Whiting D64.

D39 A red-letter **Day**

1740 Belcher *Papers* 2.304: This is a red letter day. **1780** Curwen *Journal* 2.679: Having no concern on red letter days. **1792** Dennie *Letters* 122: My Calendar has been marked with few red letter days. **1816** Pintard *Letters* 1.33: These red letter days are very sparcely scattered thro' my Calendar. **1818** Bentley *Diary* 4.543: But Thursday is also included of late years, but by no statute on the red letter days. **1819** Adams *Works* 10.382: The red letter day [July 4] in our national calendar. **1823** Pintard *Letters* 2.127: England retains numerous red letter days as they are called w^h afford intervals of rest, 182, **1832** 4.29: We shall drink y^r healths at dinner, as this is a red letter day. NED Red letter 2b.

D40 Sufficient unto the **Day** is the evil thereof

1766 AA in *Adams FC* 1.56: Sufficient to the Day is the Evil thereof. Thus says the psalmist. **1777** Fitch *New-York Diary* 122.

1789 Adams *New Letters* 23: But sufficient to the day. **1791** Scott *Journal* 291. **1792** Jay *Correspondence* 2.420. **1786** DAllison in *Blount Papers* 3.58. **1805** *Tyler Letters* 1.210. Adams *Writings* 5.355. **1819** Cobbett *Year's* 99. Barbour 46(15); *Oxford* 785; Whiting D52.

D41 There is a good **Day** a-coming

1792 Brackenridge *Modern* 16: He may not be yet skilled in the matter, but there is a good day a-coming. Cf. Whiting D49.

D42 To carry the **Day**

1807 *Salmagundi* 57: It . . . seems to be the prevailing opinion that Madame Bouchard will carry the day. TW 93(29).

D43 To come the **Day** after the battle

1810 Beecher *Autobiography* 1.183: I . . . came as near having a call as the fellow did being killed who came to the field the day after the battle.

D44 To differ as **Day** from night

1676 Williams *Writings* 5.273: Differ as much as Day from Night, and Light from Darkness. Barbour 129: Night (3); Taylor *Comparisons* 34; Whiting D37. See **L131**.

D45 To lay up (*etc.*) for a rainy **Day**

1753 Franklin *Papers* 4.482: I should think the Poor would be more careful . . . and lay up something for themselves against a rainy day. **1775** Hopkinson *Miscellaneous Essays* 1.20: And to lay by a little at the year's end, against a rainy day. **1780** Barney *Memoir* 83: Shall I keep something for a *rainy day*? **1780** *Deane Brothers Papers* 152: I thought it best to secure something before a Wet Day. **1787** *American Museum* 1.115, **1788** 3.119. **1788** *Politician* 25: To make hay while the sun shines *against* a rainy day. **1795** Ames *Letters* 1.164: A stock of merit laid up against a rainy day. **1818** Fearon *Sketches* 446: They cannot reasonably calculate . . . on laying by any thing for what is called "a rainy day." **1829** Pintard *Letters* 3.100: Sailors are a thoughtless, improvident set, it is difficult to allure them to make deposits & keep something for a rainy day. *Oxford* 663; TW 93(23).

D46 We little know what a **Day** will bring forth

1813 Fletcher *Letters* 74: How little do we know what a day will bring forth. Cf. Whiting D57.

D47 As clear as **Daylight**

1798 Cobbett *Porcupine* 10.43: A conclusion as clear as day-light, **1799** 11.57: It proves as clear as day-light. **1806** *Port Folio* NS 1.11, **1815** 3NS 5.436. **1821** Adams *Writings* 7.135: As clear as daylight. TW 93(1).

D48 To knock someone's **Daylights** out

1819 Peirce *Rebelliad* 49: And knock the rulers' daylights out. Barbour 46; TW 94(2).

D49 To make **Daylight** shine through someone

1774 *Boston Gazette* in Thornton *Glossary* 1.239: He would make Daylight shine thro' 'em. **1777** JWoodhull in *Clinton Papers* 1.590: The Ensign Having his sword Drawn, says he whould make the Day Light shine true him. NED Daylight 1c; TW 94(3). See **S524.**

D50 As sober as **Deacons**

1820 Pintard *Letters* 1.3531: We w[alk]ed off at 10, as sober as Deacons. TW 94(2).

D51 As steady as a **Deacon**

1812 Randall *Miser* 16: She stays at work for her father as steady as a deacon.

D52 To make a **Deacon** swear

1768 Freneau *Poems* 1.21: Discover'd what might make a deacon swear. Cf. TW 295: Preacher. See **A94, Q3, S72.**

D53 Enough to raise the **Dead**

1708 Cook *Sot-Weed* 9: Such Peals the Dead to Life wou'd bring. **1775** APollok in Iredell *Correspondence* 2.604: After waiting a considerable time screaming enough to raise the dead. TW 94(4).

D54 Let the **Dead** bury their dead

1815 Dow *Journal* 340: A worldling replied to him, "let the dead bury their dead." Whiting *NC* 291(4).

D55 Speak well of the **Dead** (*varied*)

1692 Bulkeley *Will* 89: It is in this case an excellent rule, *de vivis nil nisi verum, de mortuis nil nisi bonum.* **a1700** Hubbard *New England* 94: For according to the old rule "de mortuis nil nisi lene," speak well of the dead. **1734** *New-York Weekly Journal* in *Newspaper Extracts*(*I*) 1.400: *De mortiis nihil nisi bonum, de absentibus nihil nisi verum.* **1754** MGraves in *Fitch Papers* 1.4: De mortuis & absentibus nil nisi bonum. **1768** CChauncey in Stiles *Itineraries* 444: My maxim is, nil nisi bonum de mortuis. **1774** JEliot in *Belknap Papers* 3.61: General Molineux is dead . . . *Nil nisi bonum de mortuis.* **1781** Pickering *Life* 2.88: "De mortuis nil nisi bonum" is a maxim to which I never subscribed. **1785** Freneau *Poems* (*1786*) 367: There is an old adage our poets have read, That nothing but good should be spoke of the dead. **1788** *American Museum* 3.380: the adage [Latin only]. **1791** Smith *Life and Correspondence* 2.344: The dead can never vindicate nor defend themselves. Therefore, of *them*, is given the counsel, *nil nisi bonum.* **1796** *Federal Orrery* in Buckham *Specimens* 2.244: An ancient maxim of philosophic humanity [Latin only]. **1797** Tyler *Algerine* 1.33-4: It must have given him pain to *speak evil even of the dead.* **1798** Cobbett *Porcupine* 8.76: in general a good maxim [Latin only]. **1798** RTroup in King *Life* 2.433: *De mortuis nil nisi bonum* is a maxim as applicable to him as if he was in his grave. **c1800** Dennie *Lay Preacher* 180: Athens is no more, and, recollecting an old adage, we will not insult her ashes. **1806** Fanning *Narrative* 68: The good old adage which says, "we should never speak ill of the dead." **1809** Bates *Papers* 2.109: a good old maxim [Latin only]. **1810** Rush *Letters* 2.1034: Doctor Franklin used to say, "The maxim of not speaking evil of the dead should be reversed. We should speak evil *only* of the dead, for in so doing we can do them no harm." **1813** Eaton *Life* 9: The old precept *Nil de mortuis nisi bonum* was never intended for history or biography: adhesion to such a dictate would effectually destroy the value of both. **1813** JGJackson in Knopf *War of 1812* 2.72: *De mortus.* **1816** *Port*

Folio 4NS 1.149: To alter the old adage *De mortuis nil nisi bonum*, to *de mortuis nil nisi verum*. *Oxford* 761; TW 94(3).

D56 None so **Deaf** as those who will not hear

1766 JParker in Franklin *Papers* 13.18: For none so deaf as those who will not hear. **1791** S.P.L. *Thoughts* 167. Barbour 46; *Oxford* 172; Whiting D75. See **B206.**

D57 As awful as **Death**

1805 Asbury *Journal* 2.474: A ceremony awful as death.

D58 As bitter as **Death**

1652 Williams *Writings* 6.239: It was as bitter as death to me. Whiting D79.

D59 As black as **Death**

1824 Neal *American Writers* 66: Black hair — "black as death." TW 95(1).

D60 As certain as **Death**

1760 GClough *Journal* in *Historical Collections of the Essex Institute* 3(1861) 198: This is as certain as death itself is. **1795** Bayard *Journal* 53: How uncertain is everything but death. **1805** JReynolds in *Ruffin Papers* 1.91: I will pay Robinson tonight: as certain as death. **1814** Harmon *Sixteen Years* 167: I begin to think there is little certainty of any thing in this World except disappointments and Death, **1816** 185. Cf. *Oxford* 789; TW 95(18); Whiting D81. See **D76.**

D61 As certain as **Death** and taxes (rates)

1789 Franklin *Writings* 10.69: But in this world nothing can be said to be certain, except death and taxes. **1803** *Yankee Phrases* 87: As certain as death, or as rates. **1822** Lee *Diary and Letters* 201: He looks like death and rates. Barbour 46(1); *Oxford* 580: Nothing. See **R30.**

D62 As cold as **Death**

1756 Franklin *Papers* 6.365: Finding them [sheets] as cold as death. **1802** Dow *Journal* 131: Her hands seemed as cold as death. TW 94(4).

D63 As cruel as **Death**

1772 Freneau *Poems* 1.64: Cruel as death. See **G156.**

D64 As hungry as **Death**

1809 Freneau *Poems* 1.167: North's friends down swarming . . . Hungry as death.

D65 As inevitable as **Death**

1777 Hamilton *Papers* 1.212: War . . . "was as inevitable as death." [Quoted from a letter by Franklin.]

D66 As pale as **Death**

1769 *Johnson Papers* 6.754: He was pale as death. **1787** *American Museum* 1.47. **1797** Cobbett *Porcupine* 5.40. a**1814** Dow *Journal* 406. a**1820** Biddle *Autobiography* 159. **1824** Doddridge *Notes* 181: Pale as death with rage. *Oxford* 608; TW 95(9).

D66a **Death-pale**

1801 Nichols *Jefferson* 7: His death-pale cheek.

D67 As poor as **Death**

1757 Carter *Diary* 1.158: This latter still as poor as death and always in a quiet fever.

D68 As sick as **Death**

1764 JA in *Adams FC* 1.33: Powder that make them as sick as Death. TW 85(13).

D69 As silent as **Death**

1775 Schaw *Journal* 119: All was silent as death. **1788** Humphreys *Works* 253: It was silent as the house of death. **1797** Mann *Female* 240: The night was silent as death. **1803** WGrave in *Steele Papers* 1.368. **1816** Ker *Travels* 154: All was silent as the hour of death. **1819** Noah *Travels* 306. **1819** Royall *Letters* 198. **1832** Pintard *Letters* 4.7. *Oxford* 733; TW 95(14). See **G160.**

D70 As solemn as **Death**

1793 Asbury *Journal* 1.770: Solemn as death! **1812** Knopf *War of 1812* 5(1) 203. TW 95(15).

D71 As still as **Death**

1778 Wister *Journal* 171: They halted. All as still as death. **1791** Bartram *Travels* 217: All around is now as still as death. **1812** Maxwell *Poems* 21. **1815** JHewson in *Lincoln Papers* 211: We was as still as death. **1833** Floy *Diary* 32. **1837** Hone *Diary* 1.259. Barbour 46(2); Whiting D83.

D72 As true as **Death**

1825 Neal *American Writers* 197: All the dates are true—true as death. TW 95(20).

D73 Better **Death** than a slave's life (*varied*)

1637 Williams *Writings* 6.15: Better an honorable death than a slave's life. c1680 Radisson *Voyages* 161: I will venter choosing to die like a man then live like a beggar. 1777 JDuché in Washington *Writings* 9.382: Perhaps it may be said, that it is "better to die than be Slaves." This indeed is a splendid maxim in theory. 1804 RQuinn in *Barbary Wars* 4.203: Death is always superior to slavery. Whiting D95, 239. See **F291.**

D74 **Death** and the cobbler

1680 FJWinthrop in *Winthrop Papers(B)* 4.288: Soe yᵗ at yᵉ breaking vp of yᵉ Generall Court here I loock for nothing else (as yᵉ proverbe) but death & yᵉ cobler.

D75 (**Death**) cancels all debts

1742 *Georgia Records* 23.275: [He] died lately after a farther Expence; & has thereby cancell'd all Debts. *Oxford* 174; Tilley D148.

D76 **Death** is certain, but not the time (*varied*)

a1700 Hubbard *New England* 257: But man knoweth not his time. 1723 *New-England Courant* 105(1.2): *Death is certain, but the Time very uncertain.* 1765 Ames *Almanacs* 367: Nothing more certain than Death, or more uncertain than the Time. 1779 JFogg in *Sullivan Journals* 93: Man knoweth not his time. 1791 Bartram *Travels* 322: All men must surely die, Tho' no one knows how soon. 1796 Paine *Decline* 2.652: Nothing, they say, is more certain than death, and nothing more uncertain than the time of dying. *Oxford* 571; Whiting D96. See **D60.**

D77 **Death** is certain (common) to all

1634 Wood *New-England* 10: Death being certain to all. 1692 Randolph *Letters* 7.407: Like Death spareing none. 1764 Watts *Letter Book* 213: Least any Accident, or Death the common Lot of all Mortals, should have overtaken his friend, 229: Treatment, that has no Alleviation unless like Death it is common to all. 1771 Carter *Diary* 1.565: Death is not only certain in ourselves but also in Every living creature. 1790 Pickering *Life* 2.466: Death, you know, is the common lot of all mankind; and none can escape the stroke. *Oxford* 10; Whiting D97. See **D175, M15.**

D78 **Death** is the gate of life

1792 *Universal Asylum* 9.120: Mors Janua Vitæ. *Death is the gate of life, they say.*

D79 **Death** takes all (*varied*)

a1656 Bradford *History* 1.443: Thus these too great princes, and their pastor, left this world near aboute one time. Death makes no difference. 1717 Wise *Vindication* 41: Death observes no Ceremony, but Knocks as loud at the Barriers of the Court, as at the Door of the Cottage. 1762 Ames *Almanacs* 328: Death levels all, the Wicked and the Just; Man's but a Flower, and his end is Dust. 1769 Woodmason *Journal* 161: Death You know has no respect of Persons. 1785 Bailey *Journal* 202: All powerful rum, which in this country, like death, levels all distinctions. 1788 Alden *Epitaphs* 3.92: High and low, rich and poor are death's equal prey. 1790 *Universal Asylum* 4.216: Rum, like death, is a universal leveller. 1801 *Port Folio* 1.352: Death cuts down all, both great and small. *Oxford* 10, 174; Whiting D101. See **G80, 162.**

D80 **Death** takes no bribes

1742 Franklin *PR* 2.336: Death takes no bribes. Tilley D149. Cf. Whiting D103.

D81 There is **Death** in the pot

1777 Baldwin *Journal* 112: Blazing Hot with death in the pot. 1803 Asbury *Journal* 2.401: There has been *death in the pot* here, 1806 498, 1810 633, 1813 726, 733. 2 Kings 4.40; Lean 1.509.

D82 To be at **Death's** door

c1680 Radisson *Voyages* 84: I had no desire to doe anything, seeing myselfe so insnared at death's door amongst the terrible torments. 1714 Plumstead 160: They should thereby be recovered from their fainting fits, who were now at death's door. 1736 *Georgia Records* 21.232. 1755 GFisher in

W&MCQ 17(1908) 107. **1763** Laurens *Papers* 3.461. **1765** JParker in Franklin *Papers* 12.409: A sweating Fever and Ague . . . that rendered him quite at Death's Door. **1769** JWatts in *Aspinwall Papers* 2.619: At death's door with a flux. **1770** Carter *Diary* 1.402: It also almost led him to death's door in a fit of sickness. **1778** Lee(W) *Letters* 2.484. **1778** Washington *Writings* 10.345. **1782** NGreene in Reed *Life* 2.380: Poor fellow, he has been at death's door for a long time. **1783** Lee(W) *Letters* 3.921. **1787** Washington *Writings* 29.210. **1788** Jefferson *Papers* 12.539, 14.276. **1788** Jones *History* 2.125: The rebellion was supposed to be at death's door. **1789** Jefferson *Papers* 15.187. **1795** Murdock *Triumphs* 41. **1810** Mackey *Letters* 107. **1812** *Austin Papers* 1.212. **1816** Pintard *Letters* 1.29, **1817** 73. **1819** Jefferson *Writings* 19.22: These reduced me to death's door, **1821** 18.315. **1826** Pintard *Letters* 2.273. **1830** Cooper *Letters* 2.5, **1835** 3.173, **1846** 5.166, **1848** 296, **1849** 6.36: A lady at death's door. *Oxford* 174; Whiting D107.

D83 To be loved to **Death**

1803 Asbury *Journal* 2.380: They would love me to death, **1814** 756: I would not be loved to death. Cf. TW 96(24). See **K17**.

D84 To dread like **Death**

1775 JAdams in *Warren-Adams Letters* 1.75: This Negociation I dread like Death. Cf. Whiting D110.

D85 To see **Death** on one's cape

1774 Carter *Diary* 2.854: And I saw his death on his cape.

D86 To stick like grim **Death** to a dead cat

1804 *Literary Magazine and American Register* 2.178: He stuck to him like grim Death to a dead cat. TW 96(27).

D87 Out of **Debt** is out of danger

1772 Franklin *Writings* 5.442: Out of Debt, as the Proverb says, was being out of Danger. Barbour 47(1); *Oxford* 601-2; Tilley D166.

D88 To pay the **Debt** of (to) nature (*varied*)

1650 Bradstreet *Works* 295: Two years and more, since nature's debt he paid. **1702** Mather *Magnalia* 2.10: He did, at length, pay one debt, namely, that unto *nature,* by death. **1707** Makemie *Writings* 165: Their Bodies are paying their debt to the Dust. **1731** Chalkley *Journal* 242: *Death was a Debt due to Nature, and that we must all pay it.* **1738** *Georgia Records* 22¹.325: The Loss of so valuable a Friend demands a Debt of Nature, which Grief usually pays. **1765** Watts *Letter Book* 337-8: 'Tis a Debt we are every Day apaying. **1768** MGoosley in *Norton Papers* 63. **1774** Carter *Diary* 2.834. **1776** Freneau *Poems* 1.246: Death as a debt to nature must be paid. **1778** GMorris in *Clinton Papers* 3.460: Paid the last Debt to nature. **1778** Reed *Life* 1.361: Paid the great debt of nature. **1779** WWhite in *PM* 1(1877) 436. **1781** HKnox in Kirkland *Letters* 2.82: To pay his last debt to nature. **1781** WSSmith in Webb *Correspondence* 2.369. **1782** Freneau *Prose* 83. **1783** *Washington *Writings* 26.82: He has paid the debt which we all owe, and sooner or later shall be called upon to discharge. **1783** Williams *Penrose* 293: He had paid his debt to nature. **1787** Webb *Correspondence* 3.77: He is cut off in the flower of his age. True 'tis a debt we must all pay. **1790** BRush in *Belknap Papers* 3.472. **1791** Long *Voyages* 152. **1792** ABrown in *Belknap Papers* 3.522. **1793** Barlow *Works* 1.244: to. **1793** EHazard in *Belknap Papers* 2.341. **1794** Alden *Epitaphs* 4.186: Weep not my friend, o'er me, the debt is paid. **1797** Washington *Writings* 35.434: The debt of nature . . . sooner or later, must be paid by us all. **1799** Mackay *Letters* 10: Doctᴿ. Wilson paid Natures debt a few days ago. **1799** *Washington *Writings* 37.109. **1800** Bates *Papers* 1.54. **1800** MJRandolph in Jefferson *Family Letters* 182: to. **1801** JCollins in *Blount Papers* 3.473. **1802** Chester *Federalism:* to. **1804** JCowdery in *Barbary Wars* 5.159: to. **1804** *Port Folio* 4.198: His last great debt is paid—poor Tom's no more! **1805** Claiborne *Letter Books* 312. **1805** WSSmith in Smith *Journal and Correspondence* 2(2) 186. **1806** Hitchcock *Works* 139. **1807** Janson *Stranger*

51, 108. **1807** Maxwell *Mysterious* 8.136: First must Elvira pay great nature's debt. **1807** *Monthly Anthology* 4.615. **1807** *Port Folio* NS 4.133, **1810** 2NS 4.514. **1813** Adams *Writings* 4.489. **1813** Luttig *Journal* 110. **1814** Valpey *Journal* 12. **1815** Andrews *Prisoners' Memoirs* 106: You've paid the debt we all must pay. **1815** Freneau *Poems* (*1815*) 1.134: That prison, called the grave, pays nature's debt. **1817** Short *Letters* 355. a**1826** Woodworth *Melodies* 47: When death dissolves the *firm*, my love, We'll pay the only *debt* we owe. **1831** Cooper *Letters* 2.139: I was sorry to see that Mr. Simond has paid the great debt. **1833** Floy *Diary* 42: I will one day have to undergo the bitter pains of death. I must pay the debt to Nature. **1853** Fletcher *Letters* 244: But she has gone to her long home . . . and paid the debt we have all to pay sooner or later. *Oxford* 614; Whiting D116.

D89 **December** and May
1734 *South Carolina Gazette* 192: In this our Town I've heard . . . That cold December does make Love to May. *Oxford* 518; Whiting J14. See **A138, J16.**

D90 To clear the **Decks**
1803 Bentley *Diary* 3.6: Then clear the Decks for a hot action. Colcord 54; TW 96.

D91 As certain as the **Decrees** of heaven
1797 WBlount in *Blount Papers* 3.174: I said . . . it was as certain as the Decrees of Heaven.

D92 **Deeds** and words
1656 JBrewster in *Winthrop Papers*(B) 2.77: If I were of ability to Make it knowen by dedes, as words. *Oxford* 175, 187; Whiting W642. See **W333.**

D93 Gentle **Deeds** make the gentleman
1702 Mather *Magnalia* 1.107: That saying of old Chaucer . . . "to do the genteel deeds, that makes the gentleman." *Oxford* 299; Tilley G67; Whiting D131. See **G32.**

D94 Great **Deeds** live
1767 Ames *Almanacs* 387: Great deeds live, all things else die. Tilley D183.

D95 One **Deed** is worth a thousand speeches
1767 Ames *Almanacs* 382: To prove a friend, experiences teaches, One deed is worth a thousand speeches.

D96 As swift as a **Deer**
1787 Freneau *Poems* 2.337: Care, swift as deer—as tempests strong. Barbour 47(3); Svartengren 377; TW 96(2).

D97 As wild as **Deer**
1786 Smith *Diary* 2.206: And you know that the American Whites are as wild as the Deer of their Forests. Barbour 47(6).

D98 Avoid the wounded **Deer** and hooked fish
1774 Schaw *Journal* 67: Our human proverb, "Avoid the wounded deer and hooked fish."

D99 To run like **Deer**
1818 WLewis in Jackson *Correspondence* 6.463: Whether the Kentuckians . . . ran like frightened deer. **1819** Faux *Memorable Days* 212: The pigs . . . seem more than half wild, and at the approach of man fly, or run like deer at the sight of an Indian rifle. Barbour 47(4, 5); *Oxford* 688; TW 96(5).

D100 The best **Defence** is offence (*varied*)
1775 WHDrayton in Gibbes 2.174: It is a maxim, that it is better to attack than to receive one. c**1790** Brackenridge *Gazette* 97: I say the best defence is offence. **1799** *Washington *Writings* 37.250: Make them believe, that offensive operations often times, is the *surest*, if not the *only* (in some cases) means of defence. Barbour 47.

D101 **Delays** are dangerous
1636 THewson in *Winthrop Papers*(A) 3.235: Delays breadeth Divers Dangers. a**1700** Hubbard *New England* 483: Where present distress doth urge delays may be as dangerous as denials. **1704** WWhiting in *Winthrop Papers*(B) 5.218: Delays in this case may be dangerous. **1707** WDudley in *Baxter Manuscripts* 9.241: The Souldiers say Delays come to nothing. **1728** Talcott *Papers* 2.417: Long delays may be dangerous. **1738** PLivingston in *Colden Papers* 8.257: Delay may be dangerous. **1749**

Franklin *PR* 3.350: Dangers unthoughtof will attend Delay. **1753** LMcGillvery in McDowell *Documents* 1.378-9. **1754** WShirley in *Baxter Manuscripts* 12.252. **1756** *Johnson Papers* 9.421. **1769** Brooke *Emily* 98: There is danger in delay; she has a thousand proverbs on her side. **1775** JDavid in *Naval Documents* 1.610, 1057. **1776** *Blockheads* 12: Delays of this kind may prove fatal. **1776** Washington *Writings* 5.205. **1777** WBlount in *Blount Papers* 1.6. **1777** Hamilton *Papers* 1.277: Delay will ruin them. **1777** JWard in *Bowdoin Papers* 1.404: Delays we have ever found attended with misfortune. **1777** Washington *Writings* 9.121. **1779** WDowne in *Baxter Manuscripts* 18.286: It is an Old and very true Maxim . . . and so the event prov'd. **1780** PWadsworth in *Baxter Manuscripts* 18.290. **1781** FShaw in *Baxter Manuscripts* 19.248. **1783** *Clinton Papers* 8.182. **1786** RO'Bryen in Jefferson *Papers* 9.619: Delays breed danger. **1787** *Blount Papers* 1.377. **1788** Cathcart *Journal* 306. **1791** Washington *Diaries* 4.154: To show the danger which might result from delay. **1794** RBlackledge in *Blount Papers* 2.441: As you Know delays bread Daingers. **1795** *Washington *Writings* 34.154. **1798** Ames *Letters* 1.228: Every day's delay is perilous. **1801** TTingey in *Barbary Wars* 1.435. **1805** Smith *Letters* 49. **1806** CMead in Claiborne *Letter Books* 4.83: Death is in delay. **1809** Weems *Marion* 198: Dreading the dangers of delay. **1818** Royall *Letters* 118. **1819** Baldwin *Letters* 303. **1820** Welby *Visit* 338: Here again we proved that. **1820** Wright *Views* 180. **1828** *Yankee* 80: There's danger in long delay. *Oxford* 176; Whiting D157.

D102 Delights dwell as well in the cottage as the palace

1775 Committee of Deer Island [Maine] in *Naval Documents* 1.910: We trust delights dwell as well in the humble Cottage as In the most splendid Palace.

D103 Mathematical **Demonstrations** can no man gainsay

1739 RFry *Scheme* in *Colonial Currency* 3.259: We have a common Proverb, *Mathematical Demonstrations can no Man gainsay.* Cf. TW 132: Figures (4).

D104 There is something rotten in **Denmark**

1781 HGates in Jefferson *Papers* 4.501: Is there a Rotteness in the State of Denmark? **1806** AJackson in Claiborne *Letter Books* 4.54: There [is] something rotten in the State of Denmark. **1807** Jackson *Correspondence* 1.181: The delay . . . has the appearance "that there is something *rotten* in the *state of Denmark,*" **1812** 215: Is there nothing rotten in Denmark? **1812** VHorne in Knopf *War of 1812* 3.128: I fear there is something rotten in denmark. Barbour 47.

D105 To be out of one's **Depth**

1738 Stephens *Journal(I)* 1.237: Fearing to be out of my Depth, I stopt here and said no more. NED Depth 13.

D106 As dry as the **Desert**

1809 Freneau *Poems(1809)* 1.256: Huge volumes as dry as the deserts of Zaara. Svartengren 190; TW 315. Cf. TW 97.

D107 **Despair** never pays any debts

1767 JParker in Franklin *Papers* 14.329: Yet I know Dispair never pays any debts.

D108 As black as the **Devil** (old Nick)

1801 TPierce in Vanderpoel *Chronicles* 388: Here the graces that adorn a lady . . . and are as black as the devil. **1806** Morris *Diary and Letters* 2.484: The French Revolutionists are painted in them as black as the devil. **1809** Weems *Marion* 110: Tom is a negro, and as black as Old Nick. Lean 2.808; TW 97(1). See **O23.**

D109 As black as the **Devil's** arse

1774 Harrower *Journal* 76: I have at this time, a great high Gire Carline as Black as the D——s A—se spinning for me.

D110 As dull as the **Devil**

1785 GHandley in Jackson *Papers* 7: We have nothing . . . new here, as dull as the devil. Svartengren 53.

D111 As happy as if the **Devil** had me

1793 EWinslow in *Winslow Papers* 399: They came together this heat and, as Forrest used to say, made me as happy as if the Devil had me.

D112 As if the **Devil** (*etc.*) were after one (*varied*)

1777 *New-York Gazette* in *Newspaper Extracts*(*II*) 1.475: The rebel army . . . ran . . . as if the devil was after them. **1781** JCochran in *PM* 5(1881) 231: For astray we are going as fast as the Devil can drive us. **1805** Dow *Journal* 230: The young woman was turbulent, I told her Old Sam would pay her a visit, 248: He ran, and I after him, crying, "run, run, Old Sam is after you." **1806** JWBlagrove in *M&WCQ* 2S 9(1929) 271: Driving through the streets as if the devil sent them along. **1809** Weems *Marion* 195: My men . . . went off as if the d——l had been behind them. **1814** Palmer *Diary* 42: [They] run for their muskets as tho' the Devil was after them. **1821** Doddridge *Dialogue* 47: Back he ran as if old nick were arter him. **1832** Cooper *Letters* 2.303: And away the old woman went, as if the devil was after her. *Oxford* 591; TW 270; Tilley N161.

D113 As proud as the **Devil**

1766 DFowler in *Wheelock's Indians* 103: I am accounted a Devil or Proude as the Devil. TW 97(4). See **L250.**

D114 As sure as the **Devil** is in Dublin (London)

1801 Weems *Letters* 2.172: Otherwise sure as the Devil's in Dublin, I shall be dragg'd under. **1803** Davis *Travels* 430: As sure as the devil is in *London*. Cf. TW 97(6); Whiting *Devil* 212(38).

D115 As wicked as the **Devil**

1779 Rodney *Letters* 324: As those termed Speculators are . . . as Active and wicked as the Devil himself. **1814** Valpey *Journal* 12: Blankets that was as full of Lice as the Devil is of wickedness. Barbour 48(13).

D116 Away goes the **Devil,** *etc.*

1809 *Port Folio* 2NS 2.430: Away goes the devil, when he finds the door shut against him. *Oxford* 24; TW 98(18).

D117 The bigger the **Devil** the better soldier

1819 Pintard *Letters* 1.209: The bigger devil the better soldier is the general maxim.

D118 The blue **Devils**

1783 Van Schaack *Letters* 348: I am . . . perfectly free from blue devils. **1791** JWebb in Webb *Correspondence* 3.170: I really have the Blue Devils bad enough. **1807** *Salmagundi* 165: When Langstaff . . . gives audience to the blue devils from his elbow-chair. **1810** Jefferson *Writings* 12.372. **1815** Freneau *Poems*(*1815*) 2.133. **1816** Paulding *Letters*(*I*) 2.13: I could entertain a score or two of blue devils. **1818** Cobbett *Year's* 60: Just the weather to give drunkards the "blue devils." **1819** Drake *Works* 328: You're vexed and beset with blue devils. But a change in your diet will banish the blues. **1821** Freneau *Last Poems* 51: *Blue devils from blue laws create.* **1826** *Austin Papers* 2.1483: So many persons labour under (what is called) the *Blue Devils*, Horrors Hippo or whatever else you may please to call those fits of Apathy. **1826** Duane *Colombia* 426: But here are genii, by the Spaniards called *Los Diablos Azulos*, in our language the *Blue Devils*. NED Blue devil 2a; Partridge 69-70. See **B232, W119.**

D119 The **Devil** and his dam

1682 Claypoole *Letter Book* 86: Thou mightst send to the devil and his dam too, he cared not. Whiting D181.

D120 The **Devil** can quote Scripture (*varied*)

1691 *Humble Address* in *Andros Tracts* 2.258-9: Their use of Law is only like the Devil's use of Scripture, *to pervert it, and do mischief therewith.* **1692** Mather *Wonders* 187: The Devil will make a deceitful and unfaithful use of the *Scriptures* to make his *Temptations* forceable, 188: When the Devil would perswade men to vile *Actions,* he'l quote Scriptures for them. **1769** Davis *Colonial Virginia Satirist* 61: The Devil himself to serve a turn has it in his power to tell a truth, and has often done so. **1799** Carey *Porcupiniad* 2.26: The devil can quote scripture to his purpose. *Oxford* 180; TW 98(17).

D121 The **Devil** finds work for the idle (*varied*)

1808 AAdams in Massachusetts Historical Society *Proceedings* 66 (1936-41) 136: It is a true saying that the devil will find work for those who have not any employment. **1818** Hall *Travels* 278: But says a proverb, Those whom the devil finds idle, he sets about his own work. **1819** Cobbett *Year's* 213: It is an old saying, that, if the Devil finds a fellow idle, he is sure to set him to work. *Oxford* 180; Whiting D182.

D122 The **Devil** hates holy water (*varied*)

1705 Ingles *Reply* 26: Being as much affraid of his Secret & Sinister Designs when Discovered as a witch is of holy water or a school boy is of a whipping. **1779** JEliot in *Belknap Papers* 3.143: He loves me as the Devil doth righteousness. **1783** Williams *Penrose* 130: To hate and detest them as the Devil hates holy water. **1803** Davis *Travels* 448: I love that fellow as the devil loves holy-water. **1815** Freneau *Poems(1815)* 1.86: Palsies and gouts shall at your mandate fly As Satan does when holy water's nigh. *Oxford* 182; TW 99(23); Whiting D208.

D123 The **Devil** is a hog

1819 Faux *Memorable Days* 296: But if she did scratch and poker me, I would knock her down, and the devil's a hog, if I would not kill her. Cf. *Oxford* 181; Tilley D306.

D124 The **Devil** is God's ape

1676 Williams *Writings* 5.46: The *Devill* will be *Gods Ape* in most things. *Oxford* 181; Tilley D247.

D125 The **Devil** is kind to his own

1811 Taggart *Letters* 375: The devil is always kind to his own. Barbour 48(10); *Oxford* 181; TW 99(21).

D126 The **Devil** is not so black as he is painted (*varied*)

1777 TNelson in Jefferson *Papers* 2.3: They say the Devil is not so black as he is painted. **1782** Freneau *Poems* 2.144: 'Till they all get as black as they paint the old Boy. **1790** Maclay *Journal* 232: I could hardly find it in my heart to paint the devil so bad. **1791** Burroughs *Memoirs* 274: The devil is not so

bad as his picture. *Oxford* 182; Whiting D189.

D127 The **Devil** is the father of lies

1694 Makemie *Writings* 83: Satan, the Father of Lyes. **1747** Stith *History* 259: It was put into his Mouth by the Father of Lies; for a fouler Lye himself never told. **1777** Moore *Diary* 1.397: All the powers of darkness and the father of liars at their head. **a1793** Scott *Journal* 26: One of the grand false hoods of the father of lies. **1811** Weems *Gambling* 35: The Devil . . . that father of lies. **1817** Tyler *Prose* 340: It is edited by the father of lies. Whiting D186.

D128 The **Devil** is the root of all evil

1733 Chalkley *Journal* 260: The Devil, who is the Root of all Evil.

D129 The **Devil** owes one a spite (shame)

1703 Mather *Diary* 1.487: The Divel owes me a Spite. **1742** *Byrd Letters* in *VHM* 37(1929) 115: I Suppose that what is commonly meant in Saying the Devil owes one a Shame. **1796** Barton *Disappointment* 51: The devil has ow'd me a spite this long time. Whiting D192.

D130 The **Devil** take the hindmost

1742 *Georgia Records* 23.333: Land Alianable . . . would bring in the Stock Jobbing Temper, the Devill take the Hindmost. **1782** Freneau *Poems* 2.172: The de'il may take them who are farthest behind. **1808** Quincy *JQuincy* 146: The Presidential term will have expired, and then away to Monticello, and let the —— take the hindmost. **1809** *Port Folio* 2NS 1.74: And d—n the hindmost. **1824** *Tales* 1.157: The troops . . . hurried away . . . with a precipitation which seemed to say "De'il tak the hindmost." **1834** Paulding *Letters(II)* 157: And as the old Proverb says "the D——l take the hindmost." *Oxford* 183; TW 99(25), 234-5(14). See E81.

D131 The **Devil** to pay

1747 GClinton in *Colden Letters* 3.403: I have had yᵉ devil and all to pay here. **1762** *Johnson Papers* 3.923: Fortunes are made by some (People), and the Devil to pay among the Merchants, **1764** 11.10. **1770**

Adams *Legal Papers* 3.190: There will be the *devil to pay* between the Towns People and the Soldiers, or *blood shed.* **1770** *Johnson Papers* 7.351: [There was] the Divil to pay between the Soldiers and the [Sons of] L——. **1777** Moore *Diary* 1.452: There might be both the Devil and Piper to pay. **1778** Winslow *Broadside* 153. **1779** Bowen *Journals* 2.541. **1780** Shaw *Journals* 77: Were I writing to any friend but a *reverend* one, I should say, the Devil has been to pay in this quarter. **1781** Witherspoon *Works* 4.473. **1783** RBlount in *Blount Papers* 1.55. **1787** Adams *Diary* 327: The d——l will be to pay if I have not some stock of law. **1787** WBlount in *Blount Papers* 1.236. **1788** Bowen *Journals* 2.567. **1789** AThomas in *Blount Papers* 1.522. **1790** Mason *Papers* 3.1192. **1791** Morris *Diary* 2.123. **1795** DCobb in *Bingham's Maine* 1.551: The devil is to pay among the demo's. **1796** Barton *Disappointment* 60. **1801** *Farmers' Museum* 104: Till all shall think the devil's to pay, From Bennington to Canada. **1803** Austin *Constitutional* 70: To use a vulgar expression, "the devil was to pay among the tailors." **1804** *Port Folio* 4.14. **1806** Fessenden *Modern Philosopher* 133: For, gentlemen, the devil's to pay, That you forsake the good old way. a**1820** Biddle *Autobiography* 406. a**1826** Woodworth *Melodies* 172. *Oxford* 184; Whiting D194. See **O24.**

D132 The **Devil** to pay and no pitch hot

1744 Hamilton *Itinerarium* 83: It was *the devil to pay and no pitch* hot? An interrogatory adage metaphorically derived from the manner of sailors who pay their ship's bottoms with pitch. Colcord 99; *Oxford* 184; TW 99(27).

D133 The **Devil** upon two sticks

1812 Randall *Miser* 10: I have heard of the devil upon two sticks. Whiting D206.

D134 The **Devil** was sick, the Devil a monk would be, *etc.*

1752 Joseph Robson, *An Account of Six Years Residence in Hudson's Bay* (London, 1752) Appendix 56: *The devil was sick—the devil a monk would be: The devil was well—the devil a monk was he.* **1775** Carter *Diary*

2.919: I believe as he gets well he will make the Spanish Proverb good, The Devil whilst sick, a monk would be. *Oxford* 184; TW 100(37).

D135 The **Devil** will be busy (*varied*)

1740 Belcher *Papers* 2.304: But fall back fall edge, I have nothing to do in that matter, yet the Devil will be busy. **1800** JMcHenry in Gibbs *Memoirs* 2.423: The devil, who is never idle.

D136 The **Devil** will have a chapel where God has a church

1637 LDowning in *Winthrop Papers(A)* 3.421: But, it feard, as the ould proverb: the divell will haue a chapell whear god hath a church. *Oxford* 309; Tilley G259; Whiting *Devil* 207(8).

D137 The **Devil** will play at small game rather than stand out (*varied*)

a**1731** Cook *Bacon* 320: Tho' Carron, yet De'll takes his Due. At smallest Game, he'll take a Bout, Rather than unconcern'd stand out. **1777** Curwen *Journal* 1.401: For as the old proverb has it 'tis better to play at a small game than stand out. **1787** *Belknap Papers* 1.472: The Devil will play at *small game* rather than be idle. *Oxford* 631; Tilley G21.

D138 The **Devil** wipes his breech with poor folks' pride

1743 Franklin *PR* 2.369: The D——l wipes his B——ch with poor Folks Pride. *Oxford* 184; Tilley D271.

D139 Enough to blow the **Devil's** horns off

1803 Davis *Travels* 147: [The wind] is enough to blow the devil's horns off.

D140 Fight **Devil** fight baker

1784 POliver in Hutchinson *Diary* 2.403: And so fight D—— fight B——. **1807** Irving(P) *Journals* 49: Pull d—— pull baker. *Oxford* 653; TW 101: Dick; Whiting *Devil* 210(17). See **D244.**

D141 Go to the **Devil** and shake yourself

1803 Bentley *Diary* 3.4: Tune, Go to the Devil and shake yourself. **1813** Knopf *War of 1812* 5(2) 141: Go to the Devil and shake yourself.

D142 He must needs go whom the **Devil** drives (*varied*)

1660 Hull *Diary* 193: He must needs go whom the Devil drives. **1689** Randolph *Letters* 6.313: the Old proverb. **1702** Mather *Magnalia* 2.524. **1720** Walter *Choice Dialogue* 6: I know my friends foretold (according to a good old Proverb more than twice thirty years old) that I must needs go, &c. **1776** JMcKesson in *Clinton Papers* 1.434: I fear none of you would have enough of the Devil, to drive. **1778** Smith *Memoirs(II)* 328: There is a Needs must — it is impossible for them to act wisely — they have a Choice only of one bad step instead of another. **1787** *Belknap Papers* 1.472: He must run whom the Devil drives. **1803** Ames *Letters* 1.329: When *somebody* (a Jacobin too) drives, we must run. **1824** *Tales* 2.35: For "needs must when somebody drives" — you understand. *Oxford* 560; Whiting D199.

D143 Raise no **Devil** that you cannot lay (*varied*)

1714 Talbot *Letters* 133: There's nothing but Pawawing and Conjuring to raise a Devil they cannot lay again [at a Quaker meeting]. **1766** *Johnson Papers* 12.4: They woud be Glad to Lay the Devil they Raisd. **1781** Oliver *Origin* 76: They never considered how easy it is to raise the D——l, & how hard to lay him. **1792** Hamilton *Papers* 11.442: They forget an old but a very just, though a coarse saying — That it is much easier to raise the Devil than to lay him. **1793** Brackenridge *Modern* 235: The Captain saw that it was a difficult matter to lay the devil he had raised. **1793** ZSwift in *American Antiquarian Society Proceedings* NS 4(1885-7) 371: Many wild furious democrats . . . wish to raise the Devil. **1804** Taggart *Letters* 133: It is a vulgar proverb, that it is easy to raise the devil but difficult to bury him. **1815** Brackenridge *Modern* 663: It is said to be an easy thing to raise the devil, but to lay him, requires all the art of the free-mason with a wand, circle, and a black cat. *Oxford* 663; TW 98(15).

D144 Talk of the **Devil** and his imps appear

1728 Byrd *Dividing Line* 65: He swore enough in the Night, to bring the Devil into the Room had not the Chaplain been there. **1796** Barton *Disappointment* 10: Talk of the devil and his imps appear — as the saying is. Barbour 48(8); *Oxford* 804; TW 98(16).

D145 Though the **Devil** is up early, God is up before him

1676 Williams *Writings* 5.276: Mr. J. Dod used to say, *though the Devil was up early, God was still up before him*.

D146 To call the **Devil** one's uncle

1830 Ames *Mariner's* 188: I would not have "called the devil my uncle."

D147 To change the **Devil** into an angel of light (*varied*)

1777 BHarrison in *Thomson Papers* 410: You may as soon change the Devil into an Angel of Light as a C[onnecticu]t man into any thing else. **1778** JMVarnum in *Sullivan Letters* 2.41: Lord North and the Devil have made a League to appear in the borrowed Garb of Ithuriel. **1830** PWilliams in Porter *Negro Writing* 300: Satan . . . often appears under the garb of an angel of Light. Tilley D231; Whiting 561.

D148 To cheat the **Devil**

1752 *Johnson Papers* 9.87: Major Drum, I fear will cheat the Devil once more. **a1788** Jones *History* 2.362: A trading Dutchman will cheat the Devil if he can. **1800** Cobbett *Porcupine* 11: 262: But I know of no man who surpasses Rush in what is vulgarly called, cheating the devil of a lie.

D149 To eat the (**Devil**) and sup his broth

1783 Williams *Penrose* 266: Thes Indians wad devoor the auld Whaapnab himsel, gin he were weel cooked, and sup his broth after that. Barbour 47(2); *Oxford* 215; Tilley D291.

D150 To foil the **Devil** with his own weapons

1807 *Salmagundi* 88: If we were his enemies, we might justify it by the old maxim of "foiling the devil with his own weapons." Cf. TW 98(11); Whiting *Devil* 209(13). See **W84**.

D151 To give the **Devil** his due

1769 Winslow *Broadside* 135: We'll give the

Devil his Due. **1772** Paterson *Glimpses* 121: We must e'en give the dev'l his due. **1775** Freneau *Poems* 1.133. **1780** *Royal Gazette* in *Newspaper Extracts(II)* 4.239: Yet give the Devil and his Imps their due. **1781** Freneau *Poems* 2.97: 'Twas wrong to rob the devil of his due. **1787** *Columbian Magazine* 1.392: Why not allow the poor devil his due. **1787** Trumbull *Autobiography* 148. **1789** *Columbian Magazine* 3.646. **1793** WLSmith in Hamilton *Papers* 14.339. **1796** FMartin in *Blount Papers* 3.19: Let the Devil have his due. **1798** Adams *New Letters* 137: Give the devil his due, but by no more than he deserves to his charge. **1799** Jefferson *Writings* 10.109. **1803** JJackson in Milledge *Correspondence* 98. **1804** Brackenridge *Modern* 395. **1809** Fessenden *Pills* 45. **1809** Weems *Marion* 161. **1814** Palmer *Diary* 58. **1815** Freneau *Poems(1815)* 1.65: My keys I render up to you, Which are, in fact, the devil's due. **1816** Paulding *Letters(I)* 1.170. **1817** Adams *Writings* 6.204. **1819** Kinloch *Letters* 1.137: To give him his due, in that spirit of charity, which our old proverb expresses. Barbour 48(4); *Oxford* 304; TW 100(31).

D152 To give the **Devil** one to take the other

1820 Durand *Life* 50: I'd give the devil one if he'd take the other. Whiting D209.

D153 To have the **Devil's** own time

1815 Brackenridge *Modern* 693: I had de devil's own time, bad luck to dem.

D154 To keep the **Devil** under a bushel

1812 Taggart *Letters* 378: Mr. Gallatin has hitherto kept the devil under a bushel, but now he is going to show him to us. Cf. TW 28.

D155 To look as the **Devil** over Lincoln

c1777 Sargent *Loyalist* 108: For they know that the devil will watch over Lincoln [a play on General B. Lincoln's name]. **1780** *Royal Gazette* in *Newspaper Extracts(II)* 4.671: And make a bow and take a look Like Satan over Lincoln. *Oxford* 183; Tilley D277; Whiting D212.

D156 To play the (very) **Devil**

1764 Watts *Letter Book* 244: The Woman has playd the Devil at Greenwych & run away. **1770** *Johnson Papers* 7.484: Playing the Devil with the Traders. **1777** TNelson in Jefferson *Papers* 2.3: They play the very Devil with the Girls and even old Women to satisfy their libidinous appetites. **a1788** Jones *History* 2.120. **1778** JWebb in Webb *Correspondence* 2.135. **1794** WGrove in *Steele Papers* 1.125. **1813** Jackson *Correspondence* 1.430. TW 100(33).

D157 To run (scamper) as if the **Devil** were in one

1741 *Johnson Papers* 1.11: They turned Tale and Ran as if the Devil was in them. **1769** Woodmason *Journal* 154: They scamper'd away as if the Devil had been in them. **1776** Rodney *Letters* 122: When the Firing ceased their Troops began to land and ours to Run as if the Devil was in them. **1785** Hunter *Quebec* 101: He would scamper off as if the devil was in him. TW 100(38).

D158 To see the **Devil**

1737 Franklin *Drinkers* 2.175: He's seen the Devil. Partridge 743.

D159 To whip the **Devil** round the stump

1776 Carter *Diary* 2.1028: It was only an artifice to whip the devil round the stump. **1786** EHazard in *Belknap Papers* 1.427: This is not what the Virginians call "whipping the devil round a stump." **1798** Cobbett *Porcupine* 8.248: The House of Representatives sit . . . whipping the devil round the post. **1799** Carey *Porcupiniad* 2.11: *Whipping the devil round the post.* **1809** Weems *Marion* 159: The rogues were drinking brandy . . . but by way of whipping the devil round the stump, they called it *water;* that is, *apple water,* **1822** *Letters* 3.334: Some fair sales—some, whipping the Devil round the stump by *raffles.* **1840** Cooper *Letters* 4.28. Barbour 48(11); TW 100(36).

D160 What is got over the **Devil's** back, *etc.*

1677 Hubbard *Indian* 2.256: What hath been gotten over the Back of the evil Fiend is lost under his Belly, according to the Proverb. **1726** Sewall *Letter-Book* 2.236: And upon this occasion, the Truth of that Saying, What is gotten over the Devil's back, is spent under his belly, comes to mind. **1796** Cobbett *Porcupine* 4.222: It is an old saying, and all old sayings are true, **1797** 6.69: It may not be amiss to remind him of a maxim . . . that *what is got over the devil's back goes under his belly,* **1799** 11.48: It is perfectly right, that what is "gotten over the devil's back should go under his belly. **1805** Sewall *Parody* 35: That n'eer can prosper got o'er Satan's back. Barbour 47(1); *Oxford* 329; TW 100(35).

D161 When the **Devil** goes fishing, *etc.*

c1800 Tyler *Island* 22: Strong temptation — when the devil goes a fishing — he baits his hook with handsome girls. Cf. Whiting W530.

D162 As busy as a **Devil's Needle**

1797 HKnox in *Bingham's Maine* 2.864: He is well, and as busy as a devils needle.

D163 As calm as **Dew**

1803 *Yankee Phrases* 87: My slumbers were calmer than dew.

D164 As sweet as **Dew**

1789 *Columbian Magazine* 3.437: Eloquence sweet as the dew on the fields.

D165 To vanish like morning **Dew**

1780 *Washington *Writings* 19.482: The flattering prospect . . . is vanishing like the Morning Dew, 20.317, 327. Whiting D223.

D166 As mild as **Dewdrops**

1818 Royall *Letters* 120: He is as mild as the dew drops.

D167 **Diamond** cut diamond

1777 Winslow *Broadside* 151: It is diamond cut diamond, fight on until we die. **1804** Irving *Corrector* 77: Diamond cut diamond was the word; Each spread his wily net. **1806** Fanning *Narrative* 48. **1812** Melish *Travels* 72: You thought to play a Yankee trick upon me, but this is diamond cut diamond for you! **1817** Weems *Franklin* 87. *Oxford* 185; TW 101(6); Tilley D323.

D168 A **Diamond** of the first water

1773 Quincy *Memoir* 100: Dulany is a diamond of the first water. NED Water 20b.

D169 A rough **Diamond**

1791 Paine *Works* 48: The rough diamond of the human mind. Barbour 48(1); *Oxford* 685; TW 101(1).

D170 To sparkle like **Diamonds**

1822 Royall *Letters* 239: They [eyes] sparkle like diamonds. Taylor *Comparisons* 34.

D171 As even as **Dies**

1783 Williams *Penrose* 84: Her teeth even as dies. Cf. TW 102(1).

D172 As level as a **Die**

1822 Weems *Penn* 157: A grand extended surface, level as a die. Svartengren 271.

D173 As true as a **Die**

1828 *Yankee* 252: As true as a die. Lean 2.885; Svartengren 371.

D174 The **Die** is cast [The following is a selection from 90 occurrences of the phrase]

1765 Watts *Letter Book* 407: The Die is thrown & we must hope the best. **1768** Eliot *Letters* 430: *Jacta est alea.* We must wait the event. **1773** JAdams in *Warren-Adams Letters* 2.403: The Dye is cast: The People have passed the River and cutt away the Bridge. **1775** *Norton Papers* 373-4: The dye seems now to be cast for America a gold chain or a wooden leg. **1776** Washington *Writings* 4.319: I should long ere this have put every thing to the cast of a Dye. **1784** Jefferson *Papers* 7.509: The die is thrown here and has turned up war. **1795** Adams *Memoirs* 1.141. **1799** Eaton *Life* 106: The die will be cast against us. **1801** DCobb in *Bingham's Maine* 2.1110: The political die is cast. **1808** Wirt *Letters* 1.255: But the die is cast — and the question is how to carry on the game. **1809** Jefferson *Writings* 12.341: The die is cast, and we have only to regret what we cannot repair. **1812** Hitchcock *Social* 25: Will see her die of fortune cast. **1812** Jackson *Correspondence* 1.235, **1844** 6.286, 321, **1845** 379. Barbour 44(2); *Oxford* 186; TW 102(3); Tilley D326. See L224.

D175   All must **Die** (*varied*)

1617 JRolfe in *VHM* 10(1902) 137: All must die. **1745** *Louisbourg Journals* 33: It's Appointed for all Men once to Die. **1769** Woodmason *Journal* 161: We must all dye. **1770** Carter *Diary* 1.505: All men must die, but I hardly believe any one with a regular Pulse. **1812** Randall *Miser* 40: All must die. **1822** Stansbury *Pedestrian* 20: The old adage, *"man must die at one time or another."* Oxford 10; Whiting D243. See **D77, M15.**

D176   Never say **Die**

1814 Palmer *Diary* 80: Then look out blow her up boys never say die. Barbour 49(2); *Oxford* 563; TW 102(3).

D177   We are born to **Die**

1748 Laurens *Papers* 1.171: We are born to die. *Oxford* 555; Tilley B140.

D178   We **Die** but once (*varied*)

1775 EInman in Murray *Letters* 211: I told them . . . we could die but once. **1781** Moore *Diary* 2.437: It is appointed for all men once to die. **1809** Weems *Marion* 55: A man can die but once. **1818** Hall *Travels* 243: You can die but once. *Oxford* 503; Whiting D242.

D179   There is a **Difference** between staring and stark mad

1753 *Independent Reflector* 144: In a Word, there's a great Difference between staring and stark-mad. **1788** Wingate *Letters* 10: There is a difference between staring and stark mad. *Oxford* 187; Tilley D334.

D180   **Diligence** is the mother of good luck

1736 Franklin *PR* 2.138: Diligence is the Mother of Good-Luck, **1758** *WW* 342. **1770** Ames *Almanacs* 412: Dilligence is the mother of good luck, and God giveth all things to industry. *Oxford* 102: Care; Tilley D338.

D181   After **Dinner** mustard

1807 JAdams in *Adams-Warren Correspondence* 432: Your thirty-first chapter, Madam, is like mustard after dinner, as our friends the French say; or like a volunteer toast after a feast, when the original list is exhausted, 451. *Oxford* 6; Tilley M809.

D182   Not to be a **Dinner** for someone

1775 FLLee in *Naval Documents* 2.1086: We do not think the whole of these raw Irish will make a dinner for our troops. Whiting D251. See **B313.**

D183   To make two **Dips** to a bawbee

1793 Freneau *Prose* 306: Forget not . . . you would have been difficulted to make *twa dips to a baubee*. NED Bawbee, a Scots coin worth a half penny; Dip 7, a farthing candle.

D184   As cheap as **Dirt**

1811 Weems *Gambling* 32: Cheap as dirt. **1812** Hitchcock *Social* 81: As *cheap as dirt*. TW 102(2).

D185   As plenty as **Dirt**

1769 *Johnson Papers* 12.745: Dollars are here now as plenty as dirt.

D186   **Dirt** will rub off when it is dry

1774 Franklin *Writings* 6.258: Splashes of Dirt thrown upon my Character, I suffered while fresh to remain. I did not chuse to spread by endeavouring to remove them, but rely'd on the vulgar Adage *that they would all rub off when they were dry.*

D187   Throw **Dirt** against heaven and it will return on one's own head

1753 *Independent Reflector* 349: He that throws Dirt against Heaven, may expect to have it return on his own Head. *Oxford* 766-7; Tilley H356.

D188   Throw **Dirt** enough and some will stick (*varied*)

1703 *Penn-Logan Correspondence* 1.247: Where bias may be already, at least some dirt sticks. **1705** Ingles *Reply* 20: Having Learnt of Macchiavell: to thro Dirt enough hoping Some of it may Stick. **1733** Franklin *Papers* 1.334: But approve well of that old Saying, *Throw Dirt enough, and some will stick.* **1765** TWharton in Franklin *Papers* 12.95: In the present Instance they endeavor to throw dirt at others. **1766** Mecom in *Franklin-Mecom* 93: As considering when a great Deal of Durt is flung some is apt to stick. **1766** Franklin *Papers* 13.488: Dirt thrown on a Mud-Wall may stick and incorporate; but it will not long adhere to polish'd Marble. **1768** *Pennsylvania Journal* in *Newspaper Extracts(I)* 7.226: It has been an old saying, "Cast dirt plentifully and some of it will stick." **1770** WSJohnson in *Trumbull Papers* 1.455: To throw as much dirt as possible, in hopes that some will certainly stick. **1780** Mecom in *Franklin-Mecom* 205: I fear there is two much truth in that comon saying, where much Dirt is thrown some will stick. *Oxford* 189; Tilley D349.

D189 Discount is good pay

1780 *New-York Gazette* in *Newspaper Extracts(II)* 4.208: The old and fair Maxim, *that Discount is good Pay.*

D190 Discretion is the better part of valor (*varied*)

1747 Franklin *PR* 3.103: Courage would fight, but Discretion won't let him. **1764** *Paxton Papers* 145: Here Corin adopts the opinion of Old Falstaff, thinking "the better part of valour is discretion." **1791** Belknap *History* 2.90: Dunbar's prudence . . . got the better of his courage, and he retired. **1804** Irving *Corrector* 67: The better part of valor is discretion. **1807** *Emerald* 2.291: The better part of valour is discretion. **1814** JRussell in Clay *Papers* 1.920. **1816** Adams *Writings* 6.45: My discretion got the better part of my valor. **1818** GBadger in *Ruffin Papers* 1.204: I recollect Sir John Falstaff's maxim that. **c1820** Bernard *Retrospections* 197. **1826** Jones *Sketches* 1.127: Thinking with . . . Hudibras and many others less candid, that "prudence is the better part of valor." **1830** Ames *Mariner's* 208: [He] being apparently a disciple of the illustrious Falstaff, and believing that "the better part of valor was discretion." **1832** Barney *Memoir* 54: They possessed "the better part of valour," discretion. Barbour 49; *Oxford* 189; TW 103, 297; Tilley D354.

D191 Desperate Diseases must have desperate remedies (*varied*)

1646 Winslow *Hypocrisie* 66: Extream evils must have extreame remedies. **1735** WByrd in *VHM* 36(1928) 120: It must have been a desperate one [distemper], to require so desperate a Remedy. **1726** *Melancholy State* in *Colonial Currency* 3.142: Desperate Diseases call for extraordinary Remedies. **1739** RFry *Scheme* in *Colonial Currency* 3.277: We have a common saying, *A desperate Disease must have a desperate Cure.* **1774** Franklin *Writings* 6.274: No considerate Person . . . can approve of desperate Remedies, except in desperate Cases. **1776** *Washington *Writings* 6.402: Desperate diseases require desperate Remedies. **1777** WDuer in Jay *Correspondence* 1.139: Such is the desperate situation of affairs that nothing but desperate remedies can restore these people to reason. **1778** Carver *Travels* 397: Desperate disorders require desperate remedies. **1794** DAllison in *Blount Papers* 2.428: In dangerous Cases Powerful remedies ought to be applied. **1797** UTracy in Gibbs *Memoirs* 1.539: It must be remembered that desperate cases require desperate remedies. **1798** Cobbett *Porcupine* 8.76: Desperate diseases require violent remedies. **1799** Barlow *Works* 1.380: The novelty of applying an old desperate remedy where there was no disease. **1819** Royall *Letters* 200: It was a desperate case, and required a desperate remedy. **1831** Smith *Letters* 330: Extraordinary cases require extraordinary remedies. *Oxford* 178; TW 56(2), 103. Cf. Whiting C68.

D192 Oppose a Disease at its beginning

1768 Dickinson *Letters* 49: *Venienti occurrite morbo.* Oppose a disease at its beginning. See **B348.**

D193 To be Disguised (i.e., drunk)

1725 JMinot in *Baxter Manuscripts* 10.345: [They] never Disguise themselves at all & many of them will not drink any. **1763** *Johnson Papers* 4.43: He . . . might possibly be disguised in Liquor. **1792** PHall in Porter *Negro Writing* 65: I would not here be understood a brother in disguise, for such an one hath no business on a level floor. *Oxford* 190; Whiting D255.

D194   New **Dish** fresh appetite

1692 Randolph *Letters* 7.405: Every New Dish Creates A fresh Appetite in A Glutton.

D195   To dip in the **Dish**

1723 *Winthrop Papers*(B) 6.405: But I now finde those that dip't in the dish wth me have betrayed me. NED Dip *v.* 1, *absol.*

D196   To get a **Dish**

1737 Franklin *Drinkers* 2.174: He's got a Dish. Partridge 224; Tilley D368.

D197   To have thrown in one's **Dish** (*varied*)

1637 *Winthrop Papers*(A) 3.463: Would itt nott be a greater tryall to haue [torn] ge castt in a mans dish. **1697** Calef *More Wonders* 38: How often have I had this thrown into my dish. **1767** Smith *Life and Correspondence* 1.407: One Mr. Dunlap, a Printer, who is constantly thrown in our dish by the Presbyterians. **1817** Weems *Franklin* 97: And severe sarcasm . . . has been often thrown into the parson's dish. *Oxford* 190; Tilley T155. See **W145.**

D198   To meet in a **Dish**

1732 Betty Pratt [age 10] in *VHM* 26(1918) 288: To be as perfect strangers, not to know each other tho' if by accident (as they say) we were to meet in a dish.

D199   To feel like a **Dish-clout**

1822 Gallatin *Diary* 212: I feel like a wrung out dish-clout. NED Dish-clout b. Cf. Barbour 50; Svartengren 393; TW 103.

D200   As flat as **Dish-water**

1781 JLovell in *Adams FC* 4.196: As Flat as Dishwater. Cf. Apperson 218; Partridge 224; Taylor *Comparisons* 37.

D201   There is no **Disputing** about tastes

1786 EHazard in *Belknap Papers* 1.441: *De gustibus non est disputandum.* **1788** Adams *Diary* 421: De gustibus non est disputandum; there's no disputing about the choice of a wife. **1795** EHazard in *Belknap Papers* 2.351: [Latin only]. **1802** *Port Folio* 2.312: [Latin only]. **1808** RSmith in King *Life* 5.95: But de gustibus &c &c. **1811** *Port Folio* 2NS 5.37: "There is no disputing about tastes," said one of the ancient philos-

ophers. **1811** Taggart *Letters* 366: [Latin only]. **1813** *Port Folio* 3NS 2.62: [Latin only]. a**1820** Tucker *Essays* 35: [Latin only]. **1821** Knight *Poems* 2.26: [Latin only]. **1823** Bierce *Travels* 87: [Latin only]. *Oxford* 2; Tilley D385. See **A18, E89.**

D202   A **Distinction** without a difference

1776 Curwen *Journal* 1.268: I fancy "here is a difference without distinction" meaning a distinction without a difference. **1780** PSchuyler in Sparks *Correspondence* 2.411: The distinction I have drawn . . . is not one without a difference. **1787** Tyler *Contrast* 54: A true Yankee distinction, egad, without a difference. **1799** Adams *Works* 8.632: A distinction without a difference. NED Distinction 3b.

D203   **Distrust** is the mother of security

1776 *Heath Papers* 2.8: Distrust is the mother of security, **1782** 3.371. Cf. *Oxford* 671; Tilley R72.

D204   To be in one's last **Ditch**

1779 Lee *Papers* 3.370: Great Britain is at her last ditch. **1821** Jefferson *Writings* 1.132: Driven to the last ditch by the universal call for liberty. NED Ditch *sb.*[1] 5.

D205   To die in the last **Ditch**

1779 Rush *Letters* 1.238: Britain I hope will soon enjoy the heroic pleasure of dying in the *last ditch*. **1779** AScammell in Kirkland *Letters* 1.64: They seem to be determined to die in the last ditch. **1788** *American Museum* 3.49: Though some patriots are for dying in the last ditch, it is certainly better not to perish at all. **1796** Barlow *Letters* 138. **1806** Jackson *Correspondence* 1.153: I will die in the last Ditch before I would yield a foot to the Dons, **1808** 192: Or die nobly in the last ditch. **1809** Taggart *Letters* 331: Varnum will die in the last ditch of democracy. **1814** Jackson *Correspondence* 2.116: I am . . . prepared to meet him And die in the last ditch before he shall reach the city. **1821** Jefferson *Writings* 15.312. NED Die *v.*[1] 5, Ditch *sb.*[1] 5.

D206   As plenty as **Ditch-water**

1758 *Johnson Papers* 2.871: Liquor was as

plenty among them as Ditch Water. Cf. Whiting D267.

D207 Divide and conquer (*varied*)

1694 Scottow *Narrative* 295: His Maxime . . . divide, and Overcome. **1705** Beverley *History* 106: The Machevellian Principle, Divide & Impera. **1708** Johnston *Papers* 24: That known Maxim, Divide & impera. **1754** Plumstead 310: [Latin only]. **1757** Davis *Colonial Virginia Satirist* 21: [Latin only]. **1759** Smith *Life and Correspondence* 1.220: The Maxim [Latin only], **1760** 245: The Quakers, who love to divide in order to rule our Church, 274: [Latin only]. **1768** Dickinson *Letters* 6: To divide, and thus to destroy, is the first political maxim. **1774** JAllen in Izard *Correspondence* 28: [Latin only]. **1774** WBollan in *Bowdoin Papers* 1.363: The ancient maxim [Latin only]. **1775** *New York Journal* in *Newspaper Extracts(I)* 11.26: Divide and impera was their motto. **1775** Thacher *Journal* 21: The maxim adopted by our enemies is, "*Divide and conquer.*" **1778** Moore *Diary* 2.38: *Divide and rule.* **1778** *New Jersey Gazette* in *Newspaper Extracts(II)* 2.180: rule. **1779** Lee (W) *Letters* 2.690: The old maxim [Latin only]. **1780** Rush *Letters* 1.259: The old maxim of dividing and conquering does not apply to the present circumstances of America. **1781** Peters *Connecticut* 277: [Latin only]. **1781** *Trumbull Papers* 2.249: [Latin only], 4.248: [Latin only]. **1789** WGrayson in Henry *Life* 3.391: [Latin only]. **1790** Bentley *Diary* 1.177: Divide et impera is found a salutary, and moral truth. **1791** Maclay *Journal* 393: [Latin only]. **1792** Barlow *Works* 1.172: [Latin only]. **1792** Freneau *Prose* 284: "Divide and govern" is a maxim consecrated by the experience of ages. **1792** Morris *Diary* 2.583: Adopt the Rule — Divide and reign. **1793** Wayne *Correspondence* 253. **1796** Cobbett *Porcupine* 4.274: They have the Machiavelian maxim, "divide and you govern," continually in their eye. **1796** WTathim in Hamilton *Papers* 20.154: the ill judged maxim. **1798** Gadsden *Writings* 281: Give to the French for their motto of "*Divide and Conquer,*" United we are and we will stand. **1802** Port *Folio* 2.100. **1807** *Emerald* 2.203: [Latin only]. **1807** Taggart *Letters* 222: The Gallic maxim. **1809** Freneau *Poems* 3.292: To divide, and to rule by the florentine law. **1809** Kendall *Travels* 1.172: [Latin only]. **c1810** Randolph *Virginia* 211: [Latin only]. **1834** Jackson *Correspondence* 5.289, **1835** 321, **1842** 6.177. *Oxford* 190-1; Tilley D391.

D208 Do as I say, not as I do

1817 Weems *Franklin* 97: Don't do as I do, but do as I say. *Oxford* 191; Whiting D281. See **E104**.

D209 Do as you would be done by

1668 *The Letter Book of Peleg Sanford* (Providence, R.I., 1928) 47: The Goulden Rule . . . doe as yo would be done unto. **1676** Williams *Writings* 5.24: That Golden Rule, Do as thou would'st be done by. **1681** Willard *Ne Sutor* 6: The golden Rule . . . doing as we would be done by. **1689** Bulkeley *People's Right* 70: Tis a golden Rule, That which you would that others should do to you, do you the same to them. **1702** Mather *Diary* 1.465: I will do no otherwise than I would be done to. **1709** Lawson *Voyage* 244. **1713** Chalkley *Forcing* 376: That royal Law, which says, *Do to all Men, as you would that they should do unto you.* **1716** Mather *Diary* 2.379. **1719** *Addition* in *Colonial Currency* 1.393: That rule, *As ye would that Men should do unto you, do ye also to them likewise.* **1720** JColman *Distressed State* in *Colonial Currency* 1.404. **1725** JMinot in *Baxter Manuscripts* 10.343. **1731** *Commerce of Rhode Island* 1.22: How far soe much artifice may consist with dealing as wee would be dealt by I leave you to judge. **1734** Plumstead 270. **1735** Franklin *Papers* 2.39. **1751** *New York Weekly Post Boy* in *Newspaper Extracts(I)* 3.18. **1753** *Beekman Papers* 1.193. **1762** Laurens *Papers* 3.168. **1766** JParker in Franklin *Papers* 13.411. **1769** Lloyd *Papers* 2.718. **1769** Shaw *Letter Book* 209. **1770** *Pennsylvania Gazette* in *Newspaper Extracts(I)* 8.100. **1772** Lloyd *Papers* 2.729. **1773** Adams *Legal Papers* 2.65. **1774** *Pennsylvania Gazette* in *Newspaper Extracts(I)* 10.231. **a1775** Churchman *Account* 76.

1775 *New York Journal* in *Newspaper Extracts(I)* 11.27. **1777** AA in *Adams FC* 2.358. **1777** Winslow *Broadside* 189. **1778** *New Jersey Gazette* in *Newspaper Extracts (II)* 2.101. **1778** Smith *Works* 2.56. **1779** Lee(W) *Letters* 2.649. **1781** Moore *Diary* 2.363. **1781** *New Jersey Gazette* in *Newspaper Extracts(II)* 5.172, 175, 210. **1782** Mason *Papers* 2.714. **1783** Van Schaack *Letters* 293. **1787** Adams *Diary* 318. **1787** PCarr in Jefferson *Papers* 11.299. **1792** Brackenridge *Modern* 140. **1794** Paine *Age of Reason* 1.598. **1795** Bayard *Journal* 63. **1797** Beete *Man* 17. **1797** Morris *Diary and Letters* 2.270: I respect the golden rule, and do not admire on some occassions the society of a third person. **1797** Smith(EH) *Diary* 30: He meant at least to do unto others as they did unto him. **1798** DAllison *Blount Papers* 3.221. **1798** GMinor in *VHM* 30(1922) 244. **1799** Asbury *Journal* 2.214. **1799** *Washington Writings* 37.194. **1803** Austin *Constitutional* 115. **1805** Parkinson *Tour* 441. c**1813** Dow *Journal* 333. **1816** MCarey in *Lewis and Clark Expedition* 628. **1819** Brackenridge *South America* 1.179. **1819** Peirce *Rebelliad* 7: That golden rule, "Do as you are done by." **1823** Jackson *Correspondence* 3.202. a**1824** Marshall *Kentucky* 1.19: He "will do unto others, as they do unto him." **1824** Blane *Excursion* 224. **1824** Doddridge *Notes* 51. **1829** Cooper *Letters* 1.367. Barbour 50(1, 2); *Oxford* 191; Whiting D274.

D210   Do or die

1819 Peirce *Rebelliad* 53: Let us do or die! **1822** Bache *Notes* 92: Ready to do or die. *Oxford* 192; Whiting D276.

D211   He who cannot Do as he would must do what he can (*varied*)

1778 Asbury *Journal* 1.264: When a man cannot do what he would, he must do what he can. **1778** *Washington Writings* 13.79: If he cannot do as he wishes, he must do what he can. **1802** Dow *Journal* 150: So I must do as I could if I could not do as I would, **1805** 244: The wind being high . . . that I could not be landed where I would, so I must where I could. *Oxford* 191; Whiting D285, W276.

D212   Once well Done is twice done (*varied*)

1729 JBelcher in Talcott *Papers* 1.171: Once well done is twice done. **1741** Franklin *PR* 2.296: Well done, is twice done. **1761** *Boston Gazette* in *Olden Time* 2.31: Once well done is twice done. **1793** *Washington Writings* 33.198: A thing but half done is never done, and well done is, in a manner done forever. *Oxford* 878; Tilley T153. See **G48**.

D213   To Do one over

1800 Adams(TB) *Letters* 133: It has fairly done us over, as the saying is. DA do 2(3).

D214   Well Done is better than well said

1737 Franklin *PR* 2.168: Well done is better than well said. *Oxford* 192, 702; Tilley S123. Cf. Whiting D281.

D215   What is Done cannot be undone (*varied*)

1782 Adams *D and A* 3.90: But what is done, is irrevocable. **1783** Shippen *Journal* 158: What is past cannot indeed be undone. **1791** *Washington Writings* 31.433: What has been done cannot be undone. **1801** Asbury *Letters* 3.200: What is done, cannot be done over again. **1815** GMorris in King *Life* 5.470: Whatever has been done is done and the Consequences will follow in their own Course without Impediment or Deviation from what we may do or attempt. **1835** Floy *Diary* 145: What is done cannot be undone. *Oxford* 199; Whiting D287. See **G66, P32**.

D216   What is worth Doing is worth doing well

1780 AA in *Adams FC* 3.293: If it is worth doing at all, it is worth doing well. **1795** *Washington Writings* 34.153: It is a *fixed* principle with me, that whatever is *done* should be *well done*. This maxim . . . **1814** Wirt *Bachelor* 3: The maxim that "whatever is worth doing, is worth doing well." **1828** Jones *Sketches* 2.243-4: An excellent maxim . . . what is worth doing at all is worth doing well. *Oxford* 921; TW 104(4).

D217   Dock Square compliment

1785 JEliot in *Belknap Papers* 3.283: I . . . will ever esteem it a pleasure, without a Dock Square compliment, to answer . . .

every question you see fit to ask. Cf. NED *Compliment* 3, quote 1854.

D218 Beware of the young **Doctor** and the old barber

1733 Franklin *PR* 1.314: Beware of the young Doctor and the old Barber. *Oxford* 927; Tilley B72.

D219 Do not misinform your **Doctor** or your lawyer

1737 Franklin *PR* 2.169: Don't misinform your Doctor nor your Lawyer. *Oxford* 371; Tilley P261.

D220 The three **Doctors**: Diet, Quiet and Temperance

1761 Ames *Almanacs* 319: The three Doctors, Diet, Quiet and Temperance are the best Physicians. *Oxford* 622; Whiting L175. See **P101, T31.**

D221 As fat as a **Doe**

1803 *Yankee Phrases* 87: I late was as fat as a doe.

D222 As nimble as **Does**

1815 *Port Folio* 3NS 5.448: As nimble as does. Lean 2.858; Svartengren 159. Cf. Whiting D293.

D223 As sleek as a **Doe**

1792 Pope *Tour* 15: And sleek was her Skin as a Doe.

D224 As artful as a **Dog**

1775 JHarvey in *Blount Papers* 1.3: Shes artful as a dog.

D225 As ashamed as a **Dog**

1801 Trumbull *Season* 156: I . . . feel as ashamed as a dog. TW 105(8).

D226 As demure as a **Dog**

1821 Knight *Poems* 2.153: Could fawn as demure as a dog.

D227 As drunk as a **Dog**

1868 RAbbott in *Ruffin Papers* 4.197: He was drunk all the time at court, as a dog. Barbour 51(15); TW 105(11).

D228 As naked as **Dogs**

1757 RWall in McDowell *Documents* 2.317:

[They are] almost starved and as naked [as] Doggs. Whiting *NC* 397(20).

D229 As sick as a **Dog**

1827 Watterston *Wanderer* 103: I am as sick at the stomach as dog, so I am. Barbour 52(42); Taylor *Comparisons* 72; Tilley D440; Whiting *NC* 397(24).

D230 **Dog-cheap**

1731 *Weekly Rehearsal* in Buckingham *Specimens* 1.123: To sell wind (dog-cheap too). **1798** *Echo* 189: Edmund was willing to sell him dog-cheap. **1798** TPierce in Vanderpoel *Chronicles* 369. **1800** *Echo* 273. **1806** Fessenden *Modern Philosopher* 78: A few cargoes of American liberty, which we will sell you dog cheap. **1807** *Salmagundi* 273. **1811** Graydon *Memoirs* 298. **1822** Weems *Letters* 3.331. **1833** Cooper *Letters* 2.372. **1840** Hone *Diary* 1.477: Cotton is dog-cheap. TW 195(9).

D231 A **Dog** barks (bays) against the moon

1656 Hammond *Leah* 15: Those that shall blemish Virginia any more, do but like the Dog bark against the Moon. **1753** *Independent Reflector* 127: His Noise . . . will have much the same Influence upon you, as hath the Barking of a Dog upon the Moon. **1819** *Port Folio* 4NS 8.94: But, though curs may bay the Moon, its light shall still beam forth unclouded. **1828** JSkinner in *Ruffin Papers* 1.465: Making in effect the President to use his own terms "a mere dog to bay the moon." *Oxford* 30; Tilley D449; Whiting M654. See **M232.**

D232 **Dog** eats dog

1749 *Johnson Papers* 1.239: Let dog eat dog & Ind[n] fight with Ind[n]. **1797** Cobbett *Porcupine* 7.228: In these degenerate days dog eats dog. **1819** Murphey *Papers* 1.128: And that bringing two Suits upon one Bond . . . merely for the purpose of getting Fees, is in the Language of Peter Browne, *Dog eating Dog*. TW 106(24). See **D235.**

D233 The **Dog** in the manger

1674 Josselyn *Account* 45: Like the dog in the manger. **1729** DDunbar in *Baxter Manuscripts* 10.453: It looks like y[e] dog in y[e] Manger (I beg pardon for the comparison) that would not let the Horse eat hay or eat it himself. **1738** RStaunton in *Letters from Hudson Bay* 271: He . . . was an honest man which as they termed it would neither eat oats himself nor suffer any other within his knowledge . . . as if they had said he would not be a rogue himself nor suffer any other within his knowledge to be so. **1741** Stephens *Journal(I)* 2.265: But we have some ill-conditioned People, who verify the Saying of a *Dog in a Manger*. **1761** *New York Mercury* in *Newspaper Extracts(I)* 4.524-6: Poor Cæsar's Antagonist is likely to be found in a worse State than the Dog in the Manger. **1775** Adams *D and A* 2.190. **1775** TWilling in Adams *Works* 2.454. **1779** Mason *Papers* 2.524. **1792** Freneau *Poems* 3.105: Yon dog of the manger, how stately he struts. **1793** HWilliamson in *Blount Papers* 2.237, **1795** 548: He Complains much of Frye, who has like the Dogg in the Mainger not yet done the Work. **1801** Story *Shop* 109: Like fabl'd dog, who in the manger lay. **1810** *Port Folio* 2NS 4.74: [A] yelping dog in a manger, who neither eats himself nor will let others eat. **1829** Cooper *Letters* 1.296, **1833** 2.369. Barbour 51(3); *Oxford* 195; Whiting H565.

D234   The **Dog** returns to his vomit

1636 ETrelawny in *Trelawny Papers* 80: Not Returning with the *Dogg to his Vomitt, nor with the sowe to her wallowing in the Mire.* **1642** SGorton in Winslow *Hypocrisie* 10: You should doe them wrong, in not resuming your vomit into its former Concoction againe. **1643** Williams *Writings* 1.385: And like the Dog, lickt up their vomit of former loosnes and profanes of lip and life. **1646** Winslow *Hypocrisie* 38-9: They doe not say plainly that our Magistrates are dogs, but compare them to dogs in resuming their vomit into its former concoction. **1652** Williams *Writings* 7.81: Like a *Dog*, they vomit up the filth which (after their stomach is eased) they return unto, and lick up by new *Commissions*. **1653** Wigglesworth *Diary* 27: I told him of the dog returning to his vomit and the sow to her wallowing &c. **1677** Hubbard *Indian* 1.60: And returning back to his old Vomit. **1702** Mather *Magnalia* 2.406: He return'd unto his vomit

and his quagmire, until the sentence of death at last fell upon him. **1756** Johnson *Writings* 3.555: Return with the dog to his vomit. **1764** G. C. *Little Looking Glass* 74. **1772** *New-York Gazette* in *Newspaper Extracts(I)* 9.149: Send your hounds back again . . . to lick up their nauseous vomit. **1813** JRandolph in Quincy *JQuincy* 330: The canine race in New York have returned to their vomit. **1814** Kerr *Barclay* 25: As a dog returneth to his vomit, so a fool returneth to his folly. Prov. xxvi, 11. **1816** Adams *Writings* 6.15: She has . . . returned to her own vomit. **1829** Wirt *Letters* 2.272: It seems to me now very much like "the dog returning," &c. I do not say "the sow returning to her wallowing in the mire." **1843** Paulding *Letters(II)* 348. *Oxford* 196; Whiting H567. See **S349, 543.**

D235   **Dog** will not eat dog

1792 Brackenridge *Modern* 70: The maxim is, dog will not eat dog. **1814** Kerr *Barclay* 193: Making use of the following vulgar expression—"dog won't eat dog." **1818** Royall *Letters* 170. *Oxford* 194-5; TW 106(25). See **C75, D232, F23.**

D236   A **Dog's** life, hunger and ease

1671 TBatts in Clayton *Writings* 74: Yesterday . . . we lived a Dog's life, hungry & Dased. **1676** Williams *Writings* 5.206: All this is no more than hunger and Ease, the Dogs Life also. *Oxford* 197; Tilley D521. See **D264.**

D237   A **Dog's** trick

1800 Delano *Narrative* 299: This cautious and repulsive policy is owing probably to some *dog's tricks* which were successfully played on them, 301: As I have said something respecting *dog's tricks*, which the English privateers have played upon them. *Oxford* 197; Tilley D546.

D238   **Dogs** in office

1804 Irving *Journals* 1.100: This it is to deal with *Dogs in office*. Cf. *Oxford* 408; Tilley J17. See **J11.**

D239   **Dogs** jump at a dirty pudding

1777 *The Downfall of Justice*, 2nd ed. (Danvers, 1777 [Phostat Americana]) 6: 'Tis said that scornful dogs sometimes jump at a dirty pudding. *Oxford* 393; Whiting D310. See **P238, T150.**

D240 **Dogs** love you the better for kicking them

1810 Cuming *Sketches* 263: If any of them [Indians] displease us, we take them out of doors and kick them a little, for they are like dogs, and so will love you the better for it. *Oxford* 758-9; Tilley S705.

D241 **Dogs** show their teeth when they dare not bite

1791 S.P.L. *Thoughts* 167: Dogs shew their teeth when they dare not bite.

D242 Enough to make a **Dog** sick

c1790 Brackenridge *Gazette* 107: Enough to make a dog sick. Cf. Whiting *NC* 397(29).

D243 Every **Dog** has his day

1777 JSewall in Gerry *Letters* 1.271: Every dog they say has his day. **1782** Freneau *Poems* 2.186: For fools may write and knaves must have their day (**1786** ed.: For fools must prate and dogs must have their day). **1787** *American Museum* 2.595: "Sit omnibus hora," each dog has his day. **1787** *Anarchiad* 47. **1789** RPutnam in Cutler *Life* 1.447: The saying is. **1791** S.P.L. *Thoughts* 77. **1799** Carey *Porcupiniad* 2.35. **1800** *Echo* 271: Every Dog may have his day. **1803** *Port Folio* 3.54. **1805** *Echo* 179: Our lying Dogs at length have got their day. **1806** *Port Folio* NS 1.340. **1807** Bowne *Letters* 219: If it were not for using a most homely proverb, I would say "Every dog has his day." **1807** *Salmagundi* 269. **1812** Woodworth *Beasts* 25: Why, dogs, you know, will have their way. **1816** Paulding *Letters*(*I*) 1.60: Every nation, like every dog, has its day. **1819** *Port Folio* 4NS 7.248. **1820** *Fudge Family* 39: Every dog should have his day. **1830** Ames *Mariner's* 159: One of their [sailors'] proverbs, namely, "every dog must have his day, and every b——h two Sunday afternoons," is commonly explained by supposing that in another world, captains and mates will go to sea before the mast and so *vice versa*. Barbour 51(16); *Oxford* 195; Whiting D306.

D244 Fight **Dog**, fight bear

1764 *March of the Paxton Men* in Franklin *Papers* 11. (after p.70): Fight Dog! fight Bear! *Oxford* 256; Tilley D467. See **D140.**

D245 Give a **Dog** an ill name, *etc.*

1723 *New-England Courant* 102(1.1): The old Proverb I had often heard, *Give a Dog an ill Name, and he is half hang'd.* **1807** Janson *Stranger* 299: It is an old saying, "give a dog a bad name, and hang him." **1823** King *Life* 6.518: To disserve an argument, which we do not like, or cannot answer, it is a common practice to give it a bad name. *Oxford* 302; TW 106(29).

D246 He that lies down with **Dogs**, *etc.*

1733 Franklin *PR* 1.315: He that lies down with Dogs, shall rise up with fleas. Barbour 52(32); *Oxford* 460-1; Tilley D537.

D247 Like a **Dog** in a chain

1705 RCarter in *VHM* 5(1897) 43: Lett ye feinds grate their teeth if they will, —be but like a dog in a Chain.

D248 Like a **Dog** in a dancing-school

1776 CLee in Washington *Writings* 4.457: I am afraid that I shall make a shabby figure, without any real demerits of my own. I am like a Dog in a dancing school.

D249 Like a **Dog** with his tail between his legs (*varied*)

1739 Belcher *Papers* 2.246: Such a thing would . . . make him clap his tail between his legs, & leer home like a dog, as he is. **1779** FWade in Rodney *Letters* 320: The Doct. . . . sneaked off like another curr with his tail between his legs. **1813** Bates *Papers* 2.262: But seeing that All our Dogs had clapt their tails between their legs and cryed. **1815** *Port Folio* 3NS 6.91: He ran . . . like a slinking hound with his tail between his legs. Barbour 52(36); TW 107(38), 365(4).

D250 Like **Dogs** that had been stealing sheep

1775 Webb *Correspondence* 1.68-9: The Poor Dogs [soldiers] were forced to Come back like Dogs that had been stealing sheep. **1809** Weems *Washington* 25: They . . . pass each other, with looks cold and shy as sheep-thieving curs. **1817** MBayard in Pintard *Letters* 1.51: The chief actors getting intelligence escaped in the night like dogs that had been engaged in sheep killing. Cf. Barbour 51(25); TW 107(37).

D251 A living **Dog** is better than a dead lion
1677 Hubbard *Indian* 1.166: A living Dog is better than a dead Lion. **1776** Freneau *Poems* 1.244: More I esteem, and better is by far A dog existing than a lion dead. **1784** WHooper in Iredell *Correspondence* 108: And as the saying is, a live dog is better than a dead lion. **1788** Freneau *Prose* 193: The Hebrew record tells us in a certain place, that "a living dog is better than a deceased lion." **1805** Brackenridge *Modern* 582: Solomon says. **1816** Fidfaddy *Adventures* 141: A living *dog* to *lion* dead, King Solomon prefers. **1830** Ames *Mariner's* 33: The axiom. Barbour 51(7); *Oxford* 476; Whiting D317. See **G6.**

D252 None but **Dogs** and foreigners (go out in the sun)
1819 Brackenridge *South America* 1.294: It was formerly a saying, that during the siesta, none but dogs and foreigners were to be seen in the street. Lean 1.19. (Cf. Noel Coward: "Mad dogs and Englishmen go out in the mid-day sun" in *Oxford Dictionary of Quotations*, 2nd ed. [1966] 157.)

D253 A sad **Dog**
1765 *Johnson Papers* 11.833: Sherlock is a most sad dog. NED Dog 3b; Partridge s.v. sad.

D254 To be hanged like a **Dog**
1752 Ames *Almanacs* 234: A thousand such Witnesses are not sufficient to hang a Dog. **1770** Adams *Legal Papers* 2.427: I heard some Body say *hang him like a dog*. **1773** Smith *Memoirs(I)* 160: I had rather be shot like a Gent, than carried to Town tarred feathered & hang'd like a Dog. **1776** Burr *Memoirs* 1.104. **a1778** Jones *History* 1.381. **1792** Brackenridge *Modern* 84: It was not the way, at that time, to hang, as you would a dog. **1799** JCathcart in *Barbary Wars* 1.309. **1807** Weems *Murder* 8: I see that you are to be hung as certainly as ever a dog was,

1809 *Marion* 5, 187, 231, 238, **1811** *Gambling* 31: The hangman . . . launches him into eternity like a soul-less dog. TW 107(41); Whiting H574.

D255 To be tossed like a **Dog** in a blanket
1699 Ward *Trip* 38: With these sort of cogitations I past away my Time, being tost about by Waves like a *Dog* in a *Blanket*. NED Blanket 2, Toss 9.

D256 To cringe like **Dogs**
1688 JPipon in *Baxter Manuscripts* 6.425: If they be severely dealt with, they shall cringe Like dogs. Cf. Whiting H578.

D257 To die like a **Dog**
1763 Laurens *Papers* 3.319: Their fellow Soldiers died like Dogs. **1807** Weems *Murder* 38: He struggles in the shameful halter, dying the death of a dog. *Oxford* 185-6; Whiting D321.

D258 To follow like a **Dog**
1819 Gallatin *Diary* 137: She follows him like a dog.

D259 To go to the **Dogs**
1702 Mather *Magnalia* 1.358: At last he roared out, "That he was damned, and that he was a dog, and that he was going to the dogs forever." So he cried and so he died. **1742** Belcher *Papers* 2.425: [They] are both gone to the dogs. **1771** Carter *Diary* 1.556: And no proper notion of Gratitude which will carry him to the dogs sooner or later. **1774** Seabury *Letters* 60. Barbour 52(46); *Oxford* 208; TW 107(39). See **B351.**

D260 To help a lame **Dog** over a stile
1637 Morton *New English Canaan* 314: Where upon this man of much recconing . . . helpes the lame dogge over the stile. **1791** S.P.L. *Thoughts* 167: Few are inclined to "help a *lame* dog over a stile." *Oxford* 368; Whiting D327.

D261 To keep a **Dog** and bark oneself
1791 S.P.L. *Thoughts* 167: Shall I keep a dog, and bark myself. *Oxford* 416-7; TW 106(26).

D262 To kill one's **Dog**

1737 *Pennsylvania Gazette* in DA dog 8(1): He's kill'd his Dog [is drunk].

D263 To kill someone like **Dogs**

1724 *Baxter Manuscripts* 23.165: Thinking to kill us all like dogs. 1752 McDowell *Documents* 1.243: Kill his People like Dogs. 1766 WLithgow in *Baxter Manuscripts* 24.133: They [Indians] say it's better for them to Die lick men, then to be kill'd lick Dogs, 137. TW 108(52).

D264 To lead a **Dog's** life

1781 Hamilton *Papers* 2.539: Its a dog of life when two dissonant tempers meet. 1791 Freneau *Poems* 3.57: Imprisoned by Neptune, he lives like a dog. 1792 GClymer in Hamilton *Papers* 12.522: They complained of having led a dog's life. 1811 Graydon *Memoirs* 329: The tented field, which dog's life as it is, I had become fond of. 1813 *Port Folio* 3NS 2.485. 1831 Longfellow *Letters* 1.361. Barbour 52(47); Tilley D521; Whiting D330. See **D236.**

D265 To scold like a **Dog's** tail

1778 SHodgkins in Hodgkins *Letters* 240: She [a baby] is a Scolding at me like a dogges tal.

D266 To take a **Dog** by the ears

a1700 Hubbard *New England* 476: Lest by interposing in a strife that was not within their reach, they should but take a dog by the ears. Whiting H594. Cf. Tilley W603. See **W261.**

D267 To turn (put) out a **Dog**

1704 Knight *Journal* 58: The weather was so stormy none but she would have turned out a Dogg. 1772 Winslow *Diary* 29: My aunt says . . . this day is 10 degrees colder than it was yesterday; and moreover, that she would not put a dog out of doors. Partridge 231; TW 108(57).

D268 To work like a **Dog**

1787 *American Museum* 1.485: A man for his victuals must work like a dog. Barbour 52(50); TW 108(58).

D269 To yaw about like a **Dog** in a fair

1803 Davis *Travels* 451: You yaw her about like a dog in a fair. Mind your port helm! *Oxford* 195; Tilley D494.

D270 Two **Dogs** with one bone

1809 Irving *History* 2.28: You might as well look for unanimity and concord between two lovers with one mistress, two dogs with one bone, or two naked rogues with one pair of breeches. *Oxford* 850; Whiting W500.

D271 While two **Dogs** are fighting for a bone, *etc.*

1766 JParker in Franklin *Papers* 13.264: While . . . two Dogs were fighting for a Bone, the Third would run away with it. 1784 Gadsden *Writings* 212: Verifying the coarse proverb, while two dogs are fighting for a bone, a third comes and runs away with it. *Oxford* 850; Whiting D334.

D272 You can't teach an old **Dog** new tricks (*varied*)

1806 Randolph(J) *Letters* 14: There is an old proverb, "You cannot teach an old dog new tricks." 1812 Randall *Miser* 37: It is hard to teach old dogs new tricks. 1820 Wirt *Letters* 2.113: According to an elegant and favorite saying of J.W's, that "old dogs don't learn new tricks," 1824 182: Wickham has an uncourtly saying that "old dogs do not learn new tricks." Barbour 52(51); *Oxford* 805; TW 105(6). See **B182.**

D273 Not worth a **Doit**

1792 Morris *Diary* 2.571: This Tactick, which from the moment of such avowal was no longer worth a Doit. *Oxford* 193: Dodkin; Tilley D430.

D274 As bright as a **Dollar**

1820 Hodgson *Letters* 1.210: He came out, to use my friend's expression, as bright as a dollar. Barbour 53(2); TW 108(2).

D275 First catch a **Dolphin**

1801 *Farmers' Museum* 55: A recipe in an old book on the art of cookery: "How to dress a dolphin, first *catch a dolphin*, &c." *Oxford* 262. See **T284.**

D276 Till **Doomsday**

1785 JAdams in Jefferson *Papers* 8.577: He will wait till Doomsday and it will never come. a1788 Jones *History* 1.118: Here the matter rested and is likely to rest till dooms-day. **1791** Hamilton *Papers* 9.549: You may think this as remote as a *certain day*, that pious people talk so much about. **1811** Weems *Letters* 3.39. **1822** Watterston *Winter* 34. Barbour 53; TW 109; Whiting D346.

D277　At the wrong **Door**
1710 JUsher in *Baxter Manuscripts* 9.306: I Suspend him, comeing in att wrong door under notion of a Mandate, & affrontt to yo͏ʳ office. **1713** Wise *Churches* 147: You beg at the wrong door. You Beg without a Brief. Whiting D348.

D278　The back **Door** robs (the house)
1676 Williams *Writings* 5.403: They do but by a *jugling Hocas pocas*; a *back dore*, &c. rob all others of their *points*, Ribbons, and Laws. Barbour 53(4); *Oxford* 25; Tilley B21.

D279　**Doors** and walls are fools' paper
1733 Franklin *PR* 1.316: Doors and walls are fools paper. Tilley W17; Whiting *NC* 410: Fool (5).

D280　To eat one out of **Doors**
1807 *Salmagundi* 325: Enriched them with a numerous and hopeful offspring, who eat them out of doors. Whiting H614, quote 1469. See **H343.**

D281　To lie at one's **Door**
1705 NSaltonstall in *Saltonstall Papers* 1.279: Pray consider what lyes at your doore, and do not deale so unhandsomely with Y͏ʳ. patient friend. **1794** DAllison in *Blount Papers* 2.428: This is laid at my door. **1803** Monroe *Writings* 4.91: The whole responsibility . . . would have lain at my door. NED Door 6. Cf. Tilley D561.

D282　As dead as a **Door-nail**
1783 Hopkinson *Miscellaneous Essays* 1.232: And dead as any nail in door. **1801** *Port Folio* 1.48: When I lie dead as door-nail. **1813** Paulding *Letters(II)* 37: And drank all the New York Delegation, as dead as Door-nails. Barbour 63(1); *Oxford* 170; Whiting D252.

D283　To sleep like a **Dormouse**
1796 Dennie *Lay Preacher* 53: Let the sloth and the dormouse sleep, but let man be "up and doing." **1797** Cobbett *Porcupine* 5.149: That patriotism, which slept like a dormouse. Whiting D353.

D284　As faithful as a **Dove**
c1800 Paine *Works* 126: Now, warm and faithful as the cooing dove. Whiting T542.

D285　As gentle as a **Dove**
1814 Wirt *Bachelor* 76: As gentle and piteous as the tender dove. Barbour 54; Whiting *NC* 400(1).

D286　As innocent as a **Dove**
1780 AA in *Adams FC* 3.288: Can the Innocence of the dove or the wisdom of a more subtle animal screne him from all these foes? **1796** Barton *Disappointment* 27: He thinks me as innocent as a dove. Svartengren 6; TW 110(3). See **S103.**

D287　As true as a **Dove**
1806 Tyler *Verse* 143: I was *onest* and true as a dove. *Oxford* 840: Turtle; Whiting T542.

D288　The **Dove** has no gall
1702 Mather *Magnalia* 1.437: If it were *metaphorically* true (what they *proverbially* said) of Beza, that "he had no gall." **1703** Taylor *Christographia* 324.68: The harmless dove . . . is reported to have no gall. Whiting D364.

D289　From **Dover** to Berwick
1654 Johnson *Wonder-Working* 108: He crosses the Angles of *England* from *Cornewall* to *Kent*, from *Dover* to *Barwick*. *Oxford* 47; Whiting B260.

D290　**Dover Court:** all speakers and no hearers
1783 Williams *Penrose* 337: So that it was become a Dover Court (all Speakers and no hearers). **1787** Smith *Diary* 2.181: I warn'd them to be ready with their Questions to avoid a Dover Court. *Oxford* 200; Tilley D575. See **T19.**

D291　As soft as **Down**
1772 Paterson *Glimpses* 115: And soft as

down in Cherub's wing. Barbour 54(2); Taylor *Comparisons* 76; Whiting *NC* 400.

D292 To be going **Downhill**

1799 CPinckney in Moultrie *Memoirs* 1.354: Having reached forty-seven years, and consequently going down hill, as the saying is. NED Downhill.

D293 To be on a cold **Drag**

1766 JVining in Rodney *Letters* 27; It therefore appears that our friend R.H. is upon a cold drag. **1790** Maclay *Journal* 261: It all seemed uphill or like a cold drag with the Philadelphians. Cf. NED Cold 12, Drag 6.

D294 To eat like a **Dragon**

1787 AMaclaine in Iredell *Correspondence* 2.164: But he eats like a dragon. NED Dragon[1] 2c.

D295 As swift as a **Dream**

a1786 Ladd *Remains* 70: My life flies swifter than a dream.

D296 A **Dream** of a dry summer

1702 Mather *Magnalia* 2.595: This proved as vain as a dream of a dry summer. *Oxford* 202; Tilley S966.

D297 **Dreams** are false

1754 Ames *Almanacs* 252: Dreams like notorious Liars are generally false, but may speak truth now and then. **1774** Fithian *Journal and Letters* 110: Dreams indeed are vain & false. *Oxford* 202; Whiting D387.

D298 **Dreams** go by contraries

c1725 Byrd *Another Secret Diary* 456: I believe that Dreams . . . are to be taken by the contrarys. *Oxford* 202; Whiting S951.

D299 To vanish as **Dreams**

1802 JHaywood in *Steele Papers* 1.258: I will cherish the hope, that those lowering clouds . . . will vanish as dreams, and be succeeded by a refulgent Noon. **1812** Maxwell *Poems* 14: Oh! empty dreams, soon vanish'd into air!

D300 **Drink** is the source of all evil

1789 Washington *Writings* 30.263: Drink, which is the source of all evil. Cf. *Oxford* 185; Tilley D324.

D301 **Drink** it to save it

1801 PBuckner in *W&MCQ* 2S 6(1926)192: Sam'ls horse broke another bottle of whisky; we then determined to drink up the balance to save it.

D302 To **Drink** more than one has bled

1681 Sewall *Diary* 2.16*: Her death puts in mind of the Proverb wherein we say such an one hath drunk more than he hath bled to-day. **1737** Franklin *Drinkers* 2.174: Has drunk more than he has bled. Whiting D406.

D303 A **Drop** in (of) the bucket

1678 RWilliams in *Hinckley Papers* 21: All lands and all nations are but a drop of a bucket in the eyes of that King of kings. **1702** Taylor *Christographia* 222.77-8: All the power in the World, is but a drop of his bucket. **1750** JMayhew in Thornton *Pulpit* 50: Civil tyranny is usually small in the beginning like the "drop of a bucket." **1766** Franklin *Papers* 13.42: What remain'd in their Hands was but like a Drop of the Bucket compar'd to what was now in the Hands of the Commons, **1768** 15.63: A drop in the bucket. **1775** Adams(A) *Letters* 32: The loss of Charlestown affects them no more than a drop of the bucket. **1778** GMott in *Clinton Papers* 2.760: Only Eleven Cattle the week before last which was like a Drop of the Bucket, for 500 or six hundred men. **1779** *Washington *Writings* 16.125. **1786** Jefferson *Papers* 9.448: What we were authorized to offer being to this but as a drop to a bucket. **1787** *American Museum* 2.40: The loan-office was only a drop in the bucket, compared with this ocean of private credit. **1792** Paine *To Addressers* 2.507. **1792** Wayne *Correspondence* 77. **1793** *Washington *Writings* 33.21-2. **1794** TSedgwick in Callender *Political Register* 1.373: Gentlemen may *argue* and *argue* about this drop in the bucket compared with the ocean. **1797** Callender *Annual Register 1796* 29. **1798** Gadsden *Writings* 283: A Trifle, a mere drop in the Bucket. **1810** Wirt *Letters* 1.284. **1812** JMorrison in Knopf *War of 1812* 6(4) 147. **1813** LCass in Knopf *War of 1812* 2.226: This will add but a drop to the bucket. **1847** Cooper *Letters*

5.194: On which he will not fail to make $20,000 . . . —a drop in the bucket of his speculations, however. Barbour 55(1); TW 111(1).

D304 A Drop in the ocean

1639 HPeter in *Winthrop Papers(A)* 4.140: I need not cast my drop into your ocean. **1652** Williams *Writings* 7.166: All the *Wisedome* that is in us is but a *drop* to the *Ocean* of that which is in the *Father* of *mercies*. **1756** *Colden Letters* 9.167: The money . . . would be no more felt by the rich than a drop of water is in the Sea. **1776** JSewall in *Naval Documents* 3.496. **1777** WHDrayton in Gibbes 3.79: The . . . expenses . . . are but as drops of water in the ocean. **1781** AA in *Adams FC* 4.135: You will find your own [knowledge], but as a grain of sand, a drop in the ocean. **1782** Freneau *Poems* 2.138: Or what is a drop when compared to the main. **1812** JWilled in Knopf *War of 1812* 2.52. *Oxford* 204-5; TW 111(1); Tilley D613.

D305 To have a Drop in one's eye

1813 Weems *Drunkard* 60: Has got a drop in his eye. TW 111(5).

D306 Continual Dropping wears away stones (*varied*)

1702 Mather *Magnalia* 1.437: The *spirit* of Mr. Stone, as worn out by the *continual dropping* of their contention.—*Gutta cavat Lapidem*, **1706** *Diary* 1.525: But who can tell, what may be the Effect of a *continual Dropping?* **1758** Franklin *WW* 343: Constant Dropping wears away Stones. **1770** Ames *Almanacs* 413: Constant dropping wears away stones. **1784** POliver in Hutchinson *Diary* 2.398: *Gutta cavat lapidem.* **1793** Coke *Journals* 182: But constant dropping, 'tis said, will wear out a stone. **1796** *Washington *Writings* 35.126: Drops of Water will Impress (in time) the hardest Marble. **1797** Weems *Letters* 2.87: By the continual dropping of water the Stones are worn away. **1797** Carey *Plumb* 8: It is a trite observation . . . that incessant dropping of water will wear away the hardest stone. **1801** Cobbett *Porcupine* 10, postscript p.3: By continual dropping water will wear away the hardest marble. **1804** Hamilton

Law Practice 1.810: Drops of water, in long and continued succession, will wear out adamant. **1811** Barlow *Works* 1.559: Till, unlike the *gutta saepe cadendo*, they were found not to wear into that rock. **1816** Paulding *Letters(I)* 2.200: It is like the wearing away of the solid rock by drops of water. **1819** Wright *Views* 111: Ages are required to mould him by imperceptible degrees, as the water smooths the rock over which it flows. Barbour 55; *Oxford* 141; Whiting D412. See **T265.**

D307 A Drug (in the market) (*varied*)

1648 LDowninge in *Winthrop Papers(A)* 5.293: For shop paye is nowe the druge. **1656** Bradford *History* 2.44: It may prove a drugg in time. **1720** Walter *Choice Dialogue* xix: A Drugg in the Market of Literature. **1720** EWigglesworth *Letter* in *Colonial Currency* 1.436: Something . . . which great plenty hath made a Drug of. **1731** *Commerce of Rhode Island* 1.15: All soarts of goods being now a drugg. **1741** ?WDouglass *Second Letter* in *Colonial Currency* 4.126. **1743** *Georgia Records* 23.487. **1745** Stephens *Journal(II)* 2.185. **1747** Franklin *Papers* 3.151. **1750** *Beekman Papers* 1.107. **1756** Laurens *Papers* 2.325, 383, **1762** 3.134. **1773** EPendleton in *Letters to Washington* 4.203, 236. **1775** JWarren in *Warren-Adams Letters* 1.176. **1776** DCobb in *Bingham's Maine* 1.427. **1778** Paine *American Crisis* 1.131. **1779** JClay in *Norton Papers* 422: I have dispos'd of all the goods . . . Except the Medicines, which are a *drug.* **1782** *Belknap Papers* 1.152: Bibles are now a drug in the shops at Portsmouth. **1786** Denny *Journal* 279. **1787** SJones in *Baxter Manuscripts* 21.371. **1796** JPrescott in *Blount Papers* 3.83. **1801** Dorr *Letters* 248, 267: Teas being a drug, 287: Ginseng . . . its now a drug. **1805** WHiggins in *Barbary Wars* 6.106. **1816** Lambert *Travels* 2.155. *Oxford* 205; TW 112.

D308 As empty as a Drum

1775 Freneau *Poems* 1.164: But empty as the interior of his drum. Whiting *NC* 400(1). Cf Barbour 55(1).

D309   As tight as a **Drum-head**
1807 *Weekly* 2.95: Shall strain every nerve just as tight as a drum-head. Svartengren 264; TW 112.

D310   There are more old **Drunkards** than old doctors
1736 Franklin *PR* 2.139: There's more old Drunkards than old Doctors. Tilley D630.

D311   Like a **Duck** in thunder
1807 *Salmagundi* 33: He rolls up his eyes, as M' Sycophant says, "like a duck in thunder." *Oxford* 210; TW 113(10).

D312   To drink with the **Ducks**
1830 Ames *Mariner's* 201: Wearing a Scotch bonnet . . . would, in our service, subject the wearer to "drinking with the ducks," or getting his "*back* rations" in the gangway. *Oxford* 203; TW 112(1); Whiting D427.

D313   To milk the **Ducks**
1815 Humphreys *Yankey* 21: 'Tend table, and milk the ducks. Whiting D429.

D314   A full **Due**
1785 Perkins *Diary* 2.275: McDonald Sails for Lunenburg, where it Seems he is removed for a full due. [For good and all.]

D315   To play at **Duke** and no duke
1776 Lee *Papers* 2.123: In short we are playing at Duke & No Duke, and throwing everything into confusion and anarchy, 179: The inconveniences of the complex play we are acting of Duke and No Duke are numberless.

D316   To dine with **Duke Humphrey** (*varied*)
1728 Byrd *Dividing Line* 244: We had made clean Work in the morning and were in Danger of dining with St. Anthony, or his Grace Duke Humphrey. **1795** *Tablet* 4: Expect to day Duke Humphry's fare. **1803** *Port Folio* 3.91: To dine with Duke Humphrey, or, in other words, to go without food, 224, **1811** 2NS 5.62: The sheriff resolutely persisted in dispensing him nothing but duke Humphrey's fare. **1815** *Reviewers* 56: Treating them now and then, with a Duke Humphrey dinner. **1820** Irving *Sketch Book*

292. *Oxford* 188; TW 113; Tilley D637. See S24.

D317   Downright **Dunstable**
1803 *Port Folio* 3.97: He [a country man in the city] is *downright dunstable* in his style. NED Dunstable lc; *Oxford* 209; Whiting D441.

D318   To be in the (doleful) **Dumps**
1714 Hunter *Androboros* 32: Here he comes again in very pensive Mood and doleful Dumps. **1758** Winslow *Broadside* 127: In doleful Dumps cry'd "Oh!" **1775** AInnes in *Naval Documents* 2.467: All his friends are . . . in the Dumps. **1780** *Deane Brothers Papers* 154: We are in doleful Dumps. **1781** JEliot in *Belknap Papers* 3.211: To keep you out of the dumps. **1788** May *Journal* 73: I don't intend to . . . get into the dumps. **1788** *Politician* 49. **1789** *Columbian Magazine* 3.196: Tho' in the darkest dumps you view 'em. **1812** Cooper *Letters* 1.27. Barbour 56; *Oxford* 208; Tilley D640.

D319   As plump as a **Dumpling**
1764 EFitch in Lloyd *Papers* 2.656: She looks as round & plump as a Dumplin. Barbour 56(1); Svartengren 183.

D320   As round as a **Dumpling**
1816 Paulding *Letters(I)* 2.162: [She is] as round as a dumpling. Barbour 56(1); Svartengren 279; Whiting *NC* 401.

D321   As black as **Dung**
1779 TRoberts in *Sullivan Journals* 242: The timber land Black as Dung.

D322   As wet as **Dung**
1815 Humphreys *Yankey* 20: I am all dripping wet as dung. Svartengren 302.

D323   As dry as **Dust**
1834 Floy *Diary* 63: Oftentimes we come across a book of which the matter is as dry as dust. Barbour 56(2); *Oxford* 206; Tilley D647; Whiting *NC* 401(1).

D324   **Dust** thou art, *etc.*
1793 Freneau *Prose* 306: Forget not thou art made of dust (says the eastern proverb) that thou may'st continue humble. **1802** Alden *Epitaphs* 5.116: *Dust thou art, and unto*

dust shalt thou return, **1811** 1.87: Dust we are, and unto dust we must return. Barbour 56(3); Whiting E22.

D325 To bite the **Dust**

1814 Freneau *Poems* 3.356: And bite the dust, with many a groan. TW 113(2).

D326 To kick up a **Dust**

1768 *New-York Gazette* in *Newspaper Extracts(I)* 7.119: It now suits their Purpose to kick up a Dust. **1768** JParker in Franklin *Papers* 15.214: Those . . . kicking up a Dust by their haughty Behaviour. **1769** Adams(S) *Writings* 1.381: Preparation was made that very day for *a dust that was to be kick'd up* in the Evening. **1770** Adams *Legal Papers* 2.416: R. said he hoped if these were before Importers Doors there be a Dust beat up. **1773** *Johnson Papers* 8.690: Pains was taken to kick up [MS burned] Dust against any New Members. **1774** Adams *Works* 4.70. **1774** *Pennsylvania Packet* in *Newspaper Extracts(I)* 10.333. **1775** JHuntington in *Trumbull Papers* 1.498: General Putnam will knock up a dust. **1778** EWinslow in *Winslow Papers* 30: They must kick up a hell of a dust in the Jersies. **1782** Freneau *Poems* 2.194. **1784** Pynchon *Diary* 202. **1785** EHazard in *Belknap Papers* 1.416. **1791** Jefferson *Writings* 8.207: The press . . . will have shown you what a dust Paine's pamphlet has kicked up here. **1795** Cobbett *Porcupine* 2.92. **1796** TPickering in McHenry *Letters* 171: Many of the whites . . . seek an opportunity of kicking up a dust with the Indians. **1797** Gadsden *Writings* 278: There may be some dust attempted to be kicked up amongst those of that nation. **1805** Bentley *Diary* 3.194: They do not make such a dust in Salem as they have done in the last past months. **1805** Dow *Journal* 225, 227. **1809** Lindsley *Love* 11. **1812** Hitchcock *Social* 178. **1818** Adams *Memoirs* 4.83: It would certainly stir up a dust. **1818** Royall *Letters* 135: Go into the kitchen . . . and kick up a dust with her about the dinner. TW 113(4).

D327 To lick the **Dust**

1677 Hubbard *Indian* 1.201: God shall . . . bring down their Enemies to lick the Dust before them. **1778** TMcKean in Rodney *Letters* 273: Americans licking the dust from the feet of a British Minister. **1781** *New Jersey Gazette* in *Newspaper Extracts(II)* 5.182. **1789** *American Museum* 5.371: To lick up the dust at the footstool of his imperial throne. *Oxford* 429-30; Whiting E25.

D328 To shake the **Dust** from one's feet

1643 Williams *Writings* 1.331: The Apostles . . . were to turne and to shake the dust of their feet. **1704** Knight *Journal* 65: Shaking the dust from their Heels left the good woman and her Child among the number of the wicked. **1781** Peters *Connecticut* 125: He *shook off the dust of his feet* against them, and departed, 176. **1801** Story *Shop* 22: So 'gainst her kick the dust off from your feet. **1812** Burr *Journal* 2.401. **1846** Paulding *Letters(II)* 437: After my short visit to the City, whence I departed Shaking mud from my feet, and thinking of Sodom and Gomorrah. *Oxford* 719; Whiting D446.

D329 To throw **Dust** in someone's eyes

1781 PMazzei in Jefferson *Papers* 5.376: [It] has afforded matter . . . to throw dust in the eyes of many people. **1797** Jefferson *Writings* 9.384, **1808** 12.105. **1832** Cooper *Letters* 2.358. *Oxford* 209; Whiting D445.

D330 ("What a **Dust** I raise" said) the fly upon the wheel

1782 Adams *Works* 7.527: What a dust we raise, said the fly upon the chariot wheel. **1795** Freneau *Poems* 3.127: To a Political Shrimp, or, Fly upon the Wheel. **1800** Adams *New Letters* 230: See says the fly upon the wheel, What a dust I raise. **1815** Adams *Writings* 5.327: We have stood in great need of the *"fly on the coach wheel"* — that is, of the secretary to the commission, **1817** 6.218: He . . . now affects to have been the very fly upon the wheel at the restoration. **1820** Pintard *Letters* 1.271: In the mean time like the fly on the coach wheel. *Oxford* 271; Tilley D652.

D331 Double **Dutch**

1803 Davis *Travels* 413: "What the devil language is that? Is it double *Dutch* coiled against the sun?" . . . "It is *Welch*." TW 114(2).

D332   The **Dutch** are proverbial for cleanliness

1814 *Port Folio* 3NS 3.253: The cleanliness of the Dutch in their houses is proverbial, and is sometimes curiously contrasted with the neglect of their persons. See **C193**.

D333   Dutch courage

1809 Irving *History* 2.152: It was not a murderous weapon . . . but a little sturdy stone pottle, charged to the muzzle with a double dram of true Dutch courage. **1813** Weems *Drunkard* 76: One of the fools, in taking his dose of Dutch courage, had gone so deep into the whiskey bottle, that he was quite on the staggers, when the fight began. **1815** Porter *Journal* 1.183: Her captain had taken a good stock of Dutch courage. **c1820** Bernard *Retrospections* 165: And his was no Dutch courage, no constitutional apathy or blindness to danger. TW 114(1).

D334   The **Dutch** have taken Holland

1815 Waterhouse *Journal* 88: And because the Dutch have taken Holland. Partridge 251.

D335   To beat the **Dutch**

1775 *Essex Gazette* in *Historical Collections of the Essex Institute* 3(1861) 228: Our cargoes of meat, drink and clothes beat the Dutch. **1820** GCutler in Vanderpoel *Chronicles* 200: It beats the Dutch. Barbour 56; TW 114(3).

D336   As the **Dutchman** says

1777 Fitch *New-York Diary* 236: [It] is an extreem cold morning for the time of season (as the Dutchman says). **1786** JQAdams in Smith *Journal and Correspondence* 2(1) 105: You will have much more leisure, and I hope I shall profit by it, (as the Dutchman says).

D337   Do your **Duty** and be afraid of none

1749 *Colden Letters* 9.7: Do your Duty & you need be affray'd of none.

D338   (**Dwarfs** on giants' shoulders)

1694 Scottow *Narrative* 303: They were of lower stature then our first Reformers . . . yet having the advantage of standing upon their Gigantine Shoulders, they had the opportunity of seeing further, then those Giants did. *Oxford* 209; Whiting D449.

E

E1 To **Each** his own

1713 Wise *Churches* 35: The Golden Rule (*Quo dat Suum Cuique*). **1783** Gordon *Letters* 486-7: *Suum cuique*, I think is the king of Prussia's motto. **1813** *Port Folio* 3NS 2.62: Let each enjoy his own. TW 115; Tilley M209.

E2 As swift as **Eagles**

1650 Bradstreet *Works* 364: Swifter than swiftest Eagles so were they. Barbour 56(3); Whiting E142.

E3 The **Eagle** soars at the sun

1732 Belcher *Papers* 1.115: And have told him, the eagle soars at the sun, 203: How does the soaring eaglet beam from his eyeballs in a sort of rivalship with the dazzling rays of light itself. *Oxford* 210; Whiting E1.

E4 An **Eagle** will not catch flies

1645 Wheelwright *Writings* 213: Thinking no *Eagle* would catch such flyes. **1687** Taylor *Poems* 40: What shall an Eagle t'catch a Fly thus run. **a1700** Hubbard *New England* 436: But the design was too low for the said Governor to attempt, as he was advised by the worthy Governor of the Massachusetts — Aquila non capit muscas. **1702** Mather *Magnalia* 2.105: He was endued with a certain soaring and serious greatness of soul, which rendered *fly-catching* too low a business for him. **1732** Belcher *Papers* 1.126: Always remember *Acquila non captat muscas*, **1734** 2.142: The first head I declaimed on when I entred the College was *Aquila non captat muscas*. **1809** Irving *History* 1.292: *The Eagle always despiseth the Beetle fly. Oxford* 211; Whiting E2.

E5 An **Eagle's** mind never fits a raven's feather

1708 Saffin *His Book* 170: An Eagles mind n'er fitts a Ravens Feather, To dare, and to be able to Suit Together.

E6 By the **Ears** [The following is a selection from 80 occurrences of the phrase]

1646 WPynchon in *Winthrop Papers(A)* 5.90: Fale together by the eares for smaler matters. **1647** SDanforth in Silverman 114: Many this month I doe fore-see Together by the eares will be. **1651** Williams *Writings* 6.211-2: They all fell together by the ears; yet no blood spilt, **1652** 4.183: And so therewith the *world* set together by the eares. **a1656** Bradford *History* 1.299. **c1680** Radisson *Voyages* 104: [It] made us goe together by the ears, 171: We weare soone together by the ears. **1692** Randolph *Letters* 7.400. **1702** Mather *Magnalia* 1.528. **1728** Parkman *Diary* 71.204. **1758** *Johnson Papers* 13.108: We and the English would get by the ears very soon. **1767** Adams *D and A* 1.335: Friend and Friend are all set together by the Ears. **1774** JEliot in *Belknap Papers* 3.63: [It] will soon bring him & us by the ears. **1784** Hamilton *Papers* 3.513: To keep them by the ears. **1788** Washington *Writings* 29.474. **1806** *Weekly* 1.24: Get by the ears. **1818** Royall *Letters* 174: The other widow amuses herself at their expense, and often has them almost by the ears. **1837** Paulding *Letters(II)* 198. *Oxford* 716; Whiting E13.

125

E7 In at one **Ear** and out at the other

1802 *Port Folio* 2.73: Went into one ear and out of the other. **1805** WGarnett in *Ruffin Papers* 1.80: The excuses . . . seems as the saying is to have gone in at one ear and come out at the other. **1807** *Emerald* 2.292: It goes in at one ear and out at the other. Barbour 57(3); *Oxford* 402; Whiting E4.

E8 Over (to) the **Ears** in debt

1798 Adams *Writings* 2.279: He was over the ears in debt. **1812** Hitchcock *Social* 82: Plung'd half his townsmen *to their ears* in debt. Cf. Whiting E7. See **H129**.

E9 To be led by the **Ears**

1782 Rush *Letters* 1.275: The British nation is a huge mob. They are led by their ears. Whiting E9. See **N97**.

E10 To blush behind the **Ears**

1816 Smith *Life* 110: What he said . . . was sufficient to make any modest woman blush behind her ears, if such a thing is possible.

E11 To hang one's **Ears**

1741 Stephens *Journal(II)* 1.11: It was observable some of the principal among our notable Enterprizers in the Work of Reformation, hung their Ears pretty much upon Receipt of a Letter. Tilley E22.

E12 To have (something) about one's **Ears**

1637 JHigginson in *Winthrop Papers(A)* 3.405: We are like to have all the Indians in the countrey about our ears. **1646** TStoughton in *Winthrop Papers(A)* 5.106: Though I pulled the world about my eares. **1692** Randolph *Letters* 7.383: The country . . . are ready to pull his house down about his ears, **1700** 637: It . . . would have brought ye state as well as the church upon my Eares. **1766** WFranklin in Franklin *Papers* 13.256: I should have had my House pull'd down about my Ears, 269: An explosion . . . tumbled their House about the Conjuror's Ears. **1775** Hutchinson *Diary* 1.503: If the town had been beat about your ears from the heights of Charlestown. **1776** *Battle of Brooklyn* 28: You have brought old Ireland about your ears. **1780** Hamilton *Papers* 2.418: A violent storm [figurative] in which our house is tumbling about our ears. **1783**

James Moody *Narrative* (2nd ed., London, 1783) 16: I will instantly pull down your house about your ears. **1816** Paulding *Letters(I)* 1.83: His house is just on the point of tumbling about his ears. **1830** Cooper *Letters* 1.422: We should soon draw the whole fabric about our ears. TW 115(6). See **H342**.

E13 To hearken with the left **Ear**

1624 Davenport *Letters* 12: [They] looke upon me with a squint eye, and hearken to my sermons with the leaft eare. Cf. NED Left 2.

E14 To make one's **Ears** tingle (*varied*)

1767 TBChandler in Johnson *Writings* 1.408: To hear the character of the rest . . . would make the ears of any sober heathen to tingle. **1782** Baldwin *Life and Letters* 41: I suppose the twiching of your right Ear gave you notice what we are about. **1849** Cooper *Letters* 6.97: The *two Dutches* must have set her ears ringing. *Oxford* 212; TW 115(7); Whiting E12.

E15 To prick up one's **Ears**

1739 Stephens *Journal(I)* 1.431: And pricked up their Ears at this News. NED Ear *sb.*[1] lc.

E16 To turn a deaf **Ear**

1646 Winslow *Hypocrisie* 102: To such wee never turn a deafe eare. a1700 Hubbard *New England* 489: Lent a deaf ear. **1713** Wise *Churches* 146. **1740** Stephens *Journal(I)* 1.489, **1744** 2.165. **1752** LGrant in McDowell *Documents* 1.237: To give a deaf Ear, **1754** 492, 533. **1766** JParker in Franklin *Papers* 13.18. **1767** Woodmason *Journal* 16. **1768** JJohnson in *Wheelock's Indians* 139. **1769** Davis *Colonial Virginia Satirist* 58: lent. **1769** Franklin *Papers* 16.193-4. **1771** Adams *Legal Papers* 1.160. **1773** Franklin *Writings* 6.49. **1774** Hopkinson *Miscellaneous Essays* 1.81. **1777** Hamilton *Papers* 1.247. **1777** Smith *Memoirs(II)* 115, **1778** 289, 341. **1782** AA in *Adams FC* 4.342. a1788 Jones *History* 2.28. **1793** Ingraham *Journal* 79, 88. **1801** Story *Shop* 50: Delia turns a deafen'd ear. **1802** JCathcart in *Barbary Wars* 2.323: lent. **1806** *Weekly* 1.92. **1808** Adams *Works* 6.539. **1812** JWatson in

Knopf *War of 1812* 6(1) 230. **1816** *Port Folio* 4NS 1.298, 2.183. **1817** Young *Life* 155. a**1820** Tucker *Essays* 36. **1820** Wright *Views* 176. **1824** Blane *Excursion* 214. **1824** *Tales* 1.212. Barbour 57(6); *Oxford* 172; Whiting E14.

E17 As opposite as **East** from west

1741 Stephens *Journal(I)* 2.252: Finding him . . . as opposite to my Sentiments as East is from West. Cf. Barbour 57(1).

E18 **Eat,** drink and be merry, *etc.*

a**1700** Hubbard *New England* 103: This counsel was easy to be taken . . . to eat, drink, and be merry, while the good things lasted. **1736** *Melancholy State* in *Colonial Currency* 3.139: Let us eat and drink to day, for to morrow we die. **1750** Fairservice *Plain Dealing* 34: Let us eat and drink for To-morrow we die. c**1770** Smith *Works* 1¹.219: As the Apostle says . . . "Let us eat and drink, for to-morrow we die." **1775** Hopkinson *Miscellaneous Essays* 1.45: A man hath no better thing under the sun than that he should eat, drink, and be merry. **1779** *New Jersey Gazette* in *Newspaper Extracts(II)* 3.197: The maxim of Epicurus, *eat, drink and divert yourselves, for after death there is no pleasure.* **1789** Jefferson *Papers* 15.395: Eat, drink, and be merry in our day. **1797** Perkins *Diary* 4.4: Like the Rich fool in the Gospel having much goods laid up for many years, they will take their ease eat drink & be merry. **1805** WGarnett in *Ruffin Papers* 1.66: But are more inclined to take for their guide the maxim of "a penny saved is a penny got" than that of "let us eat drink and be merry for tomorrow we die." **1813** Jefferson *Writings* 12.271: [They] have consumed it in eating, drinking, and making merry in their day. **1823** Beecher *Autobiography* 1.497: Let us eat and drink, for to-morrow we die. Whiting E36.

E19 **Eat** till one sweats and work till one freezes

1674 Josselyn *Account* 182: Of the *English* there are that can eat till they sweat, and work till they freeze. **1699** Ward *Trip* 52: It being no rarity there, to see a Man *Eat* till he

Sweats, and *Work* till he *Freezes. Oxford* 215.

E20 **Eat** to live and not live to eat

1733 Franklin *PR* 1.314: Eat to live, and not live to eat. **1807** *Emerald* 2.71: You live to eat, I only eat to live. **1827** Jones *Sketches* 2.108: People eat here [Turkey] to satisfy nature: in America often for the sake of eating. *Oxford* 215; Whiting E37. Cf. Barbour 57.

E21 Governor **Eaton** said it

1702 Mather *Magnalia* 1.154: It became a proverb for incontestable truth, "Governor Eaton said it."

E22 At a low **Ebb**

1754 Lloyd *Papers* 2.522: Poor Boston . . . is reduc'd to a pretty low Ebb. NED Ebb 2b.

E23 **Ebb** and flood (flow) (*varied*)

1756 *Johnson Papers* 2.532: Mens hopes are ebbed & a flood of fears are driving in. **1775** NGreene in Ward *Correspondence* 146: Human Affairs are ever like the Tide constantly upon the Ebb and flow. **1780** EPendleton in Madison *Papers* 2.142: I hope 'tis the beginning of a Flood tide in our Southern Affairs after the long Ebb we have experienced. **1787** Jefferson *Papers* 11.45: There are ebbs as well as flows in this world. **1793** WBlount in *Blount Papers* 2.325: In good time My Popularity had ebbed and flowed several Times. **1796** DAllison in *Blount Papers* 3.11: Altho they all Ebb and Flow yet I find every Ebb occasions a greater flood than the succeeding [i.e., preceding] one. NED Ebb 1; Whiting E39, 42.

E24 As black as **Ebony**

1723 *New-England Courant* 103(1.1): As black as Ebonie. **1789** Brackenridge *Gazette* 317: Teeth as white as ebony. **1815** Porter *Journal* 1.228: Black as ebony. **1830** Pintard *Letters* 3.167: A superb Dutch Cass or Wardrobe nicely carved, as black as ebony with age. TW 116.

E25 Make every **Edge** cut

1779 JWilliams in Gibbes 3.118: Let no pains be spared to make every edge cut. TW 116(1).

E26 To cut with a double **Edge**

1705 Beverley *History* 70: This was a Misfortune that cut with a double Edge. Cf. NED Double-edged.

E27 As safe as an **Eel** in an eel-pot

1771 *Trial of Atticus* 67: I had him as safe as an eel in an eel-pot.

E28 As slippery as an **Eel**

1676 Williams *Writings* 5.106: As slippery as Eeles. **1787** Cobbett *Porcupine* 5.129: Were he as slippery as the eel . . . he could not escape her. **1823** Jefferson *Writings* 15.450: They were not . . . aware of the slipperiness of the eels of the law. Barbour 57; *Oxford* 743; Svartengren 24; Whiting E45.

E29 As used as **Eels** are to skinning

1812 Melish *Travels* 444: But they seemed to be used to it [ague] as the fisherwoman's eels were to skinning. *Oxford* 582.

E30 To hold an **Eel** by the tail

1694 *Connecticut Vindicated* 119: The [if] that all this is propounded with, makes it like a wet *Eele*, hard to take any hold on. **1720** Walter *Choice Dialogue* xiv: To use an old Latin Scrap, I learnt at School, Citius Anguillam Cau[da] teneas. **1787** JWadsworth in King *Life* 1.221: You may as well catch an Eel by the tail. *Oxford* 378; Svartengren 34f., 360; Whiting E48.

E31 To squirm like **Eels** in a basket

1790 Maclay *Journal* 225: He and Fitzsimons are now squirming like eels in a basket. NED Squirm 1a. Cf. TW 117(12).

E32 As full as an **Egg** is of meat

1689 Taylor *Poems* 58: As full of Sin I am, as Egg is of meate, **c1700** 422: They are as full as is an Egge of meate. **1785** Washington *Writings* 28.98: Your . . . friend is . . . as full of spirits as an egg shell is of meat. **1787** Smith *Diary* 2.215: And as full as an egg. *Oxford* 293; TW 117(3); Tilley K149. Cf. Whiting E50.

E33 As if one trod on **Eggs**

1764 Franklin *Papers* 11.435: You trip over these Matters, as if you trod upon Eggs. TW 118(11).

E34 As like as one **Egg** is to another

1805 Sewall *Parody* 9: As like each other . . . as one egg to another. Svartengren 330; Tilley E66; Whiting *NC* 403(2).

E35 As sure as **Eggs** and bacon

1796 Tyler *Verse* 48: Zounds, as sure as eggs and bacon. Cf. TW 118(5).

E36 An **Egg** today is better than a hen to-morrow

1734 Franklin *PR* 1.356: An Egg today is better than a Hen to-morrow. Barbour 57(1); *Oxford* 50; Tilley E70.

E37 Of no worth **Egg** or bird

1783 Williams *Penrose* 257: You never was of any worth, Egg or Bird. *Oxford* 318; Tilley E77.

E38 To look for **Eggs** in a mare's nest

1815 Humphreys *Yankey* 21: Next time, send me to look for eggs in a mare's nest. *Oxford* 512; TW 118(13).

E39 You can eat an **Egg** after anybody

1785 Hunter *Quebec* 27: I'll take care to have . . . spoons for my eggs, which you may eat after anybody. [Of dirty surroundings and food poisoning.] Cf. *Oxford* 17; Tilley A296.

E40 As dark as **Egypt**

1822 Royall *Letters* 240: There they lay . . . as dark as Egypt, **1826** *Sketches* 214. **1840** Paulding *Letters(II)* 280. Barbour 57-8; TW 119.

E41 To spoil the **Egyptians**

1832 Harriet Beecher [Stowe] in Beecher *Autobiography* 2.278: Father is . . . begging, borrowing, and spoiling the Egyptians. *Oxford* 767; Whiting E57.

E42 **Elbow-grease**

c1825 Tyler *Prose* 103: The scullion was . . . polishing with his elbow grease the shoes. *Oxford* 219; TW 119(1); Tilley E103.

E43 **Elbow-room**

1637 Morton *New English Canaan* 306: Land . . . which was so large it would suffice for Elbow roome for more then were in all the Land by 700000. **1647** Ward *Simple*

Cobler 3: To find elbow-roome for our pha-natick Doctrines and practises. **1654** Johnson *Wonder-Working* 132. **1666** Alsop *Maryland* 64. **1692** Bulkeley *Will* 195: We must, we will have elbow room, to act by Will and Doom. **1702** Mather *Magnalia* 2.324: So that they might have elbow-room enough in the world. **1728** Byrd *Dividing Line* 5, **1736** in *VHM* 36(1928) 354. **1739** Ames *Almanacs* 129: Give me the week for Elbow Room to guess in, **1761** 318. **1771** Jefferson *Papers* 1.63. **1775** Murray *Letters* 222: New York, where there will be more elbow Room. **1778** Case *Poems.* **1780** Witherspoon *Works* 4.392. **1788** Jefferson *Papers* 13.416: This last event has given him three quarters of the globe elbow-room. **1790** Hamilton *Papers* 6.545. **1817** Wirt *Letters* 2.33: A new place where they will have elbow room enough to play at large. **c1819** Beecher *Autobiography* 1.395: We have never had sufficient elbow-room in this holy state. **1824** Flint *Recollections* 35: He wanted elbow-room, did not wish to have a neighbour within three miles of him. **1844** Jackson *Correspondence* 6.339: You have sufficient energy to give yourself elbow room, 348. DA elbow 3; TW 119(2).

E44 To be at one's **Elbow** (s' end)
1734 Belcher *Papers* 2.458: They are at their wit's end (tho' the devil is alwayes at their elbows). **1782** Baldwin *Life and Letters* 79: What a happy Fellow you are, Beauty, Religion and children at your elbows end. NED Elbow 4a.

E45 To be out at **Elbows**
1789 Morris *Diary* 1.335: For both these Gentlemen are not a little out at Elbows. **1790** Maclay *Journal* 311: Every one out at elbows in his circumstances. **1791** Morris *Diary* 2.159. **1809** JRandolph in Kirkland *Letters* 2.122: I too am out at elbows, a little. **1854** Paulding *Letters(II)* 544: My memory is so much out at the elbows that I can hardly trust it with regard to remote facts relating to myself. *Oxford* 601; Tilley E102.

E46 To be up to one's **Elbows**
1787 GTurner in Webb *Correspondence* 3.78: I am . . . in Business up to the Elbows.

1788 RHaswell in *Columbia* 55: Captain Kendrick had been for several weeks up to his elbos in morter building a brick chimne. NED Elbow 4b.

E47 To lift one's **Elbow**
1818 Robertson *Letters* 57: He was in the habit of lifting his elbow. NED Suppl. Elbow 4g; Partridge 381.

E48 Out of one's **Element**
1798 Drinker *Journal* 331: He is like the rest of us, out of his element. *Oxford* 219; Tilley E107.

E49 The **Emperor** is king of kings, *etc.*
1647 Ward *Simple Cobler* 48: There is a quadrebulary saying, which passes current in the Westerne world, That the Emperour is King of Kings, the Spaniard King of Men, the French, King of Asses, the King of *England*, King of Devills . . . Then *Spaine* can make men, or the Emperour Kings. *Oxford* 219; Tilley E110.

E50 The **End** crowns all
1703 *Penn-Logan Correspondence* 1.252: The end has usually crowned all. **1778** Shaw *Journals* 50: So true is that hackneyed remark, *Finis coronat opus.* **1778** Smyth *Tour* 2.441: [Latin only]. **1787** *American Museum* 2.338: [Latin only]. **1794** Jay *Correspondence* 4.135: Whether *finis coronat opus* the president, senate, and public will decide. **1796** Cobbett *Porcupine* 3.243: [Latin only]. **c1800** Dennie *Lay Preacher* 120: [Latin only]. **1804** Asbury *Journal* 2.436: The *end* is all. **1813** *Beauties of Brother Bull-us* 93: [Latin only]. **1813** Wirt *Letters* 1.350: [Latin only]. **1840** Cooper *Letters* 4.88: [Latin only]. *Oxford* 220; Whiting E75.

E51 The **End** justifies the means (*varied*)
1657 Wigglesworth *Diary* 103: Now the end is better than the means. **1723** Symmes *Utile* 29: He that requires the End, requires the means. **1746** *Law Papers* 2.279: I look not so much at ye meanes so the good end may be obtain'd. **1780** *Lee Papers* 3.439: The famous Jesuitical Maxim that ends will justify [themselves]. **1782** Deane *Papers* 5.104: I

never was a disciple of those who assert that the end justifies the means. **1788** Adams *Diary* 445: Zealots . . . who . . . justify unworthy means by the sanctity of the end, **1805** *Writings* 3.110: The end too must go some way . . . to justify the means. **1805** Bentley *Diary* 3.191: The end sanctions the means. **1807** *Weekly* 1.266, 2.135: One of the fundamental principles of jacobinism. **1809** Asbury *Journal* 2.603: The end is to sanctify the means. **1811** Burroughs *Memoirs* 325: He ever appeared to think it laudable . . . to use the most nefarious means to obtain a favorite [end], if the means and ends were immediately connected. **1816** Fidfaddy *Adventures* 68. **1817** *Port Folio* 4NS 3.219-20: A false and pernicious maxim. **1831** WPope in Jackson *Correspondence* 4.297. *Oxford* 220; TW 120(1).

E52 The latter **End** of a feast, *etc.*

1686 Dunton *Letters* 243: And remembering the old Proverb, That the latter End of a Feast is better than the beginning of a Fray. *Oxford* 52: Tilley E114. Cf. Whiting C388.

E53 On the **End** of one's pen

1771 *Commerce of Rhode Island* 1.365: Bad Tidings still hangs on the end of my Penn.

E54 There is an **End** to all things (*varied*)

c1680 Radisson *Voyages* 129: But there is an end to all things. **1773** Habersham *Letters* 232: There is a period to everything. **1782** *Washington *Writings* 25.269. **1797** Drinker *Journal* 304: All things must have an end! **1819** Weems *Letters* 3.243: And all things & Ills will have an end. *Oxford* 231; TW 120(4); Whiting T87. See **E91**.

E55 To be at the **End** (length) of one's tether

1740 Stephens *Journal(I)* 1.544: But I must not run beyond the Length of my Tedder. **1755** *Johnson Papers* 2.261: I have exerted my self in every Shape to the utmost of my Tether. **1775** JWarren in *Adams-Warren Letters* 1.153: Our House are adjusting the ceremonies . . . and then will end our tether. **1776** Adams *D and A* 3.445: He has nearly reached the End of his tether. **1777** Heath *Memoirs* 144: He found that he had got to

the end of his tether of evasion. **1778** JPreble in Preble *Genealogical Sketch* 107. **1778** Smith *Memoirs(II)* 292: With Respect to this Province the Congress may perceive the End of their thread. **1780** Adams *Correspondence* 177. **1780** *New-York Gazette* in *Newspaper Extracts(II)* 5.107: Affairs here have got to the end of the rope. **1781** JWarren in Massachusetts Historical Society *Proceedings* (1932-36) 259: Rodney has gone the length of his tether. **1783** Williams *Penrose* 56. **1785** Adams *Works* 8.355. **1786** Smith *Diary* 2.103. **1787** Freneau *Poems* 2.354. **1787** Jefferson *Papers* 11.611: Mr. Grand is at the length of his tether in advancing [funds] for us. **1787** Pickering *Life* 2.278: Franklin has got to the end of his tether. **1787** Tyler *Contrast* 78. **1788** EHazard in *Belknap Papers* 2.37: The poor Anti-feds. seem to have got almost to "the length of their tether," as Governour Hutchinson said. **1816** Paulding *Letters(I)* 2.180: He got to the length of his tether. *Oxford* 221; TW 120(5), 368.

E56 To come out at the little **End** of the horn

1781 BFranklin in Adams *Works* 7.478: Thus I was drawn in at the broad end of the horn and must squeeze out at the narrow end as well as I can. **1787** *Massachusetts Centinel* in Buckingham *Specimens* 2.45: It is a good maxim which inculcates the practice of *"entering at the little end of the horn."* **1801** *Farmers' Museum* 46: And how the former all forlorn, Crept through the small end of the horn. **1801** Weems *Letters* 2.166. **1805** *Baltimore Evening Post* in Thornton *Glossary* 1.544. **1811** Weems *Gambling* 33. **1814** JBrace in Vanderpoel *More Chronicles* 104-5: I never can begin a round sentence but what I come out of the little end of the horn. **1817** *Massachusetts Spy* in Thornton *Glossary* 1.544. **1817** Weems *Letters* 3.196: 15 years ago this same Mr. Bertrand was as conceited a Virginia Fop as ever squeezed himself out at the little end of a horn. **1821** Doddridge *Dialogue* 48. **1847** Paulding *Letters(II)* 450: They had rather Scott should come out of the little end of the Horn than the Big one. Barbour 58(7); TW 120(8).

E57 To have the worst (better) **End** of the staff (*varied*)

1654 Johnson *Wonder-Working* 182: Mattachuset had the worst end of the staff. 1720 Carter *Letters* 44: It appears he hath much the better end of the staff. 1778 Paine *American Crisis* 1.150: They have taken every thing up at the wrong end. 1815 Waterhouse *Journal* 97: During all this time, we found we had got hold of the heaviest end of the timber. *Oxford* 221; TW 120(10); Whiting E89.

E58 To make both **Ends** meet

1756 JChivillette in McDowell *Documents* 2.180: If I can make both Ends meet. 1766 JParker in Franklin *Papers* 13.311: I hardly think Benny will make both Ends meet, 411, 1767 14.98, 296, 1768 15.214, 289, 1769 16.43. 1774 Seabury *Letters* 58: To enable him to make both ends of the year meet, as we say. 1776 Shaw *Journals* 11: Everything is extravagantly dear, so that a subaltern must live close to bring both ends of the month together. 1780 JA in *Adams FC* 3.276. 1780 *Beekman Papers* 3.1367. 1784 JThomas in *Moose Fort Journals* 257. 1787 Washington *Writings* 29.212: My estate for the last 11 years has not been able to make both ends meet. 1788 Jefferson *Papers* 13.202. 1789 AThomas in *Blount Papers* 1.515. 1790 Adams *New Letters* 43: We shall not make both ends meet, as they say. 1803 Wirt *Letters* 1.95: In Virginia, the most popular lawyer in the State merely makes the ends of the year meet. 1818 *Port Folio* 4NS 5.316. 1819 Faux *Memorable Days* 139. 1827 Paulding *Letters(II)* 89: If a man can . . . make both ends meet at the end of the year. *Oxford* 77; TW 121(12).

E59 To the **End** of the chapter

1720 Carter *Letters* 5: The tobacco you had sold of mine I was very well contented with and shall be glad to find you held out to the end of the chapter.

E60 An open **Enemy** (foe) is better than a treacherous friend (*varied*)

1740 Franklin *PR* 2.249: An open Foe may prove a curse; But a pretended friend is worse. 1775 EPhelps in *Connecticut Histori-*

cal Collections 175: One enemy in the city is worse than ten outside. 1776 NCooke in American Antiquarian Society *Proceedings* NS 36(1926) 303: An Enemy in our bosom has it in his power to do us more mischief than one without. 1777 *Trumbull Papers* 2.83: Internal enemies are always to be considered as the most dangerous, and to be watched with the greatest attention. 1778 Clay *Letters* 79: Internal Enemies are the worst. 1778 Galloway *Diary* 42: Private enemies worse than open ones. 1793 Jackson *Papers* 79: An internal enemy will be far worse than a foreign one. 1796 DHumphreys in *Barbary Wars* 1.136: Foe, under the mask of friendship. 1797 Paine *Correspondence* 2.1389: They had rather have . . . America for an open enemy than a treacherous friend. 1805 Eaton *Life* 310: I like an open enemy better than a treacherous friend. c1810 Randolph *Virginia* 195: A more dangerous, because a domestic enemy [slaves]. 1823 WBrady in Jackson *Correspondence* 3.210: A lukewarm supporter, will do more mischief than an open enemy, 1824 261: I love a candid, open enemy, but a hypocritical friend, who professing friendship acts the hidden enemy, I dispise. *Oxford* 50; Whiting E97, F365.

E61 There is no little **Enemy** (*varied*)

1733 Franklin *PR* 1.316: There is no little enemy, 1775 *Writings* 6.431: The Italian adage, that there is no *little enemy*. 1777 *Archibald Robertson . . . His Diaries*, ed. H. M. Lydenberg (New York, 1930) 121: It will serve as a lesson in future never to despise any Enemy two much. 1806 Plumer *Memorandum* 479: I answered an enemy dispised often proves dangerous. *Oxford* 221; Whiting E99.

E62 Your **Enemies** tell you your faults

1691 ?CMather *Bills of Credit* in *Colonial Currency* 1.195: Fas est et ab Hoste Doceri. 1740 Stephens *Journal(I)* 1.602: [Latin only]. 1756 Franklin *PR* 6.321: Love your Enemies, for they tell you your Faults. 1763 Gadsden *Writings* 59, 1765 67: [Latin only]. *New Jersey Gazette* in *Newspaper Extracts(II)* 1.525: this maxim [Latin only]. 1783 Van Schaack *Letters* 215: [Latin only]. **1797**

Gadsden *Writings* 267: [Latin only]. **1801** Ames *Letters* 294: [Latin only]. **1807** *Weekly* 2.257: A maxim which was not thought unworthy of the policy of the wisest nations of antiquity [Latin only]. Ovid *Metam.* iv.428; *Oxford* 222; Tilley E137.

E63 In plain **English** [The following is a selection from 75 occurrences of the phrase] **1634** EHowes in *Winthrop Papers(A)* 2.164: Give me leave in plaine English the second tyme this springe to present my vnfeigned respects to you in a few lynes. **1689** Randolph *Letters* 4.307: They are in plain English an hypocritall wicked & By-gothed poeple, **1700** 7.608: To write plaine English upon this Subject. **1702** Mather *Magnalia* 2.548: I did in plain English tell him the dishonesty of the matter. **1732** Belcher *Papers* 1.474: The plain English of this is that I will have the ore deliver'd me according to agreement. **1756** Laurens *Papers* 2.389: The plain English is they would be glad to have it in their power to buy or let it alone. **1772** *Bowdoin Papers* 1.298: But to speak plain English. **1775** *Deane Brothers Papers* 3: I am very scant in l'Argent or in plain English in Money. **1776** Curwen *Journal* 1.288: In plain english, my purse is nearly emptied. **1780** JSewall in Curwen *Journal and Letters* 265: No man there dares write upon political subjects in *plain English*. **1783** Hopkinson *Miscellaneous Essays* 1.222: This is certainly very plain English, and incapable, one would suppose, of misconstruction. **1788** *Politician* 10: I always curses and swears in plain English. **1795** Burr *Correspondence* 39: In plain English, I am sick. **1797** Beete *Man* 17: They can't understand plain English. **1809** Adams *Works* 9.621: In plain English, Great Britain is the first sinner. **1811** *Port Folio* 2NS 5.165: In as plain English, as smiles could speak, **1813** 3NS 2.495: Telling my story in *plain English* without . . . scraps of Latin or French. **1815** Humphreys *Yankey* 29: You don't understand plain English. **1822** Pintard *Letters* 2.130: Young ardent minds, who for the sheer fun of it are disposed, in plain English, to raise the Devil. NED English 4; Tilley E152; Whiting E103.

E64 **Englishmen** feel but cannot see **1735** Franklin *Papers* 2.14: For Englishmen feel but cannot see; as the Italian says of us, **1747** 3.188: It is said the wise Italians make this proverbial Remark on our Nation, viz. *The English FEEL but they do not SEE.*

E65 **Enough** is as good as a feast **a1656** Bradford *History* 1.303: When they had maize (that is, Indian corne) they thought it as good as a feast. **1770** Munford *Candidates* 41: Enough's as good as a feast. **1807** *Emerald* NS 1.88. *Oxford* 224; Whiting E115.

E66 More than **Enough** is a feast **1809** Irving *History* 1.176: According to the favourite Dutch maxim, that "more than enough constitutes a feast." Cf. *Oxford* 544; Tilley M1152.

E67 Better be **Envied** than pitied **1639** EWinslow in *Hutchinson Papers* 1.124: I have too often used a foolish proverb, I had rather be envyed than pittyed. *Oxford* 51; Whiting E133.

E68 **Equals** should choose equals **1821** Knight *Poems* 1.67: Equals should equals choose, non vain desire Of wealth, or lineage, quench love's holy fire. *Oxford* 516; Tilley E178; Whiting M175.

E69 As dark as **Erebus** **1796** JJackson in Milledge *Correspondence* 39: A heart as dark as Erebus. **1801** Paulding *Letters(II)* 11: And the night as dark as Erebus. NED Erebus; Svartengren 237. Cf. TW 121.

E70 As pure as **Ermine** **1822** Watterston *Winter* 56: If he be as pure as ermine, or as spotless as a vestal. Cf. Whiting E140.

E71 A sleeveless (fruitless) **Errand** **1674** FJWinthrop in *Winthrop Papers(B)* 4.277-8: Whether it may not be a litle kinde of reflection vpon me to appear with a sleeveless errand. **1709** *Penn-Logan Correspondence* 2.322: A sleeveless errand. **1739** Belcher *Papers* 2.248: He is going on a fruitless errand. **1762** Watts *Letter Book* 37:

[He] has been sent of a very sleeveless Errand, 1763 128. **1781** Hopkinson *Miscellaneous Essays* 2.163. **1790** Maclay *Journal* 186: [He] had some sleeveless things to say, 277. **1791** Morris *Diary* 2.329. **1816** *Port Folio* 4NS 1.287. **1821** Pintard *Letters* 2.52. **1832** JRandolph in Jackson *Correspondence* 4.419. *Oxford* 743; Tilley E180; Whiting S384.

E72   Many **Estates** are spent in the getting, *etc.*

1733 Franklin *PR* 1.315: Many estates are spent in the getting, Since women for tea forsook spinning and knitting, **1758** *WW* 345: as above *and* And Men for Punch forsook Hewing and Splitting. **1770** Ames *Almanacs* 412: Since women for tea forsook spinning and knitting and men for punch forsook hewing & splitting, many fair estates are spent in the getting. *Oxford* 509.

E73   As volatile as **Ether**

1818 Wirt *Letters* 2.75: She . . . is as volatile as ether.

E74   The **Ethiopian** cannot change his skin or the leopard his spots (*varied*)

1676 Williams *Writings* 5.425: The *Spots* of the *Leopard,* and the *Blackness* of the *Neger* comes not by Accident. **1706** *Penn-Logan Correspondence* 2.153: But can the leopard change his skin? **1716** Sewall *Diary* 3.93: Mr. Pemberton's Text, Can the Ethiopian —. **1720** *Letter* in *Colonial Currency* 2.234: We may not reasonably Expect the Ethiopian to change his skin, or voracious Tygers, to divest themselves of their savage Nature, and become mild and gentle. **1729** Ames *Almanacs* 60: The Blackmoor may as eas'ly change his Skin As Men forsake the ways they'r brought up in. **1743** Belcher *Papers* 2.448: Can the Ethiopian change his skin or the leopard his spots? **1750** *Massachusetts* in *Colonial Currency* 4.448: *Can the Ethiopian change his Skin?* **1769** Davis *Colonial Virginia Satirist* 64. **1782** JWarren in *Warren-Adams Letters* 2.183: But even Fortune cannot change the Spots of the Beast, or alter the Skin of the Ethiopian. **1797** PHall in Porter *Negro Writing* 71: A nation (that I have somewhere read of) called Ethiopeans,

that cannot change their skin. **1798** Adams *New Letters* 127: But the Ethiopen could not Change his Skin, and the spots of the Leopard have been constantly visible, tho sometimes shaded, 159: But the Ethiopean cannot Change his skin. **1809** JSidney in Porter *Negro Writing* 362: The Ethiopian cannot change his skin. **1814** Adams *Writings* 5.55. *Oxford* 456; Tilley E186, L206; Whiting E153.

E75   To wash an **Ethiopian** (*etc.*) white

1652 Williams *Writings* 5.58: *Time* hath and will discover that such a *Blackamore* cannot be washed in the *blood of Christ,* 7.173: The holy Spirit . . . washeth white some Blackamores, and changeth some *Leopards spotts.* **1694** *Connecticut Vindicated* 110: The New-labour-in vain; a washing a white man; as if he were a blackmore, to make him white, when as he never was otherwise. **1702** *Penn-Logan Correspondence* 1.103: It all looks like washing the blackamoor white. **1707** Mather *Letters* 75: The attempts of our councilors to blanch Ethiopians and blacken honest men. **c1720** Byrd *Another Secret Diary* 284: But to make them fair will be as hopeless an experiment as to wash the Negro white. **1749** Franklin *PR* 3.340: Who then would set the crooked Tree aright, As soon may wash the tawny Indian white. **1766** JParker in Franklin *Papers* 13.327: I find it all as Vain, as washing the Blackmoor white. **1767** *Johnson Papers* 5.719: Washing the Negro white, labour in vain. **1771** SHood in *Bowdoin Papers* 1.273: There is no washing the blackmoor white. **1776** Lee *Letters* 1.173: As well . . . might a person expect to wash an Ethiopian white, as to remove the taint of despotism from the British Court. **1798** *Washington *Writings* 36.474: You could as soon scrub a blackamore white, as to change the principles of a profest Democrat, 498: It is not easier to change the principles of the *leaders* of such measures, than it would be to wash a blackamoor white. **1813** GMorris in King *Life* 5.359: Your efforts to wash the Blackamoor white. **1830** Ames *Mariner's* 300: Trying to get discounts, compared to which washing a negro white is a hopeful and profitable piece of business. *Oxford* 868.

E76 As bare as **Eve's** backside
c1703 Byrd *Another Secret Diary* 202: I see her spreading out her arms with her elbows as bare as Eve's backside. Cf. Lean 2.805.

E77 Great **Events** are brought about by small beginnings (*varied*)
1773 Rush *Letters* 1.81: Great events have been brought about by small beginnings, **1812** 2.1137: "Great events from little causes" will be reversed, should he be chosen. TW 122(2). See **C99, 189.**

E78 **Everybody** is nobody
1796 Cobbett *Porcupine* 3.425: Constituents are every body, and *every body is nobody.* Lean 3.455. See **B377.**

E79 One cannot please **Everybody**
1742 *Georgia Records* 23.282: But . . . it is not posable to please all men kind. **1779** *Washington *Writings* 15.97: To please every body is impossible; were I to undertake it I should probably please no body. **1792** Asbury *Journal* 1.734: We cannot please everybody. *Oxford* 633; Whiting M124.

E80 What **Everybody** says must be true
c1825 Tyler *Prose* 98: I s'pose what every body says must be true. *Oxford* 841; Whiting M309. See **M82.**

E81 **Every man** for himself
1706 *Penn-Logan Correspondence* 2.129: Every man is for himself, and so in thy case thou wilt find it. **1755** JCargill in *Baxter Manuscripts* 24.37: So I told them to Shift Every man for himself so set out for home. **1773** *Johnson Papers* 8.874: Every bodys first principle is to take care of themselves. **1775** Morison *Journal* 30: Our . . . situation reduced us to the sad necessity for every man to shift for himself. **1795** DYancey in *VHM* 30(1922) 224: The old adage might well be applied in many cases. Every man for himself, etc. **1808** *Emerald* NS 1.482: Every one for himself. **1811** Burroughs *Memoirs* 145: Every man shift for himself. **1819** Waln *Hermit* 14: *Sauve qui peut* is the watch-word. **1820** *Fudge Family* 62: *Sauve qui peut.* **1822**

Watterston *Winter* 150: Every man is a Cæsar; and therefore every man is for himself. **1823** Jefferson *Writings* 15.437: The word among the herd of kings, was *"sauve qui peut."* Each shifted for himself, and left his brethren to squander and do the same as they could. **1832** Barney *Memoir* 25: *Sauve qui peut* was . . . the principle that governed every individual. *Oxford* 229; TW 234(14); Whiting M73. See **D130, N120.**

E82 **Every man** for himself, and God for us all
c1680 Radisson *Voyages* 133: Heere every one for himselfe & God for all, 194. **1697** Chalkley *God's Great Love* 338: It is a common Expression now a Days, *Every Man for himself, and God for us all.* **1776** Carter *Diary* 2.1027: God for us all, and every man for himself. **1778** JCantine in *Clinton Papers* 3.697. **1781** *New Jersey Gazette* in *Newspaper Extracts(II)* 5.237: It is a baneful and an accursed maxim. *Oxford* 229; TW 235(15); Whiting M73.

E83 **Every man** has a pope in his belly
1689 Bulkeley *People's Right* 79: We often say, that *every man has a pope in his belly,* **1692** *Will* 161: But men that carry both a king and a pope in their bellies find no such difficulty there. Tilley P479.

E84 **Every man** has his price
1769 Franklin *Papers* 16.21: "Every man has his price." **1777** AWhipple in *Correspondence of Esek Hopkins* (Rhode Island Historical Society, Providence, 1933) 81: You was char'g was [*for* with] Saying that there was no man but what could be bought. **1778** AA in *Adams FC* 3.48: It was a Saying of a very corrupt Statesman that every Man had his price, had Sir Robert *etc.* **1778** PPayson in Thornton *Pulpit* 338: Such maxims of policy as. a**1778** Jones *History* 2.11. **1791** NHazard in Hamilton *Papers* 9.535: Walpole said. **1794** Wansey *Journal* 169: I used to think Walpole's assertion, "That every man had his price," was too severe a satire on mankind. **1806** *Weekly* 1.90. **1807** Jefferson *Writings* 11.325: The prophet, who no doubt is a scoundrel, and only needs his price. **1857** WEdwards in *Ruffin Papers*

2.562: I am not yet willing to concur with Walpole that . . . *Oxford* 229; TW 235(16).

E85 **Every man** is nearest akin to himself
1804 *Port Folio* 4.213: In Latin it is a common proverb, *Egomet sum proximus mihi;* or, as we express it in English, "Every man is nearest a-kin to himself." Cf. Tilley S356.

E86 **Every man** knows his own business best
1847 Paulding *Letters(II)* 451: But it is my maxim that every man Knows his own business best. *Oxford* 230; Tilley M130.

E87 **Every man** to his trade (*varied*)
1723 Symmes *Utile* 46: Every Man to his Trade, wherein he's to be believed. **1804** Brackenridge *Modern* 357: Reversing the maxim, that every man is to be trusted in his own profession. *Oxford* 230; TW 235(19).

E88 **Every one** ought to mend one
1729 Franklin *Papers* 1.115: Every one ought to mend one. **1751** Sherman *Almanacs* 256: Let's every one mend our Ways, and we shall soon see better Days. *Oxford* 230; Whiting M113.

E89 **Every one** to his taste (*varied*)
1767 Ann Hulton, *Letters of a Loyalist Lady* (Cambridge, Mass., 1927) 7: But everyone to their taste. **1775** Schaw *Journal* 135: Every man to his mind, all's one to me. **1794** Drinker *Journal* 234: Different persons have different tastes. **1813** *Port Folio* 3NS 2.408: *Chacun a son goût.* **1835** Floy *Diary* 154: But every one to his notion. *Oxford* 230; TW 235(18). See **A18, D201.**

E90 **Every thing** has a beginning
1750 Sherman *Almanacs* 219: Every thing hath a beginning. **1774** Harrower *Journal* 56: You know every thing must have a beginning. **1791** Paine *Rights of Man* 1.285: Every thing must have had a beginning. *Oxford* 232; Whiting E164. See **M16.**

E91 **Every thing** has an end, except a pudding, which has two
1832 Ames *Nautical* 8: The lecture had finally an end like every thing else on earth except a pudding, which has two. *Oxford* 231; Tilley E121. See **E54.**

E92 **Every thing** has two handles
1810 Bentley *Diary* 3.550: But it was forgotten that every thing has two handles. *Oxford* 545; Tilley T193.

E93 **Every thing** is beautiful in its season
a1700 Hubbard *New England* 296: But every thing is beautiful in its season. **1788** *Politician* 12: Every thing is beautiful in its season, you know. *Oxford* 232; Tilley S190. Cf. Whiting T88, 116.

E94 **Every thing** is for the best
1758 Washington *Writings* 2.172: But everything, I hope, is ordered for the best. **1817** Royall *Letters* 95: All things happen for the best. Whiting *NC* 404(1).

E95 **Every thing** tells
1814 Wirt *Bachelor* 84: There is no bow, no smile, no familiar enquiry that is thrown away. According to the cant phrase, *every thing tells.*

E96 Not **Every thing** told one is true
1770 CCarroll in *MHM* 13(1918) 58: You must not take Everything to be true th[t] is told you. Cf. *Oxford* 43; Whiting B221.

E97 All **Evils** cure themselves
1790 Maclay *Journal* 216: All evils, it is said, cure themselves. **1794** Rush *Autobiography* 231: All evils cured by evil. Diseases cure each other. Cf. *Oxford* 464.

E98 Better prevent an **Evil** than attend it
1689 JNelson in *Baxter Manuscripts* 5.26: It is much better to prevent and meet an evil then to Attend or Waite it.

E99 Better suffer a great **Evil** than do a small one.
1767 Ames *Almanacs* 388: Better suffer a great evil than do a small one. *Oxford* 55; Tilley I23.

E100 **Evil** to him that evil thinks
1776 Malmedy in Lee *Papers* 2.353: *Honi soit qui mal y pense.* **1788** *Politician* 8: Evil to them that evil thinks. **1793** *Echo* 83: An old Proverb, "Evil to him that evil thinks." **1826** Audubon *1826 Journal* 106: [French only]. *Oxford* 397; Whiting S197.

E101 He that does **Evil** shuns the light (*varied*)

1702 Mather *Magnalia* 2.547: A fellow that had "shunn'd the light, because his deeds were evil." **1747** *Commerce of Rhode Island* 1.56: He hated the Light because his Deeds were Evil. **1807** Maxwell *Mysterious* 8.127-8: Just actions seldom shun the faithful light, And guilt seeks covert 'neath concealments shade. *Oxford* 194; Tilley I26; Whiting E184. See **W340**.

E102 Of two **Evils** choose the least

1714 PDudley in *Winthrop Papers(B)* 6.284: Of two evils choose the least. **1723** Mather *Letters* 362: Never till now was that rule contested, of two evils, choose the least. **1734** *New-York Weekly Journal* in *Newspaper Extracts(I)* 1.399: He followed . . . a known Proverb *of two Evils choose the least.* **1742** Johnson *Writings* 1.106. **1750** *Massachusetts* in *Colonial Currency* 4.452. **1755** *Johnson Papers* 1.646: We must . . . submit to one Inconveniency to avoid a greater. **1762** BPratt in *Colden Letters* 6.115: The last of these two Evils is the Greatest. **1771** HHusband in Boyd *Eighteenth Century Tracts* 357. **1773** Carroll *Correspondence* 1.351: Between two such evils what choice have we left? The choice of the least. **1774** Boucher *View* 344: I recommend it only as the least of two evils. **1774** Smith *Memoirs(I)* 176. **1776** Cresswell *Journal* 172: I am obliged to do the first as the lesser evil of the two. **1776** Lee *Papers* 2.38. **1776** Paine *Common Sense* 1.5. **1776** WWest in *Naval Documents* 3.955. **1778** Smith *Memoirs(II)* 407: To fly to N. England as the least of two Evils. **1778** Webb *Correspondence* 2.119. **1779** *New Jersey Gazette* in *Newspaper Extracts(II)* 3.286: The common saying. **1779** Van Schaack *Letters* 239: You have only a choice of evils. **1779** Washington *Writings* 17.98: That the common cause may not encounter the greater evil, while we attempt to avoid the lesser. **c1780** Bailey *Journal* 7. **1780** Baldwin *Life and Letters* 61: We chose the latter as being least of the evils. **1780** Jones *Letters* 43: Of the evils that present themselves we think we choose the least. **1780** PMazzei in Jefferson *Papers* 3.359. **1781**

EPendleton in Madison *Papers* 3.234: It is ever good policy when evils are inevitable to choose the lesser. **1781** Peters *Connecticut* 57: By way of preferring the lesser to the greater evil. **1784** Adams *Works* 8.183. **1784** Reed *Life* 2.413: And even good men were obliged to concur in it as the lesser evil. **1785** GAtkinson in *Moose Fort Journals* 261. **1785** Hunter *Quebec* 33-4. **1785** Jefferson *Papers* 9.35: The Loss of their Vessel and Cargo being the lesser Evil. **1785** Lee *Letters* 2.339. **1785** *Sans Souci* 14: Of two evils, plays must be considered the least. **1786** *Washington Writings* 28.370: I submit to this imposition as the lesser evil, 29.35: The lesser evil, where there is a choice of them, should yield to the greater. **1786** WWhiting in American Antiquarian Society *Proceedings* NS66 (1956) 152. **1788** JWarren in *Warren-Gerry Correspondence* 211: A choice only of the least evil. **1789** EGerry in *Warren-Gerry Correspondence* 215: I have selected a certain positive evil; whether it be the least of the two, I am yet to learn. **1790** TBland in Henry *Life* 3.418. **1792** Jefferson *Writings* 8.345: They naturally join those whom they think pursuing the lesser evil. **1793** Barlow *Works* 1.305: Perhaps a full treasury would be the greatest evil of the two. **1793** *Washington Writings* 33.45. **1794** Hamilton *Papers* 17.484. **1795** CGerrard in *Blount Papers* 2.555. **1797** Baily *Journal* 385. **1797** Callender *Annual Register 1796* 262. **1797** UTracy in Gibbs *Memoirs* 1.439. **1797** *Washington Writings* 35.357: As the lesser evil of the two. **1798** Asbury *Journal* 2.149. **1798** Cleveland *Letters* 37: Of the two evils I have made choice of the former as the smallest. **1799** DCobb in *Bingham's Maine* 2.993. **1799** Monroe *Writings* 3.159: I . . . may have avoided one evil by preferring a worse one. **1799** *Washington Writings* 37.329. **1800** Baldwin *Life and Letters* 425: Be of the opinion of Laribe, of two evils to take neither. **1800** Cobbett *Porcupine* 11.362: Says the proverb. **1800** Hamilton *Works* 10.401. **1800** RO'Brien in *Barbary Wars* 1.380. **1800** SSewall in Otis *Letters* 1.212. **1800** UTracy in McHenry *Letters* 484. **1801** Bayard *Papers* 130: [It] was acquiesced in as the least of evils to which we were exposed,

131: On the principle of chusing the least of evils. **1801** Nichols *Jefferson* 8: We chuse the smaller evil. **1801** RPeters in King *Life* 3.371: *Why,* I cannot tell unless it be on the principle of the man who had to choose a wife, either one or the other, of a tall or short woman; and he took the short one on the old adage, *of two evils choose the least.* **1808** Cleveland *Letters* 127. **1808** Jefferson *Writings* 12.151: Withdrawing from the greater evil, a lesser one has been necessarily encountered. **1809** Claiborne *Letter Books* 4.287: The latter it seems is thought by Congress the least evil. **1809** Jefferson *Writings* 16.357: A choice between two evils. **1810** Adams *Lectures* 1.269. **1810** JPearson in *Steele Papers* 2.621: I . . . think I shall adopt the measure — as a choice of evils. **1811** Adams *Writings* 4.265: Those were the greatest of two evils. **1811** Morris *Diary and Letters* 2.529. **1812** SDexter in Otis *Letters* 1.319: Only a choice of evils. **1812** Stoddard *Sketches* 57. **1815** Andrews *Prisoners' Memoirs* 141. **1816** Adams *Writings* 6.89: One yields compliance as the least of two evils. **1817** Barker *How to Try a Lover* 9: Wouldnt it be a lesser evil? **1817** Jefferson *Writings* 18.298: On the axiom that a less degree of evil is preferable to a greater. **1819** Faux *Memorable Days* 1.275: And sanctioned their marriage as the least of two unavoidable evils. **1819** Noah *Travels* 8: Of the evils . . . it most fortunately happened that I experienced the least of the two. **1820** *Austin Papers* 1.352: I consented to accept of the lesser evil to avoid the greater. a**1820** Biddle *Autobiography* 289. **1820** Wright *Views* 180: One of two evils. a**1824** Marshall *Kentucky* 1.249: The least of probable evils, 2.339: It was but a choice of evils — they considered Burr as president, the least of the two. **1825** Jefferson *Writings* 16.148: A temporary yielding to the lesser evil. **1840** Cooper *Letters* 4.98: Bad is the best, but there is a choice between evils. Barbour 59(7); *Oxford* 233; Whiting E193.

E103 We must not do **Evil** that good may come of it

1689 Bulkeley *People's Right* 59: We must not do evil that good may come of it. *Oxford* 562; Tilley E203.

E104 **Example** is above precept

1702 Taylor *Christographia* 244.20: *Exempla docent.* **1709** Chalkley *Loving Invitation* 369: *Example,* which, as the Proverb says, is above Precept. **1725** JMinot in *Baxter Manuscripts* 10.346: Example is before precept wth them. **1765** Watts *Letter Book* 373: As Example goes far beyond Precept all the World over. **1802** Dow *Journal* 130: [A] contribution . . . which I refused, knowing that example goes before precept. *Oxford* 233-4; TW 122. See **D208.**

E105 **Exceptions** prove the rule

1802 Ames *Letters* 1.306: Admitting these exceptions to exist, which prove the rule, not detract from it. **1803** UTracy in McHenry *Letters* 522: The few exceptions seem only to confirm the general rule. **1807** *Monthly Anthology* 4.275: If M'Fingal is an exception, that exception only proves the rule. **1808** Grant *Memoirs* 2.213: An exception that only confirms the rule. **1857** WEdwards in *Ruffin Papers* 2.562: Do the exceptions prove the rule? *Oxford* 234; TW 122(1).

E106 There are **Exceptions** to every general rule (*varied*)

1691 Fitzhugh *Letters* 262: Yet I am of opinion this case of your's is an Exception from the said generall Rule. **1702** Mather *Magnalia* 2.260: He was a notable exception to the general rule, 465. **1713** Wise *Churches* 132: There is no General Rule, but has its Exception. **1728** Byrd *Dividing Line* 70: And were there any exceptions to this Rule. **1745** Johnson *Writings* 3.471: We commonly say there is no general rule without some exception. **1764** *Paxton Papers* 181: We have learn'd many (when at School) Exceptions to a special Rule. **1769** Brooke *Emily* 239. **1770** Adams *Legal Papers* 3.234: This is plainly . . . a general rule, which, like all others of the kind must have its exceptions. **1775** Carter *Diary* 2.926: For General Principles are like General rules, subject to multitudes of Exceptions. **1776** Deane *Papers* 1.224. **1777** Shaw *Journals* 30: I mention this as an instance that there are some exceptions to that almost general rule, that Churchmen are Tories. **1780** D'Amours in Jefferson *Papers* 4.67. **1784** Shaw *Journals* 183. **1788** Coke *Journals* 85: Some exceptions are . . . to be made to this general rule. **1788** Ledyard *Russian Journey* 214: There are few exceptions to this general Rule. **1791** *Universal Asylum* 6.152. **1792** Bentley *Diary* 1.388: This evening as an exception to a general rule I attended the evening Lecture. **1797** Cleveland *Letters* 22. **1797** Hamilton *Papers* 20.522: I think it pedantry to admit no exceptions to any general rule. **1798** King *Life* 2.471: It will be an exception to a good Rule. **1799** Adams(TB) *Letters* 97: I ask pardon of those who may be exceptions to the general rule. **1799** Carey *Plumb* 16: A sort of lusus naturæ, a sui generis hurled into existence to belie all general rules. **1800** Dow *Journal* 90. **1804** Plumer *Memorandum* 213: He is a very extraordinary man & is an exception to all rules. **1805** Paine *Another Callender* 2.987: With as few exceptions as any general rule will admit of. **1806** Dow *Journal* 274. **1806** Fessenden *Modern Philosopher* 105: But this is only one exception to a general rule. **1808** Hitchcock *Poetical Dictionary* 87: There must, however, be exceptions in this as most other cases. **1810** Adams *Lectures* 2.97, 158: But the exceptions . . . are so numerous that they outnumber the rule. **a1811** Henry *Account* 52. **1812** Adams *Writings* 4.424. **1812** Lee *Memoirs* 2.37. **1814** Adams *Memoirs* 3.96: However general a rule that might be, an exception might be considered proper. **1814** Jefferson *Writings* 14.142: There is no rule without exceptions; but it is false reasoning which converts exceptions into the general rule. **1815** *Kennon Letters* 38.159. **1817** Weems *Franklin* 106: Franklin appears to have been a favoured exception from this general rule. **1818** Adams *Writings* 6.413: To this rule, as to all others, there are exceptions. **1819** Waln *Hermit* 36. **1820** Bernard *Retrospections* 74: Fennell was an exception to this rule. **1833** Jackson *Correspondence* 5.145: I hope this may be an exception from the general rule. *Oxford* 687-8; TW 122-3(2), 313(2).

E107 **Exchange** is no robbery

1737 *Georgia Records* 22^1.53: Such an Exchange is no Robbery. **1813** Fletcher *Narrative* 16: [He] said *exchange was no robbery*. *Oxford* 234; TW 123.

E108 A bad **Excuse** is better than none (*varied*)

1686 Dunton *Letters* 30: A bad Excuse, you know, Brother, is better than none. **1786** *Belknap Papers* 1.443: A poor one [government] is better than none at all. **1807** *Emerald* 2.229: A bad excuse . . . according to the proverb is worse than none. **1821** Wirt *Letters* 2.132: Yet the old fellow's look had a glimpse of passing cunning as much as to say, "A bad excuse is better than none." *Oxford* 26; Tilley E214.

E109 **Experience** is dear bought (*varied*)

1639 *Winthrop Papers(A)* 4.99-100: When experience (which usually costs deare) teach you to improve it in the right kinde. **1654** Johnson *Wonder-Working* 207: [They] have been forced to pay pretty roundly to Lady Experience for filling their heads with a little of her active after-wit. **1732** Byrd *Progress* 324: I was very sorry he had bought that experience so dear. **1741** *Georgia Records* 23.17: As by dear bought experience 'tis found to be here. **1776** Curwen *Journal* 1.284: Sharp's the word, and I am trained in the school of experience. **1777** HKnox in American Antiquarian Society, *Proceedings* NS 56(1946) 219: Experience is a good master and I hope we have not purchas'd it at too dear a rate. **1778** *Clinton Papers* 2.851: Experience is better, if not too dear bought. **1779** *New Jersey Journal* in *Newspaper Extracts(II)* 3.632: The dear bought experience we have had. **1783** Deane *Papers* 5.151: And [I] shall in my future course, being taught by dear bought experience, avoid politics with as much care as the seamen of old did Scylla and Charybdis. **1797** JJay in King *Life* 2.182: It seems Experience must generally be purchased, and sometimes at a high price. **1815** Palmer *Diary* 149: Experience is a good Schoolmaster—if we pay not too Dear for being taught. I have heard of one A. Palmer jun^r's haveing been on a Cheese Voyage—to Philadelphia where Dear bought Experience was taught him to perfection. Cf. *Oxford* 234, 235. See **W346.**

E110 Experience is the best rule to walk by
1779 *Washington *Writings* 16.167: Experience . . . is the best rule to walk by.

E111 Experience is the mother of wisdom
1788 *American Museum* 3.183: If it is true, that experience is the mother of wisdom, history must be an improving teacher. Barbour 69(4); *Oxford* 235; Tilley E221.

E112 Experience keeps a dear school, *etc.*
1743 Franklin *PR* 2.373: Experience keeps a dear school, yet Fools will learn in no other, **1758** *WW* 349: and scarce in that. **1770** Ames *Almanacs* 413: Experience keep a dear school but fools will learn in no other, and scarce in that. **1797** Foster *Coquette* 161: I have heard it remarked, that experience is the preceptor of fools. **1809** Weems *Marion* 177: "Experience," says Dr. Franklin, "*is a dear school; but fools will learn in no other,* and hardly in that." Barbour 59(2); *Oxford* 234-5. Cf. Tilley E220.

E113 Experience makes men wise
1774 Andrews *Letters* 356: As experience makes men wise. **1785** PWright in Jefferson *Papers* 9.101. **1801** *Port Folio* 1.256: Experience . . . makes folks wise.

E114 Experience teaches
a1656 Bradford *History* 1.52: Experience haveing taught them many things. **1666** Alsop *Maryland* 19: *Experientia docet.* **1719** *Addition* in *Colonial Currency* 1.371: Common sayings declare, that . . . *Experience is the best School-master.* **1751** *Appendix* in *Colonial Currency* 4.468: Experience teacheth irresistably, 479: But nothing teacheth like *Experience.* **1766** Adams *D and A* 1.300: *Experientia docet.* **1771** Habersham *Letters* 133: [Latin only]. **1779** Shaw *Journals* 55, 61: [Latin only]. **1782** Trumbull *Satiric Poems* 208: Alas, great Malcolm cried, experience Might teach you not to trust appearance. **1783** Baldwin *Life and Letters* 165: [Latin only]. **1803** Weems *Letters* 2.278: Experience, the best of teachers.

1811 Graydon *Memoirs* 347: Experience is the best of schools. **1818** *Adams-Waterhouse* 142: [Latin only]. **1818** Hall *Travels* 251: Experience begins to teach. **1818** Watterston *Letters* 7: Experience, it is said, is the best school of wisdom. **c1820** Bernard *Retrospections* 297: The old saying that "experience teaches." **1833** Dunlap *Diary* 3.751: Experience will never teach. **1833** Wirt *Letters* 2.412: It is this that makes that large experience which is the great school of wisdom. Barbour 60; *Oxford* 234-5; TW 123(1). See **O40.**

E115 Avoid Extremes
a1700 Hubbard *New England* 185: Extremes are to be avoided. **1750** JMayhew *Discourse* in Bailyn *Pamphlets* 1.247: Extremes are dangerous. **1770** Paterson *Glimpses* 78: Extremes should be avoided. Cf. *Oxford* 235; TW 123(2); Tilley E224; Whiting E203.

E116 Extremes meet (*varied*)
1762 Watts *Letter Book* 48: But as extremes meet we may possibly the sooner have a peace for it. **1797** Foster *Coquette* 181: One extreme commonly succeeds another. **c1800** Rush *Autobiography* 71: As extremes meet in a point. **1810** Bentley *Diary* 3.498: Six children of these enthusiasts were apprehended for stealing in the time of service last Sunday. The extremes meet. *Oxford* 235; TW 123(1).

E117 No Extremes last long
1634 Wood *New-England* 4: It is an Axiome in Nature, Nullum violentum est perpetuum. No extreames last long. *Oxford* 235; Tilley E222. See **M265, N112.**

E118 An Eye for an eye, *etc.*
1814 Jackson *Correspondence* 2.29: An Eye for an Eye, Toothe for Toothe and Scalp for Scalp, 45. Whiting E208.

E119 The Eye is index to the mind
1781 AA in *Adams FC* 4.215: I did not study the Eye that best Index to the mind. Barbour 60(10); Lean 4.119; *Oxford* 237: Face; Tilley Fl. See **F2.**

E120 The **Eye** of the master will do more work than his hands

1744 Franklin *PR* 2.399: The Eye of a Master, will do more Work than his Hand, **1755** 5.474: The Master's Eye will do more Work than both his Hands, **1758** *WW* 344 [as **1755**]. **1770** Ames *Almanacs* 412: The diligent eye of the master will do more work than both his hands. Barbour 60(9); *Oxford* 236; TW 124(6).

E121 An **Eye** to the main chance (*varied*)

1716 Johnston *Papers* 155: They should be forced away, and oblidgd to live Elsewhere upon the mainchance. **1768** *New York Journal* in *Newspaper Extracts*(I) 7.114: It will tend to take off the public Attention from the Main Chance. **1787** Tyler *Contrast* 35: Keep your eye upon the main chance, 37: Be a good girl, and mind the main chance, 38, 96: I did not care what his principles or his actions were, so long as he minded the main chance, 97: Women understand the main chance, 113: Be a man of punctuality and mind the main chance. **1788** *Politician* 24: I must mind the main chance. **1797** Beete *Man* 24-5: Old Screwpenny shall be notorious for only minding the main chance. **1810** Cary *Letters* 180: I am getting on, not losing sight of the "main chance" all the way. **1850** Cooper *Letters* 6.220: My business . . . being to look after the main chance. *Oxford* 500; TW 124(13); Tilley E235. See **R51.**

E122 **Eyes** and priests bear no jests

1735 Franklin *PR* 2.6: Eyes and Priests Bear no Jests, **1739** 221. *Oxford* 411; Tilley E242.

E123 He who buys needs a hundred **Eyes,** *etc.*

1745 Franklin *PR* 3.7: He who buys had need have 100 Eyes, But one's enough for him that sells the Stuff. *Oxford* 96; Tilley N85.

E124 Keep your **Eyes** wide open before marriage, *etc.*

1738 Franklin *PR* 2.194: Keep your eyes wide open before marriage, half shut afterwards. *Oxford* 419.

E125 Many **Eyes** see more than one

1698 Bulkeley *People's Right* 59: *Plus vident*

oculi quam oculus. Many eyes see more than one: and a weak eye may chance to see that which a better over-looks. Barbour 60(5); *Oxford* 850; Tilley E268.

E126 One **Eye** of the master, *etc.*

1809 *Port Folio* 2NS 2.548: One eye of the master sees more than four eyes of his servant. *Oxford* 236; Tilley E243.

E127 To be all one's **Eye**

1778 Moore *Diary* 2.92: And take him pris'-ner in a week, But that was all my eye, sir. *Oxford* 10; TW 124(3).

E128 To be cheated out of my **Eyes**

1810 Dwight *Journey* 52: Mr W—— is so much afraid of making trouble that he will . . . let them cheat him out of his eyes, & say nothing. Cf. TW 125: Eye-teeth (2).

E129 To cost (sell) one's **Eyes**

1634 AWhite in Clayton C. Hall, ed. *Narratives of Early Maryland* (New York, 1910) 34: Every thing bore so high price, that nothing could be had but it Cost us our eies. **1634** Wood *New-England* 67: The *French,* (who will sell his eyes, as they say, for beaver).

E130 To have a brass **Eye**

1737 Franklin *Drinkers* 2.175: He's Got a brass Eye.

E131 To have **Eyes** bigger than bellies

c1680 Radisson *Voyages* 128: They eate as many wolves, having eyes bigger then bellies. Barbour 60(6); *Oxford* 235; Tilley E261; Whiting E212.

E132 To keep an **Eye** to windward

1804 HCampbell in *Barbary Wars* 5.96: At the same time Keep an Iye to windward. Colcord 209.

E133 To keep one's **Eyes** open

1821 MStokes in Murphey *Papers* 1.185: They acted as the common saying is "with their eyes open." TW 124(14).

E134 To keep one's **Eyes** open wider than one's mouth

1721 Wise *Word* 170: I hope our Eyes will be opened wider than our Mouths. *Oxford* 419.

E135 To look (see) with a jaundiced **Eye**

1777 Carter *Diary* 2.1125: I was going to return that all things look Yellow to the jaundiced eye. **1781** JWadsworth in Deane *Papers* 4.527: Caused you to see every thing with a jaundiced eye. *Oxford* 410; Tilley A160.

E136 To love as one's **Eyes**

1812 Maxwell *Poems* 26: Her husband lov'd her as his eyes. Whiting E221. See **A105.**

E137 To put in one's **Eye** and still see

1692 Bulkeley *Will* 129: But what any man gets for restitution by these laws, he may put in his eye and not see the worse. **1783** Williams *Penrose* 193: All de Monix [moneys] is dare I vil put in mine eye, and dan Ick sal see, too! *Oxford* 11; TW 124(19); Tilley W503.

E138 To say black is his **Eye**

1637 Morton *New English Canaan* 299: There is not one has more cause to complaine, or can say black's his eie. **1733** Franklin *Papers* 1.325: No Man can say, *Black is* (the white of) *their Eye.* *Oxford* 64; Tilley 252; Whiting E223.

E139 To wet one's **Eye**

1733 Byrd *Journey* 270: Here our thirsty companions raised their drooping spirits with a cheerful dram, and having wet both eyes, we rode on. Cf. Partridge 261, 946. See **C192, W134.**

E140 What the **Eye** does not see, the heart does not rue

1692 Bulkeley *Will* 132: That which the eye sees not, the heart rues not. **1821** Pintard *Letters* 2.31: What the eye does not see the heart does not covet. *Oxford* 236; Whiting E216.

E141 To hang by the **Eyelids**

1780 PSchuyler in *Clinton Papers* 5.644: So that the Vermont business still hangs by the Eye lids. **1792** Morris *Diary* 2.366: Being in the whole eighteen Days that it had hung by the Eyelids. TW 125.

E142 To be an **Eyesore**

1762 Watts *Letter Book* 331: The Vessel . . . became an Eye Sore to me by her long delay. **1781** Oliver *Origin* 88: They were, what is vulgarly called an Eye Sore to the Inhabitants of Boston. Whiting E227.

E143 To have (cut) one's **Eye-teeth**

1770 *Johnson Papers* 7.670: His Lordship . . . must have his Eye Teeth & be a good State pilot in the Bargain. **1782** Lee *Papers* 4.25: He seems a sensible young man, and upon my word (according to the vulgar saying) he seems to have all his eye teeth about him. **1816** Paulding *Letters(I)* 1.79: The folks were just cutting their eye-teeth. TW 125(1).

F

F1 **Face** and heart do not correspond

1759 Adams *D and A* 1.68: Her face and Hart have no Correspondence. Barbour 60(1); Whiting C173, F2.

F2 The **Face** is the index of the mind *(varied)*

1702 Taylor *Christographia* 180.33: The old maxim *Vultus est index animi.* **1752** *Johnson Papers* 9.87: Villain is wrote in his Face. **1772** Habersham *Letters* 163: Mine [portrait] has certainly a very gruff and surly Appearance, especially about the Mouth, which my Friends say is not like me, and I should be very sorry, that it was an Indication of my Heart. *Oxford* 237; Tilley Fl. Cf. Whiting W265. See E119.

F3 A fair **Face** but a foul bargain

1730 Ames *Almanacs* 67: A Fair Face but a foul Bargain. Tilley F2.

F4 A good **Face** needs no Band, *etc.*

1666 Alsop *Maryland* 23: For in our vulgar Resolves 'tis said, *A good face needs no Band, and an ill one deserves none. Oxford* 319; Tilley F6.

F5 To fly in the **Face** of (something)

1734 *New-York Weekly Journal* in *Newspaper Extracts(I)* 1.399: *He flys in the face of his Superiours.* **1781** DMorgan in Jefferson *Papers* 5.219: Threatened them should they attempt to fly in the face of the Law. *Oxford* 270; TW 126(5).

F6 To have a **Face** of brass

1653 ASadleir in Williams *Writings* 6.249: It seems you have a face of brass, so that you cannot blush. **1788** *American Museum* 4.394: A young fellow is taught, that, to qualify himself for the company of the fair sex, he should rub a little brass on his face, as the expression is, lest he should be laughed at as too modest. Tilley F8.

F7 To make (wear) a long **Face**

1775 AMcDougall in *Naval Documents* 2.645: The Whigs make long Faces, **1776** HParker 3.617: Long Faces in the Congress because they are Almost out of hopes of taking [Quebec]. **1777** EDyer in Sullivan *Letters* 1.540: They now ware long faces, they hang their heads, they are mute, **1778** 2.49: The number of D—m——d Long Faces they are oblidged to wear in Parliament. **1780** *New Jersey Gazette* in *Newspaper Extracts (II)* 4.314: Something is the matter, which causes long faces. **1796** ANeale in *Blount Papers* 3.90: The Inhabitants of this place wear very long faces. NED Face 6b.

F8 To put a bold **Face** on a bad cause *(varied)*

1662 in *American Historical Record* 1(1872) 7: Then he standing up set a bold face on a bad cause. **c1680** Radisson *Voyages* 84: I had no desire to doe anything . . . but must shew a better countenance to a worse game. **1691** *Wyllys Papers* 325: A good face is set upon it. **1748** Franklin *PR* 3.255: To Friend, Lawyer, Doctor, tell plain your whole Case; Nor think on bad Matters to put a good Face: How can they advise, if they see but a Part. **1781** *New Jersey Gazette* in *Newspaper*

Extracts(II) 5.245: To put a good face upon a bad bargain. *Oxford* 319; Whiting F10.

F9   To smile in one's **Face** and plunge a dagger in his heart

?1807 Jackson *Correspondence* 1.175: But not in the yankee stile of base duplicity, by smiling in the face of an enemy and plunging a dagger in his [heart]. *Oxford* 444-5; Tilley F16.

F10   Two **Faces** in one hood (*varied*)

1669 Morton *New-Englands Memoriall* 84: As that divers faces were not carried under a hood. **1676** Williams *Writings* 5.417: *Fox* herein carries two faces under one hood. **1744** *Georgia Records* 24.262: Just & honest & Not Carrying two faces instead of one. **1783** Freneau *Poems* 2.220: Thrice happy thou, who wore a double face. **1814** Kerr *Barclay* 75: You are a damn'd Judas, a turn coat, and a two-faced man. *Oxford* 850; Whiting F13.

F11   **Facts** are facts

1760 Montresor *Journals* 236: But facts are facts.

F12   **Facts** are stubborn things

1748 Eliot *Essays* 41: Facts are stubborn Things, which will not bow nor break. **1770** Adams *Legal Papers* 3.269: Facts are stubborn things, **1777** *Works* 9.470. **1778** Curwen *Journal and Letters* 174: Facts are of a stubborn nature, and bend not to our wishes. **1786** [BAustin] *Observations on the Pernicious Practice of the Law* (Boston, 1819) 32: Facts are Stubborn Things. *Oxford* 238.

F13   **Facts** speak for themselves

1780 *Washington *Writings* 17.423: [Appears. and] facts must speak for themselves. **a1788** Jones *History* 1.153: Facts speak for themselves, 2.254. **1792** Belknap *Foresters* 121: Facts will speak for themselves.

F14   **Facts** speak louder than words

a1788 Jones *History* 2.212: Facts speak louder than words. **1792** Hamilton *Papers* 12.188: Facts . . . speak louder than words, and, under certain circumstances, louder even than oaths. TW 126(1).

F15   The **Fag-end**

1702 Mather *Magnalia* 2.504: In that "fag-end of the world." [Apparently Providence, R.I.]. **1806** *Weekly* 1.26: The fag end of the gang. **1818** Drake *Works* 252: You're at the fag-end of the feast. NED Fag-end.

F16   **Fair** and softly

1750 JAyscough in *Colden Letters* 4.223: That he may be prepared to meet the Assembly, which he proposes to do fair and softly. **1776** JA in *Adams FC* 1.382: We are obliged to go fair, and softly. **1793** Brackenridge *Modern* 236: Fair and softly, said the Captain. **1796** Cobbett *Porcupine* 2.442: Fair and softly, good master, *Surgo ut Prosim.* **1804** Brackenridge *Modern* 375: Soft and fairly, said the peace officers. **1817** Royall *Letters* 100. *Oxford* 238; Whiting F17.

F17   Long **Fair,** long foul

1812 Melish *Travels* 184: The elements indicated a change of weather, and recollecting the highlandman's prognostication, "long fair, long foul," I felt by anticipation a dreary tail to my journey.

F18   **Fair-weather** birds, *etc.*

1773 *New-York Gazette* in *Newspaper Extracts(I)* 9.476: *Fair-weather Birds.* **1782** JWereat in Jackson *Papers* 5: We shall find many fair-weather friends. **1794** GChristie in Callender *Political Register* 1.101: Not the fair-weather patriots of the present day, but the patriots of *seventy-five.* **1809** Weems *Letters* 2.426: If we are to laugh & be gay only when our plans succeed and money is pouring in upon us in torrents, what poor imbecile fair weather birds we must be! **1811** TBurr in Burr *Correspondence* 221: He is a fair-weather friend, in truth. **1830** Pintard *Letters* 3.152: I am no fair weather Christian. TW 127.

F19   To pin one's **Faith** on another's sleeve

1732 *South Carolina Gazette* 183: [I'm] No profligate Sinner, nor pragmatical Saint, I'm not vain of my Judgment, nor pinn'd on a Sleeve. **1734** Johnson *Writings* 3.39: Not to pin their faith upon any man's sleeve. **1776** HLaurens in Lee *Papers* 2.227: Pin not your faith upon my sleeve, but act the part which an Honest Heart . . . shall dictate. **1783** BHarrison in Madison *Papers* 4.11: They . . . therefore pin their faith on other mens sleeves, many of whom . . . lead them to wrong measures. **1784** Van Schaack *Letters* 294: We call this, "pinning our faith upon another's sleeve." **1789** Ames *Letters* 1.47: I was cautioned against pinning my faith on any man's sleeve. **1789** Monroe *Writings* 1.352: "Not to pin my faith upon the sleeve of any man," was one of my earliest lessons. **1792** EHazard in *Belknap Papers* 2.296: It must be a pleasing circumstance, especially when it is considered that, as many people pin their faith upon the reviewer's sleeves, it may increase the sales. **1819** Adams *Memoirs* 4.207: We should not have the appearance of pinning ourselves too closely upon her [England's] sleeve. *Oxford* 626; Tilley F32.

F20 The **Falling out** of lovers is the renewal of love

1701 Sewall *Letter-Book* 1.263: And bring with you one or two Christian friends . . . that so we may try to give an instance of the Truth of that old Proverb, *Amantium Irae Amoris Redintegratio est.* **1780** AA in *Adams FC* 4.13: As the poet says, "The falling out of Lovers is the renewal of Love." **1797** Cary *Letters* 120: "The falling out of lovers," etc. You may remember the old adage. **1808** *Emerald* NS 1.174: The old adage—The falling out of faithful friends renewing is of love. **1820** Jefferson *Writings* 15.283: Two or three years' trial will bring them back, like quarrelling lovers to renewed embraces, and increased affections. *Oxford* 242; Whiting V9.

F21 Common **Fame** is a liar

1779 Webb *Correspondence* 2.178: Common fame in General is, you know, a dam'd lyar. **1795** Freneau *Prose* 348: *Fame*, we all know, is often a liar. *Oxford* 137; Tilley F44.

F22 **Familiarity** breeds contempt

1680 Radisson *Voyages* 104: The long familiarity we had wth one another breeded contempt. **1734** Plumstead 258: For the common people . . . would be very apt to grow too familiar and despise the men whom

they find upon a level with themselves. **1787** Adams *Works* 5.289: How is it possible that a man should not acquire a contempt for death, from his familiarity with it? **1789** *Columbian Magazine* 3.254: Too much familiarity breeds contempt. **1813** Cutler *Life* 2.127. **1803** Morris *Diary and Letters* 2.442: The truth of the old adage. **1805** Silliman *Travels* 2.53-4: Familiarity with danger appears almost always to produce negligence and indifference to those who are exposed to it. **1809** *Port Folio* 2NS 1.233: That "too much familiarity begets contempt," has long been recognized as a sound maxim. Barbour 61; *Oxford* 243; Whiting H426.

F23 A great **Famine** when wolves eat wolves

1733 Franklin *PR* 1.315: Great famine when wolves eat wolves. *Oxford* 353: Winter; Tilley W509. See **D235, W230.**

F24 So **Far,** so good

1769 JParker in Franklin *Papers* 16.78: So far, so good. **1776** Margaret Morris, *Her Journal,* ed. John W. Jackson (Philadelphia, 1949) 51. ?**1796** Weems *Letters* 2.13. **1797** Beete *Man* 7. **1799** Carey *Porcupiniad* 2.20. **1827** *Austin Papers* 2.708. **1832** Pintard *Letters* 4.40. **1839** Paulding *Letters(II)* 266. *Oxford* 749; TW 127(1).

F25 **Far-fetched** and dear bought (is good for ladies)

1720 EWigglesworth *Letter* in *Colonial Currency* 1.421: We simple Country People being mightily pleas'd with fine things far fetcht and dear bought. **1721** ?TPaine *Discourse* in *Colonial Currency* 2.285: *But far fetch'd and dear must be the articles of our Adorning.* **1793** Brackenridge *Modern* 229: Hence the proverb, "far-fetched, and dear bought, is good for ladies." **1798** Latrobe *Journal* 83: *"Far fetched and dear bought,"* as the proverb says, are epithets that human pride has made almost synonomous with *excellent, valuable,* and *useful. Oxford* 173; Whiting F58.

F26 Who wouldn't sell a (**Farm**) and go to sea?

1826 Audubon *1826 Journal* 25: When

drenched to the skin, he [the captain] laughs and says, "Who wouldn't sell a handsome plantation and go to sea!" Colcord 160-1; *Oxford* (2nd ed.) 573; Partridge 741; sea.

F27   If the **Farmer** fails all will starve

1721 Wise *Word* 186: You must keep up your Farmers heart; for if he fails, you are in danger to starve all. Cf. Lean 3.509: husbandman.

F28   Not care a **Fart**

1826 Audubon *1826 Journal* 50: Without caring a f—— . . . I know you blushed when the single letter F came to your sight, unaccompanied. I will soon relieve you . . . I intended to write *Fig* in full but my rascally pen was not supplied with material sufficient. NED Fart 1b. Cf. Whiting F60-62.

F29   To set a **Fart** against a north-west wind

1734 Belcher *Papers* 2.41: As for his protest, if he shou'd set a f——t against a N.W. wind, how then? Whiting *NC* 405.

F30   **Farthings** long saved amount to pounds at last

1749 Franklin *PR* 3.350: Farthings long sav'd amount to Pounds at last. Cf. *Oxford* 798-9; Tilley P201, 213.

F31   Not a **Farthing** to bless oneself with

1784 Freneau *Prose* 105: [I] found not a farthing to bless myself with. *Oxford* 156: Cross; Whiting P115.

F32   Not care a (brass) **Farthing**

1747 GClinton in *Colden Papers* 3.365: I did not care a farthing. a1767 Evans *Poetry* 152: But I'll proceed, nor care one farthing. 1770 *Johnson Papers* 7.334: one. 1770 Munford *Candidates* 18. 1771 BMoore in *Norton Papers* 193: one. 1776 Adams *Works* 9.396. 1777 Munford *Patriots* 480. 1782 Freneau *Poems* 2.195. 1785 Adams *D and A* 3.176. 1787 AAdams in Smith *Journal and Correspondence* 1.121. 1787 *Anarchiad* 120: I shuldnt cair a bras nor a Copper fardin. 1797 Adams *Works* 8.555. 1801 Story *Shop* 39: He cares not one brass farthing. 1802 Paine *To the Citizens* 2.925. 1810 Stebbins *Journal* 28. 1813 JAdams in *Adams-Jefferson Letters* 2.333, 1818 *Works* 10.298. 1824

Neal *American Writers* 34. NED Farthing 2; Partridge 267.

F33   Not regard a **Farthing**

1823 JAdams in Otis *Letters* 1.175: I would not regard it as a farthing.

F34   Not value a **Farthing**

1717 Lloyd *Papers* 1.217: Not any fear of Mr. E.'s prosecution . . . (which I value not a farthing).

F35   Not worth a **Farthing**

1688 WByrd in *VHM* 25(1917) 257: Not worth a farthing. 1702 Taylor *Christographia* 252.7-8: Their Outside array is not worth a farthing. 1747 Johnson *Writings* 1.129. 1771 *Johnson Papers* 8.114. 1772 Hearne *Journey* 315. 1778 WMalcom in Leake *Lamb* 207. 1787 Smith *Diary* 2.216. 1788 *Columbian Magazine* 2.468. 1789 CHoward in McGillivray *Letters* 224. 1791 Morris *Diary* 2.185. 1796 Cobbett *Porcupine* 3.274: Not worth a brass farthing. 1798 JHopkinson in Gibbs *Memoirs* 2.49. 1806 *Port Folio* NS 2.305, 1807 4.242. *Oxford* 81; Whiting F65.

F36   To owe no man a **Farthing**

1737 Franklin *Drinkers* 2.175: [He] Owes no Man a Farthing.

F37   To play **Fast** and loose

1692 Bulkeley *Will* 145: We may observe how these men dodge and play fast and loose, that a man knows not where to have 'em. 1705 Ingles *Reply* 157: To play fast and loose. 1726 Sewall *Diary* 3.372. 1776 Lee *Papers* 1.255. 1782 JMatthews in Gibbs *Memoirs* 2.200: I wish he may not be playing a fast and loose game. 1802 Hamilton *Works* 10.432. 1843 FBlair in Jackson *Correspondence* 6.236: Their watchword of "Tipp and Ty," . . . might be translated appropriately into . . . "fast and loose" to use the commonest expression. *Oxford* 630; TW 127(1).

F38   The **Fat** is in the fire

1723 Symmes *Utile* 50: All the Fat's in the Fire. 1801 Weems *Letters* 2.214: All the fat's in the fire again, 1802 228. 1815 Barney *Memoir* 282. Barbour 62(2); *Oxford* 247; Whiting F71.

F39 To live on the **Fat** of the land

1764 Habersham *Letters* 22: Knox has lived on the Fat of the Land in England. **1768** Ames *Almanacs* 392: His lofty Steed, loaded with the Fat of the Land. **1779** *Commerce of Rhode Island* 2.80. **1819** Noah *Travels* 141. **1826** Royall *Sketches* 200. Barbour 62(1).

F40 As certain as **Fate**

1778 Paine *American Crisis* 1.150: As certain as fate. **1812** Melish *Travels* 62. TW 128(1).

F41 As fixed as **Fate**

1812 Knopf *War of 1812* 5(1) 203: As fixed as fate.

F42 As steady as **Fate**

1797 Freneau *Poems* 3.164: Steady as fate, unmov'd will you appear. Cf. TW 128(2).

F43 As swift as **Fate**

1797 Freneau *Poems* 3.147: Then, swift as fate, her pace defied.

F44 As fast as **Father Luke** takes snuff

1794 Cobbett *Porcupine* 1.147: As fast as Father Luke takes snuff.

F45 Box it about till it come to (my **Father**)

1692 Mather *Letters* 45: And when you have so knocked me down, in a specter so unlike me, you will enable me to box it about among my neighbors, till it come, I know not where, at last. *Oxford* 303; Tilley F85.

F46 The **Father** to the bough, the son to the plough

1713 Wise *Churches* 61: The *Kentish Yeomantry* . . . secured their fair Estates of Lands in Fee and Free-holds forever from all Forfeiture by Felony, according to their Country proverb, *The Father to the Bough, The Son to the Plough.* **1764** Hutchinson *History* 1.377: [The] customs of gavelkind, one of which is, "the father to the bough, the son to the plough." *Oxford* 248; Whiting F76.

F47 Happy is he whose **Father** was born before him

1787 Cutler *Life* 1.222: Happily for him he had a father born before him. *Oxford* 351-2; Tilley F740.

F48 Like **Father,** like son

1774 Ames *Almanacs* 451: The truth of the old saying, *"like father, like son."* **1776** Carter *Diary* 2.1001: But now, like father, like Son, I wonder everybody can't go to hell by themselves without endeavouring to carry their Children there. Barbour 62(2); *Oxford* 248; Whiting F80. See **M258.**

F49 **Fatigue** is better than a bed of down

1809 Pinkney *Travels* 131: Fatigue, however, according to the proverb, is better than a bed of down.

F50 **Favor** is deceitful and beauty is vain

1754 Plumstead 318: Favor is deceitful and beauty is vain (Prov. 31.30). Lean 2.677, 3.463.

F51 The **Favor** of the great is no inheritance

1733 Franklin *PR* 1.314: The favour of the Great is no inheritance. Tilley K81. See **S108.**

F52 One should prize small **Favors** (*varied*)

1640 MCole in *Winthrop Papers(A)* 4.235: We ought to prise small favors they come from the same love of god that great ons doe. **1802** Ames *Letters* 1.311: Grateful for little favors. **1822** Weems *Penn* 40: You are thankful for small favours. **1832** Ames *Nautical* 159: "The smallest favors will be gratefully acknowledged," as the advertisements say. **1856** Paulding *Letters(II)* 575: We ought to be as grateful for small evils as small favours. Barbour 62; TW 128(1).

F53 To curry **Favor**

1740 *Colden Letters* 7.336: To curry favour with you. **1741** Stephens *Journal(I)* 2.209: And therefore this was done to curry Favour with his Excellence. **1764** Franklin *Papers* 11.297. **1769** Smith *Memoirs(I)* 58. **1775** WLee in *Naval Documents* 1.473. **1775** Washington *Writings* 3.450-1. **1789** Boucher *Autobiography* 110. **1793** Jefferson *Writings* 9.254. **1793** Paine *Correspondence* 2.1327. **1796** Cobbett *Porcupine* 3.267, **1797** 7.300: Old Toper to *currying horses* was bred; But, tired of so humble a life, To *currying favour* he turned his head, And's now *curried* himself by his wife. **1808** Hitchcock *Poetical Dictionary* 88. **1810** Weems

Letters 3.3. **1812** Hitchcock *Social* 18. **1820** Simpson *Journal* 73, **1821** 302. **1827** Watterston *Wanderer* 194. *Oxford* 210; Whiting F85.

F54 **Fear** made the first gods
1676 Williams *Writings* 5.365: As the old saying is, primos in Orbe Deos, &c. Fear made the first Gods. Whiting D385.

F55 **Fear** makes people loving
1775 AA in *Adams FC* 1.232: I have often heard that fear makes people loving.

F56 The **Fear** of God is the beginning of wisdom
1632 EHowes in *Winthrop Papers(A)* 3.66: As the feare and Love of God is the begininge of true Wisdome. **1731** Chalkley *Journal* 250: *The true Fear of God,* which the wise King Solomon says, *Is the Beginning of Wisdom.* **1779** Franklin *Writings* 7.381: *The fear of the Lord is the beginning of Wisdom.* Barbour 62(2); Whiting B194.

F57 Either a **Feast** or a famine (fast)
1767 *Commerce of Rhode Island* 1.203: But hope will mend, as its the Consequence of this place, either a feast or a fast. **1770** Hearne *Journey* 85: It may justly be said to have been either all feasting, or all famine. **1770** Munford *Candidates* 24: It's always a feast or a famine with us. **1792** Asbury *Journal* 1.732: He who sometimes suffers from a famine will the better know how to relish a feast. **1802** RLake in *Blount Papers* 3.549: After a Feast comes a Famine. **1812** *Kennon Letters* 33.277: Give you a feast and then let a fast follow. *Oxford* 251; Whiting *NC* 406(1).

F58 To relish a **Feast** but not love the reckoning
1812 Taggart *Letters* 384-5: They may relish war as a feast, yet do not love to pay the reckoning. *Oxford* 528; Tilley F149.

F59 As light as a **Feather**
c**1765** JTrumbull in *Monthly Anthology* 2. (1805) 247: And jump'd from bed, as light as a feather. c**1775** *Connecticut Journal* in Buckingham *Specimens* 1.314: His heart light as a feather. **1784** Freneau *Poems*

2.279. **1795** Murdock *Triumphs* 54. **1796** Barton *Disappointment* 47. c**1800** Rush *Autobiography* 162. **1804** Brackenridge *Modern* 442. **1801** TPickering in Cabot *Letters* 396. a**1811** Henry *Account* 195. **1812** Hitchcock *Social* 86. Barbour 63(5); *Oxford* 462-3; Whiting F94.

F60 A **Feather** (plume) in one's cap
1703 Taylor *Poems* 186: The Feather in the Tabernacle's Cap, **1722** 373: Stick them as feathers in thy Cap my king. **1730** DDunbar in *Baxter Manuscripts* 11.33: [It] was but a feather in my Hatt. **1753** Franklin *Papers* 4.467: For a Feather in the Cap is not so useful a thing . . . as a Pair of good Silk Garters. **1754** RDinwiddie in Washington *Writings* 1.82. **1764** Watts *Letter Book* 255. **1767** TWharton in Franklin *Papers* 14.29. **1775** Deane *Papers* 1.75: And give place to men who do not think it degrading to serve their country though they have not the highest feather in their cap. **1779** Angell *Diary* 41. **1779** JFogg in *Sullivan Journals* 95. **1779** JWarren in *Warren-Adams Letters* 2.106. **1783** RRLivingston in Hamilton *Papers* 3.434: I consider it as a feather that would have graced my cap. **1790** ADonald in Jefferson *Papers* 16.592. **1792** *Belknap Papers* 2.306: You have . . . congratulated me on a certain academical feather which has lately been stuck in my cap. **1793** Ingraham *Journal* 172. **1799** Carey *Plumb* (4). **1806** Fessenden *Modern Philosopher* 114. **1807** Bates *Papers* 1.143: You have stuck a feather in the cap of my vanity. **1807** MWarren in *Adams-Warren Correspondence* 454. **1809** Weems *Marion* 158: One of the finest plumes that I ever expected to feather my cap with, *Washington* 108. c**1810** Randolph *Virginia* 208: [It] gave Dunmore a false éclat, a feather for his vanity. **1811** Graydon *Memoirs* 118. **1813** JSloane in Knopf *War of 1812* 3.166: This will be a fresh plume in the enemies crown. **1815** Adams *Works* 10.115. **1815** Morris *Diary and Letters* 2.583: No candidate can wear to the polls a finer feather than the words No Taxes, handsomely pinned to his hat. a**1824** Marshall *Kentucky* 1.337: His adherents were pleased to stick this new plume in his cap. **1833** Jackson *Correspondence* 5.213: If you succeed it

will be a lasting feather in your cap. **1834**
Baldwin *Diary* 326: The agency . . . would
be something of a feather in my cap. Barbour 62(1); *Oxford* 251-2; TW 129(5); Tilley F157.

F61 Fine **Feathers** make fine birds

1783 *Washington *Writings* 26.40: Do not
conceive that fine Clothes make fine Men,
any more than fine feathers make fine Birds.
1785 Adams(A) *Letters* 258: The observation did not in general hold good, that fine
feathers make fine birds. **1803** Davis *Travels*
386. **1809** *Kennon Letters* 32.164: You
know. Barbour 62(3, 4); *Oxford* 258; TW
129(3). See **C209, 232.**

F62 The last **Feather** will sink the camel

1793 WJackson in *Bingham's Maine* 1.298:
It is certainly true that the last feather will
sink the camel. **1817** Pintard *Letters* 1.98:
The weight of another feather w^d break my
back. *Oxford* 443; TW 129(6).

F63 Like a **Feather** in the wind

1702 Taylor *Christographia* 229.11-3: Christ
. . . Will blow the old Serpent . . . away as a
feather in the Winde. Cf. Whiting F105. See
C108.

F64 Not a **Feather** the worse

1824 *Tales* 1.53: The carriage . . . is never a
feather the worse.

F65 Not care a **Feather**

1802 *Port Folio* 2.216: Quashee no care — no
not a feather. Cf. Whiting F96.

F66 Not weigh a **Feather**

1776 FLLee in Burnett *Letters* 1.417: The
. . . happiness of America, compared with
which, the interests of Britain, is as a feather
in the scale. **1781** Oliver *Origin* 103: The
Power of *Great Britain* did not weigh a
Feather in their Consideration. **1789**
RTroup in Hamilton *Papers* 5.361: He . . .
he has not the weight of a feather with any
body. **1792** HJackson in *Bingham's Maine*
1.69. **1817** Pintard *Letters* 1.98. Barbour
62(1); *Oxford* 251-2; TW 129(9); Whiting
F98.

F67 To fly like a **Feather**

1741 Ames *Almanacs* 148: It comes, it goes,
it fly's like a Feather.

F68 To knock one down with a **Feather**

1796 Cobbett *Porcupine* 4.131: As the old
women say, you might have knocked me
down with a feather. Barbour 63(7); *Oxford*
433; TW 130(15).

F69 To rise at a **Feather**

1794 Jefferson *Writings* 9.296: Being so
patient of the kicks and scoffs of our enemies,
and rising at a feather against our friends,
1815 14.290: Accustomed to rise at a feather
themselves and to be always fighting. NED
Feather 10b.

F70 To show the white **Feather**

1820 Simpson *Journal* 105: Chastellain
showed the White Feather. *Oxford* 885; TW
130(17).

F71 **February's** kiss

1777 Carter *Diary* 2.1080: I did imagine
February would give us her wonted kiss
before she parted with us. Cf. Dunwoody 94;
Oxford 541; Tilley M1110.

F72 All **Fellows** at football

1634 Wood *New-England* 76: But as all are
fellowes at foot-ball, so they all meete friends
at the kettle. **1711** Sewall *Diary* 2.303: Mr.
Bridgham declining to sign, saying it was not
fit for him to sign with persons so much
above him; I said pleasantly, We are at Football now; and then he presently signed. *Oxford* 9; Tilley F182.

F73 Hail **Fellow** well met

1699 Ward *Trip* 68: But are never known to
offer any Indignity to their Kings, who are
Hail Fellow well met with his Subjects. **1713**
Wise *Churches* 41: When men are without
Law, and all *hail Fellows*, not well but badly
met. **1787** *American Museum* 2.90. **1798**
Echo 191: The sire, and the brats, are "hale
fellows, well met." **1800** Dorr *Letters* 206.
1807 *Salmagundi* 10: He tempers, so happily, the grave and ceremonious gallantry of
the old school with the "hail-fellow"
familiarity of the new. **1815** Waterhouse
Journal 13. **1832** Ames *Nautical* 209. **1837**

Hone *Diary* 1.235, **1840** 464. *Oxford* 342; TW 130(1); Whiting H16.

F74 A good **Fence** makes good neighbors
1640 ERogers in *Winthrop Papers(A)* 4.282: A good fence helpeth to keepe peace betweene neighbours. **1815** Brackenridge *Modern* 787: Good fences . . . *preserve good neighbourhoods.* Barbour 63(2). Cf. *Oxford* 494; Tilley N109. See **N46.**

F75 To be on one side of the **Fence** or the other
1830 ABalch in Jackson *Correspondence* 4.116: I shall always be found on one side of the fence or the other. TW 130(5).

F76 To be on the **Fence**
1837 AHuntsman in Jackson *Correspondence* 5.446: *I believe he is on the fence, and it is uncertain which side he will drop.* Barbour 63(5); TW 130(1).

F77 No **Fencing** against a flail
1734 Johnson *Writings* 3.54: There is no fencing against a flail. *Oxford* 253; Tilley F185.

F78 The Alabama (*etc.*) **Fever**
1817 JGraham in *Ruffin Papers* 1.198: The *Alabama Feaver* rages here with great violence and has *carried off* vast numbers of our citizens. **1822** *Austin Papers* 1.469: In Short nothing is Spoken of but the Texas fever, **1825** 2.1020: The emigrating or Texas *fever* prevails. **1830** GSpruill in *Ruffin Papers* 2.18: I suppose you have not felt the *Goldmine* fever. **1848** Cooper *Letters* 6.8: The California fever still runs high, though I fancy the expectation of getting rich in a month is a good deal abating. **1859** JJones in *Ruffin Papers* 3.20: I have two or three valuable friends who have recently been taken with the Southern fever. DA southern 3(9); *Oxford* 98; TW 54(2), 368.

F79 The **Fewer** the better
1762 *Johnson Papers* 10.563: But if Determin^d to Go down the fewer the better. Whiting *NC* 406. Cf. Whiting M679. See **M241.**

F80 As fine as a **Fiddle**
1802 Chester *Federalism* 10: Build a grave yard and paint it as fine as a Dutch fiddle. **1802** Irving *Jonathan* 28: With her courtiers, fine as a fiddle. **1803** *Yankee Phrases* 37: Although, as a fiddle they're fine. **1815** Humphreys *Yankey* 37: I am as fine as a fiddle — and e'en-a-most as musical tu. Barbour 63(1); *Oxford* 266; TW 130(1).

F81 To hang up one's **Fiddle**
1809 Wirt *Letters* 1.264: The man who can read Locke for an hour or two, and then lay him down and argue feebly upon any subject, may hang up his fiddle for life. TW 131(4).

F82 To look like a **Fiddle**
1792 JBoit in *Columbia* 389: This day the Ship was completely rig'd, Hold stowed, and in every respect in readiness for sea. She look'd like a *fiddle!* Cf. *Oxford* 266; TW 130-1(1, 2).

F83 As fuddled as a **Fiddler**
1837 Cooper *Letters* 3.267: They say *Sir Thomas* gets as fuddled as a fiddler. Cf. *Oxford* 206; TW 131(1); Whiting *NC* 407.

F84 He that dances must pay the **Fiddler**
1740 Belcher *Papers* 2.298: As the dance is over, the next thing is to pay the fidler 15 or £ 200,000. **1787** WSSmith in Smith *Journal and Correspondence* 1.195: If people will dance they must pay the fiddler. Barbour 64; TW 131(2). See **D10, P174.**

F85 A **Fiddlestick** for them
1830 Ames *Mariner's* 191: A fiddlestick for the pair of them. NED Fiddlestick 2.

F86 Not care a **Fiddlestick**
1807 *Salmagundi* 184: As we do not care a fiddle-stick . . . for public opinion. NED Fiddlestick 2.

F87 Out of old **Fields** comes new corn
1679 Fitzhugh *Letters* 66: For out of old fields must come the new Corn. Whiting F128.

F88 A **Fig** for (whatever)
1702 Taylor *Christographia* 201.25: A Fig for Foes. **1775** *Essex Gazette* in Buckingham *Specimens* 1.219: A fig for all care. **1777** Munford *Patriots* 466: A fig for our lives . . .

A fig for the English. **1784** Chipman *Writings* 21: learning. **1787** Tyler *Contrast* 28: sentiment. **1788** *Politician* 43: your Latin, 64: both Constitutions. **1790** Dennie *Letters* 40: care. **1797** Beete *Man* 33: his name. **1801** *Port Folio* 1.48: inspiration, **1805** 5.55: the doctor, **1806** NS 1.93: care. **1812** JBrace in Vanderpoel *More Chronicles* 144: Miss Shedden. **1813** Paulding *Lay* 77: your musty professors. **a1815** Freneau *Poems* 3.305: the pay, 309: the sweat on his brow. **1815** *Port Folio* 3NS 5.204: admirals. **1816** Paulding *Letters(I)* 2.33: Doctor Hutton. **1824** *Tales* 1.iv: the world's opinion, 2.14: the phrase. **1826** WBiglow in Buckingham *Specimens* 2.291: Harvard College. *Oxford* 255; Whiting F136.

F89   Not care a Fig

1769 Woodmason *Journal* 154: He didn't care for them a Fig. **1779** Sargent *Loyalist* 97: Nor car'd for friends a fig. **1789** Maclay *Journal* 125, **1790** 242, **1791** 368. **1800** Adams *Writings* 2.464. **1801** Story *Shop* 53. **1807** Jefferson *Family Letters* 317. **1808** Hitchcock *Poetical Dictionary* 81. **1809** Lindsley *Love* 41. **1809** Weems *Marion* 242. **1810** *Kennon Letters* 32.269. **1812** Hitchcock *Social* 83. **1816** Fidfaddy *Adventures* 22, 139. **1816** Lambert *Travels* 1.480. **1817** Weems *Franklin* 146, 202. **1818** Adams *Memoirs* 4.66. **1837** Jackson *Correspondence* 5.473: If they can make money they care not a fig how the administration gets on. **1837** Paulding *Letters(II)* 202, **1841** 313. TW 132(2). Cf. Whiting F137.

F90   Not give a Fig

1773 JBoucher in *MHM* 8(1913) 185: You would not give a Fig for Me. **1787** Adams *Diary* 338, n.3. **1801** Weems *Letters* 2.206, **1802** 224, **1804** 292, **1805** 311. **1813** *Kennon Letters* 35.19. **1836** Clifford *Letters* 73. TW 132(3).

F91   Not worth a Fig

1801 Story *Shop* 23: This ode ain't worth a single fig. **1805** Sewall *Parody* 16: They prove not worth a fig. **1807** Weems *Letters* 2.366, **1809** 392, **1810** 3.18. **1828** MJenkins in *Ruffin Papers* 1.435. **1828** *Yankee* 7. *Oxford* 255; Whiting F137.

F92   To call a Fig a fig

1774 Seabury *Letters* 71: I must have the privelege of calling a fig, —a Fig; an egg, —an Egg. *Oxford* 98; Tilley S699. See **S354.**

F93   Not care a Fig's end

1832 Ames *Nautical* 203: [Care] not a fig's end. NED Fig *sb.*[1] 4.

F94   He that Fights and runs away may live to fight another day

1774 Willard *Letters* 30: Two of those desperate warriors, who have run away, that they may live to fight another day. **1781** Oliver *Origin* 38: He liv'd to fight another Day Without being forc'd to run away. **1782** Sargent *Loyalist* 144: And sure 'tis right, When in a fright, To fly without delay: For now my men May fight again, Upon some other day. **1792** Belknap *Foresters* 197: Several of the hunters . . . were obliged to take to their heels, that they might "live to hunt another day." **1803** *Steele Papers* 1.364: I am indebted for the perfect establishment of my health which like the courage of the man who fights and runs away, will enable me to do better in future. **1804** Irving *Corrector* 115. **1806** Fessenden *Modern Philosopher* 216. **1809** *Port Folio* 2NS 1.253: The man who fights, and runs away, May live to fight another day; But, he that is in battle slain, Will never live to fight again, 2.263: [compares these lines from *Hudibras*: For those who fly may fight again, Which he can never do, that's slain]. **1816** Lambert *Travels* 1.478. **1816** *Port Folio* 4NS 2.26. **1819** Faux *Memorable Days* 1.76: Where my uncle Henry . . . lived, loved, fought, ran away, and lived to fight another day. **1827** Jones *Sketches* 2.14: Each one decides that it is best "to live to fight another day." *Oxford* 256; TW 132(1); Whiting F141.

F95   To live like Fighting-cocks

1825 Pintard *Letters* 2.181: They live like fighting cocks to what I did. *Oxford* 256; TW 132. See **G19.**

F96   Figures will not lie

1739 RFry in *Colonial Currency* 3.278: *All Mankind well knows that Figures will not lye.* **1831** Cooper *Letters* 2.140: Figures cannot lie, **1838** 3.347. Barbour 64; TW 132(4).

F97 To miss a **Figure**

1819 TWBarnes *Memoirs of T. Weed* (Boston, 1884) 12: They have missed a figure, for we now complete twelve months. TW 132(2).

F98 So much **Finery**, so much poverty

1745 Ames *Almanacs* 183: So much Finery, so much Poverty, **1754** 252: Finery and Poverty go together.

F99 At one's **Fingers'** ends

1721 *Letter* in *Colonial Currency* 2.253: The first Lesson . . . which every Poor Tyro . . . has at his Finger's ends. **1741** Franklin *PR* 2.293: She had her Lesson at her Fingers Ends. **1740** *Georgia Records* 23.177. **1753** Laurens *Papers* 3.430. **1767** Woodmason *Journal*: I have . . . all the Offices at my fingers Ends. **1783** Curwen *Journal* 2.919: [He] has it [the Bible] almost at his fingers ends. **1786** Tilghman *Letters* 138. a**1788** Jones *History* 2.209: [He] had hypocrisy, art, and dissimulation, at his fingers' ends. **1797** JMcHenry in Hamilton *Papers* 21.48. **1809** *Port Folio* 2NS 2.423. **1811** Graydon *Memoirs* 86: The whole body of Roman poetry . . . might have been at my finger-ends. **1822** Robertson *Letters* 182. *Oxford* 259; Whiting F150.

F100 By one's **Fingers'** ends

1755 *Johnson Papers* 2.244: He has the Summer past by his fingers Ends Supported them [his family]. NED Finger-end b.

F101 Every **Finger** a fish-hook

1784 Shaw *Journals* 137: "These fellows," said he, "are St. Peter's children,—every finger a fish-hook, and their hand a grapnel." *Oxford* 693. Cf. Whiting H60.

F102 One's little **Finger** is thicker than another's loins

1692 Bulkeley *Will* 192: They cry out against Sir Ed. Andross, but their little finger is thicker than his loins. **1774** Franklin *Writings* 6.300: Let them feel that your little finger is thicker than the loins of all your ancestors. 2 Chron. 10.10; NED Finger 1b.

F103 To be **Finger** cold

1781 [Jan. 25] Curwen *Journal* 2.723: Air like what we in New England call finger cold. NED Finger 15.

F104 To be **Finger** next the thumb

1734 Belcher *Papers* 2.147: He is finger next the thumb with S[r] R. W. *Oxford* 258; Tilley T645.

F105 To burn one's **Fingers**

1718 Byrd *Another Secret Diary* 329: I believe he'll have a care how he burns his fingers any more in this business. **1728** JAlexander in *Colden Letters* 1.259: And for that purpose had Endeavoured to make them burn their fingers. **1741** Stephens *Journal(I)* 2.105: Fearing lest I should . . . burn my own Finger. **1758** DColden in *Colden Papers* 5.220. **1764** CChauncy in Stiles *Itineraries* 441. **1764** Watts *Letter Book* 248: The old Man . . . is afraid of burning his fingers. **1769** *Commerce of Rhode Island* 1.276-7: And if you happen to burn your fingers in Rhode Island, I think it ungenerous to blame me for it in Jamaica. **1769** Woodmason *Journal* 154. **1773** TNelson in *Norton Papers* 299. **1773** Trumbull *Satiric Poems* 94: The child that plays with fire, in pain Will burn its fingers now and then. **1774** Franklin *Writings* 6.301. **1782** EPendleton in Madison *Papers* 5.440: Medlars often get their fingers burnt. **1788** May *Journal* 88. **1789** Paine *Correspondence* 2.1279. c**1825** Tyler *Prose* 75: An . . . incident . . . which had . . . taught him not to burn his fingers with meddling with women's matters. Barbour 64(4); *Oxford* 259; Tilley F240. Cf. Whiting F157.

F106 To have one's **Finger** in the pie (*varied*)

1713 Johnston *Papers* 121: Busy restless tempers who would have a finger in everything. **1756** EHubbart in Franklin *Papers* 7.70: The Parson and the Deavel have a finger in the Pye you know. **1794** EHazard in *Belknap Papers* 2.350: Most of their committee have had a finger in the pye. **1802** *Port Folio* 2.380: But Beelzebub, or proverbs lie, Must have a finger in each pie. **1809** JCampbell in *Ruffin Papers* 1.123: A great many being of opinion that he had a hand in the pye. **1812** Hitchcock *Social* 82: The lawyer too must *dabble in the pye. Oxford* 258; TW 133(3).

F107 To have one's Fingers itch

1879 JHarvey in *Blount Papers* 1.519: My fingers itch to be at the business. *Oxford* 259; Tilley F237.

F108 To have someone between Finger and thumb

1769 *Johnson Papers* 6.575: We w^d have them all between our Finger & Thumb here in the City.

F109 To lick one's Fingers

1810 Rush *Letters* 2.1038: You will often lick your fingers in reviewing the days and hours you are now spending in the highly cultivated society of Edinburgh. NED Lick 1b.

F110 To lie and cool one's Fingers

1721 Carter *Letters* 94: For the rest, I reckon he may lie and cool his fingers. Cf. NED Cool *v.*[1] 3.

F111 To love one's little Finger, etc.

1796 Barton *Disappointment* 50-1: I love your little finger better than Raccoon's whole body. *Oxford* 490; Tilley F227.

F112 To put one's Finger in his eye

1814 Kerr *Barclay* 70: The Esquire was continually harping it over, putting his fingers in his eyes—or something like it. *Oxford* 258; Whiting F155.

F113 To put one's Finger in the fire, etc.

1819 Faux *Memorable Days* 1.39: And give you this toast, That President Madison be no more like General Washington than puté finger in the fire, and haul it out again. Cf. *Oxford* 657; Whiting F157.

F114 To slip through one's Fingers (hands)

1745 *Georgia Records* 24.356: The Colonel seems to be sliping through his Lordships . . . Hands as Water does. **1765** Watts *Letter Book* 372: If this Money had not slipt thro' his Fingers. **1838** Paulding *Letters(II)* 222: But he has slipped through my fingers. TW 133(5).

F115 To stick to one's Fingers

1767 JWatts in *Aspinwall Papers* 2.597: I

can assure you none of it [flour] sticks to my fingers. Barbour 64(5).

F116 To wear (work) one's Fingers to the bone

1815 Humphreys *Yankey* 67: I will wear these fingers to the bone! **c1825** Tyler *Prose* 63: I work my fingers to the bone.

F117 To wind someone round one's Finger

1743 *Georgia Records* 24.184: Watson could wind Parker round his finger. **1809** Weems *Marion* 34: I can wind him round my finger like a pack-thread. *Oxford* 847; TW 133(9).

F118 With a wet Finger

1713 Wise *Churches* 110: [They] will now finish their Work with a wet Finger. *Oxford* 881; Whiting F160.

F119 With one's Finger(s) in one's cheek (mouth)

1755 AStephen in *Letters to Washington* 1.160: Or then perhaps be Obliged to Return with our fingers in our Cheeks. **1786** AMaclaine in Iredell *Correspondence* 2.139: Mr. G. Hooper is now there, and will come back with his finger in his mouth. **1795** DCobb in *Bingham's Maine* 1.517: I shall go down there with my finger in my mouth. *Oxford* 258.

F120 As hot as Fire

c1700 Taylor *Poems* 402: And doth persue as hot as sparkling fire. **1785** Hunter *Quebec* 76: I . . . went to bed as hot as fire. Barbour 65(6); Whiting F170.

F121 As mad as Fire

1809 Lindsley *Love* 36: He mad like fire! **1820** Weems *Letters* 3.290: The People all mad as fire for a very recent imposition. **1862** JBrodnax in *Ruffin Papers* 3.254: I know you would get mad as fire. TW 134(4).

F122 As opposite as Fire to water

1714 Hunter *Androboros* 27: As opposite as Fire to Water. Lean 2.860.

F123 As red as Fire

1787 *American Museum* 1.47: Sue look'd as red as fire. Whiting F171.

F124 **Fire** and water are good servants but bad masters (*varied*)

1677 Hubbard *Indian* 2.174: One of those three bad Masters, the Fire, the Water, or the barbarous Heathen. **1702** Mather *Magnalia* 1.92: Ten times has the *fire* made notable ruins among us, and our *good servant* been almost our *master*. **1783** Williams *Penrose* 80: Fire and Water are no friends to Man unless under a strict limitation. **1787** *Belknap Papers* 1.469: We had an awful proof of the old observation that "fire is a good servant, but a bad master." **1800** Gadsden *Writings* 300: The art of oratory with fire and water are good servants, but terrible masters. **1808** Adams *Works* 6.533: Like fire, they are good servants, but all-consuming masters. Barbour 65(4); *Oxford* 259; TW 134(8); Tilley F253. Cf. Whiting F188. See **S308.**

F125 **Fire** in the straw

1646 SSymonds in Hutchinson *Papers* 1.247: Not being able suddenly to discerne the poyson in the sweet wine, nor the fire wrapt up in the straw. *Oxford* 167; Tilley F272; Whiting F195.

F126 **Fire** treads snow

1793 Drinker *Journal* 216: "The fire treads snow," as 'tis said.

F127 Liquid **Fire**

1806 Asbury *Letters* 3.343: They can live without slavery, or liquid fire, **1812** *Journal* 2.707: Two innkeepers . . . declare against selling liquid fire. DA liquid fire.

F128 A little **Fire** may kindle a great matter

1699 Mather *Diary* 1.285: As not knowing, how great a matter a little Fire may kindle. **1739** Talcott *Papers* 2.174: How great a matter may a little fire kindle. **1815** Bentley *Diary* 4.309: Behold how great a matter a little fire kindles. **1816** CCHester in Vanderpoel *More Chronicles* 191: Nancy's text . . . was — "Behold how great a matter a little fire kindleth." James 3.5; Whiting S559. See **C99.**

F129 One **Fire** drives out another

1637 Morton *New English Canaan* 267: One

fire they say drives out another. Barbour 64(2); *Oxford* 596; TW 134(9); Tilley F277.

F130 There is **Fire** in the smoke

1794 Asbury *Journal* 2.21: There was fire in the smoke. *Oxford* 568; Whiting F194. See **S263.**

F131 To be between two **Fires**

1777 Smith *Memoirs(II)* 162: Put him between two Fires, 214. **1780** Jefferson *Papers* 3.478: Being situated between two fires. **1782** Adams *Works* 7.618. a**1788** Jones *History* 1.218. **1795** WShort in Monroe *Writings* 2.268. NED Fire 14.

F132 To come to fetch **Fire**

1732 Belcher *Papers* 1.213: But he seem'd to come hither to fetch fire, & not to do business. **1831** JRuffin in *Ruffin Papers* 2.31: I shall be glad to see you in March: *do not come for a chunk of fire*. Barbour 65(8); *Oxford* 254; Whiting F201.

F133 To go like **Fire**

1806 Asbury *Journal* 2.494: Went off like fire. **1817** Young *Life* 141: His words went like fire through the assembly. Cf. Whiting F203, 204. See **B373, F162, W159.**

F134 To go through **Fire** and water

1776 Hodgkins *Letters* 215: We whar obliged to go through fire & wharter. **1779** Asbury *Journal* 1.296: If it be through fire and water, **1780** 329: Keep me through the fire and water, **1799** *Letters* 3.177: She went through the fire and water of affliction unhurt. **1815** Harmon *Sixteen Years* 198: By flattering their vanities . . . they may be made to go through fire and water. *Oxford* 259; Whiting F209.

F135 To know enough to keep out of **Fire** and water

1758 Adams *D and A* 1.52: Knowledge eno' to keep out of fire and Water, is all that I aim at. **1779** JHill in *Baxter Manuscripts* 17.263: [They were] only Compos Mentis sufficient to keep themselves out of Fire and Water. **1787** Tyler *Contrast* 34-5: They us'd to say . . . that if a woman knew how to make a pudding, and to keep herself out of fire and water, she knew enough for a wife. **1797**

Mann *Female* 55: Hence the shrewd saying—"*Learning keeps him out of fire and water.*" **1799** Tyler *Prose* 304: A daughter, who could scarce keep out of fire and water. TW 134(16).

F136 To rake up the **Fire**

1821 JAdams in *Adams-Jefferson Letters* 2.576: You may . . . hope to be the last to take your flight and to rake up the fire as father Sherman who always staid to the last and commonly two days afterward used to say, "that it was his office to sit up and rake the ashes over the coals."

F137 To strike **Fire** out of flummery

1763 Watts *Letter Book* 173: But you might as well have struck fire out of Flummery, indeed I believe they want all. Cf. NED Flummery.

F138 To strike **Fire** out of ice

1775 Smith *Works* 2.281: You might more easily "strike fire out of ice." *Oxford* 260; Tilley F284.

F139 To take **Fire** into one's bosom

1777 SAdams in *Warren-Adams Letters* 1.292: Can a man take Fire into his Bosom, and not be burnd? Whiting F208.

F140 **Fire-new**

1790 Freneau *Prose* 257: As you will now . . . receive your printing materials fire-new (as the phrase is) from Europe. TW 134(5).

F141 All is **Fish** that comes to net

1692 Bulkeley *Will* 84: Yet they have been too ready to follow Such unprofitable counsel, as would bring fish to their nets. **1780** Asbury *Journal* 1.343: All is fish that comes to the net. *Oxford* 264-5; Whiting F221.

F142 As mute as a **Fish**

1781 WSLivingston in Webb *Correspondence* 2.342: The Line march'd the next Day Southward—Mute as Fish. **1783** Williams *Penrose* 338: Off she went, mute as a Fish. **1788** *Columbian Magazine* 2.219: Their tongues were mute as fishes. **1794** WHeth in Hamilton *Papers* 16.570. **1798** Cobbett *Porcupine* 10.42. **1812** CANorton in Knopf *War*

of 1812 3.38. *Oxford* 552; Tilley F300. Cf. TW 135(2); Whiting F222.

F143 Better catch small **Fish** than none

1735 *Georgia Records* 21.18: I thought t'was better to catch Small fish than none. Barbour 65(2); *Oxford* 51; Tilley F303.

F144 **Fish** and visitors stink in three days (*varied*)

1736 Franklin *PR* 2.137: Fish and Visitors stink in 3 days, **1767** *Papers* 14.299-300: Not to become tiresome Guests at the End of Three Days at farthest. Barbour 65(6); *Oxford* 287; Tilley F310.

F145 **Fish** begin to taint at the head

1674 Josselyn *Account* 9: The first part that begins to taint in a fish is the head [literal]. *Oxford* 263; Tilley F304.

F146 The great **Fish** devour the less

1643 Williams *Writings* 1.142: *What* Habacuck *once spoke, mine eyes Have often seene most true, The greater fishes devoure the lesse, And cruelly pursue,* **1644** 3.398: The *Fishes* . . . hurt and devoure each other, and the greater devour the lesse, 424: The greater [fishes] taking, plundering, swallowing up the lesser. **1705** Ingles *Reply* 24: I neither suffer ye greater Fish to eat up ye Lesser. **1719** Chalkley *Journal* 100: They living upon one another in the Sea, the great Fishes on the small ones. **1731** *Money* in *Colonial Currency* 2.432. **1740** *Letter* in *Colonial Currency* 4.11: The Pleasure which . . . the great Fish of the Sea, take in devouring the less. **1775** AA in *Adams FC* 1.329. **1775** Moore *Diary* 1.135: The fate of these petty rogues is . . . like that of the little fish that are occasionally devoured to fatten and keep alive the larger ones. **1785** JAdams in *Warren-Adams Letters* 2.269. **1806** Hitchcock *Works* 34: Then let him God's last end express, Why the great fish destroy the less? *Oxford* 333; Whiting F232.

F147 He that would catch **Fish** must venture his bait

1757 Franklin *PR* 7.80: He that would catch Fish, must venture his Bait. See N113.

F148 It will be good **Fish** when it's caught

1692 Bulkeley *Will* 127: And that will be good fish when catch'd, for *omnia eo spectantia — vestigia cerno, nulla retrorsum.* **1720** Carter *Letters* 19: As for the bad debt, 'twill be good fish when it's caught. *Oxford* 319; Tilley F317.

F149 Like a **Fish** out of water

1652 Williams *Writings* 7.68: As a *Fish* out of the *water.* **1702** Mather *Magnalia* 1.370: He was even "like a fish out of the water," 508: Our Whiting . . . would have thought himself a fish out of his element, if he had ever been at any time any but in the *Pacifick* Sea. **1742** Johnson *Writings* 3.456. **1775** Webb *Correspondence* 1.51: Your Gentleman is as uneasy as a fish out of Water. **1778** Joslin *Journal* 348: I have longed to be at work as much as Ever a fish Did to be out of Warter. **1792** Brackenridge *Modern* 13. **1793** Jefferson *Writings* 1.387. **1832** Barney *Memoir* 155: Having passed the previous summer . . . very much, as the proverb has it, "like a fish out of water." **1838** Fletcher *Letters* 159. Barbour 66(8); *Oxford* 264; Whiting F233.

F150 Neither **Fish** nor flesh (nor fowl, nor good red herring)

c1692 *Wyllys Papers* 347: And so is neither flesh nor good fish. **1772** Hearne *Journey* 280: The flesh . . . must have a very disagreeable taste, neither resembling fish, flesh, nor fowl. **1799** Cobbett *Porcupine* 10.210: The *True American* is a non-descript animal . . . it is neither fish, flesh, nor good red-herring. **1830** Ames *Mariner's* 279: The English language will soon become "neither fish, flesh, nor red herring." *Oxford* 264; Whiting F235.

F151 There are as good **Fish** in the sea as ever came out of it

1809 *Port Folio* 2NS 2.131: There is as good fish in the sea as ever was taken out. **1810** *Kennon Letters* 32.276: The old saying. Barbour 66(12); *Oxford* 263-4; TW 135(7).

F152 To catch like **Fish** at a bait

1781 Asbury *Journal* 1.414: And they catch at them like fish at a bait. *Oxford* 263; Whiting F230.

F153 To cry stinking **Fish**

1666 Alsop *Maryland* 24: I have a thousand *Billings-gate* Collegians that will give in their testimony, *That they never knew a Fishwoman cry stinking Fish.* **1718** TLechmere in *Winthrop Papers*(B) 6.387: No man who has fish to sell will say "it stinks." *Oxford* 569; TW 136(10).

F154 To drink like a **Fish**

1832 Ames *Nautical* 183: [It] will compel every man to "eat like a beast and drink like a fish." Barbour 66(15); *Oxford* 203; TW 136(12).

F155 To have other **Fish** to fry

1736 Gyles *Memoirs* 18: But he had other Fish to Fry. **1745** Stephens *Journal*(II) 2.193: Whilst I had other Fish to Fry at home, 256. **1802** *Port Folio* 2.104. **1803** Wirt *British Spy* 241: He . . . answered me in the cant of the country, that he "had other fish to fry." **1815** Humphreys *Yankey* 88. **1817** Baldwin *Letters* 229: It is time to begin to think of *frying other fish.* **1826** Audubon *1826 Journal* 301. **1830** Ames *Mariner's* 4: In consequence of my then having "other fish to fry," but as my frying pan has subsequently been upset and all my fat thrown into the fire by a frolic of Fortune. Barbour 66(17); *Oxford* 265; TW 136(13).

F156 (To make) **Fish** of one and flesh of another

1814 Wirt *Bachelor* 15: Fish of one and flesh of another. *Oxford* 264; Tilley F314.

F157 To swim like a **Fish**

a1820 Biddle *Autobiography* 76: He . . . swam like a fish. *Oxford* 794; TW 136(14).

F158 As calm as a **Fishpond**

1794 Wansey *Journal* 8: The sea is now as calm as a fish pond. Cf. TW 244: Mill-pond.

F159 **Fisherman's** walk, *etc.*

1803 Davis *Travels* 435: A fisherman's walk; two steps and overboard. *Oxford* 265; TW 136.

F160 To talk like a **Fish-woman** (*varied*)

1753 TBChandler in Johnson *Writings* 1.166: Without sinking into the language of fishwomen. **1798** Adams *New Letters* 144: He can . . . be as low and vulgar as a fish woman. **1813** Jackson *Correspondence* 1.314: It is the character of the . . . *soldier* not to quarrel and brawl like the fishwoman. a**1820** Biddle *Autobiography* 170: Calling me every vile name she could think of. No fishwoman . . . could equal her. See **B167**.

F161 One's **Flag** is out

1737 Franklin *Drinkers* 2.175: His Flag is out.

F162 To spread like a **Flame**

1790 WShort in Jefferson *Papers* 17.17: This spread like a flame through Paris. Cf. Whiting F251. See **B373, F133, W159**.

F163 Fire away, **Flannagan**!

1783 Freneau *Poems*(*1786*) 321: It was nothing but Fire away Flannagan! DA fire v. 3(1); *Oxford* 259.

F164 A **Flap** with a fox tail

1676 Williams *Writings* 5.171: Flap me in the mouth with a *Fox Tail*. **1740** Belcher *Papers* 2.354: Don't think I am to be turn'd of with the flap of a fox tail. *Oxford* 266; Tilley F344.

F165 A **Flash** in the pan

1792 Morris *Diary* 2.465: Brémond . . . tells me that their Majesties flash'd in the pan Yesterday Morning. **1798** Dunlap *Diary* 1.227: Milnes left a farce for me to look at called a "Flash in the pan." **1808** HGOtis in Quincy *JQuincy* 165. **1809** Weems *Marion* 22: A mere flash in the pan. Barbour 67(1); NED Flash v.[1] 5c.

F166 To go like a **Flash**

1809 Weems *Marion* 84: Gose away like a flash, **1811** *Letters* 3.39: Books which in *one* place w[d] go off *like a flash,* w[d] in another lie till doom's day on the shelves, **1813** *Drunkard* 72: *I wants, when I go, to go like a flash.* TW 137(3).

F167 To come out **Flat-footed**

1826 JMarable in Jackson *Correspondence* 3.300: It is as much as his Friends can do to keep him from coming out as he says flat footed. NED Flat-footed 2; TW 137.

F168 To give one the **Flats**

1790 Maclay *Journal* 348: It gave my friend Thomas Fitzsimons the flats, for he hardly said a word afterward. DA flat 4.

F169 Keep **Flax** from fire (*varied*)

1736 Franklin *PR* 2.138: Keep flax from fire, youth from gaming. **1786** *Washington Writings* 29.108: Fire, where there is inflamable matter, very rarely stops. *Oxford* 267; Tilley F351; Whiting F182.

F170 Sow **Flax** in the mire, *etc.*

1749 Eliot *Essays* 55: I met with an Old English Rhyming Proverb, Viz. To have great Crops of Flax, and Barley. *Sow Flax in the Mire, Sow Barley in the Fire.*

F171 As close as **Flea** to rug

1801 Story *Shop* 71: With lip to ear, as close as flea to rug. Magdalen King-Hall, *Gay Crusader* (New York, 1934) 328. Cf. TW 138(4). See **B350**.

F172 As nimble as **Fleas**

1831 Cooper *Letters* 2.110: They are as nimble as fleas and about as honest. Svartengren 161.

F173 As snug as a **Flea**

1778 Hopkinson *Miscellaneous Essays* 3 (part 2) 170: Sir William he, snug as a flea. **1809** Weems *Marion* 163-4: As snug as fleas in a sheep skin. TW 138(4). See **B350**.

F174 A **Flea** in one's ear

1773 *Johnson Papers* 13.622: Piernaas sent him off wth a flea in his Ear. **1776** WWhipple in *Naval Documents* 4.631: They will be . . . sent back with a flea in the ear. **1782** Freneau *Poems* 2.117: Cornwallis returns with a flea in his ear. **1784** Franklin *Writings* 9.262: [He] was sent home with a Flea in his Ear. **1788** *Politician* 32. **1793** Freneau *Poems* 3.106. **1798** RTroup in King *Life* 2.466: The Secretary, who dismissed him with a flea in his ear. **1809** Irving *History* 1.98: The adventurous Hudson . . . returned down the river—with a prodigious flea in his ear. **1819** Peirce *Rebelliad* 75: Old Sikes . . . in the Council Hall appears With two great fleas in both his ears. *Oxford* 267-8; Whiting F259.

F175 Hardly enough to drown a **Flea**

1788 May *Journal* 28: We got a little sprinkling — hardly enough to drown a flea, however.

F176 To make a **Flea** an elephant

1652 Williams *Writings* 4.469: [It] usually hath been found, that as in multiplying glasses a *Flea* is made an *Elephant*. *Oxford* 270-1: fly; Tilley F398.

F177 To skin a **Flea** (louse) for its hide and tallow

1803 Davis *Travels* 374: You *New Jersey Men* are close shavers; I believe you would skin a louse. **1819** Faux *Memorable Days* 1.40: Being one of those Yankees . . . who . . . are said to skin a flea for its hide and tallow. Barbour 67(2); *Oxford* 267; TW 138(8). See **F188.**

F178 A **Flea-bite** (-biting)

1644 Williams *Writings* 3.13: We must not let goe for all the flea bitings of the present afflictions. **a1656** Bradford *History* 1.24: Their former afflictions were but as flea-bitings in comparison. **1722** Winslow *Broadside* 115: No more than Flea bites them they minded not. **1775** Washington *Writings* 4.125: One hundred thousand dollars will be but a flea-bite to our demands at this time. **1807** *Port Folio* NS 4.416. **1808** Adams *Writings* 3.240: I still esteem it as no more than the bite of a flea to the bite of a rattlesnake. **1815** Humphreys *Yankey* 56. **1816** UBrown in *MHM* 10(1915) 281: This Mountain . . . is but a mere flea bite to travel over, to the Mountains . . . in Virginia. NED Fleabite, Flea-biting; Whiting F266.

F179 **Flea catchers** are in haste

1734 Ames *Almanacs* 94: The Flea Catchers are in great haste. *Oxford* 580: Nothing; Tilley N251. See **T59.**

F180 To be more for the **Fleece** than the flock

1757 Inhabitants of Gorham in Smith *Journal* 145: He [an unpopular pastor] is more for the fleece than he is for the flock. **1786**

Pemberton *Life* 226-7: The man . . . censuring their ministers for being more concerned for the fleece than for the flock. **1789** *Belknap Papers* 2.125: He shews that he is not "after the fleece, but the flock" (a very favourite expression on such occasions).

F181 A **Flemish** account (voyage)

1756 RDemere in McDowell *Documents* 2.151: I fancy there will be but a Flemish Account given. **1766** JParker in Franklin *Papers* 33.526: He . . . has made a Flemish Voyage as we say: His Behaviour has not been as good abroad as it should have been. **1770** Carter *Diary* 1.495: If I don't mistake my riverside account of Corn will be a flemmish one, **1771** 546: This makes 19 dead and 13 alive out of 32 yeaned — A very flemmish account. **1793** Washington *Writings* 33.147: Unless this is done there will be a flemish account of it when it is wanted for use. **1830** Ames *Mariner's* 211: Rodil . . . took the liberty to shoot a dozen or so daily, so that when the place surrendered, there was but a "Flemish account" of these wooly headed warriors. NED Flemish 3.

F182 All **Flesh** is grass

1643 Williams *Writings* 1.323: *For all flesh is grass.* **1649** *Simplicities Defence* in Force *Tracts* 4.6.116: All flesh is grass. **1653** Keayne *Apologia* 1: All flesh is as grass that must wither and will return to the dust. **1656** Williams *Writings* 6.299. **1658** TEaton in *Winthrop Papers*(B) 2.478. **1676** Williams *Writings* 5.351. **a1700** Hubbard *New England* 281. **1774** *Essex Journal* in Buckingham *Specimens* 1.300: All flesh is hay. **1778** Moore *Diary* 2.92. **1789** Hopkinson *Miscellaneous Essays* 3 (part 2) 201: That flesh is grass, and subject to decay. **1794** Asbury *Journal* 2.10, **1797** *Letters* 3.166. **1811** *Port Folio* 2NS 5.539. **1817** JHewson in *Lincoln Papers* 220: All flesh is as grass, and all the glory of man as the flower of grass, and the grass withereth, and the flower thereof falleth away. **1821** Knight *Poems* 1.165. Whiting F271.

F183 The **Flesh** is weak (frail)

1785 Pemberton *Life* 200: The flesh is weak. **1791** A North Carolina Planter in Boyd

Eighteenth Century Tracts 500: You're but a man! a' flesh is frail. **1801** Asbury *Letters* 3.197: All flesh is frail. *Oxford* 268; Whiting F272. See **S370**.

F184   The **Flesh-pots** of Egypt

1699 College Oration in *W&MCQ* 2S 10(1930) 326: Returne to the . . . Flesh potts of Egypt. **1776** *McIntosh Papers* 24: Some . . . Lust after the old flesh potts. **1782** ERandolph in Madison *Papers* 5.29: In the attempt to corrupt us with the flesh-pots of Egypt. **1783** EPendleton in Madison *Papers* 7.51: Some Gentlemen . . . seem to long for the Flesh Pots of Egypt, particularly some cheese & Porter. **1812** Jefferson *Writings* 18.12-3: The flesh-pots of Egypt could not suddenly be forgotten, even in this new land of Canaan. **1817** Tyler *Prose* 352. **1820** Simpson *Journal* 177: The Flesh Pots of Egypt do sometimes obtrude themselves on my thoughts. **1832** Ames *Nautical* 133. NED Flesh-pot.

F185   As hard as **Flint**

c1700 Taylor *Poems* 437: Methinks my heart is harder than a flint. **1815** CGoddard in *Smith Papers* 5.70: My heart would be harder than a flint. **1815** Jackson *Correspondence* 3.460: Hard as the flint was Jackson's heart. **1819** *Musings* 45: Your hearts are hard, as hard as is the warrior's flint. **1822** Freneau *Last Poems* 110: Divorced from hearts as hard as flint. Barbour 67; *Oxford* 352; Whiting F284.

F186   As hardy as a **Flint**

1780 JA in *Adams FC* 3.305: Your delicate Charles is as hardy as a flynt.

F187   As unfeeling as a **Flint**

1812 Hitchcock *Social* 60: Of hearts unfeeling as a flint.

F188   To skin a **Flint** (*varied*)

1766 JWayles in *VHM* 66(1958) 304: [He is] a skin flint in every sence of the word. **1801** Weems *Letters* 2.191: 'Tis astonishing that a Gentleman . . . sh'd as a skin'd flint be niggardly to me. **1807** *Salmagundi* 201: The fool . . . who, in skinning a flint worth a farthing, spoiled a knife worth fifty times the sum. **1817** Weems *Letters* 3.208: Chiefly

among the skin flint Dutch, I got 12000$ subscrib[d]. **1838** *New England Merchants* 185: This morning the queen sent for on shore to commence trade. Found it like skinning flints. *Oxford* 267; Whiting F286. See **F177**.

F189   To claim the **Flitch** of bacon

1782 EHazard in *Belknap Papers* 1.146: I expect he will claim the flitch of bacon, if the war should end soon enough. **1798** Cary *Letters* 143: They have fully earned the famous *Flitch of Bacon*. *Oxford* 269; Whiting D440.

F190   One **Flock** one shepherd

1696 Sewall *Diary* 1.441: And so revive that joyful Proverb in the world, One flock, one Shepherd.

F191   As old as the **Flood**

1843 Paulding *Letters(II)* 351: Descended from a family as old as the Flood. *Oxford* 588.

F192   As level as a (house) **Floor**

1766 Bartram *Diary* 45: The avenue is as level as a floor from bank to bank. **1768** Coffin *Memoir* 53: A great deal of the road was pitch pine land, like a house floor. **1788** May *Journal* 105: [The land] appeared as level as a floor. **1800** Harmon *Sixteen Years* 36: A plain . . . is as level as a House floor, **1805** 90. **1835** Longfellow *Letters* 1.51: The road is most excellent, Macadamised and as level as a floor. TW 139(2).

F193   As flat as a **Flounder**

1783 Jefferson *Papers* 6.350: The high head is made as flat as a flounder. **c1790** Brackenridge *Gazette* 22: When I fall down as flat's a flounder. **1815** Humphreys *Yankey* 86: I'll knock him down, flat as a flounder! *Oxford* 267; TW 139(1). Cf. Whiting P194.

F194   As blithe as **Flowers** in May

1787 *Columbian Magazine* 1.636 [He was] blythe as flowers in May. See **B219**.

F195   As fresh as **Flowers**

c1770 Paterson *Glimpses* 181: Fresh and gay As flowers in May. **1801** Story *Shop* 126: A damsel . . . fresh as flowers of May. **1801** Weems *Letters* 2.164: My hopes were coming up fresh and fair as the flowers of Spring. *Oxford* 287; Whiting F306.

F196 A fair **Flower** springs out of a dunghill

1807 *Salmagundi* 95: Many a fair flower, however, springs out of a dunghill. Eden Phillpotts, *Tales of the Tenements* (London, 1910) 176: Like a flower on a dung-heap.

F197 The fairest **Flower** fades the soonest

1775 Ward *Correspondence* 102: The fairest Flower sometimes fades the soonest. *Oxford* 270; Tilley F391; Whiting F317.

F198 As light as a **Fly**

1784 Shippen *Journal* 186: My heart has been as light as a fly all day. *Oxford* 463; Whiting F331.

F199 As thick as **Flies**

1780 *New Jersey Gazette* in *Newspaper Extracts(II)* 4.629: Pretend not to see them, tho' thicker than flies. Whiting F332.

F200 The **Fly** and the flame (*varied*)

a1700 Saffin *His Book* 191: So long the foolish Fly, plays with the flame, Till her light wings are Singed with the same. **1778** Adams(S) *Writings* 4.53: Little Insects will be for ever playing about the glimmering Light of a farthing Candle. **1790** Morris *Diary* 2.63: She . . . may perhaps singe her Wings while she flutters round that Flame. **1797** Freneau *Poems* 3.189: To A Night-fly Approaching a Candle. **1805** Taggart *Letters* 168: Two or three butterflies which will always hover around the candle. **1812** Hitchcock *Social* 135: We mongrel bards, who spout and vapour Like *millers* round a burning taper. **1816** Paulding *Letters(I)* 2.233: To catch some little unwary moth that flutters round his expiring taper. *Oxford* 271; Whiting B623.

F201 A **Fly** in the ointment

1642 Winthrop *Journal* 1.66: One dead fly spoils much good ointment. **a1700** Hubbard *New England* 380: There are dead flies in the apothecary's best ointment. **1726** Sewall *Letter-Book* 2.207: I Look upon it as a dead fly in the precious Ointment. **1735** Belcher *Papers* 2.193: I say the god of this world stands ready with 10,000 wicked suggestions to serve as flies in our ointm^t. **1773** Stiles *Diary* 1.341: Except as to that Flie in the Oyntment, the Disposition to exaggerate. **c1800** Dennie *Lay Preacher* 172: Like the dead insect in the ointment, they cause the whole to send forth an odious and putrid savour. **1818** M'Nemar *Kentucky* 27: The truth . . . was like a dead fly in the ointment of the apothecary, to the Calvinists. **1809** Weems *Letters* 2.392: The truth is my Dr Sir, as *"one dead fly will cause the Apothecary's Ointment to stink."* **1811** Rush *Letters* 2.1103: The opposite vice to integrity is like the fly in the pot of ointment. It spoils a host of virtues. **1817** Weems *Letters* 3.175: As to Davies, My dear Sir, why sh^d there be a dead fly in such a pot of Arabian spices! **1822** *Penn* 37: By excess of folly to throw *"dead flies into the apothecary's sweetest ointment."* Barbour 67(1); *Oxford* 270; Tilley F400.

F202 A **Fly** may disturb the sleeping lion

1813 Claiborne *Letter Books* 6.276: A fly you know brother may disturb the sleeping lion. Cf. Whiting F258.

F203 More **Flies** are caught with honey than vinegar (*varied*)

1744 Franklin *PR* 2.396: Tart Words make no Friends: a spoonful of honey will catch more flies than a Gallon of Vinegar. **1800** *Austin Papers* 1.54: A french proverb Says that flys are not Caught with Vinegar. **1812** Jay *Correspondence* 4.361: A Spanish proverb says: "We cannot catch flies with vinegar." **1820** Faux *Memorable Days* 2.108: The experience of ages proves that an ounce of honey is worth a ton of vinegar. **1821** Adams *Writings* 7.171: None of the honey which the profligate proverb says is the true fly-catcher. Barbour 68(3); TW 140(4); Tilley F403; Whiting F335.

F204 Not worth a **Fly**

1708 Taylor *Poems* 234: If not, no Life's in mee that's worth a Fly. *Oxford* 270; Whiting F345.

F205 Not worth a **Fly** wing

1697 Taylor *Poems* 124: Whose best at best as mine's not Worth a Wing Of one poore Fly. Cf. Whiting F355, 356.

F206 As white as **Foam**

a1786 Ladd *Remains* 46: Your souls are whiter than the ocean foam. Whiting F361.

F207 A **Foe** vanquished is a foe no more

1795 Cobbett *Porcupine* 2.63: That maxim in war, "a foe vanquished is a foe no more," ought even to operate with him who calls himself the vanquisher.

F208 Live with your **Foe** that he may be your friend

1777 Smith *Memoirs(II)* 94: If he did recollect it despised the Rule Live with your Foe so that he may one Day be your Friend. *Oxford* 222: Enemy.

F209 To be lost in the **Fog**

1799 *Port Folio* 2NS 7(1812) 339: In the clear atmosphere of America, a lingering messenger is still said to be "lost in the fog." NED Fog *sb.*^{2} 2b. Cf. TW 141(1).

F210 Fat **Folks** can't bear malice

1759 Franklin *Papers* 8.414: You fat folks can't bear malice. 1783 AMacaulay in *W&MCQ* 11(1902) 188: She . . . entertained us with a degree of good nature which is peculiar to Fat people. Tilley F419.

F211 Lazy **Folks** take the most pains (*varied*)

1735 Franklin *Papers* 2.20: But tho' it be true to a Proverb, *That Lazy Folks take the most Pains.* 1792 *Universal Asylum* 8.344: Lazy folks are ever in a hurry. *Oxford* 395; Tilley F420.

F212 Threatened **Folks** live long

1702 Mather *Magnalia* 1.73: The *threatened folks* have *lived so long. Oxford* 815; TW 236(35). Cf. Whiting W49.

F213 Young **Folks** think old folks to be fools, *etc.*

1787 Tyler *Contrast* 113: Young folks think old folks to be fools; but old folks know young folks to be fools. 1807 *Emerald* 2.133: Young folks think old folks are fools, but old folks know young ones to be so. *Proverb. Oxford* 927-8; TW 236(41).

F214 One's **Folly** recoils on his own head

1820 Wright *Views* 221: His folly recoils upon his own head. NED Head 35. See **C377, M191, N51, P182, S281, T222.**

F215 Answer a **Fool** according to his folly

1721 Wise *Friendly Check* in *Colonial Currency* 2.247: *Answer a fool according to his Folly, least he be Wise in his own conceit,* Prov.26. 1737 Talcott *Papers* 2.481: It would not have done to have answered a fool according to his folly. 1763 WSJohnson in Johnson *Writings* 3.265: I do not wish anybody to answer this fool according to his folly. 1806 Adams *D and A* 4.37: I thought it would be as well for once to set a brazen face against a brazen face and answer a fool according to his folly. Whiting F391.

F216 As fat as a **Fool**

1817 Wirt *Letters* 2.23: I am . . . as our friend Pope says, "as fat as a fool." Barbour 68(8); *Oxford* 247; TW 142(2).

F217 As merry as a **Fool**

1786 Ledyard *Russian Journey* 106: And as merry as a fool.

F218 As the **Fool** thinketh, so the bell clinketh

1723 Symmes *Utile* 36: As the Fool thinketh, so the Bell Clinketh. *Oxford* 276; Tilley F445.

F219 Better marry a quiet **Fool** than a witty scold

1762 Ames *Almanacs* 327: Whether it is not better to marry a quiet Fool than a witty Scold. Tilley F494.

F220 A **Fool** always finds a greater fool to admire him

1797 Cobbett *Porcupine* 5.92: His admiration of which is easily accounted for, on the maxim, that "a fool always finds a greater fool to admire him." Lean 4.60. Cf. *Oxford* 275.

F221 A **Fool** and his money are soon parted

1699 Ward *Trip* 39: Which, I think, plainly proves Two old *Adages* true, *viz. That a Fool and his Money is soon parted.* 1772 Ames *Almanacs* 440: The proverb ought to run "a fool and his words are soon parted, a man of genius and his money." 1789 Brown *Better* 40: This excellent axiom. 1791 S.P.L.

Thoughts 77. **1792** Pope *Tour* 10: I began like *Strap* to moralize, with only this Difference, he said "A Fool and his Money is soon parted:" I used the word Horse instead of Money. **1819** Noah *Travels* 260. **1834** Floy *Diary* 88: He is to pay $8. "A fool and his money &c." Barbour 68(1); *Oxford* 273; Tilley F452.

F222 A **Fool** can ask more questions, *etc.*
1690 *Further Quaeries* in *Andros Tracts* 1.195: There be a truth in the Proverb, That a Fool may ask more than a Philosopher can answer. **1787** *American Museum* 2.44: I have often heard it said, that *"a fool may start a question, which a wise man cannot answer."* **1793** EHazard in *Belknap Papers* 2.323: A fool can ask more questions in a day than a wise man can answer in a month. *Oxford* 274; TW 142(7).

F223 A **Fool** is known by his much laughing
1787 *Columbian Magazine* 1.551: A fool is known by his much laughing. Whiting F400.

F224 A **Fool** may speak the truth
1773 Asbury *Letters* 3.16: A fool may speak the truth sometimes. *Oxford* 274-5; Tilley F449. See **C157.**

F225 A **Fool** never makes a good husband
1807 Weems *Murder* 26: In no instance . . . was ever more completely verified the old saying—"*A fool never makes a good husband!*"

F226 A **Fool's** bolt (is soon shot)
1676 Williams *Writings* 5.136: And their *Fools Bolt shot.* **1784** Curwen *Journal* 2.993: Received . . . from my free speaking Landlady a fools bolt. *Oxford* 276; Whiting F408. See **B250.**

F227 A **Fool's** paradise
a1656 Bradford *History* 1.382: Which brought others as well as them selves into a fools paradise. **1676** Williams *Writings* 5.368: The Quakers and their fools Paradise. **1683** Randolph *Letters* 6.139: Into what a fooles paradise I am betrayed, **1686** 190. **1759** Ames *Almanacs* 295: Now many Castles in the Air are built, whose Makers go

to Fools Paradise, described by Milton. **1787** *American Museum* 1.157. **1811** Adams *Writings* 4.245: I suppose it is in the paradise of fools, **1814** 5.26: The Empire of Napoleon is in the Paradise of Fools, **1816** 544: One would imagine that the American legation at London was the moon of Ariosto, or Milton's Paradise of Fools. *Oxford* 277; Whiting F411.

F228 **Fools** are the tools of knaves
1789 Maclay *Journal* 84: Although it is a common observation that fools are the tools of knaves. Cf. Tilley K144.

F229 **Fools** build and wise men purchase
1820 Faux *Memorable Days* 2.120: There is an old adage, that "fools build, and wise men purchase." **1860** PCameron in *Ruffin Papers* 3.68: Fools build houses, etc. Barbour 68(9); *Oxford* 278; Tilley F553.

F230 **Fools** can gain wealth
1804 *Monthly Anthology* 1.196: According to the Spanish proverb, fools can gain wealth.

F231 (**Fools**) live poor to die rich
a1700 Saffin *His Book* 98: His desire is to live poor, to Dye Rich. *Oxford* 278; Tilley F539.

F232 **Fools** make feasts and wise men eat them
1733 Franklin *PR* 1.314: Fools make feasts and wise men eat 'em, **1745** 3.8, **1758** *WW* 345. **1758** Ames *Almanacs* 284: Some Fools make Feasts, for wise Men to eat, **1770** 413. **1784** Franklin *Writings* 9.243: The first part of the Proverb is thereby verified, that *Fools make Feasts.* I wish in this Case the other were as true, *and wise Men eat them.* *Oxford* 278; Tilley F540.

F233 **Fools** rush in where angels fear to tread (enter)
1789 Iredell *Correspondence* 2.277: Rash presumption illustrates the line, "Fools rush in where angels fear to tread." **1819** Brackenridge *South America* 2.236: An era contemptible, perhaps, in the eyes of the impatient visionary, who in the language of Burke, "rushes in where angels fear to en-

ter." Barbour 68(12); Pope *Essay on Criticism* iii 66.

F234 Fools should never meddle with edge-tools

1788 DHumphreys in *American Museum* 3.279: Yet fools Should never meddle with edge-tools. *Oxford* 120; Tilley J45. See **C147**.

F235 Fools speak and show their want of wit

1750 Sherman *Almanacs* 253: Fools often speak and shew their want of wit. Cf. Whiting F401, 441. See **H160**.

F236 Fools will be meddling

a**1814** Dow *Journal* 406: But fools *will be meddling. Oxford* 279; Tilley F546. Cf. Whiting F397.

F237 Fools will have their way, *etc.*

c**1800** Tyler *Island* 11: Fools will have their way & wise men let them. Cf. Whiting F443. See **W292**.

F238 Fortunate **Fools** have no need of wisdom

1769 JParker in Franklin *Papers* 16.75: They are Scots Lads: and if they be *fortunate Fools,* they will have no Need of Wisdom. Hislop 97; Tilley F536. Cf. *Oxford* 312; Whiting G236.

F239 He has a **Fool** for his master who teaches himself

1741 Franklin *PR* 2.292: He that teaches himself, hath a fool for his master. *Oxford* 806; Tilley F490.

F240 He is a **Fool** that makes his doctor his heir

1733 Franklin *PR* 1.312: He's a Fool that makes his Doctor his Heir. *Oxford* 276; Tilley F483; Whiting H326.

F241 He is a **Fool** who undresses before he is going to bed

1733 Franklin *PR* 1.316: The old Man has given all to his Son: O fool! to undress thy self before thou art going to bed. *Oxford* 656; Tilley D570. Cf. Whiting B182.

F242 He that has neither **Fools,** *etc.*

1736 Franklin *PR* 2.138: He that has neither

fools, whores nor beggars among his kindred, is the son of a thunder gust, **1747** 3.102: 'Tis a strange Forest that has no rotten Wood in't And a strange Kindred that all are good in't. *Oxford* 278; Tilley F557, cf. F49.

F243 It is hard to deal with a **Fool**

1811 Burroughs *Memoirs* 157: I found the old adage, "It is hard to deal with a fool," most sensibly verified. Cf. *Oxford* 275; Tilley F486; Whiting F425.

F244 On a **Fool's** errand

1776 *Blockheads* 17: Who can help laughing at what a *tom fool's* errand we have been sent on. **1776** MOgden in Burr *Memoirs* 1.95: Winds is sent home on a fool's errand. **1778** Gordon *Letters* 400. **1804** Irving *Corrector* 90. **1808** Barker *Tears* 152. **1814** JSBayard in McHenry *Letters* 613. NED Errand 2c; Whiting F410.

F245 One **Fool** makes many

1791 S.P.L. *Thoughts* 77: One Fool makes many. **1827** Watterston *Wanderer* 122: One fool makes many, is an old adage. *Oxford* 274; TW 142(9).

F246 Playing the **Fool** at times is a pleasure

1788 Adams *Diary* 401: But there is a pleasure in playing the fool at times. *Oxford* 569; Whiting M350.

F247 To bray a **Fool** in a mortar

1806 *Weekly* 1.76: The old proverb which speaks of braying a fool in a mortar. **1863** FRuffin in *Ruffin Papers* 3.348: Bray a fool in a mortar, says Solomon, and he will be a fool still. Whiting F454.

F248 To play the **Fool**

1702 Taylor *Christographia* 131.90-1: Such as neglect Christ play the Foole, 213.62-3: Davids feare made him play the foole. **1786** McGillivray *Letters* 125: It was to play the fool. NED Fool *sb.*[1] 2b.

F249 Better slip with **Foot** than tongue

1734 Franklin *PR* 1.352: Better slip with foot than tongue. *Oxford* 55-6; Tilley F575.

F250 The cloven **Foot** appears (*varied*)

1654 Johnson *Wonder-Working* 203: The

162

divel shewed his horns in that book. **1763** Laurens *Papers* 3.350: Must not every Officer . . . see the cloven foot. **1765** Watts *Letter Book* 402: His Successors . . . discover'd the Cloven Foot. **1766** Mason *Papers* 1.68: The Cloven foot has been too plainly seen to be again concealed. **1768** Franklin *Papers* 15.243. **1768** JJohnson in *Wheelock's Indians* 133: The Indians . . . have let too much of their Cloven foot appear. **1774** Seabury *Letters* 145: Now the mask is off: now the cloven foot is thrust out into open light. **1775** Lee(W) *Letters* 1.142, **1778** 2.456: Every step they take leaves a visible mark of the cloven foot. **1783** CColden in *Clinton Papers* 8.222: Times that has given opertunity . . . to those who had a Cloven foot to Put it forward. **1783** BHarrison in Madison *Papers* 6.11: A certain preamble will point out the cloven footed monster. **1785** *Massachusetts Centinel* in Buckingham *Specimens* 2.33. **1796** Cabot *Letters* 111: If the devil is in company, it is always best to see his cloven foot. **1801** Hamilton *Works* 10.423: His old party . . . have shown the cloven foot of *rank Jacobinism.* **1806** WChipman in *Winslow Papers* 556: You shall not be known except by the "cloven foot," which I suspect will always betray you in whatever you write. **1807** *Weekly* 2.140. **1809** Weems *Washington* 62: Government had shown the cloven hoof. **1844** Jackson *Correspondence* 6.258, **1845** 367. *Oxford* 129, 182; Tilley D252. Cf. Whiting H454.

F251 His **Foot** is too big for his shoe

1652 Shepard *Hints* 159: The Elder's foot is now too big for his shoe. Cf. TW 42: Breeches(1).

F252 To have one's **Foot** in the fire

1809 Bates *Papers* 2.58: He has his foot in the fire. Cf. Whiting F476.

F253 To have one **Foot** in the grave

1759 Smith *Life and Correspondence* 1.224: A poor old servant of the Church, who had already one foot in the grave. **1764** *Paxton Papers* 260: Time in this World is but short, you have one foot in the Grave and the other almost in. **1775** Carter *Diary* 2.938. **1775** JEliot in *Belknap Papers* 3.86: We esteem

her to be an old woman with one leg in the grave. **1779** Adams(S) *Writings* 4.132: He has his foot on the Grave & with Pleasure views it. **1790** Morris *Diary* 1.428: *Quere* whether the Proverb of one Foot in the Grave be not of flemish Extraction. **1794** JDayton in Callender *Political Register* 1.121. **1796** Barton *Disappointment* 93: I . . . have one foot in the grave and the other scarcely out. **1798** Pickering *Review* 161. **1802** Chester *Federalism* ii. **1809** Fessenden *Pills* 2: Dame Columbia . . . Has one foot fairly in her grave. **1809** Weems *Marion* 3. **1819** Jefferson *Writings* 15.221, **1821** 342, **1825** 16.119: With one foot in the grave, and the other uplifted to follow it. Barbour 69(4); *Oxford* 596; Whiting F474. See **B329, G25.**

F254 To occupy six **Feet** of earth

1802 Paine *To the Citizens* 2.922: [He] left me to occupy six foot of earth in France. *Oxford* 738; Whiting F472.

F255 To pull **Foot**

1775 Bowen *Journals* 2.468: The cruisers all pulled foot and harbored. TW 143(4).

F256 To put one's **Foot** in it

1790 Maclay *Journal* 235: No man ever had a more complete knack of putting his foot in a business than this same Elsworth. **1817** in Buckingham *Specimens* 2.97: One-who-puts-his-foot-in-it. Barbour 69(6); TW 143(6).

F257 To put the best **Foot** (leg) foremost

1744 Stephens *Journal(II)* 2.56: Mr. Parker put the best leg foremost after his Sickness. **1770** Hearne *Journey* 111: The only effect it had on them, that of making them put the best foot foremost. **1787** Baldwin *Life and Letters* 259-60. **1789** Jefferson *Papers* 14.662: They will naturally set the best foot foremost. **1804** Dow *Journal* 209: I have seen some men and women in courtship put the best foot foremost, and the best side out. **1809** Irving *History* 1.180: leg. **1811** *Port Folio* 2NS 5.3: I ought to put my best foot foremost, according to the vulgar apophthegm. **1817** Weems *Letters* 3.204. **1837** Paulding *Letters(II)* 194. **1843** Cooper *Let-*

Foot

ters 4.349. *Oxford* 47; TW 143(5); Whiting L191. See **S197**.

F258 To put the wrong Foot foremost
1808 Asbury *Journal* 2.576: Put the wrong foot foremost. **1822** Randolph(J) *Letters* 246: Mr Speaker B. . . . set off wrong foot foremost. See **L102**.

F259 To stand on one's own Feet
1791 TJefferson in Adams *Works* 8.510: Paine's pamphlet stood on its own feet. Whiting F481.

F260 To be a Football (varied)
1702 Mather *Magnalia* 2.462: She would . . . be tost about the house like a foot ball. **1774** WAntill in Smith *Life and Correspondence* 1.499: But let Philosophy, let the Love of Mankind soar above these foot-balls of Fortune. **1782** Adams *Works* 8.9: America . . . has been a football between contending nations. **1786** Ledyard *Russian Journey* 94: My last letters . . . left me in the Metropolis of France, the verry football of chance. **1797** Cobbett *Porcupine* 6.55: A mere football to be kicked about at the pleasure of every petty European tyrant. **1810** Adams *Writings* 3.449: We are made the common football of Europe. **1814** *Port Folio* 3NS 4.586: It is a play thing, a foot ball, kicked from street to street. **a1824** Marshall *Kentucky* 2.263: [The state constitution] would have been the thing its enemies wanted it to be, a football for state demagogues to kick about at pleasure. **1845** Paulding *Letters(II)* 398: Resist *influence* — or you will be a mere Foot-Ball in the hands of Politicians and Congressmen. NED Football 3; TW 143(3). See **H134**.

F261 To bounce like a Football
1808 M'Nemar *Kentucky* 61: He must . . . bounce from place to place like a foot-ball. Cf. TW 143(2).

F262 To play at Football
1794 Cobbett *Porcupine* 1.148: Was it well done, Gentlemen, first to play at football with a poor pamphlet. **1816** Paulding *Letters(I)* 2.143: Those laborious idlers, who play at football with worlds.

F263 Force shits upon reason's back
1736 Franklin *PR* 2.141: Force shites upon Reason's Back.

F264 To repel Force with force (varied)
1612 Strachey *Historie* 26: To drawe our swordes, *et vim vi repellere*. **1754** JGlen in McDowell *Documents* 1.525: We are to repel [Force] with Force, this is the Language of the Law of Nations, it is the Voice of Nature. **1762** GLeHunte in *Colden Letters* 6.164: And that he would Repel Force by Force. **1770** Carter *Diary* 1.398: He would have had a right to resist force by force. **1772** Andrews *Letters* 325, **1774** 347. **1774** Boucher *View* 395: To oppose force to force. **1775** WLee in *Naval Documents* 1.472: Force . . . should meet with Force. **1775** Gibbes 2.109. **1798** Hamilton *Works* 10.281-2. **1812** BWhiteman in Knopf *War of 1812* 2.10. Whiting F491.

F265 Forewarned, forearmed
1685 FHooke in Belknap *History* 1.347: The old proverb is, forewarned forearmed. **1736** Franklin *PR* 2.141: Forewarn'd, forearm'd, unless in the case of Cuckolds, who are often forearm'd before warn'd. **1778** *Washington *Writings* 10.265: To forewarn, and consequently forearm me, against a secret enemy. **1780** JThaxter in *Adams FC* 3.413: It forewarns and if well read it forearms. **1784** Reed *Life* 2.414. **1787** *Anarchiad* 120: Fourwarned! fourarmed! **1788** Washington *Writings* 30.21, 96: Preparation should be the sure attendant upon forewarning. **1797** Cobbett *Porcupine* 6.241. **a1804** Humphreys *Works* 88. **1819** Pintard *Letters* 1.218. *Oxford* 280; Whiting W49.

F266 Forgive and forget [The following is a selection from 70 occurrences of the phrase]
1653 Keayne *Apologia* 63: It is a question whether a Christian be bound or that God requires it at their hands fully to forgive and finally forget all sinful unkindnesses. **1702** Mather *Magnalia* 1.55: The Indians would never *forget* or *forgive* this injury. **1705** Beverley *History* 226: The *Indians* never forget nor forgive an Injury. **1707** Makemie *Writings* 196: The Jersey Piper, called Forget and Forgive. **1752** Parkman *Diary* 75.131: He

164

asked whether we should not strive to forget as well as forgive. **1761** *Johnson Papers* 10.317: [Indians] never forget, nor forgive. **1767** GCroghan in Franklin *Papers* 14.271: [Indians] never forget and seldom forgive. **1773** Quincy *Memoir* 81: May Heaven forgive, but *the people* never forget them. **1774** Adams *Legal Papers* 1.137: No man . . . can ever forget such an Indignity, tho he may forgive it. **1787** Jefferson *Papers* 11.90: Forget and forgive my errors. **1788** Washington *Writings* 30.20. **1801** McHenry *Letters* 499: To forget and forgive . . . is a Christian duty. **1813** Jefferson *Writings* 14.27. **1822** Watterston *Winter* 110: The scriptures enjoineth us to forget and forgive. **1823** Jackson *Correspondence* 3.208: Therefore believing this . . . *I have forgive, I cannot forget,* **1844** 6.275. Barbour 69(3); *Oxford* 281; Whiting F497.

F267 A **Fortress** (and a maidenhead) which parleys will surrender

1734 Franklin *PR* 1.354: Neither a Fortress nor a Maidenhead will hold out long after they begin to parly. **1763** JAplin in Bailyn *Pamphlets* 1.275: A fortress that can be brought to a parley will surrender. *Oxford* 124; Whiting C71.

F268 **Fortunatus's** wishing cap

1787 Jefferson *Papers* 12.23: Fortunatus's wishing cap was always the object of my desire. Cf. *Oxford* 281.

F269 **Fortune** and her wheel (*varied*)

a**1700** Hubbard *New England* 379: The affairs of the world are carried in a moveable wheel, wherein it is oft found that what is highest in one season is laid quite underneath soon after. **1701** INorris in *Penn-Logan Correspondence* 1.44: Till all things now on the wheel are settled here to his peace and comfort. **1742** Stephens *Journal(II)* 1.54: And that he thought the Wheel was turning, by wch. he might again rise into Power. **1748** Franklin *Papers* 3.330: For Fortune's Wheel is often turning. **1750** Sherman *Almanacs* 250: At will, while fortune turns the wheel, That life's a lott'ry mankind feel. **1765** JParker in Franklin *Papers* 12.112: I shall wear them sometimes for the

Sake of contemplating on the changes of Fortune's Wheel. **1767** WSJohnson in *Trumbull Papers* 1.241-2: Who will rise or fall in this (if I may be allowed the expression) rapid whirl of fortune's wheel. **1769** Davis *Colonial Virginia Satirist* 55: By falling from the top of fortune's wheel. **1775** Paine *Farmer Short* 2.1086: But fortune, whose perpetual wheel Grinds disappointment sharp as steel. **1776** Fithian *Journal* 159: He is on the lowest part of Fortune's Wheel. **1780** ANash in Jefferson *Papers* 3.463: They are putting their last stake in the wheel of fortune. **1780** MWarren in Massachusetts Historical Society *Proceedings* 65(1932-36) 237: The wheel of politics as well as the wheel of fortune moves rapidly. **1781** Hamilton *Papers* 2.594: The wheel of fortune will have too much part in determining. **1781** JThaxter in *Adams FC* 4.199: I am not too envious to wish any one success in this Wheel of Fortune. **1782** Trumbull *Satiric Poems* 181: Dame Fortune's wheel has turned so short, It plung'd us fairly in the dirt. **1790** AGerry in *Warren-Gerry Correspondence* 243: Our second trial in the wheel of fortune [a lottery ticket]. **1792** Adams *New Letters* 84: Such is the wheel of fortune. **1794** Rowson *Charlotte* 2.84: Why do we see fools and knaves at the very top of the wheel, while patient merit sinks to the extreme of the opposite abyss? **1797** Cobbett *Porcupine* 5.9: You will preserve your hatred and I my contempt, till fortune gives her wheel another turn. **1798** *Codman Letters* 79: The wheel of fortune is going round, and the next turn may produce better, but as likely as perhaps more so, *a total loss.* **1806** Fessenden *Modern Philosopher* 2: Although Dame Fortuna was by ancient mythologists, represented as a whimsical being, cutting her capers on the periphery of a large wheel, I am justified in accomodating her goddeship with a ladder, by virtue of . . . *Poetica Licentia.* **1806** *Weekly* 1.113: 'Till fortune's wheel presents a prize. **1807** Janson *Stranger* 161: Such is sometimes the turn of the wheel of fortune. **1808** CJPeters in *Winslow Papers* 609: The happy turn in the wheel of fortune. **1814** Wirt *Bachelor* 116: Are we alone . . . exempt from the revolution of Fortune's wheel? **1817** Scott *Blue*

Lights 45: These watch the turn of fortune's wheel. **1820** Tudor *Letters* 337: He has suddenly risen on the wheel of fortune. **1822** Freneau *Last Poems* 63: To build your hopes on *Fortune's wheel* Is folly in the extreme. *Oxford* 282; Whiting F506.

F270 Fortune attends the unrighteous

1804 WBainbridge in *Barbary Wars* 3.410: It appears in this climate that fortune attends the *u*[*n*]*righteous*. Cf. *Oxford* 281-2; Tilley F600.

F271 Fortune favors the bold (*varied*)

1677 Hubbard *Indian* 1.234: *Audaces fortuna juvat.* **1748** JAyscough in *Colden Letters* 4.84: Three old Proverbs, on this occasion occur to my Memory (viz) . . . Fortune assists the bold. **1752** *Johnson Papers* 9.86: Fortune will favour the Brave. **1769** Davis *Colonial Virginia Satirist* 64: Fortune, quæ semper javet fatuis, also exerts herself in their behalf. **1775** BArnold in *Naval Documents* 2.1078-9: Fortune has so far been favourable & is generally so to the brave. **1776** Mackenzie *Diary* 1.85: Fortune however favoured the bold. **1789** JWarren in *Warren-Gerry Correspondence* 236: Let us . . . beleive . . . that Fortune with all her Caprices will favour the Resolute. **1815** Freneau *Poems(1815)* 1.46: The motto is, in latin words, "Dame Fortune helps the bold."* *Fortuna fortibus favet. **1816** Pintard *Letters* 1.24: Fortune favors the enterprising. *Oxford* 282; Whiting F519.

F272 Fortune is blind

1777 Izard *Correspondence* 325: A few more such instances of her [Fortune's] discernment will convince me that she is not so blind, as some folks would make us believe; and I think there are some grounds to suspect, without doing her any great injustice, that the old English proverb may be applied to her. [There is an omission here, so that the proverb is missing.] **1794** Rowson *Charlotte* 2.84: Fortune is blind. **1807** *Port Folio* NS 4.92: Fortune, they say, is blind. *Oxford* 282; Whiting F521.

F273 Fortune is fickle (*varied*)

1650 Bradstreet *Works* 210: Now up and down, as fortune turns her hand. **1749** Franklin *PR* 3.350: And Fortune is as fickle as she's fair. **1759** Adams *D and A* 1.111: Fortune is a capricious Goddess. She diverts herself with Men. **1760** RStewart in *Letters to Washington* 3.197: But as I hitherto have been no Favorite of Fortune's I did not think it prudent to trust to any of her superficial smiles. **1764** *Beekman Papers* 1.466: Curse the old Whore Mother fortune bestowing her daughter on me in my Old Days. [He is referring to ill luck in trade.] **1764** JWatts in *Aspinwall Papers* 2.519: Barre I find has fallen as fast as he rose. Dame Fortune is sometimes very capricious, still we woo her. **1778** ECornell in Sullivan *Letters* 2.258: I have ever known her to be fickle, NGreene 404: Fortune is a fickle Jade and often gives us a tumble when we least expect it. **1779** Curwen *Journal* 2.580-1: Fortune having for some months since almost invariable denyed me the pleasing smile, but his Deityship is to a proverb Capricious, and that is my solace. **1780** JAdams in *Adams-Warren Letters* 2.131: Fortune . . . is a great changeling, and frowns upon one, sometimes in half an hour after having lavished upon him her Smiles and Favors. **1782** NGreene in Reed *Life* 2.387: Fortune has many capricious turns—we often think she is most bountiful where there is least merit, but her Ladyship will do as she pleases. **1790** JHarmar in Denny *Journal* 541: Miss-*Fortune*, the slippery jade. **1800** Bentley *Diary* 2.349: How capricious is fortune, says the world. **1800** Eaton *Life* 179: Fortune began to play into my hands, and the fickle Goddess has almost persuaded me that she will not immediately change sides. **1814** Palmer *Diary* 20: Fortune is a slipery jade. *Oxford* 282; Whiting F523.

F274 Fortune knocks once at every man's door

1809 *Port Folio* 2NS 2.431: Fortune knocks once, at least, at every man's door. *Oxford* 282; Tilley F608.

F275 Fortune may fail us, *etc.*

1776 Heath *Memoirs* 36: It is a military axion, that "fortune may fail us, but a prudent conduct never will."

F276 The **Fortune** of the sea
1720 Byrd *London Diary* 367: However, it is the fortune of the sea. Cf. NED Fortune 1d. See **W25.**

F277 More by **Fortune** than forecast
1728 Byrd *Dividing Line* 148: [He] did at length, more by Fortune than forecast, hire a clumsy Vehicle. 1812 Bayard *Papers* 199: In the affairs of this world good fortune has more for men than good sense. Cf. Whiting H101, 104, 106. See **L255.**

F278 One's best or worst **Fortune** is a wife
1816 Freneau *Last Poems* 5: A man's best fortune or his worst's a wife, A steady friendship, or continual strife. *Oxford* 48; Whiting F539, T105. See **H75, W148.**

F279 As cunning as a **Fox**
1756 Washington *Writings* 1.305: Their cunning is only to be equalled by that of the Fox. 1764 *Paxton Papers* 169: For he was as cunning as a fox. 1776 SAdams in *Warren-Adams Letters* 1.199: The Cunning of the fox. Barbour 70(3); TW 145(2).

F280 As sly as a **Fox**
1836 Floy *Diary* 224: And accordingly walked as sly as a fox to try and espy her in the room. Barbour 70(7); Whiting F590.

F281 As subtle as **Foxes**
1676 Williams *Writings* 5.450: They be as subtle as *Foxes*.

F282 The **Fox** is the finder
1774 Carter *Diary* 2.838: I am mistaken in that fellow Northern, if the fox has not been the finder. Barbour 70(8); *Oxford* 284; Tilley F634a.

F283 The **Fox** that has lost his tail, *etc.*
1789 PButler in Iredell *Correspondence* 2.264: Perhaps I am something like the fox in the fable, having lost my own tail, I wish North Carolina to do likewise. *Oxford* 285; Tilley F646.

F284 Many **Foxes** grow grey, but few grow good
1749 Franklin *PR* 3.337: Many Foxes grow grey, but few grow good. *Oxford* 284-5; Tilley F638. Cf. Whiting F596.

F285 The sleeping **Fox** catches no poultry
1743 Franklin *PR* 2.371: The sleeping Fox catches no poultry. Up! Up! 1758 WW 341. 1770 Ames *Almanacs* 412. Barbour 70(1); *Oxford* 742; Tilley F649; Whiting *NC* 411(9). See **C73.**

F286 To put on the **Fox's** skin
1638 THooker in *Winthrop Papers(A)* 4.75: To do mischief this way . . . somtyme he putts on the foxes skynn as the proverb is. *Oxford* 467-8; Tilley L319.

F287 When **Foxes** meet there is destruction among the fowls
1818 Adams *Memoirs* 4.163: He said there was an Italian proverb that when the foxes meet there was sure to be destruction among the fowls.

F288 To be out of **Frame**
1701 RLivingston in *Winthrop Papers(B)* 5.67: Our governm^t here being much out of frame. Whiting F607. See **S391.**

F289 He that lives by **Fraud** is in danger of dying a knave
1748 Ames *Almanacs* 212: He that lives by Fraud is in Danger of dying a Knave. Cf. *Oxford* 292, 476; Tilley F770, L392; Whiting F611.

F290 The more **Free** the more welcome
1788 *Politicians* 7: You may make free and welcome, for the more free the more welcome, as the old saying is.

F291 Better die **Freemen** than live slaves
1775 Willard *Letters* 101: Better to be buried freemen, than live to be slaves. 1776 WBingham in *Deane Brothers Papers* 28: Better die the last of Freemen, than bear to live the first of Slaves. 1778 Case *Poems* 5: I'll die a freeman, e'er I'll live a slave. Cf. Whiting D239. See **D73, L111.**

F292 A **French** compliment
a1700 Hubbard *New England* 494: But that was but a French compliment.

F293 **French** gold has conquered more than their swords
1751 RBunning in McDowell *Documents* 1.149: It has often been a Proverb that the

French Gold has conquered more than their swords. Cf. Whiting G296.

F294 To take French leave

1767 *Norton Papers* 25: Yo. took a French leave. **1775** Eddis *Letters* 122: Many of our friends have found it expedient to take a French leave. **1778** *Wyllys Papers* 463: Our Allies have shewed us a French trick — left us, when we most needed their assistance. **1780** JLaurens in Sparks *Correspondence* 2.403: Taken French leave. **1783** *American Wanderer* 118, 229. **1783** JWarren in *Warren-Gerry Correspondence* 165: You have really in the true Modern Stile taken a French Leave of us. **1784** Baldwin *Life and Letters* 216. **1784** EWinslow in *Winslow Papers* 228. **1786** *Belknap Papers* 1.423. **1786** McGillivray *Letters* 125. **1787** TBlount in *Blount Papers* 1.317: Rucker . . . took French leave, as the saying is. **1792** Dennie *Letters* 97. **1796** Cobbett *Porcupine* 4.26, 48. **1797** Paine *Works* 180: 'Till the dim taper takes French leave to doze. **1801** Bowne *Letters* 76: My candle . . . took French leave to doze, **1806** 214. **1806** Plumer *Memorandum* 390-1: You have a saying that applies to leaving company without ceremony, that you call "French leave." **1807** Irving(P) *Journals* 53. **1808** JAdams in *Adams-Cunningham Letters* 36. **1810** RPeters in Jay *Correspondence* 4.339: This will . . . produce my French-leave of all sublunary things. **1810** *Port Folio* 2NS 3.318. **1813** Bayard *Papers* 485. **1813** *Beauties of Brother Bull-us* 85: In Paris, they call this taking French leave. **1813** Paulding *Lay* 70. **1816** Pintard *Letters* 1.27: Doctor Carmichael took a French and unexpected leave of us last Saturday. **1818** Baldwin *Letters* 276: I took a kind of French leave. **1818** *Cary Letters* 269. **1824** *Tales* 2.134. **1826** Duane *Columbia* 588. *Oxford* 287; TW 146.

F295 A Frenchman will be a Frenchman

1798 *Politicians* 17: [It] is only fulfilling the old saying, that a Frenchman will be a Frenchman all over the world, and all the days of his life.

F296 Friday is an unlucky day

1782 TShaw in Shaw *Letter Book* 329: Friday (always called an unlucky day). **1819** Cobbett *Year's* 133: All the foolish country sayings about *Friday* being an *unlucky day* to begin anything fresh upon. Tilley F679.

F297 A Friend in need is a friend indeed (*varied*)

1640 EWinslow in *Winthrop Papers(A)* 4.193: But alas however a Friend loves at all times, now is the time of tryall. **1739** Belcher *Papers* 2.228: I remember my m^r wrote me for a copy that trite saying, *A friend in need is a friend indeed.* **1740** Stephens *Journal(I)* 1.497: What Sort of Behaviour then he must have shewn among them, not to find one Friend in this Time of Need, who would appear to give him kind Assistance. **1754** Parkman *Diary* 76.139: The Friend at a Pinch, Lieutenant Tainter brought a Load of Wood. **1763** *Johnson Papers* 10.954. **1770** Munford *Candidates* 34: as the proverb says. **1771** *Johnson Papers* 12.883: As nothing can afford me more real pleasure than Serving my freind in time of Need. **1776** Margaret Morris, *Her Journal,* ed. John W. Jackson (Philadelphia, 1949) 52. **1777** Deane *Papers* 5.555: One of our proverbs says. **1779** Gadsden *Writings* 163. **1780** Sargent *Loyalist* 113: A friend like this, in time of need. **1782** RHopkins in *MHM* 23(1928) 297: I have oft heard. **1788** *Politician* 7: A friend indeed is a friend in need, as the saying is. **1789** *Columbian Magazine* 3.182. **1792** Pope *Tour* 85: Young Washington a former Friend in Need. **1798** Murdock *Politicians* 9: The old saying. **1799** Asbury *Journal* 2.213. **1815** Adams *Writings* 5.419: The navy proved itself the friend in need. **1815** Palmer *Diary* 137, 146. **1830** Jackson *Correspondence* 4.208, 212. Barbour 71(1); *Oxford* 289; Whiting F634.

F298 A Friend nearby is better than a brother far off

1682 ERawson in *Hinckley Papers* 63-4: A friend, Solomon saith, is nearer than a brother. **1686** Dunton *Letters* 91: For (says he) *There is a Friend that is nearer than a Brother.* **1771** Winslow *Diary* 11: My old friend, who being *near by* is better than a brother far off. **1781** WHeath in *Clinton Papers* 7.623: It is natural in times of distress, to call on those nearest to us. Happy when we can find a friend. Such, you are sensible the wise man tells us, is better than a brother far off. **1812** Colby *Life* 1.153: But found that I had a friend that sticketh closer than a brother. See **B337, N44.**

F299 **Friends** must part

1640 EHowes in *Winthrop Papers*(*A*) 4.242: Friends must sometymes parte, that they may againe renew theire frindshipp. **1685** Dunton *Letters* 10: But dearest friends must part. **1775** *Jacksons and Lees* 1.300. **1784** Smyth *Tour* 1.285: Sooner or later, all, even the dearest of friends, must part. *Oxford* 290; TW 146(4); Whiting F639.

F300 He is my **Friend** that grinds at my mill

1800 Weems *Letters* 2.144: My little hopper drops not a grain but into your grinder. **1809** *Port Folio* 2NS 2.429: He is my friend that grinds at my mill. *Oxford* 289; Tilley F705.

F301 I'll pledge my **Friends,** *etc.*

1652 Joshua Coffin, *Sketch of the History of Newbury, Newburyport, etc.* (Boston, 1845) 55: I'll pledge my friends, And for my foes, A plague for their heels, And a poxe for their toes. [The user of this rhyme was fined for swearing in Salem Court, despite his claim that it was "the proverb used in the west country."]

F302 Kiss and be **Friends**

1775 Franklin *Writings* 6.326: They should kiss and be Friends. **1782** Pickering *Life* 1.355: They had now kissed and made up. **1789** Boucher *Autobiography* 81: We never in our lives went to sleep without kissing and being friends. **1815** Humphreys *Yankey* 63: Let us buss and be friends. **1827** Watterston *Wanderer* 107: Come ge's a kiss, and mak friens. *Oxford* 429; Tilley W649.

F303 An old **Friend** is better than a new one

1766 JParker in Franklin *Papers* 13.535: Knowing that an Old Friend was better than a new One. Whiting F650, 668. See **S166, W295, 322.**

F304 There are three faithful **Friends,** *etc.*

1738 Franklin *PR* 2.192: There are three faithful friends, an old wife, an old dog, and ready money. **1758** Ames *Almanacs* 283: There are three faithful Friends: an old Wife, an old Dog, and ready Cash.

F305 To have a **Friend** at court

1702 Mather *Magnalia* 1.261: If at any time he should want a *friend* at court, they would improve all their interest for him. **1809** Weems *Marion* 85: It was *good to have a friend at court.* a**1811** Henry *Account* 77: Now our mess had "friends at court." **1812** WThornton in *Steele Papers* 2.675: I really think a Friend *at Court* Is but a kind of Friend *in sport. Oxford* 289; TW 146(11); Whiting F633.

F306 To lose a **Friend** rather than a joke

1773 Ames *Almanacs* 443: Some people will lose their best Friend rather than miss cracking a Joke — yet cannot bear one themselves. *Oxford* 54; Tilley F708, J40. See **W248.**

F307 Trencher **Friends**

1826 Pintard *Letters* 2.213: Never Mayor had so many (trencher) friends. *Oxford* 828; Tilley F762.

F308 **Friendship** is like wine, *etc.*

1811 Jefferson *Writings* 13.77: I find friendship to be like wine, raw when new, ripened with age, the true old man's milk and restorative cordial. *Oxford* 589; Tilley F755. See **W222.**

F309 There is no **Friendship** in trade

1784 Adams(S) *Writings* 4.310: No Friendship in Treaties . . . is almost as proverbial as *No Friendship in Trade.* **1792** THPerkins in *Cabot Family* 1.388: You quote the old adage that there's no friendship in trade. **1795** Cobbett *Porcupine* 2.60. **1800** Dennie *Letters* 177: The *friendship* of trade is proverbial. **1812** Melish *Travels* 543. TW 146(1).

F310 As cold as a **Frog**

1802 Morris *Diary and Letters* 2.424: [The President] is as cold as a frog. Barbour 72(1); Svartengren 314; Whiting *NC* 412(2).

F311 Like a **Frog** upon a gridiron

1796 Cobbett *Porcupine* 3.266: He writhed and winced and jumped about, as the

French say, like a frog upon a gridiron. Cf. *Oxford* 369: Hen; Whiting *NC* 412(7). See **H86, T160.**

F312 Like **Frogs** after a heavy rain

1795 JSchenck in *Blount Papers* 2.581: A numer of Advocates have come forward like frogs after a havy shower of Rain. TW 376: Toad (3).

F313 **Froth** always swims on the surface

1800 RSpaight in *Blount Papers* 3.356: Froth you know always swims on the surface. See **P255.**

F314 Let the **Fruit** hang till it is ripe

1773 SAdams in *Naval Documents* 3.209: I am taught the Rule of Prudence to let the fruit hang till it is ripe. Cf. Whiting F688.

F315 Out of the **Frying-pan** into the fire

1681 Claypoole *Letter Book* 59: That will be out of the frying pan into the fire. 1685 Dunton *Letters* 16: But it was very near making good the Proverb, "out of the Frying-Pan into the fire." 1686 24. 1692 Bulkeley *Will* 248: We shall then but leap out of the pan into the fire. c1700 Taylor *Poems* 428: Would you fain aspire Out of the Frying Pan into the Fire? 1738 Stephens *Journal(I)* 1.89: Whereas they would find themselves abundantly more enslaved, and make good the Proverb. 1745 Pote *Journal* 16: Having Exactly fulfiled yᵉ old English proverb and jumpt. 1760 GClough *Journal* in *Historical Collections of the Essex Institute* 3(1861) 197: I believe he jumped out of the frying pan into a greater fire [suicide]. 1774 Bartram *Report* 152: Thus was the proverb verified with respect to thes fish jumping out of the Frying pan into the fire. 1786 JLibbey in *Belknap Papers* 3.312: According to the old proverb. 1793 *Washington Writings* 32.484: I should get out of the frying pan into the fire. 1796 Cobbett *Porcupine* 4.53: This was making use of a culinary figure, jumping. 1800 Gadsden *Writings* 293. 1801 *St. Clair Papers* 1.227. 1809 Weems

Marion 20. 1814 *Kennon Letters* 37.151. 1814 Palmer *Diary* 42: Dost thou think that the Yankies are such fools as to Jump out of the pan into the fire? 1816 Fidfaddy *Adventures* 47: as the saying is. 1817 Barker *How to Try a Lover* 9: It would only be out of the fire into the frying-pan. 1817 Royall *Letters* 114: Thus he fell out of the pan into the fire. 1819 *Port Folio* 4NS 7.349. 1845 Paulding *Letters(II)* 404: I came to Town . . . to get cool, but have only jumped out of the frying Pan into the fire. Barbour 72; *Oxford* 292-3; Whiting F696. See **F155** (1830).

F316 The **Fuel** removed the fire will expire

1819 Pintard *Letters* 1.217: I hope that the fuel being removed the Fire will expire, and the aliment withheld that the malady will become extinct. *Oxford* 293; Tilley F786. See **C101.**

F317 To add **Fuel** to the fire

a1750 *Washington Writings* 1.16: That's only adding Fuel to fire. 1757 DPepper in McDowell *Documents* 2.390. 1764 Watts *Letter Book* 291: A Dissolution . . . would only have added fuel to Fire in the uneasy temper of Mind the Province is. 1771 Carter *Diary* 2.631: And as it was adding fire to flames I did not expect it Could live. 1777 Shaw *Journals* 39: And the good news from the northward adds fuel to the flame. 1796 Cobbett *Porcupine* 3.350: To add fuel to the flame. 1807 JMadison in *Bowdoin Papers* 2.383: flame. 1814 Gallatin *Diary* 31, 1816 86. *Oxford* 293; TW 148.

F318 To see the **Fur** fly

1814 *Niles Register* in DA fur b: You will soon see "the fur fly." TW 148.

F319 To glow like **Furnaces**

1759 Adams *D and A* 1.77: They came out glowing like furnaces. Whiting F704.

F320 To push on like **Fury**

1804 Weems *Letters* 2.297: I mean to push on like Fury thro' the *Interiors* of N. & S. Carolina. TW 148(2).

G

G1 Light **Gains** heavy purses

1744 Franklin *PR* 2.398: Light Gains heavy Purses. **1801** Weems *Letters* 2.165: Light profits make heavy purses. *Oxford* 463; Whiting G4. See **L178**.

G2 No **Gains** without pains

1745 Franklin *PR* 3.6: No gains without pains, **1758** *WW* 342. Barbour 134; *Oxford* 572-3; TW 149(2).

G3 Small **Gain** from ill-gotten gear

1791 North Carolina Planter in Boyd *Eighteenth Century Tracts* 498: Sma' gain frae sic ill-gotton gear. Whiting *Scots* 1.180: Good. See **G115**.

G4 As bitter as **Gall**

1736 Franklin *PR* 2.139: Things that are bitter, bitterer than Gall. **1777** JHarvie in Jefferson *Papers* 2.35: That would restrain me if the Service was as bitter as Gall. **1782** Freneau *Poems* 2.139: Your hearts are as black, and as bitter as gall. **1807** *Salmagundi* 267: Mons. Charron says they are descended from the Gauls — bitter enough. Barbour 73; Svartengren 303; Whiting G8.

G5 **Gall** or honey

1755 Davis *Colonial Virginia Satirist* 25: Laws contriv'd to plague & puzzle them . . . Yielding gall instead of honey. Tilley H556; Whiting G12. See **H266, W321**.

G6 A living **Gallant** is better than a dead husband

1712 Byrd *Another Secret Diary* 226: Remember that a liveing Gallant is better than a dead Husband. See **D251**.

G7 **Gallapagos** mutton

1815 Porter *Journal* 1.173: Tortoise meat (which by them was called Gallapagos mutton). See **A63, B18, M168**.

G8 **Galley-news**

1813 Palmer *Diary* 7: I'm fearful it is only Gulley news, **1814** 12: Much Galley news in circulation regarding the Cartel. **1815** Waterhouse *Journal* 145: Such like stories were told to us . . . When discovered to be false, they were called *galley-news* or galley *packets*. Colcord 85; NED Galley 8, Galley-packet, *Suppl.* Galley 8, Galley yarn. See **C17**.

G9 To work like a **Galley-slave**

1809 Pinkney *Travels* 2: He continued to work, to use his own expression, like a galley-slave for five years. **1816** Pintard *Letters* 1.18: I have toiled like a galley slave to be prepared for the first meeting of the Society. *Oxford* 917. Cf. TW 338. See **N43, S247**.

G10 The **Gallows** groans for someone

1752 LGrant in McDowell *Documents* 1.263: A monstrous Sett of Rogues for the major Part of whom the Gallows groans. *Oxford* 295; Tilley G15.

G11 To dance under the **Gallows**

1777 JWoodhull in *Clinton Papers* 1.604: Hoped to see the Capt. Henged in two months time and he would Dance under ye gallows.

G12 The **Game** (*etc.*) is not worth the candle

c1710 Byrd *Another Secret Diary* 250: To lament the length of your courtship after you are in possession of your wishes, looks as if you thought the Game not worth the Candles. **1741** Belcher *Papers* 2.374: Nor will the game pay for the candle. **1752** Carter *Diary* 1.101: And yet the play in this Case is not worth the Candle, **1772** 2.679: Such a play must be worth more than any candle, **1775** 929: It may be easily seen, that the play will be worth the candle, as the saying is. **1778** JPreble in Preble *Genealogical Sketch* 107: The game they have been playing . . . is not worth the candle. **1778** Smith *Memoirs(II)* 429: My Opinion always was, Le Jeu ne vaut pas la Chandelle. **1825** Wirt *Letters* 2.196: But this I could overcome if I could persuade myself that the play was worth the candle. **1840** Hone *Diary* 1.463: The greatest doubt is *si le jeu vaut la chandelle.* Oxford 295; TW 150(2).

G13 The **Game** is scarce worth the chase
1797 Morris *Diary and Letters* 2.265: The game is scarce worth the chase.

G14 The **Game** is up

c1720 Byrd *Another Secret Diary* 283: Let me therefore conjure you dear Couzen til the dreadfull age of 31 (when you know a woman's game is up) to mix 9 grams of folly with one of wisdom. **1776** Washington *Writings* 6.347: The game will be pretty well up, 398: The game is pretty near up. **1777** Curwen *Journal and Letters* 106: The tories here believe the American game of independency is nearly up. **1777** BLincoln in Gerry *Letters* 1.261. **1777** Pickering *Life* 1.143: The game is nearly over with them. **1778** Curwen *Journal and Letters* 166. **1778** TWalker in American Antiquarian Society *Proceedings* NS 41(1931) 153. **1779** Lee *Letters* 2.54. **1781** Deane *Papers* 4.283. **1782** JThaxter in *Adams FC* 4.359. **1785** HCruger in Van Schaack *Letters* 408. **1787** JAdams in *Adams-Jefferson Letters* 1.202. **1797** *Columbian Centinel* in Buckingham *Specimens* 2.73. **1798** Codman *Letters* 71. **1813** Jefferson *Writings* 13.262. **1815** Adams *Memoirs* 3.167, **1820** 4.502. **1820**

Robertson *Letters* 127, 270. **1825** Neal *American Writers* 216. **1828** *Yankee* 77. TW 150(4). See **J33**.

G15 So the **Game** goes
1777 Joslin *Journal* 334: We got to Elijah Williams and went to bed and So the game goes. Whiting G22. See **W345**.

G16 To play a double **Game**
1777 *Washington *Writings* 7.144: The next are endeavouring to play a dble. game. **1781** ACampbell in Jefferson *Papers* 4.363: Which shews the double game that People have been carrying on. **1795** GOgg in *Blount Papers* 2.481, 553: Playing the double game. NED Game 5a.

G17 To play another at his own **Game** (*varied*)
1756 Laurens *Papers* 2.83: Which has put it in the power of the Planters to play upon the Sellers their own Game. **1776** Deane *Papers* 1.397: *Omnia tentanda* is my motto, therefore I hint the playing of their own game on them. **1807** Cabot *Letters* 374: It is completely within the power of the British government to beat us at our own game. *Oxford* 36; TW 150(5); Tilley W204. See **W84**.

G18 To play the same **Game**
a1778 Jones *History* 2.230: Washington thought he could play the same game, dance the same jig.

G19 As strong and fierce as **Game-cocks**
1809 Weems *Marion* 102: They, from high keeping, as strong and fierce as game cocks or butcher's bull dogs. Cf. TW 150(1). See **F95**.

G20 As grey as a **Gander**
c1725 Byrd *Another Secret Diary* 458: Her very Heart-breakers . . . turn'd as grey as a Gander. Whiting G375. See **G127**.

G21 **Gaping** is catching
1783 *Belknap Papers* 1.247: They say gaping is catching: perhaps marrying is. Lean 2.29: Yawning.

G22 As familiar as one's **Garter**
1790 Maclay *Journal* 299: Fate, familiar as

her garter, ended the difficulty. Lean 2.827; Shakespeare, *Henry V* I i 47.

G23 Between the **Garters** and the girdle

1709 Lawson *Voyage* 57: The Savages well knowing, how much Frailty possesses the *Indian* Women, betwixt the Garters and the Girdle.

G24 To the last **Gasp**

1743 Stephens *Journal(II)* 2.5: Cash being now run almost to the last Gasp. NED Gasp 1b.

G25 To the **Gates** of death

a1649 Shepard *Autobiography* 360: After I had bin next vnto the gates of Death by the Pox the yeare before. **1682** JWhiting in *Mather Papers* 466: My wife hath been nigh to the gates of death. **1696** JPaine in *Mayflower Descendant* 8(1906) 183: Brought her . . . to the very gates of the grave. **1717** Mather *Diary* 2.495. **1748** Brainerd *Memoirs* 401. **1768** EWheelock in *Wheelock's Indians* 232: Lately raised from the Gates of Death. NED Gate *sb.*[1] 3b. See **B329, F253**.

G26 Tell it not in **Gath,** *etc.*

1644 Williams *Writings* 3.385: O let not this be told in *Gath,* nor heard in *Ashkalon!* **1647** in Stiles *Itineraries* 356: We wish it be not tould in Gath & published in Ashkalon. **1650** Bradstreet *Works* 362: In *Gath* let not this thing be spoken on, Nor published in streets of Askalon. **1704** Sewall *Letter-Book* 2.18: And it has been done: But tell it not in Gath. **1713** Wise *Churches* 29: I wish I could whisper it so low that the Echo might never Rebound to *Gath* or *Askelon.* **1725** CMather in *Mather Papers* 461: This I have not hitherto *told in Gath.* **1744** WVesey in Johnson *Writings* 1.119, **1754** 178: Tell it not in Gath! Much less into the ears of our dear mother-country. **1776** Marshall *Diary* 68. **1776** SWest in Thornton *Pulpit* 307. **1777** Gordon *Letters* 340: Publish it not in Britain, tell it not in the streets of Westminster. **1778** Case *Poems* 14: In *Europe* let it n'er be known, Nor publish it in Askelon. **1778** Curwen *Journal* 1.434: Tell it not in Gath. **1790** EPendleton in *MHM* 46(1951) 76: Tell it not in Gath! **1791** Burroughs

Memoirs 275. **1799** Weems *Philanthropist* 20: O tell it not in England, publish it not in the streets of London. **1800** Eaton *Life* 146: Tell it not in Gath. **1804** Irving *Corrector* 59. **c1806** Beecher *Autobiography* 1.155. **1809** Fessenden *Pills* 75: Tell it not in Gath. **1809** Weems *Washington* 43. **1819** Waln *Hermit* 163: Tell it not in Paris; publish it not in the streets of London, **1828** Jones *Sketches* 2.265: Tell it not in Gath. **1832** Maria Stewart in Porter *Negro Writing* 137. *Oxford* 297; Whiting G41. See **D7**.

G27 To run the **Gauntlet**

1756 Laurens *Papers* 2.349: We fear she must run the Gauntlet amongst the Islands, 373: The *Brislington* will run the Gauntlet by going to the West Indies, **1757** 427: But if she touches at your Island must run the Gauntlett by the Swarms of Privateers We hear infest you. **1775** Bowen *Journals* 2.443: He run gauntlet and passed the *Merlin*. **1777** JClay in *Norton Papers* 422: I had great confidence in . . . an Experienced Commander in running the gantlope. **1781** BFranklin in Adams *Works* 7.478. **1802** Barlow *Letters* 192: I could not avoid running the gauntlet of all their dinners. **1809** Adams *Correspondence* 101. **1811** VHorne in Knopf *War of 1812* 3.22: It has yet to run the gauntlet in the House. **1811** Weems *Gambling* 33: Running the gauntlet through hungry hordes of thieves and pickpockets. **1814** Kerr *Barclay* 177: Running the gauntlet from one judiciary to another, 192. **1815** Dow *Journal* 342. **1817** Weems *Franklin* 149: There run the gauntlet through so many ruinous charges. *Oxford* 689; TW 151.

G28 To take up (throw down) the **Gauntlet**

1774 WSJohnson in Smith *Life and Correspondence* 1.488: I shall not . . . take up the Gauntlet. **1779** *New-York Gazette* in *Newspaper Extracts(II)* 4.111: You seem to throw the gantelope to all around you, and, Quixote like, are for raising up enemies to combat with. **1791** Paine *Rights of Man* 1.278: Throwing the gauntlet. **1792** Barlow *Works* 1.104: The gauntlet might have been thrown. **1793** Jefferson *Writings* 9.211: thrown down. **1798** 10.2: thrown down.

1806 *Weekly* 1.126: The Spaniards had the gauntlet thrown. **1812** DMcArthur in Knopf *War of 1812* 5(1) 64: thrown. **1813** Jefferson *Writings* 13.385: Took up, **1814** 14.213: Throwing down to us the gauntlet of war, **1815** 309: His taking up at length the gauntlet against England. **1817** Robertson *Letters* 14: taken up, **1819** 101: taken up. *Oxford* 297; TW 151.

G29 To be a **Gazing-stock**

1788 Scott *Journal* 236: I sat down . . . after having stood as a gazing stock among them, perhaps several minutes. NED Gazing-stock.

G30 When the **General** trembles, the soldier quakes

1814 GMorris in Otis *Letters* 2.183: When the General trembles the Soldier must quake. Cf. Whiting H252, 253.

G31 **Genius** is not an inheritance

1770 *Johnson Papers* 7.713: Providence has not thought fit to make genious an Inheritance as the Law does Money. Cf. *Oxford* 382; Whiting G43.

G32 He is a **Gentleman** that acts what is gentle

1718 JUsher in *Saltonstall Papers* 1.323: He is a getleman thatt acts which is gentele. *Oxford* 299; Tilley G67, 71; Whiting D131, G46, M54. See **D93**.

G33 **Gentleness** in the manner, but substance in the thing

1811 Claiborne *Letter Books* 6.10: The good old maxim, "Gentleness in the manner, but substance in the thing."

G34 To be before **George**

1737 Franklin *Drinkers* 2.175: He's Been before George.

G35 From **Georgia** to New Hampshire (*varied*)

1766 Adams *Works* 3.476: In every colony, from Georgia to New Hampshire. **1774** TBland in *Naval Documents* 1.1: Every American . . . from Nova Scotia to Georgia. **1775** in *Baxter Manuscripts* 14.255: All the Colonies from Nova scotia to geordia. **1775** Willard *Letters* 94: Nova Scotia to Georgia, 97: Halifax to Georgia. **1779** Brackenridge *Gazette* 135: Georgia to New-Hampshire. **1785** Adams *Works* 8.304: Georgia to New Hampshire. **1798** *Remarks on the Jacobiniad* 2.v: Georgia to Maine, 47: Georgia's limits to the district of Maine. **1808** Adams *Works* 6.530: Georgia to New Hampshire. **1808** *Port Folio* NS 6.76: Georgia to Maine, **1812** 2NS 7.156: Maine to Georgia. **1814** Alden *Epitaphs* 2.157: Maine to Georgia. **1815** Adams *Works* 10.165: New Hampshire to Georgia. **1815** Kerr *Barclay* 192: This cause . . . has run the gauntlet, as it were, from Maine to Georgia. **1816** *Port Folio* 4NS 1.402: Maine to Georgia, 2.188: The Province of Maine offers to them the fogs of Britain, and by visiting Georgia they may bask in the heat of the torrid zone. **1817** Scott *Blue Lights* 54: Little recks he the manners strange, Of wintry Maine or Georgia's range. **1821** Hodgson *Letters* 2.263: Maine to Georgia. **1824** Neal *American Writers* 79: Georgia to Maine, **1825** 109: Georgia to Maine. **a1826** Woodworth *Melodies* 159: Maine to Georgia. TW 90: Dan. See **D6**.

G36 As poor as a **Georgian**

1740 *Georgia Records* 22^2. 394: It's become proverbial (this way) to say (as poor as a Georgian).

G37 As pale as a **Ghost**

1794 DJarratt in *W&MCQ* 3S 9(1952) 384: He looked pale as a ghost. **1804** Irving *Journals* 1.104: He turnd as pale as a ghost. **a1855** Beecher *Autobiography* 2.359. Barbour 74(1); Whiting G54.

G38 As white as a **Ghost**

1821 Knight *Poems* 1.40: The sinner's white as a bleach'd ghost. Barbour 74(3); Svartengren 230; TW 151(2).

G39 To give up the **Ghost**

1644 BArnold in *Winthrop Papers(A)* 4.432: And another (sayd he) of his sonns lyeth now ready to give vp the ghoust. **a1649** Shepard *Autobiography* 392: And so gave up the ghost. **c1680** Radisson *Voyages* 30: I should have given freely up the ghost to be freed from their clawes. **a1700** Hubbard *New England* 322: Their hopes of trade gave up the ghost. **c1703** Byrd *Another Secret Diary* 209: No woman after she has given up the Ghost can keep a secret more faithfully than he conceals his Intrigues. **1750** Winslow *Broadside* 167. **1755** AStiles in Stiles *Itineraries* 568: Our hopes from the Camp appear too like y[e] Giving up the Ghost. **1781** *St. Clair Papers* 1.560. **1783** Williams *Penrose* 82. **1785** AMoore in Jefferson *Papers* 7.17: The remainder of your game have given up the Ghost. **?1786** Freneau *Poems* 2.302. **1791** FAmes in Hamilton *Papers* 9.56. **1792** *Washington Writings* 32.101: She [a mare] gave up the ghost. **1804** *Port Folio* 4.343. **1815** Weems *Adultery* 164. **1816** Freneau *Last Poems* 6. **1817** Randolph (J) *Letters* 198. **1818** Gallatin *Diary* 125. **a1820** Tucker *Essays* 229. **1827** Longfellow *Letters* 1.242. **1832** Barney *Memoir* 55: These toasts were repeated, until "John Barleycorn" gave up the ghost, or, in other words, until the bottoms were emptied. **1838** Paulding *Letters(II)* 234: I am afraid your newly planted trees will go near to giving up the ghost, **1847** 461: I find my Socks, shirts, and Pocket Handkerchiefs, are every day giving up the Ghost. Barbour 74(1); Whiting G55.

G40 As strong as **Gibraltar**

1774 JLovell in Quincy *Memoir* 181: And now it is boasted they are as strong as Gibraltar. **1776** Heath *Memoirs* 52: Although the post before mentioned was made as strong as Gibralter. **1825** Jones *Sketches* 1.59: It [Gibraltar] deserves the distinction, which makes its name a proverb, when we speak of strength. Barbour 74; Whiting *NC* 414(3).

G41 The **Gift** of (the) gob (gab)

1714 Hunter *Androboros* 5: He had a good Gift of the Gob. **1791** North Carolina Planter in Boyd *Eighteenth Century Tracts* 491: Trowth, I hae nae sic gift o' gab. **1807** *Salmagundi* 148: Every man who has what is here called the gift of gab, that is, a plentiful stock of verbosity, becomes a Soldier outright. **1815** Waterhouse *Journal* 106: He had "the gift of gab." **1817** Scott *Blue Lights* 128: Endowed with a tolerable "gift of the gab." **1820** *Harvard College Rebel-*lion 74: Gift of the gab. Barbour 72(2); *Oxford* 301; Tilley G99.

G42 **Gifts** blind the wise

1632 EHowes in *Winthrop Papers(A)* 3.74: The wise man saith; guifts blinde the wise. *Oxford* 301; Whiting G66.

G43 **Gifts** burst rocks

1736 Franklin *PR* 2.140: Gifts burst rocks. Tilley G106. Cf. *Oxford* 301.

G44 What is freer than a **Gift**?

1792 Belknap *Foresters* 122: What is freer than a gift? *Oxford* 579; Whiting G86.

G45 To pick the **Gilding** off of gingerbread

1782 Gadsden *Writings* 187: These [people] may be consulted occasionally to pick the guilding off of ginger bread or some such trifling matter. NED Gingerbread[2]; *Oxford* 800.

G46 To look white about the **Gills**

1818 Robertson *Letters* 57: He looks white about the Gills, as if he was in the habit of lifting his elbow. TW 152.

G47 Better to **Give** than to receive (*varied*)

1647 Ward *Simple Cobler* 41: And it is much better to doe good than receive. **1702** Mather *Magnalia* 1.122: That lesson of our Lord, "that it is better to give than to receive." **1744** Johnson *Writings* 3.459: It is . . . a maxim of eternal truth, that it is more blessed to give than to receive, 460, **c1763** 2.573: The maxim . . . that it is more blessed to give than to receive. **1763** AA in *Adams FC* 1.9: We are told that the giver is more blessed than the receiver. Barbour 75(2); *Oxford* 53; Whiting G93.

G48 He **Gives** twice that gives soon

1650 Davenport *Letters* 85: *Bis dat qui cito dat.* **1695** NSaltonstall in *Saltonstall Papers* 1.232: [Latin only]. **a1700** Hubbard *New England* 483: [Latin only]. **1732** Belcher *Papers* 1.131: I will have it as much in my thoughts to do him every good office as if he was my own son, and as soon as possible — *bis dat qui cito dat.* **1742** Franklin *PR* 2.334: [Latin only]. **1747** GWhitefield in Franklin *Papers* 3.144: [Latin only]. **1752** Franklin *PR* 4.250: *Bis dat qui cito dat:* He gives twice that gives soon; i.e. he will soon be called upon to give again. **1809** *Port Folio* 2NS 2.262: *Bis dat, qui cito dat;* he gives twice who gives quickly. Barbour 75(1); *Oxford* 304-5; Whiting G76. See **D212.**

G49 To **Give** as good as one gets

1811 Lee *Diary and Letters* 140: I gave him as good as he sent. *Oxford* 303; TW 152(1). See **G113.**

G50 To **Give** as well as take

1790 TJefferson in Mason *Papers* 3.202: I think it necessary to give as well as take in a government like ours. **1797** Cobbett *Porcupine* 5.416: Give and take, is a good old maxim. **1804** Paine *Remarks* 2.958: Give and take is *fair* play. *Oxford* 303; Whiting G84. Cf. Tilley G121.

G51 To stick in one's **Gizzard**

1798 Cobbett *Porcupine* 8.59: The editors . . . were troubled with something sticking about their gizzards. **1798** Gadsden *Writings* 284: This Hamburg Trade . . . seems to stick in the Gizzard of G.Bn. **1806** Milledge *Correspondence* 134: That affair sticks much in my gizzard. **1820** GCutler in Vanderpoel *Chronicles* 207: "I can't forget that excellent saw, it sticks in my gizzard yet." The boy ran down to the Captain crying out—"I have found where the saw is—it sticks in the Carpenter's gizzard!" Tilley G131. See **C349, L190.**

G52 As brittle as **Glass**

1793 Smith *Works* 1¹.59: More brittle than glass. **1807** *Yankee Phrases* 87: But pleasures are brittle as glass. **1820** Simpson *Journal* 204: Hatchets . . . are as brittle as Glass. *Oxford* 305; Whiting G109.

G53 As clear as **Glass**

1812 Melish *Travels* 342: The water is as clear . . . as glass. a**1814** Dow *Journal* 411: Yet remains clear and sound as the crystal glass. **1821** Freneau *Last Poems* 34: The matter is as clear as glass. Barbour 75(1); *Oxford* 125; Whiting G111.

G54 As smooth as **Glass**

1643 Williams *Writings* 1.135: *And calmes*

as smooth as glasse. **1776** Curwen *Journal* 1.208: The country and Sea, "*as smooth as a piece of bristol glass.*" **1789** Boucher *Autobiography* 174: The sea as smooth as glass. **1790** Maclay(S) *Journal* 36. **1791** Morris *Diary* 2.197. **1793** JMacdonell in Gates *Five Fur Traders* 100. **1806** Fanning *Narrative* 41. **1810** Schultz *Travels* 2.101. **1812** Melish *Travels* 342. Barbour 75(4); Whiting G118.

G55 As tranquil as **Glass**

1807 Irving(P) *Journals* 91: Its surface tranquil as glass.

G56 As transparent as **Glass**

1776 Cresswell *Journal* 149: Transparent as glass. **1818** Cary *Letters* 259: The river as smooth and transparent as glass. TW 153(4). See **C336.**

G57 **Glass,** *etc.* are easily cracked and never well mended

1750 Franklin *PR* 3.454: Glass, China, and Reputation, are easily crack'd, and never well mended. **1816** Smith *Life* 20: A female character, when once gone, is like a broken looking-glass, which can never be made whole. Barbour 75(2). Cf. *Oxford* 907-8.

G58 He that whines for **Glass** without G, *etc.*

1746 Franklin *PR* 3.62: He that whines for Glass without G Take away L and that's he. *Oxford* 495. Cf. Tilley G138.

G59 One **Glass** is enough, *etc.*

1824 *Tales* 2.55: They say one glass is enough, two is too much, and three is not half enough.

G60 One's **Glass** is run

1674 JLeverett in *Hutchinson Papers* 2.197-8: My time . . . I must need accompt to be short, little sand being to run in my glass. **1748** Wolcott *Papers* 481: My Glass is So near runn out. **1763** Watts *Letter Book* 147: My Glass is run. **1781** ETilghman in Rodney *Letters* 420: Your Sand I am told seems nearly run out, mine is very nearly. **1797** *Heath Papers* 3.397: I am now arrived at threescore years of age, and I know that my glass is nearly run. *Oxford* 305; Tilley G132.

G61 The **Glory** of the world passes away

1776 POliver in Hutchinson *Diary* 2.110: *Sic mutat gloria mundi.* **1777** JBoucher in *MHM* 10(1915) 28: *Sic transit Gloria Mundi.* **1777** JSewall in Gerry *Letters* 1.271: [Latin only]. **1780** JPemberton in Kirkland *Letters* 2.70: So passeth away as a Shadow this World's Glory. **1780** JSewall in *Winslow Papers* 61: [Latin only]. **1785** WSmith in King *Life* 1.110: [Latin only]. **1787** WSmith in Jefferson *Papers* 12.243: [Latin only], **1788** 13.517: [Latin only]. **1788** *Columbian Magazine* 2.432: [Latin only]. **1802** *Port Folio* 2.40: [Latin only]. **1803** Austin *Constitutional* 303: [Latin only]. **1807** *Port Folio* NS 4.4: [Latin only]. **1808** Taggart *Letters* 304: [Latin only]. **1813** JAdams in *Adams-Jefferson Letters* 2.356: [Latin only]. **1814** Alden *Epitaphs* 2.53: [Latin only]. **1815** Adams *Works* 10.148: *Sic transit gloria.* **1816** Fidfaddy *Adventures* 141: Some say that glory here below, Is *transient* in its nature. **1821** JAdams in *Adams-Jefferson Letters* 2.574: Sic transit Gloriola (is there such a Latin Word?) mundi. **1822** Watterston *Winter* 155: [Latin only]. **1840** Cooper *Letters* 4.11: [Latin only]. Barbour 76; Whiting G156.

G62 To fit like a **Glove**

1779 Lee *Letters* 2.147: No glove ever fitted his hand better than this character does the Man. **1783** *American Wanderer* 29: Affability, which fits easy as your glove upon persons of genuine breeding. Barbour 76(2); TW 153(2).

G63 More die by **Gluttony** than by the sword (*varied*)

1754 Ames *Almanacs* 252: More die by Gluttony, than perish by the Sword. **1777** JA in *Adams FC* 2.209: Our Frying Pans and Gridirons, slay more than the Sword. *Oxford* 306; Whiting G167. See **K47.**

G64 To strain at a **Gnat** and swallow a camel

1640 TLechford in *Transactions of the American Antiquarian Society* 7(1885) 275: They will strain at gnats . . . but I . . . pray that I may never swallow such camels as departe from Christ. **1676** Williams *Writ-*ings 5.362: The blind *Quakers* . . . swallow down a fly & a Camel too. **1691** Sewall *Diary* 1.342: One sign of a hypocrit was for a man to strain at a Gnat and swallow a Camel. **1712** CToppan in Sewall *Letter-Book* 1.421: Perceiving that some of the Ceremonies were Camels too big for them to Swallow, told them that they should be left to their Liberty. **1734** Johnson *Writings* 3.66. **1764** Watts *Letter Book* 318: Tho' our Governors were Condemn'd for swallowing Gnats, they themselves swallow Camels. **1768** Woodmason *Journal* 42. **1772** McClure *Diary* 32. **1775** WBradford in Madison *Papers* 1.139: To strain at a Gnat or swallow a camel as best suits his purpose. **1779** Bailey *Journal* 151. **1781** AA in *Adams FC* 4.176: A Body who too often strain at a knat while they gulph down a camel with great facility. **1781** EWinslow in *Winslow Papers* 70, **1785** 282: Even in this Province [Nova Scotia], where they "swallow camels without a hiccup." **1787** Adams *Writings* 1.33. **1791** Henry *Life* 3.645. **1796** Cobbett *Porcupine* 3.277. **1799** Carey *Porcupiniad* 2.iii: Would it not be vastly worse than straining at gnats, after having swallowed not only camels, but mammoths. **1801** Sewall *Parody* 162: And while an insect strains their squeamish caul, Down goes a monstruous camel—bunch and all. **1809** Weems *Washington* 63: If he could but prevail on the young Mammoth to take down a tax, though no bigger than a *Gnat*, he should soon bring him to swallow a *Camel!* **1811** Adams *Writings* 4.136: As if it were calculated for the federal swallow (for which no camel is too big). **1817** DClinton in King *Life* 6.84: After swallowing the National Bank and the Cumberland Road &c., it was not to be supposed that Mr. Madison would strain at Canals. **c1820** Bernard *Retrospections* 18. **1824** Jefferson *Writings* 16.13. **1828** *Yankee* 131. **1832** JRandolph in Jackson *Correspondence* 4.427: But John Bull gullible as he is cannot swallow such a camel as this with his whole pack upon his back. Barbour 76(3); *Oxford* 778-9; Whiting G178. See **C329.**

G65 **Go** farther and fare worse

1819 Welby *Visit* 226: We drove past; for-

getting "farther on you may fare worse."
1824 *Tales* 2.104: You shall judge for yourself, if a man mayn't go further and fare
worse. *Oxford* 306; Whiting G183.

G66 Once **Gone** always gone

1776 Harrower *Journal* 143: And once gone
always gone. Cf. Tilley O41. See **D215.**

G67 What **Goes** in must come out

1776 *Blockheads* 9: What *goes in must come
out*, 17: *When what is in will out*. Cf. Whiting *NC* 414.

G68 To give one the **Go-by**

1704 JDudley in *Winthrop Papers*(B)
5.248: The enemy would give mee the go-by
there. **1762** *Johnson Papers* 10.554: To
those He was able very properly to give the
go by. **1779** AA in *Adams FC* 3.249. **1780**
Adams *Correspondence* 152, *Works* 7.247.
1818 Murphey *Papers* 1.121. a**1824** Marshall *Kentucky* 2.357: That sinister motive
in legislation, which gives correct principles,
"the go by," (a legislative phrase). TW 154.
See **S251.**

G69 As false as **God** is true

1794 Paine *Age of Reason* 1.555: [It] is as
fabulous and as false as God is true. c**1796**
JWendell in Wendell *Letters* 283: Things as
false as God is true. *Oxford* 243; Whiting
G192.

G70 As sure (true) as there is a **God** in
heaven

1758 EHersey in *Adams-Jefferson Letters*
2.374: As sure as there is a God in Heaven.
1768 Adams *Legal Papers* 1.327: As true as
a God in Heaven, **1770** 2.417: As sure as
there was a G— in heaven. **1789** Maclay
Journal 71: *As sure as God was in the firmament*. *Oxford* 840; Whiting G194.

G71 **God** and Mammon cannot dwell
together

1719 Chalkley *Journal* 99: God and Mammon cannot dwell together. Tilley G253.
See **M66.**

G72 **God** bless you!

1811 *Port Folio* 2NS 6.356: The year 750, is
commonly reckoned the era of the custom of
saying "God bless you," to one who happens

to sneeze, *etc.*, **1817** 4NS 3.121: When a
person sneezes, it is usual to say, *God bless
you:* as much as to say, may God so bless you
as that portends, *etc. Oxford* 289; Whiting
C245.

G73 **God** deliver me from my friends, *etc.*

1790 Rush *Letters* 1.534: I am led to conclude this narrative with the famous Spanish
prayer: "God deliver me from myself and
my friends." **1824** Neal *American Writers*
50: Heaven save us from our friends! *we* will
take care of our enemies. **1845** WLewis in
Jackson *Correspondence* 6.387: To save
Polk from his friends, believing that he
could take care of his enemies. *Oxford* 176;
Whiting G219.

G74 **God** gives all things to industry

1755 Franklin *PR* 5.474: God gives all
Things to Industry, **1758** *WW* 342.

G75 **God** gives and God takes away

1771 Carter *Diary* 1.543: The Lord Gave
and taketh away and blessed be his name for
all things, **1775** 2.935: God gave and God
hath taken away and blessed be the name of
the Lord. **1801** Dorr *Letters* 295: God is
just, he giveth and taketh away. **1820** Cottle
Life 382: But since it's God who gave—he
takes away. **1828** Jackson *Correspondence*
3.401: He that giveth hath a right to take
away. Whiting G206.

G76 **God** heals and the doctor takes the fees

1736 Franklin *PR* 2.142: God heals, and the
Doctor takes the Fees, **1744** 398. *Oxford*
310; Tilley G190.

G77 **God** helps them that help themselves

1736 Franklin *PR* 2.140: God helps them
that help themselves, **1758** *WW* 341. **1770**
Ames *Almanacs* 412: God helps them that
help themselves. **1775** AA in *Adams FC*
1.280: as King Richard said. **1775** JAdams
in *Warren-Adams Letters* 1.120: Heaven
helps those who help themselves, 128: God,
153. **1776** Lee *Letters* 1.168. **1777** AA in
Adams FC 2.358: That saying of king Richard often occurs to my mind. **1777**
Adams(S) *Writings* 3.387: I will never forget
because it exactly coincides with my religious opinion and I think it warranted by

holy writ, that "God helps those who help themselves," **1780** 4.189: says an eminent writer. **1780** Franklin *Writings* 8.146: The Proverb says . . . And the world too in this Sense is very godly, **1782** 391: The surest way to obtain liberal aid from others is vigorously to help ourselves. **1802** *Port Folio* 2.313: Remember with the sage Dr. Franklin, the Sancho Panza of America, that. **1812** Melish *Travels* 351: As poor Richard says in his almanack. **1819** JStory in Adams *Writings* 6.301, n.[1] : The old proverb asserts that, **1822** 7.194-5: The old prudential maxim that. Barbour 77(4); *Oxford* 310; TW 154(3). See **H199.**

G78   God is a good man

1702 Mather *Magnalia* 1.284: When the rude Cornish men saw how miraculously the vessel had escaped, they said, "God was a good man to save them so." *Oxford* 310; Tilley G195; Whiting G213.

G79   God is above all (law)

1644 Williams *Writings* 2.166: God is above Law. **1776** Hutchinson *Diary* 2.6: God is above all. See **K19, P230, 288.**

G80   God (*etc.*) is no respecter of persons

1763 Griffith *Journal* 250: The Lord, with whom there is no respect of persons. **1791** AHShippen in *Adams FC* 4.204: The Dr. appears to be no respecter of persons. **1797** PHall in Porter *Negro Writing* 71. **1811** Asbury *Journal* 2.664. **1814** Littell *Festoons* 110: It is said that the Almighty is no respecter of persons. **1817** Weems *Franklin* 144: That divine philosophy, which commands its disciples to be "no respecters of persons." Whiting G216. See **D79, G162.**

G81   God knows: I don't

1794 *Commerce of Rhode Island* 2.466: But what port I shall arive to God only noes for I dont, I am sure. Partridge 338.

G82   God loves a cheerful giver

1809 Weems *Marion* 191: *God loves a cheerful giver, and so do I . . . a willing soldier.* Whiting G222.

G83   God made the country and man made the town

1800 Rush *Letters* 2.824: God made the country—man made cities. **1816** Paulding *Letters(I)* 1.74: "God made the country, and man made the town." *Oxford* 311; TW 235(2).

G84   God sends curst cows short horns

1676 Williams *Writings* 5.276: The Proverb is here true, *God hath sent curst Cows short Horns.* *Oxford* 162; Whiting G234. See **C323.**

G85   God sends meat and the Devil cooks

1735 Franklin *PR* 2.5: Bad Commentators spoil the best of books, So God sends meat (they say) the devil Cooks. **1745** Pote *Journal* 56: This put me in mind of y[e] old Proverb, God Sent meat and y[e] D——l Cooks. **1785** Franklin *Writings* 9.402: The sailors have therefore a saying that. **1790** Freneau *Poems* 3.42: That God gives them meat, but the devil sends cooks. **1806** *Port Folio* NS 1.96: Though the Lord sends you victuals, the Devil sends cooks. **1809** Pinkney *Travels* 17: The old proverb that God sent meats, and the d——l cooks, is verified in every kitchen in France. *Oxford* 312; TW 228(2). See **M139.**

G86   God speed the plough

1732 Belcher *Papers* 1.143: God speed the plough, **1742** 2.428: And now what can you do on your part to help to speed the plough? a**1786** Ladd *Remains* 22: Trade should revive, the plough protected speed. **1818** JAdams in *Adams-Jefferson Letters* 2.531: And I say, God speed the Plough, and prosper stone Wall. *Oxford* 763; Whiting G239.

G87   God tempers the wind to the shorn lamb

1780 JSewall in *Winslow Papers* 60: "God," said Maria, "tempers the wind to the shorn Lamb." **1788** AA in Adams *D and A* 3.214: I think that God will suit the wind to the shorn Lamb, **1799** *New Letters* 212: Providence, who knows how as Sterne says, to. **1801** GMorris in King *Life* 4.13: And rely much on the scriptural Assurance that Heaven tempers the Wind to the shorn

Lamb. **1801** Paine *Works* 345: In tempering the wind to the shorn lamb. **1807** Janson *Stranger* 61: A saying not more trite than true. **1809** *Port Folio* 2NS 1.143: Sensitive as the shorn lamb to the bleak and wintry wind, **1810** 4.149: [duly ascribed to Sterne]. **1813** AAdams in *Warren-Adams Letters* 2.384: Sterne tells us. **1817** Royall *Letters* 98. **1821** *Austin Papers* 1.398. **1822** Weems *Penn* 159: There is generally the presence of him who *"tempers the air to the shorn lamb."* Barbour 77(6); *Oxford* 312-3; TW 154(6).

G88 The **Gods** are slow but sure paymasters
1750 Sherman *Almanacs* 250: The gods are slow but sure paymasters. *Oxford* 310; Tilley G197.

G89 The **Gods** themselves may be taken with gifts
1787 Adams *Works* 6.215: According to the heathen proverb, "the gods themselves may be taken with gifts." See **G43.**

G90 If **God** blesses a man, his bitch brings forth pigs
1736 Franklin *PR* 2.143: If God blesses a Man, his Bitch brings forth Pigs. *Oxford* 311; Tilley G261.

G91 If **God** is with us, who can be against us?
1629 *Hutchinson Papers* 1.52: If God be with us who can be against us? **1751** *Georgia Records* 26.242. **1775** SLangdon in Thornton *Pulpit* 256. **1775** RRichardson in Gibbes 2.220: If God is for us, we have nothing to fear. **1812** Asbury *Letters* 3.465: We will not, if God be with us leave a hoop behind. Whiting G252, *NC* 415 (14).

G92 In **God's** good time
1677 Hubbard *Indian* 2.176-7: The Issue of which we as yet wait to hear in Gods good Time.

G93 Out of **God's** blessing into the warm sun
1612 Strachey *Historie* 24: To bring them (to invert our English Proverb) out of the warme Sun, into Gods Blessing. **1718** Sewall *Letter-Book* 2.93: It would be no Gain to go out of Gods Blessing into the warm Sun. *Oxford* 602; Whiting G256.

G94 Serve **God**, serve Devil
1699 Ward *Trip* 36: All Hands in a *Calme* to *Pray* or Pick *Okum*, but to work in a *Storm*, serve God serve Devil. **1824** EPatchell in Jackson *Correspondence* 3.263: But I believe [he] has ever since been a praying "good God, good Devil," not knowing whoes hand he might fall into. Lean 4.93. Cf. Whiting G258.

G95 They are well guided whom **God** guides
1790 ESteele in *Steele Papers* 2.760: Remember your Maker, and ask him to guide you: it is a good old saying, "they are well guided whom he guides, and he leaves them that don't ask him, to their own ways." *Oxford* 340: guided.

G96 To fear **God** and have no other fear
1789 Shippen *Journal* 288: Which I answered with the old adage I fear God & I have no other fear.

G97 To hang **God's** bible at the Devil's girdle
1647 Ward *Simple Cobler* 8: He . . . will for a need hang Gods Bible at the Devills girdle.

G98 What **God** made for a jackass cannot be made a fine horse
1823 *Austin Papers* 1.582: That which God made for a Jack Ass can not be educated so as to make a fine Horse. Cf. Whiting F37. See **P323.**

G99 Whom **God** (Jupiter) would destroy he first makes mad
1704 *Penn-Logan Correspondence* 1.319: Quos perdere vult Jupiter prima dementat. **1740** WDouglas *Discourse* in *Colonial Currency* 3.350: The old Saying, *Quem Deus vult perdere, prius dementat.* **1760** Johnson *Writings* 3.566: [Latin: Jupiter]. **1768** Franklin *Papers* 15.193: [Latin only]. **1769** *Bowdoin Papers* 1.141: [Latin only]. **1774** Franklin *Writings* 6.173: Divine Providence first infatuates the power it designs to ruin. **1775** Carter *Diary* 2.956, 960: [Latin only]. **1775** Lee(W) *Letters* 1.168: [Latin only]. **1775** Quincy *London Journal* 465: [Latin only]. **1776** Carter *Diary* 2.1045, 1065: [Latin only]. **1776** Moore *Diary* 1.322: the old adage [Latin only]. **1776** *New York*

Journal in *Naval Documents* 5.1028: [Latin only]. **1776** Serle *Journal* 80: [Latin only]. **1777** Hutchinson *Diary* 2.135: [Latin only]. **1784** Jay *Correspondence* 3.134: The old adage [Latin only]. **1789** Stiles *Diary* 3.358: [Latin only]. **1796** Morris *Diary and Letters* 2.232: [Latin only]. **1797** Tyler *Algerine* 2.211: Well does the Latin poet exclaim [Latin only]. **1798** Cobbett *Porcupine* 8.171: [Latin only]. **1800** Ames *Letters* 1.283: [Latin only]. **1806** Paine *Remarks* 2.615: *Those whom God intends to destroy he first renders mad.* **1807** Taggart *Letters* 222: the adage [Latin only]. **1809** HWDesaussure in Quincy *JQuincy* 191: The truth of the maxim [Latin only]. **1811** Taggart *Letters* 350: [Latin only]. **1813** GMorris in King *Life* 5.359: [Latin only]. **1815** Jefferson *Writings* 14.285: [Latin only]. **1816** *Port Folio* 4NS 2.27: *Quos Deus* . . . or rather *Quem Jupiter.* **1819** Kinloch *Letters* 1.129: The Latin proverb says, that Heaven begins by depriving those of their senses, whom it means to destroy. **1838** Jackson *Correspondence* 5.546: Who god wills for distruction he first maketh *mad.* **1862** HNash in *Ruffin Papers* 3.242: Whom the Gods intend to destroy, they first make mad. Barbour 77(13); *Oxford* 313; Tilley G257.

G100   With God all things are possible

1712 Mather *Letters* 117: However, take it again; all things are possible with God! **1741** Belcher *Papers* 2.406. **1776** Fithian *Journal* 242: Nothing is impossible with God. **1826** Beecher *Autobiography* 2.62: All things are possible with God. *Oxford* 580; Whiting G269.

G101   Goffe, Whalley, or the Devil

1794 Stiles *Three Judges* 34: Hence it is proverbial in some parts of New-England, in speaking of a champion at athletic and other exercises, to say that none can beat him but Goffe, Whalley, or the Devil.

G102   All is not Gold that glisters, *etc.*

1636 EHowes in *Winthrop Papers(A)* 3.272: All is not gold that glisters like it, and he that would learne to distinguish, may pay too deare for his knowledge. **1645** Williams *Writings* 7.37: Hypocrites, (which may but glister, and be no solid gold). **1690** WByrd in *VHM* 26(1918) 251: Some thinking all had been gold that glister'd. **1702** Mather *Magnalia* 2.546: People, who thought "all was gold that glittered." **1705** Beverley *History* 30: For they, taking all to be Gold that glister'd, run into the utmost Distraction. **1722** *New-England Courant* 55(2.1): But (*Simile non est Idem*) all is not Gold that Glisters. **1748** JAyscough in *Colden Letters* 4.84: glistens. **1779** Brackenridge *Gazette* 133: glitters. **1779** Lee(W) *Letters* 2.610: glisters. **1780** Asbury *Journal* 1.337: shines. **1790** Maclay *Journal* 328: glitters. **1810** Asbury *Letters* 3.433: shines. **1810** Lee *Diary and Letters* 104: glitters. a**1814** Dow *Journal* 405: glitters. **1820** Faux *Memorable Days* 2.58: glitters. Barbour 77(1); *Oxford* 316; Whiting G282.

G103   As bright as Gold

1696 Taylor *Poems* 110: More bright than gold (my Love). Whiting G284.

G104   As precious as Gold

1653 Keayne *Apologia* 28: [It is] a little thin pocket book . . . which I esteem more precious than gold. Whiting G290.

G105   As pure as Gold

1805 WBainbridge in *Barbary Wars* 6.174: Whose heart is as pure as gold refined a thousand times. **1811** *Adams-Waterhouse Correspondence* 67: I rejoice in the Governor's Spirits. He will come out of the Furnace double refined. **1821** Beecher *Autobiography* 1.459: Pure as gold. Barbour 77(3); Whiting G291. See **G108**.

G106   As yellow as Gold

1674 Josselyn *Account* 63: As yellow as Gold. **1709** Lawson *Voyage* 150: Wings as yellow as Gold. **1765** Ames *Almanacs* 367: Butter, as yellow as Gold. **1771** Adams *D and A* 2.30: Butter, as yellow as Gold. Barbour 77(5); Svartengren 252; Whiting G294.

G107   Gold (money) grows (not) on trees

1750 WChancellor in *PM* 92(1968) 471: Africa, where tis so falsly said, that Gold grows on the Trees. **1774** GSimpson in *Let-*

ters to Washington 5.71: Neither S[r] do I Beleive that your orchads Bears Gold of Tree kind. **1787** *American Museum* 2.383: When the new government is established, "money will grow upon the trees." Barbour 122(11); TW 248(8).

G108 **Gold** is tried in the fire

1702 Mather *Magnalia* 1.373: He . . . came forth as "gold that had been tried in the fire." **1771** CCarroll in *MHM* 13(1918) 254: As gold becomes purer by passing oftener thro' the Chymist's fire. **1801** Sewall *Poems* 176: As gold try'd by fire, leaves the dross all behind. **1804** TLear in *Barbary Wars* 4.471: You will come out as gold tried in the fire. **1808** Eaton *Life* 404: Your reputation may come from the ordeal *like gold seven times tried by the fire. Oxford* 315; Whiting G298. See **G105.**

G109 **Gold** may be bought too dear

1691 ?CMather *Bills of Credit* in *Colonial Currency* 1.192: Unless men (according to the Proverb) should *Buy Gold too Dear.* **1769** JParker in Franklin *Papers* 16.138: But a man may buy Gold too dear. **1775** Paine *Cupid* 2.1117: Gold . . . may be bought too dear. **1796** Morris *Diary and Letters* 2.222: says the proverb. *Oxford* 95; Whiting M147.

G110 More **Gold** than grace

1801 Asbury *Journal* 2.311: There is more gold than grace. Whiting G414.

G111 **Good** cannot come from evil

1778 JMVarnum in Sullivan *Letters* 2.42: It is a common Maxim, tho not true, "that good cannot come from Evil." *Oxford* 562; Tilley E203.

G112 **Good** often comes out of evil

1767 Eliot *Letters* 407: Good often comes out of evil. Cf. Tilley I35.

G113 To give one as **Good** as he brings

1709 Byrd *Secret Diary* 35: She gave me as good as I brought. Whiting G366. See **G49.**

G114 Too **Good** to be true

1745 *Louisbourg Journals* 7: I fear too good News (for us) to be true. **1776** JBoucher in *MHM* 9(1914) 57: I fear, this is too good

news to be true. **1777** Cresswell *Journal* 184: This is too good news to be true, 246, 251: Afraid it is too good to be authentic. **1778** Serle *Journal* 303. **1800** Adams(TB) *Letters* 118. **1814** Bentley *Diary* 4.283. **1814** Palmer *Diary* 38, 88, 90: This is too good for all of it to be true. **1815** GSalisbury in American Antiquarian Society *Proceedings* NS 20 (1909) 220. **1816** PRobertson in *W&MCQ* 11(1931) 63. *Oxford* 831; TW 155(4).

G115 (Ill-gotten) **Goods** seldom descend to the third heir

a1700 Hubbard *New England* 498: But goods gotten after that rate seldom descend to the third heir, as heathens have observed. **1702** Mather *Magnalia* 2.399: *Vex gaudet Tertius Haeres. Oxford* 399; Whiting G333. See **G3.**

G116 The more **Goods** at market the cheaper

1784 Gadsden *Writings* 213: Certainly the more goods at market the cheaper we may get such articles as we want. Cf. Whiting P368.

G117 The **Goodness** of a thing is known when it is wanting

1656 JBrewster in *Winthrop Papers*(B) 2.76: As oft tymes it faulles out soe that the goodnes of a thing is not soe well knowen as when it is wanting & longe absent from vs. *Oxford* 922; Tilley W924. See **V5, 6, 7, W18, 103.**

G118 To keep shop on **Goodwin** Sands

1748 Franklin *PR* 3.252: Sell-cheap kept Shop on Goodwin Sands, and yet had Store of Custom. *Oxford* 328; Whiting S272.

G119 All one's **Geese** are swans

1702 *Penn-Logan Correspondence* 1.170: If his swan do not prove a goose. **1722** Taylor *Poems* 375: The Worlds geese are white swans In its account. **1725** Franklin *Papers* 1.71: Our *Geese* are but *Geese* tho' we may think 'em Swans. **1782** Lee *Papers* 4.28: All his own Geese are Swans, all his pewter silver and all his drayhorses are mountain Arabs. **1789** Boucher *Autobiography* 101, **1798** in *MHM* 10(1915) 121. **1801** Sewall *Poems* 246: Some people's geese are swans (so says The proverb trite and old), **1805** *Parody* 32. **1807** *Monthly Anthology* 4.336: In this country, where all our geese are swans, and our swans, alas! too often turn out geese. *Oxford* 298; TW 156(4). Cf. Whiting G387.

G120 As dizzy as a **Goose**

1737 Franklin *Drinkers* 2.175: He's As Dizzy as a Goose. Apperson 154; Tilley G346.

G121 As fierce as a **Goose**

1803 Davis *Travels* 412: He looks as fierce as a goose with one eye. Svartengren 92; Tilley G347.

G122 A **Goose** for dinner on Michaelmas Day

1778 Hutchinson *Diary* 2.219: A goose for dinner on Mich[aelmas] Day, occasioned an observation—that otherwise money would be wanted before the year was out.

G123 A **Goose's** breast-bone (as a weather prognostic)

1807 Drinker *Journal* 411: If we are to judge by the Goose's breast-bone, according to Capt. Antony, we shall have a hard winter. Dunwoody 36.

G124 Older than a white **Goose**

1674 Josselyn *Account* 101: Whereupon the proverb, Older than a white *Goose*.

G125 To kill the **Goose** that lays the golden eggs

1764 OThacher *Sentiments* in Bailyn *Pamphlets* 1.497: The good wife in the fable who killed her hen that every day laid her a *golden egg*. **1765** DDulany in *MHM* 7(1912) 56: The sanguine genius of one of the *Anti-American* writers, brings to my mind the fable of the boy and the hen that laid *golden eggs*. He is not content to wait. **1765** Watts *Letter Book* 406: Very like the old Woman dissatisfy'd with an Egg a day killd the poor Hen to have them all at Once. **1768** Franklin *Papers* 15.188: To kill the goose which lays the golden eggs. **1781** Jefferson *Papers* 5.313: The taking them was ripping up the hen which laid the golden eggs, 6.35: hen, **1785** 8.229: hen. **1796** MCarey in Weems *Letters* 2.17: You . . .

can not have forgotten the fable of the goose with golden eggs, **1797** 80. **1798** Cobbett *Porcupine* 8.100: Impatience would lead them to save the proprietors of houses, goods, and land, *exactly as the boy did with the golden-egg goose.* **1801** Weems *Letters* 2.171: But you can preach about the Boy and Goose with golden eggs. **1805** Parkinson *Tour* 424: Resembles the boy in the fable killing his goose that laid golden eggs. **1806** Latrobe *Journal* 134. **1814** ACHanson in *MHM* 35(1940) 359. **1826** Royall *Sketches* 119. Barbour 78(3); *Oxford* 422-3; Whiting G386.

G126 To cut the **Gordian** knot

1650 Bradstreet *Works* 254: Where the Prophetick knot he [Alexander] cut in twain. **1652** Williams *Writings* 7.206: *Alexander's sword* will cut all *Gordian* knots. **1668** FDrake in Mather *Magnalia* 2.113: Confess the world a gordian knot agen. **1679** BTompson in Jantz 158. **1687** Fitzhugh *Letters* 218: For about a month since, that Gordian knot was tyed betwixt them, that nothing but Death will separate. **1713** Wise *Churches* 66: We find . . . such heaps of *Gordian Knots*, **1721** *Word* 192. **1739** *Georgia Records* 22².138: The Gordian Knot which he cannot untie. **1740** Byrd *Another Secret Diary* 31: And by Three the Gordian knot was tyed. **1742** Belcher *Papers* 2.433. **c1765** JTrumbull in *Monthly Anthology* 2(1805) 248: Tied up in wondrous Gordian knot, They neither can untie nor cut [marriage]. **1765** Watts *Letter Book* 399: Providence in mercy has reserv'd the power of dissolving it as Alexander did the Gordian Knot, by cutting the thread. **1774** AA in *Adams FC* 1.179. **1775** Lee *Papers* 1.224, 3.300: A Goddian Knot . . . will baffle all thy powers of art. **1776** Deane *Papers* 1.227. **1776** Moore *Diary* 1.192. **1776** Stiles *Diary* 2.21. **1785** Jefferson *Papers* 8.406: The knot which you thought a Gordian one will untie itself before you. **1787** Adams *Diary* 328. **1789** Washington *Writings* 30.188. **1791** Adams *Writings* 71. **1795** Hamilton *Papers* 19.23. **1796** Cobbett *Porcupine* 3.378: untie. **1804** Adams(A) *Letters* 393. **1807** *Weekly* 1.223. **1809** Irving *History* 1.63. **c1810** Randolph *Virginia* 169. **1810** Schultz

Travels 2.134: Chaste as the virgin queen before the Gordian knot is tied, yet indulgent as the Cyprian goddess for ever after. **1811** *Port Folio* 2NS 6.590, **1812** 8.198: A woman . . . seduced me into a Gordian tie, from which . . . nothing but the hand of death can extricate me. **1813** Asbury *Journal* 2.731: King Gordius had well-nigh been amongst us; but the knots were untied peaceably. **1814** Kerr *Barclay* 305: A gordian knot; a monster that cannot easily be subdued; this knot cannot be cut asunder, but by the two edged sword of justice. **1814** Wirt *Bachelor* 153. **1821** Jefferson *Writings* 1.136. **1822** Wirt *Letters* 2.141, **1824** 173. *Oxford* 328-9; TW 211(2).

G127   Gosling-gray

1821 Knight *Poems* I 45: When oaks are gosling-gray. Whiting G375. See **G20**.

G128   As true as the Gospel

c1680 Radisson *Voyages* 197: Att wch they weare astonished, believing it to be true as ye Christians the Gospell. **1777** Munford *Patriots* 470: As true as the gospel. **1778** Moore *Diary* 2.91: This was believ'd as gospel true. **1779** Freneau *Poems* 2.8. **c1780** Witherspoon *Works* 4.391. **1811** Graydon *Memoirs* 14. *Oxford* 840; Svartengren 371; Whiting G399. See **H256**.

G129   As valid as the Gospel

1744 *Georgia Records* 24.255: This was allowed of by the Court Martial as Valid as The Gospel.

G130   As light as Gossamer

1764 AA in *Adams FC* 1.37: Were I not then light as the Gosemore. Whiting G402.

G131   As soft as Gossamer

1821 Knight *Poems* 1.149: Soft as gossamer the breast.

G132   The wise men of Gotham

1741 Stephens *Journal(II)* 1.24: Among our wise men of Gotham. **1781** Oliver *Origin* 148: They duped the Clergy, they duped the People & they duped the wise men of *Gotham* in *England*. **1791** Paine *Rights of Man* 1.318: He has put . . . all wise men of Gotham on the other side. **1798** Morris

Diary and Letters 2.340: These wise men of Gotham. **1803** JJackson in Milledge *Correspondence* 97: And for one of your wise men of Gotham, a Member of the Legislatures. **1805** Taggart *Letters* 148: Our warm wise men of Gotham. *Oxford* 899. Cf. Whiting G406. See **C369**.

G133   Once in Grace always in grace

1803 Dow *Journal* 177: [He] believed once in grace and always in grace, **1804** 198: The old doctrine, *"once in grace always in grace,"* 351.

G134   Against the Grain

1675 WLeete in *Winthrop Papers(B)* 2.578: [It] doth run hard against the graine of nature to be so surrendred. **a1700** Hubbard *New England* 258: Which went so against the grain with Mr. Vane . . . that he refused to put it to vote. **1702** *Penn-Logan Correspondence* 1.84: Much against the grain. **1722** Byrd *Another Secret Diary* 374. **1726** Lloyd *Papers* 1.274: [It] is contrary to the grain. **1747** Johnson *Writings* 1.128, **c1763** 2.566: Forced to go against the grain of nature. **1764** Watts *Letter Book* 295. **1771** Hamilton *Papers* 1.7: Do but rub her 'gainst the grain. **1772** Paterson *Glimpses* 98. **1777** JBoucher in *MHM* 9(1914) 327. **1777** JWarren in *Warren-Gerry Correspondence* 83-4. **1778** *New Jersey Gazette* in *Newspaper Extracts(II)* 2.244. **1792** Morris *Diary* 2.395. *Oxford* 6-7; TW 158. See **H13**, **S449**.

G135   A Grain of caution is worth a pound of medicine (*varied*)

1780 *Commerce of Rhode Island* 2.111: One Grain of Caution is worth a Pound of Medicine. **1805** Ames *Letters* 1.345: A grain of prevention, say the wise, is worth a ton of remedy. See **O44**.

G136   To take with a Grain of salt

1645 Wheelwright *Writings* 210: Taken *cum grano salis*. **1777** Smith *Memoirs(II)* 2.61: These accounts are to be taken cum grano, **1778** (II) 375: taken cum grano. **1786** Van Schaack *Letters* 422: [Latin only]. **1789** Adams *Diary* 463: It must be understood, as they say, with a grain of salt. **1789** *Columbian Magazine* 3.126: [Latin only].

1802 Tyler *Prose* 390: [Latin only]. **1805** Brackenridge *Modern* 516: These strictures must be taken "with a grain of salt." **1830** Ames *Mariner's* 71: [Latin only]. Barbour 79(2); *Oxford* 330; Tilley G402; Whiting *NC* 470: Salt(4).

G137 To puff and blow like a **Grampus**

1744 Black *Journal* 1.132: To see A person come puffing and blowing like a Grampus before a Storm. *Oxford* 330; TW 158. See **P236.**

G138 To shoot one's **Granny**

1832 Ames *Nautical* 23: They have "shot their granny," which is, I take it, the English for the "reductio ad absurdum" of the logicians. TW 158(3).

G139 To seem to stand awry like **Grantham Steeple**

1717 Wise *Vindication* 89: Nay the best we can meet with without vanity or Envy, that not only seemingly like *Grantham* Steeple, but really it stands awry. *Oxford* 331; Tilley H396.

G140 The **Grapes** are sour

c1700 Byrd *Another Secret Diary* 260: I did never think the Fruit the less beautifull, for being out of my reach. **1702** Mather *Magnalia* 1.31: Sometimes find fault that "the grapes are not ripe." **1720** Walter *Choice Dialogue* xvi: A man is very apt (as the Fox in the Fable) to call it sowre stuff, because it is out of his Reach. **1748** Smith (John) *Diary* 170: My returns have rather been like Sour Grapes, than suitable. **1780** JThaxter in *Adams FC* 3.341. **1784** POliver in Hutchinson *Diary* 2.415: The grapes, I know as well as the fox did, that they are sour. **1786** JQAdams in Smith *Journal and Correspondence* 2(1) 117: Old bachelors too are very apt to talk of sour grapes. **1788** Washington *Writings* 30.98: The Fable, in which the Fox is represented as undervaluing the grapes he could not reach. **1792** Ames *Letters* 1.123. **1796** Cobbett *Porcupine* 4.123: These writings are now become *dirty water!* Say rather, *sour grapes,* **1797** 6.81. **1805** Parkinson *Tour* 733. **1808** Jefferson *Writings* 16.310. **1810** Beecher *Autobiography* 1.230: An argument of vexation, somewhat analogous to that of the fox after vain exertions to reach the grapes. **1816** *Port Folio* 4NS 1.489. **1822** Gallatin *Diary* 197: It is a case of sour grapes. **1822** EMitchell in *Ruffin Papers* 1.263: Without any particle of that feeling which influenced the fox to aver respecting the grapes that they were sour I can say that I thank God I have no children. **1825** WBingham in Murphey *Papers* 1.305. **a1826** Woodworth *Melodies* 156. Barbour 79(2); *Oxford* 331; Whiting F597.

G141 One cannot gather **Grapes** of thorns, *etc.*

1652 Williams *Writings* 4.166: We cannot expect *grapes* from such *briars,* nor *figs* from such *thistles,* **1676** 5.392: No *grapes* will be gathered of these *Thorns,* nor *Figs* of these *Thistles.* **1704** Chalkley *Journal* 47-8. **1711** JDummer in *W&MCQ* 3S 24 (1967) 418: The thorns have yielded me grapes, and the thistles figs. **1718** Chalkley *Observations* 450, **1720** *Considerations* 518, **1725** *Journal* 154, 157. **1743** *Franklin-Mecom* 38. **1753** *Independent Reflector* 219: As easily will Figs grow upon Thorns or Grapes upon Thistles. **1782** JJay in Van Schaack *Letters* 320: From such "thorns no man could expect to gather grapes." **1788** *American Museum* 3.562. **1789** *Columbian Magazine* 3.298. **1790** *Herald of Freedom* in Buckingham *Specimens* 1.324: Can the figtree bear olive berries, or the vine figs. **1796** Dennie *Lay Preacher* 57: My readers will gather grapes from my thorns. **1807** *Weekly* 1.224: When grapes shall grow on brambles, then, Expect *good* measures from *bad* men. **1810** *Tyler Letters* 1.246. **1819** Brackenridge *South America* 1.49. **1819** Cobbett *Year's* 129. *Oxford* 331; Whiting G421.

G142 Strong enough to bear up a **Grape-shot**

1830 Ames *Mariner's* 24: Coffee, strong enough to bear up a *grape shot.* Cf. Whiting *NC* 494: Wedge(4).

G143 As green as **Grass**

1709 Lawson *Voyage* 134: Poison . . . as green as Grass. Barbour 79(4); *Oxford* 336-7; Whiting G422.

G143a Grass-green

1672 Josselyn *New-Englands Rarities* 109: Color . . . of a sad Grass green, 130: One Leaf of a Grass Green colour, **1674** *Account* 115. **1772** Hearne *Journey* 390: Others with beautiful grass-green legs. **a1786** Ladd *Remains* 135: This grass-green hill. **a1814** Dow *Journal* 479: The fourth an Emerald, and is of grass green. Whiting G422a.

G144 As long as Grass grows and water runs

1750 The Raven in McDowell *Documents* 1.75: As long as Grass grows and Water runs. DA grass 4d; TW 159(2). See **R92, S527.**

G145 Grass will grow (grows) in the streets

1727 JWentworth in *Baxter Manuscripts* 10.414: Trade . . . stagnated to that Degree that the grass in Boston streets will soon appear. **1797** Lee *Diary and Letters* 40: Antwerp . . . and now grass grows in the streets.

G146 Grass will not grow on an oft-beat path

1769 Woodmason *Journal* 145: The Path was too oft beat for any Grass to grow except the Field could be lock'd up. [A promiscuous woman is childless.] Barbour 79(2); *Oxford* 331; Tilley G414.

G147 No Grass grows to my heels

1740 Belcher *Papers* 2.311: No grass grows to my heels. **1812** BFStickney in Knopf *War of 1812* 6(1) 204: The grass does not grow under my feet, day or night. Barbour 80(5); *Oxford* 331; TW 159(6).

G148 To be turned out to Grass

1792 Ames *Letters* 1.123: From the account of the votes . . . I think I shall be turned out to grass. NED Grass *sb.*[1] 5.

G149 To bloom and die like Grass

1744 Mather Byles, *Poems on Several Occasions* (Boston, 1744) 58: He blooms and dies like grass. Cf. Whiting G436.

G150 To go to Grass

1807 *Balance* in Thornton *Glossary* 1.370: He will have to go to grass, as the saying is. **1819** Peirce *Rebelliad* 66: Thucydides may go to grass. Barbour 79(1); TW 159(4).

G151 To wither like Grass

1642 SGorton in Winslow *Hypocrisie* 24: Which . . . like the grasse shall wither. Cf. Whiting G435, 436.

G152 While the Grass grows the steed starves

1748 Eliot *Essays* 41: *While the Grass grows the Steed starves.* **1775** Committee of Deer Island [Maine] in *Naval Documents* 1.910: Reflectings on that Proverb—While the grass Grows the Cattle Starve. **1788** *Politician* 8: While the grass grows the mare starves—the horse, I mean. **1845** Jackson *Correspondence* 6.368: While the grass grows the steed starves. **1848** Paulding *Letters(II)* 475-6, **1856** 565. *Oxford* 331-2; Whiting G437.

G153 As feeble as a Grasshopper

1784 Smith *Diary* 1.58: She is as feeble as a Grasshopper. Cf. Whiting *NC* 417: poor.

G154 As thick as Grasshoppers

1815 Bentley *Diary* 4.347: Tales thick as grasshoppers.

G155 As cold as the Grave

1819 Pintard *Letters* 1.233: I c[d] not . . . obtrude myself on a new and strange lady, cold as the grave, & wrapped up in her own self & her darling plants. Barbour 80(1); Whiting *NC* 417(1).

G156 As cruel as the Grave

1778 Galloway *Diary* 61: They are Cruel as the grave. **1780** Curwen *Journal* 2.607: Party rage . . . is cruel as the grave. **1782** JA in *Adams FC* 4.324: Jealousy is as cruel as the Grave, and Envy as spightful as Hell. **1802** Dow *Journal* 148: How guarded we should be against the spirit of jealousy! which is as cruel as the grave! Song of Songs 8.6. See **D63.**

G157 As dark as the Grave

1758 Smith *Works* 1[2].136: Dark as the grave. **1809** Weems *Marion* 89: A veil, dark as the grave, is thrown over future events. TW 160(4).

G158 As secret as the Grave

1779 *Adams FC* 4.193, n.3: Secret as the Grave, **1785** *Works* 8.279: Keep this as secret as the grave. **1793** Hamilton *Papers* 14.467, 545. **1822** Adams *Memoirs* 6.112. TW 160(7).

G159   As serious as the **Grave**

1801 Sewall *Poems* 165: While each long phiz was serious as the grave.

G160   As silent as the **Grave**

1778 TPaine in Deane *Papers* 3.99: A public man . . . ought to be as silent as the grave. **1778** *Washington *Writings* 12.149: They stole off as silent as the grave, 157. **1784** WShort in Jefferson *Papers* 7.236. **1785** Jefferson *Writings* 19.6: In the silence of the grave. **1804** GDavis in *Barbary Wars* 4.271. **1807** Weems *Murder* 38: Tho silent as the grave that waited to receive her. **1812** Melish *Travels* 447. **1815** *Port Folio* 3NS 5.258. **1816** Ker *Travels* 283. *Oxford* 733; Svartengren 386; TW 160(8). See **D69, T175.**

G161   As stern as the **Grave**

1781 WSSmith in Webb *Correspondence* 2.363: We shall look as stern as the grave upon him.

G162   The **Grave** is a place of perfect equality

1782 Freneau *Prose* 73: The market house, like the grave, is a place of perfect equality. *Oxford* 459; Tilley G428. See **D79, G80.**

G163   He has dug his **Grave** and must lie in it

1844 Hone *Diary* 2.700: He has dug his own grave and must lie in it. Cf. *Oxford* 502: Bed.

G164   To dig one's **Grave** with his teeth

1789 *Columbian Magazine* 3.431: To dig my own grave with my teeth. **1820** Pintard *Letters* 1.338: More, says the old proverb, dig their graves with their Teeth than their Tankard. Barbour 80(3); *Oxford* 187; TW 160(10).

G165   As sleek (slick) as **Grease**

1803 *Yankee Phrases* 87: Sleek as grease. **1811** *Massachusetts Spy* in Thornton *Glossary* 1.316: I should pass Slick as grease, cf. 2.809. Barbour 80(1); TW 160(1).

G166   To fret in one's **Grease**

1733 Belcher *Papers* 1.369: They have been fretting in their grease for three years past. *Oxford* 292; Whiting G443.

G167   He that is **Greedy** is never happy

1824 *Austin Papers* 1.992: A greedy man can never be happy, the loss of a cent makes him miserable. Whiting M52, 53.

G168   As merry as a **Greek**

1724 Mather *Letters* 397: And that the ancient Greeks began with small cups at their merry meetings (in which they would be as *merry as Greeks*). **1775** Stiles *Diary* 1.516: He . . . is gay & merry as a Greek. *Oxford* 528; Tilley M901. Cf. Taylor *Comparisons* 57. See **G174.**

G169   To be all **Greek** to one (*varied*)

1794 Asbury *Journal* 2.14: But it seemed as if my discourse had almost as well have been Greek. **1807** *Port Folio* NS 1.368: 'Tis Greek to me. **1817** Royall *Letters* 87: The conversation (which was all Greek to me) was interrupted by the old farmer, **1818** 125: They stuff it with such a number of outrageous hard words, that I could understand Greek sooner, **1826** *Sketches* 60: They pay no more attention to you than if you were muttering Greek. Barbour 80; *Oxford* 336; TW 161(2). See **H175.**

G170   When **Greek** meets Greek then comes the tug of war

1804 Irving *Journals* 1.69: "When Greek meets Greek then comes the tug of war." **1815** *Port Folio* 3NS 5.300: For Greek meeting Greek, comes the hard tug of war. **1818** Hall *Travels* 220: But when "Greek meets Greek," the careless fastening of a vizor-clasp may decide the contest. c1820 Bernard *Retrospections* 57: And "When Greek meets Greek," etc. *Oxford* 336; TW 161(3).

G171   **Greek** faith

1674 Josselyn *Account* 181: No trading for a stranger with them, but with a *Grecian* faith, which is not to part with your ware without ready money. **1702** Mather *Magnalia* 2.558: The Indians observing but a *Greek faith* in the slow fulfilments of their promises. Tilley F31. See **P313, R65.**

G172 The **Greek** calends

1678 CMather in *Mather Papers* 383: Which may . . . bee before the Greek Calends. **1713** Wise *Churches* 110: Till the Greek Calends come about. **1778** Gadsden *Writings* 154: *Ad Graeca Calendas.* **1790** Dennie *Letters* 31: I shall defer my application to it till the *winter vacation,* or, in the words of Augustus the Lacedemonian, *ad Graecas Calendas.* **1804** Adams *Memoirs* 1.296: This I suppose will be ad Kalendas Græcas. *Oxford* 336; TW 53. See **L43.**

G173 Three **Griefs** enough to kill a man

1702 Mather *Magnalia* 1.224: The Italian proverb, "To wait for one who does not come; to lye a bed not able to sleep; and to find it impossible to please those whom we serve; are three griefs enough to kill a man."

G174 As merry as a **Grig**

c**1790** Tyler *Contrast* 36: I don't see why she should not be as merry as a grig. **1790** Morris *Diary* 1.384: [He] is as merry a Grig as lives. **1801** Story *Shop* 47, 155. **1824** *Tales* 2.59. **1833** Baldwin *Diary* 232. *Oxford* 527; TW 162. See **G168.**

G175 As grey as **Grimalkin**

1821 Knight *Poems* 2.186: You'll die an old maid, grey as our grimalkin. Cf. Lean 2.838.

G176 To **Grin** and bear it

1774 MOgden in Burr *Memoirs* 1.47: I grinned and bore it. **1778** Kemble *Papers* 1.150: What am I to do?—Why, wretch, Grin and bear it. **1799** Carey *Plumb* 47. **1801** SFelton in American Antiquarian Society *Proceedings* NS 69(1959) 133. **1805** Brackenridge *Modern* 605. **1818** Gallatin *Diary* 120. Barbour 81; *Oxford* 339; TW 162(1).

G177 (Not) to see through a **Grindstone**

1807 *Emerald* NS 1.88: *Without seeing through a grindstone,* I could see he did not like this. TW 162(3). See **M175.**

G178 To bring **Grist** to one's mill

1637 Morton *New English Canaan* 283: There hee would be a meanes to bringe sacks to their mill. **1691** *Revolution* in *An-* *dros Tracts* 1.116: The greedy Officers would hereby have Grist to their Mill, 161, 168. **1765** GSims in Boyd *Eighteenth Century Tracts* 188: The hardships we suffer . . . for Benton to bring grist to his own mill. **1776** Smith *Memoirs(II)* 39: To draw Grist to his Mill. **1779** Moore *Diary* 2.174. **1787** *American Museum* 2.595: All nature seems proud to bring grist to our mill. **1800** Cobbett *Porcupine* 11.295: I told the "True American," . . . that more of the same grist might easily be gotten at the same mill. **1805** Brackenridge *Modern* 623: Occasioning a double douse, Of grist to this your mill, you goose. *Oxford* 339; TW 162. See **F141, 300.**

G179 Not advance a grey **Groat**

1785 Curwen *Journal* 2.1035: [I shall not] willingly advance a grey groat. NED Grey 8.

G180 Not amount to a **Groat**

1772 Carter *Diary* 2.730: It is my 3d plannet that governs and I shall not this year amount to a Groat.

G181 Not care a **Groat**

1792 Freneau *Poems* 3.106: Though the low-born may chatter, I care not a groat. NED Groat 2c.

G182 Not matter a **Groat**

1753 *Independent Reflector* 430: Which after all matter'd not a Groat. **1768** Adams(S) *Writings* 1.204: It was not a groat's matter which of them had the honor of it.

G183 Not value a **Groat**

1777 JBurgoyne in Moore *Diary* 1.461: Nor reason valued at a groat.

G184 Not worth a **Groat**

1636 JWinter in *Trelawny Papers* 90: [He is] I think not worth a groat. **1690** Fitzhugh *Letters* 271: For I think your precious factor not worth a groat. **1700** JConverse in *Baxter Manuscripts* 9.99: All he hath, Is thought not to be worth A Groat. **1777** TCollins in Rodney *Letters* 194: I think at present that the Militia will not be worth a groat in a little time. **1790** JBarrell in Webb *Correspondence* 3.153. **1792** *Echo* 35. **1807** Weems *Letters* 2.366: Knowledge, alas! not worth a groat. *Oxford* 339; Whiting G474.

G185 He that sits on the **Ground** seldom falls lower

1792 Scott *Journal* 315: He that sits upon the ground seldom falls lower. *Oxford* 461; Whiting G479. See **N114.**

G186 As weak as a **Grub**

1826 Jones *Sketches* 1.152: It has left Turkey weak as a grub, with its coat just shed.

G187 To swallow **Gudgeons**

1636 THewson in *Winthrop Papers(A)* 3.235: Neither standeth it with the Credit of Mr. Johnsons frends to swallow such Guggions. *Oxford* 791; Tilley G473.

G188 As clean as a **Gun**

1733 Byrd *Journey* 266: I prescribed him a gallon or two of chicken broth, which washed him as clean as a gun.

G189 As sure as a **Gun**

1764 *Paxton Papers* 176: For plain it is, and sure's a Gun Four contain four, three, two and One. **1794** Brackenridge *Gazette* 241: As sure's a gun. **1809** Lindsley *Love* 8: Jest found, sure as guns. **1809** Weems *Marion* 109: Lost, as sure as a gun. **1815** *Port Folio* 3NS 5.298. *Oxford* 789; TW 164(2). See **R80.**

G190 To blow great **Guns**

1764 Carter *Diary* 1.260: The snow and ice in Storms of Great Guns. **1769** HBarnes in Murray *Letters* 124: The wind blew like guns. **1803** Davis *Travels* 427: It blows great guns. **1818** Gallatin *Diary* 134. **1845** Hone *Diary* 2.726. *Oxford* 70; TW 164(9).

G191 To marry the **Gunner's** daughter

1803 Davis *Travels* 418: Marry him to the gunner's daughter [*i.e.,* flog]. *Oxford* 514; TW 164-4. See **M196.**

G192 According to **Gunter**

1713 Wise *Churches* 80: This is the way . . . as the Square or Rule most agreeable with Gunter, to take the Dimensions, Length and Breath of our Candidates [for the ministry] by. **1839** Ames *Mariner's* 129: It was not "according to Gunter." TW 165.

G193 As plain as **Gunter's** line

1713 Chalkley *Journal* 79: They were as plain as *Gunter's Line,* or as 1, 2, 3. NED Gunter 1.

G194 **Guts** can sometimes do more than brains

1742 Belcher *Papers* 2.422: Gutts can sometimes do more than brains. Cf. *Oxford* 341; Tilley G485.

G195 (Not) fit to carry **Guts** to a bear

1789 Brackenridge *Gazette* 313: Just fit to carry guts to a bear. **1816** *Port Folio* 4NS 2.89: A member of the Boston assembly . . . left in a pet, declaring . . . that not one of the members was fit to carry *offals* to a bear. *Oxford* 104; TW 165.

G196 One's **Guts** are in his brains

1721 *The Little-Compton Scourge* in *New-England Courant* after 1: For your Works declare, your Guts are in your Brains. *Oxford* 341; Tilley G484.

G197 To fret one's **Guts** to fiddle-strings

1772 CCarroll in *MHM* 14(1919) 284: Mr. Aston has fretted his Guts to Fiddle strings about Mr. Lucas's Pranks. *Oxford* 287.

H

H1 Hab nab

1656 Hammond *Leah* 7: Beware them, for it is not only hab nab whether ye go to a good service or a bad, but scandalous to your selves to be so seduced. NED Hab; *Oxford* 342; Whiting H1. See **H229.**

H2 Habit (Custom, Use) is a second nature

1797 Makemie *Writings* 182: Habit becomes fixed like a second nature. **1757** Smith *Works* 1^2.96: Custom . . . is justly called a second nature. **1776** WStewart in *Naval Documents* 5.70: I . . . asked him whether . . . if we pursued it much longer it would not become a second Nature to Us. **1777** Wister *Journal* 114: It verifies the old proverb, that "Use is second nature." **1782** MRidley in *W&MCQ* 3S 20(1963) 106: Habit becomes second nature. **1785** Hunter *Quebec* 26: Custom everywhere becomes a second nature. **1787** *Columbian Magazine* 1.463: An assumed character by habit, may be strengthened into a second nature. **1792** Barlow *Works* 1.112-3: When a person was repeating to Fontenelle the common adage *l'habitude est la seconde nature,* the philosopher replied, "*Et faites moi la grace de me dire, quelle est la premier.*" **1797** Mann *Female* 138: Use soon becomes a second nature. **1806** Randolph(J) *Letters* 18. **1807** Janson *Stranger* 298. **1807** *Salmagundi* 399-400: As the ingenious Linkum Fidelius profoundly affirmeth. **1809** Irving *History* 1.278: It would be impossible to suppress a practice which . . . had become second nature. **1810** Cuming *Sketches* 312: The truth of the old adage, that *custom is second na-*

ture. **1820** Weems *Letters* 3.269. *Oxford* 162; TW 166; Whiting C646.

H3 Habit makes all things agreeable

1770 Adams *Legal Papers* 3.160: Habit makes all things agreeable. **1770** Quincy *Memoir* 32: Habit makes all things agreeable: what at first was irksome soon becomes pleasing. **1772** Copy-book in *Wheelock's Indians* opp. 276: Custom makes things familiar and Easy. **1785** Hopkinson *Miscellaneous Essays* 2.159: But habit reconciles every thing. **1800** Eaton *Life* 141: Habit reconciles mankind to every thing, even humiliation; and custom veils disgrace. TW 88: Custom. See **C387, U14.**

H4 Habits are hard to break

1758 Franklin *Papers* 8.215: I hear the reader say, Habits are hard to break. **1792** Belknap *Foresters* 119: Old habits are not easily broken. Whiting C645. See **C385.**

H5 To be under the **Hackle**

1819 Jackson *Correspondence* 2.446: Genl. Mitchel is under the Hackle for smuggling affrican slaves. See **F311, H86.**

H6 As deaf as a **Haddock**

1803 *Yankee Phrases* 87: And she, like a haddock, grew deaf. Svartengren 175. Cf. TW 40: Braddock; Whiting *NC* 418.

H7 Had-I-wist

1623 EHowes in *Winthrop Papers(A)* 3.292: I . . . give caution for a good beginning and foundation, that hereafter it may not be said Pœnitet, or had-I-wist. *Oxford* 342; Whiting H9.

H8   As thick as Hail

1637 Morton *New English Canaan* 271: And that there shafts were let fly as thick as haile at him. **1775** DWard in Ward *Correspondence* 48: The Small Pox was as thick as hale. **1809** Weems *Washington* 90: Cannon-balls . . . fell upon it thick as hail, **1816** *Letters* 3.169: And it does make my heart bleed to see . . . the fat-back[d] Dutchmen, sowing thick as hail their seed for the bread that perisheth. **1818** CBeecher in Vanderpoel *Chronicles* 187: Mop-sticks & broomsticks thick as hail . . . Shall fall on your devoted pate. **1823** Weems *Letters* 3.355: Here have the bullets been flying thick like hail. Whiting H13. See **H12.**

H9   To fly like Hail

1676 Tompson *Poems* 59: Like haile arrows and bullets flew. **1702** Mather *Magnalia* 1.53: Arrows that flew like hail. **1725** Wolcott *Poetical Meditations* 60: With winged Arrows like a shower of Hail. **1745** Pote *Journal* 4: Bullets flew among us Like hail from y[e] heavens. **1775** JChester in Webb *Correspondence* 1.64: Musket Balls were flying about our Ears like hail. **1775** *Pennsylvania Packet* in *Naval Documents* 1.607. **1821** Freneau *Last Poems* 46: When beams and shingles flew, like hail. TW 166(3); Whiting H14.

H10   To rattle like Hail

1775 SMott in *Naval Documents* 2.320: The grape Shot ratled round me Like hail. Cf. Whiting H14.

H11   To run down like Hail

1740 Murray *Letters* 48: The tears run down her Cheeks like hail.

H12   As thick as Hailstones

1666 Alsop *Maryland* 63: The Bullets flew about their ears as thick as Hail-stones usually fall from the Sky. **1775** Webb *Correspondence* 1.64: Double headed Shot flew as thick as Hail Stones. **1786** Humphreys *Works* 33.253: Then thick as hail-stones from an angry sky. Whiting H13. See **H8.**

H13   Against the Hair

c1780 Witherspoon *Works* 4.390: I would advise every man . . . however smooth and gentle a Scotchman may appear, not to take him *against the hair,* as the saying is in their own country. *Oxford* 7; Whiting H36. See **G134, S449.**

H14   A Hair of the same dog

a1820 Tucker *Essays* 233: They tried the "hair of the same dog," as the topers say. **1843** Paulding *Letters(II)* 337: Whose evils are only expected to cure themselves, by the application of the hair of the Same dog whose teeth gave the wound. Barbour 82(11); *Oxford* 343; Whiting H21.

H15   More than (numberless as) the Hairs of one's head

1744 Brainerd *Memoirs* 137: They appeared more in number than the hairs of my head. **1811** Weems *Gambling* 10: Proofs numberless as the hairs of thine head. Whiting H24.

H16   Not change a Hair

1812 Hitchcock *Social* 34: All don't change realities a hair. Cf. Whiting H25-30.

H17   Not hurt a Hair (of one's head)

1752 JFrancis in McDowell *Documents* 1.251: Without hurting a Hair of him. **1769** WSJohnson in *Trumbull Papers* 1.332: We will not hurt a hair of your heads. **1798** Murdock *Politicians* 28: I would nae injure a hair of his head. TW 167(16).

H18   To a Hair

1744 Hamilton *Itinerarium* 160: The pedlar seemed to understand his business to a hair. **1778** WMalcom in *Clinton Papers* 3.668: Your remarks. . . correspond with my opinion to a hair. **1780** *New-York Gazette* in *Newspaper Extracts(II)* 5.107. **1787** Freneau *Poems* 2.350: His boat was his own — and he knew to a hair. **1788** *Politician* 3. **1807** *Salmagundi* 183. **1809** *Port Folio* 2NS 1.185. **a1811** Henry *Account* 89. **1815** Freneau *Poems(1815)* 1.32. **1817** Weems *Franklin* 130: [They] will answer this character to a hair. TW 167(7).

H19 To have one's **Hair** stand on end

1796 Cobbett *Porcupine* 4.140: At the very idea of which my hair stands on end. TW 167(15).

H20 To shave the **Hair** off one's teeth

1809 Lindsley *Love* 26: The black barded jews'll shave the hair off my teeth. Cf. *Oxford* 721; Tilley E76.

H21 To split **Hairs**

1767 Lloyd *Papers* 2.707: If you are for Splitting Hairs. **1793** Jefferson *Writings* 9.87: E. R. found out a hair to split. **1794** Adams *Writings* 1.247: Splitting hairs of etiquette. **1803** *Port Folio* 3.135. **1813** JWilkinson in Jackson *Correspondence* 1.286: I have no disposition to split Hairs or make difficulties. **1814** GMorris in Otis *Letters* 2.184: The Federalists may . . . deliberate and hesitate and split Hairs about Right and Wrong. **1817** Adams *Writings* 6.263: The Republicans could split hairs of principle. **1818** Hall *Travels* 201. c**1825** Tyler *Prose* 67. *Oxford* 164; TW 167(17).

H22 A **Hair('s)** breadth

c**1700** Taylor *Poems* 396: If of the Law one hair breadth short it fall, **1702** *Christographia* 218.11: It should ascend another haire breadth more, **1703** 339.26-7: From which it cannot vary a hair breadth. **1704** Knight *Journal* 9: To lodg my tongue a hair's breadth more on one side of my mouth than tother. **1740** *Letter* in *Colonial Currency* 4.9: Souls can't be made to see a Hair's Breadth beyond the circle of self. **1744** Hamilton *Itinerarium* 36: Hair's. **1751** Wolcott *Papers* 31: hairs. **1773** Quincy *Memoir* 69: hair. **1776** RMorris in Deane *Papers* 1.332: hair's. **1778** WChipman in *Winslow Papers* 23: hair. **1781** Adams *Works* 7.364: hair's. **1781** Jefferson *Papers* 4.637: hair's. **1783** JWarren in *Warren-Adams Letters* 2.231: hair. **1785** Hunter *Quebec* 27: hairs. **1788** Humphreys *Works* 272: hair's. **1790** Jefferson *Papers* 16.601: hair. **1790** Maclay *Journal* 177: hair. **1791** JAdams in *Warren-Adams Letters* 2.327, n.1: hair's. **1798** Cobbett *Porcupine* 10.10: Than see a *Jury* strain a point but the breadth of a hair against him. **1798** EWin-slow in *Winslow Papers* 429: hair's. **1800** TPierce in Vanderpoel *Chronicles* 377: hair's. **1801** Asbury *Journal* 2.290: hair's. **1812** Lee *Memoirs* 2.175: hair. **1813** Adams *Writings* 4.479: hair's, **1817** *Memoirs* 3.525: hair's. **1823** Jefferson *Writings* 18.322: hair's. **1826** Royall *Sketches* 123: [He] was within a hair's breadth of being hung. **1827** *Austin Papers* 2.1565: hairs. **1830** Longfellow *Letters* 1.337: hair's. *Oxford* 151; Whiting B526.

H23 **Half** a loaf is better than no bread

1693 IMather in *Andros Tracts* 2.310: It is an old proverb, That *half a Loaf is better than no Bread.* **1721** *Boston News-Letter* in Buckingham *Specimens* 1.9: According to the Proverb . . . half a Loafe was better than no Bread. **1765** JOtis *Vindication* in Bailyn *Pamphlets* 1.562: Unless the gentleman will contend that half a loaf is equal to a whole one. **1775** SMoylan in *Naval Documents* 2.434. **1777** JChester in Huntington *Papers* 370. **1778** Smith *Memoirs(II)* 423: I . . . said Great B would never think Half a Loaf equal to a whole one. **1781** MWillet in Stark *Memoir* 222: It is a true old saying that. **1789** Lee *Letters* 2.499: I hope that if we cannot gain the whole loaf, we shall at least have some bread. **1790** Maclay *Journal* 326. **1794** *Echo* 123: What proverbs old have said, That, a**1807** 203. **1830** JOverton in Jackson *Correspondence* 4.153. **1833** Wirt *Letters* 2.407: Rather give me the half loaf than no bread at all. **1839** Paulding *Letters(II)* 271: You must therefore be satisfied with half a loaf, and console yourself with the old Proverb. Barbour 112: Loaf; *Oxford* 344; Whiting H39. See **H28.**

H24 **Half** the truth is often a great lie

1758 Franklin *PR* 7.353: Half the Truth is often a great Lie. **1789** Adams *Diary* 464: Half the truth is oftentimes a great falsehood. *Oxford* 344. See **T273.**

H25 One **Half** the world does not know how the other half lives

1755 Franklin *PR* 5.467: It is a common Saying, that One Half of the World does not know how the other Half lives. **1786** Hunter *Quebec* 257: In short, half the world do not know how the other half live. **1797** Mann *Female* 114. Barbour 83(5); *Oxford* 344-5; TW 414(7).

H26   To see with **Half** an eye

1683 *Mather Papers* 105: Wee may see with halfe an eye which way they intend to drive poor England. **c1737** *Colden Letters* 9.302: [He] said any one with half an eye can see with what Success an appeal is like to be attended. **1745** Johnson *Writings* 3.470: We can't but see with half an eye. **1746** *Georgia Records* 25.52. **1786** Jefferson *Papers* 10.245. **1786** Smith *Diary* 2.59. **1806** *Port Folio* NS 1.39: Those who *understand* the American newspapers must do it with half an eye. **1814** Kerr *Barclay* 272: A man with half an eye could see through the deception. TW 124: Eye(22).

H27   To go off **Half-cocked**

1815 WWirt in *W&MCQ* 22(1913) 251: Why can't you quit this way you have of going off half cock'd? **1821** Doddridge *Dialogue* 50: I go off half-cocked sometimes. **1844** Jackson *Correspondence* 6.340: He goes off at half bent, 341: But some times [he] goes off at half cock. Barbour 83; TW 168.

H28   **Half-pay** is better than no pay

c1770 ADunbar in American Antiquarian Society, *Proceedings* NS 19 (1908) 71: Half pay is better than no pay. Cf. *Oxford* 751: Somewhat; Whiting S462. See **H23.**

H29   To give up one's **Half-penny**

1737 Franklin *Drinkers* 2.176: He drank till he gave up his Half-Penny. Tilley H50.

H30   To be **Half-seas** over

1724 Mather *Letters* 397: Began with small cups . . . and then call for large ones when they were half seas over. **1737** Franklin *Drinkers* 2.177: He's Half Seas over. **1744** Hamilton *Itinerarium* 81: He was more than half seas over in liquor. **1774** Fithian *Journal and Letters* 226: But Mr Lane was (as they say) "Half Seas over," **1775** *Journal* 55. **1780** Marshall *Diary* 258: Giving us a relation of the conduct at times of Daniel Whitelock, when half or quite over (in the seaman's term). **1788** *American Museum*

4.490. **1796** Bentley *Diary* 2.182: He had not his sea legs, but the Sea sickness on horseback, & was more than half-seas over. **1798** Ames *Diary* 78. **1806** Fanning *Narrative* 93. **1810** Cuming *Sketches* 231-2. **1819** Waln *Hermit* 121. **1844** ERWare in *New England Merchants* 314: Steward ran away yesterday . . . back half seas over. *Oxford* 344; TW 168.

H31   To be **Half-shaved**

1813 Weems *Drunkard* 60: Half-shaved. NED Suppl. Half-shaved.

H32   It is merry in **Hall** when beards wag all

1697 Sewall *Letter-Book* 1.184: I have no more at present in my hands: And the Proverb is Tis merry in the Hall, when beards wag all. *Oxford* 528; Whiting H46.

H33   As high as **Haman**

1845 FBlair in Jackson *Correspondence* 5.238: [quoting Jackson] The leaders I will hang as high as Haman. TW 168.

H34   Like *Hamlet* minus the Prince of Denmark

1817 Gallatin *Diary* 117: It was like "Hamlet" minus the Prince of Denmark. *Oxford* 345.

H35   As dead as a **Hammer**

1803 *Yankee Phrases* 87: I soon shall be dead, as a hammer. Barbour 83; TW 168(1).

H36   **Hammer** and tongs

1759 CWhittelsey in Stiles *Itineraries* 583: And so we go at it hammer and tongs. *Oxford* 346; TW 168(3).

H37   One must be either **Hammer** or anvil

1785 Jefferson *Papers* 8.568: Every man here must be either the hammer or the anvil, **1786** 9.591: Every man must be the anvil or the hammer. Whiting *NC* 419(3).

H38   As easy as kiss your **Hand**

1811 Weems *Gambling* 16: Just as easy as kiss your hand. *Oxford* 213; TW 168(1).

H39   From **Hand** to mouth

1656 Hammond *Leah* 16: They . . . make hard shift to subsist from hand to mouth.

1732 Belcher *Papers* 1.113: A poor Govr who lives but from hand to mouth. 1732 Byrd *Progress* 348. 1747 Stith *History* 56: Such Provisions as . . . served them from Hand to Mouth, 82: Careless of every thing, but just from Hand to Mouth, 107. 1761 EWheelock in *Wheelock's Indians* 17: They are used to live from hand to Mout (as we speak). 1762 Eliot *Essays* 172: To write as poor Men live, from Hand to Mouth. 1769 Gadsden *Writings* 82: Buying from hand to mouth. 1770 Johnson *Writings* 1.465: Money comes in from hand to mouth, so that we get along pretty comfortably. 1773 Franklin *Writings* 6.31: We govern from Hand to Mouth. 1774 Andrews *Letters* 344: The poor (who always liv'd from hand to mouth), i.e. depended on one day's labour to supply the wants of another. 1776 Carroll *Correspondence* 1.169. 1777 Huntington *Papers* 389. 1777 JHuntington in *Trumbull Papers* 3.196. 1777 Smith *Journal* 236. 1778 *Trumbull Papers* 3.323. 1778 Washington *Writings* 10.392, 459, 11.277. 1780 Madison *Papers* 2.145: Our army is living from hand to mouth. 1780 GSchaick in *Clinton Papers* 5.762, 7.100, 111. 1780 Washington *Writings* 19.295, 1781 22.366: What we are now likely to draw from the several States will be from hand to mouth. 1791 EDenny in *St. Clair Papers* 2.256. 1792 Wayne *Correspondence* 129. 1802 PCasso in *Blount Papers* 3.489. 1810 Weems *Letters* 3.3. 1816 Lambert *Travels* 2.147: It may be truly said that he lives only from hand to mouth. 1820 Adams *Memoirs* 5.221. 1822 Bache *Notes* 169: They all live, literally, from hand to mouth. 1841 Cooper *Letters* 4.113: This is a hand to mouth country and government, 1850 6.147, 226. *Oxford* 474; Whiting H54.

H40 Help **Hands,** for I have no lands

1745 Franklin *PR* 3.5: Help, Hands; For I have no Lands, 1758 *WW* 342. *Oxford* 368; TW 169(5).

H41 Let not one's right **Hand** know, *etc.*

1766 JDevotion in Stiles *Itineraries* 457: My Right Hand shall not know what my Left Hand does. 1797 Graham *Vermont* 69: That divine precept of the Gospel, "*Not to*

let his left hand know what his right hand did." Barbour 83(4); Whiting H61.

H42 A light **Hand** makes a heavy pocket

c1820 Bernard *Retrospections* 81: A light hand makes a heavy pocket. [Ascribed to Franklin.]

H43 Many **Hands** make light work

1637 IStoughton in *Winthrop Papers(A)* 3.436: But many hands make light work. 1674 Josselyn *Account* 182: Many hands make light work, many hands makes a full fraught, but many mouths eat up all. 1797 Brackenridge *Modern* 325. 1818 Cleveland *Letters* 194. 1830 Ames *Mariner's* 253: So many hands can be employed that it is done very quick. Barbour 83(10); *Oxford* 509; Whiting H62.

H44 Not to know one's right **Hand** from his left

1793 Scott *Journal* 351: Many of them seemed not to know their right hand from their left. *Oxford* 677; Tilley H74.

H45 One **Hand** for the owners and one for yourself

1799 *Port Folio* 2NS 7.130: Always keep one hand for the owners, and one for yourself. Colcord 93; TW 169(8).

H46 One **Hand** washes the other

1836 Hone *Diary* 1.203: Persons in business . . . who make, as the saying is, "one hand wash the other." Barbour 83(11); *Oxford* 347; Tilley H87.

H47 Put not your **Hand** in a dog's mouth

1790 Maclay *Journal* 201: A man ought not to put his hand in a dog's mouth, and trust to his generosity not to bite it.

H48 Strike, but conceal the **Hand**

1812 Stoddard *Sketches* 65: "Strike, but conceal the hand" is no less a maxim among them, than with some of their more civilized contemporaries.

H49 To act (carry) with a high **Hand**

1792 McGillivray *Letters* 348: None but myself . . . can act with a high hand among those chiefs. 1801 Asbury *Letters* 3.211:

Matters had been carried with such a high hand. TW 169(13). Cf. Whiting H72.

H50 To be at one's own **Hand**

1815 Brackenridge *Modern* 735: That like Noctra Mullin's dog, he had been at his own hand, these six weeks. NED Hand 25i.

H51 To be **Hand** and glove

1777 *Deane Brothers Papers* 108: Figuet and Lefeber Are hand and Glove together on this Occasion. **1784** FHopkinson in Jefferson *Papers* 7.20: You may now see those very men who hang'd Roberts and Carlisle hand and glove with the friends of Roberts and Carlisle. **1789** Brown *Better* vi: *Roscius* . . . was hand-in-glove with *Tully*. **1798** *Washington *Writings* 37.71: As familiar with them all . . . as the hand is with the glove. **c1800** Tyler *Island* 12. **1801** Dorr *Letters* 293, **1802** 327. **1805** *Echo* 177: We're hand and glove with atheist Paine. **1806** *Weekly* 1.26. **1822** Robertson *Letters* 195. **1847** Paulding *Letters(II)* 465-6, **1851** 519. *Oxford* 346; TW 169(10).

H52 To be on the losing **Hand**

1704 SPartridge in *Winthrop Papers(B)* 5.183: But alwayes be upon yᵉ looseing hand. NED Hand 4b.

H53 To be on the mending **Hand**

1674 GManning in *Baxter Manuscripts* 6.42: Mine is I hope upon the mending hand, **1677** 169: My Wound is now at ye mending hand. **1724** Bobin *Letters* 178. **1766** Rowe *Diary* 105: [He] thinks he is on the mending hand. **1775** GSimpson in *Letters to Washington* 5.98. **1780** WPaterson in Burr *Memoirs* 1.211. **1789** WGrayson in Henry *Life* 3.389: I am now afflicted with a diarrhoea, though I hope I am on the mending hand. **1806** Webb *Correspondence* 3.227. NED Hand 4b; Tilley H93.

H54 To bear one in **Hand**

1642 Winslow *Hypocrisie* 9: Bearing the world in hand, **1646** 44: These may beare the world in hand that they allow ministration of Justice. **1647** SSymonds in *Winthrop Papers(A)* 5.125: To beare people in hand of multitudes to be of their mind. **1654** Johnson *Wonder-Working* 202. **a1656**

Bradford *History* 1.378: He bore them in hand he could doe great matters, 2.196. **1681** IMather in Willard *Ne Sutor* a4ᵛ. *Oxford* 34; Whiting H65.

H55 To bite the **Hand** that feeds him (*varied*)

1681 FJWinthrop in *Winthrop Papers(B)* 4.295: I like not those spirits that overmuch fawne & croutch whilst they are takeing from the hand, yet when they have opportunety will snekingly & cruelly bite. **1792** Hamilton *Papers* 12.107: It is thought ungrateful for a man to bite the hand that puts bread in his mouth. **1796** Cobbett *Porcupine* 3.347: I never snapped at the hand that gave me bread. **1797** Beete *Man* 27: A fellow that I . . . nurtured in my bosom, viper like, to bite the hand that fostered him. **1798** Carey *Plumb* 37. **1829** MBarney in Jackson *Correspondence* 4.45: Many of your own friends . . . who . . . had stung the bosom which warmed and the hand which fed them. Barbour 83(5, 6); *Oxford* 62; Whiting NC 419(2). See **H182.**

H56 To gather with the **Hands,** *etc.*

1791 *Universal Asylum* 7.14: What they gather with their hands they kick away with their feet.

H57 To get (have) the upper **Hand**

1650 Bradstreet *Works* 312: How some when down, straight got the upper hand, 320: The Persians got the upper hand. **a1656** Bradford *History* 2.52: At length gott the upperhand. **1692** Mather *Wonders* 104: The *Spiritual Wickednesses in High Places,* have manifestly the Upper hand of us. **1733** Johnson *Writings* 3.21, **1754** 1.196: They have the upper hand. **1755** *Johnson Papers* 9.204. **1764** SPowel in Morgan *Journal* 29: His Amor Patriæ maintains the upper hand. **1766** SPurviance in Stiles *Itineraries* 555. **1770** Franklin *Papers* 18.41. **1775** Willard *Letters* 215-6. **1782** Trumbull *Satiric Poems* 181. **1788** McGillivray *Letters* 199. **1791** Morris *Diary* 2.122, 238. **1793** Perkins *Diary* 3.248: have. **1794** Ames *Letters* 1.143. **1794** Jefferson *Writings* 9.291: having. **1795** Morris *Diary and Letters* 2.84: had. **1798** Drinker *Journal* 317: Griswold had the advantage, or upper hand. **1802** Chester *Federalism* 22. **1804** TPickering in Cabot *Letters* 339. **1806** Hitchcock *Works* 20: gain, 77. **1809** Weems *Marion* 189. **1813** Adams *Works* 6.312, **1814** in *Adams-Jefferson Letters* 2.435. **1819** Peirce *Rebelliad* 48. **1845** Paulding *Letters(II)* 392: It appears to me that the Pharisees are getting the upper hand in this Country. *Oxford* 856; Whiting H74.

H58 To get (have) the whip **Hand**

1739 RPartridge in Kimball 1.117: The English have got the whip hand of both the other Powers. **1750** Fairservice *Plain Dealing* 34: They have the whip hand of us. **1775** Rodney *Letters* 58. **1787** Mary C. Dewees, *Journal of a Trip to Philadelphia* (Crawfordsville, Ind., 1936) 10. **1833** Dunlap *Diary* 3.741. *Oxford* 884; TW 169(15).

H59 To give (lend) a helping **Hand**

1741 Stephens *Journal(I)* 2.239: [He] seemed determined to go through stitch, and give his helping Hand to every Design formed in opposition to the Honourable Trust. **1742** *Georgia Records* 23.351: You will lend an helping Hand. **1752** *Johnson Papers* 9.96: lend. **1776** *Clinton Papers* 1.445. Whiting H81.

H60 To kiss the **Hand** that boxes one's ears

1782 Paine *American Crisis* 1.227: It is kissing the hand that boxes his ears. See **R116**.

H61 To make a poor (*etc.*) **Hand**

1720 Byrd *London Diary* 369: The wind blew fresh against us that we could make but a poor hand of it. **1740** Parkman *Diary* 72.103: The Ground was so Strong . . . that they made but a poor Hand of [plowing]. **1741** Stephens *Journal(II)* 1.20. **1748** *Beekman Papers* 1.62: bad, **1753** 184: bad. **1756** JBeamer in McDowell *Documents* 2.95: great. **1760** *Beekman Papers* 1.357: I Expect to make a better hand by What I have shiped to London. **1769** Patten *Diary* 87: My wife and I went a Chestnuting but made a poor hand of it. **1761** Lloyd *Papers* 2.595: bad. **1766** JParker in Franklin *Papers* 13.474. **1766** Shaw *Letter Book* 172. a**1770** Johnson *Writings* 1.38. **1770** Carter *Diary* 1.384: better. **1775** Honyman *Journal* 30:

This young parson made but a poor hand of [his sermon]. **1775** Mason *Papers* 1.225. **1775** Washington *Writings* 4.126: lame. **1777** Perkins *Diary* 1.154. **1779** ECornell in Sullivan *Letters* 2.490: They make but a bad hand of travelling. **1782** Perkins *Diary* 2.116: pretty good, **1785** 270. **1786** Washington *Diaries* 3.56: indifferent. **1788** Perkins *Diary* 2.441: tolerable, **1790** 3.26: great, 41: There is Some ponds . . . where our Salmon Fishermen have usually made a hand of gitting the Salmon, **1791** 82, **1802** 4.425: dull. **1805** Dow *Journal* 248: I will make a hand of it. TW 170(19); Tilley H99.

H62 To put one's **Hand** in the lion's mouth

1761 *Boston Gazette* in *Olden Time* 2.30: Put your Hand in the Lion's Mouth, then get it out if you can. **1804** SRuffin in *Ruffin Papers* 1.59: Remember an old proverb which will well apply to you, "Your hand is in the Lion's mouth, and you must get it out as easily as possible," **1829** 524: However, as my hand is in the "*lion's mouth,*" I must get it out with as little damage as possible. *Oxford* 346; TW 177(14); Tilley H82.

H63 To put one's **Hand** to the plow, *etc.*

1741 ?WDouglass *Second Letter* in *Colonial Currency* 4.115: They have put their Hands to the Plough, &c. **1747** JRutherford in *Colden Letters* 3.334: And as you've now put your hand to the plow you must keep it going, 359: But as you have put your hand to the plough give me leave to add two or three more latin words tu ne cede malis, sed contra audentior ito. **1747** Stith *History* 203: He desired, that having put their Hands to the Plough, they would not now look back, or be weary of well-doing. **1749** *Georgia Records* 25.401: As we have put our hands to the Plough We are Yet willing . . . to prosecute our Designs as far as we can. **1754** HBarclay in Johnson *Writings* 4.25: You have put your hand to the plow, and I know not how you can now look back. **1758** TPownall in *Baxter Manuscripts* 13.141. **1759** JBoucher in *MHM* 7(1912) 12. **1762** Adams *D and A* 1.232. **1766** JParker in Franklin *Papers* 13.535: I can't bear . . . after I have put my Hand to the Plough, to turn back in the Day of Battle. **1775** PVandervoort in *Naval Documents* 1.1295. **1777** Paine *American Crisis* 1.71: We have put . . . our hands to the plough and cursed be he that looketh back. **1783** *Commerce of Rhode Island* 2.181-2: Shearman has put his hand to the plow, and will go thro with his Buisness. **1785** JStuart in *Kingston* 103. **1794** TBlount in *Blount Papers* 2.361. **1798** Adams *New Letters* 178: Every hand should be put to the plough. **1798** *Washington Writings* 36.510. **1813** Fletcher *Narrative* 23. **1813** DHumphreys in Smith *Papers* 1.128. **1814** JLyman in Otis *Letters* 2.185. Whiting H83.

H64 To receive with one **Hand** and pay with the other

1762 Watts *Letter Book* 3: I am to receive with one hand & pay with tother. **1785** Washington *Writings* 28.118: I shall receive with one hand and pay with the other, if I may be allowed to use the phrase. **1816** Paulding *Letters(I)* 2.181: He only receives it in one hand to pay it out with the other. Whiting *NC* 419(4).

H65 To wash one's **Hands** of something

1643 RSaltonstall in *Saltonstall Papers* 1.132: We labour to wash our hands wholly of this dessigne. **1689** JPynchon in *Baxter Manuscripts* 9.51: Wee doe now wash our hands of it. **1740** *Georgia Records* 22².479: From the whole I wash hands. **1765** *Johnson Papers* 11.678. **1775** Deane *Papers* 1.73. **1776** JAdams in *Warren-Adams Letters* 1.248. **1783** Franklin *Writings* 9.93. **1786** MByles in *Winslow Papers* 329: I . . . inclose the papers and wipe my hands of it. **1786** WHooper in Iredell *Correspondence* 2.141: Suffer me to do justice, — if you will not, I wash my hands clean — I wish others could. **1796** Barton *Disappointment* 17. **1797** ASpencer in Webb *Correspondence* 2.204. **1806** *Weekly* 1.151: To wash their hands of Burr. **1807** Mackay *Letters* 71. **1809** Adams *Works* 9.623. **1813** JRandolph in Quincy *JQuincy* 333. **1815** Humphreys *Yankey* 46. **1817** Weems *Franklin* 128: They washed their hands of a bad bargain. **1820** Cooper *Letters* 1.56. **1832** Barney *Memoir* 141. **1832** Cooper *Letters* 2.258,

1833 6.320. Barbour 83(2); *Oxford* 868; Whiting H87.

H66 To wish in one **Hand** and spew in the other, *etc.*

1798 Cobbett *Porcupine* 9.191: You may wish in one hand and spew in the other, and see which will be full first. **1798** Carey *Porcupiniad* 2.10: [Quotes the above and adds this note]: Cobbett has shewn some regard for decency in this expression, which is far more chaste than in its genuine form — the form in which this gentleman uses it in his colloquial style. The word *spew* is not used on those occassions. The one that takes its place begins with the same letter. *Sat verbum sapienti.* Tilley H106.

H67 Two **Hands** in a dish and one in a purse

1811 *Port Folio* 2NS 5.374: Two hands in a dish and one in a purse. *Oxford* 851; Tilley H123.

H68 To give a **Handle**

1777 Smith *Memoirs(II)* 154: I was sorry the Congress of 1774 had given a Handle to suppose nothing less would satisfy us. TW 170(4).

H69 To take by the smooth **Handle**

1787 Jefferson *Papers* 11.271: The plan . . . being to take things by the smooth handle, **1825** *Writings* 16.111: Take things always by the smooth handle. TW 170(8).

H70 **Handsome** is that handsome does

1774 Schaw *Journal* 57: Handsome is, that handsome does. **1791** S.P.L. *Thoughts* 77. Barbour 12: Beauty(1); *Oxford* 348; TW 171(1).

H71 To **Hang** and then judge

1713 Wise *Churches* 146: That illegal Way of Hanging men and then Judging them. Whiting H95. Cf. *Oxford* 459.

H72 **Hanging** (burning) is too good for someone

1777 WGilly in *Baxter Manuscripts* 15.90: Asking if those Rebels did not think hanging was too good for them. **1780** GBurnham in *Baxter Manuscripts* 18.95-6: Jones . . . abused your Deponent very much threatning that Burning was too good for him. **1822** Lee *Diary and Letters* 200: Hanging is too good for such a villain. TW 171.

H73 No **Hanging** for thinking

1760 WFranklin in Franklin *Papers* 9.190: There is no hanging a Man for his Thoughts. **1764** RBland *Colonel* in Bailyn *Pamphlets* 1.343: The proverb which tells us that a man cannot be hanged for *thinking.*

H74 *Hans en kelder* ("Jack in the cellar")

1723 Mather *Letters* 365: And this *Hans en kelder* was a mere apostle (when doing the part of an Apollyon) to his wretched votaries. *Oxford* 351, 408; Tilley J18.

H75 The good or ill **Hap** of a good or ill life, *etc.*

1745 Franklin *PR* 3.8: The good or ill hap of a good or ill life, Is the good or ill choice of a good or ill wife. **1775** Paine *Reflections* 2.1118: 'Tis confessed on all hands that the weal or woe of life depends on no one circumstance so critical as matrimony. *Oxford* 48, 323; Whiting F539, T105. See **F278, W148.**

H76 What **Happens** once may happen again

1815 Waterhouse *Journal* 63: An Englishman's fears may tell him, that what once happened, may happen again. Whiting *NC* 420.

H77 **Happiness** does not consist in riches alone

1792 MDavenport in *M&WCQ* 2S 9(1929) 270: Happiness does not consist in Riches alone. Lean 4.89: Riches. Cf. Barbour 123(16). See **W79.**

H78 **Happy** go lucky

1815 Palmer *Diary* 200: Happy go lucky has at lengh recieved the smile of fortune. TW 171; Tilley H141.

H79 Leave not the **Harbor** in a gale

1815 Freneau *Poems(1815)* 1.154: Perhaps the proverb may be stale, But heed the meaning of the tale, *"Leave not the harbor in a gale."*

H80 **Hardest** fend off

1713 Sewall *Diary* 2.384-5: Were provoked by Capt. Belcher's sending Indian Corn to Curasso. The Select-men desired him not to send it; he told them, the hardest Fend off! If they stop'd his vessel, he would hinder the coming in of three times as much. **1777** Carter *Diary* 2.1091: But W[ashington] sent word hardest send [*for* fend] off, had wanted[?] no truce with him. **1789** McGillivray *Letters* 216: If my Conjecture proves true, why let the Hardest fend off. **1808** *Emerald* NS 1.482: No, no, every one for himself, "hardest, fend off." **1816** Wirt *Letters* 1.415: And after that, "the hardest must fend off." **1851** Cooper *Letters* 6.258: And if the fight must come, the hardest fend off. Colcord 74; TW 171.

H81 As mad as a March **Hare**

1708 Cook *Sot-Weed* 17: No Hare in March was ever madder. **1799** Freneau *Prose* 432: The man's mad—mad as a March hare. **1804** Brackenridge *Modern* 431: As mad as a March hare. **1806** Fessenden *Modern Philosopher* 18. **1806** *Port Folio* NS 1.30. **1809** Fessenden *Pills* 101. **1809** Weems *Marion* 110. **1815** Humphreys *Yankey* 55. **1818** CBeecher in Vanderpoel *Chronicles* 185: And if they did oppose her there, As mad she'd be as a March hare. Barbour 84(2); *Oxford* 497; TW 171-2; Whiting H116.

H82 Don't hunt two **Hares** with one dog

1734 Franklin *PR* 1.353: Don't think to hunt two hares with one dog, **1737** 2.170: He that pursues two Hares at once, does not catch one and lets t'other go. *Oxford* 688; Tilley H163; Whiting F440.

H83 He is happy that learns by other men's **Harms** (*varied*)

1619 RCushman in Bradford *History* 1.88: But rather desire to larne by other mens harmes. **1620** JHuddleston in Bradford *History* 1.272: The old rule which I learned when I went to schoole . . . That is, Hapie is he whom other mens harmes doth make to beware. **1633** EHowes in *Winthrop Papers(A)* 3.115: Faelix quem faciunt aliena pericula, etc. **a1700** Hubbard *New England*

73: Advising them to beware, according to the old rule, by other men's harms. **1729** Chalkley *Journal* 229: Is not that Maxim good? *Let others Harmes learn us to beware, before it be too late.* **1734** Franklin *Papers* 1.359: [Latin only], **1743** *PR* 2.373: [Latin only], **1749** 3.335: Wise Men learn by others Harms, Fools by their own. **1751** Parkman *Diary* 75.124: We ought to learn by the Evils which others suffer'd ourselves to beware. **1758** Franklin *WW* 346. **1767** Adams *D and A* 1.337: Happy is he whom other Mens Errors, render wise . . . Felix quem faciunt aliena Pericula cautum. **1768** Dickinson *Letters* 50: Happy are the Men, and *happy the people who grow wise by the misfortunes of others.* **1775** Izard *Correspondence* 110: [Latin only]. **1779** JFogg in Sullivan *Journals* 98: [Latin only]. **1780** RPeters in Pickering *Life* 1.267: "Learn to be wise by others' harms" is a good maxim. **1790** Adams *Works* 6.227: [Latin only]. **1797** Graham *Vermont* 3: [Latin only]. **1798** Jefferson *Family Letters* 151: The errors and misfortunes of others should be a school for our own instruction. **1809** JAdams in *Adams-Cunningham Letters* 74: Happy they who are made cautious by others' dangers. *Oxford* 58; Whiting E197, M170.

H84 To die in **Harness**

1848 Cooper *Letters* 5.286: Old Quincy Adams died. He died in harness, falling in a fit in his place, in Congress. *Oxford* 186.

H85 To hang one's **Harp** upon the willow(s)

1781 AA in *Adams FC* 4.215: My harp was so hung upon the willows. **1787** Baldwin *Life and Letters* 390: Friends . . . are hanging their harps upon the willows. **1812** Taggart *Letters* 409: He might have hung his harp on the willow. **1817** Adams *Works* 10.237: All harps upon the willow, we sat down to a *triste* dinner. *Oxford* 349; Tilley H174.

H86 To be under the **Harrow**

1778 *Washington *Writings* 13.334: If he is innocent, 'tis cruel to keep him under the harrow. **1795** Adams *Memoirs* 1.128: Allis is under the harrow, and obliged to comply

with the Captain's will. **1816** Fidfaddy *Adventures* 47: We must be put under the harrow again. **1865** PCameron in *Ruffin Papers* 4.25: There is a party in the North . . . that would be glad to see us put under saws and harrows. TW 376(8). Cf. *Oxford* 826; Whiting T344. See **F311, H5.**

H87 As dead as **Harry** the Eighth

1764 HWilliamson in *Paxton Papers* 345: The Proprietor is no more; by 26 very decent and very modest Resolves of the House, you conceive him as dead as Harry the Eighth.

H88 To settle the **Hash**

1788 *Politician* 23: If the case lies there, that settles the harsh. **1807** Weems *Murder* 3: A stunning knock to the ground settled the hash. **1809** Fessenden *Pills* 114: To settle fighting Europe's hash. **1809** Weems *Marion* 47. **1824** *Tales* 2.19. **1841** Hone *Diary* 2.557, **1842** 597. NED Suppl. Hash 3b; TW 172.

H89 As much **Haste** as good speed

1786 Gordon *Letters* 613: I . . . shall make as much haste as good speed. **1824** *Tales* 1.143: The messengers made at least as much haste as good speed. Cf. *Oxford* 355-6; Tilley H200.

H90 **Haste** makes waste

1753 Franklin *PR* 4.405: Haste makes Waste. **1761** *Boston Gazette* in *Olden Time* 2.30. **1779** WLee in Deane *Papers* 3.389: Hasty measures are often injurious. **1785** HLaurens in Hamilton *Papers* 3.606: Haste would make havoc. **1791** *Universal Asylum* 7.15. **1806** Plumer *Memorandum* 529-60: My *Register* ought to have been called the *Waste* book—for I write in too much haste. Barbour 85(2); *Oxford* 356; Whiting H162.

H91 Make **Haste** slowly

1734 Belcher *Papers* 2.98: Often revolve in your mind the great Lord Coke's motto, *Prudens qui patiens* and that of the excellent Judge Hale's, *Festina lente.* **1744** Franklin *PR* 2.396: Make haste slowly. **1756** in Stiles *Itineraries* 1: [Latin only]. **1765** JOtis *Vindication* in Bailyn *Pamphlets* 1.565: [Latin only]. **1780** Jay *Correspon-*

dence 1.343: the old adage *festina lente* (see also 2.30, 353, 4.385, 435 [Latin only]). **1782** EHazard in *Belknap Papers* 1.150 (see also 2.90, 217: [Latin only]). **1787** JJay in Jefferson *Papers* 11.314: But the maxim of *festina lente* does not suit our southern sanguine Politicians. **1787** Mason *Papers* 2.822: motto, 918: Maxim. **1788** BLincoln in Sparks *Correspondence* 4.224: We must make haste slowly. **1789** Brackenridge *Gazette* 84: [Latin only]. **1790** PWingate in *Belknap Papers* 3.459: We go *slow* fast enough. **1791** *Universal Asylum* 7.155: [Latin only]. **1798** AHamilton in Murray *Letters* 315: [Latin only]. **1798** HJackson in *Bingham's Maine* 2.945: "To make haste slowly" is a good maxim. **1800** Weems *Letters* 2.135: [Latin only], **1802** 225: [Latin only]. **1804** Adams *Writings* 3.27: The old and wholesome adage [Latin only]. **1806** Randolph(*J*) *Letters* 17: There is another excellent rule . . . "make haste slowly." **1809** Irving *History* 1.240: I rather think it may be ascribed to the immemorial maxim of this worthy country . . . not to do things in a hurry. **1809** Weems *Letters* 2.415: [Latin only]. **1810** Bates *Papers* 2.166: The "hatons nous lentement" . . . is a faculty which we shall never acquire. **1810** Randolph(*J*) *Letters* 81: [Latin only]. **1814** Adams *Works* 6.512: [Latin only]. **1815** *Port Folio* 3NS 5.148: "Festina lente" — go on slowly. **1816** JAdams in *Adams-Jefferson Letters* 2.503: [Latin only], **1819** 533: [Latin only]. **c1825** Tyler *Prose* 113: *Festina lente,* hasten slowly. **1827** Wirt *Letters* 2.239: But I am not going to kill myself "for a' that:" *festina lente.* Barbour 85(3); *Oxford* 501; TW 172(1).

H92 Marry in **Haste** and repent at leisure

1637 Morton *New English Canaan* 336: And had done that on a sodaine which they repented at leasure. **1734** Franklin *PR* 1.354: Marry'd in Haste, we oft repent at Leisure; Some by Experience find these Words misplac'd, Marry'd at Leisure, they repent in Haste. **1829** *Yankee* 123: Nor ever to marry in a hurry and repent at leisure. Barbour 85(1, 4); *Oxford* 515; TW 172(2). Cf. Whiting H158, 159.

H93 More **Haste** than good speed

a1700 Hubbard *New England* 517: But in the way making more haste than good speed, he fell down. **1702** Mather *Magnalia* 1.184: There was more *haste* than good *speed* in the attempt, 2.586-7: With more *haste* than good *speed.* **1712** Sewall *Diary* 2.333, **1720** 3.274, 275. **1724** Mather *Diary* 2.748. **1728** Byrd *Dividing Line* 42: They could not forbear paying too much regard to a Proverb — fashionable in their Country, — not to make more hast than good Speed, 287. **1739** Stephens *Journal(I)* 1.315. **1770** Carter *Diary* 1.424. **1777** Gordon *Letters* 352. **1779** CPinckney in Moultrie *Memoirs* 1.328. **1786** Washington *Writings* 29.125: The old proverb. **1789** Brackenridge *Gazette* 84: Festina lente; make no more haste than good speed, is the proverb. **1790** Maclay *Journal* 177. **1790** Washington *Writings* 31.41. **1791** *Universal Asylum* 7.14. **1830** Pintard *Letters* 3.154. *Oxford* 543; Whiting H167.

H94 The more **Haste** the worst speed

1787 *American Museum* 2.478: *The more haste makes the worst speed.* **1800** NBarrell in Webb *Correspondence* 2.209: Most haste, least speed. **1826** Longfellow *Letters* 1.169: "The more haste, the worse speed" is a true maxim when applied to a man sitting down to write a letter. *Oxford* 356; Whiting H168.

H95 As thick as **Hasty** pudding

1775 Winslow *Broadside* 141: And there we see the men and boys As thick as hasty pudding. **1809** Lindsley *Love* ii: And there we saw the boys and galls as thick as haster pudden. **1822** Watterston *Winter* 62: Lawyers and doctors, thick as hasty pudding. TW 173.

H96 As black as a **Hat**

1637 RRyece in *Winthrop Papers(A)* 3.361: His fleshe and kydnes were as blacke as a hatte. **1772** Adams *Legal Papers* 1.277: The ground . . . is black as a Hat. **1775** Freneau *Poems* 1.132: This night he will vomit as black as my hat. **1791** Delano *Narrative* 85. **1801** Story *Shop* 27. **1802** *Port Folio* 2.272: With heart . . . as black as hat.

1807 *Salmagundi* 138: my. 1817 Royall *Letters* 110: your, 115: your. 1821 Knight *Poems* 2.181: my. 1826 Royall *Sketches* 59: your. Svartengren 242; TW 173(2).

H97 To have on one's little **Hat**

1737 Franklin *Drinkers* 2.175: He's Got on his little Hat.

H98 To keep under (the) **Hatches**

1689 Plumstead 121: They had their enemies under hatches. 1689 Randolph *Letters* 4.288: The honest party, who are by all meanes kept under Hatches. 1775 Washington *Writings* 4.105: The . . . cramped state of our treasury, which keeps us for ever under the hatches. 1816 WEdwards in *Ruffin Papers* 1.185: Emigration and all its concomitants will always keep us under the Hatches. Colcord 95; NED Hatch *sb.*[1] 4.

H99 As thick as **Hatchel-teeth**

1782 Trumbull *Satiric Poems* 168: Nor cut your poles down while I've breath, Tho' raised more thick than hatchel teeth.

H100 As sharp as a **Hatchet**

1770 MGoosley in *Norton Papers* 127: My face . . . is almost as Sharp as a Hatchet. Cf. Svartengren 420.

H101 As thin as a **Hatchet**

1803 *Yankee Phrases* 87: Till I, like a hatchet, grow thin. See **K45.**

H102 To bury the **Hatchet**

1724 Corlair[?] in *Baxter Manuscripts* 23.161: Lay down the Hatchet and bury itt for ever. 1727 JGyles in *Baxter Manuscripts* 10.408-9: Y^e tribes have sent a Messag . . . to bury ye hatchet. 1753 Skigunsta in McDowell *Documents* 1.445: We buried the bloody Hatchet under Ground. 1758 Lower Cherokees in McDowell *Documents* 2.429: The Kinikee Indians have buried the Hatchet. 1760 *Johnson Papers* 3.212: I now burry the bloody Hatchet in the bottomless pitt. 1763 JBoucher in *MHM* 7(1912) 162-3. 1766 *Johnson Papers* 12.229, 1774 8.1051: They Pretended to bury the hatchet [not Indians and figurative]. 1778 Carver *Travels* 91: Cause the bloody hatchet to be deep buried under the roots of the great tree of peace. 1778 JKendall in Kirkland *Letters* 2.44. 1779 JAllan in *Baxter Manuscripts* 17.430. 1779 Washington *Writings* 15.54: He has taken up the Hatchet with us, and we have sworn never to bury it. 1783 THutchinson in Hutchinson *Diary* 2.390: The disposition here seems to be to bury the hatchet. 1785 Lee *Letters* 2.342: By effectually "burying the hatchet" as our Aborigines express the idea. a1788 Jones *History* 2.12. 1790 Pickering *Life* 2.465. 1790 Smith *Works* 2.306. 1791 Belknap *History* 1.225. 1792 Brackenridge *Modern* 57: You have only to talk of burying hatchets under large trees. 1792 ABrown in *Belknap Papers* 3.538. 1793 Jefferson *Writings* 16.381. 1794 Jay *Correspondence* 4.147: To use an Indian figure, may the hatchet henceforth be buried for ever. 1795 Wayne *Correspondence* 380. 1797 Hawkins *Letters* 98, 185, 186. 1804 Brackenridge *Modern* 409: There was some talk of *brightening* the chain, and *burying the hatchet,* 1805 538, 608: The hatchet was buried deep, and an oak tree, figuratively speaking, was planted on it. 1807 Janson *Stranger* 25. 1808 *Salmagundi* 455: If I know our trio, we have . . . no hatchet to bury. 1809 Weems *Marion* 22. 1813 Wirt *Letters* 1.359: Let us bury the hatchet for past omissions. 1816 Jackson *Correspondence* 2.259: On my part the hatchet is buried in oblivion, 1819 422. 1825 *Austin Papers* 2.1221: Let us bury the hatchet [and] smoke the pipe of peace. Barbour 85-6; DA hatchet 4a; *Oxford* 92-3; Thornton *Glossary* 1.424; TW 173-4. See **T173.**

H103 To take up the **Hatchet**

1720 JAdams in *Baxter Manuscripts* 9.462: The Indians . . . as they term it took up the hatchet. 1754 Old Hop in McDowell *Documents* 1.488: I . . . am now provoaked to take up the Hatchett of War. 1756 McDowell *Documents* 2.97, 98, 203, 1757 420. 1778 JAllan in *Baxter Manuscripts* 16.64, 1779 362, 18.33: [Pierre Tomma] It was a pity . . . for us to Take up the Hatchet for America. 1781 Jefferson *Writings* 16.373. 1791 Belknap *History* 2.222. 1793 Jefferson *Writings* 16.381, 1807 11.345,

361, **1808** 12.37, **1813** 14.23, 18.141. NED Hatchet 2; *Oxford* 187.

H104 The **Haughty** in prosperity are meanest in adversity

1775 Smith *Memoirs(I)* 231: So trew it is that the Haughty in Prosperity will be mean in Adversity, **1786** *Diary* 2.42: A strong Instance of an Old Remark that the Haughty in Prosperity are the meanest in Adversity.

H105 As hungry as **Hawks**

1728 Byrd *Dividing Line* 189: Our absent Men, who came to the Camp as hungry as Hawks, **1732** *Progress* 345: This airing made us as hungry as so many hawks. **1740** *Letters* in *VHM* 37(1929) 31: People . . . are poor & hungry as Hawks. **1822** Freneau *Last Poems* 73: If hungry as a famished hawk. TW 174(6).

H106 To be between **Hawk** and buzzard

1637 Morton *New English Canaan* 336: They stood betwixt Hawke and Bussard: and could not tell which hand to incline unto. **1677** WWinthrop in *Winthrop Papers(B)* 4.417: And for the other, which has bin allwayes betweene hauke and buzzurd. **1692** Randolph *Letters* 7.351: Newcastle in delaware bay, lying between hauk and Buzard, has been made a free port. **1729** Byrd *London Diary* 39: Affairs have been so long between hawk and buzzard that I have not known which to call it. **1775** JAdams in *Warren-Adams Letters* 1.88: We are between Hawk and Buzzard [getting nothing done]. **1776** Reed *Life* 1.230: So that we may be properly said to be between hawk and buzzard. *Oxford* 359; TW 175(11).

H107 To tell (know) a **Hawk** from a handsaw

1801 *Farmers' Museum* 102: And tell a handsaw from a hawk. **1808** Paine *Works* 399: Else, they will never know "A hawk from a handsaw." **1824** *Tales* 1.72: I have heard . . . of persons, who, when the wind was eastwardly, did not know a hawk from a hand-saw. **1834** Paulding *Letters(II)* 141: They can . . . "tell a hawk from a handsaw." *Oxford* 434; TW 174(3).

H108 To watch like a **Hawk**

1803 Austin *Constitutional* 257: In Massachusetts, the treasury department is watched with hawk-eyed attention. **1822** Watterston *Winter* 36: His eye was black and piercing as an hawk's. Barbour 86(2); TW 175(12).

H109 Between **Hay** and grass

1763 *Johnson Papers* 4.246: Then thou wilt be week and feable, as the Saying is between hay and grass. TW 159: Grass(3).

H110 He has **Hay** upon his horn

1812 Wirt *Letters* 1.348: Mr. Warden . . . remarked . . . "Take care of him, he has hay upon his horn" . . . "Jock, rich in wit and Latin too, Cries, '*Habet fœnum in cornu.*' " **1813** Jefferson *Writings* 13.221: If nature had planted the *fœnum in cornu* on the front of treachery. *Oxford* 359; Tilley H233.

H111 Make **Hay** while the sun shines

1637 Morton *New English Canaan* 305: Hee, resolving to make hay whiles the Sonne did shine. **1701** *Penn-Logan Correspondence* 1.74: Make hay while the sun shines, **1709** 2.349. **1721** WDouglas in *Collections of the Massachusetts Historical Society* 4S 2(1854) 167: Guiding myself by the maxim of *Hoc age* and of making hay while the sun shines. **1727** Ames *Almanacs* 53: When Titan shines now make your Hay, Men live by Work & not by Play, **1743** 162: Make Hay while you may. **1748** PCollinson in *Colden Letters* 4.103. **1765** Watts *Letter Book* 342. **1766** Jay *Correspondence* 1.5. **1769** Smith *Memoirs(I)* 71. **1776** *Blockheads* 8: a very good maxim. **1785** WBlount in *Blount Papers* 1.170: There's an old Proverb which says. **1787** *Belknap Papers* 1.474. **1788** *Politician* 25: It is better to make hay while the sun shines *against* a rainy day. **1792** *Echo* 35: And pat another proverb meets my eye, While the sun shines, spread out your hay to dry. **1793** Ingraham *Journal* 1. **1797** Cobbett *Porcupine* 6.354. **1803** *Port Folio* 3.60: In de sun make de hay. **1804** JPerkins in *Cabot Family* 2.522. **1830** Wirt *Letters* 2.293. **1849** Paulding

Letters(II) 500. Barbour 86(3); *Oxford* 501; Whiting H206.

H112   As tall as a **Haypole**

1803 *Yankee Phrases* 87: As tall as a hay pole her size. Cf. TW 240: Maypole(2).

H113   To dance the **Hays**

1785 Jefferson *Papers* 7.637: Engld. Ireld. and Scotld. may dance the hays. NED Hay *sb.*[4] 1b.

H114   All **Heads** and no heads

1813 Asbury *Letters* 3.491: All heads and no heads. See **M115, O12.**

H115   At **Heads** and points

c1800 Tyler *Island* 11: That if you men lay heads and points like hogs in a distillery yard, we'll put every man in his right place in a twinkling. **1806** Weems *Letters* 2.355: Tis a confounded thing Mr Carey that two Gentlemen . . . shou'd yet be so eternally at heads and points. TW 176(3).

H116   From **Head** to foot

1760 JRigbie in *MHM* 36(1941) 49: He . . . cursed me from head to foot. *Oxford* 832; Whiting H215. See **T202.**

H117   He has a **Head** and so has a pin (beetle)

1811 Wirt *Letters* 1.306: He has a head, and so has a pin. **1815** Waterhouse *Journal* 189: O Caleb! Caleb! thou hast a head and so has a beetle. *Oxford* 360; Whiting *NC* 421(2).

H118   The **Head** and the members need each other

1720 JColman *Distressed State* in *Colonial Currency* 1.407: *Shall the Head say to the Members, we have no need of thee, or shall the Members say to the Head in like manner?* Whiting H214. See **H147.**

H119   **Heads** or tails

1782 CGadsden in Gibbes 3.243: 'Tis heads or tails with us, and the stake, I am afraid, is no less than the whole State. NED Head 3b.

H120   **Head** over ears

1822 Adams *Writings* 7.284: George is plunged head over ears in the *Fortunes of Nigel.* **1846** Hone *Diary* 2.777: I am head over ears in the election.

H121   **Head** over heels

1775 Hopkinson *Miscellaneous Essays* 1.36: [It] would have surprised any body to see how many . . . tumbled out, helter skelter, head-over-heels, in the gushing stream. **1778** *Washington *Writings* 10.449: We shall be plunged into it as we were last year head over heels. **1793** EWinslow in *Winslow Papers* 405: We are to be . . . kicked to the Devil head over heels. **1816** Paulding *Letters(I)* 2.233: Mine honest, sanguine, and head-over-heels friend, brother Jonathan. **1824** Neal *American Writers* 61: We went up to him, reverently—they, head-over-heels. TW 177(12). See **H177.**

H122   **Heads** I win, tails you lose

1814 GMorris in King *Life* 5.369: To play old John Carpenter's Game of tossing up— Heads I win, Tails you lose. *Oxford* 361; TW 176(5).

H123   His **Head** is full of Bees

1737 Franklin *Drinkers* 2.174: His Head is full of Bees. *Oxford* 360; Whiting H239.

H124   If your **Head** is wax, don't walk in the sun

1749 Franklin *PR* 3.342: If your head is wax, don't walk in the Sun. *Oxford* 360; Tilley H249.

H125   Keep your **Head** cool and feet dry

1769 Read *Correspondence* 36: It is an old maxim in favor of health "that you keep your head cool and feet dry," and a very just one. *Oxford* 207, 419; Tilley F576, 579; Whiting *NC* 421(3).

H126   Little **Head** great wit

1735 *South Carolina Gazette* in Elizabeth C. Cook, *Literary Influences in Colonial Newspapers* (New York, 1912) 240: According to the old Proverb, of little head great Wit. Tilley H261; Whiting *NC* 421(6).

H127   Not to know if one is on his **Head** or feet (heels)

1716 Church *History* 2.39: He bid them . . . Not to trouble themselves, whether he came upon his head or feet. **1776** TField in *VHM* 10(1902) 182: We none of us know whether we stand on our Heads or our Heels. **1825** Jones *Sketches* 1.34-5: Before he had recovered sense enough to know whether his head or feet were uppermost. **1827** Watterston *Wanderer* 161: I didn't know whether I was on my head or feet. TW 176(7).

H128 An old **Head** on young shoulders

1785 Van Schaack *Letters* 407: Don't think I expect to place an old head upon young shoulders. **1794** Drinker *Journal* 256: But we can't put old heads on young shoulders. **1805** Weems *Letters* 2.314: Oh when shall we see Old Heads upon young shoulders. *Oxford* 589-90; TW 176(4).

H129 Over **Head** and ears

1676 Williams *Writings* 5.191: We . . . are over head and Ears in Debt to God. **1680** F-JWinthrop in *Winthrop Papers(B)* 4.287: I am over head & eares in comon censure. **1723** *New-England Courant* 111(1.2): All Batchelors over Head and Ears in Love. **1731** Belcher *Papers* 1.55: I am . . . going to plunge myself over head and ears in obligation and debt to your Lordship. **1734** *New-York Weekly Journal* in *Newspaper Extracts(I)* 1.398: (in Debt). **1741** *Georgia Records* 23.185: To be over Head & Ears in scurrilous & notorious Falshood. **1750** *Massachusetts* in *Colonial Currency* 4.439: To deceive the People into Debt over Head and Ears. **1755** *Johnson Papers* 1.614: The Indians are arrived and I am head & Ears engaged with them. **1756** Laurens *Papers* 2.304: in debt. **1763** Watts *Letter Book* 142: in Debt. **1765** JBoucher in *MHM* 7(1912) 296: in Debt. **1774** Willard *Letters* 37: in debt. **1778** NGreene in Kirkland *Letters* 1.55: Poor fellow he is over head and Ears in Love. **1778** SHodgkin in Hodgkin *Letters* 242: Brother is over head & ears in work. **1779** JChester in Huntington *Papers* 141: in Business. **1781** RMorris in Deane *Papers* 4.402: But Congress are pressing their business on me, and I shall soon be plunged over head and ears. **1786** Gordon *Letters* 535: in business. **1787** *Belknap Papers* 1.488: He is over head and ears in the

Ohio. **a1788** Jones *History* 2.121: in debt, 322: in debt. **1789** Boucher *Autobiography* 93: in debt. **1792** Belknap *Foresters* 164: Bull now found himself soused over head and ears in that "deep ditch", the law. **1795** Murdock *Triumphs* 19: in love. **1797** Foster *Coquette* 23: And here I am again over head and ears in the hypo. **1805** Mackay *Letters* 185: in love. **1809** Sumter *Letters* 52: Mr. S. also is well but head & ears in Machinery. **1809** Weems *Marion* 156: in love. **1810** SSwan in *New England Merchants* 32: I do not wish to go over head & ears into speculation. **c1813** Dow *Journal* 320: in debt. **1815** Adams *Works* 10.148: I had been plunged head and ears in the American revolution. **1816** Paulding *Letters(I)* 2.102: in debt. **a1820** Latrobe *Journal* 247: in love. **1822** Watterston *Winter* 80: in love. **1828** Smith *Letters* 239: in debt. **1831** Pintard *Letters* 3.208: I am over head & ears in Savings Bank duty. **1834** Baldwin *Diary* 254: He was head and ears in love. **1837** Paulding *Letters(II)* 207: in debt. *Oxford* 603; TW 176-7(1). See **E8**.

H130 Plotting **Heads,** *etc.*

1719 *Present Melancholy* in *Colonial Currency* 1.359: We think . . . that *Plotting Heads, Proud Hearts, and Idle hands* will never maintain a People.

H131 To be knocked in the **Head**

1689 *Baxter Manuscripts* 9.24: By means of som Discuragment from Haverill all is knockt in y[e] head. **1764** JParker in Franklin *Papers* 11.415: That was knock'd in the Head. **1776** Burd *Letters* 82: But it [Convention] made a great Noise in Philadelphia, and if not intirely knocked in the head, is at least postponed. **1789** Boucher *Autobiography* 29: Mr Younger failed, which effectually knocked on the head all my hopes of becoming a merchant, 64: He knocked the whole project on the head. **1799** Dorr *Letters* 196: The whole business would be knocked in the head. **1807** Mackay *Letters* 87: Should a war take place our prospects are all knocked in the head. NED Knock 3b.

H132 To comb his **Head** with a three-legged stool

1795 Murdock *Triumphs* 30: If I don't comb his head with a three-legged stool, there is no snakes in Ireland. *Oxford* 134; Tilley H270.

H133 To eat one's **Head** off

1777 JAdams in *Warren-Adams Letters* 1.333: My Horses are eating their Heads off. **1820** Welby *Visit* 321: Though their heads were large they had pretty well *eaten them off* (as prize cattle are sometimes known to do in other parts of the world). NED Eat 4b.

H134 To give one's **Head** for a football

1790 Maclay(S) *Journal* 53: That if Pringle could find a Road there, then he Shirley would Give them his head for a foot ball. TW 143(4). See **F260.**

H135 To give one's **Head** in a hand-basket

1714 Sewall *Diary* 3.23: Govr said he would give his head in a Hand-Basket as soon as he would pass it.

H136 To hang one's **Head** like a bulrush

1775 JLovell in *Essex Institute Historical Collections* 13(1875) 172: The Villains in this Town hang their Heads like Bullrushes. **1776** BTupper in *Naval Documents* 5.124: The Torrys here begin to hang their heads like Bull rushes. NED Bulrush 3.

H137 To hold one short by the **Head**

1777 RBoyd in *Clinton Papers* 2.4: [I] think if you can hold him a little short by the Head he may prove serviceable. NED Short C 6b.

H138 To keep one's **Head** (chin) above water

1692 Mather *Wonders* 77: So long, New-England will at least keep its head above water. **1739** Belcher *Papers* 2.228: I don't believe he would stick at any thing . . . to keep his head above water, **1743** 447: Tho' he does all (& strange things) to keep his head above water. **1751** JWaller in *VHM* 59(1951) 475: I scarcely can . . . keep my chin above water. **1766** JParker in Franklin *Papers* 13.327: It is hard for me, who can hardly keep myself above Water. **1771** *John-*

son Papers 8.92: He is likely to get his head above water again. **1790** Maclay *Journal* 178: I have, however, kept its head above water so far. **1806** Wilson *Letters* lxvi: We are just getting our heads above water. *Oxford* 418; TW 177(17).

H139 To knock one's **Head** against the wall

1692 Bulkeley *Will* 105: A man had as good knock his head against the wall as meddle in it. Cf. *Oxford* 688; Tilley H273.

H140 To lug (*etc.*) in **Head** and shoulders

1775 MLewis in Webb *Correspondence* 1.102: New York was, according to custom, lugged in Head & Shoulders by Col. Gadsden. **1787** Stiles *Diary* 3.275: Texts of scripture which were haled in by the head & shoulders at every other sentence, whether applicable or not. **1794** Chipman *Writings* 395: They have been brought in by the head and shoulders, and with the strength of a Hercules, as a comic writer observes on a like occasion. **1797** Paine *Prosecution* 2.727: And those often dragged in head and shoulders, **1807** *Examination* 2.858: This, as Swift said on another occasion, is *lugged in head and shoulders. Oxford* 360; Tilley H274. See **N27.**

H141 To make neither **Head** or tail of

1775 Lee *Papers* 1.208: I can make neither head or tail of it myself. **1775** MLewis in Webb *Correspondence* 1.103: A man must be endued with a spirit of Divination to make Head or Tail of it. **1781** Jackson *Papers* 1: A story I can make neither head or tail of. **1793** *Washington *Writings* 32.401: Butlers . . . reports are such as I can neither make head or tail of. **1797** Paine *Examination* 2.869. **1826** Audubon *1826 Journal* 296. *Oxford* 360; Whiting H244.

H142 To make one shorter by the (a) **Head**

1775 *Naval Documents* 1.854: They would shorten his Ambition of Despotism By the head. **1793** JBoit in *Columbia* 428: At this place we first heard of the War and troubles in Europe, and that poor Louis was a head shorter. **1799** Freneau *Poems* 3.230: He made them shorter—by a head. NED Short 2.

H143 Two **Heads** (are better than one)

1743 *Boston Evening Post* in *Newspaper Extracts(I)* 2.161: The *Querist* . . . has evidently put together two Heads, as one, perhaps out of Regard to the Old Proverb. Barbour 86(9); *Oxford* 851; Whiting H250.

H144 Up to the **Head** and ears

1763 *Johnson Papers* 4.40: I am swallowed up to the Head & ears in Mortar Stone and Timber. *Oxford* 855-6.

H145 A weak **Head** and a good heart

1767 *Johnson Papers* 5.682: To make an offer of the poor abilities of a weak head and a good Heart. **1800** Dow *Journal* 103: It argues a sound heart, but a weak head. Cf. Whiting H248.

H146 When the **Head** is becacked the body's beshit

1714 Hunter *Androboros* 6: It is an Old Maxim, et c'est Escrit, Au trou de mon cul, look there you'll sie't, When the Head is Be—ck't the Body's Beshit. . . . But 'tis strange how Notions are chang'd of late, For 'tis a New Maxim, but an odd one, That Ce que perd a nos culs dois nous garnir latete.

H147 When the **Head** is sick the members are out of frame (*varied*)

1637 BGurdon in *Winthrop Papers(A)* 3.386: The hed is scicke and all the memburs out of frame. **1637** Morton *New English Canaan* 293: But if one head from thence be tane away The Body and the members will decay. **1702** Taylor *Christographia* 253.49-51: For every member of the body hath its life and growth in Common with the Whole body, but all Come from the Head. **1721** Wise *Word* 163: When our Head is spoiled, the Members of the Body will soon Languish. **1724** Jones *Virginia* 151: I need not relate the fable of the head and the members. **1788** *American Museum* 3.338: They are the head, and will take care that the members do not perish. **1807** Fraser *Letters and Journals* 249: It is a true observation of yours that when the head fails the Body soon goes to wreck. *Oxford* 359; Whiting H254. See **H118.**

H148 **Health** is before wealth

1718 Chalkley *Letter* 473: *Intemperance destroys the Health of the Body, which we generally esteem before Wealth.* **1795** Morris *Diary and Letters* 2.111: What is riches without health? Barbour 87(1); *Oxford* 363; Whiting H261.

H149 **Health** is sweet, though the pill be bitter

1654 SSymonds in *Winthrop Papers(B)* 2.130: Health you know is sweet, though the pill that procureth it be bitter. *Oxford* 63; Tilley M558, P327. See **P138.**

H150 To be struck all of a **Heap**

1756 Laurens *Papers* 2.269: The advice of War Struck our planters all of a heap. **1790** Maclay *Journal* 173: I feel so struck of an heap, I can make no remark on the matter. **1817** Weems *Franklin* 122: They sink down . . . doubled or *folded together,* or as we say, "all in a heap." *Oxford* 781; TW 178.

H151 Be swift to **Hear** and slow to speak

1699 Williams *Writings* 6.327: My study is to be swift to hear, and slow to speak. Whiting H263.

H152 **Hear** and bear

1638 THooker in *Winthrop Papers(A)* 4.76: Only goe not to Conitticut: we heare and beare . . . We heare still and bear, 77, 78: They are realityes which passengers dayly relate, and we heare and beare.

H153 **Hear** and see and say the best

1712 Danforth *Poems* 188.201-4: Whoso desires that He himself, And others live at Rest, Must Hear and See, with Charity, And wisely Say the best. *Oxford* 362; Whiting H264.

H154 **Hear** before you blame

1798 Adams *New Letters* 178: Hear before you blame, is a good maxim. See **P29.**

H155 **Hearing** is the truth

1718 JUsher in *Saltonstall Papers* 1.324: Had any told me of Such a thing I could not beleive itt. Butt hearing is the truth. Cf. *Oxford* 710: Seeing; TW 321(1).

H156 A blithe **Heart** makes a blooming look
1812 Melish *Travels* 89: They [eyes] were very pretty, and she had a blooming look, the indication of a *blythe heart*, according to the Scots proverb. *Oxford* 68; Tilley H301.

H157 Faint **Heart** never won fair lady
1777 HLivingston in Webb *Correspondence* 1.198: The old Proverb says a faint heart never wins a fair lady. **1787** Tyler *Contrast* 60: Remember a faint heart never — blisters on my tongue — I was going to be guilty of a vile proverb. **1797** Freneau *Prose* 373. **1800** Cobbett *Letters* 111: Says the old proverb. **1805** Weems *Letters* 2.328, **1811** *Gambling* 16: they say. **1817** Pintard *Letters* 1.101: Faint heart never won fair lady, nor man neither as experience has perfectly convinced me. Barbour 87(5); *Oxford* 238; TW 178(2).

H158 **Heart** and hand
1781 DMerit in *Baxter Manuscripts* 19.191: We will Joine with you, heart & hand. **1828** FNash in *Ruffin Papers* 1.457: Mears told me to assure you he was heart and hand in the cause. **1837** Jackson *Correspondence* 5.503: Donelson was heart and hand with them. *Oxford* 363; Tilley H339.

H159 The **Heart** is all
1809 Weems *Marion* 122: But daddy says as how the heart is all, 156. [Size alone does not count.]

H160 The **Heart** of a fool is in his mouth, *etc.*
1733 Franklin *PR* 1.316: The heart of a fool is in his mouth, but the mouth of a wise man is in his heart. *Oxford* 901; Tilley M602; Whiting M260. See **F235.**

H161 **Heart** of oak
1770 Munford *Candidates* 41: So my heart of oak, **1777** *Patriots* 455: Were you not a heart of oak. *Oxford* 364; Tilley H309.

H162 **Hearts** of gold
1777 Winslow *Broadside* 151: As for the British soldiers, they fought like hearts of gold. Barbour 87(10).

H163 A light **Heart** and a thin pair of breeches, *etc.*
1794 Drinker *Journal* 247: And he appeared to have a light heart, and the other requisites to go through the world. **1809** Irving *History* 1.116: A light heart and *thin pair of breeches*, Will go through the world, my brave boys. TW 178(5).

H164 A merry **Heart** does good like a medicine
1789 Adams *New Letters* 11: A merry Heart does good like a medicine, 22. **1797** Foster *Coquette* 124: Since the wisest of men informs us, that "a merry heart doth good like a medicine." Proverbs xvii 22. Cf. Tilley H320a.

H165 One's **Heart** is at (into) his mouth
1666 Alsop *Maryland* 37: Their hearts are at their mouths. **1801** SFelton in *American Antiquarian Society, Proceedings* NS 69 (1959) 131: My heart almost leap't into my mouth for fear. *Oxford* 364; TW 178(12).

H166 One's **Heart** is better than his head
1813 Dow *Journal* 315: I replied there were some good mistaken men whose hearts were better than their heads.

H167 The stoutest **Heart** must fail at last
1776 Paine *Forester's Letters* 2.77: You have had a long run, and the stoutest heart must fail at last.

H168 To have more at one's **Heart**, *etc.*
1828 Lucretia Bancroft in *American Antiquarian Society, Proceedings* NS 14(1900) 131: My mother would sometimes tell me in a plaiful manner, I should never have more at my heart than I should throw off at my heels. Cf. Whiting H296.

H169 To move a **Heart** of stone, *etc.*
1660 Saffin *His Book* 184: Enough to make a Marble Heart to weep. **1692** Mather *Wonders* 102: It would break a heart of stone, to have seen what I have lately seen. **1699** Ward *Trip* 38: And their *Streets*, like the *Hearts* of the *Male Inhabitants* are paved with *Pebble*. **c1700** Taylor *Poems* 426: With us! alas! a Flint would melt to see A Deadly foe, in such a Case as wee. **1702**

Mather *Magnalia* 1.74: An heart of stone must have dissolved into *Tears*. **1734** Winslow *Broadside* 85: A Sight I think enough to make a Heart of Stone to ake. **1748** PDeLancey in *Colden Letters* 8.351: Every one who saw him was mov'd & indeed he would have mov'd a heart of Stone. **1750** JParson in *Law Papers* 3.353. **1754** Hopkinson *Miscellaneous Essays* 3 (part 2) 3: Oh! could I boast to move with equal art The human soul and melt the stony heart. **c1760** JHowe in Belknap *History* 3.282: Screaming . . . enough to penetrate a heart of stone. **1770** Winslow *Broadside* 47: This would melt a stony Heart, That these two Lovers so must part. **1774** JA in *Adams FC* 1.131: It is enough . . . to melt an Heart of Stone, 157, **1775** 192: Enough to melt a Stone, 241: Enough to melt an Heart of stone, **1776** 2.23. **1781** Moore *Diary* 2.494: In a manner to rend a heart of stone. **1786** *Washington Writings* 29.44: Enough to pierce a heart of adamant. **1787** JPJones in Jefferson *Papers* 12.97: Your cause would move a heart of flint! a**1788** Jones *History* 2.79: Petitions . . . that would have melted a heart of stone. **1789** Anburey *Travels* 1.101: Pierced a heart of stone. **?1796** MBlount in *Blount Papers* 3.96: It would have mov'd a stone almost to have been with her. **1801** Otis *Letters* 1.149: Enough to melt a heart of stone. **1809** Weems *Washington* 47: Sufficient to excite sympathy in hearts of flintiest stone. **1818** Adams *Memoirs* 4.77: In the care of public moneys, it seems as if one were required to have a heart of stone. **1818** Fessenden *Ladies Monitor* 37: A heart of adamant cannot but shew Some kindness to so delicate a beau. **1823** Longfellow *Letters* 1.41: An instance . . . enough to melt any heart! heart did I say! Not a heart of flesh but a heart of stone. Barbour 87(11); TW 179(18); Whiting H277. See **S417.**

H170 To take **Heart** at (of) grace
1686 NMather in *Mather Papers* 62: The Papists take heart at grass. **1830** Ames *Mariner's* 208: The Spaniard finally took heart of grace. *Oxford* 364; Whiting H297.

H171 A warm **Heart** and a cool head
1781 Oliver *Origin* 15: A Man of a warm

Heart & a cool Head is to be urged with the Weapons of Reason only. Barbour 83: Hand(2); *Oxford* 132: Cold hand.

H172 **Heaven** favors strong batallions
1811 Graydon *Memoirs* 136: General Lee . . . treated their solemnities with ridicule, telling them, in the spirit of the ancient fable of Hercules and the waggoner, that *Heaven was ever found favourable to strong battalions. Oxford* 652: Providence; TW 297.

H173 To go to **Heaven** in a swing (?string)
1781 Oliver *Origin* 23: Some, who chose to go to Heaven in a Swing, stay'd behind to enjoy the Halter. *Oxford* 308; Tilley H353.

H174 To move **Heaven** and earth
1777 Lee *Letters* 1.320: They have taken infinite pains, according to custom, to move heaven and earth in their favor. **1781** Lee *Papers* 3.456: I would have moved heaven and earth. **1784** WChipman in *Winslow Papers* 175. **1788** FHopkinson in Jefferson *Papers* 13.39, **1789** 14.376, 699. **1795** EBoudinot in Kirkland *Letters* 2.109: The Demos are moving Heaven & Earth to . . . create some confusion. **1797** *Washington Writings* 35.358. **1809** Adams *Correspondence* 429. **1829** Cooper *Letters* 1.355. **1830** Jackson *Correspondence* 4.177. TW 179(2).

H175 To be all **Hebrew** to one
1775 Digges *Adventures* 1.140: It is all Hebrew to me. TW 179. See **G169.**

H176 Durn (Damn) the **Heels** that let the body suffer
1777 Munford *Patriots* 481: But durn the heels, thinks I, that lets the body suffer; so off I ran. Cf. TW 179(1); Whiting H325. See **H183.**

H177 **Heels** over head
a**1731** Cook *Bacon* 322: Heels over Heads, away they trot. **1784** *Deane Brothers Papers* 207: J. W. goes on at his usual Rate heels Over head, I fear his Ruin is Near. **1809** Wirt *Letters* 1.263: I was soon heels over head among "innate ideas." **1811** ADavie in *Steele Papers* 2.648: He turned heels over head and injured one of his legs. **1824** *Aus-*

tin Papers 1.745: People are heels over head in debt. Whiting H323. See **H121**.

H178   To cool one's Heels

1798 Cobbett *Porcupine* 8.11: So that our Envoys . . . were suffered to cool their heels and blow their nails from the 27th of September to the 8th of October. *Oxford* 143; Tilley H391. See **S145**.

H179   To kick one's Heels

1776 Lee *Papers* 2.260: They will no longer remain kicking their heels at New York. NED Heel *sb.*[1] 17; *Oxford* 422.

H180   To kick up one's Heels

1817 Wirt *Letters* 2.11: The inpression that you were absent from Winchester on this visit, and were kicking up your heels in Washington. Cf. NED Heel *sb.*[1] 23.

H181   To lay one by the Heels

1639 JUnderhill in *Winthrop Papers(A)* 4.143: But the lord soferd him so to misdemen him slfe as he is likli to li by the hielse this too month. **1647** Ward *Simple Cobler* 44: Were I a Constable bigge enough, I would set one of them by the heeles, to keep both their hands quiet. **1652** Williams *Writings* 4.38: To lay a Faithfull *Prophet* . . . by the heels. **1738** Stephens *Journal(I)* 1.172: He . . . was taken out of Court, not without being threatened to be laid by the Heels. **1741** *Georgia Records* 23.61: He would lay me by the Heels for it, as a Saucy Fellow. **1775** Mason *Papers* 1.259: They are now all fast by the heels in the goal of Frederick Town. NED Heel *sb.*[1] 18.

H182   To lift one's Heel against the hand that fed him

1776 Deane *Correspondence* 350: A certain emigrant intriguer . . . has . . . in the most public and ungrateful manner lifted his heel against the hand that has long and generously fed and supported him. NED Heel *sb.*[1] 3. See **H55**.

H183   To take to one's Heels

1787 Tyler *Contrast* 57: I was glad to take to my heels and split home. **1821** Royall *Letters* 203: I took to my keels [*for* heels]

and did hook it. *Oxford* 801; Whiting *NC* 422. Cf. Tilley H394. See **H176**.

H184   To turn up the Heels

1687 *Wyllys Papers* 302: [This] is but the turning the heels of the Law upward, and to make that Law a very peice of Non sence. NED Heel *sb.*[1] 23.

H185   To plough with another's Heifer

1789 Maclay *Journal* 34: I have, by plowing with the heifer of the other House, completely defeated them. *Oxford* 635; Whiting C504.

H186   As black as Hell

1785 EWinslow in *Winslow Papers* 291: My prospects black as H— —. **c1814** Freneau *Poems* 3.372: And cry'd "Like hell his heart is black." Whiting H329.

H187   As deep as Hell

1781 Smith *Works* 2.154: Deep as hell. *Oxford* 175-6; Whiting *Devil* 231.

H188   As false as Hell

1785 AAdams in Jefferson *Papers* 8.653: The account is as false . . . as Hell, but I will substitute one not less expressive and say, false as the English. *Oxford* 243; TW 180(5); Tilley H398.

H189   As hungry as Hell

1775 Freneau *Poems* 1.168: Hungry as hell. Whiting *Devil* 232.

H190   From Hell, Hull and Halifax, *etc.*

1777 Curwen *Journal* 1.375: 'Tis the beggars prayer from Hell Hull and Halifax good Lord deliver us. *Oxford* 367; Tilley H399.

H191   Hell, Hackney or New Orleans

1814 Palmer *Diary* 82: My prayer is that our Government may send the prisoners in the states to Hell, Hackney or New Orleans. Cf. *Oxford* 367; Tilley H399.

H192   Hell is full of good intentions

1809 *Port Folio* 2NS 2.549: Hell is very full of good meanings and good intentions. Barbour 88(3); *Oxford* 367; Tilley H404; Whiting *NC* 423(15).

H193 In **Hell** one should pay court to the Devil

1800 DCobb in *Bingham's Maine* 2.1017: The proverb is too true "that if a man is in Hell his best interest is to pay court to the Devil."

H194 To go to **Hell** or Kentucky

1820 Faux *Memorable Days* 2.13: Long ago it was said, when a man left other States, he is gone to hell, or Kentucky.

H195 To have a little **Hell** of one's own

1796 Cobbett *Porcupine* 3.356: Then, as the saying is, he will have a little hell of his own. *Oxford* 887; Tilley M417.

H196 To kick up **Hell** and Tommy

1809 Lindsley *Love* 40: Kick up hell and leetle Tomy. TW 180(11).

H197 To rake **Hell** with a fine-tooth comb

1834 Floy *Diary* 122: The Whigs had searched in every direction for votes . . . They raked hell with a fine-tooth comb. TW 77: Comb(2). Cf. *Oxford* 664.

H198 There is no **Help** for sickness

1790 Maclay *Journal* 198: As the saying is, "There is no help for sickness." Cf. Whiting D78. See **A50, R54.**

H199 Impossible to **Help** those who will not help themselves

1789 Morris *Diary* 1.153: It is impossible to help those who will not help themselves. *Oxford* 368; Whiting H340. See **G77.**

H200 To send the **Helve** after the hatchet

1721 Wise *Word* 170: And so away that goes after the rest, like the helve after the Hatchet. 1774 TYoung in Leake *Lamb* 91: It would be sending the hatchet after the helve. *Oxford* 368; Tilley H413; Whiting A255, *NC* 423.

H201 As busy as a **Hen** with one chick

1785 Gordon *Letters* 525: I am now full as busy as a hen with one chick. Barbour 89(4); *Oxford* 93; Tilley H415. Cf. TW 181(6, 19).

H202 As mad as a wet **Hen**

1821 Doddridge *Dialogue* 47: Mad as a wet hen. Barbour 89(6); TW 181(4).

H203 He that is born of a **Hen,** etc.

1809 *Port Folio* 2NS 2.549: He who is born of a hen must scrape for a living. *Oxford* 136; Tilley H420.

H204 A **Hen** that crows, etc.

1674 Josselyn *Account* 193: They [hens] use to crow often, which is so rare a thing in other Countries, that they have a proverb *Gallina recinit* a Hen crows. 1734 Franklin *PR* 1.356: Ill thrives that hapless Family that shows A Cock that's silent, and a Hen that crows: I know not which lives more unnatural Lives, Obeying Husbands, or commanding Wives. 1783 Freneau *Poems* 2.237: And a hen crow'd at midnight, my waiting man says. Barbour 96(6); *Oxford* 368; TW 194: House(7). See **S21.**

H205 To be pecked by a (speckled) **Hen**

1723 *New-England Courant* 112(1.2): They are Hen-peck'd at Home. 1783 JEliot in *Belknap Papers* 3.262: It is a wonder if his girl don't prove a *speckled hen* that will peck him.

H206 To sell a **(Hen)** in a rainy day

1793 Brackenridge *Modern* 225: It is therefore like selling a fowl in a rainy day, to attempt negociating with an ignorant man. *Oxford* 713; Tilley H427; Whiting *NC* 424(16).

H207 To be **Hen-hearted**

1808 Hitchcock *Poetical Dictionary* 66: A hen-hearted lover. Whiting H349.

H208 (As strong as) **Hercules**

1800 Cobbett *Porcupine* 11.262: Mr. Mierken is the Hercules of Philadelphia; that his amazing strength is proverbial. Whiting H358.

H209 To know **Hercules** by his foot

1686 Dunton *Letters* 77: And given a short account what they are, which may serve only ex pede Hercules. 1766 Gadsden *Writings* 54: *Ex pede Hercules.* 1788 Jefferson *Papers* 13.364: Ex pede Herculem. 1789

Morris *Diary* 1.45: [Latin only]. **1792** Brackenridge *Modern* 103: Because, *ex pede Herculem*, you may know what I can do by this essay. **1792** GMorris in Hamilton *Papers* 11.261: [Latin only]. **1797** Callendar *Annual Register 1796* 232: You may know Hercules, says the proverb, by the print of his foot. **1809** *Port Folio* 2NS 2.324: [Latin only], **1811** 6.430: [Latin only], **1814** 3NS 4.599: [Latin only]. **1814** Wirt *Bachelor* 43: [Latin only]. **1819** Verplanck *State* 147: "*Ex pede Herculem*," said the ancient artist, "I can tell Hercules from his toe." Jones 41.

H210   To put **Hercules** to the distaff

1743 Stephens *Journal(II)* 2.11: And found him like Hercules among the distaff pretending to have a Strong Feaver upon him. **1786** AAdams in Jefferson *Papers* 9.278: For troubling you with such trifling matters is a little like putting Hercules to the distaff. *Oxford* 370.

H211   Neither **Here** nor there

1769 WNelson in *Norton Papers* 105: That's neither here nor there; as Dr. Amson used to say, that is, who cares? **1769** Woodmason *Journal* 151: Thats neither Here nor there. **1783** Williams *Penrose* 210. **1792** Brackenridge *Modern* 94: As to his being a member of the philosophical society, it could be neither here nor there with a lady. **1807** *Port Folio* NS 4.287. *Oxford* 561; TW 182(2).

H212   Now **Here**, now there

1773 Wheatley *Poems* 30: Now here, now there, the roving Fancy flies. Whiting N179.

H213   To out **Herod** Herod

1804 Brackenridge *Modern* 346: He must out Herod Herod in all that is scurrilous. **1815** Adams *Writings* 5.438: It would be a sort of murder of the innocents that would out-Herod Herod. **1817** King *Life* 6.79: They have in fact outheroded Herod. **1827** Watterston *Wanderer* 126. *Oxford* (2nd ed.) 481; TW 182.

H214   As dead as a (red) **Herring**

1714 Hunter *Androboros* 34: Dead as a Herring. **a1731** Cook *Bacon* 320: The Gen'ral thus (as Herring dead). **1782** Trumbull *Satiric Poems* 159: When once his corse is dead as herring. **1790** Freneau *Prose* 269: They are to all intents and purposes as dead as a red herring. *Oxford* 170; TW 182(2).

H215   As plenty as **Herrings**

1761 Adams(A) *Letters* 5: They are as plenty as herrings. NED Herring 2: Thick. Cf. TW 182(1).

H216   Like **Herrings** in a barrel

1619 RCushman in Bradford *History* 1.87: They were packed together like herings. **1777** Cresswell *Journal* 244: A number of people being crowded together in to so small a compass almost like herrings in a barrel. **1795** DCobb in *Bingham's Maine* 1.540: We should be stow'd as thick as herrings in a barrel. *Oxford* 371; Tilley H445. Cf. TW 318: Sardines.

H217   To haul a **Herring** off a gridiron

1832 Ames *Nautical* 37: A dozen of whom would not, to use the contemptuous language of the Yankee sailors, "haul a herring off a gridiron."

H218   **Herring-pond**

1766 Gadsden *Writings* 73-4: On the other side of the great herring pond. Thornton *Glossary* 1.431; TW 182.

H219   Not to find **Hide** nor hair

1815 Humphreys *Yankey* 78: I can't find hide nor hair on him. **1816** Fidfaddy *Adventures* 70: I will leave him neither hide nor hair, root or branch. TW 183(1).

H220   Those that **Hide** can find

1766 Gadsden *Writings* 73: According to the old proverb, they that hide can find. *Oxford* 372; Whiting F149.

H221   **Hilsborough** paint (treat)

1774 Andrews *Letters* 338: This morning the *remarkable cleanliness* of your uncle Joe's door was obliterated by the application of what was formerly called *Hilsborough paint* [either tar or excrement—uncle Joe was suspect as a possible friend of "government"], 370: Last night they gave Scott a *Hilsborough treat*, and not content with disfiguring the outside of his shop . . . open'd his chamber window and emptied several buckets full into it . . . such beastly practises.

H222   As old as the Hills

1828 Wirt *Letters* 2.246: This may be as old as the hills, for aught I know, 249. Barbour 90(6); *Oxford* 588; TW 183(3).

H223   To be loose in the Hilts

1737 Franklin *Drinkers* 2.175: He's Loose in the Hilts. Cf. *Oxford* 484; Partridge 392; Tilley H472.

H224   To be off the Hinges

1700 INorris in *Penn-Logan Correspondence* 1.22: After much teasing, and sometimes almost off the hinges. **1702** Mather *Magnalia* 2.106: All things . . . seem to be off the hinges. **1836** Floy *Diary* 229: Jo read this, and when he got to the latter part, I thought he would have gone off his hinges. *Oxford* 586; Tilley H473.

H225   To give one the Hip

1763 *Commerce of Rhode Island* 1.103: After you left this our old Lodgings became vacant, which has almost given me the hip. NED Hip *sb.*[3]; Partridge 392.

H226   To have one on the Hip

1701 Taylor *Christographia* 67.82: He then hath them upon the hip. **1798** WPinkney in McHenry *Letters* 300: The Directory have us "on the hip." **1815** *Port Folio* 3NS 5.581: We've got the daring vaunters on the hip. *Oxford* 374; Whiting H392.

H227   Hit or miss

1797 Asbury *Journal* 2.125: At last (hit or miss, Providence is all) into the path we came. **1806** Dow *Journal* 274: This appears to me to be wrong in any person to form their mind hit or miss. *Oxford* 374; TW 184.

H228   As white as Hoar-frost

1834 Floy *Diary* 77: Every wool on his conical shaped head was as white as the hoar frost. Cf. TW 147: Frost(1).

H229   Hob or (and) nob

1774 Ames *Almanacs* 451: The Courtly Vice of Corrupting *Hob or no Hob* into Hob

or Nob. **1774** Schaw *Journal* 80: Our hostess . . . gave her hob and nob with a good grace. **1807** *Weekly* 2.29: Hob or Nob. c**1825** Tyler *Prose* 172: Come hob and nob, which do you prefer—white or red? *Oxford* 342; Tilley H479; Whiting H1. See **H1.**

H230   To play Hob with

c**1790** Brackenridge *Gazette* 59: Afraid he might play hob with her. TW 181.

H231   One's Hobby-horse [The following is a selection from 87 occurrences of the phrase]

1650 Bradstreet *Works* 147: His Hobby striding did not ride but run. **1767** Stiles *Itineraries* 460-1: For a while his hobby horse rode away with him and who is there that is not hobby horsical at Times? **1769** *Norton Papers* 111-2: You might have mounted on your hobby, with it's head directed towards the *City of Williamsburg.* **1769** Read *Correspondence* 32: My marsh, which may . . . be . . . called my hobby-horse. **1776** Paine *To Quakers* 2.57: If you . . . mean not to make a political hobby-horse of your religion. **1778** Rowland in Deane *Papers* 4.77: Peace, everlasting Peace, is my hobby-horse and my pride. **1782** JA in *Adams FC* 4.353: In this country [Holland], as in all others, Men are much Addicted to "Hobby Horses." These Nags are called in the Language of the Dutch "Liefhebbery," as they are called in French "Marotte." **1783** Baldwin *Life and Letters* 132: Electricity is his Hobby Horse. **1786** Adams *Works* 9.546: In your [Count Sarsfield's] kind letter of the 26th of January, you ask an explanation of that expression of the Massachusetts, "a rider of hobby-horses." In the original of the word hobby-horse, it signified a little horse, the same with pony in English, or *bidet* in French. The English then transferred it to Irish and Scottish horses, *cheval d'Irlande* and *d'Écosse.* From this horse it was transferred to those little wooden horses which are made for children to ride on for their amusement. It is defined "a stick on which boys get astride and ride;" "*un bâton par lequel les enfans vont à cheval.*" It is defined in Latin, arundo longa, a reed or cane; for the boys in want of better instruments made use of these. From these originals it has been used, I do not know whether metaphorically or poetically, to signify any favorite amusement of grown men of all ranks and denominations, even sages and heroes, philosophers and legislators, nobles, princes, and kings. All nations, I believe, have some word appropriated to this meaning. There is one in French, which I once knew familiarly, but have forgotten. The Dutch have a proverb, *"Jeder heeft zyn speelpop,"* "every one has his hobby-horse." For example, the hobby-horse of Mr. Lionet was the anatomy of caterpillars; that of Mr. Ploos Van Amstell, to collect drawings, &c. The Italians say, *"Quel legno o bastone che i fanciulli si mettono fra gambe e chiamano il loro cavallo."* The Dutch proverb is very true; every man has a staff which he puts sometimes between his legs and rides, and calls it his hobby-horse. It is in this sense the hobby-horse of many curious persons, to become acquainted with singular and extraordinary characters. It has ever been my hobby-horse to see rising in America an empire of liberty, and a prospect of two or three hundred millions of freemen, without one noble or one king among them. a1788 Jones *History* 2.341: Committees and popular meetings are his delight, his greatest pleasure, his hobby horse. 1791 Belknap *History* 1.iii: This employment was (to speak in the style of a celebrated modern author) his "hobby horse." 1792 Hamilton *Papers* 11.444: I would mount the hobby horse of popularity. 1807 Janson *Stranger* 210: The president persists in riding his naval hobby-horse. 1807 *New-England Palladium* in Buckingham *Specimens* 2. 168-9: Hobby-horsical riding has always been free. 1813 Jefferson *Writings* 13.225: A navy has always been his hobby-horse. 1815 Adams *Works* 10.127: My hobby-horse was a navy. 1816 Paulding *Letters(I)* 2.22: But Oliver . . . ran his hobby-horse against my Kentucky pony, and unhorsed my imagination in a twinkling. 1819 Wright *Views* 74: The child rides the hobby, while the hobby too often rides the man. 1820 LWil-liams in Banks *Maine* 197: The Missouri question . . . will be conjured up into a kind of political hobby horse. 1823 TJefferson in *Adams-Jefferson Letters* 2.599: I am fortunately mounted on a Hobby, which indeed I would have better managed some 30 or 40 years ago, but whose easy amble is still sufficient to give exercise and amusement to an Octogenary rider. NED Hobby, *sb.*[1]. Hobby-horse 6; *Oxford* 375.

H232   Hobson's (Scogan's) **choice**

1637 Morton *New English Canaan* 278: Heres Scogans choise for Scilla, and none other, 281: And Scogans choise tis better [than] none at all. **1713** Wise *Churches* 90: A kind of Hobsons Choice *One of these, or None.* **1776** ARoberts in *PM* 7(1883) 460: We had Hobsans choice this or none. **1792** *Washington *Writings* 32.264: The Season made it almost Hobson's choice, him or none. **1793** Wayne *Correspondence* 235: I have therefore called this place *Hobson's Choice.* **1797** FAmes in Gibbs *Memoirs* 1.498: It is *Hopson's Choice* or no other road lies open. **1798** *Washington *Writings* 36.394: It was a Hobson's choice. **1800** FAmes in King *Life* 3.293: Therefore it is, excuse me, Hopson's choice to write to you. **1814** Tilly Buttrick, Jr., *Voyages, Travels and Discoveries,* ed. Reuben G. Thwaites (Cleveland, 1904) 55: This place we named Hobson's choice, (that or none). **1821** Beecher *Autobiography* 1.458: No number ought to be made up of Hobson's choice, "that or none." a1824 Marshall *Kentucky* 2.83: Hobson's choice [a place]. **1832** Barney *Memoir* 231: Be confined to "Hobson's choice." *Oxford* 375; TW 184.

H233   To play Hocus-pocus

1701 Taylor *Christographia* 28.17-9: Fine jingles, that would only please the Eare, or play the Hocus-Pocus with the Soule promising without performing. NED Hocus-pocus 1b.

H234   As dull as a Hoe

1803 *Yankee Phrases* 87: But now I am dull, as a hoe. Barbour 91; TW 184.

H235 To agitate one's **Hoe-cake**

1806 Milledge *Correspondence* 134: You . . . are correct on the subject, which is now agitating our hoe cake. Cf. DA hoe-cake.

H236 As dirty as **Hogs**

1793 Ingraham *Journal* 152: They . . . eat everything without caution or examination as dirty as hogs. Barbour 91(3); Whiting *NC* 425(2). See **P112**.

H237 As drunk as a **Hog**

1801 Story *Shop* 121: I'm as drunk as a hog. **1813** Weems *Drunkard* 117: Her husband reeling about on the green . . . as drunk as a brewer's hog. Whiting *NC* 425(3). Cf. Whiting S955. See **S346, W135**.

H238 As fat as a **Hog**

1709 Lawson *Voyage* 44: He is as fat as a Hog. Barbour 91(4); TW 184(1). See **P113**.

H239 As greedy as a **Hog**

1765 DFowler in *Wheelock's Indians* 95: Gready as a Hog that been kept in a Pen two Days without it's Swill. Whiting *NC* 425(6).

H240 As nasty as **Hogs**

1765 DFowler in *Wheelock's Indians* 94: My Cooks are nasty as Hogs. Cf. TW 184(4).

H241 **Hog** and hominy

1776 WHooper in Murray *Letters* 239: I might . . . eat my Hogg and Hominee without anything to make me afraid. **1802** *Port Folio* 2.64: I think I see Each with his "hog and hominy," 392: At some remote Virginia inn . . . Where nought but hog and hominy is found. **1815** *Reviewers* 38: They vegetate the remainder of the year on hog, hominy and apple whiskey. **1817** Scott *Blue Lights* 142: At Saturday suppers [in Connecticut], the never-failing repast of baked beans was as regularly administered as the "hog and hominy" of North Carolina. **1824** Doddridge *Notes* 88: "Hog and hominy" were proverbial for the dish of which they were the component parts. **1824** Lee *Diary and Letters* 220: Your *good* old-fashioned hog and hominy people. **1831** RLove in Jackson *Correspondence* 4.376: We cannot grow Cotton or Tobacco, our employment being

as the old saying is, we can make plenty of Hog and Hominy, and then sit down and eat it. Barbour 92: Hominy; DA hog 9b.

H242 A **Hog** swimming cuts his own throat

1806 TPickering in King *Life* 4.494: He was like a hog swimming over a river who would cut his own throat. **1809** Fessenden *Pills* 51: Then when a hog is not content With his own native element, — Beyond his depth attempts to float, He cuts with clumsy hoof, his throat. Brown *Collection* 7.469: 7739; TW 88: Current, 284: Pig(9).

H243 A **Hog** will run forward

1761 Rowe *Diary* 384: I suppose tis Harder to Break their Views as tis to Stop a Hog that Runs Right forward, 399: But no Arguments or Reason will turn a Hog from Running forward.

H244 **Hogs** see the wind

a**1725** Byrd *Another Secret Diary* 455: They can see Death hovering o're a Family as plain as Hogs see the Wind. *Oxford* 625; Tilley P311; Whiting *NC* 479(2).

H245 Ill driving black **Hogs** in the dark

1748 Franklin *PR* 3.255: 'Tis very ill driving black Hogs in the dark. *Oxford* 204; Tilley H500.

H246 No **Hog** can trespass on his master's ground

1809 Irving *History* 1.241: Noe man's owne hogg (as men use to say) can trespass upon his owne master's grounde.

H247 To bring one's **Hogs** (pigs) to a fair (*etc.*) market

1689 *Appeal* in *Andros Tracts* 3.197: Had we not brought our *Hogs* (and all our other *Cattle* too) to a fair market? **1709** Lawson *Voyage* 78-9: They may thank their Friends of *New-England*, who brought their Hogs to so fair a Market [literal]. **1713** Wise *Churches* 141: Four score Years has brought (not our Hogs, but) our Innocent Flock to a fair Market. a**1731** Cook *Bacon* 320: He driving Hogs, need run, ('tis said) Tho' brought to Market ne'er so bad. **1732** Franklin *Papers* 1.279: The Pork-seller, who it seems has *brought his Hogs to a fine Market*. **1764** JWatts in *Aspinwall Papers*

2.537: Lady Susan . . . has brought her pigs to a fine market to be sure. **1777** Curwen *Journal* 1.303: I . . . have brought my wares to a wretched poor market. **1787** *Belknap Papers* 1.472: The Devil always brings his pigs to a bad market. **1788** *Politician* 8: Or else old father will bring his pigs to a fine market, as the old proverb goes. **1798** Cobbett *Porcupine* 9.258: He has brought his hogs to a fine market. **1804** Weems *Letters* 2.299: Well I've brought my Pigs to a fine market truly, **1809** *Marion* 139: [They] brought *their pigs to a bad market*. **1815** Humphreys *Yankey* 19: You've brought your pigs to a fine market. **1818** Fearon *Sketches* 176: Lawyers, doctors . . . would, to use an American phrase, "come to a bad market." **1822** Weems *Penn* 43: My pigs are all brought to a fine market! Barbour 140(13); *Oxford* 376; TW 284(14).

H248 To go the whole **Hog**

1830 Ames *Mariner's* 91: They "go the whole hog" in all of them, 186. **1831** JCoffee in Jackson *Correspondence* 4.309: At suitable season, I expect he will go the whole hog round. **1832** Ames *Nautical* 179. **1834** MVanBuren in Jackson *Correspondence* 5.275: I have sent them a whole-Hog toast, 283: Grundy told me the other day he would go the whole *hog* for you. **1837** Hone *Diary* 1.242-3: Or, to use an expression which was brought into the American vocabulary about the same time that he [Jackson] assumed the crown and sceptre, he goes "the whole hog" in insulting the feelings of that part of the American people who have yet remaining some veneration for their country's institutions, 262: "I reckon," as Brother Jonathan says, "to go the whole hog," to use a Yankee expression, **1838** 321: The Speaker appointed . . . a chairman and three other thorough whole-hog men. Barbour 91(14); *Oxford* 307; TW 184(9).

H249 To run like a scalded **Hog**

1807 Janson *Stranger* 11: She did to be sure run off like a scalded hog.

H250 To sleep like a **Hog**

1809 Weems *Marion* 61: He go sleep like von hog. Whiting H408. See **P127**.

H251 To mend a small **Hole** by covering the whole garment

1787 Jefferson *Papers* 11.480: This proposes to mend a small hole by covering the whole garment.

H252 To pick a **Hole** (in one's coat)

1632 EHowes in *Winthrop Papers*(A) 3.76: Though there are here a thousand eyes watchinge ouer you to pick a hole in your coats. **1684** Mather *Diary* 1.89: Is it not very bitter . . . to hear . . . little but the *idle chat* whereby Holes are pick'd in the Coats of other and absent and honest Men? **1699** SWillis in *Winthrop Papers*(B) 6.51: Where Major Palmes . . . seems much inclined to pick holes in his neighbours coates. **1729** Ames *Almanacs* 65: Were I disposed to pick holes in his Coat, I should leave him in a ragged Condition. **1732** Franklin *Papers* 1.243: There are Holes enough to be pick'd in your Coat as well as others. **1756** SAngell in Kimball 2.232: Sum of the Boston Ranglers have begun to Pick hooles in Our Campain. **1759** Franklin *Papers* 8.398: No man should be oblig'd to produce his Deeds for his Adversaries to pick Holes in. **1769** Woodmason *Journal* 139: Any thing will serve for a Pretext to Pick Holes. **1776** *McIntosh Papers* 23: If they could pick a hole in my Conduct. **1789** Burd *Letters* 154: But I am as certain that he would pick a hole in my Coat in a short time afterwards. **1800** Gadsden *Writings* 303: A generous public *above picking holes* will use these powers discreetly, **1801** 307: Without any captious hole-picking. *Oxford* 623; TW 185(5).

H253 To beat (*etc.*) (all) **Hollow**

1769 *Johnson Papers* 6.575: We Shall Carry our Election All Hollow against the Miscreants. **1782** Madison *Papers* 5.416: The Pensylvanians alledge that the cause is going hollow in their favor. **1783** *American Wanderer* 158: The mortal would have beat her hollow. **1785** MByles in *Winslow Papers* 265: Miss Miller . . . is allowed by your connoiseurs in beauty to beat Miss Polly Prince all hollow. **1788** *Belknap Papers* 2.11: They intend, if they cannot get a clear vote to carry it, "all hollow," as the phrase is. **1790**

Maclay *Journal* 253: We . . . finally carried the business hollow. **1796** WVMurray in McHenry *Letters* 199: So we beat him hollow. **1801** DRoss in *Bingham's Maine* 2.1111. **1803** Davis *Travels* 325: There are no snakes if *Philadelphia* does not beat *Charleston* hollow. **1807** *Weekly* 2.95. **1809** Lindsley *Love* 8. **1809** Pinkney *Travels* 217: France beats it hollow in rural scenery. **1815** Adams *Works* 10.125: Now I have him all hollow. **1816** Bentley *Diary* 4.429. **1816** Paulding *Letters(I)* 2.24. **1818** Royall *Letters* 121. **1819** Waln *Hermit* 184. **1826** Pintard *Letters* 2.310: The election . . . has been carried all hollow. **1847** Paulding *Letters(II)* 465. TW 186(1).

H254   Court Holy-bread

1637 Morton *New English Canaan* 246: These servants at first arived at new Plimmouth, where they were entertained with Court holy bread by the Brethren. NED Court holy bread. Cf. *Oxford* 148; Whiting H419.

H255   To be all Holy-day with one

1796 Weems *Letters* 2.59: It seems, I must throw in my petition with respect to the lottery, in a given time or it will be all holyday with me. Cf. *Oxford* 228; Tilley S548.

H256   As true as Holy Writ

1794 Dennie *Letters* 144: You will laugh at my opinion but it is as true as holy Writ. TW 186; Whiting B281. See **G128.**

H257   Home is home be it never so homely

1723 Symmes *Utile* 18: Home is Home, be it never so Homely. **1776** Curwen *Journal* 1.284: Home is home be it ever so homely. **1783** Williams *Penrose* 293: The old Proverb was truly fulfilled, "Home is home, &c." **1791** S.P.L. *Thoughts* 77. **1805** Asbury *Journal* 2.456: Home is home. **1813** Harmon *Sixteen Years* 158: Home is home, let it be ever so homely! **1814** JMcDowell in *W&MCQ* 8(1899) 226: According to the old adage I love my home however homely above all places else. **1815** Humphreys *Yankey* 19-20: Hum is hum, be it ever so humbly. **1826** Longfellow *Letters* 1.172. **1826** LSheldon in Vanderpoel *Chronicles* 64.

1832 Clifford *Letters* 37: Home is home though ever so homely. *Oxford* 379; Whiting H420.

H258   To one's long Home

1657 JGreen in Wigglesworth *Diary* 115: God would come . . . and send them packing to their long home. **1674** Saffin *His Book* 23: He's gone to his Long home. **a1700** JPaine in *Mayflower Descendant* 8(1906) 181. **1702** Mather *Diary* 1.451, *Magnalia* 2.150: That passage, Eccles. xii.5, "Man goeth to his long home." **1703** Sewall *Letter-Book* 1.288, **1712** *Diary* 2.332: Major Walley . . . seems to be hastening to his Long home, **1717** *Letter-Book* 2.67, 77, **1725** 187. **c1725** Byrd *Another Secret Diary* 456: The poor soule is not far from his long home. **1733** Belcher *Papers* 1.339. **1766** JBoucher in *MHM* 7(1912) 302. **1775** JBalfour in *Letters to Washington* 5.144: It had like to have carry'd me to my long Home. **1775** JChester in Webb *Correspondence* 1.89: Sent the enemy . . . to their long homes. **1777** Fitch *New-York Diary* 148: Indeed great numbers had already arrived at their long home. **1781** Oliver *Origin* 109: Had the Assembly finished their Sessions, & returned to their *long* Homes, it is probable that Rebellion herself would have returned to *her long* Home with them. **1786** RO'Brien in *Barbary Wars* 1.4, **1790** in Jefferson *Papers* 18.443. **1790** JWinthrop in *Warren-Adams Letters* 2.321: Following her husband to his long home. **1791** Rush *Letters* 1.601: This afternoon Miss Bullock's remains were consigned to their long home. **1795** Cobbett *Porcupine* 2.99. **1796** Dow *Journal* 29. **1798** RO'Brien in *Barbary Wars* 1.247. **1801** ANMcLeod in Gates *Five Fur Traders* 148. **1805** Irving *Journals* 1.251. **1807** *Monthly Anthology* 4.362: The butchers retire to their long homes. **1809** Colby *Life* 1.36. **1809** Weems *Washington* 170. **1810** Wilson *Letters* cxvi. **1812** Asbury *Letters* 3.464. **1814** Valpey *Journal* 12. **1824** Flint *Recollections* 237, 294. *Oxford* 479-80; Whiting H422.

H259   To return Home as wise as one went

1740 Stephens *Journal(I)* 1.595-6: They returned home again this Afternoon, as wise as they went. **1788** May *Journal* 67: They came from home moneyless and brainless and have returned as they came. *Oxford* 379; Whiting H424.

H260   To come short **Home**

1677 Hubbard *Indian* 2.93: Sundry of them [did] come short Home. NED Short C 8e [did not come at all].

H261   **Homer** sometimes nods

c1650 Shepard *Hints* 159: *Aliquando bonus dormitat Homerus.* **1754** Johnson *Writings* 1.198: [Latin only]. **1777** JLovell in Sparks *Correspondence* 1.414: *Aliquando dormitat* did not appear an unnatural charge against Homer. **1790** *Columbian Magazine* 4.90: [Latin only]. **1805** *Monthly Anthology* 2.170: *Homer sometimes dozes.* **1808** *Emerald* NS 1.409: [Latin only]. **1810** *Port Folio* 2NS 3.49: Unlike Homer, the writer never nods. **1814** Wirt *Bachelor* 41: But Hippocrates sometimes nodded as well as Homer, **1822** *Letters* 2.147: [Latin only]. **1832** Ames *Nautical* 141: "Aliquando bonus Homerus dormitat," is good Latin, and if old Homer himself is allowed to "catch a noddy" occasionally, why not the humble writer of these Reminiscenses? Barbour 92; *Oxford* 379; Whiting H427.

H262   As coarse as **Hominy**

1815 John Pickering, *A Vocabulary or Collection of Words and Phrases* (Boston, 1815) 48: Hence a vulgar comparison — As *coarse* as hominy.

H263   As hard as a **Hone**

1807 *Weekly* 1.209: Her heart is harder than a hone.

H264   **Honesty** is the best policy

a1700 Saffin *His Book* 18: Honiesty is the best Pollicy. **1753** *Independent Reflector* 221: It will be found, that Honesty is the best Policy. **1753** Sherman *Almanacs* 239, **1755** 255: Plain down right Honesty, is the Beauty and Elegancy of Life. **1765** TBChandler in Johnson *Writings* 1.357: When I was young I was taught to believe that honesty is the best policy, the truth of

which maxim I could wish to see once put to the trial. **1776** JWarren in *Warren-Adams Letters* 1.221. **1777** Franklin *Writings* 7.8. **1778** Hamilton *Papers* 1.441: I look upon the old proverb . . . to be so generally true. **1778** Paine *American Crisis* 1.121: Let it teach you policy, if it cannot honesty. **1779** WDuer in Deane *Papers* 3.335. **1779** Franklin *Writings* 7.381. **1779** Paine *Deane* 2.165. **1781** Sullivan *Letters* 3.322. **1784** JDickinson in *St. Clair Papers* 1.585: the old saying. **1784** Hamilton *Papers* 3.495. **1785** Jefferson *Papers* 8.42: A wise man, if nature has not formed him honest, will yet act as if he were honest: because he will find it the most advantageous and wise part in the long run. **1785** Mrs. JTemple in *Bowdoin Papers* 2.43: A proverb truely verified in my husband. **1785** *Washington *Writings* 28.336: an old adage, **1786** 517: I can only repeat what I have formerly told my countrymen in a very serious manner "that honesty will be found, on every experiment, the best policy." **1787** Adams *Diary* 322: says nature. **1787** *American Museum* 2.108. **1787** *Washington *Writings* 29.302: Honesty in States, as well as Individuals will ever be found the soundest policy. **1789** Maclay *Journal* 104: on the whole. **1791** Bartram *Travels* 223: The truth of the old proverb. **1791** *Universal Asylum* 6.98. **1792** Belknap *History* 3.160: Honesty at home is the only foundation for credit abroad. **1794** Monroe *Writings* 2.153-4: There is but one kind of policy which is safe, which is the *honest policy*. **1796** *Washington *Writings* 35.235: I hold the maxim no less applicable to public than to private affairs, that honesty is always the best policy. **1797** Cobbett *Porcupine* 5.201: that good old proverb. **1797** Gadsden *Writings* 273: Honesty is the best and truest policy. **1797** Hawkins *Letters* 223: in politics as well as private life. **1797** *Washington *Writings* 36.4. **1798** DBarrow in *W&MCQ* 3S 20(1963) 449. **1805** Brackenridge *Modern* 618: the adage. **1808** *Emerald* NS 1.433. **1808** Hitchcock *Poetical Dictionary* 86: the proverb [there follows a discussion of the validity of the proverb]. **1809** Irving *History* 1.200: As to nations, the old maxim, that "honesty is the best policy," is a sheer and ruinous mistake. **1814** Carroll *Correspondence* 2.306. **1817** WColeman in King *Life* 6.52: the old fashioned maxim. **1819** Pintard *Letters* 1.225. **1820** Weems *Letters* 3.299. **1824** Neal *American Writers* 30: after all. **1827** Jackson *Correspondence* 3.369. **1833** Floy *Diary* 3. **1833** Jackson *Correspondence* 5.224, **1841** 6.122. Barbour 92(1); *Oxford* 380; TW 186(1).

H265   As sweet as **Honey** (and the honeycomb)

1644 Williams *Writings* 3.58: Thy words, which are sweeter then the honey and the honey-combe, **1652** 7.78. **1701** Taylor *Christographia* 35.10: Sweeter than hony rhimes, **1703** 395.90-1: Sweeter than the honey, and the Honey Comb. Ps.19.10. **1742** Johnson *Writings* 3.454. **1769** Capt. Martin in Silverman 257. **1817** Young *Life* 18. Barbour 92(2); *Oxford* 793; Whiting H430.

H266   **Honey** and gall, *etc.*

c**1705** Byrd *Another Secret Diary* 233: They have a luscious sweetness in the mouth, but are gall and poison in the stomach. **1755** Franklin *PR* 5.474: When you taste Honey, remember Gall. **1779** Adams(S) *Writings* 4.132: His Words are like Honey, but there is a large Mixture of Poison. **1795** Adams *Writings* 1.475: It is not improbable but the trial of honey will be substituted for that of vinegar. **1804** Dow *Journal* 210: After the knot was tied . . . and the honey is all gall and vinegar. **1819** Drake *Works* 309: To honey thou shalt change their gall. *Oxford* 381; Whiting H433. See **G5, W321.**

H267   **Honey** and pie

1782 Baldwin *Life and Letters* 100: The family—so alarmed that they were quite softened into Honey & Pie, **1783** 141: Took Tea by Invitation at Mʳˢ Judge Yates, all Honey & Pye. Cf. TW 187(1).

H268   **Honey** is sweet but the bee has a sting

a**1700** Hubbard *New England* 100: But whatever were the honey in the mouth of that beast of trade, there was a deadly sting in the tail. **1758** Franklin *PR* 7.354: The

Honey is sweet, but the Bee has a Sting. *Oxford* 39; Whiting H436.

H269   All **Honor** and no porridge, *etc.*

c**1800** Tyler *Island* 13: All honour and no porridge is a luncheon for a Camellian. Cf. *Oxford* 382-3; Tilley H573.

H270   Give **Honor** where honor is due

1777 SAdams in *Warren-Adams Letters* 1.375: May Honor be given to whom Honor may be due. **1834** Floy *Diary* 50: Loudon must be a man of taste . . . and disposed to give all credit where any credit is due. Lean 3.504. Cf. *Oxford* 382; Tilley H571.

H271   **Honors** change manners

1741 Franklin *PR* 2.297: Honours change Manners. *Oxford* 383; Tilley H583.

H272   There is **Honor** among thieves

1799 Eaton *Life* 116: There is honor among thieves. **1802** *Port Folio* 2.120: Honour 'mongst thieves. **1806** *Weekly* 1.139: An old maxim;—"Honor among"—you know the rest. **1809** *Port Folio* 2NS 2.401. **1816** Paulding *Letters(I)* 2.187: a sacred maxim. a**1820** Biddle *Autobiography* 274: the old saying. **1824** *Tales* 1.125: There is such a proverb as. Barbour 93(1); *Oxford* 382; TW 187. See **T45.**

H273   By **Hook** or by crook

c**1645** JCotton in Williams *Writings* 2.43: By hook or crook. **1732** Belcher *Papers* 1.490: By hook or by crook. **1783** *Washington *Writings* 26.242. **1783** Williams *Penrose* 169, 344. **1794** *Washington *Writings* 34.9. **1797** Cobbett *Porcupine* 6.286. **1797** OWolcott in Gibbs *Memoirs* 1.566. **1798** *Echo* 160: By hook or crook. **1801** Story *Shop* 54: By hook and crook. c**1810** AJFoster *Jeffersonian America* 155: By hook or crook. **1816** Fidfaddy *Adventures* 56. **1819** *Hallowell Gazette* in Banks *Maine* 132. **1820** Irving *Sketch Book* 460: In that ingenious way which is commonly denominated "by hook and by crook." **1821** Freneau *Last Poems* 44: Has made his way by *hook* and *crook.* **1822** Smith *Letters* 156: By hook and by crook, as the saying is. *Oxford* 382; Whiting H458.

H274   A gilded (silver) **Hook**

1790 *Universal Asylum* 5.167: Never swallow a gilded hook. **1810** Schultz *Travels* 1.19: We have already seen several salmon *jumping*, but have not been able to catch any, except with a *silver hook. Oxford* 14; Tilley H591.

H275   On one's own **Hook**

1792 Belknap *Foresters* 101: Adventurers who came into the forest on their own hook, and had no assistance. **1812** *Boston Gazette* in DA hook 2b: Rodgers himself says he went upon his own hook. **1832** Hone *Diary* 1.69: Some troops are marching about the street, "upon their own hook," I suppose, **1841** 2.571: Urging his flock to come out at the election "upon their own hook." **1852** CWard in Clifford *Letters* 255: It is written, as the Vermont soldier fought — "on my own hook." *Oxford* 383; TW 187-8(4).

H276   To throw all over **Hoop**
1753 DSchyler in *Colden Letters* 4.412: We most give them what they ask for or Els they will throw all over hoop again.

H277   To go **Hoop** for something
1721 Carter *Letters* 101: He will insist so long, I believe, that he may go hoop for his loading. NED Hoop *v.*[2], Whoop.

H278   He that lives upon **Hope** dies farting
1736 Franklin *PR* 2.138: He that lives upon Hope, dies farting, **1758** *WW* 342: will die fasting. Barbour 93(2); TW 188(2); Tilley H609. See **H283.**

H279   **Hope** deferred makes the heart sick
1733 Talcott *Papers* 1.285: As hope deferred makes the heart sick. **1735** WByrd in *VHM* 36(1928) 210: The worst of it is those Hopes sicken a little at their being so long deferr'd. **1788** NCoffin in *Baxter Manuscripts* 22.343: that saying of very great antiquity. **1796** Weems *Letters* 2.15. **1811** Adams *Writings* 4.7: Their hopes have been deferred until their hearts are sick. **1813** Colby *Life* 1.202. **1814** Jackson *Correspondence* 1.438. **1814** Palmer *Diary* 124: Hope deferd is like a lingering consumption, it wastes away our lives by degrees, and will end only in Death. **1817** *Port Folio* 4NS

4.176: Hope has been deferred until the heart is sick. **1818** [JSloan], *Rambles in Italy* (Baltimore, 1818) 39: That "sickness of the heart which arises from hope deferred." **1825** WStrange in *Ruffin Papers* 1.323. **1828** Longfellow *Letters* 1.276. **1830** JOverton in Jackson *Correspondence* 4.154. **1832** Ames *Nautical* 50. Barbour 93(3); *Oxford* 384; TW 188(3); Whiting H473.

H280   **Hope** is a sovereign balsam
1784 WHooper in Iredell *Correspondence* 2.108: Hope, however, is a sovereign balsam.

H281   **Hope** of gain lessens pain
1734 Franklin *PR* 1.353: Hope of gain Lessens pain. *Oxford* 294; Tilley G6.

H282   If it were not for **Hope** the heart would break
1810 *Kennon Letters* 32.173: You know it is said if it was not for hope, the heart would break, **1812** 33.268: How true is the old saying. *Oxford* 384; Whiting H475.

H283   One cannot live on **Hope**
1796 Hamilton *Papers* 20.334: For one cannot always live on hope. 'Tis a thin diet at best. *Oxford* 475. See **H278.**

H284   To live in **Hope,** if one dies in despair
1809 *Kennon Letters* 32.162: However, as the negroes say, I lives in hopes, and I hope I shan't die in dispair. **1811** MMarshall in Frances M. Mason, *My Dearest Polly* (Richmond, Va., 1961) 207: I frequently put myself in mind of the old proverb of living in hope if I die in dispaire. **1814** Palmer *Diary* 84: We must live, and hope but we may die in dispair. Whiting *NC* 426.

H285   **Hop-in-hoy,** half woman, half boy
1721 Wise *Friendly Check* in *Colonial Currency* 2.247: *Then to play-hop-in-hoy, Half Woman, and half Boy.* Tilley H480.

H286   As thick as **Hops**
1777 JBurgoyne in Moore *Diary* 1.459: From Canada as thick as hops. **1789** Dunlap *Darby's Return* 110: As thick as hops. **1796** Barton *Disappointment* 95. **1801** Story *Shop* 65: Sighs as thick as hops. **1809**

Weems *Marion* 46: Nanny houses were springing up thick as hops. **1819** Peirce *Rebelliad* 72: Boys and girls, as thick as hops. **1834** Floy *Diary* 67. Barbour 93; *Oxford* 246; TW 188(1).

H287 As hard as **Horn**

1748 Franklin *PR* 3.247: Blisters . . . as hard as Horn. TW 188(1); Whiting H481.

H288 As loud as a French **Horn**

1823 Weems *Letters* 3.354: "Hallo! hallo there!" . . . roared old M'Gregor, loud as a French horn. Whiting H482.

H289 **Horns** of cuckoldry

1644 Winthrop *Journal* 2.162: She . . . said she would make him wear horns as big as a bull. **1666** Alsop *Maryland* 98: Herds of Deer are as numerous in this Province of *Mary-land,* as Cuckolds can be in *London,* only their horns are not so well drest and tipt with silver as theirs are. **1682** J. W. *Letter* 4: A — —'s wife has been most notorious . . . by putting the Horns on her Husband, 5: All which . . . can tell how to adorn their Husbands Heads with a Forked Coat of Arms. **1709** Lawson *Voyage* 41: He seldom misses of wearing greater Horns than the Game he kills. **1731** Franklin *Papers* 1.220: This is the second Brace of Bucks that have been caught by the Horns this Fall. **1731** *Weekly Rehearsal* in Buckingham *Specimens* 1.116-7: That ornament of hair, which is styled the *Horns* . . . was certainly first calculated by some good-natured lady to keep her spouse in countenance. **1734** Belcher *Papers* 2.37: As he is very scant & strait lac'd I believe his horns won't sprout much. **1735** Franklin *Papers* 2.24: And so durst not marry, for fear of those dishonourable Decorations of the Head, which they think it the inevitable Fate of a Fumbler to wear. **1743** Ames *Almanacs* 163: Horns will sprout in less Time than Mushrooms. **1747** Stith *History* 81: But their Horns were too short, and they themselves narrowly escaped a greater Mischief. **1767** Ames *Almanacs* 387: A fine growing season—for horns. **1769** Davis *Colonial Virginia Satirist* 53: To have given an unsuspicious husband invisible horns. **1772** Carroll

Copy-Book 212: The Cornelian family (to use Molière's expression) is become in point of numbers truly alarming. **1774** Ames *Almanacs* 449: *Herodotus* tells us that "in Cold Countries Beasts have very seldom Horns, but in Hot, they have very large ones." This might bear a very pleasant Application! **1775** 457: As it is rare since the Days of a certain Roman Emperor, for hornsmiths to have the sanction of the Senate, some of our Daughters of Liberty must inform who are the best workmen. **1775** Tilghman *Memoir* 92-3: The Onandago Tribe . . . look upon horns as the emblem of strength, Virtue and Courage. This name might have made a suspicious man very unhappy, and made him feel his Temples every now and then for the sprouting honours. **1776** *Blockheads* 11: You may expect a pair of horns grow out of your head as large as your old bulls. **1779** Perkins *Diary* 1.255: The Soldiers rode Mr. Wicks, a Soldier, on their Shoulders with a large pair of Horns over his Head, which is said to be a Custom with them, After one of their Comrades are married. **1782** Paine *American Crisis* 1.227: The bride . . . who has placed on his head the ensigns of her disgust. **1782** Trumbull *Satiric Poems* 193: Great Loring, famed above laymen, A proper Priest for Lybian Ammon, Who, while Howe's gift his brow adorns, Had match'd that deity in horns. **1784** Freneau *Poems* 2.278: That Venus has horns we've no reason to doubt. **1787** DHumphreys in *American Museum* 1.488: See the cuckolds arise! See the horns that they rear. . . . Ere younger Cymon's horns began to grow. **1789** Brackenridge *Gazette* 317: I put horns on Traddles head. **1789** Brown *Better* 45: Vengeful she becomes and bold, Hence the *growing* ill of horns. **1789** Morris *Diary* 1.252: So to mark my Attention to her as eventually to confer on him the cornuted Badge, **1790** 360-1: Monsieur at length goes away . . . and we take the opportunity to decorate his Brow with the connubial Graces of the Country. **1793** Bowen(?) *Journals* 2.595: A brace of proud antlers Your brows may adorn And a hundred to one but you'll Double Cape Horn. [This is from a song which begins "As you mean to set sail For the Land of Delight."] **1795** Cobbett *Porcupine* 2.55: I question much whether they do not look upon a pair of antlers as an honourable mark of distinction, **1798** 8.186: It was quite natural for her to choose as the first object of her favours, a French *sans-culotte,* who . . . qualified the *keeper* to make his appearance amongst his *horned* herd. **1801** Sewall *Poems* 251: He [an ox] glories in what C——lds blush at—his horns. **1805** Brackenridge *Modern* 500: But she saw *horns*. Horns! said she. What can this mean? Mean, said the Captain, every one knows the meaning of the emblem. Antlers is a common place figure for cuckoldom. **1808** Barker *Tears* 184: Do your brows branch by anticipation? 185: Those horns have sounded an alarm to the girl's modesty. **1809** JAdams in *Adams-Cunningham Letters* 94: You committed adultery the night before and put horns upon your husband. **1811** Graydon *Memoirs* 257: He laboured under that "curse of great ones," in having the "forked plague" fixed on him by Sir William. **1816** Lambert *Travels* 1.292: The husbands . . . content themselves with increasing the number of their *horned* brethren. **1818** Hall *Travels* 90: Deem'st thou, that first of men, the nuptial horn Thy brow hath glorified? **1819** Peirce *Rebelliad* 62: Thus Logic fairly lost his breeches; Although, it seems, for them he got A pair of horns and petticoat. **1821** Doddridge *Dialogue* 47: I once saw a couple of horns set up on two poles [at a wedding], **1824** *Notes* 106: Another method of revenge which we adopted when the chastity of the bride was a little suspect was that of setting up a pair of horns on poles, or trees, on the route of the weddingg party. This was a hint to the groom that he might expect to be complimented with a pair of horns himself. *Oxford* 385; Whiting H483.

H290 Neither **Horn** nor hoof

1647 Childe *New Englands Jonas* in Force *Tracts* 4.3.6: He had neither horn nor hoofe of his own, nor any thing wherewith to buy his children cloaths. NED Horn 2b.

H291 Soft in the **Horn** and hard in the hoof

1804 Irving *Corrector* 89: Soft in the horn and hard in the hoof, like the Devil's Jack Ass. Spanish Proverb.

H292 To be **Horn-mad**

1721 *Wyllys Papers* 399: I reckon [he] wil be horn mad at it. **1787** *American Museum* 1.137: He is horn mad, and runs bellowing like a bull [jealous]. **1805** Weems *Letters* 2.315: They will run horn mad if you vex 'em in the life of Wash. **1815** Humphreys *Yankey* 55: The man is . . . horn-mad. *Oxford* 385; Whiting H496.

H293 To be on the **Horns** of a dilemma

1754 Johnson *Writings* 1.205: I . . . bring the two horns of a dilemma to stare you in the face. **1798** Adams *Writings* 2.332: It is an uncomfortable dilemma, from both horns of which it is in these times impossible to escape. **1805** *Monthly Anthology* 2.78: To force their opponents upon one of the horns of this dilemma. **1814** Morris *Diary and Letters* 2.562: They hang up our masters on the horns of this dilemma. **1820** TJefferson in *Adams-Jefferson Letters* 2.562: We have so lived as to fear neither horn of the dilemma. **1834** PCameron in *Ruffin Papers* 2.109: I am still upon the horns of doubt and uncertainty as to my location. **1842** Paulding *Letters(II)* 316: The Whig Leaders, who stand guard at each horn of the Dilemma. *Oxford* 385; TW 189(13).

H294 To blow one's own **Horn**

1815 Ames *Diary* 280: I should fear he would soon burst with so hard blowing his own horn. Barbour 93(2); *Oxford* 70; TW 189(11); Whiting H490. See **T258.**

H295 To pull (*etc.*) one's **Horns**

1676 Williams *Writings* 5.35: He pluckt in his horns. **1691** *Wyllys Papers* 327: The high flown men began to hang down yᵣ heads and pul in yᵣ horns. **1702** Mather *Magnalia* 2.645: Nor that they ever advised him to pull in his *horns,* from goring the sides of New-England. **1721** Carter *Letters* 79: We must haul in our horns and live as we can afford. **1732** Belcher *Papers* 1.462. **1738** *Georgia Records* 22¹.119: Such . . .

must of necessity draw in their horns. **1749** JColden in *Colden Letters* 4.178. **1783** Williams *Penrose* 323: I now began to draw in my horns. **1785** Coke *Journals* 39: drew. **1786** Adams(A) *Letters* 310: drew. **1797** Dunlap *Diary* 1.87: I should adopt measures that would make him (using a vulgar expression) "hawl in his horns." **1801** Sewall *Poems* 251. **1807** *Weekly* 2.192: haul'd. **1808** Hitchcock *Poetical Dictionary* 24. **1835** Hone *Diary* 1.189: haul. Barbour 93; *Oxford* 201; Whiting H491.

H296   As fierce as a **Hornet**
1796 Latrobe *Journal* 104: This dangerous fly [the bald-face hornet] is proverbially fierce. Cf. TW 189-90.

H297   As mad as a **Hornet**
1835 Floy *Diary* 185: Every time he would suggest something concerning the matter I would get as mad as a hornet. Barbour 93-4; TW 189-90.

H298   To raise (*etc.*) a **Hornet's** nest (about one's ears)
1768 *Johnson Papers* 6.238: [They] will indeavor to raise the whole nest of Hornets . . . at home again[st] him. **1777** RMorris in Deane *Papers* 2.35: For they will thus raise a Nest of Hornets that they do not expect. **1778** Smith *Memoirs(II)* 421: [They] would have a Hornets' Nest about their Ears if they did not soon mend their Manners. **1784** *Adams-Waterhouse Correspondence* 4: It has stirred up a Nest of Hornets against the Authors of it. **1792** Belknap *Foresters* 158. **1801** Cutler *Life* 2.44: He will have a hornet's nest of Jacobins about his ears. **1806** *Weekly* 1.131. **1809** *Port Folio* 2NS 2.535. **1812** Burr *Journal* 2.321: By going to New Orleans, I may go plump into a hornet's nest. **1814** Jefferson *Writings* 14.68: To bring such a nest of hornets on me. **1816** Paulding *Letters(I)* 2.73. **1820** Adams *Memoirs* 5.16: To bring down a hornets' nest of printers upon me, **1822** 6.48. **1822** Jefferson *Writings* 15.391: Into what a nest of hornets would it thrust my head! **1822** Weems *Penn* 186: He was sure to stir up a hornet's nest of angry hard-visaged puritans. **1831** JRandolph in Jackson *Corre-*

spondence 4.386: If you had not . . . come out and stirred that nest of hornets. **1843** Paulding *Letters(II)* 330: He will bring a Nest of Hornets about your Ears. *Oxford* 869; TW 190(3); Tilley W79. See S539.

H299   Better be a **Horse** than a cart
1803 *Port Folio* 3.175: There is an old proverb, which says, "it is better to be a horse than a cart."

H300   Enough to knock a **Horse** down
1796 Lee *Diary and Letters* 12: [A] rascal who stinks of garlic enough to knock a horse down. Cf. TW 191(21).

H301   (Enough) to tire a **Horse**
1744 Hamilton *Itinerarium* 71: In general there was such a medley of Dutch and English as would have tired a horse.

H302   A galled **Horse** will wince
1676 Williams *Writings* 5.75: They would cry out (especially *W.E.* like a *galled horse* winching), 136: The *gall'd Horse* endures not rubbing. **1692** Bulkeley *Will* 93: But this precarious, usurped and tyrannical authority of theirs is the galled place that will not endure to be touched in word or deed without a kick. **1705** Ingles *Reply* 18: Every Body knows y^t a Gal'd horse will winch. **1714** Hunter *Androboros* 6: Let the Gall'd Horse wince, our Withers are unwrung. **1723** *Wyllys Papers* 402: If you touch a galde horse hee will flinch. **1733** Franklin *Papers* 1.327: They delight (to use their own Phrase) in *touching gall'd Horses* that they may see 'em *winch*. **1775** POliver in Hutchinson *Diary* 1.574. **1778** Paine *Deane* 2.115: The gentlemen seem to wince before they are touched. **1779** WHumphreys in Deane *Papers* 4.15. **1794** UTracey in Callender *Political Register* 1.85: Whenever a subject of that kind was touched, there were certain gentlemen in that House, who shook their backs, *like a sore backed horse*, 86(JM'Dowell): He adverted to the simile of the sore-backed horse, and said, that he believed his back to have been rubbed harder in the last war than that of the gentleman. *Oxford* 686; Whiting H505.

H303 He keeps a good **Horse** that can travel well afoot

1737 Franklin *PR* 2.168: He that can travel well afoot, keeps a good horse. Barbour 94(9).

H304 He that leads his **Horse** may well go afoot

a1772 Madison *Papers* 1.16: He may well go afoot who leads his Horse in his hand. Prov. *Oxford* 864; TW 191(24).

H305 **Horse,** foot and dragoons

1827 WClements in Murphey *Papers* 1.359: I immediately turned over to you, Horse foot and Dragoons. 1837 Jackson *Correspondence* 5.503: The Biddleites and Bankites are in the state routed horse foot and Dragoons. *Oxford* 386; Tilley H655.

H306 A **Horse** of another color

1798 *Aurora* in Thornton *Glossary* 1.453: [That] is a horse of another colour. Barbour 94(3); *Oxford* 387; TW 190(3).

H307 A **Horse** taught and a woman to teach

1733 Franklin *PR* 1.315: A taught horse, and a woman to teach, and teachers practising what they preach. *Oxford* 386; Tilley H636.

H308 A **Horse** thinks one thing, and he that saddles him another

1754 Franklin *PR* 5.184: The Horse thinks one thing, and he that saddles him another. *Oxford* 598; Tilley H667; Whiting B101.

H309 It is a bad **Horse** that will not carry his own provender

1816 *Emigrant's Guide* 26-7: A homely proverb asserts, "It is a bad horse that will not carry his own provender." *Oxford* 651; Whiting H521.

H310 Like a **Horse** in a mill

1782 Freneau *Poems* 2.194: We are doomed to drive on, like a horse in a mill. *Oxford* 386. Cf. TW 190(10); Tilley H697.

H311 Live **Horse** and thou shall get grass

1745 *Johnson Papers* 1.34: That's fulfilling the old Pr[overb] Live horse and y^u shall gett grass. *Oxford* 474. Cf. Whiting G437.

H312 One may lead a **Horse** to water, *etc.*

1692 Bulkeley *Will* 148: Can a man make his horse drink unless he will. 1766 Franklin *Papers* 13.8: As the proverb says, though one man may *lead* a horse to water, ten can't *make him drink.* 1785 Mason *Papers* 2.834: I believe such an Experiment wou'd prove simular to the old vulgar Adage, of carrying a Horse to the Water. They may pass a Law to issue it, but twenty Laws will not make People receive it. Barbour 95(21); *Oxford* 449; Whiting H541.

H313 One may steal a **Horse** while another may not look over the hedge (*varied*)

1650 Williams *Writings* 6.203: Uncas might better steal many horses then Wenekunat look over the hedge. 1698 JUsher in *W&MCQ* 3S 7(1950) 106: Se how one that robs Shall be favord more than a lookeron. 1767 Franklin *Papers* 14.319: The old saying is as true now as ever it was, *one man may better steal a horse, than another look over the hedge.* 1771 Ames *Almanacs* 421: One may steal a Horse while another may not look over the Wall. 1771 TWalker in American Antiquarian Society, *Proceedings* NS 41(1931) 143: Some men had better steal an Horse than others look over the Hedge. 1778 Lee(W) *Letters* 2.370. 1780 Reed *Life* 2.247: The old proverb is frequently verified in me. 1816 Fidfaddy *Adventures* 125: One may steal a horse, while another is hanged for looking over a hedge. 1838 Hone *Diary* 1.347: True it is that these men may "steal a horse when we cannot look over the hedge." *Oxford* 772; Whiting M283.

H314 A short **Horse** is soon curried

1816 Fidfaddy *Adventures* 48: A short horse is soon curried. Barbour 94(4); *Oxford* 727-8; Whiting H525.

H315 Though you ride, remember the **Horse** goes on foot

1782 Freneau *Prose* 71-2: An adage very frequent with the Turks, viz. "Though you ride, remember the horse goes on foot."

H316 To be drawn asunder by wild **Horses**

1710 Sewall *Diary* 2.284: Govr says, He will

be drawn asunder with wild Horses before he will be thrust upon as last year, 288. Whiting H526.

H317 To eat like a **Horse**

1728 Byrd *Dividing Line* 243: This man had an odd Constitution, he eat like a Horse. **1785** Hunter *Quebec* 103: We eat like horses. Barbour 94(17); Whiting H532.

H318 To lie faster than a **Horse** can trot

1822 Lee *Diary and Letters* 203: He will lie gratuitously farther [*for* faster] than a horse can trot. Barbour 94(8); TW 190(7).

H319 To ride a free **Horse** to death

1778 Paine *People of Pennsylvania* 2.280: It was riding a free horse to death. **1809** Weems *Marion* 192: Never ride a free horse to death. **1816** DCameron in Murphey *Papers* 1.90: This *new* trouble to you is indeed a verification of the old proverb—"that a free Horse is always rode to death." Barbour 94(7); *Oxford* 768; Whiting H520.

H320 To ride (*etc.*) the high **Horse**

1787 WSmith in Jefferson *Papers* 12.390: They feel themselves on the high Horse of power. **1791** Ames *Letters* 1.108: What did we Yankees do but mount the high horse, and scold in heroics? **1796** Hamilton *Papers* 20.52: Laurance rather rides a high horse upon the occasion. **1801** FAmes in King *Life* 4.2: But Democracy rides the high horse, 76: Virginia rides the great horse. **1811** Graydon *Memoirs* 285: Not one of the prisoners had been more upon his high horse. **1817** Adams *Memoirs* 4.28: Clay had already mounted his South American great horse. **1818** Wirt *Letters* 2.77: A fellow who . . . is perpetually on his high horse, may make a very good centaur, but he will not do long for a man. Barbour 94(18); *Oxford* 676; TW 192(36). See **R138.**

H321 To snort (snore) like a **Horse**

1803 Davis *Travels* 327: My bed-fellow . . . snorted like a horse. **1850** Cooper *Letters* 6.139: He . . . snores like a troop of horses. Whiting H533.

H322 To work (*etc.*) for a dead **Horse**

1732 Byrd *Progress* 317: Which he per-

formed as lamely as if he had been to labor for a dead horse. **1755** Laurens *Papers* 2.45: We shall have been working for a dead Horse for a Year or two past. **1776** JWarren in *Warren-Gerry Correspondence* 47: Tho' this is working, as the proverb is, for a dead Horse. **1779** *New Jersey Journal* in *Newspaper Extracts(II)* 3.257: Which (to use a phrase well understood) is paying for a *dead horse.* **1824** Neal *American Writers* 64: No man likes working for a dead horse. *Oxford* 916; TW 192(40).

H323 To work like a **Horse**

1775 Lee *Papers* 1.199: For I work like ten post Horses. **1776** Gordon *Letters* 605: The soldiers working like horses night and day. **1785** WChipman in *Winslow Papers* 278: A man who . . . will work like a horse. **1785** Hunter *Quebec* 62. **1801** JJackson in Milledge *Correspondence* 71. **1809** Weems *Marion* 61: They are working away like horses. **1812** Burr *Journal* 2.436: Working and sweating like a horse. **1818** Wirt *Letters* 2.72: *Read law like a horse.* **1816** Paulding *Letters(I)* 2.163. **1819** Welby *Visit* 251. **1840** Paulding *Letters(II)* 285: It comes rather hard to work like a horse and be abused like a pickpocket for my pains, **1855** 555. Barbour 95(20); *Oxford* 917; TW 192(39).

H324 Win the **Horse** or lose the saddle

1765 Franklin *Papers* 12.199: Win the Horse or lose the Saddle. **1793** HWilliamson in *Blount Papers* 2.282: Harris . . . and you . . . may possibly resolve *to win the Horse or lose the Saddle,* to get a large price or none. **1802** Chester *Federalism* 13. *Oxford* 892; Whiting H522.

H325 As dead as **Horse-blocks**

1806 Fessenden *Modern Philosopher* 198: Till dead as horse-blocks. Cf. Lean 2.820: Block.

H326 A **Horse-laugh**

c**1725** Byrd *Another Secret Diary* 473: Voracio . . . only answer'd her with a very ingenious Horse-laugh not having time to wast upon idle Repartees. **1769** Ames *Almanacs* 402: A Horse laugh is as far from Chearful-ness as Sowerness is from Sorrow or Religion. **1775** Curwen *Journal* 1.87. **c1780** Bailey *Journal* 4. **1788** *Belknap Papers* 2.12. **1797** Smith(EH) *Diary* 32. **1800** Cobbett *Porcupine* 11.336. **1806** Fessenden *Modern Philosopher* 58: From a simple attempt to excite a simper, to a violent effort to raise a horse laugh. In short, we ever have, and always will, *laugh by rule.* **1807** *Weekly* 1.268. **1809** *Port Folio* 2NS 2.190. **1822** Watterston *Winter* 131. TW 191(23).

H327 To reckon without one's **Host**
c1680 Radisson *Voyages* 188: We left that inn wth out reckoning wth our host [literal]. **1708** Sewall *Letter-Book* 1.371: Thus I Reckon; but if reckoning without my Host, I reckon wrong; your Adjusting the Account, will gratify. **1744** RWolcott in *Law Papers* 1.242-3: Mr Hosmanden is a Gentleman of a Great deal of Assurance but I hope in this matter he has Reckend without his Landlady. **1775** GWashington in *Naval Documents* 2.930: I reckoned without my Host. **1776** Paine *Common Sense* 1.44. **1776** Shaw *Journals* 12: In this, however, I reckoned without my host, for the price of every thing is raised to an extravagant height. **1783** Williams *Penrose* 255. **1785** Washington *Writings* 28.248, **1788** 30.146: You are reckoning without your host, as the phrase is. **1797** Baily *Journal* 418. **1800** Cobbett *Porcupine* 12.145. **1807** *Weekly* 2.395. **1808** *Kennon Letters* 31.195: I had, if I may be permitted to quote an old adage, reckoned without my host. **1809** WCunningham in *Adams-Cunningham Letters* 145. **1812** Melish *Travels* 307. **1816** Paulding *Letters(I)* 1.41. **1819** Welby *Visit* 226. **1832** Ames *Nautical* 34. *Oxford* 667; Whiting H550.

H328 Soon **Hot** and soon cold
c1816 Durang *Memoir* 110: Their disposition is like my own, soon hot and soon cold. *Oxford* 752; Whiting H554. See **L229.**

H329 As white as a **Hound's** tooth
1783 Williams *Penrose* 295-6: A smart Privateer with a bottom as white as a Hound's tooth. Barbour 95(1).

H330 To keep with the **Hound** and run with the hare (*varied*)
1755 Davis *Colonial Virginia Satirist* 26: To keep with the hound, while they run with the hare. **1798** Cobbett *Porcupine* 10.18: Holding with the hare, and running with the hounds. **1820** HSGTucker in *W&MCQ* 10(1901) 11: Surely the Northern People think he can "keep with the hounds, and run with the Hare." **1832** JRandolph in Jackson *Correspondence* 4.410: *His holding with the Hare and running with the hounds* has damned him. **1845** Jackson *Correspondence* 6.371: Those who during the late struggle ran with the *hair,* and *cryed* with the *hounds.* Barbour 95(2); *Oxford* 689; Whiting H586.

H331 The darkest **Hour** is just before day (*varied*)
1776 Curwen *Journal* 1.286: The darkest part of the night immediately preceeds the break of day. **1776** SHodgkins in Hodgkins *Letters* 220: Many times the darkest time is jest before day. **1780** Thacher *Journal* 220: It is always darkest just before day light. **1797** PHall in Porter *Negro Writing* 74: The darkest is before the break of day. **1800** Dow *Journal* 90: But the darkest hour is just before the break of day. **1814** Jackson *Correspondence* 2.35: It is an old adage . . . that the darkest hour of all the night is Just before day. **1822** *Austin Papers* 1.494: According to the old addage it is never so dark as before day. *Oxford* 168; TW 193.

H332 **Hours** were made for slaves
1819 Cobbett *Year's* 180: "Hours were made for slaves," is an old saying.

H333 He that lives in a glass **House** should not throw stones (*varied*)
1710 JDummer in *W&MCQ* 3S 24(1967) 411: I should not out of common prudence cast stones at my Neibour's windows, when my own are made of glass. **1712** Danforth *Poems* 189.217-8: Would you not have your Glass-house broke, Then throwing stones forbear. **1736** Franklin *PR* 2.141: Don't throw stones at your neighbours, if your own windows are glass. **1778** Paine *American Crisis* 1.134: "He who lives in a glass

house," says a Spanish proverb, "should never begin throwing stones." **1779** Lee *Letters* 2.9: You will do well to advise your friend to observe the Spanish Proverb for the future, "that he who lives in a glass house, should not begin to throw stones." **1794** JAdams in Smith *Journal and Correspondence* 2(2) 129: Your [AAS's] proverb that a tenant of a glass house should never throw stones at the passengers in the street, has great and sound sense. **1803** Wirt *British Spy* 233: This has been called "throwing stones at other people's glass houses," and the person who communicated those letters . . . is politely reminded that he himself resides "in a glass house." **1807** DMcKeehan in *Lewis and Clark Expedition* 406: Did your Excellency never attend to the advice given to those who have glass houses? **1813** Jefferson *Writings* 19.203: It is not for those who live in glass houses to set the example of throwing stones. **1821** Royall *Letters* 203. **1825** Jackson *Correspondence* 3.283: A man who dwell[s], as he does, in a glass house, ought never to cast stones. Barbour 96(5), 138(5-7); *Oxford* 360; TW 194(4). Cf. Whiting H218. See **T64**.

H334 A **House** divided cannot stand

1704 Chalkley *Journal* 42: My Mother would often say, *A House divided could not stand.* **1735** *Wyllys Papers* 414: A house Divided Cannot Stand. **1750** JOulton in *Baxter Manuscripts* 12.85: This puts me in mind of y^t Saying, A house divided Ag^st it self Cannot Stand. **c1765** Winslow *Broadside* 185. **1773** GSimpson in *Letters to Washington* 4.217: But what must becom of that house that devids against its Self? **1776** JHabersham in Gibbes 2.259. **1787** *American Museum* 2.384. **1790** Maclay *Journal* 298. **1793** GMorris in Sparks *Correspondence* 4.431: A sound maxim from an excellent book. **1812** AAdams in *Adams-Warren Correspondence* 502: A house divided against itself, — and upon that foundation do our enemies build their hopes of subduing us. May it prove a sandy one to them! **1822** Stansbury *Pedestrian* 153. **1830** Jackson *Correspondence* 4.205, 208, **1831** 254, 276:

I repeat the adage is true, "that a House divided cannot stand," **1831** 318, **1840** 6.82: says the scriptures, **1843** 204: The scripture has been fulfilled. Barbour 95(1); *Oxford* 428; Whiting K62.

H335 A **House** without woman and firelight, *etc.*

1733 Franklin *PR* 1.312: A house without woman and Firelight, is like a body without soul or sprite.

H336 If the **House** is on fire, no matter where it kindled

1783 Rush *Letters* 1.307: The house is on fire — it is no matter *where* it kindled or *who* blew the flame. Cf. Chaucer *Troilus* iii 855-9.

H337 A little **House** well filled, *etc.*

1735 Franklin *PR* 2.5: A little House well fill'd, a little Field well till'd, and a little Wife well will'd, are great Riches. *Oxford* 470; Tilley H779; TW 193(2).

H338 One **House** filled is better than two spoiled

1805 Bentley *Diary* 3.161: One house filled was better than two spoiled. *Oxford* 54-5; Tilley H570.

H339 One's **House** is his castle

1692 Bulkeley *Will* 226: Our houses are no castles against their warrants. **1761** Adams *Legal Papers* 2.125: A Man, who is quiet, is as secure in his House, as a Prince in his Castle, 142: A man's house is his castle; and while he is quiet, he is as well guarded as a prince in his castle. **1768** Dickinson *Letters* 45: The common law . . . ever regarded a man's *house* as his castle, or a place of perfect security. **1770** Adams *Legal Papers* 2.412: A Man's house is his Castle, and he may defend it by himself alone or with such as he calls to assist him, **1774** 1.137: An Englishmans dwelling House is his Castle. **1774** W. H. Drayton in Gibbes 2.21: Thus were the houses, the castles of English subjects, preserved inviolate (Sir Edward Coke). **1774** Seabury *Letters* 62: My house is my castle. **1781** Oliver *Origin* 84: He repaired to his House, as his Castle. **1792** Jefferson *Writings* 17.332: Is that spirit of independence and sovereignty which a man feels in his own house, and which Englishmen felt when they denominated their houses their castles, to be absolutely subdued? **1797** Cobbett *Porcupine* 7.50: And if I dare to defend my "castle." **1802** Austin *Literary Papers* 142: His house in a double sense is the owner's castle. **1802** Irving *Jonathan* 52: When an actor is on the stage, he is in his own house—it is his castle. **1807** *Monthly Anthology* 4.18. **1816** Paulding *Letters(I)* 2.6: His castle—every man's house is his castle, you know,—ergo, every house is a castle. **1822** Bache *Notes* 110. **1824** Flint *Recollections* 125: We had fearful evidence that they considered their master's house as his castle. **1848** Clifford *Letters* 177: Every House is a castle. Barbour 95(2); *Oxford* 389; TW 193(1).

H340 Set not the **House** on fire to roast eggs

1645 Shepard *Hints* 159: And not set the whole house on fire to roast their own Egs. **1751** Franklin *PR* 4.86: Pray don't burn my House to roast your Eggs. *Oxford* 717; Tilley H757. See **B48.**

H341 A smoky **House** and a scolding wife, *etc.*

1788 *American Museum* 3.125: A smoky house and a scolding wife, Are two of the greatest ills in life. *Oxford* 817; Whiting T187.

H342 To bring an old **House** upon one's head (ears)

1713 Wise *Churches* 152: They may chance to bring, if not an Old, a New House upon their heads. **1746** *Law Papers* 2.316-7: I doubt we have brôt an old house on our Heads but god deliver us. **1783** Williams *Penrose* 131: I began to think I had brought an Old house over my head by having this Indian left with me. **1789** *Columbian Magazine* 3.102: Which generally brings "an old house over my head" as the saying is. **1800** *Echo* 270: He pulls an *old house* round his ears. **1804** Burr *Correspondence* 148: If the compliment should be returned, I should bring an old house about my ears. *Oxford* 654; Tilley H756. See **E12.**

H343 To eat one out of **House** and home

1807 Mackay *Letters* 61: These two bears will eat & drink him out of house & home. **1830** Ames *Mariner's* 93: Eat Josh "out of house and home." Barbour 96(8); *Oxford* 215; Whiting H614. See **D280.**

H344 To lose the **House** rather than break the window

1806 JWilkinson in Claiborne *Letter Books* 4.60: Shall we lose the house because we will not break the window?

H345 To turn one out of **House** and home

1816 Paulding *Letters(I)* 2.211: Let's turn Uncle Sam out of house and home. Whiting H613.

H346 To turn the **House** out at the windows (*varied*)

1783 JDickinson in Read *Correspondence* 381: The servants may turn the house out at the windows. **1833** Hone *Diary* 1.88: One of our tremendous great New York affairs, where the house is turned out of doors and the money turned out of pocket to furnish two hours' entertainment for a large party. **1836** *Diary of Millie Gray* (Houston, Texas, 1967) 82: Sister Susan spent the morning with me. The house turned out of the windows *she says*. *Oxford* 390; Tilley H785.

H347 As broad as the **House-floor**

a**1656** Bradford *History* 1.70: A seale as broad as the house flore.

H348 A good **Housewife** is more of a goose than a sheep

1775 Ames *Almanacs* 456: A good housewife commonly is no sheep—more of a goose. Cf. *Oxford* 730; Tilley S412.

H349 As dead as a **Hub**

1757 Adams *D and A* 1.90: The Action is as dead as a Hubb.

H350 Up to the **Hub**

1815 Humphreys *Yankey* 33: I've bin up to the hub, and didn't flinch. a**1855** Beecher *Autobiography* 1.116: They were Congregational up to the hub. DA hub²; NED Hub¹ 2; Thornton *Glossary* 1.457-8.

H351 To take **Huff**

1756 Washington *Writings* 2.500: Otherwise he takes huff, thinks his wisdom and merit affronted, and so marches off. NED Huff 2b. See **S303**.

H352 **Hugger-mugger**

1692 Bulkeley *Will* 186: But keeping it [a proclamation] in hugger-mugger, and making a great talk of it, it was possible to beguile some. **1779** WHarper in *Clinton Papers* 4.714: The popell are very uneasy at Justice . . . being huger mugered do. **1787** *Anarchiad* 120: Not huggermuggerly in the dark, but openlye. **1806** Taggart *Letters* 195: Several other things nugger muggerd in secret. *Oxford* 391; Whiting H628.

H353 "I wish I could see," quoth blind **Hugh**

1678 WWinthrop in *Winthrop Papers(B)* 5S8.411: I told Cowell you would bring him a hors, and he sayes, "I wish I could se him, quoth blind Hue. **1679** Danforth *Poems* 179.39-40: The Sun from th'Lyon will make retreit, In truth 'twould joy a blind man much to se it. Whiting H629, M51.

H354 To eat **Humble-pie**

1766 JParker in Franklin *Papers* 13.493: He got foul of an Humble-Pie, and wrote me a Note that he would return. **1775** DCobb in *Bingham's Maine* 1.402: He must eat humble pye. **1793** *Echo* 107: Eat humble-pye. *Oxford* 391; TW 195. See **P108**.

H355 As light as a **Humming-bird**

1798 HKnox in *Bingham's Maine* 2.912: Render my heart as light as an humming bird. Cf. TW 195.

H356 **Hunger** breaks through stone walls (*varied*)

1700 Taylor *Poems* 153: Love like to hunger'll break through stone strong Walls. **1750** *Massachusetts* in *Colonial Currency* 4.437-8: Hunger will break through *Brick Walls*. **1774** AA in *Adams FC* 1.148: Least hunger should break thro the Stone walls. **1774** Quincy *Memoir* 210: Your perseverance will occasion in time that hunger which will break through stone walls. **1777** JMVarnum in Washington *Writings*

10.184: According to the saying of Solomon, hunger will break thro' a Stone Wall. **1778** MDavis in *Baxter Manuscripts* 15.398. **1779** Ledyard *Journal of Cook's Last Voyage* 107: Passions which . . . like hunger would pervade stone walls. **1781** Adams *Correspondence* 481: Hunger will break down all ordinary fences. **1811** Burroughs *Memoirs* 113: It is said. **1812** Adams *Writings* 4.332. **1815** Andrews *Prisoners' Memoirs* 44: It is maxim strikingly true, that "hunger will break through a stone wall;" and it is equally true, that it will break through all moral obligations. **1815** Palmer *Diary* 176: It's an old saying that hunger will go through a Stone Wall, and this saying was veryfied. **1815** *Reviewers* 9. *Oxford* 392; Whiting H637.

H357 **Hunger** is the best sauce (*varied*)

1690 SDavis in *Baxter Manuscripts* 5.146: Our provetions was very shorte Indian Corn & acorens. Hunger mad it very Good & God Gave it strentgth to norrish. **1705** Beverley *History* 178: They have no other Sauce but a good Stomach, 185: Their Sauce to this dry Meat, (if they have any besides a good Stomach) is only a little Bears Oyl. **1728** Byrd *Dividing Line* 216: [Wild pigeons'] Flesh is far from being white and tender, tho' good enough upon a March, when Hunger is the sauce. **1731** TMcCliesh in *Letters from Hudson Bay* 160: We seldom want for the best of sauce, which is a good stomach. **1733** Byrd *Journey* 281: The whole company ate their venison without any other sauce than keen appetite. **1734** *Letter* in *Colonial Currency* 3.9: *Hungry Persons will be tempted to eat Trash, if they can't get wholesome Food.* **1750** Franklin *PR* 3.441: Hunger is the best Pickle. **1776** ARoberts in *PM* 7(1883) 458: It was an agreeable repast, a good stomach supplying the place of sauce. **1788** RHaswell in *Columbia* 17: We made an excessive hearty meal to which we added a good salit and a long voyage proved the best seasoning it could be dressed with. **1791** Long *Voyages* 119: Hunger needs not the borrowed aid of sauce. **1794** Wansey *Journal* 30: We wanted no sauce, hunger supplying the best of the kind. **1810** Cuming *Sketches* 56: I now proved that "hunger is a good sauce." **1812** Maxwell *Poems* 36: Hermits don't care much what they eat, And appetite can make it sweet. **1819** Noah *Travels* 163: Hunger gave me an appetite. **1827** Jones *Sketches* 2.122: Our appetites giving the best seasoning to the food. Barbour 96; *Oxford* 392; Whiting H642. See **S447**.

H358 **Hunger** looks in at the window, *etc.*
1737 Franklin *PR* 2.168: At the working man's house Hunger looks in but dares not enter, **1758** *WW* 342.

H359 **Hunger** never reasons
1803 Austin *Literary Papers* 239: Hunger never reasons. Whiting H641. See **B142**.

H360 **Hunger** never saw bad bread
1733 Franklin *PR* 1.313: Hunger never saw bad bread. Cf. Tilley B628.

H361 **Hunters** never grow rich
1819 Thomas *Travels* 43-4: It has long been remarked, that *hunters never grow rich*.

H362 A good **Hunter** will not hold out always
1766 *Johnson Papers* 12.164: I am well recoverd of my late Illness, but much torn down, a good hunter will not hold out always. Cf. Tilley F23, H670.

H363 A **Hurrah's** nest
1830 Ames *Mariner's* 53: Your intestines are twisted by a bilious cholic into what sailors, when speaking of a *melange* of entangled ropes, call a "hurra's nest." Colcord 104; TW 196.

H364 A **Husbandman** is the first partaker, *etc.*
1754 RWolcott in *Fitch Papers* 1.12: It is an old Observation that the Husbandman is first partaker of the fruits of the Earth. *Oxford* 394; Tilley H842.

H365 To cut off the **Hydra's** head
1777 WKillen in Read *Correspondence* 267: The apprehending these Tories is really like cutting off the hydra's head. *Oxford* 361; Tilley H278.

I

I1 To dot the **I's** and cross the t's

1809 Fessenden *Pills* xi: The doctor . . . wanted somebody to dot his i's and cross his t's. **1820** Beecher *Autobiography* 1.435: As to the strokes of the *t,* and dots of the *i,* and everything of verbal improvement, only make improvement, and no matter how much. **1820** *Fudge Family* 87: The *i*s should be dotted, and *t*s should be cross'd. **1828** Jackson *Correspondence* 3.423: I neither attempt to dot my i's nor X my t's, **1845** 6.421: He has nobly advised the Government and the people to satisfy the proposals offered by me, without dotting an i, or crossing a t. **1846** Beecher *Autobiography* 2.521: Please note that this is my first letter. I have crossed the t's and dotted the i's. *Oxford* 200; TW 197(2).

I2 As chaste as **Ice**

1804 *Echo* 201: As chaste as ice. Lean 2.813; Svartengren 14. See **S284.**

I3 As cold as **Ice**

1728 Byrd *Dividing Line* 188: We quarter'd near a Spring of very fine Water . . . as cold as Ice. **1788** *Columbian Magazine* 2.662: That fire is cold as ice. **1807** Plumer *Memorandum* 638: His heart is hard as adamant & cold as Greenland ice. **1815** Andrews *Prisoners' Memoirs* 22. **1817** JGraham in *Ruffin Papers* 1.193-4: That man's heart must be as cold as the ice at the north pole who feels no regret at parting from friends. **1824** *Austin Papers* 1.843. **1850** Cooper *Letters* 6.244: Legs . . . as cold as ice. Barbour 96-7; *Oxford* 132; Whiting I1.

I3a **Ice-cold**

1809 Weems *Washington* 190: His ice-cold lips. Whiting I1a.

I4 As slippery as **Ice**

1728 Byrd *Dividing Line* 269: The Leaves that cover'd the Hills as slippery as Ice. **1788** *Politician* 34: She's as slippery as ice, tho' not quite so cold. Barbour 97(2); Lean 2.873; Svartengren 273; Whiting NC 429(3).

I5 As smooth as **Ice**

1849 Paulding *Letters(II)* 498: However we got on as smooth as Ice. Whiting NC 429(4).

I6 To break the **Ice**

1623 Letter in Bradford *History* 1.321: You have been instruments to breake the ise for others. **1633** JHopkins in *Winthrop Papers(A)* 3.105: Yet he that brake the yce never wantes his honour. **1665** Williams *Writings* 6.321: My first breaking of the ice in amongst them. **1687** *Hinckley Papers* 160: By breaking the ice, and making way for a numerous increase. **1699** College Oration in *W&MCQ* 2S 10(1930) 335: Two famous Bishops . . . who has broke the Ice to the other Bishops. **1702** Mather *Magnalia* 1.68: The *ice* was now broken, by the American offers of a retreat. **1704** MIngles in *VHM* 7(1899) 392. **1706** Sewall *Letter-Book* 1.339. **1740** Belcher *Papers* 2.528. **1747** *Georgia Records* 25.203, **1749** 370. **1772** *Johnson Papers* 8.423. **1772** Smith *Memoirs(I)* 113, **1774** 198. **1781** WHeron in Parsons *Life* 431: In order to break the ice (as says the vulgar adage). **1781** RMorris in *Thomson Papers*

462. **1783** Rush *Letters* 1.309. **1787** Washington *Writings* 29.313: You have I find broke the Ice. **1795** Jay *Correspondence* 4.163. **1800** Adams *New Letters* 244. **1800** Trumbull *Season* 65: I hope now the ice is broken and you have found that you *can* write. **1801** RO'Brien in *Barbary Wars* 1.415. **1810** Smith *Letters* 84. **1811** Graydon *Memoirs* 64. **1816** Smith *Letters* 133. **1822** Stansbury *Pedestrian* 248: An elderly lady broke the ice of conversation. **1829** LTazewell in Jackson *Correspondence* 4.16: Mere general declarations . . . may not be sufficient to break the ice, with which a British statesman is always encrusted. *Oxford* 83; TW 197(7).

I7 When **Ice** is hot
1779 Moore *Diary* 2.237: He take this city —yes, when ice is hot. Cf. *Oxford* 260, 711; Tilley W128.

I8 As cold as **Ice-plant**
c1800 Paine *Works* 126: Cold as ice-plant. NED Ice-plant.

I9 As chaste as an **Icicle**
1807 *Salmagundi* 26: Miss Diana Wearwell, who is as chaste as an icicle. **1822** Adams *Writings* 7.198: Chaste as an icicle. Lean 2.813.

I10 As cold as an **Icicle**
1824 Adams *Memoirs* 6.308: Clay had become cold as an icicle. Barbour 97; TW 197(1).

I11 **Idleness** is the greatest prodigality
1745 Franklin *PR* 3.7: Idleness is the greatest Prodigality, **1758** *WW* 341: Wasting Time. **1819** Peirce *Rebelliad* 7: Now time wastes me and vice versa . . . I waste time.

I12 **Idleness** is the mother of evil (*varied*)
c1680 Radisson *Voyages* 147: Idlenesse is the mother of all evil. **1730** Chalkley *Youth* 554: Idleness . . . is the Mother of many Mischiefs. **1731** *Trade* in *Colonial Currency* 2.367: Idleness is the leader of most kinds of Vices. **1741** Talcott *Papers* 2.359: Idleness (ye Mother of all mischief). **1763** Griffith *Journal* 17: Idleness is the nursery of vice. **1766** Ames *Almanacs* 376: Poverty is the

fruit of idleness. **1769** Brooke *Emily* 32: Idleness being the root of all evil. **1776** SWest in Thornton *Pulpit* 297-8: To punish idleness, that parent of innumerable evils. **1787** *Columbian Magazine* 1.699: The proverb, "Idleness is the parent of want, and of pain." **1788** AChurch in Jefferson *Papers* 14.210: Idleness . . . "is the root of all evil." **1811** Graydon *Memoirs* 74: If want of occupation, as we are told, is the root of all evil, my youth was exposed to very great dangers. **1814** Wirt *Bachelor* 22: Idleness is the mother of vice and disease. **1839** Jackson *Correspondence* 5.562: Indolence is the mother of mischief. Barbour 97(1); *Oxford* 396; Whiting I6. See **M37, T253.**

I13 **Ifs** and ands
1723 RStaunton in *Letters from Hudson Bay* 89: He replied with a great many ifs and ands. **1748** Parkman *Diary* 73.419: I was ready to throw up the Precincts Votes without any Ifs and and's. *Oxford* 396; Tilley I16.

I14 **Ifs** and buts
1819 Robertson *Letters* 42: He will be sliding in his emphatic appellatives of *ifs* and *buts*. NED But *sb.*[1].

I15 **Ignorance** is the mother of devotion
1654 Johnson *Wonder-Working* 98: Ignorance say the Papist is the Mother of devotion. **1705** Beverley *History* 211: According to the *Romish* Maxim, *Ignorance is the Mother of Devotion*. *Oxford* 396; Tilley I7.

I16 **Ignorance** of the law excuses no one
1755 Sherman *Almanacs* 253: Ignorance of the Law doth not excuse one. **1774** WHDrayton in Gibbes 2.44: *Ignorantia legis neminem excusat.* **1778** Washington *Writings* 12.288: As directed by General Orders, an Ignorance of which is the worst of all possible Excuses. **1792** Barlow *Works* 1.80: That barbarous maxim of jurisprudence, *That ignorance of the law is no excuse for the offender,* 209: [Latin only]. **1807** *Emerald* 2.267: [Latin only]. **1808** *Salmagundi* 469: A sage maxim of law—"Ignorantia neminem excusat"— and the same has been extended to literature. **1830** Ames *Almanacs* 241: The maxim

"ignorantia neminem excusat," ignorance of the law excuses nobody. *Oxford* 396; Whiting I9.

I17. Ignorance tends to happiness

1812 Stoddard *Sketches* 310: The old observation, that "ignorance tends to happiness." Cf. *Oxford* 396; TW 198.

I18 The Iliad in a nutshell

1702 Mather *Magnalia* 1.399: *An Iliad in a nut-shell.* 1713 Wise *Churches* 103: You have the main of this History contained, like *Homers Iliads* in a Nut shell. 1775 Curwen *Journal* 1.78: 'Tis observed that Homer's illiad is in a nutshell. NED Nutshell 3. See N131.

I19 Ill is mingled with the good

1791 Hamilton *Papers* 8.531: 'Tis the lot of every thing human to mingle a Portion of ill with the good. See R153.

I20 Ill will speaks good of no one

1767 Ames *Almanacs* 387: Ill will speaks good of no one. *Oxford* 401; Tilley I41. Cf. Whiting I18.

I21 To look like Images of rye-dough

1732 Franklin *Papers* 1.245: They looked . . . but (excuse the Simile) like so many blue wooden Images of Rie Doe. *Oxford* 402; Tilley I42.

I22 To sit like dead Images

1772 Griffith *Journal* 409: In a plain dress sit in their religious meetings like dead images. Cf. Whiting I23.

I23 First Impressions are the most lasting (*varied*)

1786 Van Schaack *Letters* 422: I know by experience that *first impressions* are not to be implicitly adopted. 1791 HJackson in *Bingham's Maine* 1.112: First impressions are the most lasting. 1818 *Port Folio* 4NS 6.284: Early impressions are said to be the most lasting. 1821 Simpson *Journal* 373: First impressions are lasting. Barbour 97; *Oxford* 262.

I24 Give him an Inch and he'll take an ell

1680 Randolph *Letters* 3.63: Hee gives an Inch of power; you take an Ell. 1714 Hunter *Androboros* 27: Law or Custom make an Inch an Ell very fair allowance; you, it seems, want an Ell to an inch. 1720 ?ECooke *Reflections* in *Colonial Currency* 2.118: If we tamely give up one Inch, we shall (according to the Proverb) find by sad Experience we shall loose an Ell. 1781 Oliver *Origin* 74: The *Inch* was given to them, and they well knew . . . that they could take the *Ell* when it best suited them. 1786 Mecom in *Franklin-Mecom* 286: I dont know but I deserve to be cencered of those unreasonable Persons to whom if you give an Inch they will take an Ell. 1788 JForbes in Adams *Diary* 371, n.3: The old proverb—"give 'em an inch and they'll take an ell." 1807 HGray in Otis *Letters* 1.285: If you give them an Inch, they want an Ell. 1814 *Kennon Letters* 37.146: There is an old adage . . . it is said give some people an inch, and they will take an ell. Barbour 97(1); *Oxford* 303; Whiting I33.

I25 An Inch breaks no square

1671 Sewall *Letter-Book* 1.20: For you know, [an] inch breaks no square in a load of Logs. *Oxford* 403; Whiting I30.

I26 Not see (an Inch) beyond one's nose (*varied*)

1744 Black *Journal* 1.405: A Person, who otherwise has his Sight Limited to the Length of his Nose. 1774 Seabury *Letters* 112: Every man who can see one inch beyond his nose. 1779 JBoucher in *MHM* 10(1915) 35: I have never been able to see an Inch before my Nose. 1800 NAmes in *DHR* 10(1899) 81: If they would see an inch before their nose. 1811 Quincy *JQuincy* 217: The evils are distant, at least twice the length of the nose, and that is half as far again as the majority of those who call themselves politicians deign to examine. 1814 JAdams in *Adams-Jefferson Letters* 2.427: I dare not look beyond my Nose into futurity. 1815 Adams *Writings* 5.372: Could they have seen, to use a vulgar expression, far enough before their noses. 1815 Freneau *Poems* (*1815*) 1.132: An envoy should be chose, Who *could not see beyond his nose.* 1817 Adams *Works* 10.248: Ruggles's foresight reached not beyond his nose. c1825 Tyler *Prose* 78: And he who boasts the keenest sight Can't see an inch beyond his nose. *Oxford* 709; Tilley N220. See B393.

I27 Not trust an **Inch** beyond one's nose

1820 Faux *Memorable Days* 2.126: And, besides, the saying of the late General, "I would not trust any man an inch beyond my nose who would set an example of sabbath-breaking." Cf. *Oxford* 843; Tilley T557.

I28 To die (*etc.*) by **Inches**

1754 Mrs. Browne in *VHM* 32(1924) 314: He had better kill them all at once than to let them dye by Inches. **1763** Laurens *Papers* 3.307: The . . . women & Children must yet famish by inches. **1772** *New-York Gazette* in *Newspaper Extracts*(*I*) 9.149: He lives but on a rack and dies by inches [figurative]. **1773** *New-York Gazette* in *Newspaper Extracts*(*I*) 10.29: Murder his little wife, as it were by inches. **1778** Washington *Writings* 10.328: He was perishing by inches. a**1788** Jones *History* 2.233: This was murdering a man by inches. **1792** BMarston in *Winslow Papers* 708: Starving by inches. **1798** Asbury *Journal* 2.152, **1803** *Letters* 3.271, **1807** *Journal* 2.534. *Oxford* 186.

I29 Little **Incidents** produce great events

1778 Adams *D and A* 2.78: It is thus that little Incidents produce great Events. Cf. *Oxford* 42; Tilley B264. See **C99.**

I30 No **Inconvenience** without a convenience

1781 Oliver *Origin* 62: The vulgar Maxim, *that there is no Inconvenience without a Convenience* now took place. Lean 4.150. Cf. Whiting I34. See **C282.**

I31 To make **Indentures**

1737 Franklin *Drinkers* 2.176: He makes Indentures with his Leggs. *Oxford* 403; Tilley I63. See **V26.**

I32 As dirty as an **Indian**

1803 Davis *Travels* 43: You are as dirty as an *Indian*.

I33 (As lazy as an **Indian**)

1702 Mather *Magnalia* 2.663: *Secondly*, they [the Indians] are sluggards to a proverb; they are for any way of living rather than work. **1806** *Port Folio* NS 1.97: The unconquerable laziness of the savage, unless driven to exertion by extreme necessity, is proverbial.

I34 **Indians** will be Indians

1766 HCalvin in *Wheelock's Indians* 51: Indians will be Indians.

I35 An **Indian** feast

1737 Franklin *Drinkers* 2.175: He's been at an Indian Feast.

I36 An **Indian** gift (present)

1728 Byrd *Dividing Line* 122: They offer'd to give us Silk-Grass baskets . . . which we Modestly refused, knowing that an Indian present, like that of a Nun, is a Liberality put out to interest, and a Bribe plac'd to the greatest Advantage, 123: An Indian Present like those made to Princes, is only a Liberality put out to Interest, & a bribe placed to the greatest Advantage. **1764** NAmes in *Ames Almanacs* 25: We Americans well know what is meant by an Indian gift, that is to make a present but expect more in return than we give. **1754** Hutchinson *History* 1.394: An Indian gift is a proverbial expression, signifying a present for which an equivalent is expected. **1793** Ingraham *Journal* 130: I have often heard when a person gave something away with an expectation of a return it was termed an Indian gift; this saying cannot be more completely verified than among these people. TW 199(5).

I37 As blue as **Indigo**

1795 Drinker *Not So Long Ago* 83: His feet almost as blue as indigo. Barbour 98; TW 199.

I38 **Industry** need not wish

1739 Franklin *PR* 2.224: Industry need not wish, **1758** *WW* 342. Champion 613(30).

I39 **Industry** pays debts, *etc.*

1742 Franklin *PR* 2.338: Industry pays Debts, while Despair encreases them, **1758** *WW* 342.

I40 As weak as an **Infant**

1768 Woodmason *Journal* 38: As weak as any Infant. TW 199(4).

I41 To know no more than a new-born **Infant**

1783 Williams *Penrose* 294: All of which we

knew no more of than a new born infant. TW 12: Babe(7).

I42   Ingatestone market

1699 Ward *Trip* 57: They have a *Charter* for a *Fair* at *Salem* but it Begins, like *Ingerstone* Market, half an Hour after Eleven a clock, and ends half an Hour before Twelve. Lean 1.84.

I43   Say I am Ingrateful, say anything

1694 *Connecticut Vindicated* 115: It was an old Saying: *Say I am Ingrateful and say any thing.* Cf. *Oxford* 98; Tilley M435.

I44   He that Injures cannot forgive

1793 Rush *Letters* 2.717: He knows that he has injured me, and therefore he cannot forgive me.

I45   To pocket an Injury

1764 Watts *Letter Book* 220: And the terrible Insults & Injurys we have receivd be quietly pocketed. **1775** Cresswell *Journal* 74: Obliged to pocket the affront. *Oxford* 626; Tilley I70.

I46   As black as Ink

1666 Alsop *Maryland* 25: His Brat as black as Ink. **1677** Hubbard *Indian* 1.176: A thick Humor, as black as Ink, **1677** Sewall *Diary* 1.43: A female Quaker . . . her face as black as ink. **1691** Taylor *Poems* 67, **1693** 87, **1707** 222: A Bugbare State: as black as any inke. **1709** Lawson *Voyage* 38, 153. **1743** Colden *Letters* 3.26. **1757** PDemere in McDowell *Documents* 2.428: He was as black as Ink. **1776** Moore *Diary* 1.299. **1797** Smith(EH) *Diary* 371. **1821** Simpson *Journal* 304. Barbour 98; *Oxford* 63; Whiting I43.

I47   Ins and outs

1763 Franklin *Papers* 10.304: I hear of Ins and Outs and Ups and Downs, and know neither why nor wherefore. **1770** MGoosley in *Norton Papers* 144: There will be ins and outs. NED In *sb.* 2.

I48   To be high in the Instep

1826 Pintard *Letters* 2.250: Madame Pell . . . is pretty high in the instep, being the g^d daughter of Judge Duane. *Oxford* 372; Whiting I48.

I49   To add Insult to injury

1775 PLee in *Naval Documents* 1.611: Looked upon . . . as an Insult to the Injurys Offered. **1781** WJackson in *Adams FC* 4.219: After adding insult to injury. **1781** Oliver *Origin* 56: It was adding Contempt to Insult. **?1791** Henry *Life* 3.625. **1795** DCobb in *Bingham's Maine* 1.539. **1804** Jackson *Correspondence* 1.107. **1804** WPVanNess in Hamilton *Works* 10.470. **1805** Ames *Diary* 292. **1812** Quincy *JQuincy* 253: It was both an insult and an injury. **1812** Taggart *Letters* 395. **1814** *Smith Papers* 2.210-1: We have borne insult superadded to injury. *Oxford* 405; TW 200.

I50   Interest rules the world

1809 *Port Folio* 2NS 2.550: That great saint, Interest, rules the world.

I51   Interest will not lie

1686 Dunton *Letters* 78: And do make good the Truth of that old Proverb, That Interest will not lie. **1720** ?ECooke *Reflections* in *Colonial Currency* 2.119: If it be a true Maxim, that Interest will not lie. **1720** EWigglesworth *Letter* in *Colonial Currency* 1.437: It is commonly accounted a true Saying, that *Interest will not lye.* **1721** Wise *Word* 54: It is a very sure Maxim, viz. *Self Interest will neither Cheat or Lye: For that this is the String in the Nose (thro' the World) which governs the Creature.* **1729** *Modest Enquiry* in *Colonial Currency* 2.342: *Interest,* they say, *will not Lie.* **1731** *Trade* in *Colonial Currency* 2.419: It is a sure Maxim, viz. Self-Interest will neither cheat or lye. *Oxford* 405; Tilley I86.

I52   Not abate an Iota

1740 Stephens *Journal(I)* 1.599: [He] resolved not to abate one Iota of what he thought due to the Civil Magistrate. NED Iota 2. See J50.

I53   An Irish hint

1769 Madison *Papers* 1.43: I believe there will not be [the] least danger of my getting an Irish hint as they call it. DA Irish 2(4).

I54   The wild Irish

1637 Morton *New English Canaan* 134: The Natives of New England are accustomed to build their houses much like the wild Irish. **1637** Williams *Writings* 6.34: Or turn wild Irish themselves [the Pequot Indians]. **1728** Byrd *Dividing Line* 102: And, like the Wild Irish, find more Pleasure in Laziness than Luxury, 262: Like the wild Irish, they would rather want than work. **1815** Jefferson *Writings* 14.337: The wild Irish . . . had gotten possession of the valley between the Blue Ridge and North Mountain. **1815** *Reviewers* 27: Hunting down the wild Irish. TW 200(1).

I55   As many as **Irishmen** in Newfoundland

1782 Perkins *Diary* 2.161: The woman also Secreted my Orders . . . & by some means took Copys of them & threatned to Set up as many of them on the Trees as there is "Irishmen in Newfoundland."

I56   An **Irishman's** (Paddy's) hurricane

1803 Davis *Travels* 428: "It is almost like an *Irishman's* hurricane." "Right up and down." **1819** Welby *Visit* 154-5: We are now first experiencing a calm attended by a heavy swell of the sea; — the sailors call this "Paddy's Hurricane." Colcord 47: Calm; TW 200(1).

I57   As hard as **Iron**

1818 Royall *Letters* 168: Those most pleased with fictitious distress, have hearts as hard as iron. Barbour 99(1); Whiting I55.

I58   As strong as **Iron**

1771 Chester *Papers* 113: Tendrils would grow Strong Like Iron, 115: They would be as Strong as Iron. **1821** Beecher *Autobiography* 1.459. Whiting I56.

I59   **Iron** sharpens iron, *etc.*

1805 Plumer *Memorandum* 327: *As iron sharpeneth iron so doth the countenance of a man his friend.* **1817** Young *Life* 117: I could say. *Oxford* 406; Whiting I58.

I60   Strike while the **Iron** is hot

1682 Claypoole *Letter Book* 145: I thought best to strike the iron while it was hot. **1701** *Penn-Logan Correspondence* 1.54: The iron is now hot; therefore strike. **1725** WDummer in *Baxter Manuscripts* 10.307: It will become us to Strike while the Iron is hot. a**1731** Cook

Bacon 321. **1734** DHorsmanden in *Colden Letters* 2.110. **1740** *Byrd Letters* in *VHM* 37(1929) 28. **1763** Franklin *Papers* 10.215. ?**1766** SAuchmuty in Johnson *Writings* 1.381. **1781** Oliver *Origin* 67: The Iron was now hot. **1789** *Massachusetts Centinel* in Buckingham *Specimens* 2.52. **1792** Morris *Diary* 2.391. **1792** JJWilmer in *MHM* 19(1924) 230. **1793** Freneau *Poems* 3.112: And struck — while his iron was hot. **1801** TTingey in *Barbary Wars* 1.435. **1803** Rush *Letters* 2.856. **1814** ACHanson in *MHM* 35(1940) 361: We should strike every moment while the furnace is in blast & the iron can be kept hot. **1816** Fidfaddy *Adventures* 80. **1816** Freneau *Last Poems* 18. **1823** Doddridge *Logan* 10. Barbour 98(2); *Oxford* 781; Whiting I60.

I61   To have many **Irons** in the fire, *etc.*

1753 PCollinson in Franklin *Papers* 4.455: Our Friend Cave has so many Irons in the Fire Some will burn. **1758** Adams *Earliest Diary* 76: I have so many Irons in the Fire, that everyone burns. **1765** Watts *Letter Book* 377: The Old saying is a very wise one, about the Irons, some will grow cold. **1776** WWhipple in Burnett *Letters* 1.479: There are so many irons in the fire, I fear some of them will burn. **1777** JAdams in Jefferson *Papers* 2.21: We have too many Irons in the Fire. **1778** SAOtis in Otis *Letters* 1.22. **1781** Oliver *Origin* 64: Thus by having so many Irons in the Fire not only some, but all of them were burnt. **1789** McGillivray *Letters* 219. **1790** WShort in Jefferson *Papers* 16.403: There are (to make use of a vulgar expresion) irons heating or perhaps heated in the fire. **1796** MCarey in Weems *Letters* 2.20, 52: I hope to have leisure to attend to as many irons as you may chuse to clap in the forge. **1797** Morris *Diary and Letters* 2.273: One must not have too many irons in the fire at once. **1802** BSmith in *Blount Papers* 3.520: I have Irons enough in the Fire. **1813** Baldwin *Letters* 89: I have too many irons in the fire. **1829** Pintard *Letters* 3.96: The old adage of "too many irons in the fire," is an abominable lie. **1845** Paulding *Letters(II)* 406, **1846** 435. Barbour 98-9; *Oxford* 509-10; TW 201(6).

I62   When **Italy** wants poison, *etc.*

a1700 Saffin *His Book* 35: *A Proverb, or Prophisie of an Observant Statist:* When Italie Doth poyson want And Traytoᵣˢ are in England Scant When Spain's not proud, and hates a Punke And Hollanders Cease to be Drunke When France is of Commotion free The World without an Earth shall be. Tilley I104.

I63   To shun like the **Itch**

1795 Cobbett *Porcupine* 2.42: Though sober sensible people shun him . . . as they would the itch or the halter.

I64   As white as **Ivory**

1686 Dunton *Letters* 217: She had . . . Teeth as white as ivory. **1744** Black *Journal* 2.45: Teeth white as Ivory. **1774** Bartram *Report* 164: Talons white as Ivory. **1826** Royall *Sketches* 200: teeth. *Oxford* 884; Whiting I68.

I65   The **Ivy** destroys the oak

1689 Randolph *Letters* 6.323: Adhereing to that only as the Ivy doth the oake imbrace it till it by degrees grows up to the top and than destroys it.

J

J1 A good **Jack** makes a good Jill

1750 Sherman *Almanacs* 251: A good jack makes A good gill. **1804** *Port Folio* 4.233: An old adage, "Bonum dux bonum facit militem," which has been translated "A good Jack makes a good Gill." *Oxford* 321; Tilley J1.

J2 **Jack** and Jill

1748 Franklin *PR* 3.259: If Jack's in love, he's no judge of Jill's beauty. **1775** Curwen *Journal* 1.33: Ragged and saucy Jacks and Jills. **1805** Irving *Journals* 1.166: He has also an invincible propensity to *familiarize* names and Jack's and Jill's every body he speaks of. *Oxford* 407; Whiting J2.

J3 **Jack** is become the gentleman

1779 Shaw *Journals* 54: Jack is become the gentleman, and, to keep up the farce, he must appear as such. Cf. *Oxford* 409; Whiting J9.

J4 A **Jack** of all trades

1707 Lord Cornbury in Makemie *Writings* 265: He is a Jack of all Trades; he is a Preacher, a Doctor of Physick, etc. **1721** *New-England Courant* 1(1): *Homo non unius Negotii:* Or *Jack of all Trades.* **1786** JQAdams in Smith *Journal and Correspondence* 2(1) 119: Death appears to be a jack-of-all-trades. **a1788** Jones *History* 2.14: Robertson was . . . in short, a Jack-at-all-trades. **1812** Hitchcock *Social* 57: In . . . in short, a jack at *ev'ry trade.* **1812** Melish *Travels* 335. **1815** Brackenridge *Modern* 791. **1816** Paulding *Letters(I)* 1.84. **1820** Faux *Memorable*

Days 2.120: A New England man succeeds in a new country, because he is a jack-of-all-trades. **1824** *Tales* 1.51: A race of men, fast fading away . . . going under the denomination of "jacks of all trades." **1827** Watterston *Wanderer* 155. **1828** *Yankee* 85. *Oxford* 408; TW 202(1).

J5 A **Jack** of all trades and good at none (*varied*)

1721 *Boston News-Letter* in Buckingham *Specimens* 1.8: Jack of all Trades, and it would seem, Good at none. **1723** *New-England Courant* 100(2.1): They can, like Children, play *Jack of all Trades,* tho' they understand none. **1777** Marshall *Diary* 140: The want of workmen, obliges me to be a jack of all trades, as the saying is, and good at none. **1792** Brackenridge *Modern* 4: A Jack of all Trades, is proverbial of a bungler, **1793** 226: It does not do to be a jack of all trades. **1796** Cobbett *Porcupine* 3.406: A *Jack* of all trades, and *master* of none. **1800** Freneau *Prose* 437: *Jacks of all trades,* said I, I never liked. **1801** *Port Folio* 1.38: It is an old and true adage, that "a Jack of all trades is good at none." Barbour 99; *Oxford* 408; TW 202(2).

J6 **Jack** will never make a gentleman

1787 *Columbian Magazine* 1.557: Jack ne'er will make a gentleman. *Oxford* 409; Tilley J2.

J7 Never a **Jack** without a Jill

1721 *The Little-Compton Scourge* in *New-England Courant,* after 1: Never a *Jack* without a *Jill.* 1785 Tilghman *Letters* 36: They say there was never a Jack in the World that could not find a Jill. 1791 S.P.L. *Thoughts* 77: Every Jack has his Gill. *Oxford* 408; Whiting J7.

J8 To make one's Jack

1817 Royall *Letters* 95: I will try to beguile the time in amusing myself with "mine host" and hostess, who I dare say, expect to make their Jack out of me. DA Jack 12d. Cf. TW 203(3).

J9 To play Jack a (on, of) both sides

1663 WHooke in *Mather Papers* 124: Of ones playing Jack a both sides. a1700 Hubbard *New England* 71: Squanto . . . began to play the Jack on both sides. 1793 Freneau *Prose*: A jack of both sides. 1809 Irving *History* 2.91: He played the perfect jack-of-both-sides. 1809 Weems *Marion* 240: To play *jack a both sides. Oxford* 408; Tilley J21.

J10 Jack Hooter

1703 Taylor *Christographia* 360.54-6: And yet are noe more Concerned with Christ, than Jack Whooter (as the Howle is proverbially called). NED Hooter.

J11 Jacks-in-office

1742 Franklin *PR* 2.334: Two upstart Jacks in Office, proud and vain, Come riding by, and thus insult the Swain. *Oxford* 408; Tilley J17. See **D238.**

J12 Before one can say Jack Robinson

1785 EWinslow in *Winslow Papers* 310: Before I could say "Jack Robinson." 1809 Lindsley *Love* 9: Before you'll say Jack Robinson. 1826 Wirt *Letters* 2.217: Before I have had time to say "Jack Robinson," my whiskers have turned grey. 1832 JRandolph in Jackson *Correspondence* 4.423: as the saying is. *Oxford* 40; TW 202(3). See **B252, J44, P42.**

J13 To dust one's Jacket

1806 *Balance* in Thornton *Glossary* 1.487: To dust his jacket. Barbour 99; *Oxford* 409; Tilley J13.

J14 To be jammed like Jackson

1803 Davis *Travels* 414: He'll get jammed

like *Jackson* between the fly of the ensign and the mizzen-shrouds. Colcord 108.

J15 Whistle to a Jade and he will pay you with a fart

1674 Josselyn *Account* 122-3: I believe my reward will be according to *Ben Johnsons* proverb, Whistle to a Jade and he will pay you with a fart, Claw a churl by the britch and he will shit in your fist. See **C184.**

J16 January and May

1772 Paterson *Glimpses* 120: He'd look, joined to a lass so gay, Like January wed to May. 1809 Weems *Marion* 92: There is such a strange January and May sort of contrast between your locks and your looks as quite confuses me. *Oxford* 518; Whiting J14. See **A138, D89.**

J17 At the Jaws of death

1794 JPrice in *Blount Papers* 2.363: Sylby . . . has been at the very Jaws of death. NED Jaw *sb.*[1] 5. Cf. Whiting D107. See **D82-83.**

J18 As fine as a Jay

1813 Weems *Drunkard* 120: Is there any . . . who, though fine as a Jay, has no valuable ideas for his *brain.* Cf. Whiting J17.

J19 Jenny's whim

1775 POliver Jr in Hutchinson *Diary* 1.572: I want to know where Jenny's whim is in London. We know where it is here. [A young man in Boston is writing to a friend in London.] Partridge 951: Whim [female pudend].

J20 To (at) Jericho

1713 Wise *Churches* 86-7: There is no reason to send such Youths to *Jerico* with *Davids* messenger. 1809 Weems *Marion* 109: Chased general Gates to Jericho, and to the d — —l for what I care. 1815 *Port Folio* 3NS 5.436: I wish you and your cause were at Jericho. *Oxford* 410; TW 203.

J21 To have been to Jericho

1737 Franklin *Drinkers* 2.175: He's Been to Jerico. Partridge 436.

J22 As white as Jersey veal

1800 Cobbett *Porcupine* 11.276: I could

probably have talked very learnedly about *"bleeding as white as Jersey veal."*

J23   To be going to Jerusalem
1737 Franklin *Drinkers* 2.175: He's Going to Jerusalem. Partridge 437.

J24   A Jest (joke) in earnest (*varied*)
a1700 Hubbard *New England* 420: It is bad jesting about matters of life and death. **1807** *Emerald* NS 1.88: I thought the remark was *"too true to make a jest on."* **1822** Adams *Memoirs* 6.13: By way of a joke in earnest. *Oxford* 411; Tilley J44; Whiting P257. See **W315.**

J25   Ill Jesting with joiner's tools
1752 Franklin *PR* 4.252: It is ill Jesting with the Joiner's Tools, worse with the Doctor's. *Oxford* 411; Tilley J45. See **T190.**

J26   As black as Jet
1634 Wood *New-England* 95: Black as jet. **1637** Morton *New English Canaan* 165: Their eies . . . are black as iett, 206. **1672** Josselyn *New England Rarities* 123. **1686** Dunton *Letters* 217: Eyes. **1688** Clayton *Writings* 59: teeth, 95: feathers. **1775** JHarvey in *Blount Papers* 1.3: teeth. **1783** Williams *Penrose* 84: hair, 267, 327: plant. **1789** Anburey *Travels* 1.137. **1797** Freneau *Poems* 3.146. **1807** *Port Folio* NS 3.334: hair. **1826** Duane *Colombia* 496: His eyes were as black as his hair, and both black as glistening jet. Whiting J29.

J26a   Jet-black
1772 RCNicholas in *Norton Papers* 262: Jet black. **1778** Carver *Travels* 474, 511. **1778** Thacher *Journal* 174. **1781** Jefferson *Notes* 71: A daughter, jet black. **1781** *New Jersey Gazette* in *Newspaper Extracts(II)* 5.229. **1784** Smyth *Tour* 1.51. **1787** Tyler *Contrast* 23. **1788** Ledyard *Russian Journey* 209. **1789** Boucher *Autobiography* 77. **1793** Campbell *Travels* 71. **1793** Ingraham *Journal* 33. **1797** Hawkins *Letters* 175. **1805** Burr *Correspondence* 211. **1806** Pike *Travels* 202. **1807** Bentley *Diary* 3.319. **1816** Ker *Travels* 121. **1816** Paulding *Letters(I)* 1.117. **1818** Royall *Letters* 155. **c1820** Bernard *Retrospections:* The jet-black of the African. **1820** Hodgson

Letters 1.158. **1824** Doddridge *Notes* 44. **1826** Jones *Sketches* 1.108. Whiting J29a.

J27   As rich (wealthy) as a Jew
1783 Williams *Penrose* 186: Could it make us as Rich as ten Jews. **a1788** Jones *History* 1.336: As rich as a Jew, 350. **1800** Weems *Letters* 2.144: The Good Lord grant I may see you as rich as a Hebrew Jew. **1805** Brackenridge *Modern* 570. **1806** Fanning *Narrative* 17. **1808** Hitchcock *Poetical Dictionary* 82. **1809** Weems *Marion* 119, 230: As wealthy as a Jew. **1812** Randall *Miser* 35. TW 204(2).

J28   No Jew can get his bread in Boston
1781 Oliver *Origin* 48: This Business was so notable a School to teach the Art of tricking & foreswearing that it became proverbial *"that no Jew could get his Bread in Boston."*

J29   One Jew is equal to a Genoese, *etc.*
1777 Curwen *Journal* 1.400: This city [Bristol] remarkable to a proverb for sharp and hard dealings. There runs a proverb, I write from report, One jew is equal to a Genoese, and one Bristolian to 2 jews. Cf. Lean 1.23, 91.

J30   To be worth a Jew's eye
1804 Weems *Letters* 2.298: My life may be worth a Jew's eye to you. *Oxford* 921; TW 204.

J31   To swear like a Jew-Turk
1778 NGreene in Webb *Correspondence* 2.231: Wadsworth is at Philadelphia swearing like a disappointed *Jew Turk.* See **T290.**

J32   A Jewel in a dunghill
1643 Williams *Writings* 1.352: His Jewels are most precious to him though in a Babilonish dunghill, and his Lillie sweet and lovely in the Wildernes commixt with Briars. **1773** Carroll *Correspondence* 1.357: They always suggest to my mind the idea of the jewel buried in a dunghill.

J33   The Jig is up
1777 *Maryland Journal* in Thornton *Glossary* 1.494: The jig is over. **1778** BGEyre in *PM* 5(1881) 477: The Gig is up with us. **1787** Smith *Diary* 2.177: I think this Man's Jigg is up. **1800** *Aurora* in Thornton *Glossary*

1.494: The Federal Jigg is up. TW 204(2).
See **G14**.

J34   Joan is as good as my lady in the dark
(*varied*)
1721 ?TPaine in *Colonial Currency* 2.284:
Were it not for the different Seats they sit in,
one would scarce know Joan *from* my Lady
by Daylight. **1722** Byrd *Another Secret Diary*
377: I must take the liberty to differ both
from my ingenious correspondent, and the
Proverb, and believe Women so very unlike
one another, that they are not the same so
much as in the dark. **1791** S.P.L. *Thoughts*
77: Joan is as good as my lady in the dark.
Oxford 412; Tilley J347-8. See **C57, D15**.

Job (1)

J35   As patient as Job (*varied*)
1637 Morton *New English Canaan* 278: And
so patient As Job himselfe, 281: Hee had
need have . . . as much patience as Iob that
should come there. **1652** Williams *Writings*
7.100: In *patience as Job*. **1658** TEaton in
Winthrop Papers(B) 2.479: Like holy Job
for patience he excel'd. **1737** Custis *Letters*
61: A man had need to have the patience of
Job and the life of Methusala to wait upon
them. **1743** Ames *Almanacs* 170: Enough to
plague ye patience of Jobe. **1763** *Commerce
of Rhode Island* 1.103: One must have the
patience of Jobe. **1769** Woodmason *Journal*
148: Patience of a Job. **1776** JAdams in *Warren-Adams Letters* 1.232: The Patience of
Job. **1778** JSewall in Curwen *Journal and
Letters* 208: The situation . . . is enough to
have provoked Job's wife, if not Job himself.
1778 JTracy in *Baxter Manuscripts* 16.90:
Job's patience was nearly exhausted. **1783**
SWinslow in *Winslow Papers* 152: You must
have the patience of Job. **1785** Hunter *Quebec* 57: It's enough to try the patience of Job.
1787 *American Museum* 1.379: The patience of Job. **1788** *Politician* 21: Isn't this
enough to try Job's patience? **1789** *Columbian Magazine* 3.103: If I had the patience
of Job. **1797** Cobbett *Porcupine* 5.65. **1807**
Port Folio NS 4.207: The patience of Job.
1813 Weems *Drunkard* 81: Not Job with all
his patience . . . could possibly avoid being
insulted by them. **1815** Palmer *Diary* 214:

We want the patience of Job. **1817** Weems
Letters 3.215: But to be run . . . round &
round the circumference of a Bee-gum like a
Dog in chase of his tail, is enough to try the
patience of ten Jobs. **1821** Knight *Poems*
2.182: Your coldness is more than Job's patience could bear. **1835** *New England Merchants* 166: Requires the patience of Job to
deal with these negroes, 167: It certainly
would try Job's patience if he were here. **1845**
Paulding *Letters(II)* 401: You have con-
siderably more patience than Job, **1847** 466:
I have not the patience of Job. *Oxford* 613;
Whiting J45.

J36   As poor as Job
1756 WJohnson in Johnson *Writings* 1.239: I
shall return home as poor as Job. **1777** Cresswell *Journal* 251: I am as poor as Job, but not
quite so patient. **1789** EHazard in *Belknap
Papers* 2.108. **1794** JHaywood in *Blount
Papers* 2.424. **1816** *Port Folio* 4NS 1.532.
1818 Royall *Letters* 143. **1821** Freneau *Last
Poems* 35: As poor as Job (and all agree
That none could be more poor than he). *Oxford* 638; Whiting J46.

J37   As poor as Job's cats
1810 Fletcher *Letters* 11: I tried to appear
like a gentleman, when I was as poor as Job's
Cats. TW 204(3).

J38   As poor as Job's turkey
1817 Scott *Blue Lights* 76: Art thou as that
turkey poor, Which at Uz, by famine died*.
*137: This is one of the many scripture tradi-
tions, current in New England, serving to
illustrate the extreme poverty to which the
patient Job was reduced. To be as poor as
Job's turkey, has passed into a proverb. **1830**
Ames *Mariner's* 184: The situation of Job's
turkey, without a feather to fly with. **1843**
Paulding *Letters(II)* 351: Descended from a
family . . . as poor as Job's Turkey. Barbour
100(1); TW 205(4).

J39   (Enough) to make Job swear
1778 Lee *Papers* 3.279: The calumny . . .
would make Job himself swear like a Virginia
Colonel. **1792** HWilliamson in *Blount Papers* 2.182: The Patience of Job could hardly
prevent him from swearing at such Jack
Asses. **1798** Murdock *Politicians* 10: You

would make a man with a happier disposition than Job, swear. **1805** Weems *Letters* 2.324: If Job were in my situation he w^d outcurse a Boatswain of a British Man of War. Cf. Whiting J45. See **A94**.

J40 A Job's comforter
1728 Chalkley *Journal* 223: I had one of *Job's* comforters. **1778** SHodgkins in Hodgkins *Letters* 236: So he is but one of Job's comforters. *Oxford* 412; Whiting J47.

Job (2)

J41 To do one's Job
1778 JThaxter in *Adams FC* 3.56: I think he has done his job this time. NED Job *sb.*² 4b.

J42 To give up as a bad Job
1824 WRuffin in *Ruffin Papers* 1.302: They haven't answered one of them and I have given it up as a bad job and quit. TW 205(2).

J43 A Joe Bunker
1776 Shaw *Journals* 10: This creates a new and not a small expense, which, however, must be met, unless a person has a mind to be looked upon as a *Joe Bunker,* that is, a fellow without a soul. DA Joe 2(2).

J44 As soon as one can say John Smith Pease
1770 Carter *Diary* 1.418: The rain . . . left us almost as soon as a man could say John Smith Pease. Cf. TW 202: Jack (3). See **J12**.

J45 From John a Groat's to Land's End
1805 Silliman *Travels* 2.228: A well-educated American may travel from London to John a Groat's house, and thence to Land's-end, and everywhere pass for a Londoner. *Oxford* 441; TW 205. See **D6, G35**.

J46 John-a-Nokes
1755 Laurens *Papers* 1.279: No one of the Bakers will buy of it & to retail it out by the Barrel to John an Oakes & J. Stiles is poor work. **1773** Trumbull *Satiric Poems* 78: Or she'll be awkward when she's bigger, And look as queer as *Joan of Nokes*. **1800** *Echo* 272: Their President and Congress folks, Are only *Tom,* and *John-a-nokes*. *Oxford* 412; Tilley J66.

J47 To be a big John
1772 *New-York Gazette* in *Newspaper Extracts(I)* 9.70: Mr. A. Z. . . . would give us to understand that he is one Big John, of great consequence in the world. Cf. DA big 5b(7): big Ike (1907).

J48 To be with Sir John Goa
1737 Franklin *Drinkers* 2.175: He's Been with Sir John Goa.

J49 To be out of Joint
1721 Wise *Word* 217: When things are out of Joynt. **1801** Perkins *Diary* 4.329: The Death of a Man of Business put everything out of Joint. *Oxford* 414; Whiting J54.

J50 Not a Jot
1743 Stephens *Journal(II)* 1.154: And so I did; but was not a Jot the wiser for what passed, 203-4: Without mending the matter one Jot, 2.25, **1745** 199: Our Busy Bodies were not a Jot wiser than before. NED Jot *sb.*¹. See **I52**.

J51 Not care a Jot
1791 Morris *Diary* 2.194: There are many of these patriots who don't Care a Jot for Consequences. NED Jot *sb.*¹. Cf. Whiting J57.

J52 Jove laughs at the perjuries of lovers
1796 Smith(EH) *Diary* 183: Jove laughs at the perjuries of lovers. *Oxford* 414; Tilley J82; Whiting G201. See **L248**.

J53 He that would Joy and sorrow mix, *etc.*
1759 RWolcott in *Collections of the Connecticut Historical Society* 3(1895) 329: In 1675 began the Narrhaganset war. The English made small success and many losses untill the Fort Fight, Decr 19th, 1675, and the next year end the war with victory. From hence they had this proverb: Hee that would joy and sorrow mix Join 75 with seventy-six.

J54 No Joy without alloy
1773 *Commerce of Rhode Island* 1.429-30: Providence has wisely ordained that [no] Situation in this world shall be without its Alloy. **1786** Drinker *Journal* 172: But there is no joy, *sans alloy,* **1789** *Not So Long Ago* 67. **1790** *Cary Letters* 71: Every joy has its alloy.

Oxford 414; Tilley J85. Cf. Whiting J59. See **N106, R145.**

J55   A Judas kiss
1720 Byrd *London Diary* 400: And saluted them with a Judas's kiss. **1789** Brown *Power* 1.118: Like *Judas* with a kiss *betray*. **1808** Eaton *Life* 415: Bonaparte, like Judas, kisses to betray. **1811** Claiborne *Letter Books* 5.327: But their smiles are deceptive & Judas like they will kiss, & then betray him. *Oxford* 414; Whiting J68.

J56   As grave as any Judge
1819 Wirt *Letters* 2.96: I will promise to be on my best behavior, —that is to say, "as grave as any judge." *Oxford* 749; Tilley J93.

J57   As sober as a Judge
1775 Harrower *Journal* 131: And spent the evening as sober as a Judge. **1804** Irving *Corrector* 104: Went to bed sober as a judge. **1813** Weems *Drunkard* 122: For the monkey . . . keeps as sober as a judge. Barbour 100; *Oxford* 749; TW 205-6(2).

J58   Be Just before you are generous
1826 WVans in *Codman Letters* 374: "Be just, before you are generous," is my maxim. *Oxford* 416.

J59   Justice and mercy
1682 Claypoole *Letter Book* 176: Yet with justice we must have some mercy. **1771** *Trial of Atticus* 78: As justice never appears so triumphant, as when qualified with clemency and mercy. *Oxford* 526; Whiting J81, M508.

J60   Justice (vengeance) has iron heels and leaden feet (*varied*)
1677 Hubbard *Indian* 2.63: But as is usually said *Justice Vindictive* hath Iron Heels, though Leaden Feet. **1691** *Humble Address* in *Andros Tracts* 2.258: Divine Vengeance has leaden Heels but Iron Hands. **1740** Belcher *Papers* 2.298: Altho' Justice seems to have leaden heels. *Oxford* 309: God; Tilley G182.

J61   Justice is blind
1782 Jay *Correspondence* 2.181: Although we are told that Justice should be blind, yet there are no proverbs which declare that she ought also to be hungry. Lean 4.22. See **F272.**

K

K1 **Keep** what you've got, *etc.*

1790 *Columbian Magazine* 4.90: *Keep what you've got, and catch what you can.* Agreeably to the prudent directions of this excellent old proverb, *etc.* Whiting C112, quote c1516.

K2 To **Keep** oneself to oneself

1682 Randolph *Letters* 6.128: If Mr. Cranfeild had kept himselfe to himselfe. **1765** DFranklin in Franklin *Papers* 12.303: But keep my self to my self and so I did. **1790** Maclay *Journal* 253: I had better keep myself to myself with regard to him. NED Keep 44b; Partridge 450; TW 207.

K3 Who can **Keep** what will away?

1672 WWinthrop in *Winthrop Papers(B)* 4.390: For whoe can keepe y^t which will away. *Oxford* 377-8; Whiting H413.

K4 The **Kernel** and (or) the shell (*varied*)

1689 SStow in *Winthrop Papers(B)* 6.24: I hope my friends . . . will overlook, & not cast away a good kernel for som spots that may be on ye outside of ye nut. **1745** Brainerd *Memoirs* 197: There are some that love to feed on the kernel, rather than the shell. **1775** Asbury *Journal* 1.168: Satan will help us to the shell, if we will be satisfied without the kernel. **1779** JFallon in *Clinton Papers* 4.463: The Kernel is never to be thrown away for the shell, 467: This proves that . . . the shell is often broken through for the Kernel. **1788** WCarmichael in Jefferson *Papers* 13.91: Endeavors to break the Shell that I might enjoy the kernel. **1810** Adams *Lectures* 1.203: The art of collecting the kernel from the shell. *Oxford* 215; Whiting N190, 191.

K5 A **Kettle** of fish (*varied*)

1807 *Salmagundi* 94: The Doctor . . . has employed himself . . . in stewing up many a woful kettle of fish, 217: Flourish of two-penny trumpets and rattles . . . —air. "O what a fine kettle of fish." **1816** Paulding *Letters(I)* 1.41: Making a pretty kettle of fish of it. **1818** Wirt *Letters* 2.69: 'Till the moment comes, when a loose shoe on Morgan Rattler, or some disorder of a girth or stirrup-leather will spoil the whole kettle of fish. Barbour 101(2); *Oxford* 421; TW 207(1).

K6 To shine like a **Kettle**

1807 *Salmagundi* 116: His face in dancing shone like a kettle.

K7 The used **Key** is always bright

1744 Franklin *PR* 2.398: The used Key is always bright, **1758** *WW* 341. **1770** Ames *Almanacs* 412: The used Key is always bright. *Oxford* 857; Tilley K26.

K8 More **Kicks** than coppers

1816 Paulding *Letters(I)* 2.9: People are always more rational and enlightened where banks are plenty, and will take "kicks and coppers," with great thankfulness, provided they come together. **1824** Neal *American Writers* 71: One gets more kicks than coppers in it. **1828** *Yankee* 246: More Kicks than Coppers. **1830** Ames *Mariner's* 28: Receiving from them more thumps and kicks than coppers. *Oxford* 541; TW 208(3).

K9 To be **Kicked** upstairs (*varied*)

1780 Curwen *Journal* 2.693: Tis probable by late Chancellor's friendship he will be kicked upstairs. **1784** WShort in Jefferson *Papers* 7.18: My Office would be a Fall upstairs. NED Kick 5b, Upstairs 1b. See **S399**.

K10 To be of the same **Kidney** (*varied*)

1756 *Johnson Papers* 2.451: The best actions of Persons not of their own Kidney. **1775** Washington *Writings* 3.450: The officers . . . are nearly of the same kidney with the Privates, 4.126: To have two of this kidney. Apperson 339; Partridge 455; Tilley K31.

K11 Like **Kilkenny** cats

1826 Duane *Colombia* 95: And when the heroes, like the Kilkenny cats, disappeared. *Oxford* 256. Cf. Taylor *Comparisons* 52.

K12 **Kill** or cure

1684 [July 15] in Daniel B. Updike, *Richard Smith* (Boston, 1937) 118: These doge days makes men mad, I thinke, but I hope violent distempers will not hould longe. Either mend or kill. **1713** Wise *Churches* 130: Kill or cure. **1792** Morris *Diary* 2.342: Nothing but violent Remedies can operate and these must either kill or cure. **1798** OWolcott, Jr., in Hamilton *Papers* 21.397: The dose will kill or cure. *Oxford* 422; TW 87: Cure (1). See **M13**.

K13 **Kill-devil**

1674 Josselyn *Account* 26: Wanneston . . . drank to me a pint of kill-devil *alias* Rhum at a draught. **1699** Ward *Trip* 52: *Rum,* alias *Kill Devil* is as much ador'd by the *American English,* as a dram of *Brandy* is by an old *Billingsgate.* **1728** Byrd *Dividing Line* 92: Most of the Rum they get . . . is so bad and unwholesome, that it is not improperly call'd "Kill-Devil." NED Kill-devil 2; Partridge 455.

K14 Up **Killick**

1776 DCobb in *Bingham's Maine* 1.414: Upon which the fleet immediately up Killeck and stood out to sea. Colcord 111; TW 208.

K15 To be paid in one's own **Kind**

1782 TBosomworth in McDowell *Documents* 1.281: Mrs. Bosomworth payed him in his own Kind. NED Kind 15b. See **C250**.

K16 **Kindness** begets kindness

1819 Faux *Memorable Days* 1.184: Kindness begets kindness. Cf. Tilley K50.

K17 To kill with **Kindness**

1716 Mather *Letters* 214: We killed one another with kindness, and put nature out of the course. **1737** Custis *Letters* 61: Capt Friend killd them with kindness. **1771** Murray *Letters* 141. **1774** JA in *Adams FC* 1.164: I shall be kill'd with Kindness. **1790** TBlount in *Blount Papers* 2.94. **1799** WSSmith in Smith *Journal and Correspondence* 2(2) 161: With respect to the black horse, they are about killing him, as they do others, with kindness. **1817** JAdams in *Adams-Jefferson Letters* 2.508: Enemies who mean to . . . kill me with kindness. **1817** Mason *Memoir* 157: The good people of Boston will kill the President with kindness, 163. c**1820** Bernard *Retrospections* 23. **1822** Robertson *Letters* 183: We had nearly killed him out of pure kindness. **1824** Neal *American Writers* 30. Barbour 102(2); *Oxford* 423; TW 208. See **D84**.

K18 As happy as a **King**

1795 Murdock *Triumphs* 53: He more happy dan a king. *Oxford* 527; TW 208(1). See **L215, P287**.

K19 The **King** can do no wrong

1647 WPynchon in *Winthrop Papers(A)* 5.135: If his subjects will sticke to his lawes . . . the king cannot wrong them. **1681** RChamberlain in JSJenness, *Transcripts of Original Documents* (New York, 1876) 92: It would have bin against Law & a wrong (which yᵉ King cannot do). **1740** Stephens *Journal(I)* 2.47: I know it is said in *England* . . . that the King can do no Wrong. **1750** JMayhew in Thornton *Pulpit* 94. **1764** JOtis *Rights* in Bailyn *Pamphlets* 1.448: a maxim. **1769** Eliot *Letters* 446: If the King can do no wrong, his ministers may. **1773** Carroll *Correspondence* 1.251: The maxim of the British Constitution. **1774** Adams *Works* 4.77. **1776** SWest in Thornton *Pulpit* 316:

How often have we been told. **1786** *Columbian Magazine* 1.183. **1786** WWhiting in American Antiquarian Society, *Proceedings* NS 66(1956) 153: A Maxim in Monarchial Governments. **1798** Adams(S) *Writings* 4.336: In England . . . a Maxim. **1789** RLee in Henry *Life* 3.403: In England they say. **1791** Paine *Rights of Man* 1.339: It is laid down as a maxim. **1792** Barlow *Works* 1.31. **1794** Stiles *Three Judges* 207. **1806** *Port Folio* NS 2.85: A maxim of the law in England, **1816** 4NS 2.203: According to the English law, the king can do no wrong—a modest expression of the fact, that he can do nothing. **1818** Watterston *Letters* 15. *Oxford* 425; Tilley K61. See **G79, P230, 288.**

K20 **King** Log
1786 *Massachusetts Centinel* in Buckingham *Specimens* 2.41: And blockheads and knaves hail the reign of King Log. *Oxford* 477; Tilley L409.

K21 The **King** never dies
1689 Bulkeley *People's Right* 68: In Judgement of Law, The King never dyes. **1734** Plumstead 246: From whence doubtless is that maxim in our English law: "The king never dies," that is, the regal authority never dies. *Oxford* 426. See **L56.**

K22 The **King** of France with forty thousend men, *etc.*
1774 Andrews *Letters* 347: The old adage—" the king of France, &c'a" **a1788** Jones *History* 2.184: "The King of France with forty thousand men Went up the hill, and so came down again." **1813** in Knopf *War of 1812* 5(2) 185: This letter might easily have been comprized in the old saying of the King of Frances' troops—"The British marched their troops up to Fort Meigs, and then marched down again." *Oxford* 426.

K23 The **King's** cheese is half wasted in parings
1735 Franklin *PR* 2.7: The King's cheese is half wasted in parings: But no matter, 'tis made of the people's milk. **1797** Calender *Annual Register 1796* 74: These observations confirm an old proverb, that *the king's*

cheese goes half away in parings. *Oxford* 427; Tilley K79.

K24 The **King's** debts must be first paid
1691 ?CMather *Bills of Credit* in *Colonial Currency* 1.195: It is a known Maxim of Law in England . . . that of Debts, *The King's must be first paid.*

K25 **Kings** and bears often worry their keepers
1733 Franklin *PR* 1.312: Kings and Bears often worry their keepers, **1739** 2.219. *Oxford* 428; Tilley K85.

K26 **Kings** have long arms
1752 Franklin *PR* 4.247: Kings have long Arms, but Misfortune longer: Let none think themselves out of her Reach. **1756** RDemere in McDowell *Documents* 2.223: He is a great and powerfull King; his Arm is long and reaches far. **1788** Ledyard *Russian Journey* 209: Then begun in Proverbs to tell me "that Sovereigns had long Arms." *Oxford* 425; TW 208(5).

K27 To clip the **King's** English
1722 Franklin *Papers* 1.40: *Clip the King's English,* **1737** *Drinkers* 2.176: Clips the King's English. **c1810** Foster *Jeffersonian America* 189: A very good-humoured person [Matthew Lyon] who was used to clip the King's English. *Oxford* 427; Tilley K75.

K28 To distort (*etc.*) the **King's** English
1808 Paine *Works* 386: After twisting and distorting the King's English. **1815** *Reviewers* 67: The reviewers think that no other than their own nation have a right to *twistify* the "King's English." *Oxford* 427; Whiting K44.

K29 To have seen the French **King**
1737 Franklin *Drinkers* 2.176: He's Seen the French King.

K30 To live like **Kings**
1812 *Kennon Letters* 33.269: They live like little Kings. Whiting K58. See **P290.**

K31 To treat one like a **King**
1804 Dow *Journal* 185: He gave me what I wanted and treated me like a king. **1807** As-

bury *Journal* 2.547: We were entertained like kings. TW 209(7). See **L289.**

K32   The two **Kings** of Brentford

1775 Curwen *Journal* 1.53: Brentford . . . 'Tis celebrated for the residence of the two Kings in the Witty Duke of Buckingham's Satyrical Comedy called the Rehearsal. **1777** JWereat in *McIntosh Papers* 71: They have given us two Kings of Brentford. **1802** *Port Folio* 2.268: This loving pair of synonymies grin at each other, like the two kings of Brentford. **1818** Cobbett *Year's* 290: The *two kings of Brentford,* whose cordiality was . . . so perfect, that they smelt to the same nosegay. Lean 1.133.

K33   In the **Kingdom** of the blind the one-eyed man is king

1732 *South Carolina Gazette* 181: And that . . . their own One Eye gave them a Right to preside among the Blind. **1808** Grant *Memoirs* 2.159: He found himself . . . the one-eyed king in the kingdom of the blind. *Oxford* 428; Tilley E240; Whiting M263.

K34   As cute as a **Kingfisher**

1824 *Tales* 2.49: That young devil's limb is as 'cute as a kingfisher.

K35   To **Kiss** and tell

1809 Lindsley *Love* 15: Me no de kiss and tell secret of de fair sex. *Oxford* 429; TW 209.

K36   **Kissing** goes by favor

1739 Belcher *Papers* 2.236: For it's said kissing goes by favour. **1775** AA in *Adams FC* 1.321: There is an old adage kissing goes by favour that is daily verified. **1781** Curwen *Journal* 2.746. **1793** JHarmar in Denny *Journal* 466. **1797** JPerkins in *Cabot Family* 2.508: says the proverb. **1815** Barney *Memoir* 284. **1817** *Cabot Family* 2.554. **1837** Smith *Letters* 378: Every thing goes by favor. *Oxford* 430; TW 209.

K37   A fat **Kitchen,** a lean will

1733 Franklin *PR* 1.315: A fat kitchen, a lean Will, **1758** *WW* 345: makes a. Barbour 102; Tilley K110; Whiting *NC* 433.

K38   **Kitchen** physic

1660 Shepard *Hints* 161: Kitchen physick

[food good for ill people]. *Oxford* 430; Tilley P260.

K39   As yellow as a **Kite's** foot

1688 Clayton *Writings* 60: Tobacco . . . a bright Kite's foot colour. **1757** Carter *Diary* 1.160: None turned as yellow as a kite's foot. *Oxford* 925; TW 209(1); Whiting K74.

K40   To set up a **Kite** to keep the hen-yard in order

1787 Jefferson *Papers* 12.357: They are setting up a kite to keep the hen yard in order. Cf. *Oxford* 285: fox.

K41   As playful as a **Kitten**

1789 Dunlap *Father* 21: Playful as the kitten yet unstained with blood. Barbour 103(4); *Oxford* 632; TW 209(7).

K42   **Knaves** and nettles are akin, *etc.*

1748 Franklin *PR* 3.250: Knaves and Nettles are akin; Stroak 'em kindly, yet they'll sting. Tilley N133.

K43   There is **Knavery** in all trades

1826 Duane *Colombia* 140: There is a little knavery in all trades. *Oxford* 431-2; Tilley K152. See **T244.**

K44   To be **Knee-high** to a toad

1814 *Portsmouth Oracle* in DA knee 3b: One . . . who, as farmer Joe would say, is "about knee high to a toad." TW 210.

K45   As thin as a **Knife**

1824 Gallatin *Diary* 250: A huge farm-horse —who is as thin as a knife. See **H101.**

K46   Never a good **Knife** made of bad steel

1755 Franklin *PR* 5.472: There was never a good Knife made of bad Steel.

K47   To die of **Knife** and fork

1791 Rush *Autobiography* 206: [He] told me that Revd. Dr. Manning "had died of his knife and fork," that is of eating too much. NED Knife and fork. Cf. Whiting K91. See **G73.**

K48   To whet a **Knife** to cut one's own throat

1804 MLewis in *Lewis and Clark Expedition* 180: Men . . . whetting knives to cut their own throats. *Oxford* 882. See **P182.**

K49 Knight of the post

1643 SGorton in Winslow *Hypocrisie* 33: Calling him a knight of the post. **1778** Paine *American Crisis* 1.108: The new knight of the windmill and post. **1781** Peters *Connecticut* 232. **1784** Gadsden *Writings* 238: This *mere Knight of the Post*, this *Marplot*. **1787** Adams *Works* 6.154: Calumniators and informers (such as we call "Knights of the Post.") **1813** Paulding *Lay* 161: A distinguished freebooter of the new order of knights of the post. *Oxford* 432-3; Tilley K164.

K50 Soft Knocks enter hard blocks

1738 Churchman *Account* 57: He again asked me, if I knew the meaning of a common saying of those parts [New Jersey] who were used to the business [splitting wood], " 'Tis soft knocks must enter hard blocks:" I told him I knew it well; but there was some old wood that was rather decayed at heart, and to strike with a soft or gentle blow at a wedge in such blocks, would drive it to the head without rending them, and the labour would be lost, when a few smart lively stroks would rend them asunder. Whereupon he laid his hand on my shoulder, saying, "Well, my lad; I perceive thou art born for a warrior, and I commend thee." Whiting *NC* 433.

K51 As tough as a Knot

1779 Carroll *Correspondence* 2.29: Fine hardy fellows, as tough as the knots of an old seasoned oak. Cf. Barbour 103(4).

K52 To seek a Knot in a bulrush

1637 *Winthrop Papers(A)* 3.465: Which the Answerer would have understood well enough, if he had not beene minded to seeke a knot in a rush. **1652** Williams *Writings* 4.58: But what *knot* in a *Bulrush* is that? 59, 60. **1686** Dunton *Letters* 91: He is a very conscientious Man . . . and so great a Critick, that he wou'd even find a knot in a Bulrush. *Oxford* 433; Whiting K98.

K53 To tie the Knot

1772 *Norton Papers* 254: To tie the knot soon with a young Lady. **1804** Dow *Journal* 210: After the knot is tied . . . thus the *dear* becomes *cheap*. Barbour 103(3); TW 211(4).

K54 Know thyself

1772 WBradford in Madison *Papers* 1.73: "Gnothi se auton" was the celebrated maxim of the antients. **1779** Van Schaack *Letters* 192: The maxim—*nosce te ipsum*. **1787** Adams *Works* 4.393: Know thyself is as useful a precept to nations as to men. **1789** *Columbian Magazine* 3.96: "*Nosce teipsum*"—Know thyself. **c1790** Brackenridge *Gazette* 111: The Gnothi Seauton of the Greeks is his motto. **1798** *Echo* 155: Gnothi Seauton. **1811** Murphey *Papers* 1.51: this is true Wisdom. **1812** *Port Folio* 2NS 8.540: a precept of no less importance to a nation than to individuals. **1816** Jefferson *Writings* 18.297: The precept. **1816** *Port Folio* 4NS 1.168: That first of knowledge. **1834** Floy *Diary* 45: Which shows how necessary it is to know oneself. *Oxford* 435; Whiting K100.

K55 To Know enough to walk in when it rains (*varied*)

1801 *Farmers' Museum* 102: Of wit I brag not, yet brains Enough to walk in, when it rains. **1811** Jefferson *Writings* 18.268: You have seen an order of scavans, really well informed, who, notwithstanding, scarcely know how to escape from a shower of rain when it happened to beset them. **1832** Ames *Nautical* 48: People who have "wit enough to go below when it rains." Barbour 150(2); *Oxford* 903: Wit; TW 211(2); Tilley F537.

K56 Knowledge is power

1806 Rush *Letters* 2.935: The well-known aphorism that "knowledge is power." **1816** Paulding *Letters(I)* 1.168: *Knowledge is power*, 2.23: "Knowledge is power," said the great Ham—I beg pardon, Bacon. **1818** Hall *Travels* 326. **1821** Jefferson *Writings* 18.313. **1828** *Yankee* 150. **1834** JMCorr in Porter *Negro Writing* 148: For "knowledge is light—knowledge is power." **1847** Paulding *Letters(II)* 456. Barbour 104(2); *Oxford* 436-7. See **M210, W81**.

L

L1   A **Labor** of love

1629 *Winthrop Papers(A)* 2.100: Thy Labour of love, **1646** 5.95: In both I see your labour of love, **1660** (*B*) 2.515, **1661** 3.392. **1672** WGoffe in *Mather Papers* 141, **1677** 159. **1682** *Hinckley Papers* 63. **1717** Sewall *Letter-Book* 2.67: I humbly Thank your Excellency for your Labour of Love in following our worthy Pastor to his long home yesterday, though it snow'd so fast. **1725** Chalkley *Journal* 162. **1740** *Georgia Records* 22².328. **1785** Adams(A) *Letters* 274-5. **1809** Weems *Washington* 140. **1814** Bentley *Diary* 4.256. **1848** Cooper *Letters* 5.278: This book is not a labour of love, but a labour. TW 212(1).

L2   To have one's **Labor** for his pains

1691 ?CMather *Bills of Credit* in *Colonial Currency* 1.190: The Gentlemen get but their labour for their pains. **1710** IMather in *Saltonstall Papers* 1.297: The Commissioners have nothing but their labor for their paines. **1725** JPritchard in *Baxter Manuscripts* 10.327. **1755** Franklin *Papers* 6.22. **1761** POliver in Eliot *Essays* 246. **1764** Morgan *Journal* 156: They would only have their labour as a Reward for their Pains. **1775** Adams(S) *Writings* 3.192-3. **1787** JQAdams in Smith *Journal and Correspondence* 2(1) 131-2. **1789** Brown *Power* 2.135-6: He will reap his labour for his pains. **1811** Weems *Gambling* 31: He is . . . obliged to take his pains for his pay. **1816** Paulding *Letters(I)* 1.162: He who looked further generally got his labour for his pains. **1824** Prince *Journals* 128: So we had our toil and danger for our pains. *Oxford* 438; TW 212(2).

L3   To have one's **Labor** (to labor) in vain

1639 Masconomet in *Winthrop Papers(A)* 4.104: The Creeke commonly called Labour in Vane Creeke. **1682** Plumstead 100: If I could helpe to drive home any of these nails I should think it labor not in vain. **1694** *Connecticut Vindicated* 110: The New-labour-in vain, 113. **1695** NSaltonstall in *Saltonstall Papers* 1.239: I have labored . . . in vain. **1717** Mather *Diary* 2.472. **1733** Byrd *Journey* 303. **1737** *Georgia Records* 21.347, 370. **1741** DHorsmanden in *Colden Letters* 2.225. **1741** Stephens *Journal(I)* 2.137, **1744** (*II*) 2.103. **1747** *Georgia Records* 25.182, 200. **1747** Johnson *Writings* 3.193. **1750** *Georgia Records* 26.103, **1751** 158. **1755** *Fitch Papers* 1.181. **1757** RDemere in McDowell *Documents* 2.310: My Labour has not been imployed in vain. **1762** *Johnson Papers* 3.639. **1762** Watts *Letter Book* 17: It would be Labour lost to attempt it, 105. **1766** Franklin *Papers* 13.78. **1767** *Johnson Papers* 5.719. **1772** Asbury *Journal* 1.28, **1773** 71, **1774** 133. **1774** Freneau *Poems* 1.106. **1775** Asbury *Journal* 1.168, **1777** 238. **1777** Washington *Writings* 10.148. **1778** Smith *Works* 2.58. **1780** Adams *Works* 9.510. **1786** ?JGreen in Porter *Negro Writing* 412. **1788** *American Museum* 3.93. **1792** Washington *Writings* 32.215. **1793** Ingraham *Journal* 10. **1795** *Washington *Writings* 34.153. c**1800** Rush *Autobiography* 80. **1806** Barlow *Works* 1.519: labored. **1812** SHopkins in Knopf

War of 1812 5(1) 282. **1814** Kerr *Barclay* 248. **1817** Young *Life* 78. **1820** Cottle *Life* 385. **1823** Murphey *Papers* 1.284. *Oxford* 438; Whiting L11.

L4   To lose one's Labor

c1645 JCotton in Williams *Writings* 2.63: And found all your labour lost. **a1656** Bradford *History* 2.209-10: He was to loose his labour. **1708** Talbot *Letters* 118: We have lost our Labour. **1716** JKnight in *Letters from Hudson Bay* 65: To prevent their losing of their labour. **1726** Hempstead *Diary* 171. **1753** JGlen in McDowell *Documents* 1.403, **1756** 2.157. **1775** Digges *Adventures* 2.54: It was all lost labour. **1775** Hutchinson *Diary* 1.415. **1777** JWard in *Bowdoin Papers* 1.412. **1778** STen Broeck in *Clinton Papers* 4.34: It is only Lost Labour. **1781** AA in *Adams FC* 4.191: His generous Labour is not lost. **1783** Jones *Letters* 104. **1784** WHooper in Iredell *Correspondence* 2.100. **1787** *Washington Writings* 29.244: My labour is lost. **1800** Paine *Correspondence* 2.1410. **1805** Adams *Memoirs* 1.327. **1807** Rush *Letters* 2.959: Who after this can refrain from crying out with the parrot, "I have lost my labor"? **1810** Adams *Writings* 3.530: [It] is but labor lost. **1815** Humphreys *Yankey* 63. **1819** Peirce *Rebelliad* 60: He found it labor lost. **1833** Jackson *Correspondence* 5.214: They have found by experience that their abuse of you is labour lost. *Oxford* 485; Whiting L11, T442.

L5   The Laborer is worthy of his hire

1644 Williams *Writings* 3.304: But (say they) is not the *Labourer* worthy of his hire? **1646** *Hutchinson Papers* 1.245: The scripture saith the labourour is worthy of his wages. **1652** Williams *Writings* 7.163: But is not the *Labourer* worthy of his *Reward?* **1694** Makemie *Writings* 80: The workman is worthye of his Meat, and else where, is worthy of his Hire. **1698** HAshurst in *Winthrop Papers*(B) 6.42. **1713** Chalkley *Forcing* 382: Reward. **1741** *Letter* in *Colonial Currency* 4.95: If their Labour is worth the Hire. **1745** Johnson *Writings* 3.476. **1753** *Independent Reflector* 431: But if that *Labourer is unworthy of his Hire.* **1776** SWest

in Thornton *Pulpit* 301: It is a maxim of eternal truth that the laborer is worthy of his reward. **1797** Beete *Man* 27. **1798** Allen *Vermont* 483. **1801** *Port Folio* 1.276: For the Workman is worthy of his meat. **1802** Chester *Federalism* 11. **1835** Floy *Diary* 145: Saw scribbled on the wall of the Jury room, "The laborer is worthy of his hire: 12½ cts." Barbour 104; *Oxford* 439; Whiting W655.

L6   To kick down the Ladder

1783 JFMercer in Madison *Papers* 6.376: That ct. [court] was about to realize the case of those kicked down the ladder by wch. they had been elevated. *Oxford* 421; Tilley L26.

L7   As docile as Lambs

1808 Hitchcock *Poetical Dictionary* 106: Makes us . . . as docile as lambs. TW 213(8).

L8   As gentle as Lambs

1797 Cobbett *Porcupine* 6.55: The American youth are now as gentle as lambs. **1803** Jackson *Correspondence* 1.70: But as soon as I got upon my legs, from the fierceness of lyons, the[y] softned down to the Gentleness of lambs. **1806** JRutledge in Otis *Letters* 1.281: As gentle as a Lamb. **1813** Weems *Drunkard* 81. Barbour 104(2); *Oxford* 298; Whiting L28.

L9   As meek as a Lamb

c1700 Taylor *Poems* 391: Mercy . . . Comes as meeke as any Lamb. **1740** *Georgia Records* 22².477: As Humble & as Meek as Lambs. **1805** Sewall *Parody* 29: Meek as the lambkin. Barbour 104(4); *Oxford* 298; Svartengren 64; Whiting L31.

L10   As mild as a Lamb

1782 Lee(W) *Letters* 3.887: Adams . . . is mild as a Lamb. **1787** Freneau *Poems* 2.341: When Snip was in sight, he was mild as a lamb. *Oxford* 298; Whiting L32. See S121.

L11   As patient as a Lamb

1776 AA in *Adams FC* 2.106: He . . . is as patient as a Lamb.

L12   As pure as a Lamb

1820 *Fudge Family* 11: I'm innocent yet, as

pure as a lamb. Cf. Barbour 104(6); TW 212(6).

L13   As quiet as a Lamb

1770 Adams *D and A* 1.354: Make the Americans as quiet as Lambs. **1777** JTrumbull in *Heath Papers* 2.86: Connecticut will be quiet as lambs. **1797** Tyler *Prose* 215. **1801** *Farmers' Museum* 278. **1826** Audubon *1826 Journal* 243. **1826** Austin *Literary Papers* 28. **1833** Jackson *Correspondence* 5.216: We will . . . have Mr. Biddle and his Bank as quiet and harmless as a *lamb* in six weeks. Lean 2.865; *Oxford* 298; TW 213(11).

L14   A Lamb here, a lion there

1774 Jones *Journal* 58: For tho' when among us they are lambs, found them *lions* at home. **1799** Humphreys *Works* 142.611: In peace a lamb, in fight a lion fierce. Whiting L38. See **L162.**

L15   To bear something like a Lamb

1770 *Johnson Papers* 7.388: Gout, which he bears like a Lamb.

L16   To commit the Lamb to the wolf

1692 Bulkeley *Will* 249: And so the lamb will be committed to the custody and guardianship of the wolf. **1783** JAdams in *Warren-Adams Letters* 2.207: They have committed a Mistake in committing the Lamb so unreservedly to the Custody of the Wolf, **1790** *Works* 9.571: [This] is *"committere agnum lupo."* **1797** Cobbett *Porcupine* 6.73: Pennsylvania had too much virtue . . . to vote *a French wolf the guardian of her sheep.* **1814** Adams *Works* 6.512: This . . . *"committere agnum lupo."* It is to commit the lamb to the kind guardianship and protection of the wolf! **1818** 10.338. *Oxford* 907; Whiting W460, cf. **L48.**

L17   To die like a Lamb

1716 Hempstead *Diary* 58: Joshua Died . . . like a Lamb. Whiting L41, quote c1370.

L18   To go like Lambs to Smithfield

1786 Dunlap *Diary* 1.5: My fellow traveller seem'd to think them going like lambs to smithfield. Whiting L41, quote c1390.

L19   Lame Duck Alley

1792 Rush *Autobiography* 219: Chestnut Street was now called "Lame Duck Alley." DA lame 2b; NED Duck *sb.*[1] 9.

L20   To smell of the Lamp

1637 Morton *New English Canaan* 322: Hee doe not make use of any notes for the helpe of his memory; for such Things, they say, smell of Lampe oyle. **1702** Mather *Magnalia* 2.92: They still smelt of the *lamp.* **1721** *Boston News-Letter* in Buckingham *Specimens* 1.10: Your Letter . . . and Rhyme . . . smell more of the Ale Tub than the Lamp. **1753** *Independent Reflector* 347: Theirs is an illiterate kind of Wit that smells of the Lamp. **1781** Oliver *Origin* 96: *Their* Address had a great Proportion of that fœtid Smell of the Lamp, which generally evaporated from their Pulpit Discourses. *Oxford* 745; Tilley C43, L44.

L21   The Land flowing with milk and honey (*varied*)

1657 Wigglesworth *Diary* 102: Who brought them . . . into a good land flowing with milk and hony. **1665** AMoray in *W&MCQ* 2S 2(1922) 160: The settling in a wilderness of milk and honey. **1685** Mather *Letters* 18: It came from the upper Canaan that flows with milk and honey. **a1700** Hubbard *New England* 22, 52-3. **1702** Mather *Magnalia* 1.44: The *land flowing with milk and honey,* 52, 437: The land that flows with what is better than milk and honey. **1754** Plumstead 293. **1771** Woodmason *Journal* 287. **1772** Boucher *Autobiography* 83: The promised land which, in the best sense of the phrase, flows with milk and honey [his prospective wife!]. **1779** Adams *D and A* 2.380: There was a rich Stream of Benevolence flowing like Milk and Honey, thro all his [Sterne's] works. **1781** Oliver *Origin* 149. **1783** Van Schaack *Letters* 334: Let us content ourselves with the milk and honey of our *native* country, without a latent wish for the leeks and onions of the old. **1785** Washington *Writings* 28.206: Abound, as in the Land of promise, with milk and honey. **1802** Humphreys *Works* 99.98: Let milk and honey flow the happy land. **1805** Irving *Journals* 1.160. **1807** Janson *Stranger* 259:

He was led to believe that . . . the new world flowed with milk and honey, 453. **a1808** Burr *Correspondence* 228: He is now all milk and honey. **1808** Hitchcock *Poetical Dictionary* 40. **1810** GHeriot in *Winslow Papers* 653: We . . . hope in a short time to live like little Irish Kings, in a Land overflowing with milk and honey. **1812** Hitchcock *Social* 131: Would witness with their *milk and honey*, A general overflow of money. **1813** Barlow *Letters* 272: He is sucking the milk and honey from three colleges. **1817** Tyler *Prose* 338: Ohio . . . that "land of milk and honey." **1818** Cobbett *Year's* 301. **1822** Weems *Penn* 160: An earthly Canaan of their own, flowing with the milk and honey of peace and quiet. **1824** Flint *Recollections* 41: If once they could arrive at the land of milk and honey, supplies would come of course. *Oxford* 531; Whiting M549.

L22   The **Land** of liberty

1819 Flint *Letters* 168: On such occasions, they exclaim, *"this is a free country"* or a *"land of liberty,"* adding a profane oath, 169: or an allusion to the *land of liberty.*

L23   The **Land** of Nod

1702 Sewall *Diary* 2.62: Right conducts me to Wooburn through the Land of Nod. **1796** Cobbett *Porcupine* 3.266: After this trip to the Land of Nod, let us return to our Stenographer. **1798** *Echo* 152: And far before me stretch'd the land of Nod. **1801** Story *Shop* 89: Doctor Dodd, Whose friendship swung him to the land of Nod. **1818** Beecher *Autobiography* 1.376: The land of Nod (a dark unexplored place nobody knows where). **1832** Longfellow *Letters* 1.391: Even now I write you from the borders of the Land of Nod. *Oxford* 441; TW 213(2).

L24   The **Land** of pumpkins

1769 *Johnson Papers* 6.638: Since yʳ return from the Land of Pumpkins. DA land 6b(14), where the first reference to Connecticut is in 1829.

L25   The **Land** of the living

1647 Davenport *Letters* 81: You are yet in the land of the living. **1718** JGyles in *Baxter Manuscripts* 9.442: You ar in the Land of yᵉ

Liveing. **1728** Sewall *Letter-Book* 2.254. **1768** JParker in Franklin *Papers* 15.288. **1775** WGriffin in *Naval Documents* 2.1025: I am still in being. I dare not say in the [lan]d of the Living for I dare not shew my Nose. **1788** AA in *Adams FC* 3.46. **1780** Angell *Diary* 105. **1786** Franklin *Writings* 9.547. **1793** JBarr in *Blount Papers* 2.334. **1804** Mackay *Letters* 150. **1809** *Kennon Letters* 32.159. **1812** Fletcher *Letters* 54. **1814** WRuffin in *Ruffin Papers* 1.145. **1817** WCrawford in Milledge *Correspondence* 164. **1820** GLambert in *Winslow Papers* 703. Job xxviii 13; NED Land 2c.

L26   To see how the **Land** lies

1728 Byrd *Dividing Line* 13: Mr. Eden was much better inform'd how the Land lay than he. **1776** Burr *Memoirs* 1.85: Find out how the land lay. **1811** Graydon *Memoirs* 127: Where he probably came to see how the land lay. **1820** Robertson *Letters* 138. Colcord 113; NED Land 1c; TW 213-4(3).

L27   To kiss the **Landlady** for good luck

1733 Byrd *Journey* 265: We fortified ourselves with a beef-steak, kissed our landlady for good luck. Cf. *Oxford* 496; Tilley L575.

L28   If the **Landlord** lives the tenant starves

1728 Talcott *Papers* 2.428: In this poore Country if the Landlord Liveth the Tenant Starveth.

L29   It is a long **Lane** that has no turning (*varied*)

1778 Paine *American Crisis* 1.153: It is a long lane that has no turning. **1803** UTracy in McHenry *Letters* 522: It is a long road which never turns. **1811** Wirt *Letters* 1.309: Well, it is a long lane that has no turn. **1815** Palmer *Diary* 214: Good fortune will come along by and by. It is a long lane that never turns. Barbour 105; *Oxford* 480; TW 214. See **T101, W190**.

L30   To speak the same **Language**

1773 *Commerce of Rhode Island* 1.465: The purchasers seem to understand each other this year better than we ever knew, for they seem all to speak the same Language, and to know the conversation that passed between us and either of them. Barbour 105(1); Berrey 16.5, 171.3, 181.8, *etc.*

L31 As blithe as a **Lark**

1795 Murdock *Triumphs* 81: My heart is as blythe as a lark's. **1817** Pintard *Letters* 1.46: Blighsome as a Lark, **1826** 2.254: Dear Sister is a blightsome as a Lark on the occasion of moving to her own house. *Oxford* 527; TW 214(1).

L32 As bright as a **Lark**

1850 Cooper *Letters* 6.113: I am as bright as a lark. TW 214(2).

L33 As cheery as a **Lark**

1826 Royall *Sketches* 103: A doudy drab . . . as cheery as a lark. TW 214(3).

L34 As gay as a **Lark**

1785 Adams(A) *Letters* 233: As gay as a lark. **1787** WSSmith in Smith *Journal and Correspondence* 1.177: Yesterday I was as gay as a lark. **1801** *Farmers' Museum* 97. **1811** Weems *Gambling* 44. **1812** Adams *Memoirs* 2.393. **1815** *Port Folio* 3NS 5.448. **1834** Lee *Diary and Letters* 237, **1837** 247. Barbour 105(1); *Oxford* 527; TW 214(5).

L35 As good-humored as a **Lark**

1816 Paulding *Letters(I)* 2.162: [She is] good-humoured as a lark.

L36 A **Lark** is worth a kite

1806 *Port Folio* NS 1.416: What says the old proverbial strain? "A lark is worth a kite." *Oxford* 454; TW 214(8); Whiting L189.

L37 To rise with the **Lark**

c**1800** Tyler *Island* 27: Arose with the lark. *Oxford* 38; Whiting L85.

L38 To sing like a **Lark**

a**1767** Evans *Poems* 143: And, like a lark, sang all the way. Barbour 105(3); *Oxford* 736; TW 214(12).

L39 **Last** but not least

1798 Bentley *Diary* 2.293: The New Year's Wish of the Gazette says of Salem, "Tho' often last, she's never least, And fame & fortune to secure Tho' very slow, she's very sure." **1818** Drake *Works* 252: But Willy has it—"last not least." Barbour 105(1); *Oxford* 442; Tilley L82.

L40 Better **Late** than never

1630 MWinthrop in *Winthrop Papers(A)* 2.219: I must nowe veryfy that proverbe better late then not at all. **1664** JMason in *Winthrop Papers(B)* 2.424: But better late than never. c**1680** Radisson *Voyages* 103. **1718** Sewall *Letter-Book* 2.83: Nunquam sera est ad bonos mores via. Possibly our English, Better late than never, may explain this Latine Proverb. **1732** Belcher *Papers* 1.234: That trite saying. **1745** *Pepperrell Papers* 409. **1761** *Beekman Papers* 1.385. **1761** *Boston Gazette* in *Olden Time* 2.31. **1765** RNeave in Read *Correspondence* 27: I think the old proverb "of it's being better late than never to mend" a very good one. **1770** *Beekman Papers* 1.524. **1776** CTufts in *Adams FC* 2.18. **1776** Ward *Correspondence* 187: The old Proverb. **1780** Sullivan *Letters* 3.201. **1783** Williams *Penrose* 171. **1786** *Belknap Papers* 1.447: the old maxim. **1786** RPeters in Jefferson *Papers* 9.350. **1786** Washington *Writings* 28.471: an adage not less true, or less to be respected because it is old, **1797** 36.8. **1799** WSmith in Gibbs *Memoirs* 2.238. **1809** King *Life* 5.159. **1811** Adams *Memoirs* 2.246, **1817** 3.507. **1825** Paulding *Letters(II)* 75. **1828** GBadger in *Ruffin Papers* 1.433. **1849** Paulding *Letters(II)* 503. Barbour 105(2); *Oxford* 54; Whiting L89.

L41 (Never) too **Late** to mend

1778 *Clinton Papers* 2.839: But it is too late to mend a bad Day's Work. Barbour 105(4); *Oxford* 563; TW 215(2).

L42 As thin as a **Lath**

1785 Smith *Diary* 2.22: He was 6 Feet high & as thin as a Lath. c**1810** AJFoster *Jeffersonian America* 243. **1810** Mackay *Letters* 90: James Wallace thinner than a lath. **1834** Floy *Diary* 114: I cannot do much, being thin as a lath. TW 215.

L43 Till **Latter Lammas**

1713 Wise *Churches* 110: Till Latter Lammas. *Oxford* 444; Tilley L90. See **G172.**

L44 **Laugh** and grow fat

1798 Drinker *Journal* 337: It made him think of an old saying, "Laugh and grow fat." **1828** Wirt *Letters* 2.247: *C'est egal—* So *vive la bagatelle* again! which, being rendered, signifieth "laugh and be fat." A proverb so full of wisdom that I wonder it escaped Solomon. *Oxford* 444; TW 215(1).

L45 **Laugh** if you are wise

1787 *Columbian Magazine* 1.550: *Ride si sapis*, the old apothegm, *Laugh if you are wise.*

L46 Let them **Laugh** that win

1765 Watts *Letter Book* 370: It is generally thought, however (says he) let them laugh that win. **1783** JEliot in *Belknap Papers* 3.261: I will laugh too, agreably to the old maxim, Let him laugh who wins. **1788** *American Museum* 3.382. **1792** Belknap *Foresters* 12. **1796** Barton *Disappointment* 82. **1797** Cobbett *Porcupine* 7.46, **1798** 8.10. **1814** *Port Folio* 3NS 4.225: Let Russians smile, — "they laugh who win." **1826** WBiglow in Buckingham *Specimens* 2.290: Oh! ye may grin and laugh who win. *Oxford* 445; Whiting L91.

L47 Let those **Laugh** who lose

1801 Baldwin *Life and Letters* 432: Let those who lose, laugh. TW 215(2).

L48 To gather (pluck) **Laurels**

1758 *Washington *Writings* 2.260: We stop'd at the Laurel Hill this Winter; not to gather Laurels, by the by, desirable in their effects. **1805** SRuffin in *Ruffin Papers* 1.77: Your choice of a profession by which you expect to gain a livlihood, and no doubt pluck some laurels in your travels through the different wilderness of this worlds pilgrimage. TW 215.

L49 To lie (lay) in **Lavender**

1734 Belcher *Papers* 2.140: His lady's fortune will lye in lavender to grow. **1807** JNiblock in *Ruffin Papers* 1.113: [He] has been for some time been laid up in Lavender but this evening seems to have recovered. *Oxford* 447-8; Tilley L96.

L50 Any **Law** is better than no law

1772 GCroghan in *St. Clair Papers* 1.262: Every one will agree, any Law is beter than No Law. Cf. Whiting L109.

L51 Good **Laws** are occasioned by evil manners

1652 Williams *Writings* 7.180: That true *Apothegme* or saying, *Ex malis moribus bona leges:* Good Laws occasioned by Evill manners. **a1700** Hubbard *New England* 535: *Ex malis moribus nascuntur bonae leges:* Laws are not the worse by being occasioned by evil men or evil manners. **1718** Sewall *Diary* 3.203: I said Twas a shame that a Law should be needed; meaning *ex malis moribus bonae Leges*. *Oxford* 233: Manners; Tilley M625.

L52 In **Law** nothing is done without money

1732 Belcher *Papers* 1.112: Yet you know there's nothing to be done in the law without money. *Oxford* 447; Whiting L110.

L53 The **Law** doesn't stand upon trifles

1701 EKimberly in *Winthrop Papers(B)* 5.84: *De minimis non judicat lex.* **1786** Hopkinson *Miscellaneous Essays* 2.262: *De minimi non curate lex*—in English, the law don't stand upon trifles. **1797** Tyler *Prose* 219: De Minimis curat Lex. **1801** *Port Folio* 1.370: De Minimis non curat lex.

L54 **Laws** are like cobwebs, *etc.*

1692 Bulkeley *Will* 228: And their majesties laws are but cobwebs, which they break through at pleasure. **1703** Taylor *Christographia* 461.84-6: The Laws of their Kingdoms are like Copwebs that catch little flies, but are Snapt in pieces by the greater. **1713** Steere *Daniel* 67: Then Blessed are the Rich, the Great & Noble, Whose Stations are above those Cob-web Laws, Which keep in Awe the Low and vulgar Crowd. **1732** Belcher *Papers* 1.211: Thus the laws seem only cobwebs for little weak rogues. **1734** Franklin *PR* 1.356: *Laws* like to *Cobwebs* catch small Flies, Great ones break thro' before your eyes. **1776** AA in *Adams FC* 2.67: We catch flies and let the wasps go. **1784** Gadsden *Writings* 232: Our laws are like cobwebs, they catch small flies, but let wasps and hornets break through. **1797** *Blount Papers* 3.585: Laws may then be truly compared to cobwebs—equal to the catching of small flies—[br]oke through by the wasps. **1798** Cobbett *Porcupine* 10.37: It is an old maxim with those who wish to decry all sorts of subordination, that "the laws are *cobwebs,* which hold the *weak,* but which *the strong break through."* **1814** *Port Folio* 3NS 3.361: Solon, who compared laws to cobwebs through which the great flies break while the little ones are caught. **c1825** Tyler *Prose* 126: Here comes one of those overgrown flies which buzz through the cobwebs of the law. *Oxford* 446-7; Whiting L106.

L55 Laws are silent amid arms

1692 Bulkeley *Will* 95: A dispensing power . . . makes a *tempus belli, cum leges silent.* **1770** SCooke in Thornton *Pulpit* 166: Inter arma silent leges. **1770** Plumstead 333: [Latin only]. **1773** Carroll *Correspondence* 1.338: [Latin only]. **1774** Adams(S) *Writings* 3.162: [Latin only]. **1776** Deane *Papers* 1.224: [Latin only]. **1781** Oliver *Origin* 118: [Latin only]. **1808** Bates *Papers* 1.263: Laws are silent amidst arms. **1808** Jefferson *Writings* 12.183: the maxim of the law itself, that *inter arma silent leges.* **1815** Andrews *Prisoners' Memoirs* 108: *Inter armis lages silent,* "the laws are silent amid arms." *Oxford* 205; Tilley D624. Cf. Whiting L105.

L56 Laws may sometimes sleep, but never die

1734 *New-York Weekly Journal* in *Newspaper Extracts(I)* 1.362: There is a Saying, *That Laws may sometimes sleep, but never die.* **a1788** Jones *History* 2.133: I am told the law never dies. Cf. *Oxford* 426: King. See **K21.**

L57 The **Laws** of the Medes and Persians

1678 Saffin *His Book* 24: By laws more sure than Mede or Persian. **1682** Steere *Daniel* 35: He cannot change, nay shall not, nor is able, The *Medes* and *Persians* Law's unalterable. **1719** Wise *Vindication* 104: Their alteration is not so firm, as the Laws of the *Medes* and *Persians.* **1728** Ames *Almanacs* 55: A much more strong and uncontrolled Law, Than any Mead or Persian ever saw. **1724** Jones *Virginia* 127: Ill customs in time . . . are established as firm as Median laws. **1760** *Letter* in Bailyn *Pamphlets* 1.269: Edicts, which like the laws of the *Medes* and *Persians* were to alter not. **1774** Adams *D and A* 2.98: The resolutions of the Congress shall be the laws of the Medes and Persians, **1774** *Works* 4.34: Was it not regarded as the laws of the Medes and Persians? **1774** Boucher *View* 362: Like the laws of the Medes and Persians, that is unalterable. **1774** CLeffingwell in *Deane Correspondence* 140: Laws like unto those of the Medes and Persians, which must not be altered. **1776** SWest in Thornton *Pulpit* 275: It is like the laws of the Medes and Persians—it altereth not. **1786** Shaw *Journals* 227: A people whose manners and customs may be considered like the laws of the Medes and Persians, which altered not. **a1788** Jones *History* 2.20: Their decrees, like those of the *Medes* and *Persians,* were irreversible, unimpeachable, and irrevocable. **1790** Baldwin *Life and Letters* 294: The resolve shall be like those of the Medes & the Persians unalterable. **1795** Cobbett *Porcupine* 2.90: Lovers' vows are like the laws of the Medes and Persians. **1802** Croswell *New World* 43: If but two principles can be maintain'd, Unalt'rably like laws of Medes and Persians. **1804** Hamilton *Law Practice* 1.829: A precedent like the laws of the Swedes and Persians, never to be changed. **1808** Asbury *Journal* 2.576: Make a decree but not of the Medes and Persians, **1809** *Letters* 3.422: Rules are not like the laws of the Medes and Persians. **1809** *Port Folio* 2NS 1.430: Nothing more certain, and which shall endure, Than laws of Medes and Per-si-ans more sure, 2.264: As irrevocable as the laws of the Medes and the Persians, **1810** 4.66: Laws . . . like those of the Medes and Persians . . . made unalterable. **1812** Hitchcock *Social* 54: And, like Persian rules of state, As irrevocable as fate. **1813** Kennon *Letters* 34.335: As immutable as the laws of the Medes and Persians. **1818** Royall *Letters* 164: And these [rules] were as firm and steadfast as the laws of the Medes and Persians. **1819** MChester in Vanderpoel *Chronicles* 190: Everything here is . . . as fix'd as the laws of the Medes and Persians. **1819** Noah *Travels* 190: Their mandate [is] as imperative as the law of the Medes and Persians. **1820** Simpson *Journal* 179: His

Edicts are as absolute and unalterable as those of the "Medes and Persians." *Oxford* 446; Whiting L104.

L58 No good **Law** will please all men

1676 WSherwood in *VHM* 1(1893) 168-9: Noe good Law can be so made to please all men. Cf. *Oxford* 633; Tilley P88.

L59 The strictest **Law** is the greatest oppression

1747 *New-York Evening Post* in *Newspaper Extracts(I)* 2.397: It is an old Maxim, *The strictest Law is the greatest Oppression.* Cf. *Oxford* 235; Tilley R122.

L60 (Lazy) **Lawrence**

1824 Doddridge *Notes* 131: A person who did not perform his share of labor . . . was designated by the epithet of *Lawrence,* or some other title still more opprobrious. *Oxford* 448-9; TW 215.

L61 A cunning **Lawyer** beats the Devil

1817 *Port Folio* 4NS 4.83: Thus 'tis we say, though quite uncivil, A cunning lawyer beats the devil!

L62 A good **Lawyer** is seldom a good neighbor

1710 Mather *Bonifacius* 163: There has been an old Complaint, *That a Good Lawyer seldom is a good Neighbour.* **1737** Franklin *PR* 2.168: A good Lawyer, a bad Neighbour. *Oxford* 447; Tilley L124.

L63 **Lawyer** and liar are synonymous terms

1720 ?ECooke *Reflections* in *Colonial Currency* 2.116: Lawyer and Liar are synonimous Terms. *Oxford* 447.

L64 As poor as **Lazarus**

1783 EWinslow in *Winslow Papers* 128: I am always poorer than Lazarus. Svartengren 342. Cf. Lean 2.865: ragged.

L65 **Laziness** travels so slowly that poverty soon overtakes him

1756 Franklin *PR* 6.328: *Laziness* travels so slowly, that *Poverty* soon overtakes him, **1758** *WW* 342. **1770** Ames *Almanacs* 412: Laziness always travels so slow that Poverty soon overtakes him.

L66 As clear as **Lead**

1793 *Echo* 91: In short, I think 'tis proved, as clear as lead, That Louis Capet ought to lose his head.

L67 As cold as **Lead**

1708 Taylor *Poems* 239: But now, like lead I Cold and Heavy lie. Whiting L119.

L68 As heavy as **Lead**

1787 *American Museum* 2.203: One whose head Was not so heavy near as lead. **1803** Davis *Travels* 142: His heels, As lead were heavy. **1812** *Kennon Letters* 34.228: My heart is as heavy as lead. Barbour 106(2); *Oxford* 449; Whiting L123.

L69 There is **Lead** in Mendon Hills

a**1700** Hubbard *New England* 23: But as it is proverbially said of some parts of England, they do not every where abound with mines, though there be lead in Mendon [Mendip] Hills.

L70 To sink like any **Lead**

?**1722** Winslow *Broadside* 115: Over they turns, and sunk like any lead. Whiting L133.

L71 **Lead** or drive (draw) (*varied*)

1690 GSaltonstall in *Winthrop Papers(B)* 5.8: They were for driving and he was for drawing. **1727** JMyatt in *Letters from Hudson Bay* 122: They are a people that may be led but not drove. **1734** Belcher *Papers* 2.175: For the people here... may be drawn but will not be driven. **1753** *Georgia Records* 26.426: A Failing too common with these People, who are neither to be led nor driven. **1756** ALewis in McDowell *Documents* 2.167: They are like the Devil's Pigg they will neither lead nor drive. **1765** *Johnson Papers* 11.737: A very proud . . . pople . . . Easey Lead Butt hard to Drive. **1779** GMorris in *Clinton Papers* 3.420: It is easier to lead men than to drive them at all times. *Oxford* 449; Tilley L138. See **C237**.

L72 **Leading-strings**

1743 *Georgia Records* 23.470: Ebenezer [a town] next we see grown to such Maturity as to need no farther Leading Strings here-

after. **1771** Smith *Memoirs*(*I*) 100: A Fool &
in Leading Strings. **1779** Paine *Peace* 2.190:
At best it is but in leading strings and fit
rather for the cradle than the cabinet. **1782**
Gordon *Letters* 468: I abhor the idea of
being in leading strings or pinning our faith
upon others' sleeves. **1786** Baldwin *Life and
Letters* 262: They must learn the Strings by
which Delila like, they can lead about &
controul the morose Samsons of America.
1789 WCarmichael in Jefferson *Papers*
14.501: A Woman here will guide him as an
Infant in Leading Strings. **1790** Morris
Diary 1.500. **1794** Rowson *Charlotte* 1.58:
Have you a mind to be in leading strings all
your lifetime? **1798** Adams *Writings* 2.302.
1800 Tatham *Tobacco* 112. **1802** Paine *To
the Citizens* 2.928. **1803** Austin *Constitutional* 67: Spurn at the leading strings of
interested bigots. **1808** Adams *Works* 6.539:
Presidents must break asunder their leading
strings. **1809** Weems *Marion* 7: Or dream of
going to heaven but in *their* leading strings.
1815 Jefferson *Writings* 14.257. **1816** Paulding *Letters*(*I*) 1.50. **1818** Fessenden *Ladies
Monitor* 30: The things, Who dangle in a
lady's leading strings. **1819** JHolmes in
Banks *Maine* 176. **1837** Jackson *Correspondence* 5.449: I am neither superannuated,
or yet in leading strings, as they . . . pro-
claim to the world. NED Leading-string.
See **A113**.

L73   As many (numerous) as **Leaves** on the
trees

1764 *Johnson Papers* 11.228: They had as
many men as there were leaves on the trees.
1806 Pike *Travels* 104: Besides, you white
people are like the leaves on the trees for
numbers. **1808** Jefferson *Writings* 16.426:
We are as numerous as the leaves of the
trees. **1812** JWatson in Knopf *War of 1812*
6(1) 230: We are as . . . numerous as the
leaves on the trees of the forest. Whiting
L136.

L74   To fade like a **Leaf**

1642 SGorton in Winslow *Hypocrisie* 24:
Which shall fade as a leafe. **1653** Wigglesworth *Diary* 10: For I fade as a leaff. Whiting L145.

L75   To shake like a **Leaf**

1643 Williams *Writings* 1.210: I shake as a
leafe. **1777** Asbury *Journal* 1.245: Shook like
a leaf. **1783** Williams *Penrose* 300. **1803**
Davis *Travels* 318. Barbour 106(2); TW
216(6); Tilley L140; Whiting L146. See
A128.

L76   To tremble like a **Leaf**

1800 Hamilton *Law Practice* 1.729: He . . .
trembled all over like a leaf. Barbour 106
(2); Whiting L147. See **A128**.

L77   To wither away like a **Leaf**

a**1820** Drake *Works* 280: Hope . . . Shall
wither away as a leaf on the tree. Cf. Whiting *NC* 435(6): fade.

L78   To take a **Leaf** out of another's book

1818 Gallatin *Diary* 129: He has taken a leaf
out of his master's book. *Oxford* 798; TW
216-7(1).

L79   To turn over a new **Leaf**

1721 Sewall *Diary* 3.286: I . . . desired him
to pray with us, that might redeem the
Time, and turn over a new Leafe; which he
did. **1740** Stephens *Journal*(*I*) 1.605: But he
hoped in a few Months to see a new Leaf
turned over. **1801** Adams *Writings* 2.508:
Human nature is turning over a new leaf.
1801 WMStewart in *W&MCQ* 3S 10(1953)
112. **1807** *Weekly* 1.194. ?**1812** JEarly *Diary*
in *VHM* 36(1928) 331. **1814** Adams *Memoirs* 2.571. **1823** Longfellow *Letters* 1.65.
1824 *Tales* 1.229, 2.221. Barbour 106; *Oxford* 846; TW 217(2); Whiting L148.

L80   A small **Leak** will sink a great ship

1745 Franklin *PR* 3.5: Beware of little
Expences, a small Leak will sink a great
Ship, **1758** *WW* 345. **1804** Dow *Journal* 392:
One leak will sink a ship. Barbour 106; *Ox-
ford* 450; Tilley L147.

L81   A **Leap** in the dark

1741 Stephens *Journal*(*I*) 2.89: I was determined not to take a leap in the Dark. **1760**
JBoucher in *MHM* 7(1912) 24: Let's E'en
take our Chance: 'Tis all a Leap into the
Dark, as Hobbes said of Death. **1810** ELor-
rain in Murphey *Papers* 1.37: I made a
Leap in the dark in coming to Louisiana.

1815 JMay in *Ruffin Papers* 1.160. *Oxford* 450; Tilley L148; Whiting *NC* 435.

L82 Never too old to **Learn**

1783 Williams *Penrose* 123: A man is never too old to learn. *Oxford* 563; Tilley L153; Whiting O30.

L83 **Learning** has no enemy but ignorance

1797 Mann *Female* 99: The maxim— *"Learning has no enemy but ignorance."*

L84 **Learning** is better than house and land

1797 Freneau *Poems* 3.170: When house and lands are gone and spent, Then learning is most excellent—(So says a proverb through the world well known). 1815 *Port Folio* 3NS 6.161-2: A maxim . . . "Learning is better than house and land." *Oxford* 389; TW 217(2). See **W237**.

L85 **Learning** makes a good man better, *etc.*

1758 Ames *Almanacs* 283: Learning makes a good Man better, but a bad Man worse. *Oxford* 451.

L86 **Least** said is soonest mended

1698 JUsher in *W&MCQ* 3S 7(1950) 101: Least Saide, Soone amended a noli me Tangere. 1741 Belcher *Papers* 2.373: For my part, *rebus sic stantibus*, I think least said is soonest mended. 1769 Lloyd *Papers* 2.717. 1779 Brackenridge *Gazette* 147: That salutary maxim. 1780 JThaxter in *Adams FC* 3.340: But the least said is best. 1788 TPaine in Jefferson *Papers* 13.588: *"Least said is soonest mended,"* and nothing said requires no mending. 1795 Cobbett *Porcupine* 2.78: the truth of that good old proverb. 1804 Paine *Remarks* 2.958. 1806 EWinslow in *Winslow Papers* 552. 1824 Longfellow *Letters* 1.97: The maxim is a true one—"the least said,—the soonest amended." 1828 Pintard *Letters* 3.6: They are both no more, the least said the better. Barbour 107; *Oxford* 472; TW 217. See **L180**.

L87 Those who say they care **Least** care most

1733 Belcher *Papers* 1.373: It's a common saying in the world, when people say they care least they care most.

L88 As tough as **Leather**

1805 *Port Folio* 5.336: Her joints are as supple and tough as new leather. Barbour 107 (2); *Oxford* 834; Whiting L160. See **W140**.

L89 To be on one's upper **Leathers**

1776 GSaltonstall in *Deane Brothers Papers* 17: To give so much Masts & Canvass as to make the Vessell go, as the Sailors Phrase is, on her upper leathers. Cf. NED Upper *sb.* 1c; Partridge 928.

L90 **Leave** is light

1757 Franklin *Papers* 7.222: *Leave* they say is *light*. *Oxford* 453; Whiting L165.

L91 To hang (fasten) like a **Leech**

1796 Cobbett *Porcupine* 4.323: You had tasted the sweets of plunder, and you hung to it like a leech. 1796 Latrobe *Journal* 40: He had fastened upon me like a leech. TW 217(2).

L92 To stick like a **Leech**

1770 Paterson *Glimpses* 74: They stick to him like leeches. 1780 Lee(W) *Letters* 3.786: I will answer for both of them sticking leeches to yᵉ charge. 1789 *Columbian Magazine* 3.313: Stick close as a leech to the stove. Barbour 107; TW 217(3).

L93 On a **Lee** shore

1784 Freneau *Poems* 2.270: On the devil's lee shore were eternally cast. 1800 Eaton *Life* 140: The Danes are running on a lee shore here. 1803 RO'Brien in *Barbary Wars* 2.357: As our affairs are Verging on to a Lee shore. Colcord 116; NED Lee shore. Cf. Whiting L188.

L94 **Leeks** and onions

1775 WWatson in *Naval Documents* 2.1107: An uneasy sett of fellows who . . . are longing for the Leeks & Onions of Connecticut. 1788 Sullivan *Letters* 3.567: Some few . . . longed for the onions of Egypt [the good old days].

L95 To (the) **Leeward**

a1800 Bowen *Journals* 1.30: I was all to leeward in my pl[ans]. a1814 Dow *Journal* 418: It is a rarity that a young woman goes to the leeward with a broken ***. Colcord 116; TW 217.

L96   A **Left-handed** (something or other)

1734 *New-York Weekly Journal* in *News-paper Extracts*(I) 1.374: Members who had no private left-Handed Views. **1795** Cobbett *Porcupine* 2.151: Nothing was to be heard but their malicious left-handed complaints. **1796** *Washington *Writings* 35.122: This . . . is a left-handed way to make money. **1807** *Salmagundi* 307: Although we are indebted to the world for little else than left-handed favors. **1809** Irving *History* 2.230: Nor did he omit . . . to bestow some thousand left-handed compliments upon the sovereign people. **1813** *Adams-Waterhouse Correspondence* 89: This Malady or rather this Ailment is vulgarly yclept, left handed Wisdom and sometimes crooked Wisdom. **1814** Wirt *Bachelor* 9: This left-handed defence of us, by the critic. **1816** Paulding *Letters*(I) 2.211: He had a queer left-handed way of showing [his good qualities], that one half of the time people took them for faults. **1819** Adams *Memoirs* 4.423: But he was a cunning man. His wisdom was left-handed. **1832** Barney *Memoir* 1-2: The King, upon whom he had bestowed many a *left-handed blessing*. TW 217-8. Cf. Tilley L578. See **S186**.

L97   As long as one's **Leg**

1816 UBrown in *MHM* 10 (1915) 364: [I] am presented with a tax bill so long as my leg. Svartengren 283. See **A115**.

L98   As right as one's left **Leg**

1807 *Salmagundi* 78: Linkum as right as my left leg. *Oxford* 677; TW 218(3).

L99   To be on one's last **Legs**

1767 EWheelock in *Wheelock's Indians* 56: He knows he is upon his last legs. **1788** *Politician* 25: I shall be upon my last legs. **1827** Watterston *Wanderer* 209: He has run through his means . . . and is now empathically [sic] on his last legs. Barbour 107(3); *Oxford* 443; TW 218(5).

L100   To be tied by the **Leg**

1759 *Washington *Writings* 2.337: I am now tied by the Leg and must set Inclination aside. **1781** ABrasher in *Clinton Papers* 6.690: I look only to the means of preserving a family from starving . . . which if I had

done before, and not permitted myself to be tied by the leg.

L101   To pull one's **Leg**

1821 Gallatin *Diary* 184: I really think father, in a covert way, pulls his leg. NED Leg 2; Partridge 476.

L102   To stand on one's own **Legs**

1653 Keayne *Apologia* 27: I must have stood upon my own legs or fallen into greater straits, 28: So that I begin . . . to stand upon my own legs. a**1656** Bradford *History* 1.127: They must then looke to stand on their owne leggs. a**1700** Hubbard *New England* 238. **1740** Belcher *Papers* 2.274, **1741** 365, 418, 420: So you must stand upon your own legs. **1741** *Georgia Records* 23.8. **1741** Stephens *Journal*(II) 1.18. **1745** *Georgia Records* 24.440: Poor white people . . . can Stand once upon their own Legs, **1749** 25.368-9. **1776** Adams *Works* 9.384: We must . . . stand upon our own legs or fail. **1786** Smith *Diary* 2.65: It may give him a Discharge, & leave me upon my own Leggs. *Oxford* 770; Tilley L194. See **F259**.

L103   To give **Leg-bail**

1774 Sargent *Loyalist* 125: Pay your debts at the tavern by giving leg-bail. **1775** Freneau *Poems* 1.136: I gave them leg-bail in a terrible shower. **1806** Fanning *Narrative* 199: We had given them the slip, and meant to show them a yankee trick, by giving them leg-bail, 207. **1809** Weems *Marion* 204: The rest, by giving good *leg-bail*, made their escape. *Oxford* 454; TW 218.

L104   To get the **Length** of one's foot

1776 Lee *Papers* 2.247: You really in the vulgar phrase seem to have got the length of their foot. **1787** Cutler *Life* 1.302: Though Duer assures me I have got the length of his foot. *Oxford* 456; Tilley L202.

L105   He has a short **Lent** who must repay at Easter

1738 Franklin *PR* 2.193: He that would have a short Lent, let him borrow Money to be repaid at Easter, **1758** *WW* 348: Those have a short Lent . . . who owe Money to be paid at Easter. *Oxford* 728; Tilley L204.

L106   The **Less** said the better

1789 Baldwin *Life and Letters* 400: The less is said and done upon the Subject the better for his character. TW 218.

L107   A **Liar** is always a coward

1807 Randolph (J) *Letters* 39: A liar is always a coward.

L108   A **Liar** needs a good memory

1702 Mather *Magnalia* 2.473: A lyar, we say, had need have a good memory. **1722** *New-England Courant* in Buckingham *Specimens* 1.76: *Oportet mendacem esse memoriam. A liar . . . had need have a good memory.* **1797** Cobbett *Porcupine* 6.82: A liar ought to have a good memory. **1805** Paine *Another Callender* 2.986: Liars ought to have good memories. Barbour 108(1); *Oxford* 457-8; Tilley L219.

L109   **Liberty** is sweet

1637 JWhite in *Winthrop Papers(A)* 3.335: As Liberty is sweet soe is it apte (as it is with sweet meats) to allure men to Excess. **1807** Janson *Stranger* 323: Liberty, to be sure, is sweet. Cf. *Oxford* 458; Tilley L223.

L110   **Liberty** often degenerates into licentiousness

1762 Watts *Letter Book* 101: And sweet Liberty often degenerates into Licentiousness. Cf. *Oxford* 458, 831; Tilley L225, 226; Whiting L224-6.

L111   **Liberty** ought to be dearer than life

1786 WWhiting in American Antiquarian Society, *Proceedings* NS 66(1956) 158: Whose maxim is that a mans Liberty ought to be dearer to him then his Life. Cf. *Oxford* 456; Whiting F612, 613. See **F291**.

L112   **Liberty Hall**

c**1816** Durang *Memoir* 55: We instantly put on the air of consequence and entered Liberty Hall. NED Hall 11; *Oxford* 458.

L113   A **Lie** stands on one **Leg**, truth on two

1735 Franklin *PR* 2.8: A Lie stands on 1 leg, Truth on 2. **1767** Ames *Almanacs* 387: A lye stands upon one leg, truth upon two. Barbour 108(3); Tilley L235.

L114   A **Lie** with a latchet

1647 Ward *Simple Cobler* 49: When I hear a lye with a latchet, that reaches up to his throat that first forged it. *Oxford* 460; Tilley L238.

L115   To cram a **Lie** down one's throat

1755 Indian Trader in McDowell *Documents* 2.60: The Lie being cramed down the Second Man's Throat. NED Throat 3c. Cf. *Oxford* 460; Tilley T268.

L116   To **Lie** faster than one speaks

1732 Belcher *Papers* 1.232: For he commonly lyes faster than he speaks. Cf. *Oxford* 829; Tilley T400.

L117   To **Lie** is better than to stand, *etc.*

1787 Hopkinson *Miscellaneous Essays* 2.317: It is a common saying among the poor of Indostan, that to lie is better than to stand, to sleep is better than to wake, but death is best of all, for it delivers them from the cruelty of their nabobs.

L118   As large as **Life**

1815 Dow *Journal* 341: A stone "image," large as life, denoting great antiquity. **1816** Fidfaddy *Adventures* 2: Suffer events as large as life. Barbour 108(2); *Oxford* 442; TW 219(3).

L119   He that loses his **Life**, *etc.*

1643 RSaltonstall in *Saltonstall Papers* 1.134: The German Proverb, which saith, He that loseth his life in an unnecessary quarrel or danger dies the Devills Martyr.

L120   **Life** has no peer

1630 *Winthrop Papers(A)* 2.204: Of all outward things life hath no peer. Cf. Whiting L246.

L121   **Life** is a span

1668 EWeld in Alden *Epitaphs* 3.42: The life of man Is like a span. **1808** Hitchcock *Poetical Dictionary* 25: Our day is at best but a span. *Oxford* 461-2; Tilley L251.

L122   **Life** is short

1802 *Port Folio* 2.123: Life is short. **1806** Hitchcock *Works* 30: The life of man is short, they say, 31. **1809** Asbury *Journal*

2.615: Life is short. *Oxford* 19; TW 220(10). Cf. Whiting L245. See **A122**.

L123   A **Life** of leisure and a life of laziness are two things

1746 Franklin *PR* 3.65: A Life of leisure and a life of laziness, are two things, **1758** *WW* 343.

L124   A short **Life** and a merry one

1697 Chalkley *God's Great Love* 345: It is better to live a merry Life and short. **1702** Mather *Magnalia* 1.173: To lead "a short life and a merry." **c1725** Byrd *Another Secret Diary* 472: Among men of tast & Spirit, who choose a merry life and a short. **1796** Cobbett *Porcupine* 3.391. **1803** Davis *Travels* 380. **1818** Fearon *Sketches* 281: Yet to all men whose desire only is to be rich, and to live a short life but a merry one, I have no hesitation in recommending New Orleans. **1824** Flint *Recollections* 324: The present is their day, and "dum vivimus, vivamus," in other words "a short life and a merry one," their motto. *Oxford* 728; TW 220(1).

L125   To be the **Life** and soul of (whatever)

a1770 Johnson *Writings* 1.39: He was . . . the life and soul of the whole affair. **1784** Smyth *Tour* 2.160: Major Lewis was also the life and soul of the troops. **1814** *Kennon Letters* 36.236: Kennon is usually the soul and body [of the party]. **1818** Royall *Letters* 143: His wife . . . (is) the life and soul of the Bluff. **1823** Bache *Notes* 236: Perez was the soul of the party. NED Life 5.

L126   To love as (one's) **Life**

a1672 Bradstreet *Works* 396: Commend me to the man [her husband] more loved than life. **1720** Walter *Choice Dialogue* 2: Blasphemies he loves as his Life. **1747** Stith *History* 72: [He] loved them as his Life. **1807** JAdams in *Adams-Warren Correspondence* 337: My wife and children, whom I loved more than my own life. Whiting L252.

L127   Where **Life** is concerned no delay is too long

1692 Bulkeley *Will* 233: And, *In vita hominis nulla cunctatio longa*, where the life of man is concerned, no delay for due deliberation &c. is too long.

L128   While there is **Life** there is hope

1781 Webb *Correspondence* 2.365: While life remains there is room for hope. **1790** Adams *Works* 9.569: And believe me yours *dum spiro* &c. **1793** Drinker *Journal* 218, **1793** *Not So Long Ago* 70. **1800** WFaris in *MHM* 28(1933) 234: While there is life thare is hopes. **1802** Harmon *Sixteen Years* 58: But where there is *life* there is generally *hope* also. **1804** *Monthly Anthology* 1.275: While there is life, there may be hope. Barbour 109(13); *Oxford* 462; TW 220(15).

L129   To help at a dead **Lift**

1653 Keayne *Apologia* 56: But I kept this private to myself . . . knowing this would help me at a dead lift. **1679** BTompson in Jantz 158: To help this province at a dead lift. **1688** Fitzhugh *Letters* 246: An handsom Cupboard of plate . . . is a sure friend at a dead lift. **1700** WWinthrop in *Winthrop Papers(B)* 6.69. **1747** Johnson *Writings* 3.193. **1762** Watts *Letter Book* 6: The Tipling Soldiery that used to help us out at a dead lift are gone to drink it in a warmer Region. **1775** Freneau *Poems* 1.192: To help a sinner at so dead a lift. **1780** *New-York Gazette* in *Newspaper Extracts(II)* 5.107: There's something that tells me—who's at a dead lift. **1791** Dennie *Letters* 88: My Spirits . . . are ready, as Sancho phrases it, to help me at a dead lift. **1811** Taggart *Letters* 375. **1831** Beecher *Autobiography* 2.250: I spent sixteen of the best years of my life at a dead lift in boosting. *Oxford* 367-8; Tilley L271. See **S141**.

L130   As clear as **Light**

1644 Williams *Writings* 3.109: It is cleare as the light. **1778** Paine *American Crisis* 1.125: What we have now to do is as clear as light. **1821** JRogers in *Ruffin Papers* 1.248: The theory is clear as light to my apprehension. Svartengren 363; Whiting L259.

L131   To differ as **Light** from darkness (*varied*)

1676 Williams *Writings* 5.273: Differ as much as . . . Light from Darkness. **1728** Byrd *Dividing Line* 127: But Orion had done all; which was as Opposite to Truth, as Light is to darkness, or Modesty to Impudence. **1777** JWereat in *McIntosh Papers* 67: As diametrically opposite to truth as Light to darkness. **1793** Rush *Letters* 2.741: A disease on the cause and cure of which they differed as widely as light differs from darkness. Cf. Lean 2.860: Day. See **D44**.

L132   To stand in one's own Light

1775 Willard *Letters* 165: Dr. Smith . . . who seldom stands in his own light. **1796** Weems *Letters* 2.34: With all due submission I think you stand prodigiously in your own light. **1809** Sumter *Letters* 41: It was foolish . . . to stand so much in her own light. *Oxford* 770; Whiting L264.

L133   A Lightening before death

1769 JParker in Franklin *Papers* 16.202: On Monday Morning he seemed better than for some Time before, but it was only a little lightning before Death. *Oxford* 463; Tilley L277.

L134   After Lightning comes thunder

1789 Brown *Power* 1.25: After the lightning comes the thunder. *Oxford* 464; Tilley L281.

L135   As quick as Lightning

1687 Taylor *Poems* 40: Though mine Affections Quick as Lightning fly. **1764** Franklin *Papers* 11.382: Quick as the Flashes of Lightning. a**1767** Evans *Poems* 97: Quick as the lightning darts from pole to pole. **1776** Case *Poems* 3: Quick as lightning. **1777** *Pennsylvania Evening Post* in *Newspaper Extracts(II)* 1.264. **1778** Carver *Travels* 484. **1781** *New Jersey Gazette* in *Newspaper Extracts(II)* 5.182. **1785** Adams(A) *Letters* 234. **1785** Adams *Works* 8.258: The King replied, as quick as lightning. **1787** *American Museum* 1.59: The perception of a woman is as quick as lightning. **1791** Bartram *Travels* 114. **1793** Campbell *Travels* 14. c**1800** Paine *Works* 218: Quick as heat lightning—and as harmless too. **1803** Paine *Lines* 2.1102: Quick as the lightning's vivid flash. **1807** JAdams in *Adams-Warren Correspondence* 327. **1808** M'Nemar *Kentucky* 21: Quick as the lightning's flash. a**1811**

Henry *Account* 41. **1814** Palmer *Diary* 93: He went head long down stairs quicker than a chain of lightning through a goosbury bush. **1815** Porter *Journal* 2.136. **1830** Cooper *Letters* 2.5. Barbour 109(8); Whiting L268.

L136   As swift as Lightning

a**1786** Ladd *Remains* 45: Swift as lightning's rapid flash. **1797** Baily *Journal* 278: Our boat passed by as swift as lightning. **1809** Weems *Marion* 117. Barbour 109(3); Whiting L269.

L137   To fly (etc.) like Lightning

1754 Johnson *Writings* 4.14: It flies like lightning. **1769** *Johnson Papers* 6.595: This News went to Albany like lightning. **1771** Hearne *Journey* 228: When he put it to his mouth it apparently slipped down his throat like lightning. **1774** Stiles *Diary* 1.485. **1775** AA in *Adams FC* 1.204. **1775** Pickering *Life* 1.63. **1777** Wister *Journal* 129: He darted like lightening out at the front door. **1778** AScammel in Pickering *Life* 1.204: spread. **1781** Oliver *Origin* 58: It echoed to their Shores with the Rapidity of Lightning. **1789** Anburey *Travels* 1.113: dart. **1794** Adams *Writings* 1.254: darted. **1799** Freneau *Prose* 412: ran. **1808** Fraser *Letters and Journals* 76: Thus skimming along like lightning. **1812** Luttig *Journal* 38: went off. **1815** *Port Folio* 3NS 6.214. **1816** Ker *Travels* 96-7: darted. **1819** Noah *Travels* 292: pass. **1822** Randolph(J) *Letters* 239: I mounted Wildfire . . . and came home like a flash of lightning. **1822** Watterston *Winter* 27: darted. TW 222(16).

L138   Every Like is not the same

1674 Josselyn *Account* 88: *The proverb old is here fulfill'd in me, That every like is not the same you see.* *Oxford* 464; Tilley A167, L288.

L139   Like for like

1794 DJarratt in *W&MCQ* 3S 8(1952) 364: He wished to return the parson like for like. **1796** Smith(EH) *Diary* 120: On the common principle of "Like for like," I should be justified in sending you a short letter. NED Like C2.

Like

L140 Like produces like

1803 Paine *To the Citizens* 2.928: *Like will always produce like.* **1822** Weems *Penn* 6: Like generally begets like. *Oxford* 464; TW 222(2).

L141 Like to like (*varied*)

1783 Williams *Penrose* 246: Like to like. **1818** Fessenden *Ladies Monitor* 128: Like seeks its likeness, block-heads marry fools. **1835** Floy *Diary* 153: Of course I liked him somewhat the better, as like loves like. *Oxford* 465; Whiting L272.

L142 Like it or lump it

1791 S.P.L. *Thoughts* 77: As you like it, you may lump it. *Oxford* 464; TW 223(1).

L143 As pale as a **Lily**

1822 Weems *Penn* 39: Pale as a blighted lily. TW 223(1).

L144 As white as a **Lily**

1799 Carey *Porcupiniad* 2.35: It's colour is as lily white. Barbour 110(3); Whiting L279.

L144a Lily-white

1650 Bradstreet *Works* 142: My lilly white when joyned with her red. **1786** Winslow *Broadside* 195. **1787** Tyler *Contrast* 48: The faces of the beaux are of such a lily-white hue. **1788** *Politician* 47: gloves. **1792** Smith *Life and Correspondence* 2.361: hand. **1809** *Port Folio* 2NS 2.375: hands. **1809** Weems *Marion* 42: hands. **1813** Gerry *Diary* 212: cheek. **1814** Littell *Festoons* 6: That lily-white, that rosy red. **1821** Knight *Poems* 2.72: robe. Whiting L279a.

L145 A **Lily** among thorns

1781 Asbury *Journal* 1.404: He is a lily among thorns. Whiting L280.

L146 Lime makes the father rich, *etc.*

1795 Adams *D and A* 3.225: The German farmers say that Lime makes the father rich, but the Grandson poor—i.e. exhausts the Land. Lean 1.416; *Oxford* 465.

L147 As straight as a **Line**

1751 James Birket, *Some Cursory Remarks* (New Haven, 1916) 64: Streets . . . all Straight as a Line. **1774** Schaw *Journal* 83: Palmetto tree . . . as straight as a line. **1778**

Paine *American Crisis* 1.125: The way to it is as straight as a line. *Oxford* 778; Whiting L301.

L148 To chalk a **Line**

1782 *Washington Writings* 25.223: I . . . wish that Congress would chalk a line for me to walk by in the business. NED Chalk *v.* 4c.

L149 As pale as **Linen**

1793 Campbell *Travels* 307: Pontinac turned as pale as linen.

L150 Choose not **Linen**, girls or gold by candle-light

1737 Franklin *PR* 2.168: Fine linnen, girls and gold so bright, Chuse not to take by candle-light. *Oxford* 122; Tilley W682.

L151 To wash one's dirty **Linen**

1809 Fessenden *Pills* 45: To "wash his dirty linen." NED Linen 3a; *Oxford* 863.

L152 As bold as a **Lion**

1650 Bradstreet *Works* 243: O're mountains, rocks and hills as lions bold. **1654** Johnson *Wonder-Working* 30: Bold as Lions. **1776** JThaxter in Stiles *Letters* 43: Fellows, who went like the righteous bold as Lions. **1777** Moore *Diary* 1.429: Come on, my brave boys, now as bold as a lion. **1777** Munford *Patriots* 470. **1782** Trumbull *Satiric Poems* 181. **1784** Chipman *Writings* 22. **1825** Austin *Literary Papers* 117. **1844** Paulding *Letters(II)* 362. *Oxford* 72; Whiting L305.

L153 As brave as a **Lion**

1824 Pintard *Letters* 2.154: He was a gallant lad & brave as a lion. Barbour 110(1); TW 224(2).

L154 As fierce as a **Lion**

1650 Bradstreet *Works* 166: My heart sometimes as fierce as Lion bold. **1676** Williams *Writings* 5.450: As fierce and Cruel as Lyons. Barbour 110(2); *Oxford* 72; Whiting L305, 311.

L155 As strong as a **Lion**

1650 Bradstreet *Works* 364: Stronger than Lions ramping for their prey. **1814** Wirt *Bachelor* 76: As strong and as brave as a young lion. **1826** Pintard *Letters* 2.226: He is as muscular & strong as a little Lion. TW 224(2); Whiting L324.

L156 If one plays with a **Lion**, let him beware of its paw

1797 Foster *Coquette* 82: If she will play with a lion, let her beware of his paw, I say.

L157 If the **Lion** says the lamb is a fox, it must be so

1653 Keayne *Apologia* 48: For if the lion will say the lamb is a fox, it must be so, the lamb must be content to leave it. **1789** RPutnam in Cutler *Life* 1.447: It is dangerous to quarrel with that power who may determine a fox's ears to be horns. Lean 3.509.

L158 The **Lion** and the lamb

1785 Adams(S) *Writings* 4.314-5: Will the Lion ever associate with the Lamb or the Leopard with the Kid? 343. **1797** Hamilton *Papers* 20.515: The *Lion* and the *Lamb* are to lie down together. **1802** WEaton in *Barbary Wars* 2.197: When the Lyon and the lamb shall lie down together, 298. **1812** Jefferson *Writings* 13.119: The lion and the lamb lie down in peace together. **1814** Palmer *Diary* 114: The time may yet come when the Lamb and the Lion shall lye down in peace together. **1820** Jefferson *Writings* 15.263. **1827** Watterston *Wanderer* 67: The lion seemed to repose with the lamb; the eagle to sport with the dove; and oil to unite with water. Cf. Isa. 11.6.

L159 A **Lion** in God's cause

1727 Danforth *Poems* 175.87-8: 'Gainst Sin did Lions in God's Cause appear, But in their own, they Lambs for Meekness were. *Oxford* 504; Whiting L333. See **L162**.

L160 A **Lion** in the way

1720 *Letter* in *Colonial Currency* 2.238: Their would not be so many Lyons and Bears, in the Plain way to your releif. **1777** JLovell in Sparks *Correspondence* 1.414: I never ask myself whether there may not be a lion in the way. **1786** JAdams in *Warren-Adams Letters* 2.276: I never heard or read of Sluggards, who saw so many fantastical Lions in the way, as our People appear to have seen since the Peace. **1793** Brackenridge *Modern* 168. **1796** Weems *Letters*

2.31: Much rather had I have met the Nemean Lyon in my path than that cold frosty monosyllable. **1824** *Tales* 2.41. *Oxford* 466-7; Whiting L330.

L161 The **Lion's** mouth

1770 Carter *Diary* 1.374: I will not put myself out of the way at any time from keeping out of a Lion's mouth. **1832** Barney *Memoir* 102: It would be running foolishly into the lion's mouth. *Oxford* 467; Whiting L332.

L162 Of **Lions** to make lambs

1803 Jackson *Correspondence* 1.70: But as soon as I got upon my legs, from the fierceness of lyons, they softned down to the Gentleness of lambs. Whiting L333. See **L14, 159**.

L163 To beard the **Lion**

1689 Randolph *Letters* 6.315: It would be better to take a lion by the beard than to demand money of this incensed people. **1797** Callender *Annual Register 1796* 23: We cannot as yet take the British Lion by the beard. **1828** Jackson *Correspondence* 3.427: The coalition have "bearded the lion in his den." *Oxford* 35; TW 224(12).

L164 To fight like **Lions**

a**1788** Jones *History* 1.292: They fought like lions. **1813** Wirt *Letters* 1.358: We should have fought like lions. Whiting L345.

L165 To roar like a **Lion**

1752 *Independent Reflector* 109: I beseech you to roar like a Lion against those useless Curs. Barbour 110(4); Whiting L358.

L166 To see (show) the **Lions**

1740 *Byrd Letters* in *VHM* 37(1929) 33: When He comes to England . . . you will be so good as to shew Him the Lions, & introduce him into other good Company. **1778** BWentworth in *Winslow Papers* 35: I'd seen the Lions and other great curiosities in this vast metropolis. **1789** [1777] Anburey *Travels* 2.31: [A captured British officer said to an old woman staring at him]: "So, you old fool, you must come out and see the lions." [To which she replied]: "Lions! lions! I declare now I think you look more like lambs!" **1820** Hodgson *Letters* 1.372: My steam-boat companions went to see the Lions. **1835** Smith *Letters* 356: These crowds, at least in Washington, go to see the lion and nothing else. *Oxford* 468; TW 224(16).

L167   To throw at a **Lion** with corks
1745 JMitchell in *Colden Letters* 8.316: And to trust to them entirely, is only *Leonem subere excipere,* (as the Latins say) to throw at a Lyon with Corks instead of Stones.

L168   Wake not the sleeping **Lion**
c1825 Tyler *Prose* 128: Do not let us by futile altercations wake the sleeping lion. *Oxford* 863; Tilley L317.

L169   To keep a stiff upper **Lip**
1815 *Massachusetts Spy* in Thornton *Glossary* 1.509: I kept a stiff upper lip. **1832** Wirt *Letters* 2.377: Be it known to you, I can keep as stiff an upper lip as most people. Barbour 111(3); *Oxford* 774; TW 225(4).

L170   To speak from the **Lips** but not the heart
1755 *Johnson Papers* 1.629: They have spoke as [?*for* us] fair outwardly, but while their Lips were smooth, their Hearts were full of Poison against us, **1764** 4.467-8: He . . . Expected they would speak from their hearts, and not their Lips, **1774** 12.1089: They were amusing them with Speeches from the Lips only, 1090: It is from their Lips only, and not from their Hearts. **1780** Pierre Tomma in *Baxter Manuscripts* 18.339: Our Language to the Britains is from our Lips only, but when we address the Americans & French its from our hearts. **1792** Putnam *Memoirs* 337: I . . . speak to you from my Heart, not from my Lip's only. **1794** Savery *Journal* 85: We do not speak it with our lips only, it is the language of our hearts. TW 178(3); Whiting L376.

L171   **Lip**-labor
1652 Williams *Writings* 7.75: *Hypocrites* pray but in a *form* and *lip-labour.* Whiting L378.

L172   **Lip** service
1795 Dennie *Letters* 145: This . . . has pro-

cured me a host of friends, not lip service friends. TW 225(6).

L173   To be on the black **List**
1775 AA in *Adams FC* 1.194: His name . . . was upon the black list. NED Black list, Suppl. Black list. See **B264.**

L174   **Listeners** seldom hear good of themselves
1722 Franklin *Papers* 1.41: I met indeed with the common Fate of *Listeners,* (who *hear no good of themselves*), **1759** 8.313: Another Instance confirming the old Adage, That Listners seldom hear any Good of themselves. **1812** Adams *Writings* 4.292: Listeners they say seldom hear anything good of themselves. *Oxford* 468; TW 225.

L175   Better a **Little** with content, than much with contention
1747 Franklin *PR* 3.105: Better is a little with content than much with contention. **1790** Adams *New Letters* 37: Better is a little with contentment than great Treasure; and trouble therewith. Whiting L388. See **M251, W78.**

L176   Better risk a **Little** than lose the whole
1780 UHay in *Heath Papers* 3.25: On the principle of its being better to risque a little than lose the whole. See **N113.**

L177   Every **Little** helps
1787 EHazard in *Belknap Papers* 1.477: A guinea is a guinea, and every little helps, **1789** 2.195. **1794** RBlackledge in *Blount Papers* 2.442: Every Little helps. **1796** WHeth in Hamilton *Papers* 20.347: Every little may help. *Oxford* 228; TW 225(2). See **S360, 377.**

L178   Every **Little** makes a mickle
1732 Franklin *Papers* 1.242: Every little makes a mickle, **1737** *PR* 2.165, **1758** *WW* 345: Many a Little makes a Mickle. **1812** Hitchcock *Social* 167: And a great many *littles,* you must be sensible, make a *great* deal. **1814** Palmer *Diary* 118: Many a little makes a mickle — as the old saying is. *Oxford* 508; Whiting L402. See **G1, M154.**

L179 He who gains **Little** gains much

1802 Weems *Letters* 2.225: He who gains *little,* gains *much.*

L180 **Little** said tends to peace

1814 Palmer *Diary* 231: For little said will tend to peace. Cf. *Oxford* 472; Whiting L399. See **L86.**

L181 Speak **Little** do much

1755 Franklin *PR* 5.471: Speak little, do much. Whiting W642. See **W309.**

L182 Those who do **Little** expect the most

1801 Story *Shop* 108: Now, says a proverb, of which there's a host, "Those, who but little do, expect the most."

L183 To say **Little** but think the more (*varied*)

1779 Galloway *Diary* 165: So [I] said little to her but I think the more. **1782** Hopkinson *Miscellaneous Essays* 1.260: Yet tho' he disdains to murmur, he thinks, nevertheless, the more. **1819** ASBCabell in *VHM* 47(1939) 152: Wirt and Carrington say nothing, but like the widower's parrot, they, I suppose, think the more. *Oxford* 701; TW 319: Say (1); Whiting M685. Cf. Thompson *Motif-Index* 6.567-8.

L184 Where **Little** (much) is given, little (much) is required

1787 EHowell in *MHM* 24(1929) 28: To whom little is given little is required. **1800** Adams *New Letters* 235: Where much is given, much is required. Cf. Whiting L401, M790.

L185 You'd do **Little** for God if the Devil were dead

1763 Franklin *Papers* 10.303: *Why God no kill the Devil?* It [the answer] is to be found in the Scottish Proverb; *Ye'd do little for God and the Deel were Dead. Oxford* 191; Tilley L371.

L186 As sure as one is **Living**

1783 Williams *Penrose* 249: As sure as we are living. **1831** ABalch in Jackson *Correspondence* 4.315: You will see this prophecy verified as sure as you live. *Oxford* 789; TW 225(2). See **A68.**

L187 **Live** and learn

1784 *Belknap Papers* 2.373[24] : But we must, as the old saying is, "live and learn." **1790** Freneau *Poems* 3.26: Here strives to live — and learn. **1792** Brackenridge *Modern* 126: as the saying is. **1811** *Kennon Letters* 32.344. Barbour 111(1); *Oxford* 473; TW 225-6(4).

L188 **Live** and let live

1785 Adams *Works* 8.300: The honest old principle of "live and let live," **1790** 9.569: The old maxim. **1796** Weems *Letters* 2.10: the generous rule. **1799** *Washington Writings* 37.357: Live and let live is, in my opinion, a maxim founded in true policy; and is one I am disposed to pursue. **1801** Weems *Letters* 2.170: the old adage, **1809** *Marion* 173: the royal law, **1811** *Gambling* 12: That Golden saying. **1832-3** Cooper *Letters* 6.323: We shall be half-a-dozen of live-and-let-live sort of fellows. Barbour 111(3); *Oxford* 473; TW 226(7).

L189 The longer we **Live** the more we learn

1815 Palmer *Diary* 214: I find the longer we live the more we learn of human Nature. TW 226(5); Tilley L393.

L190 To stick in one's **Liver**

1759 Franklin *Papers* 8.313: It sticks in his liver, I find. See **C349, G51.**

L191 To have the **Loaf** under one's arm

1773 *New York Gazetteer* in *Newspaper Extracts(I)* 10.30: It was common for him to say, that now he had got the loaf [his wife's estate] under his own arm, that he would cut it as it pleased him.

L192 **Loaves** and fishes

1765 JWatts in *Aspinwall Papers* 2.575: I am much mistaken if he leaves his successor much to do about the Loaves and Fishes than can be cleared off, **1774** 2.712: Those loaves and fishes are a convenient diet. **1779** AA in *Adams FC* 3.207: It begins to be considered as rather burdensome and no loaves and fishes to be caught. **1779** *New Jersey Gazette* in *Newspaper Extracts(II)* 3.85-6: But I fear too many are following for the loaves and fishes. Take them away and few will follow the empty dishes. **1780** Lee *Papers* 3.446: I might have partook of the loaves and the fishes which wou'd have been at their disposal. **1783** Lee(W) *Letters* 3.940: There has been such a scuffle for the loaves and fishes. **1783** Madison *Papers* 7.90: The hungry suitors for the loaves & fishes of the Administration. **1787** Adams *Works* 5.18: Divided . . . into factions for the loaves and the fishes, 257: Scrambling for loaves and fishes. **1789** EHazard in *Belknap Papers* 2.122: Yet it will not do to be out of the way when the loaves and fishes are dividing, lest it should be thought I have eaten and am satisfied, and my share should be given to somebody who is hungry. **1790** Maclay *Journal* 206: I ever thought since I knew him that he was a loaf-and-fish man. **1791** Adams *Works* 8.508: The Stone House faction will be sure of all the loaves and fishes. **1791** Paine *Rights of Man* 1.282: This government of loaves and fishes. **1796** Barton *Disappointment* 95: We'll now feast on, —the loaves and fishes. **1798** *Newburyport Herald* in Buckingham *Specimens* 2.330: The loaves and fishes which they suppose those in office receive. **1799** Jefferson *Writings* 10.124: The loaves and fishes which arise out of war expenses, **1801** 253: If they could have continued to get all the loaves and fishes . . . they would continue to eulogize. **1802** *Port Folio* 2.271: So the dull *Democrat,* his dosing keeps, And till the *loaves* and *fishes* call him, *sleeps,* **1803** 3.64: No harpies, but our own, Shall gorge the public loaves and fish. **1806** *Weekly* 1.84: To taste the loaves and fishes. **1808** Hitchcock *Poetical Dictionary* 83: Can deal out the fishes and loaves to their minions. **1812** VHorne in Knopf *War of 1812* 3.128: [The] turnings of Political trimers to engross the loaves & fishes. **1814** Adams *Works* 6.502: They follow and hosanna for the loaves and fishes. **1826** WBiglow in Buckingham *Specimens* 2.290: When Adams was named for the office he claimed By the greedy for loaves and for fishes. *Oxford* 476; Whiting L414.

L193 Lob's dominion

1830 Ames *Mariner's* 125: A beverage which an English sailor on board very appropriately characterized as *"lob's dominion,* two buckets of water and an old shoe." Cf. *Oxford* 476-7; Tilley L403.

L194 As red as a Lobster

1821 Knight *Poems* 2.152: Her lips like a lobster so red. Svartengren 248; TW 226.

L195 As dead as a Log

1801 *Port Folio* 1.143: Would suck till dead as log. **1806** Fessenden *Modern Philosopher* 226: As dead as a log. Cf. TW 227(2).

L196 As motionless as Logs

1813 Weems *Drunkard* 82: Some literally *dead drunk,* and motionless as logs. Svartengren 384.

L197 As still as a Log

1745 JBartram in *Colden Letters* 3.131: For there y[e] pain & cramp seemed y[e] worst which engaged me to ly as still as A log.

L198 To lie like Logs

1709 Lawson *Voyage* 190: They lie as unconcern'd, as if they were so many Logs of Wood.

L199 To go to Loggerheads

1755 Laurens *Papers* 1.304: Some of them went to Loggerheads. **1764** *Beekman Papers* 1.469: It will not do for me to go to Loggerheads with them. **1768** *Johnson Papers* 6.112. **1769** Woodmason *Journal* 150, 158. **1775** NGreene in *Naval Documents* 2.576: Here we are at Loggerheads, 899: Lord Dunmore is at Logger heads with the Virginians. **1785** *Massachusetts Centinel* in Buckingham *Specimens* 2.35. **1787** Adams *Works* 6.57. **1787** ADonald in Jefferson *Papers* 12.427. a**1788** Jones *History* 1.22. **1792** Belknap *Foresters* 180. **1801** DRoss in *Bingham's Maine* 2.1138: Almost at loggerheads who shall have the most. **1803** Paine *To Mr. Jefferson* 2.1101: Some Feds, Who, in their wisdom got to loggerheads. **1805** Plumer *Memorandum* 270. **1806** Jefferson *Writings* 11.126: The whole were to be set to loggerheads to destroy one another. **1810** Mackay *Letters* 108: Our cabinet at Washington is at Loggerheads. **1815** Humphreys *Yankey* 33: If ever we Yankeys cum to loggerheads, we'll show whose heads are hardest. TW 227.

L200 To chop **Logic**

1800 Ames *Letters* 1.289: The democrats would trust to the rights of man and chopping logic. **1802** Cutler *Life* 2.65: Bacon is often up, chopping his logic, but never without exciting ridicule. **1804** Brackenridge *Modern* 368: What harm, in letting pedants chop logic . . . in the seminaries. **1807** Weems *Murder* 6: [He] talks politics, and chops logic. *Oxford* 122; Whiting L424.

L201 **Log-rolling**

1820 Flint *Letters* 215: Combinations are formed for effecting particular purposes. These are called *log rolling*; a very significant metaphor, borrowed from the practice of several farmers uniting in rolling together large timber to be burnt. **1822** Murphey *Papers* 1.251: Intrigue and Bargaining (they call it Log-Rolling here) are at the Bottom of everything. a**1824** Marshall *Kentucky* 2.179: [It] became quite common, and notorious, under the denomination of "log rolling" — alluding to an agricultural practice of exchanging help to each other among neighbours, for the purpose of clearing the logs off the new land. **1829** Jackson *Correspondence* 4.109: That flagicious *logg-rolling legislation*, **1832** 4.465: To stop this corrupt log-rolling system of legislation, **1833** 5.165: The log rolling system of Internal Improvements. TW 227(6).

L202 **London** lickpenny

1776 Curwen *Journal* 1.165: London . . . is, in the peasant phrase, a sad lickpenny. *Oxford* 478; Whiting L429.

L203 **London** measure

1647 Ward *Simple Cobler* 24: In a word, whatever Christianity or Civility will allow, I can afford with *London* measure. NED London.

L204 The **Longer** the worse

1640 TGostlin in *Winthrop Papers(A)* 4.212; I see the longer the worser. *Oxford* 481; Whiting L430.

L205 Long **Looked** for comes at last

1603 TFones in *Winthrop Papers(A)* 1.149: Long looked for comes at last, so sayth our English Proverb. **1741** Stephens *Journal(I)* 2.233: Long wish'd for came at last. **1831** Pintard *Letters* 3.269: Long looked for come at last. *Oxford* 480; Tilley L423.

L206 **Look** before or find yourself behind

1735 Franklin *PR* 2.5: Look before, or you'll find yourself behind. *Oxford* 484; Tilley L433. Cf. Whiting L436.

L207 To **Look** before one leaps

1694 Makemie *Writings* 38: Look before they Leap. **1761** *Boston Gazette* in *Olden Time* 2.30: Look before you leap. **1779** *Washington Writings* 17.144: It was of magnitude sufficient to have made a wise and just people look before they leaped, **1788** 29.510-1: [This] will make all, except desperate men, look before they leap into the dark consequences of rejection. **1810** Colby *Life* 1.54. **1815** JPerkins in *Cabot Family* 2.550: All men sh'd look a little before they take commercial leaps. **1820** Pintard *Letters* 1.319. **1828** *Yankee* 226. **1847** Paulding *Letters(II)* 458: the Old Proverb, **1849** 500. Barbour 112(2); *Oxford* 482; Whiting L435.

L208 To **Look** on is easy

1812 *Port Folio* 2NS 7.130: It's very easy to look on. If you had as much to do as I have, you'd not work any smarter than I do. Whiting W648.

L209 **Lookers-on** see more of the game *(varied)*

1669 WHubbard in *Saltonstall Papers* 1.157: Standers by may be admitted to see more than persons engaged. **1780** Deane *Papers* 4.245: Being but a passenger, I have leasure for observation and . . . am able to see as much of the game as some who play the great hands. **1790** *Universal Asylum* 4.155: A looker on often sees more of the game than those who play. **1799** *Washington Writings* 37.399: A bye stander sees more of the game, generally, than those who are playing it. **1813** Jefferson *Writings* 13.259: I know from experience that profitable suggestions sometimes come from lookers on, 262. **1815** RPeters in Jay *Correspondence* 4.382: At *our* age we are lookers-on, and see the game better than those who play it. *Oxford* 483; Tilley S822.

L210 As smooth as a **Looking-glass**

1773 Franklin *Writings* 6.156: Making . . . the pond . . . as smooth as a looking-glass. **1775** Schaw *Journal* 116: A Sea smooth as a looking glass. See **M189.**

L211 It is one's **Look-out**

1769 Smith *Memoirs(I)* 56: Watts said briefly it is your Look out. TW 228(1).

L212 As crazy as a **Loon**

1812 *The Sophomore* (Warren, Rhode Island, 1812) 15: He was as crazy as a Loon. Barbour 112; TW 228(1).

L213 As drunk as a **Lord**

1744 Hamilton *Itinerarium* 17: The landlady looked after every thing herself, the landlord being drunk as a lord. **1784** Smyth *Tour* 2.312: All as drunk as lords. **1813** Weems *Drunkard* 83, 121. Barbour 112(1); *Oxford* 206; TW 229(1); Tilley L439. See **P286.**

L214 As fine as a **Lord**

1790 Maclay *Journal* 257: Hartley, fine as a lord, met us. Cf. *Oxford* 258; Tilley L443.

L215 As happy as a **Lord**

1822 Watterston *Winter* 22: I am as happy as a lord. TW 229(3). See **K18, P287.**

L216 As merry as my **Lord**

1759 LWood *Journal* in *Essex Institute Historical Collections* 19(1882) 66: And there we Lodgd that Knight as merry as me Lord [a little drunk].

L217 As rich as my **Lord**

1782 SHenderson in *Blount Papers* 1.28: And then Sir am Rich as My Lord. Barbour 112(2); Svartengren 341.

L218 New **Lords** new laws

1775 WEmerson in Hodgkins *Letters* 27: New lords, new laws. **1783** James Moody, *Narrative* (2nd ed., London, 1783) 24: Under new masters, it is hoped, General Arnold has learned new maxims. **1821** Doddridge *Dialogue* 48: But new lords have new laws. *Oxford* 564; Whiting L453.

L219 Give **Losers** leave to speak (*varied*)

1690 WByrd in *VHM* 26(1918) 248: You ought to give ye Loosers leave to Speake. **1692** Bulkeley *Will* 223: So that losers have not leave to speak, or if they do, it is but an aggravation. **1707** Makemie *Writings* 196: I hope it will be no Crime, for Losers to speak. **1746** *Georgia Records* 25.98: People that have been Injur'd its an old Saying have a Right to Speak. **1753** *Independent Reflector* 126: The Sufferer has more than a bare Proverb, to intitle him to complain: 'Tis his legal and indubitable Right, to expostulate the Matter with becoming Animation and Freedom. **1785** DHartley in Jefferson *Papers* 8.587: An English proverb says Losers have a right to complain. *Oxford* 485-6; Whiting L470.

L220 **Losers** are apt to complain

1763 Watts *Letter Book* 117: Loosers are apt to complain, **1764** 285: The Looser is seldom content or satisfyd. Lean 4.38; NED Loser 2.

L221 (Buy and sell) and live by the **Loss**

1749 *Johnson Papers* 1.236: I believe many of the Traders will be Obliged to live by the Loss and not the Profit of their Summers Works. *Oxford* 95; Tilley L459.

L222 The **Loss** of one is the gain of two, *etc.*

1801 TTingey in *Barbary Wars* 1.435: "The Loss of one is the gain of two And the choice of twenty more." Barbour 112(1); *Oxford* 486; TW 229(2); Tilley M337.

L223 Better **Lost** than found

1739 Stephens *Journal(I)* 1.308: [I] concluded that he were better lost than found. *Oxford* 54; Whiting L465. See **R130.**

L224 The **Lot** is cast

1637 Morton *New English Canaan* 292: So now the lott is cast. a1700 Hubbard *New England* 180: But though the lot was cast into the lap, the matter was otherwise disposed by the Lord, 334. NED Lot 1d. See **D174.**

L225 Not care a **Louse**

1780 Sargent *Loyalist* 110: She did not care a louse. NED Louse 1b. Cf. Whiting L474.

L226 Not value a **Louse**

1764 *Paxton Papers* 181: For us, we value not a Louse, A Seat in the Assembly House. Cf. NED Louse 1b; Whiting L474.

L227 Not worth a **Louse**

1742 Belcher *Papers* 2.426: It's generally thôt Trinkalo's not worth a louse. *Oxford* 488; Whiting L475.

L228 For **Love** or money

1647 JJones in *Winthrop Papers*(*A*) 5.159: If love or money would have procured a horse in these parts. **1683** Claypoole *Letter Book* 189: I may serve thee . . . for love and not money. **1724** Talbot *Letters* 158: People . . . can't get them here for love or money. **1734** Belcher *Papers* 2.29. **1735** Chalkley *Journal* 277: Sailors were hard to be got . . . either for Love or Money. **1740** *New-York Weekly Journal* in *Newspaper Extracts*(*I*) 2.38. **1748** Eliot *Essays* 17: Dung, which cannot be had for Love nor Money. **?1757** TBacon in *MHM* 6(1911) 234. **1774** Jones *Journal* 101. **1775** AA in *Adams FC* 1.249: Not a pin is to be purchased for love nor money. **1775** Huntington *Papers* 17. **1775** Schaw *Journal* 217. **1777** JAdams in *Warren-Adams Letters* 1.333. **1777** FBoardman in *Naval Documents* 4.1487. **1780** JEliot in *Belknap Papers* 3.189, **1783** 265: Preachers are so scarce that love or money will not procure them to supply our pulpits. **1785** Hunter *Quebec* 75. **1793** Asbury *Journal* 1.747: The gentleman refused to receive us for love, money, or hospitality's sake. **1793** Campbell *Travels* 299. **1797** JTaylor in Monroe *Writings* 3.387. **1802** Dow *Journal* 127, 136, **1805** 244: And rode on a cart, as a chair could not be obtained for love, nor hired for money, 260. **1805** Parkinson *Tour* 30. **1807** *Port Folio* NS 4.208. **1808** Fraser *Letters and Journals* 110. **1815** Weems *Letters* 3.131: Dr Ewell will not sell his Med. Compan. for love or money. **1817** Cobbett *Year's* 25, **1819** 191. **1821** Pintard *Letters* 2.76. **1823** Bierce *Travels* 83: [I] tried love and money . . . without effect. Barbour 113(14); *Oxford* 493; Tilley L480; Whiting L484.

L229 Hot **Love** soon cool

1747 Johnson *Writings* 1.123: Their hot love

may soon cool. *Oxford* 388; Whiting L484. See **H328.**

L230 In **Love** and war no time should be lost

1777 Munford *Patriots* 451: In love and war no time should be lost. **1784** Washington *Writings* 28.2: Favorable moments in war, as in love, once lost are seldom regained.

L231 **Love** and lordship hate companions

1737 Franklin *PR* 2.167: Love and lordship hate companions. **1811** Rush *Letters* 2.1108: "Where love enters," you know, "he will rule alone, And suffer no co-partner in his throne." *Oxford* 488; Whiting L495.

L232 **Love** at first sight

1777 Wister *Journal* 95: He fell violently in love with Liddy at first sight. **1807** Tyler *Verse* 161: This comes from loving at first sight. **1809** Lindsley *Love* 44. **1809** Weems *Marion* 28: There must be truth in the old saying of *"people's falling in love at first sight."* **1822** Watterston *Winter* 80: We girls . . . are apt to fall in love at first sight. *Oxford* 493; Whiting L496.

L233 **Love**, cough and a smoke cannot be hid

1737 Franklin *PR* 2.167: Love, Cough, and a Smoke, can't well be hid. *Oxford* 488; Tilley L490.

L234 **Love** is blind

1646 JParker in *Hutchinson Papers* 1.174: But love thinks noe ill and yet not blind. **a1700** Saffin *His Book* 191: If Cupid then be blinde. **1735** Ames *Almanacs* 99: Hatred is blind as well as Love. **a1767** Evans *Poems* 47: And there th'unerring archer blind. **1774** AA in *Adams FC* 1.176: The villan, the urchin is deaf as well as blind. **1777** Munford *Patriots* 498: Love, tho' blind, by instinct finds his way. **1809** Freneau *Poems*(*1809*) 2.29. Barbour 113(7); *Oxford* 490; Whiting C634.

L235 **Love** is next neighbor to pity

1787 DHumphreys in *American Museum* 1.487: For love to pity is next neighbour. *Oxford* 628; Tilley P370.

L236 Love is strong as death
1644 Williams *Writings* 3.335: *Love* is strong as *death.* **1764** *Paxton Papers* 254: For Love, Solomon says, is stronger than Death. TW 230(9); Whiting L523.

L237 Love is too dainty a food to live upon
1794 *Washington *Writings* 33.501: Love is too dainty a food to live upon *alone.* Whiting *NC* 439(7). Cf. Tilley M226; Whiting L575-6.

L238 Love makes fools of all
1772 Paterson *Glimpses* 94: Love makes fools of all. Cf. Tilley L558; Whiting L533.

L239 **The Love of money is the root of all evil (*varied*)
1677 Hubbard *Indian* 2.252: Covetousness was and will be the Root of all Evil in every Age of the World. **c1680** Radisson *Voyages* 232: But, O covetousnesse thou art yᵉ cause of many evils. **a1700** Hubbard *New England* 100: The love of money is the root of all evil. **1708** Talbot *Letters* 117: Money . . . the want of that is the root of all Evil. **1718** Chalkley *Observations* 441: *The Love of Money, is the Root of all Evil;* i.e. the inordinate Love of it, and seeking after it. **1719** *Addition* in *Colonial Currency* 1.377, **1720** 2.234: The want, as well as the love of money, is in some sense the root of all evil. **1721** Wise *Word* 7, 168. **1732** Belcher *Papers* 1.211: What won't mankind be guilty of thro' the cursed love of lucre? **1734** *Letter* in *Colonial Currency* 3.45, **1748** 4.360-1, **1750** 440: Covetousness being the Root of all Evils. **1750** Sherman *Almanacs* 219. **1751** *Appendix* in *Colonial Currency* 4.477: The Love, or rather the *Lust* of Money, is the *Root* of all *Evils.* **1773** *Johnson Papers* 8.984: It shall be put into Doctor Deases Slay when he arrives, as well as the Box of the Root of all Evil. **1777** Gordon *Letters* 349. **1777** CTufts in *Adams FC* 2.345: Money is the Root of all Evil. **1778** AA in *Adams FC* 3.6: We are told by the best authority that. **1778** Lee *Letters* 1.439: I know the root of this evil is in the redundance of money. **1780** SHoward in Thornton *Pulpit* 380. **1786** Paine *On Government* 2.406-7: The love of gold and silver may produce covetousness, but covetousness, when not connected with dishonesty, is not properly a vice. It is frugality run to an extreme. **1788** *Politician* 24: That stupid proverb, money is the root of all evil. **1790** EHazard in *Belknap Papers* 2.237: I suspect the root of all evil is at the bottom of this business. **1797** Cobbett *Porcupine* 6.303: *Money,* that cursed root of all evil. **1798** *Echo* 190: And still scarcer with us is that "Root of all evil," That widow of Mammon and child of the Devil. **1801** *Port Folio* 1.69: Covetousness is the root of all evil. **1803** *Steele Papers* 1.364: It was said by some wise man. perhaps Soloman, that money is the root of all evil. **1805** Weems *Hymen* 35. **1806** *Port Folio* NS 2.112: Money, they say, is evil's root. **1808** Rush *Letters* 2.963: Covetousness. **1809** *Port Folio* 2NS 2.86: Covetousness. **1812** Melish *Travels* 232, 531. **1814** Colby *Life* 1.208. **1816** Ker *Travels* 76: In quest of that detested root of all evil, and the only object of our hearts. **1816** Paulding *Letters(I)* 2.167: This is the true significance of money being the root of all evil. **1816** Smith *Life* 19. **1825** *Salem Observer* in *Olden Time* 1.64: Those who bitterly complain of the great dearth of "the root of all evil." Barbour 113(16); *Oxford* 150; Whiting C491.

L240 Love's labor lost
1813 *Port Folio* 3NS 2.630: All this was literally love's labour lost. TW 230(10).

L241 **No **Love like a mother's
1814 *Kennon Letters* 36.235-6: [A mother], whose love for her offspring is proverbially greater than any other affection.

L242 **No **Love to a person unknown
1694 Scottow *Narrative* 312: It hath bin an old saying: *Ignoti nulla Cupido: No Love to a person unknown, and consequently as little hatred.* Cf. *Oxford* 854-5; Whiting U5.

L243 **There are no ugly **Loves, *etc.*
1737 Franklin *PR* 2.168: There are no ugly Loves, nor handsome Prisons. *Oxford* 490; TW 230(12); Tilley L454; Whiting L550.

L244 **There is no **Love lost between them
1777 *New Jersey Gazette* in *Newspaper Ex-*

tracts(*II*) 1.521: There never was any love lost between him and the family of Brunswick. **1778** Gadsden *Writings* 153: There is no love lost between him and I. **1803** Davis *Travels* 408. **1804** *New England Merchants* 19: There is no Love lost on either side. **1809** Lindsley *Love* 17. **1815** Waterhouse *Journal* 19. **1835** Floy *Diary* 196: He loves me, and there is no love lost, it is reciprocated. **1847** Cooper *Letters* 5.231. *Oxford* 492; Tilley L644.

L245 **Love** me little, love me long

1790 *Universal Asylum* 5.84: The proverbial saying, "Love me little, but love me long." **1791** S.P.L. *Thoughts* 77: Love me little love me long. *Oxford* 492; Whiting L568.

L246 **Love** me, love my dog

1775 JAdams in *Warren-Adams Letters* 1.89: But you must love his Dogs if you love him, and forgive a thousand whims. **1776** Gordon *Letters* 323: Love me, love my dog. **1791** S.P.L. *Thoughts* 167. **1797** Ames *Letters* 1.217. **1797** Cobbett *Porcupine* 7.85: says the old precept, **1798** 8.31: that's my motto. **1811** Adams(A) *Letters* 404: As if you love me, proverbially, you must love my dog. Barbour 52: Dog(37); *Oxford* 492; Whiting L569.

L247 **Love** well, whip well

1733 Franklin *PR* 1.313: Love well, whip well. Barbour 113(1). See **R114**.

L248 It is lawful for **Lovers** to lie (*varied*)

a1700 Saffin *His Book* 157: If it be Ever lawfull to lye, it is for a Lover. **1796** Ames *Letters* 1.198: Between friends (as between lovers) a promise is but wind. **1847** Paulding *Letters(II)* 452: Knowing by experience that the promises of Editors are pretty much on a par with the oaths of lovers. *Oxford* 414; Whiting G201, L527, 578. Cf. Tilley J82, L570. See **J52**.

L249 **Lubberland**

c1680 Radisson *Voyages* 151: Imagining that the larks will fall in their mouths roasted. **1759** Eliot *Essays* 134: Unless you can promise Mountains of Gold, and that the Colony that engages in it shall immediately be turned to *Lubber-Land*. **a1772**

Franklin *Writings* 5.536: Till England becomes another Lubberland, where it is fancied that streets are paved with penny-rolls, the houses tiled with pancakes, and chickens, ready roasted, cry, "Come eat me," **1782** 8.607: In short, America is the Land of Labour, and by no means what the English call *Lubberland*, and the French *Pays de Cocagne*, where the streets are said to be pav'd with half-peck Loaves, the Houses til'd with Pancakes, and where the Fowls fly about ready roasted, crying, "*Come eat me!*" **1810** TRJoynes in *W&MCQ* 10(1901) 222: Where they want, I *suppose*, to find land that will produce loaves of bread already baked, and hams of bacon already boiled [of lazy settlers in Kentucky]. **c1820** Bernard *Retrospections* 51: Here was an English agriculturalist just arrived, a firm believer in the doctrine of ready-roasted pigs squeaking "Come, eat me." NED Lubber-land; *Oxford* 495.

L250 As proud (haughty) as **Lucifer**

1692 Randolph *Letters* 7.409: The Collector as proud as Lucifer. **1783** Williams *Penrose* 300: As proud as Lucifer. **1789** EHazard in *Belknap Papers* 2.108: The man . . . is . . . as proud as Lucifer. **1796** Cobbett *Porcupine* 4.217: They can be as haughty as Lucifer, and they can be as mean. **1812** Randall *Miser* 19. **1818** Royall *Letters* 144: This Widow of 70 . . . ignorant and proud as Lucifer. **1822** Watterston *Winter* 36: As proud as Lucifer, and as silent as Pythagoreans. Barbour 114; *Oxford* 651; Whiting L587. See **D113**.

L251 As wise as **Lucifer**

1812 Randall *Miser* 45: There is time enough yet to be as wise as Lucifer.

L252 Better **Luck** next time

1771 *Johnson Papers* 7.1154: Johnson's Boy is turned out to a Girl, better luck I hope next time. *Oxford* 54; TW 231(1).

L253 The **Luck** of a lousy calf

1769 Anne Blair in *W&MCQ* 16(1907) 176: Who knows the luck of a Louisa Calf [a girl should go where there are eligible young men]. TW 231(3). Cf. *Oxford* 496; Tilley L574.

L254 **Luck** will turn

1761 HSmith in Lloyd *Papers* 2.601: Tho' my luck does not seem to have turn'd as yet. Barbour 114(3); TW 231(2).

L255 More by **Luck** than cunning

1782 Lee *Papers* 4.11: A fortunate purchase that I made (more by luck than cunning). 1791 DLewis in Otis *Letters* 1.33: More by good Luck then good Conduckd. *Oxford* 321; Tilley C225. Cf. Whiting H101, 104, 106. See **F277.**

L256 To give one his **Lugs**

1691 Fitzhugh *Letters* 290: I dare venture to give her my Lugs, if in ten years he comply with £20 of the purchase. Cf. NED Lug *sb.*² 2c; TW 115: Ear(2).

L257 Throw your **Lumps** where your love lies

1791 S.P.L. *Thoughts* 77: Throw your lumps where your love lies. Cf. *Oxford* 475; Tilley L541.

L258 To leave in the **Lurch** [The following is a selection from 72 occurrences of the phrase]

1664 Bradstreet *Works* 71: Leave those in the lurch. 1694 *Connecticut Vindicated* 117: *Our* Goliah *leaves us in the Lurch.* 1702 NNoyes in Mather *Magnalia* 1.19: Tradition leaves us in the lurch. 1722 *New-England Courant* in Buckingham *Specimens* 1.74: The rhyming spirit left him in the lurch. 1745 Stephens *Journal(II)* 2.226. 1756 AGarden in *Colden Letters* 5.90: Then I steal a day & leave my Partner in the Lurch. 1766 Paterson *Glimpses* 27: You . . . will be . . . so enchanted with some Dulcinea, that poor pilgarlic will be left in the lurch. 1777 JA in Adams *FC* 2.224: To leave the Continent in the Lurch. 1780 Sargent *Loyalist* 7: And leave religion weeping in the lurch. 1784 Jefferson *Papers* 6.471, 567. 1788 Washington *Writings* 29.474: Left sadly in the lurch. 1809 Fessenden *Pills* 74. 1816 Dow *Journal* 348: The captain ran away with my passage money and things, which left me in the lurch. 1818 Pintard *Letters* 1.142: Since my being injured by Doctor Brown who left me in the lurch for $500. 1821 Knight *Poems* 1.39: And those who leave quite in the lurch, Their own good long-established church. *Oxford* 452-3; TW 231.

L259 To bring to the **Lure**

1637 JWister in *Trelawny Papers* 108: The Company that Came with Narias Haukin hath brought all the rest to their lure, 1639 164: Yf the rest do not turne him to their lure. Whiting L589.

L260 **Lying** rides upon debt's back

1741 Franklin *PR* 2.295: Lying rides upon Debt's back, 1758 *WW* 348. Barbour 114(2); *Oxford* 497.

L261 To have a **Lynx's** eye

1779 Moore *Diary* 2.238: Who finds them out must have a lynx's eye. 1807 *Port Folio* NS 4.207: The piercing eyes of a lynx. TW 231; Whiting L596.

M

M1   As the **Maggot** bites

1777 Munford *Patriots* 484: He says he is a tory, or no tory, a whig or no whig, just as the maggot bites. **1777** EOswald in Webb *Correspondence* 1.357: The whole army . . . wait orders for marching to Peekskill, or perhaps farther down, just as the maggot may bite. **1786** Cutler *Life* 2.239: I have got a new maggot in my head, which sometimes bites pretty smartly. *Oxford* 498; TW 232(3).

M2   To have **Maggots** in the brain

1701 Charles Wolley, *A Two Years Journal* (London, 1701), ed. E. B. O'Callaghan (New York, 1860) 32: Their primitive Beverage of water, which . . . breed no Worms in the Belly nor Maggots in the Brain. **1750** AHamilton in *MHM* 59(1964) 209: You mean the maggots in your brain and mine. **1762** JHalsey in *Wheelock's Indians* 253: I have known many a Maggot get into his Brain and get out again. **1790** Putnam *Memoirs* 237: This maggot I know is in the head of Some people. **1812** *The Sophomore* (Warren, Rhode Island, 1812) 7: I wonder what has filled his head with maggots now. **1817** *Portland Gazette* in Banks *Maine* 389: The famous construction . . . was originally a maggot of his brain. **1818** Adams *Memoirs* 4.145: It was nothing but a maggot in the brain of Hassler, **1821** 5.286: Some maggot in the brain. TW 232(2).

M3   As greedy as a **Magpie**

1819 Cobbett *Year's* 236: The Magpie's greediness, impudence, and cruelty are proverbial; so are those of the Parson.

M4   As jocund as a **Magpie** over a mutton

1637 Morton *New English Canaan* 314: This man . . . was as jocund on the Matter as a Magpie over a Mutton. Cf. Whiting P173, 174.

M5   To chatter like a **Magpie**

1720 Taylor *Poems* 362: Preaching without it's as a Magpies chatter. **1744** Hamilton *Itinerarium* 116: Mons. de la Moinnerie chattered like a magpie in his own language. **1775** JHarvey in *Blount Papers* 1.3: And chatters like a pie. **1809** Weems *Marion* 159. **1815** Brackenridge *Modern* 698: They [fowls] are said to *chatter;* as for instance the magpie, 780: They might gabble like magpies. Barbour 114; TW 232; Whiting P179. See **P107.**

M6   Like **Mahomet's** tomb

1634 Wood *New-England* 99: Hanging her like *Mahomet's* tombe, betwixt earth and heaven. *Oxford* 498-9; TW 247.

M7   As peevish as an old **Maid**

1728 Byrd *Dividing Line* 87: Tho' Orion was as peevish as an old Maid all the way. Cf. Svartengren 95-6.

M8   Let not the **Maid** become the mistress

1784 Gadsden *Writings* 237: I mention this now to put the state on their guard, *lest the maid became the mistress.* Whiting H92.

M9 Never kiss the **Maid** if you can kiss the mistress

1783 Adams *Works* 8.56-7: I had rather be master than servant, on the same principle that men swear at Highgate, —never to kiss the maid when they can kiss the mistress. 1784 Shaw *Journals* 135: Never kiss the maid when he can kiss the mistress, unless he likes the maid best. *Oxford* 275; Tilley M1021.

M10 Old **Maids** lead apes in hell (*varied*)

1735 Franklin *PR* 2.5: Old Maids lead Apes there, where the old Batchelors are turn'd to Apes. c1750 Winslow *Diary* 119-20 [notes]: Miss Rebecca Salisbury (1731-1811) who was married in 1757, was told by a rejected suitor: "The proverb old—you know it well, That women dying maids, lead apes in hell," to which she replied: "Lead apes in hell—tis no such thing; The story's told to fool us. But better there to hold a string, Than here let monkeys lead us." [No source is given.] 1769 Anne Blair in *W&MCQ* 16(1907) 176: I most shrewdly suspect I very reluctantly shall join that set of animals destin'd to lead apes. 1789 Brown *Better* 23: And if I deny him then bid me depart, And lead apes in the regions below. 1795 Bayard *Journal* 90: Miss Dancer . . . is much of an old Maid . . . and I really think, if any of our sex is ever honour'd with a sight of his Old Majesty, she may be. 1801 *Port Folio* 1.32: She . . . wisely preferred leading one ape on earth To perhaps a whole dozen in hell. 1805 Weems *Hymen* 19: And a saving antipathy to *apes*. 1807 *Salmagundi* 249: The girls he courted until they grew old maids, or married out of pure apprehension of incurring certain penalties hereafter. 1812 *Port Folio* 2NS 7.405: But Miss Jackanapes May be forc'd to lead apes, Like other old maids, as they tell; And I, by the Lord, If her heart be but thaw'd, Will be her head monkey in h-ll, 8.201: The threat which he [?Puttenham] adds, of their dying *single wymmen,* and leading apes, 1816 4NS 2.377: Not content with allowing some of us to "lead apes" in the next world, he would make us mothers of them in this. 1819 Pintard *Let-

ters* 1.178: There must remain a larger proportion of the present race of females, destined to lead apes in tother country. 1827 Watterston *Wanderer* 122: An antique belle, who has reached the grand climacteric, and is making a desperate effort to avoid the misery of leading apes in Tartarus. *Oxford* 590: Tilley M37; Whiting in *Englische Studien* 70(1936) 337-51; G. B. Needham in *Journal of American Folklore* 75(1962) 106-19.

M11 To splice the **Main-brace**

1813 Valpey *Journal* 10: All Hands was called to Splice the Main Brace at Noon. We fired a salute of seventeen guns and then we went to drinking. 1816 *Port Folio* 4NS 2.447: The *main-brace* we'll splice and our glasses we'll fill. 1825 Jones *Sketches* 1.79: An extra allowance of grog, (called splicing the main brace). Colcord 174; *Oxford* 767; TW 233.

M12 **Make** or break

1784 Gadsden *Writings* 237: It will Make Or Break Us. TW 233. Cf. *Oxford* 385.

M13 **Make** or mar

1713 Wise *Churches* 73: The Marring or Making of our Churches, 130: Make or Mar. 1784 FDana in Gerry *Letters* 1.442: And there seems to be in many places a rage for mending or rather marring it. *Oxford* 501; Whiting M24. See **K12, M146.**

M14 The **Malt** is above the water

1737 Franklin *Drinkers* 2.177: The Malt is above the Water. Tilley M57. Cf. *Oxford* 503; Whiting M28.

M15 All **Men** are mortal

1716 *Considerations* in *Colonial Currency* 1.338: All Men are Mortal. 1754 JInnes in *Letters to Washington* 1.42: All men are mortale and Subject to common frailty. 1771 *Johnson Papers* 8.299: We are all Mortall. 1788 Adams *Diary* 369: But we are all mortal. *Oxford* 10; Tilley M502. Cf. Whiting D243. See **D77, 175.**

M16 All **Men** must have a beginning

1713 Wise *Churches* 85: All men must have

a beginning. Whiting M65, cf. E164. See
E9.

M17 As a **Man** is, so is his praise
1741 Talcott *Papers* 2.359: For as is a man
so is his praise. Cf. *Oxford* 643; Tilley
P540.

M18 As drunk as an honest **Man** could wish
1776 Cresswell *Journal* 175: As drunk as an
honest man could wish, **1777** 201: As drunk
as any honest man aught to be.

M19 Bad **Men** hurt a good cause
1793 Bentley *Diary* 2.39: We are obliged to
forget on occasions . . . that bad men hurt a
good cause.

M20 Better a **Man** without money than
money without a man
1734 Ames *Almanacs* 95: It is better to have
a man without money than money without
a man. *Oxford* 506-7; Tilley M361.

M21 Better **Men** better times
1751 Ames *Almanacs* 230: Better Men better Times.

M22 A blind **Man** is no judge of colors
1693 Calef *More Wonders* 164: But how the
tempter appeared to him . . . is as far beyond my cognizance, as for a blind man to
judge of colours. **1742** Johnson *Writings*
3.448: [They] have no notion what it is to
be true Christians; any more than a man
born blind, what it is to see, or what light or
colors are. **1775** HLaurens in *Naval Documents* 2.217: Many had judged of the
Scheme as blind Men do of Colours. **1787**
Mason *Papers* 3.925: It would be as unnatural to refer the choice of a proper character for chief Magistrate to the people as it
would, to refer a trial of colours to a blind
man. **1833** Floy *Diary* 23: But even supposing they had the most correct ideas (which
is almost supposing the same as that a blind
man knows colours or that the King of Siam
knows what ice is). *Oxford* 68; Whiting xv,
M50.

M23 Dead **Men** tell no tales
1797 Cobbett *Porcupine* 7.195: You know,
Mr. P. that *dead men never tell tales.* **1804**
Brackenridge *Modern* 378: Dead men tell

no tales. **a1824** Marshall *Kentucky* 2.134:
He . . . was as careful as he had been of the
Spaniards, "that they should tell no tales."
Barbour 116(30); *Oxford* 171; Whiting
M56.

M24 Deal with all **Men** as though they were
rogues (*varied*)
1738 Curwen *Journal and Letters* 11: My
dealings with sundry people here have . . .
confirmed me in the maxim to treat all
persons as if they were dishonest. **1754** Carter *Diary* 1.113: There's no believing mankind. **1834** Jackson *Correspondence* 5.309:
The old adage, "deal with all men as tho
they were rogues." Cf. Tilley F34, M503,
534; Whiting M31.

M25 Deliver me from the **Man** of one business
1732 Belcher *Papers* 1.201: The Italian
adage may also serve for your instruction, —
Deliver me from the man of one business.
Cf. *Oxford* 58; Tilley W395.

M26 A drowning **Man** will catch at a straw
(*varied*)
1720 ?ONoyes *Letter* in *Colonial Currency*
2.12: Their Case being almost desperate,
they were glad to lay hold of any thing to
save themselves from Drowning. **1733** Belcher *Papers* 1.496: I see the party are still
willing (as drowning men) to catch at straws
or firebrands. **1733** Talcott *Papers* 1.281:
Being ready to Catch att every Twig in hope
to escape Drowning. **1758** Franklin *Papers*
8.75: This seems like a drowning Man
catching at a Straw. **1766** WDunlap in
Franklin *Papers* 13.86: There is nothing
more natural than for a *drowning Man* to
catch at the most distant Twig. **1771** *New
York Journal* in *Newspaper Extracts(I)*
8.401: The unhappy Youth . . . was then
like a drowning Man, willing to catch at a
Straw. **1775** BRomans in *Naval Documents*
2.1048: You catch at my word "superficial," as drowning people do at straws. **1780**
New Jersey Gazette in *Newspaper Extracts*
(*II*) 5.99: Our negro-masters . . . like
drowning men, will catch at every twig, at
every shadow, to prolong . . . their reign.
1785 Adams(A) *Letters* 268-9: This nation

(will) catch at every straw that swims. **1796** Smith(EH) *Diary* 195: To the drowning wretch, a straw appears as an anchor of safety. **1802** Chester *Federalism* 19: The adage of "*a drowning man's catching at straws.*" **1806** Hitchcock *Works* 143: As drowning men, to bear their bodies up, Seize sticks and leaves, that on the waters glide. **1813** JAdams in *Adams-Jefferson Letters* 2.350: They can scarcely hold their heads above water. They catch at Straws and Shadows to avoid drowning. **1814** William Rotch *Memorandum* (Boston, 1916) 45: We are like drowning men, catching at every straw that passes by. *Oxford* 205; Whiting M137. See **S483.**

M27 A drunken **Man** gets no harm

1702 Mather *Magnalia* 2.394: There is a lying proverb, "A drunken man gets no harm." We have seen the judgments of God upon *drunkards* most wofully confuting that lye. **1816** Lambert *Travels* 2.103: A drunken man is never in danger. *Oxford* 206; Tilley M94.

M28 Enough to make a dumb **Man** swear

1798 Murdock *Politicians* 18: By J——s, it is enough to make a dumb man swear. Cf. *Oxford* 696: Saint; Tilley S28. See **A94.**

M29 Every **Man** may err (*varied*)

1692 Bulkeley *Will* 131: Only it must be remembered, that *humanum* est errare. **1721** Philo Patræ in *Saltonstall Papers* 1.343: It is a Saying as true as old, *Humanum est errare*—and never is a man more likely to err, than when under the influence of ill resentments. **1763** *Colden Letters* 6.274: Does not every man err every day? **1765** CWhittelsey in Stiles *Itineraries* 588: [Latin only]. **1784** Van Schaack *Letters* 295: *et nescire* [Latin only]. **1787** PMallett in *Blount Papers* 1.311: The best of men may err. **1788** *American Museum* 3.381: [Latin only]. **1798** Heath *Memoirs* iii: It is the lot of man to be fallible. *Oxford* 225: Err; Tilley E179. See **M68.**

M30 Evil **Men** evil times

1756 Sherman *Almanacs* 250: Evil men occasion evil times.

M31 A good **Man** is a mixed man

1702 Mather *Magnalia* 1.124: The French have a saying, That *Un honeste homme, est un homme mesle!*—a *good* man is a *mixt* man. Cf. Cotgrave s.v. Mellé.

M32 Great **Men** must be obliged

1733 Belcher *Papers* 1.368: But great men must be oblig'd.

M33 Happy **Man** be his dole

1809 Weems *Washington* 134: Happy man be his dole. **1811** Wirt *Letters* 1.309: Well, happy man be his dole, say I! *Oxford* 352; Whiting M96.

M34 Hate not the **Man**, but his vices

1730 Ames *Almanacs* 67: Hate not the man, but his vices. *Oxford* 358; Tilley P238.

M35 He deserves no **Man's** good word, *etc.*

1702 Mather *Magnalia* 1.224: Nor has a certain proverb in Asia been improper in America, "He deserves no man's good word, of whom every man shall speak well."

M36 He that steals the old **Man's** supper does him no wrong

1737 Franklin *PR* 2.166: He that steals the old man's supper, do's him no wrong. *Oxford* 924; Tilley M181. See **N74, S531.**

M37 An idle **Man** is the Devil's play fellow

1766 Ames *Almanacs* 377: An idle man is the d——l's playfellow. **1769** Davis *Colonial Virginia Satirist* 56: An idle man, say the Arabians, is the devil's companion. *Oxford* 395. See **I12, T253.**

M38 It is not good for **Man** to be alone

1792 Belknap *History* 3.178: To experience the truth of that adage, "It is not good for man to be alone." **1797** Dunlap *Diary* 1.51: O what to Man so pleasant is, as fellowship of man. Tilley M203. See **W254.**

M39 Judge a **Man** by his works

1701 Taylor *Christographia* 53.94-5: Everyone is known by his works. **1819** Wright *Views* 163: Judge a man by his works, it is said, but to judge a nation by its works was no adage. *Oxford* 917; Whiting W654.

M40 A **Man** after one's own heart

1743 JBartram in *Colden Letters* 3.3: Desireing me to Call & see thee for I should find thee a man after my own heart. **1770** Munford *Candidates* 39: You are a man after my own heart. **1818** GBadger in Murphey *Papers* 1.120: He is indeed a "man after your own heart." Tilley M215.

M41 **Man** and mouse

1836 Longfellow *Letters* 1.553: The Brig Hollander . . . went down in sight of her port, and was lost "with man and mouse," 556: The vessel . . . went to the bottom "with man and mouse." NED Mouse 2b.

M42 The **Man** in the moon

1646 TStoughton in *Winthrop Papers(A)* 5.105: I received from my adversarie many impertinent things . . . as about a world in the moone bec[ause] a moone in the world: and a man in the moone. **1706** FJWinthrop in *Winthrop Papers(B)* 5.358: Conceites to have such faggots in cold wether as the man in the moone carryes on his back warmes very little. **c1720** Byrd *Another Secret Diary* 265: And if there be a man in the moon, doubtless he had the same design upon you. **1780** *New-York Gazette* in *Newspaper Extracts(II)* 5.105: And thought myself snug as the man in the moon. **1790** *St. Clair Papers* 2.140: Of what is passing in your quarters . . . we know as little as the man in the moon. **1792** Paine *To the Attorney-General* 2.512: It is as consistent that you obtain a verdict against the Man in the Moon as against me. **1793** Freneau *Prose* 311: Whether the Man in the Moon, (as is vulgarly expressed) be her husband. **1797** Callender *Annual Register 1796* 22: Basden might as well land in Philadelphia and seize the compting house of Mr. Swanwick, as belonging to *the man in the moon.* **1803** *Yankee Phrases* 87: And thought not of danger, nor harm, Any more than a man in the moon. **1806** Fessenden *Modern Philosopher* 53: E'en fairly knock the man in the moon down, 240: You will perceive that what is vulgarly called the *man in the moon* is a prodigious volcano. **1807** *Salmagundi* 75, 185-6: We care just as much . . . as we do about the man in the moon and his whim-whams, 213: They no more suspected me of being Launcelot Langstaff than they suspected me of being . . . the man in the moon. **1809** Fessenden *Pills* 73: Vulgarly called the *man in the moon.* **1809** Irving *History* 1.80, 82. **1814** Taggart *Letters* 430: A subject of which he could know as much as the man in the moon. *Oxford* 504; Whiting M138.

M43 The **Man** is fire, the woman tow, *etc.*

1809 *Port Folio* 2NS 2.431: The man is fire; the woman tow; and then the devil comes to blow the coals. *Oxford* 259; Whiting F182.

M44 A **Man** is generally the last that hears ill of himself

1748 Laurens *Papers* 1.198: As a man is generally the last that hears Ill of himself. Cf. *Oxford* 159: Cuckold; Tilley C877.

M45 A **Man** is known by his company

1780 AA in *Adams FC* 4.28: It is an old observation that a Man is known by his company. **1794** Morris *Diary and Letters* 2.59: If it be just to judge a private man by his friends, it is not amiss to estimate a public man by his foes. Barbour 115(5); *Oxford* 138; Tilley M248. See **C271.**

M46 **Man** is the only animal that is hungry with his belly full

1776 HGates in Massachusetts Historical Society, *Proceedings* 67 (1941-44) 141: Man is the only Animal that is Hungry with His belly full.

M47 A **Man** knows not what he can do till he tries (*varied*)

1795 Murdock *Triumphs* 49-50: But a man don't know what he can do, until he is put to the push. **1812** Adams *D and A* 3.152: No man knows what he can bear till he tries . . . As has been said before, human nature never knows what it can endure before it tries the experiment. **1819** Cobbett *Year's* 144: A man knows not what he can do 'till he tries. **1838** Paulding *Letters(II)* 211: A man knows not what he can do till he tries. *Oxford* 436; TW 236(29).

M48 A **Man** may be wise for another, and a fool for himself

1831 Austin *Literary Papers* 52: A man may be wise for another, and a fool for himself. *Oxford* 274; Whiting F404.

M49 A **Man** may kiss his cow

1802 *Port Folio* 2.312: According to the elegant proverb of Dr. Franklin, "a man may *kiss his cow.*" *Oxford* 228-9; Whiting M71.

M50 A **Man** must ask his wife whether he is to be rich

1721 Wise *Word* 221: It is a common saying, that a Man must ask his Wife whether he shall be Rich? 1822 Weems *Penn* 12: As a man must ask his *wife,* whether he is to be a rich man or a beggar; so, a child must ask his *mother,* whether he is to be a wise man or a fool, a saint or a demon for ever. Cf. *Oxford* 819, 905; Tilley L169; Whiting M155.

M51 A **Man** must be a physician at forty or a fool

1783 Van Schaack *Letters* 347: 'Tis a common observation, founded in much truth, that a man must be his own physician at forty, or a fool. 1787 Adams(A) *Letters* 341: It is an old adage, that a man at thirty must be either a fool or a physician. *Oxford* 275; Tilley M125.

M52 A **Man** of straw

1705 Ingles *Reply* 158: He Sets up a Man of Straw of his own to pelt at. 1754 BNicoll in Johnson *Writings* 4.200: In wisely setting up a man of straw, a mere chimera and imagination. 1770 Adams(S) *Writings* 2.45. 1802 Ames *Letters* 1.311: I am, in health, a man of straw. 1803 MCutler in *Essex Institute Historical Collections* 39(1903) 322: The Constitution is become a mere man of Straw. 1809 JAdams in *Adams-Cunningham Letters* 193: A Republican would dress up a man of straw to divide the Federalists. 1817 Gallatin *Diary* 105. NED Straw *sb.*[1] 2e. Cf. *Oxford* 506; Tilley M294.

M53 A **Man** of wax

1822 Freneau *Last Poems* 74: But now! to please both *White & Black,* A man must be —*a man of wax. Oxford* 196; Tilley D453.

M54 A **Man** of words and not of deeds, *etc.*

1758 *Franklin-Mecom* 67: A man of words and not of deeds Is like a garden full of weeds, 68: A man of deeds and not of words Is like a garden full of — —I have forgotten the rhyme, but remember 'tis something the very reverse of perfume. Barbour 115(11); *Oxford* 915; Tilley M296.

M55 A **Man** or a mouse

1680 Randolph *Letters* 3.62: One year, may bee a man, the next a Mouse. a1731 Cook *Bacon* 323: In Peace a Man, in War a Mouse. 1796 Washington *Writings* 35.279: Speculators . . . may be men one day, and mice the next. 1805 Sewall *Parody* 41-2: [The] well known proverb—"Be a man or a mouse." *Oxford* 506; TW 234(6); Tilley M297.

M56 **Man** proposes, but God disposes

1654 Johnson *Wonder-Working* 75: Man purposes, but God disposes. a1656 Bradford *History* 1.444: Man may purpose, but God doth dispose. 1661 LDowning in *Winthrop Papers*(B) 3.53: But God must dispose and wee must submit. 1676 Sewall *Diary* 1.25: *Homo prop. Deus disp. Omnia,* 1716 *Letter-Book* 2.51: As we profess, so we experience, that man purposes, but GOD Disposes all things. 1763 Griffith *Journal* 136: We see sometimes, when man appoints, the Lord disappoints. 1773 Mrs. STurner in *Norton Papers* 321-2: It is an old observation noticed by every body, that Man appoints, & God disappoints. 1779 Hutchinson *Diary* 2.280. 1802 Perkins *Diary* 4.431: But man appoints & God disappoints. 1815 Gallatin *Diary* 77: *Homme propose mais Dieu dispose.* 1821 Howison *Sketches* 281: Aye, man appoints, and God disappoints. *Oxford* 506; Whiting M162.

M57 The **Man** shall have his mare again

1692 Randolph *Letters* 5.84: Neal did hear and see said Randolph drink frequently a health to the Man that should have his Mare again, 89: He makes it his Business to drink healths frequently to the man that should have his Mare again (a by-word by them used to signify King James's return to the Crowne). *Oxford* 504; Tilley A153.

M58 The **Man** with no business is the busiest man

1774 Webb *Correspondence* 1.40: I have frequently heard that a man without any business is the most busy man in the world. *Oxford* 395; Tilley F420. See **W335.**

M59 **Man's** extremity is God's opportunity

1776 SHodgkins in Hodgkins *Letters* 220: It has been observed that mans extremity was Gods oppertunity. *Oxford* 507; Tilley M471.

M60 **Men** and melons are hard to know

1733 Franklin *PR* 1.316: Men and Melons are hard to know. Tilley M867: Woman.

M61 **Men** are blind in their own case

a1700 Hubbard *New England* 363: So apt are men to be blinded in their own case, and forbid others to steal, while themselves are committing sacrilege. *Oxford* 67; Whiting M205. See **M69.**

M62 **Men** are everywhere the same

1792 Barlow *Works* 1.170: The adage, That men are every where the same. See **N15.**

M63 **Men** are saved not by faith, but by the want of it

1754 Franklin *PR* 5.184: In the Affairs of this World Men are saved, not by Faith, but by the Want of it, 1758 *WW* 344. Lean 4.8. Cf. Tilley F34.

M64 **Men** may meet, mountains never

1742 Franklin *PR* 2.336: Men meet, mountains never. 1818 Hall *Travels* 73: Though mountains could not meet, men might. *Oxford* 290; Tilley F738.

M65 A merciful **Man** is merciful to his beast (*varied*)

1783 Heath *Memoirs* 373: For if the merciful man be merciful even to his beast, how much more ought a great and brave man to feel for the unfortunate of his own species. 1828 *Yankee* 175: The Yankees are proverbially kind to their cattle. 1832 Ames *Nautical* 131: The merciful man is merciful to his beast. TW 234(10).

M66 No **Man** can serve two masters

1713 Steere *Daniel* 65: What tho' no man can serve two Masters well, The Supream God, and the Inferiour Mammon. 1745 Pote *Journal* 28: And found I must Endeavor to Serve two masters and please them both. 1748 *Word* in *Colonial Currency* 4.362: They cannot serve two Masters in one Capacity, and as they love Money, they must consequently hate their Country, 1750 440: They could not serve two Masters; but they actually served Mammon, and pretended to serve God. 1769 CGadsden in Woodmason *Journal* 265. 1775 JBoucher in *Naval Documents* 3.393: They seem desirous to serve two Masters. 1775 Marshall *Diary* 40: I had insisted on the impropriety of serving two masters. 1776 Carter *Diary* 2.1057: He cannot serve God and Mammon. 1776 JDickins in Asbury *Journal* 1.215. 1782 Jay *Correspondence* 2.344. 1794 Adams *Writings* 1.178. ?1806 *Austin Papers* 1.118: To comply . . . was as impossible as to serve God and Mammon. 1810 Weems *Letters* 3.27, 1811 55, 57, 1815 *Adultery* 152: For as *no man can serve two masters,* so no woman can love two men. 1820 Pintard *Letters* 1.336, 339. 1835 Jackson *Correspondence* 5.338. *Oxford* 569; Whiting M227. See **G71.**

M67 No **Man** is a hero to his valet

1801 JTaylor in *Steele Papers* 1.242: "No man appears great," I believe it is somewhere said, or possibly "No man is a hero in the eyes of his valet de chambre." 1809 Tyler *Yankey* 54: The Duke de Rochefoucault observes that no man was ever a hero in the eyes of his valet-de-chambre. 1811 Graydon *Memoirs* 137: No man is a hero to his valet de chambre. 1825 Smith *Letters* 202: It is said, that no man is a great man, when seen near. *Oxford* 570; Tilley M517.

M68 No **Man** is without faults (*varied*)

1653 Keayne *Apologia* 2: For all men have their weaknesses and the best societies of men have their imperfections. 1732 Franklin *PR* 1.246: *For there are none without their Faults, no not one.* 1751 *Appendix* in *Colonial Currency* 4.462: All Mankind have Faults. 1791 OHWilliams in Hamilton *Pa-*

pers 10.369: Infallibility is the attribute of no man. **1805** Morris *Diary and Letters* 2.474: Nobody human is perfect, and . . . every change is hazardous, **1815** 587: Nothing human can be perfect. **1822** Jackson *Correspondence* 3.179: They both have been taken with the Bank-mania, which has realized the adage that there are no great men without their weaknesses. *Oxford* 229; Whiting L255, M235. See **M29.**

M69 No **Man** may be a judge in his own cause

1645 JCotton in Williams *Writings* 2.25: Mr. *Williams* may be Judge in his own cause, himselfe hath been persecuted without mercy. **1646** Winslow *Hypocrisie* 67: And let them not bee parties and judges. **1708** Sewall *Diary* 2.226: I told Mr. Bromfield, I should not meddle in it, I must not be a Judge in my own Cause. **1758** CCarroll in *MHM* 10(1915) 149: No man is a Judge in his own cause. **1762** Adams *D and A* 1.231: This Maxim that a Man shall not be Judge in his own Cause. **1766** Jay *Correspondence* 1.5: Give me leave to remind you of the old law maxim, that a man's evidence is not to be admitted in his own cause. **1773** Carroll *Correspondence* 1.349: Hence, the maxim, "no man ought to be a judge in his own castle." **1798** Adams *Writings* 2.263. **1817** Baldwin *Letters* 216: It was making him *a judge in his own cause.* *Oxford* 415: Judge; Whiting M244. See **M61.**

M70 No wise **Man** dies without a will

1713 JDudley in *Winthrop Papers*(B) 6.267: The English saying is, No wise man dyes without a will. Cf. Whiting M229.

M71 An old **Man** in a house is a good sign

1744 Franklin *PR* 2.399: An old Man in a House is a good Sign. *Oxford* 590; Tilley M347.

M72 An old young **Man** will be a young old man

1735 Franklin *PR* 2.10; An old young man, will be a young old man, **1745** 3.7: Old young and old long. **1812** Rush *Letters* 2.1142: From necessity I conformed to the Spanish proverb of "being *old* when I was

young, that I might be *young* when I was old," by living temperately. *Oxford* 593; Tilley O36.

M73 One **Man** is as good as another

1819 Flint *Letters* 169: Or the favourite maxim that one man is as good as another. Tilley M343, 351.

M74 One **Man's** meat is another man's poison (*varied*)

1776 AA in *Adams FC* 2.94: What is meat for one is not for another. **1800** Dow *Journal* 90: For what is one's meat is another's poison. **1805** *Echo* 179: Since one man's poison is another's meat. **1811** *Port Folio* 2NS 5.374. c**1820** Bernard *Retrospections* 124: In physics we find the source of life to one being is death to another. Barbour 116(53); *Oxford* 552; Tilley M483.

M75 A poor **Man** is a mean man

1825 Pearse *Narrative* 57: I have heard it used almost as a proverb, that "a poor man is a mean man." Cf. Whiting *NC* 410: Poor folks.

M76 The poor **Man** walks to get meat, *etc.*

1735 Franklin *PR* 2.6: The poor man must walk to get meat for his stomach, the rich man to get a stomach to his meat. *Oxford* 639; Tilley M366.

M77 A quarrelsome **Man** has no good neighbors

1746 Franklin *PR* 3.62: A quarrelsome Man has no good Neighbours.

M78 So many **Men,** so many minds (*varied*)

a**1656** Bradford *History* 2.367: Diverse were mens minds and oppinions. a**1672** Bradstreet *Works* 250: And he that story reads, shall often find; That severall men, will have their severall mind. **1731** Franklin *Papers* 1.194: That the Opinions of Men are almost as various as their Faces; an Observation general enough to become a common Proverb, *So many Men so many minds.* **1765** Rush *Letters* 1.21: It is yet "quot homines tot sententiae." **1775** JWarren in *Warren-Adams Letters* 1.190: Many men, you know, are of many minds. **1778** Murray *Letters* 273-4: As many men of many minds have done before her. **1789** *Columbian Magazine* 3.403: Many men of many minds. **1791** S.P.L. *Thoughts* 77: Many men of many minds. **1809** Weems *Marion* 3: God . . . has made many men of many minds. **1815** Brackenridge *Modern* 642: When all voices are heard, there may be found as many opinions as there are voices. Quot hominum, tot capitum. **1824** Cooper *Letters* 1.110: Though opinions are as various as men's minds. **1831** Wirt *Letters* 2.324: Many men of many minds — I may be wrong in the opinion. *Oxford* 525; Whiting M202.

M79 Take it as the poor (wise) **Man** took his wife

1721 Wise *Word* 192: You must do by your Bills, as all Wise Men do by their Wives; Make the best of them. **1777** Rodney *Letters* 171: Be that as it may, you must take it as the poor man took his Wife. *Oxford* 802; Tilley M65, cf. B326. See **B160.**

M80 To kick a **Man** when he is down (*varied*)

1634 Wood *New-England* 23: The Beare perceiving him to be such a coward as to strike him when he was down. **1770** Munford *Candidates* 42: Nobody but a fool would kick a fallen man lower. **1803** Clay *Papers* 1.94: It is natural for some characters to worship the rising sun; but I do not therefore conclude that it is generous to kick at the fallen. **1809** Weems *Marion* 98: When a poor fellow is going down hill, it is but too common, they say, for every body to give him a kick. **1821** *Austin Papers* 1.451: Some Characters . . . who was very Unfriendly to your Father in his greatest distress and as the old saying is, was allways ready to give a kick when theay found he was going down hill. *Oxford* 374; TW 207(2).

M81 To wait for dead **Men's** shoes

1714 WWinthrop in *Winthrop Papers*(B) 6.282: A Leiftenant Governer has nothing to do in the Gover^mt, unless the Governor . . . should dye, and thay that wait for such shoose may go barefoot. **1776** AA in *Adams FC* 2.106: I remember the old proverb, he who waits for dead mens shoes may go barefoot. **1852** FNash in *Ruffin Papers* 2.371: I admit it is not the thing to be waiting for dead mens shoes — we sometimes slip our own too soon. *Oxford* 171; Whiting M325.

M82 What all **Men** say must needs be true

1750 Sherman *Almanacs* 253: It must needs be true which all men say, Better have money to receive than pay. **1760** Montresor *Journals* 236: What all the world says must be true. **1796** Cobbett *Porcupine* 4.130: What everybody says must be true. *Oxford* 841; Whiting M309. See **E80.**

M83 When all **Men** say you are an ass, it is time to bray

1809 *Port Folio* 2NS 2.429: When all men say you are an ass, 'tis time to bray. *Oxford* 10; Tilley M531.

M84 Why does the blind **Man's** wife paint herself?

1736 Franklin *PR* 2.140: Why does the blind man's wife paint herself? *Oxford* 68; Tilley M446.

M85 A wise **Man** wonders at nothing

1778 Adams(S) *Writings* 4.75: It is said a wise Man wonders at Nothing.

M86 Wise **Men** are not always wise

a**1700** Hubbard *New England* 437: But wise men are not always wise. **1804** Brackenridge *Modern* 377: Captain, said he, *Nemo omnibus horis sapit* . . . no man is wise at all times. Cf. *Oxford* 571; Whiting M234.

M87 Wise **Men** may receive benefit by hearing fools

1691 JEaton in *Baxter Manuscripts* 5.306: Somtims wise men may Receive benift by her^g fools. *Oxford* 274; Whiting F404, M340.

M88 Wise **Men** speak most where they intend to do least

a**1700** Hubbard *New England* 435: Sometimes wise men will speak most where they intend to do least. Cf. Whiting W643.

M89 Wise **Men** think twice before they act once

1761 *Boston Gazette* in *Olden Time* 2.30: Wise Men think twice before they act once. Lean 4.158.

M90 Young **Men** may die, but old men must die

1645 "Thomas Dudley" in Jantz 34: Younge men may dye, but old men, these dye must. 1709 Chalkley *Loving Invitation* 362: A common Proverb, *i.e. The Young* (may live, and they) *may die, but the Old must die.* 1756 Hopkinson *Miscellaneous Essays* 3(part 2) 10: That old age *must,* and blooming youth *may* fall. 1824 *Ruffin Papers* 1.319: If the old must die, the young may die. *Oxford* 927; TW 236(37); Whiting M354.

M91 To steal a **Manchet** out of the brewer's basket

1737 Franklin *Drinkers* 2.174: Has Stole a Manchet out of the Brewer's Basket. Tilley M621.

M92 **Manners** differ in different countries (*varied*)

1784 Adams(A) *Letters* 200: Manners differ exceedingly in different countries. 1819 Thomas *Travels* 75: It has been justly said, that "manners change with climes." *Oxford* 147; Whiting T63.

M93 **Manners** make the man (*varied*)

1742 Franklin *PR* 2.334: Money and good Manners make the Gentleman. 1764 Watts *Letter Book* 262: Candor & steady Manners form the Man. 1806 *Port Folio* NS 2.80: Manners Make The Man. Barbour 117(1); *Oxford* 508; Tilley M1051; Whiting M362, 628.

M94 Tell me thy **Manners** and I'll tell thy fortune

1754 Ames *Almanacs* 251: Tell me thy Manners and I'll tell thy Fortune. *Oxford* 508; Tilley M630.

M95 **Many** are called, but few chosen

1791 Bentley *Diary* 1.264: Many are called, but few chosen. Whiting M365.

M96 As cold as **Marble**

1786 Trumbull *Autobiography* 109: The heart which does not melt before it, must be still harder and more cold than marble. 1800 Burr *Correspondence* 58: Her heart is as cold as marble. 1807 JAdams in *Adams-Warren Correspondence* 445: But the lady was as cold as marble. 1816 Smith *Life* 106: His sermon was flat as the canvas, and cold as the marble, 283. Svartengren 314; Whiting M368.

M97 As durable as **Marble**

1814 Jackson *Correspondence* 2.112: Established a fame for themselves as durable as marble.

M98 As white as **Marble**

1801 *Farmers' Museum* 90: Fingers, like the marble white. TW 237-8.

M99 To steal a **March**

1776 WPurviance in *Naval Documents* 5.743: I am Very anxtius to Steale a march on that Vilan. 1782 EDouglas in *PM* 1 (1877) 47: Our Indians stole a march upon them. Barbour 117; *Oxford* 712; TW 238(2).

M100 **March** comes in like a lion, *etc.*

1740 Ames *Almanacs* 138: March, this year, ends like a Lamb. 1740 Byrd *Another Secret Diary* 44: March came in like a lion with a strong wind. 1747 Smith *Journal* 270 (March 31): There has been no high winds this month—no lion-like days. 1759 Ames *Almanacs* 294: March comes in like a Lyon, this Year. 1760 GClough *Journal* in *Historical Collections of the Essex Institute* 3(1861) 196: And thus the month ends as of old said "March, hack ham, comes in like a lion and goes out like a lamb." 1766 Deane *Diary* in Smith *Journal* 316: The Year comes in like a lion. 1780 Smith *Journal* 281 (March 2): Blustering day, lion-like March, 1782 282(March 23): Lion-like March. 1788 Adams *Diary* 389: The month [March] comes in like a lion, and according to the farmer's proverb it must go out like a lamb, 400: The weather for a day or two past has been very mild and pleasant; verifying the vulgar saying, mentioned at the beginning of the month. **1794** Drinker *Journal* 222: March is going out like a Lion. **1813** RPeters in Quincy *JQuincy* 367: You have anticipated the month of March by coming in like a lion; but it is not likely that you will go out like a lamb. **1833** Pintard *Letters* 4.129: Dear Mother says March comes in like a Lion. Barbour 117(1); Dunwoody 95; *Oxford* 511; TW 238(2).

M100.1   March windy and April rainy, *etc.*
1733 Franklin *PR* 1.314: March windy, and April rainy, Makes May the pleasantest month of any. Dunwoody 95; *Oxford* 895; Tilley M644.

M100.2   To live to climb **March Hill**
1832 Pintard *Letters* 4.17: If I live to climb March Hill, I trust to be relieved by milder weather. *Oxford* 519: May-hill; Tilley M772.

M100.3   The gray **Mare** is the better horse
1716 TMcCliesh in *Letters from Hudson Bay* 45: In case the gray mare should prove the better horse. **1732** Bryd *Progress* 321: The gray mare is the better horse in that family, **1733** *Journey* 304. **1787** *Columbian Magazine* 1.642. **1788** *American Museum* 3.187-9: *The Gray Mare the Better Horse* [title of a poem]. **1789** Brackenridge *Gazette* 314. **1789** *Columbian Magazine* 3.495. **1791** S.P.L. *Thoughts* 77-8: The gray mare should be the better horse. **1797** Tyler *Algerine* 1.55: The old adage. **1800** ANMcLeod in Gates *Five Fur Traders* 129. **1802** *Port Folio* 2.102: Origin of the Grey Mare's Being The Better Horse [an anecdote purporting to explain the proverb], 222: The metamorphoses of "grey mares" into "better horses." **1809** Irving *History* 1.248: The governor's spouse, who . . . was . . . "the better horse." **1824** *Tales* 1.141: If I were to be as serious as a man with a gray mare in his house—(out upon all gray mares, I say, at board or at manger)—I could not alter one tittle of my tale. *Oxford* 338; Whiting M376.

M100.4   He that speaks ill of the **Mare** will buy her
1742 Franklin *PR* 2.337: He that speaks ill

of the Mare, will buy her. *Oxford* 762; Tilley M648.

M101   Tell that to the **Marines**
1830 Ames *Mariner's* 238: Tell that to the marines. Barbour 118; *Oxford* 807; TW 238.

M102   To be beside the **Mark**
1770 Franklin *Papers* 17.358: This is all beside the Mark. NED Mark *sb.*[1] 7e.

M103   To miss the **Mark**
a1700 Hubbard *New England* 518: But it missed the mark. **1719** JBridger in *Baxter Manuscripts* 10.121: The Agent missed his mark very much. Tilley M669.

M104   To overshoot the **Mark**
1742 Stephens *Journal(II)* 1.37: Made them overshoot their mark. **1763** Watts *Letter Book* 212: The good folks at Home are quite overshooting the Mark about Trade here. **1781** TPickering in *Clinton Papers* 7.257. **1788** Stiles *Diary* 3.326. NED Overshoot 2b. Cf. *Oxford* 727; TW 238(1).

M105   To mend one's **Market**
1709 Sewall *Diary* 2.250: If she should have Mr. Stoddard, she would mend her market. **1776** Curwen *Journal* 1.284: I doubt whether I should mend my market by removing. NED Market 4c.

M106   Marriage and hanging come by destiny
1637 Morton *New English Canaan* 281: But marriage and hanging (they say) comes by desteny and Scogans choise tis better [than] none at all. *Oxford* 350; Whiting W164. See **M117**.

M107   As merry as a **Marriage** bell
1834 Longfellow *Letters* 1.453: May all go "merry as a marriage bell." Byron *Childe Harold* iii 21. Cf. TW 398: Wedding(1).

M108   Better to **Marry** than burn
1731 Belcher *Papers* 1.63: He falls in with that part of the Apostle's advise, Better to marry than burn, and that marriage is honourable & the bed undefiled, **1732** 168: It's better to marry than to burn. **1783** JEliot in *Belknap Papers* 3.241: It is better to marry

surely than to *freeze*. **1790** Humphreys *Works* 230. **1796** Dennie *Lay Preacher* 6. **1801** *Farmers' Museum* 96. Whiting W162.

M109 Like **Master** like man

1692 Bulkeley *Will* 219: And hence, *Like master like man,* their officers are for the most part like themselves. **1788** *Politician* 47: Like master, like man, as the old saying is. **1789** Dunlap *Father* 36: They say. **1791** Long *Voyages* 106: It is *tel maitre, tel valet,* the bourgeois must work as hard as the engagés. **1801** Story *Shop* 63. **1806** *Port Folio* NS 1.226. **1806** *Weekly* 1.86. *Oxford* 517; Whiting M408. See **C34, O13.**

M110 The **Master's** eye (makes the horse fat)

1686 Dunton *Letters* 177: Yet I remembered that . . . the Masters Eye makes the Horse fat. **1714** Plumstead 168: And other good husbandry which the master's eye and presence would from time to time carefully bestow on it. **1771** Carter *Diary* 2.641: Hardly any work has been done or indeed could be done, even making great allowances for the want of the master's eye, **1776** 1020: So that the master's eye is wanting with him which did not use to be. **1813** Mrs. RJackson in Jackson *Correspondence* 1.273: The stock wants there master's eye. *Oxford* 517; TW 239(1).

M111 Those that are good for their **Masters** are good for themselves

1730 Chalkley *Youth* 556: A common Maxim . . . *Those that are good for their Masters, are good for themselves.*

M112 To be **Master** in one's own house

1629 TFones in *Winthrop Papers(A)* 2.79: I . . . cannot I see now be master in myne owne howse. *Oxford* 229; Tilley M123.

M113 To be one's own **Master**

1790 *Cary Letters* 80: Though, as the vulgar saying is, you will be your own master.

M114 To grow great with one's **Master's** decay

1640 JLuxford in *Winthrop Papers(A)* 4.180: I have not with soome growe great with my m[aste]rs decay. Cf. *Oxford* 242: Falling master.

M115 Where all are **Masters,** *etc.*

1783 Williams *Penrose* 155: All had now become masters and nobody left to throw the water out of the Longboat, as the Sailors term it. Lean 4.189. Cf. *Oxford* 230; Tilley A341, M412; Whiting H429. See **H114, O12.**

M116 Though the **Mastiff** be gentle, *etc.*

1757 Franklin *PR* 7.84: Tho' the Mastiff be gentle, yet bite him not by the Lip. *Oxford* 518; Tilley M744.

M117 **Matches** are made in heaven (*varied*)

1686 Dunton *Letters* 208: There is a Proverb, Sir, which tells us, *Matches are made in Heaven.* **1804** Dow *Journal* 209: Some people have an idea, that all matches are appointed. **1823** Bierce *Travels* 116: To see such a brute united with so lovely a woman was enough to prove that matches are not made in Heaven. Barbour 118; *Oxford* 514; TW 239. See **M106.**

M118 A **Matter** of moonshine

1777 *Washington *Writings* 7.395: As if it was a matter of Moonshine whether they came to day, to morrow, a Week, or a Month hence, 8.124: It is almost a matter of moonshine whether they are completed or not, **1778** 13.57, **1798** 36.190: Where or how the houses . . . may be fixed, is, to me, . . . a matter of Moonshine. **1818** WLewis in Jackson *Correspondence* 6.463: Whether the Kentuckians . . . ran like frighted deer, or faught like bull dogs, is to him a mere matter of moon-shine. *Oxford* 542; TW 249-50(2). Cf. Whiting M666.

M119 As blooming as **May**

1788 *American Museum* 4.189: Columbia . . . blooming as May.

M120 As fine as **May**

1799 Freneau *Poems* 3.269: And dizzen'd out as fine as May.

M121 As sweet as **May**

1775 Freneau *Poems* 1.203: Fair as the day, and sweet as May.

M122 Wet **May** makes short corn, *etc.*

1752 RJackson in Eliot *Essays* 92-3: That Wheat and Rye bear Drought much better than Grass is an old Observation preserved in one of the *English* proverbs. *Wet May, makes short Corn and long Hay, Dry May, makes long Corn and short Hay.* As the old *English* Proverbs contain Truth and good Sense, founded on due Observation and Experience, I have a Fondness for them. Cf. Lean 1.361,363.

M123 **May** bees don't fly in November

1807 *Emerald* NS 1.88: "That *may be* Sir;" but "*may bees* do not fly in November." *Oxford* 518.

M124 As straight as a **May-pole**

1822 Watterston *Winter* 37: He was as straight as a may-pole. 1830 Longfellow *Letters* 1.347: I shall not despair of seeing you in Brunswick ere long—as strait as a may-pole. Cf. TW 240; Tilley M778.

M125 As upright as a **May-pole**

1792 Belknap *Foresters* 79: They stood upright as a maypole. Cf. TW 240; Tilley M778.

M126 What is bad for **Me** may be bad for thee

1759 RWolcott in *Collections of the Connecticut Historical Society* 3(1895) 335: According to the proverb What is bad for me may be bad for thee, by turns. Cf. *Oxford* 395; Tilley T371; Whiting T349.

M127 Always taking out of the **Meal-tub**, *etc.*

1758 Franklin *WW* 346: Always taking out of the Meal-tub, and never putting in, soon comes to the Bottom. 1770 Ames *Almanacs* 413. *Oxford* 12; Tilley B552; Whiting *NC* 443-4.

M128 To be **Mealy-mouthed**

1776 The Sentinel in *Naval Documents* 3.1011: This is not a season to be mealy-mouthed, or to mince matters. Whiting M436.

M129 By fair **Means** or foul

1718 NBurwell in *W&MCQ* 7(1898) 44: He had better go by fare means than fowl, for go he shall. 1728 Byrd *Dividing Line* 250: Two of them [horses] . . . would not advance a foot farther, either by fair means or foul. 1752 JFrancis in McDowell *Documents* 1.252: Burgess is taken either by fair Means or foul. 1759 CCarroll in *MHM* 10(1915) 239: If not by fair means at least by foul. TW 240(1); Whiting M437.

M130 The golden **Mean**

1637 Morton *New English Canaan* 116: The Middell Zone betweene the two extreames is best, and it is therefore called *Zona temperata* and is in the golden meane, 119: Therefore let us leave these two extreames . . . and indeavour to finde out this golden meane, so free from any one of them. 1753 *Independent Reflector* 293: A Man of Sense and Impartiality will, however, preserve the golden Mean. 1756 Johnson *Writings* 2.339: It is good to keep the golden mean and hold moderation. 1761 Adams(A) *Letters* 5: Men neglect the golden mean. 1761 Smith *Works* 2.380. 1767 Johnson *Writings* 1.410: To endeavour to preserve the golden mean between all extremes. 1769 Brooke *Emily* 22. 1773 GClymer in Quincy *Memoir* 118. 1773 SDeane in Webb *Correspondence* 1.17. *Oxford* 317; Tilley M792. Cf. Whiting M739-48, 451-61. See **M144, W64**.

M131 **Measure** for measure

1774 *Pennsylvania Packet* in *Newspaper Extracts(I)* 10.334: Return *measure* for *measure, heeped up* and *pressed dowm.* 1777 Smith *Memoirs(II)* 277: I will answer for his returning Measure for Measure. 1798 Murdock *Politicians* 6: I am determined always to give measure for measure. *Oxford* 520; Tilley M800.

M132 The **Measure** you mete shall be measured to you again

1689 Bulkeley *People's Right* 70: The measure that you mete may be measured to you again. 1745 Johnson *Writings* 3.470: With what measure we mete to others it should be measured to us again. Whiting M467.

M133 Not the **Measure** but the man

1762 Watts *Letter Book* 102: But if I guess right, it is not so much the Measure as the

Man in your Brothers Case. **1811** Adams
Writings 4.225: The hackneyed . . . adage
about measures and not men, **1813** 487:
Measures and not men has been sometimes
a favorite maxim among Republicans.
Lean 2.920, 4.45.

M134 Beware of **Meat** twice boiled, *etc.*
1733 Franklin *PR* 1.313: Beware of meat
twice boil'd, and an old foe reconcil'd, 316.
Oxford 667; Tilley H378; Whiting E96.

M135 Much **Meat,** much malady
1754 Ames *Almanacs* 252: Much Meat,
much Malady. *Oxford* 549; Tilley M829.

M136 Those who had the **Meat** should pick
the bone
1793 *Echo* 75: For 'tis in politics a maxim
known, *That those who've had the meat
should pick the bone. Oxford* 217.

M137 To be **Meat** for one's master
1792 Brackenridge *Modern* 107: There is
no Teague O'Regan at this house. We have
meat for his master. *Oxford* 522; Tilley
M837.

M138 To be one's **Meat** and drink
1781 MWillett in *Clinton Papers* 7.253: For
to Chastize the Wretches who trouble our
frontier, for this campaign, I am determined to make my meat and my Drink.
1784 Pemberton *Life* 163: It is their meat
and drink to do the Lord's will. *Oxford* 521;
Tilley M842. Cf. Whiting M478.

M139 To like the **Meat** but not the cook
1680 Randolph *Letters* 3.62: She likes the
meate, but can't abide the Cook. See **G85.**

M140 To take **Meat** before grace
1816 Paulding *Letters(I)* 2.207: His mother
made a blunder, and mistook meat before
grace, for grace before meat.

M141 Neither **Meddle** nor make
1721 Wise *Word* 196: We will neither meddle nor make with them. *Oxford* 522; Tilley M852.

M142 To be bad **Medicine**
1805 Ordway *Journal* 184: They think that

we are bad medicine and say that we must
be killed. DA bad 2(7).

M143 To swallow one's own **Medicine**
1804 King *Life* 4.424: May the Inventors be
obliged to swallow their own Medicine. TW
241(2). Cf. Whiting M489.

M144 There is a **Medium** in all things (*varied*)
1783 HWilliamson in Iredell *Correspondence* 2.38: Is it not clear that virtue consists in a medium? **1787** Hamilton *Papers*
4.215: There is a medium in everything.
1805 Brackenridge *Modern* 560: There is a
medium in all things. *Oxford* 520; Whiting M464. See **M130, W64.**

M145 When the **Members** quarrel the
whole body must suffer
1782 Jay *Correspondence* 2.330: Whenever
the members quarrel the whole body must
suffer. Cf. Whiting H219.

M146 **Mend** or end
1804 Asbury *Letters* 3.286: Mend it or end
it, 302: Many that will not be mended will
be ended, or mended and ended both. *Oxford* 525; Tilley M874. Cf. Whiting M500.
See **M13.**

M147 One **Mend-fault** is worth two findfaults, *etc.*
1735 Franklin *PR* 2.10: One Mend-fault is
worth two Findfaults, but one Findfault is
better than two Makefaults. Cf. *Oxford*
526.

M148 A **Mercury** is not made of every wood
1690 Palmer *Account* in *Andros Tracts*
1.44: *Ex quovis Ligno non fit Mercurius.*
1713 Wise *Churches* 76: *Exonni Ligno, non
fit Mercurius.* **1755** Davis *Colonial Virginia
Satirist* 23: [Latin only]. **1784** *Universal
Asylum* 9.[1792] 168: The old saying [Latin
only]. **1787** Adams *Works* 8.465: [Latin
only], **1808** 6.531-2: Mercuries ought not,
indeed, to be sculptured out of every kind
of wood. NED Wood *sb.*[1] 6i; *Oxford* 227-8;
Tilley M893.

M149 **Mercy** to a few is cruelty to many
1747 Pote *Journal* 163: But am Under obligation to accord with ye old Proverb Viz y^e

Tender mercys of ye wicked are cruel. **1799** CLee in Adams *Works* 9.21: Mercy to a few is cruelty to many. *Oxford* 526.

M150   Good to be **Merry** and wise

?1710 Byrd *Secret Diary* 106: We were merry and wise and went to bed in good time by my means. **1714** Hunter *Androboros* 12: If 'tis good; To be Merry and Wise. 'Tis the Dev'l to be Sullen and Mad. **1758** HRoberts in Franklin *Papers* 8.85: When they are inclin'd to be merry . . . to be Merry and Wise. **1781** JThaxter in *Adams FC* 4.186: We were merry and wise. **1787** *Columbian Magazine* 1.551: I . . . love to be *merry* as well as *wise*. *Oxford* 527; Whiting M514.

M151   **Method** in one's madness

1796 Latrobe *Journal* 42: There is so much method in his madness. **1801** *Farmers' Museum* 284: This romance, like the incoherence of Hamlet, has "method in madness." **1817** Randolph(J) *Letters* 194: I was quite delirious, but had method in my madness. **1830** Ames *Mariner's* 9. **1846** WLewis in Jackson *Correspondence* 4.258. *Oxford* (2nd ed.) 422; TW 241.

M152   As old as **Methuselah**

1782 Trumbull *Satiric Poems* 168: Should I live long as old Methus'lah. **1815** Humphreys *Yankey* 34: Till I'm as old as Methusalem. **a1855** Beecher *Autobiography* 1.39: Live as long as Methusaleh. Barbour 119; *Oxford* 588; Svartengren 149; Whiting M526.

M153   **Meum** and tuum

1607 Newport's *Discoveries* in *Transactions and Collections of the American Antiquarian Society* 4(1860) 61: Neither is there scarce that we call *meum et tuum* among them, save only the kings know their own territoryes. **1670** Williams *Writings* 6.348-9: Matters of propriety and *meum* and *tuum* between the King and his subjects. **1692** Bulkeley *Will* 112: As for their other laws of a common nature, relating to *meum et tuum*, in sea and land affairs. **a1700** Hubbard *New England* 110: That so *meum* and *tuum* that divide the world, should not

disturb the peace of good Christians. **1708** Johnston *Papers* 24: Set the Clergy together by the Ears about *Meum* & *Tuum*, **1711** 72: Law Suits and Disputes about *Meum* & *Tuum*. **1719** *Addition* in *Colonial Currency* 1.392: In matters of *Meum* and *Tuum* as they're called. **1730** Chalkley *Youth* 555. **1752** Johnson *Writings* 2.424: A notion of *meum* and *tuum,* and thence a very quick sense of justice and injustice. **1753** *Independent Reflector* 118. **1755** Johnson *Writings* 1.223. **1772** *Johnson Papers* 12.953. **1774** Dickinson *Writings* 477: The question of "meum vel tuum." **1784** *Belknap Papers* 2.373[14]. **1787** Adams *Works* 6.203: They will rise in arms . . . about common affairs of meum and tuum. **1788** JCutting in Jefferson *Papers* 13.663. **1789** Stiles *Diary* 3.343. **1805** Brackenridge *Modern* 619, **1815** 708: But as to those duties or professions which require some discrimination of meum and tuum, they ever remain totally incompetent. **1815** Weems *Letters* 3.133: That's the meum & tuum of the right stamp & I am ready to give it the right hand of a hearty welcome. **1823** Bierce *Travels* 89: The distinction of "meum et tuum," or my property and yours, should be kept up. **1824** Blane *Excursion* 55: [It] thus destroyed the reverence for the *meum* and *tuum*. **1824** *Tales* 2.15: You must promise to have all invidious distinctions between *meum* and *tuum* abolished. **1827** Watterston *Wanderer* 111: [He] had lost all knowledge of the distinction between *meum* and *tuum*. **1830** Ames *Mariner's* 192: To make them understand the difference between *meum* and *tuum*. *Oxford* 529; TW 242; Whiting M571.

M154   Many **Mickles** make a muckle

1793 *Washington *Writings* 32.423: A Scotch addage, than which nothing in nature is more true "that many mickles make a muckle," 33.192: There is no addage more true than an old Scotch one, that "many mickles make a muckle," **1794** 33.390: There is an old Scotch adage, than which none in the whole catalogue of them is more true or more worthy of being held in remembrance, viz. NED Mickle B 4; Whiting L402. Cf. *Oxford* 508. See **G1, L178**. See Introduction, p. xvii above.

M155   As black as **Midnight**

1796 CPowell in *W&MCQ* 12(1903) 225: A cloud . . . as black as midnight. Barbour 119(1); TW 242(1). See **N70**.

M156   As dark as **Midnight**

1805 Silliman *Travels* 1.93: As dark as midnight. Barbour 119(1); Whiting M530. See **N71**.

M157   As solemn as **Midnight**

1826 Royall *Sketches* 227: All was as solemn as midnight.

M158   As still as **Midnight**

1809 JAdams in *Adams-Cunningham Letters* 124: The Newspapers are as still as midnight, 1811 in *Adams-Waterhouse Correspondence* 1.69: As still as Midnight. Whiting M532. See **N72**.

M159   **Might** overcomes right (*varied*)

a1700 Hubbard *New England* 375: For ofttimes might overcomes right, according to the proverb. 1702 Taylor *Christographia* 201.1-3: O! what a thing is Might right mannag'd! 'Twill That Proverb brain, whose face doth ware this paint (Might ore goe's Right). 1786 Washington *Writings* 28.486: Upon such principles, *might*, not *right*, must ever prevail. 1789 *Norton Papers* 485: So that might aided by golden influence prevail over right. 1798 Ames *Diary* 123: Might will overcome Right. 1809 Weems *Washington* 60: What signifies *right* against *might!* 1818 TDawes in King *Life* 6.154: The false maxim that *might is right*. 1825 Pearse *Narrative* 57: Power gives right. Barbour 119(2); *Oxford* 530-1; Whiting M534.

M160   With **Might** and main

1622 *Mourt's Relation* 16: They ran away with might and mayne. 1632 EHowes in *Winthrop Papers(A)* 3.101: The divell . . . setts upon you with all his might and maine. 1703 Sewall *Diary* 2.79: None being by, his bold sworn Attorneys push it on with might and main. 1705 JHigginson in *Baxter Manuscripts* 9.211. 1710 Johnston *Papers*

58. ?1722 Winslow *Broadside* 115: Come padling down with all their might and main. a1731 Cook *Bacon* 321. 1734 Belcher *Papers* 2.155. 1752 Carter *Diary* 1.92. 1764 RBland *Colonel* in Bailyn *Pamphlets* 1.311: One who was resolved to trudge, with might and main, through dirt and mire. 1764 Franklin *Papers* 11.385. 1722 Hearne *Journey* 324: They may with truth be said to cry with all their might and main. 1774 JNewell in *VHM* 11(1903) 248. 1778 *New Jersey Gazette* in *Newspaper Extracts(II)* 2.124. 1790 Jefferson *Papers* 16.89: I could wish therefore that he could apply with might and main to these two languages. 1794 DJarratt in *W&MCQ* 3S 9(1952) 386. 1795 *Tablet* 43. 1801 Story *Shop* 96. 1802 *Port Folio* 2.248. 1805 Weems *Hymen* 19: "Marry and raise up soldiers might and main." 1806 Fessenden *Modern Philosopher* 239. 1806 *Weekly* 1.101. 1809 Irving *History* 2.67, 205. 1811 Burroughs *Memoirs* 301: That I should be turned out of town by might and main. 1817 Drake *Works* 159. 1822 Watterston *Winter* 130. 1823 Wirt *Letters* 2.158: I have turned into the practice of the law, might and main, 1828 243: My two brothers and my son-in-law have turned into cropping might and main. 1832 Cooper *Letters* 2.321, 1836 3.228: About twice as many have sold as of Slidell's book, but they are puffing away at him, might and main. *Oxford* 530; Whiting M537.

M161   As sweet as **Milk**

1733 Byrd *Journey* 290: The river . . . rolling down its waters, as sweet as milk. Whiting M544.

M162   As white as **Milk**

1691 Taylor *Poems* 67: Remain, though wrought for Saints as white as milk, 1692 75: But this thy Web more white by far than milke, 1695/6 106: And whiter far than Milke. 1702 Mather *Magnalia* 1.396: Whiter than milk. 1709 Lawson *Voyage* 152: As white as milk. 1716 Taylor *Poems* 326, 1718 342. 1750 PKalm in Franklin *Papers* 4.47: It is white as milk or snow. 1775 JHarvey in *Blount Papers* 1.3: Her lips as milk are white. 1779 AHubley in Sullivan *Journals* 148. 1791 Delano *Narrative* 86.

1801 Story *Shop* 15: Far whiter than foaming milk. **1802** Cutler *Life* 2.72: A dish somewhat like a pudding — inside white as milk or curd. Whiting M545.

M162a   Milk-white

1622 *Mourt's Relation* 82: A milke white foule. **1672** Josselyn *New England Rareties* 58: In winter they are milk white, 132, 133 **1686** Taylor *Poems* 30, 33, **1687** 40, **1688** 47, **1689** 52, **1691** 72, **1692** 74, 75, **1697** 123, **1699** 145, **c1700** 394, 401, 431, **1701** *Christographia* 34.49, **1703** 461.88, **1712** *Poems* 276, **1715** 314, 316. **1716** JPaine in *Mayflower Descendant* 9(1907) 137. **1717** Taylor *Poems* 334, **1718** 342, **1720** 365, **1723** 378. **1753** JPerkins in Franklin *Papers* 4.449. **1765** Timberlake *Memoirs* 64. **1774** Cresswell *Journal* 32. **1772** Freneau *Poems* 1.70, 104. **1773** De Brahm *Report* 246. **1778** Carver *Travels* 101. **1784** EHazard in *Belknap Papers* 1.380. **a1786** Ladd *Remains* 154. **1791** Bartram *Travels* 102. **1792** Pope *Tour* 15. **1793** Campbell *Travels* 54, 131, 217. **1793** Ingraham *Journal* 41, 42. **1794** Tyler *Verse* 29. **1795** *Tablet* 4. **1802** Chester *Federalism* 39. **1805** Silliman *Travels* 2.154. **1806** *Port Folio* NS 1.88. **1815** Brackenridge *Modern* 798. **1818** Evans *Pedestrious* 306. **a1826** Woodworth *Melodies* 103. Whiting M545a.

M163   Milk and cider

1807 Jackson *Correspondence* 1.164: It [a letter] is of a doubtful hue, a milk and cider thing, **1813** 421: It really brought nothing but milk and cider recommendations. DA milk (e).

M164   Milk and water

1776 Lee *Papers* 1.377: But for the same apathy ... towards what the milk and water people call reconciliation. **1783** JArmstrong in Madison *Papers* 6.349: Milk & Water Stile. **1789** PButler in Iredell *Correspondence* 2.265: A few *milk-and-water* amendments have been proposed. **1789** Mason *Papers* 3.1164. **1792** Jefferson *Writings* 1.318: This Constitution was a shilly shally thing, of mere milk and water. **1792** *Washington *Papers* 31.494: Not such a milk and water thing as I expect to see.

1793 Jefferson *Writings* 1.386: Our Government is good for nothing, is a milk and water thing. **1794** Livingston *Democracy* 10. **1796** *Polar Star* in Buckingham *Specimens* 2.299: It is a milk-and-water paper. **1797** UTracy in Gibbs *Memoirs* 1.537. **1803** RTroup in King *Life* 4.203: Jefferson's milk and water communication on this subject is not generally liked. **1809** Fessenden *Pills* 101: The mincing, milk and water measures of our late administration. **1810** Jefferson *Writings* 12.292. **1813** Jackson *Correspondence* 1.428: With all such damd. milk and water observations, which is well calculated to raise mutiny in the minds of the men. **1813** RPeters in Quincy *JQuincy* 368. **1817** Robertson *Letters* 15. **1822** Gallatin *Diary* 227. **1823** JLowell in Otis *Letters* 2.253: The desertion of the milk & water Federalists. Thornton *Glossary* 2.580; TW 244(11).

M165   The Milk of human kindness

1774 Lee(W) *Letters* 1.92: Too much of the milk of human kindness in them. **1788** Shaw *Journals* 280: They seem to possess much of the milk of human kindness. *Oxford* (2nd ed.) 423-4.

M166   To cry for shed (spilt) Milk

1757 Laurens *Papers* 2.502: Tis too late to cry for shed milk. **1782** Jay *Correspondence* 2.329: As Putnam used to say, "it is not worth while to cry about spilt milk." Barbour 119(1); *Oxford* 159; TW 243(5).

M167   Milk-warm

1800 Adams *Letters on Silesia* 192: The bath waters are about milk-warm. **1810** TRJoynes in *W&MCQ* 10(1901) 149: The waters in the spring are ... more than milk-warm. Whiting M550.

M168   Mill news

1777 Wister *Journal* 69: No passengers came by the house, except to the Mill, & we don't place much dependence on Mill news. *Oxford* 565; Tilley N143; Whiting M552. See **C17, G8.**

M169   A Miller, a thief (*varied*)

1680 Randolph *Letters* 3.63: And doe not like the Miller; he's a theife. **1770** Carter

Diary 1.429: And if we should reckon the cheating of Miller's the nibbling of wheat, **1771** 574: While Millers are no honester and we are to pay them for thieving from us. *Oxford* 532; Whiting M560.

M170   As calm as a **Millpond**

1789 Anburey *Travels* 1.4-5: The sea . . . was now become as calm as a mill-pond. **a1841** Trumbull *Autobiography* 59: Calm as a mill-pond.

M171   As smooth as a **Millpond**

1793 Ingraham *Journal* 206: The sea . . . smooth as a millpond. **1803** Ellicott *Journal* 212: The sea almost as smooth as a mill pond. **1831** Murphey *Papers* 1.393. **1832** JRandolph in Jackson *Correspondence* 4.424. **1841** Clifford *Letters* 128. *Oxford* 747; TW 244(2). See **P227.**

M172   As still as a **Millpond**

1796 Ames *Letters* 1.199: The sea of politics . . . is as still as a mill-pond.

M173   As hard as the nether **Millstone**

1754 Smith *Works* 1¹.7: Harder than . . . the nether millstone. TW 224(1).

M174   To be a **Millstone** about one's neck

1777 JA in *Adams FC* 2.262: They will hang like a Mill stone about their Necks, **1780** *Works* 7.184: This debt would be a heavier millstone about their necks than that of England. **1780** Franklin *Writings* 8.25: Their Debt . . . hangs like a Millstone upon the Neck of their Credit. **1795** Morris *Diary and Letters* 2.91. **1796** Smith(EH) *Diary* 168. **1801** *Codman Letters* 228. **1804** Adams *Writings* 3.59: The cost of the Louisiana purchase hangs like a mill stone upon the neck of our commerce. **1808** Rush *Letters* 2.984. **1809** Adams *Writings* 3.314: They will hang like millstones on the neck of Mr. Madison's measures. **1809** Jefferson *Writings* 12.276: That form will forever be a millstone round our necks. **1811** LWTazewell in Monroe *Writings* 5.173. **1815** Morris *Diary and Letters* 2.577. **1834** Paulding *Letters(II)* 147: They have got a millstone about their necks, in the shape of a Bank, **1839** 250, **1850** 510: A portion of the democracy of New-York . . . has at length

found itself with the millstone of fanaticism about its neck. Barbour 120; Whiting M565.

M175   To see as far into a **Millstone** as another

c1800 Tyler *Island* 25: I can see as far into a millstone as he who picked it. **1807** *Salmagundi* 30: Dick . . . who can see as far as anybody — into a millstone, 289: Mr. Ichabod Fungus; who I soon saw was at his usual trade of prying into millstones. **1815** *Port Folio* 3NS 5.428: J. R. W. cannot only see as far into a millstone as any other man, but much farther. **1816** Paulding *Letters(I)* 1.81: A knowing man who saw deep into mill stones, 2.63: I do believe he can see further into a millstone than most people. **1833** Cooper *Letters* 2.371: He has got a glass eye, and thinks he can see [better] into a mill-stone. *Oxford* 532; Whiting M566. See **G177.**

M176   To sink like a **Millstone**

1765 Adams *Legal Papers* 1.95: Many a Case, has sunk like a Millstone to the Bottom of the Ocean.

M177   A contented **Mind** is a feast (*varied*)

1676 Tompson *Poems* 49: And the best *Sawce* to every Dish, *Content*. **1718** Chalkley *Observations* 411: The meek and contented Mind hath (according to a good general Maxim) a continual Feast. **1772** Copy-book in *Wheelock's Indians* opp. 276: A contented mind is a contented Feast. *Oxford* 142; Tilley M969. Cf. Whiting C412.

M178   The **Mind** makes the man

1823 *Austin Papers* 1.639: *The mind makes the man. Oxford* 533.

M179   A sound **Mind** in a sound body

1783 Van Schaack *Letters* 222: *Mens sana in corpore sano.* **1785** Jefferson *Papers* 8.407: A strong body makes the mind strong. **1795** Smith(EH) *Diary* 80: [Latin only]. **1795** Wansey *Journal* x: [Latin only]. **1812** Holcombe *First Fruits* 155: A sound mind in a sound body. **1821** BWaterhouse in *Adams-Waterhouse Correspondence* 148: [Latin only]. **1833** Wirt *Letters* 2.409: For what is the *mens sana* without the *corpore* *sano?* Juvenal *Satires* x 356; *Oxford* 755; Tilley M974.

M180   **Mine** is better than ours
1756 Franklin *PR* 6.320: *Mine* is better than *Ours.*

M181   Enough to make **Ministers** swear
1775 Freneau *Poems* 1.124: It's enough to make ministers swear. See **A94, P23.**

M182   A **Minister** should know nothing but his Bible
1702 Mather *Magnalia* 1.459: The French proverb, *Un ministre ne doit Savoir que sa Bible*—"A minister should know nothing but his Bible."

M183   As black as a **Mink**
1778 Carver *Travels* 465: "As black as a mink," being a proverbial expression in America. TW 245(1).

M184   As lean as a **Mink**
1801 Story *Shop* 27: He's . . . lean as a mink.

M185   If you are not sure of a **Minute,** *etc.*
1738 Franklin *PR* 2.195: Since thou art not sure of a minute, throw not away an Hour, 1758 *WW* 343. Cf. TW 245(1).

M186   He that has seen one **Miracle,** *etc.*
1674 Josselyn *Account* 108: The *Italian* hath a proverb, that he that hath seen one miracle, will easily believe another, 150.

M187   **Miracles** (wonders) will never cease
1766 Copley *Letters* 48: But I shall be Married as I find Mericle[s] have not ceas'd. 1780 Jay *Correspondence* 1.444: Miracles have ceased. 1799 Cobbett *Porcupine* 10. 211: Miracles will never cease. 1802 Asbury *Journal* 2.340: Wonders will never cease. 1805 AM'Caine in *Ruffin Papers* 1.83: Wonders, 1807 113: Miracles. 1809 *Kennon Letters* 31.305: Will "marracles ever be done ceasing." 1815 WCNicholas in *W&MCQ* 27(1918) 206: Miracles. 1820 Robertson *Letters* 112: Wonders, 1821 160-1: Wonders. 1822 Lee *Diary and Letters* 198: Wonders. 1826 Pintard *Letters* 2.309: Wonders, 1833 4.170: Wonders. *Oxford* 912; TW 410(2).

M188   In the **Mire**
1756 JEliot in Stiles *Itineraries* 480: Ineffectual struggling doth but sink a man the deeper into the mire. 1765 TWharton in Franklin *Papers* 12.359: In every Step they take they plunge themselves further into the mire. 1777 King *Life* 1.25: God help them out of the mire in his own good time. 1783 ANash in Iredell *Correspondence* 2.36: So we all say, but this won't get the cart out of the mire. 1812 Hitchcock *Social* 28. *Oxford* 534; Whiting M573, cf. C59.

M189   As smooth as a **Mirror**
1814 Brackenridge *Views* 228: The river as smooth as a mirror. Cf. TW 246. See **L210.**

M190   No **Mischief** but had a priest or a woman at the bottom
1779 Hamilton *Papers* 2.168: The proverb is verified—"there never was any mischief but had a *priest* or a woman at the bottom." *Oxford* 572; Tilley M1000-1. See **P206.**

M191   One's **Mischief** returns on his head
1746 *Boston Evening-Post* in *Newspaper Extracts(I)* 2.305: You must receive it as . . . *your own Mischief returning on your Head.* *Oxford* 162; Tilley C924. Cf. Whiting D342. See **C377, F214, P182.**

M192   **Misery** loves company
1775 TGilbert in *Naval Documents* 1.279: Misery Loves Compy. 1778 Smith *Memoirs (II)*286: Both were astonished at the Falsehood of those Calumnies which they imputed to Fear and a Desire of Company in their approaching Misfortunes. 1785 Pynchon *Diary* 221: What a fine thing it is to have company in streights. 1806 Dunlap *Diary* 2.383: It is generally supposed that fellowship in suffering lightens pain. 1814 Palmer *Diary* 19. 1815 King *Life* 5.449: Crime and misery love company. 1816 *Port Folio* 4NS 1.295. 1817 Adams *Writings* 6.157: There is an old vulgar saying that. 1817 Baldwin *Letters* 236: Misery always wants company. 1832 Pintard *Letters* 4.74: tis s^d. Barbour 120; *Oxford* 138; Whiting W715.

M193 Misery makes strange bedfellows

1813 Adams *Writings* 4.456: The principle of Shakespeare's Trinculo, "Misery acquaints a man with strange bed fellows." *Oxford* 535; TW 246(1). See **P226, T227.**

M194 Misfortunes seldom come alone (*varied*)

1722 Franklin *Papers* 1.22: Until one Misfortune comes upon the Neck of another. c1725 Byrd *Another Secret Diary* 466: One misfortune treading, like Count Marino's Duns, upon the heals of another. 1779 JFogg in Sullivan *Journals* 93: Misfortunes, according to the ancient whim, seldom come singly. 1782 JNoyes in *Baxter Manuscripts* 19.456. 1791 TBurr in Burr *Memoirs* 1.301: We certainly see the old proverb very often verified. "That misfortunes never come singly," that poor little woman is a proof. 1793 MDusenbury in Iredell *Correspondence* 2.401: The fever is all around us, and one calamity seldom comes alone. 1793 Ingraham *Journal* 40. 1794 Jefferson *Writings* 18.193: Good things, as well as evil go in a train. 1798 *Washington *Writings* 36.350: One trouble . . . frequently draws on another. 1800 Cobbett *Porcupine* 11.405: says the proverb. 1802 DCarmick in *Barbary Wars* 2.294: Misfortunes, they say, come together. 1803 Burr *Correspondence* 136: That good and ill fortune never come in single strokes, but in sequences, you have heard since you were four years old. 1806 *Port Folio* NS 2.321: When misery comes, it comes not singly. 1810 Dwight *Journey* 56: One misfortune follows another. 1810 Rush *Autobiography* 338: We complain that sorrows seldom come alone. 1817 Baldwin *Letters* 222: *Misfortunes never come singly.* 1822 Watterston *Winter* 31: His misfortunes, like every body else's, came not singly. 1815 Palmer *Diary* 216: Dont let us forbode Mishaps, they always come fast enough. 1823 Gallatin *Diary* 245: Troubles do not come singly. 1832 Barney *Memoir* 277: Gloomy fancies, like misfortunes, seldom come in single file. Barbour 121(3); *Oxford* 535; TW 246(1); Whiting H139.

M195 A **Miss** is as good as a mile

1788 *American Museum* 3.382: A miss is as good as a mile. 1794 Drinker *Journal* 254: The miss of an inch is said to be as good as a mile. Barbour 121; *Oxford* 535; TW 246.

M196 To be married to **Miss Roper**

1796 Cobbett *Porcupine* 4.39: Tied to the gang-way, or, as the sailors call it, married to *miss roper*. Cf. TW 164-5. See **G191.**

M197 To go off (vanish) like a **Mist**

1775 Huntington *Papers* 249: Doctor Sprague . . . thinks her Disorder will go off like a Mist. 1777 Smith *Memoirs(II)* 175: And their decietful Delusions will vanish like a Mist before the Noon Day Sun. Whiting M594. See **A60, S262.**

M198 Mistrust is the mother of safety

c1680 Radisson *Voyages* 110: Mistrust is the mother of safety, 196: Mistrust nevertheless is the mother of safety.

M199 Not avail a **Mite**

1748 *Word* in *Colonial Currency* 4.368: It will not avail one *Mite*. Whiting M599.

M200 Not suffer a **Mite**

1718 JBridger in *Baxter Manuscripts* 9.419: No person would suffer a Mite in their Estates. Cf. Whiting M597-611.

M201 To cast in one's **Mite**

1774 Jones *Journal* 68-9: Mrs. Henry, knowing well the disposition of the Indians, cast in her mite. NED Mite[2] ic.

M202 To handle without **Mittens**

1710 Sewall *Letter-Book* 1.406: Thus being handled without mittens. 1733 Belcher *Papers* 1.279: I wou'd handle him without mittens. 1780 BTallmadge in Webb *Correspondence* 2.252. 1800 HJackson in *Bingham's Maine* 2.1085: He will be handled without mittens by all the friends of Mr. Adams. *Oxford* 348; TW 247(3).

M203 Mocking is catching

1791 S.P.L. *Thoughts* 77: Mocking is catching. *Oxford* 351, 537; Tilley H131, S152. Cf. Whiting M612.

M204 As sweet as **Molasses**

1803 *Yankee Phrases* 87: As sweet as molasses her lips. Lean 2.880; Svartengren 306.

M205 (As blind as a **Mole**)

1657 Wigglesworth *Diary* 103: Such blind moles as goe up and down the world and see no god in the world. *Oxford* 67; Taylor *Comparisons* 19; Tilley M1034; Whiting NC 445.

M206 He that wants **Money** wants all things

1781 *Deane Brothers Papers* 158: You may apply the old adage "He that wanteth Money wanteth all things." 1803 Davis *Travels* 206: The man who wanted money, was in want of every thing, 313. Tilley M1046.

M207 Lend **Money** to an enemy, *etc.*

1740 Franklin *PR* 2.254: Lend Money to an Enemy, and thou'lt gain him, to a Friend and thou'lt lose him. Barbour 122(18); *Oxford* 455; Tilley F725.

M208 Make **Money** honestly if you can, but make money

1815 *Reviewers* 20: One of John Bull's favorite axioms is . . . "make money honestly *if you can,* but make money."

M209 **Money** answers all things

1719 *Addition* in *Colonial Currency* 1.377: The Wise Man says *Money answers all things,* 1720 2.97: *Money answers all things.* 1721 Wise *Word* 14. 1725 Wolcott *Poetical Meditation* 12: Money answers every thing, but a Guilty Conscience Sting. 1731 *Trade* in *Colonial Currency* 2.368, 1740 3.398: (as the Wise Man tells us), 1750 4.440-1. 1777 POliver in Hutchinson *Diary* 2.150. 1780 *Belknap Papers* 1.57. 1795 Bentley *Diary* 2.128. *Oxford* 538; Tilley M1052.

M210 **Money** is power

1741 Ames *Almanacs* 148: Laws bear Name, but Money has the Power. 1789 Ames *Letters* 1.39: Money is power. TW 248(4). See **K56, W81.**

M211 **Money** is sweeter than honey

1735 Franklin *PR* 2.7: Nothing but Money, Is sweeter than Honey. Tilley H544, quote 1578.

M212 **Money** is the sinews of trade

1731 *Money is the Sinews of Trade* in *Colonial Currency* 2.431.

M213 **Money** is the sinews of war

1690 F-JWinthrop in *Winthrop Papers(B)* 4.303: Any mistake in those sinews of war will greatly hinder & weaken the force of yor armes. 1721 Wise *Word* 14: It is an old Saying and a true one, Scil. *Money is the Sinews of War.* 1732 Belcher *Papers* 1.159: As money is the sinews of war, so it is of government. 1750 *Massachusetts* in *Colonial Currency* 4.440. 1775 Carter *Diary* 2.945. 1777 ZAdams in *Adams FC* 2.215. 1777 Washington *Writings* 8.112. 1779 *New Jersey Gazette* in *Newspaper Extracts* (*II*) 3.653: To destroy our currency in hope to cut the sinews of our defensive war, 1781 5.235. 1782 Huntington *Papers* 454. 1789 Humphreys *Works* 334: Money, the nerve of war, was wanting. 1800 Paine *Correspondence* 2.1414: It used to be said in England that. 1806 Morris *Diary and Letters* 2.483. 1815 Jefferson *Writings* 14.356: Our money, the nerve of war. 1816 *Port Folio* 4NS 1.170: The sinew of war is likewise the life-blood of literature. 1819 Brackenridge *South America* 2.190. *Oxford* 539; TW 248 (5).

M214 **Money** makes the mare go (*varied*)

1771 *Johnson Papers* 8.13: Nothing makes the Mare go like the Visibles [money in hand]. 1781 JA in *Adams FC* 4.248: I have no Money to make the dull Jacks go. 1787 Tyler *Contrast* 35: It is money makes the mare go. 1808 *Port Folio* NS 6.80: 'Twas money that made the old mare go. 1815 Brackenridge *Modern* 777. Barbour 122(9); *Oxford* 529; TW 248(6). Cf. Whiting M627.

M215 **Money** once gone never returns

1771 Copley *Letters* 138: But remember money once gone never returns.

M216 **Money** will do anything (*varied*)

1683 IMather in *Mather Papers* 106: Butt in England Money will do much. 1753 Franklin *PR* 4.405: He that is of opinion Money will do every Thing, may well be suspected of doing every Thing for Money. **1775** Paine *Cupid* 2.1116: Money will do any thing. **1776** Deane *Papers* 1.212: As money purchases everything in this country. **1785** Washington *Writings* 28.185: Money we know will fetch anything, and command the services of any man. **1812** Melish *Travels* 72: I know money will procure any thing. Lean 4.50; Cf. *Oxford* 537, 538, 540; Whiting M633.

M217 To pour out **Money** like water (*varied*)

1811 Fletcher *Letters* 37: What money I let you have goes as free as water, I value the dollars no more than chips. **1823** Sumter *Letters* 100: In fact my dear money goes like water. **1834** Hone *Diary* 1.142: My money frequently poured out like water. **1837** RTaney in Jackson *Correspondence* 5.492: And money will be poured out like water to accomplish the object of the Bank. TW 395(17).

M218 To take **Money** out of one pocket and put it in another

1768 JParker in Franklin *Papers* 15.58: It was taking Money out of one Pocket to put it in to'ther.

M219 To throw good **Money** after bad

1690 Fitzhugh *Letters* 274: And consequently good money thrown after bad. **1751** Wolcott *Papers* 50-1: I was not willing to throw away good Money after bad. **1792** Belknap *Foresters* 149: Why should I keep on throwing away good money after bad. **1797** *Washington *Writings* 36.13: The appearance of throwing good money after bad. *Oxford* 819.

M220 As mischievous as a **Monkey**

1813 Paulding *Lay* 203: In Spain it has passed into a proverb; and to say that a man is "as mischievous as a collegian or a monkey," conveys an idea of a superlative pickle.

M221 As nimble as a **Monkey**

1795 Murdock *Triumph* 49: If I had not been as nimble as a monkey. Cf. Svartengren 158: agile; Whiting NC 446(1).

M222 From the **Monkey** to the rat

1779 JFogg in Sullivan *Journals* 97: The whole party [of soldiers] from the monkey to the rat, had armed themselves with almost every species of the vegtable creation.

M223 The higher a **Monkey** climbs the more we see his tail (*varied*)

1738 *Georgia Records* 22¹.166: But Monkeys in climbing will always discover something not fit to name. **1802** Chester *Federalism* 26: The higher they climb, the more they show—themselves. **1747** Cooper *Letters* 5.194: The higher a monkey climbs the more we see his tail. *Oxford* 372; Whiting A144.

M224 Like a **Monkey** in a china shop

1787 Hopkinson *Miscellaneous Essays* 2.164: After he had fatigued himself with mischief, like a monkey in a china shop. *Oxford* 90: Bull; TW 46: Bull(5).

M225 To grin like a **Monkey**

1809 Weems *Marion* 159: Some of them grinned in my face like monkies, **1813** *Drunkard* 133: The red-faced populace looking on the while, and grinning like monkeys. **1818** Evans *Pedestrious* 320. **1822** Watterston *Winter* 105: The three negroes . . . grinning like monkeys. TW 248(2).

M226 The more **Months** the more 40s

1766 MBeckwith in *W&MCQ* 23(1914) 260: But noe matter, according to the old proverb—The More months, the more 40s.

M227 To be happy by the **Month**

1779 Ledyard *Journal of Cook's Last Voyage* 141: Where our extrinsic virtues might gain us another short space of being wondered at, and doing as we pleased, or as our tars expressed it of being happy by the month. Cf. *Oxford* 351.

M228 To have a **Month's** mind

1787 Tyler *Contrast* 57: I had a month's mind to buss her. *Oxford* 541; Tilley M1109.

M229 As changeable as the **Moon** (*varied*)

1780 JMecom in *Franklin-Mecom* 200: But

if the Artists that have taken y[r] Face have varied . . . it will appear as changeable as the moon. **1782** Jay *Correspondence* 2.317: Those unstable ones who, like the moon, change once a fortnight. **1798** Adams *New Letters* 145: [Fashions] are as various as the Changes of the moon. **1824** Mason *Memoirs* 287: The prospects of the candidates are more changeable than the moon. **1834** Baldwin *Diary* 274: He is as full of changes as the moon. Barbour 123(11); *Oxford* 114; Whiting M647, 655.

M230 As red as the **Moon**

1791 Delano *Narrative* 97: His face was as round and as red as the moon. Whiting M649.

M231 The **Moon** is made of green cheese

1723 *New-England Courant* 95(1.1): 'Twere easy to make him believe, that the Moon is made from green Cheese. **1772** SGardiner in Bailey *Journal* 97: [Any] more than they can prove the sun to be green cheese. **1774** Carroll *Copy-Book* 223: If my country men judge me incapable of serving them in a public station for believing y[e] moon to be made of green cheese. **1788** *Columbian Magazine* 2.696: I am sure I cannot divine, if the *moon and green cheese* were not used to betoken disparity. **1790** Winslow *Broadside* opp. 210: Demonstrate clearly, that the moon is cheese. **1800** WCobbett *Letters* 50: They will not . . . be able to persuade John Bull, that the moon is made of green cheese. **1807** *Salmagundi* 190: She held the story of the moon's being made of green cheese as an abominable slander on her favorite planet. **1811** *Port Folio* 2NS 5.285: The moon is not moulded out of green-cheese. **1815** Brackenridge *Modern* 779: He had said the moon was made of green cheese. **1815** Palmer *Diary* 133: We might as well look for cheese in the moon, 142. **1816** Paulding *Letters(I)* 1.195: The moon was only a great *Welsh* cheese, about the size of a cartwheel. *Oxford* 542; Whiting M659.

M232 To bay (howl against) the **Moon**

1777 JEliot in *Belknap Papers* 3.103: It is a rare thing to meet with any body here with- out some *lofty titles* to declare their merit, Colonel A, Major B, Captain C., denominates every puppy that "bays the moon." **1797** Graham *Vermont* 139: They hear him *"howl against the moon,"* and spit his venom forth against every institution held sacred. Barbour 123(2); *Oxford* 541; Whiting M654. See **D231**.

M233 To fish for the **Moon**

1806 Hitchcock *Works* 127: Turns out like Welshmen fishing for the moon. Cf. *Oxford* 542; Whiting M666.

M234 To see two **Moons**

1722 Franklin *Papers* 1.40: *See two Moons,* **1737** *Drinkers* 2.176: He sees two Moons.

M235 As mild as a **Moonbeam**

1818 Fessenden *Ladies Monitor* 36: Mild as a moon beam in the month of May. TW 249.

M236 A **Moonlight** flitting

1793 Campbell *Travels* 282: A moon-light flitting is thought of. *Oxford* 542; TW 249.

M237 To hold to one's **Moorings**

1801 JCathcart in *Barbary Wars* 1.456: We cannot hold to our moorings.

M238 As straight as a **Moose's** course

1792 Belknap *History* 3.120: [The moose's] course through the woods is straight, to a proverb.

M239 The **More** one gets the more he wants

1761 *Johnson Papers* 3.515: The more they get the more they ask. **1775** Ward *Correspondence* 68: A Miser . . . the more money he gets, wa[nts] the more. **1788** *Politician* 25: The more we have the more we want. **1798** Manning *Key* 9: In short he is never easy, but the more he has the more he wants. Barbour 124(2); *Oxford* 543; Tilley M1144; Whiting C115, G305, M675.

M240 **More** than meets the ear (*varied*)

1717 Byrd *Another Secret Diary* 301: [I] had reason to beleive there was more in the Paper, than was expresst in Black and White. **1788** Washington *Writings* 30.96: More is meant than meets the ear. **1810** Adams *Lectures* 1.199: The rhetoricians

. . . meant more than meets the ear. **1824** *Tales* 2.98: There was more in all this than met the ear. TW 250: Ear(2).

M241 The **More** the merrier, *etc.*
1786 JCurrie in Jefferson *Papers* 10.108: The more the merrier but the fewer the better cheer. **1815** *Kennon Letters* 38.366: Well the more the merrier thay say; and happy is the man who has his quiver full [of children]. **1853** Fletcher *Letters* 246: I . . . [will] most surely be with you, and the more the merrier. Barbour 123-4; *Oxford* 544; Whiting M679. See **F79.**

M242 To grasp **More** than one can hold
1654 Johnson *Wonder-Working* 197: [This] hath caused many towns to grasp more into their hands then they could afterward hold. **1703** JDudley in *Baxter Manuscripts* 9.156: The English in these parts having already grasp'd more than they can plant or defend. *Oxford* 331; Whiting F435, M774. See **A78, M294.**

M243 As fair as the **Morn**
1777 Hopkinson *Miscellaneous Essays* 3(part 2) 166: Fair as the morn was she. Whiting *NC* 446: Morning(1).

M244 As sweet as **Morn**
c1792 Paine *Works* 79: And here her life . . . be sweet as morn.

M245 As beautiful as **Morning**
1806 Tyler *Verse* 143: She's as *bucheous* as morning in May.

M246 A bright **Morning** followed by a dark day, *etc.*
a1700 Hubbard *New England* 233: But ofttimes a bright morning is followed with a dark and obscure evening. **1721** *Boston News-Letter* in Buckingham *Specimens* 1.9: It is often observed, a bright Morning is succeeded by a dark Rainy Day. **1812** Randall *Miser* 28: The pleasantest morning, is sometimes followed by the darkest night. *Oxford* 297; Whiting M687.

M247 In the **Morning** drink one dram, *etc.*
1777 Fitch *New-York Diary* 97: I arose very early in the Morning & paid a strict Attention to a perticular French Proverb . . . (viz)

"In the Morning to Drink one dram Eat one piece of Garlic & Smoak one Pipe of Tobacco."

M248 A louring **Morning** before a lightsome day
1677 Hubbard *Indian* 1.179: A louring Morning before a lightsome Day. **1776** SKennedy in *PM* 8(1884) 115: It often happens that a cloudy morn precedes a clear day. *Oxford* 128; Whiting M686.

M249 A serene **Morning** succeeds a stormy night
1720 ?ECooke *Reflections* in *Colonial Currency* 2.111: A *Serene Morning* succeed a *Stormy Night.* Whiting M692.

M250 Some praise at **Morning** what they blame at night
1747 Ames *Almanacs* 196: Some praise at Morning, what they blame at Night. Cf. Whiting E158.

M251 A dry **Morsel** with quietness is sweet
1649 Williams *Writings* 6.165: Oh how sweet is a dry morsel and a handful with quietness from earth and heaven. Whiting M700. See **L175, W78.**

M252 As meek as **Moses**
1652 Williams *Writings* 7.100: In meekness as Moses. **c1737** *Colden Letters* 9.336: For Moses meek as he was libelled Cain & who is it that has not libelled the Devil? **1776** JAdams in *Warren-Adams Letters* 1.232: The Meekness of Moses. **1787** *American Museum* 1.379: The meekness of Moses. **1804** *Echo* 301: Meek as Moses. **1826** Royall *Sketches* 337: As meek as Moses. Barbour 124(2); Taylor *Comparisons* 57; Whiting *NC* 446.

M253 As thick as **Mosquitoes**
1638 Williams *Writings* 6.99: I sometimes fear that my lines are as thick and over busy as the musketoes.

M254 To catch napping, as **Moss** caught his mare
a1731 Cook *Bacon* 320: When Death at's Chamber door came rapping, As *Moss*

caught Mare, took Bacon napping. *Oxford* 111; Tilley M1185. See **N14.**

M255 To see a **Mote** in another's eye, *etc.*

1618 *Winthrop Papers*(*A*) 2.228; Hypocrite, first cast out the beam that is in thine owne eye. **1653** Keayne *Apologia* 47: For all these are but leaden rules to walk by and often lead into errors and mistakes, making a mote in some men to be a mighty beam and another man's mountain . . . to be looked at as a small molehill. **1718** JCustis in Byrd *Another Secret Diary* 290: Give me leave to bee soe free with you Sʳ as to remove yᵉ cursed moat from before yʳ eys. **1740** Franklin *PR* 2.251: In other men we faults can spy, And blame the mote that dims their eye; Each little speck and blemish find; To our own stronger errors blind, **1767** *Papers* 14.319: There are those who can *see a mote in their brother's eye, while they do not discern a beam in their own.* **1778** JLovell in *Adams FC* 2.404: The Parable of the Beam and Mote. **1783** Van Schaack *Letters* 211: Take care of the beam in your own eye, but do not expose the moat in that of others. **1789** *Columbian Magazine* 3.96: First cast the beam out of thine own eye, and then thou shalt see clearly to take the mote out of thy brother's eye. **1797** Cobbett *Porcupine* 5.339: Don't you think that *Americanus* . . . ought . . . to have first removed the beam from his own eye, lest the sin should lie at his own door. **c1800** Dennie *Lay Preacher* 170: With a beam in their own eyes, they go groping about to discover a mote in their neighbour's. **1803** Austin *Constitutional* 76: A man must cast out the beam in his own eye, before he attempts to pull out the mote which is in his brother's eye. **1803** Davis *Travels* 162: They could spy a mote in the eye of their neighbour, and not perceive the beam in their own. **a1814** Dow *Journal* 410: They . . . view a mote until it looks as large as a mountain. **1816** Webster *Letters* 393: Let the English remove the beam from their own eye before they attempt to pull the mote from ours. **1819** Cobbett *Year's* 180: This America . . . is the beam in the eye . . . of every despot. **1829** Jackson *Correspon-*

dence 4.53: Whose principal business it is to run about the country and point to the mote in their brother or sister's eye without being conscious of the beam that lirks in their own. *Oxford* 545; Whiting M710.

M256 Every **Mother's** son

1650 Bradstreet *Works* 227: And on their ground they die each Mothers Son. **c1680** Radisson *Voyages* 132: It was well that the river swelled, for not a mother's son of us could else escape. **1757** Davis *Colonial Virginia Satirist* 31: Every Mooders son of dem. **1764** JA in *Adams FC* 1.48: The Character of every Mothers Daughter of them is as yet problematical to me. **1782** *New Jersey Gazette* in *Newspaper Extracts*(*II*) 5.384. **1782** Trumbull *Satiric Poems* 130. **1786** *Anarchiad* 6. **1787** Tyler *Contrast* 56. **1789** *American Museum* 5.298. **c1790** Brackenridge *Gazette* 62, **1793** *Modern* 166: With speed each mother's son of them [fleas] goes. **1793** JSmith in Smith *American Poems* 233: And ev'ry mother's son soon *kick the bucket.* **1794** Livingston *Democracy* 20. **1795** *Echo* 133. **1804** Irving *Journals* 1.94, **1809** *History* 2.35, 142, 202, 205. **1810** Schultz *Travels* 1.97. **1813** Weems *Drunkard* 80: And running down into the sea were drowned every mother's pig of them. **1817** Scott *Blue Lights* ix. **1819** Peirce *Rebelliad* 76. **1830** JOverton in Jackson *Correspondence* 4.152. **1832** Ames *Nautical* 133. *Oxford* 546; Whiting M719.

M257 Light-heel'd **Mothers** make leaden-heeled daughters

1745 Franklin *PR* 3.8: Light-heel'd mothers make leaden-heel'd daughters. *Oxford* 463; Tilley M1198.

M258 Like **Mother,** like daughter

1644 Williams *Writings* 3.275: Is not this as the Prophet speaks, Like *mother,* like *daughter?* 345: Like Mother, like Daughter. *Oxford* 546; Whiting M720. See **F48.**

M259 **Mother Cary's** chickens

1784 AAdams in Adams *D and A* 3.165: The Sailors call them Mother Carys Chickens, and that they portend wind. Colcord 132; *Oxford* 546; TW 251.

M260 Mother Rowlandson's removes

1778 Curwen *Journal* 1.448-9: [The number of his moves] amounts since my arrival
in England to just the number of Mother
Rowlandson's removes, of which having
taken minutes will, I fancy, not fail under
the earnest hand of a judicious friend to
make a suitable appendix to the next edition of that curious performance, 1781
2.787: By my present residence I have
arrived at my 19th removal, and am in a
fair way, should life continue, of exceeding
the celebrated Mother Rowlandson who her
history records, as you well know, to have
experienced 24. 1786 EHazard in *Belknap
Papers* 1.444: From the time I went to college till my settlement at Dover I had near
as many removals as Mother Rowlandson
(this is a New England comparison, and will
make Mrs. Hazard laugh).

M261 Mother Tapley's boys

1770 Adams *Legal Papers* 3.212: They are
nothing said he, but a parcel of boys; I
hastily replied, yes, Mother Tapley's boys.
Q. What did you mean by that? *A.* I meant
boys as big as I am. [The speaker was a
man; the editors have no clue to the reference.]

M262 One's Mother tongue

1650 Bradstreet *Works* 274: They had for-
got their mother tongue. 1676 Williams
Writings 5.242: *Hebrew* being their Mother
Tongue, 389: Latin . . . was his *Mother
Romane Tonge.* . . . His *Mother English.*
1690 Danforth *Poems* 145.33: His own
Mother-Tongue beside. 1699 College Ora-
tion in *W&MCQ* 2S 10(1930) 324: The
Comliness of our own Mother tongue. 1723
New-England Courant 100(1.2): 'Tis pity
you should quite forget Your Mother
Tongue. 1751 Franklin *Papers* 4.104. 1753
Smith *Works* 1².205: They greatly con-
demn the practice of neglecting the mother-
tongue. 1761 EWheelock in *Wheelock's
Indians* 17. 1764 *Paxton Papers* 310: The
Number of Students greatly decrease, . . .
and generally return Home with their Heads
stuff'd full of Vulgar Phrases, instead of
that native Purity of their Mother Tongue

they brought with them. 1770 *Norton Pa-
pers* 132. 1777 JA in *Adams FC* 2.307. 1777
Curwen *Journal* 1.388. 1781 JA in *Adams
FC* 4.114, 1782 283. 1783 Hopkinson *Mis-
cellaneous Essays* 2.4: After the youngster
hath been taught to spell, read, and write,
in his mother tongue, he ascends the first
step of learned education. 1783 Williams
Penrose 289. 1787 Shaw *Journals* 247. 1788
Sullivan *Letters* 3.567: Having the holy
Scripture continued to us in our mother
Tongue. 1792 *Echo* 45. 1793 Ingraham
Journal 67. 1796 Hawkins *Letters* 20. 1798
Webster *Letters* 173: It is of particular importance that the principles and structure
of our mother tongue should be clearly defined. 1802 Harmon *Sixteen Years* 55. 1805
Brackenridge *Modern* 580. 1805 Harmon
Sixteen Years 93. 1805 Paine *To the Citizens* 2.950: As to falsehood, it is become so
naturally their [the Federal news-papers]
mother tongue, especially in New England.
1805 Webster *Letters* 262: As a preliminary
step [I] have been learning Anglo-Saxon,
the mother tongue of the present English.
1808 Fraser *Letters and Journals* 84. 1809
Kendall *Travels* 1.120. 1810 Schultz *Travels*
1.118: Those who could not read their own
mother tongue. 1811 Graydon *Memoirs*
180. 1813 Jefferson *Writings* 13.346: Separate it [American English] in name as well
as in power from the mother-tongue. 1814
Littell *Festoons* 70. a1820 Tucker *Essays* 20:
[English] will be the mother tongue, in less
than two centuries, of more than half the
number of people probably now living in
the whole world! 1820 Pintard *Letters*
1.347. 1830 Ames *Mariner's* 119, 278.
Whiting M722.

M263 Mother-in-law and daughter-in-law,
etc.

1810 *Port Folio* 2NS 3.314: Mother-in-law
and daughter-in-law are a tempest and a
hailstorm. *Oxford* 546.

M264 Mother-wit

1702 Mather *Magnalia* 1.207: They have as
much *mother-wit* . . . as the rest of mankind. c1800 Tyler *Island* 30: I have mother
wit enough to find out . . . I am unfit for

office. a1804 Humphreys *Works* 208: With nature's mother-wit, **1815** *Yankey* 40. Whiting M723. Cf. *Oxford* 601; Tilley O87. See **O41.**

M265   The violent **Motion** must break

1652 Williams *Writings* 4.12-3: The Maxime is most true . . . .: the *violent* motion must break. *Oxford* 581; Whiting T195. See **E117, N112.**

M266   As big as a **Mountain**

1793 Brackenridge *Modern* 165: Who had a mind as big's a mountain. Whiting *NC* 446(1).

M267   As stable as a **Mountain**

1784 Pickman *Letters* 138: I thought it stable as the Mountains. Cf. Svartengren 262: firm.

M268   If the **Mountain** will not come to Mahomet, *etc.*

1733 Belcher *Papers* 1.373: In short, if the mountain can't go to Mahomet, I believe Mahomet must come to the mountain. **1778** AWayne in *Thomson Papers* 439: We shall like Mahomet and the Mountain, go to the Clothing if the Clothing won't come to us. **1783** JAdams in *Warren-Adams Letters* 2.189: The Mountain shall come to Mahomet or Mahomet shall go to the Mountain. **1801** Jefferson *Writings* 10.237: Since the mountain will not come to them, they had better go to the mountain. **1808** *Port Folio* NS 6.413: When the mountain would not come to Mahomet, Mahomet felt it no disgrace to proceed to the mountain. **1813** *Kennon Letters* 34.335: I have read somewhere . . . that when Mahomet could not make the mountain come to him, he went to the mountain. **1824** *Tales* 1.151: Here is an old proverb put to shame with a witness —"Mahomet would not go to the mountain, and the mountain has actually come to Mahomet." **1826** Jones *Sketches* I 88. *Oxford* 547; TW 252(1).

M269   The **Mountain** was in labor and brought forth a mouse (*varied*)

1685 IWisewall in *Hinckley Papers* 144: In poet's language [*parturiunt mo*]ntes nasci-

tur *ridiculus mus.* **1692** Bulkeley *Will* 203: *Sic parturiere montes.* **1699** Ward *Trip* 47: And finding nothing but a *Cheese,* laugh'd as heartily at their Disapointment, as the *Mob* in the Fable at the *Mountain-Mouse.* **1713** Wise *Churches* 125: It is even another fit or Paroxism of the Mountains bringing forth, as the Poet says, *Parturiunt montes* &c. **1720** *Letter* in *Colonial Currency* 2.235: The mountain would bring forth a mouse. **1720** Walter *Choice Dialogue* ii: The Mountain groans in Travail, and brings forth a Mouse. **1721** ?TPaine *Discourse* in *Colonial Currency* 2.294: His own proverb [Latin only]. **1721** Wise *Word* 22: Thought I, this is Ridiculous mus all over. **1739** *South Carolina Gazette* 164: [Latin only]. **1740** Belcher *Papers* 2.515: You'll sing with the poet of old [Latin only]. **1741** *Letter* in *Colonial Currency* 4.88: This Mountain may bring forth a Mouse, as the other did a Viper. **1758** Ames *Almanacs* 283: Expectation waits to know, Whether the Mountain bears a Mouse or no. **1764** RBland *Colonel* in Bailyn *Pamphlets* 1.310: Fling him into labor with another criticism and make him bring forth, like the mountain in the fable. **1765** Watts *Letter Book* 378: It looks big, may it not prove the Mountain in labour, may the offspring be Noble. **1767** BGale in Stiles *Itineraries* 492. **1767** Paterson *Glimpses* 29: [Latin only]. **1774** Adams *D and A* 2.139: Don't let America look at this Mountain, and let it bring forth a Mouse. **1774** JConnolly in *Letters to Washington* 5.9. **1774** Seabury *Letters* 81: Like the country people in the fable, we stood all attentive to the *throes* and *pangs* of the *labouring* mountain . . . [which] produced, not a silly mouse . . . but a venomous brood of scorpions. **1776** Serle *Journal* 121: *Parturiit Mons.* **1777** WDuer in *Clinton Papers* 1.565: [Latin only]. **1778** Curwen *Journal* 1.495: [It] appears to be a mountain bringing forth a mouse. **1778** Serle *Journal* 308: [Latin only]. **1781** Baldwin *Life and Letters* 55: Our productions are too fine to be compared with a *ridiculus mus.* **1782** Paine *American Crisis* 1.214. **1783** Gordon *Letters* 501: They came, and the mouse appeared upon the green cloth [not the great event expected]. **1783** Shaw *Journals* 101. **1784** GMorris in Hamilton *Papers* 3.499: The Mountain labored long and hard, & then outpopp'd Captain Peale. **1787** *American Museum* 2.47. **1787** ALee in Shippen *Journal* 251. **1787** Paine *Prospects on the Rubicon* 2.623: At last the mountain has brought forth a Dutch mouse. **1787** JWhite in *Blount Papers* 1.330: If the issue should prove the "mountains in labour." **1788** *Columbian Magazine* 2.290. a**1788** Jones *History* 1.356: [Latin only]. **1789** *Columbian Magazine* 1.701: *Mons peperit murem* . . . A mountain has brought forth a mouse. **1791** Adams(A) *Letters* 353: But, after all, the bluster will scarcely produce a mouse. **1795** Cobbett *Porcupine* 2.92. **1796** Smith(EH) *Diary* 182. **1797** Cobbett *Porcupine* 6.334: The mountain has laboured—I see no production. **1799** Carey *Plumb* 21. **1802** *Port Folio* 2.165. **1803** Cabot *Letters* 335: [It] should not pass as a thing worthy the mountain's labor. **1807** *Salmagundi* 90. **1812** Bayard *Letters* 23: The fable of the mountain I fear will no apply. If the birth should be equally harmless, I should be satisfied that it should be equally ridiculous. **1814** Kerr *Barclay* 310. **1814** JMcDowell in *W&MCQ* 8(1899) 225: [Latin only]. **1815** Ames *Diary* 279-80: In conclave, bro't forth a mouse. **1817** Wirt *Letters* 2.27: [Latin only]. **1827** Watterston *Wanderer* 200: It is the mountain in labor! **1841** Cooper *Letters* 4.121: [Latin only]. *Oxford* 547; Whiting H388.

M270 To attempt to remove **Mountains** is in vain

1777 Burd *Letters* 98: It is in vain to attempt to remove Mountains. Whiting M726.

M271 To make a **Mountain** of a molehill (*varied*)

1643 RVines in *Winthrop Papers(A)* 4.420: The truth is the over pleading the case . . . which made the moale hill seeme a mountayne. **1652** Williams *Writings* 4.458: It now questions no *Difference* between the *Mountaines* and the *Molehills*. **1653** Keayne *Apologia* 47: For all these are but leaden rules to walk by and often lead into errors

and mistakes, making . . . another man's mountain . . . to be looked at as a small molehill. c**1700** Taylor *Poems* 409: Your Mites are Molehills, Molehills Mountains bee. **1734** Johnson *Writings* 3.66: Raise mole-hills into mountains. **1741** *Georgia Records* 23.185: To magnify Molehills into Mountains. **1749** Franklin *PR* 3.350: Molehills, if often heap'd, to Mountains rise. **1766** AA in *Adams FC* 1.54: I hope there will not be any more Mountains arise to hinder me. Mole hills I always Expect to find, but them I can easily surmount. **1767** Franklin *Papers* 14.107. **1770** *Bowdoin Papers* 1.244: Things are viewed through a false medium and mole-hills appear mountains. **1771** Boucher *View* 218: [It] would be, in comparison, as the measure of a mountain is to that of a mole-hill. **1777** Wister *Journal* 114: These saucy creatures are forever . . . metamorphosing mole-hills into mountains. **1778** Hutchinson *Diary* 2.203: Every mole-hill was a mountain. **1778** LPintard in Webb *Correspondence* 2.102. **1781** Oliver *Origin* 29: A disordered Optick will swell a Molehill to the Bulk of a Mountain. **1794** DCarthy in *Blount Papers* 2.366. **1799** Freneau *Prose* 407: All these frights were only as a mole-hill by side of a mountain. **1802** Bowne *Letters* 145. **1805** Paine *Another Callender* 2.981: It works under ground like a mole, and having thrown up its little mole-hills of dirt, blows them with its pestiferous breath into mountains. **1807** *Salmagundi* 108, 203. **1811** Adams *Memoirs* 2.520. **1816** Asbury *Letters* 3.546. **1816** *Emigrant's Guide* 51: Every molehill of dissension . . . is magnified into a mountain of insurrection. **1821** Freneau *Last Poems* 45. **1825** *Austin Papers* 2.1187. **1827** Watterston *Wanderer* 201: The mountain and the molehill. Barbour 124; *Oxford* 547; TW 252(2).

M272 To make a **Mountain** of a mouse

1803 RIzard in *Barbary Wars* 3.382: What a mountain they have made of a mouse.

M273 As lean as a **Mouse**

1836 Floy *Diary* 232: He was as lean as a mouse.

M274   As quank(?) as **Mice**

a1731 Cook *Bacon* 325: The friendly cordial Advice, Made both the Wolves, as quank as Mice.

M275   As quiet as **Mice**

1836 Floy *Diary* 208: I gave 3 or 4 of them tremendous boxes on their ears, and then they were as quiet as mice. Barbour 124(4); Svartengren 384; TW 252(3).

M276   As silent as a **Mouse**

1809 Freneau *Poems(1809)* 2.28: He was as silent as a mouse. NED Mouse 2a; Svartengren 387.

M277   As still as a **Mouse**

1798 *Echo* 160: How Daniel kept the lions still as mice. **1801** Story *Shop* 30: Still as a mouse sat Wisdom. **1802** Weems *Letters* 2.260: While 2 editions of a Quarto bible are oblig^d to steal thro the country with as little noise, as so many mice thro' a pantry. **c1816** Durang *Memoir* 63: Being quartered on charity, we whare as still as a mouse all night. **1817** Royall *Letters* 81. **1818** CBeecher in Vanderpoel *Chronicles* 185. **1820** *Cary Letters* 284. **1821** Doddridge *Dialogue* 48. Barbour 124-5; TW 252(5).

M278   As whist as a **Mouse**

1771 *Trial of Atticus* 67: The noise itself was as whist as a mouse. Svartengren 387; TW 252(7).

M279   The **Mouse** by diligence bit in two the cable

1735 Franklin *PR* 2.5: By diligence and patience, the mouse bit in two the cable, **1758** *WW* 343: ate in two, **1771** *Papers* 18.160: By Diligence and Patience the Mouse ate in twain the Cable. *Oxford* 548; Whiting M738.

M280   A **Mouse** can build a home without timber

1771 Adams *D and A* 2.14: Dr. Cooper quoted another Proverb from his Negro Glasgow—a Mouse can build an Home without Timble [?*for* Timber].

M281   The close **Mouth** catches no flies

1742 Franklin *PR* 2.334: Speak and speed: the close mouth catches no flies. Barbour 125(1); *Oxford* 127; Tilley M1247.

M282   A close **Mouth** makes a wise head

1865 EConigland in *Ruffin Papers* 4.46: I am not unmindful of the maxim "A close mouth makes a wise head." Barbour 125(2).

M283   Keep your **Mouth** wet, feet dry

1733 Franklin *PR* 1.317: Keep your mouth wet, feet dry. Tilley F579.

M284   **Mouths** and hearts consent

1695 NSaltonstall in *Saltonstall Papers* 1.232: Their mouths (and I hope their hearts consent therewith) are abundantly open. *Oxford* 364; Whiting M754.

M285   To be down in the **Mouth**

1691 Mather *Letters* 28: But before the month was out, they grew down in the mouth. **1692** Bulkeley *Will* 241: Some are quite down in the mouth. **1749** JColden in *Colden Letters* 4.178. **1757** Laurens *Papers* 2.437. **1764** Allen *Extracts* 58. **1777** JBoucher in *MHM* 9(1914) 332: Doctor Nelly is a little down in the mouth. **1777** Hutchinson *Diary* 2.135: Dr Franklin is down in the mouth. **1782** NGreene in Reed *Life* 2.470. **1789** Dunlap *Father* 48. **1798** Drinker *Journal* 319: Ye Democrats are down in the mouth, as some term it, by the accounts from France. **1801** Trumbull *Season* 126. **1812** DCWallace in Knopf *War of 1812* 2.207: The Tamanies are completely down in the Mouth here. **1820** Weems *Letters* 3.278. **1834** PMurphey in *Ruffin Papers* 2.133. **1835** Floy *Diary* 148: Not very well and very much down in the mouth. TW 253(2).

M286   To be sweet **Mouths**

1807 Fraser *Letters and Journals* 254: They are sweet mouths thieves lyers and in short have every bad quality. NED Sweet 3.

M287   To fall into one's **Mouth**

1782 Lee(W) *Letters* 3.887: The business will bye and bye fall into your mouth. Tilley M1261.

M288   To get one's **Mouth** full of yellow clay

1803 Davis *Travels* 238: *Die come in every*

part of the world . . . black man! white man! all one day or another get their mouth full of yellow clay! 386: I wished that my first wife had not got her mouth full of yellow clay. Cf. *Oxford* 224-5; Tilley E166.

M289 To have one's **Mouth** nailed up

1743 RTemple in Lloyd *Papers* 1.354: As the failure is on Our parts my mouth is Nail'd up. Cf. Whiting M765.

M290 To make a poor **Mouth**

1777 Cresswell *Journal* 216: My companion and brother Scape begin to make a poor mouth; indeed we are both poor enough but it does no good talking about it. 1787 EHazard in *Belknap Papers* 1.477: I suspect that "giving up the idea of *profit*" is what we call *making a poor mouth*. NED Mouth 3m; TW 253(7).

M291 To make one's **Mouth** water

1722 Taylor *Poems* 372: It is a feast so sweet . . . That makes the very Angells mouths to water. 1778 JAdams in *Warren-Adams Letters* 2.73: To expect that the Coffers of the American Banker here, would not make some Mens Mouths water. *Oxford* 501; TW 253(5).

M292 To make up one's **Mouth**

1784 Gadsden *Writings* 235: Continue here . . . until you have made up your mouth, (as the phrase is). *Oxford* 502; Whiting M761. Cf. TW 253(4).

M293 To sweeten one's **Mouth**

1773 *Commerce of Rhode Island* 1.432: Bardin has sweetned my mouth with a purse of Pistoles. Cf. Whiting H69.

M294 He that contends for too **Much** may lose all

1817 Weems *Franklin* 133: Learning . . . that by . . . contending for too *much*, they might possibly lose *all*. Whiting M774. Cf. *Oxford* 9. See **A78, M242.**

M295 **Much** in little

1643 Williams *Writings* 1.86: They . . . comprise much in little. 1651 NMather in *Mather Papers* 3: Here is much in little roome. 1710 Mather *Bonifacius* 157: I shall wrong it, if I say, *Tis Much in a Little;* I

must say, *Tis All at Once.* 1716 Sewall *Letter-Book* 2.55: There is *Multum in parvo.* 1779 *Commerce of Rhode Island* 2.58: Accept much Love I say in a little. 1784 EWinslow in *Winslow Papers* 219: [Latin only]. 1797 Smith(EH) *Diary* 401: The great difficulty . . . is to say much in a small space. Multum in parvo should be my motto; but I fear that parvum in multo will be more descriptive of my performance. 1833 Baldwin *Diary* 222: Papers, which, instead of being *multum in parvo,* are parvum in multo. 1834 Floy *Diary* 110: [Latin only]. Whiting M783.

M296 Too **Much** of one thing is good for nothing (*varied*)

1784 EWinslow in *Winslow Papers* 227: Too much of one thing is good for nothing. 1786 Ledyard *Russian Journey* 106: As Poor Richard says "Too much of one thing is good for nothing." 1791 S.P.L. *Thoughts* 168. 1807 *Salmagundi* 253: Our publisher . . . has begged so hard that we will not overwhelm him with too much of a good thing, that we have . . . cut short the residue of uncle John's amours. 1822 Bierce *Travels* 53: I thought too much of a good thing was more than enough. 1827 *Ruffin Papers* 1.387: You know there may be too much even of a good thing. 1827 Wirt *Letters* 2.231: A good thing may be too often repeated. 1830 Ames *Mariner's* 170: There certainly is such a thing as having too much of a blessing. *Oxford* 831; TW 369(15); Whiting M793.

M297 As clear as **Mud**

1809 Lindsley *Love* 8: Darn my skin, 'f you wouldnt dewe it clear as mud. 1815 Humphreys *Yankey* 32: You are tarnation bright —clear as mud. 1816 Paulding *Letters(I)* 2.34: As clear as *mud,* —as we used to say of Doctor ——'s metaphysics. Barbour 125(1); Svartengren 362; TW 253(1).

M298 To be as deep in the **Mud** (dirt) as another is in the mire

1744 Hamilton *Itinerarium* 129: Had he had the same cunning as some others of his brethren who doubtless are as deep in the dirt as he is in the mire. 1783 Lee(W) *Let-*

ters 3.916: Franklin is publicly charged with being as Deep in the Mud as Mr. Silas Deane is in the Mire. **1835** Floy *Diary* 147: The case being that of seduction; the "lady" as deep in the mud as her suitor in the mire. TW 253(2).

M299 As obstinate as a **Mule**

1776 *Echo* 11: The *old prig* is as obstinate as a mule. **1782** Franklin *Writings* 8.432: Muley Istmael (a happy name for a prince as obstinate as a mule). **1794** Gordon *Letters* 574. **1805** Brackenridge *Modern* 624: Not by maxims of his rule, So much as obstinacy of mule. **1813** Paulding *Lay* 168. **1826** Duane *Colombia* 259: In every other country the obstinacy of the mule is a sort of proverb. **1827** Watterston *Wanderer* 101: The other was as obstinate as a Spanish mule. Svartengren 101; TW 254(4). Cf. Whiting M800.

M300 As stubborn as a **Mule**

1809 Weems *Washington* 46: Mule-stubborn in acting. **1816** Fidfaddy *Adventures* 56: Stubborn as a mule. **c1820** Bernard *Retrospections* 347: As stubborn as a mule, and therefore a Vermonter. Barbour 126(13); TW 254(6).

M301 In the **Multitude** of counsellors there is safety

1746 *New-York Weekly Post Boy* in *Newspaper Extracts*(*I*) 2.322: *In the multitude of Council there is Safety,* **1747** 357: In the Multitude of Commissioners is the greatest Safety. **1782** Franklin *Writings* 8.506: As another Text observes, that in *"the Multitude of Counsellors there is Safety."* **1788** Jay *Correspondence* 3.304. **1806** Fessenden *Modern Philosopher* 195. **1807** *Salmagundi* 295. **1832** Barney *Memoir* 12: The saying of the wisest man of the world. *Oxford* 691.

M302 **Mum's** the word

a1731 Cook *Bacon* 326: So Mum's the Word about this matter. **1783** Lee *Letters* 2.278: I was going to write a word or two about politics but—Mum for that. **1785** JRussell in *Belknap Papers* 3.296: I want to express myself freely on a certain subject; but mum! **1785** *Washington Writings* 28.124: Therefore Mum, **1793** 33.24: But

mum on this head, **1797** 36.93: And therefore, Mum, on that topic. **c1800** Tyler *Island* 22: But mum's the word. **1809** *Kennon Letters* 31.306. *Oxford* 551; Whiting M803, W602. See **W317.**

M303 As dry as a **Mummy**

1821 Knight *Poems* 2.186: You'll die an old maid . . . Dry as a mummy.

M304 **Mumpsimus** for sumpsimus

1723 Mather *Diary* 2.693: Their zeal transported some of them so far (on the behalf of *Mumpsimus*) that they would not only use the most opprobrious Terms, and call the Singing of these Christians, a worshipping of the Devil, but also they would run out of the Meeting-house at the Beginning of the Exercise. **1795** Coffin *Memoir* 71-2: Rev. Emerson said a popish Bishop had long used the word *mumpsimus* after having received the Eucharist, thus dismissing the assembly, his son having learned proper Latin, told him he should say sumpsimus. I will not give up my old mumps for your young sumps. *Oxford* 114; Tilley M1314.

M305 **Murder** will out

1705 Ingles *Reply* 27: Murder will out, 156: Well as I s'd before murder will out. **1771** Woodmason *Journal* 115. **1794** Ames *Letters* 1.145. **1807** *Salmagundi* 200: But the murder is out. **1813** Weems *Drunkard* 63. **1817** Barker *How to Try a Lover* 9: The murder's out. **1820** Simpson *Journal* 114. **1825** WBingham in Murphey *Papers* 1.304: Things will out at last. **1825** Neal *American Writers* 216. **1832** Ames *Nautical* 101: Murder will out some time or some how or other. *Oxford* 551; Whiting M806. See **T128, 274.**

M306 As humble as a **Mushroom**

1806 FTudor in Massachusetts Historical Society, *Proceedings* 65 (1932-36) 177: After this he was as humble as a mushroom.

M307 To spring up like **Mushrooms**

1807 *Salmagundi* 100: An immense army had sprung up, like mushrooms, in a night. **1831** WPope in Jackson *Correspondence* 4.298: That State-Banks will . . . spring up like mushrooms. TW 255.

M308   As sweet as **Musk**

1695/6 Taylor *Poems* 106: Thy Typick Holiness, more sweet than Muske. Lean 2.880; Svartengren 307.

M309   Enough to make a **Musselman** turn Christian

1778 WMalcom in *Clinton Papers* 2.834: This is enough to make a musleman turn christian—it puts one mad—I know it might be otherwise. Cf. *Oxford* 848; Tilley T609.

M310   What **Must** be, must be

1774 Carter *Diary* 2.826: What must be, must be. **1808** *Kennon Letters* 31.198: Well as Tom Tough says "What must be, must," **1812** 34.230: As poor Tom Tough says, "In Providence I'll trust; for do you see, what must be must." *Oxford* 552; TW 255. Cf. Whiting N61.

M311   As pungent as Tewkesbury **Mustard**

1816 *Port Folio* 4NS 2.234: A biting sarcasm, not less pungent than Tewkesbury mustard. *Oxford* 809. Cf. Tilley M1333.

M312   As strong as **Mustard**

1782 *New Jersey Gazette* in *Newspaper Extracts(II)* 5.382: For *North,* you know, talk'd strong as mustard. Svartengren 391; Tilley M1332.

M313   As thick as **Mustard**

1757 Tyler *Contrast* 72: They came on as thick as mustard. *Oxford* 809, quote 1598; Tilley M1333.

M314   **Mustard** makes a weak man wise

1799 Tyler *Verse* 94: I love no flowers, but the flowers of Mustard; And that I love, because, the proverb cries, That mustard makes a very weak man wise.

N

N1   As happy as a **Nabob**

1824 Longfellow *Letters* 1.73: So that I am as happy as a Nabob.

N2   As rich as a **Nabob**

a1788 Jones *History* 2.179: As rich as a Nabob.

N3   Drive the **Nail** that will go

1741 *Georgia Records* 22².490: I do all I possibly can, to drive the Nail that will go. **1764** Watts *Letter Book* 255: We shall not be unmindfull of the Doctor when any Nail will go. **1783** *American Wanderer* 137: The *argumentum ad hominem,* in plain English, the driving the nail that will go. **1792** Wendell *Letters* 279: [He is] very industrious and drives the nail that will go. This is character. *Oxford* 204; Tilley N14.

N4   On the **Nail**

1753 *Independent Reflector* 107: Not a Dram should be drawn, but for Cash upon the Nail. **1796** Weems *Letters* 2.42: I got but 90 Dol. on the nail. **1797** Cobbett *Porcupine* 5.61: We are aware of his terms — (cash on the nail). **1802** Weems *Letters* 2.243. **1832** Ames *Nautical* 46: We moderns . . . require to be paid "ready praise down on the nail." *Oxford* 553; TW 57(2), 256(4).

N5   To blow one's **Nails**

1798 Cobbett *Porcupine* 8.11: So that our Envoys . . . were suffered . . . to blow their nails from the 27th of September to the 8th of October. NED Nail 3b. Cf. Whiting N2.

N6   To clinch the **Nail**

1783 Scattergood *Journal* 29: I was concerned to endeavor to clinch the nail. NED Nail 7c.

N7   To drive a **Nail** in one's coffin

1805 Paine *To the Citizens* 2.951: He has driven another nail in the coffin of the federal faction. **1807** Weems *Letters* 2.370: Every such blow drives a nail in her coffin! *Oxford* 553; TW 256(5).

N8   To drive the **Nail** home, *etc.*

1682 Plumstead 100: If I could help to drive home any of these nails I should think it labor not in vain. **1705** Ingles *Reply* 157: He thinks he has drove ye nail to ye head. **1739** Stephens *Journal(I)* 1.266: It behooved me, if I could not go the Length I would, to drive the Nail as far as it would go. **1791** Jefferson *Writings* 8.137: The nail will be driven as far as it will go peaceably, and farther the moment that circumstances become favorable. *Oxford* 204; Tilley N15; Whiting N8.

N9   To hit the **Nail** on the head

1622 *Mourt's Relation* 144: Though thorow my slender iudgement I should misse the marke, and not strike the naile on the head. **1765** Burd *Letters* 7: Though I hardly think that after all, you have hit the Nail upon the head. **a1775** Churchman *Account* 102: Thou hast hit the nail on the head! **1789** Brackenridge *Gazette* 316: The saying hits th' nail on th' head. **1813** Paulding *Letters(II)* 33. **1819** Peirce *Rebelliad* 30. **1820**

Harvard College Rebellion 68: Mrs. Hedge and myself thought "the nail was hit fair." **1848** Cooper *Letters* 5.314. Barbour 127(4); *Oxford* 374-5; Whiting N9. See **B185.**

N10 A good **Name** is better than bread (riches)

1739 *Georgia Records* 22².149: A good Name is better than bread. **1772** STurner in *Norton Papers* 247: To quote Solomon . . . that a good Name is better than Riches. Barbour 127; *Oxford* 322; Whiting N12.

N11 A good **Name** once lost seldom comes again

a1700 Saffin *His Book* 132: A good Name being once Lost, seldom or Never comes or returns againe. Lean 3.388; Whiting N13. See **R62, W370.**

N12 His **Name** is up, he may lie abed till noon (*varied*)

1792 *Universal Asylum* 8.252-3: Our good country folks, when they mean to say a man's fame is spread abroad . . . say *his name is up,* or *he has got his name up* . . . When a man's name is up, he may lie a-bed till noon. **1805** Taggart *Letters* 150: You know when a man gets the name of rising early he may lie in bed until noon. **1805** Weems *Letters* 2.314: Up fame, up fortune or, *vulgariter,* When a man's name is up *he* may go to bed. **1812** Maxwell *Poems* 82: Tho' Leander has manag'd to get up his name. **1826** Pintard *Letters* 2.258: The Spanish proverb says "Get a good name and you may go to sleep." Barbour 127(4); *Oxford* 554; Tilley N26, 28. Cf. TW 257(3).

N13 To have a bad **Name** is a bad thing

1723 *New-England Courant* 78(1.1): It is a common saying, *that it is a bad thing to have a Bad Name.* Cf. Whiting N11.

N14 To be taken (caught) **Napping**

1776 SAdams in *Warren-Adams Letters* 1.280: The Congress will soon be taken napping. **1781** Jefferson *Papers* 4.609: Some time hence perhaps the enemy may be again taken napping. **1816** Fidfaddy *Adventures* 28: Uncle Sam will never be caught napping. *Oxford* 110-1; TW 257. See **M254.**

N15 Human **Nature** is the same everywhere (*varied*)

1774 Seabury *Letters* 46: The passions of human nature are much the same in all countries. **1778** Serle *Journal* 279: Human nature is the same every where. **1781** Peters *Connecticut* 73: Human nature is every where the same. **1792** Brackenridge *Modern* 31: Human nature is human nature still. **1812** Hitchcock *Social* 34: Nature remains exactly what it is: Man has a human, not an angel's phiz. TW 258(5). See **M62.**

N16 It is the **Nature** of the beast

1834 Floy *Diary* 68: I am an extravagant fellow in books, but such is the nature of the beast, as the saying is. *Oxford* 556.

N17 **Nature** abhors a vacuum

1760 Ames *Almanacs* 304: Nature abhors a vacuum too, they say. **1806** *Port Folio* NS 2.192. **1818** Evans *Pedestrious* 290: Aristotle says that she [Nature] abhors a vacuum. *Oxford* 355; TW 258(4)

N18 You may toss out **Nature** with a pitch-fork, *etc.*

1623 JPory in James *Three Visitors* 7: Horace, "Naturam expellas furca licet," etc. **a1700** Hubbard *New England* 125: "Naturam expellas," &c. **1713** Wise *Churches* 120: *Naturam Expellas furca Licet usque Recurrit.* **1792** Brackenridge *Modern* 148: According to the maxim— *Naturam expellas bifurca, usque recurret;* You may toss out nature with a pitchfork, she will still come back upon you. **1794** Adams *Memoirs* 1.51: [Latin only]. **a1820** Tucker *Essays* 264: [Latin only]. *Oxford* 106; Tilley N50. Cf. TW 258(11).

N19 Great **Necessities** call out great virtues

1780 AA in *Adams FC* 3.269: Great necessities call out great virtues. See **O10.**

N20 **Necessity** became a law

1741 Stephens *Journal(I)* 2.144: There was no longer any Room for dallying, for Necessity became a Law. **1815** AJDallas in Jackson *Correspondence* 2.212: But the case of necessity which creates its own Law, must not be confounded with the ordinary case of military service, **1817** 333: Cases of necessity, creates their own rule, and where they really exist, forms an exception from the Genl. rule.

N21   Necessity has compulsion in it (*varied*)
a1656 Bradford *History* 1.54: As necessitie was a taskmaster over them, so they were forced to be struck. 1692 Mather *Wonders* 176-7: *Necessity* has a wonderful compulsion in it. 1776 JHewes in *Naval Documents* 3.672: Necessity, dire Necessity induced us to make that infringment of one of our own Laws.

N22   Necessity has (knows) no law
1674 JNorton in *Winthrop Papers(B)* 3.421: Puts me to a kind of necessitie, which as it hath no law, so it hath no shame. a1700 Hubbard *New England* 50: And necessity, they said, having no law, they were constrained to be silent. 1726 Lloyd *Papers* 1.271: But necessity has no law. 1734 Franklin *PR* 1.357: *Necessity* has no Law; I know some Attorneys of the name. 1738 Stephens *Journal(I)* 1.110. 1746 RWolcott in *Law Papers* 2.341. 1747 GClinton in *Colden Letters* 3.359. 1747 *Law Papers* 3.174. 1751 *Appendix* in *Colonial Currency* 4.474: Has Necessity any Law? 1755 Franklin *PR* 5.472: *Necessity* has no Law; Why? Because 'tis not to be had without Money. 1755 Sherman *Almanacs* 254. 1764 JA in *Adams FC* 1.48. 1770 Hearne *Journey* 83. 1773 *New-York Gazette* in *Newspaper Extracts(I)* 9.588. 1774 Smith *Memoirs(I)* 203, 223. 1775 Gordon *Letters* 316: *Necessitas non habet legem.* 1776 FRhinelander in Van Schaack *Letters* 54: Necessity knows no law. 1777 King *Life* 1.29. 1778 Hutchinson *Diary* 2.235. 1778 Sullivan *Letters* 2.20: knows, 428: A Maxim older than the Congress. 1780 Baldwin *Life and Letters* 60: It is a well known Maxim that . . . necessity knows no Law. 1780 Washington *Writings* 19.491. 1782 PSchuyler in *Heath Papers* 3.352: knows. 1783 Baldwin *Life and Letters* 142: knows. 1784 Adams(A) *Letters* 161, 252; Necessity is without law. 1785 *Belknap Papers* 1.331. 1786 Hunter *Quebec* 230. 1786 WWhiting in American Antiquarian Society, *Proceedings* NS 66(1956) 141: That antient Maxim (viz) Necessity

knows no Law. a1788 Jones *History* 1.320. 1788 SHParsons in *St. Clair Papers* 2.71: [Latin only]. 1788 *Politician* 22: [Latin only]. 1796 GOgg in *Blount Papers* 3.53. 1798 *Codman Letters* 71. 1799 Eaton *Life* 103. 1807 Mackay *Letters* 78. a1811 Henry *Account* 61. 1814 Randolph(J) *Letters* 158: I know that they are worth more, but "necessity, &c." 1824 Doddridge *Notes* 112. 1856 Paulding *Letters(II)* 565: [Latin only]. Barbour 127(2); *Oxford* 556-7; Whiting N51.

N23   Necessity is the mother of invention
1681 Fitzhugh *Letters* 103: Necessity as 'tis the Mother of Invention, so it is the Nurse of Industry. 1736 Gyles *Memoirs* 31: Necessity is the Mother of Invention. 1736 *New-York Gazette* in *Newspaper Extracts(I)* 1.454. 1750 PKalm in Franklin *Papers* 4.50: But the necessity, that has been the beginning of several useful things, made them try all. 1764 Watts *Letter Book* 262. 1766 *Johnson Papers* 5.13, 1770 7.477. 1772 Hearne *Journey* 264: The methods practiced by this poor creature to procure a livelihood . . . are great proofs that necessity is the real mother of invention. 1775 JBarrell in Webb *Correspondence* 1.114. 1777 AA in *Adams FC* 2.340. 1777 IAllen in *Collections of the Vermont Historical Society* 1(1870) 130. 1777 Carroll *Correspondence* 1.209: is said to be. 1777 Gordon *Letters* 362. 1777 Huntington *Papers* 389: The Proverb says. 1784 Smyth *Tour* 2.112: Innovations and improvements, which in fact necessity compelled me to discover and adopt. 1789 Boucher *Autobiography* 108: Necessity may perhaps be the parent of eloquence, as it is said to be of other gifts of genius. 1791 JBoit in *Columbia* 371. 1797 Foster *Coquette* 49. 1798 Allen *Vermont* 330. 1800 Tatham *Tobacco* 58: Necessity (that very prolific mother of invention). 1801 Bowne *Letters* 59: Necessity is the nurse of all the great qualities of the mind. 1804 *Port Folio* 4.143: Necessity may be the mother of *lucrative* invention, but it is the death of poetical. 1805 Brackenridge *Modern* 578. 1807 *Emerald* 2.409: says the proverb. 1807 *Salmagundi* 203: This prolific body may not improperly

be termed the "mother of inventions." **1808**
Emerald NS 1.433. **1812** Melish *Travels*
347. **1819** Robertson *Letters* 75: Never . . .
was an old adage verified with more justness. **1824** Doddridge *Notes* 94: It may be
truly said that, 114. **1825** Austin *Literary
Papers* 107. Barbour 127(1); *Oxford* 558;
TW 258(1). See **W17**.

N24   Necessity must speak

1802 JShaw in *Barbary Wars* 2.75: Necessity must speak.

N25   Necessity never made a good bargain

1735 Franklin *PR* 2.6: Necessity never made
a good bargain. Tilley N63. Cf. Whiting
N41.

N26   Neck and heels

1689 JSwayne in *Baxter Manuscripts* 9.68:
We have punished several of y^m by laying
neck & heeles & fineing. **1730** JGrover in
Baxter Manuscripts 11.45: They woold
carry them to the Fort lay them neck and
heels, and detain them. **1769** Woodmason
Journal 146: Both Neck and Heels would be
risqued. **1777** Smith *Memoirs(II)* 85: They
openly declared they would tie the Whig
part[y] Neck and Heels if Mr. Carleton
came down. **1784** JCoffin in *Winslow Papers*
203: And Mr. Hardy thrown neck & heels,
with his party, into the River. **1807** *Salmagundi* 116: I found Will had got neck and
heels into one of his travellers stories. **1821**
Pintard *Letters* 2.5: Mr. Sherred . . .
wanted . . . to turn my family out neck &
heels to make room for Tom Herring. **1822**
Jackson *Correspondence* 3.156: I hope and
trust before this reaches you he has been
turned out neck and heel. **1828** TTurner in
Ruffin Papers 1.453: I have no defence, but
also to lug the subject matter neck and heels
into my conversation and correspondence.
TW 259(2); Tilley N65.

N27   Neck and shoulders

1730 Franklin *Papers* 1.180: A long insipid
trifling Tale . . . drawn in by Neck and
Shoulders. **1779** Lee(W) *Letters* 2.673: So
vague a charge . . . and so foolishly brought
in neck and shoulders, **1783** 3.908: I . . .
should be dragged in neck and shoulders.
1820 *Fudge Family* 56: The . . . Admirals

appear to be dragged in here somewhat
neck and *shoulders*. Tilley H274. See **H140**.

N28   Neck or nothing

1765 Franklin *Papers* 12.199: Neck or nothing. **1776** Carter *Diary* 2.1015: For everybody wants to be ahead and aims at it Neck
or Nothing as it is commonly said. **1781** Jean
de Neufville in *Adams FC* 4.188: Throwing
his last Stake, Neck or Nothing. **1781** Oliver
Origin 103. **1791** S.P.L. *Thoughts* 167.
1802 Chester *Federalism* 13, 17. **1803** *Port
Folio* 3.182. **1804** Irving *Corrector* 104.
1816 Paulding *Letters(I)* 2.128: A hap-haz-
ard, neck-or-nothing voyage, 154: [He]
went neck or nothing. **c1820** Bernard *Retrospections* 211: That reckless, dare-devil,
neck-or-nothing enterprise. **1828** *Yankee*
226. *Oxford* 558; TW 259(4).

N29   On one's Neck

1699 Taylor *Poems* 136: The Storm will
Cease then, all lies on my neck. **1773** *Johnson Papers* 8.841: I had Caghnawagey
parties on my Neck. NED Neck *sb.*[1] 3c;
Whiting N43.

N30   To break the Neck of

1751 *Georgia Records* 26.221: We have now
broke the Neck of it, and can give . . . a reasonable Assurance of bringing this Culture
to answer their warmest Winter. NED Neck
sb.[1] 5b.

N31   To slip (pluck) one's Neck out of the
collar

1619 RCushman in Bradford *History* 1.89:
He . . . plucked his neck out of the collar,
yet at last his foote is caught. **a1656** Bradford *History* 1.92: So he might slip his own
neck out of the collar. **1769** CCarroll in
MHM 12(1917) 281: He thought to have
slipped his neck out of the collar. **1770** *Johnson Papers* 7.577: The Duke of Grafton has
slipped his neck out of the Collar. *Oxford*
558; Tilley N69.

N32   Need makes the old wife trot

1708 Taylor *Poems* 234: Need makes the
Old Wife trot. *Oxford* 558-9; Whiting N54.

N33 As sharp as a **Needle**

1819 Wright *Views* 120: She is as sharp as a needle [bright]. *Oxford* 720; Whiting N66.

N34 Like the **Needle** to the pole (*varied*)

1719 Byrd *Another Secret Diary* 363: And I shall as naturally obey her call as the needle dos the attraction of the Loadstone. **1733** Belcher *Papers* 1.284: As the needle is ever pointing to its beloved pole, so is your fond father to his Ascanius, **1740** 2.272: As the needle to its beloved North, so my thoughts point towards you. **1767** *Washington Writings* 2.466: As certain as the Needle will settle to the Poles, **1778** 10.338: I . . . pursued the great line of my duty . . . as pointedly as the needle to the pole. **1801** *Farmers' Museum* 85: All Democratic wishes roll, As true as needle to the Pole, 111. **1802** *Port Folio* 2.216: True as the needle to the pole. **1816** Fidfaddy *Adventures* 23: O as true as a needle, a fine Beast to ride to Elections on. TW 259. Cf. Barbour 128(3).

N35 To look for a **Needle** in a haystack (*varied*)

1674 Josselyn *Account* 63: As a man should seek for a needle in a bottle of Hay. **1748** Laurens *Papers* 1.195: One may as well look for a Needle in a Bundle of Hay as for any Taylor in London. **1779** WRogers in Sullivan *Journals* 262: But agreeably to the old adage it was similar to looking for needles in a hay stack. **1808** *Salmagundi* 449: So that if I want to find any particular article, it is, in the language of a humble but expressive saying—"looking for a needle in a haystack." **1815** Waterhouse *Journal* 193: But he might as well have sought a needle in a hay-mow. Barbour 128(2); *Oxford* 559; Whiting N71.

N36 Two **Negatives** make an affirmative

1686 Dunton *Letters* 115: I know two Negatives makes an Affirmative. **1777** Curwen *Journal* 1.401: Like two negatives in Algebra, added together, you know, produce an Affirmative. *Oxford* 851; Tilley N101.

N37 **Neglect** kills injuries, revenge increases them

1749 Franklin *PR* 3.345: Neglect kills In-juries, Revenge increases them. Tilley N102.

N38 **Neglect** may breed great mischief

1758 Franklin *WW* 344: A little Neglect may breed great Mischief. See **W16.**

N39 As black as a **Negro**

1796 Barton *Disappointment* 34: You may tawk an tawk till you're as black as a nager. Barbour 129(2); TW 261: Nigger(1).

N40 The better you use the **Negroes,** the worse they will use you

1815 Asbury *Journal* 2.772: The better you use the Negroes the worse they will use you. Cf. Whiting C259.

N41 A **Negro** and a cedar chest is a Bermuda girl's fortune

1790 JMeigs in Stiles *Itineraries* 537: It is a proverbial expression among us that "A Negro & a Cedar Chest is a Bermuda Girl's Fortune." [Meigs was a Connecticut man then living in Bermuda.]

N42 **Negroes** have no souls

1806 Dow *Journal* 286: "Negro what do you praise God for? Negroes have got no souls." Cf. *Oxford* 910: Woman; Tilley W709. See **W288.**

N43 To work like a **Negro**

1785 Hunter *Quebec* 62: The men work like Negroes. **1803** Davis *Travels* 383: I . . . worked like a new negur. Barbour 129(7); TW 262: Nigger(17). See **G9, S247.**

N44 A good **Neighbor** is a desirable thing

1790 Jefferson *Papers* 17.211: A good neighbor is a very desireable thing. Whiting N76. See **F298.**

N45 He dwells far from **Neighbors** who must praise himself

1666 Alsop *Maryland* 24: I dwell so far from Neighbors, that if I do not praise my self, no body else will. *Oxford* 560; Whiting N79. See **P272.**

N46 Love your **Neighbor,** yet don't pull down your hedge

1754 Franklin *PR* 5.184: Love your Neighbour; yet don't pull down your Hedge. *Oxford* 494; Tilley N109. See **F74.**

N47 Neighbor's fare

1773 JWGisberne in Lee(W) *Letters* 1.74: You say you can only promise me *Neighbour's Fare* for my Tobaccoo. 1786 WGrayson in Jefferson *Papers* 9.654: It was but neighbor's fare that Connecticut should be treated as we had been before. NED Fare *sb.*[1] 8, quote 1727.

N48 When one's Neighbor's house is on fire, *etc.*

1643 *Winthrop Papers(A)* 4.406: Let the Latin Proverb be attended as well as the Germaine and that will tell us that *res nostra agitur, paries cum proximus ardet.* 1666 Davenport *Letters* 264: [Latin only]. 1677 Hubbard *Indian* 2.268: He that will not help to quench the Fire in his Neighbours House, may justly fear to lose his own. c1737 *Colden Letters* 9.337: It is an old & wise caution *that when our Neighbours house is on fire we ought to take care of our own.* 1768 Lee *Letters* 1.26: It being a common observation, does not lesson the value of it, that a prudent man should lend his assistance to extinguish the flames which had invaded the house of his next door neighbour, and not coldly wait until the flame had reached his own. 1769 Woodmason *Journal* 257: When their own House was on Fire, they then thought on their Neighbours. 1774 WBollan in *Bowdoin Papers* 1.363: Supposing the old Maxim *proximus ardet* would not take place in the Colonies. 1791 Jefferson *Papers* 18.578: Yet when neighbors' houses are afire, our own is always in danger. *Oxford* 561; Whiting N85.

N49 To feather one's Nest

1654 Johnson *Wonder-Working* 221: Every bird to feather his own nest. 1692 Bulkeley *Will* 84: Yet they have been too ready to follow such unprofitable counsel, as would bring . . . feathers to their nests, 89: If I would but temporize I could . . . feather my nest too. 1713 Wise *Churches* 63: We have . . . Built a fair Nest well feathered. 1726 Sewall *Letter-Book* 2.238: A few dealers (who have learnt the feathering of their own Nests in the Fogs of our Confusion and unrighteousness) may be hereby promoted.

1768 *Boston Evening Post* in Buckingham *Specimens* 1.148: But feather your nests for they're bare enough yet. 1768 Dickinson *Writings* 427. 1779 HGriffith in *Aspinwall Papers* 2.792. 1782 *Heath Papers* 3.354. 1788 Freneau *Poems* 2.379: With a girl and a bottle he feather'd his nest. 1792 Jefferson *Papers* 1.290. 1792 Morris *Diary* 2.378. 1802 Chester *Federalism* 17, 36. 1803 *Port Folio* 3.60. 1804 Paine *Remarks* 2.960. 1808 Hitchcock *Poetical Dictionary* 70. c1813 Dow *Journal* 308: And gone to Missisippi to feather his nest. 1841 Hone *Diary* 2.521. Barbour 128(2); *Oxford* 252; TW 260(3).

N50 The Net is set in vain in the sight of the birds

1644 Williams *Writings* 3.84: Surely in vaine the Net is laid in the sight of the Saints (heavenly Birds). *Oxford* 403; Whiting N88. See S279.

N51 To be taken in one's own Net

1754 Johnson *Writings* 1.194: With the net which he hath privily spread for others will his own foot be taken. 1773 *New-York Gazette* in *Newspaper Extracts(I)* 9.508-9: [Let him] take heed lest he fall into the net he spreads for others. 1790 Morris *Diary* 2.70: If she should omit this I shall be handsomely catched in my own Net, 1791 176: If she does not take Care she will in trying to catch me find herself caught. 1831 JBranch in Jackson *Correspondence* 4.280: They were taken in their own nett. Lean 4.195; *Oxford* 561; Tilley F626. See C377, P182, S281.

N52 As hot as a Nettle

1809 Lindsley *Love* 10: Hot as a nettle [angry].

N53 To sit upon Nettles

1744 Hamilton *Itinerarium* 43: They set in for drinking, to which I was averse and therefor sat upon nettles. NED Nettle *sb.*[1] 2; TW 260. See P160, T70.

N54 A New-England man is a go-to-meeting animal

1817 Scott *Blue Lights* 136: It is part of the definition of a New-England man, that he is a go-to-meeting animal. Cf. DA go-to-meeting 2b.

N55 **New England** trick, see **T241.**

N56 Whoever believes a **New-England** saint shall be sure to be cheated

1699 Ward *Trip* 45: And it is a Proverb with those that know them, *Whoever believes a* New-England Saint *shall be sure to be Cheated. And he that knows how to deal with their Traders, may deal with the Devil and fear no Craft.*

N57 A **New Englander** answers one question with another (*varied*)

1807 MWarren in *Adams-Warren Correspondence* 364: I answer by asking another question, which it has been said is common among New Englanders. **1809** Tyler *Yankey* 106-8: [A New England man replies to questions by asking others]. **1816** JAdams in *Adams-Jefferson Letters* 2.464: Would you go back to your Cradle and live over again Your 70 Years? I believe You would return me a New England Answer, by asking me another question "Would you live your 80 Years over again?" **1825** Longfellow *Letters* 1.125: And my last letter so full of questions, and illustrating thereby the true spirit of New England. Cf. Partridge 734: Scotch fashion.

N58 As empty as a **New-English** purse

1647 Ward *Simple Cobler* 51: Time . . . is an empty thing, as empty as a *New-English* purse, and emptier it cannot be.

N59 A **Newfoundland** spell

1803 Davis *Travels* 442: "How long has he been there?" "Half the watch, Sir. He is taking a *Newfoundland* spell."

N60 **New Jersey** trick, see **T241.**

N61 **New York** trick, see **T241.**

N62 Bad **News** flies fast (*varied*)

1620 JHuddleston in Bradford *History* 1.273: Bad news doth spread it selfe too farr. **1637** LDowning in *Winthrop Papers(A)* 3.367: Ill newes selldome wants messingers (in our climat). **1755** Lloyd *Papers* 2.527: As bad news flies fast. **1780** PMazzei in Jefferson *Papers* 3.458: Bad news have long legs. **1814** Wirt *Bachelor* 132: As the old saying is, *bad news comes soon enough.* **1823** Sumter *Letters* 101: You see how quick bad news comes. **1840** Cooper *Letters* 4.59: As I know bad news flies swiftly. Barbour 128(1); *Oxford* 400; TW 261(2).

N63 Good **News** from a far country, *etc.*

1758 JKirkpatrick in *Letters to Washington* 3.80: As News from a far Country is a proverbial proof—how much more from a person of Your Rank & Distinction? **1775** Curwen *Journal* 1.21: Like good news from a far Country it was a most joyful Sound. **1780** Curwen *Journal and Letters* 255: Solomon never uttered more truth, or discovered more knowledge of mankind, than in the following proverb: "Good news from a far country is as cold water to a thirsty soul." **1796** JEllegood in *Winslow Papers* 423: News from afar, says the Royal Preacher, is like water to the thirsty Hart. Prov. 25.25.

N64 **News** from the tree of Cracovie

1780 JAdams in *Warren-Adams Letters* 2.131: The News Mongers of Paris assemble commonly under this Tree, so that it is become proverbial to call false News Les Nouvelles de l'arbre de Cracovie—News from the Tree of Cracovie.

N65 No **News** is good news

1754 Johnson *Writings* 4.26: I may always depend that no news is good news. **1760** INorris in Franklin *Papers* 9.43: I hope the old Saying "that No News is good News" may be our Case. **1774** Bowen *Journals* 2.402, 440. **1776** Carter *Diary* 2.1023: It is generally said that, 1094. **1776** RHLee in Lee *Papers* 2.124. **1788** Jefferson *Papers* 13.642. **1788** *Washington *Writings* 30.161: The English adage. **1798** Jefferson *Writings* 9.444. **1837** Lee *Diary and Letters* 245, 247: As the saying is. Barbour 128(3); *Oxford* 572; Tilley N152; Whiting *NC* 451(3).

N66 To have always **New Year**

1783 Freneau *Poems* 2.202: By my soul, I suspect they have always new year. Cf. *Oxford* 123: Christmas; Tilley C372.

N67 More **Nice** than wise

1733 Franklin *PR* 1.312: More nice than wise. **1773** Bowen *Journals* 2.366: Some . . . are much more nice than wise. *Oxford* 543-4; Tilley N158.

N68 In the **Nick** of time

1682 WJones in *Mather Papers* 613: Just in the nick of tyme. **1689** *Account* in *Andros Tracts* 2.197: Just in that Neck of time. **1689** Hutchinson *History* 1.319: Had it not been just at the nick. **1690** *Further Quaeries* in *Andros Tracts* 1.201: At the same nick of Time. **1692** Bulkeley *Will* 153: And therefore now was the nick of time for them. **c1700** Taylor *Poems* 406. **1700** Mather *Diary* 1.369. **1701** Sewall *Letter-Book* 1.256: Just at such a Nick of Time. **1702** Mather *Magnalia* 1.59, 2.556: At the very nick of time, 566. **1714** Johnston *Papers* 144: Att that nick of time. **a1731** Cook *Bacon* 324. **1734** Winslow *Broadside* 85. **1763** Laurens *Papers* 3.253. **1769** *Johnson Papers* 7.301. **1776** Curwen *Journal* 1.108. **1780** JScott in *Clinton Papers* 6.254: Just at the nick of time. **1782** Trumbull *Satiric Poems* 164: at. **1785** EGerry in King *Life* 1.87. **a1788** Jones *History* 1.291. **1790** Asbury *Journal* 1.630. **1791** *Echo* 14. **1795** Murdock *Triumphs* 27. **1798** *Washington Writings* 37.20. **1805** Sewall *Parody* 46. **1809** Irving *History* 1.xxv, 250, 2.127, 149. **1811** Randolph(J) *Letters* 87: at. **1813** *Port Folio* 3NS 1.47. **1817** Barker *How to Try a Lover* 6. **1818** Weems *Letters* 3.238: At the spot & nick of time. **1821** JAdams in *Adams-Jefferson Letters* 2.571. **1824** Neal *American Writers* 61. **1824** *Tales* 1.51,150. **1826** Gallatin *Diary* 264. Barbour 128; *Oxford* 565; Tilley N160.

N69 **Nick** and froth

1637 Morton *New English Canaan* 328: And so hee handles the matter as if hee dealt by the pinte and the quarte, with Nic and Froth. NED Nick *sb.*[1] 11; Tilley N162.

N70 As black as **Night**

1768 Freneau *Poems* 1.4: Guilt, black as night, **1775** 153: Doubts, black as night, **1780** 2.38: And, black as night, the hell born refugee! **1797** John Burk *Bunker-Hill* (New York, 1891) 52. **1808** Clubb *Journal* 16: Corrupted men, black as night. **1812** Woodworth *Beasts* 69. **1816** Freneau *Last Poems* 12: The Bride will look as black as night. Barbour 129(1); Svartengren 246; TW 262(1). See **M155.**

N71 As dark as **Night**

1707 Taylor *Poems* 222: Into this Lowest pit more darke than night, **1721** 369: Would make its Vision darke as dark as night. **1747** Ames *Almanacs* 198: A Scene as dark as night. **1780** Sargent *Loyalist* 18. **1781** Smith *Works* 2.154. **1800** Humphreys *Works* 172.322: Rides dark as night and louring as a storm. **1806** Alden *Epitaphs* 5.91. Barbour 129(1); Whiting N103. See **M156.**

N72 As still as **Night**

1788 May *Journal* 57: We moved as still as night. **1801** Adams *Works* 9.581: All is still as night in this region. Tilley N165. See **M158.**

N73 Good **Night,** Nicholas

1770 Carter *Diary* 1.463: If so good night to you Nicholas, both with Corn and Tobacco. *Oxford* 323; Tilley N170.

N74 To be easy all **Night,** let your supper be light

1750 Sherman *Almanacs* 257: To be easy all Night, Let your Supper be light. Whiting *NC* 451-2. Cf. Whiting S913. See **M36, S531.**

N75 The **Nightingale** sings with breast on thorn

1705 Taylor *Poems* 202: My Bird like to a Nightinggaile in th'Spring With breast on sharpest thorn, thy praise shall sing. *Oxford* 566; Whiting N112.

N76 To sing like a **Nightingale**

c1800 Tyler *Island* 27: Sung like a nightingale. Whiting N114.

N77 Nimble **Ninepence**

1801 Weems *Letters* 2.167: But the Scotch Merchants, who are your best marksmen at a dollar on the wing, will tell you that there's nothing like the nimble ninepence, 171: Remember the Nimble Ninepence is

better than the slow shilling. *Oxford* 567.
See **S142.**

N78 As drunk as **Ninepins**
1813 Paulding *Letters(II)* 36: Thereby
making them as drunk as nine pins.

N79 To fall (go) like **Ninepins**
1763 Watts *Letter Book* 212: Like Nine pins
says Hudibras, One Merchant knocks down
·another. **1779** Lee *Letters* 2.153: This cap-
ture will be sufficient to humble the british
Merchants like falling ninepins. **1781** *New
Jersey Gazette* in *Newspaper Extracts(II)*
5.212: This is their last cast; if they do not
succeed, they go like ninepins. TW 262.

N80 **Nineteen** (sixteen) to a (the) dozen
1821 Doddridge *Dialogue* 45: I'll work your
jacket nineteen to a dozen, **1824** *Notes* 98.
1824 Neal *American Writers* 68: Knock up
the whole alphabet of American writers, sixteen to the dozen. Cf. *Oxford* 813, 823; Tilley T227.

N81 Every **Nit** will make a louse
1755 in *New England Quarterly* 20(1947)
187: Every nit will make a louse. **1823** Doddridge *Logan* 11: I would kill all, nits will
be lice. *Oxford* 568; Tilley N191; Whiting
NC 452(3).

N82 Not to take **No** for an answer
1779 JChester in Webb *Correspondence*
2.159: He would not take no for an answer.
1800 Trumbull *Season* 62: Mr. Phelps
would hardly take no, for an answer. **1814**
Adams *Writings* 5.120: If they will take no
for an answer. **1815** Asbury *Journal* 2.774:
Mother Long would by no means take a
nay. **1815** Humphreys *Yankey* 55. **1815** Palmer *Diary* 220. **1840** ERWare in *New
England Merchants* 291. TW 263.

N83 To bring a **Noble** to ninepence
1716 Mather *Diary* 2.410: Had he lived, he
had soon brought a Noble to Nine-pence.
1732 Belcher *Papers* 1.213: And to be continually spending, & in no way of getting, I
have told him will soon bring a noble to 9ᵈ.
Oxford 86; TW 263. Cf. Whiting S244.

N84 A **Nod** is as good as a wink (to a blind
horse)
1806 *Port Folio* NS 1.39: A vulgar proverb,
A nod is as good as a wink, &c. *Oxford* 575;
TW 263(1).

N85 To make a great **Noise**
1813 Bentley *Diary* 4.177: He certainly
does, as the phrase is, make a great noise.
NED Noise 6.

N86 To make a **Noise** about a turd
1769 Woodmason *Journal* 154: They'll
blunder and make a Noise about a Turd.

N87 As clear as the **Noon-day**
1676 Williams *Writings* 5.466: As clear as
at Noon-day. **1725** Sewall *Diary* 3.353: [It]
made the Cause clear as the Noonday. **1749**
Georgia Records 25.470: It is to me as clear
as the Noon day. TW 263(4). See **S511.**

N88 As open as **Noon-day**
1741 Stephens *Journal(I)* 2.84: These Mys-
teries unfold themselves, which I know must
in a short Time be as open as the Noon-day.
Cf. Lean 2.859.

N89 As opposite as **North** and south
1777 JA in *Adams FC* 2.176: Characters as
opposite as North and South. Cf. Whiting
N123. See **P221.**

N90 As old as the **North star**
1789 *Columbian Magazine* 3.184: The
thought is as old as the north star.

N91 As plain as the **Nose** on one's face
c**1775** Hopkinson *Miscellaneous Essays* 3
(part 2) 159: The law is as plain as the nose
on your face. **1775** Paine *Farmer Short*
2.1088: I'll prove it by as plain a case, As is
the nose upon your face. **1780** *New-York
Gazette* in *Newspaper Extracts(II)* 5.105:
Till each prov'd as plain as the nose on his
face. **1782** *New Jersey Gazette* in *Newspaper
Extracts(II)* 5.384: As plain as nose on a
man's face. **1787** *Anarchiad* 44: 'Tis plain
as nose in face is. **1792** Belknap *Forester* 32.
1801 Paulding *Letters(II)* 8. **1806** Fessenden
Modern Philosopher 191: Unless the *cause
. . . .* Is nine times plainer than his nose is.
1806 *Weekly* 1.167: 'Tis plain on the nose of

your Jacobin phiz. Barbour 130(8); *Oxford* 629; TW 263(1). See **S283.**

N92   **Big Nose** (big virility)

c1720 Byrd *Another Secret Diary* 270: It may be you make this Inference from the bigness of his nose which amongst the women is a hopeful mark of every good quality, **c1725** 458: Gloriana wou'd infallibly wed a man with a great nose in his face, and have into the bargain all the advantages, which . . . are promis'd by that comely Feature. Maria Leach, ed., *Dictionary of Folklore, Mythology, and Legend* (New York, 1950) 2.803; Partridge 570: A long nose is a lady's liking.

N93   **In spite of one's Nose**

c1680 Radisson *Voyages* 181: And by that means gatt ground in spight of their noses. Whiting N125. See **T194.**

N94   **A Nose of wax**

1652 Bradford *Dialogue* 5: They may . . . make a nose of waxe of the rest. **1676** Williams *Writings* 5.149: Calling it *a dead Letter, a Nose of wax, a leaden Rule,* 200: A Nose of wax, a *Leaden Rule,* a *dead Letter.* **1692** Bulkeley *Will* 119: I think no man should make arbitrary laws, which, like a nose of wax or leaden rule, may be twisted which way a man will. **1694** Makemie *Writings* 56: Calling it [Scripture] a nose of Wax, Pen & Ink Divinity. **1701** Taylor *Christographia* 15.50-1: This would . . . have made the threatening a nose of Wax. **1713** Johnston *Papers* 131: A Minister at this rate, was but a mere nose of wax, a vile worthless thing. **1721** *Letter* in *Colonial Currency* 2.262: Declare our . . . Laws, to be but a *Nose of Wax.* **1734** Johnson *Writings* 3.81. **1764** *Paxton Papers* 253: What a Nose of Wax, the Word Loyalty has been made to serve the vile Purposes of all the Insurrections that have been rais'd against the Sovereign. **1764** Watts *Letter Book* 309. **1785** Adams *Works* 8.346: Pitt is but a tool . . . a nose of tender virgin wax. **1788** EHazard in *Belknap Papers* 2.14. **1789** Brackenridge *Gazette* 329. **1800** Gadsden *Writings* 290. **a1814** Dow *Journal* 484: Conscience, like a nose of wax, may be put into any

shape. **1815** Brackenridge *Modern* 639. **1833** Cooper *Letters* 2.380: We have a fair specimen of the effect of the nose-of-wax system. *Oxford* 577; Tilley H531, L104, N226.

N95   **To bite off one's Nose to spite one's face**

1784 Gadsden *Writings* 202: Is not this biting our nose to spite our face? **1795** Cobbett *Porcupine* 2.22: It was almost literally biting off the nose to be revenged on the face. **1820** *Fudge Family* 41: They've too much sense, it plainly shews To bite the face and spite the nose. **1832** Barney *Memoir* 117: The man who, according to the children's fable, *"bit his own nose off to spite his face!"* Barbour 130(9); *Oxford* 163; TW 263-4(2).

N96   **To hold (keep) one's Nose to the grindstone** (*varied*)

1647 Ward *Simple Cobler* 44: If I be not much deceived, that *Salus Populi* suffered its nose to be held to the Grindstone. **1692** Mather *Wonders* 155: She would hold his Nose as close to the Grindstone as ever it was held since his name was Abbot. **1758** Franklin *WW* 344-5: A Man . . . may keep his Nose all his Life to the Grindstone, and die not worth a Groat at last. **1770** Ames *Almanacs* 412. **1792** DHuger in Hamilton *Papers* 11.542: The mild punishment of having his Nose ground off at the Grindstone. **1803** Davis *Travels* 319: There's no snakes in *Virginia,* if I don't bring his nose to the gridiron. **1804** Brackenridge *Modern* 386: A mans nose is just as much upon the grind-stone as it was before the revolution. **1826** Anderson *Diary* 257. **1832** Ames *Nautical* 133. **1846** Paulding *Letters(II)* 420, 435. Barbour 130(10); *Oxford* 578; Whiting N128.

N97   **To lead one by the Nose**

1697 WByrd in *W&MCQ* 3S 2(1945) 62: He should be able to lead that worthy Gentleman by the nose. **1721** *Letter* in *Colonial Currency* 2.238: Men . . . will suffer themselves to be led by the Nose, 261. **1736** Murray *Letters* 35: People . . . so stupid as to be led by the nose. **1747** *New-York*

Evening Post in *Newspaper Extracts(I)* 2.399: Tho' the ignorant sort (which is the greatest part) as generally taken by the Nose. **1753** *Independent Reflector* 147. **1753** Wolcott *Papers* 275. **1765** *Johnson Papers* 11.818. **1767** Ames *Almanacs* 388. **1768** Franklin *Papers* 15.221: My countrymen, we are all by the nose. **1775** Moore *Diary* 1.43. **1789** Jefferson *Papers* 15.456. **1790** *Universal Asylum* 5.40. **1800** RLioton in Gibbs *Memoirs* 2.391: I must now endeavour to lead Mr. Adams by the nose. **1804** Irving *Corrector* 90. **1807** *Salmagundi* 239. **1809** Fessenden *Pills* 39. **1817** *Port Folio* 4NS 4.434. **1819** Waln *Hermit* 91. **1821** Howison *Sketches* 300-1: The people . . . are led about like a pig by the nose. *Oxford* 449; TW 264(6). See **E9.**

N98 To pay through the **Nose**

1805 Sewall *Parody* 24: We paid for't thro' the nose. **1811** Burroughs *Memoirs* 4: This scene of merriment I enjoyed to the full, but soon paid for it through the nose. **1819** Cobbett *Year's* 162: He must lay in his store at the beginning of winter, or he must buy through the nose. *Oxford* 615; Tilley N234.

N99 To put one's **Nose** out of joint

1637 Morton *New English Canaan* 281: Hee that playd Proteus (with the helpe of Priapus) put their noses out of joynt, as the Proverbe is. **1781** JA in *Adams FC* 4.265: His Nose is out of Joint. **1782** *Belknap Papers* 1.148. **1814** Wirt *Bachelor* 90: You have entirely put the nose of politics and foreign news out of joint. **1837** Paulding *Letters(II)* 199. **1842** Cooper *Letters* 4.328, **1850** 6.195, 230. Barbour 130(6); *Oxford* 577; TW 264(9).

N100 Under one's own **Nose**

1755 *Johnson Papers* 1.640: But to come here even under your own Noses to do the same. **1775** *London Chronicle* in *Naval Documents* 1.1183: The Yankies . . . destroyed the light-house twice under his very nose. **1775** *New York Journal* in *Naval Documents* 1.585: All this was done in sight, and as we may say, under the noses of the whole fleet and army. NED Nose 7b.

N101 To the **Notch**

1764 AA in *Adams FC* 1.13: Our pale Face . . . keeps at the old notch and . . . may be say'd to be a little better. **1787** Tyler *Contrast* 103: He was up to the notch — ha, ha, ha. TW 265.

N102 A **Note** above Ela

1708 Saffin *His Book* 170: You have therein tun'd yoᵣ Song a Note above Ela. **1721** Carter *Letters* 80: Your next paragraph is a note above Elah, sure. You were . . . looking upon me as one of your dependents and inferiors. Whiting E58.

N103 To change one's **Note**

1691 *Humble Address* in *Andros Tracts* 2.249: *The Parsons obliged to change their note.* **1728** Byrd *Dividing Line* 52: I fancy the Pocoson you must struggle with tomorrow will make you change your Note, and try what Metal you are made of. **1764** *Paxton Papers* 163. **1769** Eliot *Letters* 438. **1776** PCallbeck in *Naval Documents* 3.628. **1778** Smith *Memoirs(II)* 402. **1785** Curwen *Journal* 2.1036. **1789** Boucher *Autobiography* 125. **1783** Ingraham *Journal* 200. Tilley N248. See **T280.**

N104 Blessed is he that expects **Nothing,** *etc.*

1739 Franklin *PR* 2.221: Blessed is he that expects nothing, for he shall never be disappointed. **1762** *Johnson Papers* 3.958-9: I am now to Console myself in this Beatitude, "Blessed is [he] who Expects nothing for he shall never be Disappointed. **1773** SEve in *PM* 5(1881) 192: Happy is the man that expects nothing for he shall not be disappointed. **1776** Curwen *Journal and Letters* 59: *"Blessed is he* (saith Pope) *that expecteth nothing, for he shall never be disappointed;"* nor a more interesting truth was ever uttered. **1784** POliver in Hutchinson *Diary* 2.409. **1792** JStuart in *Kingston* 284. **1812** Claiborne *Letter Books* 6.116: That State which the Scripture represents to be desirble. — "Happy is the man who expects nothing, for if he gets nothing he will not be disappointed." **1826** Audubon *1826 Journal* 59: Expect not too much and thou shalt not be disappointed. *Oxford* 66; TW 265(4).

N105 Lose **Nothing** for want of asking

c1725 Byrd *Another Secret Diary* 465: In which they're turn'd loose upon the Sex with this thriving motto, Loose nothing for want of asking. *Oxford* 485; Tilley A346.

N106 **Nothing** comes unmixed

1786 EHaynie in *MHM* 36(1941) 208: I find the truth of the saying, that nothing comes to us unmixt. See **J54, R145.**

N107 **Nothing** is difficult to willing minds, *etc.*

1775 JMacpherson in Read *Correspondence* 116: To willing minds nothing is difficult, and to a victorious army nothing is impossible. *Oxford* 580; Whiting N157.

N108 **Nothing** is done while anything remains to do

1780 Lee *Letters* 2.170: Nothing is done whilst any thing remains to be done. 1806 Fessenden *Modern Philosopher* 113: For 'tis a maxim, ever true That naught is done if aught's to do. 1819 Kinloch *Letters* 1.326: Bonaparte thinking . . . that nothing was done, while any thing remained to be effected. Whiting N156.

N109 **Nothing** is ill-spoken till it is ill-taken

1723 *New-England Courant* 112(1.2): Some peaceable Fools would have us believe, that nothing is *ill spoken till it is ill taken*. *Oxford* 878-9; Tilley S730, T31.

N110 **Nought** is never in danger

1815 Humphreys *Yankey* 21: They say, *nought* is never in danger. *Oxford* 582; Whiting N140.

N111 **Nothing** should be bought, *etc.*

1793 *Washington *Writings* 32.423: There is one rule, and a golden one it is, that nothing should be bot. that can be made, or done without.

N112 **Nothing** that is violent can be lasting

1791 S.P.L. *Thoughts* 77: Nothing that is violent can be lasting. *Oxford* 581; TW 265(12); Tilley N321. See **E117, M265.**

N113 **Nothing** venture, nothing have (*varied*)

1748 JAyscough in *Colden Letters* 4.84:

Three old Proverbs, on this occasion occur to my Memory (viz) Nothing venture nothing have. 1782 AA in *Adams FC* 4.345: I recollected the old adage. 1786 Freneau *Poems(1786)* 174: Where nothing is ventur'd no laurels are won. 1789 *Belknap Papers* 2.202: Perhaps my fortune may be, "Nothing venture, nothing have," which I would reverse thus, "Nothing venture, nothing lose." Barbour 191(2); *Oxford* 581; Whiting N146. See **F147, R90.**

N114 **Nothing** will exempt from the arrest of death

1702 Mather *Magnalia* 1.494: But, *Contra Vim Mortis*—Nothing will exempt from the arrest of *death*. *Oxford* 173; Whiting D78. See **R54.**

N115 Of **Nothing** nothing can be made

1716 Johnson *Writings* 2.198: *Ex nihilo nihil fit.* 1744 JDumbleton in Silverman 326: Tho' sage Philosophers have said, *Of nothing, can be nothing made.* 1744 Stephens *Journal(II)* 2.114: [Latin only]. 1746 Franklin *Papers* 3.88: [Latin only]. 1755 JBowdoin in Franklin *Papers* 5.489: *Ex nihilo nihil fit* cannot be true; for matter which it is granted had no existence, must have been formed either out of the divine substance, or *ex nihilo.* 1756 Adams *D and A* 1.28: Nothing can proceed from Nothing. 1763 Watts *Letter Book* 154: [Latin only]. 1816 Jefferson *Writings* 14.381: It is vain for common sense to urge that *nothing* can produce but *nothing.* 1827 Watterston *Wanderer* 138: [Latin only]. Barbour 131; *Oxford* 579; Whiting N151.

N116 Thank you (God) for **Nothing**

1734 Belcher *Papers* 2.461: Thank him for nothing. 1745 Stephens *Journal(II)* 2.206: Which put me in mind of *Thank ye for nothing.* 1787 *Columbian Magazine* 1.392: So thank you for nothing. 1801 JJackson in Milledge *Correspondence* 71: Thank God for nothing. 1815 Humphreys *Yankey* 34: you. *Oxford* 809. TW 265(6).

N117 Those who have **Nothing** can lose nothing

1814 King *Life* 5.399: Those who have

nothing can lose nothing. *Oxford* 580; Whiting N142. See **G185**.

N118 **Now** or never

1686 CMather in *Mather Papers* 390: Now or Never. **1707** FWainwright in *Baxter Manuscripts* 9.237: Now is the time or Never. **1764** Watts *Letter Book* 245. **1774** JHawley in Adams *Works* 9.641. **1776** PSchuyler in Sparks *Correspondence* 1.108. **1776** Shaw *Journals* 20. **1777** Munford *Patriots* 463. **1778** *Clinton Papers* 3.112. **1779** CPinckney in Gibbes 3.111. **1788** *Columbian Magazine* 2.229. **1795** Tyler *Verse* 46. **1796** Cobbett *Porcupine* 3.354. **1800** *Cary Letters* 160. **1806** *Port Folio* NS 1.87. **1809** Weems *Letters* 2.425. **1810** JMason in King *Life* 5.224. **1815** Freneau *Poems(1815)* 1.135. c**1819** Beecher *Autobiography* 1.404. **1824** *Tales* 2.102: It's a now-or-never business. **1833** Longfellow *Letters* 1.422. *Oxford* 583; Whiting N178.

N119 Odd **Numbers** are lucky

c**1725** Byrd *Another Secret Diary* 467: I believe that all odd numbers are lucky except the fatal number of 13. NED Odd 2, quote 1598; *Oxford* 496.

N120 Take care of **(Number)** one

1736 Gyles *Memoirs* 13[misnumbered]: A Word or a Wink was enough to excite me to take care of One. **1741** *Georgia Records* 23.71: Tis a professed Maxim with him . . . To take care of One. **1801** Story *Shop* 51: Bet and Moll look'd out for number one. **1809** Woodworth *Poems* 237: Like others, you "take care of number one." **1815** *Port Folio* 3NS 6.527: Selfo the harvest's all thine own, The golden adage strained, By taking care of number one Thou hast thy million gained. *Oxford* 583; TW 270(5). Cf. Tilley O50. See **E81**.

N121 To lose the **Number** of one's mess

1814 Palmer *Diary* 48: Diseases are geting more prevalent . . . I very much fear if they Keep us here through the Summer that the majority of us will lose the number of our mess, 99: I realy pity You as I know some of you will Loose the number of your mess. Colcord 130; NED Number 4c; TW 266(1).

N122 As demure as any **Nun**

1772 Paterson *Glimpses* 121: He looks demure as any nun Tho' meanest fellow under sun.

N123 As stupid as a **Nun**

1774 Fithian *Journal and Letters* 233: And yet I am blamed for being stupid as a Nun.

N124 As sound as a **Nut**

1803 *Yankee Phrases* 87: As sound as a nut. TW 266(6).

N125 As tight as a **Nut**

1803 Davis *Travels* 410: She [a ship] was tight as a nut.

N126 A hard **Nut** to crack

1739 Stephens *Journal(I)* 1.453: Wherefore that Nut was a little too hard for us to crack. **1745** Franklin *Papers* 3.26: Fortified towns are hard nuts to crack, **1775** *Writings* 6.409: This is a harder nut to crack than they imagined. Barbour 131(1); *Oxford* 353; TW 266(9).

N127 **Nut-brown**

1775 (MWarren) *The Group* (Boston, 1775) 15: I wedded nut brown Kate. **1776** *Pennsylvania Journal* in Buckingham *Specimens* 1.292: His nut-brown Maid. **1780** Hamilton *Papers* 2.455: A little *nut brown maid* like you. **1783** Williams *Penrose* 84. **1792** Pope *Tour* 15: Nut brown were her Locks. **1796** Barton *Disappointment* 51. **1798** Paine *Works* 267: lass. **1809** Weems *Washington* 34: ale. **1827** Longfellow *Letters* 1.219: The Basque girls are very beautiful—they are literally "nut-brown maids." Whiting N189.

N128 **Nuts** to apes (monkeys)

1787 Adams *Works* 6.167: They cannot be diverted like apes, by throwing the nuts of the executive power among them, **1811** *Adams-Waterhouse Correspondence* 67: How many hot Nuts for the Monkeys you will see, I know not. *Oxford* 583-4; Tilley N363.

N129 To be **Nuts** to (for) one

1802 Irving *Jonathan* 19: This was all nuts to his merry persecutors. **1811** Wirt *Letters* 1.299: All this was nuts to me. **1817** Royall *Letters* 112: This was nuts for me. **1836**

Hone *Diary* 1.195: It was nuts for him to be the organ of Mr. Lynch's attack upon his quondam associate. *Oxford* 583-4; TW 266(8).

N130 To make wooden Nutmegs

1822 Jackson *Correspondence* 3.167: A fit subject to be turned to the Trade of making wooden Nutmegs to impose upon the world with. NED Nutmeg 1, Wooden nutmeg.

N131 In a Nutshell

1770 Franklin *Papers* 17.60: The true Art of governing the Colonies lies in a Nut-Shell. **1804** Brackenridge *Modern* 446: Why not, at least, put the Acts of assembly in a *nut shell?* **1815** *Port Folio* 3NS 5.432: To bring the case within a nutshell. **1824** Pintard *Letters* 2.160: A subject . . . condensed in a nutshell. **1841** Webster *Letters* 520: The same may be said of our popular proverbs, many of which contain important truth in a nutshell. Barbour 180: Thing(13); TW 267(3). See I18.

N132 The Nymph may be chaste that has never been tried

1737 Franklin *PR* 2.167: And the nymph may be chast that has never been tryd. Cf. *Oxford* 911; Tilley W681; Whiting W484.

O

O1 As sturdy as an **Oak**

c1814 Freneau *Poems* 3.353: Sturdy as the mountain oak. Whiting O5; Whiting *NC* 453(2).

O2 To have (*etc.*) the laboring **Oar**

1702 *Penn-Logan Correspondence* 1.111: That is what I have the laboring oar against. **1743** RPartridge in Kimball 1.233: The labouring Oar will then be upon him. **1752** *Johnson Papers* 9.89: Besides the labouring Oar will now be on Mr. Beekman. **1753** Wolcott *Papers* 323. **1778** WMalcom in Leake *Lamb* 206: You know there [are] but few, that will take the labouring oar, tho' many that will follow, and shove along. **1781** Witherspoon *Works* 4.473: The laboring oar lies upon you. **1792** *Washington Writings* 32.84: The enclosed will . . . throw the labouring Oar upon Mr. H—. **1804** WEaton in *Barbary Wars* 5.35: As they have the laboring oar, it seems but reasonable they should enjoy the honor. **1821** Jefferson *Writings* 1.75-6: I saw . . . that the laboring oar was really at home, 86: I took the laboring oar. Colcord 135; NED Labouring ppl. a 4.

O3 To lie on one's **Oars**

1751 Wolcott *Papers* 74: They Keep us Lying upon our oars. **1755** Laurens *Papers* 2.42: We shall think it best to lye upon our Oars for a few days, **1756** 118: We lay upon our Oars some days. **1766** Franklin *Papers* 13.298. **1778** JSewall in Curwen *Journal and Letters* 207: A number of gentlemen . . . have been lying on their oars to see which way the game would finally go. **1784** Putnam *Memoirs* 224. **1784** Smith *Diary* 1.92. **1785** EGerry in Jefferson *Papers* 8.516. **1789** JBridge in Adams *Diary* 391, n.2. **1790** Jefferson *Papers* 16.537: They have for some time been resting on their oars, **1796** *Writings* 9.337: Republicanism must lie on its oars. **1798** Cobbett *Porcupine* 8.159. **1798** Jefferson *Writings* 18.204. **1808** Hitchcock *Poetical Dictionary* 74: Horse-jockies and inn-keepers were compelled to lie upon their oars on Sunday. **1810** Delano *Narrative* 561. **1810** *Port Folio* 2NS 3.170: By the beer keg he rally'd, but lay on his oars. **1813** WBarbee in Knopf *War of 1812* 3.215. **1824** Neal *American Writers* 35: We would seriously admonish all young writers . . . never to lie upon their oars. **1824** HSeawell in *Ruffin Papers* 1.292: We . . . are waiting upon "our Oars" for the arrival of further testimony. **1832** Barney *Memoir* 76: He was compelled, in the nautical phrase, to "lie on his oars" for many successive weeks. **1834** TAshe in *Ruffin Papers* 2.110: I am ambitious of floating upon my own oars. **1834** Clifford *Letters* 71: I am upon my oars until tuesday night. Colcord 135; TW 268(2).

O4 To put in one's **Oar**

1744 Black *Journal* 2.46: Every One of the Young Ladies put in an Oar and helpt her out. **1760** Adams *D and A* 1.176: She must put in her Oar. **1765** Adams(S) *Writings* 1.204: One of the ferrymen . . . *put in his oar* and said. **1771** Adams *D and A* 2.50. Colcord 135; *Oxford* 585; Whiting O12.

319

O5 To quit the **Oar**

1784 HWilliamson in *Blount Papers* 1.151: I can hardly get my own Concent to quit the Oar in this Place.

O6 To sow one's wild **Oats**

1650 Bradstreet *Works* 157: When my wild oates were sown & ripe and mown. 1768 JParker in Franklin *Papers* 15.144: Had he attempted to sow his Wild Oats while single. 1783 Williams *Penrose* 236. 1797 Foster *Coquette* 98: Yet I intend after a while (when I have sowed my wild oats) to make a tolerable one [wife]. 1820 *Fudge Family* 31. 1822 Gallatin *Diary* 201: I have sown about one-half or, say, three-quarters of my wild oats. c1825 Tyler *Prose* 142. 1830 Pintard *Letters* 3.200, 203. 1848 Paulding *Letters(II)* 471: I am convinced that so long as we have room for expansion, and the People can sow their wild oats all over the continent, we can't be ruined. *Oxford* 889; TW 268(2).

O7 To take to one's **Oats**

1783 Williams *Penrose* 339: He'el be taking to his Qats [*for* oats] ere long again. Cf. TW 268(1).

O8 Compelled **Oaths** are not binding (*varied*)

1769 Brooke *Emily* 103: She has . . . observed that indiscreet engagements are better broke than kept. 1779 SAlexander in *Baxter Manuscripts* 18.36: The said oath which he was Compeled To Take was not binding upon him. 1782 Trumbull *Satiric Poems* 125: And vows extorted are not binding In law, and so not worth the minding. a1788 Jones *History* 2.8: The oath was taken by compulsion, and was of course unjust, illegal, not binding. 1793 AJames in *MHM* 38(1943) 349: But the saying is, I gave my consent when obliged. a1811 Henry *Account* 136: A constrained oath, as theirs would be, could not be binding. 1812 Maxwell *Poems* 32: The oath? It was a sin to take it, And therefore can be none to break it. 1832 Longfellow *Letters* 1.383: Which promise, like all promises *extorted by violence,* I consider as by no means obligatory. *Oxford* 585; Whiting O13.

O9 He that cannot **Obey** cannot command (*varied*)

1734 Franklin *PR* 1.356: He that cannot obey, cannot command. 1771 GWilson in *St. Clair Papers* 1.258: I . . . was not fit to Command if not Willing to obay. 1776 Smith *Works* 1².23: It was wisely considered that he who had so well learned to obey, was fittest to command. 1797 Tyler *Algerine* 1.28: He must learn to obey, before he is fit to govern. 1809 Irving *History* 1.236: Adding at the same time a profound maxim . . . that "he who would aspire to *govern,* should first learn to *obey.*" 1813 RLucas in Knopf *War of 1812* 3.180: For Alexander the great, observed emphatically: "That he would conquer others, must first learn to conquer himself." 1816 Asbury *Letters* 3.545: If a man is not . . . practiced in obedience to know how to serve, he will never know how to command. c1825 Tyler *Prose* 103: The good old maxim "First learn to serve and then you will know how to govern." *Oxford* 136; TW 78; Tilley M714, S246; Whiting M228.

O10 Great **Occasions** make great men

1816 Fidfaddy *Adventures* 108: Hence we say "great occasions make great men." See N19.

O11 The **Occasion** makes the thief

c1680 Radisson *Voyages* 196: The occasion makes the thief, 221. *Oxford* 600; Whiting E27. See **O33.**

O12 All **Officers** and all men

1788 May *Journal* 95-6: The company with whom I am to ascend the Ohio is composed of all officers and all men: consequently every . . . matter . . . has to be stated and discussed an hour or so before it can be determined how it shall be. Cf. Whiting H429. See **H114, M115.**

O13 Good **Officers** make good soldiers

1777 AA in *Adams FC* 2.347: Good officers will make good Soldiers. See **C34, M109.**

O14 As smooth as **Oil**

1677 Hubbard *Indian* 2.218: He found their Words *smoother than Oyl,* a1700 *New England* 448: But though his words were smoother than oil, yet . . . in his heart were drawn swords. a1731 Cook *Bacon* 324: Words, as smooth as Oil. 1812 "Tristram Trap'em" in Otis *Letters* 2.25: With tongue as smooth as oil. 1826 Austin *Literary Papers* 31: The Hudson was a sea of glass, smooth as oil. *Oxford* 747; Whiting O23.

O15 More **Oil** than corn

1740 Stephens *Journal(I)* 2.26: The first Compliment he bestowed was, that he thought what I had read contained more Oil than Corn.

O16 **Oil** and water do not mix (*varied*)

1783 Jones *Letters* 122: Like oil and water jumbled together they will soon separate. 1800 Adams *New Letters* 239: Oil & water might as well mix, as the Fathers harmonize. 1815 Adams *Works* 10.139: I wish I could amalgamate oil and water. c1820 Bernard *Retrospections* 114: Oil and water would not be a more incongruous mixture. 1821 Knight *Poems* 1.33: Till oil and water natures mingle, Pride and religion must live single. TW 269(2).

O17 The **Oil** of hickory

1753 *Independent Reflector* 303: And effect by the Oil of Hickory, what could not be obtained by the Verdict of my Peers. NED Hickory 8(11). Cf. *Oxford* 587; Tilley O28.

O18 To consume midnight **Oil**

1796 Dennie *Lay Preacher* 8: Much midnight oil must be consumed. 1810 Adams *Lectures* 1.100: The future orator must consume the last drop of his midnight oil. *Oxford* 92; Tilley O31.

O19 To pour (*etc.*) **Oil** on the fire

1645 TJenner in *Winthrop Papers(A)* 5.15: I think Counsell to the contrary doth rather (like oyle on the fire) enflame them. 1652 Williams *Writings* 4.499: A *Tenent* in *England* most unseasonable, as powring Oyle on those *Flames* which . . . *Parliament* . . . had begun to quench. a1656 Bradford *History* 1.411: All reprofes were but as oyle to the fire. 1727 Parkman *Diary* 71.190-1: Thus did he . . . keep up the flame by throwing in oil when he pretended to cast in

water to quench it. Barbour 131(4); *Oxford* 587; Whiting O24.

O20 To pour **Oil** on troubled waters

1786 Rush *Letters* 1.390: His presence and advice, like oil upon troubled waters, have composed the contending waves of faction. 1795 HKnox in *Bingham's Maine* 1.573: The Presidents letter had the effect of oil to quiet a troubled ocean. 1818 Grant *Memoirs* 2.133-4: It was like oil poured on agitated waters, which produces a temporary calm immediately round the ship. 1814 Gallatin *Diary* 27, 1815 73. *Oxford* 587; TW 269(4).

O21 Too much **Oil** extinguishes the light

a1700 Hubbard *New England* 520: Too much oil extinguishes the light it should maintain.

O22 Clout the **Old** as the new is dear

1783 EInman in Murray *Letters* 287: I took the old method to Clout the auld as the new was dear [fix over an old dress].

O23 As black as **Old Nick**

1764 *Paxton Papers* 177: By which, they with a Magic Trick Could shew white Folks as black's Oldnick. *Oxford* 591; TW 270; Tilley N161. See **D108**.

O24 **Old Nick** to pay

1819 Peirce *Rebelliad* 18: He thought th'Old Nick must be to pay. See **D131**.

O25 The **Olive** branch (of peace) [The following is a selection from 85 occurrences of the phrase]

1652 Williams *Writings* 4.476: With *Olive branches* of *civill peace*. 1682 Randolph *Letters* 3.162: The Agents return home with an Olive branch, 1686 4.92: Coming with such an olive branch in my mouth. a1700 Hubbard *New England* 576: Which made them return like Noah's dove with an olive branch of peace in their mouths and hands. 1761 Laurens *Papers* 3.74: Holding the Olive branch in one hand & the [sword] of cruel War in the other. 1764 Watts *Letter Book* 288: The reasons, one hand the Olive, tother the Dart. 1774 GClymer in Quincy *Memoir* 146: Many . . . are for offering the olive-branch to the mother country. 1775

Adams *Works* 9.356: To hold the sword in one hand and the olive branch in the other. **1775** Franklin *Writings* 6.400: You know it was said that he [Lord North] carried the sword in one hand, and the olive branch in the other; and it seems he chose to give them a taste of the sword first. **1776** Stiles *Diary* 2.32: But when what some People, Tories, may call the Olive-plant is handed to us at the point of the Bayonet, This is doubtless the Olive Leaf; but it comes too late. **1778** JThaxter in *Adams FC* 3.18: The Olive Branch seems to be held out, but . . . it rests upon the Sword, 46. **1780** Adams *Correspondence* 295: As to the olive branch, the seed is not yet sown that is to produce the tree that will bear it, in *Warren-Adams Letters* 2.155: The beauteous olive Branch will never decorate my Brows. **1783** *Washington *Writings* 26.118: The Speech of his Britainic Majesty is strongly indicative of the Olive branch. **1791** Pickering *Life* 2.484: While I carried the sword in one hand, I should wish to hold the olive-branch in the other. **1801** Delano *Narrative* 364: I will here remark, that the olive branch, or a branch of a green tree or bush, is an emblem of peace. **a1804** Humphreys *Works* 55.162: The sword and olive-branch in either hand. **1809** Rush *Letters* 2.1018: Mr. Jackson is arrived in our country . . . I hope with an olive branch in his mouth. **1813** Miss DHayes in *VHM* 49(1941) 219: And then may the American Eagle Soar high and build her downy Nest in the Olive branch. **1814** Bayard *Letters* 37, *Papers* 313: If the olive branch be presented to us by one hand, a cup of humiliation and disgrace will be held out in the other. **1825** Jefferson *Writings* 16.141-2. **1827** Cooper *Letters* 1.210. Whiting O32.

O26 As plain as **1**, 2, 3
1713 Chalkley *Journal* 79: They were as plain as *Gunter's* Line, or as 1, 2, 3. See **A7**.

O27 To lose by **One** what you get by another
1763 *Beekman Papers* 1.449: You will Lose by One what you git by Another. Cf. *Oxford* 487; Tilley H809; Whiting H634. See **S158**.

O28 The more **Onions** are cursed the more they grow
1722 *New-England Courant* 25(1.1): As the Connecticut Trader once said of his Onions, *The more they are curs'd, the more they grow.* Cf. *Oxford* 284: Fox; Tilley F632.

O29 Too many **Opinions** mar any plan
1777 Reed *Life* 1.347: I would further add that too many opinions will mar any plan. Cf. *Oxford* 763. See **C285.**

O30 **Opportunities** are everything in love and war
1777 Reed *Life* 1.354: For in love and war, opportunities are everything.

O31 **Opportunity** is a precious companion
1797 Mann *Female* 61: *Opportunity is a precious companion.*

O32 **Opportunity** is the great bawd
1735 Franklin *PR* 2.9: Opportunity is the great Bawd. *Oxford* 599; Tilley O70.

O33 **Opportunity** makes the thief
1734 *Letter* in *Colonial Currency* 3.45: The *homely Proverb,* That Opportunity makes the Thief. *Oxford* 600; Whiting E27. See **O11.**

O34 To play **(O)possum**
1794 DAllison in *Blount Papers* 2.428: I have lain and possumed as ColO. Blount says. **1823** Weems *Letters* 3.353: Two of whom, in the language of that day *played possum,* 354: The two English soldiers who had *played possum,* agreed to creep up to the fire. **1824** Blane *Excursion* 134: Hence it is a common saying in America, when any one is pretending or counterfeiting, that he is "playing possum." **c1840** Clark *Letters* 67: I really think my friend, the Rev. Mr. Clark, has been "playing possum." **1845** Cooper *Letters* 5.66: Still he plays possum. TW 271(6).

O35 As true as an **Oracle**
1775 JA in *Adams FC* 1.290: Your Words are as true as an oracle. Cf. *Oxford* 761; TW 271.

O36 As yellow as an **Orange**
1807 JAdams in *Adams-Warren Correspon-*

dence 402: The whole seven provinces became as yellow as an orange [Holland, and thus a pun of sorts]. **1812** Melish *Travels* 444: One of the women here . . . as yellow as an orange. TW 271.

O37   Obey **Orders** or break owners
1782 Gordon *Letters* 476: You will be safe, though you break orders that would break your owners. **1802** Dorr *Letters* 320: Ahhere to the Vulgar Adage (nevertheless true) Obey Orders or break Owners. TW 271.

O38   The **Ostrich** (partridge) hides its head
1782 Van Schaack *Letters* 320: Like the ostrich, who hides her head to prevent the pursuer from knowing where she is. **1786** Jefferson *Papers* 10.117: Like the foolish Ostrich who when it has hid it's head, thinks it's body cannot be seen. **1811** Wirt *Letters* 1.302: Joe Cabell . . . told me, when I enjoined secrecy upon him, that I resembled the ostrich, hiding his head while his whole body was exposed to the world. **1849** Paulding *Letters(II)* 493: Do they think they can protect themselves . . . like a covey of Partridges by hiding their heads in a Brush heap. *Oxford* 600; Tilley O83.

O39   An **Ounce** of decision is worth a pound of doubt
1809 Irving *History* 1.221: And when an ounce of hair-brained decision is worth a pound of sage doubt.

O40   An **Ounce** of experience is better than a pound of science
1748 Eliot *Essays* 15: It used to be the Saying of an old Man, *That an Ounce of Experience is better than a Pound of Science.* *Oxford* 601; TW 272(3). See **E114.**

O41   An **Ounce** of mother wit is worth a pound of clergy
1771 Adams *D and A* 2.13: Dr. Cooper mentioned an old Proverb that an Ounce of Mother Wit is worth a Pound of Clergy, **1794** *Works* 1.463: An ounce of mother wit is worth a pound of clergy. **1805** Brackenridge *Modern* 617: And the truth of it is eternal, "An ounce of mother wit is worth a pound of clergy." *Oxford* 601; Tilley O85. See **M264.**

O42   An **Ounce** of prevention is worth a pound of cure
1735 Franklin *Papers* 2.12: *An ounce of Prevention is worth a Pound of Cure,* **1750** 4.63: 'Tis an old Saying, **1784** *Writings* 9.272-3: An English Proverb. **1796** Carey *Plumb* 13: The old adage. **1805** Weems *Hymen* 35: is better than. c**1825** Tyler *Prose* 68: pound of remedy. **1830** Ames *Mariner's* 281: a homely and trite proverb. Barbour 132; *Oxford* 646; TW 272(2). See **P275.**

O43   An **Ounce** of proof is worth a ton of assertions
1781 JJay in Deane *Papers* 4.295: An ounce of proof is worth a ton of assertions. **1804** Freneau *Prose* 452: An ounce of proof was better than a pound of profession.

O44   An **Ounce** of Prudence (discretion) is worth a pound of wit
1771 Adams *D and A* 2.13-4: Mr. Otis mentioned another which he said conveyed the same Sentiment — an Ounce of Prudence is worth a Pound of Wit. This produced a Dispute, and the sense of the Company was that the Word Wit in the 2nd. Proverb, meant the faculty of suddenly raising pleasant Pictures in the Fancy, but that the Phrase Mother Wit in the first Proverb meant natural Parts, and Clergy acquired Learning — Book Learning. **1772** Carter *Diary* 2.729: And got there about 5 minutes before the storm, which convinced me that an ounce of discretion is worth a pound of wit. *Oxford* 601; Tilley O85. See **G135.**

O45   An **Ounce** of wit that is bought, *etc.*
1745 Franklin *PR* 3.9: An ounce of wit that is bought. Is worth a pound that is taught. *Oxford* 601; Tilley O87. See **W242.**

O46   As hot as an **Oven**
1744 Franklin *Papers* 2.440: Rooms, compar'd to ours, as hot as ovens. **1845** Beecher *Autobiography* 2.501: I . . . slept on the settee in the dining room, hot as an oven and thronged with misqueties. Whiting O58.

O47   As grave as an **Owl**
1799 BHoward in *VHM* 30(1922) 248: I

would look as grave as an owl. Svartengren 60.

O48 As stupid as an **Owl**

1809 Fessenden *Pills* 101: As stupid as owls. **1816** Paulding *Letters(I)* 2.121: I found him as stupid as an owl. **1830** Ames *Mariner's* 119. TW 272(7).

O49 Not to be scared at an **Owl**

1809 Lindsley *Love* 10: Don't think tewe come paddy over a Suffield boy, I never was scart at an owl in all my born days. TW 411(2). Cf. *Oxford* 475.

O50 An **Owl** in an ivy bush

c1770 Tyler *Verse* 5: Or like an Owl in Ivy Bush Yea such a doleful wretch am I. *Oxford* 604; TW 273(4).

O51 An **Owl** is the Welshman's nightingale

1819 Pintard *Letters* 1.198: I made no reply, but like the Welshman's Nightingale, the Owl, I paid it off in thinking. Cf. *Oxford* 879-80; Tilley A233.

O52 To bring **Owls** to Athens

1612 Strachey *Historie* 55: Bring Owles to Athens. **1679** Josselyn *Account* 97: What does this man to bring *Owls* to *Athens?* *Oxford* 604; Tilley O97. See **C225, S482.**

O53 As big as an **Ox**

1809 Irving *History* 2.247: He had a heart as big as an ox. Barbour 133(1); TW 273(3).

O54 As patient as **Oxen**

1809 Fessenden *Pills* 101: As patient as oxen.

O55 Muzzle not the **Ox** that treads the corn

1713 Chalkley *Forcing* 382: Thou shalt not muzzle the Ox that treadeth out the Corn. **1766** Franklin *Papers* 13.513: That precept of the good book, *Thou shalt not muzzle the mouth of the ox that treadeth out the corn,* **1782** *Writings* 8.584. **1792** Brackenridge *Modern* 45: It is a good maxim and a scriptural expression. **1794** Paine *Age of Reason* 1.524. **1802** Chester *Federalism* 11. Barbour 133(7); *Oxford* 552; Whiting O78.

O56 As happy as **Oysters**

1808 Hitchcock *Poetical Dictionary* 46: And free from prisons, courts, and cloisters, Be happy as a race of oysters.

O57 As passive as **Oysters**

1809 Fessenden *Pills* 101: As passive as oysters.

O58 **Oysters** (*etc.*) are not good in months without an R

1774 Adams *D and A* 2.132: He told us of a Law of this Place [Philadelphia], that whereas oysters, between the Months of May and Septr. were found to be unwholesome food, if any were brought to Markett they should be forfeited and given to the Poor, *Adams FC* 1.110: There is a vulgar Saying, that Claims are unwholesome in every Month of the Year, which has not an R. in it. This common Sentiment receives much Credit from the Facts here related [deaths in June ascribed to eating clams]. **1776** Carter *Diary* 2.1062: Who would eat oysters up in July said the Mighty man. **1824** Doddridge *Notes* 98: It was a customary saying that fur is good during every month in the name of which the letter R occurs. *Oxford* 605; Tilley O117; Whiting *NC* 454(3).

O59 (Not) worth an **Oyster-shell**

1774 Adams(S) *Writings* 3.132: Whether . . . all the Trade . . . would . . . be worth an Oyster-Shell. Whiting O95.

P

P1 To be on (mind) one's **P's** and Q's

1784 EHazard in *Belknap Papers* 1.378: I assure you he stands very much upon his P's and Q's. **1792** Belknap *Foresters* 73: They did not make their P's and Q's exactly to his mind. **1814** Palmer *Diary* 26: Told him if he minded his P's and Q's he might possible get home soon. **1819** ASBCabell in *VHM* 47(1939) 148: Your Uncle Wirt still keeps you all on your Ps and Qs. Barbour 134; *Oxford* 606; TW 274.

P2 A slow **Pace** goes far

1633 EHowes in *Winthrop Papers(A)* 3.115: A slowe pace goes farre. *Oxford* 750; Tilley P3; Whiting P1.

P3 **Pack** and package

1685 FHooke in Belknap *History* 1.347: They . . . are removed both pack and packidge. See **B24, S2.**

P4 To know as little as a **Pack-horse**

a1788 Jones *History* 2.22: Though Mayor . . . knew as little of the laws of the land . . . as any common pack-horse in the country.

P5 **Pad** (in the straw)

1672 WGoffe in *Mather Papers* 126: There is a pad in the straw which God will in due time descover. **1674** Josselyn *Account* 150: Oh I see the pad, you never heard nor saw the like. *Oxford* 606; Whiting P3.

P6 Serve him as **Paddy** did the drum

1803 Davis *Travels* 448: I'll serve him . . . as *Paddy* did the drum. I'll give the fellow a good baiting.

P7 **Paint** costs nothing

1824 Blane *Excursion* 499: The inhabitants [of New England] may be supposed firm believers in the old Dutch proverb, that "paint costs nothing." Champion 115(185); Lean 4.79.

P8 As thin as a **Pair** of tongs

1850 Hone *Diary* 2.898: I am weak, very, and thin as a pair of tongs. Svartengren 186.

P9 Not touch one with a **Pair** of tongs

1646 Winslow *Hypocrisie* 52: I will not touch them with a paire of Tongues, 54. *Oxford* 833; TW 274-5(2).

P10 One **Pair** of heels is worth two of hands

1731 Cook *Bacon* 322: One Pair of Heels, worth Two of Hands. *Oxford* 607; Tilley P34.

P11 To show a fair (clean) **Pair** of heels

1654 Johnson *Wonder-Working* 111*: They . . . shewed the English a fair pair of heeles. **1736** Gyles *Memoirs* 14: I resolv'd to show them a pair of Heels. **1763** *Johnson Papers* 10.791: [They] had no other way to get clear of them but by showing them a clean pair of Heels. *Oxford* 729; Whiting P15.

P12 To bear (away) the **Palm**

1776 Tilghman *Memoirs* 139: The Virginia and Maryland Troops bear the Palm. **1787** Stiles *Diary* 3.274-5: Others not yet born may bear away the Palm. **1788** Ledyard *Russian Journey* 253: The delphic god bore the palm. **1794** DCobb in *Bingham's Maine* 1.465: The frank generous and hospitable

manners of Bostonia must have the palm.
1811 Graydon *Memoirs* 37: Lewis bore away
the palm from everyone that dared enter
against him. **1820** *Harvard College Rebellion* 74. **1828** Jones *Sketches* 2.231. **1828**
Longfellow *Letters* 1.282: For beauty, our
American ladies bear away the palm. **1831**
Pintard *Letters* 3.242. TW 275. Cf. *Oxford*
608; Whiting P17.

P13 To grease one's **Palm,** *etc.*

1765 GSims in Boyd *Eighteenth Century
Tracts* 186: So long as they perceive you
have any money to grease their fists with.
1790 Freneau *Poems* 3.9: Eternal squabblings grease the lawyer's paw, 49: New salaries grease unworthy paws. **1791** RO'Brien
in *Barbary Wars* 1.28: There is no doing any
business . . . without first palming the ministry. **1796** Cobbett *Porcupine* 3.385: That a
vain man should condescend to cajole the
mob, to grease the hands of the leaders.
1806 Plumer *Memorandum* 369: You must
grease the fists of Bonaparte with your gold.
1808 Eaton *Life* 416: Both these nations
have an itching palm for this country. **1816**
Adams *Writings* 6.46: Tacit ticklings of the
pirates' palms. **1818** Gallatin *Diary* 119:
One of the footmen (whose palm I greased).
Oxford 332; Whiting H69.

P14 To yield the **Palm**

1798 RSpaight in *Blount Papers* 3.259: But
I hope that Tom will not yield the palm to
him. NED Palm *sb.*[1] 3.

P15 As flat as a **Pancake**

1774 Schaw *Journal* 52: A poor duck,
squeezed as flat as a pancake. **1784** Hopkinson *Miscellaneous Essays* 1.336: Why your
head is as flat as a pancake. **1801** *Farmers'
Museum* 96: Your nose full as flat as a pancake or flatter. **1823** Sumter *Letters* 110:
Some change has taken place which has
rendered me as flat as a pancake without
being much thinner. Barbour 134; *Oxford*
267; TW 275; Tilley P39.

P16 As round as a **Pancake**

1782 Freneau *Poems* 2.132: Made center,
and circles as round as a pancake.

P17 **Pandora's** box

1677 Hubbard *Indian* 2.252: Opened this
Pandora's Box. **1707** Taylor *Poems* 226:
Pandora's Box would peps the theft with ire.
1708 Cook *Sot-Weed* 1: Plagues worse then
fill'd *Pandora's* box. **1714** PDudley *Objections* in *Colonial Currency* 1.241: This *Pandora's Box* once opened, 280, 311, **1720**
2.114: Having fill'd his Pandoras Box. **1745**
RWolcott in *Law Papers* 2.149: This fort
like Pandoras box is full of all Mischeif to us.
1761 Adams *D and A* 1.191. **1764** WNelson
in *Norton Papers* 31-2. **1764** CTufts in
Adams FC 1.38-9. **1766** JParker in *Franklin
Papers* 13.394: There was one Comfort left
even in Pandora's Box. **1774** AA in *Adams
FC* 1.177: Opened the pandoræn Box. **1774**
TBaldwin in Lee *Papers* 1.127: Woful experience has shewn us that it is the Residence of Pandora, whose baneful Box was
first open'd here; this, we know, was never to
be shut again. **1774** Miss ESmith in *Adams
FC* 1.103. **1774** MWarren in *Adams FC*
1.103: O're the Broad deep pour'd out Pandora's Box. **1775** Smith *Memoirs(I)* 248.
1780 Freneau *Poems* 2.28. **1784** Gadsden
Writings 203-4, 217, 221, 222. **1785** Washington *Writings* 28.145: This man has participated of the qualities of Pandora's box,
and has spread as many mischiefs. **1787**
NWebster in *Bowdoin Papers* 2.180. **1788**
American Museum 4.30. **1790** EPendleton
in *MHM* 46(1951) 75: The appointment of
Colonel Mercer to be the Pandora of the
Box. **1791** Gordon *Letters* 564. **1791** Maclay
Journal 378-9. **1792** Freneau *Poems* 3.66.
1792 Hamilton *Papers* 11.436, **1795** 19.76.
1796 JJackson in *Milledge Correspondence*
39. **1796** Latrobe *Journal* 35: This Pandora's
box of questions. **1799** DCobb in *Bingham's
Maine* 2.951. **1799** Jay *Correspondence*
4.254: I often think of Pandora's box; although it contained every kind of evil, yet it
is said that *hope* was placed at the bottom.
1800 Bowne *Letters* 29: I believe Pandora
opened her box upon him when he first
came into existence. **1803** Austin *Constitutional* 139. **1804** Plumer *Memorandum* 104.
1809 Fessenden *Pills* 126. **1809** Weems
Marion 128, *Washington* 217: A very Pandora's box, replete with every curse. **1810**

RPeters in Jay *Correspondence* 4.340: Turn Pandora's box bottom upwards, and get hope out first, 343. **1810** *Port Folio* 2NS 3.72: But to foul stinks that cities stifle, Pandora's box is but a trifle. **1810** WThornton in *Steele Papers* 2.631. **1811** Graydon *Memoirs* 389: To restore the freedom of the seas, and destroy that Pandora's box of human ills, Great Britain. **1814** *Port Folio* 3NS 4.584: Open the pandorean box. **1821** Knight *Poems* 2.76. **1822** Adams *Writings* 7.260: Opened a Pandora's box of democracy in Germany. **1826** Duane *Colombia* 266. **1830** Ames *Mariner's* 9. *Oxford* 608; Tilley P40.

P18   As pale as Paper

1825 Jones *Sketches* 1.17: His face is as pale as paper.

P19   As thin as Paper

1826 Pintard *Letters* 2.258: I am pretty near worn as thin as this paper. Whiting P23.

P20   As white as Paper

1796 Cobbett *Porcupine* 3.58: He was white as paper, **1797** 4.362: The remorseless Doctor Rush shall *bleed* me till I am white as this paper. **1806** Adams *D and A* 4.67: A face as pale or rather as white as a Sheet of paper. Svartengren 231; TW 275(1); Whiting P24.

P21   As dry as Parchment

1804 Irving *Journals* 1.44: The skin as dry as parchment. Whiting P26.

P22   To be fitted out by the Parish

1803 Davis *Travels* 13: She seemed fitted out by the parish; there was not a rope on board strong enough to hang a cat with. Cf. NED Parish 7: parish-rigged. See **C183.**

P23   Enough to make a Parson swear

1777 Gordon *Letters* 347: They are enough to make a parson angry, but not enough to make him swear. **1814** Palmer *Diary* 237: Such bustle fuss and stir is there Enough to make a Parson swear. **1817** JRandolph in King *Life* 6.88: [It] might make a person [*?for* parson] swear. TW 295: Preacher. See **M181.**

P24   Never spare the Parson's wine nor the baker's pudding

1733 Franklin *PR* 1.312: Never spare the Parson's wine, nor the Baker's pudding, **1738** 2.197.

P25   The Parson of Pancras

1666 Alsop *Maryland* 68: But stop (good Muse) lest I should, like the Parson of *Pancras*, run so far from my Text in half an hour, that a two hours trot back again would hardly fetch it up. Cf. Tilley P65.

P26   The Parthian flees and fights (varied)

1810 Adams *Lectures* 1.56: Wit, like the ancient Parthian, flies while it fights, **1824** *Memoirs* 6.263: His Parthian shaft at me. **1831** Jackson *Correspondence* 4.301: There has been another Parthian flight from this city who . . . has attempted to throw his darts behind him, 304, 313. **1832** Wirt *Letters* 2.376: In the Parthian shot you gave me on your departure from Richmond. *Oxford* 610; Tilley P80.

P27   As plump as a Partridge

1672 Josselyn *New-England Rarities* 157: [Women] as plump as partridges. **1772** *Bowdoin Papers* 1.302: Yʳ little girl is as plump as a partridge. **1791** TBurr in Burr *Memoirs* 1.299. **1803** *Yankee Phrases* 87. **1806** Adams(TB) *Letters* 175. **1820** Irving *Sketch Book* 464. **1821** Pintard *Letters* 2.33, **1826** 219: He is very elastic on his feet & plump as a partridge. *Oxford* 611; Svartengren 184; TW 276(1).

P28   As wild as a Partridge

1834 Jackson *Correspondence* 5.281: I found . . . little Rachel . . . as wild as a little partridge. Cf. TW 276(3).

P29   Hear both (all) Parties (sides)

1646 *Simplicities Defence* in Force *Tracts* 4.6.29: Else you had heard both sides speak before you had judged. **1646** EWinslow in *Winthrop Papers(A)* 5.87: The truth is hearing both sides speake. **1682** Claypoole *Letter Book* 93: I must hear both parties. **1708** Talbot *Letters* 118: I have heard all sides and Parties, what can be said pro or con. **1736** Talcott *Papers* 2.12: I can't Judge in a case that I have not opportunity to hear boath parties. **1739** Parkman *Diary* 72.37: My Advice was That it was not fit for them to expect a Judgment of the Case unless both sides are fully heard. **1775** Smith *Memoirs(I)* 218: To stick to the Rule *Audi Alteram Partem.* **1779** Deane *Papers* 3.285: *Audi alteram partem.* Hear the other side is a standing maxim of justice. **1779** Van Schaack *Letters* 195: Hear all, —judge for yourself. **1780** Adams *Works* 7.315: [Latin only]. **1782** JBowdoin in *Baxter Manuscripts* 20.119: In the present case, only one of the Parties has been heard. **1788** *Deane Brothers Papers* 223: Your Candor will prevent your deciding on any Subject, without hearing both parties. **1804** Claiborne *Letter Books* 1.336: Hear all parties, but think and act for yourself. **1805** JRodgers in *Barbary Wars* 6.303: It is customary I believe, for the Impartial Judge to hear the evidence of both Parties. **1810** Claiborne *Letter Books* 5.29: [Latin only]. **1813** *Port Folio* 3NS 1.398: [Latin only]. **1814** Jefferson *Writings* 14.135: [Latin only]. **1819** Brackenridge *South America* 2.48: The good old rule [Latin only]. **1826** *Austin Papers* 2.1470: Hear boath sides then you can better Judge. **1850** Paulding *Letters(II)* 514: [Latin only]. *Oxford* 362; Whiting P42. See **H154.**

P30 When one **Party** is willing the match is half made

1767 Franklin *Papers* 14.336: In matrimonial matches 'tis said when one party is willing the match is half made. Cf. Charles Dickens, *David Copperfield* (1849-50), chapter 5: Barkis is willin'.

P31 Drive one **Passion** out by letting another in

1770 Jefferson *Papers* 1.36: I expect he will follow the good old rule of driving one passion out by letting another in. Cf. *Oxford* 597: Nail; Whiting N6.

P32 What is **Past** cannot be recalled

1755 *Johnson Papers* 1.791: It's past, and not now to be recall'd. **1777** Washington *Writings* 9.7: What is past cannot be recalled. **1777** Wister *Journal* 113: But we cannot recall the past. **1783** Freneau *Poems*

2.233: Then forget what is past. **1798** Adams *New Letters* 142: What is past cannot be remedied. **1799** *Washington *Writings* 37.117: Things passed may be regretted but can never be recalled. **1815** *Bulger Papers* 72. *Oxford* 611; Whiting D287, P45. See **D215.**

P33 He that can have **Patience** can have what he will

1736 Franklin *PR* 2.140: He that can have Patience, can have what he will. Tilley P102. See **T124.**

P34 **Patience** and shuffle the cards

1793 McHenry *Letters* 142: "Patience and shuffle the cards." *Oxford* 612; Tilley P105.

P35 **Patience** is a virtue

1724 Chalkley *Journal* 129: I saw that Patience was an excellent Virtue. **1776** Smith *Memoirs(II)* 44: But there certainly is Virtue in Patience. **1781** JArmstrong in Reed *Life* 2.335. **1783** Washington *Writings* 27.1: Patience is a noble Virtue, and when rightly exercised, does not fail of its Reward. **1784** Adams(A) *Letters* 166: Patience, patience, patience, is the first, second, and third virtue of a seaman. **1787** WSSmith in Smith *Journal and Correspondence* 1.127. **1788** WCarmichael in Jefferson *Papers* 13.91. **1796** CPowell in *W&MCQ* 12(1903) 230. **1807** *Salmagundi* 407: Patience is a virtue but little known in the Cockloft family. **1826** Royall *Sketches* 98: Patience, a virtue of so much service to us in this uncertain world. Barbour 135(2); *Oxford* 613; Whiting P56.

P36 **Patience** perforce

c**1680** Radisson *Voyages* 103: But patience perforce. **1804** Irving *Journals* 1.100: *Patience par force* must be my motto. **1826** Duane *Colombia* 42: I had learned, among other wise saws, the Spanish proverb *patiencia por force*. *Oxford* 613; Whiting P60.

P37 As old as **Paul's**

1807 Tyler *Verse* 159: Lard! it is as old as poles [*for* Paul's]. *Oxford* 588; Tilley P119.

P38 No **Pay** but good words

1737 Hempstead *Diary* 319: No pay yet but good words. Cf. Barbour 136. See **W332.**

P39   A bad **Paymaster** is him that pays be-forehand

1786 *Washington *Writings* 28.370: I have had some reason to remember an old adage, that one of the bad paymasters is him that pays before hand. *Oxford* 614; Tilley W845.

P40   A good **Paymaster** is lord of another man's purse

1736 Franklin *PR* 2.137: The good Pay-master is Lord of another man's Purse, **1748** *Papers* 3.307: Remember this Saying, **1785** *Writings* 9.289: Says the Proverb. *Oxford* 323; Tilley P130.

P41   As alike as two **Peas**

1763 Jefferson *Papers* 1.7: You never saw two peas more alike than our yesterday and today. **1773** Trumbull *Satiric Poems* 88: Two peas were never more alike. **c1800** Tyler *Island* 22: I know a case like this as two peas, poor man. **1815** Humphreys *Yankey* 59: It wood be as unpossible . . . as it wood to find two peas, or pumkins jest alike in all perticklars. **1820** Faux *Memorable Days* 2.132: We are both as much alike on this subject as pea to pea. *Barbour* 136; *Oxford* 851; TW 277(3). See **P65.**

P42   Before you could say **Peas**

1824 *Tales* 2.49: The sail was split to rags before you could say peas. See **B252, J12, 44.**

P43   **Pea-green**

1786 Adams(A) *Letters* 298: The curtains of pea green. **1811** Adams *Writings* 4.29: Pea green liveries. **1818** Gallatin *Diary* 134: He is pea-green, **1823** 243: Lucius is now pea-green [Lucius had been seasick both times]. TW 277(2).

P44   Put another **Pea** in the pot

1803 Davis *Travels* 441: "How fair the breeze!" "Yes, we may put another pea in the pot." Cf. *Oxford* 617; Whiting P103.

P45   To hop like a parched **Pea**

1798 TGFessenden in Buckingham *Specimens* 2.218: My heart . . . hopped like a pea, that is parching. TW 277(4, 8).

P46   To sell like green **Peas** in spring

1810 Weems *Letters* 3.25: It sold like green peas in spring. Cf. TW 277(6).

P47   A bad **Peace** is better than a good war (*varied*)

1748 Wolcott *Papers* 478: Yet Some Say, an Unjust peace is better than a Just Warr. **1775** Franklin *Writings* 6.371: Even a bad Peace was preferable to the most successful War, **1782** 8.454: There has never been, nor ever will be, any such thing as a *good War,* or a *bad Peace,* **1783** 9.74: In my opinion, there never was a good War, or a bad *Peace,* 96, **1786** 492-3. **1787** Adams *Works* 5.101: Solderini thought "a lean peace better than a fat war." *Oxford* 416; Tilley P150, 154.

P48   He that would live in **Peace**, *etc.*

1736 Franklin *PR* 2.143: He that would live in peace and at ease, Must not speak all he knows, nor judge all he sees. *Oxford* 474; Tilley P140.

P49   In **Peace** prepare for war (*varied*)

1755 LGrant in McDowell *Documents* 2.75: The only best Time to prepare for Warr, is in Time of Peace, or before the evil Day comes. **1766** Franklin *Papers* 13.55: *Pax quaeritur Bello.* **1771** *Johnson Papers* 8.35: We follow the old Maxim to Maintain Peace; for we are arming Whilst we Nego-tiate. **1774** AA in *Adams FC* 1.161: The Maxim in time of peace prepair for war, 165. **1777** Adams(S) *Writings* 3.354: A good old Maxim, *In Peace prepare for War.* **1779** SShaw in Leake *Lamb* 219: To be in a con-dition of sustaining war properly, is one of the surest means of procuring an advanta-geous peace. **1780** *Washington Writings* 19.410: It is an old maxim, that the surest way to make a good peace is to be well pre-pared for War. **1781** Jay *Correspondence* 2.67: To prepare vigorously for war is the only sure way of preparing for a speedy and valuable peace. **1781** *Washington Writings* 23.181. **1782** Lee *Letters* 2.266: The surest way to procure speedy and honorable peace is to be well prepared for war. **1782** *Washington Writings* 25.115: There is nothing which will so soon produce a speedy and honorable Peace as a State of preparation for War, 166: Being in a state of perfect preparation for war, is the only sure and infallible means of producing Peace. **1785** Lee *Papers* 2.334. **1799** Eaton *Life* 107: How often is the maxim repeated in America, "to preserve peace, be prepared for war"? **1799** RGHarper in Bayard *Papers* 84: The best way to gain peace, is to be prepared for war. **1813** DHumphreys in *Smith Papers* 1.128: The only way to obtain Peace, is to be prepared for all *Contingencies,* even the *worst.* **1820** Robertson *Letters* 142: To make an honourable peace, we must be prepared for war. **1837** Jackson *Correspondence* 5.505: the adage, "in peace prepare for war." *Oxford* 616; Tilley T300. Cf. Whiting W152.

P50 **Peace** blooms and war consumes

1800 Adams *Letters on Silesia* 21: The old proverb, *Friede nusert, und krieg verzehrt* —(Peace blooms, and war consumes).

P51 **Peace** breeds plenty, *etc.*

1654 Johnson *Wonder-Working* 71: Verily, Cold, Purity, Peace and Plenty run all in one channell. a**1700** Saffin *His Book* 136: Worldly peace breeds plenty, plenty breeds pride, & pride breeds contention, & war where with comes Ruine. **1744** Franklin *PR* 2.401: War begets Poverty, Poverty Peace; Peace makes Riches flow, (Fate ne'er doth cease.) Riches produce Pride, Pride is War's Ground; War begets Poverty, &c. The World goes round. **1794** WCooper in King *Life* 1.562: Remember that *Peace* makes *Plenty, War* makes *Poverty.* a**1820** Tucker *Essays* 328: The proverb that "war begets poverty, poverty peace." **1816** Adams *Writings* 5.462: That peace should be followed by plenty, is of very old experience. But that plenty should operate as a great national calamity, requires a public debt of a thousand million sterling, and a banking system to be accounted for. *Oxford* 616; Whiting P68.

P52 As gaudy as a **Peacock**

1789 Maclay *Journal* 41: The Dutch Minister . . . gaudy as a peacock. Svartengren 221.

P53 As gim as a **Peacock**

1796 *Massachusetts Spy* in Thornton *Glos-*

sary 1.iii: [Gentlemen] dressed as gim as peacocks. NED Gim: smart, spruce.

P54 As proud as a **Peacock**

1731 *Weekly Rehearsal* in Buckingham *Specimens* 1.120: The pride of a peacock. **1796** Adams *Writings* 2.56, n.3: As proud as a peacock. Barbour 136(1); *Oxford* 651; Whiting P280.

P55 (As vain as a **Peacock**)

1771 *Johnson Papers* 8.322: So much vanity . . . as to point at the Notion of the wandering Peacock. Barbour 136(1); TW 278(3).

P56 A **Peacock** has gay feathers, but black feet

1664 Bradstreet *Works* 49: It is reported of the peakcock that, prideing himself in his gay feathers, he ruffles them up; but spying his black feet, he soon lets fall his plumes. **1813** *Kennon Letters* 34.337: To be like a peacock, ashamed to show her feet. Lean 4.134; *Oxford* 616; Whiting P74.

P57 To look for **Pears** from an elm

1807 *Port Folio* NS 4.207: To use the homely proverb of Sancho, "looking for *pears* from an *elm.*" *Oxford* 20. Cf. TW 278. See **T62.**

P58 To cast **Pearls** before swine

1640 EHowe in *Winthrop Papers(A)* 4.241: I allwayes forbeare to contradict the wilfull, tis to . . . cast pearles to swyne. **1693** Calef *More Wonders* 146: Our Saviour expressly cautions his disciples that they do not throw their pearls before swine. **1694** *Connecticut Vindicated* 89: *Cast not your Pearls before Swine.* **1762** JEttwein in Laurens *Papers* 3.101: All the Pearls are thrown before the Swine & Dogs. **1768** *New-York Gazette* in *Newspaper Extracts(I)* 7.84: Like throwing pearls before a certain kind of animals. **1769** Davis *Colonial Virginia Satirist* 59. **1775** AA in *Adams FC* 1.321. **1775** AMiddleton in Gibbes 2.136: jewels. **1778** Paine *American Crisis* 1.120: To be cast like a pearl before swine. **1781** JEliot in *Belknap Papers* 3.204, 633d. **1793** Savery *Journal* 39: It was like casting pearls before swine, they turn again and rend you. **1796** DAllison in *Blount Papers* 3.41. **1799** Adams(TB) *Letters* 97. **1805** Brackenridge *Modern* 583. **1807** Paine *On* *the Question* 2.1012. **1807** *Weekly* 2.255. **1807** Weems *Murder* 27, **1809** *Marion* 81. **1818** Pintard *Letters* 1.110. **1826** Royall *Sketches* 162. **1830** Ames *Mariner's* 302, **1832** *Nautical* 9. **1833** Pintard *Letters* 4.127: As it is, I will not harshly say that it w^d be casting away pearls, but it w^d not be read. Barbour 136(2); *Oxford* 617; Whiting P89.

P59 To sow **Pebbles** when one may get wheat

1809 Weems *Letters* 2.407: Why in God's name shou'd we be sowing pebbles when we may get good wheat? Cf. Whiting D375.

P60 To turn a **Pebble** into a diamond

1816 Adams *Writings* 6.41: No labor will ever turn a pebble into a diamond. See **A119, P323.**

P61 To cry **Peccavi**

1769 *Johnson Papers* 7.69: He has cried peccavi. **1774** JTemple in *Bowdoin Papers* 1.358: They will cry *peccavi.* **1792** Belknap *Foresters* 49. **1793** Jefferson *Writings* 1.409: [It] might perhaps be calling *peccavi* before he was charged. **1798** Freneau *Poems* 3.215: To the tune of peccavi, a Solo will play. **1811** Graydon *Memoirs* 248. *Oxford* 158; TW 278; Tilley P170.

P62 To be in a **Peck** of troubles

1774 *Pennsylvania Packet* in *Newspaper Extracts(I)* 10.334: So wilt thou involve thyself in a *peck* of troubles. **1774** TYoung in Leake *Lamb* 91: They are in a peck of troubles. **1783** Van Schaack *Letters* 283: in a pack of troubles. **1790** Morris *Diary* 2.80. **c1800** Dennie *Lay Preacher* 167: He is an overgrown Pharoah, not, as it is vulgarly expressed, in a peck, but in a Red Sea, of troubles. **1803** *Port Folio* 3.92. **1809** Irving *History* 1.258: Its valiant commander . . . answers the vulgar, but expressive idea, of "a man in a peck of troubles." **1837** Cooper *Letters* 3.291, **1849** 6.70. *Oxford* 618; TW 279(1).

P63 To eat a **Peck** of salt together

1769 Woodmason *Journal* 152: We have eaten many a Peck of Salt together and why

should We fall out about Trifles. NED Peck *sb.*[1] 1b; *Oxford* 40; Whiting F626.

P64 To eat one's **Peck** (pound) of dirt

1784 AAdams in Adams *D and A* 3.158: If we do not die of Dirt now we shall at least eat our peck. **1819** Beecher *Autobiography* 1.424: The proverb is, "Every one must eat his pound of dirt." It might be a maxim, every one must write his quire of nonsense. *Oxford* 214; TW 279(2).

P65 To a **Pee** (?*for* Tee)

1801 Asbury *Letters* 3.228: Snelthen and me fit to a pee. See **P41, T1.**

P66 Pay for **Peeping**

1781 AA in *Adams FC* 4.164: But pay for peeping is an old adage and so have I. Lean 4.205.

P67 A **Peg** higher

1682 ERawson in *Hinckley Papers* 64: They . . . drew up the governor into a frame that seemed to me a peg higher. TW 279(1).

P68 A **Peg** lower

1772 SSpring in Burr *Memoirs* 1.42: If you are let down a peg lower, you may tell me of it. Barbour 130: Notch; *Oxford* 799-800; TW 279(3).

P69 **Pelion** on Ossa

1717 Mather *Letters* 246: But on the twenty-fourth day of the month comes Pelion upon Ossa. Another snow came on which almost buried the memory of the former. **1784** Freneau *Poems* 2.279: And the giants of old, that assaulted the skies With their Ossa on Pelion, shall freely confess That all they attempted was nothing to this, **1790** 3.24: With Pelion piled on Ossa. **1798** *Remarks on the Jacobiniad* 2.20: The very *Pelion* and *Ossa* of puns, piled one upon another. **1806** Adams *D and A* 4.13. **1814** Freneau *Poems* 3.327. **1818** Adams *Works* 10.342: As the giants heaped Pelion upon Ossa. **1818** Adams *Writings* 6.528: Pelion has been heaped upon Ossa to put down poor old Hickory. **1818** Watterston *Letters* 119, **1827** *Wanderer* 178: Heaping thought upon thought, *subjecto Pelio Ossam. Oxford* 600; TW 271.

P70   A **Pennsylvania** hurricane

c1820 Bernard *Retrospections* 250: A "Pennsylvany hurricane," like a "Caroliny swamper," was indeed a common term, nearer home, for a sublime Munchausenism —vulgarly speaking a long lie. DA Pennsylvania 2(11).

P71   As clean as a **Penny**

1723 *New-England Courant* 93(1.2): They are all (even to a Woman) from *the old and tough* to the *young and tender,* as *clean as a—Penny.* 1783 Hopkinson *Miscellaneous Essays* 1.230: Will keep them clean as any penny. *Oxford* 125; Svartengren 321; Tilley P188; Whiting *NC* 456(4).

P72   A bad **Penny** returns

1766 AA in *Adams FC* 1.55: Like a bad penny it returned to me again. *Oxford* 26; TW 280(6).

P73   In for a **Penny,** in for a pound

1785 *Washington Writings* 28.140: In for a penny, in for a pound is an old adage. 1816 Paulding *Letters(I)* 2.180: the old saying. *Oxford* 402; TW 280(4).

P74   No **Penny,** no paternoster

1652 Williams *Writings* 7.164: No longer *penny* no longer *Paternoster,* no longer *pay,* no longer *pray.* 1750 Sherman *Almanacs* 218: No Penny no Pater-noster. *Oxford* 573; Whiting P116.

P75   Not worth a **Penny**

1782 Freneau *Poems* 2.154: You said all our paper was not worth a penny. Whiting P118.

P76   A **Penny** for your thoughts

1787 *American Museum* 2.203: You bid a penny for my thoughts. 1807 *Emerald* NS 1.88: A penny for your thought. 1821 Gallatin *Diary* 184. Barbour 137(2); *Oxford* 619; Whiting P122.

P77   A **Penny** saved is a penny got

1699 *College Oration* in *W&MCQ* 2S 10(1930) 327: A penny sav'd is a penny gott. 1732 Franklin *Papers* 1.241-2: You know a penny sav'd is a penny got. 1749 *Law Papers* 3.329: Sometimes a penny Saved—not always. 1758 *New American Magazine* in *Newspaper Extracts(I)* 4.256. 1770 Habersham *Letters* 93: An old home Spun Adage. 1779 Franklin *Writings* 7.382. 1787 *American Museum* 1.118: It is a well known maxim . . . that a penny saved is a penny gained. 1787 *Anarchiad* 120: A penny saved is as good as a penny arned. 1788 *Politician* 24. 1792 *Universal Asylum* 9.293: "A penny saved is a penny gained," was his favorite proverb. 1792 *Washington Writings* 32.262: There is no Proverb in the whole catalogue of them more true, than that a penny saved, is a penny got, 1793 307: There is, certainly, no proverb more true, 442. 1795 *Tablet* 18: That "scoundrel maxim." 1797 *Washington Writings* 35.377: no adage more true. 1805 WGarnett in *Ruffin Papers* 1.66. 1818 Evans *Pedestrious* 147: Nothing is more true than the adage that a penny saved is a penny earned. 1830 Ames *Mariner's* 34: the maxim. Barbour 137(3-5); *Oxford* 619; Tilley P206.

P78   A **Penny** saved is two pence clear (got)

1737 Franklin *PR* 2.165: *A Penny sav'd is Twopence clear.* 1787 *American Museum* 1.68: A penny saved, is two pence got. 1819 *Port Folio* 4NS 7.329: The mercantile wisdom of "a penny saved is two-pence got." TW 279-80; Tilley P207.

P79   **Penny** wise, pound foolish

1747 Franklin *PR* 3.105: D. wise, = £ foolish. 1770 CCarroll in *MHM* 12(1917) 367: You will be Penny wise & Pound foolish. 1778 Paine *American Crisis* 1.127: has been the ruin of thousands. 1779 *New Jersey Journal* in *Newspaper Extracts(II)* 3.594. 1782 Paine *American Crisis* 1.202: Or, in proverbial language, that she could not bear to pay a penny to save a pound; the consequence of which has been, that she has paid a pound for a penny. 1784 Adams(A) *Letters* 192. 1787 AMaclaine in Iredell *Correspondence* 2.184: the old saying. 1802 *Port Folio* 2.223. 1803 Davis *Travels* 176: in popular language. 1805 Weems *Letters* 2.313: *Penny,* prudent—*pound,* prodigal. 1807 *Salmagundi* 201: If a man was to throw away a pound to save a beggarly penny. 1809 Fessenden *Pills* vi: A penny-grasping, pound-losing policy, 101: Penny wise, pound foolish poltroons. **1809** Weems *Marion* 246: God preserve our legislature from such "*penny wit and pound foolishness,*" **1820** *Letters* 3.294. Barbour 137(12); *Oxford* 620; TW 280(5). See **C104.**

P80 To turn an honest **Penny**

1798 Cobbett *Porcupine* 8.131: To turn an honest penny, their temple has been let out for a school. *Oxford* 847; TW 280(7).

P81 A well spent **Penny** that saves a groat

1749 Franklin *PR* 3.337: 'Tis a well spent penny that saves a groat. *Oxford* 619; Tilley P210. Cf. Whiting P123. See **C360.**

P82 At a great **Pennyworth** pause a while

1739 Franklin *PR* 2.219: At a great Pennyworth, pause a while, **1758** *WW* 345. *Oxford* 317; Tilley B79.

P83 To have a **Pennyworth** for one's penny

1720 Carter *Letters* 3: 'Tis no small satisfaction to me to have a pennyworth for my penny. **1779** Curwen *Journal* 2.517: So that in commercial language I've not had my pennorth for my penny. Whiting P131.

P84 Good **People** are scarce

1788 *Politician* 31: Good people, they say, are scarce. *Oxford* 322: Man; Tilley M521.

P85 The **People** love to tap a new barrel

1702 Mather *Magnalia* 2.543: Mr. Parker used to say, "The people love to tap a new barrel." Cf. Whiting C392, P134.

P86 As hot as **Pepper**

1812 Melish *Travels* 186: For drink we had *new* peach brandy as hot as pepper. Barbour 138; TW 280.

P87 **Pepper** is black

1723 Symmes *Utile* 44: *The Tune of,* Pepper is Black. Claude M. Simpson, *The British Broadside Ballad and its Music* (New Brunswick, N.J., 1966) 575. Cf. *Oxford* 620-1; Whiting P139.

P88 As hot as **Pepper-porridge**

1806 Fessenden *Modern Philosopher* 251: All piping hot, as pepper-porridge. NED Pepper 5.

P89 As hot as **Pepper-pot**

1765 JWatts in *Aspinwall Papers* 2.580: Even tho' he should be as hot as pepper pot itself. DA pepperpot.

P90 To avoid like a **Pest** (pestilence)

1741 *Georgia Records* 23.105: Men . . . he once avoided as the Pest of the place they lived in. **1776** WCarmichael in Deane *Papers* 1.354: Some in consequence avoided me as the Pest. **1778** Galloway *Diary* 41: I am fled from as a Pestilence. **1795** Adams *Memoirs* 1.80: This Maulde was avoided like a pestilence. **1797** Foster *Coquette* 255: By the virtuous part of the community, I am shunned as the pest and bane of social enjoyment. **1809** Adams *Correspondence* 331: I was avoided like a pestilence. Whiting P151. See **P193, S104.**

P91 Hoist with one's own **Petard**

1817 Adams *Writings* 6.170: 'Tis sport to see "the engineer hoist with his own petard." *Oxford* 376; Shakespeare *Hamlet* III iv 206.

P92 To rob **Peter** to pay Paul

1657 *Hutchinson Papers* 2.5: It is to take from Peter and give it to Paul. **1768** JJZubly in Stiles *Itineraries* 598: I cannot believe that it is right to rob Peter to pay Paul. **1777** Adams *Works* 9.470: The robbing of Peter to pay Paul. **1780** *Clinton Papers* 6.392. **1781** NGreene in Gibbes 1.195-6. **1816** Paulding *Letters(I)* 1.45. Barbour 138; *Oxford* 680; Whiting P154.

P93 **Petticoat** government

1788 *Politician* 54: You might as well be under the Devil's government as petticoat government. **1791** JHoskins in *Columbia* 235: His wife of course must be the Empress for they are intirely subject to a petticoat government the women in all cases taking the lead. **1792** Belknap *Foresters* 113: That humiliating condition, which . . . was formerly called *petticoat-government.* **1803** Austin *Literary Papers* 235. **1806** Dow *Journal* 298. **1809** Irving *History* 1.248. **1809** Lindsley *Love* 58. **1811** Dow *Journal* 531: His miss . . . has such influence, that he may be styled the "Petticoat Prince." **1813** *Port Folio* 3NS 2.485. **1837** Paulding *Letters(II)* 205, **1846**

420: For Petticoat Government is nothing compared with Petticoat Literature. Cf. NED Petticoat 4b.

P94 Put the **Petticoat** on the man, *etc.*

a1814 Dow *Journal* 412: [They] according to the vulgar saying, *put the petticoat on the man and wear the breeches themselves.* See **B319.**

P95 To puzzle a **Philadelphia** lawyer

1788 *Columbian Magazine* 2.182: In speaking of a difficult point, they say, *it would puzzle a Philadelphia lawyer* [in London]. **1803** *Balance* in Thornton *Glossary* 2.659: It would (to use a Yankee phrase) puzzle a dozen Philadelphia lawyers to unriddle the conduct of the democrats. **1809** Lindsley *Love* 40: You'd puzzle a philadelphia lawyer. **1816** Paulding *Letters(I)* 2.44-5: It would puzzle a Philadelphia lawyer to make a romance out of a log-hut. **1832** Ames *Nautical* 132: A jacket that it would "puzzle a Philadelphia lawyer" to get in and out of. NED Suppl. Philadelphia lawyer; TW 282(2).

P96 To appeal from (**Philip** drunk to Philip sober)

1797 HKnox in Sparks *Correspondence* 4.494: We must appeal from them, mad and drunk with power as they may be, to the time when they shall have regained their senses. *Oxford* 16; Whiting A85.

P97 To be among the **Philistines**

1722 Franklin *Papers* 1.40: *Among the Philistines,* **1737** *Drinkers* 2.176: He's Been among the Philistines.

P98 **Philosophers** may be bred, but poets must be born

1812 Hitchcock *Social* 196: It is a common saying, that *Philosophers may be bred, but Poets must be born. Oxford* 636: Poet; Tilley P451; Whiting *NC* 460.

P99 As scarce as the **Phoenix** egg

1715 JHepburn *American Defence* in American Antiquarian Society, *Proceedings* 59(1949) 116: The Reader will find them almost as scarce to be found as the *Phenix Egg.* Cf. *Oxford* 664; Tilley P256.

P100 **Physic** after death

1748 Franklin *PR* 3.254: Physic after death they give. *Oxford* 6; Tilley D133; Whiting L168.

P101 Live temperate and defy the **Physician**

1761 Ames *Almanacs* 319: Live temperate and defy the Physician. *Oxford* 252; Whiting M459. See **D220, T31.**

P102 **Physician,** heal thyself

1703 Taylor *Christographia* 416.69-70: He is Scorned on the Cross with A Physician, heale thyselfe. **1722** Mather *Letters* 349: I will not think it enough to say, *Medice, Cura teipsum;* but I will rather look up to the Lord our Healer for you. **1774** Fithian *Journal and Letters* 215: Physician heal thyself. **1827** Jones *Sketches* 2.42. *Oxford* 622; Whiting L171.

P103 Three **Physicians**

1772 Mrs. STurner in *Norton Papers* 247: I flatter myself that your health is by this time perfectly restored since you have taken Three Physicians, to be of your Household [the recipient has just been married]. Cf. Barbour 138; *Oxford* 622; Whiting L175.

P104 In a **Pickle**

c**1680** Radisson *Voyages* 34: I viewing myselfe all in a pickle. **1691** *Humble Address* in *Andros Tracts* 2.245: They are in this pickle about it. c**1700** Taylor *Poems* 396: Ile'st se in what a pickle he is in, 430: In what a wofull Pickle, Lord, we bee. **1702** Mather *Magnalia* 2.617: The enemy were now in a pitiful pickle. **1721** Wise *Friendly Check* in *Colonial Currency* 2.246: They are in hazard of falling into Old King *James's* Pickle. **1732** Belcher *Papers* 1.158: a fine, 215: a wretched, 231: a sad, **1734** 2.158: a fine, **1739** 205: a fine. **1771** Madison *Papers* 1.63: In such a pickle then I stood. **1774** *Pennsylvania Journal* in *Newspaper Extracts(I)* 10.348. **1777** Munford *Patriots* 495: a most woeful. **1779** Bailey *Journal* 146: a most woful, **1782** 187: This woful. **1783** Williams *Penrose* 119: a fine. **1784** Gadsden *Writings* 204: a fine. **1787** Bailey *Journal* 214. **1787** Jefferson *Papers* 12.72: a terrible, 147. **1801** Story *Shop* 46: so dire a. **1801**

Trumbull *Season* 155: a pretty. **1803** Davis *Travels* 407: a pretty. **1819** Peirce *Rebelliad* 21: a doleful. **1822** Watterston *Winter* 15. **1824** Neal *American Writers* 64. **1827** Watterston *Wanderer* 161. *Oxford* 623; TW 282.

P105 As great as two **Pickpockets**

1805 Sewall *Parody* 9: Great as two pickpockets [close friends]. TW 282.

P106 The **Picture** of ill luck

1767 *Johnson Papers* 5.746: I am really what you may call the picture of Ill luck. *Oxford* 623; TW 283(8).

P107 To chatter like a **Pie**

1806 *Weekly* 1.16: And chatter like a Pie. Whiting P179. See **M5.**

P108 To eat cold **Pie**

1809 Kendall *Travels* 3.28: *And the English obliged to eat cold pie.* Cf. *Oxford* 391; Partridge 150: Choking; TW 195. See **H354.**

P109 A **Piece** of one's mind

1817 Royall *Letters* 97: I'll tell him a piece of my mind. TW 283(2).

P110 As pale as **Pieces-of-Eight**

1762 *Johnson Papers* 3.960: Some look as pale as pieces of Eight. NED Piece 13c.

P111 As short as **Pie-crust**

1815 Humphreys *Yankey* 36: Crusty! Short as pie-crust! Techy and snappish. TW 283(2).

P112 As dirty as a **Pig**

1795 TParkin in *MHM* 7(1912) 364: [He was] as dirty as a pig. Barbour 139(4). Cf. TW 184: Hog(4). See **H236.**

P113 As fat as a **Pig**

1825 Pintard *Letters* 2.182: My little namesake as fat as a pig. **1830** Fletcher *Letters* 117: I reckon you will get as fat as a little pig this winter. **1845** Cooper *Letters* 5.13: Mrs. Jay looks like a girl—fat as a pig. Barbour 139(5); TW 283(2). See **H238, P234.**

P114 As snug as **Pigs** in the sty

1814 Palmer *Diary* 40: Stowe away under the Table snug as pigs in the Stye. Cf. *Oxford* 749; Tilley P296. See **P124.**

P115 As stupid as a **Pig**

1807 Janson *Stranger* 180: I do not agree with the vulgar saying, "as stupid as a pig." I have, from observation, found swine the most sagacious quadrupeds of the farm. Cf. Svartengren 133: Ignorant.

P116 In a **Pig's** whisper

1803 Davis *Travels* 431: I would, Sir, in a pig's whisper, if I did not think he would sue me at *Cowes.* Cf. TW 285: pig's whistle.

P117 A **Pig** in armor

1809 Fessenden *Pills* 60: And feels as awkward, when misplaced, A silly pig in armour cased. *Oxford* 376: Hog; Tilley H489.

P118 **Pigs** play upon organs

c1720 Byrd *Another Secret Diary* 265: All this together made a sort of musick like an Organ . . . from whence without Controversy came that good old saying of Piggs playing upon Organs. *Oxford* 624; Tilley P306.

P119 **Pigs** that sleep together become fond

1801 Weems *Letters* 2.216: Pigs, they say, by sleeping together contract a fondness for each other. *Oxford* 624; Tilley P313.

P120 To bleed like a **Pig**

1775 Moore *Diary* 1.33: The fellow, bleeding like a pig, roared out. **1805** Drinker *Journal* 398: He bled like a pig, as the saying is. Partridge 627.

P121 To buy a **Pig** in a poke

1732 *South-Carolina Gazette* in *W&MCQ* 3S 19(1962) 604: Never buy a pig in a poke. **1786** Drinker *Journal* 171: Little Dan came this morning with a load on his back, Not a Pig in a poke, but a cat in a sack. **1788** Washington *Writings* 30.144: I am not fond of buying a Pig in a Poke (as the phraze is), **1791** 31.421: To buy, to borrow an old adage, "A Pig in a Poke." **1797** Tyler *Algerine* 2.23. **1805** Brackenridge *Modern* 583: purchasing. **1809** Irving *History* 1.208: the good old vulgar maxim. **1809** Weems *Marion* 112: Selling their liberties for a *pig in a poke.* **1815** Brackenridge *Modern* 650: The blow . . . which was aimed at a pig in a poke, which a man was carrying home. **1828** *Yankee* 258: None but a fool would buy a pig in a poke. *Oxford* 95; Whiting P187. See **C72.**

P122   To have the wrong **Pig** by the ear

1793 *Echo* 58: They've caught the wrong pig by the ear. *Oxford* 756; TW 284(17); Whiting S540. See **S351.**

P123   To let the **Pig** out of the bag

1800 *Constitutional Telegraphe* in Buckingham *Specimens* 2.311: Dennie . . . has let the "Pig out of the bag." **1821** Howison *Sketches* 284: I let the pig out of the bag. See **C85.**

P124   To live like a **Pig** in a sty

1756 *Johnson Papers* 9.403: At present I live like a pig in a stye of Poles, and my fare differs but little from such. Cf. Whiting S967. See **P114.**

P125   To live like **Pigs** in clover

1795 *Echo* 217: Four weeks they liv'd like pigs in clover. **1813** *Boston Gazette* in Thornton *Glossary* 2.664: And live henceforth like pigs in clover. TW 284(16). Cf. *Oxford* 129. See **C215.**

P126   To roar like a stuck **Pig**

1783 Williams *Penrose* 300: Owen . . . roar'd like a stuck pig. Cf. Svartengren 390; TW 284(21).

P127   To sleep like a **Pig**

1785 Hunter *Quebec* 70: I slept as sound as a pig. **1822** GHowland in *New England Merchants* 125: They . . . slept like pigs all night [drunk]. Whiting H408: Hog. See **H250.**

P128   To squeal like a **Pig**

1793 Brackenridge *Modern* 234: He would imagine sometimes that the devil was in himself, and would squeel like a pig. TW 284(21).

P129   To stare like a **Pig**

1754 Mrs. Browne in *VHM* 32(1924) 313: They all stared at him like Pigs. **1817** Tyler *Prose* 326: The cashier . . . stared like the pig in the proverb. *Oxford* 771; TW 284(22).

P130   The worst **Pig** often gets the best pear

1809 *Port Folio* 2NS 2.549: The worst pig often gets the best pear. *Oxford* 921: Hog; Tilley P162. See **W115.**

P131   (To send one for) **Pigeon's** milk

1805 Irving *Journals* 1.234: N.B. no *pidgeons milk*. NED Pigeon's milk 2.

P132   To coo like **Pigeons**

1798 *Cary Letters* 143: The . . . couple cooing away like two pigeons. NED Coo 3, 4.

P133   To be either a **Pike** or a gudgeon

1821 Jefferson *Writings* 15.332: It will be as in Europe, where every man must be either pike or gudgeon. Cf. Tilley A261, H62.

P134   As plain as a **Pikestaff**

1712 Taylor *Poems* 280: Although the matters thou hast thine allowd, Plain as a pike Staffe bee. **1714** Hunter *Androboros* 34: Is not that a Hand as plain as a Pike Staff? **1766** *Johnson Papers* 5.8: It is as plaine as a Spike Staff. **1804** Brackenridge *Modern* 395. **1811** Wirt *Letters* 1.308. c**1825** Tyler *Prose* 67. *Oxford* 629; TW 285(1). Cf. Whiting P2.

P135   (Poor) **Pilgarlic**

1744 Hamilton *Itinerarium* 135: And haul poor pill-garlick with great rapidity thro' the pond. **1756** *Johnson Papers* 9.472: Thank god for all things Capt Eyre a Majority Wrexaell a Company poor pell garlick nothing, **1771** 8.63: As for Us we are poor pill Garlixs, no one to Converse with but the Indian Nobility. **1776** Song in *Naval Documents* 4.491: Now off goes Pilgarlick with his men in a fright. **1789** Ames *Letters* 1.34: I, Pilgarlic, sat entranced. **1789** *Columbian Magazine* 3.403: Poor Pill Garlic was in a dismal plight. **1810** *Port Folio* 2NS 3.170. **1834** Floy *Diary* 92: I never saw such a pill garlick of a looking, soft-talking fellow. NED Pilgarlic; Whiting G38.

P136   **Pilgrims** in a vale of tears

1685 JWilson in Jantz 149: We pilgrims are, this is a vale of tears. **1812** Maxwell *Poems* 25: But I, poor pilgrim in this vale of tears. Whiting P200.

P137   A **Pilgrimage** (of woe)

1791 Hamilton *Papers* 9.26: The little adverse circumstances that must attend us in this pilgrimage. **1806** Hitchcock *Works* 18: Their existence, here below, Is but a pilgrimage of woe. *Oxford* 461; Whiting P201, W663.

P138 Bitter **Pills** procure sound health

1630 *Winthrop Papers*(*A*) 2.205-6: Bitter pills helpe to procure sounde healthe. *Oxford* 63; Tilley P327; Whiting D393. See **H149.**

P139 To gild the **Pill**

1763 JBoucher in *MHM* 7(1912) 157: I need not have my Pills gilded. **1769** WBollan in *Bowdoin Papers* 1.133: How far this wou'd change the med'cine farther than gilding the pill I leave to you. **1774** Boucher *View* 336: A pill thus gilded we swallow without hesitation. **1780** Kemble *Papers* 2.304: In short, soften the Pill and gild it in the best manner you can. **1790** CGore in King *Life* 1.386. **1815** *Bulger Papers* 139: We shall succeed in gilding the bitter pill. *Oxford* 625, 786; Tilley P325.

P140 To swallow a bitter **Pill** (*varied*)

1721 Carter *Letters* 71: The Northern Neck business is like to prove a bitter pill to me. **1742** Stephens *Journal*(*II*) 1.128: Tho I swallow'd many a bitter Pill from his Insolence, **1743** 212: This bitter Pill stuck so, that 'twas hard to Swallow. **1775** Franklin *Writings* 6.360: The Pill might be bitter, but it would be salutary, and must be swallow'd. **1776** Lord Stirling in Sparks *Correspondence* 1.173. **1781** Jefferson *Papers* 5.633: Genl. Phillips either swallowed this Pill of Retaliation or made an Apology for his rudeness. **1783** JJones in Jefferson *Papers* 6.428: The impost . . . was with some a bitter pill, but finding it must be swallowed, they ceased at length to make opposition. **1786** Jefferson *Papers* 9.396, 404, 434: He said the renunciation of this interest was a bitter pill which they could not swallow. **1812** Jackson *Correspondence* 1.245: It is a bitter pill to have to act with him but . . . I will swallow [it]. Tilley P326.

P141 To sweeten the **Pill**

1782 Madison *Papers* 5.187: The Declaration of Congress . . . will . . . sweeten the pill. **1807** Jefferson *Writings* 11.137: This

would not sweeten the pill to the French. *Oxford* 625, 786; Tilley P325.

P142 As stiff as a **Pillar**

1775 RTPaine in Gerry *Letters* 1.81: You may be able to stand stiff as a pillar in our new government. Whiting P203.

P143 A **Pillar** of the church

1816 Colby *Life* 2.9: And become a pillar in the church of God. NED Pillar 3b.

P144 To consult one's **Pillow**

1809 Weems *Marion* 63: Having consulted his pillow, he had made up his mind to defend the place. **1810** Schultz *Travels* 2.25: I shall consult my pillow, and resolve to-night. *Oxford* 799; Tilley C696.

P145 To sew **Pillows** under the elbows

1652 Williams *Writings* 4.477: *Sows pillowes* under all *ellbowes,* makes the *Heart* of the *Righteous sad. Oxford* 625; Tilley P329.

P146 As bright as a new **Pin**

1794 PHolland in *Bingham's Maine* 1.230: In a few hours, our speechless, dying man was as bright as a new pin. Partridge 554; Svartengren 219.

P147 As neat as a new **Pin**

1787 *Columbian Magazine* 1.636: [He was] neat as a new pin. **1814** Wirt *Bachelor* 159: She has me as clean and neat as a new pin. **1824** Tyler *Verse* 208. Barbour 140(2); *Oxford* 557; Svartengren 219; TW 285(1).

P148 Not a **Pin** matter

1729 Franklin *Papers* 1.116: When, perhaps, it mayn't be a Pin Matter whether they ever do so or no. NED Pin *sb.*[1] 18.

P149 Not care a **Pin**

1780 *Royal Gazette* in *Newspaper Extracts* (*II*) 4.611: Nor car'd a Pin for Wayne. **1798** Ames *Letters* 1.236: I care not a pin. **1834** Cooper *Letters* 3.59: I care not a pin for Mr. Jackson, Mr. Van Buren, or Mr. Any one else. *Oxford* 102; TW 286(7).

P150 Not care a **Pin's** head

1821 Knight *Poems* 2.160: I care not a pin's head about ye. Cf. TW 286(9); Whiting P218.

P151   Not care a **Pin's** point

1803 Ames *Letters* 1.334: We the people care not a pin's point for it. NED Pin *sb.*[1] 3c.

P152   Not give a **Pin**

1778 Galloway *Diary* 44: I wou'd not give a pin. **1782** Hamilton *Papers* 3.192: You would not give a pin. Whiting P210.

P153   Not signify a **Pin**

1819 Peirce *Rebelliad* 13: 'T does not signify a pin.

P154   Not value a **Pin**

1668 EWeld in Alden *Epitaphs* 3.46: As not to value me a pin. **1822** Watterston *Winter* 50: I don't value a pin. Cf. TW 286(9).

P155   Not worth a **Pin**

1729 Ames *Almanacs* 61: The *Almanack's* not worth a pin. **1777** TDavis in *Innes (James) and his Brothers* 61: Life wou'd not be worth a Pin. **1779** Winslow *Broadside* 191. **1821** Jefferson *Writings* 1.134: Without secreting . . . a pin's worth to themselves. Barbour 140(3); *Oxford* 626; Whiting P213.

P156   On a merry **Pin**

1779 Hutchinson *Diary* 2.288: S[r] John upon a merry pin. *Oxford* 528; Whiting P215.

P157   A **Pin** a day is a groat a year

1737 Franklin *PR* 2.165: A Pin a day is a Groat a Year. **1802** *Port Folio* 2.24: That liberal and classical maxim, "A pin a day is a groat a year." *Oxford* 626.

P158   A **Pin** for (whatever)

1723 *New-England Courant* 110(2.1): A Pin for Platforms say I. NED Pin *sb.*[1] 3b.

P159   Stick a **Pin** there

1781 *Belknap Papers* 1.103: When a common person would say *Stop* . . . and a quoter of poetry "Stick a pin there." TW 286(11).

P160   To be upon **Pins**

1811 Adams *Memoirs* 2.246: He had been upwards of a fortnight upon pins until yesterday. Barbour 140(6); *Oxford* 626. See **N53, T70.**

P161   To come down a **Pin**

1776 Moore *Diary* 1.238: It shows their willingness to come down a pin.

P162   To hear a **Pin** drop

1814 Smith *Letters* 113: It was so still you might have heard a pin drop on the pavement. **1817** Weems *Franklin* 199: Whenever he opened his lips, you might, as the saying is, *have heard a pin drop.* **1820** Wright *Views* 265: A silence so profound that the drop of a pin might have been heard. **1842** Hone *Diary* 2.630: A stillness prevailed . . . such that you might literally "hear a pin drop." *Oxford* 363; TW 286(10).

P163   To come to the **Pinch**

a1700 Hubbard *New England* 125: Yet when it came to the pinch and upshot of the trial, 453: So as when it came to the pinch. **1770** Munford *Candidates* 27: When it comes to the pinch. Whiting P220.

P164   Upon (at) a **Pinch**

1705 Beverley *History* 35: And sometimes also upon a Pinch they wou'd not disdain to dig them up again to make a homely Meal of after they had been buried. **1741** Stephens *Journal(I)* 2.272: By such means they have an Opportunity of sliding two or three Negroes now and then at a Pinch into their Plantations. NED Pinch 4; Whiting P219.

P165   As straight as a **Pine**

1782 Bailey *Journal* 189: The husband standing . . . straight as the pine tree of Kennebeck. TW 286(1).

P166   No one can cut down a **Pine** and live to see the stump rotten

1792 Belknap *History* 3.81: The stumps and roots of the mast pine are very durable. It is a common saying, that "no man ever cut down a pine, and lived to see the stump rotten."

P167   A **Pint** is a pound the world over

1792 Bentley *Diary* 1.391: A pint is a pound the world over. ["A pint is a pound the whole world round," is familiar to me from childhood, but is in none of the ordinary reference books.]

P168 Not care a **Pipe** of tobacco

1769 Woodmason *Journal* 154: I care not a Pipe of Tobacco.

P169 The **Pipes** of peace

1705 Beverley *History* 187: They call them the Pipes of Peace. NED Pipe *sb.*[1] 10b; *Oxford* 627.

P170 To clear one's **Pipes**

1733 Byrd *Journey* 265: After the major had cleared his pipes.

P171 To put up one's **Pipes**

1637 Morton *New English Canaan* 302: And either hee must put up his pipes and be packing, or forsake Ionas posture. *Oxford* 657; Tilley P345.

P172 No longer **Pipe**, no longer dance

1702 Mather *Magnalia* 2.550: I see, no longer pipe, no longer dance. **1705** Ingles *Reply* 22: No longer pipe, no longer dance. **1734** Belcher *Papers* 2.146. *Oxford* 569; Tilley P346.

P173 As drunk as a **Piper**

1770 Carter *Diary* 1.491: When no Piper was ever drunker. **1796** Barton *Disappointment* 72: As drunk as a piper. **1813** Weems *Drunkard* 122. Svartengren 199; TW 287(1).

P174 To pay the **Piper**

1779 Galloway *Diary* 179: I will not pay the piper for others. **1785** JCurrie in Jefferson *Papers* 8.342: The Dutch must pay the piper. **1797** Callender *Annual Register 1796* 38: Why do you continue to pay the piper, without ever getting a tune? **1809** Weems *Washington* 67: As that most undutiful child had always led off the dance . . . she should pay the piper. **1816** Paulding *Letters(I)* 1.85: Honest Jack-come-last, who, as usual, pays the piper, **1834** *Letters(II)* 155: Then we shall see whether the people who insist upon dancing are willing to pay the Piper at once. Barbour 64: Fiddler; *Oxford* 615; TW 287(2); Tilley P349. See **D10, F84.**

P175 To break like **Pipestems**

1798 EWinslow in *Winslow Papers* 430: The stoutest of Elms & Maples were broke like pipestems. TW 287(2).

P176 **Piping** hot

1765 Adams *Legal Papers* 1.99-100: Pretended Complaint of Allen piping Hot. **1779** Gordon *Letters* 417: News you know is always best piping hot. **1781** Shaw *Journals* 88. **1782** Adams *D and A* 3.73: To come piping hot from Versailles. **1782** EPendleton in Madison *Papers* 5.220: A story we have piping hot from Philada. **1784** Gadsden *Writings* 217. **1788** *American Museum* 3.542: Baked, and, as it were, piping hot from the classical oven. **1801** Story *Shop* 71: Some old rascals come forth piping hot. **1807** *Weekly* 2.32. **1809** Fessenden *Pills* 94: Whipped syllabub and pepper-pot, By Jacobins served piping hot. **1809** *Kennon Letters* 32.80: He is bran piping hot from Richmond. **1816** Fidfaddy *Adventures* 90: When I imagine I have him piping hot for battle. **1826** Jones *Sketches* 1.180: The coffee is brought piping hot. Whiting P224.

P177 To swear like a **Pirate**

1800 TPierce in Vanderpoel *Chronicles* 383: [It] would make you swear like a pirate. Whiting *NC* 459. See **T249.**

P178 As busy as **Pismires**

1775 JWarren in *Warren-Adams Letters* 1.68: We are as busy as you ever saw pismires on a mole hill. TW 287.

P179 To **Piss** backward

1742 Belcher *Papers* 2.441: How came it to pass, after the matter is got so well forward, that you incline to piss backward?

P180 To **Piss** on one and shit on the other

1770 Franklin *Papers* 17.331: Be quiet, says the Wag in the Story, I only p[iss] o[n] you: I sh[it] o[n] t[he] o[the]r.

P181 As easy as **Pissing** abed

1739 Franklin *PR* 2.217: 'Tis as easy as pissing abed. Svartengren 348.

P182 To fall into the **Pit** one digs for another

1608 Wingfield *Discourse* in *Transactions and Collections of the American Antiquarian Society* 4 (1860) 84: It pleased God to cast him into the same disgrace and pitt that he prepared for another. **1652** Williams

Writings 4.209: Carnal policy ever fals into the pit it digs and trips up its own heels. **a1656** Bradford *History* 1.414: Ps:7.15. He hath made a pitte, and digged it, and is fallen into the pitte he made. **1677** Hubbard *Indian* 1.131: They themselves fell into that Pit they were digging for others, 2.224-5, **a1700** *New England* 517: What Solomon long since declared . . . "He that diggeth a pit, shall fall into it." **1775** *Deane Correspondence* 340: They know a public hearing must . . . tumble them into the pit they have (like moles) been digging for me. **1775** WHDrayton in Gibbes 2.68: I shall now precipitate them into their own pit. **1776** Marshall *Diary* 77. **1778** Smith *Memoirs(II)* 360: They may fall into the Pit they dug for the Multitude, 362: What a Pitt have they dug for themselves. **1793** EChurch in *Barbary Wars* 1.50. **1800** Cobbett *Porcupine* 11.300: Thus, you see, reader, that my enemies have fallen into their own pit. **1810** JWinthrop in *Warren-Adams Letters* 2.368. **1822** Pintard *Letters* 2.122. **1829** Jackson *Correspondence* 4.31: But these satelites of Clay . . . are falling into the pitts dug for Major Eaton, **1830** 208, 211, **1831** 281, 328, 346, 349, **1837** 5.509: I hope Mr. Van Buren sees this and will . . . permit those who have dug the secrete disguised pit to fall into it. *Oxford* 187; Whiting P232. See **C377, F214, K48, M191, N51, S281.**

P183 As black as **Pitch**

1825 Pinkney *Works* 216: Some old witch, as black as pitch. Barbour 141(1); *Oxford* 63; Whiting P233.

P183a **Pitch-black**

1819 Latrobe *Journal* 232: Pitch-black faces. TW 287(2).

P184 As dark as **Pitch**

1707 Taylor *Poems* 222: As dark as Pitch. **1797** Baily *Journal* 426: It was . . . dark as pitch. **1809** Weems *Marion* 85. **a1811** Henry *Account* 37: The night became dark as pitch. **1812** Melish *Travels* 257. Barbour 141(2); *Oxford* 63; Whiting P234.

P184a **Pitch-dark**

1785 Hunter *Quebec* 145: It was so pitch-dark that I could not see an inch before me. TW 287(4).

P185 It is hard to touch **Pitch** and not be defiled

1707 Makemie *Writings* 181: It is hard to touch pitch, and not be defiled therewith. **1780** AA in *Adams FC* 3.353: Who can touch pitch and not be defiled? Barbour 141(3); *Oxford* 834; Whiting P236.

P186 To make one's **Pitch**

1764 Hutchinson *History* 1.22: Here Mr. Newell and some of his friends made their pitch. DA pitch n^1 2b; NED *sb.*^{2} 11; TW 288(1).

P187 A cracked **Pitcher**

1797 SMorris in Cobbett *Porcupine* 6.300: The Lord had given him a chosen vessel to be the comfort of his old age (a crack'd pitcher, he meant, Peter). Partridge 637.

P188 The **Pitcher** will go to the well once too often (*varied*)

a1731 Cook *Bacon* 322: So Pitcher now, you see, is broke. **1777** Shaw *Letter Book* 223: But don't you think the Pitcher will go to the well once too often? **1802** *Port Folio* 2.272: And now dear boys remember well the story of the pitcher, And while you may, get out o'the way of that curs'd thing the *snitcher.* **1817** Adams *Writings* 6.265: *Tant va la cruche à l'eau qu'à la fin elle se casse,* was an old French proverb long before Washington's mother was born. *Tant va la cruche à l'eau qu'à la fin elle s'emplit,* is the variation of Beaumarchais's Basile in the *Marriage of Figaro.* But whether the pitcher is broken or whether it is filled, it was made to go to the water, and go to the water it must. Break it also must, a little sooner or little later, etc. Barbour 141(1); *Oxford* 628; Whiting P323.

P189 To rain **Pitchforks**

1815 Humphreys *Yankey* 55: I'll be EVEN with you, if it rains pitchforks—tines downwards. Barbour 141-2; TW 288(2).

P190 High **Places** are slippery

1684 Claypoole *Letter Book* 237: High places are slippery, and more snares attend him that governs than him that suffers. Cf. Whiting H47, P247, R191.

P191 He that is born to the **Plack** will never win the bawbee

1815 Brackenridge *Modern* 695: "He that is born to the plack will never win the babee," is a proverb in the old Saxon language. NED Bawbee, Plack[1] c. Cf. *Oxford* 629.

P192 More **Plague** than profit

1776 Huntington *Papers* 302: If they stay in Service they are (to use a vulgar Phrase) more Plague than Profit.

P193 To shun like the **Plague** (contagion)

1801 Story *Shop* 64: Shun them as you would the plague. **1831** JWilliams in Jackson *Correspondence* 4.230: [They] shuned him as they would contagion. See **P90, S104.**

P194 He that uses **Plain-dealing** dies a beggar

1652 JClark in *Collections of the Massachusetts Historical Society* 4S 2(1854) 17: To use plain dealing with all men, although I verifie the Proverb, and die a begger. *Oxford* 629; Tilley P382.

P195 A **Planter's** pace

1694 Clayton *Writings* 105: A planters pace is a Proverb, wch is a good sharp hand gallop. DA planter 1b.

P196 Too small a **Plaster** for so great a sore

1701 Sewall *Diary* 2.47: I dissented from it as too small a Plaister for so great a Sore. Cf. Lean 4.135; *Oxford* 630; Tilley S646.

P197 To break the **Platter**

1819 Peirce *Rebelliad* 73: 'Tis no great matter How, when, or where, the little slut First broke the platter [lost her virginity].

P198 Fair **Play** and above-board

1818 *Port Folio* 4NS 5.316: It was all fair play and above-board. Lean 3.462; NED Above-board.

P199 Fair **Play** is a jewel

1809 Irving *History* 2.151: That noble maxim . . . that "fair play is a jewel." **1809** Lindsley *Love* 7: Fair play's a jewel. *Oxford* 239; TW 289(4).

P200 Fair **Play** is bonny play

1805 Brackenridge *Modern* 520: Fair play is bonny play. Lean 3.462: is good play.

P201 **Please** and prosper

1805 Weems *Letters* 2.313: I subjoin 2 or 3 old sayings for your young tooth—"*Please,* and, *Prosper.*"

P202 Never **Pleased,** full nor fasting

1734 Johnson *Writings* 3.41: He is neither pleased, full nor fasting. *Oxford* 563; Tilley W265.

P203 Flee **Pleasures** and they'll follow you

1738 Franklin *PR* 2.193: Fly Pleasures, and they'll follow you, **1758** *WW* 343. **1788** *Columbian Magazine* 2.263: Fame and Pleasure, like a Shadow, fly from those who pursue them, and like it always await those who seem to shun them. *Oxford* 272; Tilley L479; Whiting C526, *NC* 459.

P204 **Plenty** is strength

1758 *New American Magazine* in *Newspaper Extracts*(I) 4.200: Every body knows plenty is strength.

P205 **Plenty** makes poverty

1684 Clayton *Writings* 4: A place where plenty makes poverty, Ignorance ingenuity, & covetousness causes hospitality. *Oxford* 634; Tilley P427.

P206 There is never a **Plot,** *etc.*

1741 DHorsmanden in *Colden Letters* 2.225: The Old Proverb has herein also been verified That there is Scarce a plot but a priest is at the Bottom of it. *Oxford* 572; Tilley M1000. See **M190.**

P207 He that by the **Plow** would thrive, *etc.*

1747 Franklin *PR* 3.106: He that by the Plow would thrive, Himself must either hold or drive, **1758** *WW* 344. **1770** Ames *Almanacs* 412. **1779** Franklin *Writings* 7.381-2. *Oxford* 635; TW 290.

P208 A **Plowman** on his legs, *etc.*

1746 Franklin *PR* 3.63: A Plowman on his Legs is higher than a Gentleman on his Knees, **1758** *WW* 346. Barbour 143.

P209 To eat like **Plowmen**

1699 Ward *Trip* 52: They have wonderful *Appetites,* and will Eat like *Plough-men;* tho very *Lazy,* and *Plough* like *Gentlemen.*

P210 As neat as **Plush**

1802 *Port Folio* 2.268: Neat as plush, **1808** NS 6.301: He could make a bargain as *neat as plush.*

P211 To be out of **Pocket**

1814 JJackson in Jackson *Correspondence* 6.444: I fear you will be a Negro out of Pocket. NED Pocket 3a.

P212 To have one in his **Pocket**

1770 Smith *Memoirs(I)* 93: That without Doors it would be supposed that the Govr was in their Pocket. **1791** Morris *Diary* 2.114: Better he be vexed than carry me about in his Pocket. NED Pocket 3d.

P213 To pick one's **Pocket**

1772 *Commerce of Rhode Island* 1.413: This trade will only pick your Pockit. NED Pick *v.*[1] 9.

P214 A **Point** at a herring

1809 *Port Folio* 2NS 2.109: These poor devils get nothing to eat but *plantains,* and perhaps are sometimes favored with a *point at a herring,* **1811** 2NS 5.339: Their food [consists] of cassada bread, yams, and roasted plantains, seasoned perhaps with a salted herring, which answers the purpose of being *pointed at. Oxford* 641; TW 293(10).

P215 To carry one's **Point**

1747 GClinton in *Colden Letters* 3.334: But one thing I can tell them I don't doubt but carry my point even to turn out y[e] C. J. TW 290(2).

P216 **Poison** is killed by boiling, *etc.*

1803 Austin *Literary Papers* 239: As the sailors say, "Poison is killed by boiling, and what will not poison you will fatten you."

P217 There is **Poison** in sweet wine

1647 SSymonds in *Winthrop Papers(A)* 5.125: Not being able suddenly to discerne the poyson in the sweet wine. Cf. Whiting P289.

P218 To hate like **Poison**

1807 *Salmagundi* 130: Poor Jeremy hates them as he does poison. *Oxford* 357; TW 290(3); Tilley P459.

P219 As snug as a **Poker**

1780 Barlow *Letters* 33: I have taken lodgings in an old Dutchman's bedroom, as snug as a poker. **1783** EWinslow in *Winslow Papers* 82: A house . . . where we are as snug as pokers.

P220 As stiff as a **Poker**

1815 Humphreys *Yankey* 34: And won't I stan by 'em tu, stiff as a poker? **1822** Watterston *Winter* 65: As stiff as a poker [dead]. **1826** Jones *Sketches* 1.92: Marines . . . stiff as a poker. **1834** Floy *Diary* 95: But it is so much worse when there is a bile on both knees so as to make them nearly as stiff as pokers. Barbour 143(2); *Oxford* 774; Svartengren 262; TW 290-1(1).

P221 As far as **Pole** from pole (*varied*)

1781 Barlow *Works* 2.36: Far as pole from pole. **1792** Adams *Writings* 1.113: Many of them differing widely as the poles. **1807** Bowen *Journals* 2.615: Our Political oppinions are as opposite as the Poles. **1812** BStoddert in *Steele Papers* 2.685: Between Marshall & Clinton the difference is as wide as the poles are asunder. Whiting *NC* 460. See **N89.**

P222 As straight as a **Pole**

1801 Story *Shop* 26: She is . . . as straight as a pole. Whiting P290.

P223 To be under bare **Poles**

1804 Bentley *Diary* 3.125: He is now, as he expressed it, under "bare poles." Colcord 29.

P224 **Policy** avails more than force

1797 Brackenridge *Modern* 293: Policy oftentimes avails more than force. *Oxford* 637; Tilley P462. See **W238.**

P225 **Politeness** costs little

1765 Timberlake *Memoirs* 96: Politeness (which costs but little, and often does a great deal). *Oxford* 125: Civility. See **W311.**

P226   Politics makes strange bedfellows

1839 Hone *Diary* 1.404: But party politics, like poverty, bring men "acquainted with strange bedfellows." Taylor *Proverb* 12, 20; TW 291. Cf. *Oxford* 525. See **M193, T227.**

P227   As smooth as a Pond

1848 Cooper *Letters* 5.281: The lake was smooth as a pond. TW 291(1). See **M171.**

P228   Poor and proud (*varied*)

1634 Wood *New-England* 73: Although they be thus poore, yet is there in them the sparkes of naturall pride. **1722** *New-England Courant* 55(2.1): Pride and Poverty agree but very ill together. **1746** *Georgia Records* 25.51: Pride and Poverty have a great while went hand in hand. **1763** Griffith *Journal* 95: The men appeared to us . . . poor, proud, and exceedingly lazy. **1764** *Johnson Papers* 4.341: I . . . Never See So Much pride & poverty before. **1773** SEve in *PM* 5 (1881) 192: Poverty without pride is nothing, but with it, it is the very deuce. **1779** Bailey *Journal* 158: John marched along in all the pride of poverty. **1786** Stiles *Diary* 3.227. **1786** ETrist in Jefferson *Papers* 10.167. **1798** Murdock *Politicians* 27: "Is there a country on earth turns out so many learned men as Scotland?" "Nor poorer nor prouder." **1809** *Port Folio* 2NS 1.426: The hateful association of beggarly pride and groveling poverty. **1809** Tyler *Yankey* 162. **1812** Stoddard *Sketches* 131: They still remain in all the pride of poverty. **c1820** Bernard *Retrospections* 110: He was as proud as he was poor. *Oxford* 639; Whiting M267, P381, 394.

P229   The Poor are friendless

1779 Galloway *Diary* 56: The poor are allways friendless. Whiting P295, 335.

P230   A Pope and a mountebank are above all law

1809 Pinkney *Travels* 70: One of them . . . made me a very pleasing apology, repeating at the same time a French proverb — that a pope and a mountebank were above all law. See **G79, K19, P228.**

P231   The Pope resides at Rome

1745 *Georgia Records* 24.406: The thing is

as much a Secret, as that The Pope Resides at Room. See **Q7.**

P232   To let off a Pop-gun in a thunderstorm

1791 Maclay *Journal* 400: To speak in the present roar of business was like letting off a pop-gun in a thunder-storm.

P233   The Populace are fickle

1775 Boucher *Autobiography* 136: The populace, who, we need not tell you, are even [*for* ever] proverbially fickle and false. Whiting P134. See **R61.**

P234   As fat as Pork

1803 *Yankee Phrases* 87: My body was fatter than pork. Svartengren 183; Whiting P308. See **P113.**

P235   As fat as a Porpoise

1766 AA in *Adams FC* 1.57: She is fat as a porpouse. TW 292(1).

P236   To puff (blow) like a Porpoise

1791 Maclay *Journal* 379: Dr. Hutchinson came in, greasy as a skin of oil and puffing like a porpoise. **1827** Watterston *Wanderer* 200: Our friend . . . blowing like a porpoise. TW 292(3). See **G137.**

P237   To try one's Possibles

1797 Perkins *Diary* 4.56: I cannot Say how I can effect it, but must try my Possibles. Cf. NED Possible B 1c.

P238   Any Port in a storm

1775 JWarren in *Warren-Adams Letters* 1.153: We are in a storm and must make a port. **1796** Barton *Disappointment* 52: Any port in a storm. **1804** Asbury *Letters* 3.294, **1807** *Journal* 2.552, **1809** 617. Barbour 144; *Oxford* 15; TW 292. See **D239, T150.**

P239   To carve large Portions out of other men's estates

1653 Keayne *Apologia* 26: It is an easy matter for others to carve large portions out of others men's estates and tell what they might or should do. Cf. *Oxford* 163; Whiting L62, T217.

P240   Possession is eleven points of the law (*varied*)

a1700 Hubbard *New England* 307: In such

kind of possessions the *premier seisin* is the best title, 432: To which he could lay no other claim but by the law of possession, or *premier seisin*. **1712** TBanister in *Trelawny Papers* 403: It may be very difficult to dispossess him, on Accompt of a Law of Possession now in force in this Country. **1713** Wise *Churches* 37: That acknowledged Maxim, *in Eequali Jure, melior est Condition Possidentis*, When two plead an Equal Right, he is in the best Condition who is in Possession. **1766** Montresor *Journals* 367: They declare that possession is Eleven points in the Law. **1769** Adams *Legal Papers* 2.82: We are in Possession and Possession is a good Title, untill a Person demands who has an absolute Right. **1779** Lee *Letters* 2.44: Possession is eleven points of the Law. **1788** *American Museum* 3.382: Possession is equal to eleven points in law. **1792** Belknap *Foresters* 8: It is a maxim, you know, 162. **1797** Baily *Journal* 366: Possession in this country being not only nine parts but the *whole* of the law. **1802** Chester *Federalism* 10: Possession is seven points of the law. **1808** *Port Folio* NS 6.319: Possession is at least nine (some *dicta* say eleven) points of the law. **1816** Lambert *Travels* 1.499: nine points. *Oxford* 640; Tilley P488; Whiting P311.

P241   As blind as a **Post**
1779 Gordon *Letters* 416: They are as blind as a post.

P242   As deaf as a **Post**
1822 Watterston *Winter* 52: As deaf as a post. **1847** Paulding *Letters(II)* 461: And the fellow turns out as deaf as a Post. Barbour 144(1); *Oxford* 172; Svartengren 173-4; TW 292(1).

P243   As firm as a **Post**
1798 Cobbett *Porcupine* 10.43: America will . . . remain *firm; firm* as a post. Svartengren 261. Cf. Whiting P312.

P244   As still as a **Post**
1810 Schultz *Travels* 2.142: He stands as still as a post. TW 292(3).

P245   Between you and me and the **Post**
1796 Tyler *Prose* 219: Between you and I, *and the post*. **1809** *Kennon Letters* 32.80:

But this, as Mrs. Higginbotham says, is between you, myself and the post, 85. **1817** Wirt *Letters* 2.27: To say the truth, (between you and me and the post). *Oxford* 57; TW 293(5).

P246   From **Post** (pillar) to pillar (post)
1692 Bulkeley *Will* 87: But the people were but a tennis ball for them to toss from post to pillar. **1765** Watts *Letter Book* 323: And a meer Post & Pillar too he must be, to take two Months to travel from your Neighbourhood, 352: Was the Drawer to play hide & seek from post to pillar? **1778** JChester in Huntington *Papers* 97: I have been drove about so from pillar to post lately. **1779** Paine *Deane* 2.124: We were driven about from pillar to post. **1781** JHall in *W&MCQ* 23(1914) 46: He . . . drove the Enemy out of Richmond, & so on from Pillar to post. **1781** DJameson in Madison *Papers* 3.215: Being driven from Post to pillar to secure my person. **1783** Adams *Works* 8.81: I have been . . . danced about from "post to pillar." **1790** Maclay *Journal* 261: I ran this morning like a foot-boy from post to pillar. **1818** *Port Folio* 4NS 6.237: They have been bandied about from pillar to post. **1849** Paulding *Letters(II)* 501: We are always Knocking our heads against the Post, endeavouring to avoid the Pillar. *Oxford* 625; Whiting P313.

P247   The earthen **Pot** and the brazen pitcher
1771 Franklin *Papers* 18.25: Little regarding the Story of the Earthen Pot and Brazen Pitcher. *Oxford* 212; Whiting P319.

P248   The **Pot** (calls the) kettle (black)
1807 *Salmagundi* 93: The Doctor's abusing poor Toney Pasquin brought forcibly to our recollection the vulgar cant about the pot and the kettle. Barbour 144(2); *Oxford* 421; TW 293(3).

P249   To admit one to be **Pot** or kettle
1783 Pynchon *Diary* 161: Mr. Fr. tells Mr. Parker that he designedly went from home to see whether Mr. S. would admit him to be pot or kettle, as he said he was. Cf. *Oxford* 212; Whiting P319.

P250 To be **Pot** and can

1789 *American Museum* 5.297: We shall be pot and can in the general conviction. *Oxford* 160: cup; Whiting C921.

P251 To go to **Pot**

1721 Wise *Word* 200: They must go to Pot. a1731 Cook *Bacon* 321: And so make *Traytors* go to Pot. 1740 Ames *Almanacs* 139: The Pope goes to Pot. 1747 Franklin *Papers* 3.139: And like Brands pluck'd out of the Flames, in which they were going to pot. 1779 Gordon *Letters* 414. 1779 Hopkinson *Miscellaneous Essays* 3(part 2) 183: Connecticut must go to pot. 1783 Freneau *Poems* 2.234. c1790 Brackenridge *Gazette* 61. 1792 *Echo* 35: Those whom valiant Brady sent to pot, 331. 1792 *Universal Asylum* 9.21. 1801 Story *Shop* 28, 86, 123: When death gives the word, we must all go to pot. 1804 Brackenridge *Modern* 373: All my laudanum . . . all gone to pot, or rather the pots gone with them, 442: There are chimney sweepers, who think all will go to pot, when they drop off. 1807 Weems *Letters* 2.366: For Feds and Dems must all to pot, If love be absent there. 1813 Paulding *Lay* 114. 1819 Peirce *Rebelliad* 47, 49, 76. 1821 Freneau *Last Poems* 46. 1822 *Austin Papers* 1.470: Many whome you left roleing in affluence are gown to pot. 1824 *Ruffin Papers* 1.307. Barbour 144(4); *Oxford* 308; TW 293(5); Tilley P504.

P252 To have neither **Pot** nor pan, *etc.*

1732 Franklin *Papers* 1.238: The couple describ'd in the Scotch Song, who had "Neither Pot nor Pan But four bare Legs together." *Oxford* 513-4; Tilley M1146. Cf. Lean 2.925; Whiting T140.

P253 To make the **Pot** boil

1778 Wister *Journal* 161: Never mind what I say, I have enough to make the pot boil. 1837 TCameron in *Ruffin Papers* 2.168: Col. Jones was to see me to day, he says, that lad is "boiling his pot in Raleigh." 1846 Paulding *Letters(II)* 432: It is my design to resume my Pen, both as a resource for Killing Time, and making the Pot Boil. *Oxford* 72; Tilley P505.

P254 Touch **Pot**, touch penny

1764 Franklin *Papers* 11.284: Our lowest untaught Coblers and Porters feel the Force of it in their own Maxim . . . Touch Pot, touch Penny. 1797 Cobbett *Porcupine* 5.199: The old proverb, *Touch pot, touch penny.* 1824 *Tales* 1.13. *Oxford* 833; Tilley P506.

P255 When the **Pot** boils the scum rises

1777 JEliot in *Belknap Papers* 3.104: When the pot boils, the scum will arise. 1779 Adams *D and A* 2.367: Otis says when the Pot boils the Scum rises to the Top. 1798 Cobbett *Porcupine* 10.30: When the political pot boils, the scum rises to the top. 1804 Taggart *Letters* 134: The faster the pot boils the sooner it will throw off the scum, 1806 177: It may be a means of causing the scum to settle to the bottom. Lean 4.186. See **F313.**

P256 As small as **Pot** herbs for the pot

c1700 Taylor *Poems* 398: As if each Word . . . Should hackt a sunder be, and Chopt As small as Pot herbs for the pot. Svartengren 290; Whiting W688.

P257 **Pot-luck**

1776 Washington *Writings* 4.220: Take Pott Luck with me to day. 1787 Tilghman *Letters* 145: I hope her *Pot luck* will always be as good as it is at present. c1810 Foster *Jeffersonian America* 134. 1819 Faux *Memorable Days* 1.189. 1826 Anderson *Diary* 244: To take as he says *pot luck*—and generally at his table the *luck* is bad. 1827 Watterston *Wanderer* 189. TW 294.

P258 To be **Pot-valiant**

1696 NSaltonstall in *Saltonstall Papers* 1.249: By foolish if not pot-valiant firing. 1777 *New Jersey Gazette* in *Newspaper Extracts(II)* 1.523: Every country village . . . you will find crowded with pot-valiant heroes and fire-side companions. 1806 Fanning *Narrative* 115: Jones never did, nor never would fight, except he was nearly drunk. The English generally believing this to be the case with him, called him a pot-valiant fellow. 1819 Drake *Works* 325: The very

345

proverb says—*pot-valiant*. c1825 Tyler *Prose* 148. NED Pot-valiant.

P259 They that are out will **Pout**

1741 Belcher *Papers* 2.387: And Old Grub-street says, They that are out will pout.

P260 As poor as **Poverty**

1650 Bradstreet *Works* 158: Were I as poor as poverty would be. 1788 *Politician* 69: As poor as poverty.

P261 **Poverty** and peace, *etc.*

1814 Fletcher *Letters* 80: Poverty and peace is better than plenty with contention. Cf. Whiting P336.

P262 **Poverty** is a crime

1806 Claiborne *Letter Books* 4.36: The rich . . . are too apt to view poverty, even honest poverty, as a Crime. Cf. Barbour 145(2); *Oxford* 642; Tilley P526; Whiting P331.

P263 **Poverty** is subject to temptation

1780 JDodge in Jefferson *Papers* 3.522: As poverty is always subjection to temptation, I fear their good intentions may be seduced. Cf. *Oxford* 642; Tilley P521.

P264 **Poverty** wants some things, *etc.*

1735 Franklin *PR* 2.8: Poverty wants some things, Luxury many things, Avarice all things. *Oxford* 643; Tilley P530.

P265 When **Poverty** comes in at the door, *etc.*

1790 *Universal Asylum* 5.84: When poverty comes in at the door, love flies out at the windows. 1796 Barton *Disappointment* 56: It's an old saying, and I think a true one:— When poverty comes in at the door, love flies out at the window. 1812 THPerkins in *Cabot Family* 1.419: The latter . . . did not believe that when "Poverty looked in at the door Love would fly out of the window." Barbour 145(3); *Oxford* 642; Tilley P531; Whiting *NC* 462(3). Cf. Whiting L526, P343.

P266 As dry as **Powder**

1740 Custis *Letters* 84: The dirt being as dry as powder. Barbour 145(1).

P267 Not worth **Powder** and shot

1800 Weems *Letters* 2.137: Many things are not worth powder and shot. TW 295(3).

P268 Not worth the **Powder** to blow one to hell

1823 *Austin Papers* 1.582: All the government in the world would not make them worth the powder that it would take to blow them to Hell. Barbour 145(2); TW 294(2).

P269 **Practice** makes perfect

1761 Adams *D and A* 1.192: Practice makes perfect. 1780 *New Jersey Gazette* in *Newspaper Extracts(II)* 4.315: But practice hath made them more perfect. 1785 PWright in Jefferson *Papers* 9.101. 1787 *American Museum* 1.117: Practice alone makes perfect. 1794 Ames *Letters* 1.159: Practice has made Boston perfect. 1810 Weems *Letters* 3.30. 1819 Waln *Hermit* 179. 1831 Jackson *Correspondence* 4.350. 1848 Cooper *Letters* 5.261. Barbour 145; *Oxford* 856; TW 295. Cf. Whiting U8, 9. See **U13.**

P270 To **Practise** what one preaches (*varied*).

1702 Mather *Magnalia* 1.357: And as far as he could, he practised what he professed. 1733 Franklin *PR* 1.315: Teachers practising what they preach. 1747 *New-York Evening Post* in *Newspaper Extracts(I)* 2.378: We hear them condemning their practice in every Sermon they Preach. 1763 Griffith *Journal* 83: Hypocrites, professing one thing, and practising another. 1764 Hutchinson *History* 1.95: His practice was agreeable to his principles. 1766 JParker in Franklin *Papers* 13.326: Good Humour in such Fortune as mine is . . . much easier preach'd than practised, 342: It is far easier to preach that Doctrine, than to practise it. 1775 SMorris in *Naval Documents* 2.61: I preach philosophy to you but do not practice it myself. 1777 Pickering *Life* 1.186: I confess, 'tis easier to preach than practise the lessons of wisdom. 1777 HWinthrop in *Warren-Adams Letters* 1.284: It is much easier to Preach Fortitude and Patience under Sufferings than to Practice them. 1778 Lee *Letters* 2.471: I hope you will in one instance prove like the priests—practice differently from what you preach. **1778** JWarren in *Warren-Adams Letters* 2.46: This is the doctrine I preach and practise. **1779** Asbury *Journal* 1.302: I was amazed to think how such a contrariety of preaching and practice could be found in the same man. **1779** Lee *Letters* 2.639: You can't say that my practice and preaching are different. **1786** Adams(A) *Letters* 300: You . . . so perfectly practise what he preached. **1791** Burr *Memoirs* 1.306: I prescribe, however, what I do not practice. **1791** Jefferson *Writings* 8.146: Heresies preached now, to be practised hereafter. **1796** Weems *Letters* 2.38. **1812** Quincy *JQuincy* 252: I have preached and practised. **1813** *Beauties of Brother Bull-us* 43-4. **1815** Wirt *Letters* 1.395: You see how natural it is for old men to preach, and how much easier to preach than to practice. **1816** *Port Folio* 4NS 1.54: Those who preach what they do not practice. **1817** Young *Life* 86: I did not dare to preach that to others, which I would not practice myself. **1818** Hall *Travels* 107: The Government of the United States not only preaches, but practises economy. **1820** Pintard *Letters* 1.338: Simplicity in food is easier preached than practiced. **1826** WVans in *Codman Letters* 374: You preach one thing, and practice another. *Oxford* 643; TW 295. Cf. Whiting P359.

P271 **Praise** little, dispraise less
1754 Franklin *PR* 5.184: Praise little, dispraise less.

P272 Self **Praise** is a shame (*varied*)
1637 Morton *New English Canaan* 61: If I should commend myself to you, you reply with this proverb, — *Propria laus sordet in ore*. **1747** Franklin *PR* 3.101: To praise himself Vincenna knows a shame. **1778** JWindee in *Clinton Papers* 2.685: There need no regard [be] paid to what I have said of Myself because the old saying is, self praise is No commendation. **1803** Davis *Travels* 388: Though self praise is no praise. **1817** Adams *Writings* 6.279: Let another praise you and not your own lips. Barbour 146(2, 3); *Oxford* 507; Whiting M173, P351. See **N45.**

P273 **Prayers** and provender hinder no journey
1744 Franklin *PR* 2.397: Prayers and Provender hinder no Journey. *Oxford* 645; Tilley P556.

P274 Cold **Preachers** make bold sinners
1710 Mather *Bonifacius* 94: And the Saying of a Modern also, not to be forgotten; *Cold Preachers make Bold Sinners*.

P275 **Prevention** is better than cure (*varied*)
1772 TScammell in *Baxter Manuscripts* 14.152-3: That no time might be lost, and from experience finding tis much easier to prevent than remedy. **1785** Washington *Writings* 28.281-2: Disorders [illness] oftentimes, are easier prevented than cured, **1786** *29.109: It is better to prevent misfortunes, than to apply remedies when they have happened. **1786** WWhiting in American Antiquarian Society, *Proceedings* NS 66(1956) 152: That antient maxim (viz) to prevent is better than to cure. **1792** Belknap *Foresters* 123: It is better to prevent an illness than to cure it. **1792** *Washington *Writings* 32.265: It is easier to prevent evils than to apply remedies after they have happened, **1798** 36.464: It being easier, at all times, to prevent an evil, than to provide a remedy for it. **1826** Pintard *Letters* 2.257: Prevention is better than cure. *Oxford* 646; TW 296; Tilley P569. See **O42.**

P276 To kick against the **Pricks**
1637 Wheelwright *Writings* 176: So saith the Apostle, it is hard to kicke against the pricks. **1651** Williams *Writings* 6.225: It is a dismal battle for poor naked feet to kick against the Pricks, **1652** 4.26: It is hard for you to kick against the Pricks, 515: It is a dismall Battle for poore naked *feete*. **1769** Adams(S) *Writings* 1.380. **1772** RAtkinson in *VHM* 15(1907) 353. **1774** *Pennsylvania Gazette* in *Newspaper Extracts(I)* 10.233. **1780** GLeaycraft in *Clinton Papers* 5.922. **1784** Hamilton *Papers* 3.529. **1800** CGoodrich in Gibbs *Memoirs* 2.373. **1801** Weems *Letters* 2.171. **1802** Chester *Federalism* 33. **1814** *Austin Papers* 1.243. **1816** Adams *Writings* 6.59. *Oxford* 421; Whiting P377.

P277 **Pride** breakfasted with plenty, *etc.*
1757 Franklin *PR* 7.82: *Pride* breakfasted with *Plenty,* dined with *Poverty,* supped with *Infamy,* **1758** *WW* 347. *Oxford* 646.

P278 **Pride** gets into the coach, *etc.*
1758 Franklin *PR* 7.353: *Pride* gets into the Coach, and *Shame* mounts behind. *Oxford* 647; Whiting P385.

P279 **Pride** is as loud a beggar as want
1770 Ames *Almanacs* 413: Pride is as loud a beggar as want. *Oxford* 647.

P280 **Pride** that dines on vanity sups on contempt
1752 Franklin *PR* 4.250: Pride dines upon Vanity, sups on Contempt, **1758** *WW* 347.

P281 **Pride** will have a fall (*varied*)
1725 Wolcott *Poetical Meditations* 7: Pride goes before Destruction And haughtiness before a fall. **1730** Talcott *Papers* 1.214: It's likely this haughty look is before a fall. **1767** Ames *Almanacs* 387: Pride will have a fall. **1776** Deane *Papers* 1.99: For if a fall generally follows a haughty spirit, his end is near. **1782** AA in *Adams FC* 4.328: Pride commeth before Humility and a haughty Spirit before a fall. **1797** Smith(EH) *Diary* 286: And pride must have a fall. Barbour 146; *Oxford* 647; Whiting P393.

P282 To put one's **Pride** in his pocket
1837 Hone *Diary* 1.234: I must put my pride in my empty pocket and hope for better times. TW 296(2).

P283 To swallow one's **Pride**
1821 Pintard *Letters* 2.6: How much pride have I to swallow. Cf. *Oxford* 636; Tilley I70. See **W323**.

P284 Like **Priest** like people
a**1700** Hubbard *New England* 358: That they might be "like priest like people." **1745** RRutherford in *Baxter Manuscripts* 11.307: The scripture Aphorism, like priest like people. **1792** *Universal Asylum* 7.344: Like people, like priest. **1813** Asbury *Journal* 2.732. **1814** Kerr *Barclay* 59. **1834** Floy *Diary* 46. *Oxford* 647; Whiting P135.

P285 The **Priest** will christen his own child first
1790 Maclay *Journal* 194: The priest will christen his own child first. *Oxford* 610; Tilley C318.

P286 (As) drunk (as a **Prince**)
1776 Cresswell *Journal* 175: I was . . . most princely drunk. Lean 2.823; Svartengren 196. See **L213**.

P287 As happy as a **Prince**
1769 Woodmason *Journal* 155: They are as happy as Princes. **1779** JLivermore in Sullivan *Journals* 189: Every soldier . . . appearing as happy as a prince. **1784** PHolland in *Bingham's Maine* 1.210. **1785** Hunter *Quebec* 78, 136. **1791** Asbury *Journal* 1.666: As happy as princes in a palace. **1805** Irving *Journals* 1.224, 309. **1812** Holcombe *First Fruits* 82: [They] were much more happy than any number of graceless princes. **1813** Barlow *Letters* 272. **1835** Floy *Diary* 181: Towards evening I was as happy as a Prince and more so. Svartengren 77. See **K18, L215**.

P288 A **Prince** is above the law
1822 Freneau *Last Poems* 79: *He* is a prince *above the Law.* Cf. Lean 2.713: King; Whiting K42. See **G79, K19, P230**.

P289 To be treated like **Princes**
1821 Simpson *Journal* 216-7: They were treated like princes. See **K31**.

P290 To live like a **Prince**
1775 Tilghman *Memoir* 92: The Gen[1]. . . . lives like a prince. **1780** *New Jersey Gazette* in *Newspaper Extracts(II)* 5.80: You live like a prince. **1785** Hunter *Quebec* 150. **1806** EWinslow in *Winslow Papers* 553. **1816** Lambert *Travels* 2.147. **1826** Jones *Sketches* 1.193. **1826** Royall *Sketches* 170. TW 297. See **K30**.

P291 As plain as **Print**
1806 *Weekly* 1.84: This truth, as plain as print. TW 296(2).

P292 As black as a **Printer's** devil
1810 *Port Folio* 2NS 4.292: Go in linen as black as a printer's devil. NED Devil 5a.

P293 To break **Priscian's** head

1628 FWinthrop in *Winthrop Papers(A)* 1.393: Contra inbellem Prissianum bellum gerebat, et furioso verborum gladio caput ejus vulnerabat. **1686** Dunton *Letters* 147: Which I remember by that very remarkable token of your Taxing me once with breaking Priscians Head in making false Latin. **1713** Wise *Churches* 78: Priscians head will in likehood be kept bleeding from one Generation to another, by reason of some unlucky Strokes. **1750** AHamilton in *MHM* 59(1964) 208. *Oxford* 82-3; Whiting P404.

P294 **Procrastination** is the thief of time

1784 GMorris in Hamilton *Papers* 3.569: Procrastination is the Thief of Time says Doctor Young. **1787** MWarren in *Warren-Gerry Correspondence* 200: Procrastination —not only thief but murderer of time. **1788** Jefferson *Papers* 14.365. **1804** GDavis in *Barbary Wars* 4.110: I can only say, that procrastination is ever attended with serious evils. **1808** JCaldwell in Murphey *Papers* 1.25: Young tells us. **1817** *Port Folio* 4NS 4.60. **1821** BWaterhouse in *Adams-Waterhouse Correspondence* 151. Barbour 146; *Oxford* 648; TW 296-7.

P295 **Procrustes's** bed

1781 Jefferson *Notes* 160: Introduce the bed of Proscrutes then, and as there is danger that the large men may beat the small, make us all of a size, by lopping the former and stretching the latter. *Oxford* 648; Tilley P597.

P296 **Prodigality** begets necessity

1786 Franklin *Writings* 9.496: The truth of those proverbs which teach us, that *Prodigality begets necessity.* Whiting P405.

P297 **Promises** and pie-crusts were made to be broken

1789 *American Museum* 5.297: Considering promises as pipe [sic]-crusts. **1791** S.P.L. *Thoughts* 77: Promises and pye-crust are made to be broken. **1827** Watterston *Wanderer* 70: His promises according to an old adage, were like pie-crusts, made to be broken. **1848** EAEmmerton in *New England Merchants* 412: I hope his promises may not bear too close a resemblance to pie crusts;

made only to be broken. *Oxford* 649; Tilley P605.

P298 To **Promise** and not perform (*varied*)

1640 JWinter in *Trelawny Papers* 218: The people heare promyse well but pay yll. **1664** Bradstreet *Works* 71: Friends who . . . promise much, and perform nothing. **1688** JMoodey in *Mather Papers* 372-3: Some men that make fair p[ro]mises, but are very short in p[er]formances. **1691** *Wyllys Papers* 335: Great promises [were] made by y[m] but no performance folowed. **1699** NStone in *Hinckley Papers* 306: Their promises have been better than their performances. **1704** *Penn-Logan Correspondence* 1.292: He promises well, but performs nothing. **1707** *Winthrop Papers(B)* 5.391: The other great matter was great promises not performed. **1732** Byrd *Progress* 315: She promised much, though at the same time intended to perform little. **1736** *Georgia Records* 21.305: Meeting with many promises and few performances, **1737** 461: They all Promise very fare & will I hope Perform as well. **1750** JBuckles in McDowell *Documents* 1.37: The French have made them large Promises, but never performed them. **1757** Carter *Diary* 1.140: [He] promises much but does little. **1757** PDemere in McDowell *Documents* 2.429: They promise a great Deal . . . and . . . perform but little. **1764** Carter *Diary* 1.277: It promised much, but very little fell, only a mere turnip shower. **1766** JParker in Franklin *Papers* 13.527: He promises fair, but performs but little. **1770** Munford *Candidates* 23: You all promise mighty fair, but the devil a bit do you perform. **1780** Deane *Papers* 4.233: Promises without [payment] are lighter than air, and proper only to help to furnish the limbs of vanity. **1781** Webb *Correspondence* 2.345: Her promises great —and her exertions a Puff. **1783** Lee *Letters* 2.281: But as usual, much is talked of & but little done. **1788** *Deane Brothers Papers* 236: Great mens Promises are Often words of Course. **1788** JTrumbull in Jefferson *Papers* 12.622: Brown who promises, but I am afraid will not perform. **1790** Morris *Diary* 1.579: He promises fairly. Qu: as to the Performance? **1796** Cobbett *Porcupine* 3.412: He that promises every thing pays nothing, and he that promises nothing pays every thing. **1798** MJRandolph in Jefferson *Family Letters* 154: She deals much in promises but very little in deeds. **1805** WEaton in *Barbary Wars* 5.456: He had promised much and fulfilled nothing. **1806** EWinslow in *Winslow Papers* 552: I am loaded with fair promises . . . but unluckily the appetites of my family require Beef & Bread. **1809** Henry *Travels* 260: They promised more than they performed. **1815** Humphreys *Yankey* 21: It is not my way . . . to promise more than I can perform. Barbour 147; *Oxford* 649; Tilley P602; Whiting M779, P409.

P299 The **Proof** of the pudding is in the eating

1769 Lloyd *Papers* 2.720: The old saying may with propriety be applied here Vizt. the proof of the puding is in the Eating. **1784** *Washington *Writings* 27.367: The proof of the pudding must be in the eating. **1792** Brackenridge *Modern* 89: And we judge of the pudding not by the maker, but the eating. There is a proverb that establishes this. Barbour 147; *Oxford* 650; TW 297(2); Whiting E172.

P300 Touch my **Property** touch my life

1819 Brackenridge *South America* 1.167: Their maxim was, *Touch my property, touch my life.*

P301 A **Prophet** is not without honor save in his own country

1632 EHowes in *Winthrop Papers(A)* 3.77: A prophet hath small honour in his owne Contrie. **1672** RSaltonstall in *Saltonstall Papers* 1.160: It were a thousand pitties that such a Prophet should be without honour in his own Countrey, and among his own Acquaintance. **1702** Mather *Magnalia* 1.260, 2.146. **1766** Smith *Life and Correspondence* 1.404: It is seldom a "prophet has honor in his own country." **1773** Rush *Letters* 1.82: A prophet, you know, has no honor in his own country. **1774** Carter *Diary* 2.880: In me is verified the saying that. **1774** Stiles *Diary* 1.443: He was a prophet in his own Country. **1776** Carter Diary 2.1057. **1780** AA in *Adams FC* 3.298, **1785** *Letters* 251. **1788** *Columbian Magazine* 2.211: The hackneyed

proverb, that *no man is a prophet in his own country.* **1793** Gadsden *Writings* 258. **1798** *Echo* 151: The maxim . . . "Ne'er where they're known, do prophets honor find." **1800** Adams(A) *Letters* 258: It was truly gratifying to find . . . that a Prophet could meet with honour in his own native soil. **1803** Davis *Travels* 34: Observing that no man was a prophet at home. **1804** *Literary Magazine and American Register* 1.246: The adage, "that a prophet has no honour in his own country." **1805** Silliman *Travels* 1.67: But you know where it is that the prophet is usually without honour. **1809** Irving *History* 1.112: For adventurers, like prophets, though they make great noise abroad, have seldom much celebrity in their own countries. **1813** *Port Folio* 3NS 2.421. **1817** Weems *Franklin* 106. **1822** Jackson *Correspondence* 3.159: The scriptures tell us, "a prophet has no honour in his own country." **1822** Watterston *Winter* 137: It is o'er true I find that the prophet gets na credit in his ain country. *Oxford* 650; Whiting P416.

P302 One cannot live upon **Prospects**

1806 Dunlap *Diary* 2.381: But it has long been ascertain'd that people cannot live much less grow rich upon prospects.

P303 **Prosperity** discovers vice, adversity virtue

1751 Franklin *PR* 4.86: Prosperity discovers Vice, Adversity Virtue.

P304 **Prosperity** makes friends, adversity tries them

1827 Pintard *Letters* 2.384: Prosperity makes friends, adversity tries them. Barbour 147; *Oxford* 650; Tilley P611; Whiting P418.

P305 Once a **Prostitute,** always a prostitute

a**1824** Marshall *Kentucky* 2.229: "Once a prostitute, and always a prostitute," is a fair mode of argument—at least among politicians. *Oxford* 594: Whore; Tilley W321.

P306 **Prudence** looks before as well as behind

1812 Jay *Correspondence* 4.363: Prudence

looks all around — *before* as well as behind. Cf. Chaucer *Troilus* v 744-9.

P307 He that can't sing *Psalms,* let him pray

1797 Cobbett *Porcupine* 6.104: Mr. Swanwick's toast puts me in mind of the pious old precept: "he that can't sing psalms, let him pray."

P308 In a **Pucker**

1741 Stephens *Journal(I)* 2.272: In his Discourse [he] was got into such a Pucker about Freewill, Election *etc* that it was past my Understanding. TW 297.

P309 To give one cold **Pudding**

1837 PCameron in *Ruffin Papers* 2.168: Ask Alice in your next letter if she has not had a *Beau.* I am under the impression as Grandmother Kirkland would say, that she has given him cold pudding. *Oxford* 133; Tilley P622.

P310 Too much **Pudding** (will choke a dog)

1804 Wirt *Letters* 1.122: Certainly I shall write no more Spies; "too much pudding &c." *Oxford* 831.

P311 A long **Pull,** a strong pull, *etc.*

1815 Humphreys *Yankey* 36: Now, I take a long pull, a strong pull, and, mayhap, a pull altogether. **1817** Weems *Letters* 3.189: However it is likely I shall give you a long pull, a strong pull & a pull all together. **1818** Fearon *Sketches* 145: A long pull, a strong pull, and a pull altogether. **1820** Weems *Letters* 3.267. *Oxford* 480; TW 297.

P312 To have a **Pull** at the halyards

1803 Davis *Travels* 436: "What say you to a pull at the haliards?" "I fear there are no haliards in the bottle."

P313 **Punic** faith

1750 *Massachusetts* in *Colonial Currency* 4.453: Our *Punic Faith* Is Infamous, and branded to a Proverb. **1754** Plumstead 308: Punic faith! unless perhaps Gallic is become sufficiently proverbial. **1764** Hutchinson *History* 1.53: Indian fidelity is proverbial in New-England, as Punick was in Rome. **1770** *New York Journal* in *Newspaper Extracts(I)* 8.295: The *Punic* perfidy of many of the in-

habitants of New York. **1775** JLaurens in Kirkland *Letters* 2.16: Men . . . sufficiently infamous to have their Name substituted to the Punick, in the contemptuous Proverb, which makes their shame immortal. **1775** JPrince in Gibbes 2.193. **1777** Lee *Letters* 1.250: A people to whom the term Punica fides may be applyed. **1778** Curwen *Journal* 1.432: French faith [is] now like punic of old. **1778** JWarren in *Heath Papers* 2.223: Punic or Greek faith, so long the subject of ridicule in ancient and modern history, must drop into oblivion. **1789** Humphreys *Works* 335: Hence we were in danger of having our faith become as proverbial as that of Carthage, and our name the scorn of the earth. **1794** Wansey *Journal* 189: American faith will become as infamous and proverbial as Punic faith. **1810** Jefferson *Writings* 12.375: The *Punica fides* of modern Carthage [England]. *Oxford* 654. See **G171, R65.**

P314 To fight like **Punk**

1782 *New Jersey Gazette* in *Newspaper Extracts(II)* 5.384: And fight like punk by land and water. **1789** *American Museum* 5.298: Their proneness to fight like punk. Cf. DA punk.

P315 As good-conditioned as a **Puppy**

1737 Franklin *Drinkers* 2.176: He's As good conditioned as a Puppy. Cf. TW 298(1).

P316 No **Purchase** no pay

1692 in *Baxter Manuscripts* 5.376: Ther may be men Enough found to doe yᵉ worke no purchas no pay. **1787** JChurchman in Jefferson *Papers* 11.397: To renew the old contract "no purchase no pay." **1793** Perkins *Diary* 3.252. *Oxford* 573.

P317 An empty **Purse** is a poor travelling companion

1784 *Belknap Papers* 1.335: An empty purse is a poor travelling companion. Cf. *Oxford* 219-20; Tilley P648-9, 665.

P318 The heavier the **Purse,** the lighter the head

1750 *Massachusetts* in *Colonial Currency* 4.443: And often the heavier the Purse, the lighter the Head. Barbour 148(1); *Oxford* 366; Whiting P454.

P319   Light **Purse,** heavy heart (*varied*)
1733 Franklin *PR* 1.312: Light purse, heavy heart. **1809** Weems *Letters* 2.410: Heavy pockets, and light hearts. *Oxford* 463; Whiting P444.

P320   A light **Purse** is a heavy curse
1745 Franklin *PR* 3.5: A light purse is. a heavy Curse. Cf. Whiting P450.

P321   The longest **Purse** will prevail (*varied*)
1764 NDonnell in *Baxter Manuscripts* 13.351: [It] will . . . Enable the longest Purse and not the Justest Cause to prevail. **1778** PPayson in Thornton *Pulpit* 338: Such maxims of policy as . . . that "the longest purse, and not the longest sword, will finally be victorious." See S547.

P322   An open **Purse** would be safe (*varied*)
1780 Reed *Life* 2.246: My people behave with a regularity of discipline beyond anything I ever saw in militia. A flock of chickens would go untouched through the camp. **1784** Van Schaack *Letters* 365: A purse of gold hung up in the public streets, would be safe from our inhabitants as it used to be in the great Alfred's time. **1805** Irving *Journals* 1.370: And (as we had often been told before) a man might travel through the country [Switzerland] with his purse open in his hand in perfect safety. Whiting P69.

P323   You can't make a silk **Purse** out of a sow's ear
1804 Brackenridge *Modern* 392: There is no making a silk purse out of a sow's ear. **1820** Tudor *Letters* 31: To say, with Sancho, "You cannot make a silk purse from a pig's-ear." **1848** Cooper *Letters* 5.329: New York always reminds me of the silk purse and the sow's ear. Barbour 148(4); *Oxford* 733; TW 298(2). Cf. Whiting S316. See **A119, G99, P60.**

P324   To keep (hold) the **Purse-strings**
1768 Dickinson *Letters* 43: No free people ever existed . . . without keeping, to use a common, but strong expression, "the purse strings," in their own hands. **1792** Jefferson *Writings* 1.307: They held the purse strings. NED Purse-string.

P325   Thank you, good **Puss,** starved my cat
1809 *Port Folio* 2NS 2.550: Thank you, good puss, starved my cat. Cf. *Oxford* 419; Tilley T96, 97.

P326   A (**Pyrrhic**) victory
1777 Lee *Letters* 1.322: But Gen. Howe may say with Pyrrhus, such another victory will ruin me. **1839** Paulding *Letters(II)* 243: But a few more such victories and Pyrrhus is undone. *Oxford* 658.

Q

Q1   Q in the corner

1807 *Salmagundi* 29: Fungus is . . . one of our "Q in a corner fellows." NED Q I 3, also Suppl.

Q2   As fast as a **Quail**

1808 AAdams in Massachusetts Historical Society, *Proceedings* 66 (1936-41) 136: She . . . runs as fast as a quail.

Q3   (Enough) to provoke a **Quaker's** oath

1780 Sargent *Loyalist* 112: It would provoke a Quaker's oath, To see such lads miscarry. Cf. *Oxford* 696: Saint; Tilley S28. See **A94, D52, S72.**

Q4   Those who interpose in **Quarrels** often wipe a bloody nose

1740 Franklin *PR* 2.251: Those who in quarrels interpose, Must often wipe a bloody nose.

Q5   A bad **Quarter** of an hour

1817 Gallatin *Diary* 99: I had a *mauvais quart d'heure*, **1820** 164: Poor Pozzo passed a bad quarter of an hour with mamma. NED Quarter 1b.

Q6   Good for the **Quarter,** but not for the course

1778 HLaurens in Sparks *Correspondence* 2.120: I know my countrymen are good for the quarter, but I have doubts of their going the course. Cf. DA quarter 9b(5).

Q7   **Queen Mary** is dead

1700 NSaltonstall in *Saltonstall Papers* 1.267: Cap. Forbes ship is come lately from England and (They Say) brings news that Queen Mary is certainly Dead [Mary had been dead six years]. *Oxford* 659: Anne, Elizabeth. See **P231.**

Q8   Ask no **Questions** and be told no lies

1775 JAdams in *Warren-Adams Letters* 1.156: Of Mr. McPherson's Errand . . . ask no Questions and I will tell you no false News. **1783** Williams *Penrose* 298: If I did not ask too many Questions they would tell me the fewer lies. **1815** Humphreys *Yankey* 62: Don't quiz me with questions, and I'll tell you no lies. *Oxford* 20; TW 300(3).

Q9   To pop the **Question**

1785 Pynchon *Diary* 225: But he is to pop the question to her at night. **1787** Tyler *Contrast* 36: When I popp'd the question to her she did look a little silly. **1814** JBrace in Vanderpoel *More Chronicles* 106: I had an inclination once or twice to have "popped the question" but could not summon sufficient courage. TW 300(1).

Q10   To have the **Quickstep**

1776 JHaslet in Rodney *Letters* 138: Mr. Wilson [is] not well this fortnight, his step, like mine, too Quick. **1778** Joslin *Journal* 350: I am not well for I have got the Quick Step. Berrey 130.10, 894.1.

Q11   A **Quid** pro (for) quo

1699 JNoyes in *Trumbull Papers* 1.203: Giving them quitt for quo. **1712** Sewall *Diary* 2.366: Then there would be *Quid pro Quo*. **1755** Johnson *Writings* 1.211: You do not talk of *Quid pro quo*. **1780** *Clinton Pa-*

pers 5.764. **1780** Gordon *Letters* 442. **1785** Adams *Works* 8.274: There must be *quid pro quo* . . . This is more than a *quid* for your *quo*. **1788** EHazard in *Belknap Papers* 2.23, **1789** 138. **1788** Mason *Papers* 3.1066. **1792** *Universal Asylum* 9.218. **1796** Morris *Diary and Letters* 2.223. **1798** Gadsden *Writings* 283: A *Quid* for the very advantageous *Quo* she has for us. **1803** *Port Folio* 3.38. **1805** Brackenridge *Modern* 502. **1809** Claiborne *Letter Books* 4.353. **1811** Graydon *Memoirs* 120. **1815** Jefferson *Writings* 14.298: By a strange *quid pro quo*. **1818** Adams *Writings* 6.473. **1820** *Fudge Family* 33. **1822** Wirt *Letters* 2.140. **1831** Cooper *Letters* 2.60. **1836** Clark *Letters* 36, 94.

Q12   To give a Quietus

1666 Alsop *Maryland* 67: Until the rottonness of their circular habitation give them a *Quietus est*.   **1749** NSparhawk in· *Baxter Manuscripts* 12.23: S^r W^r will give him His quietus. **1817** Weems *Franklin* 122: [It] gave him his quietus. *Oxford* 660; Tilley Q16.

Q13   To ooze through one Quill

1805 Sewall *Parody* 9: Betwixt us jointly claiming but *one* will, And always meekly oozing thro' *one* quill. *Oxford* 627: Piss; Tilley Q17.

R

R1 R is the canine letter

1682 CMather in *Mather Papers* 388: But the Insolent Tobias R. (there are Three or Four Names equally applicable to that Canine Initial Letter!). *Oxford* 661; Whiting R1.

R2 As lean as Rabbits

1804 Weems *Letters* 2.298: You w^d find them as lean as so many rabbits in the Dog days. Cf. *Oxford* 661; Tilley R2.

R3 A Rabbit is fat three days in the week, *etc.*

1811 Sumter *Letters* 80: He wants to know if Mary M is always like a rabbit fat 3 days in the week & poor the other three. *Oxford* 661; Tilley R2.

R4 To breed like Rabbits

1807 *Salmagundi* 123: As they always bred like rabbits, the family has increased and multiplied like that of Adam and Eve.

R5 To buy the Rabbit

1741 ?WDouglass *Letter* in *Colonial Currency* 4.78: This is *Ruffian* like, by Superiority of Numbers, to endeavour to make honest People *buy the Rabbit.* **1755** Davis *Colonial Virginia Satirist* 22: 'Tis hard to leave an antient habit, 'Tis harder still to buy the Rabbit. TW 301(6).

R6 The Race is not to the swift nor the battle to the strong

1671 MPray in *Winthrop Papers*(B) 3.109: My soul knoweth . . . the race is not to the swift nor the battel to the strong. **1677** Hub-bard *Indian* 2.259: But as it is said, the Battle is not always to the Strong, nor the Race to the Swift, but Time and Chance hath strangely interposed to the prolonging of our Miseries, **a1700** *New England* 450: But the battle is not always to the strong, no more than the race to the swift; time and chance happens to them all. **1745** ?CHansford in *VHM* 74(1966) 446: The Battle is not always to the Strong. **1745** Winslow *Broadside* 119. **1755** *Johnson Papers* 1.539: The Battle is not always to the strong. **1770** Carter *Diary* 1.383. **1771** TPownall in *Bowdoin Papers* 1.271. **1775** AA in *Adams FC* 1.222. **1776** HGates in Massachusetts Historical Society, *Proceedings* 67(1941-44) 149: May Him who gives the Race to the Slow, and The Battle to the Weak, prosper Our Arms. **1776** JPage in Jefferson *Papers* 1.470. **1776** Shaw *Journals* 25. **1776** JTrumbull in Sparks *Correspondence* 1.282. **1777** Clay *Letters* 34: The Battle is not always to the Strong. **1777** Hutchinson *Diary* 2.171. **1778** RWalker in Webb *Correspondence* 2.5. **1779** JFogg in Sullivan *Journals* 101: "The battle is not to the strong," is a proverb fully verified in this expedition. **1787** Brackenridge *Gazette* 256. **1788** Ledyard *Russian Journey* 245. **1792** Brackenridge *Modern* 154. **1795** ABrown in *Belknap Papers* 3.590: The race is not to the swift, nor success to the powerful. **1800** Adams *Letters on Silesia* 173. **1809** *Port Folio* 2NS 1.528. **1809** Weems *Marion* 141: The good book tells us, "*the race is not always to the swift.*" **1810** Maclay *Letters* 109: Though the "race is not always to the swift." **1812** JQAdams in

American Antiquarian Society, *Proceedings* NS 23(1913) 123: Winning the race from the swift, and wrestling the battle from the strong. **1812** Hitchcock *Social* 197: Solomon affirms that. **1813** Dow *Journal* 315. **1832** Ames *Nautical* 135. *Oxford* 661; Whiting R240.

R7   At **Rack** and manger

1728 Byrd *Dividing Line* 153: The Carolina Men liv'd at Rack & Manger. *Oxford* 661; Whiting R5.

R8   As hot as an old **Radish**

1809 Irving *History* 1.284: Governor Kieft, who, though in temperament as hot as an old radish.

R9   As limber as a (wet) **Rag**

1813 Weems *Drunkard* 99: Then pale and limber as a rag. **1832** Smith *Letters* 337-8: I feel this morning, to use a very vulgar, but very expressive comparison, as limber as a wet rag. Barbour 149(1, 2); TW 302(1).

R10   To take the **Rag** off the bush

1810 *Austin Papers* 1.176: Dr. J. W. takes the rag off the bush a door below your old place of residence. **1810** *Norfolk Gazette* in DA bush 5(1): This "takes the rag off the bush" so completely, that we suppose we shall hear no more . . . about the Chesapeake business. Barbour 150(4); TW 302(7).

R11   As lean as a **Rail**

1766 AA in *Adams FC* 1.56: I am lean as a rale. **1790** Freneau *Poems* 3.44: As lean as a rail. Cf. Barbour 150: skinny; TW 302(1): Thin.

R12   It never **Rains** but it pours

1755 Franklin *Papers* 6.175: You will say, It can't rain, but it pours. **1775** Carter *Diary* 2.948: I remember to have read a Proverb that it never rains but it pours, **1777** 1113: It never rains now but it Pours. **1794** Drinker *Journal* 232: "It can't rain but it showers," a silly old adage. **1814** Randolph(J) *Letters* 151: If I had answered them [letters], I should enclose them to you; but they *poured* in this morning, according to the proverb. Barbour 150; *Oxford* 663; TW 303(1).

R13   As poor as **Rakes**

1723 *New-England Courant* 112(1.1): As *poor as Rakes*, and *had not a Groat to buy them a Breakfast*. Svartengren 186; Whiting *NC* 465(2). Cf. *Oxford* 350; Whiting R23.

R14   A reformed **Rake** makes the best husband

1797 Foster *Coquette* 76: But is it not an adage generally received, that *"a reformed rake makes the best husband"*? 83: "A reformed rake," you say, "makes the best husband;" a trite, but a very erroneous maxim. Lean 3.402.

R15   To plow with a **Ram's** horn

1819 Faux *Memorable Days* 1.169: It seems (as we say at Somersham) as though it was ploughed with a ram's horn, or the snout of a hog, hungry after grubs and roots. Cf. Whiting R26.

R16   To pay with a **Ram skin**

c**1813** Dow *Journal* 313: Though he thought of paying with a "ram skin," as the saying is —i.e. deliver up all.

R17   To have swallowed a **Ramrod**

1824 *Tales* 1.68: He sat as bolt upright (to use a common simile,) as if he had swallowed a ramrod. Cf. TW 303.

R18   Not care a **Rap**

1797 Beete *Man* 29: I would not care a rap halfpenny about him. *Oxford* 664.

R19   A **Rap** on the knuckles

1766 SPurviance in Stiles *Itineraries* 558: He rec'd such a Rapp o'er the knuckles as . . . has . . . silenc'd him. **1778** Deane *Papers* 3.10: He did not incline to subject himself to any further censures, or, as he expressed it, "raps over the knuckles" for meddling in the affair. NED Knuckle 2b.

R20   As dead as (a) **Rat**

1755 Davis *Colonial Virginia Satirist* 24: Or to be shot, as dead as Rat. Svartengren 145. Cf. TW 303(2).

R21   As poor as a **Rat**

a**1788** Jones *History* 2.356: Where he lives as

poor as a rat. Barbour 151(4); *Oxford* 638; TW 304(4). See **C181.**

R22 As weak as a **Rat**

1803 *Yankee Phrases* 87: And lean and as weak, as a rat. NED Rat *sb.*[1] 2c; Svartengren 393.

R23 As wet as a drowned **Rat**

1631 *Winthrop Papers*(*A*) 3.16: We came to our iourneys end as wet as drounded rats. **a1731** Cook *Bacon* 322: Tho' like drown'd Rat wet. **c1775** Hopkinson *Miscellaneous Essays* 3(part 2) 160: I was wet to the skin, like an half-drowned rat. **1782** Bailey *Journal* 187: If I may be allowed to assume the vulgar dialect, she resembled a drowned rat. **1783** Williams *Penrose* 152. **1785** Denny *Journal* 266: They having received a plentiful quantity of wet that occasioned a near resemblance to drowned rats. **1799** TPierce in Vanderpoel *Chronicles* 373. **1804** Brackenridge *Modern* 374: [They] were as wet as rats. Barbour 151(7); Svartengren 302; TW 304(6). Cf. Whiting R36.

R24 One **Rat** brings another

1805 Brackenridge *Modern* 547: For as one rat brings another, so lawyer brings lawyer. See **T54.**

R25 A **Rat** that has but one hole (is in danger)

1821 Dalton *Travels* 147-8: But you, gentleman prairie owners, are like a rat that has but one hole to go out and come in at. *Oxford* 548; Whiting M739.

R26 **Rats** abandon (*etc.*) a sinking ship

1755 Franklin *Papers* 6.305: You won't pump Ship, because 'twill save the Rats as well as yourself. **1780** Moore *Diary* 2.344: It is a common saying at New York, that the ship must be near sinking when the rats are leaving it. **1799** Adams(TB) *Letters* 87: To desert the Government and abandon it to its fate, as Rats will a ship just before she sinks. **1803** Davis *Travels* 12: A report being circulated that the rats had left the vessel when in harbour, Coster Pearman concluded that they had done it by instinct; and as an opinion prevails among sailors that a ship on such an event, never gets safe to her port of destination, the booby gave himself up for lost. **1812** Jefferson *Writings* 13.149: I think the old hulk in which you are, is near her wreck, and like a prudent rat, you should escape in time. **1819** RKing in Banks *Maine* 130: This is a ship wrecked party, and . . . the Rats are daily quitting their old friends & forming new ones. **1823** Adams *Memoirs* 6.186: A ship which . . . the very rats have abandoned. **1841** JCatron in Jackson *Correspondence* 6.90: Henry Clay is . . . not likely to embark in a ship from which he saw the grayest rats in philda. . . . . running. Barbour 151(5); *Oxford* 664-5; Tilley M1243.

R27 **Rats** flee from a falling house

1782 Trumbull *Satiric Poems* 186: Like rats that fly from house that's falling. **1796** CGoodrich in Gibbs *Memoirs* 1.341: When old rats leave a house, it has always been considered as a bad omen. **1806** *Weekly* 1.26: He ran like a rat From a house falling flat. *Oxford* 664-5; Tilley M1243.

R28 To be like a **Rat** in trouble

1737 Franklin *Drinkers* 2.177: He's Like a Rat in Trouble. Cf. Partridge 688.

R29 To smell a **Rat**

1714 Hunter *Androboros* 5: You smell a Rat. **a1731** Cook *Bacon* 315: They in the Letter smelt a Rat. **1747** Laurens *Papers* 1.38. **1776** CTufts in *Adams FC* 2.18. **1777** Cresswell *Journal* 250. **1777** Munford *Patriots* 489. **1787** Tyler *Contrast* 74. **1790** *Universal Asylum* 5.169: A . . . customer smelt the rat, **1791** 6.252. **1801** *Port Folio* 1.232. **1807** *Salmagundi* 30. **1809** Weems *Marion* 135. **1817** Wirt *Letters* 2.12. **1819** Peirce *Rebelliad* 75. **1825** Neal *American Writers* 128. **1832** Ames *Nautical* 131. *Oxford* 745; TW 304(10).

R30 As sure (certain) as **Rates**

1798 *Echo* 155: I've beat old Brackenridge as sure as rates. **1803** *Yankee Phrases* 87: As certain as death, or as rates. **1815** Humphreys *Yankey* 55: As sure as rates. *Oxford* 580; TW 304(1). See **D61.**

R31 As black as a **Raven**

1750 Franklin *PR* 3.444: Those Tresses as the Raven black. **1791** Bartram *Travels*

138: As black and shining as a raven, 306: Hair . . . black as a raven. **1822** Weems *Penn* 149: Hair, black as the raven's breast. **1826** Royall *Sketches* 300. Svartengren 244-5; Whiting R42.

R32 **Raw-head** and bloody bones

1637 Morton *New English Canaan* 320: Hee made Fairecloaths Innocent back like the picture of Rawhead and blowdy bones. **1775** Curwen *Journal* 1.30: Their imaginative description of raw head and bloody bones. **1775** Moore *Diary* 1.8: In vain are their scare-crows, raw-head and bloody bones, held up to deter us from taking the most effectual means for our security. **1776** Hopkinson *Miscellaneous Essays* 1.95: And *raw-head* and *bloody-bones* shall come out of France to devour them, 96. **1776** JWarren in *Warren-Gerry Correspondence* 18: A Hobgoblin that frights more people than raw head and Bloody Bones. **1781** Oliver *Origins* 65. **1798** Cobbett *Porcupine* 8.100. **1799** Jefferson *Writings* 10.78: Stories of raw-head and bloody bones, **1804** 444: Imaginary caricatures, which existed only in the land of the raw head and bloody bones, being created to frighten the credulous. **1807** *Salmagundi* 34: A hungry-looking Gaul . . . who is doubtless the original of the famous "Raw-head-and-bloody-bones" so potent in frightening naughty children, 404. **1808** Taggart *Letters* 303: Our wry faces, our raw head and bloody bone and all that. **1810** Jefferson *Writings* 12.362, 372. **1810** *Port Folio* 2NS 4.337. **1810** Rush *Letters* 2.1062: I was her "raw head and bloody bones." **1817** TJefferson in *Adams-Jefferson Letters* 2.513: Hancock and the Adamses were the rawhead and bloody bones of tories and traitors, **1818** *Writings* 1.281. **1822** Bache *Notes* 81. **1824** Jefferson *Writings* 16.40-1: They hold up this raw-head and bloody-bones *in terrorem* to us. **1827** Longfellow *Letters* 1.232. **1828** MJenkins in *Ruffin Papers* 1.436. **1831** JCoffee in *Jackson Correspondence* 4.310: Mr. Ingham . . . cries out, *War, bloodshed, death* and *raw head* and *bloody bones*. **1843** Paulding *Letters(II)* 325: The Public I think is quite tired of raw-head and bloody bones romance. *Oxford* 665; TW 176: Head(8).

R33 As sharp as a **Razor**

1789 JSmith in *The Columbian Muse* (New York, 1794) 110: And sharp as a razor, blows the northern gale. Barbour 151(2); *Oxford* 721; Svartengren 255; Whiting R53.

R34 He outrages **Reason** who sings out of season

1806 *Port Folio* NS 2.399: "He most of all doth outrage reason, Who fondly singeth out of season." A proverb that in sense, surpasses The brains combined of stags and asses. Cf. Lean 3.415; NED Season 16.

R35 Like **Reason,** like law

1728 Talcott *Papers* 2.429: The ancient maxim, the like reason, the like Law.

R36 There is **Reason** in roasting eggs

1815 Humphreys *Yankey* 55: It has bin said by them of old time, "there is reason in roasting eggs." *Oxford* 666; TW 305(2).

R37 No **Reasoning** with the belly

1805 Brackenridge *Modern* 544: There was "no reasoning with the belly." *Oxford* 45; Tilley B286, 287. See **B142.**

R38 To have a **Receipt** from the drummer

1782 Perkins *Diary* 2.164: He did not own his being a Soldier, but his back has a Receipt from the Drummer. See **G191.**

R39 No **Receiver,** no thief

1656 Hammond *Leah* 13: As the Proverb is, where there are no receivers, there are no thieves. **1716** *Considerations* in *Colonial Currency* 1.346: The Proverb tells us . . . *that if there were no Receivers, there would be no Thieves.* **1738** RStaunton in *Letters from Hudson Bay* 267: If there would or was not to be any receivers there certainly would be no theft, 271: An old proverb in England which is that. *Oxford* 573; Whiting R60.

R40 The **Receiver** is as bad as the thief

1716 *Considerations* in *Colonial Currency* 1.346: The Proverb tells us, That *the Receiver is as bad as the Thief.* **1767** Franklin *Papers* 14.318: Our proverb too says truly, that *the receiver is as bad as the thief,* **1770** 17.39: The old and true saying. **1780** EHazard in *Belknap Papers* 1.35: The receiver of stolen goods is as bad as the thief. **1788** *American Museum* 4.31: The receiver of stolen goods, is as bad as the thief. **1826** WVans in *Codman Letters* 373: It is a maxim in Law, The Receivers of stolen goods are as bad as the thief. *Oxford* 667; Tilley R52.

R41 Right **Reckonings** make long friends (*varied*)

1776 Paine *Common Sense* 1.37: A firm bargain and a right reckoning make long friends. **1817** Tyler *Prose* 323: Short reckonings make long friends — Poor Richard. **1827** Prince *Journals* 398: Must I again remind you of the old adage I have so often repeated "Frequent reckonings make firm friends." **1832** Jackson *Correspondence* 4.443: Remember the old adage, "that short settlements makes long friends." *Oxford* 728; TW 305; Whiting R61.

R42 **Red-hair** is inclined to lewdness

1732 Byrd *Progress* 327: Her complexion, being red-haired, inclined her so much to lewdness. Lean 2.308-11; NED Red-haired, quote 1726.

R43 As slender as a **Reed**

1774 Adams *D and A* 2.117: Slender as a Reed, 121: Thin and slender as a Reed.

R44 As weak as a **Reed**

1774 Boucher *View* 351: They were rendered weak, *as a reed that is shaken in the water.* **1818** JBooth in *Kingston* 387: I am weaker than a brused reed. Cf. Whiting R69.

R45 A **Reed** shaken with the wind

1670 Plumstead 58: The first particular enquiry is whether they went to see "a reed shaken with the wind"? The expression is metaphorical and proverbial. Cf. Whiting R73.

R46 The **Reed** (osier) yields to the blast (*varied*)

1776 *St. Clair Papers* 1.375: The osier keeps its footing when the oak is torn up by the roots. **1803** Ellicott *Journal* 291: This change is very severe on the firm constitutions of our northern citizens, which like strong oaks in a tempest, are broken off or torn up by the roots, while weak constitutions like flexible reeds, yield to the tempest, and rise when the storm is over. **1807** AAdams in *Warren-Adams Letters* 2.352: I bend to the blast. It passes over for the present and I rise again. **1808** M'Nemar *Kentucky* 71: Your pliant soul must yield, like a reed before the wind. *Oxford* 584; Tilley O3; Whiting R71. See **W168.**

R47 To be a broken **Reed** (*varied*)

1664 Bradstreet *Works* 71: They prove like the reeds of Egypt that peirce instead of supporting. **1669** Morton *New-Englands Memoriall* 50: He proved but a staff of Reed to the Plantation of Plimouth. **a1700** Hubbard *New England* 257: But as a broken reed for a State to lean upon, 498-9: Thus they that trust to an unfaithful friend do but wade in unknown waters, and lean on a broken reed, which both woundeth as well as deceiveth those that rely thereon. **1720** Mather *Letters* 308: Those on whom I had most reliance proved broken reeds. **1755** *Johnson Papers* 1.693: We have advanced on the faith of ye others . . . (I fear a broken Reed). **1769** JParker in Franklin *Papers* 16.73. **1776** *Blockheads* 15. **1778** Sullivan *Letters* 2.225: His dependence must be upon a Reed, who has faith in their distant Support. **1779** Moore *Diary* 2.237. **1779** *Washington Writings* 14.266: They are leaning upon a broken reed. **1781** ALee in *Warren-Adams Letters* 2.170: I wish they may prove neither broken reeds, nor Spears to peirce us. **1782** Gordon *Letters* 463: Her husband is a broken reed. **1782** Jay *Correspondence* 2.452: We shall lean on a broken reed, that will sooner or later pierce our hands. **1782** Trumbull *Satiric Poems* 185: For know those hopes can ne'er succeed That trust on Britain's breaking reed. **1789** Morris *Diary* 1.131. **1795** OWolcott, S^r., in Gibbs *Memoirs* 1.214-5: The nation which depends upon treaty for its security, leans upon a reed. **1807** *Weekly* 1.193: Dependence on them . . . Is leaning on a broken reed, Which has already pierc'd your hand. **1809** Fessenden *Pills* 9: We conceive that a broken reed to lean upon is better than no support. **1812** Hitchcock *Social* 62. **1815**

Bulger Papers 76: Trusting only, what a reed to lean on, that *"something would turn up."* **1821** Hodgson *Letters* 2.327. **1828** *Ruffin Papers* 1.458: Thank Heaven! the trust is not entirely upon a fragile reed. 2 Kings 18.21; *Oxford* 88; Whiting R70. See **S397.**

R48   To take a **Reef** in the mainsail

1802 Asbury *Letters* 3.241: You have taken a reef in the mainsail. **1805** JButler in *Barbary Wars* 6.153: Dam-n my *eyes* if I don't take a double reef in *your* Top Sails. Colcord 149; NED Reef *sb.*[1] 1.

R49   To get the **Reins** off one's neck

a**1656** Bradford *History* 1.55: Getting the rains off their neks, and departing from their parents. Cf. NED Rein *sb.*[1] 2b; *Oxford* 448.

R50   To give (keep) the **Reins**

1750 *Georgia Records* 26.40: Stephens . . . has given the Reins out of his Hands. **1818** *Adams-Waterhouse Correspondence* 142: My Advice . . . is, to keep the Reins in your own hands, till you are married. *Oxford* 86; Tilley B671.

R51   Be careful how you touch another's **Religion,** *etc.*

1742 Franklin *PR* 2.337: You will be careful, if you are wise; How you touch Men's Religion, or Credit, or Eyes. **1771** Adams(S) *Writings* 2.276: Ne lude cum sacris is a proverb. *Oxford* 411; Tilley R64. See **E121.**

R52   No **Remedy** but patience

1682 Claypoole *Letter Book* 93: I know no remedy but patience. **1689** Randolph *Letters* 6.310: Patience is the best remedy. **1750** RPartridge in Kimball 2.98: I know of no Remedy but Patience. **1752** TBosomworth in McDowell *Documents* 1.280: There is no other Remedy, but waiting the Event with Patience. **1763** Griffith *Journal* 140-1. **1778** LPintard in Webb *Correspondence* 2.142. **1779** Bailey *Journal* 147: We had no other remedy except patience, and a very slender dose of that excellent drug. **1785** Adams *Works* 8.259: We must submit to what we cannot alter. Patience is the only remedy. **1794** Savery *Journal* 90: Patience then be-

comes our only remedy. *Oxford* 612-3, 670; Tilley P107-8, R71; Whiting P55.

R53   The **Remedy** (cure) is worse than the disease

1633 EHowes in *Winthrop Papers(A)* 3.135: The Cure wilbe worse then the disease. a**1656** Bradford *History* 2.153: This remedy proved worse than the disease. **1661** F-JWinthrop in *Winthrop Papers(B)* 4.269. **1702** Mather *Magnalia* 2.492. **1728** Byrd *Dividing Line* 276. **1734** *Letter* in *Colonial Currency* 3.31: The Disease was bad; but the Remedy, I think, is worse, 110: A Remedy for our Difficulties, which is already found much worse than the Disease. **1747** JStoddard in *Law Papers* 3.97. **1763** Watts *Letter Book* 163. **1764** NDonnell in *Baxter Manuscripts* 13.351: The Remedy proposed is more than adequate (indeed much Worse) than the disease. **1766** JParker in Franklin *Papers* 13.341. **1771** HBarnes in Murray *Letters* 142: Perhaps you will say the remedy may be as bad as the disease. **1774** Boucher *View* 359: A remedy . . . almost as dangerous as the disease. **1774** Chandler *Friendly Address* 37: A remedy of this kind is ten thousand times worse than the disease. **1777** Cresswell *Journal* 200. **1779** *New Jersey Gazette* in *Newspaper Extracts(II)* 3.211. **1782** Lee *Papers* 4.13: The preventive must be almost worse than the disease. **1785** Lee *Letters* 2.383. **1787** BHarrison in Washington *Writings* 29.279. **1787** Ledyard *Russian Journey* 189. **1792** Jefferson *Writings* 1.323: The President said the remedy would be worse than the disease. **1793** Washington *Writings* 33.12: In which case correction cannot retrieve either, but often produces evils which are worse than the disease. **1794** DAllison in *Blount Papers* 2.428: Cure. **1794** ?TPCarnes in Callender *Political Register* 1.356. **1799** JMason in Otis *Letters* 1.173: By a remedy scarcely short of the Disease. **1815** Brackenridge *Modern* 780. **1817** Short *Letters* 360: The remedy he thought as bad as the disease. **1819** Adams *Memoirs* 4.370: The greatest danger is of the application of remedies worse than the disease. **1820** Simpson *Journal* 124: The remedy may be nearly as bad as the disease.

1835 Hone *Diary* 1.171, 180. *Oxford* 671; Tilley R68; Whiting *NC* 466.

R54 There are **Remedies** for everything but death

1788 Freneau *Prose* 117: As the saying is, there are remedies for every thing but death. *Oxford* 670; Tilley R69; Whiting M484. See **A50, H198, N114.**

R55 Three **Removes** are as bad as a fire

1758 Franklin *WW* 344: Three Removes is as bad as a Fire. 1770 Ames *Almanacs* 412. 1785 Hopkinson *Miscellaneous Essays* 2.154-5: And proved that the losses and destruction incident to two white-washings are equal to one removal and three removals are equal to one fire. 1790 Freneau *Poems* 3.49: Whoever 'moves must suffer loss. *Oxford* 817; TW 306. See **T234.**

R56 One **Renegade** is worse than ten Turks

1732 Franklin *Papers* 1.261: Hence one Renegade is (as the Proverb says) worse than 10 Turks. 1775 *New York Journal* in *Newspaper Extracts(I)* 11.34: As it is a proverb among the Turks that one renegadoe is worse than ten Turks, so it has been one among the Christians, that one apostate is worse than ten infidels. 1801 *Port Folio* 1.114: One renegado, says the old proverb, is worse than ten Turks. Cf. NED Renegade 1, Renegado 1.

R57 To **Repent** too late

1646 EWinslow in *Winthrop Papers(A)* 5.87: If you doe, I conceive you will also too late repent it, 88: Since we followed your examp[le] in one partic[ular] which wee too late repent. 1650 Bradstreet *Works* 145: Lest we too late this rashness do repent. 1700 PDudley in *Winthrop Papers(B)* 5.518: They have often repented it when too late, 1707 390. 1709 Lawson *Voyage* 246. 1721 Wise *Word* 201. 1730 Talcott *Papers* 214: All New England may repent when 'tis too late. 1744 Stephens *Journal(II)* 2.182. 1755 *Johnson Papers* 1.823. 1756 *Beekman Papers* 1.271. 1760 Adams *D and A* 1.138. 1761 *Beekman Papers* 1.386, 1767 512. 1772 Wheatley *Poems* 75. 1777 Lee(W) *Letters* 1.270. 1811 Burroughs *Memoirs* 133. Whiting R84. See **A141.**

R58 **Repentance** may be too late

1788 *American Museum* 3.172: Caution is never too late: repentance may be. 1807 *Weekly* 1.224: Repentance comes a day too late. Lean 4.89; *Oxford* 672; Whiting R86.

R59 There's no **Repentance** in the grave

1805 Alden *Epitaphs* 5.230: There's no repentance in the grave. Cf. Whiting R86, S335.

R60 To buy **Repentance** too dear

1689 *Appeal* in *Andros Tracts* 3.194: Whether any good man has done any other than buy Repentance at a dear rate. 1728 Byrd *Dividing Line* 308: A Princess for a Pair of Red Stockings can't, surely, be thought buying Repentance much too dear. 1740 Franklin *PR* 2.252: He is the greatest fool that lays it out in a purchase of repentance, 1758 *WW* 346: 'Tis foolish to lay out Money in a Purchase of Repentance. *Oxford* 672; Tilley R81-2.

R61 **Republics** are ungrateful (*varied*)

c1776 Hutchinson *History* 1.277: Instances of gratitude in a multitude, or in the body of a people are so rare. 1779 BArnold in Sparks *Correspondence* 2.291: Congress have stamped ingratitude as a current coin. 1779 JJay in Hamilton *Papers* 2.183: Republics are always jealous, seldom liberal, never grateful, and not always just, and yet . . . the least evil of all Governments. 1782 *St. Clair Papers* 1.576: I have seen it somewhere laid down as a maxim that "kings *may* be ungrateful, but republics *must* be." 1783 Washington *Writings* 26.462: Ingratitude has been experienced in all Ages, and Republics in particular have ever been famed for the exercise of that unnatural and Sordid Vice. 1785 MWarren in *Warren-Adams Letters* 2.260: I answer, when Republics are Famed for their Gratitude and the Multitude learn to Discriminate. 1786 Franklin *Writings* 9.528: It has formerly been said, that Republicks are naturally ungrateful, 1788 695: The reproach thrown on republics, that *they are apt to be ungrateful.* 1798 Gerry *Letters* 2.96: We both know that republics were never remarkable for the constancy of their attachment. 1793

ABrown in *Belknap Papers* 3.561: But you have put it beyond the power of malice to speak at his grave of the ingratitude of republics. **1795** Cobbett *Porcupine* 2.341: The ingratitude of republics and republicans has long been proverbial. **1795** Freneau *Prose* 346, 347, 348: *Republics have ever been famed for ingratitude.* **c1800** Dennie *Lay Preacher* 147. **1805** Brackenridge *Modern* 588: The ingratitude of a republic, has, somhow, or other, come to be taken for a truth. **1808** JHaywood in *Steele Papers* 2.552: As Republics ever were and it is likely will remain ungrateful. **1811** Graydon *Memoirs* 374: Let it no longer be said that the people are ungrateful, or that virtue in republics goes unrewarded. **1815** Barney *Memoir* 284. **1818** Hall *Travels* 203: Behold, says Prejudice, the gratitude of republicks! **1822** Adams *Writings* 7.191: If ever there was a citizen of a *Republic* who had reason to complain of the *ingratitude* of his country, I am not that man. **1825** *Austin Papers* 2.1048: This . . . has proved to the world that republics are not ungrateful. **1828** Pintard *Letters* 3.19. **1844** Mason *Memoir* 16: Another item in the history of the ingratitude of republics. **1844** Paulding *Letters(II)* 361: As to the Old Colonel, he is the best proof in the world that the charge so often brought against Republics is without foundation, for had not our Country once been grateful for his former Services, they would have sent him to the Devil long ago. TW 306. Cf. *Oxford* 90; Whiting P134. See **P233.**

R62 **Reputation** is a jewel whose loss cannot be repaired

1797 Foster *Coquette* 202: No woman . . . can be indifferent to reputation. It is an estimable jewel, the loss of which can never be repaired. See **N11, W370.**

R63 **Revenge** is sweet

a1656 Bradford *History* 2.247: Revenge was so sweete unto them. **1702** Mather *Magnalia* 2.452: Revenge! revenge! sweet is revenge! 554: The prospect of a *sweet revenge.* **1728** Byrd *Dividing Line* 291: Nor was this Revenge sweeter to him than a Griskin of it was to the Doctor, who of all worldly food conceives this to be the best. **1733** Winslow *Broadside* 83: we often hear. **1742** Belcher *Papers* 2.421: The wicked Lord Rochester said, revenge was a sweet morsel. **1764** *Paxton Papers* 116: you know. **1777** JChester in Washington *Writings* 7.3: They are determined to have sweet revenge. **1785** JAdams in *Warren-Adams Letters* 2.269. **1803** Davis *Travels* 392. **1808** JAdams in *Adams-Cunningham Letters* 44: His revenge has been sweet, and he has rolled it as a delicious morsel under his tongue. **1809** Weems *Marion* 213. Barbour 152; *Oxford* 673; TW 306.

R64 To go to one's **Reward**

1810 Asbury *Journal* 2.656: Bloodgood has also gone to his reward, **1814** 767: My aged friends . . . have gone to their reward. TW 306.

R65 **Rhode Island** faith

1787 *American Museum* 2.287-8: Rhode Island faith in particular is become superlatively infamous, even to a proverb. See **G171, P313.**

R66 Without **Rhyme** or reason

1728 Byrd *Dividing Line* 131: A Letter . . . wherein without Rhyme or Reason, they took care to celebrate Firebrand's Civility. **1753** *New York Weekly Post Boy* in *Newspaper Extracts(I)* 3.325: To beat her Brains out without Rhime or reason. **1771** Sewall *Poems* 50: And *rhyme* with *reason* wages impious war. **1782** Rush *Letters* 1.279: Men who were never moved by beauty or harmony or by rhyme or reason. **1784** Gadsden *Writings* 221. **1786** ?RPeters in Jefferson *Papers* 9.350: We'll give our *reason* not our *rhime.* **1792** Morris *Diary* 2.584: All this Rhyme is not without some Reason. **1795** Bentley *Diary* 2.128. **1801** Story *Shop* 57: Who . . . can guide their rhyme or reason. **1804** JStuart in *Kingston* 326. **1806** Fessenden *Modern Philosopher* 259: If rhyme or reason could avail any thing. **1809** Irving *History* 1.43: This learned Theban, who is as much distinguished for rhyme as reason. **1818** Weems *Letters* 3.238: Contrary to all rhyme or reason. **1819** Drake *Works* 309, 329: Between merry rhyme and dull reason.

1820 RWaln *American Bards* (Philadelphia, 1820) 31: His rhyme and reason. 1824 Tyler *Verse* 189: As, 'gainst all reason, rhyme and rule. 1841 Hone *Diary* 2.553: There was rhyme, but no reason in it. *Oxford* 674; Whiting R103.

R67 One's **Rib**

1792 ABrown in *Belknap Papers* 3.534: I have presented your salutations to my Rib. 1797 EHazard in *Belknap Papers* 2.363: My rib unites with me in affection for yourself. 1797 Tyler *Prose* 219: My own dear rib. NED Rib *sb.*[1] 3. Cf. Whiting *NC* 467.

R68 To stick by the **Ribs**

1824 Doddridge *Notes* 90: Tea and coffee were the only slops, which in the adage of the day "did not stick by the ribs." *Oxford* 773; Tilley R101.

R69 To be too free with Sir **Richard**

1737 Franklin *Drinkers* 2.177: He's Been too free with Sir Richard.

R70 He that will increase in **Riches**, *etc.*

1787 *American Museum* 1.462: The old adage will ever hold true, "He that will increase in riches, must not hoe corn in silk breeches."

R71 The more **Riches** the less wisdom

1750 *Massachusetts* in *Colonial Currency* 4.443: Generally speaking, the more Riches the less Wisdom. Cf. *Oxford* 898; Whiting W390.

R72 **Riches** bring cares

1807 Maxwell *Mysterious* 31.33: Riches bring cares, and affluence is need, When virtue's wanting. *Oxford* 675; Whiting R117. See **W79.**

R73 **Riches** consist in having few wants

c1810 Randolph *Virginia* 197: The maxim that genuine riches consisted in having few wants. Cf. *Oxford* 674; Whiting S867.

R74 **Riches** have wings

1730 Chalkley *Youth* 560: Riches . . . very soon are on the Wing. 1748 *Word* in *Colonial Currency* 4.363: Riches . . . are said to take to themselves Wings and flee away. 1754 Plumstead 319: Riches take to themselves wings. 1792 Paine *To Addressers* 2.505: "Riches make themselves wings, and fly away." *Oxford* 675; Whiting R116.

R75 To seek **Riches** in a beggar's cottage

1702 Taylor *Christographia* 134.95: No man will Seek Riches in a beggers Cottage.

R76 Good **Riddance** (to bad ware, rubbish)

1771 *Essex Gazette* in *Olden Time* 4.22: A good Riddance of bad Ware. 1782 Adams *Works* 7.658: A good riddance for us. 1782 Curwen *Journal* 2.820: 'Tis too troublesome an inmate not to say a good riddance. 1799 Adams *Writings* 2.394: Of H[ichborn] you have at length a good riddance. 1810 Stebbins *Journal* 14: Good riddance. 1815 Humphreys *Yankey* 88: Good riddance to bad rubbidge! 1836 Floy *Diary* 248: Sold the horse for $80; good riddance, 261. Barbour 152-3; *Oxford* 323.

R77 As leaky as a **Riddle**

1772 Carter *Diary* 2.648: His single covering to my adjoining building though not more than a week done is as leaky as a riddle. Barbour 153; *Oxford* 732: Sieve; TW 333(1): Sieve; Tilley S435. See **S200.**

R78 Come **Riddle** come raddle

1807 Fraser *Letters and Journals* 253: I have a small Touch of come riddle come Raddle.

R79 Where there is stony **Riding** there's good abiding

1773 McClure *Diary* 140: He . . . cited the adage, "Where there is stoney riding, there's good abiding."

R80 As sure as a **Rifle**

1776 *Virginia Gazette* in *Naval Documents* 3.1187: As sure as a rifle (and that, they will know, is pretty sure) Commodore Hopkins will pay them a visit. See **G189.**

R81 As true as a **Rifle**

1829 Wirt *Letters* 2.269: He is a fine fellow, as true as a rifle. Cf. TW 306.

R82 To run a (the) **Rig**

1764 AA in *Adams FC* 1.13: Than having run my rig, think it time to draw towards a close. 1780 CPhelps in *Clinton Papers* 6.162: If your Excellency . . . will suffer me to be so injured . . . I have run a fine rig. **1802** Dow *Journal* 156: One began to run the rig upon me, asking me how much money I had got. *Oxford* 688.

R83 Do no **Right** and take no wrong

1822 Adams *Memoirs* 6.39: "Do no right and take no wrong," I have heard was the English sailor's motto. *Oxford* 192; Tilley R126.

R84 Extreme **Right** is extreme wrong

1721 *Letter* in *Colonial Currency* 2.253: Summum Jus, est Summa Injuria. Extream Right is Extream Wrong. *Oxford* 235; Tilley R122.

R85 **Right** is a stubborn thing

1750 Wolcott *Papers* 20: Right is a Stuborn thing, **1751** 43: There is no deneying men Right it is a stuborn thing.

R86 A **Right** to one's own opinion

1797 Adams *New Letters* 119: Everyone has a right to their own opinion. **1801** Perkins *Diary* 4.336: As every one has a right to an Opinion of their own. Cf. *Oxford* 599; Tilley O69.

R87 As stiff as a **Ring-bolt**

1737 Franklin *Drinkers* 2.177: He's as Stiff as a Ring-bolt.

R88 Soon **Ripe**, soon rotten

1699 Ward *Trip* 53: The *Women*, like Early *Fruits*, are soon *Ripe* and soon *Rotten*. **1702** Mather *Magnalia* 1.254: The proverb, "soon ripe, soon rotten," has often been too *hastily* applied unto *rathe ripe wits*, in young people. **1790** Bentley *Diary* 1.183: A general maxim respecting education . . . soon ripe, soon rotten. **1828** *Yankee* 288: Soon ripe, soon—. Barbour 153; *Oxford* 752; Whiting R142.

R89 He must **Rise** betimes that would please everyone

1666 Alsop *Maryland* 20: There is an old Saying in English, *He must rise betimes that would please every one*. *Oxford* 678; Tilley N86.

R90 One must **Risk** to win

1832 Jackson *Correspondence* 4.475: *You must risque to win*. See **N113**.

R91 All **Rivers** run into the sea

1760 Franklin *Papers* 9.247: It is . . . a very general opinion that *all Rivers run into the Sea*. *Oxford* 679; Tilley R140; Whiting F289.

R92 As long as the **Rivers** run

1700 Sewall *Letter Book* 1.241.-2: Your Excellencies Performance herein will cause a Current of thankful Praises to spring up amongst his people; which shall flow as long as the Merrimack or Hudson's River shall pay tribute to the ocean. **1756** RDinwiddie in McDowell *Documents* 2.103: As long as the Rivers run, or the Trees grow. Cf. Tilley R140. See **G144, S527**.

R93 To set a **River** (*etc.*) on fire

1807 *Salmagundi* 289: He seemed to entertain strong doubts as to the objects of the Society in the invention of these infernal machines — hinted a suspicion of their wishing to set a river on fire. **1812** Maxwell *Poems* 63: Let's set fire to Chesapeek Bay; Or suppose we drink up the Atlantic. **1825** Neal *American Writers* 206: For he was never the man to set rivers on fire. *Oxford* 717; TW 307-8(3). See **W350**.

R94 As whole and sound as a **Roach**

1805 *Port Folio* 5.78: I found myself . . . as whole and sound as a roach. c**1825** Tyler *Prose* 169: [He] declared himself as sound as a roach. TW 308.

R95 Bad **Road** and good land

1774 Jones *Journal* 87: It might be called bad road and good land. *Oxford* 321: Good land; Tilley L50.

R96 The shortest **Road** to men's hearts is down their throats

1814 Adams *Works* 6.505: As I have heard, "the shortest road to men's hearts is down their throats." **1831** ABatch in Jackson *Correspondence* 4.315: The shortest road to the hearts of half mankind is down their throats. Barbour 194: Way(7); *Oxford* 871-2; TW 194: Heart(20).

R97 A **Roanoke** entertainment

1733 Byrd *Journey* 304: We had a true Roanoke entertainment of pork upon pork, and pork again upon that.

R98 To pay the **Roast**

1778 Lee(W) *Letters* 1.329: Their Agents know the Treasury is to pay the roast, 336: Where others were to pay the roast. NED Roast, 1c, quote 1680.

R99 To rule the **Roast**

1637 Morton *New English Canaan* 288: This private counsell, given him by one that knew who ruled the rost. *1654* Johnson *Wonder-Working* 132: This woman . . . had the chiefe rule of all the roast. *1671* DRussell in Silverman 118: They'll King it over all, and rule the Rost. *1692* Bulkeley *Will* 87: They rul'd the roast. *1721* Wise *Word* 174. a*1731* Cook *Bacon* 314: Berkeley, Ruler of the Roast. *1739* Belcher *Papers* 2.222. *1763* Watts *Letter Book* 168. *1770* Franklin *Papers* 17.221. *1778* Curwen *Journal and Letters* 209. *1781* WGrayson in Reed *Life* 2.354. *1781* JLovell in *Adams FC* 4.163. *1782* Freneau *Poems* 2.158: 'Tis strange that they always would manage the roast. *1789* *Columbian Magazine* 3.494. *1791* Morris *Diary and Letters* 1.383. *1791* *Universal Asylum* 6.226. *1794* Morris *Diary and Letters* 2.60. *1796* *Echo* 224. *1797* Cobbett *Porcupine* 5.417: When the married lady . . . rules the conjugal roast, 7.197: He foresaw Sambo would soon rule the roast. *1797* Tyler *Prose* 219. *1802* Chester *Federalism* 9: The danger of republicans ruling the roast. *1807* *Weekly* 1.191. *1813* Freneau *Poems* 3.316. *1817* Scott *Blue Lights* 103. *1819* Drake *Works* 302. *Oxford* 687; Whiting R152. See **R131.**

R100 To cry **Roast** meat

1781 Adams *Works* 7.492: I wish . . . he had eaten his chicken without crying roast meat. *1795* Cobbett *Porcupine* 2.62: I hope we shall have too much sense to run about crying roast meat. *Oxford* 158; Tilley M849.

R101 To give one **Roast** meat and beat him with the spit

1763 Gadsden *Writings* 26: We can by no means think, that because a gentleman has given us roast meat, he has therefore a right to beat us with the spit. *Oxford* 680; Tilley M147.

R102 **Robbers** must exalted be, *etc.*

1748 Franklin *PR* 3.248: Robbers must exalted be, Small ones on the Gallow-tree, While greater ones ascend to Thrones, But what is that to thee or me? Whiting L456, M94. See **C128.**

R103 As round as a **Robin**

1784 Hopkinson *Miscellaneous Essays* 1.250: As round aye, as round as a robin. *1821* Pintard *Letters* 2.61: Mrs C. is very thin & looks like a shade alongside yʳ enbonpoint sister who is as round as a Robin, 75.

R104 Many talk of **Robin Hood** who never shot in his bow

1736 Franklin *PR* 2.140: As many Men do talk of Robin Hood Who never did shoot Arrow in his Bow. *Oxford* 761; Whiting R156.

R105 Songs of **Robin Hood**

1782 Franklin *Writings* 8.443: Your common people in their ale-houses sing the twenty-four songs of Robin Hood, and applaud his deer-stealing and his robberies on the highway. *Oxford* 803; Whiting R157.

R106 To go round **Robin Hood's** barn

1797 Weems *Letters* 2.76-7: I can sell them abundantly fast without the trouble of going round Robin Hood's barn. *1799* *Port Folio* 2NS 7(1812) 339: To follow a winding road is going, "round about Robin Hood's barn." Barbour 154; TW 308.

R107 As firm as a **Rock**

1759 Ames *Almanacs* 291: Firm as a Rock. *1766* Bartram *Diary* 54: The water . . . seeming as firm as A rock. *1774* WTudor in *Adams FC* 1.149. *1776* JLangdon in *Naval Documents* 5.704: They ever have been firm as Rocks, near relatives to the Yankees. *1777* JAdams in *Warren-Adams Letters* 1.293. *1781* EPendleton in Madison *Papers* 3.34. *1792* RTroup in Jay *Correspondence* 3.430. *1796* Barton *Disappoint-*

ment 29. **1802** Chester *Federalism* 18: They've got Bishop into office as firm as a rock. **1809** Irving *History* 2.140: Here stood stout Risingh, firm as a thousand rocks. **1809** Weems *Marion* 80: Firm as a rock of granite. **1812** Lee *Memoirs* 1.181. **a1815** Freneau *Poems* 3.309. **1816** Adams *Memoirs* 3.277. **1829** Smith *Letters* 282. **1831** Jackson *Correspondence* 4.383: Virginia . . . is as firm as a rock, 384. **1847** Cooper *Letters* 5.240, **1848** 387. *Oxford* 261; TW 308-9(2).

R108 As hard as a **Rock**

1650 Bradstreet *Works* 175: The prince of plumbs, whose stone's as hard as Rock. **1723** Symmes *Utile* 49: His Face, is harder than a Rock. **1737** RNorton in *Letters from Hudson Bay* 228: Froze as hard as a rock. **1745** Brainerd *Memoirs* 238. **1775** Freneau *Poems* 1.175. **1786** Hunter *Quebec* 236: My bed was hard as a rock. **1816** Freneau *Last Poems* 17: The heart of the Blacksmith, as hard as a rock. **1818** Bentley *Diary* 4.516. **1821** Freneau *Last Poems* 38: With hearts as hard as granite rock. Barbour 154(2); Svartengren 156; TW 309(3). See **S454**.

R109 As solid as a **Rock**

1789 Jefferson *Papers* 15.335: They must be packed as solid as rock to avoid being destroyed. **1791** Henry *Life* 3.626: Our government and national existence . . . are as solid as a rock. Whiting *NC* 467(3). Cf. Whiting R160.

R110 As steadfast as a **Rock**

1804 Delano *Narrative* 471: And assisted in searching for the boat, which we found lying on the bottom as stedfast as a rock.

R111 As unshaken as a **Rock**

1831 Jackson *Correspondence* 4.342: Old faithful Pennsylvania remains as unshaken as a rock.

R112 The **Rock** one will split on

1734 DHorsmanden in *Colden Letters* 2.105: I think twil be the Rock of Rocks that the Deluded man will Split upon. **1765** Watts *Letter Book* 402: But what is *reasonable* when we come to the Point will be the Rock I am afraid we shall split upon.

1781 Jefferson *Papers* 4.398: If there be a rock on which we are to split, it is the want of muskets, **1787** 12.445. **1802** *Port Folio* 2.17: Upon this rock . . . your newly launched bark will most probably split. Colcord 151; NED Rock *sb.*[1] 2a; TW 309(8).

R113 To go up like a **Rocket** and fall like the stick

1782 Paine *American Crisis* 1.197: As he rose like a rocket, he would fall like a stick, **1783** *Rhode Island* 2.360. **1818** Mason *Memoir* 199: Tom Paine, in speaking, or rather writing of some one, says, "He went up like a rocket and came down like the stick." *Oxford* 308.

R114 Spare the **Rod** and spoil the child

1740 Byrd *Letters* in *VHM* 37(1929) 107: When the question lys between Sparing the Rod or Spoiling the child. **1774** Carter *Diary* 2.903: So that Solomon was a damned fool when he said spare the rod and spoil the child. **1818** Fessenden *Ladies Monitor* 84: You spare the rod, and you may spoil the child, And yet the rod has many children spoil'd. **1820** Irving *Sketch Book* 458: the golden maxim. Barbour 154; *Oxford* 759; Whiting Y1. See **L247**.

R115 To have **Rods** in pickle (soak)

a1731 Cook *Bacon* 313: For Fortune, that is ever fickle, And always has some Rods in Pickle. **1788** WSmith in King *Life* 1.310: England will feel the end of the rod which is in soak for him. **1799** Carey *Plumb* 47: in soke. **1807** TTodd in Clay *Papers* 1.296: in soak. **1816** Smith *Life* 350: in pickle. **1820** Simpson *Journal* 131: in pickle. **1846** MVan Buren in Paulding *Letters*(*II*) 429-30: But I have a rod in pickel for some of them. *Oxford* 682; Tilley R157.

R116 To kiss the **Rod**

1654 Johnson *Wonder-Working* 222: And kiss thy rod. **c1656** Bradstreet *Works* 18: Walk in his Law, and kisse his Rod. **1672** Williams *Writings* 6.361: Your humble kissing of his holy rod. **1701** Taylor *Poems* 154: I'll kiss the Rod. **1707** GSaltonstall in *Winthrop Papers*(*B*) 5.411. **1755** Davis *Colonial Virginia Satirist* 22. **1756** Smith

Works 2.101-2. **1759** CCarroll in *MHM* 10(1915) 246: Where is the man of spirit that can behold the rod lifted up, tremble and kiss the hand of him that holds it? **1766** Mason *Papers* 1.72. **1770** Carter *Diary* 1.472: The inspired pen of many a writer seems to recommend that we should kiss the rod of affliction. **1771** JTemple in *Bowdoin Papers* 1.284: Like a Spaniel [they] meanly cringed, & kiss'd the rod that whip'd 'em. **1774** Willard *Letters* 34: The greatest boasters among us will kiss the rod. **1775** Ames *Almanacs* 452. **1775** Jefferson *Papers* 1.270: And kiss the rod with which he deigns to scourge us. **1776** Adams *Works* 9.396: For the past, I kiss the rod. **1776** Washington *Writings* 4.455: They . . . kissed the rod that should be held out for chastisement. **1777** Cresswell *Journal* 262: They kiss the rod that so tyrannically strikes them. **1777** Rush *Letters* 1.130. **1779** AA in *Adams FC* 3.185. **1781** *Washington *Writings* 21.320. **1783** *American Wanderer* 109. **1791** Scott *Journal* 303. **1793** *Echo* 57: And school-boy like, most humbly kiss the rod. **1794** "Franklin" in Hamilton *Papers* 17.175. **1797** PHall in Porter *Negro Writing* 75. **1797** Hamilton *Papers* 20.525. **1797** *Tyler Letters* 1.196. **1799** Adams *Writings* 2.440. **1801** Eaton *Life* 190: Then bid us kiss the rod! *This is the price of peace.* **1804** Alden *Epitaphs* 4.234: We check our grief and kiss the rod. **1804** *Echo* 312: Half Europe kiss the iron rod. **1806** Dunlap *Diary* 2.386. **c1810** Foster *Jeffersonian America* 153. **1815** *Port Folio* 3NS 5.41. **1819** Noah *Travels* 422. **1820** Cottle *Life* 384, 385. **1826** Pintard *Letters* 2.266, 285. *Oxford* 430; TW 309(1); Whiting Y3. See **H60.**

R117 To make a **Rod** for one's own back (*varied*)

1681 SBradstreet in *Mather Papers* 478: The great Conservators . . . in the Bay, are making rods for their own backs, & the backs of others. **1686** Sewall *Diary* 2.23*: And now God was whiping them with a Rod of their own making. **1697** Calef *More Wonders* 40: The devils could get nothing, but, like fools, a scourge for their own backs. **1701** Taylor *Christographia* 9.53-5: He hath . . . made a [rod] for his own back,

and found out a Stone that hath broken his own Head, **1703** 323: Such make but a rod for their own back. **1774** Willard *Letters* 22. **1776** Paine *Common Sense* 1.6: The public will be secured by the prudent reflection of not making a rod for themselves, **1778** *People of Pennsylvania* 2.300: They . . . are making a rod for themselves and their heirs. **1790** Maclay *Journal* 257: I have no objection to see them whipped with their own rod. *Oxford* 681-2; Whiting S652. See **R139, S395, 431.**

R118 To rule with a **Rod** of iron

1728 Byrd *Dividing Line* 6: This Gentleman, it seems, ruled them with a Rod of Iron. **1822** Gallatin *Diary* 211: Madame du Cayla absolutely rules him with a rod of iron. *Oxford* 687.

R119 As nimble as the **Roe**

1650 Bradstreet *Works* 166: My comely legs as nimble as the Roe. Cf. Lean 2.858: doe.

R120 As swift as a **Roe**

1725 Wolcott *Poetical Meditations* 65: Mason swift as the chased Roe. **1809** Weems *Marion* 77: Swifter than a roe buck. Svartengren 377; Whiting R170.

R121 A rich **Rogue** is like a fat hog, *etc.*

1733 Franklin *PR* 1.313; A rich rogue, is like a fat hog, who never does good til as dead as a log. *Oxford* 376, 795; Tilley M1005.

R122 **Rogues** hang together

1797 Cobbett *Porcupine* 5.204: That . . . all the world may exclaim, *"See how rogues hang together,"* 9.360: I have always thought that rogues hang together better than honest men.

R123 Set a **Rogue** (thief) to catch a rogue (thief)

1676 PWalker in Jantz 55: Imploy a wily Roag to cach a thefe. **1702** Mather *Magnalia* 2.574: Set a thief to catch a thief. **1708** Cook *Sot-Weed* 24: I set one Rogue to catch another. **1775** Moore *Diary* 1.135: [They] have herein verified the ancient aphorism, viz.: *set a rogue to catch a rogue.* **1778** Lee(W) *Letters* 2.495: You know the common saying, "Set one Rogue to catch another." **1779** *Belknap Papers* 2.24-5: It seems to be constructed on the old maxim, "Set a rogue to catch a rogue." Barbour 179: Thief(2); *Oxford* 810; TW 309, 386(6). See **T41.**

R124 When **Rogues** fall out, honest men may come to their dues (*varied*)

1740 Stephens *Journal(I)* 2.55: And it is allowed to be a never-failing Maxim, that the *Indians* falling out with one another, never forebodes any Ill to us. **1742** Franklin *PR* 2.336: When Knaves fall out, honest Men get their goods: When Priests dispute, we come at the Truth. **1774** JWarren in *Warren-Adams Letters* 1.23: If they quarrel in the settlement of that matter, we may avail ourselves of the old Proverb. **1777** Adams(S) *Writings* 3.370: I am informed that General Carleton and his Brother have been very ill used and are greatly disgusted with the British Court. That Lord George Sackville and all the Scotch hate them, and they him. You remember the old Proverb. **1795** DLyman in *Winslow Papers* 415: The saying will be well verified there, When Rogues fall out &c. **1798** HGOtis in *Warren-Adams Letters* 2.335: Or whether the five Kings will squabble with each other, so that "honest men may come to their dues." **1838** Jackson *Correspondence* 5.545: You must recollect the old adage, "When rogues fall out, truth is revealed, and honest men get justice." *Oxford* 810-1; Whiting T83.

R125 A **Roland** for one's Oliver

1775 ACary in *Naval Documents* 3.228: Give the deluded publisher a Rowland for his Oliver. **1778** RIzard in Deane *Papers* 3.209: But I sent him a Roland for his Oliver. **1778** *New Jersey Gazette* in *Newspaper Extracts(II)* 2.29: [He] has already had such a *Rowland* for his *Oliver.* **1778** JSewall in Curwen *Journal and Letters* 208. **1800** Freneau *Prose* 433: I know you can give *Oliver* a *Roland.* **1802** Adams *D and A* 3.317: I made it a rule to return him a Rowland for every Oliver. **1803** *Port Folio* 3.77. **1808** TPickering in McHenry *Letters* 547. **1809** Quincy *JQuincy* 181: Give to any and all men . . . what politicians call a

Rowland for their Oliver. **1806** Fessenden *Modern Philosopher* 215: In case any of our Olivers chance to meet with a Rowland, 226: Swore he'd be our Oliver's Rowland. **1809** JTrumbull in King *Life* 5.154. **1811** Graydon *Memoirs* 349. **1811** Wirt *Letters* 1.314. **c1820** Bernard *Retrospections* 133. *Oxford* 682; TW 309-10.

R126 **Rome** was not built in a day

1646 *Hutchinson Papers* 1.236: Rome was not built in a day. **1676** Tompson *Poems* 60: *Rome* took more time to grow than twice six hours. **1711** Johnston *Papers* 78: Rome was not built in a day. **1773** Winslow *Diary* 72. **1776** AA in *Adams FC* 2.47. **1779** Van Schaack *Letters* 189: Remember that the greatest works have arisen from the smallest beginnings; but this was not done in a day. Rome, the mistress of the world, was founded by a few vagrants. **1785** *Sans Souci* 14. **1788** Parsons *Life* 530. **1812** Adams *Works* 10.24: Washington city was not built in a day, any more than Rome. **1814** *Port Folio* 3NS 4.218. **1817** Royall *Letters* 95: As if she actually intended to give the lie to the old proverb, that "Rome was not built in a day." **1837** Clark *Letters* 95. Barbour 154(1); *Oxford* 683; Whiting R183. See **W362.**

R127 To fiddle while **Rome** is burning

1798 Ames *Letters* 1.235: Congress fiddles while our Rome is burning.

R128 When in **Rome** do as the Romans do (*varied*)

c1680 Radisson *Voyages* 85: Many flemings wondered, & could not perceive how those could love me so well; but the pleasure caused it, as it agrees well wth the Roman proverbe, "doe as they doe." **1718** SShute in *Baxter Manuscripts* 9.376: You know the Old saying, Cum Fueris Romae Romano Vivito More. **1766** AA in *Adams FC* 1.55: My advice to you is among the Romans, do as the romans do. **1783** Williams *Penrose* 174: When a man is in Rome he must comply with the Roman customs or he will lead a miserable life there. **1796** Lee *Diary and Letters* 11: I quieted my conscience with the old saying, "When you are among the heathen, do as the heathen do." **1800** Cleveland *Letters* 59: I am now a Dane, and must do as the Danes do. **1803** Davis *Travels* 356-7: A man of sense will conform with the customs of every country, (and at *Rome,* as my Lord *Chesterfield* elegantly observes, kiss either the *Pope's* great toe, or his b—k—e). **1813** Bayard *Papers* 487: Quand on est a Rome il faut faire commes des Romains. **1816** *Port Folio* 4NS 2.289: Every one was obliged to uncover his head as they passed, and we did as Rome did [in Spain]. **1819** Waln *Hermit* 41: When you are in Rome—you know. **1826** Duane *Colombia* 89: It is best to "do as they do in Rome." **1826** Jones *Sketches* 1.120. **1828** Pinkney *Works* 165: The soul, "at Rome," conformed and was a Roman. **1849** Paulding *Letters(II)* 502: Instead of following the safe rule of doing in Turkey as the Turks do. Barbour 154(2); *Oxford* 683; TW 210(2). Cf. Whiting D273, R184.

R129 As ragged as **Rooks**

1809 Weems *Marion* 224: We were all as ragged as young rooks. Cf. NED Ragged a^1 1c.

R130 One's **Room** is better than his company (*varied*)

1724 Jones *Virginia* 87: Felons . . . whose room they had much rather have than their company. **1728** Byrd *Dividing Line* 57: Tho' he did no other good but favour us with his Room instead of his Company. **1776** JSmith in *Naval Documents* 3.725: His room will prove much more agreeable than his Company. **1781** BFranklin in Adams *Works* 7.476: [They] had rather at present have the General's absence than his company. *Oxford* 683; TW 310(3). See **L223.**

R131 To rule the **Roost**

1769 ABlair in *W&MCQ* 16(1907) 175: They say, she rules the Roost. **1821** Knight *Poems* 2.170: That man his marriage-day will rue, When partlet rules the roost. **1831** Cooper *Letters* 2.76: In ten years, the picture will be very different—In twenty we rule the roost. **1841** Hone *Diary* 2.545, **1850** 905. Barbour 154; TW 310. See **R99.**

R132 To destroy (*etc.*) **Root** and branch

1705 Beverley *History* 34: So that the Indians . . . formed a Stratagem to destroy them Root and Branch. **1761** *Johnson Papers* 3.520: To extirpate them Root and branch. **1777** JA in *Adams FC* 2.329, **1778** 3.57: They must be eradicated Root and Branch, **1780** 414. c1812 Putnam *Memoirs* 115. **1815** Asbury *Letters* 3.525. **1837** TBenton in Jackson *Correspondence* 5.519: But as I wish to make "a root and branch business of it." TW 311(1).

R133 As disagreeable as a **Rope** to a thief

1788 May *Journal* 81: The roar of a cannon is as disagreeable to an Indian as a rope is to a thief. Cf. *Oxford* 683; Whiting R194. See **T42.**

R134 Avoid talking about **Ropes** (in the house of a man that was hanged)

1801 *Port Folio* 1.318: This careless writer surely forgot the French proverb, to avoid talking about *ropes* on certain occasions. *Oxford* 684; TW 311(8).

R135 Give one enough **Rope** and he'll hang himself (*varied*)

1698 JUsher in *W&MCQ* 3S 7(1950) 106: Theres a saying give Men Rope enough, they will hang themselves. **1780** AA in *Adams FC* 3.406: Give an extensive cord, and you know the adage. **1782** Lee(W) *Letters* 3.887: Give a Rogue rope enough & he will soon hang himself. **1799** *Washington Writings* 37.323: I am persuaded that if a rope, a little longer had been given him, he would have hung himself up something worse. **1802** Paine *To the Citizens* 2.910: Give them rope enough and they will put an end to their own insignificance. **1804** Dow *Journal* 217: Here I must observe the truth of the maxim, "Give the devil rope enough and he will hang himself." **1805** Paine *To Mr. Hulbert* 2.977. **1806** *Austin Papers* 1.112: Give such men tether enough and they will hang themselves. **1818** Royall *Letters* 177: As a friend of mine once said, "all the common people want rope enough," **1821** 225: All your citizens want is rope. Barbour 155(1); *Oxford* 683; TW 311(2).

R136 (Not to know) the **Ropes**

1774 JA in *Adams FC* 1.131: He is ignorant of every Rope in the Ship. Barbour 155(3); Colcord 152; *Oxford* 435; TW 311(3).

R137 **Rope**(s) of sand

c1645 JCotton in Williams *Writings* 2.39: Both which hang upon that ground like ropes of sand. ?1689 ?Mather *Vindication* in *Andros Tracts* 2.59-60: This 'tis to make *Ropes of Sand!* 1754 JGlen in McDowell *Documents* 1.478: They . . . consider us as a Rope of Sand, loose and inconnected. 1764 Johnson *Writings* 3.281: It is . . . a pretty well twisted rope of sand, which . . . crumbles into dust. 1774 Adams(S) *Writings* 3.131: They were a Rope of Sand in Reality. 1774 Asbury *Journal* 1.127. 1775 Adams *D and A* 2.190: We shall become a Rope of Sand. 1775 Asbury *Journal* 1.159. 1775 NGreene in Ward *Correspondence* 153. 1775 TWilling in Adams *Works* 2.454. 1776 JHawley in Gerry *Letters* 1.161. 1776 Serle *Journal* 117: The American Rope of Sand is beginning to fall in Pieces. 1777 JTrumbull, Jr., in *Trumbull Papers* 3.200. 1778 Adams *D and A* 2.304. 1779 Deane *Papers* 3.274. 1779 Sullivan *Letters* 2.529: My Line when extended and for this purpose, is not unlike a rope of Sand. 1779 JWarren in *Warren-Adams Letters* 2.92: We are a rope of Sand without any Cement. 1781 Jones *Letters* 78. 1781 RMorris in *Clinton Papers* 7.139: That our Union is a rope of Sand. 1782 Heath *Memoirs* 345. 1782 *Washington *Writings* 24.347: We are no better than a rope of Sand and are as easily broken asunder. 1783 Adams *Works* 8.78. 1783 ALee in Madison *Papers* 6.273: He had rather see Congress a rope of sand than a rod of Iron. 1783 Van Schaack *Letters* 337. 1785 *Washington *Writings* 28.93. 1788 Rush *Letters* 1.495. 1789 AYates in *W&MCQ* 3S 20(1963) 241. 1800 Adams *Works* 9.87. 1801 *Columbian Centinel* in Buckingham *Specimens* 2.85. 1807 EGerry in *Adams-Warren Correspondence* 498. 1807 Weems *Letters* 2.369. 1808 Bentley *Diary* 3.343. 1809 Weems *Marion* 80: Loose as a rope of sand. 1810 RTroup in *W&MCQ* 3S 13(1947) 216. 1810 *Tyler Letters* 1.245. 1811 Graydon *Memoirs* 358.

1813 Morris *Diary and Letters* 2.553: The buzz of political speculations by those who "ropes of sand can twist." 1814 *Smith Papers* 3.168: [It] is like attempting to drag Field Pieces with ropes of Sand. 1815 Adams *Works* 10.109: You say . . . that "I built upon the sand." . . . I had no material for a foundation, but a rope of it. 1815 Asbury *Letters* 3.524. 1815 Waterhouse *Journal* 210. a1824 Marshall *Kentucky* 1.256: It was, they said, a rope of sand —a sovereign without subjects. 1832 JRandolph in Jackson *Correspondence* 4.422: But if as I believe and *fear* this Rope of Sand, miscalled the federal Governmant, shall go to pieces, 499. *Oxford* 684; TW 311(1).

R138 To be on the high **Rope**(s)

?1711 Byrd *Secret Diary* 269: He was on the high rope and gave me back my papers, 1719 *London Diary* 322: I found him on the high rope but at last he agreed to write a letter by me. 1758 Franklin *Papers* 8.100: Tho' the Proprietaries are at present on the high Ropes. 1767 *Beekman Papers* 1.514: Since he is Upon his high Ropes dont abate him one farthing. 1771 CCarroll in *MHM* 13(1908) 252. 1790 Morris *Diary* 2.57: The Baron is as usual on the high Ropes of royal Prerogative. 1802 Barlow *Letters* 187. 1808 Jefferson *Writings* 1.488: The letter of Canning . . . was written in the high ropes and would be stinging to every American breast. *Oxford* 372; Tilley R175. See **H320.**

R139 To twist **Ropes** to hang oneself

1809 Fessenden *Pills* 70: You're twisting ropes to hang yourselves! See **R117, S295, 431.**

R140 As beauteous as the **Rose**

1802 Humphreys *Works* 97.10: The wilderness bloom beauteous as the rose.

R141 As blooming as a **Rose**

1719 Byrd *Another Secret Diary* 408: P-lly . . . Blooming like Rose, and bright Lilly. 1787 Adams *Diary* 297: The eldest daughter . . . blooming as a rose. 1798 Adams *New Letters* 135: Blooming as a rose in June. TW 311(1).

R142   As fresh as a **Rose**

1776 JA in *Adams FC* 2.75: She . . . looks as fresh as a Rose. **1778** Lee(W) *Letters* 2.505: The young lady is as fresh as a rose. *Oxford* 668; Whiting R198.

R143   As red and white as a **Rose**

1801 Story *Shop* 26: As red and white as a rose. Barbour 155(5); Whiting R199.

R143a   **Rosey-red**

1771 Hamilton *Papers* 1.6: A rosey-red o'er spread her face. Whiting R199a.

R144   As sweet as a **Rose**(bud)

1772 Paterson *Glimpses* 115: Sweet as the Rosebud in the Spring. **1788** May *Journal* 90: I found her as sweet as a rose. **1851** Clark *Letters* 127: And all came safe, and sweet as a rose in June. Whiting R201.

R145   No **Rose** without a thorn

1734 Franklin *PR* 1.352: You cannot pluck roses without fear of thorns, Nor enjoy a fair wife without danger of horns. **1759** Murray *Letters* 101: Your Roses are mix'd with thorns. **1777** POliver in Hutchinson *Diary* 2.128: But every species of roses hath its disagreeable prickles. **1786** Jefferson *Papers* 10.451: We have no rose without its thorn. **1787** Adams *Diary* 357-8: I might in that manner pluck the rose, without pricking my finger with the thorn. **1787** WSSmith in Smith *Journal and Correspondence* 1.162-3: I have often wondered when people have their choice, they do not as frequently pick up a rose, as meddle with a thorn, 173: Persons who seem disposed to pluck the thorn rather than the rose. **1791** Cary *Letters* 87: Our journey is strewed with thorns as well as roses. **1794** *Washington Writings* 33.359: Mr. Bl—ts Agency will, it is feared, be more productive of thorns than roses. **1795** Cobbett *Porcupine* 2.308: Independence . . . is not a rose without a thorn. **1798** McHenry *Letters* 308: Places where there are more thorns than roses. **c1800** Paine *Works* 116: For you, its roses bloom, "without a thorn." **1802** Humphreys *Works* 104.283-4: Nor deem him hostile who of danger warns, Who leaves the rose, but plucks away its thorns. **1807** *Emerald* 2.71: A rose without a thorn. **1807** Maxwell *Mysterious* 17.164-5: With blooming beauties, like the budded rose, which only serv'd to hide the thorn beneath. **1808** *Emerald* NS 1.130: The *Rose* without a thorn. **1815** Adams *Writings* 5.264: It is probably from the thorns of their dissentions that we have plucked the rose of peace, **1817** 6.194: There are roses as well as thorns in the paths of public life. **1820** Robertson *Letters* 270: There is no rose without a thorn. **1828** *Yankee* 288: We can't get rosy-posies without sometimes being wounded by thorns . . . I have mentioned this old maxim. Barbour 155(3); *Oxford* 684, Whiting R204, 206. See **J54, N106.**

R146   To beat old **Rose**

1815 Humphreys *Yankey* 87: But these marvellous cummings together, beat old Rose in the gun-room. Cf. Tilley R183.

R147   To blush like a **Rose**

1772 Paterson *Glimpses* 116: Modestly blushing as the Rose. NED Blush *v.*[1] 3, quote c1532; Whiting *NC* 468(6).

R148   To pluck a **Rose**

1800 WVMurray in American Antiquarian Society, *Proceedings* NS 12(1897) 248: Mrs. M. having occasion to pluck a rose as is usual with delicate women after a ride of 22 miles. *Oxford* 623; Tilley R184.

R149   **Sub Rosa** [The following is a selection from 37 occurrences of the phrase]

1747 Laurens *Papers* 1.23. **1766** Montresor *Journals* 345. **1772** Adams *D and A* 2.71. **1775** JEliot in *Belknap Papers* 3.83: The *sub rosa* paragraph afforded me much diversion. **1781** RCranch in *Adams FC* 4.179: Sub rosae. **1783** Baldwin *Life and Letters* 153. **1784** Smith *Diary* 1.6: It is imagined Shelburne visits the Court now Sub Rosa. **1802** *St. Clair Papers* 2.558. **1812** Adams *Memoirs* 2.425. **1816** JAdams in *Adams-Jefferson Letters* 2.486. **1822** Watterston *Winter* 20.

R150   Under the **Rose** [The following is a selection from 61 occurrences of the phrase]

1707 JWinthrop in *Winthrop Papers*(B) 5.389. **1708** INorris in *Penn-Logan Correspondence* 2.255: To speak my mind under the rose. **1713** WBassett in *VHM* 23(1915) 360. **1717** JWinthrop in *Mather Papers* 682. **1764** *Beekman Papers* 1.476. **1770** Carter *Diary* 1.521: But this under my own rose. **1775** JA in *Adams FC* 1.214. **1775** *Washington *Writings* 4.97 [and 11 times subsequently]. **1779** NGreene in Webb *Correspondence* 2.209. **1779** Jefferson *Papers* 3.13. **1779** *New Jersey Gazette* in *Newspaper Extracts(II)* 3.54: We were in hopes at first of keeping Van Kirk under the rose, but the secret is out. **1783** Williams *Penrose* 299: This part of the game was plaid off under the rose. **1790** Jefferson *Papers* 3.13. **1798** Cobbett *Porcupine* 8.85: While these Baltimore *federalists* were mumping their morsel quietly under the rose. **1809** Irving *History* 2.122. **1812** Jackson *Correspondence* 1.237 [and 8 times subsequently]. **1817** *Port Folio* 4NS 3.201: *To speak a thing under the rose;* and *under the rose be it spoken;* are phrases of some difficulty, though the sense of them be well enough understood; they mean *secretly;* but the query is, how they came to imply that. The clergyman wears a rose in his hat; and in confession what is spoken in his ear, is in effect under the rose, and is to be kept secret, as being under the seal of confession. **1819** Robertson *Letters* 105: One hot roll eaten under the rose. **1832** Longfellow *Letters* 1.382. *Oxford* 854; TW 312(9). See **T63.**

R151 Under the **Rose** a merkin

1682 J. W. *Letter* 9: They should have Roses clapt upon their Merkins; which is the original of our new Proverb, *Under the Rose a Merkin.* Cf. NED Merkin.

R152 **Rough** and ready

1746 Cooper *Letters* 5.163: Our passage from Providence was not "rough and ready" but rough and rainy. DA rough-and-ready; NED Rough-and-ready; *Oxford* 685.

R153 **Rough** and (or) smooth

1775 JMacpherson in Read *Correspondence* 116: I wish for the roughs as well as the smooths of a soldier's life. **1799** Denny *Journal* 476: I am determined to make the best

of what offers—rough or smooth. *Oxford* 685; Whiting R220. See **I19.**

R154 There's the **Rub**

1774 Adams *Works* 4.40: Ay, there's the rub, **1775** *Adams FC* 1.332: There's the Rub. **1785** *Sans Soucie* 9. **1788** Belknap *Papers* 1.500: Ay, 2.76: Ay. **1794** DAllison in *Blount Papers* 2.445: And save me perhaps from some hard rubs. **1795** Smith(EH) *Diary* 94: Aye. **1798** Manning *Key* 42: Ah here is the rub. **1799** Moultrie *Memoirs* 1.335. **1800** Gadsden *Writings* 288: Here is the rub. **1814** JAdams in *Adams-Jefferson Letters* 2.436: Aye! **1814** Kerr *Barclay* 356: Ay, ay. **1815** Humphreys *Yankey* 60: But how to get there, that is the rub. **1821** *Adams-Waterhouse Correspondence* 152: Aye! **1826** Jones *Sketches* 1.95. **1841** Cooper *Letters* 4.114: I think he will flinch at the rub. *Oxford* 686; Shakespeare *Hamlet* III i 65: Aye, there's the rub; TW 313. See **S428.**

R155 To beat the **Rub**

1813 Knopf *War of 1812* 5(2) 11: We only want an opportunity to "get our hands in," that we may "beat the rub."

R156 To throw (find) **Rubs** in one's way

1740 Stephens *Journal(I)* 2.37: I told him that I should be so far from throwing any Rubs in his Way, that I should do my part in getting his Appointment fulfilled, **1745** *Journal(II)* 2.260: No wonder (if that was the Case) why we of this Colony should find some Rubs in our way, to prevent matters running so smoothly on. NED Rub *sb.*[1] 3.

R157 To meet **Rubbers**

1776 *Pennsylvania Journal* in *Newspaper Extracts(II)* 1.27: And I am mistaken if they don't meet some severe rubbers. NED Rubber *sb.*[1] 1b.

R158 To pass the **Rubicon**

1774 Chandler *Friendly Address* 30: The Rubicon has been passed. **1774** Hutchinson *Diary* 1.139: If we have not passed the Rubicon this winter, we never shall. **1776** Deane *Papers* 1.444. **1776** Paine *Common Sense* 1.45. **1776** Sullivan *Letters* 1.196. **1777** Burd *Letters* 100: It is as bad as passing the

Rubicon. **1778** Mason *Papers* 1.435. **1779** Chipman *Writings* 31. **1781** Adams *Correspondence* 517. **1781** Jay *Correspondence* 2.62: But take Spain as she is, if she could be prevailed upon to pass the Rubicon, that is, to acknowledge . . . our independence. **1781** Oliver *Origin* 103. **1782** Freneau *Prose* 82. **1783** Jones *Letters* 99. **1787** Paine *Prospects on the Rubicon* 2.623. **a1788** Jones *History* 1.36. **1788** Washington *Writings* 29.431: With *some,* to have differed in sentiment, is to have passed the Rubicon of their friendship. **1789** Jefferson *Papers* 15.459: It will be against that which shall first pass the Rubicon of reconciliation with the other. **1789** Maclay *Journal* 120, 326. **1789** Morris *Diary* 1.145: These poor Fellows have passed the Rubicon with a Witness. **1798** Cabot *Letters* 159. **1802** Adams *D and A* 3.314. **1802** *Port Folio* 2.31. **1803** Austin *Constitutional* 197. **1806** Plumer *Memorandum* 444. **1808** Grant *Memoirs* 2.124. **1811** Graydon *Memoirs* 157: The step was considered wise, although a passage of the Rubicon, and calculated to close the door to accomodation. **1812** Adams *Memoirs* 2.381. **1812** Hitchcock *Social* 172: The work . . . had passed the *Rubicon* of inspection. **1816** Fidfaddy *Adventures* 43. **1819** Adams *Memoirs* 4.450: We had crossed the Rubicon without looking before or behind us. **1819** Adams *Works* 4.8. **1829** MBarney in Jackson *Correspondence* 4.45. **1845** Cooper *Letters* 5.89: And now he considers himself as past the Rubicon, on the side of safety. *Oxford* 684; TW 313.

R159   As ruddy as **Rubies**

1695 Taylor *Poems* 106: In Bodie ruddier than Rubies.

R160   **Ruby-red**

1798 TGFessenden in Buckingham *Specimens* 2.217: The ruby red tint. NED Ruby-red; Whiting R224.

R161   It is a poor **Rule** that will not work both ways

1837 Cooper *Letters* 3.281: There is a healthful axiom which says, "It is a poor rule that will not work both ways." Barbour 156; TW 313(1). See **W67.**

R162   **Rule** of thumb

1787 *Columbian Magazine* 1.247: And rifled by the rule of thumb. *Oxford* 687; Tilley R203.

R163   The **Ruler** shows the man

1777 Moore *Diary* 1.384: 'Tis an old and true observation, *Magistratus indicat Virum,* "the Ruler shows the Man."

R164   In the long **Run**

1747 WSJohnson in Johnson *Writings* 1.121: It will do him no good in the long run. *Oxford* 480.

R165   He that **Runs** fastest is the best

1736 Gyles *Memoirs* 15: He was the best Man that could run fastest. *Oxford* 689; Whiting R239.

R166   He that **Runs** may read

1642 SGorton in Winslow *Hypocrisie* 15: That he that runs may read them. **1644** Williams *Writings* 3.369: He that *runs* may *read* and tremble at. **1720** JColman *Distressed State* in *Colonial Currency* 2.80. **1740** Byrd *Letters* in *VHM* 37(1929) 32: Writ in so plain a Hand, that he that runs might read it. **1753** *Independent Reflector* 271. **1776** MEarle in *Naval Documents* 3.702: In plain and express Terms, that he who runs might read. **1783** RPeters in *Thomson Papers* 178: This would be a lesson according to the old adage, he that *runs may read,* and I am sure if we do not *read* in case of another war, we shall *run,* as the Corporal told the Colonel. **1797** *Washington Writings* 35.457: Our cause is plain; they who run may read it, **1798** 36.497: His object, to those who are not determined to be blind, may be read as they run. **1799** Carey *Plumb* 17. **1799** *Washington Writings* 37.323. **1811** JHamm in Knopf *War of 1812* 3.11: In such energetic & plain language that he that runs may read. **1827** Jones *Sketches* 2.157. *Oxford* 689-90; Whiting R236.

R167   As straight as a **Rush**

1744 Hamilton *Itinerarium* 80: His wig was

remarkably weather beaten, the hairs being all as streight as a rush. Apperson 605; Lean 2.877; NED Rush *sb.*[1] 2b; Svartengren 276; Whiting R241.

R168   As thick as **Rushes**

1792 Freneau *Poems* 3.74: Where lords and knights, as thick as rushes grow.

R169   Not care a **Rush**

1676 Tompson *Poems* 50: Merchants car'd not a rush. **1798** *Echo* 155: He does not care a rush. **1816** Paulding *Letters(I)* 1.231. **1835** Cooper *Letters* 3.177. Whiting R245.

R170   Not give a **Rush**

1753 *Johnson Papers* 1.392: I would not give a Rush for it. Whiting R247.

R171   Not regard a **Rush**

1710 Sewall *Letter-Book* 1.406: Regards nor Coin nor Life a Rush. Whiting R248.

R172   Not signify a **Rush**

1750 *Johnson Papers* 1.302: Without any one act y[t] Synifies a rush to their Country. **1779** Lee *Letters* 2.103: Our vigor will signify not a rush. NED Rush *sb.*[1] 2a, quote 1884.

R173   Not value a **Rush**

1809 Irving *History* 2.222: That . . . he valued not a rush. Whiting R247, 251.

R174   Not worth a **Rush**

1675 JCalkins in *Hutchinson Papers* 2.206: Yet is not all hee hath done worth a rush. **1765** JOtis *Vindication* in Bailyn *Pamphlets* 1.563: All other municipal laws that are worth a rush. **1773** Trumbull *Satiric Poems* 77: And sure there's nothing worth a rush in That odd, unnatural trick of blushing. **1779** EHuntington in Webb *Correspondence* 2.232: Money is good for nothing here, no not a Rush. **1787** TBlount in *Blount Papers* 1.362. **1800** Cobbett *Porcupine* 11.217: The family and character of Rush would have remained with me, objects of as perfect insignificance as the poverty-bred plant, the name of which he bears, and the worthlessness of which is proverbial. **1807** Morris *Diary and Letters* 2.502. **1816** Paulding *Letters(I)* 2.183. **1819** Welby *Visit* 205. TW 314(3); Whiting R250.

R175   To tremble like a **Rush**

1803 Davis *Travels* 318-9: I trembled like a rush.

R176   Scratch the **Russian** and find the Tartar

1823 Gallatin *Diary* 229: Very true the saying is, "Scratch the Russian and find the Tartar." *Oxford* 706.

R177   To rub off some of one's **Rust**

1767 *Johnson Papers* 5.844: I admit him to my own Table . . . with a Design to rub off some of his Rust. Cf. Whiting R254.

R178   The **Rutland** wriggle

1816 Paulding *Letters(I)* 1.235: [He] walked with the genuine *Rutland wriggle;* that is to say, on tiptoe, and with a most portentous extension of the hinder parts. DA Rutland (2).

S

S1 To be beyond the **Sabbath** (*varied*)

1757 JFitch in *Mayflower Descendant* 2(1900) 174: [In camp they had to work on Sunday] But Vary Little Resemblence of the Sabath. Indeed one of yᵉ Sentries Said that yᵉ Sabath was Taken Up & Put Into yᵉ Stors at Albony & Not to Be Sufferd to Com Up Here till yᵉ Fort was Finsihd. **1800** Harmon *Sixteen Years* 37: There is no Sabbath in this Country. **1824** Flint *Recollections* 173: It is a common proverb of the people, that when we cross the Mississippi, "we travel beyond the Sabbath." TW 315. See **S529.**

S2 **Sack** and pack

1813 Luttig *Journal* 117: And left the fort sack and pack. See **B24, P3.**

S3 A **Sack** is tied faster before it is filled

1811 *Port Folio* 2NS 1.53: His wits are like a sack, which the French proverb says, is tied faster before it is filled than when it is full. Barbour 156(1); *Oxford* 59; Tilley S2.

S4 To fall like a **Sack**

1802 RSpaight in *Blount Papers* 3.508: But having lost my activity, I fell like a *Sack*. Cf. Whiting S7.

S5 As black as **Sackcloth**

1685 Taylor *Poems* 24: Heavens Curtains blancht with Sun, and Stars of Light Are black as sackcloath to his Garments bright.

S6 The **Saddle** is laid on the wrong horse

1776 Adams(S) *Writings* 3.308: To use a homely Proverb, the Saddle has been laid, or

attempted to be laid on the wrong horse. Tilley S16, quote 1659.

S7 To be in the **Saddle**

a1700 Hubbard *New England* 182: Being contented the elders should sit in the saddle, provided they might hold the bridle, as some have expressed it. **1756** *Johnson Papers* 2.529: You are fairly in the Saddle, and must make the Seat easy. **1777** Smith *Memoirs(II)* 160: The Whiggs are fixing themselves in the Saddle. Barbour 156(2); TW 315(5).

S8 To put the **Saddle** on the right horse

1692 Bulkeley *Will* 87: Let the saddle lay upon the right horse. **1705** Ingles *Reply* 27: That so yᵉ Saddle might be put upon yᵉ right horse. **1756** *Johnson Papers* 2.398: I'll put the saddle on the right horse. **1764** *Paxton Papers* 116: That is as the Proverb is, not putting the Saddle on the right horse. **1766** *Johnson Papers* 5.37. **1774** Quincy *Memoir* 134. **1774** Smith *Memoirs(I)* 178, **1775** 220. **1777** Adams(S) *Writings* 3.397: I hope . . . to use the homely Proverb, the Saddle laid on the right Horse. **1781** Witherspoon *Works* 4.473. **1782** EPendleton in Madison *Papers* 4.443: Let them answer . . . who alone might have saddled the right horse. **1796** Cobbett *Porcupine* 3.421: And, as the saying is, "clapped the saddle on the right horse." **1803** *Port Folio* 3.376: The Plaintiff has not put the saddle on the right horse [a pun]. **1813** TJefferson in *Adams-Jefferson Letters* 2.337: It has been hoped you would leave such expectations as would place every saddle on it's right horse. *Oxford* 690-1; TW 315(2).

S9 Safe and sound

c1680 Radisson *Voyages* 165: If we were not surprized we should come safe and sound wth out hurt to the french. **1764** Watts *Letter Book* 318: Your Liquor in my Custody is all hitherto safe & sound. **1769** JParker in Franklin *Papers* 16.57. **1770** Bowen *Journals* 1.246. **1775** JWadsworth in Webb *Correspondence* 1.125: The widow is safe and sound. **1788** Bowen *Journals* 2.569. **1790** Freneau *Poems* 3.35: Then homeward trudged—half drunk—but safe and sound. **1796** Barton *Disappointment* 13. **1804** WGarnett in *Ruffin Papers* 1.55: I have arrived quite sound and safe. **1808** Barker *Tears* 151. **1815** Otis *Letters* 2.170. **1816** Murphey *Papers* 1.85. **1816** Paulding *Letters(I)* 1.104. **1817** Royall *Letters* 79, 112. **1817** Scott *Blue Lights* 63. **1834** Floy *Diary* 93. **1834** WLewis in Jackson *Correspondence* 5.277: His Bank is sound and safe. **1834** Longfellow *Letters* 1.429. **1843** Cooper *Letters* 4.400, **1845** 5.26, **1851** 6.268. *Oxford* 691; Whiting S10.

S10 The Safety of the people is the supreme law

1636 JWhite in *Winthrop Papers(A)* 3.322: Salus populi suprema lex was wonte to [be] the Rule. **1644** Winthrop *Journal* 2.185: The parliament had taught us, that salus populi is suprema lex, **1645** 240: As if salus populi had been the transcendent rule to walk by. **1653** JHaynes in *Winthrop Papers(B)* 2.464: That ould principle [Latin only]. **1721** *Letter* in *Colonial Currency* 2.253: Salus Populi est Suprema Lex. The Good of a People is the highest Law. **1750** *Some Observations* in *Colonial Currency* 4.414: That Maxim . . . *Salus Populi est suprema Lex,* i.e. The Safety of the People is the ultimate End of Society. **1751** *New York Weekly Post Boy* in *Newspaper Extracts(I)* 3.109: [Latin only]. **1766** Adams *Works* 3.479: The public good, the *salus populi,* is the professed end of all government. **1775** *New York Journal* in *Newspaper Extracts(I)* 11.26: [Latin only]. **1779** *New Jersey Gazette* in *Newspaper Extracts(II)* 4.43: [Latin only]. **1781** Peters *Connecticut* 40: They voted themselves an independent people, and commenced despots, pleading the old adage [Latin only]. **1796** Morris *Diary and Letters* 2.219: The public safety being the supreme law of princes. **1810** Jefferson *Writings* 12.421: Rendered the *salus populi* supreme over the written law, **1821** 1.122: It saves the Republic, which is the first and supreme law.

S11 As yellow as Saffron

1709 Lawson *Voyage* 154: Fat . . . as yellow as Saffron. **1778** Hutchinson *Diary* 2.176: Bliss . . . is as yellow as saffron with the jaundice. Barbour 156; Whiting S11. Cf. TW 315.

S12 To be under full Sail

1796 Bentley *Diary* 2.197: A Brother under full sail, came to invite me to an installation. NED Sail *sb.*[1] 3c.

S13 To fetch up with a wet Sail

1783 Williams *Penrose* 239: I have fetched you up with a wet Sail at last, so that the difference lies only in the departure. Cf. NED Wet 6d.

S14 To have one's top-gallant Sails out

1737 Franklin *Drinkers* 2.177: He's got his Top Gallant Sails out.

S15 To lower one's Sails

1759 CWhittelsey in Stiles *Itineraries* 582: It will lower his Sails somewhat, or else oblige him to tell a Fibb. NED Sail *sb.*[1] 3. Cf. TW 315(2); Whiting S14. See **T209.**

S16 To be (all) plain Sailing

1785 WWhite in Smith *Life and Correspondence* 2.154: It is plain sailing and there can be no errors. **1804** Brackenridge *Modern* 367: All is plain sailing now, 389: All plain sailing with him. **1827** Gallatin *Diary* 272: All will now be plain sailing. Colcord 142; NED Plain sailing.

S17 Good Sailors are tried in a storm

1767 JParker in Franklin *Papers* 14.97: Every One can sail the Sea in fine Weather, good Sailors are try'd in a Storm.

S18 A Sailor has a sweetheart in every port

1745 *Boston Evening Post* in Buckingham

Specimens 1.138: There is no safety in *matrimony*, especially for Sailor's wives. Their husbands may have sweethearts at every port they go to. **1803** Davis *Travels* 424: Adams . . . had, like a true sailor, found a mistress in a foreign port. Stephen Leacock, *My Remarkable Uncle and other Sketches* (1942) (Toronto, 1965) 34: The Jolly Jack Tar is supposed to have "a wife in every port."

S19 **Sailors** are never easy till they get rid of money

1760 *Johnson Papers* 13.195: Like Sailors, who, when they have mony, are never Easy till they get rid of it. Cf. *Oxford* 692.

S20 To take a **Sailor's** leave

1783 Williams *Penrose* 286-7: I took a Sailors leave of my Wife and the rest, leaving them all in tears abruptly, and away we went.

S21 A whistling **Sailor,** a crowing hen, *etc.*

1830 Ames *Mariner's* 247: Whistling at sea is never tolerated except in a calm. "A whistling sailor, a crowing hen and a swearing woman ought all three to go to hell together," so say the *old salts. Oxford* 155, 368; TW 174(7). See **H204.**

S22 Enough to provoke a **Saint**

1787 Hopkinson *Miscellaneous Essays* 2.163: Yet it is enough to provoke a saint. **1811** Sumter *Letters* 79: I have vexation enough to spoil the temper of a Saint & I am not a Saint. **1814** Palmer *Diary* 88: Is not this enough to provoke a Saint? Cf. *Oxford* 696. See **A94, D52, Q3.**

S23 Young **Saint,** old devil

c1675 Saffin *His Book* 16: So that this Honour's your undoubted Due, Of being a young Saint, and an Old one too. **c1700** Taylor *Poems* 407: Young Saint, old Divell. **1702** Mather *Magnalia* 1.592: There has been a trite proverb, which I wish indeed were so threadbare as to be never used more, *Angelicus Juvenis, senibus Satanizat in Annis,* which, though it were pity it should ever speak English, has been Englished — "A young saint, an old devil." I remember Erasmus believes the devil himself was the author of that proverb. This I am sure, the

proverb was none of Solomon's, *etc.* Barbour 157(2); *Oxford* 928; Whiting S19.

S24 To dine with **St. Anthony**

1728 Byrd *Dividing Line* 244: [We] were in Danger of dining with St. Anthony, 318: [They] made a Saint *Anthony's* Meal, that is, they supp't upon the Pickings of what Stuck in their Teeth ever since Breakfast. Partridge 722. Cf. NED Dine 1b. See **D316.**

S25 Like **St. George,** always a horseback and never rides

1738 Franklin *PR* 2.195: Defer not thy well doing; be not like St. George, who is always a horseback, and never rides on, **1755** *Papers* 6.86-7: And he remains like St. George in the Sign, always a Horseback, and never going on. *Oxford* 693-4; Tilley S42.

S26 **St. Monday**

1766 Franklin *Papers* 13.516: St. Monday, and St. Tuesday, will cease to be holidays, **1768** 15.107: St. Monday is generally as duly kept by our working people as Sunday, **a1772** *Writings* 5.538: *Saint Monday* and *Saint Tuesday* will soon cease to be holidays. **1788** *American Museum* 4.32: In those manufacturing towns in England, where the Sundays are spent in idleness, or frolicking, little or no work is ever done on the ensuing day; hence it is called St. Monday. *Oxford* 695.

S27 As big as **St. Paul's** church

1787 Ledyard *Russian Journey* 140: I have a heart as big as St Pauls church.

S28 **St. Swithin's** day

August 28, **1816** Adams *Memoirs* 3.438: There was not one of the forty days from St. Swithin's, to a certainty, without rain: so that the old prediction seems to have been this year made good. *Oxford* 696; Tilley S62.

S29 (On **St. Valentine's** day) every bird has chose his mate

1730 Ames *Almanacs* 66: But every Bird has chose his Mate The joyful Spring to Celebrate. *Oxford* 696; Whiting S26.

S30 No **Salary** but (*without*) service

1789 Maclay *Journal* 47: I spoke seriously to Fitzsimons, saying the old proverb must be reversed. Here it was, "Be no service, but salary." Cf. Whiting S168.

S31   To be the Salt of the earth

1689 Bulkeley *People's Right* 71: Those among us who *are the salt of the earth.* **1731** Belcher *Papers* 1.89: Gent^m of his learning & piety may properly be call'd the salt of the earth. **1747** *Law Papers* 3.106: As to money Quantity avails little when the Quality is become like Salt that has lost its Savour. **1777** Carter *Diary* 2.1089: For verily our salt has lost its savoryness. **1802** OWolcott in *Steele Papers* 1.261. **1816** JAdams in *Adams-Jefferson Letters* 2.485: He is a *Mountain of Salt* of the Earth. **1844** Paulding *Letters(II)* 369: They say honest men are the Salt of the Earth. Barbour 157(3); Whiting S38.

S32   To be worth one's Salt

1788 Marshall *Diary* 185: Although all the good she does is not worth half the salt she eats. **1800** Dorr *Letters* 236: Long . . . is not worth his salt. Barbour 157(4); *Oxford* 922; TW 316(5).

S33   To earn one's Salt (varied)

1776 JMcKesson in *Clinton Papers* 1.434: They seldon earn the salt they eat at any kind of Labour. **1779** *New Jersey Journal* in *Newspaper Extracts(II)* 3.309: That [the surplus cash] of the private soldiers' (to make use of an old expression) will not procure even salt for their porridge. **1816** Paulding *Letters(I)* 2.25: I cannot earn salt to my porridge, if I had any. **1820** Short *Letters* 388: His conviction that he should never be able to earn salt to his bread. Barbour 157(5); TW 316(4). Cf. *Oxford* 922.

S34   To eat without Salt

1778 Moore *Diary* 2.23: And eat up an army without salt or gravy. **1799** DRoss in *Bingham's Maine* 2.960: My old neighbours woud think me a delicious morsel without either salt or mustard. NED Salt *sb.*[1] 2a; *Oxford* 214; Whiting S39.

S35   To throw Salt

1813 Bayard *Papers* 492: The Countess remarked that he was fond of throwing salt into his conversation. NED Salt *sb.*[1] 3c.

S36   To throw Salt on a (black)bird's tail

1678 CMather in *Mather Papers* 383: If I could but either fling salt on the tail of Time, or gett the wind and tide to be favorable to my designs. **1744** Hamilton *Itinerarium* 87: He . . . ran out of doors so fast that we could never throw salt on his tail again. **1809** Fessenden *Pills* 114: Like cunning boy, who would not fail, In putting salt on blackbird's tail. **1809** Irving *History* 1.295: In an ineffectual attempt to catch swallows by sprinkling fresh salt upon their tails. *Oxford* 697; Whiting S40.

S37   To be up Salt River

1844 Paulding *Letters(II)* 360: I am comparatively an idle man, since being rowed up Salt River. Barbour 157; NED Suppl. Salt River; TW 317.

S38   A Salve for every sore

1652 Bradford *Dialogue* 7: These juglers provid a salve for every sore. **1799** Carey *Porcupiniad* 2.27: But the vast wealth of Spanish shore, would be a salve for ev'ry sore. *Oxford* 698; Tilley S84.

S39   Old Sam

1807 JEarly in *VHM* 34(1926) 300: I opened the fire and put them [a string of beads] in to let her know I wanted to burn old Sam up [he is exhorting a young lady against worldly vanity]. TW 317; Whiting *Devil* 247.

S40   If such (is) the Sample, what is the sack?

1799 Carey *Porcupiniad* 2.18: With the old miller, they'll cry "alack! If such the sample, what's the sack?" *Oxford* 690: Sack.

S41   As strong as Samson

1637 Morton *New English Canaan* 278: So stronge as Sampson and so patient as Job himselfe, 281: And hee had need have Sampsons strenght to deale with a Dallila. **1804** *Echo* 301: As strong as Sampson. Barbour 157; Svartengren 391; Whiting S52.

S42   As instable as Sand

1780 *New-York Gazette* in *Newspaper Exstacts(II)* 5.106: What's life, my Tabitha? Instable as sand. Svartengren 25.

S43   As numerous as the Sands

1753 Washington *Diaries* 1.49: My Force is

as the Sand upon the Sea Shore. **1769** Franklin *Papers* 16.46: As numerous as the Sands of the Sea. **1775** Freneau *Poems* 1.175: Numerous as sands that strew the Atlantic shore. **1790** *Universal Asylum* 4.171: Sins more numerous than the grains of sand upon our shores. **1799** Humphreys *Works* 147. 785-6: Who count the sands by eddying whirlblasts driv'n, Or number all the stars that rise in heav'n? **1811** Weems *Gambling* 6: Numerous as the sands of the sea. Whiting S54, 55. See **S409.**

S44 As thick as **Sand**

1777 *Clinton Papers* 1.773: And the Regulars would come up as thick as Sand. Whiting S55.

S45 To build on the **Sand**

1708 Sewall *Diary* 2.227: Mr. Stoddard preaches a good Sermon against building on the Sand. Barbour 157(1); *Oxford* 698-9; Tilley S88.

S46 To write on the **Sand**(s)

1766 Franklin *Papers* 13.299: 'Tis like writing on the Sands in a windy Day. **1767** *Johnson Papers* 5.513: Like Writing in the Sand. NED Sand *sb.*² 2c, Write 1c; Tilley W114.

S47 As cunning as **Satan**

1797 Freneau *Poems* 3.191: As cunning as Satan, and fond of disputes. Cf. Whiting *Devil* 211(38).

S48 **Satan** reproves sin

1750 Fairservice *Plain Dealing* 42: It does not favour to see Satan reprove Sin, for one Devil is too proud to be cast out by another. **1805** Sewall *Parody* 39: 'Tis *Satan*, sir, rebuking *sin*. *Oxford* 699; TW 318(5).

S49 As smooth as **Satin**

1819 Verplanck *State* 208: *Large* is the word with him, yet smooth as satin. Barbour 158; TW 318(1).

S50 **Saturday** comes but once a week

1803 Davis *Travels* 438: Saturday night comes but once a week, so here's to sweethearts and wives. Cf. *Oxford* 123; TW 69(1).

S51 To be served with sour **Sauce**

1762 *Johnson Papers* 3.738: It will be sower sause to them. **1780** Gordon *Letters* 443: The ministerial sugar plumbs . . . will have sour sauce served up to them. NED Sauce 1b; *Oxford* 793; Whiting M746, S64, 65, 942.

S52 To be served with the like **Sauce**

1674 GManning in *Baxter Manuscripts* 6.43: They have served them the lieke Sause. *Oxford* 699; Whiting S66.

S53 What is **Sauce** for a goose is sauce for a gander

1757 Davis *Colonial Virginia Satirist* 32: They say whats good for the Goose is good for the Ganders. **1764** Franklin *Papers* 11.380: *What is Sauce for a Goose is also Sauce for a Gander,* **1771** 18.78: So that agreeable to the Proverb, what was then thought Sauce for the Goose, is now found to be Sauce for the Gander. **1805** *Echo* 179: Nor does the adage in this case hold true, "That sauce for goose is sauce for gander too." **1815** Humphreys *Yankey* 55: What is sairse for the goose, is sairse for the gander. Barbour 158; *Oxford* 699; TW 318.

S54 As big as **Saucers**

1795 Freneau *Prose* 352: Were his eyes as big as a saucer. **1822** Watterston *Winter* 57: His eyes stretched to the dimensions of two saucers. TW 318-9. Cf. Whiting S68.

S55 **Saul** among the prophets

1732 Franklin *Papers* 1.246: Ever since which *Saul also has been among the Prophets,* and our Disputes lie dormant. **1770** HHusband in Boyd *Eighteenth Century Tracts* 268: It catched every Man, good or bad, as Saul was catched among the Prophets. **1782** JEliot in *Belknap Papers* 3.232: I never thought of a *ryme*, but Saul will run among the prophets some*times*. *Oxford* 700; Tilley S104.

S56 **Save** and have

1737 Franklin *PR* 2.165: Save and have. *Oxford* 700; Tilley S107.

S57 Think of **Saving** as well as getting

1743 Franklin *PR* 2.372: If you'd be

wealthy, think of saving more than of getting, **1758** *WW* 345.

S58 To work like a **Sawyer**

c1775 Hopkinson *Miscellaneous Essays* 3 (part 2) 158: He likewise related his case to the lawyer In such agitation, he worked like a sawyer.

S59 Easier **Said** than done

1712 Mather *Letters* 127: The projection of anglicising our Indians is much more easy to be talked of than to be accomplished. **1793** Morris *Diary and Letters* 2.38: This is not quite so easily done as said. Barbour 156(1); *Oxford* 212; Whiting S73.

S60 No sooner **Said** than done

1769 Anne Blair in *W&MCQ* 16(1907) 178: No sooner said than done. **1773** Trumbull *Satiric Poems* 33: So said, so done. **1788** *Politician* 26. **1802** Cutler *Life* 2.78. **1814** Palmer *Diary* 93. **1815** Brackenridge *Modern* 785. Barbour 157(2); *Oxford* 574; TW 319(3).

S61 **Saying** and doing are two things (*varied*)

1697 Chalkley *God's Great Love* 332: 'Tis not by Saying, but by Doing, that we are justified. **1756** Franklin *PR* 6.331: *Saying* and *Doing*, have quarrel'd and parted. **1809** *Port Folio* 2NS 2.429: Saying and Doing do not dine together. **1831** Wirt *Letters* 2.363: But saying and doing are two things. Barbour 158(2); *Oxford* 702; Whiting S83.

S62 Though I **Say** it that should not say it

1764 Franklin *Papers* 11.292: That threadbare Form of Words *Though we say it that should not say it.* **1786** *Anarchiad* 113: Though I say't that should not say't. **1788** *Politician* 48. **1809** *Kennon Letters* 32.79-80: Although as poor old cousin Betty Fitzhugh used to say: I say that you should not. **1815** *Port Folio* 3NS 6.160. **1815** *Reviewers* 21: For thogh Sally says it, that should not say it. **1826** Longfellow *Letters* 1.200. *Oxford* 814; Whiting S74.

S63 One **Scale** sinks as the other rises

1809 Bates *Papers* 2.68: For one scale sinks

as the other rises. Cf. *Oxford* 89; Whiting B575.

S64 To make oneself **Scarce**

1777 Fitch *New-York Diary* 213: Who Inform'd me that Majr: Brown had made himself scarce. NED Scarce 6.

S65 As red as **Scarlet**

1803 Davis *Travels* 307: Sins, red as scarlet. **1821** Royall *Letters* 232: Her face was as red as scarlet, from the heat and rage together. Lean 2.867; Svartengren 6, 246-7.

S66 **Scheming** seldom has success

1761 Adams *D and A* 1.217: But scheming seldom has success.

S67 Clear the old **Score** before beginning the new

1720 ?EWigglesworth *Country-Men's Answer* in *Colonial Currency* 1.411: It should seem . . . Wise and Prudent . . . to clear the old Score, before we begin a new one. Tilley S147. Cf. TW 320.

S68 A false **Scot**

a1656 Bradford *History* 2.135: Amongst the company was a false Scott. Lean 1.243; *Oxford* 243; Whiting S98.

S69 The **Scotch** fiddle

1810 Wilson *Letters* cxiii: Their persons covered with filth, and frequently garnished with the humours of the Scotch fiddle; from which dreadful disease, by the mercy of God, I have been most miraculously preserved. **1826** JRandolph in Quincy *JQuincy* 421: I have not catched the literary "Scotch fiddle." NED Fiddle 4c: the itch.

S70 A **Scotch** (Scots) mist

1728 Byrd *Dividing Line* 143: There fell a Sort of Scots Mist all the way. **1750** Hempstead *Diary* 560: In the foren [forenoon] a Scotch mist. **1778** Curwen *Journal* 1.466: I took leave, the sky denouncing more than a Scotch mist that in event proved only a drisle, 511: A drisle, which truly proved as inconvenient [as] a Scotch mist being thoroughly drencht, **1780** 2.642, 668: A shower, that proved almost a Scotch mist, **1783** 902, 946. **1815** Waterhouse *Journal* 175: Here reigns more than two thirds of the year, the

Scotch mist, which is famous to a proverb. **1824** Austin *Literary Papers* 4: He always leaves a Scotch mist behind him. By many a wet jacket do I remember him. **1826** Duane *Colombia* 362: The clouds, in which we travelled, had proved to us a *"Scots mist."* **1834** Floy *Diary* 77: Coming home I was sprinkled through and through by a Scotch mist, **1835** 168. NED Mist *sb.*[1] 1c; *Oxford* 705; Tilley M1016.

S71   A Scotch prize

1776 HFisher in *Naval Documents* 4.854: Luckily for them . . . [they came] aboard again . . . or they would have caut a Scotch Prize and be Damn'd to them. NED Scotch 4.

S72   As cruel as a Scotchman

1815 Waterhouse *Journal* 55: *"Cruel as a Scotchman,"* has become a proverb in the United States. Cf. Lean 1.243.

S73   To stick together like Scotchmen abroad

1807 Janson *Stranger* 15: They stick together like Scotchmen abroad.

S74   The three Scourges of mankind, *etc.*

1728 Byrd *Dividing Line* 9: That it was a Place free from those 3 great Scourges of Mankind, Priests, Lawyers, and Physicians. Cf. Tilley P261.

S75   To come up to the Scratch

1824 Neal *American Writers* 55: Although, to come up to the scratch, manfully we confess. *Oxford* 706; TW 320(1).

S76   Scratch me, and I will scratch you (*varied*)

1779 Gordon *Letters* 414: Gen'l Heath and the Boston Officers have been scratching one another. **1793** Freneau *Prose* 298: "Scratch me and I will scratch you, Sawney." **1797** Cobbett *Porcupine* 7.117: It is so much like the *scratch for scratch* of the vulgar. **1813** TJefferson in *Adams-Jefferson Letters* 2.389: These families are canonised in the eyes of the people on the common principle "you tickle me, and I will tickle you." *Oxford* 706; Whiting K1.

S77   To Scratch for (something)

1620 RCushman in Bradford *History* 1.119: For the rest . . . we may goe scratch for it. Cf. TW 320.

S78   Between Scylla and Charybdis (*varied*)

1643 AOttley in *Winthrop Papers(A)* 4.365: I am fallen into the twoe daungers Sylla and Carybdis. **1686** Fitzhugh *Letters* 189-90: I am more afraid of falling upon Scylla to avoid Charybdis. a**1700** Hubbard *New England* 277: And so apt are the best of men oft times to come in danger of Scylla, that they be sure to keep clear of Charybdis. **1705** Sewall *Diary* 2.148. **1747** *Georgia Records* 25.184. **1750** *Law Papers* 3.414: Incidit in Scyllam Qui Vult Vitare Charybdim. **1772** Chester *Papers* 181: Those dreadful Scylla's and Charybdis's, the Florida and Bahama Banks, those Bug Bears to the fancy of our navigators. **1775** SAdams in *Warren-Adams Letters* 1.192: You have Scilla and Charybdis to avoid. **1775** WHDrayton in Gibbes 2.56: [Latin only]. **1776** JWarren in *Warren-Gerry Correspondence* 32. **1780** Gordon *Letters* 445. **1781** AA in *Adams FC* 4.184. **1781** Deane *Papers* 4.313: They must see Scylla on one side and Charybdis on the other, 344, 389. **1782** Gadsden *Writings* 192: Carried us through so many Scyllas and Charybdas. **1782** Lee *Letters* 2.267: Take care . . . that they carry the vessel of the state clear from Charybdis . . . [and] do not wreck it upon Scylla. **1783** *Belknap Papers* 1.234. **1783** Deane *Papers* 5.151: [I] shall . . . avoid politics with as much care as the seamen of old did Scylla and Charybdis. **1784** WEllery in Kirkland *Letters* 2.97: Through the Scylla, and Charibdis of Import & Commutation. **1785** Adams *Writings* 1.19, n.1: This is escaping Scylla to fall into Charybdis. **1785** Jefferson *Papers* 9.70: This will be worse than running on Scylla to avoid Charybdis. **1787** Ledyard *Russian Journey* 139. **1788** EHazard in *Belknap Papers* 2.68-9: It is almost impossible to keep clear of both Scylla and Charybdis. **1793** CAdams in Adams *Writings* 1.146. **1795** Hamilton *Papers* 19.96: To avoid Sylla may we not run upon Charybdis? **1795** *Washington Writings* 34.266: This government in relation to

France and England may be compared to a ship between the rocks of Scylla and Charibdas, 285. **1797** Cobbett *Porcupine* 7.402. **1797** Gadsden *Writings* 272: A Caesar and Pompey, a Scylla and Charybdis. **1797** Jefferson *Writings* 18.202: Finding the strait between Scylla and Charybdis too narrow for his steerage, he has preferred running plump on one of them. **1799** *Washington *Writings* 37.246. **1804** GDavis in *Barbary Wars* 4.276: Thus *in voiding Sylla, we are nearly on Charibdis.* **1804** JVaughan in Burr *Memoirs* 2.265: The Sylla of oligarchy, or Charybdis of disorganization must be the portion of our government. **1805** Irving *Journals* 1.176: The . . . risk . . . of running on Scylla when they avoided Charbydis. **1806** *Weekly* 1.62: In steering from Scylla, they would dash on Charybdis. **1807** Janson *Stranger* 89. **1812** *Port Folio* 2NS 7.532: [Latin only]. **1814** JBrace in Vanderpoel *More Chronicles* 109: Good heavens shall I steer clear of Scylla and Charybdis, the prejudices of either. **1816** *Port Folio* 4NS 2.26: [Latin only]. **1817** Beecher *Autobiography* 1.337. **1817** *Port Folio* 4NS 4.409: I may have avoided Scylla, only to be thrown on Charybdis. **1819** Kinloch *Letters* 1.279. **1819** Wright *Views* 54. **1822** Adams *Writings* 7.296: You know there is a Scylla as well as a Charybdis. **1833** Jackson *Correspondence* 5.5: Calhoun finds himself between Scylla and Caribdis and is reckless. *Oxford* 707; Whiting S101. See **S280, W35.**

S79   As inconstant as the Sea

1821 Knight *Poems* 2.185: Thou'rt inconstant as the sea.

S80   As unstable as the Sea

1772 Freneau *Poems* 1.64: Unstable as the sea. Whiting S107. See **W51.**

S81   As wide as the Sea

1727 Talcott *Papers* 1.98: We look't . . . upon the breach made to be as wide as the sea. Svartengren 286; Whiting *NC* 471(4).

S82   If you would learn (to pray) go to Sea

1774 Schaw *Journal* 31: If you have a mind to learn, they say, go to Sea. *Oxford* 451; Tilley S173.

S83   In crossing the Sea we change the climate not the soul

1766 BKent in Franklin *Papers* 13.49: The Old saying non Animam mutat, qui trans mare Currunt, 431: An old Observation, on which I much rely viz [Latin only]. **1781** EBenson in Jay *Correspondence* 2.153: the adage [Latin only]. **1783** Curwen *Journal* 2.955: [Latin only]. **1789** Morris *Diary and Letters* 1.21: Horace tells us that in crossing the sea we change our climate not our souls, **1797** 2.303: Horace is perfectly right [Latin only]. *Oxford* 114, 836; Tilley P374, T477.

S84   The Sea and the gallows refuse none (*varied*)

1699 Ward *Trip* 35: A Man on Board cannot but be thoughtful on two Destinies, *viz.* Hanging and Drowning: For withinside you have *Rope* and without *Water* enough to effect either. So that it often put me in mind of the old Proverb, *The Sea and the Gallows refuses none.* **1781** Oliver *Origin* 138: For what the Sea refuses the Gallows accepts of. *Oxford* 707; Tilley S178.

S85   Sea-green

1773 De Brahm *Report* 246: A beautiful Sea-green. **1792** Paine *Works* 60: Their sea-green caves. **1809** Irving *History* 2.109: His standard . . . consisting of a huge oyster *recumbent* upon a sea-green field. **1814** Dow *Journal* 479. TW 321(4).

S86   To lade the Sea with an acorn bowl (*varied*)

1702 Taylor *Christographia* 226.3: And lade the Sea dry with an acron bowle, *Poems* 165: How should an acorn bowle the Sea lade dry? **1809** Weems *Washington* 79: Sir Peter . . . was . . . tickled with the idea of measuring the *Atlantic* ocean with a *quart pot, etc.* **1831** in Porter *Negro Writing* 282: If they can "drain the ocean with a bucket." *Oxford* 707; Tilley S183. Cf. Whiting S110, 112.

S87   To be worth a Sea-bream's eye

1672 Josselyn *New-England Rarities* 228: Their eyes are accounted rare meat: Whereupon the proverbial comparison, "It is worth a sea-bream's eye." NED Sea-bream.

S88   As fat as Seals

1774 *Commerce of Rhode Island* 1.494: The Hogs they were as fatt as Seals. **1822** Randolph(J) *Letters* 253: When I *"lent"* him, he was seal fat, and in the highest condition. Whiting S117.

S89   To have one's Sea-legs

1796 Bentley *Diary* 2.182: He had not his sea legs, but the Sea sickness on horseback, and was more than half seas over. TW 321.

S90   In Season and out of season

1796 Weems *Letters* 2.6: By paying all due honor to the good old injunction, I mean, by being *instant in season and out of season,* I have . . . enlisted several Patrons. NED Season 17.

S91   There is a Season to every purpose, *etc.*

1682 Plumstead 91: The wise man tells us there is a season to every purpose, and sometimes this season comes once and no more. Whiting S120. See **T116.**

S92   Secrecy is the soul of business

1732 Belcher *Papers* 1.108: I much admire the Italian proverb, *Secrecy is the soul of business,* 203: That excellent Italian proverb, **1733** 436.

S93   If you cannot keep your own Secrets, *etc.*

1795 Cathcart *Journal* 356: If you can not keep your own secrets how can you expect I should keep them for you? *Oxford* 146: Counsel; Whiting C462.

S94   To whom you tell your Secret, *etc.*

1737 Franklin *PR* 2.170: To whom thy secret thou dost tell, To him thy freedom thou dost sell. *Oxford* 708, 808; Tilley S192.

S95   It is done Secundum usum Sarum (Massachusettensem)

1702 Mather *Magnalia* 1.83: As for there [for their] *church-order, it was generally secumdum usum Massachusettensem.* **1731** Wise *Churches* 30: That (as they say) it may be done, *Secundum usum sarum. Oxford* 708; Whiting S125.

S96   To See and be seen

1771 Wister *Journal* 79: So I had an opportunity of seeing and being seen, the former the most agreeable, to be sure. **1809** Cleveland *Letters* 138: That attraction so conspicuous at Ballstown, *to see* and *be seen.* **1813** Mason *Memoir* 74: The room was very full of people who wanted to see and be seen. *Oxford* 709; Whiting S131.

S97   A small Seed sometimes produces a large tree

1755 Franklin *Papers* 6.180: But a small Seed properly Sown, sometimes produces a large and fruitful Tree. Tilley S211. See **C99.**

S98   Seek and you shall find

1783 Jay *Correspondence* 3.95: *"Seek and you shall find"* does not, it appears, always extend to that [health] of the body. *Oxford* 711; Whiting S136.

S99   Self-preservation is the first law of Nature (*varied*)

1689 TDanforth in *Hutchinson Papers* 2.312: Nature hath taught us selfe preservation. **1691** *Humble Address* in *Andros Tracts* 2.247: Self Defence is a Principle in Nature. **1712** *Wyllys Papers* 373: The light of Nature Strongly obliges to Self Preservation. **1715** JHepburn *American Defence* in American Antiquarian Society, *Proceedings* 59(1949) 123: Self-Preservation, an Instinct of Nature belonging to all the Creatures of God. **1736** SWaldo in *Baxter Manuscripts* 11.164: The Eternal Law of Selfpreservation makes it the Indispensible Duty of every one who hath acquired . . . an Estate . . . to keep the same. **1738** RStaunton in *Letters from Hudson Bay* 265. **1745** Johnson *Writings* 3.477: The great law of nature, the law of self-preservation. **1751** *Appendix* in *Colonial Currency* 4.474: *Is not Self-Preservation the great Law?* **1756** Davis *Colonial Virginia Satirist* 17: As I have hard the Parsin call it. **1756** DPepper in McDowell *Documents* 2.298. **1764** RPeters in *Aspinwall Papers* 2.510: The people are then by the Laws of Nature oblig'd to preserve themselves. **1766** Adams *D and A* 1.331. **1771** *Pennsylvania Journal* in *Newspaper Extracts(I)* 8.622: The principal law of nature (self defence). **1772** Hearne *Journey* 288. **1774** *New Hampshire Gazette* in *Naval Documents* 1.40. **1775** JLyon in *Baxter Manuscripts* 14.312: The sacred laws of self preservation. **1775** EMusgrove in Gibbes 2.202: The nature of humanity is such that self-preservation very much prevails. **1776** WHDrayton in Gibbes 2.281: Nature cried aloud — self-preservation is the great law — we have but obeyed. **1776** JParker in Lee *Papers* 1.460: Until hurried into it by the equitable law of self preservation. **1776** *Pennsylvania Journal* in *Newspaper Extracts(II)* 1.175: The immutable law. **1776** Smith *Works* 1².25. **1776** Sullivan *Letters* 1.156: The Principal of self preservation Call'd for such a proceedure. **1776** Washington *Writings* 5.311: The propriety of it is founded on the Law of Self preservation. **1776** SWest in Thornton *Pulpit* 279: The law of self-preservation will always justify opposing a cruel and tyrannical imposition, 279-80, 283, 285, 312: The law of nature . . . a part of which . . . is the principle of self-defence. **1778** Sullivan *Letters* 2.78: Or that we are backward in revenging Injuries when dictated by self Preservation. **1780** *Royal Gazette* in *Newspaper Extracts(II)* 4.544-5: Solely on the principles of Self Preservation. **1791** JBoit in *Columbia* 367: But they soon was taught the doctrine of self-preservation. **1793** Freneau *Prose* 318. **1793** *Jackson Papers* 77: Self preservation with States as Individuals is the supreme law. **1794** *Federal Orrery* in Buckingham *Specimens* 2.238. **1800** Jefferson *Writings* 1.434: There is in every legal body of men a right of self-preservation, authorizing them to do whatever is necessary for that purpose. **1801** Weems *Letters* 2.180: Self preservation is a grand law in the economy of Man. **1808** Jefferson *Writings* 12.183: Self-preservation is paramount to all law. **1809** Lindsley *Love* 26. **1810** Jefferson *Writings* 12.418: The laws of necessity, of self preservation . . . are of higher obligation, 419: The unwritten laws of necessity, of self-preservation, and of the public safety, control the written laws of *meum* and *tuum*, 421. **1811** Burroughs *Memoirs* 289. **1814** Kerr *Barclay* 317. **1815** Andrews *Prisoners' Memoirs* 16, 56: They justified themselves on the plea of self-preservation, 135: Self-love

and self-preservation are . . . deeply rooted in the very nature of all living creatures. **1825** Neal *American Writers* 110. **1830** JRandolph in Jackson *Correspondence* 4.180. **1849** JBuchanan in Clifford *Letters* 249, 250. *Oxford* 712; TW 322.

S100 To have more **Sense** in one's little finger, *etc.*

1809 EHall in *Port Folio* 2NS 2.422: A fellow who has not as much sense in his whole corporation as your son has in his little finger. **1818** Evans *Pedestrious* 165: That mon has more sanse in his latle fanger than we've in both of oure hades. *Oxford* 903: Wit; Tilley W549.

S101 Where **Sense** is wanting, everything is wanting

1754 Franklin *PR* 5.185: Where Sense is wanting, every thing is wanting.

S102 As cunning as a **Serpent**

1784 *Belknap Papers* 1.324: My master is as cunning as a serpent about every thing except half bushels. **1808** Hitchcock *Poetical Dictionary* 22: They're cunning as serpents. **1812** Randall *Miser* 46. Barbour 161(1).

S103 As wise as a **Serpent** and harmless as a dove

1652 Williams *Writings* 4.156: *Christ* gave his *disciples* a charge to be as wise as *Serpents.* **1692** Bulkeley *Will* 247: Yet there are some among 'em, who (tho' they have but little of the dove,) yet have too much of the serpent in them. **1699** Sewall *Diary* 1.500: How hapy I were, if I could once become wise as a Serpent and harmless as a Dove. **1699** Ward *Trip* 40: But tho' they wear in their Faces the *Innocence* of Doves, you will find them in their Dealings, as *Subtile as Serpents.* **1720** Chalkley *Considerations* 514. **1722** Sewall *Letter-Book* 2.144. **1724** Chalkley *Journal* 139. **1746** Brainerd *Memoirs* 276. **1754** *Johnson Papers* 9.134: The Crafty Inhabitants . . . whose Title to that place seems rather derived from the Subtility of the Serpent, than the meekness of the Dove. **1776** AA in *Adams FC* 2.125: May you be as wise as Serpents. **1792** Alden *Epitaphs* 3.212. **1799** Beecher *Autobiography* 1.113: [He] was deficient in that wisdom of the serpent, which is compatible with the harmlessness of the dove. **1805** Asbury *Letters* 3.326: We ought to be as wise as serpents. **1805** Sewall *Parody* 29: Harmless as the dove. **1808** Hitchcock *Poetical Dictionary* 22: Harmless as doves. **1813** Asbury *Letters* 3.467. **1816** Smith *Life* 384: They were as wise as doves and harmless as serpents. **1820** Adams *Memoirs* 5.136. Not all can have the wisdom of the serpent. All can be harmless as a dove. **1825** Pearse *Narrative* 73: The Saviour's words. Barbour 161(1); *Oxford* 714; Svartengren 27; Whiting A44. See **D286.**

S104 To shun as one would a **Serpent**

1772 Griffith *Journal* 396: Warning friends and others to shun the conversation of those tinctured therewith, as they would a poisonous serpent. Whiting A45, 46. See **P90, 193.**

S105 He that serves himself has an awkward **Servant,** *etc.*

1816 Fidfaddy *Adventures* 7: He that serves himself, has an awkward servant, and a scurvy master. See **C310.**

S106 If you would have a faithful **Servant,** serve yourself

1737 Franklin *PR* 2.170: If you'd have a Servant that you like, serve yourself, **1758** *WW* 344: If you would have a faithful Servant, and one that you like, serve yourself. *Oxford* 715; Tilley S248. See **B378.**

S107 Offered **Service** stinks

1815 Bentley *Diary* 4.338: Sara . . . said offered service stunk. *Oxford* 648-9; Whiting S167.

S108 **Service** is no inheritance

1784 Franklin *Writings* 9.279: *Service is no Inheritance,* as the Proverb says. *Oxford* 716; Whiting S169. See **F51.**

S109 As fleeting as a **Shadow**

1781 AA in *Adams FC* 4.258: I know the voice of Fame to be . . . fleeting as a Shadow. Cf. Whiting S180.

S110 To be afraid of one's own **Shadow**

1718 WKeith in *Colden Letters* 1.94: The Town is become most insipid & every Man is affraid of his own shadow. **1770** *Johnson Papers* 7.309: I could wish that the Bishop . . .

were not afraid of shadows. **1774** Adams *Works* 9.351: Afraid of their own shades. **1776** BHarrison in *Naval Documents* 3.1263: We shall start at Shadows till we are undone. **1776** *Washington *Writings* 6.110: Ready to fly from their own shadows. a**1778** Jones *History* 2.119: Of so timid a disposition that if there was nothing else to frighten him, his own shadow would do so. **1797** GMorris in Cobbett *Porcupine* 6.299. **1801** Delano *Narrative* 326: I saw the man . . . frightened at his own shadow. **1806** Hitchcock *Works* 55, **1808** *Poetical Dictionary* 107: They flee from their shadow whene'er it pursues 'em. **1829** DCaldwell in *Ruffin Papers* 1.481: They are afraid of a shadow. Barbour 160(4); *Oxford* 261; Whiting S177.

S111 To catch at the **Shadow** and lose the substance (*varied*)

1632 WPeirce in Bradford *History* 2.156: We fooles catch after shadows, that flye away, and are gone in a momente. **1633** EHowes in *Winthrop Papers(A)* 3.112: *Canis dum captat* etc. which may not unfitly be applyed to them, whoe medlinge with shadowes . . . loose theire substances . . . As the Dog did. **1647** Davenport *Letters* 81: Those, who, being mislead by fancie, catch at shadowes, neglecting the substance. **1702** Taylor *Christographia* 194.23-4: They do like Esops dog, Catch at the Shadow, and let the Substance fall, 288.36-7: Now to use the type is to say, the Shadow is better than the Substance, **1703** 349.31-2: For what they did, but in the Shadow, he did in the very Substance of the thing. **1724** Chalkley *Journal* 125: We see beyond the Figure or Shadow, and are come to the Substance. **1728** Byrd *Dividing Line* 145: And finding the Shadow there I knew the Substance cou'd not be far off. **1748** *Word* in *Colonial Currency* 4.360: Fare like the *Dog* in the Fable, and so have neither the *Substance,* nor the *Shadow.* **1749** *Brief Account* in *Colonial Currency* 4.380: Like the Dog in the Fable, while they catch'd at the Shadow, they let go the Substance. **1764** *Paxton Papers* 234: But let the Cabellers have a care that they dont fare like the Dog in the Fable, and loose the Substance by grasping at the Shadow. **1768** Adams *Legal Papers* 2.199: Deluding Men with Shadows instead of

Substances. **1769** Brooke *Emily* 102: This foolish quality of preferring the shadow to the substance. **1772** Franklin *Writings* 5.446: Losing Substance for Shadow. **1774** Eddis *Letters* 86. **1774** Seabury *Letters* 130: [It] tempted us to *grasp* at the mere *shadow* of civil freedom, while we lose its real *substance*. **1776** *Blockheads* 6. **1776** Smith *Memoirs(II)* 46. **1777** Cresswell *Journal* 259: They are like the Dog in the Fable, quit the substance for an empty shadow. **1778** Murray *Letters* 273. **1779** Franklin *Writings* 7.227: This is worse than advising us to drop the Substance for the Shadow. The Dog after he found his Mistake, might possibly have recover'd his Mutton; but we could never hope to be trusted again by France. **1786** JQAdams in Smith *Journal and Correspondence* 2(1) 104. **1786** Washington *Writings* 28.474: Therefore giving the *shadow* for the substance of a debt, **1787** 29.164. **1793** EPendleton in Washington *Writings* 33.94: A Sacrifice of the substance of Justice to its shadow. **1795** Murdock *Triumphs* 39: You are in love with a substance—I only with a shadow. **1796** JAdams in Smith *Journal and Correspondence* 2(2) 147. **1807** JEarly in *VHM* 34(1926) 301: She had the substance and not the shadow. **1808** M'Nemar *Kentucky* 39: Many . . . deceive themselves with the *shadow*, and think it was the *substance*. **1811** Graydon *Memoirs* 420: The substance of justice was exchanged for its shadow. **1814** Kerr *Barclay* 290. **1814** Wirt *Bachelor* 40. **1819** Faux *Memorable Days* 1.129. **1820** Adams *Memoirs* 5.190-1. **1820** Faux *Memorable Days* 2.131. **1820** Wright *Views* 172: The shadow against the substance. **1821** Adams *Memoirs* 5.307: The serviles have the substance and the liberals the shadow. **1827** Watterston *Wanderer* 134: I love the substance, and you the shadow. **1828** Pintard *Letters* 3.34. *Oxford* 110; Tilley S951; Whiting *NC* 483.

S112 To follow like a **Shadow**

1779 NGreene in Webb *Correspondence* 2.209: This will follow you like your shadow. *Oxford* 272; Whiting S181.

S113 To pass like **Shadows**

1744 Franklin *PR* 2.398: Vain Fortune's Favours, never at a Stay, Like empty Shadows, pass, and glide away. **1780** JPemberton in Kirkland *Letters* 2.70: So passeth away as a Shadow this World's Glory. **1811** Adams *Writings* 4.27: They pass like Chinese shadows before us. Whiting S185.

S114 To wrestle (fight) with one's **Shadow**

1649 Shepard *Hints* 158: Wrastling with his shadow. **1734** Johnson *Writings* 3.93: He . . . fights with his own shadow, **1736** 129: To fight in the air with his own shadow. *Oxford* 256; Tilley S262.

S115 **Shanks'** mare

1809 Fessenden *Pills* 45: On shanks' mare. **1818** Baldwin *Letters* 276: I . . . posted away home on "Shank's horse." **1821** Knight *Poems* 2.158: You may ride shanks' mare. Barbour 161; *Oxford* 720; TW 324.

S116 As greedy as **Sharks**

1805 JPerkins in *Cabot Family* 2.528: The Privateersmen are as greedy as sharks.

S117 As hungry as a **Shark**

1795 Freneau *Poems(1795)* 352: As hungry as a shark. TW 324(1).

S118 (As voracious as a) **Shark**

1792 Delano *Narrative* 155: The violence and voracity of the shark generally are proverbial. Svartengren 182; TW 324(1).

S119 To eat like a **Shark**

1803 Davis *Travels* 418: He eats like a shark.

S120 As good (well) be hanged for a **Sheep** as a lamb

1787 AAdams in *Adams D and A* 3.205: From thence I presume the old proverb took its rise, one had as good be hanged for a Sheep as a Lamb. **1797** Dow *Journal* 44: A saying I remembered, viz: "You had as good be hanged for stealing an old sheep as a lamb." **1805** Brackenridge *Modern* 541: It was as well to be hanged for an old sheep as a lamb, 576. Barbour 161(2); *Oxford* 350; TW 324(3); Tilley S293.

S121 As mild as a **Sheep**

1785 Freneau *Poems(1786)* 373: Shepherds as mild as the sheep on their plain. Whiting S205. See **L10**.

S122 As tame as a **Sheep**

1692 Bulkeley *Will* 93: When the king's authority and government lay at the stake . . . they were as tame as sheep. Whiting S211.

S123 A black **Sheep** (in the flock)

1779 JSEustace in Lee *Papers* 3.363: Mark me for a *black-sheep*. **1781** WPopham in *Clinton Papers* 7.313: It is very shagreening to be thus marked out as black sheep. **1823** *Austin Papers* 1.717: Let us have no black sheep in our flock. Barbour 161(4); *Oxford* 65.

S124 He that makes himself a **Sheep** (lamb) the wolves will eat

1733 Franklin *Writings* 6.4: There is much Truth in the Italian saying, *Make yourselves Sheep, and the Wolves will eat you,* **1773** *Franklin-Mecom* 143: And there is truth in the Old Saying, That *if you make yourself a Sheep, the Wolves will eat you.* **1797** JBarlow in *W&MCQ* 3S 19(1962) 109: There is a proverb which is only too true, although very humiliating for humanity, *who makes himself the lamb the wolf eats.* No part of this proverb is so useful as in Barbary (cf. Barlow *Letters* 149-50). **1799** Eaton *Life* 122: "Qui se fait brebis le loup le mange." He who makes himself a sheep must expect to be devoured by the wolf. *Oxford* 502; Tilley S300.

S125 Not spoil a **Sheep** for a halfpenny-worth of tar

1689 Randolph *Letters* 5.6-7: Therefore (as yᵉ old saying is) I would not have my Country men spoile a sheep for a halfe penny worth of Tarr. **1705** *Penn-Logan Correspondence* 2.11: In privileges they are for straining the strings till they break, and in supplies according to the homely proverb for losing a sheep, &c. Barbour 162: Ship(3); *Oxford* 723; Tilley H495.

S126 Now that I have a **Sheep** and a cow, *etc.*

1736 Franklin *PR* 2.140: Now that I've a sheep and a cow, every body bids me good morrow, **1758** *WW* 343. **1787** *Columbian Magazine* 1.750: says the proverb. Barbour 161(3); *Oxford* 721; Tilley S307.

S127 One scabbed (scabby) (black) **Sheep** will infect a whole flock

1624 JSherley in Bradford *History* 1.355: We have a proverbe, One scabed sheep may marr a whole flock. **1738** Ames *Almanacs* 120: Petty Attorneys and Quack Doctors are like scabbed Sheep among a Flock, One Devours and t'other breeds the Rot. **1775** Deane *Correspondence* 297: The warm Whigs curse their Provincial Congress, as being infected with [too ma]ny scabby sheep. **1795** Cobbett *Porcupine* 2.7: Though one *scabby* sheep infects a whole flock, he does not thereby work his own cure. **1804** Brackenridge *Modern* 345: One black sheep, gives the rot to the whole herd. **1813** JHewson in *Lincoln Papers* 209: There is but one Scabby Sheep in my flock [of children]. **1828** Pintard *Letters* 3.52: And if one scabby sheep infects a whole flock what must be our condition where the *whole* flock is scabby? **1856** Paulding *Letters(II)* 570: Those do not vitiate the entire code, any more than one black Sheep Spoils a whole flock. *Oxford* 702; Whiting S217. See **A107.**

S128 To cast a **Sheep's** eye

1775 Freneau *Poems* 1.134: His landlady had on the horse a sheep's eye. **1789** Brackenridge *Gazette* 312: Who on your heart has cast a sheep's eye. **1813** Weems *Drunkard* 123: He casts a sheep's eye toward the whiskey bottle. **1815** Brackenridge *Modern* 649: You may cast a *sheep's eye* at the window as long as you please, master ram. **1820** Simpson *Journal* 88: She cast a sheeps eye toward the veteran. **1822** Watterston *Winter* 36: The ladies . . . compensated for the rudeness of the legislator, by casting a sheeps-eye at me. *Oxford* 722; Whiting S231.

S129 To die like rotten **Sheep**

1778 Smith *Memoirs(II)* 404: They die like rotten Sheep. Whiting S220, quote c1400.

S130 To drive like **Sheep**

1776 Perkins *Diary* 1.130: And reported there that the King's troops had landed upon Long Island . . . and that they drove them like sheep. a1788 Jones *History* 2.310: The poor souls . . . were driven like a flock of sheep on board the transports. Whiting S220.

S131   To fly like Sheep

1778 Case *Poems* 12: Like sheep they all before me fly. Whiting S221.

S132   To follow like Sheep

1792 Gadsden *Writings* 257: Then the rest like sheep soon follow. *Oxford* 721; Tilley S309; Whiting *NC* 472(3).

S133   To keep like Sheep in fold

1755 Davis *Colonial Virginia Satirist* 24: Your keeping them like sheep in fold. Cf. Whiting S212.

S134   To know (separate) the Sheep from the goats

1683 Randolph *Letters* 3.315: The Sheepe Shall be Knowne from the Goates. **1830** Ames *Mariner's* 16: To have separated the British goats from the American sheep. Hyamson 313; NED Sheep 2c.

S135   To run like Sheep

1755 *Washington *Writings* 1.149: The English Soldiers . . . broke and run as Sheep before the Hounds, 151: They broke and run as Sheep pursued by dogs. **1781** Jefferson *Papers* 5.623: As they broke twice and run like Sheep till supported by fresh Troops. Whiting S220.

S136   As white as a Sheet

1674 Josselyn *Account* 105: As white as a sheet. **1709** Lawson *Voyage* 50, 111. **1778** Smith *Memoirs(II)* 335: Little Snow on the low land, but the Mountains are loaded & white as a Sheet. **1803** RSomers in *Barbary Wars* 3.28. **1812** AJFoster *Jeffersonian America* 100: The President was white as a sheet. **a1820** Biddle *Autobiography* 73: His face as white as a sheet. Barbour 161(2); Svartengren 231; TW 325(2).

S137   To have one's wet Sheet abroad

1813 Weems *Drunkard* 60: [He] has got his wet sheet abroad. Cf. NED Wet 14.

S138   Two (three) Sheets in the wind

1807 Harmon *Sixteen Years* 106: Some of us (as the Irishman says) got more than two sheets in the wind. **1813** Asbury *Journal*

2.743: They were sometimes two sheets in the wind. **1835** Floy *Diary* 149: An odd-looking kind of fellow, three sheets in the wind, said it would rain all day. Barbour 162(2); *Oxford* 817; TW 325(4). See **W195.**

S139   A Sheet-anchor

1776 SWest in Thornton *Pulpit* 287: Their great sheet-anchor and main support. **1779** Lee(W) *Letters* 2.690: The old maxim, divide et impera, is still their sheet anchor. **1779** Washington *Writings* 14.90: You think it advisable to throw out a sheet anchor. **1785** Lee *Letters* 2.393: Gum rubrum astringens Gambiense . . . is the Sheet Anchor of my health. **1785** AMaclaine in Iredell *Correspondence* 2.120. **1787** Mason *Papers* 3.871. **1791** Jefferson *Writings* 8.147: It is . . . the sheet-anchor of our connection with France. **1797** SHigginson in Otis *Letters* 1.73. **1798** EWinslow in *Winslow Papers* 431: I only mean (to use an emphatical expression) they have no sheet anchor, whenever factions set 'em fairly afloat they'll drift to perdition. **1801** Adams *Writings* 2.501: I look to the *Union* of our country as to the sheet anchor of our hopes. **1802** Barlow *Letters* 186: To keep a sheet anchor for him at home. **1802** Chester *Federalism* 15. **1817** Weems *Franklin* 145. **1823** Jefferson *Writings* 15.452: These are the two sheet anchors of our Union. Whiting S234.

S140   His Shekel is not good silver

c1700 Taylor *Poems* 394: Although his Shekel is not Silver good. Cf. *Oxford* 813: Penny; Whiting F67.

S141   To be put to one's Shifts

1718 Chalkley *Letter* 480: The Children . . . were put to their Shifts. **1769** WNelson in *Norton Papers* 86: They were drove to their shifts. **1779** JAllan in *Baxter Manuscripts* 17.399: In want of, I shall be put to hard shifts. **1779** CPinkney in Moultrie *Memoirs* 1.362. **1780** *New-York Gazette* in *Newspaper Extracts(II)* 5.107. **1797** Savery *Journal* 244: They were driven to their shifts, and willing to drop the argument. **1800** Tatham *Tobacco* 143. **1805** Brackenridge *Modern* 631: If they should find themselves at their shifts, or, as we say, a dead lift. *Oxford* 723; Tilley S337. See **L129.**

S142 A nimble **Shilling**

1801 Weems *Letters* 2.177: You have no idea of the *Nimble Shilling.* NED Shilling 3d. Cf. *Oxford* 567: Ninepence. See **N77.**

S143 A splendid **Shilling**

1723 Byrd *Another Secret Diary* 385: [I] have bequeath'd my Daughter a splendid shilling, if she marrys any man that tempts her to disobedience. **1779** Galloway *Diary* 76: I wou'd Never let these people pull Me down for While I had ye splindid shilling left I wou'd be happy in spight of them. Cf. *Oxford* 163.

S144 One may not break his **Shins** over stools not in his way

1833 Jackson *Correspondence* 5.227: This letter is written to put you on your guard of this man, that you may not break your shins over stools not in your way. *Oxford* 461; Tilley G44.

S145 To cool one's **Shins**

1641 LDowning in *Winthrop Papers(A)* 4.311: His grace is like to coolle his shins ere he gets in this could weather. Cf. NED Cool *v.*[1] 5. See **H178.**

S146 To cut a **Shine**

1787 Freneau *Poems* 2.349: Dress'd, booted, and button'd, and "cutting a shine." **1819** Peirce *Rebelliad* 72: Sikes cut a shine. **1830** Ames *Mariner's* 34: Well, has your skipper begun to cut any *shines* yet? [make trouble]. TW 326(2).

S147 Don't give up the **Ship**

1814 Palmer *Diary* 95: No, sooner let me die than give up the Ship. **1816** Jefferson *Writings* 14.383: My exhortation would rather be "not to give up the ship." **1818** Royall *Letters* 124. **1825** Jefferson *Writings* 16.103: I was almost ready to give up the ship, **1826** 16.152: I should not be for giving up the ship without efforts to save her. **1830** JMcLemore in Jackson *Correspondence* 4.197. Barbour 162(1); TW 327(1).

S148 Free **Ships** (bottoms), free goods (*varied*)

1780 Adams *Correspondence* 153: The principle of free ships, free goods, *Works* 7.257:

The point of *free ships free goods.* **1780** Franklin *Writings* 8.70, 76, 80: It is likely to become henceforth the law of Nations, that *free Ships make free Goods,* 130. **1781** FDana in Adams *Works* 7.469. **1793** Jefferson *Writings* 9.199: Free bottoms make free goods, 17.348: A conventional principle *that the goods shall follow the bottom.* **1795** Hamilton *Papers* 19.304, 473, 519. **1795** WVMurray in Gibbs *Memoirs* 1.228: The old Dutch principle of *free bottoms, free goods.* **1796** Hamilton *Papers* 20.479. **1796** Monroe *Writings* 3.60: The principle that *free ships make free goods.* **1798** Adams *Writings* 2.289: *Free ships make free goods.* **1798** Cabot *Letters* 594: The principle of "free bottoms making free goods." **1798** Hamilton *Papers* 21.424. **1799** WEaton in *Barbary Wars* 1.335: Free bottoms do not make free goods. **1800** Adams *Works* 9.86. **1800** Hamilton *Works* 10.399. **1800** King *Life* 3.288: The Doctrine that "free bottoms make free goods," is in direct opposition to the ancient Law. **1800** WVMurray in McHenry *Letters* 495. **1801** GCabot in King *Life* 3.379: The doctrine of "Free Ships make Free Goods" is the most pernicious to Neutrals that cou'd be devised, 408, 415. **1801** Jefferson *Writings* 10.277, 278, 282, 283, 284. **1801** Paine *Correspondence* 2.1420, 1421. **1802** WEaton in *Barbary Wars* 2.143. **1802** *Port Folio* 2.375. **1803** Adams *Memoirs* 1.273. **1803** Austin *Constitutional* 319. **1803** King *Life* 4.261. **1803** Paine *To the Citizens* 2.946. **1805** Monroe *Writings* 4.336, 342. **?1806** King *Life* 4.586, 587. **1806** *Monthly Anthology* 3.49. **1807** Paine *On the Question* 2.1016. **1809** JTrumbull in King *Life* 5.175. **1813** Jefferson *Writings* 13.243. **1815** Adams *Memoirs* 3.229. **1823** Jefferson *Writings* 15.410: The principle of "free bottoms making free goods, and enemy bottoms enemy goods," 411, 412. **1824** Adams *Memoirs* 6.381. **1824** Anderson *Diary* 151. DA free 3; Lean 3.468; NED Free 31.

S149 He that gets a **Ship** or a wife will always have trouble

1810 *Port Folio* 2NS 3.313: He who would have trouble in this world, let him get either a ship, or a wife. *Oxford* 723; Tilley S350.

S150 A **Ship** and a lady's watch are always out of repair

1830 Ames *Mariner's* 251: A ship is like a lady's watch, always out of repair. *Oxford* 723; TW 327(2). Cf. Tilley W658.

S151 The **Ship** in harbor is safe

1806 Asbury *Letters* 3.356: The ship is so safe in harbor. Whiting S250.

S152 A **Ship** never gets safe to port that has a priest on board

1800 Dow *Journal* 107: The owner would not consent that the master should take me on board; saying, where they have priest, minister, or preacher on board, there is no prosperity or good luck. **1803** Davis *Travels* 441: I hope you are not a priest. A ship never gets safe to port that has a priest on board. Lean 2.185-6.

S153 A **Ship** under sail and a big-bellied woman, *etc.*

1735 Franklin *PR* 2.7: A Ship under sail and a big-bellied Woman, Are the handsomest two things that can be seen common. *Oxford* 724; Tilley S351.

S154 To carry one's **Ship**

1648 LDowning in *Winthrop Papers(A)* 5.290: But he had not yet arte enoughe to carye his ship [to get ahead—the man had nothing to do with the sea].

S155 To pump **Ship**

1770 Adams *Legal Papers* 3.135: He said he was pumping ship. **1817** Baldwin *Letters* x: An "Exile of Erin" . . . pumped ship so enormously that he set everything afloat. Colcord 146; Partridge 667.

S156 To be **Ship-shape**

1732 Belcher *Papers* 1.212: Methinks if Madame was here it wou'd look more ship-shape. **1783** Williams *Penrose* 189: It was not quite so Ship Shap as is the Sailors term. TW 327(1).

S157 To be **Ship-shape** and Bristol fashion

1803 Davis *Travels* 427: This is neither ship-shape, nor *Bristol* fashion. *Oxford* 724; TW 327(2).

S158 What one loses in the **Shire**, he gets in the hundred

1652 Williams *Writings* 4.304: What he looseth in the *Shire*, he gets in the *Hundredth*. *Oxford* 487: Hundred; Whiting H634. See **O27.**

S159 As pale as a **Shirt**(tail)

1775 AMiddleton in Gibbes 2.138: He turned as pale as his shirt tail. **1791** Delano *Narrative* 97: White . . . returned to us as pale as a shirt. Svartengren 235.

S160 Not to let one's **Shirt** know

1701 F-JWinthrop in *Winthrop Papers(B)* 5.78: In their close counselt there is some thing they will not let their shirts know. *Oxford* 724; Tilley S357.

S161 The **Shirt** is nearest the skin

1744 Hamilton *Itinerarium* 5: This brought the proverb in my mind, the shirt is nearest the skin. *Oxford* 556; Whiting K67. See **S233.**

S162 To take from the **Shirt** to give to the ruffle

1816 Paulding *Letters(II)* 116: [It] would lead me . . . to inquire, . . . whether the acquisition of this refinement . . . does not in reality injure society by taking away from the shirt to give to the ruffle. See **W3.**

S163 As black as my **Shoes**

1765 DFowler in *Wheelock's Indians* 94: Their Cloaths are black and greasy as my Shoes. Whiting S258.

S164 If the **Shoe** fits wear it

1773 *New-York Gazette* in *Newspaper Extracts(I)* 9.508: Let those whom the shoe fits wear it. **1780** *New Jersey Gazette* in *Newspaper Extracts(II)* 4.203: Wishing that every foot may wear the shoe that fits it. Barbour 162(7); TW 328(5). See **C29.**

S165 Not good enough to wipe his **Shoes** (*varied*)

1620 RCushman in Bradford *History* 1.142: As if they were not good enough to wipe his shoes. **1646** NWard in Winslow *Hypocrisie* 77: I hold myself not worthy to wipe his slippers. *Oxford* 922; Tilley S378, cf. L84; Whiting T215.

S166 Old **Shoes** and old friends are best

1764 Rush *Letters* 1.8: It was an observation of a royal personage, and flowed from the lips of majesty itself, "that old shoes and old friends were always the best." *Oxford* 589, cf. 213; Tilley F755. See **F303, W222.**

S167 Over **Shoes,** over boots

1742 Ames *Almanacs* 154: Over Shoes and Boots for Money and Wood. **1787** Paine *Prospects on the Rubicon* 2.623: By verifying the old English proverb, "Over shoes, over boots." *Oxford* 603; Tilley S379.

S168 To be in someone's **Shoes**

1777 JA in *Adams FC* 2.336: I should put more to risque if I were in his shoes. **1845** Jackson *Correspondence* 6.387: Just placing Col. Polk in Tylers shoes. TW 328(4). See **C233.**

S169 (To know where) the **Shoe** pinches

1709 EProut in *Saltonstall Papers* 1.290: They both make very fair weather but I think Mr. Seldens shoe pinches him. **1737** Franklin *Drinkers* 2.177: His Shoe pinches him. **1742** *Georgia Records* 23.350-1: You dont want to be shewn where the Shoe Pinches, I am sure. **1751** *New York Weekly Post Boy* in *Newspaper Extracts(I)* 3.18: Here . . . we may suppose the Shoe pinches. **1756** Laurens *Papers* 2.158: They felt where the Shoe pinch'd. **1763** Gadsden *Writings* 19: Here, and only here, the shoe pinches. **1766** *Beekman Papers* 1.498: None knows where the shoe pinshes but them that wear it. **1769** Woodmason *Journal* 272: We, who *Know* and *Feel* where the Shoe pinches, can best determine. **1779** Lee(W) *Letters* 3.701: The English proverb is a good one, "that no-body can tell better where the shoe pinches but he that wears it." **1790** Adams *New Letters* 43: Every person knows best where their own shoe pinches. **1790** Lloyd *Papers* 2.827: I know where the shoe pinches. **1798** Gadsden *Writings* 284: Here the shoe pinches with her. **1798** *Washington Writings* 36.209: There the shoe pinches. **1800** Freneau *Prose* 432: Ah! says I, every body knows where his own shoe binds him. **1814** Adams *Memoirs* 3.121: Bayard . . . appeared not to know where it was that Clay's shoe pinched

him. **1821** Jefferson *Writings* 15.342: She had better lie by . . . till the shoe shall pinch an Eastern State. **1824** Blane *Excursion* 151: "Ah! master," said the poor old negro, "No one knows where the shoe pinches, but he who wears it." Barbour 162(12); *Oxford* 725; Whiting S266.

S170 Not worthy to unloose his **Shoe-latchets**

1676 Williams *Writings* 5.141: He was not worthy to unloose the Shoe-latchet of Jesus. **1809** Tyler *Yankey* 58-9: Milton, the latchet of whose shoes . . . [Dr. Johnson] was not worthy to unloose. *Oxford* 922; Tilley L84; Whiting T215.

S171 As ever trod **Shoe-leather**

1796 Barton *Disappointment* 34: As grate a rascal, as ever trod shoe-leather. **1809** Irving *History* 2.197: And the worthiest trumpeter that ever trod shoe leather. **1815** Humphreys *Yankey* 37: About as nice and tidy a crittar as ever trod shews'-leather. a**1855** Beecher *Autobiography* 2.72: It was as finely organized a Church as ever trod shoe-leather. *Oxford* 725-6; TW 329.

S172 To spend **Shoe-leather**

1766 JParker in Franklin *Papers* 13.526: I spent as much Time and Shoe-Leather, as I might have earn'd 40s. NED Shoe-leather b.

S173 A **Shoe-licker** and an arse-kisser

1766 Adams *D and A* 1.300: Made him in Thatchers Phrase a shoe licker and an A-se Kisser of Elisha Hutchinson. NED Shoe 6c; Wentworth 10: ass.

S174 He is a silly **Shoe-maker,** *etc.*

1707 *Penn-Logan Correspondence* 2.220: He must be a silly shoemaker that hath not a last for his own foot. See **C284.**

S175 **Shoe-string** fellows

1759 Adams *D and A* 1.114: Shoe string fellows that never use Tea and would use it as [?awkwardly] as the Landlady did, **1761** 214: Oh those vile shoe string Representatives. DA shoestring 2b; NED *Suppl.* Shoe-string 1c. Cf. TW 329(2).

S176 A **Shoeing-horn**

1694 *Connecticut Vindicated* 94: All this

kindness . . . is but a meer *Shooing horn* to his design. NED Shoeing-horn 2b.

S177 Keep your **Shop** and your shop will keep you

1652 Shepard *Hints* 159: He who keeps not his shop, his shop will not keep him. **1735** Franklin *PR* 2.7: Keep thy shop, and thy shop will keep thee, **1758** *WW* 344. **1770** Ames *Almanacs* 412. **1779** Franklin *Writings* 7.382. **1819** Waln *Key* 29: Stick to your shop. *Oxford* 419; Tilley S392; Whiting *NC* 473.

S178 To run a **Shore**

1815 Palmer *Diary* 198: I Rec^d some cash, which I . . . stood very much in need of — have run entirely a Shore for Tobacco &c. **1816** Smith *Life* 235: This was the first time of my seeing a minister on shore, high and dry [the minister had risen but could not find words]. Cf. Colcord 21-2.

S179 The **Short** (long) and long (short) of it.

1691 *Humble Address* in *Andros Tracts* 2.17: The short and long of the business was. **1691** Mather *Letters* 28: The short and long, and the truth of our intelligence. **1719** *Present Melancholy* in *Colonial Currency* 1.353: And this is the very Case, the short and long of the Business. **1782** Paine *Rhode Island* 2.338: The long and short of the story. **1797** Brackenridge *Modern* 264: Just the short and the lang o' it, said Duncan, 326: That is the short and the lang o' it. **1801** Trumbull *Season* 105: The long and the short of the matter. **1807** Weems *Murder* 22: That's the long and short of it. **1814** Mrs. RKennon in *VHM* 30(1922) 300: The short and the long of this circumbendibus is; that you are to try not to get in love. **1822** Weems *Penn* 60: That's the long and short of it. **1824** *Tales* 2.37. **1826** Wirt *Letters* 2.212. NED Long B I 3; *Oxford* 478; TW 227.

S180 **Short** and sweet

1738 *Georgia Records* 22¹.171: 'Twas short and sweet. **1747** Laurens *Papers* 1.72: I have your obliging favour . . . Short & sweet. **1780** Sargent *Loyalist* 14. **1809** *Port Folio* 2NS 2.425. **1809** Weems *Marion* 212. **c1825** Tyler *Prose* 105. **1829** PBPorter in Smith *Letters* 269: If my time is short, it shall be sweet, as

the proverb says, short and sweet. Barbour 163(1); *Oxford* 727; TW 330.

S181 Like a **Shot** out of a shovel

1803 Davis *Travels* 447: Here I come to you like a shot out of a shovel! **1807** Weems *Murder* 4: He beheld a defendant . . . bourne out of the Court-house like a shot out of a shovel. TW 330(4).

S182 A long **Shot**

1763 Laurens *Papers* 3.353: I thought at the very time that this was a long shot. NED Shot *sb.*¹ 9d. Cf. TW 330(2).

S183 A random **Shot**

1757 Laurens *Papers* 2.520: Her trip hither . . . seem'd in our judgement a very random shott. **1762** Watts *Letter Book* 45: I send these few Lines a random shot to Philadelphia. Cf. NED Shot *sb.*¹ 10.

S184 To have a **Shot** in the locker

1789 Alden *Epitaphs* 5.52: One who never struck his flag, while he had a shot in his locker. **1802** Chester *Federalism* 17: He'll fight while there's a shot in the locker. **1809** Lindsley *Love* 9: May the eagle have a shot in the locker till doomsday. **1812** Otis *Letters* 1.318: They will have the privilege of paying their own expenses, there being no shot in the Locker. **1827** Jackson *Correspondence* 3.355: You must visit us next year when we will attone for this should it take the last shot in the *locker*. TW 330(7).

S185 Two **Shots** never go in the same place

1778 Heath *Memoirs* 190: "Master, you never know shot to go in the same place." Cf. Barbour 109(7): Lightning; TW 221(11). See **B361.**

S186 Over the left **Shoulder**

1760 JBoucher in *MHM* 7(1912) 20: I see I have p'd you a Comp't *over the left shoulder*. **1763** Watts *Letter Book* 170: A Namesake of mine & a sort of a relation too over the left shoulder. *Oxford* 603; Tilley S405. See **L96.**

S187 To burn one's **Shoulder**

1737 Franklin *Drinkers* 2.177: He's burnt his Shoulder.

S188 To lay one's **Shoulder** to the wheel (*varied*)

1776 Paine American *Crisis* 1.55: Lay your shoulder to the wheel. **1779** *New Jersey Gazette* in *Newspaper Extracts(II)* 4.87: Let us oblige every man to put his shoulder to the wheel, 112: Remember the fable of *Jupiter* and the *waggoner,* who, having got his waggon into a slough, prayed to Jupiter to draw it out for him — But the God reproved his sloth, and ordered him to *clap his shoulder to the wheel.* **1779** *Washington *Writings* 15.61: Every man must put his shoulder to the wheel or I am convinced it will stick. **1781** Col. Willett in *Clinton Papers* 7.80: Yet let us not forget to keep our Shoulders to the wheel by doing all we can. **1784** Rush *Letters* 1.342: In the meanwhile let each of us put our shoulders to the wheel. **1796** Weems *Letters* 2.47: I'll clap my shoulders to the wheels. **1799** Cobbett *Porcupine* 10.150: He must clap his own shoulder to the wheel. **1800** Jefferson *Writings* 10.152: These are laying their shoulders to the draught. **1805** JLee in *Jacksons and Lees* 1.547-8: Unless my wants induce me to apply my shoulders more forcibly to the wheels than I have ever done. **1807** Mackay *Letters* 76. **1817** FTudor in Massachusetts Historical Society, *Proceedings* 65(1932-36) 185: I put my shoulder to the wheel and after many a hard struggle I have rolled my wagon on. **1818** Weems *Letters* 3.232. **1820** Jefferson *Writings* 15.280: They are still putting their shoulders to the wrong wheel. **1820** Wright *Views* 267. **1822** Murphey *Papers* 1.247. **1823** *Austin Papers* 1.573: Let us . . . put our shoulders to the wheel and make our fortunes. **1829** Longfellow *Letters* 1.302. **1845** Jackson *Correspondence* 6.412. Barbour 163(2); *Oxford* 729; TW 331(3).

S189 The **Show** is over

1797 Foster *Coquette* 138: Well, Charles, the show is over, as we Yankees say. DA show 3b.

S190 If we stand the **Shower** we shan't flinch for the drops

1723 Symmes *Utile* 50: If we've stood the shower I hope we shan't flinch for the Drops.

S191 The last **Shower** is always the heaviest

1808 Rush *Letters* 2.983: The last shower with them is always the heaviest.

S192 On the wrong (better) **Side** of the hedge

c1700 Taylor *Poems* 447: If it was in't to get it out he'd 'ledge, Thou on the wrong side art the Pale or hedge. **1716** Church *History* 1.161: His side which now began to be on the better side of the hedge. *Oxford* 732; Tilley S428.

S193 On the wrong (shady) **Side** of thirty (sixty)

1756 Laurens *Papers* 2.277: Such as are on the Wrong Side 30 years of Age. **1781** Curwen *Journal* 2.795: On the wrong side of 60. **1807** *Salmagundi* 126: The younger being somewhat on the shady side of thirty. TW 332(8).

S194 There are two **Sides** to a bargain

1795 OWolcott in Gibbs *Memoirs* 1.201: There are two sides to a bargain. Cf. *Oxford* 852; TW 332(4); Tilley W827. See **W326.**

S195 There are two **Sides** to a question

1802 Adams *D and A* 3.269: There were two Sides to a question, **1811** *Writings* 4.240: There are two sides to that question. **1817** TJefferson in *Adams-Jefferson Letters* 2.513: There are two sides to every question. Barbour 164(2); *Oxford* 852; TW 332(4).

S196 To laugh on the wrong (other) **Side** of one's mouth

1791 S.P.L. *Thoughts* 167: To laugh on the wrong side of one's mouth. **1823** Weems *Letters* 3.352: We will give them a spanker that may . . . put the laugh on the other side of their mouths. *Oxford* 445; TW 333(13). See **W72.**

S197 To put the best **Side** out(wards)

1792 JHoskins in *Columbia* 279: Those natives . . . as is common with more civilized people so with them they put the best side outwards. **1804** Dow *Journal* 209: I have seen some men and women in courtship put . . . the best side out. TW 333(17). See **F257.**

S198 To tell on which **Side** one's bread is buttered

1762 JWatts in *Aspinwall Papers* 1.451: We have not seen Butter to our Bread, so of course as Napier would say, can't tell on which side our Bread is butter'd. Barbour 22: Bread(7); *Oxford* 438; Whiting S302.

S199 By a **Side-wind**

1786 WGrayson in Jefferson *Papers* 9.654: To get a side wind confirmation to a thing they had no right to. **1789** Maclay *Journal* 101: But for the House of Representatives, by a side-wind, to exalt the President above the Constitution, and depress the Senate below it, is—but I will leave it without name. **1825** Pearse *Narrative* 107: The jury may have been worked by a side wind. NED Sidewind 2, 3.

S200 As leaky as a **Sieve**

1620 RCushman in Bradford *History* 1.142: Leakie as a seive. **1777** Kemble *Papers* 1.139: Leakey as a sieve. Barbour 164(2); *Oxford* 732; TW 333(1). See **R77**.

S201 As open as a **Sieve**

1803 Asbury *Journal* 2.377: [A] chapel . . . open as a sieve.

S202 To be like a **Sieve**

1785 Asbury *Journal* 1.498: The house was like a sieve. **1798** Adams *Writings* 2.335: Our government has in fact no more retention than a sieve. Everything leaks out. *Oxford* 732; Tilley S435.

S203 To fill a **Sieve** with water

1813 GMorris in King *Life* 5.359: Your efforts . . . to fill a sieve with water. *Oxford* 870; Whiting W86.

S204 Out of **Sight** out of mind

1629 MWinthrop in *Winthrop Papers(A)* 2.92: It makes me thinke that sayinge falce out of sight out of minde. **1636** WLeigh in *Winthrop Papers(A)* 3.311: But least that proverb might seame to take place in me, out of sight out of mind, know that I make more frequent mention of you . . . then is to be expressed with pen and Inke. **1750** *Washington *Writings* 1.16: You'l not make the Old Proverb good out of sight out of

Mind. **1756** Yaha Tustanage in McDowell *Documents* 2.154. **1763** HBarclay in Johnson *Writings* 4.110. **1767** *Beekman Papers* 1.508: the Old Proverb. **1771** Winslow *Diary* 13. **1774** Adams *Works* 4.71: Although he is out of our sight, he ought not to be out of our minds. **1775** *Byrd Letters* in *VHM* 39(1931) 223: the old proverb. **1776** Shaw *Journals* 12: But, though out of sight, my dear parents, you are not out of mind. **1780** Curwen *Journal* 2.710: In me is verified. **1781** Jay *Correspondence* 2.6: The vulgar proverb, *out of sight, out of mind,* always appeared to me in the light of a vulgar error when applied to *friends and companions.* **1784** MHopkins in *MHM* 24(1929) 24: The old proverb. **1785** Tilghman *Letters* 126. **1802** Ames *Letters* 1.302: is their maxim. **1825** Smith *Letters* 205. Barbour 164(2); *Oxford* 602; Whiting S307.

S205 A **Sight** for sore eyes

1709 Lawson *Voyage* 44: It is an infallible Cure for Sore-Eyes even to see an *Indian*'s Dog fat (i.e., they are never fat). **1767** MSCranch in *Adams FC* 1.59: A Sight here rare enough to cure sore Eyes. **1850** Clark *Letters* 154: The appearance of your once-familiar "hand of write" was a gude sight for sair een, to me. Barbour 164(1); *Oxford* 732; TW 124: Eye (8).

S206 To beat someone out of **Sight**

1789 BMarston in *Winslow Papers* 370: Their High Priest . . . has beat the Archbishop of Canterbury (a Marble-head man would say) out of sight. NED Sight *sb.*[1] 10c.

S207 To live at the **Sign** of the snail

1726 Mather *Letters* 410: Perhaps, I may add, *excite* him too against loss of time, and against living at the *sign of the snail.* Cf. NED Sign 6b. See **S267**.

S208 **Signs** fail in dry times

1729 Ames *Almanacs* 63: But in Dry times great Signs do Fail. Barbour 164; TW 333.

S209 **Silence** gives consent (*varied*)

1648 *Winthrop Papers(A)* 5.255: It may be my silence about it he might take for consent. **1666** Alsop *Maryland* 87: Live in silence . . . is to give consent. **1682** Plumstead 103:

And that by a total silence and a full connivance. **1685** Sewall *Diary* 1.105: Silence gave Consent. **a1700** Hubbard *New England* 278: To which the rest of the church yielded a silent assent. **1702** NNoyes in Mather *Magnalia* 1.485: He . . . took their consent in a silentful way. **1717** Byrd *Another Secret Diary* 313: Nor dare I hope any benefit from her silence, because I fear t'is rather a sign of scorn than consent. **1723** Symmes *Utile* 55. **1727** Parkman *Diary* 71.175: God forgive wherein I in any way countenanc'd it by my Criminal silence. **1742** *Georgia Records* 24.50: His father Assenting to what he said by his Countenance & Silence. **1751** Parkman *Diary* 75.91. **1774** Adams *D and A* 2.91: The Council had the Pusillanimity to consent by their Silence. **1744** Carter *Diary* 2.818: And as men of Pleasure know that silence implies consent. **1774** Seabury *Letters* 78. **1778** *Clinton Papers* 3.744: That the Silence of Congress on this Occassion . . . may be considered as countenancing these unwarantable Measures. **1781** Stiles *Diary* 2.492. **1785** Smith *Diary* 1.223: Silence passes for Assent as in the house of Lords & Commons. **1787** WSSmith in Smith *Journal and Correspondence* 1.125. **1788** *Politician* 64. **1792** *Washington *Writings* 32.46: On the other hand, to say nothing, implies consent. **1793** GMorris in Sparks *Correspondence* 4.431: If you are silent, you assent; and if you speak, you are committed. **1794** Hamilton *Papers* 17.573: I have concluded not by my silence to give sanction to it. **1795** Adams *Writings* 1.280: Their silence was taken for consent. **1799** Barlow *Works* 1.369: His silence ought not to be construed into approbation. **1800** Cobbett *Porcupine* 11.226: Your silence on the subject will be considered as an acknowledgement of your guilt. **1803** RLivingston in King *Life* 4.311. **1805** Brackenridge *Modern* 574: [They] must mistake silence for approbation. **1807** JPerkins in *Cabot Family* 2.535. **1812** Lee *Memoirs* 1.178: Gates . . . understanding silence to be an approbation of the sentiments delivered by Stevens. **1815** *Port Folio* 3NS 5.488. **1816** Smith *Life* 183: My silence was consenting to his death doctrine for that time. **1824** Monroe *Writings* 7.40: By silence admit the truth, and, if applied to by others,

affirm it. Barbour 164(1); *Oxford* 733; Whiting S733.

S210   Silence is prudence (wisdom)

1790 Adams *New Letters* 36: There are cases where silence is prudence. **1825** Jackson *Correspondence* 3.283: Silence would have been to him wisdom. *Oxford* 898; Tilley W519. Cf. Whiting S308, 309. See **T178, W310.**

S211   To take Silence as a refusal

1746 JMason in Belknap *History* 2.201: He should take their silence as a refusal.

S212   As fine as Silk

1691 Taylor *Poems* 67: A Clew of Wonders finer far than Silke, **1695** 106: More rich than Jasper, finer far then Silke. Barbour 164(3); Whiting S310.

S213   As soft as Silk

1672 Josselyn *New-Englands Rarities* 154: Soft as silk, 165. **1820** Faux *Memorable Days* 2.73: Grass . . . soft as silk. **1825** Wirt *Letters* 1.38: My hair . . . was as clean and soft as silk. Barbour 165(6); Svartengren 266; Whiting S313.

S214   Silks and satins put out the kitchen fire

1746 Franklin *PR* 3.63: Silks and Sattins put out the Kitchen Fire, **1757** 7.80: Scarlet, Silk and Velvet, have put out the Kitchen Fire, **1758** *WW* 346: Silks and Sattins, Scarlet and Velvets, put out the Kitchen Fire. **1770** Ames *Almanacs* 413: Silks & sattins put out the kitchen fire. Barbour 164(4); *Oxford* 733-4; Tilley S452.

S215   As pure as Silver

1812 JWatson in Knopf *War of 1812* 6(1) 231: Their hearts are as pure as silver.

S216   Silver-white

1784 Smyth *Tour* 1.158: Silver-white ringlets. Whiting S323.

S217   The real Simon pure

1811 Graydon *Memoirs* 44: And that a Quaker was no other than a licensed Simon pure for his amusement. **1818** JRandolph in King *Life* 6.164: At this distance it is very difficult to know the real Simon Pure. **c1820**

Bernard *Retrospections* 328: The real Simon Pure. **1824** *Tales* 1.156. **1830** Ames *Mariner's* 102. **1834** Floy *Diary* 118: No part of the original waggon is now left but one of the hubs; that is real simon pure. **1839** WLewis in Jackson *Correspondence* 6.22: These *real Simon Pures* of the party. **1840** Hone *Diary* 1.490. **1845** Jackson *Correspondence* 6.371: Those who . . . are now pretending to be the simon pures of democracy. TW 334.

S218   As ugly as Sin

1810 Rush *Autobiography* 359: She is ugly as sin. **1836** Floy *Diary* 250: He is a shrewd looking fellow but ugly as sin. Barbour 165(5); *Oxford* 853; TW 335(8).

S219   Little Sins have small pardons

c1700 Taylor *Poems* 397: For little Sins, but little pardons have.

S220   Sin and shame go together

1664 Bradstreet *Works* 64: Sin and shame ever goe together. Whiting R101, cf. S338. Cf. *Oxford* 592.

S221   Sins and debts are always more than we take them to be

1774 Franklin *Writings* 6.202-3: I am sensible there is a good deal of Truth in the Adage, that *our Sins and our Debts are always more than we take them to be,* **1780** 8.160: I am convinced now of the justness of poor Richard's remark, that "Our debts and our sins are always greater than we think for." *Oxford* 737; Tilley S476.

S222   To Sing small

1766 JParker in Franklin *Papers* 13.309: I must sing small. **1777** TThompson in Franklin *Writings* 7.55: Small Folks must sing small. **1779** JBarrell in Webb *Correspondence* 2.195. **1780** *New Jersey Gazette* in *Newspaper Extracts(II)* 4.214: The high toned loyalists sing small. **1792** Belknap *Foresters* 203. **1793** JMorse in Gibbs *Memoirs* 1.124. **1808** Hitchcock *Poetical Dictionary* 24. **1815** Humphreys *Yankey* 34. TW 339: Small.

S223   May the Single be married and the married happy

1780 RHowe in Webb *Correspondence* 2.315-6: May the single be married, and the married happy, is an old adage to which thou hast tossed off many a Bumper.

S224   Sink or swim

1652 Williams *Writings* 4.396: What ever becomes (sinck or swim) of other mens. **1676** Tompson *Poems* 94: These Worthies three must sink or float. ?**1689** ?Mather *Vindication* in *Andros Tracts* 2.68: They cared not . . . which Sank or Swam. **1689** Sewall *Diary* 1.266. **1705** Ingles *Reply* 160. **1706** Winslow *Broadside* 21: Then Sink, or Swim; or Live, or Die. **1720** ?EWigglesworth *Vindication* in *Colonial Currency* 2.36. **1724** Sewall *Letter-Book* 2.167. **1733** Belcher *Papers* 1.394. **1750** *Massachusetts* in *Colonial Currency* 4.448: They little regard who *sinks,* if they swim. **1769** Winslow *Broadside* 133: Let sink who will, or swim, they will be blest. **1781** Oliver *Origin* 101. **1783** Freneau *Poems* 2.202: I shall make it appear, I can swim where they'll sink. **1783** Williams *Penrose* 47. **1783** JWilson in Madison *Papers* 6.171. **1790** JBarrell in *Columbia* 446. **1791** S.P.L. *Thoughts* 167. **1796** Asbury *Journal* 2.101. **1800** HJackson in *Bingham's Maine* 2.1040. **1801** Adams *Writings* 2.491-2: The nation would . . . sink or swim with their flag. **1804** *Echo* 306. **1805** TJefferson in *Bowdoin Papers* 2.241: [We] should have swam or sunk together. **1806** Fessenden *Modern Philosopher* 64. **1810** Weems *Letters* 3.2: And accosting me as a Wretch who heeds not who *sinks,* provided he *swims.* When did I ever make (a)way with your *property, swim* with the *money* & leave you to sink, **1811** *Gambling* 12: Provided he swims, no matter who sinks. **1812** Asbury *Journal* 2.693. **1814** Kerr *Barclay* 75: If I can't swim I'll sink. **1816** Adams *Memoirs* 3.429: The ministers will sink or swim all together. **1816** Jefferson *Writings* 14.383: I am willing to swim or sink with my fellow citizens. **1816** Paulding *Letters(I)* 2.157. **1819** Adams *Works* 4.8: Swim or sink, live or die, survive or perish with my country. **1821** Freneau *Last Poems* 47. **1824** *Austin Papers* 1.919. *Oxford* 737; Whiting F268.

S225 The greater the **Sinner,** the greater the saint

1768 Woodmason *Journal* 101: For it is a Maxim with these Vermin of Religion, That a Person must first be a Sinner e're He can be a Saint. **1824** *Tales* 2.6: Greater the sinner, greater the saint. **1830** Ames *Mariner's* 241: The greater the sinner, the greater the Saint. *Oxford* 336; TW 335(4).

S226 **Sir Reverence**

c1725 Byrd *Another Secret Diary* 464: She . . . plants her little Foot in the midst of a wholesome Sr. Reverence. Tilley R93. Cf. *Oxford* 701; Whiting R100.

S227 At **Sixes** and sevens

1690 Sewall *Letter-Book* 1.99: His Concerns here . . . will otherwise ly at sixes and sevens. **1770** JBoucher in *MHM* 8(1913) 175: My removal hither has thrown my affairs all in to sixes and sevens. **1772** Paterson *Glimpses* 121: Things sure in sixes are & sevens. **1781** Witherspoon *Works* 4.473. **1782** *Washington Writings* 24.140: His business . . . was . . . left at Sixes and Sevens. **1788** Jefferson *Papers* 14.369: My affairs there which were left at sixes and sevens. **1809** Irving *History* 1.vi: Old mouldy books, laying about at sixes and sevens, 2.203. **1811** *Port Folio* 2NS 5.223: The author . . . is left at sixes and sevens. **1816** Paulding *Letters(I)* 1.111. **1820** Irving *Journals(Trent)* 1.22. **1842** Cooper *Letters* 4.224, **1850** 6.227. Barbour 165(3); *Oxford* 739; Whiting S359.

S228 **Six** of one and half a dozen of the other

1830 Ames *Mariner's* 121: It is six one way, and half a dozen the other. Barbour 165(1); *Oxford* 739; TW 336(1).

S229 To throw **Sixes**

1777 TMcKean in Sparks *Correspondence* 1.448: You must . . . get the game, though you should not throw sixes. **1807** Rush *Letters* 2.944: My friends have often told me I must throw sixes (to use an allusion from the dice board). NED Six B2.

S230 To ride **Skimmington**

1732 Peter Gordon *Journal,* ed. E. M. Coulter (Athens, Georgia, 1963) 30-1: After din-ner we were diverted with cudgell playing and riding of skimingtons on account of Mrs. Coles having beat her husband. **1765** *New York Weekly Post Boy* in *Newspaper Extracts(I)* 5.565: [They] had assaulted a man they suspected of wronging his Wife by too great a Familiarity with another Woman, with an Intent to make him ride *Skimmington,* that is upon a Pole, carried on Men's Shoulders. **1768** Adams *Legal Papers* 1.327: If he had not rid her skimmington he had some other way. **1776** Willard *Letters* 323: Some have been obliged to ride Skimmington on a rail. NED Skimmington; *Oxford* 740; Tilley S504.

S231 As close as one's **Skin**

1742 Belcher *Papers* 2.433: I know our candidate would hug you as close as his skin. Cf. TW 337(1).

S232 Good to sleep in a whole **Skin** (*varied*)

1625 EAltham in James *Three Visitors* 54: But they, loving to sleep in a whole skin, laid down their arms. **1692** Bulkeley *Will* 89: If I would but temporize, I could easily sleep in a whole skin. **1728** Byrd *Dividing Line* 60: Fellows . . . whom Chance had Condemn'd to remain upon Firm Land and Sleep in a whole Skin, 61: Poor Orion began to repent & wish he had Slept in a whole Skin at the College. **a1731** Cook *Bacon* 323: Other *Ingramites* thought best, Tho' naked, in whole Skins to rest. **1746** *Georgia Records* 25.50: For the sake of sleeping in whole Skin any might hide it. **1776** SAdams in *Warren-Adams Letters* 1.280: To get money and sleep, as the vulgar Phrase is, in a whole Skin. **1777** JA in *Adams FC* 2.231: We shall sleep in a whole Skin for some Time. **c1780** Witherspoon *Works* 4.393: Allow me to continue in peace and quiet, and according to the North-British proverb, *sleep in a whole skin.* **1781** Adams *Correspondence* 365: He will rather choose to sleep in a whole skin. **c1790** Brackenridge *Gazette* 20. **1800** NBarrell in Webb *Correspondence* 3.212. *Oxford* 472; Whiting S361.

S233 The **Skin** is nearer than the shirt (coat)

1690 *Further Quaeries* in *Andros Tracts* 1.207: Suffer our *French Enemies* to come and rifle us of what is nearer to us than our very *Shirts,* our *Skins.* **1755** *Johnson Papers* 1.687: My Skin is Nearer to me than my Coat, and I would rather be subjected to the Inclemency of the Weather than have my Skin stript over my Ears. *Oxford* 556-7; TW 337(4). See **S161.**

S234   To be content with one's **Skin**

1643 Williams *Writings* 1.144: *Intra pelliculam quemque tenere suam,* That every man be content with his skin.

S235   To come off (return) with a whole **Skin**

1733 Byrd *Journey* 299: The dogs . . . by their nimbleness came off with a whole skin. **1750** *Johnson Papers* 1.272: That I might return with a Whole Skin to New York. NED Skin 5c; Whiting *NC* 476(4). See **B257.**

S236   To escape with the **Skin** of one's Teeth

1730 JGrover in *Baxter Manuscripts* 11.46: [They were] to escape, as it were, with the skin of their teeth. **1775** Andrews *Letters* 405: If I can escape with the skin of my teeth. **1775** Asbury *Letters* 3.20. **1775** RCranch in *Adams FC* 1.259. **1781** JBane in *Baxter Manuscripts* 19.267. Barbour 166(1); *Oxford* 740; TW 337(3).

S237   To jump out of one's **Skin**

1788 *Politician* 164: I cou'd jump out of my skin at the thoughts of it. **1809** Irving *History* 2.38: He almost jumped out of his skin in an ecstasy of astonishment at the noise. **1814** Palmer *Diary* 118: It seemed as if the prisoners would jump out of their skins. **1816** Ker *Travels* 352. **1821** Knight *Poems* 2.163. TW 337(6); Tilley S507. Cf. Whiting S363.

S238   The toughest **Skin** will hold out the longest

1816 UBrown in *MHM* 10(1915) 346: The Tuffest Skin shall hold out the Longest.

S239   To sit on one's **Skirts** (blankets)

1762 *Johnson Papers* 3.829: Every one of their People being 3. in number found themselves between two Stockbridge Ind[ns.] pinned down as it were with their Blankets. JA in *Adams FC* 1.165: Mr. Galloway . . . has been supposed to sit on the Skirts of the

American Advocates, **1814** in *Adams-Warren Letters* 2.396: Through the whole Revolution the Tories sat on our skirts and were a dead weight. Lean 3.344; *Oxford* 738; Whiting S367.

S240   To take hold of one's **Skirt**

a1700 Hubbard *New England* 225: They took hold of the skirt of Massachusetts. Cf. NED Skirt 3(b).

S241   To be in **Skitters**

1797 JCarson in *Blount Papers* 3.127: I am in Sciethers [skitters] whether to return the Land for tax or not. NED Skitter *sb.*[1] 2.

S242   To skin one's own **Skunks**

1813 *Portsmouth Oracle* in DA skunk 3d(1): We here choose to let Mr. Madison *"skin his own skunks."* **1838** Hone *Diary* 1.331: He intends to "skin his skunks" without their aid. TW 338(4).

S243   When the **Sky** falls we shall catch larks

1778 *New Jersey Gazette* in *Newspaper Extracts(II)* 2.53. **1812** Hitchcock *Social* 34: May food and lodging for a world supply, By trapping larks beneath a falling sky. **1812** Taggart *Letters* 383. **1819** Faux *Memorable Days* 1.78: You may as well expect the sky will fall, to catch larks. *Oxford* 740; Whiting H314.

S244   **Sky-blue**

1793 *Echo* 53: The Laws sky blue. **1809** Kendall *Travels* 1.275: These are the laws sky blue. **a1814** Dow *Journal* 479: The second, a Sapphire, which is sky blue. TW 338.

S245   To be blown **Sky-high**

1824 Neal *American Writers* 61: They have blown him up—"sky-high." **1832** Ames *Nautical* 74: The press blows them "sky high." **1836** CEStowe in Beecher *Autobiography* 2.373: Their philosophy is exploded—blown sky-high. **1839** Jackson *Correspondence* 6.4: Their credit was blown sky high, **1845** 387. TW 338.

S246   High-water **Slack**

1770 Adams *Legal Papers* 3.167: In the same mode of phraseology, if so homely an expression may be used, perhaps, as the sea-

men say, it has been high-water slack. NED
Slack *sb.*³ 2.

S247 To work like a **Slave**

1785 Hunter *Quebec* 64: These Canadian
fellows work like slaves. **1796** Barlow *Letters*
131: I work like a slave. Barbour 166; Svartengren 124; TW 338. See **G9, N43.**

S248 There will be **Sleeping** enough in the
grave

1741 Franklin *PR* 2.296: In the grave will be
sleeping enough, **1758** *WW* 341: There will
be sleeping enough in the Grave. **1770** Ames
Almanacs 412. Barbour 166-7; *Oxford* 742.
See **W336.**

S249 To laugh in one's **Sleeve**

1692 Bulkeley *Will* 84: Some of his brethren
. . . cannot but laugh in their sleeves at . . .
this Goat. **1742** *Georgia Records* 23.345: He
. . . probably laughs in his Sleeve at his own
Exploits. **1747** WDawson in *W&MCQ* 2S
20(1940) 216. **1774** Stiles *Diary* 1.500. **1779**
Deane *Papers* 3.276. c**1790** Brackenridge
Gazette 191. **1790** *Universal Asylum* 5.168.
1792 Brackenridge *Modern* 40, 175. **1793**
Ingraham *Journal* 227. **1795** Freneau *Poems*
3.120. **1796** *St. Clair Papers* 2.417. **1797**
Cobbett *Porcupine* 5.63. **1797** WVMurray in
McHenry *Letters* 235. **1800** Hamilton *Works*
10.403, **1801** in McHenry *Letters* 484: Burr
. . . will laugh in his sleeve. **1802** Irving *Jonathan* 41. **1809** Fessenden *Pills* 19. 1809 Irving *History* 2.83. **1812** Hitchcock *Social* 79.
1816 Fidfaddy *Adventures* 36: The cursed
Yankees laugh in the sleeve. **1816** Ker
Travels 95. **1816** Paulding *Letters(I)* 1.159,
2.72. **1819** *Musings* 8: And if she laugh'd
not out, laugh'd in her sleeve. **1826** Royall
Sketches 73. **1829** Cooper *Letters* 1.372.
1831 Otis *Letters* 2.297. **1832** JRandolph
in Jackson *Correspondence* 4.427. *Oxford*
445; Whiting S382.

S250 There's many a **Slip** twixt the cup and
the lip (*varied*)

1758 Washington *Writings* 2.289: Many
accidents happening (to use a vulgar saying)
between the cup and the lip. **1767** Franklin
Papers 14.251: There are Uncertainties even
beyond those between the Cup and the Lip,
1771 *Writings* 5.314: For many things happen between the Cup & the Lip, **1772** 383.
1778 Lee(W) *Letters* 1.319: I know many
things have fallen out between the Cup and
the Lip. **1780** JEliot in *Belknap Papers*
3.200: Many of your sweet effusions have
been lost between the cup & the lip, **1783**
1.216: Remember the old proverb of "many
a slip," etc. **1787** Hamilton *Papers* 4.375:
You ask if . . . Kitty Livingston is married?
You recollect the proverb. She was ready . . .
to sip the blissful cup, when alas! it slipped
through her fingers—at least for a time, if
not for ever. **1790** JMercer in *W&MCQ*
17(1908) 214: But as many things fall between the Lip and the Cup. **1814** Palmer
Diary 20: As poor Richard says, **1815** 225: As
the old saying is. **1821** MStokes in Murphey
Papers 1.185: We . . . spilt the wine between
the "cup and the lip." **1823** JStory in Mason
Memoir 277. **1830** Jackson *Correspondence*
4.376: My son . . . will be a married man,
unless a slip between the cup and the lip.
Barbour 167(3); *Oxford* 160; TW 339(2).

S251 To give one the **Slip**

1637 Morton *New English Canaan* 284: Hee
might have an opportunity to give them a
slip, instead of a tester. **1745** Stephens *Jour-
nal(II)* 2.245: He had given the Slip to his
Indian Keepers, and was fled. **1772** Perkins
Diary 1.46: The people gave the officer the
slip. **1806** Fraser *Letters and Journals* 238.
NED Slip *sb.*³ 8. Cf. Tilley S537. See **G68.**

S252 As black as a **Sloe**

1792 Pope *Tour* 15: Her eyes were as black
as a Sloe. **1818** Royall *Letters* 143: Her eyes
. . . as black as sloes; and her cheeks are like
roses. Whiting S385.

S253 **Sloth** consumes faster than labor wears

1744 Franklin *PR* 2.398: Sloth (like Rust)
consumes faster than Labour wears; the used
Key is always bright, **1758** *WW* 341. Apperson 579; Barbour 167; *Oxford* 743.

S254 **Sloth** makes all things difficult

1734 Franklin *PR* 1.353: All things are easy
to Industry, All things difficult to Sloth,
1758 *WW* 341: Sloth makes all Things difficult, but Industry all easy. Apperson 579.

S255 **Slow** and (but) sure

1759 NAmes in *DHR* 1(1890) 51: Amherst goes slow and sure. **1775** JA in *Adams FC* 1.209: Our Determinations very slow—I hope sure, **1777** 2.268: Our Fabius will be slow, but sure. **1777** Lee *Letters* 1.339: The slow, but sure moving Gates has not yet sent in his Inventory. **1778** Paine *American Crisis* 1.116: Slow and sure is sound work. **1780** HGates in Jefferson *Papers* 3.650. **1781** EPendleton in Madison *Papers* 3.311: I cordially wish they may disappoint the Omens, & verify the old Adage, by giving proofs of wisdom & stability equal to their slowness. **1782** Pynchon *Diary* 134: The affairs of peace go on still, though slowly yet surely. **1787** *Washington *Writings* 29.261, **1791** 31.217: This Jack . . . though *sure*, is *slow* in covering. **1793** EWinslow in *Winslow Papers* 399: Our province goes on in the old way slowly but tolerably sure. **1794** Jefferson *Writings* 9.287: The maxim. **1794** *Washington *Writings* 33.339: We are going on in the old way "Slow". I hope events will justify me in adding "and sure" that the proverb may be fulfilled. "Slow and Sure." **1795** Jefferson *Writings* 9.303: With a slow but sure step. **1798** Bentley *Diary* 2.293: Tho' very slow, she's very sure. **1798** Dunlap *Diary* 1.336: "Caute & timide" say I, which for your edification I translate "Slow & sure." **1799** CGoodrich in Gibbs *Memoirs* 2.288: The body of the people move slowly, but surely. **1799** Weems *Letters* 2.121. **1800** Hamilton *Works* 10.363: Slow and sure is no bad maxim. Snails are a wise generation. **1805** Silliman *Travels* 2.153. **1805** Smith *Letters* 48: My kitchen work goes on sure and slow. **1812** JWheaton in Knopf *War of 1812* 6(4) 135: Altho we move slow, we will be Sure. **1813** Weems *Letters* 3.100. **1816** Fidfaddy *Adventures* 26: Take time more slowly and surely, war is not the work of a day. **1817** Scott *Blue Lights* 45. **1818** Baldwin *Letters* 281: I go on *slowly*, —and I hope the more surely. **1819** Pintard *Letters* 1.216: The old slow & sure habits of prudence & economy. **c1820** Bernard *Retrospections* 6. **1822** Lee *Diary and Letters* 196. Barbour 167; *Oxford* 743; TW 339(1).

S256 Plough (sow) deep while **Sluggards** sleep, *etc.*

1756 Franklin *PR* 6.327: Plough deep, while Sluggards sleep, And you shall have Corn, to sell and to keep, **1758** *WW* 342. **1770** Ames *Almanacs* 412: Sow deep. Barbour 167; *Oxford* 634; Tilley B625; Whiting *NC* 459.

S257 **Smallness** is a requisite of prettiness

1788 Adams *Diary* 392: But *smallness* is said to be one of the essential requisites of *prettiness*. *Oxford* 472: Little things; Tilley T188.

S258 The **Smith's** dog sleeps under the anvil

1773 Habersham *Letters* 224: We may be like the Smiths Dog, that sleeps under the Anvill, 226. *Oxford* 746; Tilley S563.

S259 A **Smithfield** bargain

1763 Watts *Letter Book* 208: It commenc'd a Matter of friendship not a Smithfield bargain. *Oxford* 746; Tilley S564. See **W154.**

S260 To have a **Smock-tail** in one's teeth

1813 Jackson *Correspondence* 1.431: I wish they and other volunteers had a smoke tail in their teeth, with a Peticoat as a coat of mail to hand down to there offspring [of men whom J. regarded as cowards, cf. n.[3]].

S261 More **Smoke** than fire

1771 Shaw *Letter Book* 231: Their is more Smoke then Fire. **1775** JA in *Adams FC* 1.196: There is always more Smoke than Fire. **1777** Munford *Patriots* 480. **1796** Washington *Writings* 35.153: I am glad to find that more smoke than fire is likely to result from the representation of French discontent. **1803** *Port Folio* 3.151. *Oxford* 550: TW 340(4); Tilley S568.

S262 To vanish like (in) **Smoke**

1647 Ward *Simple Cobler* 12: The God of Truth will in a short time scatter them all like Smoake before the winde. **a1656** Bradford *History* 1.96: They vanish into smoke. **1753** Franklin *Papers* 5.120: All the Pleasures . . . Vanishes into Smoke. **a1770** Johnson *Writings* 1.11. **1779** JMurray in *Baxter Manuscripts* 16.289: [They] would vanish into smoke without fire. **1779** *Washington *Writings* 15.58: The Good News . . . soon evaporated, and went off like smoak. **1780** Lee(W) *Letters* 3.786: It will end in smoak. **1785** EWinslow in *Winslow Papers* 273. **1790** Maclay *Journal* 261: This business will end in smoke. **1797** Callender *Annual Register 1796* 202: Jay's treaty must vanish into smoke. **1804** Harmon *Sixteen Years* 76: Vanish like smoke in the air. **1814** Jefferson *Writings* 14.114: This first project . . . vanished in smoke. **1845** Jackson *Correspondence* 6.378. Whiting S414. See **A60, M197.**

S263 Where there is **Smoke** there is fire (*varied*)

1773 WBradford in Madison *Papers* 1.80: Where there is smoke there must be some fire. **1774** Adams *Legal Papers* 1.136: The Maxim with many is that where there is so much Smoke there is always some fire. **1778** Hutchinson *Diary* 2.183: I . . . asked him whether there could be all this smoak about Lord Chatham, and no fire? **1779** 241: There seems to have been too much smoak to be no fire. **1783** JEliot in *Belknap Papers* 3.241: Can there be so much smoke without fire? **1789** Morris *Diary* 1.3: By the Smoke, however, all Doubts are removed respecting the Existence of Fire, **1797** *Diary and Letters* 2.250-1: The old proverb, "No smoke without some fire." **1815** Waterhouse *Journal* 73: Where there is much smoke there must be some fire. Barbour 167(1); *Oxford* 568, 573-4; TW 340(1); Whiting F194. See **F130.**

S264 To go (come in for) **Snacks**

1794 RBlackledge in *Blount Papers* 2.442: Others will Want favours as well as us & Come in for Snacks of course. **1797** Washington *Writings* 36.45: I am told however that he is sanguine and some add that he is to go snacks. *Oxford* 307; Tilley S578.

S265 As slow as **Snails** (snail-slow)

1774 JA in *Adams FC* 1.162: Slow, as snails. **1799** Weems *Philanthropist* 5: Others, snail slow in progress, **1809** *Washington* 46: Snail-slow to act. Barbour 167; Svartengren 373; Whiting S415.

S266 (At a) **Snail's** gallop

1794 Ames *Letters* 1.150: To hasten their snail's gallop. NED Snail *sb.*[1] 2b; *Oxford* 747; Tilley S583.

S267 At a **Snail's** pace

1787 Freneau *Poems* 2.355: The lawyer was vext that we went a snail's pace. **1801** Jefferson *Family Letters* 206: Go at a snail's pace when you set out. **1803** Irving *Journals* 1.25, 64. **1807** Jefferson *Writings* 11.400: There is a snail-paced gait for the advance of new ideas on the general mind. **1812** Bayard *Letters* 13. **1817** Weems *Letters* 3.216. **1819** WRoane in *Ruffin Papers* 1.226. c**1825** Tyler *Prose* 97, 170. **1827** Gallatin *Diary* 267. **1835** Floy *Diary* 161. *Oxford* 747; Whiting S424. See **S207.**

S268 A **Snail** has everything on its back

1793 *Washington *Writings* 33.151: 'Till then I move like a snail with everything on my back. Tilley S580.

S269 To creep like a **Snail**

1782 Trumbull *Satiric Poems* 200: Slow moved the baggage and the train, Like snail crept noiseless o'er the plain. **1836** Floy *Diary* 256: Then the beast would take advantage and creep along like a snail. TW 340(1).

S270 Tread on a **Snail** and it will turn

1803 *Port Folio* 3.121: "Tread upon a snail, and it will turn," is a very old adage. *Oxford* 837. See **W366.**

S271 As poor as a **Snake**

1797 Freneau *Poems* 3.162: Poor as a snake, and ever vile, Shall his condition be. Barbour 168(13); Whiting *NC* 478(9).

S272 As smooth as a **Snake**

1801 Story *Shop* 27: His flesh is as smooth as a snake. Cf. Whiting *NC* 478(11).

S273 As sure as **Snakes**

1789 *Columbian Magazine* 3.182: As sure as snakes it must be *tarnation* clever fun. DA snake 7(6). Cf. TW 341(4).

S274 As thin as a **Snake**

1787 *American Museum* 1.56: I'm as thin as a snake. Barbour 168(13).

S275 The **Snake** in the grass (*varied*)

1690 F-JWinthrop in *Winthrop Papers*(*B*) 4.309: The snake never hurts more than when it lyes under a secure shade. **1692** Bulkeley *Will* 172: This is a sly, incroaching insinuation, *et latet anguis in hac herba*. **1694** Scottow *Narrative* 293: A Snake crept forth which Lay Latent in the Tender Grass. **1701** CMather *Political Fables* in *Andros Tracts* 2.332: He wished the sheep would have a care of all snakes in the grass. **1702** Talbot *Letters* 86. **1705** Beverley *History* 93. **1705** F-JWinthrop in *Winthrop Papers*(*B*) 5.290: Snakes in the grass and vipers that gnaw out the bowells of their mother. **1714** WWinthrop in *Winthrop Papers*(*B*) 6.287: If there be *anguis in herba,* it may sting him at last. **1731** *Trade* in *Colonial Currency* 2.421. **1745** Belknap *History* 2.158: Beware of snakes in the grass, and mark their hissing. **1750** Sherman *Almanacs* 258. **1753** *Independent Reflector* 187: But it will be only *latet Anguis in Herba,* 278: We receive a mortal Sting from the *wilely Serpent,* that lies *concealed* beneath a Bed of Roses. **1753** ?WLivingston in Johnson *Writings* 4.132: It will be only *latet Anguis in Herba.* **1755** *Johnson Papers* 2.138: Ye late . . . Great man is ye Snake in ye Grass. **1757** Smith *Life and Correspondence* 1.154: The valley of the shadow of death, where snakes lurk under the grass. **1761** *Boston Gazette* in *Olden Time* 2.31: A Snake in the Grass may bite before it is seen. **1776** WFranklin in Franklin *Papers* 13.500, **1768** 15.221. **1769** *Johnson Papers* 6.575. **1774** *New York Journal* in *Newspaper Extracts*(*I*) 10.465: She is pester'd with snakes in the grass. **1774** Sargent *Loyalist* 76. **1778** ERutledge in Jay *Correspondence* 1.183: An abundance of snakes that are concealed in the grass. **1791** Gordon *Letters* 563: European subtility . . . may say of it, *latet anguis in herba,* but American penetration will see that neither *latet* nor *in herba* belong to it, for that the *snake* is wholly uncovered. **1791** Maclay *Journal* 396. **1793** Gadsden *Writings* 257. **1799** Cobbett *Porcupine* 10.178. **1819** JGadsden in Jackson *Correspondence* 6.472: Like a snake in the grass, he can throw his poison only from his concealment. **1821** Adams *Memoirs* 5.290:

Under the petals of this garland of roses . . . Onis had hidden a viper. **1822** Jackson *Correspondence* 3.170: I knew Major Bowie was a snake in the grass. Barbour 167(1); *Oxford* 748; Whiting S153.

S276 There are no **Snakes,** *etc.*

1803 Davis *Travels* 126: There are no snakes in *South Carolina* if I am not up to him for this, 319: There's no snakes in *Virginia*, if I don't bring his nose to the gridiron, 325-6: There are no snakes if *Philadelphia* does not beat *Charleston* hollow. TW 341(4, 6, 7).

S277 Not care the (a) **Snap**

1824 Cooper *Letters* 1.109: I cared not the snap of a finger for perils of any sort. **1828** *Yankee* 80: I care not a snap. TW 341-2(1, 2).

S278 Not give a **Snap**

1835 Floy *Diary* 137: I would not give a snap for Carrill's. **1845** Beecher *Autobiography* 2.500: I wouldn't give a snap between them. Cf. NED Snap 15b.

S279 The **Snare** is laid out of sight of the birds

1768 JDevotion in Stiles *Itineraries* 471: The Snare is laid out of Sight of the greatest Part of the Birds. *Oxford* 403: Net; Whiting N88. See **N50.**

S280 To avoid the **Snare** and fall into the pit

1631 JHumfrey in *Winthrop Papers*(*A*) 3.52: What to avoid the snare and to sinke into the pit. See **S78, W35.**

S281 To fall (*etc.*) into one's own **Snare**

1646 Winslow *Hypocrisie* 69: Hee is falne into the snare he laid. **1738** *Observations* in *Colonial Currency* 3.210: The *Crafty* at last catch'd in their own Snare. **1756** Laurens *Papers* 2.209: We hope to god that the Snare they have prepar'd for us will become a trap to their Own destruction. **1775** RBeverly in *Naval Documents* 1.876: Such Persons . . . are most frequently catched in their own Snare. **1802** WChipman in *Winslow Papers* 465: Thus have "the wicked been taken in their own snare." **1805** Bentley *Diary* 3.184: It is a pleasure to see men caught in the snare they lay for others. *Oxford* 187; Whiting S427. See **K48, M191, N51, T222.**

S282   Not to be **Sneezed** at

1744 Wendell *Letters* 255: She's not to be sneezed at, I assure you. **1836** Floy *Diary* 214: But there were many in the back seats not to be sneezed at. Barbour 168; *Oxford* 748; TW 342.

S283   As plain as the **Snout** in Grunter's face

1806 *Port Folio* NS 2.383: I think the case Plain as the snout in Grunter's face. See **N91.**

S284   As chaste as **Snow**

1806 Hitchcock *Works* 133: They may be modest, and as chaste as snow. Lean 2.813; Svartengren 14. See **I2.**

S285   As clear as driven **Snow**

1707 Sewall *Diary* 2.203: All is . . . as clear as the Driven snow.

S286   As fair as **Snow**

1792 Brackenridge *Modern* 66: She is as fair as the wool or the snow. **1797** Cobbett *Porcupine* 6.176: Men . . . of reputation fair as mountain snow.

S287   As pure as **Snow**

1695 Taylor *Poems* 106: Purer than snow. **1777** Munford *Patriots* 498: Pure as spotless snows. **1799** Carey *Porcupiniad* 2.31: Their lives . . . pure as driven snow. **1801** Sewall *Poems* 276: Pure as virgin-snow. **1806** *Port Folio* NS 1.73: She was as pure as the unsunned snow. Barbour 168(1, 3); TW 342(4).

S288   As welcome as **Snow** in harvest

1786 Asbury *Journal* 1.513: As welcome as snow in harvest. *Oxford* 748; Tilley S590; Whiting *NC* 478(3).

S289   As white as driven **Snow**

1702 Mather *Magnalia* 1.280: Hair . . . as white as the driven snow. **1778** Carver *Travels* 101: As white as the driven snow. **1790** *Universal Asylum* 5.50, **1792** 9.414. **1801** Story *Shop* 15. **1814** Alden *Epitaphs* 3.83. Whiting S436.

S290   As white as falling **Snow**

1772 Winslow *Diary* 31: White & unsullied as the falling snow. **1775** Hopkinson *Miscellaneous Essays* 1.4: She was clad in flowing robes, white as the new fallen snow.

S291   As white as feathered **Snow**

1783 *American Wanderer* 59: Teeth . . . white as feathered snow, 206.

S292   As white as mountain **Snow**

1782 Alden *Epitaphs* 4.157: Their faces white as mountain snow. Cf. TW 342(9).

S293   As white as **Snow** [The following is a selection from 61 occurrences of the phrase]

1629 *Hutchinson Papers* 1.44: Ice shining as white as snow. **1686** Dunton *Letters* 63: His Hair's as white as Snow. **1696** Mather *Diary* 1.213: *Shee was white as the Snow in Salmon.* **1698** Taylor *Poems* 129: Pure, Cleane and bright, Whiter than whitest Snow, **1710** 261: Thy Raiment was as white as Snow or light. **1728** Byrd *Dividing Line* 151. **1765** Bartram *Diary* 31. **1769** Brooke *Emily* 284. **1770** Adams *D and A* 1.357: Her Hair is white as Snow. **1774** Fithian *Journal and Letters* 204: Her head tho' was powdered white as Snow. **1782** Freneau *Poems* 2.128. **1783** *American Wanderer* 208: Breasts, white indeed like snow. **1791** Bartram *Travels* 176: Mice . . . as white as snow. **1806** Adams *D and A* 4.14: White as Snow with foam. **1812** Maxwell *Poems* 94: Little forehead white as snow. **1813** Jefferson *Writings* 14.28: Berries . . . literally as white as snow. **1819** Faux *Memorable Days* 1.102: And her woolly head was white as snow. **1822** Weems *Penn* 19: Milk and bread, white as snow. **1826** Audubon *1826 Journal* 141: Pantaloons . . . whiter than snow. Barbour 168-9(3, 6); Whiting S437.

S293a   **Snow-white** [The following is a selection from 50 occurrences of the phrase]

1693 Clayton *Writings* 95: Feathers . . . snow white. **1734** Belcher *Papers* 2.87: Let 'em be handsomely bound in snow white vellum. **1776** Freneau *Poems* 1.250: Snow-white Northern flour. **1787** *Anarchiad* 56: His snow-white bosom. **1788** *American Museum* 3.275: Where swells the breast, the snow-white skin, 4.20: Her snow white bosom and panting breasts. **1790** JQAdams in Smith *Journal and Correspondence* 2(1) 161: Thy snow-white cheek. **1811** Weems *Gambling* 23: Her life . . . snow-white with honor, **1813** *Drunkard* 105: The breakfast-table was set, and lovely shone the snow-white diaper, **1822** *Penn* 113: Snow-white honey-comb. **1832** Ames *Nautical* 92: Two snow-white . . . *chamber pots.* Whiting S437a.

S294 As white as virgin **Snow**

1790 *Universal Asylum* 4.186: Or whiter than the virgin snow Your neck.

S295 **Snow** takes the place of manure

1798 Allen *Vermont* 482: A fall of snow . . . supplies the place of manure, and when it is gradually dissolved, vegatation shoots forth in the highest luxuriancy. Dunwoody 75; Whiting S439. See **W231.**

S296 To melt like **Snow**

1776 TDanforth in Curwen *Journal and Letters* 71: It would not be strange if the rebel interest should melt like snow in a hot sun. **1778** *Clinton Papers* 2.837: Flour we yet have in Tollerable Plenty, but it is going like Snow before the Sun. **1778** *Washington Writings* 11.457: It will melt like Snow before a hot Sun. **1796** Cobbett *Porcupine* 4.40: This, my little all . . . melted away, like snow before the sun. Whiting S445.

S297 A **Snowball** gathers by rolling (*varied*)

1690 Church *History* 2.78: Some things . . . which being rowled home like a Snow-ball . . . was got to such a bigness that it overshadow'd me. **1690** GSaltonstall in *Winthrop Papers(B)* 5.8: Mr James . . . gathers like a snow ball as he goes. **1735** Belcher *Papers* 2.198: The protesters gather daily like a snowball. **1775** *Deane Correspondence* 228: Thus rolling and gathering like a snow-ball, we approached the City. **1775** Washington *Writings* 4.167: Like a snow ball, in rolling, his army will get size, 186: His strength will increase as a snow ball by rolling, **1776** 6.402. **1777** RTPaine in Gerry *Letters* 1.221: Moneys in large sums . . . enables them to roll the snow ball of monopoly and forestalling. **1780** *Washington Writings* 20.328: Expense, which was encreasing, as it rolled on,

like a Snow ball, **1786** 29.23: A snow-ball gathers by rolling, 27, 34. **1789** *American Museum* 5.297. **1797** Washington *Writings* 35.498: The debt is accumulating like a Snow ball in rolling. **1797** Weems *Letters* 2.81: Your bag in my hands is in the snow-ball way—gathering. **1798** Cobbett *Porcupine* 8.247: Their army would augment in its progress like a ball of snow rolled down a hill. **1812** Dow *Journal* 523: Reports are as the rolling snow-ball, enlarging as it goes. **1824** Jefferson *Writings* 16.84: Like a rolling snow-ball, it had gathered volume. TW 343(3); Tilley S595.

S298 To throw **Snowballs** into hell to put out the fire

1804 Cutler *Life* 2.168: For he should just as soon think of *"Throwing snow-balls into h-ll, to put out the fire,"* as to convince Democrats by reasoning. Barbour 169(1); Whiting *NC* 478.

S299 As white as a **Snow-bank**

1784 Adams(A) *Letters* 221: His head as white as a snow-bank.

S300 Not give a **Snuff**

1787 HWilliamson in *Blount Papers* 1.265: I would not give a snuff for them. NED Snuff *sb.*[3] 2b. Cf. TW 343.

S301 Not worth a **Snuff**

1816 UBrown in *MHM* 11(1916) 234: His Survey was not worth a snuff. NED Snuff *sb.*[3] 2b. Cf. TW 343.

S302 To be in great (high) **Snuff**

1802 Irving *Jonathan* 20: We used to mount our glasses in *great* snuff. **1814** Palmer *Diary* 38: He was rowd down in great Snuff with his two swabs on his shoulders. **1827** Pintard *Letters* 2.384: We had S[t] Claas in high snuff yest[y]. TW 343(2).

S303 To take **Snuff**

1764 Ames *Almanacs* 353: Some Ladies have taken Snuff at the Gentlemen [a pun]. NED Snuff *sb.*[1] 4; *Oxford* 749; Tilley S598. See **H351.**

S304 Soft **Soap**

1827 Jones *Sketches* 2.156: Such talk is often . . . what sailors call "soft soap" and landsmen flattery. **1835** Floy *Diary* 181: With which the editors express themselves "inexpressibly pleased," besides a great deal more soft soap compliments. TW 343(4).

S305 To lather without **Soapsuds** or razor

1788 *Politician* 27: I thought how you was a going for to lather me without soap-suds or razor, as the old proverb is.

S306 The richer the **Soil,** the ranker the weeds

1751 *Appendix* in *Colonial Currency* 4.477: The Richer the Soil, the ranker and stronger the *Weeds* it produces. *Oxford* 247; Tilley W241; Whiting L61.

S307 The bravest **Soldiers** are the most civil to prisoners

1736 *Georgia Records* 21.205: The common Observation that the bravest Soldiers are generally the most Civil to prisoners. See **B300, C330.**

S308 A **Soldier,** fire, and water soon make room for themselves

1809 *Port Folio* 2NS 2.549: A soldier, fire, and water, soon make room for themselves. *Oxford* 869: Water; Tilley W119. See **F124.**

S309 **Soldiers** are seldom at a loss for talk

1777 Munford *Patriots* 477: Soldiers are seldom at a loss for talk, they say. Cf. *Oxford* 591: Old men.

S310 **Soldiers** must not complain

1777 Hodgkins *Letters* 230: But Soldiers must not Complain, 232. Cf. *Oxford* 585: Obedience.

S311 The summer **Soldier** and the sunshine patriot

1776 Paine *American Crisis* 1.50: The summer soldier and the sunshine patriot will, in this crisis, shrink from the service of their country. Cf. NED Summer *sb.*[1] 4e, Sunshine 5c.

S312 To eat with **Soldiers'** stomachs

1622 *Mourt's Relation* 29-30: Our Supper, which we eate with Souldiers stomacks, for we had eaten little all that day. Cf. Tilley S870. See **H357.**

S313 To play the old **Soldier**

1820 Robertson *Letters* 138: It was now my turn to play the old soldier a little. *Oxford* 592; TW 344(3).

S314 As wise as **Solomon**

1776 JAdams in *Warren-Adams Letters* 1.232: The Wisdom of Solomon, **1779** *D and A* 2.347: The Wisdom of Solomon, the Meekness of Moses, and the Patience of Job, all united in one Character, would not be sufficient. **1819** Peirce *Rebelliad* 28: And look'd as wise as Solomon. Barbour 169; Svartengren 26; Whiting S460.

S315 Doing **Something** is often worse than doing nothing

1792 Smith *Works* 2.566: Others . . . must be Doing Something, (although it be often worse than Nothing). Whiting *Drama* 132, 141. Cf. *Oxford* 751: Somewhat; Tilley S623.

S316 **Something** has some savor

1732 Belcher *Papers* 1.230: Yet it's a large growing Province, and something has some savour, **1733** 517: Always remember Something has some Savour, and don't despise the day of small things. *Oxford* 751; Tilley S620.

S317 **Something** is always good for something

1748 Eliot *Essays* 12: The *Dutch* proverb, who say of things that are very mean, *That something is always good for something.* Cf. *Oxford* 11; TW 345(2); Whiting S462.

S318 Marry your **Son** when you will, *etc.*

1734 Franklin *PR* 1.357: Marry your Son when you will, but your Daughter when you can. **1769** Ames *Almanacs* 403: Marry thy Sons when thou wilt, thy Daughters when thou canst. *Oxford* 516; Tilley S626. See **D20.**

S319 My **Son** is my son till he takes him a wife, *etc.*

1788 Franklin *Writings* 9.656: Whereby the old Proverb is exemplified; "My Son is my Son till he take him a Wife; But my Daughter's my Daughter all Days of her Life. Barbour 45: Daughter(1); *Oxford* 751; Tilley S628; Whiting *NC* 479.

S320 A prodigal **Son** spends what a covetous father gets

1763 Ames *Almanacs* 339: A prodigal soon [*?for* son] spends what a covetous father was a long time getting. Tilley F91.

S321 The seventh **Son** of a seventh son

c1725 Byrd *Another Secret Diary* 469: But this number never discovers its vertue so strongly as in the Seventh Son. 1797 Tyler *Algerine* 1.137: He [a doctor] was the seventh son of a seventh son, and his mother was a doctress. 1809 Kendall *Travels* 1.209: A black stone . . . through which a seventh son of a seventh son, born in the month of February, with a caul on his head, can discern every thing that lies in the depths and interior of the globe. Brown *Collection* 6.38 (222-4); Lean 2.34, 491, 539; TW 345(2).

S322 A **Son** should begin where his father left off

1786 Rush *Letters* 1.403: We have a common saying among our best farmers, "that a son should always begin where his father left off."

S323 The **Sons** of heroes are trespassers

1702 Mather *Magnalia* 1.157: The proverb of the Greeks . . . "That the sons of heroes are trespassers."

S324 A wise **Son** makes a glad father

1732 Belcher *Papers* 1.198: So shall you be a wise son, making a glad father. Barbour 169; Prov. 10.1, 15.20.

S325 No **Song,** no supper

1798 Cobbett *Porcupine* 10.54: The pauper-like fare of "No Song no Supper." *Oxford* 574. Cf. Tilley S1003a.

S326 To make a **Song** of something

1738 Franklin *PR* 2.191: A mighty matter, truly, to make a Song of. NED Song 4c.

S327 To sell for a **Song**

1750 JParsons in *Law Papers* 3.352: Their Goods Sold for a Song. 1755 Laurens *Papers* 1.292: Rice . . . will sell with us for a Song, 1756 2.63, 272, 1757 430, 463, 472: It has sold for some months past for a meer Song. 1765 Watts *Letter Book* 338. 1769 Wood-

mason *Journal* 159. 1770 *New-York Gazette* in *Newspaper Extracts(I)* 8.84. 1772 *Johnson Papers* 8.537. 1773 MGoosley in *Norton Papers* 321. 1778 *Washington Writings* 13.408: Sold his own land in a manner for a song. 1779 *Beekman Papers* 3.1345. 1779 Galloway *Diary* 172: I know it will go of[f] for a song. 1787 Washington *Writings* 29. 158: They will go for a song. 1789 Jefferson *Papers* 14.418: Life-estates sell for a song. 1790 Washington *Writings* 31.2: It is not my intention to dispose of the land for a song. 1795 Ames *Letters* 1.168. 1797 Freneau *Poems* 3.174. 1801 *Columbian Centinel* in Buckingham *Specimens* 2.88: The Exports of our country, a mere song, in value. 1806 Hitchcock *Works* 21: Barter existence for a song. 1807 Pike *Travels* 339. 1807 *Salmagundi* 31: Nor would it be the first time a house has been obtained there for a song. 1808 Hitchcock *Poetical Dictionary* 100. 1825 Neal *American Writers* 178. 1835 Floy *Diary* 166: The men are all low Irish, got for a mere song. 1841 JHowerton in Jackson *Correspondence* 6.101: Even run the risk of our lives for a mear song to settle you a plantation in this country. *Oxford* 712; TW 345(1).

S328 The **Sooner** the better [The following is a selection from 110 occurrences of the phrase]

1640 BGostlin in *Winthrop Papers(A)* 4.237: I am bownd out speedyly . . . the sooner the Better. 1647 Ward *Simple Cobler* 3: And such as will come to be gone as fast as they can, the sooner the better. 1683 Claypoole *Letter Book* 223. 1717 Mather *Letters* 236: If you do this poor sermon the honor of passing thro' the press, the sooner the better. 1734 Belcher *Papers* 2.41. 1756 EFreeman in *Baxter Manuscripts* 13.46. 1761 *Johnson Papers* 10.308: The sooner it is over the better. 1770 Adams(S) *Writings* 2.100. 1774 JA in *Adams FC* 1.130. 1777 Washington *Writings* 8.322. 1777 AWayne in *St. Clair Papers* 1.390. 1778 Paine *American Crisis* 1.108. 1781 Jefferson *Papers* 5.369: The sooner this done the better. 1785 Adams *Works* 8.333. 1789 Franklin *Writings* 10.48. 1795 Hamilton *Works* 10.126. 1798 AAdams in Smith *Journal and Correspondence* 2(2) 151. **1801** Jefferson *Family Letters* 201, **1807** *Writings* 11.367: The sooner this is done the better. **1812** Weems *Letters* 3.74: I pray you send the above *immediately*. The sooner the better. **1813** Colby *Life* 1.198: The sooner they got out of this troublesome world, the better. **1815** Asbury *Letters* 3.519. **1821** Jackson *Correspondence* 3.131: If yours and her ultimate object is to mary, the sooner the better. *Oxford* 753; TW 345.

S329　As bitter as **Soot**

1772 Hearne *Journey* 291: That [meat] which is prepared by the Southern tribes is generally as bitter as soot with smoke. Whiting S480.

S330　As black as **Soot**

1775 JHarvey in *Blount Papers* 1.3: Her hands as black as Soot. *Oxford* 63; Svartengren 244; Whiting S481.

S331　As glossy as **Soot**

1821 Knight *Poems* 2.152: Its colour as glossy as soot.

S332　A **Sop** to Cerberus

1729 Ames *Almanacs* 64: He casts a poetical "sop to Cerberus." **1761** Adams *D and A* 1.223: A sop for Cerberus. **1783** *American Wanderer* 25: The wonderful efficacy of a sop upon the Dog Cerberus. **1795** Cobbett *Porcupine* 2.104. **1817** Jefferson *Writings* 15.113: The sop to Cerberus from fable has become history. *Oxford* 753; Tilley S643.

S333　It is more easy to make **Sores** than heal them

1783 JJay in *Thomson Papers* 180: It is more easy to make sores than heal them. Cf. Whiting H259, S502.

S334　To rub old **Sores**

1733 Belcher *Papers* 1.362: But I don't desire to rub old sores. *Oxford* 678: Rip; Tilley S649. Cf. Whiting S502. See **W371.**

S335　To sip **Sorrow**

1788 Henry *Life* 3.480: You will *sip sorrow,* according to the vulgar phrase, if you want any other security than the laws of Virginia. Cf. *Oxford* 754; Tilley S661; Whiting S520, 522.

S336　To be in **Sot's Bay**

1783 Williams *Penrose* 40: They were all so snugly moored in Sot's Bay [in drunken sleep]. NED Sot *sb.*[1] 3.

S337　Not care a **Sou**

1819 Drake *Works* 351: No one cares a *sou* about them. NED Sou. See **S345.**

S338　Their **Souls** are their purses

1766 Murray *Letters* 157: The madness of the people here . . . put the merchants in fear of their Souls, I mean their purses. Chaucer *CT* I(A) 654-8. Cf. NED Purse 2b.

S339　To call one's **Soul** his own

1781 Oliver *Origin* 97: Some indeed dared to say that their Souls were their own; but no one could call his Body his own. **1801** TPierce in Vanderpoel *Chronicles* 388: I have met with many who dare not open their mouths long enough to pronounce their souls their own. **1813** Paulding *Lay* 123: Nor dare to call his soul his own. **1815** Humphreys *Yankey* 34: Do you think I'm afraid to say my soul's my own? *Oxford* 755; TW 345-6(2).

S340　To hang one's **Soul** upon the hedge

1676 Williams *Writings* 5.392: The most will hang their Souls upon the *Hedge,* and venture like the *high ways* and *hedges.* Whiting S528.

S341　Born within the **Sound** of Bow bells

1782 Freneau *Prose* 51: For all she was born within the sound of Bow bells. *Oxford* 76; Tilley S671. See **C247.**

S342　**Sounds** often terrify more than realities

1796 Washington *Writings* 34.498: *Sounds* often terrify more than realities.

S343　To spit in the **Soup**

1775 Franklin *Writings* 6.353: This to me was what the French call *Spitting in the Soup.*

S344　He that has eaten the **Sour** should eat the sweet

1707 Sewall *Diary* 2.120*: He was invited into a New Trading Voyage; being told, He had *Eaten the Sowre, he should now Eat the Sweet.* Cf. Whiting S529.

S345   Not care a **Souse**

1789 *Columbian Magazine* 3.52: I don't care a souse. NED Souse *sb.*[4] 2; Partridge 802: Sou, 803: Sous. See **S337.**

S346   As drunk as a **Sow**

1770 Munford *Candidates* 35: Here's my wife . . . as drunk as a sow. NED Sow *sb.*[1] 3c; Whiting S534, 955. See **H237.**

S347   As fruitful as a white **Sow**

1674 Josselyn *Accounts* 25: Verifying the old proverb, As fruitful as a white sow.

S348   A **Sow** must be pulled by the ears, *etc.*

1795 Wendell *Letters* 282: I often compare her to the sow you tell of that must be pulled by the ears to the trough and by the tail back again. Whiting *NC* 479(1).

S349   The **Sow** returns to her wallowing in the mire

1654 Wigglesworth *Diary* 69: O Lord leave me not to return with the sow to her wallowing in the mire. **1780** Adams *Works* 7.168: Not a single juror has ever whispered a wish to return, after being washed, to their wallowing in the mire. **1787** Ledyard *Russian Journey* 146. **1811** Weems *Gambling* 50: He returns to his old courses, just like the *washed* sow to her wallowing in the mire. **1821** Pintard *Letters* 2.12. **1823** Bierce *Travels* 102. **1830** Ames *Mariner's* 291. Whiting H567, S962. See **D234, S543.**

S350   The **Sow** teaches Minerva

1676 Williams *Writings* 5.501: It is one of the *Proverbs* of the *Ancients Sus Minervam docet.* The Sow teacheth the Goddess of *Wisdome. Oxford* 757; Tilley S680.

S351   To take the wrong **Sow** by the ear

1718 JUsher in *Saltonstall Papers* 1.324: He hath taken the Sowes by the wrong ear. **a1731** Cook *Bacon* 319: Bacon, Who by the Ear wrong Sow had taken. **1782** Freneau *Poems* 2.181: The sage who took the wrong sow by the ears. **1809** Weems *Marion* 29. **1815** Humphreys *Yankey* 33: You've got the wrong sow by the ear, (as the old proverb

says). Barbour 170(4); *Oxford* 756; Whiting S540. See **P122.**

S352   As one **Sows** so shall he reap

1679 Fitzhugh *Letters* 67: Since they alledge that as they have sown they ought to reap. **1702** Taylor *Christographia* 199.93: What you Sow, that you shall reape. **1763** Laurens *Papers* 3.548: That which we sow we must also expect to reap. **1773** Adams *Legal Papers* 1.120: The Same that we Sow, that shall we reap. **1773** Boucher *View* 305. **1793** Brackenridge *Modern* 222. **1798** Ames *Letters* 1.237: He will reap the harvest he has sowed. **1815** Waterhouse *Journal* 176. **1836** Jackson *Correspondence* 5.423: We must seed well or we never can reap well, 436. **1846** Paulding *Letters(II)* 422: I take this to be . . . a commentary on his Text, about men reaping as they sow. Barbour 117(62); *Oxford* 757; Whiting S542.

S353   One may **Sow** and another reap

1664 *Wyllys Papers* 159: One may sowe and another reape. **1775** Stiles *Diary* 1.531: Herein the Saying may be true, One soweth & another reapeth. **1780** Lee(W) *Letters* 3.786: Another is to reap the harvest from the seed we sowed at Aix. *Oxford* 597; Whiting S543. See **B367.**

S354   To call a **Spade** a spade

1692 Bulkeley *Will* 90: We must call a spade a spade. **1785** JAtkinson, *Match for a Widow* (London, 1788) 32: We don't call a spade, a spade, as you sinners do here. [The speaker is a Yankee servant in England.] **1788** HWilliamson in Iredell *Correspondence* 2.237: I expressed an honest indignation by calling a Spade a *spade.* **1795** *Tablet* 45: According to a vulgar proverb, call a spade a spade. **1804** Brackenridge *Modern* 341: They could call a spade a spade. **1807** *Salmagundi* 30: Dick maintains, in the teeth of all argument, that a spade is a spade. Barbour 170; *Oxford* 98; TW 346. See **F92.**

S355   **Spain** has bridges where there is no water

1809 Pinkney *Travels* 121-2: If Spain, as the proverb says, have bridges where there is no water, I have seen repeated instances in France where there are quays without trade.

S356 As lazy as **Spaniards**

1774 *Wyllys Papers* 445: Our Clergy have become as lazy as Spaniards.

S357 As humble as a **Spaniel**

1813 Bayard *Papers* 483: He is . . . as humble as a spaniel. Lean 2.843. Cf. Whiting S548.

S358 To play the **Spaniel** (*varied*)

1758 Franklin *Papers* 8.128: One that does not . . . play the Spaniel to great Men. 1778 Paine *American Crisis* 1.139: [They] are cringing with the duplicity of a spaniel, for a little temporary bread. a1788 Jones *History* 2.21: Behaved as submissively as spaniels. 1792 Freneau *Poems* 3.77: So, a spaniel, when master is angry, and kicks it, Sneaks up to his shoe, and submissively licks it. 1796 Cobbett *Porcupine* 3.383: And he'll lick your hand like a spaniel, 438: Amidst the applauding shouts of those who crawled to him like spaniels in the year 1783. 1801 Story *Shop* 127: Yet they are of the spaniel breed, The more they're beat the better. NED Spaniel *sb.*[1] 1a; *Oxford* 758-9; Tilley S704-5, W644; Whiting S548-50.

S359 **Spare** and have is better than spend and crave

1758 Franklin *PR* 7.354: *Spare and have* is better than *spend and crave*. Cf. *Oxford* 55; Tilley S711; Whiting S553.

S360 Every **Spark** adds to the fire

1738 Talcott *Papers* 2.49: As every spark adds to the fire. See **L177, S377.**

S361 A small **Spark** will kindle a great fire (*varied*)

1624 Davenport *Letters* 24: Quench this sparke, and so prevente a greater fire. 1637 Williams *Writings* 6.35-6: Little sparks prove great fires. 1653 Keayne *Apologia* 59: Though some blew up those sparks into a great flame. 1715 Mather *Diary* 2.333: A small spark, will sett fire to a mighty Train, when it is already prepared. 1753 JGlen in McDowell *Documents* 1.389: A small Spark if not attended to, will kindle a great Fire, 1754 532. 1770 Adams *Legal Papers* 3.94: Any little Spark would inkindle a great fire. *Oxford* 759; Whiting S561. See **C99.**

S362 He can't **Speak** well who always talks

1758 Ames *Almanacs* 283: He can't speak well, who always Talks. Cf. *Oxford* 761; Tilley P146; Whiting S590.

S363 A **Speck** will produce a storm

1785 Jefferson *Papers* 8.553: Their detention of our posts seems to be the speck which is to produce a storm. NED Speck *sb.*[1] 1d.

S364 To **Spend** as freely as one gets

a1700 Hubbard *New England* 527: That sort of men are observed to spend as freely and lightly as they get. *Oxford* 752, 764; Tilley S738; Whiting G52. See **C263.**

S365 Great **Spenders** are bad lenders

1745 Franklin *PR* 3.5: Great spenders are bad lenders. *Oxford* 764; Tilley S744.

S366 **Spick-and-span**

1765 Adams *D and A* 1.281: Spick and span. 1769 LDulany in *MHM* 12(1917) 278: A Lie, spick & span from your jesuitical forge. 1771 JA in *Adams FC* 1.75: To the total neglect of spick and span. 1806 *Weekly* 1.65: A *bran span* excellent *new* word, as we Yankees would say. 1809 Adams *Correspondence* 71: To be furnished with this pamphlet, spick and spun. 1815 Humphreys *Yankey* 28: Dressed spick and span new, from top to toe. *Oxford* 764-5; TW 346, 347; Whiting S547.

S367 The **Spider** extracts poison where the bee gathers honey

1796 Eaton *Life* 45: But it is the spider's peculiar quality to extract poison from the same flower from which the bee will gather honey. *Oxford* 39; Tilley B208.

S368 To save at the **Spigot,** *etc.*

1780 *New-York Gazette* in *Newspaper Extracts(II)* 4.208: We have saved at the Spicket, but our Tyrants draw from us the Bung. 1793 *Washington *Writings* 32.464: If for the sake of making a little butter (for which I shall get scarcely any thing) my calves are starved, and die; it may be compared to stopping the spigot, and opening the faucit, that is to say, I shall get two or three shillings for butter, and loose 20 or 30/ by the death or injury done to my calves. 1819 Waln *Hermit* 163: The old story . . . of the bunghole and the spigot. 1824 *Massachusetts Spy* in Thornton *Glossary* 2.836: This, in the language of the proverb, is saving at the spigot, and losing at the bunghole. 1827 WBolling in *VHM* 44(1936) 330: Which is like saving at the spiket and letting out at the bung. 1836 Jackson *Correspondence* 5.394: This is truly pulling out the bung and driving in the spickett. *Oxford* 759; TW 347.

S369   The good **Spinner** has a large shift

1742 Franklin *PR* 2.335: The good Spinner hath a large Shift, 1756 6.324: diligent spinner, 1758 *WW* 343: diligent. *Oxford* 765; Tilley S757.

S370   The **Spirit** is willing, the flesh is weak

1816 Smith *Life* 264: Though the spirit was willing the flesh was weak. 1824 Longfellow *Letters* 1.90: For though the "spirit is willing the flesh is weak." *Oxford* 765; Whiting S635. See **F183.**

S371   To cut **Splurges**

1816 PRobertson in *W&MCQ* 2S 11(1931) 61: The Surry bucks . . . cut considerable splurges. TW 347.

S372   It is impossible to **Spoil** what never was good

1807 *Monthly Anthology* 4.614: That class of which the vulgar saying is true—"It is impossible to spoil what never was good."

S373   To put a **Spoke** in one's wheel

1652 Williams *Writings* 4.27: My end . . . is to put a *Christian barr,* and *just* and *merciful Spoaks* in the *wheels* of such zealous reforming *Jehues.* 1766 Lloyd *Papers* 2.705: I imagine that Greens Family will be no bad Spoke in your wheel ware you to attempt Such a thing. 1782 Jay *Correspondence* 2.361: He believed *this court* had found means to put a spoke in our wheel. 1791 Ames *Letters* 1.102: Congress is so little minded in the transaction of the business of this session, that I must not confide in my drawing their attention, as a spoke in the political wheel. *Oxford* 767; TW 347.

S374   He must have a long **Spoon** that sups with the Devil

1834 HWaddell in *Ruffin Papers* 2.120: I

am well aware of the Scotch adage, that "he that sups with the Devil must hae a long spoon." Barbour 171(2); *Oxford* 480-1; Whiting S639.

S375   To be born with a silver **Spoon** in one's mouth

1780 JThaxter in *Adams FC* 3.303: I was not born with a Silver Spoon in my Mouth. 1802 Cutler *Life* 2.59: Solomon was born with a silver spoon in his mouth and a scepter in his hand. 1809 Weems *Washington* 24: Washington was not born with *"a silver spoon in his mouth."* 1845 Paulding *Letters(II)* 409, 1846 440: I alway said you were born with a great Silver Ladle in Your mouth. Barbour 171(1); *Oxford* 76; TW 348(1).

S376   To stow **Spoon-fashion**

1775 WCoit in *Naval Documents* 2.915: Five of us in the cabin, and when there, are obliged to stow spoon fashion. NED Spoon 11.

S377   Every **Spoonful** adds to the cistern

1721 Wise *Word* 18: Every Spoonful adds to the Cistern. Cf. *Oxford* 228: Every little, 231-2; Whiting *NC* 437: Little. See **L177, S360.**

S378   "There will be no **Sport** without me," *etc.*

1811 Dunlap *Diary* 2.427: Aye, aye, they understand their interest now, for, as the fellow said who was going to the gallows, "There will be no sport without me."

S379   **Spots** are soonest seen in ermine

1702 Mather *Magnalia* 1.227: Spots being soonest seen in *ermin.* *Oxford* 225. Cf. Tilley S781. See **W137.**

S380   Up the **Spout**

1815 Palmer *Diary* 144: Mr. Fellows has tucked his jacket up the Spout (HE sold it). Barbour 171; TW 348.

S381   No more than a **Sprat** in a whale's belly

1714 Mather *Diary* 2.296: What Number and Value of them we have now circulating, is, as our Gentlemen of Business express it, no more than a *Spratt in a Whale Belly.* NED Sprat *sb.*[1] 3b.

S382 To throw a **Sprat** to catch a herring

1797 Cobbett *Porcupine* 6.390: It was, as they call it, *donner un œuf pour avoir un bœuf*, or, in the language of Christians, *throwing a sprat to catch a herring. Oxford* 768; TW 348.

S383 As blooming as the **Spring**

1773 Paterson *Glimpses* 103: Why I told him you were blooming as the Spring.

S384 As mild as the **Spring**

c**1703** Byrd *Another Secret Diary* 209: He is mild as the spring.

S385 **Springes** to catch woodcocks

1751 *New York Weekly Post Boy* in *Newspaper Extracts*(*I*) 3.42: *Mere Springes to catch Woodcocks*, 58: To apply that Common Saying which he improperly mentions, *Mere Springes*, not *to catch Woodcocks*, but Votes in the ensuing Election. **1799** Adams *Writings* 2.402: The springs to catch wood-cocks . . . have been laid with . . . little art of concealmentt. **1799** Paine *Works* 318: New "springes to catch Woodcocks." **1807** *Salmagundi* 338: Advertising in the usual style of playbills, as a "springe to catch woodcocks," that between the play and farce, John will make a bow—for that night only! *Oxford* 768; Tilley S788.

S386 As brisk as bottled **Spruce**

1785 JAtkinson, *Match for a Widow* (London, 1788) 38: Though I'm as brisk and sweet upon 'em as bottled spruce, they look as tart at me as *sour grout*. [The speaker is a Yankee servant in England.] Cf. Lean 2.811: bottled ale.

S387 Like a **Spur** to an old horse

1766 JParker in Franklin *Papers* 13.394: A little more, like a Spur to an old Horse, would help somewhat in the Way. Cf. *Oxford* 768; Tilley S790.

S388 On the **Spur** of the occasion (moment)

1773 Carroll *Correspondence* 1.299: The creation of twelve peers in one day *"on the spur of the occasion."* **1777** Washington *Writings* 8.339: Upon the spur of the occasion, **1778** 11.292, 303, **1780** 19.470. **1782** JJones in Madison *Papers* 4.260: Unless for the spur of the oc[casion]. **1782** JMadison in

Stiles *Letters* 54. **1784** Sullivan *Letters* 3.367. **1786** Paine *On Government* 2.375: Suited to the spur and exigency of the moment. **1786** WWhiting in American Antiquarian Society, *Proceedings* NS 66(1956) 155. **1789** Anburey *Travels* 1.274: On the spur of the moment. **1791** *Universal Asylum* 6.215. **1792** Paine *To Addressers* 2.493: moment. **1794** Bentley *Diary* 2.86: moment. **1795** Hamilton *Papers* 19.156. **1797** Boucher *View* ii. **1800** Carroll *Correspondence* 2.240: Laws and changes suited to the spur of the occasion. **1802** Cutler *Life* 2.81: moment. **1806** Taggart *Letters* 172. **1809** Boudinot *Journey* 40. **1810** Burr *Correspondence* 315. **1811** Graydon *Memoirs* 376. **1813** *Port Folio* 3NS 1.385. **1816** JRandolph in *VHM* 49(1941) 207. **1817** Scott *Blue Lights* 127. **1818** Hall *Travels* 94. **1818** Watterston *Letters* 95. **1824** Jackson *Correspondence* 3.243. **1844** FBlair in Jackson *Correspondence* 6.259: moment. *Oxford* 769; TW 349(4).

S389 To wear the **Spurs**

1650 NWard in Bradstreet *Works* 85: And chode by *Chaucers* Boots, and *Homers Fuers*, Let Men look to't, least Women wear the Spurrs. See **B319**.

S390 Look out for **Squalls**

1802 *Steele Papers* 1.269: At the same time it might not be amiss to look out for squalls. NED Squall *sb.*³ 2b.

S391 Out of **Square**

1668 EWeld in Alden *Epitaphs* 3.35: My duties were Put out of square With thine unhandy instrument. NED Square 19. See **F288**.

S392 To break no **Squares**

1713 Wise *Churches* 138: In Rhetorick it breaks no great Squares. **1750** Sherman *Almanacs* 220: A day or two can break no great squares. **1758** GTurner in McDowell *Documents* 2.471: One Day would break no Squares. **1763** Watts *Letter Book* 119. **1813** Wirt *Letters* 1.359. *Oxford* 403; Whiting I30.

S393 Upon the **Square**

1773 Lee *Letters* 1.101: I shall still continue

pressing and remitting, until we are upon the square. TW 349; Tilley S796.

S394   Squires of Alsatia

1669 Randolph *Letters* 7.586: Such unjust practises done in a Civell Government by Such Squires of Alsatia. NED Squire 5e.

S395   To beat one with his own Staff

1692 Bulkeley *Will* 216: Thus they beat us with our own staff. Whiting S652. See **R117, 139, S431.**

S396   To keep the Staff in one's own hand

1776 ERutledge in Burnett *Letters* 1.518: I am resolved to vest the Congress with no more Power than is absolutely necessary, and to use a familiar Expression, to keep the Staff in our own Hands. **1799** Dorr *Letters* 186: Keeping the staff in my own hand. *Oxford* 418.

S397   To lean (rest) on a broken Staff

1773 JJohnson in *Wheelock's Indians* 149: If I lean upon them . . . they are like a broken staff. **1776** *Washington *Writings* 6.110: To place any dependence upon militia, is . . . resting upon a broken staff. **1783** Freneau *Poems* 2.232: The charge may be true—for I found it in vain To lean on a staff that was broken in twain. **1807** Mackay *Letters* 78: But this is a broken staff I find to rely on. *Oxford* 88; Whiting S649. See **R47.**

S398   As strong as a Stag

1767 *Johnson Papers* 5.629: I return Strong as a Stag.

S399   To be kicked up Stairs

1742 Belcher *Papers* 2.438: Could the clan think the D[r] such a simpleton as to be pleas'd with being kickt up stairs? **1775** SAdams in *Warren-Adams Letters* 1.94: C —— is kickd up Stairs [promoted]. NED Kick v.[1] 5b. See **K9.**

S400   As stiff as a Stake

1736 Gyles *Memoirs* 15: Both froze as stiff as a Stake. **1815** Waterhouse *Journal* 201: While they kept their bodies either stiff as so many stakes or in a monkeyish wriggle. **1821** Doddridge *Dialogue* 50: His whole body is as stiff as a stake. *Oxford* 774; TW 350(1).

S401   To be at a Stake

1777 Committee of Tryon County in *Clinton Papers* 2.285: The Militia is not paid, every thing at a Stacke, every thing calls aloud for your Excellency's Interposition, 287: Since that Fatal Day . . . all things within this County is at a Stake. Cf. NED Stake *sb.*[1] 2.

S402   To pluck (pull) up Stakes

1640 TLechford in *Transactions of the American Antiquarian Society* 7(1885) 275: I . . . am plucking up stakes with as much speed as I may. **1642** Winthrop *Journal* 2.84: If thou wouldst have plucked up thy stakes. **1692** Bulkeley *Will* 199: It will be good for us to pluck up our stakes and go seek our fortunes. **1694** Scottow *Narrative* 288: The plucking up of their Stakes. **1702** Mather *Magnalia* 1.96: They talked of plucking up stakes, and flying away, 559. **1742** Belcher *Papers* 2.425. **1756** *Johnson Papers* 9.412. **1758** Stiles *Itineraries* 573. **1776** JHurd in Sullivan *Letters* 1.285. **1778** Curwen *Journal* 1.431: Mrs. T. . . . is going to pluck up staves and remove. **1815** Humphreys *Yankey* 32. **1816** Fidfaddy *Adventures* 52: He pulled up stakes. **1818** Pickering *Life* 2.409: Presuming that I, wearied out by opposition and cruel treatment, should *haul up stakes,* and abandon the county to its fate. **1824** Prince *Journals* 123: The Irish watchmaker . . . has pulled up stakes and gone off with several watches. **1832** Longfellow *Letters* 1.392: Just as I had "pulled up stakes." Albert Matthews in *The Nation* 69(1899) 483-4; TW 350(3).

S403   To make (be) a Stalking-horse

1637 IStoughton in *Winthrop Papers(A)* 3.442: That upon the matter they use us as their stalking horse. **1638** Winthrop *Journal* 1.259: And made (as himself said) their stalking horse. **1676** Sewall *Diary* 1.16: I told him how dangerous it was to make the convictions wrought by God's spirit a stalking horse to any other thing. a**1700** Hubbard *New England* 296. **1704** MIngles in *VHM* 7(1899) 392. **1720** *New News* in *Colonial Currency* 2.132: *Religion* is made a *Stalking-Horse.* **1780** RHowe in *Heath Papers* 3.55: Honour . . . and integrity are only used as stalking horses. **1780** Lee(W) *Let-*

ters 3.805. **1782** Paine *Rhode Island* 2.337: It may be placed as a stalking horse, to keep something else out of sight. **1790** Adams *Works* 6.335: They were a mere stalking-horse, behind which to shoot a woodcock. **c1790** Brackenridge *Gazette* 61. **1796** Hamilton *Papers* 20.194: 'Tis the stalking horse of a certain party. **1798** Jefferson *Writings* 10.23: Pinckney is made only the stalking horse. **1802** Paine *To the Citizens* 2.922: [They] are pushing Mr. Washington forward as their stalking horse, **1803** 1432. **1816** Jefferson *Writings* 14.392, **1818** 281. NED Stalking-horse; Tilley S816. Cf. *Oxford* 670.

S404 One's old **Stamping-ground**
1813 JMiller in Knopf *War of 1812* 3.156: Brush's old stamping ground. **1821** *Austin Papers* 1.456: Your old Stamping-ground. DA stamping 1; NED Stamping 3.

S405 To be at a dead **Stand**
1647 Ward *Simple Cobler* 18: So others . . . are at a dead stand, not knowing what to doe or say. **1771** Franklin *Papers* 18.193: Dr. H. must now come to a dead Stand. NED Stand *sb.*[1] 7.

S406 If you **Stand** well, stand still
1800 Adams *Works* 9.82-3: The motto of the Hôtel de Valentindis, in which I lived at Passy was, "si sta bene, non si muove." "If you stand well, stand still, **1806** *D and A* 4.42-3. **1808** Jefferson *Writings* 12.57: [Italian only], **1816** 15.22: "Chi sta bene, non si muove," said the Italian, "let him who stands well, stand still." Whiting S668.

S407 Let him that **Stands** take heed lest he fall
a1656 Bradford *History* 1.297: God can make the weake to stand; let him also that standeth take heed least he fall. **1692** Mather *Wonders* 186: It was said, *let him that standeth take heed.* **1710** Johnston *Papers* 51. **1747** Johnson *Writings* 1.127: The Apostle's aphorism. **1788** Scott *Journal* 267. **1818** Beecher *Autobiography* 1.379: Even he that standeth is exhorted by inspiration to take heed lest he fall. Whiting S671.

S408 As bright as **Stars**
1728 Byrd *Dividing Line* 200: The Women

are bright as Stars, and never Scold, 201. Barbour 171-2; Whiting S673.

S409 As numerous as the **Stars**
1790 Pickering *Life* 2.457: For we are a great people numerous as the stars. Svartengren 399; Whiting S675. See **S43.**

S410 As thick as **Stars**
1797 Callender *Annual Register 1796* 257: Colonels sat as thick as stars in the galaxy. Taylor *Comparisons* 59.

S411 Like **Stars** on a frosty (winter's) night
1721 Letter in *Colonial Currency* 2.263: They appear in as full and Open view to us, as the Stars in a clear Frosty Night. **a1855** Beecher *Autobiography* 1.163: There was not an eye in the whole church but what glistened like cold stars of a winter's night. Cf. TW 350(7); Whiting S686.

S412 To gaze at the **Stars** and fall in the ditch
1735 Franklin *PR* 2.5: So some fond Traveller gazing at the Stars Slips in next Ditch and gets a dirty Arse. *Oxford* 297-8; Whiting S684.

S413 To shine like a **Star**
1775 Deane *Papers* 1.61: A lady of but tolerable beauty shone like a star in the midst of universal gloom surrounding. Whiting S685.

S414 As insensible as **Statues**
1784 Smith *Journal and Correspondence* 1.26: The others appeared as insensible as statues of lead or wood.

S415 As silent as **Statues**
1821 Dalton *Travels* 111: As silent as statues. Cf. TW 351(4); Tilley S834.

S416 As unmoved (immovable) as a **Statue**
1682 Steere *Daniel* 48: He like a Statue stands, fixt and unmoved. **1805** Silliman *Travels* 1.323: She stood immovable as a marble statue. Cf. Whiting S692.

S417 Enough to move a **Statue**
1774 JA in *Adams FC* 1.131: It is enough to move a Statue, *to melt an Heart of Stone.* See **H169.**

S418 To stand like a **Statue**

1811 Adams *Writings* 4.29: They stand like so many statues. **c1820** Bernard *Retrospections* 88: Our horses . . . had stood like statues. **1822** Weems *Penn* 39: Mrs. Penn stood a statue of speechless consternation. TW 351(8).

S419 When the **Steed** is stolen, *etc.*

1745 *Law Papers* 2.50: When the Stead is stolen its too late to shutt the Stable door. **1747** Franklin *Papers* 3.191: The vulgar, tho' very significant Saying, *When the Steed is stolen, You shut the Stable Door*. **1788** *Politician* 8: When the steed is stolen, shut the stable door. Barbour 10: Barn(5); *Oxford* 730-1; Whiting S697.

S420 As true as **Steel**

1823 IBaker in Jackson *Correspondence* 3.196: He was as true as steel to you. **1845** Beecher *Autobiography* 2.499: I was true as steel. Barbour 172(2); *Oxford* 840; Whiting S709.

S421 **Steel** to the back

1702 *Penn-Logan Correspondence* 1.140: Honest Griffith Owen is steel to the back. *Oxford* 773; Tilley S842.

S422 From **Stem** to stern

1794 Drinker *Journal* 245: I had him stripped and washed from stem to stern in a tub of warm soapsuds. **1805** Asbury *Letters* 3.306: The famous Abner Wood is turned Baptist from stem to stern. TW 352(2).

S423 The first **Step** is easy to take

1784 Franklin *Writings* 9.188: *Ce n'est que le premier pas qui coûte*. **1786** Henry *Life* 3.376: It is easy to take the first step, but hard to foretell what it leads to. **a1820** Tucker *Essays* 13: [French only]. **1820** Pintard *Letters* 1.273: [French only]. **1840** Cooper *Letters* 4.12: [French only]. *Oxford* 773. Cf. Tilley S846.

S424 To be a **Stepdame**

1612 Strachey *Historie* 132: Nor is Nature a stepdame unto them. **a1652** Bradstreet *Works* 393: These O protect from step Dames injury. **1792** Freneau *Poems* 3.74: Where Mother-country acts the step-dame's

part. **1816** Paulding *Letters*(*I*) 2.116: [Ireland's] stern stepdame, old England. Whiting S718.

S425 To be a **Stepfather**

1740 *Postscript* in *Colonial Currency* 4.60: The with-holding of it, is a Step Father or Step-Mothers usage. **1824** Blane *Excursion* 39: Congress . . . has acted the part of a step-father rather than of a parent. Whiting S719.

S426 To be a **Stepmother**

a1649 Shepard *Autobiography* 358: My Father married agayne to another woman who did let me see the difference betweene my own mother & a step-mother; shee did seeme not to love me but incensed my father often agaynst me. **1728** Byrd *Dividing Line* 4: A Large Swarm of Dissenters fled thither from the Severities of their Stepmother, the Church. **1769** Franklin *Papers* 16.325: They us'd to call her (their Mother Country), but her late Conduct entitles rather to the Name of Stepmother. **1776** Lee *Papers* 1.319: These horrors must be attributed . . . to a hankering not after a tender Parent, but a Beldame Step Mother whose every Act is cruelty, vengeance and insanity. **1778** Freneau *Prose* 172: Nature has, in many instances, been little better than a severe stepmother to mankind. **1804** Adams *Writings* 3.97: Nature treats us like a stepmother. **1813** *Smith Papers* 7.44: [She] is what now is & always has been miraculous, an excellent step mother. **1833** Jackson *Correspondence* 5.220: Suppose . . . that she really becomes the stepmother to your children . . . becomes the real stepmother and maltreats them. Whiting S720. Cf. Barbour 172.

S427 To be a **Stepping-stone**

1793 Jefferson *Writings* 1.349: They only esteemed it as a stepping stone to something else, **1825** 16.94: It is . . . only a stepping stone to something better, 150. NED Steping-stone 2.

S428 There's the **Stick**

1769 Adams(S) *Writings* 1.303: Aye, there's the stick. NED Stick *sb.*[4] 2. See **R154**.

S429 As many as one can shake a **Stick** at
1818 *Lancaster Journal* in Thornton *Glossary*
2.779: We have . . . as many Taverns as you
can shake a stick at. Barbour 173(6); TW
353(2).

S430 It is easy to find a **Stick** (cudgel) to
beat a dog
1652 Williams *Writings* 4.473: He that hath
a minde to beate a *Dog,* will soone finde a
cudgell, &c. **1715** Mather *Letters* 168: It appears evidently that he is looking about for a
stick to beat the dog. **1767** JParker in Franklin *Papers* 14.321: If any of them should
take it into their Head, to want to beat a
Dog, they can always find a Stick. **1769**
Woodmason *Journal* 139: The old Adage has
it *When You are minded to beat a Dog its
easy to find a stick.* **1782** Hopkinson *Miscellaneous Essays* 1.266: Your honours have an
old saying. **1832** JRandolph in Jackson *Correspondence* 4.424. *Oxford* 769; Tilley
T138.

S431 A **Stick** to break one's own head
1821 Simpson *Journal* 275: It would be the
greatest folly in me to give you a stick to
break my own head with. Apperson 601(2);
Whiting *NC* 481(7). See **R117, 139, S395.**

S432 Two dry **Sticks** will burn a green one
1755 Franklin *PR* 5.472: Two dry Sticks will
burn a green One. *Oxford* 850; Tilley S852.

S433 To put a **Sting** in the tail
1705 Beverley *History* 88: But he put a
Sting into the tail of this Law. *Oxford* 774;
Tilley S858.

S434 A **Stitch** in time saves nine
1797 Baily *Journal* 268: The vulgar proverb,
"A stitch in time saves nine." **1797** *Washington Writings* 35.354: "A stitch in time,"
to make use of a homely proverb, "will save
nine." **1809** *Port Folio* 2NS 2.56: This is the
stitch in time. Barbour 173(2); *Oxford* 775;
TW 355.

S435 Not care a **Stiver**
1811 *Port Folio* 2NS 5.48: He cares not a
stiver. TW 354(1).

S436 Not worth a **Stiver**
1801 *Spirit of the Farmers' Museum* in

Thornton *Glossary* 2.859: Vagabonds, not
worth a stiver. **1816** Fidfaddy *Adventures*
31: He was not worth a stiver. DA stiver; TW
354(2).

S437 As stupid as a **Stock**
1780 Sargent *Loyalist* 14: From thence to
bed-time stupid as a stock. NED Stock *sb.*[1]
1c, quote 1594.

S438 On the **Stocks**
1772 Lee *Letters* 1.72: With 5 children and
another it may be, two, on the Stocks, a
small estate must part with nothing, 78: Five
children already, another far advanced on
the stocks, with a teaming little Wife, are
circumstances sufficiently alarming. NED
Stock *sb.*[1] 13b.

S439 **Stock** and block
1756 Laurens *Papers* 2.167: The price is so
high with you must sink Stock & Block by
such a Remittance. **1770** *New York Gazette*
in *Newspaper Extracts(I)* 8.256: We are to
be taxed, *our Lives but small, but our Children; not only Paint, Glass, &c. but their
very Stock and block, even to their Heads.*
1775 EInman in Murray *Letters* 194: Jack
Clark has . . . offered . . . to move us stock
and block to a place of safety. **1785** Hunter
Quebec 22: You may lose stock and block.
1796 *Gazette of the United States* in Thornton *Glossary* 2.859: This story turned out to
be a falsehood, or a gross mistake, "stock
and block." **1812** Bentley *Diary* 4.138: The
late account of the burning stock and block
at Serampore. NED Stock *sb.*[1] 1e Cf. TW
354-5.

S440 **Stock** and fluke
1803 Davis *Travels* 449: If you don't take
yourself to the other side of the deck, I'll
shove you over stock and fluke. **1837** Cooper
Letters 3.296: Beall has bought out Joe Miller, stock and fluke, (Anglice stock and
farm). TW 355(5).

S441 **Stock** and lock
1789 *American Museum* 5.297: Losing our
traffic, stock and lock. See TW 226.

S442 **Stock-still**
1777 JWilkinson in *St. Clair Papers* 1.441:

He has remained stock still. **1783** Williams *Penrose* 83: He stood stock still. **1807** *Salmagundi* 8. TW 354(1); Whiting S746.

S443   To be made of **Stocks** or stones

1777 *Washington *Writings* 10.195: As if they thought Men were made of Stocks or Stones and equally insensible of frost and Snow. Lean 2.933. Cf. NED Stock *sb*.[1] 1d.

S444   As dull as **Stockfish**

1801 Mackay *Letters* 30: We all become as dull as Stockfish. Cf. NED Stockfish b.

S445   To be born without **Stocking** or shoe

1776 Bowen *Journals* 2.476: Arrived at Headquarters Monsieur Shaterano born without stocking or shoe.

S446   To throw the **Stocking**

1777 JA in *Adams FC* 2.159: Tell Betcy I hope She is married — Tho I want to throw the Stocking. NED Stocking 5b.

S447   Good **Stomachs** make good savor

c1680 Radisson *Voyages* 73: But good stomachs make good savour. See **H357.**

S448   To bring down one's **Stomach**

1767 Carter *Diary* 1.331: So that I hope his stomach is brought down. Cf. NED Stomach 8b.

S449   To go against one's **Stomach**

1744 Stephens *Journal(II)* 2.89: Which went much against my stomach to comply with for some time. Tilley S874. See **G134, H13.**

S450   To stick in one's **Stomach**

1757 *Johnson Papers* 9.825: The Murder of Jerry still sticks in y[e] stomachs of the Tuscaroras. NED Stomach 6c. Cf. Whiting S754. See **C319.**

S451   As blind as a **Stone**

1764 JA in *Adams FC* 1.33: He is . . . blind as a stone. Svartengren 173; Whiting S757.

S451a   **Stone-blind**

1743 *Boston Evening-Post* in *Newspaper Extracts(I)* 2.162: They must be stone blind. **1770** Adams *Legal Papers* 3.92: Unless all the other Witnesses were Stone-blind. **1779** JLovell in Adams *Works* 9.490. **1779** Van Schaack *Letters* 146. **1789** Curwen *Journal*

2.651. **1791** Bartram *Travels* 316. **1797** Cobbett *Porcupine* 6.190: He is either stone blind himself, or he wants to put our eyes out. **1797** Tyler *Algerine* 1.82. **1800** Cobbett *Porcupine* 11.213. **1809** Weems *Marion* 64. **1813** Paulding *Lay* 16. **c1825** Tyler *Prose* 134, 157, *Verse* 233. Whiting S757a.

S452   As cold as a **Stone**

1676 JMoody in Jantz 151: My heart as cold as Stone. **1697** Dickinson *Journal* 75: Its flesh as cold as a stone. **1700** Mather *Diary* 1.355: My heart had the Coldness of a Stone upon it. **1776** Hopkinson *Miscellaneous Essays* 1.60. **1801** Story *Shop* 27. Whiting S758.

S453   As dead as a **Stone**

1784 Coke *Journals* 18: As dead as stones. **1801** *Port Folio* 1.104: Poor Abel Was dead as any stone. Whiting S759.

S453a   **Stone-dead**

1728 Byrd *Dividing Line* 161: But all agreed twas Stone dead before Firebrand fired. **1740** Custis *Letters* 84. **1778** *New Jersey Gazette* in *Newspaper Extracts(II)* 2.485. **1783** Williams *Penrose* 80, 271. **1803** EWinslow in *Winslow Papers* 504: I am not stone dead. Whiting S759a.

S454   As hard as a **Stone**

c1680 Radisson *Voyages* 225: The eggs weare as hard as stones. **1747** Stith *History* 115: As hard as a Stone. **1776** Curwen *Journal* 1.271-2: In English we say, *as hard as a stone.* **1788** *Columbian Magazine* 2.228: A guardian's heart is hard as stone. **1801** *Farmers' Museum* 77: Their bosoms are harder than stone. **1801** Story *Shop* 68. *Oxford* 352; Whiting S763. See **R108.**

S455   He that removes **Stones** shall be hurt therewith

a1700 Hubbard *New England* 517: What Solomon long since declared, . . . "whoso removeth stones, shall be hurt therewith." Deut. 27.17; *Oxford* 671; Tilley S897.

S456   A rolling **Stone** gathers no moss (*varied*)

1721 Wise *Word* 19: And a Rock which never Rolls, in a few Ages may be over run with such a Moss, as the Prophet cloths the Rock of *Tyrus* with. **1782** Franklin *Writings* 8.372: The Proverb says wisely, *a rolling Stone gathers no moss.* **1787** JAdams in *Adams-Jefferson Letters* 1.176: For a man who has been thirty Years rolling like a stone never three years in the same place. **1790** Freneau *Poems* 3.49: And rolling stones collect no moss. **1804** *Port Folio* 4.187: Adages are commonly true, because founded on experience; "the rolling stone gathers no moss." **1812** HOtis in Otis *Letters* 2.46: This rolling stone. **1814** Wirt *Bachelor* 124. **1821** Freneau *Last Poems* 39: collects. **1824** Neal *American Writers* 56. **1830** Pintard *Letters* 3.140: Poor Lewis, he has been a rolling stone. Barbour 173-4; *Oxford* 682; Whiting M372.

S457   To leave no **Stone** unturned [The following is a selection from 78 occurrences of the phrase]

c1662 JMitchell in Mather *Magnalia* 2.100: When all stones are turned it will come to this. **1665** Hull *Diary* 217: The . . . commissioners seems to be elaborate in turning every stone to find the faults of this Colony. **1692** Mather *Wonders* 74: Wherefor he has left no *Stone unturned.* **1702** *Penn-Logan Correspondence* 1.128: They . . . leave no stone unturned to oppose it, **1705** 2.26, **1707** 197. **1708** HAshurst in *Winthrop Papers*(*B*) 6.173: But there is not one stone he hath left unturn'd to keepe him in. **1719** Byrd *Another Secret Diary* 370: I believe he'll leave no stone unturn'd to hinder me from coming back. **1727** Danforth *Poems* 175.73: They left no Stone unturn'd. **1740** Belcher *Papers* 2.311: No grass grows to my heels nor is any stone unturn'd. **1750** *Massachusetts* in *Colonial Currency* 4.448: Every Stone they can turn, they certainly will turn, in order to gain their Points. **1756** Washington *Writings* 1.294: I shall leave no stone unturned for this salutary end. **1764** Franklin *Papers* 11.378: The same Men who left no Stone unturned to blacken and abuse the former Assemblies, **1771** 18.76. **1775** JWarren in *Warren-Adams Letters* 1.35. **1776** Washington *Writings* 6.18. **1781** Oliver *Origin* 72: The Faction left no Stone un-

turned . . . to discourage the importation of british Manufactures. **1782** WQuynn in *MHM* 31(1936) 185: I shall leave no stone unturned to save a Penny. **1789** Maclay *Journal* 135: The Duchess of Devonshire leaving no stone unturned to carry Fox's election. **1795** *Washington *Writings* 34.266, **1798** 36.495. **1817** WHenderson in *Ruffin Papers* 1.192. **1844** FBlair in Jackson *Correspondence* 6.346: Calhoun would leave no stone unturned to supplant and destroy me. *Oxford* 453; TW 356(14).

S458   To mark with a white **Stone**

1824 *Tales* 1.140: This is his day . . . He will mark it, I doubt not, with a white stone. **1835** Hone *Diary* 1.175: This day must be marked with a white stone, **1842** 2.616, **1845** 730, 739. *Oxford* 512; TW 356(16).

S459   To sink like a **Stone**

1783 Williams *Penrose* 303: It sank . . . like a stone. **1804** Delano *Narrative* 467: In less than three minutes she sunk like a stone to the bottom. Whiting S784.

S460   To swim like a **Stone**

1634 Wood *New-England* 81-2: Her cumbersome ballast . . . which swomme like a stone. *Oxford* 794; Tilley S893.

S461   To throw **Stones** against the wind

1781 JSpringer in *Baxter Manuscripts* 19.102: But not nowing whether it will avvile any more than throoing Stones against the wind. *Oxford* 776; Tilley S896.

S462   To be (fall) between two **Stools**

1729 JAlexander in *Colden Letters* 1.293: So that my present Station happens to be between two Stools. **1739** *Georgia Records* 22[2]. 154: I hope I shall not fall, between 2 Stools **1756** WJohnson, Jr., in Johnson *Writings* 1.249: So that between three stools, I may after all come to the ground. **1763** FBrinley in *Saltonstall Papers* 1.438: We are betwixt Two stooles, (may Slip Through) without great care. **1772** Bowen *Journals* 1.320: Between two stools the ass falls, **1775** 2.436: Between two stools the ass comes to the ground, 453: Only between two stools our ass comes to the grounds. **1778** Joslin *Journal* 354. **1788** EHazard in *Belknap Papers*

2.23. **1791** Morris *Diary* 2.322: The other, who constantly places himself between two Stools, will never have a secure Seat. **1804** Irving *Corrector* 48: Between the two stools, Daniel's breech will shortly come to the ground. **1814** ACHanson in *MHM* 35(1940) 358: My standing is not much better with the King party—between two stools. **1819** Short *Letters* 381: As is vulgarly said, between two seats one falls to the ground. **1831** Jackson *Correspondence* 4.283: I might have found myself between two stools. *Oxford* 57; Whiting S794.

S463   To sit on the **Stool** of repentance
1809 Weems *Washington* 67: She should sit on the stool of repentance. *Oxford* 777.

S464   He must **Stoop** who cannot sit upright
1809 Lee *Diary and Letters* 82: Before he got half way to this castle he was obliged to stoop down, "as he must needs, who cannot sit upright." Cf. *Oxford* 777; Tilley D555.

S465   **Store** is no sore
1772 Habersham *Letters* 220: A store can be no sore. **1777** JChester in Huntington *Papers* 66: A Store is no sore. **1793** *Washington *Writings* 32.482: A store of what can neither waste nor spoil, will be no sore. *Oxford* 777; Whiting S796.

S466   After a **Storm** comes a calm (*varied*)
c1680 Radisson *Voyages* 206: After the storme, calme comes. **1758** Ames *Almanacs* 283: After a Bustle in the Air, The weather's very calm and fair. **1770** Carter *Diary* 1.371: It is an old observation that after a storm comes a calm but in this year 1770 it has been something inverted. **1771** WSJohnson in *Trumbull Papers* 1.477: As in nature, so in politics, a dead calm has succeeded a most furious storm. **1772** Carter *Diary* 2.655: the Proverb. **a1788** Jones *History* 2.506: the old proverb fully verified. **1791** Ames *Letters* 1.96: In public, as well as in private life, a calm comes after a storm. **1802** SFelton in *American Antiquarian Society, Proceedings* NS 69(1959) 150: As the old proverb says. **1803** Davis *Travels* 428. **1806** Asbury *Journal* 2.498: To enjoy a calm after such a storm of labour. **1814** Palmer *Diary* 40: as the old

saying is. **1814** William Rotch *Memorandum* (Boston, 1916) 27: Thus after a storm came a pleasant calm. **1819** Waln *Hermit* 181. **1850** Cooper *Letters* 6.190: After a storm, there must be a calm. Barbour 174; *Oxford* 6; TW 54. Cf. Whiting S797.

S467   One **Story** is good until another is told
1769 Adams(S) *Writings* 1.338: The proverb, however homely it may be, will be allow'd by impartial men to be just, that "one story is good, until another is told." **1806** Paine *Remarks* 2.616: It is a saying often verified by experience, that *one story is good till another is told. Oxford* 597-8: Tale; Tilley T42.

S468   To make a long **Story** short
1814 Kerr *Barclay* 73: To make short of a long story. TW 357(3).

S469   At the **Stove's** mouth
1739 RStaunton in *Letters from Hudson Bay* 299: If I know for truth that everything which is spoke or acted upon all affairs is told in public at the stove's mouth. See **G8.**

S470   If **Strangers** meddle they will get a blow
1681 Willard *Ne Sutor* 3: If strangers will needlesly be medling, they must thank themselves if they get a blow. Cf. *Oxford* 523; Tilley M493; Whiting M482.

S471   Not a **Straw's** difference
1807 *Salmagundi* 165: On these occasions there is not a straw's difference between them.

S472   Not avail a **Straw**
1808 Hitchcock *Poetical Dictionary* 65: Avail not a straw with a spirit so brave. Whiting S804.

S473   Not care a **Straw**
?1689 ?Mather *Vindication* in *Andros Tracts* 2.68: They cared not a Straw. **1763** Laurens *Papers* 3.353: They . . . care not a straw. **1789** Madame Livingstone in Shippen *Journal* 270. **1800** TBlount in *Blount Papers* 3.394. **1800** Cobbett *Letters* 48: I do not care two straws, *Porcupine* 12.109: People care not two straws. **1801** Story *Shop* 77: And car'd no more for justice, than a straw. **1803**

Davis *Travels* 433: [Not] care for me three straws. **1807** *Salmagundi* 268. **c1810** Foster *Jeffersonian America* 322: Cared not one straw. **1812** Woodworth *Beasts* 54. **1813** Freneau *Poems* 3.316, **1816** *Last Poems* 5. **1818** Fearon *Sketches* 148: Few . . . appeared to care one straw about principle. **1819** Cobbett *Year's* 172. **1819** Randolph(J) *Letters* 208: There are not two persons here that care a single straw for one another, **1821** 223. **1840** Cooper *Letters* 4.56. *Oxford* 102; Whiting S805.

S474 Not give a **Straw**

1807 *Salmagundi* 173: I would not give a straw for either of the above definitions. **1810** Adams *Writings* 3.515: I would not give a straw. Whiting S810.

S475 Not heed a **Straw**

1802 Chester *Federalism* 36: He never heeded it a straw.

S476 Not value a **Straw**

1798 Adams *Writings* 2.294, n.[1]: Their . . . decree has not hurt England the value of a straw. **1798** Webster *Letters* 183: This is a trifle that I value not a straw. **1809** Irving *History* 2.237. **1810** Adams *Lectures* 1.388. **1817** Barker *How to Try a Lover* 63. **1821** Knight *Poems* 2.125. NED Straw *sb.*[1] 7, quote 1780; TW 357(3).

S477 Not worth a **Straw**

1719 *Addition* in *Colonial Currency* 1.381: Not worth a Straw. **1725** Mather *Letters* 404: We have no intelligence worth a straw. **1741** *Colden Letters* 8.270. **1780** EHuntington in Webb *Correspondence* 2.283: Paper money is not worth a straw. **1810** Stebbins *Journal* 14. **1811** Taggart *Letters* 373. **1812** Adams *Writings* 4.286: That right is not worth a straw, **1814** *Memoirs* 3.135, **1821** 5.392. **1821** Gallatin *Diary* 192. **1823** Freneau *Last Poems* 114. **1828** WWhipper in Porter *Negro Writing* 117. **1841** Cooper *Letters* 4.114, 121. *Oxford* 779; Whiting S815.

S478 A **Straw** in one's shoe

1778 RIzard in Deane *Papers* 3.208: I can get Doctor — — . . . who is as honest an Irishman as ever attended a court with a straw in his shoe. NED Straw *sb.*[1] 5d.

S479 A **Straw** would turn the scale

1778 GMorris in Jay *Correspondence* 1.174: A straw would have turned in either scale. Cf. NED Scale *sb.*[1] 4.

S480 **Straws** (*etc.*) show which way the wind blows

1774 JGalloway in Burnett *Letters* 1.5: Straws and Feathers tell us from which Point of the Compass the Wind comes. **1783** Franklin *Writings* 9.131: Light things, indeed, as Straws and Feathers, but like them they show which way the Wind blows. **1789** Maclay *Journal* 13: From the drift of dust and feathers one finds how the wind blows, **1790** 303: From the drift of chaff and feathers it is seen how the wind blows, 343, **1791** 373. **1791** Morris *Diary* 2.239: As Dr. Franklin observes, Straws and Feathers shew which Way the Wind blows. **1799** Cobbett *Porcupine* 10.161: "Straws" (to make use of Callender's old hackneyed proverb) "straws show which way the wind blows. **1802** Morris *Diary and Letters* 2.422: Though straws and feathers be light things, they show which way the wind blows. **1807** JAdams in *Adams-Warren Correspondence* 429: A feather often shows which way the wind blows. An exemplification of this light proverb is in the 231st page. **1808** Taggart *Letters* 306: Straws and feathers sometimes show how the wind blows. **1810** Jefferson *Writings* 12.434: Such coxcombs do not serve even as straws to show which way the wind blows. **1814** JBrace in Vanderpoel *More Chronicles* 92. **1819** Short *Letters* 383: A mere feather enables you to judge how the wind blows. **1828** *Yankee* 29. **1829** Jackson *Correspondence* 4.108: It is an old addage that. Barbour 174(2); *Oxford* 779; TW 357(5).

S481 To be in the **Straw**

1721 WKeith in *Colden Letters* 1.124: My wife is now much taken up with her daughter Greme in the straw. **1776** DCobb in *Bingham's Maine* 1.424: Mrs. Cobb is now in the straw with another daughter. **1777** Cresswell *Journal* 236. **1782** Baldwin *Life and Letters* 152: She was in the straw—I did not see her, **1784** 227. **1798** Weems *Letters* 2.94: Since my last remittance I have done nothing but pay a Columbian kind attention to my dame partlet in the straw. **1799** ECarrington in *W&MCQ* 2S 18(1938) 201. **1808** Cooper *Letters* 1.12. **1813** Bentley *Diary* 4.195: His wife in the straw with the 10th child. *Oxford* 779; Tilley S920.

S482 To bring Straw into Egypt

1674 Josselyn *Account* 149: You do but bring straw into Egypt, a Countrey abounding with Corn. See **C225, O52.**

S483 To catch (etc.) at every Straw

1767 Paterson *Glimpses* 32: We lay hold of every straw . . . to alleviate whatever may appear either a slight neglect. **1781** JAllan in *Baxter Manuscripts* 19.188: [The] Torys . . . are Determined to Grasp at every Straw reather then Give up the Connection with The Britons. **1782** Paine *American Crisis* 1.214: They act like men trembling at fate and catching at a straw, 226: And thus, from year to year, has every straw been catched at, and every Will-with-a-wisp led them a new dance. **1784** Gadsden *Writings* 212: It shews how hardly pressed his honor must be to catch at such straws. **1813** Adams *Writings* 4.504-5: He is . . . sick of the war, and ready to catch at any straw to get out of it, **1814** 5.83: We are catching at the straws of such trifles. **1824** Jefferson *Writings* 16.57: Their friends were eager to catch even at straws to buoy them up. **1824** Pickering *Review* 103: Mr. Adams catches at every straw. **1827** Jones *Sketches* 2.110. **1839** Hone *Diary* 1.410: That, with a change of the Administration, are the only straws we have to catch at. NED Straw *sb.*[1] 8c. Cf. TW 233(1). See **M26.**

S484 To dart Straws against the wind

1774 Jones *Journal* 45: All that was said seemed only like darting straws against the wind, for sense of duty was lost.

S485 To hurt with a Straw

1739 Belcher *Papers* 2.237: But Waldo would take hold of a straw if he thought he could use it to hurt the Governour. Cf. *Oxford* 781.

S486 To quarrel for Straws

1788 Hamilton *Papers* 4.649: The friends should be quarrelling for straws among themselves. NED Straw *sb.*[1] 7d. Cf. *Oxford* 446; Tilley L99, W5.

S487 To step over a Straw

1708 Sewall *Diary* 2.227: I mention'd the vastness of the Gov[rs] Authority; we could not lift up hand or foot or step over a straw. Whiting S814.

S488 To stumble at Straws

1620 RCushman in Bradford *History* 1.115: Shuch as stumble at strawes allready, may rest them ther a while, least worse blocks come in the way. *Oxford* 783; Whiting S823.

S489 To throw Straws across one's path

1775 Hopkinson *Miscellaneous Essays* 1.29: They cannot let a man go on in his own way, but they must be throwing straws across his path. Cf. TW 358(7).

S490 Take a Streak of fat and one of lean

1778 AMcDougall in *Clinton Papers* 4.439: But it must take a streak of Fat and one of Lean. Apperson 205: Fat; *Oxford* 800; TW 358(1).

S491 To strive (etc.) against the Stream

1685 Sewall *Diary* 2.9*: And strive no more to swim against the stream. **1689** F-JWinthrop in *Winthrop Papers*(B) 5.499: There is noe striveinge against y[e] streame of popular resolution. **1751** EWinslow in Hutchinson *Papers* 1.258: I looked upon it as a vaine thing to strive against the streame. **1759** Murray *Letters* 92: Strugling against the Stream. **1763** RStewart in *Letters to Washington* 3.248-9: Struggling against the stream of adversity. **1784** McHenry *Letters* 83. **1789** Brown *Better* 27: To deny it would be swimming against the stream of popular applause. **1826** *Austin Papers* 2.1551: They find them selvs lost and will swim against stream as long as they can. NED Stream 2f; *Oxford* 782; Whiting S830. See **T106.**

S492 To swim (etc.) with the Stream (current)

1643 Williams *Writings* 1.339: Mr *Cotton* . . . swimming with the stream of outward credit. **1728** Byrd *Dividing Line* 139: But having no Second, he ran with the Stream.

1752 *Independent Reflector* 56: They swim with the Current. **1755** Laurens *Papers* 2.31: They who have it to sell must swim with the Current. **1771** Woodmason *Journal* 124. **1775** Boucher *View* 590. **1783** *American Wanderer* 25. **1789** Hamilton *Papers* 5.248: Men are fond of going with the stream. NED Stream 2f; Tilley S930; Whiting *NC* 482(2). Cf. Whiting W332. See **T107.**

S493   To the Stretch

1787 WSmith in King *Life* 1.212: Do let me put your friendship to the stretch on this subject. NED Stretch 1g, 4b.

S494   To harp (*etc.*) on that (*etc.*) String

1646 Winslow *Hypocrisie* 45: These men still harp on that string. **1685** WWinthrop in *Winthrop Papers(B)* 4.455: And I beleieve harping on that string may move him to do what he can. **1694** *Connecticut Vindicated* 125-6: We know who has played on this String all along. **1702** RCarter in *W&MCQ* 17(1908) 256: I have harped too much already upon this string. **1720** Sewall *Diary* 3.264: Madam seem'd to harp upon the same string. **1746** *Georgia Records* 25.47: A Letter . . . touching upon the old String, the Liberty of the Subject. **1766** Gadsden *Writings* 71: It is more prudent . . . not to touch upon that string. **1770** Franklin *Papers* 17.339. **1776** Cresswell *Journal* 167: Kirk . . . is still harping on the old string. **1778** Hutchinson *Diary* 2.225: [He] harped upon the old string under another Ministry. **1780** Witherspoon *Works* 4.381-2: the same. **1788** Dunlap *Diary* 1.26: And is't on that string you are harping? **1789** PMuhlenberg in Kirkland *Letters* 2.99: the old. **1791** Maclay *Journal* 360. **1792** Ames *Letters* 1.116: It seems to strain too much on one string. **1793** Brackenridge *Modern* 181: Who on a different string did harp. **1809** Weems *Washington* 81: the old. **1823** Wirt *Letters* 2.153: Probably, too, some of the most heated republicans and interested radicals . . . might . . . harp a little, for a time, on the same string. *Oxford* 355; Whiting S839.

S495   To have two (*etc.*) Strings to one's bow

1650 Bradstreet *Works* 218: And now a King by marriage, choice and blood. Three strings to's bow, the least of which is good.

1723 JDixon in *VHM* 66(1958) 289: But two Stringes if yᵉ one is Sry [sorry] is better yⁿ one. **1741** Stephens *Journal(I)* 2.174: But *Thompson* willing to have two Strings to his Bow. **1761** *Johnson Papers* 3.359: This is Carrying two strings to her bow. **1764** Franklin *Papers* 11.352: John seem'd willing to have as many Strings as possible to his Bow. **1755** Ames *Almanacs* 459: I fear I shall Have more than *two Strings to my Bow.* **1783** Adams *Works* 8.100: It is good to have a variety of strings to our bow. **1783** WChipman in *Winslow Papers* 111: To have as many strings to my Bow as I could I have signed a petition. **1784** Washington *Writings* 27.447: I am desireous of having more strings than one to my bow. **1787** Tyler *Contrast* 97: I shouldn't be surprised if this should be the other string to her bow. **1788** EHazard in *Belknap Papers* 2.26. **1790** *Washington *Writings* 31.140: By having two strings to my bow I may chuse the one which promises best. **1795** Cobbett *Porcupine* 2.11: *The Political Progress* has, as the girls say, more than one string to its bow. **1796** WVMurray in McHenry *Letters* 203: [They] ought to . . . run Pinckney . . . that we may have too strings. **1796** Weems *Letters* 2.55: Neither shall it interfere with our other strings of the bow. **1800** RGHarper in Otis *Letters* 1.192. **1800** JMcHenry in Gibbs *Memoirs* 2.409: Two strings to a bow is said to be better than one. **1805** *Echo* 168: The ancient proverb's wiser far . . . *"Tis best to keep two strings to every bow."* **1806** Milledge *Correspondence* 136. **1806** *Port Folio* NS 2.208. **1810** Dwight *Journey* 29: It is clever to have two or three strings to ones bow. **1815** Humphreys *Yankey* 49: And if t'other strings to my bow all fail, worst cum to worst, I'll turn fiddler. **1819** Weems *Letters* 3.247: This, together with several other strong sinewy strings to the bow. *Oxford* 852; Whiting S841. See **A120.**

S496   Little Strokes fell great oaks

1750 Franklin *PR* 3.449: Little Strokes Fell great Oaks, **1758** *WW* 343. **1770** Ames *Almanacs* 413: Little strokes fell great oaks. Barbour 175; *Oxford* 782; Tilley S941. See **C99.**

S497 To take the **Stud**

1797 RMorris in *PM* 6(1882) 111: Don't you think Mr. Ashleys leading Strings may give way, if the Commy should take the Studd? **1813** Jackson *Correspondence* 1.424: It was soon discovered that . . . they had taken the stud, had changed their course and were actually marching homewards, **1814** 435. DA stud n[1] 1b.

S498 To be in a brown **Study**

1718 Mather *Letters* 254: In short, if once you could be thrown into a Brown-study upon the matter. **c1725** Byrd *Another Secret Diary* 456: I believe too that now and then, when we fall into a Brown study, thinking on nothing. **1774** Adams *D and A* 2.97: I am often In Reveries and Brown Studies. **1801** *Port Folio* 1.87: Dozing to-day in a dark brown study. **1809** Weems *Marion* 60. **1810** Beecher *Autobiography* 1.189: I am all the while in a tormenting brown study to think what under the sun I can possibly say. **1811** *Port Folio* 2NS 5.169. **1816** Paulding *Letters(I)* 2.22: I . . . fell into an enormous brown study. **1821** Adams *Memoirs* 5.416: Mrs. Adams . . . found me to be a *brown study*. **1827** Watterston *Wanderer* 157. *Oxford* (2d ed.) 67 (cf. 3d ed. 88, 782); TW 358. Cf. Whiting S854.

S499 To be a **(Stumbling-)block** in one's way [The following is a selection from 63 occurrences of the phrase, of which 11 had "block" only]

1636 RWilliams in *Winthrop Papers(A)* 3.317: And cry to Heaven, to remove the stumbling blocks. **1641** Johnson *Wonder-Working* lxxxiv: Things going heavily on, and many blocks in the way. **c1645** JCotton in Williams *Writings* 2.97: Remooving two stumbling blocks out of his way, 171. **c1656** Bradstreet *Works* 9: When I have gott over this Block, then have I another putt in my way. **1660** JTinker in *Winthrop Papers(B)* 2.246: I judge many blocks will still be laid, & your coming delayed, unless some blocks leaped. **1661** Hutchinson *Papers* 2.70-1: And stumbling blocks appearing in our way. **1666** TPell in *Winthrop Papers(B)* 3.411. **1679** Harris *Letter* 54: Unckas would be a block in theyr way wher at they were like to

Stumble & fall. **1701** INorris in *Penn-Logan Correspondence* 1.58: [They] have been a block to our plenary comforts in him. **1702** Mather *Magnalia* 2.400: Drinking houses have been a most undoing stumbling-block of iniquity in the midst of us. **1733** Johnson *Writings* 3.26: To lay a stumbling-block before our brother. **1764** Watts *Letter Book* 284: The only stumbling block that lyes in my way is a diffidence of giving satisfaction. **1775** Hutchinson *Diary* 1.501: I . . . have . . . been blamed for throwing blocks in the way. **1778** Franklin *Writings* 7.196: That Stumbling Block to England, the Independence of America. **1784** Washington *Diaries* 2.326: Throwing stumbling blocks in their way. **1801** Jefferson *Writings* 10.241-2: The great stumbling block will be removals. **1811** Beecher *Autobiography* 1.241: When the stumbling-blocks are removed. **1815** Jefferson *Writings* 14.312: To remove the stumbling block which must otherwise keep us eternal enemies. **1822** Weems *Penn* 78: Gin and ardent spirits . . . might prove a stumbling block to him. NED Stumbling-block; *Oxford* 68-9; Whiting B355. Cf. Tilley B454.

S500 As rotten as an old **Stump**

1756 Washington *Writings* 1.486-7: The French, whose hearts are false, and rotten as an old Stump. Cf. TW 359(2).

S501 To stir one's **Stumps**

1778 Moore *Diary* 2.92: And made him stir his stumps. **1779** Huntington *Papers* 136: Let us stir our Stumps and Get this Ship out of Sight. **1801** Sewall *Poems* 241: We *cut and shuffled*, stirr'd our stumps. **1801** Story *Shop* 39. **1802** *Port Folio* 2.167. **1806** *Monthly Anthology* 3.136. **1807** *Weekly* 2.112. **1815** Humphreys *Yankey* 32. *Oxford* 775; TW 359(6).

S502 To wear to the **Stumps**

1764 Watts *Letter Book* 218: The Regulars wore to the Stumps. NED Stump *sb.*[1] 3b.

S503 In the **Suds**

1737 Franklin *Drinkers* 2.177: He's In the Sudds. **1775** Deane *Correspondence* 326: Our worthy Sheriff was all in the suds on Saturday, and went over to see the officers. **1783** Freneau *Poems* 2.203: And wishing

Hugh Gaine and his press in the suds. **1816** UBrown in *MHM* 11(1916) 234: We both [were] in the sudds pretty much, 235: He thinking that I was not out of the sudds yet. NED Suds 5; *Oxford* 784; Partridge 846; TW 359(1).

S504 As sweet as **Sugar**

1813 Gerry *Diary* 192; Sweeter than sugar. Barbour 175(1); Svartengren 306; Whiting S870.

S505 To be neither **Sugar** nor salt

1770 Ames *Almanacs* 412: God has fitted our Constitutions to the Climate we live in, turn out you Sluggard . . . Thou art neither Sugar nor Salt. *Oxford* 785-6; TW 360(2).

S506 As sweet as **Sugar-candy**

c1770 Paterson *Glimpses* 181: Sweet she as sugar candy O. TW 360.

S507 In one's birthday **Suit**

1752 *Pennsylvania Journal* in *Newspaper Extracts(I)* 3.165: She . . . was wedded to her Spouse (if not in a Wedding Suit) in her Birth Day Suit. **1783** Williams *Penrose* 84: He was . . . in his birthday suit. NED Suit 19e, Suppl. Birthday. See **B272.**

S508 In a (long) **Summer's** day

1702 Mather *Magnalia* 1.176: It would require a long summer's day to relate the miseries. **c1780** Witherspoon *Works* 4.393: A genteel, portly, well-looking fellow, as you will see in a summer's day. **1786** Jefferson *Papers* 10.445: If the day had been as long as a Lapland summer day. **1792** Belknap *Foresters* 44: He was as sly a fellow as you will meet with in a summer's day. **1806** CFoote in Beecher *Autobiography* 1.142: They are five as merry girls as you will see in a long summer's day. **1816** Paulding *Letters(I)* 1.137: [They] pay their trifle of assesment with as bad grace as any people you will see in a summer's day, 174: An old man . . . not quite as amiable as one might see of a summer[s] day. *Oxford* 786; Whiting S880.

S509 As bright as the **Sun**

1710 Sewall *Letter-Book* 1.406: And shine as bright as Noon-day Sun. **1721** Wise *Word* 2.203: It is as bright as the light at noon Day.

1740 Stephens *Journal(I)* 2.48: In the Face of Truth, as bright as the Sun. **1769** Wheatley *Poems* 65: Brighter than the Glorious Sun. **1775** JHarvey in *Blount Papers* 1.3: Bright as the Sun at Noon. Barbour 176(1); Whiting S881.

S510 As certain as the **Sun's** rising

1803 Rush *Letters* 2.870: These events are predicted in holy writ and must come to pass as certainly as the rising of tomorrow's sun. Whiting *NC* 483(4). Cf. Barbour 176(3).

S511 As clear as the **Sun**

1652 Williams *Writings* 4.186: The answer is as clear as the *Sun,* **1676** 5.264: As clear as the Noon dayes Sun. **1692** Bulkeley *Will* 154: It was clear as the sun. **1702** Taylor *Christographia* 119.76-7: Gods Decrees shines as clear as the Sun in the Firmament. **1718** Chalkley *Scruples* 461: As clear as the Sun at Noon-day. **1759** Adams *D and A* 1.90, **1768** *Legal Papers* 1.328: I'm as clear as the sun. **1768** *Pennsylvania Chronicle* in *Newspaper Extracts(I)* 7.117: at noon-day. **1768** *Washington *Writings* 2.491: [It was] as clear to me as the Sun in its meridian height. **1771** *Trial of Atticus* 71-2: the noon day. **1773** Trumbull *Satiric Poems* 64: noon-day. **1774** WHDrayton in Gibbes 2.27: at noon. **1776** Washington *Writings* 4.320: in its meridian brightness, **1778** 11.450, 13.464. **1779** *New Jersey Gazette* in *Newspaper Extracts(II)* 3.316: at noon day. **1780** PHenry in Jefferson *Papers* 3.293. **1780** Rush *Letters* 1.247: the noonday. **1780** JSearle in Franklin *Writings* 8.178: the noonday. **1782** Trumbull *Satiric Poems* 120: in noonday heavens. **1788** *Columbian Magazine* 2.467: noon-day. **1798** Adams *Writings* 2.284: a midday. **1798** *Washington *Writings* 37.76: in its Meridian brightness. **1804** Freneau *Poems* 444. **1805** WJarvis in *Barbary Wars* 5.298: noon day. **1806** *Weekly* 1.27. **1808** Hitchcock *Poetical Dictionary* 77. *Oxford* 126; Whiting S882. See **N87.**

S512 As obvious as the noonday **Sun**

1812 Knopf *War of 1812* 5(1) 174: It is obvious as the noon day sun.

S513 As plain as the **Sun**

1744 Stephens *Journal(II)* 2.85: It appears

to me as plain as the Sun. **1775** Willard *Letters* 111: As plain as the meridian sun. a**1824** Marshall *Kentucky* 2.189: Made it all as plain as a noonday sun. TW 360(4).

S514   As punctual as the **Sun**

1812 Burr *Journal* 2.362: My little *menagere* is punctual as the sun. Svartengren 372. Cf. TW 360(5).

S515   As steady as the **Sun**

1815 Humphreys *Yankey* 35: I'll be stiddy as the sun in the farmament.

S516   As sure as the **Sun** moves (shines)

1739 RFry *Scheme* in *Colonial Currency* 3.263: As sure as the Sun that moves, 277. **1790** JBarrell in Webb *Correspondence* 3.159: So sure as the Sun shines. **1819** Faux *Memorable Days* 1.105: As surely as the sun shines. TW 361(6, 7); Whiting S887.

S517   As visible as the **Sun** at noonday

1771 Woodmason *Journal* 202: Facts as visible as the Sun at Noon Day. **1794** Paine *Age of Reason* 1.581: As public and as visible as the sun at noonday.

S518   No morning **Sun** lasts a whole day

1754 Franklin *PR* 5.185: For Age and Want save while you may; No Morning Sun lasts a whole Day, **1758** *WW* 349. **1770** Ames *Almanacs* 413. *Oxford* 544; Tilley S978.

S519   The **Sun** casts its beams upon the lowest shrubs

1624 Davenport *Letters* 17: As the sun casts its beames upon the lowest shrubbs. Cf. *Oxford* 787-8.

S520   The **Sun** excels a star

1712 Taylor *Poems* 280: This feast doth fall below thine, Lord, as far As the bright Sun excells a painted Star, **1718** 339: Transcends as doth the Sun a pinking Star. Whiting S889.

S521   The **Sun** has shone upon them

1722 Franklin *Papers* 1.40: *See the Sun*, or, *The Sun has shone upon them* [drunk]. Cf. Partridge 847; Tilley S970.

S522   The **Sun** shines alike on evil and good

1805 Adams *Memoirs* 1.341: He was like the sun, and shone alike on the evil and the good. *Oxford* 787-8; Whiting S893.

S523   The **Sun** shines on dunghills and diamond mines

1797 Tyler *Verse* 69: The sun—whose high good breeding shines On dunghills, and on diamond mines. NED Sun 1e(h). Cf. *Oxford* 787; Whiting S891.

S524   To make the **Sun** shine through one

1689 IPrince in *Baxter Manuscripts* 6.486: He swore if I spake One word more he would make the Sun shine through me. **1763** Adams *Works* 3.441: And I had a sword by my side I would make the sun shine through him. NED Sun 1e. Cf. TW 94: Daylight (3). See **D49**.

S525   To seek the **Sun** with a candle

1703 Taylor *Christographia* 459.11-2: And hence saith Augustin, We Seek the Sun with a Candle. *Oxford* 788; Tilley S988. See **C23**.

S526   To worship the rising **Sun**

1776 Carter *Diary* 2.996: There is not a more seeming truth in the practice of moderns, than that of worshiping the rising sun and disregarding the setting. *Oxford* 920; Tilley S979.

S527   While the **Sun** shines or waters run

1756 The Mountain King in McDowell *Documents* 2.213: While the Sun should shine or the Waters run, 252: While the Sun did shine or the Water run. **1776** in *McIntosh Papers* 60: As Long as the Sun Shines or the Waters Run. See **G144, R92**.

S528   As clear as the **Sunbeams**

1652 Williams *Writings* 4.165: It is as cleer as the Sun beams, 236. Whiting S901.

S529   No **Sunday** over five fathoms water

1825 Jones *Sketches* 1.8: I had yet to learn the saying, common among seamen, I believe, "no Sunday over five fathoms water." Lean 1.348; TW 361(3). See **S1**.

S530   The **Sunday** disorder

1785 Pynchon *Diary* 226: All ill of the Sunday disorder—laziness.

S531   Eat few **Suppers** and you'll need few medicines

1742 Franklin *PR* 2.337: Eat few Suppers, and you'll need few Medicines. Cf. Whiting S912, 913. See **M36, N74.**

S532   He that will be **Surety** for a stranger shall smart for it

c1813 Dow *Journal* 321: And taught him the lesson — "He that will be surety for a stranger shall smart for it." *Oxford* 790; Tilley S1009.

S533   **Suspicions** are natural to the guilty

1782 Pynchon *Diary* 134: Suspicions are natural to little minds and to the guilty. *Oxford* 249; Tilley F117. See **C279, W144.**

S534   One **Swallow** makes no summer (*varied*)

1652 Williams *Writings* 4.303: One *Swallow* makes not a *Summer*. a**1656** Bradford *History* 2.351: One swallow makes no summer, as they say. **1713** Wise *Churches* 81: As the Proverb is, *Una Hirundo non facit Ver;* one Swallow makes not the Spring. **1780** Curwen *Journal and Letters* 283. **1789** Maclay *Journal* 105: One swallow does not make a summer. **1792** Morris *Diary and Letters* 1.508: The old proverb. **1850** Cooper *Letters* 6.108: Every swallow does not make a summer. Barbour 176; *Oxford* 791; Whiting S924. See **D34.**

S535   To fly like a **Swallow**

1790 Freneau *Poems* 3.30: As the deacon pursues, he will fly like a swallow. Cf. Whiting S926.

S536   As white as a **Swan**

1698 Taylor *Poems* 130: In this bright Chrystall Crimson Fountain flows What washeth whiter, than the Swan or Rose, **1699** 145: More pure, and white, than Lilly, Swan, or Rose. **1810** Adams *Lectures* 2.323: Galatea is whiter than a swan. Whiting S930.

S537   A black **Swan** (is a rare bird)

1643 Williams *Writings* 1.72: Some doe not, but they are rare Birds. **1649** Winslow *Broadside* 3: He was (we surely may say this) *Rara avis in terris*. **1690** Palmer *Account* in *Andros Tracts* 1.47: I take that to be *rara Avis in Terris*. **1708** Talbot *Letters* 119 [as 1690]. **1713** Wise *Churches* 21: We find it to be *rara Avis in Jerva*, like a black Swan in the meadow. **1722** Byrd *Another Secret Diary* 376: I can't boast that such Instances are more frequent than black swans, or humble clergymen. **1753** *Independent Reflector* 136 [as 1690]. **1763** Watts *Letter Book* 198: Doctor Clossy is a rara Avis (& he truely is so in one sense). **1744** Carter *Diary* 2.816: To be sure there may be a Rara Avis in every land; and I wish I could see a black Swan in a Virginia Merchants's Counting house. **1777** JWarren in *Warren-Adams Letters* 1.297 [as 1690]. **1779** Chipman *Writings* 30 [as 1690]. **1779** NKer in *Clinton Papers* 5.162 [as 1690]. **1780** AA in *Adams FC* 3.378: It is a *rara avis* in these days. **1781** Gordon *Letters* 456: A truly honest man is as *rara avis in terra, negroque simillima cygno*. **1788** CPinckney in King *Life* 1.336: An antifederalist would be a *rara avis* in this State. **1800** Gadsden *Writings* 298: *Raisima avis* indeed. **1811** *Adams-Waterhouse Correspondence* 64 [as 1781]. **1814** Adams(A) *Letters* 416: They are considered as black swans. **1814** Adams *Works* 6.482 [as 1690]. *Oxford* 65; Whiting S931.

S538   The **Swan** sings before its death (*varied*]

1634 Wood *New-England* 30: The Silver Swan that tunes her mournefull breath, To sing the dirge of her approaching death. **1694** Taylor *Poems* 96: Sang like a Swan his dying Song. **1702** Mather *Magnalia* 1.367: The memorable *swan-song*, 578: The *vulgar error* of the signal sweetness in the song of a *dying swan*. **1725** Wolcott *Poetical Meditations* 33: And *Swans* which take such Pleasure as they fly, They Sing their Hymns oft long before they Dy. a**1767** Evans *Poems* 110: Sad as the cygnet's moving strain, When on the·shore she dies away. **1772** Hearne *Journey* 400: It has been said that the swans whistle or sing before their death. **1778** Shaw *Journals* 52: You have no doubt seen this last weapon, this swan-like production of the expiring triumvirate. **1789** Brown *Power* 1.51: Like the dying *Swan*, sings her own *Elegy*. **1818** Evans *Pedestrious* 306: Poets feign, that the swan, in the hour of death, beguiles the pains of dissolution with the most plaintive notes. **1822** Pintard *Letters* 2.117: Gov. Clinton's admirable speech, called by his Foes his Valedictory, the notes of the Dying Swan. *Oxford* 791; Whiting S932.

S539 To stir a **Swarm** of wasps about one's ears

1776 ERandolph in Jefferson *Papers* 1.407: [I] stirred up a Swarm of Wasps about my Ears. *Oxford* 869; Tilley W79. See **H298.**

S540 By the **Sweat** of one's brows, *etc.*

1643 Winthrop *Journal* 2.92: So many enemies doth the Lord arm against our daily bread, that we might know we are to eat it in the sweat of our brows. **1648** SSymonds in *Winthrop Papers*(*A*) 5.254: What I have, is gotten by the swet of my browes. **1666** Alsop *Maryland* 48: Purchasing his bread by the sweat of his brows. **1692** Bulkeley *Will* 261: Country people, who get their living by the sweat of their brows. **1705** Beverley *History* 17: [They] seem'd . . . not to have been concerned in the first Curse, *Of getting their Bread by the Sweat of their Brows.* **1729** *Modest Enquiry* in *Colonial Currency* 2.339: He hath earned his Bread with the Sweat of his Brows. **1731** Belcher *Papers* 1.51: He was to get his bread by the sweat of his face. **1758** Smith *Works* 1².134: To earn their bread by the sweat of their brow. **1768** Quincy *Memoir* 17: By the sweat of our brow, we earn the little we possess. **1772** Carter *Diary* 2.710: Am I still to eat my bread by the severe sweat of my brows? **1774** Hopkinson *Miscellaneous Essays* 1.70: Like their first parents . . . to earn their bread with the sweat of their brows. **1777** TDanielson in *Heath Papers* 2.96: The money the honest farmer has earned with the sweat of his face. **1779** Ledyard *Journal of Cook's Last Voyage* 119: Man eateth it by the sweat of his brow. **1783** DSmall in *Baxter Manuscripts* 20.223: They have with the sweat of their Brows . . . made it capable of producing the Bread which now supports them. **a1778** Jones *History* 2.171: Though earned by the sweat of their brows. **1796** Dennie *Lay Preacher* 37: That ancient

adjudication which sentenced Adam to eat bread in the sweat of his brow. **1797** Washington *Writings* 35.498: To be purchased by the sweat of the brow. **1798** Manning *Key* 14: In the swet of thy face shall thou git thy bread. **1801** TPickering in McHenry *Letters* 505: [I shall] be contented to get my bread with the sweat of my brows. **1804** Adams *Writings* 3.97: The original curse to which man was doomed, of earning his bread in the sweat of his brow. **1811** Weems *Gambling* 21: Born to *"eat bread with the sweat of our brow."* **1814** Wirt *Bachelor* 25: In the sweat of his brow man should earn his food. **1815** *Reviewers* 45: By the . . . sweat of their brow earned the precarious meal, 64: The man . . . earns a scanty pittance by the sweat of his brow. **1816** Jefferson *Writings* 14.381: To redeem man from the original sentence of his Maker, "in the sweat of his brow shall he eat his bread." **1816** RPindell in *MHM* 18(1923) 313: I shall . . . earn my Bread as heretofore by the sweat of my Brow. **1819** Pintard *Letters* 1.194: "In the sweat of thy face shalt thou eat thy bread," was denounced on Adam. **1840** CWiley in *Ruffin Papers* 2.191: I have no time to idle: by the sweat of my brow I must make my bread. Barbour 176(1); Whiting S940.

S541 Every **Sweet** has its bitter

1797 JWTomlin in *VHM* 30(1922) 226: As every sweet has its bitter, so equally on the contrary every bitter must have its sweet. **1814** Palmer *Diary* 123: But there is no sweet without some bitter. *Oxford* 885; Whiting S942, 945. See **B197.**

S542 To **Swim** between both

a1656 Bradford *History* 2.84: They knew Mr. Allerton would be with them in it, and so would swime, as it were, betweene both, to the prejudice of both. NED Swim 1b. Cf. Whiting W95.

S543 To wallow like **Swine**

1643 Williams *Writings* 1.112: *Both turne* (*like* Swine) *to wallow in, The filth of former will,* **1652** 4.184: Wallowing and tumbling (like *Swine*) in one puddle of *wickedness* after another. See **D234, S349.**

S544   As sharp as a **Sword**

1745 Brainerd *Memoirs* 259: The word of the Lord . . . sharper than a two edged sword. Barbour 177(2); Whiting S974.

S545   At **Sword**(s) points

1781 JYounglove in *Clinton Papers* 7.35: We are now . . . about half & half almost at swordspoints. **1784** *Deane Brothers Papers* 203: Mr. Morris & Holker are at sword points. **1787** Asbury *Journal* 1.556: At sword's point with the enemy. **1812** VHorne in Knopf *War of 1812* 3.35: [They were] some time ago at swords points. **1824** *Austin Papers* 1.856: He and Price are also at Swords points. TW 363(2). See **D1.**

S546   He that takes (*etc.*) the **Sword** shall perish by the sword

1652 Williams *Writings* 4.352: All that take the *Sword* . . . shall perish by it. **a1700** Hubbard *New England* 528: Thus God ofttimes doth justly order, that he that takes the sword shall perish by the sword. **1766** JDevotion in Stiles *Itineraries* 460: He that draweth the Sword shall perish by the Sword. **1792** Belknap *Foresters* 88: They who take the sword must expect to perish by the sword. **1804** Morris *Diary and Letters* 2.463: To quote the text, "Those who live by the sword shall perish by the sword." Barbour 177(1); Whiting S978.

S547   The longest **Sword** must decide

1658 *Wyllys Papers* 126: Yᵉ Law of Pirats & Theaves, the longest Sword will cary it. **1775** Shaw *Letter Book* 270: Matters seem to draw near when yᵉ longest sword must decide the controversy. **1776** Deane *Papers* 1.227: The longest Sword must decide the dispute. Lean 3.490. See **P321.**

S548   One **Sword** keeps another in the scabbard

1747 Franklin *Papers* 3.203: For 'tis a wise and true Saying, that *One Sword often keeps another in the Scabbard.* Oxford 796; Tilley S1049.

S549   A **Sword** in a madman's hand

1676 Williams *Writings* 5.457: A choice Sword . . . in a mad mans hand. **1692** Bulkeley *Will* 189: Blind zeal is but a mischievous

thing at the best, it is *acutus culter in manu furientis.* Oxford 796; Whiting M90.

S550   The **Sword** of Damocles

1776 WBingham in *Deane Brothers Papers* 40: Like the Sword of Damocles, Suspended over them by a Single Thread. **1790** Freneau *Poems* 3.46: To view the sword, suspended by a thread. **1795** Adams *Writings* 1.388: The sword of Damocles hangs over the head that wears a crown. **1809** WCunningham in *Adams-Cunningham Letters* 119: A public exposure of his mistakes was suspended over the head of Washington like the sword of Damocles. Oxford (2d ed.) 637; Whiting S979.

S551   A two-(double-)edged **Sword**

1777 Smith *Memoirs(II)* 122: This is a double edged Sword, 250: This is a two edged Sword, **1778** 365: two edged, 424: double edged. **1780** Van Schaack *Letters* 249: It . . . is a two-edged sword which cuts both ways. **1788** EHazard in *Belknap Papers* 2.68: The *discretionary power* is a two-edged sword. **1792** PSchuyler in Hamilton *Papers* 10.580: Considering a measure of this kind as a two edged Sword. **1829** MBarney in Jackson *Correspondence* 4.45: And that *your rule* was a "two-edged sword." TW 363(3). See **W68.**

S552   When the **Sword** (of rebellion) is drawn, *etc.*

1775 Copley *Letters* 348: The people have gone too far to retract and . . . they will adopt the proverb, which says, when the Sword of Rebellion is Drawn the Sheath should be thrown away. **1777** Smith *Memoirs (II)* 94: He has thrown the Scabbard away as tho' the Event of the War was no longer dubious. **1778** Lee(W) *Letters* 457: The great Prince of Parma's observation, that when the sword is drawn in certain . . . one should never forget to throw away the scabbard. **1778** Smith *Memoirs(II)* 372: They seem to have resolved to throw away the Scabbard. **1802** Adams *D and A* 3.351: There was great Wisdom in the Adage when the Sword is drawn throw away the Scabbard. **1830** ABalch in Jackson *Correspon-*

dence 4.116: I shall draw the sword in his cause and throw away the scabbard. **1849** Cooper *Letters* 5.403: I fear, from the circular I got, that the scabbard is thrown away. *Oxford* 202; Tilley S1055.

S553   As sweet as **Syrup**

1792 Freneau *Poems* 3.105: Believe me, my dear, it is sweeter that [*for* than] syrup To taste of a title, as cooked up in Europe. Svartengren 306.

T

T1 To a **T**

1802 Drinker *Journal* 377: He is worth a handsome fortune, which will suit to a T. **1815** Humphreys *Yankey* 102: And dance a jig and hornpipe, to a T. **1819** Peirce *Rebelliad* 63: For he has added to a T The letters A + B + C. **1824** *Tales* 2.157: She can fix things to a T. **1826** Audubon *1826 Journal* 289: That suits me to a "T". TW 364. See **P65.**

T2 To knock under the **Table**

1683 Randolph *Letters* 6.140: For quietness sake I am forct to knock under the Table and allow their severall Extravigancies. NED Knock 5c, 15; *Oxford* 433; Tilley B487.

T3 To turn the **Tables** [The following is a selection from 47 occurrences of the phrase]

1694 *Connecticut Vindicated* 110: The Tables thus turned. **1699** Randolph *Letters* 7.575: He presently Turned yᶜ Tables upon them. **1710** INorris in *Penn-Logan Correspondence* 2.430: I hope the tables will be turned. **1742** Belcher *Papers* 2.422: The tables may turn. **1756** Laurens *Papers* 2.183: They have turn'd the Tables upon us. **1770** Munford *Candidates* 38: I must turn the tables on him, **1777** *Patriots* 484: The tories have a mind to turn the tables upon you. **1777** Paine *American Crisis* 1.60: Turn the tables upon yourself. **1777** Washington *Writings* 7.74: The Tables will be turned, 240: A single cast of the die may turn the tables, 9.184, **1778** 11.494. **1780** Hamilton *Papers* 2.362: The tables will soon turn.

1781 *Washington *Writings* 22.179: The table may be turned. **1803** Wirt *British Spy* 221: The tables were turned. **1811** Graydon *Memoirs* 309: The conception of General Washington . . . might . . . have handsomely turned the tables. **1812** Adams *Memoirs* 2.371: He might have turned the tables upon him. **1816** Paulding *Letters(I)* 1.41: The sea fairly turned the tables upon them. **1822** Adams *Writings* 7.289. **1831** Cooper *Letters* 2.113: Turn the tables on them directly, we cannot, for we have no one to pay. *Oxford* 847-8; TW 364(2).

T4 To haul one's **Tacks** and bowlines

1676 Williams *Writings* 5.75: I was glad to *hale* my *Tacks* & *Bolings* close home, and make my best of a *bare Wind*. Cf. NED Bowline[1] 1, Tack *sb.*[1] 5.

T5 To get upon another **Tack**

1815 Weems *Letters* 3.133: 'Tis time in all conscience to come about & get upon another tack. TW 364.

T6 **Tag,** rag, and bobtail

1774 Carter *Diary* 2.820: And if he could not get the best company he could take up with tag, Rag, and bobtail. **1776** Marshall *Diary* 73: To be signed by all (tag, longtail and bob). **1780** Drinker *Not So Long Ago* 181. **1780** Sargent *Loyalist* 31. **1781** Oliver *Origin* 153. **1783** AMacaulay in *W&MCQ* 11(1902) 182. **1787** *American Museum* 1.485. **1789** *Columbian Magazine* 3.434. **c1790** Brackenridge *Gazette* 212. **1792** Freneau *Poems* 3.70: The tag-rag-bobtail of their story. **1793** Brackenridge *Modern* 189.

1793 LHopkins in Gibbs *Memoirs* 1.105. **1796** Drinker *Journal* 294: We went back into a small ordinary room, where was tag, rag &c. **1799** UTracy in Gibbs *Memoirs* 2.232: The aid of every tag-rag who could be mustered. **1802** Weems *Letters* 2.253. **1805** DCameron in Murphey *Papers* 1.3: Besides innumerable battles between tag-rag and bob-tail too tedious to enumerate. **1805** Irving *Journals* 1.225. **1805** Jefferson *Family Letters* 269: I expect there is some tag, rag, and bobtail verse among it. **1805** Weems *Letters* 2.314: I pray God you send me not into the field in the old tag rag and bob tail[d] style. **1806** Dow *Journal* 294: And took my passage in the hold with the rag, tag, and bobtail. **1809** Irving *History* 2.165: Every Tag having his Rag at his side. **1813** *Port Folio* 3NS 2.492. **1815** Brackenridge *Modern* 638, 799. **1815** *Reviewers* 53. **1816** Smith *Life* 259. **1818** Weems *Letters* 3.238: You . . . sent me the . . . Tags, Rags, and Bobtails of the Shelves. **1821** Pintard *Letters* 2.14. **1824** Neal *American Writers* 61: All the newspapers followed — of course — all the magazines — tag, rag, and bobtail. **1827** Watterston *Wanderer* 76. **1834** Hone *Diary* 1.139: And such a set of ragtag and bobtail I never saw on board of a North River steamboat. *Oxford* 797; TW 302: Rag(4), 364; Whiting T7.

T7 The **Tail** is on the other pig

1809 Kendall *Travels* 163: "The tail has got on t'other pig."

T8 To be **Tail** foremost

1797 Brackenridge *Modern* 282: But I see they hae every thing tail foremost in this kintra. Cf. *Oxford* 624; Tilley P312.

T9 To turn **Tail**

1732 LMorris in *Colden Letters* 2.81: But as soon as Mathews's back was Turned Gaasbeck & Pawling Turnd Taile. **1745** Stephens *Journal(II)* 2.183: And turning tail, began to Condemn her obstinacy with the rest of the World. TW 365(2); Tilley T16.

T10 Nine **Tailors** make a man (*varied*)

1647 Ward *Simple Cobler* 26: It is a more common then convenient saying, that nine Taylors make a man; it were well if nine-teene could make a woman to her minde: if Taylors were men indeed . . . they would disdain to be led about like Apes, by such mymick Marmosets. **1807** *Salmagundi* 105: The tailor, though being, according to a national proverb, but the ninth part of a man. **1819** Waln *Hermit* 90: And made absolute fools of, by the ninth part of a man. *Oxford* 567; TW 365(2).

T11 To be done over **Tailor**

1810 *Austin Papers* 1.174: They told me to tell you if you wished to save deal at that place you must make great exertions or you would be done over tailor as the vulgar express it. G. F. Northall, *Folk-phrases of Four Counties* (English Dialect Society, publ. 73, London, 1894) 19: Like the tailor, done over.

T12 Don't **Take** me up before I am down

1803 Davis *Travels* 349: Don't take me up before I am down. *Oxford* 799; Tilley T30.

T13 Never tell **Tales** out of school

1786 *Anarchiad* 112: And never tell tales out of school. **1812** Hitchcock *Social* 132: And still, by tattling out of school, Counter to his appointed rule. **1826** Jones *Sketches* 1.95: I must not tell tales out of school. **1826** Longfellow *Letters* 1.194. *Oxford* 803; Whiting T35.

T14 A **Tale** of a tub

1646 Winslow *Hypocrisie* 80: Hee tels a tale of a tub. **1744** Hamilton *Itinerarium* 43: He was going on with this tale of a tub. **1752** *Colden Letters* 9.118: Such work as mine never meets with so much encouragement as a Tale of a Tub. **1799** NAmes in *DHR* 9(1898) 111: Tale of tubs to reexcite languishing War hoops! . . . Know all the tale of Tubs, *etc.* **1799** Bentley *Diary* 2.298: The news . . . is much in the fog & the tale of *the tub* has vanished. **1799** Freneau *Prose* 399: The tale of a tub with a double bottom. **1799** Iredell *Correspondence* 2.548: Government has yet received no official account of the *Tales of the Tubs* from Charleston. **1799** *Washington Writings* 37.156: What *the tale of the Tubs* turned out to be I have not heard. **1815** *Port Folio* 3NS 5.300: Yet the tale of a lake's like the Tale of a Tub. *Oxford* 803; Whiting T29.

T15 Thereby hangs a **Tale**

1799 Lusitania in Deane *Papers* 3.474: For I believe thereby hangs a tale. *Oxford* 809; Whiting T31.

T16 A twice-(thrice-)told **Tale**

1762 Watts *Letter Book* 79: Any thing I can say of our Operations must be a twice told Tale. **1782** *Belknap Papers* 1.165: A weekly paper filled with thrice-told tales. **1810** *Kennon Letters* 32.171: You know the wise Ulysses says, there is nothing so tedious as a twice told tale. Barbour 176(1); NED Twice-told². Cf. *Oxford* 802; Tilley T39.

T17 To hide one's **Talent** in a napkin

1722 Franklin *Papers* 1.13: For I never intend to wrap my Talent in a Napkin. **1733** Talcott *Papers* 1.282: The Sin & folly of hiding Our Tallent in a Napkin. **1774** Willard *Letters* 16: He has not hid his talent in a napkin. **1778** AA in *Adams FC* 3.48: A talent which . . . you did not hide in a Napkin. Luke 19.20; NED Napkin 2c. See **B372.**

T18 All **Talk** and no cider

1807 *Salmagundi* 153-4: The people . . . conscious of this propensity to talk . . . have a favorite proverb on the subject, viz., "all talk and no cider." TW 365(1).

T19 All **Talkers** and no hearers

1750 WChancellor in *PM* 92(1968) 478: It ressembles an ale house all talkers and no hearers. **1815** Palmer *Diary* 223: There Bedlam commences again, all talkers and no hearers. See **D290.**

T20 Great **Talkers,** little doers

1733 Franklin *PR* 1.313: Great Talkers, little Doers. *Oxford* 804; TW 366. Cf. Whiting C516.

T21 Too slick for **Tallow**

1817 *Port Folio* 4NS 4.397-8: You have improved vastly since I first saw you; you are getting too *slick for taller!*

T22 On the **Tapis** [The following is a selection from 46 occurrences of the phrase]

1740 Belcher *Papers* 2.311: As I have such great affairs on the tapis here. **1773** Franklin *Writings* 6.89: Bringing it all upon the *tapis.* **1776** JA in *Adams FC* 2.13: Great Things are on the Tapis. **1781** Oliver *Origin* 81: When the Stamp Act was on the Tapis, he encouraged the passing of it. **1782** JA in *Adams FC* 4.273. **1783** *Washington Writings* 26.187: It would . . . be impolitic to introduce the Army on the Tapis. **1786** Jefferson *Papers* 9.137: The commercial Arrangements which are on the Tapis between France and England. **1789** Brown *Power* 2.21: If . . . matrimony is really on the tapis. **1796** MCarey in Weems *Letters* 2.17: I believe it will be well to have four or five books on the tapis at once. **1807** *Port Folio* NS 4.414: In the future, instead of asking what is on the *tapis,* we must inquire, what is on the *anvil.* [Five U.S. Senators were named Smith.] **1819** Adams *Memoirs* 4.417: Webster was again on the tapis for the appointment. **1819** Waln *Hermit* 92: To bring themselves *sur le tapis.* **1823** JAdams in Otis *Letters* 1.174. **1850** Cooper *Letters* 6.136: I have . . . a bargain with the Hartford men on the tapis. TW 366. See **C44.**

T23 As black as **Tar**

1826 Royall *Sketches* 90: The offal of hogs fried to a cracknel, and as black as tar. **1831** Pintard *Letters* 3.226: Her blood the Dʳ say[s] was as black as Tar. Barbour 178(1); Whiting T39.

T24 **Tare** and tret

1764 Watts *Letter Book* 216: I begin to think you a bad Tare & Tret Man. NED Tare *sb.*² d.

T25 There are **Tares** among the wheat

1751 *Appendix* in *Colonial Currency* 4.477: There are *Tares* among the best Wheat. **1763** Griffith *Journal* 319: [The Devil] finds opportunity to sow tares amongst the wheat. **1780** Curwen *Journal* 2.686: But among wheat will be tares. **1792** Smith *Works* 2.559: Root out the Tares from the Wheat, **1795** 456: Tares have been scattered among the wheat. **1803** Austin *Constitutional* 137:

Extravagance . . . is the *"tare among the wheat."* NED Tare *sb.*[1] 3; Tilley W282; Whiting C361. See **W110**.

T26   To catch a Tartar

1686 Randolph *Letters* 6.168: He had caught a Tartar. **1704** *Penn-Logan Correspondence* 1.305: [They] will never leave off till they catch a *Tartar.* **1731** Belcher *Papers* 1.47. **1731** Franklin *Papers* 1.219. **1769** Woodmason *Journal* 154. **1779** RCranch in *Adams FC* 3.204. **1779** JWarren in *Warren-Adams Letters* 2.102. **1807** *Salmagundi* 17. c**1810** Foster *Jeffersonian America* 236. **1811** Graydon *Memoirs* 60. **1833** Jackson *Correspondence* 5.207: In his appointment I surely caught a tarter in disguise. **1846** Paulding *Letters(II)* 432: A fellow smoked me for a green horn from the country . . . But he caught a Tartar. *Oxford* 110; TW 366. See **Y1**.

T27   To get into Tartar (? *for* Tartarus) Limbo

1781 DHall in Rodney *Letters* 398: And I dont know but I should get into Tartar Limbo if I should attempt to leave this place without discharging.

T28   Tastes differ

1803 Davis *Travels* 53: Tastes sometimes differ. *Oxford* 805. See **A18**.

T29   Female Tears and April snow, *etc.*

1775 Freneau *Poems* 1.199: Female tears and April snow Sudden come and sudden go. Cf. Tilley W674. See **W289**.

T30   The Tears shed on your grave, *etc.*

1792 Brackenridge *Modern* 53: The tears that will be shed upon your grave, will not make the grass grow.

T31   Temperance, exercise and cheerfulness, *etc.*

1797 JMiller in Iredell *Correspondence* 2.518: Temperance and exercise are the two doctors I have long employed. **1817** Weems *Franklin* 199: Nature's three great physicians, *temperance, exercise, and cheerfulness.* *Oxford* 808. Cf. Lean 1.505; Whiting L175. See **D220, P101**.

T32   When angry count Ten (*varied*)

1786 Jefferson *Papers* 10.620: Did you count 10. distinctly between the origin of that thought, and the committing it to paper? **1786** WSmith in Jefferson *Papers* 9.555: He has only to count ten and he is prepared for the subject, 557, 612-3. **1825** Jefferson *Writings* 16.111: When angry, count ten, before you speak; if very angry, an hundred. *Oxford* 14; Whiting *NC* 361: Angry.

T33   To be tossed like a Tennis-ball

1665 JUnderhill in *Winthrop Papers(B)* 2.190: As Scoot tould mee his letter was tost upon doun like a tennisbale. NED Tennis-ball b.

T34   To strike one's Tent(s)

1807 *Salmagundi* 187: A fortunate drought obliged the enemy to strike their tents. **1817** JGraham in *Ruffin Papers* 1.195: When I write you again I shall have struck my Tent for one year. NED Strike 22.

T35   Tenterden steeple is the cause of Goodwin Sands

?1689 ?Mather *Vindication* in *Andros Tracts* 2.50: [It] is to tell us that the fall of *Tenterden steeple* was the cause of *Godwin-sands. Oxford* 808: Whiting S56.

T36   To be on Tenterhooks

1637 Morton *New English Canaan* 307: And if any man should . . . be accused of a crime . . . they might set it on the tenter hookes of their imaginary gifts, and stretch it to make it seeme cappitall. **1692** GSaltonstall in *Winthrop Papers(B)* 5.15: Tormented upon y[e] tenterhooks of expectation. c**1720** Byrd *Another Secret Diary* 272: You're always upon the Tenterhooks. **1776** JA in *Adams FC* 2.63: I hang upon Tenterhooks. **1788** Washington *Writings* 30.91: The . . . Congress . . . have hung the expectations, and patience of the Union on tenter hooks. **1827** Pintard *Letters* 2.373: I am still suspended on the Tenter hooks, waiting every moment to be summoned to court. NED Tenterhook 2; *Oxford* 808.

T37   A good Text deserves a fair margent

1647 Ward *Simple Cobler* 24: A good Text always deserves a fair Margent.

T38 Through **Thick** and thin [The following is a selection from 47 occurrences of the phrase]

a1731 Cook *Bacon* 322: Thro' thick and thin, thro' Mire and Sands. **1743** Franklin *PR* 2.373: The poor Child . . . Forc'd thro' thick and thin to trudge it along. **1765** JOtis *Vindication* in Bailyn *Pamphlets* 1.557: He seems determined to flounder on through thick and thin. **1765** Watts *Letter Book* 336: If the M[inistr]y mean to have a Man to go thro' thick & thin for them, they are exactly fitted here. **1769** Adams(S) *Writings* 1.378: A Person hardy enough to go through thick and thin to support his Calumnies. **1779** Paine *Deane* 2.129: Mr. Plain Truth . . . sticks at nothing to carry Mr. Deane through everything thick or thin. **1781** Oliver *Origin* 50: They would go *p*[*er*] *Nefas*, thro' thick without thin, to accomplish their Ends. **1783** Jefferson *Papers* 6.225: Braving all weather and plunging thro' thick and thin. **1790** Maclay *Journal* 182: Elsworth . . . supported his bill through thick and thin. **1791** S.P.L. *Thoughts* 167: I am determined, *through thick and thin,* to fulfil my promises. **1795** Adams *Memoirs* 1.136: A thick-and-thin political partisan, **1799** *Writings* 2.445: Fenno . . . believes through thick and thin in the gospel of Porcupine. **1799** AHamilton in Jefferson *Writings* 1.416: We must carry it through thick and thin, right or wrong. **1808** Taggart *Letters* 328: Our Massachusetts' Demo's would go thro thick and thin to all lengths. **1812** Burr *Journal* 2.360: I . . . resolved to keep through thick and thin. **1816** Jackson *Correspondence* 2.248: Who supported it [Government] thro thick and thin. **1818** Fessenden *Ladies Monitor* 34: And drives his courtship through thick and thin. **1846** Cooper *Letters* 5.126: I voted against those who manifested a disposition . . . to support the late bishop of this diocese, through thick and thin. *Oxford* 810; Whiting T64.

T39 As safe as a **Thief** in a mill (synagogue)

1796 Barton *Disappointment* 52: Creep under the bed, and your as safe as a thief in a synagogue. **1805** *Echo* 172: And safe they lie "as thieves within a mill." *Oxford* 691; TW 368(3).

T40 Great **Thieves** hang little ones

1775 Moore *Diary* 1.135: The great thieves, it seems, begin to hang the little ones. *Oxford* 335; Whiting T68.

T41 (Set a **Thief** to catch a thief)

1819 Brackenridge *South America* 1.243: According to the old adage, he [an outlaw] justified their expectations; he . . . effectually pursued and hunted down his old companions. Barbour 179(2); *Oxford* 810; TW 368(6). See **R123**.

T42 A **Thief** abhors the fatal tree

1809 Kendall *Travels* 1.163: Not more the skulking thief the fatal tree, Than faction's brood abhor thy sons and thee! See **R133**.

T43 A **Thief** cries Catch Thief (*varied*)

1768 Franklin *Papers* 15.221: [There is] a very common custom among pickpockets, i.e. A thief cries catch thief. **1792** Freneau *Prose* 286: The best general rule on the subject is to be taken from the example of crying "Stop thief" first. **1815** *Bulger Papers* 153: The principal of some ingenious depredators, who when in danger of detection are among the first to bawl "Stop Thief!" **a1828** Pinkney *Works* 205: A detected pick-pocket . . . bawls "Stop thief!" more lustily than anyone else. **1831** Jackson *Correspondence* 4.260: The old story—rogue, cries rogue rogue first, to draw the attention from himself, **1838** 5.555: Mr. Bell cries party, party, party, which brings me in mind of the old adage of the rogue crying rogue, rogue, etc. *Oxford* 98-9; Tilley N112, W319. See **W142**.

T44 A **Thief** had rather steal a purse than find one

1806 Paine *Challenge* 2.1009: It has been said of a thief that he had rather steal a purse than find one.

T45 **Thieves** never trust one another

a1775 *The Felon* in *VHM* 56(1948) 189: For thieves can never one another trust. See **H272**.

T46 To expect a **Thief** in every bush

1702 Mather *Magnalia* 2.563: As expecting "a thief in every bush." Tilley B739, T113; Whiting W562. Cf. *Oxford* 484.

T47 All **Things** have their changes

1653 Keayne *Apologia* 14: All things have their changes. 1754 Plumstead 319: All things are full of change. Whiting T97. See **W358.**

T48 Do not do **Things** by halves

1654 SWinthrop in *Winthrop Papers*(B) 4.216: For it is not the Maner of the Lord Protector to doe things by halves. 1747 JRutherford in *Colden Letters* 3.334; 'Tis allways dangerous to do business by halfs & always safest to go thro with it with spirit. 1785 Adams *Works* 8.292: I would not do things by halves. *Oxford* 562.

T49 Don't risk any **Thing** for nothing

1789 Adams *D and A* 3.219: We should not risk any Thing for nothing. *Oxford* 751; Whiting S462.

T50 Every **Thing** is worth what it will fetch

1739 RFry *Scheme* in *Colonial Currency* 3.276: As the old saying is, The just Value of any Commodity whatever, is what it will fetch. 1788 Washington *Writings* 30.166: Butler says "everything is worth what it will fetch," 1799 37.180: Hudibras says every thing is worth what it will fetch. *Oxford* 922; Tilley W923, 925.

T51 Four **Things** necessary to make a man

1758 *New American Magazine* in *Newspaper Extracts*(I) 4.200: That article in the religion of the Magi, that the most pleasing actions to God which man could do, was to get a child, to manure a field, and to plant a tree; and we may add a fourth axiom, to load a ship. 1793 *Belknap Papers* 2.330: It is said by somebody (I forget who) that 4 things are necessary to make a *man*: 1. That he should plant a tree. 2. That he should write a book. 3. That he should get a child. 4. That he should build a house.

T52 Little **Things** lead to great

1791 Bentley *Diary* 1.255: Little things lead to great, & frequently produce them. Cf. Whiting L402. See **C99.**

T53 One **Thing** at a time

1702 *Penn-Logan Correspondence* 1.172: One thing at a time. 1792 Brackenridge *Modern* 4: One thing at once, is the best maxim that ever came into the mind of man. *Oxford* 598.

T54 One **Thing** begets another of its species

1744 Black *Journal* 2.48: As one thing begets another of its species. *Oxford* 598. See **R24.**

T55 Take **Things** (men) as one finds them

1786 JLibbey in *Belknap Papers* 3.313: We must take mankind as we find them. 1795 Jay *Correspondence* 4.179: We must take men and things as they are, and enjoy all the good we meet with. 1795 Morris *Diary and Letters* 2.93: There is nothing perfect in this world, and we must therefore take things as we find them. 1796 Jay *Correspondence* 4.217: We must take men and things as they are, and act accordingly. 1797 Baily *Journal* 414: I determined for the future to take things as I found them, and if I could not remedy them, to be content. 1800 OWalcott, Jr., in Gibbs *Memoirs* 2.417: We must . . . take things as we find them. 1812 BFStickney in Knopf *War of 1812* 6(1) 204: We must take things as they are: not as we would have them. 1817 WGarnett in *Ruffin Papers* 1.191: We must . . . take things as they happen in this life. *Oxford* 801; TW 369(8); Whiting M171, T194. See **W352.**

T56 Take **Things** as they come

1809 Mackay *Letters* 199: There is no help for these things, we must take them as they come. 1816 TJefferson in *Adams-Jefferson Letters* 2.467: But we must take things as they come. *Oxford* 801.

T57 There is no new **Thing** under the sun

1664 Bradstreet *Works* 53: There is no new thing under the sun. 1713 Wise *Churches* 67: There are none New under the Sun. 1758 NAmes in *W&MCQ* 3S 14(1957) 594: As the Wise Man observes. 1775 BDeane in *Deane Correspondence* 271: Gen Gages's proclamation or manifesto, which is a new thing under the sun. **1776** Fitch *New-York Diary* 40. **1778** Anburey *Travels* 2.84: It is . . . a new thing under the Sun. **1778** Moore *Diary* 2.22: I can't think it is true, Tho' Solomon says it, that nothing is new. **1779** JLovell in *Adams FC* 3.151. **1788** *Politician* 3: A wise man and a king has told them. **1794** Adams *Writings* 1.226: It is to me a new thing under the sun. **1801** Jefferson *Writings* 10.229: We can no longer say there is nothing new under the sun. **1810** Morris *Diary and Letters* 2.521: How true that saying of Solomon. **1813** Adams *Memoirs* 2.467. **1813** JAdams in *Adams-Jefferson Letters* 2.330. **1814** *Port Folio* 3NS 4.553. **1815** Waterhouse *Journal* 29. **1817** Tyler *Prose* 354: The great lesson taught by Solomon. **1822** GHowland in *New England Merchants* iii. **1824** Longfellow *Letters* 1.87: I believe with Solomon. **1834** Floy *Diary* 97: What is there new under the Sun? *Oxford* 580; Whiting T146.

T58 Three **Things** breed jealousy, *etc.*
1735 Ames *Almanacs* 99: Three Things breed Jealousy. A mighty State, a rich Treasure and a fair Wife.

T59 Three **Things** only are done in a hurry, *etc.*
1810 *Port Folio* 2NS 3.313: Only three things are done well in a hurry; flying from the plague, escaping quarrels, and catching fleas. *Oxford* 580: Nothing; Tilley N251. See **F179.**

T60 Were **Things** done twice, many would be wise
1758 Ames *Almanacs* 284: Were Things done twice, Many would be wise. *Oxford* 199; Tilley T185. See **T74, 299.**

T61 When **Things** are at the worst they must mend
1738 WDouglas *Essay* in *Colonial Currency* 3.247: When Things are come to the worst, then they will mend. **1779** Lee *Letters* 2.161: When things get to their worst they must mend. **1830** Ames *Mariner's* 174: It is an old sea adage, that "when things are at the worst they are sure to mend." *Oxford* 811; Tilley T216.

T62 Can **Thistles** bear roses?
1797 Cobbett *Porcupine* 5.176: Can thistles bear roses, or can honey drop from the poisonous upas? Cf. *Oxford* 331; Tilley T233; Whiting G421. See **P57.**

T63 Under the **Thistle**
1758 HRoberts in Franklin *Papers* 8.82: Now communicate their thoughts to each other in whispers under the Thistle. See **R150.**

T64 He that scatters (sows) **Thorns** should not go barefoot
1736 Franklin *PR* 2.142: He that scatters Thorns, let him not go barefoot, **1742** 2.335: He that sows thorns, should not go barefoot, **1756** 6.327: He that sows thorns, should never go barefoot. *Oxford* 30; Tilley T235. See **H333.**

T65 A **Thorn** in one's flesh
1657 Wigglesworth *Diary* 105: But lets them be thornes in the flesh to buffet me. **1699** Mather *Diary* 1.285: I was able . . . to Discourse . . . above an Hour, on the Apostles *Thorn in the Flesh;* which I find some of the Ancients, expound of a troublesome *Headache.* **1725** Chalkley *Journal* 151: The Messenger of Satan, the Thorn in the Flesh, which the Apostle speaks of. **1797** Dunlap *Diary* 1.187. **1809** Asbury *Journal* 2.611: It was like thorns in my flesh. **1812** Holcombe *First Fruits* 148. **1830** Ames *Mariner's* 307: To stick "thorns in our flesh." Barbour 181(1); TW 370(1).

T66 A **Thorn** in one's side
1646 Bradford *History* 1.15: And been as thorns in their sides. **1648** WCoddington in *Hutchinson Papers* 1.254: Gorton will be a thorne in their and our sides. **1664** Bradstreet *Works* 72: They became prickes in their eyes, and thornes in their sides. ?**1689** ?Mather *Vindication* in *Andros Tracts* 2.70: To be Thornes in the sides of their quiet Neighbours. a**1700** Hubbard *New England* 147: Such as . . . might prove as goads in their eyes and thorns in their sides. **1703** Mather *Diary* 1.492: The Rage of that young Gentlewoman . . . is transporting her, to threaten that she will be a Thorn in

my Side. **1704** F-JWinthrop in *Winthrop Papers*(*B*) 5.262. **1716** Church *History* 1.10: He believed he should prove a sharp thorne in their sides. **1739** Belcher *Papers* 2.255. **1742** *Georgia Records* 23.445. **1759** TPownall in *Baxter Manuscripts* 13.150: A Thorn will be left in the Side of this Province. **1771** Adams *D and A* 2.42: A Thorn in his Side. **1775** NGreene in *Naval Documents* 3.181. **1778** Gadsden *Writings* 126. **1780** Jefferson *Papers* 3.259: The nearer Wiandots are troublesome thorns in our sides, 292. **1782** Lee(W) *Letters* 3.860: Keeping America a perpetual Thorn in ye side of G. B. **1785** Coke *Journals* 33. **1788** *American Museum* 3.268: As great a thorn in our side, as were the tories. **1788** Washington *Writings* 29.491: A thorn this is in the sides of the leaders of opposition. **1797** Beete *Man* 24. **1798** Adams *New Letters* 143. **1799** Eaton *Life* 119: That slave has been a thorn in my side. **1804** *Port Folio* 4.48. **1819** Cobbett *Year's* 180. **1820** Simpson *Journal* 130. **1826** JRuffin in *Ruffin Papers* 1.346. Barbour 181(1); TW 370(2).

T67 **Thorns** in the path

1783 ERandolph in Madison *Papers* 7.287: [They] are indeed thorns in the path. **1808** Jackson *Correspondence* 1.186: That Party, who for two years have been planting his path with thorns. See **B97**.

T68 To be a **Thorn**

1806 Dow *Journal* 289: My hostess, who had been a thorn to her husband for about twenty three years. **1815** Gallatin *Diary* 73: Mr. Adams is certainly a thorn; he is so absolutely "Yankee" and of a common type. NED Thorn 2.

T69 To pull a **Thorn** out of another's foot, *etc.*

a1700 Hubbard *New England* 323: They were more than a little forward to pull so troublesome a thorn out of their feet. **1701** Sewall *Letter-Book* 1.251: But both those Thorns are pulled out of their feet and left sticking in mine. **1778** Lee(W) *Letters* 2.447: Experience will prove the wisdom of taking the thorn out of the feet of others,

and putting it in his own. *Oxford* 653-4; Whiting T225.

T70 To sit (be) upon **Thorns**

1784 Washington *Writings* 27.373: A countryman of yours . . . has a fair word, and I know is sitting upon thorns from his eagerness to embrace it. **1790** JMason in Mason *Papers* 3.1195-6: The People impatient and on thorns since Wednesday. **1804** Weems *Letters* 2.297: The villanous spoilations so frequently made on the mail keep me perpetually on thorns. **1811** Graydon *Memoirs* 345: I sat upon thorns, said Izard. **1811** Randolph(J) *Letters* 98: I shall be on thorns until the arrival of the next mail. *Oxford* 814; Whiting T227. See **N53**, **P161**.

T71 To go (swear) **Through-stitch**

1741 Stephens *Journal*(*I*) 2.239: Casting off all thoughts farther of filial Duty . . . [he] seemed determined to go through stitch. **1745** JAlexander in *Colden Letters* 3.103: Both he & his mother must swear thro Stitch in Chancery to make it of any benefit to them. NED Thorough-stitch B.

T72 As quick as **Thought**

1708 Cook *Sot-Weed* 7: Quick as my thoughts. **1765** "A new song" in *W&MCQ* 3S 10(1953) 80: Quick as Thought the Ships were boarded. **1779** Curwen *Journal and Letters* 226: As quick as thought. **1809** Weems *Marion* 136, 195. **1809** Woodworth *Poems* 238: The scene is changed as quick as human thought. *Oxford* 794; Whiting T232.

T73 As swift as **Thought**

1757 Churchman *Account* 254: An angel, whose motion was as swift as thought. **a1786** Ladd *Remains* 25: Lo! swift as thought the angry flashes fly. *Oxford* 794; Whiting T233.

T74 Second **Thoughts** are best

1678 Williams *Writings* 6.395: The maxim of Queen Experience (*secunda cogitationes meliores*). **1775** Moore *Diary* 1.134: But second thoughts are ever best. **1779** AA2d in *Adams FC* 3.159: You know that second thoughts are often the best. **1782** *Belknap*

Papers 1.142: they say. **1820** Hodgson *Letters* 2.75: I am led to doubt the truth of the old proverb, that second thoughts are best. *Oxford* 708; Tilley T247; Whiting *NC* 485(2). See **T60, 299.**

T75 To change like **Thought**

1816 Jefferson *Writings* 14.382: When public opinion changes, it is with the rapidity of thought. Whiting T239.

T76 One's **Thread** is spun

1632 Bradstreet *Works* 391: My race is run, my thread is spun. **1760** *New York Mercury* in *Newspaper Extracts(I)* 4.456: Thine Eyes, dear Girl, are clos'd in Night; Thy Thread, alas! is spun. *Oxford* 815; Tilley T249.

T77 To hang upon (by) a **Thread**

1782 JA in *Adams FC* 4.361: It has hung upon a Thread, a Hair, a silken Fibre. **1786** RO'Brien in *Barbary Wars* 1.5: The American peace hangs on a thread. **1787** Washington *Writings* 29.278: The political concerns of this Country are, in a manner, suspended by a thread, 340. **1795** Monroe *Writings* 2.196: Thus the connection between the two countries hung, as it were, upon a thread. *Oxford* 343; Whiting T244.

T78 To spin a fine **Thread**

1734 Belcher *Papers* 2.32: If not, your late Assembly have spun a fine thread. *Oxford* 765; Whiting T245.

T79 They who **Threaten** are afraid

1782 Franklin *Writings* 8.469: Remembring the Adage, that *they who threaten are afraid.* Tilley T254.

T80 As thick as **Three** in a bed

1784 Asbury *Journal* 1.462: To lie as thick as three in a bed. TW 370.

T81 **Three** may accord, but two never can

1804 Claiborne *Letter Books* 2.173: *Three* may accord but *two* never can.

T82 **Three** may keep a secret, if two of them are dead

1735 Franklin *PR* 2.8: Three may keep a Secret, if two of them are dead. Barbour 159-60; *Oxford* 417; Whiting T248.

T83 To be above one's **Thumbs**

1773 MCooper in Johnson *Writings* 1.489: How to set about promoting matters is above my thumbs. NED Thumb 5i. Cf. Whiting T260.

T84 To be under one's **Thumb**

1714 Talbot *Letters* 133: [They] were kept under the Thumb for Cotton Mather. **1740** JWebbe in Franklin *Papers* 2.278: He had him therefore *under his Thumb.* **1755** Davis *Colonial Virginia Satirist* 25: I hae the press under my thumb, so that nathing can be printed. **1757** TRobinson in *W&MCQ* 2S 20(1940) 539: They may have him more under their thumbs. **1782** Adams *Works* 7.508: They have the whole affair . . . under their thumbs, **1809** in *Adams-Cunningham Letters* 163: He and his Athenæum are too much under their thumbs. Barbour 181(3); *Oxford* 820; TW 371(1).

T85 To bite one's **Thumb**

1819 Drake *Works* 338: And "bite my thumb" at Mr. Bell, 364: And biting their thumb at the farmers. **1830** Ames *Mariner's* 103: Any or all nations who shall dare to "bite their thumb" at the said sailors. *Oxford* 62; TW 371(3).

T86 To have a **Thump** over the head, *etc.*

1737 Franklin *Drinkers* 174: He's had a Thump over the Head with Sampson's Jawbone.

T87 As cold as **Thunder**

1830 Ames *Mariner's* 99: The climate is as "cold as thunder."

T88 As loud as **Thunder**

1814 Palmer *Diary* 40: And run aft singing out murder, murder, as loud as thunder. Svartengren 391; Whiting T265.

T89 As strong as **Thunder**

1794 Ames *Letters* 1.143: Government is as strong as thunder.

T90 **Thunder** first, then rain

1775 Ames *Almanacs* 458: Rain, thunder, no! thunder first, then rain! so said Socrates when he receiv'd his wife's warm fragrant shower from a Window. *Oxford* 820; Whiting T267.

T91 To come like a **Thunderbolt**

1765 Watts *Letter Book* 393: C.'s Appeal . . . came like a Thunderbolt upon us. Whiting T269.

T92 To come like a **Thunderclap**

1762 Watts *Letter Book* 102: Which came upon us like a Thunder Clap (without any warning) in the Papers. 1778 *Washington *Writings* 13.465: It is devoutly to be wished that a sad reverse of this may not fall upon them like a thunder clap that is little expected. 1829 MBarney in Jackson *Correspondence* 4.47: *Like a clap of thunder* in a clear sky your dismissal came. *Oxford* 73; TW 371(16).

T93 To come like a **Thunder-gust**

1809 Weems *Marion* 137: I saw . . . M'Donald coming up on my right, like a thunder gust. TW 372.

T94 As full as a **Tick**

1803 *Yankee Phrases* 87: Though of love I am full as a tick. Barbour 181(2); Svartengren 185, 295; TW 372(1).

T95 Like a **Tick** in a tar-barrel

1799 JCCabell in *VHM* 29(1921) 263: You observed in your letter that you should feel like a "Tick in a tar barrel" were you to enter on the subject of Politicks. See **B107**.

T96 To stick like a **Tick**

1786 WGordon in *Bowdoin Papers* 2.113: The blood suckers who . . . stick to it like ticks. 1787 *American Museum* 1.57: She stuck like a tick to her resolve. TW 372(2).

T97 One's **Ticket** is not out

1796 JJackson in Milledge *Correspondence* 43: So my Ticket is not yet out.

T98 To pass without a **Ticket**

1702 Taylor *Christographia* 275.82-3: This will pass without a Ticket, having in its own power warrant Sufficient to Satisfie all Watches.

T99 Between the **Tide** and the eddy

1792 JWentworth in *Winslow Papers* 394: I have stolen a minute, between the tide and the eddy, to make my thanks to you.

T100 The highest **Tides** produce lowest ebbs

1770 Adams *Legal Papers* 3.167: The highest tides always producing the lowest ebbs.

T101 It is a long **Tide** that never turns

1811 Weems *Gambling* 47: With the old proverb in his mouth, "it is a long tide that never turns." Cf. Lean 4.140; *Oxford* 821. See **L29, W190**.

T102 There is a **Tide** in all things

1784 Smith *Diary* 1.153: There was a Tide in Affairs, and it would soon be lost. 1799 *Washington *Writings* 37.190: There is "a tide, it is said, in all things." 1827 SFAustin in *Austin Papers* 2.1565: *There is a happy moment in the tide of all events,* and men of talent know when that moment arrives and how to use it. *Oxford* 821; Tilley T283.

T103 Those who come up with a flowing **Tide,** etc.

1798 *Washington *Writings* 36.320: For those who come up with a flowing tide, will descend with the Ebb. Cf. *Oxford* 217; Tilley T284.

T104 The **Tide** may turn

1766 JParker in Franklin *Papers* 13.528: But the Tide may turn one Time or other, 535. 1780 JA in *Adams FC* 3.301: The Tide may turn. 1784 Jay *Correspondence* 3.117: There is a tide in human affairs which, like other tides, turns only to run in an opposite direction. TW 373(1).

T105 The **Tide** stays for no man

a1656 Bradford *History* 1.125: The tide (which stays for no man). 1807 Jefferson *Family Letters* 296: The tide of business, like that of the ocean, will wait for nobody. *Oxford* 821; Tilley T323. See **T125, 143**.

T106 To swim against the **Tide**

1767 JParker in Franklin *Papers* 14.239: I shall continue to swim as it were against [the] Tide. See **S491**.

T107 To swim with the **Tide**

1676 Williams *Writings* 5.241: Carnal and

lukewarm *Laodiceans,* who can swim with the tyde, sail with every wind. **1788** *Columbian Magazine* 2.230: Tom . . . Determines with the tide to swim. Cf. *Oxford* 892; Tilley W429; Whiting W335. See **S492.**

T108 To turn (go) with the **Tide**

1699 WWinthrop in *Winthrop Papers(B)* 6.49: It is som of these men, tho thay have semed to turn with the tide a little since. **1773** TDavis in *Innes (James) and his Brothers* 34: A man is forc'd to go with the Tide. **1774** CCarroll in *MHM* 16(1921) 40: He kept on the reserve, till he saw w^h way the tide would turn; he now swims with the stream. *Oxford* 848; Tilley W439.

T109 To work double **Tides**

1778 TMcKean in Rodney *Letters* 265: I have worked double tides (as the Sailors say) all the last week, being every day in Court, and also in Congress. Colcord 68; NED Tide 14; *Oxford* 916.

T110 The **Tiger** crouches before he leaps upon his prey

1798 King *Life* 2.392: The Tiger crouches before he leaps upon his prey. **1799** RGHarper in Bayard *Papers* 91: He ought never to forget that "The tyger always crouches before he leaps on his prey." **1803** Austin *Constitutional* 124: Remember, "the tyger crouches before he leaps." **1809** Fessenden *Pills* iv: The tyger though baffled is not crippled, and crouches but to render his leap the more effectual.

T111 To fight like a **Tiger**

1773 McClure *Diary* 116: Fought lyke a tyger. **1817** Weems *Franklin* 133: [They] fought like tygers. **1819** Noah *Travels* 297. TW 373(7).

T112 As ancient (old) as **Time**

1754 Bailey *Journal* 18: An old broken mug, almost as ancient as time. **a1786** Ladd *Remains* 47: We have a custom here, as old as time. Barbour 182(6); Svartengren 149; Whiting *NC* 486(2).

T113 Beware of the third **Time**

1718 Sewall *Diary* 3.172: I told him had been there but thrice, and twice upon Busi-

nee. He said *Cave tertium.* **1787** Bentley *Diary* 1.82: Beware of the third time. **1794** Adams *Memoirs* 1.40: It is the second time I have been in jeopardy from a leaky vessel. It behooves me to beware of the third. Cf. *Oxford* 813; TW 374(6). See **T121.**

T114 It is a hurrying **Time**

1813 DDaggett in *Smith Papers* 7.49: It is now a *hurrying time,* as farmers say.

T115 No **Time** as proper as the present

1764 AA in *Adams FC* 1.37: There can be no time more proper than the present. **1774** Willard *Letters* 31: No time was so proper as the present. Barbour 182(9); *Oxford* 824; TW 373(3).

T116 There is a **Time** for all things (*varied*)

1623 EAltham in James *Three Visitors* 23: But everyone hath a time, although some sooner than others. **1739** PPelham in Copley *Letters* 3: Their is a time for all things. **1772** Boucher *Autobiography* 89: To everything there is a season; a time to labour and a time to rest. **1781** *New Jersey Gazette* in *Newspaper Extracts(II)* 5.174: is an indisputable truth. **1784** Van Schaack *Letters* 226: Solomon says. **1789** Wingate *Letters* 1. **1791** HKnox in *St. Clair Papers* 2.224. **1793** Washington *Writings* 33.148: It was one of the sayings of the wise man you know, that there is a season for all things, and nothing is more true. **1794** Jay *Correspondence* 4.37: For all things there is a season. **1797** Cobbett *Porcupine* 7.278. **1798** Washington *Writings* 36.187, 288: the saying of the wise man, **1799** 37.471. **1812** Melish *Travels* 270: A proof that there is a time for all things under the sun. **1819** Pintard *Letters* 1.229. **1827** BMcLaughlen in *Ruffin Papers* 1.401: Thinking of the old saying "Omnia tempus Halent." **1830** Pintard *Letters* 3.190. **1832** Jackson *Correspondence* 4.401: Solomon says, **1833** 5.74. *Oxford* 823; TW 374(7); Whiting T88. See **S91.**

T117 There is a **Time** to sow, *etc.*

1703 Talbot *Letters* 93: There is a time to sow and a time to reap. Whiting T314.

T118 There is a **Time** to speak, *etc.*

1691 IWisewall in *Hinckley Papers* 299:

There is a time to speak, and a time to keep silence. **1750** Sherman *Almanacs* 253: Learn when to speak and when to silent set. *Oxford* 824; Whiting T315.

T119 There is a **Time** to wink as well as to see

1747 Franklin *PR* 3.102: There's a time to wink as well as to see. *Oxford* 824; Tilley T317.

T120 There is always a first **Time**

1792 Hamilton *Papers* 12.504: But there is always "a first time."

T121 The third **Time** never fails

1832 Ames *Nautical* 105: The old proverb, "the third time never fails." Barbour 182(8); *Oxford* 813; Whiting T317.

T122 **Time** and chance happen to all men

1677 Hubbard *Indian* 1.91: But Time and Chance hapneth to all Men. **1805** Brackenridge *Modern* 631: "Time and chance happeneth to all men," and must to things. TW 374(9).

T123 **Time** and patience turn the mulberry leaf into satin

1705 Ingles *Reply* 20: Time and Patience w'ch turns yᵉ Mulberry Leaf into Satin. *Oxford* 822.

T124 **Time** and patience will set all things right

1765 Watts *Letter Book* 347: Time & patience will set all right. **1795** Asbury *Journal* 2.70: I trust that time and patience will bring all things about. *Oxford* 613; Tilley P114. See **P33.**

T125 **Time** and tide tarry (wait) for no man

1632 EHowes in *Winthrop Papers(A)* 3.74: Tyme and tide tarrieth for noe man. **1796** Barton *Disappointment* 50: You know the old saying, "Time and tide waits for no one." **1824** *Tales* 2.34: I'm in a hurry. Time and tide—you understand me. a**1826** Woodworth *Melodies* 235: *"Time never stops!"* he hoarsely cried, "For no one tarries time nor tide." **1830** JRandolph in Jackson *Correspondence* 4.175: We have lost *time* and *tide* which wait for no man. Bar-

bour 182(11); *Oxford* 822; TW 373-4(5); Whiting T318. See **T105, 143.**

T126 **Time** assuages all evils

1811 Jefferson *Writings* 13.57: I hope that time, the assuager of all evils, will heal these also. Barbour 183(14); Whiting *NC* 487(9). Cf. Tilley T322.

T127 **Time** brings all things to an end

1763 Ames *Almanacs* 339: Time brings all things to an end. Cf. *Oxford* 823; Tilley T326.

T128 **Time** brings things to light (*varied*)

1612 Strachey *Historie* 118: Tyme the true Reveylor of great thinges. **1637** Morton *New English Canaan* 266: Time, that bringes all thinges to light Doth hide this thinge out of sight. **1740** *Georgia Records* 22².459: Time, wᶜʰ: usually brings things to light. **1765** TWharton in Franklin *Papers* 12.114: As Time brings most things to light. **1787** Tilghman *Letters* 148: It [pregnancy] is one of those secrets that time will certainly bring to light. **1791** *Belknap Papers* 2.254: But time will bring forth all things. c**1810** Randolph *Virginia* 206: A truth which time never fails to bring to light. **1830** Jackson *Correspondence* 4.139: Time will unravel all things. Barbour 182(12); *Oxford* 823; Tilley T324, 333. See **M305, T141.**

T129 **Time** enough always proves little enough

1747 Franklin *PR* 3.106: *Time enough* always proves *little enough,* **1758** *WW* 341. Barbour 182(5). Cf. *Oxford* 823.

T130 **Time** flies (*varied*)

1710 JPaine in *Mayflower Descendant* 9(1907) 51: How doth time pass it flies alas For it hath eagles wings. **1739** Parkman *Diary* 72.87: How wondrous Swift my Time flys. **1784** Van Schaack *Letters* 226: *Tempus irrevocabile fugit.* **1785** Smith *Diary* 1.265: I shall bid him farewell since Time flies. **1788** *Columbian Magazine* 2.167: Time swiftly flies with anxious wings. **1789** May *Journal* 149: Yet time rolls on with rapid wings. **1792** Asbury *Journal* 1.717: Swift-winged time, O how it flies. **1792**

SJay in Jay *Correspondence* 3.433: Time has wings and altho' they will appear to me to be clogged, yet they will finally waft you back to us. **1811** *Adams-Waterhouse Correspondence* 54: How time flies. **1811** Alden *Epitaphs* 1.84: Time flies, eternity hastens. **1819** Beecher *Autobiography* 1.390: Time flies; sin hardens; procrastination deceives. **1819** Weems *Letters* 3.243: However tempus fugit and things & ills will have an end. **1820** *Port Folio* 4NS 9.516: Irreparabile time fuget. **1821** Weems *Letters* 3.320: Tempus fugit and I long to be doing. **1826** Longfellow *Letters* 1.205: But how time flies. **1829** Smith *Letters* 260: Time literally flies. Barbour 183(13); *Oxford* 823; Whiting T325.

T131 Time (hangs) heavy on his hands
1777 Carter *Diary* 2.1109: How the time goes must be agreeable to an old man, though it is often heavy on his hands. NED Hang 15b.

T132 Time is a salve for every sorrow
1786 MCarr in Jefferson *Papers* 15.626: Time (that Salve for every Sorrow). Cf. Barbour 183(4); *Oxford* 698; Tilley S84, T322, 325.

T133 Time is money
1736 Franklin *PR* 2.138: For Time he knew was better far than Gold, **1748** *Papers* 3.306: Remember that Time is Money. **1796** Dennie *Lay Preacher* 54: He threw Dr. Franklin's works into the fire for saying that "time was money." **1797** *Washington Writings* 36.112: The man who does not estimate *time* as *money* will forever miscalculate. **1810** *Port Folio* 2NS 3.254: The adage of Poor Richard. **1818** Weems *Letters* 3.220: Time is the stuff money is made of. **1828** *Yankee* 19. **1831** HStith in *Ruffin Papers* 2.49: With me, time is money, — is precious, and should not pass by unimproved. Barbour 183(15); *Oxford* 823-4; TW 374(12); Tilley T329.

T134 Time is precious (precious time) [The following is a selection from 100 occurrences of the saying]
1629 PFones in *Winthrop Papers*(A) 2.154:

Time is very precious with me. **1634** Wood *New-England* 100: Those skilfull hunters whose time is not so precious. **1639** Winthrop *Journal* 1.321: Time was very precious. **1650** Bradstreet *Works* 110: But time's too short and precious so to spend. **1676** *Wyllys Papers* 236: Spending much p^r cious time In vain Company Keeping. **1681** Mather *Diary* 1.24: I lost abundance of precious Time. **1684** EWSaltonstall in *Saltonstall Papers* 1.176: Use your precious time or any way mispend it. Consider what a precious talent time is and what a strict account you must another day give for it. **1702** Mather *Magnalia* 1.32: I have lost abundance of precious time, 499: Mispence of precious time, in tipling and talking with vain persons. **1718** Chalkley *Letter* 471: *To get from them their precious Time (which cannot be bought with Money)*, 472: *How many are spending their precious Time in Taverns*, **1734** *Journal* 272: Spending so much precious Time (which cannot be recalled). **1748** *Washington Writings* 1.7: Our time being too Precious to Loose. c**1763** Johnson *Writings* 2.559: The wasting and consumption of that precious talent, time. **1769** Brooke *Emily* 308: The time is too precious to say more. **1775** Adams *D and A* 2.172: Much precious Time is indiscreetly expended. **1775** Ames *Almanacs* 457: Nothing is more precious than time, and nothing more prodigally wasted. **1776** Washington *Writings* 5.436: The time is too precious. **1780** AA in *Adams FC* 3.293: Every moment of your time is precious, if trifled away never to be recalled. **1780** Washington *Writings* 18.371, 20.455. **1781** JEliot in *Belknap Papers* 3.213: But, alas! time to me is as precious and rare as hard money. **1785** Jefferson *Papers* 8.405: Time now begins to be precious to you, 410, **1788** 14.293. **1791** Ames *Letters* 1.95: Our time is precious, because it is short. **1794** Pemberton *Life* 294: Spending precious time at cards. **1796** Asbury *Journal* 2.76: Precious time — how it flies! **1801** Adams *Works* 9.582: Your time is too precious to be wasted. **1807** Jefferson *Writings* 11.170: Time, the most precious of all things to us. **1811** Colby *Life* 1.105: [They] were spending their precious time in ball-rooms. **1812** Melish *Travels* 399: The waste of precious time, which Dr. Franklin very appropriately terms "the stuff that life is made of." **1816** Adams *Memoirs* 3.323: Late hours, which consume so much precious time, **1821** 5.335: I had wasted precious time. **1854** Paulding *Letters(II)* 550: Shaving every morning takes up time, and ours is precious. *Oxford* 823-4; Whiting T322.

T135 Time is the mother of truth
1780 Adams *Works* 7.315: Time you know is the mother of truth. *Oxford* 824; Tilley T329a, 580.

T136 Time lost cannot be recovered (*varied*)
1738 *Georgia Records* 22¹.228: Time lost was not to be recover'd. **1748** Franklin *PR* 3.248: Lost Time is never found again, **1758** *WW* 341. **1780** Deane *Papers* 4.203: Time past is irrevocable; the present only is ours. **1783** *Washington *Writings* 26.92: Reflect that you can always waste time, but never recover it. **1804** *Austin Papers* 1.94: Time lost can never be recalled. **1806** Randolph(J) *Letters* 21: But time is, at once, the most valuable and most perishable of all our possessions; when lost it can never be retrieved. Barbour 182(5); *Oxford* 824; Whiting T307.

T137 Time proves all things
1799 Eaton *Life* 128: Time proves all things. **1831** Longfellow *Letters* 1.357: Time will prove all things. Cf. Tilley T333.

T138 Time rules all things
1788 Hopkinson *Miscellaneous Essays* 2.375: *Time rules all things.*

T139 Time will correct error
1805 Jefferson *Writings* 11.67: But time and truth will at length correct error. Cf. *Oxford* 825; Tilley T324; Whiting T326.

T140 Time will cure all things
1830 JMcLemore in Jackson *Correspondence* 4.197: Time will cure all things. Barbour 183(14); *Oxford* 823; Tilley T325; Whiting T300, 306.

T141 Time will discover truth (*varied*)
1739 Stephens *Journal(I)* 1.467: The Truth of which might in Time be discovered, **1742** (II) 1.81: Time will discover truth tho late, **1743** 189: But we must leave it to time to discover the truth. **1750** EWilliams in *Law Papers* 3.394: How that may be, Time will Discover. **1761** *Johnson Papers* 3.320: Time must determine the truth of it. **1769** SCooper in Franklin *Papers* 16.183: Time will discover. **1777** Shaw *Journals* 32: Whether or not such an event will take place, I leave to that tell-tale, Time. **1784** POliver in Hutchinson *Diary* 2.398: How it will end time will tell, 402. **1784** Smith *Diary* 1.156. **1795** "Z" in Hamilton *Papers* 19.114. **1799** Adams *Works* 9.11: Time will tell the truth. **1812** King *Life* 5.278: Time . . . reveals truth. **1825** Jefferson *Writings* 16.95-6: But time will, in the end, produce the truth. Tilley T324. Cf. Whiting T326. See **T128**.

T142 Time will (must, can) show
1767 Johnson *Writings* 1.400: Time must show. **1771** Chester *Papers* 50: Time only will show. **1771** *Commerce of Rhode Island* 1.369: What the end will be time that brings all things to pass will show. **1784** Clay *Letters* 207: Time only can shew. **1784** Smith *Diary* 1.161. **1820** Simpson *Journal* 87. TW 375(15).

T143 Time will stay for no man
1789 LParadise in Jefferson *Papers* 14.455. Time is a thing, that will stay for no man. Barbour 183(21); Tilley T334; Whiting T318. See **T105, 125**.

T144 Time will try all things
1632 *Winthrop Papers(A)* 3.103: Time will try all things. *Oxford* 825; Tilley T336; Whiting T90, 326.

T145 To be wise before one's **Time**
1795 Freneau *Poems* 3.116: The lad that's wise before his time. NED Time 15b.

T146 To murder **Time**
1756 Washington *Writings* 1.310: If . . . your Honor . . . will . . . murder a little time in writing to me. NED Kill 5, Murder 5.

T147 To take **Time** (occasion) by the fore-lock (*varied*)

1623 FWinthrop in *Winthrop Papers*(*A*) 1.285: As the poet saith Fronte capillata, post est occasio calva. **1654** Johnson *Wonder-Working* 26-7: Called by occasion, whose bauld back-part none can lay hold one. **1686** Dunton *Letters* 155: And therefore I thought it was best taking Time by the Fore-lock. **1690** IWisewall in *Hinckley Papers* 276: Neglect no time: *Post est occasio calva*, 299. **1706** F-JWinthrop in *Winthrop Papers*(*B*) 5.343: Time is pictured (& truly soe) with a little lock before & bald behinde, & if one takes not hold of that, tis gon. **1763** Laurens *Papers* 3.247: I have taken time by the forelock. **1765** Watts *Letter Book* 349. **a1770** Johnson *Writings* 1.31. **1775** Franklin *Writings* 6.405: The Ancients painted *Opportunity* as an old Man with Wings to his Feet & Shoulders, a great Lock of Hair on the forepart of his Head, but bald behind; whence comes our old Saying, *Take Time by the Forelock;* as much as to say, when it is past, there is no means of pulling it back again; as there is no Lock behind to take hold of for that purpose. **1776** HLaurens in Lee *Papers* 2.227. **1777** Gordon *Letters* 352: The opportunity seems to be lost, and *post est occasio calva.* **1777** Lee(W) *Letters* 1.284: opportunity. **1779** AYates in *Clinton Papers* 4.479. **1780** *Royal Gazette* in *Newspaper Extracts*(*II*) 5.86. **1781** Oliver *Origin* 20. **1782** Baldwin *Life and Letters* 151. **1785** JAtkinson *Match for a Widow* (London, 1788) 52. **1786** RO'Bryen in Jefferson *Papers* 9.619: Opportunity once lost is not easily recovered. **1790** Burd *Letters* 158. **1792** *Echo* 35: But best it is, as ancient proverbs say, Never to let occasion run away. **1793** Wayne *Correspondence* 263. **1798** Cleveland *Letters* 25. **1801** TGFessenden in *Farmers' Museum* 36: Old Time . . . whose foretop one might hide a cat in, But bald behind as school boys latin. **1803** Davis *Travels* 122. **1811** Adams *Writings* 4.74: Time must be taken by the forelock. **1814** Jackson *Correspondence* 2.34: You will immediately perceive the necessity of takeing time by the forelock. **c1816** Durang *Memoir* 57. **1816** Pintard *Letters* 1.36, **1820** 282:

This is litterally as the old woman said, taking time by the *Firelock*. **1821** JDodge in *Ruffin Papers* 1.253: seizing. **a1826** Woodworth *Melodies* 235: With head quite bald, except before, Where one long silver lock he wore. **1845** Jackson *Correspondence* 6.387. *Oxford* 822-3; TW 375(23).

T148 What is suitable at one **Time** will not do at another

1800 Dow *Journal* 90: What will be suitable at one time will not always do at another. Cf. *Oxford* 600-1.

T149 As regular as a **Timepiece**

1786 Smith *Diary* 2.200: And every Body as regular and punctual as a Timepiece. Cf. TW 72(4). See **C201**.

T150 To quench one's **Thirst** at any dirty puddle

1803 Davis *Travels* 381: I had before quenched my thirst at any dirty puddle [of women]. *Oxford* 283: Foul water; Tilley W92. See **D239, P238**.

T151 As dry as **Tinder**

1766 Carter *Diary* 1.313: But as to the wheat laid in the treading floor . . . now as on opening as drye as tinder. **1813** Harmon *Sixteen Years* 164: Roof of the House which is . . . as dry as tinder. Svartengren 301; Whiting T332.

T152 A **Tinker** makes two (ten) flaws in mending one

1720 Walter *Choice Dialogue* 7-8: You have managed the Cause like a *Tinker*, You have made two Flaws in your Cause, in Mending one. **1744** Hamilton *Itinerarium* 188: They made but bungling work of it, spoiling ten where they made one. *Oxford* 826; Tilley T347, 351.

T153 To swear like (a) **Tinker**

a1731 Cook *Bacon* 323: And swore like Tinker in his Rage. NED Tinker 1; Svartengren 109. Cf. TW 375.

T154 **Tit** for tat

1764 Franklin *Papers* 11.380: Or Tit *for* Tat, *in your own Way*, **1765** 12.374. **1792** Belknap *Foresters* 65: "Tit for tat, tit for tat,

He stole my chick and I broke his back."
1796 Barton *Disappointment* 31. **1808** Jefferson *Writings* 12.211: I send you tit for tat. **1809** Quincy *JQuincy* 181: What the ladies term tit for tat. **1819** Peirce *Rebelliad* 7. **a1826** Woodworth *Melodies* 160. **1844** Clark *Letters* 121: I like the *tit-for-tat* of it. *Oxford* 826; Whiting T339.

T155 Tithe and be rich
1710 Mather *Bonifacius* 141: The Jewish Proverb, *Decima, ut Dives fias;* or, *Tythe and be Rich! Oxford* 826; Tilley T357.

T156 To a Tittle
1691 RBuckley in *Baxter Manuscripts* 5.263: I would as near as may be observe my instructions to a tittle. **1740** Belcher *Papers* 2.317: All I have said to him . . . is true to a tittle. **1774** *Johnson Papers* 8.1179: He will do his Duty to a tittle, & not abate them an Inch. **1787** Jefferson *Papers* 11.46: But I have never heard a tittle of it. **1806** *Weekly* 1.126: Precisely to a tittle suits. **a1824** Marshall *Kentucky* 2.143: Whitley complied to a tittle. NED Tittle 2, a, b.

T157 Titty Tiffin, *etc.*
1813 Dunlap *Diary* 2.464: "Titty Tiffin, Keep it Stiff in; Fire drake Puckey, Make it luckey; Liard, Robin, You must bobin."

T158 As full as a Toad of poison
1686 Mather *Magnalia* 2.410: A soul as full of enmity against God as a toad is full of poison. Tilley T360.

T159 To eat a Toad and half for breakfast
1737 Franklin *Drinkers* 2.175: He's Eat a Toad and half for Breakfast.

T160 A Toad under a harrow
1733 Belcher *Papers* 1.251: The poor borderers on the lines . . . live like toads under a harrow. **1764** JWatts in *Aspinwall Papers* 2.537: A poor devil marrying above himself with independency is a toad under a harrow. **1782** Paine *American Crisis* 1.227: [They] would have the life of a toad under a harrow. **1821** Knight *Poems* 2.30: Or wheeze like toad beneath a harrow. *Oxford* 826; Whiting T344. See **F311, H86.**

T161 As hot as Toast
c1825 Tyler *Prose* 170: Hot as toast. *Oxford* 827; Svartengren 310; Whiting T346. Cf. Barbour 183.

T162 To cut as small as Tobacco
1702 Mather *Magnalia* 2.617: Damn ye, we'll cut you as small as tobacco before to morrow morning.

T163 Tobacco hick, if you be well, *etc.*
a1700 Saffin *His Book* 171: Tobacco hick if you be well will make you Sick Tobacco hick will make you well if you be Sick. *Oxford* 827; Tilley T365.

T164 Like the Tod's whelps, ae year auld and twa year war'
1794 Brackenridge *Gazette* 244: Ae year auld, and twa year war', Like the tod's whelps.

T165 Here Today, gone tomorrow
1650 Bradstreet *Works* 149: Here today and gone tomorrow. **1657** Wigglesworth *Diary* 105: Creature refreshments, which are [?here] to day, and gone to morrow. **1777** *Washington Writings* 7.198: Here to-day, and gone tomorrow. **1803** *Port Folio* 3.122: Those *here-to-day and gone-to-morrow* citizens of the world. **1827** *Austin Papers* 2.1671: It is purchased today and lost tomorrow. **1831** Wirt *Letters* 2.363: Are we not here to-day,—and gone—to-morrow? Barbour 184(3); *Oxford* 370; Whiting T350.

T166 One Today is worth two tomorrows
1757 Franklin *PR* 8.80: One To-day is worth two To-morrows, **1758** *WW* 342. Barbour 184(5); *Oxford* 827; Tilley T370.

T167 Today alive, tomorrow dead
1748 Ames *Almanacs* 210: To day *Man's* dress'd in *Gold* and *Silver* bright: Wrapt in a Shrowd before *to morrow* Night. **1761** CCarroll in *MHM* 11(1916) 69: Alive today & dead to-morrow. **1817** Tyler *Verse* 179: And such is man—his prime today, Tomorrow sees him swept away. *Oxford* 827; Whiting T351.

T168 **Today** rich, tomorrow a beggar

1777 Hopkinson *Miscellaneous Essays* 1.99: To-day, he posseses the wealth of a nabob; tomorrow, he refuses a six-pence to a beggar, lest he should himself be reduced to the want of that six-pence. **1812** *Austin Papers* 1.211: Exalted to-day rich in the things of this life, to-morrow a beggar. Whiting T354.

T169 **Today** up, tomorrow down

1664 JUnderhill in *Winthrop Papers(B)* 2.188: He soght not them but thaye him, and crid him up, hosana to daye, and down with him tomorro. **1774** Fithian *Journal and Letters* 277: We poor earthly Creatures are as to fortune & Feeling, exactly like the Nails in a turning Wheel, to Day up. to morrow Down. Cf. Whiting T353. See **U5.**

T170 To make a **Toil** of pleasure

1820 GCutler in Vanderpoel *Chronicles* 194: I suppose she thought it making a "toil of pleasure as the old man said when he buried his wife." *Oxford* 827-8; Tilley T374.

T171 **Tom Coxe's** traverse

1803 Davis *Travels* 437: "Can you play at *Tom Coxe's* traverse?" "That he can . . . He is foreverlasting up one hatchway, and down the other." TW 377.

T172 **Tom**, Dick and Harry (*varied*)

1690 Palmer *Account* in *Andros Tracts* 1.44: Neither ought the whole Government to be Subverted, because *Tom* or *Harry* are ill men. **1706** F-JWinthrop in *Winthrop Papers(B)* 5.358: Dick, Tom & Robin, who are lawyers. **1755** Johnson *Writings* 4.39: A great bundle of petitions from Tom, Dick and Harry. **1785** Washington *Writings* 28.65: Enquiries after Dick, Tom, and Harry. a**1788** Jones *History* 1.338: The signatures of Tom, Dick, and Harry, produced as vouchers. **1794** Livingston *Democracy* 10. **1800** *Echo* 271. **1800** Hamilton *Law Practice* 2.132. **1801** Paulding *Letters(II)* 7: A budget of news . . . full of information about Jack, and Tom and Harry. **1804** Irving *Journals* 1.56. **1805** Brackenridge *Modern* 471, 571: So let us all be liberal, Let one another live, Dick, Harry, Tom and Gabriel, Which ever way they

drive, 577. **1806** Dunlap *Diary* 2.407: You will certainly have your choice of "Tom and Dick." **1809** Weems *Marion* 163: Tom twigg'd it—and Dick twigg'd it—and Harry twigg'd it—and so they all twigg'd it. **1812** Hitchcock *Social* 44: By Tom, Dick, Harry, Will, and Moses. **1812** *Port Folio* 2NS 7.350. **1815** Brackenridge *Modern* 644, 662. **1815** Otis *Letters* 2. opp. 168. **1816** Paulding *Letters(I)* 2.42: Messrs. Tom, Dick, and Harry, together with their illustrious contemporaries, Tag, Rag, and Bobtail, 153. **1817** Weems *Letters* 3.198. **1818** Adams *Works* 10.351: Tom, Dick, and Harry were not to censure them and their council. **1819** Weems *Letters* 3.249. a**1826** Woodworth *Melodies* 104. **1827** Watterston *Wanderer* 76. *Oxford* 828; ATaylor in *Names* 6(1958) 51-4; TW 377.

T173 To bury the **Tomahawk**

1705 Beverley *History* 194: They use formal Embassies for treating . . . or else some other memorable Action, such as burying a *Tomahawk* . . . in token that all Enmity is bury'd with the *Tomahawk*. **1777** Carter *Diary* 2.1130: Even on my birthday taking occasion to stay away, though invited to bury his dull tomahawk. **1792** Putnam *Memoirs* 346. **1804** Ordway *Journal* 122: And bury the tomahawk and knife in the ground. **1807** *Port Folio* NS 4.349: In the phrase of the aborigines, the tomahawk is buried, and we wish not to dig it up. **1810** Schultz *Travels* 2.94. **1811** *Kennon Letters* 33.68: We will bury the Tomohawk and smoke the Calumet of peace together. **1812** Claiborne *Letter Books* 6.155: A wish, that the Tomahawk . . . may long remain buried. **1812** JWatson in Knopf *War of 1812* 6(1) 231. DA tomahawk 2b; TW 377. See **H102.**

T174 As red as a **Tomato**

1821 Knight *Poems* 2.162: Her lips, O red as a double-tomato. Taylor *Comparisons* 68.

T175 As silent as the **Tomb**

1782 AA in *Adams FC* 4.344: It is as silent as a Tomb. **1805** Silliman *Travels* 1.93: Silent as the tombs. **1827** Watterston *Wanderer* 145: All was as still and silent as the tomb. Barbour 184; Svartengren 386. See **G160.**

T176 Never put off to **Tomorrow** what may be done today (*varied*)

1690 F-JWinthrop in *Winthrop Papers(B)* 5.508: A lazy & sloathfull sence of our danger, & putting off till the morrow, is the ready way to our confusion, **1701** 6.86: You are gratly mistaken about its being put off till to-morrow. **1742** Franklin *PR* 2.333: Have you somewhat to do to-morrow; do it to-day. **1793** *Washington *Writings* 33.31: [It] serves to prove the verity of the old proverb "that nothing should be put off until the morrow that can be done today," 148: I will mention a proverb to you which you will find worthy of attention all the days of your life; under any circumstances, or in any situation you may happen to be placed; and that is, to put nothing off 'till the Morrow, that you can do to day, **1796** 35.138: And not to put things off until the Morrow which can be done, and require to be done, to day. **1797** Jefferson *Writings* 9.388: Procrastination, forever suggesting to our indolence that we need not do to-day what may be done to-morrow, **1811** 13.44: The wisdom of the maxim, never to put off to to-morrow what can be done to-day, **1812** 144-5: Instead of acting on the good old maxim of not putting off to to-morrow what we can do to-day, we are too apt to reverse it, and not to do to-day what we can put off to to-morrow. **1817** *Journey to the West* in *Essex Institute Historical Collections* 8(1866) 242: That good maxim, "Not to leave for tomorrow what can be done to-day." **1823** Jefferson *Writings* 15.419: The common lazy principle of never doing today what we can put off to-morrow, **1825** 16.111. **1826** Audubon *1826 Journal* 57: The maxim that will never cease to be good is present, and I will not put off until tomorrow what can yet be performed to-day. **a1830** Burr *Memoirs* 2.14-5: I remember a remark he [Burr] made . . . which appeared to be original and wise. There is a saying, "Never put off till to-morrow what you can do to-day." "This is a maxim," said he, "for sluggards. A better reading of the maxim is—*Never do today what you can as well do to-morrow;* be-

cause something may occur to make you regret your premature action." Barbour 184(1); *Oxford* 656; Whiting T348.

T177 **Tomorrow** never comes

1756 Franklin *PR* 6.326: *To-morrow*, every Fault is to be amended; but that *To-morrow* never comes. **1772** *Norton Papers* 229: To-morrow is a day that may never come. Barbour 184(5); *Oxford* 829; Whiting T365.

T178 A close **Tongue** makes a wise head

1796 Barton *Disappointment* 16: A close tongue makes a wise head. *Oxford* 774; TW 378(2); Whiting T380. See **S210.**

T179 He that lets his **Tongue** run before his wit, *etc.*

1768 Ames *Almanacs* 395: He that lets his tongue run before his wit cuts other mens meat and his own Fingers. *Oxford* 830; Tilley T412.

T180 His **Tongue** is hung by the middle and runs at both ends

1830 Ames *Mariner's* 223; The truth of the expression, "his tongue is hung by the middle and runs at both ends." Barbour 184(1); TW 378(1).

T181 His **Tongue** is well hung

1815 JHewson in *Lincoln Papers* 214: As his tongue was pretty well hung & had been well supplied from the Blarney Stone. *Oxford* 829.

T182 Let not your **Tongue** cut your throat

1767 Ames *Almanacs* 387: Let not your tongue cut your throat. **1832** JRandolph in *Jackson Correspondence* 4.420: He has cut his throat with his own Tongue. Cf. *Oxford* 163; Whiting T376.

T183 One's **Tongue** runs like a mill (*varied*)

1749 Hempstead *Diary* 523: Being wet within side as well as without their Tongues Run like mill clocks. **1777** Fitch *New-York Diary* 97: At about 7 I came home where I found Mr: Castlelaw's Mill (his Tongue) under briskway. **1798** Murdock *Politicians* 3: Dere two tongue go like mill clap. **1799** Ames *Letters* 1.268: My tongue would run like a mill. *Oxford* 830; TW 244(3); Tilley T388. Cf. Whiting M556, 557.

T184 A soft **Tongue** breaks the bone (*varied*)

a1700 Hubbard *New England* 175: As Solomon saith, the soft tongue breaketh the bone. **1740** Franklin *PR* 2.249: Man's tongue is soft, and bone doth lack; Yet a stroke therewith may break a man's back, **1744** 399: A soft Tongue may strike hard. *Oxford* 829; Whiting T384.

T185 To speak with two **Tongues**

1764 *Johnson Papers* 11.290: He . . . whom they all knew never to have spoke with two Tongues, as most of them did. **1772** Chester *Papers* 142: I scorn Duplicity and do not Speak with Two Tongues. **1775** ACameron in Gibbes 2.208: You was told that I spoke to the Indians with two tongues. Whiting T381.

T186 **Tongue** and heart

1755 *Johnson Papers* 2.325: They said to him your tongue speak well but your heart is false. **1758** Franklin *Papers* 8.36: He was determined his Tongue should never give his Heart the Lie. *Oxford* 364; Whiting T383. See **L170.**

T187 **Tongue** double brings trouble

1733 Franklin *PR* 1.315: Tongue double, brings trouble. Whiting T381.

T188 The **Tongue** offends and the ears get the cuffing

1757 Franklin *PR* 7.88: The Tongue offends, and the Ears get the Cuffing. Cf. *Oxford* 830; Tilley T408.

T189 The **Tongue** turns to the aching tooth

1746 Franklin *PR* 3.64: The Tongue is ever turning to the aching Tooth. **1816** Paulding *Letters(I)* 2.167: The tongue touches where the tooth aches, as the saying goes; the English of which is, that people are apt to talk of what annoys them most at the moment. *Oxford* 829; Whiting T386. See **T230.**

T190 Don't play with edged **Tools** (*varied*)

1765 Watts *Letter Book* 358: It's innocent Work to bait a Minister, but hands off of edg'd tools. **1770** Carter *Diary* 1.486: And if this letter was intended as a joke, I must

say an Irony is too edged a tool to play with. **1773** Trumbull *Satiric Poems* 93: So true the antient proverb sayeth, "Edge tools are dang'rous things to play with." **1779** Lee(W) *Letters* 2.668: It appears to me an edged Tool, that is more likely to do mischief to him that plays with it, than any body else. **1799** Freneau *Poems* 410: Never meddle with the clergy — they are edge tools. *Oxford* 120, 411; TW 378(1). See **J25.**

T191 From the **Teeth** outwards

1778 Drinker *Journal* 97: They appeared kind, but I fear it is from the teeth outwards. NED Tooth 8b; *Oxford* 806; Tilley T423. Cf. Whiting L373.

T192 He that has no **Teeth** cannot crack nuts

1795 Cobbett *Porcupine* 2.56: He that has no teeth, cannot crack nuts.

T193 If you can't bite, never show your **Teeth**

1752 *Johnson Papers* 9.94: Advise his Excellency not to show his teeth till he can bite hand [?*for* hard]. **1767** Ames *Almanacs* 388: If you can't bite, never show your teeth. *Oxford* 62; Tilley T425.

T194 In spite of one's **Teeth**

1666 Alsop *Maryland* 67: In spight of their teeth. c1680 Radisson *Voyages* 221: And must advance in spight of our teeth. **1692** Mather *Wonders* 197: Yet stay in spite of his teeth. **1723** *New-England Courant* 113(1.2): In spight of your Teeth. a1731 Cook *Bacon* 323: A Friend of Berkley's (spight of's Teeth). **1738** Stephens *Journal(I)* 1.104. **1744** Hamilton *Itinerarium* 135. **1759** Adams *D and A* 1.94: To do men good in spight of their Teeth. **1762** Johnson *Writings* 4.78. **1770** Carter *Diary* 1.354, 357. **1774** Seabury *Letters* 106. **1775** WHDrayton in Gibbes 2.142, 153, 172. **1777** Munford *Patriots* 489. **1785** EWinslow in *Winslow Papers* 291. **1787** Jefferson *Papers* 12.485: A wife who will make you happy in spite of your teeth. a1788 Jones *History* 1.240. **1788** JLangdon in King *Life* 1.328: Thereby make the people happy in spight of their teeth as the sayg. is. **1796** Cobbett *Porcupine* 3.422. **1797** Adams

Writings 2.197: In defiance of all the teeth of Livingston. **1798** Jefferson *Writings* 10.59. **1816** Paulding *Letters(I)* 2.106. **1816** *Port Folio* 4NS 1.25. **1824** Neal *American Writers* 96, **1825** 155. **1828** *Yankee* 5. **1830** Ames *Mariner's* 65. *Oxford* 766; Whiting T406. See **N93.**

T195 To cast (*etc.*) in the **Teeth**

1647 GFenwick in *Winthrop Papers(A)* 5.142: For what ever yow doe that may have the least shaddow of severitie is hightened hear and cast in your brethrens teath by those who . . . wilbe as much against yow as them. **1747** GClinton in *Colden Letters* 3.404: But they Set about it & then hit me in yᵉ Teeth of Sarahtoga & severall other things. **1782** ERandolph in Madison *Papers* 5.282: To throw the opinion of Virginia herself into her own teeth. **1816** Fidfaddy *Adventures* 36: The cursed Yankees . . . throw it in our teeth. *Oxford* 106; Whiting T408.

T196 To clear one's **Teeth**

1771 Lee *Letters* 1.53: As the Adventurer John Ballandine used to say I fear they will not "clear their teeth."

T197 To have a sweet **Tooth**

1746 Thomas Lewis, *The Fairfax Line*, ed. J. W. Wayland (New Market, Va., 1925) 33: Arthur Dubo Bumped for Indulging a Sweet tooth. **1807** Mackay *Letters* 57: We had . . . several others of the sweet Tooth Gentry to help us destroy them. **c1825** Tyler *Prose* 105: I have a sweet tooth. Barbour 185; *Oxford* 793-4; Whiting T409.

T198 To have an aching **Tooth** at someone

1637 Morton *New English Canaan* 308: Captain Littleworth (that had an akeing tooth at mine Host of Ma-re-Mount,) devised how hee might put a trick upon him. *Oxford* 3; Tilley T421.

T199 To one's **Teeth**

1638 RWilliams in *Winthrop Papers(A)* 4.35: Indians will testifie such speeches to Miantunnomues teeth. Whiting T415.

T200 To show one's **Teeth**

1786 Jefferson *Papers* 10.225: There never

will be money in the treasury till the confederacy shews its teeth. NED Tooth 8f.

T201 **Tooth** and nail

1654 Johnson *Wonder-Working* 111: [They] labor tooth & naile to maintain it. **1705** Ingles *Reply* 154: He . . . opposed it Tooth & Nail. **1717** Wise *Vindication* 58: They fell to it Tooth and Nail to drive away the Fraternity. **1750** AHamilton in *MHM* 59(1964) 209: Like two schoolboys that get at it tooth and nail. **1776** Willard *Letters* 259. **1790** JBarrell in Webb *Correspondence* 3.161. **1793** *Echo* 72: Bald Father time, with mouldy tooth and nail, In vain your fame, so bulky, shall assail. **1796** Cobbett *Porcupine* 3.407. **1806** Adams *D and A* 4.95: He reported to Sir John that I told him I would set my face against him tooth and nail. These are very vulgar Expressions and were very unnecessary, if I said them, which I doubt. **1809** Irving *History* 2.143, 188. **1816** Paulding *Letters(I)* 2.45: He . . . fell foul of the language tooth and nail, **1816** (*II*) 46: Irving and he fell tooth and nail at old recollections. **1820** Irving *Sketch Book* 108. **1830** Ames *Mariner's* 174, **1832** *Nautical* 79: Philosophers went to work, tooth and nail, to prove that the animal was known to the ancients. **1847** Paulding *Letters(II)* 467: The Deacon . . . is determined to oppose the Bill for taxing Bachelors & Widowers tooth and nail. *Oxford* 832; Whiting T417.

T202 From **Top** to bottom

1782 Tilghman *Letters* 28: I will come up and titivate you from top to Bottom. NED Top *sb.*¹ 23. See **H116.**

T203 From **Top** to toe

1723 *New-England Courant* 108(1.2): If they are made like us from Top to Toe. **1788** Smith *American Poems* 224: His dress complete From top to toe be critically neat. **1797** Morris *Diary and Letters* 2.284: The Duchess, who is English from top to toe. **1806** Hitchcock *Works* 120. **1814** Littell *Festoons* 9: On every joint from top to toe. **1815** Humphreys *Yankey* 28: Dressed spick and span new, from top to toe. **1819** Noah *Trav-*

els 192. **1824** *Tales* 1.166. NED Top *sb.*[1] 25; *Oxford* 832; Whiting T421.

T204   To dance like a **Top**

1803 *Yankee Phrases* 87: Jemima . . . Like a top, nimbly danc'd o'er our plains. TW 379(1).

T205   To sleep like a **Top**

1785 Hunter *Quebec* 25: Made us sleep like tops. **1821** Pintard *Letters* 2.10: Sat up later than usual and slept like a top. **1849** Cooper *Letters* 6.25. *Oxford* 741; TW 379(2).

T206   To turn like a **Top**

1798 *Washington *Writings* 36.213-4: He can turn it round as easy as a top.

T207   To whirl like a **Top**

1800 Ames *Letters* 1.288: The Jacobins want the government to whirl like a top. TW 379(5).

T208   As hot as **Tophet**

1819 Peirce *Rebelliad* 9: Hot as tophet. Taylor *Comparisons* 50.

T209   To lower one's **Topsails**

1720 Carter *Letters* 47: [It] of necessity must make us lower our topsails, 55. **1776** Curwen *Journal and Letters* 91: It would be . . . one advantage . . . to make them "lower their topsails," **1777** 151: [They] have . . . lowered their topsails, and talk in a less positive strain. NED Topsail b. Cf. Whiting T427. See **S15**.

T210   As dead as ten **Top-sail-sheet-blocks**

1803 Davis *Travels* 443: I knocked him down . . . as dead as ten top-sail-sheet-blocks. Lean 2.820: block.

T211   **Touch** and go

1767 Bowen *Journals* 1.149: We [are] touch and go. **1796** Weems *Letters* 2.47: That by some of them was look[d] on as rather a touch and go sort of allowance. **1838** FBlair in Jackson *Correspondence* 5.543: It is touch and go with the present Bill, **1843** 6.236: Their watchword of "Tipp and Ty," which might be translated appropriately into "touch and go," "Slip and Ty," or "fast and

loose" to use the commonest expression. *Oxford* 833; TW 379.

T212   **Touch** and go is a good pilot

1782 *Belknap Papers* 1.116: I must take for my motto, *Touch and go is a good pilot.* **1803** Davis *Travels* 438: Touch and go a good pilot. *Oxford* 833.

T213   To wipe someone down with an oaken **Towel**

1762 JBoucher in *MHM* 7(1912) 152: I sh'd certainly *demand the satisfac'n* of wiping Him down with an oaken Towel. NED Towel 3; Partridge 904.

T214   Not to see the **Town** (city) for the houses

1810 Schultz *Travels* 1.119: This town brought to my recollection the story of "a country lad coming with his father to see the town, but could never get a glimpse of it for the vast number of houses." **1815** Humphreys *Yankey* 102: But coodn't see the city, for the houses. See **W303**.

T215   All **Trades** must live

1802 Irving *Jonathan* 38: All trades must live. *Oxford* 835.

T216   Free **Trade** and sailors' rights

1812 *Columbian Centinel* in Buckingham *Specimens* 2.93: This is what is called fighting for "Sailors Rights and Free Trade." **1813** Bentley *Diary* 4.191: It was called a crime that the seamen had upon their hats, Free trade & Seamens rights. **1813** Clay *Papers* 1.773: Fighting for *"seamen's rights and free trade."* **1814** Morris *Diary and Letters* 2.573: Free trade and sailors' rights. **1814** Palmer *Diary* 80, 106, 126, **1815** Andrews *Prisoners' Memoirs* 73, 136, 137. **1815** Palmer *Diary* 129. **1815** *Port Folio* 3NS 5.580. **1815** Porter *Journal* 1.160, 2.151. **1815** STaggart in Cutler *Life* 2.332. **1815** Valpey *Journal* 48. **1815** Waterhouse *Journal* 76: We believed all that was said about *"Free trade and sailors' rights"* was all stuff and nonsense, 121. **1816** Fidfaddy *Adventures* 68, 88. **1817** Scott *Blue Lights* 61: And though for trade and seamen's rights, He dare not risk himself in fight. **1818** Woodworth *Poems* 137. **1820** Wright *Views* 178.

1826 Royall *Sketches* 241. 1830 Ames *Mariner's* 187. NED Suppl. Free trade; TW 380(4).

T217 He that has a **Trade** has an estate (*varied*)

1742 Franklin *PR* 2.333: He that hath a Trade, hath an Estate, 1756 6.321: He that has a Trade has an Office of Profit and Honour, 1758 *WW* 342: He that hath a Calling hath an Office *etc.* 1770 Ames *Almanacs* 412: He that hath a Trade hath an Estate, and he that hath a Calling hath an Office of Profit & Honor. 1772 Franklin *Writings* 5.446-7: The Proverb says; He who has a Trade has an Office of Profit and Honour. *Oxford* 835; Tilley T460, 461.

T218 No **Trade** without returns

1732 Franklin *Papers* 1.246: I began the World with this Maxim, *That no Trade can subsist without Returns,* 1750 4.70: For you know there is no Trade without Returns, 1785 *Writings* 9.331: There is no trade, they say, without returns.

T219 **Trade** is a lottery

1703 *Penn-Logan Correspondence* 1.255: It may many ways miscarry, for trade is a lottery.

T220 **Trade** must regulate itself (*varied*)

1778 Paine *American Crisis* 1.153: Trade flourishes best when it is free, and it is weak policy to attempt to fetter it. 1780 *Beekman Papers* 3.1362: I Think the Trade Will Best Reguleate it Self. Trade Must be free and Will Not be Cramped up. 1780 *New Jersey Gazette* in *Newspaper Extracts(II)* 4.275: The stale saying, *Trade must regulate itself.* 1790 Morris *Diary and Letters* 1.313: They are of opinion that trade can best regulate itself.

T221 A large **Train** makes a light purse

1742 Franklin *PR* 2.336: A large train makes a light Purse.

T222 To be caught in one's own **Trap**

1714 Hunter *Androboros* 39: 'Tis but a Trap of their Own laid for you . . . in which They Themselves are Caught. 1791 Morris *Diary* 2.214: They might easily be caught

in their own Trap. *Oxford* 561: Net; TW 381(1). See **C377, N51, P182, S281.**

T223 **Travel** where you can, but die where you ought

1674 Josselyn *Account* 215: I . . . having in part made good the *French* proverb, Travail where you canst, but dye where thou oughtest, that is, in thine own Country. Tilley T474.

T224 A **Traveller** should have a hog's nose, *etc.*

1737 Franklin *PR* 2.168: A Traveller should have a hog's nose, deer's legs, and an ass's back. *Oxford* 836; Tilley W888.

T225 A **Traveller** should never laugh till he gets to the end

1816 Paulding *Letters(I)* 2.67: A traveller ought never to laugh till he gets to the end of his day's journey, as there is no knowing what may happen by the way. Cf. Whiting E158.

T226 **Travellers** may lie by authority (*varied*)

1630 (Francis Higginson) *New-Englands Plantation* (London, 1630) Bl^{r-v}: Though as the idle Proverbe is, *Travellers may lye by authoritie.* 1634 Wood *New-England* A3: That unjust aspersion commonly laid on travailers; of whom many say, They may lye by authority, because none can controule them; which Proverb had surely his originall from the sleepy beleefe of many a home-bred Dormouse, *etc.* 1686 Dunton *Letters* 21: Tho' you are a Traveller . . . yet you have no Authority to subscribe to the Lyes . . . even of your Elder Brother, 148: In which, what I write, you may assure your self is nothing but Truth, however the Proverb may abuse poor Travellers . . . and give 'em a Licence to Lye by Authority. 1705 Beverley *History* 8: I shall be reputed as arrant a Traveller as the rest, and my Credit, (like that of Women,) will be condemn'd for the Sins of my Company. 1737 Custis *Letters* 61: I have often heard our woods men chatter strange things . . . but I allways made the same allowance for them as for other travelrs. 1747 Stith *History* 126:

But these were little credited at first, and looked upon, as mere Traveller's Tales. **1750** PKalm in Franklin *Papers* 4.47: It is a very common thing with Soldiers, Sailors and travellers, to tell what wonderful thing they have done or seen, to make a louse an Elephant, to magnify every thing, and often try to make you believe what never had happen'd but in their head. **1760** Adams *D and A* 1.171: Thus he tells Wondrous Things, like other Travellers. **1784** *Belknap Papers* 2.171: This may sound like a traveller's story, but you may depend on the truth of it. **1789** Anburey *Travels* 1.79: I am afraid you will think I usurp the privilege of a traveller, when I tell you . . . . **1790** Maclay *Journal* 248: Much of what he [Adams] said bore the air of the traveler; in fact I did not believe him. **1790** Morris *Diary and Letters* 1.278: Do not suppose I am playing the traveller. **1791** Freneau *Poems* 3.61: All is not Truth ('tis said) that travellers tell. **1795** Morris *Diary and Letters* 2.81: Making use of the traveller's privilege. **1795** James Sullivan, *History of the District of Maine* (Boston, 1795) 104: The license of travellers who delighted in returning with marvellous stories. **1797** Tyler *Algerine* 2.135: It is the privilege of travellers to exaggerate. **1803** Bowne *Letters* 181: In the Jerseys, —don't laugh at travellers' stories, —but we really rode over the peaches in the road. **1804** Brackenridge *Modern* 354: For travellers have a licence to deviate. **1807** Janson *Stranger* 208: This like most travellers' exagerations, is not true. **1807** *Salmagundi* 330: Will is much addicted to hyperbole, by reason of his having been a great traveller. **1810** Burr *Correspondence* 315: No big traveller's lies. **1815** Brackenridge *Journal* 46: The reader will be disposed to give some credit for veracity, a point in which some travellers too often fail. **1819** Waln *Hermit* 136: Travellers . . . have, from time immemorial, had a privilege granted them by courtesy . . . the privilege of *lying*. **c1820** Bernard *Retrospections* 18: Traveller's tales. **1821** Wirt *Letters* 2.124: A poor man in Virginia who, at that day, had had the good fortune to have crossed the line into Maryland, on one side, or North Carolina,

on the other . . . considered himself as fully invested with the traveller's privilege as Bruce or Munchausen. **1830** Ames *Mariner's* 40: The idea of a woman's form being good without tight lacing will be scouted as absurd and . . . regarded as a traveller's story. *Oxford* 836; TW 381(2). Cf. Whiting J27, P18.

T227 Travelling acquaints a man with strange bedfellows
1803 Davis *Travels* 62: Travelling, says *Shakespeare*, acquaints a man with strange bed-fellows. *Oxford* 535; TW 246, 291, 294. See **M193, P226.**

T228 As sweet as **Treacle**
1790 Humphreys *Works* 200: They taste of kisses sweet as treacle. **1797** Dennie *Letters* 157: But an ounce of Horace is as sweet as treacle. Svartengren 64.

T229 To like the **Treason** but hate the traitor (*varied*)
c1737 *Colden Letters* 9.308: Tho they might like the Treason they hated the Traytor. **1774** Boucher *View* 423: Though Absalom might like the treason, he could not but hate the traitor. **1777** WBingham in *Deane Brothers Papers* 98: Altho they may love the treason, they will detest the Traitor. **1778** Hopkinson *Miscellaneous Essays* 1.131: For the English hate a traitor, even though they benefit by the treason. **1780** EOswald in Leake *Lamb* 267: And tho' they "approve the treason, they'll despise the traitor." **1793** ABrown in *Belknap Papers* 3.549: I dislike treason and the traitor. **1797** Boucher *View* 243: It is a common remark, that, however acceptable the treason may be, even rebels rarely like the traitor. **1812** Knopf *War of 1812* 5(1) 179: We dispise the man, but make use of the traitor. **1839** Jackson *Correspondence* 6.6: However much they may rejoice in the Treason they will despise the Traitor. *Oxford* 426; Tilley K64.

T230 Where the **Treasure** is there will the heart be also
1630 *Winthrop Papers(A)* 2.285: Where the treasure is there will the heart be allsoe.

1718 Chalkley *Observations* 440: *For where your Treasure is, there will your Heart be also.* **1765** JWatts in *Aspinwall Papers* 2.576: A ruler, whose heart naturally will be where his treasure is. **1784** Adams(A) *Letters* 186: Where my treasure is, there shall my heart go. **1808** Eaton *Life* 417. Barbour 88: Heart (15); Whiting T451. See **T189.**

T231 As the **Tree** falls there it will lie
1762 Smith *Works* 1¹.30: As the tree falleth, there it will lie. **1822** Randolph(J) *Letters* 249: "As the tree falls, so it must lie." *Oxford* 505; Whiting T477.

T232 As the **Tree** is, so is the fruit (*varied*)
1682 Claypoole *Letter Book* 121: As the tree is, so is the fruit, and as the fountain is, so the streams. **1697** Chalkley *God's Great Love* 337: *An evil Tree cannot bring forth good Fruit,* **1718** *Observations* 451: *A good Tree cannot bring forth evil Fruit, nor can a corrupt Tree bring forth good Fruit.* **1754** ?WLivingston in Johnson *Writings* 4.160: A corrupt tree, says the greatest authority, bringeth forth corrupt fruit. **1776** Adams *Works* 9.413: Make the tree good, and the fruit will be good. **1797** Beete *Man* 1: When did a withered, rotten tree produce good fruit? **1809** Weems *Washington* 193: *A good tree,* saith the divine teacher, *bringeth forth good fruit. Oxford* 837; Whiting T465.

T233 As thick as **Trees** in the woods
1778 Smith *Memoirs(II)* 286: Ships in the River as thick as Trees in the Woods. Whiting T458.

T234 An oft-transplanted **Tree** (will not thrive)
1737 Franklin *PR* 2.169: I never saw an oft transplanted tree, nor yet an oft-removed family, That throve so well as those that settled be, **1758** *WW* 344. *Oxford* 838; Whiting T474. See **R55.**

T235 An old **Tree** cannot be transplanted
1764 Franklin *Papers* 11.110: *Old trees cannot safely be transplanted.* Cf. *Oxford* 671; Tilley T491; Whiting T474.

T236 To bark up the wrong **Tree**
1841 JHowerton in Jackson *Correspondence*
6.102: He barked up the wrong tree. Barbour 186(8); *Oxford* 30; TW 381(6).

T237 A **Tree** is judged (known) by its fruits
1634 Wood *New-England* 77: A Tree may be judged by his fruite, and disposition calculated by exteriour actions. **c1645** JCotton in Williams *Writings* 2.11: The Tree is knowne by his fruits. **1646** Winslow *Hypocrisie* 66: The tree is best knowne by its fruite. **a1700** Hubbard *New England* 353: For the tree is not known but by its fruits. **1703** Taylor *Christographia* 463.43-4: For as the tree is known by its fruits, Matt.7.17.18, So the fruits are well known by the tree. A good tree brings forth good fruit. **1704** Chalkley *Journal* 47: By their Fruits you shall know them, 154, 157. **1707** Makemie *Writings* 168, 183. **1753** *Independent Reflector* 91: *By their Fruit ye shall know them.* **1788** Jefferson *Papers* 13.521: The fruit is a specimen of the tree. **1799** Carey *Porcupiniad* 1.13. **1811** Jay *Correspondence* 4.353. **1814** Kerr *Barclay* 196. **1817** Adams *Memoirs* 3.535: He is willing to judge of the tree by its fruits. **1817** Jackson *Correspondence* 2.273: It is therefore a favourite adage of mine, "that the tree is known by its fruit." **1824** Jefferson *Writings* 16.55: He has taught us to judge the tree by its fruit. **1824** *Tales* 2.42. **1833** NPaul in Porter *Negro Writing* 286. **1835** Jackson *Correspondence* 5.328, 487, 488, **1838** 527. Barbour 186(3); *Oxford* 837; Whiting T472.

T238 A **Tree's** vigor is increased by clipping
c1820 Bernard *Retrospections* 74: But, like a tree, his vigor was only increased by clipping. Whiting C259.

T239 As flat as a **Trencher**
1814 Wirt *Bachelor* 56: This globe of earth is as flat as a trencher.

T240 In a **Trice** [The following is a selection from 30 occurrences of the phrase]
1650 Bradstreet *Works* 126: In a trice, 160. **1676** Williams *Writings* 5.242: In a trice and immediately. **1702** Mather *Magnalia* 2.613. **1767** NAmes in *DHR* 2(1891) 98. **1789** Brown *Better* 50. **1801** Alden *Epitaphs* 1.60: He in a trice Exchang'd his wigwam for a paradise. **1816** Fidfaddy *Adventures*

30. **1819** Peirce *Rebelliad* 14. Whiting T479.

T241   A New England (*etc.*) Trick

1756 *Johnson Papers* 9.447: He is capable of doing any low lifed new England tricks. **1777** Smith *Memoirs(II)* 272: This is what they call a NE Trick, **1778** 357: But had adopted R. R. L.'s Conceit of its being a New York Trick. **1781** JPhilips in Webb *Correspondence* 2.329: In short 'tis a damn'd Connecticut trick! **1790** Maclay(S) *Journal* 48: And as those people were in want of Cloathes as its said, no dout they played us a Jersey Trick. **1806** Fanning *Narrative* 199: We . . . meant to show them a Yankee trick by giving them leg bail. **1809** *Port Folio* 2NS 2.533: Yankee Tricks. This is a very significant phrase, and one in very general use, 533-4: If they had, *buckskin tricks* might in Boston, or Portsmouth, or Portland, be as proverbial as *Yankee* tricks in New-York or Philadelphia. **1812** RJohnson in Knopf *War of 1812* 6(3) 103: He has played the Grandest Yanké Trick that ever has been played on the U.S. **1812** Melish *Travels* 72: "Now, you rascal," says he, "you thought to play a Yankee trick upon me." **1813** Paulding *Lay* 188-9: A Yankey trick is applied exclusively to that finesse and keenness, which it is said distinguish the people of New-England, in bargaining and other matters. The first *Yankey trick* on record *etc.* **1815** Brackenridge *Modern* 648: There were those who thought it might be called a Yankey trick, 671. **1815** Humphreys *Yankey* 81: A pretty Yankey trick—to disguise yourself like a gentleman! **1819** Thomas *Travels* 237: The conduct of fugitives from justice and from credit, has been so immoral . . . that the phrase "a Yankee trick," has become proverbially common. **1821** Gallatin *Diary* 184: Mr. Adams has been playing more of what I call "Yankee tricks." **1822** Adams *Writings* 7.291: I hear his conduct styled a *Yankee trick.* DA Yankee 4(19). Cf. *Oxford* 926: Yorkshire. See **Y2.**

T242   No Tricks upon travellers

1777 Munford *Patriots* 502: No tricks upon travellers. **1803** Davis *Travels* 385: No tricks upon Travellers. **1817** Tyler *Prose* 341: None of your tricks upon travellers. *Oxford* 657; Tilley T521.

T243   To take one's Trick

1781 Oliver *Origin* 15: Most of whom embarqued for the *Massachusetts Bay* . . . for the Priviledge of taking their Trick at the Helm of Persecution. Colcord 196; NED Trick 9.

T244   A Trick in trade

1770 *New-York Gazette* in *Newspaper Extracts(I)* 8.255: Even suppose the Consequence not to be worse than a Trick in Trade. TW 380(2). Cf. *Oxford* 431-2. See **K43.**

T245   A Trick worth two of that

1813 Weems *Drunkard* 98: *I'll show you a trick worth two of that.* **1843** ERWare in *New England Merchants* 307: I understand a trick worth two of his. *Oxford* 839; TW 382(3).

T246   To be quick on the Trigger

1808 Weems *Letters* 2.377: I trust that all your Aids will be quick on the trigger. TW 382(2).

T247   Not to know the Trim

1778 Lee(W) *Letters* 2.430: What they will do, I can't tell, not knowing the trim since John Adams was added. NED Trim 5.

T248   To eat like a Trojan

1810 EGLutwyche in *Winslow Papers* 644: He ate like a Trojan and drank very decently. TW 382.

T249   To swear like a Trooper

1770 *Johnson Papers* 7.388: Swearing like a Trooper. **1799** Cobbett *Porcupine* 10.165: His worship cursed and damned like a trooper. **1809** Irving *History* 2.35: Divers Indians, who all swore to the fact, as sturdily as though they had been so many Christian troopers. **1813** Weems *Drunkard* 63: The Barbers and Bakers were cursing like troopers. **1816** Lambert *Travels* 1.481: She . . . swears like a trooper. **1819** Cobbett *Year's* 324: Women *got drunk,* and *swore* like troopers. **1822** Bache *Notes* 43. Barbour 187(2); *Oxford* 792; TW 382. See **P177.**

T250 To turn in like a **Trooper's** horse

1803 Davis *Travels* 397: I'll be d —— d . . . if our steward does not turn in with his boots on. He is like a trooper's horse. Partridge 911; TW 382.

T251 Dr. **Trotter**

1820 Beecher *Autobiography* 1.425: My health . . . is pretty good, though I have some of those Dr. Trotter complaints. Cf. Wentworth 555: Trot.

T252 Don't borrow **Trouble** (*varied*)

1776 Asbury *Journal* 1.207: Leave the troubles of to-morrow till to-morrow comes. **1804** Dow *Journal* 195: There are trials enough daily, without borrowing trouble from the morrow. **1813** *Kennon Letters* 35.14: I . . . try not to anticipate evils; or take trouble. **1824** Carroll *Correspondence* 2.331: This proves that it is wrong to anticipate evils which may never happen. Barbour 187(4); *Oxford* 523; TW 382.

T253 **Trouble** springs from idleness

1756 Franklin *PR* 6.324: *Trouble* springs from *Idleness; Toil* from *Ease,* **1758** *WW* 343: and grievous Toil from needless Ease. See **I12, M37.**

T254 As true as a **Trout**

1774 RAtkinson in *VHM* 15(1907) 356: I know his value, as true a trout as ever swam, as staunch a hound as ever ran. Cf. NED Trout *sb.*[1] 4; Partridge 912.

T255 To catch like a **Trout** with tickling

1797 Cobbett *Porcupine* 5.362: I gave him to understand that I was no trout, and consequently was not to be caught by tickling. NED Tickling *vbl.sb.* 3c; Tilley T537.

T256 To lay it on with a **Trowel**

1817 *Port Folio* 4NS 3.180: Praise is generally laid on with a trowel. **1824** Neal *American Writers* 61: But they have laid it on with a trowel. Apperson 354; *Oxford* 448; Tilley T539.

T257 To put one to his **Trumps**

1729 JAlexander in *Colden Letters* 1.303: [It] Did really put me to my trumps. **1740** *Georgia Records* 22[2].474: The past [year] . . . has put an Old Fellow to his Trumps.

1770 Franklin *Papers* 17.53: This put the New York People to their Trumps. **1775** Andrews *Letters* 397. **1775** Fithian *Journal* 52: But I was put to my Trumps, there is no House, I must preach among the Trees. **1781** Moore *Diary* 2.456. **1781** Witherspoon *Works* 4.473. **1783** Williams *Penrose* 111, 288. **1788** *Politician* 70. **1795** Cobbett *Porcupine* 2.219. **1800** Gadsden *Writings* 291: Her sly ladyship herself seems now to be put to her last trump. **1801** Sewall *Poems* 241. **1806** *Monthly Anthology* 3.136. **1807** *Emerald* NS 1.88. **1808** Hitchcock *Poetical Dictionary* 90: The fates are driven to their trumps. **1809** Irving *History* 2.195. **1810** PWinslow in *Winslow Papers* 648. c**1825** Tyler *Prose* 131. *Oxford* 657; TW 383(2).

T258 To blow (sound) one's own **Trumpet**

1776 SAdams in *Warren-Adams Letters* 1.212: It was not hard to oblige him to blow the Trumpet himself which they had prepared to sound his Praise. **1780** Gordon *Letters* 444: The louder you sound your trumpet the deafer they will grow. **1809** Irving *History* 2.17: "How didst thou acquire this paramount honour and dignity?" . . . "Like many a great man before me, simply *by sounding my own trumpet.*" **1812** Hitchcock *Works* 92-3: To blow one's own trumpet himself, Not only is a thing the oddest, But quite improper and immodest. **1812** EWTupper in Knopf *War of 1812* 2.105: Our troops . . . have not yet learned to trumpet their own fame before we have seen an enemy. *Oxford* 70; Tilley T546. See **H294.**

T259 To be one's own **Trumpeter**

1778 JAdams in *Warren-Adams Letters* 2.72: A Man must be his own Trumpeter. **1813** Fletcher *Letters* 72: I am to you my own trumpeter, for you can hear no other way. NED Trumpeter 2. Cf. *Oxford* 841.

T260 Put not your **Trust** in princes

1759 Franklin *Papers* 8.451: That might teach them (against Scripture) to *put their trust in Princes.* **1783** Adams *Works* 8.79: The Bible teaches us not to put our trust in princes. **1800** Adams *Letters on Silesia* 293:

Put not your trust in princes. *Oxford* (2d ed.) 525; TW 383(2).

T261 He that **Trusts** not is not deceived

1736 Franklin *PR* 2.142: There's none deceived but he that trusts. Tilley D181. Cf. *Oxford* 843; Tilley T559; Whiting E97, T494.

T262 To **Trust** (believe) no farther than one can see

1771 Jefferson *Papers* 1.62: With this gentleman I beleive no farther than I see. **1793** ECossa in *Blount Papers* 2.295: No mony No Confidence No trust not the Lenght of a mans arm. **1808** Asbury *Letters* 3.396: I will only trust such men as far as I can see them. **1816** Paulding *Letters(I)* 2.82: I wouldn't trust either quite as far as I could see him. *Oxford* 843; Tilley T557.

T263 As plain as **Truth**

1819 Murphey *Papers* 1.138: I thought it as plain as Truth itself. Cf. Whiting T503.

T264 Tell **Truth** and shame the Devil

1796 Smith(EH) *Diary* 246: Tell truth & shame the Devil, 281. **1801** Weems *Letters* 2.217: Yes Mr Carey, I can shame the Devil and say that I have often experienc^d for you those feelings which so refresh our spirits when the image of a beloved brother rises on our thoughts. **1804** Irving *Corrector* 113: Our fathers said, "Tell truth, and shame the devil." **1813** Weems *Drunkard* 79: But we must speak the truth, if it were only to shame the devil, for his villainous intermeddling in our affairs. *Oxford* 807; TW 98(4), 383(27).

T265 **Truth** filters through the stone

1802 FAmes in King *Life* 4.75: Truth however filters through the stone & reaches the folks standing below, drop by drop. See **D306.**

T266 **Truth** is mighty and will prevail (*varied*)

1715 Mather *Diary* 2.333: *Magna est veritas,* et prevalebit. **1733** Belcher *Papers* 1.361: Truth is eternal & will be finally triumphant. **1737** Johnson *Writings* 3.119: [Latin only]. **1752** TBosomworth in

McDowell *Documents* 1.307: [Latin only]. **1758** *New American Magazine* in *Newspaper Extracts(I)* 4.180: [Latin only]. **1768** WNelson in *Norton Papers* 77: We may say of it as of Truth, Magna est & praevalebit. **1770** Franklin *Papers* 17.330: [Latin only]. **1771** SAdams in *Warren-Adams Letters* 1.9: [Latin only]. **1780** JEliot in *Belknap Papers* 3.184: [Latin only]. **1781** Oliver *Origin* 137: [Latin only]. **1794** RTroup in King *Life* 1.544: Magna est probitas et prevalebit. **1794** *Washington *Writings* 33.465: Truth will ultimately prevail where pains is taken to bring it to light. **1795** HLee in Iredell *Correspondence* 2.437: Truth must at last prevail. **1795** OWolcott in Hamilton *Papers* 19.265: Trust that the truth will prevail. **1804** Claiborne *Letter Books* 2.21: As our old friend Macon used to say the cause of truth will in the end prevail. **1805** WEaton in *Barbary Wars* 5.319: Make yourself easy Sir, truth is Almighty. **1809** WCunningham in *Adams-Cunningham Letters* 98: [Latin only]. **1810** Jefferson *Writings* 12.360-1: But truth and reason are eternal. They have prevailed. **1820** Jackson *Correspondence* 3.21: I am aware that truth is mighty and will ultimately prevail. **1825** Neal *American Writers* 155. **1829** Jackson *Correspondence* 4.89. **1829** Pintard *Letters* 3.108: Truth will prevail. **1838** Jackson *Correspondence* 5.529, **1839** 6.4. *Oxford* 844; Whiting T495.

T267 The **Truth** is not to be spoken at all times

1748 *Word* in *Colonial Currency* 4.354-5: The Truth may not with Propriety be spoken at all Times. **1764** RBland *Colonel* in Bailyn *Pamphlets* 1.312: The *proverbial account* of Truth, that it is not to be spoken at all times. **1774** Lee *Letters* 1.108: I have often heard it said . . . that the truth is not at all times to be spoken. **1781** Oliver *Origin* 57: it is said. **1783** Baldwin *Life and Letters* 119: The truth is not always to be spoken. **1798** Adams *Writings* 2.296: I yet adhere to an old one [adage] that "the truth is not to be told at all times." **1802** *Port Folio* 2.153: Another maxim . . . "*Veritas non est omnibus horis loquendum.*" **1807** EGerry in *Adams-Warren Correspondence* 496: The truth is not always to be spoken or recorded. **1809** *Kennon Letters* 31.303: You know truths must not be always spoken. *Oxford* 11; Whiting S485. See **T271.**

T268 **Truth** lies at the bottom of a well

1779 Curwen *Journal and Letters* 226: The old proverb justly says, truth lies in a well, and difficult it is to draw it up. **1790** *Belknap Papers* 2.225: But perhaps *veritas latet in puteo.* **1809** JMadison in Smith *Letters* 64: Truth is at the bottom of a well, is the old saying. **1856** Paulding *Letters(II)* 569: [Truth] lies . . . much deeper than the bottom of a well. *Oxford* 844; TW 384(6).

T269 **Truth** may be blamed but cannot be shamed

1767 Ames *Almanacs* 387: Truth may be blam'd but will ne'er be sham'd. **1805** Parkinson *Tour* v: The old adage—"Truth may be blamed, but it cannot be shamed." *Oxford* 844; Whiting T507.

T270 **Truth** needs no cunning (colors)

1741 Stephens *Journal(I)* 2.206: For Truth needs no Cunning for its Support, **1744** *(II)* 2.72: But truth is never to be Cloathed with false Colours. *Oxford* 844-5; Whiting T515.

T271 **Truth** ought to be spoken

1812 Hitchcock *Social* 14: The long established maxim, that *the truth ought to be spoken* let it cut where it will. See **T267.**

T272 **Truth** seeks no corners

1644 Williams *Writings* 3.180: The rich *Mines* of *golden Truth* lye hid under *barren* hills, and in *obscure* holes and *corners*. **1736** Talcott *Papers* 1.333: Now as truth seeks no corner to hide in, so the contrary hates the light. *Oxford* 845; Whiting T512.

T273 **Truth,** the whole truth, and nothing but the truth

1764 Franklin *Papers* 11.438: Requires the Evidence to speak *the Truth,* the *whole Truth,* and *nothing but the Truth.* **1774** Seabury *Letters* 85: The *truth, the whole truth, and nothing but the truth,* 146. **1778** JA in *Adams FC* 3.79, **1779** *Works* 7.96: so far as I know it, **1807** in *Adams-Warren Correspondence* 321, **1815** *Works* 10.192: I

must tell you the truth, and nothing but the truth; but to tell you the whole truth is impossible. **1815** Wirt *Letters* 1.391: at least in this book. **1818** Adams *Works* 10.338. **1819** Thomas *Travels* 180: The report of a traveller . . . ought to embrace "the truth and the whole truth." **1819** JWalker in *Ruffin Papers* 1.224: When you pay your money to a lawyer for advice tell him the truth, the hole truth, and nothing but the truth. **1819** Waln *Hermit* 137: Some have told "the truth;" a much less number "the whole truth," and not one "nothing but the truth." **1821** Dalton *Travels* 14. **1828** Jackson *Correspondence* 3.441: But to bring forth from him . . . the whole truth, and nothing but the truth. *Oxford* 845; Tilley T590. See **H24.**

T274 **Truth** will out

1780 Gordon *Letters* 446: The truth . . . will out. **1814** Kerr *Barclay* 296: Truth will out. Barbour 188(10); *Oxford* 845; TW 384(8). Cf. Whiting S490, 491. See **M305.**

T275 **Try** before you trust

1741 Ames *Almanacs* 149: Try before you trust, **1752** 236: Trust them as you have try'd them. *Oxford* 845; Tilley T595; Whiting P429.

T276 Let every **Tub** stand on its own bottom (*varied*)

1750 Fairservice *Plain Dealing* 34: Let every Tub stand on its own Bottom. **1771** *Washington Writings* 3.67: Which means every Man would stand upon his own bottom and not a few burthened with the expense of the whole. **1776** Lee *Papers* 2.291: The two armies . . . must rest each on its own bottom. **1777** Curwen *Journal* 1.401: The remainder of the story stands on its own bottom, or in other words is doubtful. **1777** *Washington Writings* 10.148: We . . . make our preparations as if we were to depend solely upon our own Bottoms. **1778** JMVarnum in Sullivan *Letters* 2.259: A Sentiment of Dean Swift is constantly with me That every Tub should stand upon its own Bottom. **1788** *Politician* 8: Every tub must stand upon its own bottom. **1798** Cobbett *Porcupine* 10.6: as the old saying is. **1804**

Brackenridge *Modern* 418: Let the poor man's cart have fair play, and stand upon its own bottom. **1834** Paulding *Letters(II)* 143: Senators, who, as the vulgar say, legislate on their own Bottoms. Barbour 188(1); NED Bottom 10b; *Oxford* 845; TW 384(1); Tilley T596.

T277 To throw a **Tub** to a whale

1734 *New-York Weekly Journal* in *Newspaper Extracts(I)* 1.406: I have already spent too much Time on this *Bradfordian, envious pitiful* Tub. **1776** JA in *Adams FC* 2.53: [He] is throwing out his Barrells to amuse Leviathan, untill his Reinforcements shall arrive. **1776** HGates in Massachusetts Historical Society, *Proceedings* 67(1941-4) 141: Can't you throw out some tubb to these whales? **1777** WCarmichael in *MHM* 44 (1949) 13: The Ministry have made it a tub to throw out to the Whale. **1779** AMcDougall in *Clinton Papers* 4.598: This is the Tub of the Day, to divert the whales. **1781** Adams *Works* 7.379: Peace is a tub easily thrown out for the amusement of the whale. **1781** JEliot in *Belknap Papers* 3.217: The destination of the French fleet is the tub of our present diversion. **1781** Oliver *Origin* 96: They knew that the Whole Rabble must have a Tub to play with. **1782** AA in *Adams FC* 4.371: It was only a tub to the Whale. **1782** EPendleton in Madison *Papers* 4.257: A mere Tub thrown out to amuse the Whale. **1785** Jefferson *Papers* 7.643: They are throwing out another barrel for the political whales to play with. **1789** Mason *Papers* 3.1164. **1793** Brackenridge *Modern* 202: [It] is like throwing a barrel to a whale, in order to preserve the ship. **1801** Weems *Letters* 2.171: It w^d do as a barrel to the whale untill we coud get another & better plan in progress. **1802** Moultrie *Memoirs* 1.95. **1802** Paine *To the Citizens* 2.924: It is as a tub thrown out to the whale to prevent its attacking and sinking the vessel. **1809** Lee *Diary and Letters* 77: Which is but a secondary object with me: as we say in New England—a tub to catch a whale with. **1809** Weems *Washington* 30: This it seems he had drawn up as a tub for the whale. **1810** King *Life* 5.181. **1811** Claiborne *Letter Books* 6.13. **1811** Weems *Gambling* 25: Great whales must needs have their great tubs. **1813** Paulding *Lay* 40. **1814** JRandolph in Quincy *JQuincy* 350: They will be delighted with some tub for the popular whale against the next election. **1818** Jefferson *Writings* 19.259: As some tub . . . must always be thrown out to the whale, **1820** 15.280. **1820** King *Life* 6.289: The proposed compromise is a mere tub to the whale. **1825** JDesha in Jackson *Correspondence* 3.286: The management in the late Presidential election will be the tub to be thrown out to the whale for the next season. **1830** Ames *Mariner's* 280: The literary arena . . . has served as a tub to the whale for a long time. **1842** Paulding *Letters(II)* 317: Every little mite of a politician . . . has only to throw a Tub to the great Whale, the People. *Oxford* 845-6; TW 384(2).

T278 As busy as a **Tumble-bug**

1822 Watterston *Winter* 27: Dicky was . . . as busy as a tumble-bug. Cf. DA tumble-bug; NED Tumble- 1.

T279 To be out of **Tune**

1770 *Johnson Papers* 7.650: The times are out of tune. NED Tune 3b.

T280 To change (turn, alter) one's **Tune**

c**1700** Taylor *Poems* 443: But if he doth he quickly turns his tune. **1750** *Johnson Papers* 1.277: [He] altered his Tune. **1778** Smith *Memoirs(II)* 357: At coming away he seemed [to] change his Tune. **1815** Brackenridge *Journal* 53: His tune was changed. Barbour 188(4); NED Tune 4b. See **N103.**

T281 To sing a different **Tune**

1821 Freneau *Last Poems* 50: Came back, and sang a different tune. Barbour 188(4); TW 385(3). Cf. *Oxford* 736: Song.

T282 A **Tune** on one's own fiddle

1832 Ames *Nautical* 62: But says the proverb, "every one has a right to a tune on his own fiddle." *Oxford* 798.

T283 To lower one's **Turban**

1774 TRodney in Rodney *Letters* 46: But your friends ar apprized of this and will not omit to lower his Turban at this election.

T284 First catch your **Turbot**

1839 JOgden in Cooper *Letters* 3.422: But a Turbot to be cooked, must first be caught. *Oxford* 262: Hare. See **D275**.

T285 The more you stir (a **Turd**) the more it stinks

?1689 ?Mather *Vindication* in *Andros Tracts* 2.56: The more you *stur,* the more you'l *Stink.* **1714** Hunter *Androboros* 22: The more you stir it, the more 'twill stink. **a1731** Cook *Bacon* 326: The more 'tis stir'd. the more 'twill stink. **1760** Adams *D and A* 1.181: The more He stirs the worse he stinks. **1767** *Johnson Papers* 5.670-1: I thought the more he Stir'd it the worse [MS defective]. *Oxford* 775; Tilley T603; Whiting T523.

T286 Not worth a **Turd**

1706 F-JWinthrop in *Winthrop Papers*(B) 5.343: Anything else is not worth a T. **1775** CMarshall in *Naval Documents* 1.1229: He expressed himself . . . in low, obscene language . . . "That he did not value all their gondolas or Committee of Safety a —." *Oxford* 846; Whiting T526.

T287 A **Turd** is a turd

1666 Alsop *Maryland* 67: But a Dogs turd would be a Dogs turd in plain terms, in spight of their teeth. **1714** Hunter *Androboros* 22: For a T— — is a T— — all the world over. NED Turd 1, quote 1553.

T288 As mad as a **Turk**

1811 Weems *Gambling* 47: Leaving him sullen and mad as a Turk.

T289 To hate as the **Turk**

1780 *New-York Gazette* in *Newspaper Extracts*(II) 5.107: Forsooth Yankee I hate as the Turk.

T290 To swear (curse) like a **Turk**

1813 Weems *Drunkard* 99: The fellow swore like a Turk that he knew nothing of the matter, **1823** *Letters* 3.354: The Englishman . . . let him drop with such a jolt . . . as made him curse like a Turk. See **J31**.

T291 To turn **Turk**

1801 Weems *Letters* 2.171: Why will you Curse the Bible & turn Turk? **1803** Davis *Travels* 427: It was this fashion that made the people at *Constantinople* turn *Turks.* NED Turk 3b; *Oxford* 848; Tilley T609.

T292 To work (pull) like a **Turk**

1774 Fithian *Journal and Letters* 144: I was obliged to take to the Oar — & pull like a Turk. **1819** Wirt *Letters* 2.99: And then sit down and "work like Turks." Barbour 188-9; Whiting *NC* 490. Cf. TW 385(3).

T293 Worse than **Turks**

1694 *Connecticut Vindicated* 120: Worse than Turks. Whiting T529.

T294 One good **Turn** deserves another

1717 Wise *Vindication* 41: *One Good turn Requires another,* is the Common Proverb. **1766** Ames *Almanacs* 376: One good turn deserves another. **1769** Woodmason *Journal* 141: One good turn deserves another and oft begets another. **1778** *New Jersey Gazette* in *Newspaper Extracts*(II) 2.50: This old trick of *one good turn's deserving another.* **1784** McGillivray *Letters* 86: You know that. **a1788** Jones *History* 2.15. **1788** *Politician* 8: as the old saying is. **1796** MBlodget in *W&MCQ* 3S 3(1946) 287: This is doing one good turn for another. **1796** Paine *Letter to Washington* 2.696. **1797** Cobbett *Porcupine* 6.383. **1797** Smith(EH) *Diary* 30. **1819** Adams *Memoirs* 4.304. **1833** Hone *Diary* 1.98. Barbour 189(1); *Oxford* 325; Whiting T533. See **K16**.

T295 **Turnabout** is fair play

1777 WHDrayton in Gibbes 3.86: Turn about, you know, is but fair play. **1823** Adams *Memoirs* 6.131: The children say "turn about is fair play." *Oxford* 846; TW 386(1).

T296 The **Turtle**(dove) and her mate

1632 EHowe in *Winthrop Papers*(A) 3.75: Lyable to the livinge death of a Turtles solitarines that hath lost her mate. **1634** Wood *New-England* 30: Turtle-Dove, Who to her mate doth ever constant prove. **1732** Belcher *Papers* 1.237: I am glad to hear . . . that the lonely turtle had rec̃d her mate. **1796** Barton *Disappointment* 94: Constant be — as turtle-dove. *Oxford* 840; Whiting T542.

T297 Tweedledum and Tweedledee

1776 Schaw *Journal* 241: All the difference is no more than Tweedle dee and Tweedle dum. **1785** Hopkinson *Miscellaneous Essays* 2.144: Mr *Tweedledum* begins the attack with a full *discord* in a *sharp third* . . . Mr. Tweedledee replies in the *natural key*. **1795** *Tablet* 20: Sound the trumpet, beat the drum, Tweedle dee, and tweedle dum, Gird your armour cap-a-pee, Tweedle dum and tweedle dee. **1822** Lee *Diary and Letters* 196: "Strange all this difference should be Twixt Tweedledum and Tweedledee." *Oxford* 848; TW 387.

T298 Careless at Twenty, etc.

1816 Adams *Writings* 6.102: Well does he [JQA] remember your [AA's] ever affectionate admonition to him thirty years ago. "Careless at twenty is a sloven at thirty, and intolerable at forty." . . . He hopes he has not verified your proverb of progressive viciousness. Cf. *Oxford* 348; Tilley T631.

T299 One can think better at Twice than once

1790 Maclay *Journal* 294: Perhaps any man can think more and better too at twice than at once. Cf. NED Twice 1e; *Oxford* 199; Tilley T185. See **T60, 74.**

T300 As the Twig is bent the tree is inclined (varied)

1796 Washington *Writings* 35.295: It has been said, and truly, "that as the twig is bent so it will grow." **1818** Fessenden *Ladies Monitor* 75: "'Tis education forms the tender mind, Just as the twig is bent the tree's inclin'd." This hacknied adage, not more trite than true. **1818** Royall *Letters* 169. Barbour 189(1); *Oxford* 46; TW 387(1); Tilley T632.

T301 In a Twink

1817 Barker *How to Try a Lover* 6: In a twink. **1819** Drake *Works* 311: We'll settle the thing in a twink. *Oxford* 849; Whiting T547.

T302 In a Twinkling

1733 *New-York Gazette* in *Newspaper Extracts(I)* 9.589: In a twinkling. **1774** Franklin *Writings* 6.300: In a twinkling. **1781**

EJAmbler in *VHM* 38(1930) 167. **c1800** Dennie *Lay Preacher* 172. **c1800** Tyler *Island* 11. **1808** Barker *Tears* 150. **1811** Graydon *Memoirs* 20. **1816** Paulding *Letters(I)* 1.84. **1819** Noah *Travels* 84. **1822** Watterston *Winter* 80, 137. **1825** Pintard *Letters* 2.189. **1826** Audubon *1826 Journal* 51. *Oxford* 849; TW 387(1); Whiting T547.

T303 In the Twinkling of a bed-post

c1800 Tyler *Island* 11: That will set you all to right in the twinkling of a bed post. NED Bed-post; *Oxford* 849.

T304 In the Twinkling of a broomstick

1796 Barton *Disappointment* 74: I'll kick his guts out in the twinkling of a broomstick. Cf. *Oxford* 849; Tilley T634.

T305 In the Twinkling of an eye [The following is a selection from 30 occurrences of the phrase]

1643 Williams *Writings* 1.78: In the twinckling of an eye, **1676** 5.485. **1722** *New-England Courant* 35(2.2). **1745** Pote *Journal* 43: And almost In yᵉ Twinkling of an Eye, they Gave us three or four Cannon. **1761** CCarroll in *MHM* 10(1915) 337: Life is but as the Twinkling of an Eye to Eternity. **1771** Hearne *Journey* 212: I must acknowledge that in the twinkling of an eye he conveyed it to—God knows where. **1774** Adams *Legal Papers* 1.139: In a twinkling of an Eye. **1796** Cobbett *Porcupine* 3.56. **1802** Adams(TB) *Letters* 162. **1811** Weems *Gambling* 19. **1836** Floy *Diary* 215: And in the twinkling of an eye part of a beautiful white neck appeared. *Oxford* 849; TW 388(3); Whiting T547.

T306 (It takes Two to make a quarrel)

1750 *New York Weekly Post Boy* in *Newspaper Extracts(I)* 2.605: It is an old Saying, and generally a true One, that *where two differ or quarrel, there are commonly Faults on both Sides.* *Oxford* 852; TW 389(9).

T307 Two and two make four (five)

1723 *New-England Courant* 95(1.1): As plain as 'tis that Two and Two make Four. **1761** *South Carolina Gazette* 15: To this plain maxim I agree, No living man can thrive, But he that will most readily, Hold two and two count five. **1815** Brackenridge *Modern* 700: I would just as soon undertake to persuade the bulk of mankind, that they saw a bull in the firmament, as that two and two make four. Barbour 189(1); *Oxford* 849; TW 388(5).

T308 **Two** are better than one

1677 Hubbard *Indian* 1.10: There are Cases wherein *two are better than one,* and a three-fold cord is not easily broken, 2.106: Two are better than one. **1751** Wolcott *Papers* 88: Two is better than one. **1780** *Belknap Papers* 1.56: For Solomon was not mistaken when he said, "Two are better than one." **1796** Dennie *Lay Preacher* 5. **1820** Cottle *Life* 381. *Oxford* 851; Tilley T642. Cf. Whiting T548.

T309 **Two** can play at that game (*varied*)

1791 Morris *Diary* 2.328: Death is a Game which two can play at. **1816** GHowland in *New England Merchants* 93: He . . . threatened to knock me into hell, I told him, if I was well two could try at that. *Oxford* 295; TW 389(6).

T310 **Two** cannot walk together unless they be agreed

1818 M'Nemar *Kentucky* 41: It is an old proverb, that "two cannot walk together unless they be agreed."

T311 **Two** of a trade can never agree

c**1770** Tyler *Verse* 4: Two of a Trade can ne'er agree For they both mended Soles. **1771** Carroll *Copy-Book* 201: Two of a trade can never agree. **1783** Williams *Penrose* 263: Two of a trade seldom agreed. **1787** *Columbian Magazine* 1.346: The truth of the proverb I see. **1794** Cobbett *Porcupine* 1.219: They say, **1797** 5.8. **1797** Latrobe *Journal* 107: The proverb. Apperson 655; *Oxford* 851; Tilley T643.

T312 **Two** to one are odds

1781 Oliver *Origin* 69: But if two to one are odds, surely 100 to one will not make an Equality. *Oxford* 852; Tilley T644. Cf. Whiting T249.

T313 Better to live under a **Tyrant** in peace, *etc.*

1681 Williams *Writings* 6.401-2: That ancient maxim, *It is better to live under a tyrant in peace, than under the sword, or where every man is a tyrant.*

U

U1 To see one's **Uncle**

1784 EHazard in *Belknap Papers* 1.407: So the Freemason "looks very poorly." Would it not be advisable for him to go and "see his uncle"? NED Uncle 3; Partridge 924.

U2 **Uncouth** unkissed

1658 HFilmer in *VHM* 68(1960) 417: But ignotia nulla cupido, uncouth unkist. *Oxford* 854-5; Whiting U5.

U3 In **Union** is strength

1654 Williams *Writings* 6.280: Union strengthens. **1837** JForten in Porter *Negro Writing* 228: In Union is strength. Barbour 190; *Oxford* 854; TW 390.

U4 **United** we stand, divided we fall (*varied*)

1768 Dickinson *Writings* 417: United we conquer, divided we die, 432: By *uniting* We stand, by *dividing* We fall. **1772** Gerry *Letters* 1.12: United we stand, divided we fall. **1774** Lee *Letters* 1.109: Let every American remember the Liberty song: By uniting we stand, By dividing we fall, Then Steady Boys &c &c. **1775** Thacher *Journal* 21: *Unite and be invincible.* **1777** Munford *Patriots* 459: the American motto. **1783** *Belknap Papers* 1.207: The motto was, "By uniting we stand, by dividing we fall." **1783** EPendleton in Madison *Papers* 6.461: The adage so often mentioned in the commencement of the dispute. **1787** *American Museum* 2.201: Unite, or Die, 384. **1787** *Anarchiad* 63: Ye Live United, or Divided Die! **1788** *American Museum* 4.385. **1788**

Massachusetts Centinel in Buckingham *Specimens* 2.47. **1796** Cathcart *Journal* 416: In other places it is a maxim to Unite and conquer but in Algiers it is quite the contrary. Divide and conquer is here the plan. **1802** *Port Folio* 2.161. **1803** Austin *Constitutional* 312. **1807** Jackson *Correspondence* 1.166: There is but one voice — *united we stand, divided we fall.* **?1813** HBallinger in *VHM* 46(1938) 333: For as our old fathers said to the troops that once marched to the north. **1819** Peirce *Rebelliad* 50. **c1825** Tyler *Prose* 167. Barbour 190; Whiting V47. See **B363.**

U5 Now **Up,** now down

1650 Bradstreet *Works* 140: Now up, now down, transported like the Air, 320: Now up, now down, now chief, & then brought under. **1777** David *Letters* 60: For as with the fellows [fellies] of a wheele first up & then down just so in war. Whiting B575, N179.

U6 **Up** and (be) doing

1745 Stephens *Journal(II)* 2.223: So that *Up and be Doing* was current among the generality of our people. **1822** Gallatin *Diary* 218: I felt I ought to be "up and doing" and make a career for myself. Berrey 1157; Longfellow, *Psalm of Life* (1835) 1.33.

U7 **Ups** and downs

1761 HHusband in Boyd *Eighteenth Century Tracts* 220: I had some Ups and Downs. **1763** Franklin *Papers* 1.304: I hear of . . . Ups and Downs. **1763** Griffith *Jour-*

nal 243: In such ups and downs, changes and conflicts. **1780** Sargent *Loyalist* 116. **1803** Davis *Travels* 349: We have all our ups and downs in the world. **1818** Royall *Letters* 132. **1819** Drake *Works* 351: 'Tis ours, their *ups* and *downs* to trace, And laugh at *ins* and *outs* together. *Oxford* 856; Tilley U19; TW 219(6).

U8   Uptails all
1699 Ward *Trip* 55: Then *Uptails-all* and the *Devils* as busie under the *Petticoat,* as a *Juggler* at a *Fair,* or a *Whore* at a Carnival. NED Uptails; Simpson 727-8.

U9   As ugly as an Urchin
1807 *Port Folio* NS 3.3: It is ugly as an urchin.

U10   He that is not for Us is against us
1767 Franklin *Papers* 14.126: The old Saying, *He that is not for us is against us;* which I think would have been full as true a Saying if there had been a small Transposition in it, *He that is not against us, is for us.* **1824** Doddridge *Notes* 198: The Indian maxim was "He that is not for us is against us." 1 Tim. 11.23.

U11   As much Use as a dog has for a side-pocket
1824 *Tales* 2.105: She's got no more use for it than a dog has for a side-pocket, as the saying is. Lean 2.791; NED Side-pocket. Cf. *Oxford* 757: Sow; Tilley S672.

U12   Use makes everything easy
1815 Waterhouse *Journal* 18: Use makes every thing easy.

U13   Use makes perfect
1719 *Addition* in *Colonial Currency* 1.371: Common sayings declare, that *Use makes perfect.* **1778** Curwen *Journal* 1.485: Use as Proverb says makes perfect. *Oxford* 856; TW 390(2). Cf. Whiting U8. See **P269**.

U14   Use reconciles most things
1778 Lee *Letters* 1.447: But use reconciles most things. See **C387, H3**.

V

V1 To labor in **Vain**

1738 Stephens *Journal(I)* 1.117: I thought he would labour in vain, **1740** 544, **1742** *(II)* 1.110: Wherein he did not labour in vain. **1775** Lee *Papers* 1.224: If you labour in vain (as I must repeat, I think will be the case). **1790** Morris *Diary* 1.507: You will strive in Vain to parry the Blow. **1792** RPlatt in Webb *Correspondence* 3.177. **1803** *Port Folio* 3.402. **1809** JAdams in *Adams-Cunningham Letters* 85: He could only labour in vain. **1822** Murphey *Papers* 1.268. *Oxford* 438; Whiting V1.

V2 In **Valencia,** flesh is grass, *etc.*

1816 *Port Folio* 4NS 2.378: The Spanish have a proverb . . . "In Valencia, flesh is grass, grass water; The men, *women—*and the *women nothing.*" Now this worse than all—to be placed at the fag-end of a musty proverb.

V3 He that stays in the **Valley** will never get over the hill

1702 Mather *Magnalia* 1.187: Some thought that by *staying in the valley,* they took the way *never to get over the hill.* **1767** Ames *Almanacs* 386: He that stays in the valley will never get over the hill. *Oxford* 772; Tilley V11.

V4 If you would know the **Value** of money try to borrow some

1754 Franklin *PR* 5.184: If you'd know the Value of Money, go and borrow some, **1785** *WW* 347: try to borrow. **1770** Ames *Almanacs* 413: If you would know the value of money, go and try to borrow some. *Oxford* 435; Tilley M1104.

V5 The **Value** of a blessing is known by deprivation

1797 Foster *Coquette* 144: It is a common observation, that we know not the value of a blessing but by deprivation. *Oxford* 922; Tilley W924. See **G117, W18, 103.**

V6 The **Value** of friends is known by their loss

1776 WHeyward in *Naval Documents* 3.569: We know not the Value of our Friends but by their Loss. Tilley W924. See **G117, W18, 103.**

V7 The **Value** of prosperity is known by adversity

1810 Fletcher *Letters* 21: I should not have known the value of prosperity if I had not been in adversity. See **G117, W18, 103.**

V8 **Variety** gives pleasure (*varied*)

1778 JSullivan in *Heath Papers* 2.247: If pleasure consist in variety . . . it will afford you no small entertainment. **1788** Freneau *Prose* 129: [I] am convinced that it is Variety *alone that can make life desirable.* **1800** Cobbett *Porcupine* 11.215: If variety have all the charms which it is said to possess. Barbour 190; *Oxford* 858; TW 391. Cf. Whiting C144.

V9 A **Vauxhall** slice

1805 Silliman *Travels* 1.214: I was no longer at a loss for the meaning or propriety of the proverbial expression, *a Vauxhall slice;* for the ham was sliced . . . thin. NED Vauxhall, quote 1892.

V10   Veering and hauling

1799 RO'Brien in *Barbary Wars* 1.321: There will always be Veering & hauling business. NED Veer *v.*[1] 4.

V11   To be upon Velvet

1790 RPeters in Hamilton *Papers* 6.209: He knows you are not yet upon Velvet in this Way, **1791** 9.115: It is true Farmers are never on Velvet. *Oxford* 858.

V12   Full Vessels make least sound

1645 JCotton in Williams *Writings* 2.56: But full vessels make least sound. Tilley V37. See **C54.**

V13   The Vicar of Bray

1774 (PLivingston), *The Other Side of the Question* in *The Magazine of History*, Extra Number 13(1916) No. 52. 10: Let who will be King, our author is Vicar of Bray. **1783** Freneau *Poems* 2.208: And said— "Here's a health to the Vicar of Bray," And Cocked up my beaver, and—strutted away. **1806** Jefferson *Writings* 18.249: Bond . . . is, we are told, like a good Vicar of Bray, gone over to the new ministry. *Oxford* 859; Tilley V40.

V14   One Vice will expel another

1778 Paine *American Crisis* 1.108: One vice will frequently expel another. Cf. *Oxford* 597: Nail; Whiting N6. See **W53.**

V15   The second Vice is lying, the first is running in debt

1748 Franklin *PR* 3.256: The second Vice is Lying, the first is Running in Debt, **1758** *WW* 348.

V16   Vice rules where gold reigns

1767 Ames *Almanacs* 387: Vice rules where gold reigns. Tilley V46.

V17   What maintains one Vice would bring up two children

1747 Franklin *PR* 3.105: What maintains one Vice, would bring up two Children, **1758** *WW* 345. *Oxford* 500.

V18   It is harder to use Victory than to get it

1633 RSaltonstall in *Saltonstall Papers* 1.121: Tell Mr. Wilson it is a harder matter to use victory than to gett it.

V19   Victory does not stand in the number of soldiers

1677 Hubbard *Indian* 1.81: But Victory stands no more in the Number of Soldiers, than Verity in the Plurality of Voices. Cf. Whiting M801.

V20   Better be first in a **Village** (Athens) than second in Rome

1769 Woodmason *Journal* 146: Its better being the first Man at Athens, than the second at Rome. **1778** AMcDougall in *Clinton Papers* 4.244: I suspect he prefers being the first man of a village to the second in Rome. **1784** Lee *Letters* 2.297: Julius Caesar shewd his ambition as much when he preferred being the *first man* in a *small village* to the *second* in *Rome*. **1789** Adams *Works* 8.494: I am not of Cæsar's mind. The second place in Rome is high enough for me. **1814** *Port Folio* 3NS 4.211: Julius Cæsar, if we are to believe the saying ascribed to him, [said] "that he would rather be the first man in a village than the second in Rome." *Oxford* 51; Tilley V55. Cf. TW 376: Toad(4).

V21   As sharp as Vinegar

1798 Morris *Diary and Letters* 2.372: She is, as usual, sharp as vinegar. **1804** Irving *Journals* 1.38: A voice every tone of which is as sharp as vinegar. Barbour 191(1); *Oxford* 721; TW 391(1).

V22   As sour as Vinegar

1760 Adams *D and A* 1.177: His face . . . as stern as the Devil, sour as Vinegar. Barbour 191(2); TW 391(2).

V23   Vinegar is the son of wine

1652 Williams *Writings* 4.56-7: Master *Cotton* being a son of *wine* (as the Jews speak in their *Proverb*) is loath to be counted a son of *vinegar*. **1702** Mather *Magnalia* 1.157: The proverb of the Jews . . . "That vinegar is the son of wine." Champion 392.255; TW 391(3).

V24   A Viper (snake, serpent, adder) in one's bosom

1653 Wigglesworth *Diary* 57: I have . . .

been a viper in his bosom where he has nourished me. **1706** WWinthrop in *Winthrop Papers*(*B*) 6.144: They foster a snake in their bosoms that would sting them to death if he could. **1764** Franklin *Papers* 11.384: When we would guard ourselves against . . . The stinging Snakes of the Mountains, Our Maxim should be *Beware of taking them to our Bosoms*. **1767** Eliot *Letters* 406: He must have lost all principles of self-preservation, who will take a serpent into his bosom, especially when he has felt his sting, and but just escaped with his life. **1773** Boucher *View* 305: This, by being carressed and taken into our bosoms, was not found out to be our foe, till, like the serpent in the fable, it had stung us to death. **1775** NGreene in *Naval Documents* 3.181: Nourishing such a serpent in the bosom of the country. **1775** Willard *Letters* 177: She is . . . nursing vipers in her bosom. **1776** Paine *Forester's Letters* 2.64: Would it be prudent to trust the viper in our very bosoms. **1779** JFallon in *Clinton Papers* 4.470: The Quakers . . . like vipers which we have cherished in our bosoms. **1781** Reed *Life* 2.374: They are fostering some serpents in their bosom, who, when opportunity offers, will sting them to death. **1783** JFMercer in Madison *Papers* 6.376: The viper which was ready to destroy the family of the man in whose bosom it had been restored to life. **1802** Croswell *New World* 17: We harbour vipers in our bosom. **1803** Claiborne *Letter Books* 3.334: Louisianians are nurturing in their bosoms, Vultures who would not willingly leave them the path which leads to the Grave of their ancestors. **1804** AAdams in *Adams-Jefferson Letters* 1.274: The serpent you cherished and warmed, bit the hand that nourished him. **1807** *Weekly* 1.192: Indeed the wretch would not be madder, Who, in his bosom, nurs'd an adder. **1828** Jackson *Correspondence* 3.409: And displays another viper I have cherished in my bosom. *Oxford* 747; Tilley V68; Whiting A42.

V25   Old **Virginia** never tires

1816 Paulding *Letters*(*I*) 1.33: "Ould Virginia," which, according to the proverb, "never tires." TW 392.

V26   To make **Virginia** fence(s)

1737 Franklin *Drinkers* 2.177: He makes Virginia Fence, Valiant. **1774** Andrews *Letters* 334: Another came running, as the only expedient to avoid making *Virginia fences*. **1789** Anburey *Travels* 2.188: The New-Englanders have a saying, when a man is in liquor, *he is making Virginia fences*. **1795** *Tablet* 13: Vinoso . . . makes his Virginia fence at nine in the morning. **1800** Tatham *Tobacco* 11: It is in allusion to this zigzag foundation that a drunken man is said to be *laying out Virginia fences*. TW 392. See I31.

V27   To make a **Virtue** of necessity

?**1678** Mather *Letters* 6: Behold! how I make a virtue of necessity. **c1680** Radisson *Voyages* 83: But the feare of death makes vertu of necessity, 116: I thought upon it, and out of distress made a virtue. **1685** Dunton *Letters* 12: [It] forc'd him to make a vertue of Necessity. **1690** Danforth *Poems* 146.90: Virtue must turn into Necessity. **1711** *Boundary Line Proceedings* in *VHM* 5(1897) 10. **1728** Byrd *Dividing Line* 70: They therefore made a virtue of what they could not help. **1731** CCarroll in *MHM* 19(1924) 191. **1755** GFisher in *W&MCQ* 17(1908) 107. **1763** RStewart in *Letters to Washington* 3.249. **1769** Brooke *Emily* 105. **1773** SAdams in *Warren-Adams Letters* 1.20. **1775** Curwen *Journal* 1.59. **1777** RAdams in *VHM* 22(1914) 393. **1779** Adams *D and A* 2.369: I may as well make a Virtue of Necessity. **1780** HHughes in *Clinton Papers* 6.454. **1785** Smith *Diary* 1.266. **1785** JStuart in *Kingston* 112. **1789** Boucher *Autobiography* 106. **1789** Washington *Writings* 30.196: I must even make a virtue of necessity. **1793** JBard in Hamilton *Papers* 15.272. **1795** Wayne *Correspondence* 428. **1797** Cobbett *Porcupine* 9.367: The cautious Washington . . . made a virtue of necessity. **1807** Janson *Stranger* 456: Making a virtue of calamity. **1810** Cuming *Sketches* 61, 340. **1811** Graydon *Memoirs* 361. **1815** TPickering in Cabot *Letters* 563. **1816** Jackson *Correspondence* 6.462: If we cannot obtain it upon just principles, we must make a virtue of necessity. **1816** Ker *Travels* 28. **1820** Simpson *Journal* 121: I . . . made a merit of necessity. a1824 Marshall *Kentucky* 1.215. 1826 Duane *Colombia* 437: Making a merit of necessity. *Oxford* 861-2; Whiting V43.

V28 Virtue is but skin-deep

1788 *Politician* 26: Vartue is but skin deep, as the saying is. Cf. *Oxford* 38: Beauty; Tilley B170. See **B89.**

V29 Virtue is its own reward

1732 Franklin *Papers* 1.245: *Scandal,* like other Virtues, is in part its own Reward. 1734 Belcher *Papers* 2.113: Vertue (but especially religion or true piety) carries its own reward. 1745 *Law Papers* 2.179: Virtue carries its own Reward. 1754 GSaltonstall in *Fitch Papers* 1.64: Cap[t] Whitwell no doubt expects a Reward for his Virtue towards the Spaniards. 1775 GSaltonstall in *Deane Correspondence* 219: To watch six months without reward, save the virtue of so doing. 1778 *Pennsylvania Packet* in *Newspaper Extracts(II)* 2.475. 1779 Lee *Letters* 2.47: Virtue is its own and a very great reward. 1782 AA in *Adams FC* 4.376: But Modest Meritt must be its own Reward. 1782 Freneau *Poems* 2.171, 1783 226. 1786 JAdams in *Warren-Adams Letters* 2.277: The Enthusiasm for Agriculture like Virtue will be its own Reward. 1787 Ledyard *Russian Journey* 182. 1789 Brown *Power* 1.49: Virtue is represented carrying its reward with it. 1792 *Universal Asylum* 9.236: It has often been said. 1794 AChurch in Hamilton *Papers* 17.251: Virtue has not found its reward. 1800 CCarroll in McHenry *Letters* 474. 1804 Brackenridge *Modern* 382: Yet courage is virtue, and is its own reward. 1813 *Adams-Waterhouse Correspondence* 107: Yet Virtue, I firmly believe, is its own reward. 1815 Freneau *Poems(1815)* 1.154: To reap in some exalted sphere, The just rewards of virtue here. c1820 Bernard *Retrospections* 236. 1832 Ames *Nautical* 45-6: Virtue is its own reward is a maxim that might do well enough for the ancients. Barbour 191; *Oxford* 861; TW 392(2).

V30 A Voice (sound) and nothing else

1686 Dunton *Letters* 116: But considering both together you'd wonder at neither, but conclude as one did of the Nightingale,

That she's *Vox et pretera nihil,* a voice and nothing else. 1703 Taylor *Christographia* 404.56: *Vox et praeteria nihil.* 1704 *Penn-Logan Correspondence* 1.274-5: [Latin only]. 1711 Johnston *Papers* 95: A mere Empty title, Vox et preterea nihil. 1754 BNicoll in Johnson *Writings* 4.201: [Latin only]. 1768 Dickinson *Letters* 13: *Vox et praeterea nihil.* Sound and nothing else. 1775 WHDrayton in Gibbes 2.67: [Latin only]. 1775 EHazard in Deane *Correspondence* 212: [Latin only]. 1775 Van Schaack *Letters* 38: [Latin only]. 1777 *New Jersey Gazette* in *Newspaper Extracts(II)* 1.524: The business of the former is a vox et præteria nihil, a mere pensioned sinecure. 1779 Gadsden *Writings* 166: [Latin only]. 1779 DRamsay in Gibbes 3.121: The patriotism of many people is *vox et praeteria nihil.* 1783 Madison *Papers* 6.130: [Latin only]. 1784 Baldwin *Life and Letters* 219: [It] answered the description of the Irishmans owl —*vox et pratera nihil.* 1784 EHazard in *Belknap Papers* 1.378: [Latin only]. 1785 Van Schaack *Letters* 234: [Latin only]. 1789 *Columbian Magazine* 3.364: [Latin only]. 1817 Tyler *Prose* 346: This great stir is *boo et preterea nihit.* 1818 Weems *Letters* 3.238: My complaints, like drum-beating are all a mere vox et praeterea Nihil.

V31 The Voice of the people is the voice of God

1734 Plumstead 236: Thus 'tis that *vox populi est vox Dei.* 1740 *Postscript* in *Colonial Currency* 4.48: By common Consent, he means the *Vox Populi.* 1751 *Appendix* in *Colonial Currency* 4.472: Vox Populi, Vox Dei. 1769 *New York Journal* in *Newspaper Extracts(I)* 7.516: As a great Man and Poet, [Pope] observes on a similar Occasion, "The Voice of the People is, and it is not, the Voice of God. 1774 Andrews *Journal* 377: [Latin only]. 1781 Peters *Connecticut* 105: The *vox populi* established these maxims in New-England. 1782 JThaxter in *Adams FC* 4.311: It will . . . stand as an eternal Monument that the Vox Populi is the — . 1782 JWebb in Webb *Correspondence* 2.421: Indeed the *vox populi* was finely in my favor.

1787 Adams *Works* 4.404: The voice of the people is the voice of God, which the voice of a prince is not. 1787 *Columbian Magazine* 1.819: Horace was not of opinion that *vox populi* was *vox Dei*. 1787 Hamilton *Papers* 4.185: [Latin only]. a1788 Jones *History* 1.257: [Latin only]. 1789 *Columbian Magazine* 3.364: *Vox populi, vox Dei,* is a common saying: that is, what all the world think, must be right. 1789 O Wolcott, S^r., in Gibbs *Memoirs* 1.33: [Latin only]. 1790 Maclay *Journal* 346: [Latin only]. 1794 Tyler *Prose* 292: Deriding the sacred vox populi. 1795 Freneau *Poems* 3.123: [Latin only]. 1796 Ames *Letters* 1.204: *Vox populi* is, you know, always *vox sapientiae*. 1797 Boucher *View* iv: He appears . . . to think that the Vox Populi is truly Vox Dei. 1797 Graham *Vermont* 137: *Robinson* got into the chair, but not by the *vox populi*. 1801 *Echo* 289: *Vox populi* through ether rings And brings to pass surprising things. 1802 Chester *Federalism* 13: That damned motto *"vox populi suprema lex,"* 39: VOX POPULI was preached up by you a few years ago as VOX DEI. 1802 Chipman *Writings* 144: The voice of the people . . . is sometimes called the voice of God. 1803 Ames *Letters* 1.328: [Latin only]. 1803 Austin *Constitutional* 172: [Latin only]. 1806 *Weekly* 1.84: [Latin only]. 1808 Hitchcock *Poetical Dictionary* 75: The voice of the people is the voice of God. 1811 Graydon *Memoirs* 348: [Latin only]. 1813 Adams *Writings* 4.447: One of the English poets says "the People's voice is odd, It *is* and it *is not* the voice of God. 1814 Littell *Festoons* 70: Vox Populi Vox Dei. I believe the maxim to be *physically* true, but I never did, and never will believe it to be *morally* true. 1816 WEdwards in *Ruffin Papers* 1.185: [Latin only]. 1826 Audubon *1826 Journal* 119: *La voie* [*for* voix] *du peuple est la voie de Dieu*. 1832 Ames *Nautical* 197: "Vox populi vox Dei," the voice of the people is the voice of God. *Oxford* 862; Whiting V54.

W

W1 As thin as a Wafer

1729 ABeale in *Letters from Hudson Bay* 141: As thin as a wafer. **1785** Hunter *Quebec* 28: A bark canoe as thin as a wafer. TW 393.

W2 As the Wages are, such is the work

1644 Williams *Writings* 3.161: Now as the *wages* are, such is the *worke*. Lean 4.48; Tilley W3.

W3 To cut up the Waistcoat to mend the breeches

1743 Stephens *Journal(II)* 1.158: This way of proceeding appears to me somewhat like a Mans cutting up his Waste Coat to mend his Breeches. See **S162.**

W4 Wait and see

1745 Parkman *Diary* 72.382: Wait and see. *Oxford* 863; Partridge 935.

W5 To have a Waiter's post

1738 Stephens *Journal(I)* 1.96: He never would explain himself to me farther, than to say shortly, or in a little Time: From whence I found I had a Waiter's Post.

W6 To take a Walk up Ladder Lane

1830 Ames *Mariner's* 228: As for hanging, or as the sailors call it, "taking a walk up Ladder lane, and down Hemp street." TW 212. Cf. *Oxford* 308; Tilley L27.

W7 We must Walk before we can run

1794 *Washington *Writings* 33.438: We must walk as other countries have done before we can run. Cf. *Oxford* 120, 262; Whiting C202.

W8 As pale as a white Wall

1777 Smith *Memoirs(II)* 222: Who was as pale as a White Wall till it was over. Whiting W12.

W9 As white as the Wall

1775 Freneau *Poems* 1.132: He's as white as the wall.

W10 Bare Walls make giddy housewives

1685 Dunton *Letters* 11: Our Landlady was resolv'd to cross the Proverb, for tho' we had scarce any thing but bare walls, she was no giddy Housewife, but went more neat and lite in her patch't cloaths than lazy slatterns in their silks and sattins. **1704** Knight *Journal* 24: To the crossing the Old Proverb, that bare walls make giddy hows-wifes. **1796** Barton *Disappointment* 92: Remember . . . that bare walls make but giddy housewives. *Oxford* 29; Tilley W18.

W11 To go (*etc.*) to the Wall

1622 *Mourt's Relation* 152: Even the most wise, sober, and discreet men, goe often to the wall. **1778** Lee(W) *Letters* 2.385: The British Ministry are now fairly pushed to the wall. **1783** Freneau *Poems* 2.212: When loaded with laurels—they go to the wall, **1786** 303: Tho he went to the wall With his project and all. **1792** RKing in Hamilton *Papers* 12.21: He must go to the wall. **1794** Ames *Letters* 1.135: It is driving us to the wall. ?**1797** Freneau *Poems* 3.187. **1804** Brackenridge *Modern* 420. **1807** *Salmagundi* 226. **1811** Taggart *Letters* 370. **1831** Sec. Branch in Jackson *Correspondence*

4.280: I have been driven to the wall. TW 393(2); Whiting W21. See **W77**.

W12   Walls have ears

1791 S.P.L. *Thoughts* 167: Stone walls have ears. **1841** Smith *Letters* 383: "Walls," it is proverbially said, "have ears." *Oxford* 864; TW 393(1).

W13   The wooden **Walls** of Britain (England)

1702 Mather *Magnalia* 1.226: Such floating and stately castles, those "wooden walls of Great Britain." **1776** Sargent *Loyalist* 62: Britain's wooden walls defend us. **1782** Rush *Letters* 1.275: "The wooden walls of Britain" is the second toast at every foxhunter's table in England. **1796** Cobbett *Porcupine* 4.37: I had heard of the wooden walls of Old England. **1799** Barlow *Works* 1.383: It is dishonorable to make use of wooden walls and floating batteries. **1805** Dow *Journal* 261: The British appear to me to lie under an infatuation as it relates to their "wooden walls". Lean 3.339: *Oxford* 223.

W14   Wall-flowers

1814 *Port Folio* 3NS 3.256: They [unhappy females] received the name of *wall-flowers.* TW 393.

W15   Straight **Wands** appear crooked in riverlets

c1700 Taylor *Poems* 435: Straite Wands appeare Crook't in, and out, in running rivlets Clear. *Oxford* 778: Stick; Tilley S850.

W16   For **Want** of a nail the shoe is lost, *etc.*

1752 Franklin *PR* 4.248: For want of a Nail the Shoe is lost; for want of a Shoe, the Horse is lost; for want of a Horse the Rider is lost, **1758** *WW* 344. **1770** Ames *Almanacs* 412: A little neglect may breed a great mischief, for want of a nail the shoe was lost, for want of a shoe the horse was lost, for want of a horse the rider was lost, being overtaken by the enemy, all for the want of a horse-shoe nail. **1819** *Cary Letters* 236: And so . . . "All for want of a horseshoe nail a man's life was lost," which you know ancient records testify. Barbour 126(1); *Ox-*

ford 865; TW 256(8); Tilley W29. Cf. Whiting T113. See **N38**.

W17   Want is the mother of industry (care)

1765 Timberlake *Memoirs* 99: Want is said to be the mother of industry. **1766** Ames *Almanacs* 376: Want prompts the wit, and first gave birth to arts. **1776** Carter *Diary* 2.1048: But the old saying is: Want is the Mother of Care. Cf. *Oxford* 642: Poverty; Tilley P527. See **N23**.

W18   The **Want** of a thing makes the worth of it

1720 JColman *Distressed State* in *Colonial Currency* 2.69: It is a Maxim in Trade, *The Want of a Thing makes the worth of it.* *Oxford* 922; Tilley W924. See **G117, V5, 6, 7**.

W19   Want of care does more damage than want of knowledge

1746 Franklin *PR* 3.64: Want of Care does us more Damage than Want of Knowledge, **1758** *WW* 344.

W20   Fiercer **War**, sooner peace

1820 Wright *Views* 247: "Fiercer war, sooner peace" says a vulgar proverb, which, perhaps, you will call me vulgar for quoting.

W21   He who makes a good **War** makes a good peace

1810 *Port Folio* 2NS 3.313: He who makes a good war makes a good peace. *Oxford* 502; Tilley W42.

W22   In **War** beware of repeating a mistake

1811 Graydon *Memoirs* 192: But *in bello non licet bis errare,* —we should beware of repeating a mistake in war. *Oxford* 866; Tilley W43.

W23   To carry the **War** into the enemy's country (Africa)

1783 *American Wanderer* 104: I am delighted to see him carry the war into the enemy's country! 121. **1827** Jackson *Correspondence* 3.370: The war is now in africa, and we must strengthen Judge White who is refered to, **1828** 6.498: We shall "carry the War into Africa," **1831** 4.280: I . . . will carry the war into the enemy's territory. **1848** Cooper *Letters* 5.314: He . . . is for carrying the war into the enemy's country. TW 394(2).

W24 Wars bring scars

1745 Franklin *PR* 3.5: Wars bring scars. *Oxford* 868; Tilley W59.

W25 War's chance (fortune, *etc.*) is uncertain (*varied*)

1740 Stephens *Journal(I)* 1.614: This is certainly an unhappy Accident, not more however than the Chance of War often produces. **1757** *Johnson Papers* 9.816: This is the Fortune of War . . . let it not discourage you in the least. **1757** JRawlings in *MHM* 10(1915) 1: Do not bewail your misfortune, as its the fortune of war. **1762** Evans *Poems* 57: See the sad chance of all-destructive war. **1763** Griffith *Journal* 77: It is the fortune of war, although it is ours to day, it may be yours tomorrow. **1773** JWentworth in *Belknap Papers* 3.46: Yet the event of war is precarious. **1775** Curwen *Journal* 1.61: The events of war are uncertain, 92. **1775** BFranklin in *Naval Documents* 3.72: The events of War are always uncertain. **1775** Washington *Writings* 3.519: We know not what the Chance of War may be. **1776** JA in *Adams FC* 1.348: The Events of War are uncertain. **1776** *Clinton Papers* 1.241: It would be unreasonable to expect the chance of war always in our favour. **1776** RMorris in Deane *Papers* 1.138: But the fortunes of war being ever uncertain, God only knows what may be the event. **1776** RVarick in Kirkland *Letters* 2.26: The Fate of War is uncertain. It's blind as Chance. **1776** *Washington *Writings* 5.64: The events of war are exceedingly doubtful. **1777** JA in *Adams FC* 2.338: The Events of War are uncertain. **1777** TTilghman in *Thomson Papers* 425: Before the Fortune of War would have thrown an equal number . . . into our hands. **1777** HWinthrop in *Warren-Adams Letters* 2.452: The Events of Battles are so Precarious. **1777** Washington *Writings* 7.214: Those whom the fortune of War may chance to throw into my Hands, 236, 8.417. **1777** Webb *Correspondence* 3.245: The fortune of War is very uncertain. **1778** JAdams in *Warren-Adams Letters* 2.38: The Events of War are

always uncertain. **1778** Hopkinson *Miscellaneous Essays* 3(part 2) 179: Always uncertain is the fate Of war and enterprises great. **1779** *Beekman Papers* 3.1349: This is the fortin of War. **1779** Clay *Letters* 140: The chance of War is uncertain. **1779** CPinckney in Moultrie *Memoirs* 1.361: A common event of the pro and con in the fortune of war. **1780** JA in *Adams FC* 3.281: The Events of Politicks are not less uncertain than those of War. **1780** Franklin *Writings* 8.165: The Fortune of War, which is daily changing. **1781** JTrumbull, Jr., in *Trumbull Papers* 4.280: The events of war are very uncertain . . . the issue is in the hand of Providence. **1781** JWarren in Massachusetts Historical Society, *Proceedings* 65 (1932-36) 259: Various have been the fortunes of war in the South. **1781** *Washington *Writings* 21.471: The chances of War are various, **1782** 24.37: The events of War are uncertain. **a1788** Jones *History* 1.44: The events of war are uncertain. **1794** Wayne *Correspondence* 350: The fortuitious events of War are very uncertain. **1812** *Journal of Two Cruises* 123: It is the fortune of war. **1813** JQAdams in American Antiquarian Society, *Proceedings* NS 23 (1913) 157: The Fortune of War will maintain its supremacy and . . . will favour sometimes one side and sometimes the other. **1813** JHeaton in Knopf *War of 1812* 3.218: Whatever the fortune of War might have brought forth. **a1815** Freneau *Poems* 3.306: Of all uncertain things below The chance of war is doubly so. **1815** Brackenridge *Modern* 691: For in war fortune avails much. **1815** Waterhouse *Journal* 67: I am sorry, very sorry, indeed; it is *le fortune de guerre*. **1822** Stansbury *Pedestrian* 138: But such is the fortune of war. **1832** Barney *Memoir* 86: Such is the fortune of war. **1840** ERWare in *New England Merchants* 291: Now that I want a little [wine] for my arrowroot, there is none—such is the fortune of war [no war involved]. Tilley C223; Whiting C141, F533, W39. See **F276.**

W26 As fractious as a **Wasp**

1818 AAdams in Massachusetts Historical Society, *Proceedings* 66(1936-41) 148:

Little Abbe . . . has been as fractious as a wasp. Cf. *Oxford* 14; Whiting W50, 52.

W27 Wilful **Waste** makes woeful want

1767 Ames *Almanacs* 387: Wilful waste makes woful want. Barbour 193; *Oxford* 869; TW 394.

W28 **Watch** and ward

1637 Wheelwright *Writings* 161: He . . . setteth watch & ward. **1689** A Brackett in *Baxter Manuscripts* 6.493: [We are] allmost worne out wth watching & warding, **1690** 5.81: We keep a continuall Watch & Ward night & day. **1755** Davis *Colonial Virginia Satirist* 24: Let such who are so well prepar'd fall on, whilst I keep watch & ward. Lean 2.938; Whiting W57.

W29 As unstable as **Water**

1775 Boucher *View* 459: He would be *unstable as water*. **1781** AA in *Adams FC* 4.258: I know the voice of Fame to be . . . unstable as water. **1789** EHazard in *Belknap Papers* 2.101. **1791** Asbury *Letters* 3.100. **1795** JMarrant in Porter *Negro Writing* 430: Unstable as water, I returned to town. **1805** Asbury *Journal* 2.487. **1816** Adams *Writings* 6.41. *Oxford* 855; Whiting W59.

W30 As weak as **Water**

1653 Wigglesworth *Diary* 13: I have no might . . . weak as water. **1734** Belcher *Papers* 2.166: The old Toper is weaker than water boil'd and grown cool again. **1764** JA in *Adams FC* 1.33. **1778** AMcDougall in *Clinton Papers* 4.245. **1787** RTyler in *Bowdoin Papers* 2.144. **1799** Adams *Works* 9.14. TW 394(5).

W31 As welcome as **Water** in a ship

1652 Williams *Writings* 7.74: Such *temptations* come in as water into a ship, or as *dust* and *diseases* into a sound eye. **1680** Randolph *Letters* 3.61: Welcome now back againe . . . as water in a ship. Lean 2.891; *Oxford* 870; Whiting W62. See **W43.**

W32 As wet as **Water** could make one

1779 Angell *Diary* 62: I got as wet as water would make me, 64, 68. **1790** Maclay(S) *Journal* 37: [We] came to the Lake just as

the first shower was over, as wet as water could make us. Cf. Barbour 194(20); Taylor *Comparisons* 86.

W33 Can pure **Water** spring from a muddy fountain?

1811 VHorne in Knopf *War of 1812* 3.16: Can pure water spring from a muddy fountain? Cf. Barbour 193(7).

W34 Dirty **Water** will quench fire

1796 Cobbett *Porcupine* 4.121: *Dirty water will quench fire.* Barbour 193(2); *Oxford* 283; TW 394(7); Whiting W64.

W35 In fleeing from the **Water** do not run into the fire

1818 Evans *Pedestrious* 167: In fleeing from the water, let us not run into the fire. See **S78, 280.**

W36 (Not) to hold **Water**

1682 Claypoole *Letter Book* 98: That will not hold water. **1822** Adams *Writings* 7.291: Not one of them, to use an elegant phrase of the *Richmond Enquirer, will hold water.* **1839** Cooper *Letters* 3.386: My account will hold water. Barbour 194(13); TW 394(9).

W37 Standing **Waters** are most apt to corrupt

1677 Hubbard *Indian* 2.254: Standing Waters are most apt to corrupt. Cf. *Oxford* 771; Tilley P465; Whiting W85.

W38 Still (sluggish) **Waters** are deepest

1768 Smith *Works* 2.196: Still and silent waters are ever the deepest. **1821** Knight *Poems* 1.37: As sluggish waters are the deepest. Barbour 193(10); *Oxford* 774; Whiting W70.

W39 Stolen **Waters** are sweet

a1700 Hubbard *New England* 104: Thus stolen waters are sweet, and bread eaten in secret is pleasant. **1772** Boucher *Autobiography* 86: A stolen meal, which so far from being sweet, as a silly proverb pretends it is, is, I am persuaded, always joyless. **1775** Hopkinson *Miscellaneous Essays* 1.43: Stolen waters are sweet—Prov. ix. **1797** Foster *Coquette* 212: The quotation is, that "stolen waters are sweet, and bread eaten in secret is pleasant." **c1825** Tyler *Prose* 145: Well did the wise man say "Stolen waters are sweet." Barbour 193(11); *Oxford* 775-6; Tilley B626; Whiting W71.

W40 To cast **Water** into the sea (*varied*)

1633 EHowe in *Winthrop Papers*(*A*) 3.124: If I should write a volume to this purpose, it were but water, cast into the sea of your aboundant abilities. **1682** Mather *Letters* 9: I do but pour water in the sea when one of my low and dirty spirit goes to revive in you the noble inclinations. **1738** WDouglas *Essay* in *Colonial Currency* 3.246: It is like throwing of Water into the Ocean, making no sensible Alteration. *Oxford* 870; Whiting W80.

W41 To fish in troubled **Waters** (*varied*)

1637 Morton *New English Canaan* 257: And holding it good to fish in trobled waters. **1647** Ward *Simple Cobler* 2: [Satan] loves to fish in royled waters. **1669** Morton *New-Englands Memoriall* 150: [Some] hoping to fish better in troubled waters, when their bait might be taken in, and the hook not easily discerned. **1676** Williams *Writings* 5.276: The Devil is a *Fisher* longing for troubled and bloody waters. **1677** WWinthrop in *Winthrop Papers* (*B*) 4.407: He will be sure to follow you as before, thinking tis good fishing in troubled waters. **1691** *Humble Address* in *Andros Tracts* 2.241: *To trouble the Waters to make good Fishing.* **1741** HGold in Johnson *Writings* 3.135: You are guilty of fishing in troubled waters. **1753** *Independent Reflector* 145. **1764** Allen *Extracts* 66. **1766** JParker in Franklin *Papers* 13.494. **1776** Willard *Letters* 266: Fishers in troubled waters. **1779** Asbury *Journal* 1.305, **1780** 336. **1780** JChalmers in *Aspinwall Papers* 2.794: All those who are not phrentic or fitted to fish in muddy streams. **1781** Pynchon *Diary* 96: They who trouble the waters first have seldom the benefit of fishing. **1782** WGlasscock in *McIntosh Papers* 124. **1782** Paine *American Crisis* 1.227. **1794** PSchuyler in Hamilton *Papers* 15.621. **1797** Boucher *View* xlii: Of course no waters are too much troubled for such anglers to take their chance in. **1799** *Columbian Centinel*

in Buckingham *Specimens* 2.79: Your love for dabbling in troubled waters. **1804** WCunningham in *Adams-Cunningham Letters* 17: He has long angled in the dirty water of democracy. **1805** Asbury *Journal* 2.460. **1809** Weems *Marion* 46: *"The devil,"* said George Whitefield, *"is fond of fishing in muddy waters."* **1815** *Bulger Papers* 105-6. **1827** Jones *Sketches* 2.66. **1831** Pintard *Letters* 3.237: It w^d be indelicate, if not worse, at my period, to fish in troubled waters. *Oxford* 265; Whiting F242.

W42 To keep (get) in hot **Water**

1764 Watts *Letter Book* 315: The Colony will get into boiling Water. **1770** *Johnson Papers* 7.389: He might keep me in hot Water. **1776** Carter *Diary* 2.1027: He has engaged . . . to keep me in hot water this year, according to that Devil's expression. **1778** JWilliams in Deane *Papers* 2.457: I have been in hot water a great while. **1780** Franklin *Writings* 8.113: I have been too long in hot water. **1781** Lee *Papers* 2.213. **1782** Adams *D and A* 3.55: To keep Us in hot Water. **1797** FAmes in Gibbs *Memoirs* 1.498. **1797** Dunlap *Diary* 1.107: [It] only strengthens my opinion that there will be more hot water, if that woman can kindle fuel to boil it. **1809** Irving *History* 1.228-9. **1809** Weems *Marion* 46: The author . . . gets into hot water. **1813** Adams *Works* 6.289: Massachusetts may keep us in hot water. **1822** Weems *Penn* 37, 60. **1827** Pintard *Letters* 2.383: It keeps the College in hot water. **1830** Ames *Mariner's* 249. NED Hot Water 3; TW 395(13).

W43 To need **Water** in one's shoes

1692 Bulkeley *Will* 195: But this also was a mere sham. — We had great need of water in our shoes. *Oxford* 870; Tilley W126. See **W31**.

W44 To take **Water**

1816 Barney *Memoir* 285: We go into Brownsville today, where I mean to *take water,* if possible. Cf. TW 395(18).

W45 To throw cold **Water** on (something) [The following is a selection from 25 occurrences of the phrase].

1741 Belcher *Papers* 2.365: So that I don't

take it, as you do, *throwing cold water on the thing.* **1751** Franklin *Papers* 4.118: And perhaps some Governors . . . may privately throw cold Water on it. **1755** *Johnson Papers* 1.591: To throw Cold Water upon Everry thing. **1760** WFranklin in Franklin *Papers* 9.190: This Matter would have been much more forward had it not been for the cold Water thrown on it. **1782** Jay *Correspondence* 3.7: We ought not, in the common phrase, to throw cold water upon it, 54, **1785** 176: The common phrase is, throw cold water on all such ideas. **1787** Jefferson *Papers* 11.521: He threw cold water on the proposition. **1799** *St. Clair Papers* 2.480: Harrison will throw all the cold water on it he can. **1800** Jefferson *Writings* 10.175-6: [It] I fear will throw cold water on the hopes of the friends of freedom. **1804** Wilson *Letters* xxxiv: I don't want you to throw cold water, as Shakspeare says, on this notion. **1821** Jefferson *Writings* 1.14: A dash of cold water on it here and there. NED Cold water c; TW 395(19).

W46 To throw **Water** on a drowned mouse (rat)

1702 Mather *Magnalia* 1.225: It would be "to throw water upon a drowned mouse." **1797** Callender *Annual Register 1796* 229: To cast water on a drowned mouse has the appearance of ill nature. **1804** Brackenridge *Modern* 350: It would be like throwing water on a dead, or as the proverb is, a drowned rat. *Oxford* 642; Tilley W102.

W47 To trouble the **Waters** (*varied*)

1738 *Georgia Records* 22¹.206: Mr Westley . . . would endeavour . . . to trouble the Waters, that he might glide with less observance. **1784** TPownall in *Bowdoin Papers* 2.31: I love not troubled waters. **1788** JRutledge in Jefferson *Papers* 13.531: England, fond of meddling in troubled waters. **1807** *Austin Papers* 1.131: Hammond is in troubled waters at the Mines. **1822** Adams *Writings* 7.352: Those to whom troubled waters are a delight. TW 395(14). See **W41**.

W48 To watch one's **Waters**

1733 Belcher *Papers* 1.270: It's very well you'll watch Rindge's waters, **1734** 2.39: However I shall watch their waters, & I fancy they'll hardly bring their marks to bear, **1739** 235. NED Water 18c; *Oxford* 483; Whiting W78.

W49 (**Water**) over the dam

1797 JAppleton in American Antiquarian Society, *Proceedings* NS 33(1923) 9: As I said before, so say I now, "It has all gone over the dam." Barbour 193(12). Cf. *Oxford* 870.

W50 **Water seeks** (its) level

1778 GMorris in *Clinton Papers* 3.725: Money it is said and justly is like water always seeking a Level. Barbour 194(15); TW 395(20).

W51 As unstable as the **Waves**

a**1767** Evans *Poems* 10: Their joys unstable as the waves. **1792** Smith *Works* 2.566: They are as unstable as the waves. Cf. TW 395; Whiting F290. See **S80**.

W52 As wild as the **Waves**

1758 Evans *Poems* 5: Wild as the waves. Whiting *NC* 493.

W53 One **Wave** thrusts out another

1713 Wise *Churches* 77: *Imago Imaginem Expellit, Alisq; Alice Succedunt,* for as one Wave thrusts out another, so one Idea another. See **V14.**

W54 The **Waves** do not rise but when the winds blow

1760 Franklin *Papers* 9.91: The waves do not rise but when the winds blow, **1768** 15.3: Prov.

W55 As neat as **Wax**

1791 Dennie *Letters* 77: His wife as the Ladies say is as *neat as wax.* NED Wax *sb.*¹ 3b; Svartengren 219; Partridge 554.

W56 As pliable as **Wax**

1781 Peters *Connecticut* 117: They became as *children weaned,* and pliable as *melted wax.* Oxford 634; Tilley W135.

W57 As soft as **Wax**

1777 Munford *Patriots* 498: Soft as wax. Cf. Whiting W98.

W58 To melt like **Wax**

1730 Plumstead 206: As wax melteth before the fire, so they perish'd at the presence of God. **1763** Griffith *Journal* 15: My heart being melted before the Lord, as wax is melted before the fire. **1768** Eliot *Letters* 423: They will melt like wax before the sun. *Oxford* 524; Whiting W105.

W59 To stick like **Wax**

1801 *Farmers' Museum* 101: I'd stick to you, like wax forever. **1805** Brackenridge *Modern* 623: Who made a war out of a tax, On tea, and stuck to it like wax. **1810** Weems *Letters* 3.25: This book stuck to me like wax. NED Wax *sb.*[1] 3b; TW 395-6(6).

W60 (As neat as) **Waxwork**

1803 Smith *Letters* 43: All neat as wax work. **1821** Pintard *Letters* 2.57: Our castle is quite renovated internally, & quite wax work. TW 396(1).

W61 As plain as the **Way** to market

1748 Franklin *Papers* 3.308: The Way to Wealth, if you desire it, is as plain as the Way to Market.

W62 The farthest (longest) **Way** round is the shortest way home

1762 Watts *Letter Book* 28: The farthest way round according to the old adage may be the nearest way home. **1784** GMorris in Hamilton *Papers* 3.503: The Truth of that old Proverb, "the farthest Way about, is the nearest Way Home." **1789** Dunlap *Darby's Return* 111: As I've often heard the people say, The farthest round is much the shortest way. **1807** Jay *Correspondence* 4.311: My rheumatism and your gout may perhaps carry us home the farthest way round, but not in an easy chair. a**1820** Biddle *Autobiography* 142: The old proverb was brought to my mind, that "the farthest way round was the shortest way home." **1846** Paulding *Letters(II)* 434: The Potatoes arrived . . . *via* New York whither they went I presume in pursuance of the Old Proverb, that "the longest way round is the shortest way home." Barbour 194(6); *Oxford* 245; TW 396(8).

W63 He does not know the **Way** home

1737 Franklin *Drinkers* 2.175: Knows not the way Home.

W64 The middle **Way** is the best

1719 Wise *Letter* in *Colonial Currency* 2.252: *The old saying,* In medio tutissime. **1769** AWard in Ward *Correspondence* 19: It gives me great Concern you studdy So closely; their is a middle Path I Pray you may Walke in. **1776** Adams *D and A* 2.229: A Gentleman from Mass. thinks that a middle Way should be taken. **1776** HGates in Massachusetts Historical Society, *Proceedings* 67(1941-4) 138: The Middle way, the best, we sometimes call, But 'tis in Polliticks no way at all. Whiting W117. See **M130, 144.**

W65 The shortest **Way** is the best way

1728 Byrd *Dividing Line* 54: The shortest way (which in this country is always counted the best). Barbour 194(6); TW 396(9).

W66 There are more **Ways** (to the wood) than one

1651 Williams *Writings* 6.207: [You] know more ways to the wood than one. **1815** Brackenridge *Modern* 769: The ways are more than one, you know. *Oxford* 872; Whiting W121.

W67 To cut both **Ways**

1783 *Washington *Letters* 36.324: It might be made to cut both ways. TW 396(4). See **R161, S551.**

W68 To get under **Way**

1814 Bentley *Diary* 4.274: The Hotel . . . is just beginning & as the phrase is, Getting under way. Colcord 203; NED Way *sb.*[1] 38b.

W69 To go the **Way** of all flesh

1616 *Winthrop Papers(A)* 1.188: She was goeinge the way of all flesh. **1653** WGoodwin in *Winthrop Papers(B)* 2.49: For although death be the way of all flesh. **1673** SWinthrop in *Winthrop Papers(B)* 4.264: But seeing it is yᵉ way of all flesh in theis ages. **1677** Hubbard *Indian* 1.48: *I am now going the Way of all Flesh, or ready to die.* **1743** WBeverley in *W&MCQ* 3(1894) 233:

1777 Carter *Diary* 2.1073. 1788 Freneau *Prose* 176. 1808 ANewell in *Cabot Family* 2.810: I . . . am afraid however the Brig's Bottom is going the way of all flesh, I mean food for worms. 1816 Paulding *Letters(I)* 2.175: He made a bad speculation in hides, and went the way of all flesh now-a-days, (*II*) 2.62. 1829 Pintard *Letters* 3.89: Polly Coutant . . . is going the way of all flesh, of a dropsy in the chest & liver complaint. 1834 Floy *Diary* 79. 1858 Paulding *Letters(II)* 582. *Oxford* 871; TW 396(10).

W70 To go the **Way** of all the earth

1742 Belcher *Papers* 2.442: You say it's thought old Joshua is going the way of all the earth. 1792 Perkins *Diary* 3.145: I am Still alive, when almost the whole of that Body of the first Characters in the Country are gone the way of all the Earth, 1794 302. 1812 *Adams-Waterhouse* 86: We must go the Way of all the Earth. 1812 Baldwin *Letters* 66, 1817 229. 1825 Prince *Journals* 224: My horse quite sick; fear he will "go the way of all the earth." 1829 Jackson *Correspondence* 4.42. 1832 HCampbell in *Ruffin Papers* 2.58. Whiting W122.

W71 To grease the **Way**

1799 JCathcart in *Barbary Wars* 1.322: [A] promise by the way, of Greasing the way. Partridge 351. See **W112.**

W72 To laugh another **Way**

1820 Durand *Life* 74: If they had known . . . they would have laughed another way. See **S196.**

W73 To look one **Way** and row another

1682 J. W. *Letter* 2: In a word, both Teacher and Flock are like Water-men, that look one way and row another. 1686 Dunton *Letters* 70: They seldom speak and mean the same thing, but like Water-men Look one Way, and Row another. 1720 *New News* in *Colonial Currency* 2.130: Who (like *Water-men*) *look one way,* while at the same time they *row the contrary.* 1779 CTufts in *Adams FC* 3.165: The Art of looking one Way and moving another is brought to greater Perfection. 1781 Oliver *Origin* 128: But in that Town [Boston] a Man must look one Way & row another to

get any way a head. 1802 Chester *Federalism* 34: These Waterman politicians, looking one way and rowing another. 1805 Brackenridge *Modern* 614: But as men row one way, and look another, it is not so well calculated to effect the purpose, as indirect attack. 1806 Adams *Memoirs* 1.406: He too has been looking one way and rowing another. 1823 Jefferson *Writings* 15.437: Her government is looking one way and rowing another. 1832 JRandolph in Jackson *Correspondence* 4.429: They all *row* one way, although they look not two, but twenty ways. *Oxford* 484; TW 396(7); Tilley W143.

W74 The **Way** of the world

1709 *Penn-Logan Correspondence* 2.313: Way of the world. 1755 *Washington Writings* 1.139: It is the way of the World. 1762 Franklin *Papers* 10.136: Tho' according to the way of the world, having received a civility, gives one a kind of right to demand another. 1796 Cobbett *Porcupine* 3.265. 1797 Tyler *Prose* 302. 1822 Adams *Writings* 6.27: Such is the way of the world! 1825 Fletcher *Letters* 96: Like the way of the world, as I grow older and perhaps richer, my cares and concerns, and of course troubles, increase. 1828 *Yankee* 288. 1833 Floy *Diary* 10, 1834 98: I have found out something of the ways of the world since my acquaintance with her. Whiting W123.

W75 The **Way** to heaven is alike in every place

1774 Ames *Almanacs* 449: The way to Heaven is in all Places alike. *Oxford* 872; Tilley W171.

W76 The **Way** to heaven is strewed with thorns

1790 Jefferson *Papers* 16.291: The way to heaven, you know, has always been said to be strewed with thorns. Tilley W172.

W77 The **Weakest** must go to the wall

1686 Dunton *Letters* 91: And was in England, so sensible that the Weakest goes to the Wall. 1720 *Letter* in *Colonial Currency* 2.234: The weakest always go by the walls. 1733 Byrd *Journey* 289: But the true reason is, that the weakest must always go to the wall. **1765** Watts *Letter Book* 368: Business is here very languid, the weak must to the Wall. **1782** Freneau *Poems* 2.153, **1809** 3.292: Where the weakest and meekest must go to the wall. **1817** JAdams in *Adams-Jefferson Letters* 2.507: The poor . . . have always gone to the Wall. *Oxford* 873; Whiting W130, See **W11.**

W78 The greatest **Wealth** is contentment with a little

1836 Austin *Literary Papers* 78: The greatest wealth is contentment with a little. *Oxford* 873; Tilley W194. See **L175, M251.**

W79 **Wealth** and content are not always bed-fellows

1749 Franklin *PR* 3.335: Wealth and Content are not always Bed-fellows. See **H77, R72.**

W80 **Wealth** is not his that has it, but his that enjoys it

1736 Franklin *PR* 2.138: Wealth is not his that has it, but his that enjoys it. Tilley W200.

W81 **Wealth** is power

1820 Tudor *Letters* 333: The maxim, that wealth is power, is very widely known. Whiting R121. See **K56, M210.**

W82 **Wealth** makes many friends

1804 Brackenridge *Modern* 397: "For wealth maketh many friends." Barbour 195(3); Whiting R115. Cf. *Oxford* 674; Tilley R103. See **P304.**

W83 The **Wealth** of Peru, *etc.*

1698 Sewall *Diary* 1.487: [He] must needs preach once every week, which he prefered before the Gold and Silver of the West Indies. **1767** Woodmason *Journal* 24-5: [I] would give all the Mines of Peru (if I had them) for a drop of water. **1772** Boucher *Autobiography* 83: The wealth of the Indies would not purchase it. **1774** ESmith in *Adams FC* 1.103: I would not express myself in these Words to him, for the riches of Peru. **1777** ALivingston in *Clinton Papers* 2.237: It is not all the riches of India that would induce me to transact Business under the Government I now am. **1778** AA in

Adams FC 3.23: I would not exchange my Country for the Wealth of the Indies. **1779** DBrodhead in Jefferson *Papers* 3.43: He will ruin the Country had we the Wealth of Potosi to have recourse to. **1795** DAllison in *Blount Papers* 2.568: I can say that even the riches of Peru shall never again tempt me to undergo such another series of fatigue of mind. **1802** Adams(TB) *Letters* 163: For all the wealth of Golconda, I would not take the risk again. **1835** Jackson *Correspondence* 5.347: This my son is more grateful to your dear father than all the wealth of Peru. Whiting G241, 295. Cf. TW 245(2).

W84 To fight one with his own **Weapons**

1778 AA in *Adams FC* 3.6: He has . . . been foiled at his own weapons. **1784** Smith *Diary* 1.13: His own Weapons are turned against him as it happens often to Demagogues. **1799** Carey *Plumb* (3): To hope to overcome a blackguard, you must fight him with his own weapons. **1819** Bentley *Diary* 4.627: Their method of fighting the enemy with his own weapons. **1822** Jackson *Correspondence* 3.165: The right mode is to meet an enemy with his own weapons, **1825** 281, 282, **1828** 403. NED Weapon 2c. Cf. *Oxford* 36; Tilley W204. See **G17.**

W85 Better to **Wear** out than rust out (*varied*)

1702 Mather *Magnalia* 1.276: Resolving rather to wear out with using than with rusting, 370: 'Tis better to be worn out with work, than to be eaten out with rust. **1774** THutchinson, Jr., in Hutchinson *Diary* 1.151: I intend to take care your chaise does not suffer, either by use or rust. **1816** Pintard *Letters* 1.13: It is as well to wear out as rust out, **1817** 48, **1826** 2.258: Better wear out than rust out, **1827** 340: But wear out, not rust out, is my Motto, **1831** 3.308. Barbour 195; *Oxford* 56; TW 397.

W86 As lank as a **Weasel**

1809 Irving *History* 2.92: He arrived . . . lank as a starved weazel. TW 397(4).

W87 As thick as **Weasels** in a hen-yard
1816 Weems *Letters* 3.166: Bible carts had been here as thick as weasels in a hen yard.

W88 As uncertain as the **Weather**
1745 Ames *Almanacs* 179: The Weather is uncertain even to a Proverb — *As fickle as the Wind,* or *as uncertain as the Weather.* **1801** *Port Folio* 1.378: My [Weather's] inconstancy is rendered proverbial. Barbour 195(10). Cf. Whiting *NC* 493(3).

W89 Hanging **Weather**
1815 [Nov. 10] Bentley *Diary* 3.199: The weather lowry, chilly. & what we call hanging weather.

W90 To be under the **Weather**
1827 *Austin Papers* 2.1622: The fredonians is all here rather under the weather. Barbour 195(9); TW 398(1).

W91 To make fair **Weather**
1709 EProut in *Saltonstall Papers* 1.290: They both made very fair weather. **1769** Smith *Memoirs* 1.60: They deserted the Cause of Liberty and aimed to make fair Weather by gradually listing on the Side of Prerogative. **1775** *Deane Correspondence* 290: I am . . . making as fair weather as possible of this transaction, and a painful task it is. **1782** Adams *D and A* 3.98: All is fair Weather — all friendly and good humoured. **1800** Cobbett *Porcupine* 11.219: If making fair weather with men of all religions and all parties be a proof of merit. TW 398(2); Whiting W155.

W92 A **Weather-breeder**
1652 Williams *Writings* 4.432: They say, a *Winters calme* (for then *stormes* are breeding) is as bad as a *Summers storme.* **1751** James MacSparran, *A Letter Book,* ed. Daniel Goodwin (Boston, 1899), 64: A Fine Day, but I fear a weather Breeder, as yᵉ wild Geese flew to Day [Nov. 5]. **1794** Drinker *Journal* 245: The day looked like what is called a weather breeder. **1801** GCabot in King *Life* 4.11: Like the Seaman who calls a *Summer* day in the winter Season a *weather breeder* I look for storms. **1824** Doddridge *Notes* 55: We commonly had an open spell of weather during the lat-

ter part of February, denominated by some *pawwawing days* and by others *weather breeders.* TW 93: Day(20). See **W235.**

W93 (To turn [*etc.*] like) a **Weathercock**
1652 Williams *Writings* 7.168: Turned forward and backward, as the *Weather-cock.* **1781** Adams(A) *Letters* 130: I know the voice of fame to be a mere weather-cock. **1782** WHooper in Iredell *Correspondence* 2.6: Craig again shifted like the weathercock. **1788** Baldwin *Life and Letters* 399: Don't call him Copper, call him Weathercock. **1806** Hitchcock *Works* 128: His ministers . . . Turn, like a weathercock, from saint to sage. **1812** LBond in Knopf *War of 1812* 3.42: A miserable demagogue, a wretched weather Cock. **1821** JGadsden in Jackson *Correspondence* 3.133: Mr. Crawford . . . Ever fluctuating like a weathercock. *Oxford* 875; Whiting W160.

W94 To have the **Weather-gauge** of one
1783 Williams *Penrose* 325: You have had the Weather Gage of us all in this discovery, for certain. NED Gauge 5.

W95 Some are **Weatherwise,** some are otherwise
1735 Franklin *PR* 2.5: Some are weatherwise, some are otherwise. NED Weatherwise.

W96 One **Wedding** creates another (*varied*)
1818 *Cary Letters* 176: I have heard it said that one wedding generally creates another. **1824** *Tales* 2.243: It has been commonly said, that one wedding makes another. **1832** *Ruffin Papers* 2.56: They say . . . that one marriage always brings about another, I have no reason to suppose that you can have any concern in that adage. *Oxford* 875; TW 398(2).

W97 An entering **Wedge**
1761 *Boston Gazette* in *Olden Time* 2.30: A Wedge once enter'd, the Log flies. **1767** JDevotion in Stiles *Itineraries* 460: The Wedge has entered, and I expect Glut upon Glut. **1798** Bentley *Diary* 2.265: The Tabernaclers are making an entring wedge at our part of the town. **1807** Bates *Papers* 1.216: The first contract was an entering

wedge. **1820** Jackson *Correspondence* 3.21: The Missouri question so called . . . will be the entering wedge to seperate the union. NED Wedge 2. Cf. *Oxford* 811.

W98　Ill **Weeds** grow apace

1714 Plumstead 168: How soon will ill weeds spring up and grow apace in the vineyard. **1818** Wright *Views* 14: The old proverb, that "ill weeds grow apace." *Oxford* 401; Whiting W170.

W99　The **Weeds** of vice overgrow the seeds of virtue

1795 Murdock *Triumphs* 14: The greatest danger is, that the rank weeds of vice will overgrow the seeds of virtue. *Oxford* 876; Whiting W174.

W100　Six **Weeks'** sledding in March

1796 Dennie *Lay Preacher* 36: The common phrase of our country, that six weeks' sledding in March may put off the evil day of furrowing the fields. **1799** HJackson in *Bingham's Maine* 2.956: It will make good the old saying, six weeks sleding in March. **1818** Bentley *Diary* 4.505: We have an old saying, 6 weeks sledding in March. DA sledding 1b. Cf. Whiting M373.

W101　Not the **Weight** of a straw

1800 Hamilton *Law Papers* 1.721: It dont bear the weight of a single straw with me. **1806** Adams *Memoirs* 1.380: They never had on my mind . . . the weight of a straw, **1814** *Writings* 5.58: Not that I imagine that the place of negotiation will have the weight of a straw upon its result.

W102　To be worth one's **Weight** in gold, *etc.*

1699 Chalkley *Journal* 29: *I was worth my Weight in Gold.* **1754** Adams *Earliest Diary* 52: Belles Lettres which are worth their weight in gold, **1775** *Adams-Warren Letters* 1.93: Your . . . Letter . . . is worth its Weight in Gold. **1775** PTimothy in *Naval Documents* 1.1135: That man is worth his Weight in Diamonds. **1781** Peters *Connecticut* 192. **1789** Ames *Letters* 1.46: Dawes . . . seemed to be worth his weight in money. **1795** Murdock *Triumphs* 24. **1797** WVMurray in McHenry *Letters* 246: I

would give their weight in gold for late papers. **c1825** Tyler *Prose* 48. **1833** Floy *Diary* 19: If it could not be replaced I would not take for it its weight in gold, **1835** 151. Barbour 196(2); *Oxford* 922; Whiting W178.

W103　When the **Well** is dry we know the worth of water

1746 Franklin *PR* 3.62: When the Well's dry, we know the Worth of Water, **1758** *WW* 346. Barbour 194: Water(19); *Oxford* 435: Know; Tilley W922; Whiting *NC*: Water(14). See **G117, V5, 6, 7, W18.**

W104　To let **Well-enough** alone

1833 Jackson *Correspondence* 5.72: Therefore it is, that I let well enough alone, **1844** 6.265: And stated the old adage of letting "well enough alone." Barbour 196; *Oxford* 453; TW 399(1).

W105　As long as a **Welsh** pedigree

1809 Irving *History* 2.85: None of which but was as long as a Welsh pedigree or a plea in chancery. *Oxford* 479; Tilley P176.

W106　Without **Welt** or guard

1648 WBradford *Dialogue* in Alexander Young, *Chronicles of the Pilgrim Fathers* (Boston, 1841) 447: Yet the man was a plain countryman, without either welt or guard, (as the proverb is). *Oxford* 880; Tilley W274.

W107　Did you ever see a **Whale?**

1832 Ames *Nautical* 79-80: I recollect when a boy very frequently hearing old people interrupt a tough story with "Darby, did you ever see a whale?" thereby intimating that the existence of that animal, now so common and well known, was considered too absurd an idea to be entitled to a place in a serious treatise upon zoology. Cf. NED Whale 5; Partridge 947.

W108　No one can beat him but **Whalley,** Goffe, or the Devil

1807 Janson *Stranger* 53: Hence it became proverbial in New England, in speaking of a champion, to say, that no one can beat him but Whalley, Goffe, or the Devil. See **G101.**

W109 To know **What's** what

1820 *Fudge Family* 14: They know not *what's what*. Whiting W204.

W110 To separate the **Wheat** from the tares (chaff)

1776 *Washington *Writings* 5.92: No time can be misspent that is employed in seperating the Wheat from the Tares. **1777** JA in *Adams FC* 2.298: The final Seperation of the Wheat from the Chaff, the Ore from the Dross. **1795** Hamilton *Works* 10.89: I pray you . . . separate the *Wheat* from the *Chaff*. **1804** Baldwin *Life and Letters* 344: He is in the habit of separating the wheat from the chaff. **1805** Wirt *Letters* 1.138: Whose just minds readily ascertain the difference between bullion and chaff. **1810** Adams *Lectures* 1.203: The art . . . of selecting the wheat from the tares. **1813** TJefferson in *Adams-Jefferson Letters* 2.388: The . . . separation . . . of the wheat from the chaff. TW 399(3); Whiting C428, W205. Cf. Tilley W282. See **T25.**

W111 A fifth **Wheel** to a coach (wagon)

1770 *Johnson Papers* 7.653: Ye Ministers, who Seem to Me to know No More of the Mater, then they wold the use of a fifth wheel to a Coach. **1793** Read *Correspondence* 548: A fourth judge . . . may be considered like unto a fifth wheel to a coach. **1801** *Echo* 288. **1803** Davis *Travels* 429-30. **1816** Jefferson *Writings* 14.434: [He] is of no more account than the fifth wheel of a coach, **1816** 15.34: His Council . . . at best but a fifth wheel to a wagon. **1841** Hone *Diary* 2.553: Mr. Tyler was a sort of adjunct to the administration, a kind of fifth wheel to the political coach. Barbour 197 (1); *Oxford* 255: Whiting W206.

W112 To grease (oil) the **Wheels**

1677 Hubbard *Indian* 1.137: Things went on so heavily for Want of well oyling the Wheels. **1732** Belcher *Papers* 1.146: The Collector says 100 guineas shall not be wanting to grease the wheels. **1768** Woodmason *Journal* 43: Those People know how to grease Wheels to make them turn. *Oxford* 332; TW 400(2); Tilley W288. See **W71.**

W113 To stop the **Wheels** of government

1811 Graydon *Memoirs* 390: Or, in the proverbial phrase. "to stop the wheels of government."

W114 A **Wheel** (wheels) within (a) wheel (wheels)

1775 EMusgrove in Gibbes 2.203: There is a wheel within a wheel. **1778** AScammell in Sullivan *Letters* 2.33: The Different Directions of wheels within wheels, must necessarily clash with each other. **1780** AA in *Adams FC* 3.377: We have so many wheels within wheels. a**1788** Jones *History* 1.145: It is a common saying that there are wheels within wheels. **1794** Paine *Age of Reason* 1.565: A wheel within a wheel (which, as a figure, has always been understood to signify political contrivance). **1805** Sewall *Parody* 31: There's . . . "a wheel within a wheel." **1807** *Salmagundi* 152: Those complicated pieces of mechanism where there is a "wheel within a wheel." **1809** WCunningham in *Adams-Cunningham Letters* 184: This system of "a wheel within a wheel." *Oxford* 882; TW 400(4).

W115 The worst **Wheel** of the cart makes the most noise

1737 Franklin *PR* 2.169: The worst wheel of the cart makes the most noise. Barbour 197(4); *Oxford* 921; Whiting W207. See **P130.**

W116 As drunk as a **Wheelbarrow**

1737 Franklin *Drinkers* 2.174: He's Drunk as a Wheelbarrow. *Oxford* 206; Tilley W290.

W117 Another **Whet** at the ram

1815 Brackenridge *Modern* 720: But when I used the words, "Once more to the breach," . . . it was as much as to say, "another whet at the ram." Cf. NED Ram *sb.*[1] 3.

W118 (To deserve the) **Whetstone**

a**1716** Mather *Letters* 138: The pleasant mention of the whetstone on the occasion obliged the gentleman to explain himself. *Oxford* 882-3; Whiting W216.

W119 To look like a blue leather **Whetstone**
a1811 Henry *Account* 36: Johnny, you look like a blue leather whet stone. Svartengren 251. Cf. NED Blue *a* 3. See **B232, D118.**

W120 A **Whetstone** sharpens while itself is blunt
1734 Franklin *PR* 1.357: Thus like the whetstone, many Men are wont To sharpen others while themselves are blunt. *Oxford* 883; Whiting W217.

W121 Worth but a **Whiffle**
1809 Fessenden *Pills* 103: Our freedom . . . will be worth but a whiffle. Cf. NED Whiffle 1.

W122 A **Whig** can smell a turd, *etc.*
1779 Curwen *Journal* 2.529: The description of a whig as distinguished from a tory . . . "a Whig can smell a turd at a distance, a Tory not till his nose is in it."

W123 As welcome as a **Whip** to a fool's back
1680 Randolph *Letters* 3.61: Welcome now back againe; as is the whip To a fooles back. Cf. *Oxford* 883; Tilley W305.

W124 To be under the **Whip**
1815 Asbury *Journal* 2.464: The Baptists are under the whip.

W125 To go **Whip** and cut
1807 *Salmagundi* 389: And away he goes whip and cut, until he either runs down his game, or runs himself out of breath.

W126 Under (with) **Whip** and spur
1795 DAllison in *Blount Papers* 2.611: For believe me I am as hard pushed as possible under whip & spur. 1810 Jefferson *Writings* 10.247: The new appointments which Mr. A. crowded in with whip and spur. NED Whip 1d. Cf. *Oxford* 768; Tilley S790.

W127 To have the **Whip-row**
1750 *Massachusetts* in *Colonial Currency* 4.440: The . . . Sharpers had two Whip Rows in this Game. 1771 *Trial of Atticus* 46: You have the whip-row of him, as the Lawyers sometimes express it. Cf. *Oxford* 884; Tilley W307.

W128 To run like a **Whirligig**
1790 Maclay *Journal* 335: His tongue ran like a whirligig. NED Whirligig 5.

W129 To ride the **Whirlwind**
1801 WPolk in *Blount Papers* 3.470: Some of your Democratic friends who now ride the whirlwind & direct its course. NED Whirlwind 2. Cf. Whiting W334.

W130 To one's **Whiskers**
c1720 Byrd *Another Secret Diary* 275: He . . . tells 'em their Faults to their wiskers that they may parry the thrust as well as they can. Cf. Whiting B115.

W131 As clean as a **Whistle**
1788 *Politician* 28: You shou'd be shav'd as clean as a whistle. 1789 Brown *Better* 25 [It] turn'd the sleigh bottom up, as clean as a whistle. Barbour 197-8(1); *Oxford* 125; Svartengren 321; TW 400(1).

W132 As clear as a **Whistle**
1807 *Salmagundi* 83: Make a book as clear as a whistle. TW 400(2).

W133 To pay too dear for one's **Whistle**
1779 Franklin *Writings* 7.414-6: [F.'s story of his whistle]. 1809 Lindsley *Love* 44: This is paying cursed dear for a woman's whistle and after all not to get it. 1813 JRandolph in Quincy *JQuincy* 339: No State in the Confederacy has paid so dearly for the *war whistle* as the Ancient Dominion. 1814 *Port Folio* 3NS 4.539: A man is unwise who purchases pleasure too dear, or as Franklin expresses it, who pays too much for his whistle. 1815 Waterhouse *Journal* 100: "We paid dear for our whistle." 1816 CChester in Vanderpoel *Chronicles* 154: I thought I should have frozen before I undressed myself, and thus did I pay for my whistle. 1819 Noah *Travels* 340: This, as Dr. Franklin would say, "was paying dear for the whistle." 1833 Jackson *Correspondence* 5.222: To feed 400 a year for 86 killing hoggs is paying too dear for the whistle. 1845 Paulding *Letters(II)* 380: We are perpetually paying too much for the whistle. Barbour 198(4); *Oxford* 615; TW 401(6).

W134   To wet one's Whistle

1723 *New-England Courant* 87 (1.1): For having lately wet my Whistle With generous Wine. **1793** JMacdonell in Gates *Five Fur Traders* 101: It being customary . . . to wet the whistle of every Indian they met. **1819** Faux *Memorable Days* 1.175: With a brown earthen jug of cold water before them, for occasionally wetting their whistles. **1826** WBiglow in Buckingham *Specimens* 2.289: In the Hall of the News-room, their whistles to wet. *Oxford* 881; Whiting W225. See **C192, E139.**

W135   To go Whistle (for one's money)

1717 TLechmere in *Winthrop Papers(B)* 6.377: Don Belleshazar may go whistle. **1804** *New England Merchants* 18: And left the Inhabitants to whistle for their money. **1816** Paulding *Letters(I)* 2.175: The rest of the creditors whistled for their money. **1842** Hone *Diary* 2.586: And as for the rest "they might go whistle." *Oxford* 884; Whiting W226. See **H277.**

W136   To level at (hit) the White

1637 Williams *Writings* 6.49: My . . . firm persuasion of your leveling at the highest white, **1638** in *Winthrop Papers(A)* 4.2: The white which a Speech or Person levells at, **1644** 3.346: I beleeve that neither one nor t'other hit the white, yet I beleeve the *Papists* arrowes fall the nearest to it. NED White *sb.* 5, 6.

W137   White soon descries a soil

1786 Winslow *Broadside* 195: As lily white will soon descry a soil. Cf. *Oxford* 225: Ermine. See **S379.**

W138   To be White-livered

1797 Cobbett *Porcupine* 6.91: Making the "white livered" Peter Porcupine run away. **1806** Fessenden *Modern Philosopher* 205: Many white-livered dastards . . . have shown a disposition to remain neuter. Whiting W232.

W139   To be White-washed

1778 WMalcom in *Clinton Papers* 4.301: And then give them a discharge and certificate that they are white wash'd. NED Whitewash *v.* 2, Whitewashed 2.

W140   As tough as Whitleather

1785 Franklin *Writings* 9.401: Their flesh [is] tough and hard as whitleather. *Oxford* 834; Svartengren 264; TW 401. See **L88.**

W141   As solemn as a Whore at a christening

1754 WJohnson, Jr., in Johnson *Writings* 1.200: [He] received the Sacrament . . . with all the solemnity I suppose a whore would put on at a christening. Svartengren 67: demure. Cf. Barbour 198(3).

W142   Cry Whore first

1690 Palmer *Account* in *Andros Tracts* 1.53: Only you *cry Whore first.* **1705** Ingles *Reply* 25: T'is a fine thing to cry where [*for* whore] first, 27. **1771** Carter *Diary* 2.618: I told him he knew the art of crying whore first. *Oxford* 98-9; Tilley W319. See **T43.**

W143   The Why(s) and wherefore(s)

1763 Franklin *Papers* 1.304: I . . . know neither why nor wherefore. **1784** Smith *Journal and Correspondence* 1.8: I have not learnt the why and the wherefore. **1798** Adams *New Letters* 137. **c1800** Dennie *Lay Preacher* 169: The askers of whys and wherefores. **1804** Wirt *Letters* 1.112. **1806** Dunlap *Diary* 2.366. **1806** Fessenden *Modern Philosopher* 148: But Gifford comes, with why and wherefore And what the devil are you there for. **1809** Adams(A) *Letters* 401-2: The whys and the wherefores. **1815** RPeters in Jay *Correspondence* 4.383. **1816** Adams *Writings* 6.111: The why and wherefore of all things. **1816** Fidfaddy *Adventures* 44. **1817** Wirt *Letters* 2.29: I . . . had an explanation . . . of the whys and the wherefores. **c1825** Tyler *Prose* 168. **1827** Longfellow *Letters* 1.235: They will believe everything a priest tells them to, without asking why or wherefore. **1828** *Yankee* 175: The wherefore and the why of all this uproar. **1837** Jackson *Correspondence* 5.497: But the Whys, and the Wherefores, I cannot understand. **1841** Cooper *Letters* 4.150: Charlotte writes to Mary, and will tell her the whys and wherefores. Whiting W236.

W144 The **Wicked** flee when no man pursues

1771 *Trial of Atticus* 75: We can adopt the sacred passage, the *wicked flee when no man pursueth.* 1777 Fitch *New-York Diary* 156: As those called Torys, who have been frequently Observed to "Flee when none persue." 1781 Oliver *Origin* 120: Their Flight confirmed that observation made by *Solomon,* viz. *the wicked fleeth when no Man pursueth.* 1814 Palmer *Diary* 232: The wicked flee when none pursue. Barbour 198; Tilley W333; Whiting M326. See **C279, S533.**

W145 He who marries a **Widow,** *etc.*

1809 *Port Folio* 2NS 2.430: He who marries a widow will have a dead man's head often thrown into his dish. *Oxford* 514; Whiting M294. See **D197.**

W146 A **Widow** bewitched

1812 *Kennon Letters* 33.277: She is now a widow bewitched once more; for her husband is at sea. NED Widow 1d.

W147 Choose your **Wife** on Saturday

1737 Franklin *PR* 2.170: If you want a neat wife, chuse her on a Saturday. 1809 *Port Folio* 2NS 2.430: Choose your wife on a Saturday, not on a Sunday. *Oxford* 122; Tilley W378.

W148 A good **Wife** and health is a man's best wealth

1746 Franklin *PR* 3.62: A good Wife and Health, Is a Man's best Wealth. *Oxford* 326. See **F278, H75.**

W149 He that takes a **Wife** takes care

1736 Franklin *PR* 2.139: He that takes a wife, takes care. Tilley W356. Cf. *Oxford* 888. See **W357.**

W150 If you take a **Wife** from hell she will bring you back

1793 Campbell *Travels* 283: It is said if you take a wife from hell, she will bring you back if she can.

W151 Ne'er take a **Wife,** *etc.*

1733 Franklin *PR* 1.312: Ne'er take a wife till thou hast a house (and a fire) to put her in. *Oxford* 389: House.

W152 Old **Wives'** tales (*varied*)

1634 Wood *New-England* 30: Th'ominous Screech-Owle, Who tells as old wives say, disasters foule. 1650 Bradstreet *Works* 166: These are no old-wives tales, but this is truth. 1712 Mather *Letters* 114: Nor have we any but old wives' fables concerning the finding of any except a bird or so. 1713 Chalkley *Forcing* 402: Beware of filthy Dreams, and old Wives Fables. 1738 Stephens *Journal(I)* 1.190: But as this News came by a Woman, we hoped it might prove an old Woman's Story only. 1757 *Johnson Papers* 9.865: You believe every old Womans Story. 1767 Washington *Diaries* 1.235: Is not this an old woman's story? 1796 Dennie *Lay Preacher* 19: An old wives fable, 47. 1807 Janson *Stranger* 53: Interspersed with old women's tales. *Oxford* 593; Whiting W244.

W153 Scolding **Wives** and smoky houses

1795 Ames *Letters* 1.160: I admit the right a man has to seek an election, in case of a scolding wife, a smoky house, or a host of duns—three pleasant reasons. c1800 Tyler *Island* 6: Let all Citizens who are blest with smoaky houses or scolding wives proceed to the City Gates. 1819 Cobbett *Year's* 195: Even amongst the lowest of the people, you seldom hear of that torment, which the old proverb makes the twin of a smoky house. 1847 Paulding *Letters(II)* 462: I believe if I were put to it, I could stand scolding wives and Smoky Chimneys. Lean 4.161; *Oxford* 817; TW 402(1); Whiting T187.

W154 To hunt out a **Wife** as one goes to Smithfield for a horse

1775 Paine *Reflections* 2.1118: These hunt out a wife as they go to *Smithfield* for a horse. *Oxford* 880: Westminster; Tilley W276. See **S259.**

W155 A **Wife** is seen with pleasure only at the wedding, *etc.*

1786 Curwen *Journal* 1.xix: An old Greek proverb, the meaning of which is—A wife is seen with the greatest pleasure by her husband *in 2 circumstances only,* in the Wedding *and* in the Winding Sheet. Tilley W382.

W156 To play the **Wild**

1827 HWebb in *Ruffin Papers* 1.379: You must keep a pretty sharp look out or he will supplant you for the buttons have played the wild in Hillsborough. TW 402(1).

W157 To stare like a **Wildcat**

1783 Williams *Penrose* 300: Harry . . . stared like a wild Cat.

W158 To fly like **Wildfire**

1702 Mather *Magnalia* 1.179: Suspicions then flying like wild-fire about the country. **a1788** Jones *History* 2.359: It flew like wild-fire. **1791** ESeton in Hamilton *Papers* 9.102. **1804** *Echo* 299. **1806** *Weekly* 1.120: The news flew like wildfire. **1815** Waterhouse *Journal* 186. **1819** JAdams in *Adams-Jefferson Letters* 2.545: They would have flown through the Universe like wildfire. Whiting W262. See **B373, F133, 162.**

W159 To go like **Wildfire**

1788 *Politician* 49: They will set it going like wild-fire. **1836** RJohnson in Jackson *Correspondence* 5.409: The amendment embracing your suggestions went like wild fire, or the fire in the prairie. See **B373.**

W160 To rage like **Wildfire**

1812 Jackson *Correspondence* 1.244: It raged like wild fire.

W161 To run like **Wildfire**

1738 Stephens *Journal(I)* 1.243: So that it ran like Wild-fire. **1769** Woodmason *Journal* 154: They run like Wild Fire after Abraham. **1775** Lee(W) *Letters* 1.128-9: It run like wildfire in the minds of men that it was so. **1775** Willard *Letters* 233. **1779** Sargent *Loyalist* 52, **1780** 26. **1801** Asbury *Letters* 3.226: The work of God is running like fire in Kentucky. **1804** Cutler *Life* 2.161. **1816** Adams *Works* 10.198: Rejoicings had run like wildfire through the continent. NED Wild-fire 5c. Cf. Whiting F203, 204.

W162 To sell like **Wildfire**

1835 Clark *Letters* 89: It has sold like wildfire here.

W163 To spread like **Wildfire**

1775 Franklin *Papers* 6.304: And a Pannick once begun spreads like Wildfire. **1771**

HHusband in Boyd *Eighteenth Century Tracts* 361: And it spread like "Wild-fire." **1788** *St. Clair Papers* 2.99. **1789** SBlackden in Jefferson *Papers* 16.249. **1799** Burd *Letters* 197. **1799** Jefferson *Writings* 10.80: The example was spreading like a wildfire. **1817** Adams *Memoirs* 3.510: The insurrection will spread like wild-fire. **1826** Pintard *Letters* 2.240, **1832** 4.67. **1855** Fletcher *Letters* 251: The Know Nothings are spreading like wild fire. Whiting *NC* 496.

W164 To take the **Will** for the deed

1627 MWinthrop in *Winthrop Papers(A)* 1.369: Thou art pleased to axcept the will for the deede. **1645** JCotton in Williams *Writings* 2.63: The Lords acceptance of our will, and endeavour for the deed. **1653** Keayne *Apologia* 27: If it be real he is pleased to accept the will for the deed and of good actions intended to be done as if they were already done. **1677** Hubbard *Indian* 2.18: Their good Will accepted for the Deed. **1694** NSaltonstall in *Saltonstall Papers* 1.213. **1718** *Winthrop Papers(B)* 6.383. **1747** Laurens *Papers* 1.83. **1764** Lee *Papers* 1.36: You must therefore, in the vulgar language, take the will for the deed, **1767** 60. **1783** RMorris in Jay *Correspondence* 3.13. **1786** Jones *Letters* 148. **1779** AA2nd in *Adams FC* 3.223. **1793** Jefferson *Writings* 19.105: I must only pray you to take the will for the deed. **1808** EGLutwyche in *Winslow Papers* 630. **1811** HBoehm in *Kingston* 337. **1811** *Port Folio* 2NS 5.374. **1813** *Beauties of Brother Bullus* 57. **1814** *Port Folio* 3NS 4.128: to use a trite expression. **1814** Wirt *Bachelor* 82. **1820** Pintard *Letters* 1.299: The will for the deed must console us. **1826** Longfellow *Letters* 1.171. **1833** *Ruffin Papers* 2.76. **1835** Clark *Letters* 91. *Oxford* 890; Whiting W267.

W165 Those that want a **Will** seldom want an excuse

1712 Mather *Letters* 117: But people that want a will seldom want an excuse!

W166 **Will** he, nill he (willy-nilly, *nolens volens*)

1640 TLechford in *Transactions . . . of the*

American Antiquarian Society 7(1885) 275: *Nolens volens.* **1650** Bradstreet *Works* 124: Will they, nill they. **1652** Williams *Writings* 4.406: Will she nill she. **1653** Wigglesworth *Diary* 12: Will I nil I. **1674** Josselyn *Account* 28: Will'd she nill'd she, 48: Volens nolens. **1676** Tompson *Poems* 55: Will she or nill. **1676** Williams *Writings* 5.230. **1683** JMoodey in *Hinckley Papers* 117: [Latin only]. c**1693** Taylor *Poems* 84. **1740** Stephens *Journal(I)* 2.53: [Latin only], **1741** 164: [Latin only]. **1748** *Georgia Records* 25.319: [Latin only]. **1752** Johnson *Writings* 2.378: Willing or nilling. **1755** Fithian *Journal* 4: [Latin only], 25 [Latin only], 148 [Latin only]. **1775** BRomans in *Naval Documents* 2.938: [Latin only]. **1787** Adams *Diary* 335: [Latin only]. **1789** JCutting in Jefferson *Papers* 15.296: [Latin only]. **1792** Belknap *Foresters* 106: [Latin only]. **1800** FAmes in Gibbs *Memoirs* 2.369: [Latin only]. **1805** Brackenridge *Modern* 565: [Latin only]. **1807** *Salmagundi* 190: Willy-nilly. **1809** WCunningham in *Adams-Cunningham Letters* 149: [Latin only]. **1809** Fessenden *Pills* 97: [Latin only]. **1809** *Port Folio* 2NS 2.421: [Latin only]. **1819** Waln *Hermit* 162: *Willy-nilly.* c**1820** Bernard *Retrospections* 9: Willy-nilly. **1826** Jones *Sketches* 1.192: [Latin only]. **1828** Wirt *Letters* 2.251: [Latin only], **1830** 303: [Latin only]. **1844** Cooper *Letters* 4.489: Will ye, nill ye. *Oxford* 575; Whiting W277.

W167 To wear the **Willow**

c**1800** Tyler *Island* 27: [It] has left me to wear the willow. *Oxford* 874; Tilley W403.

W168 The **Willow** and the oak

1764 Hutchinson *History* 1.300: Their behavior . . . discovered they had more of the willow than of the oak in their constitutions. **1773** Boucher *View* 322: Like the willow, men of loose principles bend and yield to the stream; whilst the *righteous* . . . imitating the oak, are usually torn up by the roots and swept away by the torrent. **1814** Adams *Writings* 5.54: The willow has weathered by bending to every gale as it shifted, the storm which has prostrated the

sturdiest oaks. NED Willow 1c. Cf. *Oxford* 584; Tilley O3. See **R46.**

W169 **Willows** are weak but they bind the faggot

1754 Franklin *PR* 5.185: Willows are weak, but they bind the Faggot. *Oxford* 891; Tilley W404.

W170 **Win** and wear

1692 Bulkeley *Will* 177: Truly, *Win it and wear it,* he deserved to have it, if he could get it so. **1792** Hamilton *Papers* 11.546: If your courage is not put to the test by being put to *wear* what you have *won,* it will not be my fault. *Oxford* 892; Tilley W408.

W171 A **Winchester** wedding

1709 Lawson *Voyage* 47: To celebrate our *Winchester*-Wedding. Every one of the Bride-Maids were as great Whores as Mrs. Bride [a white man takes an Indian girl for the night], 190: There seldom being any of these *Winchester*-Weddings agreed on, without his Royal Consent. Cf. *Oxford* 880-1, 892; Tilley G366.

W172 As faithless as the **Wind**

1807 *Weekly* 1.193: A tyrant, faithless as the wind. **1818** Fessenden *Ladies Monitor* 56: Volatile and faithless as the wind. Cf. Tilley W412.

W173 As fast as the **Wind**

1783 Williams *Penrose* 249: Here's the Deel coming down the Brae as fast as the wind. Whiting W290.

W174 As fickle as the **Wind**

1745 Ames *Almanacs* 179: The Weather is uncertain even to a Proverb — *As fickle as the Wind, or as uncertain as the Weather.* **1788** EHazard in *Belknap Papers* 2.24: He is . . . as fickle as the wind; all sail, no ballast. c**1800** Paine *Works* 126. **1807** *Kennon Letters* 31.188. **1815** Harmon *Sixteen Years* 197: They like their ancestors [the French] are ficle & changeable as the wind. **1820** *Harvard College Rebellion* 75: Ripley the pious, as fickle as wind. Barbour 199(3); Whiting W291.

W175 As fleet as the **Wind**

1776 "Funeral Elegy" in *Naval Documents*

5.163: Fleeter than the wind. **1825** Wirt *Letters* 1.34: A . . . horse, fleet as the winds. Whiting W298.

W176   As free as the **Wind**

1778 Sargent *Loyalist* 59: As free as the wind. **1816** Wirt *Letters* 1.397: With my fancy and my heart both as free as the winds. *Oxford* 286; TW 403(1); Tilley A88.

W177   As inconstant as the **Wind**

1729 Chalkley *Journal* 235: Men that use the Sea, are, too generally inconstant as the Wind and Waters they wade through. NED Wind *sb.*[1] 7; Tilley W412.

W178   As swift as the **Wind**

1776 Wheatley *Poems* 98: On sixty coursers, swifter than the wind. **1817** Drake *Works* 172: As swift as the wind. Whiting W294.

W179   As uncertain as the **Wind**

1775 Adams(A) *Letters* 32: Reports . . . vague and uncertain as the wind.

W180   As unstable as the **Wind**

1758 Evans *Poems* 5: Unstable as the wind. **1799** Adams *Works* 9.14: He is . . . unstable . . . as the wind. Whiting W295.

W181   As variable as the **Wind**

1757 Ames *Almanacs* 278: Much like the Winds and Weather, how variable? how unsettled? **1785** EWinslow in *Winslow Papers* 291: My intentions variable as the wind. *Oxford* 871; Whiting W296.

W182   As various as the **Wind**

1774 THosmer in *Deane Correspondence* 154: Some of this opinion, some of that, as various as the wind. Cf. Whiting W298.

W183   As wavering as the **Wind**

c1725 Byrd *Another Secret Diary* 475: My Wandering heart . . . was more wavering than the Wind. **1797** Washington *Writings* 35.459: This resolution . . . otherwise . . . will be as wavering as the wind. *Oxford* 871; Tilley W412.

W184   As wild as the **Winds**

1769 Brooke *Emily* 21: Females wild as the winds. **1772** Freneau *Poems* 1.64: Wild as the winds. Whiting W298.

W185   Between **Wind** and water

1776 Hodgkins *Letters* 213: One of the galles . . . Received a shot Between wind & wharter. **1816** Adams *Writings* 6.4: Otis has spent his life hitting the opinions of the people of Massachusetts between wind and water. **1820** John Drayton *Memoirs of the American Revolution* (Charleston, S.C., 1821) 2.114: One shot . . . struck her between wind and water. *Oxford* 892-3; TW 404(17).

W186   He that spits against the **Wind** spits in his own face

1757 Franklin *Papers* 7.294: He that spits against the Wind, spits in his own Face. *Oxford* 766-7; TW 405(23).

W187   How blows (*etc.*) the **Wind**

1652 Williams *Writings* 4.51: Master *Cotton* is wise, and knows in what *door* the wind blows of late. **1796** Barton *Disappointment* 49: How stands the wind? **1824** *Tales* 1.195: Sits the wind in that quarter? *Oxford* 893; Whiting W308. See **W211.**

W188   If the **Wind** blows on you through a hole, *etc.*

1744 Franklin *Papers* 2.425: The Spaniards have a Proverbial Saying, *If the Wind blows on you thro' a Hole, Make your Will, and take Care of your Soul. Oxford* 894; Tilley H384.

W189   In the **Wind**

1705 Beverley *History* 74: There was something else in the Wind. **1709** *Winthrop Papers(B)* 6.187: There is certainly more in ye wind y^n wee yet know of. **1720** Carter *Letters* 10: There is but one difficulty in the wind. **1777** Munford *Patriots* 462: He has got some tory in the wind. **1786** *Anarchiad* 108. **1786** JEliot in *Belknap Papers* 3.307: Another thing in the wind, & of a very windy nature from what I know of it, "The Humane Society." **1796** Barton *Disappointment* 12. **1812** Maxwell *Poems* 29. **1814** Wirt *Bachelor* 50: I began to suspect that something was in the wind. Barbour 199(4); *Oxford* 751; TW 403(5).

W190   It's a bad **Wind** that never shifted

1830 Ames *Mariner's* 86: They say it is a

"bad wind that never shifted." Cf. Lean 1.402. See **L29, T101.**

W191   It's an ill (bad) **Wind** that blows nobody good

1739 Murray *Letters* 44: 'T is a Bad wind that blows no Body Good. **1740** Belcher *Papers* 2.298: It's a bad wind blows no body good. **c1760** JHowe in Belknap *History* 3.285: 'Tis an ill wind certainly that blows no body any good. **1776** ARoberts in *PM* 7(1883) 460: Its an ill wind that blows nobody good. **1777** JWarren in *Warren-Gerry Correspondence* 71. **1777** DNorris in Wister *Journal* 200: 'Tis an ill-wind that blows nobody no good. **1782** Gadsden *Writings* 197: 'Tis an ill wind blows no good. **1790** JMason in Mason *Papers* 3.1193: I have long since heard this Proverb and now I believe it. **1799** Mackay *Letters* 11: a cursed ill wind. **1801** Weems *Letters* 2.188: We have had the ill luck to meet one of those cursed gales which blow no body good. **1802** *Port Folio* 2.116. **1803** Davis *Travels* 12. **1811** Graydon *Memoirs* 41: The old proverb was not belied; and the benign influence of this *ill wind* was sensibly felt by us school-boys. **1811** Wirt *Letters* 1.309: It is . . . an ill wind that blows nobody luck. **1816** Paulding *Letters(I)* 2.164. **1836** Austin *Literary Papers* 91. Barbour 199(5); *Oxford* 401; Whiting W305.

W192   Large **Wind,** large allowance

1699 Ward *Trip* 36: For it's a chearful saying among Seamen, *Large Wind, Large Allowance: Starving* and *Drowning* being to them equally terrible. Lean 1.494.

W193   To be before the **Wind**

1737 Franklin *Drinkers* 2.177: He's right before the Wind with all his Studding Sails out.

W194   To be but **Wind**

a1656 Bradford *History* 1.238: But all proved but wind, for he was the first and only man that forsooke them. NED Wind *sb.*[1] 14a; Whiting W313. See **W330.**

W195   To be in the **Wind**

1830 Ames *Mariner's* 117: Wretches . . . too frequently so much "in the wind" as to be incapable of defence. NED Wind *sb.*[1] 20g; Partridge 422: In. See **S138.**

W196   To be up in the **Wind**

1800 JHale in King *Life* 3.270: At present we appear all "up in the wind." **1809** *Steele Papers* 2.612: Smith has quarrelled with Jackson and thrown the whole business *"again up in the wind,"* **1810** 640: To throw the whole business *up into the wind again.* **1850** Cooper *Letters* 6.227: Yesterday I thought a bargain closed—to-day all is in the wind again. DA wind b.

W197   To change like the **Wind** (*varied*)

1789 Asbury *Letters* 3.73: The fickle tempers . . . that may tack & change more frequent than the wind. **1797** Smith(EH) *Diary* 285: [Women] "are more changing than the *winds*" [from a song]. **1798** Adams *New Letters* 127: A Man of no sincerity of views . . . a Changling as the Wind blows. **1815** Valpey *Journal* 28: There Minds Changes as the wind. Barbour 199(2); Whiting W289, 318. See **W212.**

W198   To fly like the **Wind**

1814 Freneau *Poems* 3.361: Then back to their shipping they flew like the wind. Whiting W321.

W199   To get (take) **Wind**

1769 *Johnson Papers* 6.548: The Soldiers . . . got Wind [of something]. **1776** Washington *Writings* 6.377: If the thing should take wind, the Arms would . . . be conveyed beyond our reach. TW 403(8).

W200   To get **Wind** and tide

c1678 Mather *Letters* 7: If I could . . . get the wind and tide to be favorable to my designs. *Oxford* 892; Whiting W335.

W201   To go down the **Wind**

1653 Wigglesworth *Diary* 48: I found both bodily spirits and spiritual desires much dead and down the wind. **1677** Hubbard *Indian* 1.261: [They] perceiving that he was now going down the Wind, were willing to hasten his Fall. **1687** Mather *Letters* 19: The Turk is amazingly going down the wind. **1688** SNowell in *Saltonstall Papers* 1.183: The First goes down the wind. **1702**

Mather *Magnalia* 1.89: They have gone down the wind in all their interests, **1724** *Diary* 2.806. *Oxford* 201; Tilley W432.

W202　To go like the **Wind**

1812 Luttig *Journal* 39: The Boat swung and went down the River like the Wind in full Speed. Whiting W324.

W203　To grasp the **Wind**

1650 Bradstreet *Works* 386: More vain than all, that's but to grasp the wind. Cf. *Oxford* 36. See **A58.**

W204　To have a favorable **Wind**

1767 *Johnson Papers* 5.824: A favorable Wind blew me to a safe port. Cf. *Oxford* 893; Whiting W343.

W205　To live upon the **Wind**

1797 *Boston Gazette* in Buckingham *Specimens* 1.202: He finds it impossible to live upon the wind, and promises equally uncertain. Tilley W435. See **C114.**

W206　To pass away like the **Wind**

1657 Wigglesworth *Diary* 106: The favour of men, which passeth away like the wind. Whiting W330.

W207　To raise the **Wind**

1816 Fidfaddy *Adventures* 80: One half the Battle is won by "raising the wind," as it is called. **1817** Baldwin *Letters* 236: Will it not be best for me to endeavor to raise the wind, and get ahead of him a little? **a1826** Woodworth *Melodies* 173: It's ever been the study of mankind, In every station, how to raise the wind. **1830** Ames *Mariner's* 100. **1833** Pintard *Letters* 4.126, 144. **1834** Floy *Diary* 75: And found the youngsters raising the wind pretty high. **1845** Otis *Letters* 2.304: This is at least the third time that the wind has been raised for him. **1845** Paulding *Letters(II)* 391. *Oxford* 664; TW 404(19).

W208　To run (*etc.*) near the **Wind**

1731 *Trade* in *Colonial Currency* 2.385: When a People are obliged to run so near the Wind, it is but a small variation to make a glut or a scarcity. **1763** HSharpe in *MHM* 61(1966) 197: He was so extremely saving or as they say went so near the Wind

. . . that our Officers were obliged to be content with a Sum far short of what [was] . . . due to them. **1814** Wirt *Bachelor* 79-80: No one knew better than Mr. Surrebutter how near one might sail to the wind's eye, on those subjects without being taken aback. **1815** Waterhouse *Journal* 98: We now, to use the sailor's own expressive phrase, looked up one or two points near the wind than ever. *Oxford* 692; TW 405 (21).

W209　To sail (*etc.*) against **Wind** and tide

1702 Penn-Logan *Correspondence* 1.140: To sail against wind and tide. **1776** Moore *Diary* 1.259: It is only fighting against the wind to continue the contest. **1779** *New Jersey Journal* in *Newspaper Extracts(II)* 3.307: It will be a difficult task, more arduous than rowing against wind and tide. **1782** Trumbull *Satiric Poems* 175: Ah, Mr. Constable, in vain We strive 'gainst wind and tide and rain. **1803** Weems *Letters* 2.280: I find both Wind and Tide are still against me on every tack. **1818** Short *Letters* 375: We observe that the greatest successes in the world seem to have been where the wind & tide were both opposed to the man. Whiting W332.

W210　To sail like the **Wind**

1830 Ames *Mariner's* 206: She sailed like the wind.

W211　To see (tell) which way the **Wind** blows

1642 RJordan in *Trelawny Papers* 319: Yet seeing which way the wind hanged, any man would have shaped such a cource. **1798** Murdock *Politicians* 19: To see which way the wind blows. **1811** *Port Folio* 2NS 5.37: Every child can tell *which way the wind blows.* **1812** Bentley *Diary* 4.132: We ask of politics as we do of the wind daily, which way does the wind blow? **1815** Brackenridge *Modern* 662. *Oxford* 436; Whiting W328. See **W187.**

W212　To shift like the **Wind**

1802 Adams *D and A* 3.338: He shifted them as easily as the Wind ever shifted. Cf. NED Shift 21d. See **W197.**

W213 To slip one's **Wind**

1762 Watts *Letter Book* 101: I hope he'll slip his wind there yet & not enjoy the fruits of his undeserved, ill got wealth. **1824** *Tales* 1.15: Bolton has slipped his wind. NED Slip 26c.

W214 To stop the **Winds** from blowing

1776 *Washington *Writings* 6.420: You may as well attempt to stop the Winds from blowing, or the Sun in its diurnal, as the Regiments from going when their term is expired. Whiting W327.

W215 To talk (*etc.*) to the **Wind**(s)

1714 Hunter *Androboros* 21: But all was talking to the Wind. **1775** Webb *Correspondence* 1.48: 'Twas like talking to the Wind. **1793** Hamilton *Papers* 15.15: One may as well preach moderation to the Winds as to our zealots. **1814** TJefferson in *Adams-Jefferson Letters* 2.425: You might as well, with the sailors, whistle to the wind, as suggest precautions against having too much money. **1818** Royall *Letters* 164: He argued to the wind. **1822** Jefferson *Writings* 15.383: I expect it will be but a sermon to the wind. **1828** Jones *Sketches* 2.226: One might as well talk to the winds. *Oxford* 804; Tilley W438. See **B210.**

W216 To whirl like the **Wind**

1816 Paulding *Letters*(*I*) 2.24: A singular equipage . . . whirling along the high road like the wind.

W217 To fight (*etc.*) **Windmills**

1768 Allen *Extracts* 75: They send over Men of War & Soldiers . . . to fight Windmills. **1775** Freneau *Poems* 1.207: Against a wind-mill would'st thou try thy might. **1778** Paine *People of Pennsylvania* 2.301: It seems like fighting not against the windmill, but a butterfly. **1779** Hamilton *Papers* 2.22: Even to have attacked *windmills* in your Ladyship's service. **1799** Jefferson *Writings* 10.129: Who would have conceived in 1789, that within ten years we should have to combat such windmills! **1817** Robertson *Letters* 10: The remainder of my life will be spent in fighting windmills. **1826** Beecher *Autobiography* 2.85: Combats

with windmills in the fog of distant ages. NED Windmill 4b. Cf. *Oxford* 894; Tilley W455.

W218 To get (go) to **Windward**

1752 *Beekman Papers* 1.155: It may Again be [my] good fortune to Git to winderd of you . . . you would have been Easy to have got to winder of me . . . You are so feared I shall git to Windered of you. **1782** Adams *Works* 8.5: Great Britain has . . . gone to the windward of the other European powers. TW 405(2).

W219 Good **Wine** needs no bush

1666 Alsop *Maryland* 23: So the French Proverb sayes *Bon Vien il n'a faut point de Ensigne*, Good Wine needs no Bush. **1803** Davis *Travels* 117: Good wine, as we landlords say, requires no bush. *Oxford* 326; TW 405(1); Whiting T47.

W220 He that loves **Wine** wants no woes

1650 Bradstreet *Works* 154: From pipe to pot, from pot to words and blows, For he that loveth wine, wanteth no woes. See **W285.**

W221 In **Wine** is truth

1755 Franklin *PR* 5.471: When the Wine enters, out goes the Truth, **1779** *Writings* 7.436: *In vino veritas*, dit le sage. *La vérité est dans le vin.* **1788** in *Olden Time* 4.57: In good wine there is truth. **1804** Irving *Corrector* 113: *In vino veritas* . . . Poor C[heetah]m drank too hard; and told the — truth, **1809** *History* 2.35: And to be more sure of their veracity, the sage council previously made every mother's son of them devoutly drunk, remembering an old and trite proverb, which it is not necessary for me to repeat. **1819** Cobbett *Year's* 144: It is a saying that "in *wine* there is *truth*." *Oxford* 896; TW 406(2).

W222 Old **Wine** is better

1808 Asbury *Journal* 2.572: He saith the old wine is better. *Oxford* 589, 593; Tilley F755, W740. See **F303, 308, S166, W295.**

W223 When **Wine's** in wit's out

1813 Eaton *Life* 409: He governed his glass with little jealousy; and at such times, as is usual, his "wit was out." **1813** Weems *Drunkard* 67: *When wine's in, the wit's out,"* says the proverb. **1824** *Tales* 1.216: As the old saying goes, 2.35. **1835** Longfellow *Letters* 1.521: It has a strong affinity with our own; as may be seen by the following old saying: *Dutch* Waneer de wyn is in den man, Dan is de wysheid in de Kan. Engl[ish]: Whene'er the wine is in the man Then is the wisdom in the can. *Oxford* 895; Whiting W360.

W224 **Wine** has drowned more men than the sea

1763 Ames *Almanacs* 339: Wine has drowned more Men than the Sea. Tilley W477.

W225 **Wine** inspires wit

1819 Cobbett *Year's* 144: It is a saying that *"wine* inspires *wit."* *Oxford* 895; Tilley W491.

W226 To be under one's **Wing**

a1656 Bradford *History* 1.242: Massasoyt took shelter allready under their wings. **1702** Taylor *Christographia* 224.27-8: For they are all under the Wing of his Almightiness. **1731** Belcher *Papers* 1.36: Take him under your wing to Court. **1788** Jefferson *Papers* 13.422: I present myself then under the wing of Kitty, tho' she thinks herself under mine. **1826** *Austin Papers* 2.1462. **1827** Gallatin *Diary* 265. NED Wing 3b, 15; Tilley W495.

W227 To have one's **Wings** clipt

1730 DDunbar in *Baxter Manuscripts* 11.50: Until their wings are clipt. **1749** *Colden Letters* 3.121: All with a very small exception wish to have the wings of the De-Lancey family clipt. **1755** *Johnson Papers* 2.156. **1777** Thacher *Journal* 108: Thus have we clipped the right wing of General Burgoyne, 112: Burgoyne must feel the clipping of another wing. **1783** HLaurens in Adams *Works* 8.53. **1793** EChurch in *Barbary Wars* 1.46: They can most effectually clip our Eagle's Wings. *Oxford* 127; Tilley W498.

W228 Quick as a **Wink**

c1793 Paine *Works* 120: Quick, as the wink

of Heaven's electrick eye. Barbour 199; TW 406(1). Cf. Whiting W365.

W229 To tip the **Wink**

1809 Irving *History* 2.83: His trusty followers . . . tipped each other the wink. TW 406(9).

W230 A hard **Winter** when bear eats bear

1806 UTracy in King *Life* 4.501: *It is a hard winter, my masters, when bear eats bear.* *Oxford* 353: Wolf; Tilley W509. See **F23.**

W231 Snowy **Winter,** plentiful harvest

1733 Franklin *PR* 1.317: Snowy winter, a plentiful harvest. Cf. Dunwoody 90; Tilley W507. See **S295.**

W232 **Winter** never rots in the sky

1677 IWiswall in *Baxter Manuscripts* 6.148: Because we ordinarily say that winter never rottes in ye skye; and the usuall time for Snow is in this [January] and the next month. **1817** Bentley *Diary* 4.434: Winter does not rot in the sky. *Oxford* 897; Tilley W512.

W233 **Winter** spends what summer lends

1744 Ames *Almanacs* 174: The winter spends what the summer lends. *Oxford* 897; Whiting W373.

W234 **Winter's** back is broken

1833 [March 10] Longfellow *Letters* 1.410: Winter at length is over; or as people say in these parts, "its back is broken." Dunwoody 91.

W235 A **Winter's** calm is as bad as a summer's storm

1652 Williams *Writings* 4.432: They say, a *Winters calme* (for then *stormes* are breeding) is as bad as a *Summers storme.* See **W92.**

W236 To **Winter** one and summer one

1713 Wise *Churches* 82: Unless the Association will take them home, and both Winter and Summer them. **1800** Cobbett *Porcupine* 11.146: I know the sovereign people of Philadelphia; I have wintered them and summered them, as the man said by his hogs. TW 407.

W237 **Wisdom** is better than rubies, *etc.*

1702 Taylor *Christographia* 134.74: Wisdom is better than Rubies. **1754** Sherman *Almanacs* 258: Wisdom and knowledge are preferable to gold and silver. Tilley W526. See **L84.**

W238 **Wisdom** is better than weapons of war

1677 Hubbard *Indian* 1.176: *Solomon* said of old, *Wisdom is better than Weapons of War.* Cf. Tilley W527. See **P224.**

W239 **Wisdom** is in age

1797 Cobbett *Porcupine* 4.370: "Wisdom is in age;" but, it seems, this maxim does not hold good with respect to nations. Cf. Whiting A70.

W240 The **Wish** is father to the thought

1783 Van Schaack *Letters* 321: My "wish is father to the thought." *Oxford* 43; TW 407; Tilley B269.

W241 **Wishes** and wailings mend nothing (*varied*)

1624 EAltham in James *Three Visitors* 39: It cannot be mended with wishes and wailings. 1640 TGostlin in *Winthrop Papers(A)* 4.212: Wishes and teares have both one propertie they shew ther love but want the remedye. Cf. Whiting W402.

W242 Bought **Wit** is best

1787 *American Museum* 1.188: Bought wit is often best, and abides longest. **1813** AEdwards in Knopf *War of 1812* 3.198: Have in mind, the old adage "bought wit is the best." *Oxford* 78; TW 407(2). Cf. Whiting W420. See **C45, W246.**

W243 Good **Wits** jump (*varied*)

1640 EHowes in *Winthrop Papers(A)* 4.241: We use to say good witts iumpe, though heads touch not. a1700 Hubbard *New England* 117: Or else good wits, as they use to say, did strangely jump very near together, into one and the same method and idea of church discipline. **1702** Mather *Magnalia* 2.543-4: Out of the curiosity to see how men's wits jumpt in prosecuting the same text. **1769** Woodmason *Journal* 142: How oddly things will jump together oftentimes! **1813** Adams *Writings* 4.482: It is strange to observe, as the proverb says, how "great wits jump together." *Oxford* 326-7; Tilley W578.

W244 One's **Wits** are a wool-gathering

1640 EHowes in *Winthrop Papers(A)* 4.241: I have sent you a booke . . . that will sett your witts on wollgatheringe. **1688** Taylor *Poems* 46: Wits run a Wooling over Edens Parke. **1718** Mather *Letters* 258: The famous action of the Czar . . . I have rarely told unto any people who have not presently had their wits a-wool-gathering. **1807** *Salmagundi* 397: By it were the heads of the simple Gothamites most villainously turned, their wits sent a wool-gathering. Barbour 201; *Oxford* 905; TW 412(7); Tilley W582.

W245 To be at one's **Wit's** end [The following is a selection from 38 occurrences of the phrase]

1659 WHooke in *Winthrop Papers(B)* 2.593: We are eene at our witts end. **1683** JRichards in *Mather Papers* 500: Which will . . . put them to their witt's end what to doe. **1691** *Humble Address* in *Andros Tracts* 2.244: To be at their Wits end. **1699** Taylor *Poems* 136: The Seamen they Bestir their stumps, and at wits end do weep. **1702** Mather *Magnalia* 1.194: Brought them all to their wit's ends. **1744** Brainerd *Memoirs* 184: I was . . . driven to my wit's-end. **1773** *New-York Gazette* in *Newspaper Extracts(I)* 9.570. **1776** *Washington Writings* 4.449: They were at their Wits' end. **1778** Smith *Memoirs(II)* 358: At their Wits End to furnish an Army for this Campaigne. **1778** Paine *American Crisis* 1.110: The nation is put to its wit's end. **1783** Adams *Works* 8.130: The monoyed men at their wit's end, **1786** in *Warren-Adams Letters* 2.275: I am driven to my wits' ends. **1800** Gadsden *Writings* 291: At her slippery wit's end. **1811** Adams *Memoirs* 2.298. **1823** Gallatin *Diary* 231. **1824** *Tales* 2.143: [It] drove him . . . to his very wit's end. *Oxford* 905; Whiting W412.

W246 To buy **Wit** too dear

1728 Ames *Almanacs* 55: Wit bought with

the price of Woe is a little too dear. **1806**
Fessenden *Modern Philosopher* 227: Thus
the doctor bought wit But paid dear for it.
1806 Hitchcock *Works* 152: Since few
within our hemisphere, Would choose to
purchase wit so dear. **1833** Jackson *Corre-*
spondence 5.225: Bought wit is the best
when not bought too dear. *Oxford* 78; Tilley W546; Whiting W405, 420. See **E109.**

W247   To live by one's Wits

1750 Franklin *PR* 3.450: Many would live
by their Wits, but break for want of Stock,
1758 *WW* 343: Many without Labour,
would live by their Wits only, but they
break for want of Stock. Tilley W581.

W248   To love Wit better than one's friend

1791 Adams *Works* 9.573: But they say that
you "love wit better than your friend." *Ox-*
ford 54: Jest; Tilley J40. See **F306.**

W249   As cross as a Witch

1787 Tyler *Contrast* 77: Why as to the matter of looks, you look as cross as a witch.
1810 Dwight *Journey* 35: The old woman
cross as a witch. Svartengren 95.

W250   To run on like a Salem Witch

1808 *Port Folio* NS 6.301: He . . . quoted
Boston *newspaporials,* and *run on* like a
Salem witch.

W251   To sail like a Witch

1835 Cooper *Letters* 3.178: If you see Bal-
lard get the trim of his ship, for there is no
doubt that she sailed like a witch, under
him. TW 407(3).

W252   A Witch can go to sea in an eggshell

1830 Ames *Mariner's* 246-7: A real old tar
after scraping out the meat of a boiled egg,
invariably breaks the shell to pieces, "that
the witches may not go to sea in it." Wayland D. Hand, ed., *Popular Beliefs and*
Superstitions from North Carolina in
Brown *Collection* 7.120.5621; Lean 2.148.
Cf. *Oxford* 692; Tilley S175.

W253   With a Witness

1705 Ingles *Reply* 24: Here's an Abusive
spirit wth a witness. **1713** Chalkley *Forcing*
380: Oh! high, base, and Antichristian

Practice with a Witness. **1744** RPartridge
in Kimball 1.255. **1753** ?WLivingston in
Johnson *Writings* 4.151: One would . . .
imagine the business was done, and that
with a witness. **1765** Watts *Letter Book*
373: There is a Movement in your Administration sure enough with a Witness. **1770**
Franklin *Papers* 17.38: There it appears
with a Witness. **1776** Cresswell *Journal* 143:
This is persecution with a witness. **1776**
Paine *Foresters' Letters* 2.68: Now Cato,
thou hast nailed thyself with a witness! **1778**
Heath Papers 2.208. **1778** *New Jersey Ga-*
zette in *Newspaper Extracts(II)* 2.71. **1779**
Lee(W) *Letters* 2.524. **1783** Williams *Pen-*
rose 265. **1789** Anburey *Travels* 1.136.
1798 Adams *Works* 8.618: They are now
taking vengeance on you with a witness.
1814 Kerr *Barclay* 346: Here then is wickedness and malice with a witness. **1824**
Tales 1.151: Here is an old proverb put to
shame with a witness. **1845** ERWare in *New*
England Merchants 328: This was a predic-
ament with a witness. NED Witness 14; *Ox-*
ford 905; Tilley W591.

W254   Woe to him that is alone

1692 Mather *Wonders* 197: You know who
says, *Wo to him that is alone.* a**1700** Hubbard *New England* 186: For wo to him that
is alone, 465: saith Solomon. **1702** Mather
Magnalia 2.655. *Oxford* 906; Tilley W598;
Whiting W434. See **M38.**

W255   Woe to the land when the king is a
child

1777 AHutchinson in *Collections of the*
Vermont Historical Society 1(1870) 79: Wo
to thee, O land, when thy king is a child.
Oxford 428; Whiting W436.

W256   As hungry as a Wolf

1792 Pope *Tour* 62: I am as hungry as a
Wolf. **1812** Burr *Journal* 2.322: I am as
hungry as a wolf, 449. Barbour 200(2);
Svartengren 181; TW 408(7). Cf. Whiting
W440.

W257   As ragged as Wolves

1812 Lee *Memoirs* 2.459: The rest [soldiers]
were as ragged as wolves. NED Ragged
a.^1 1.

W258 One may tame **Wolves** but never break their nature

1654 Johnson *Wonder-Working* 106*: Experience hath taught the savage Indians . . . that they may . . . bring Wolves to be tame, but they cannot breake them of their ravening nature. Cf. Tilley W616. See **W265.**

W259 To cry "**Wolf**"

1803 Jefferson *Writings* 10.440: Our wandering brethren whom the cry of "wolf" scattered in 1798. **1856** Paulding *Letters(II)* 571: But the wolf so often cried came at last. *Oxford* 158-9; Tilley W609; Whiting *NC* 498(4).

W260 To eat like **Wolves**

1833 Pintard *Letters* 4.179: For she has a nurse & maid & 3 children, who eat like wolves. Cf. NED Wolf 5b.

W261 To have (hold) a **Wolf** by the ears

1650 Bradstreet *Works* 311: *Antigonus* now had a Wolf by th'Ears, To hold her still, or let her go he fears. **1689** TDanforth in *Hutchinson Papers* 2.312: We have a wolfe by the ears. **a1700** Hubbard *New England* 144: They knew not well how to refuse, nor accept; not much unlike them that hold a wolf by the ears. **1707** INorris in *Penn-Logan Correspondence* 2.240: I account that part . . . as holding a wolf by the ears. **1820** Jefferson *Writings* 15.249: We have the wolf by the ears, and we can neither hold him, nor safely let him go. *Oxford* 906; Tilley W603. Cf. Whiting H594. See **D266.**

W262 (To keep) the **Wolf** from the door

1702 Mather *Magnalia* 1.122: Distressed by the "wolf at the door." **1820** Paulding *Letters(II)* 61: Yet I have managed to keep the wolf from the door. *Oxford* 418; Whiting W468.

W263 To skulk like **Wolves**

1741 HBarclay in *Colden Letters* 8.280: They proceed . . . and disperse themselves and skulk about like Wolfs for their prey.

W264 A **Wolf** in sheep's clothing (a lamb's skin) [The following is a selection from 44 occurrences of the phrase]

1637 Morton *New English Canaan* 341: Wolfes in Sheeps clothing. **1646** Winslow *Hypocrisie* 64: Nor see the Lion under his Lambeskinne of *simplicity and peace.* **1652** Williams *Writings* 4.521: That excellent *Fable* or Similitude of a Wolfe getting on a *Sheepes*-skin. **1654** Johnson *Wonder-Working* 4: Wolves in sheepes cloathing, 77: Wolves . . . Who in sheepes cloathing would the weake beguile. **1656** Hammond *Leah* 5. **1669** Morton *New-Englands Memoriall* 139-40: He had a piercing Judgement to discover the Wolf, though cloathed with a sheep-skin. **1676** Williams *Writings* 5.400: That Scripture of *Wolves coming in Sheeps cloathing.* **1699** Mather *Diary* 1.324, 329. **c1700** Taylor *Poems* 454: Unless the Lyons Carkass secretly Lies lapt up in a Lamblike skin. **1702** Mather *Magnalia* 1.466: The *bishop* in *sheeps' cloathing,* 2.545, 546. **1703** Taylor *Christographia* 354.34: Quakers, Wolves in Sheeps woole, **1711** *Poems* 274: Elfes Vizzarded, and Lambskinde Woolves hence goe. **1713** Chalkley *Forcing* 380: Inwardly ravening Wolves, who have got only the Sheeps Cloathing outwardly. **1728** Byrd *Dividing Line* 68: Nor is it less strange that some Wolf in Sheep's cloathing arrives not from New England to lead astray a Flock that has no shepherd. **1729** Franklin *Papers* 1.133: I discern the Wolf in harmless Wool. **1764** *Paxton Papers* 181: And are mere Wolves, in Lambs disguise. **1774** JWarren in *Warren-Adams Letters* 2.405-6: It is the Wolves in Sheeps Cloathing who do the mischief. **1775** Harrower *Journal* 123: She being realy a Wolf cloathed with a lambs skin. **1791** Asbury *Journal* 1.695. **1798** Cabot *Letters* 169: The French are wolves in sheep's clothing. **1808** AHunn in Clay *Papers* 1.337: Tremble, ye wolves in sheep-skins! **1826** *Austin Papers* 2.1331: The Woolf has put on the sheeps Clothing. Barbour 200(1); *Oxford* 907; Whiting W474.

W265 The **Wolf** sheds his coat, but never his disposition

1755 Franklin *PR* 5.472: The Wolf sheds

his Coat once a Year, his Disposition never. **a1814** Dow *Journal* 408: But shortly after marriage the wolf sheds his coat. Tilley W616. See **W258.**

W266 To put a **Wolf's-head** upon a man
1777 Smith *Memoirs(II)* 153: I asked whether my Answer were to be minuted . . . observing that as it was easy to put a Wolf's Head upon a Man Caution would be expedient unless they meant to be fair & Candid. NED Wolf's-head.

W267 Dally not with others' **Women** or money
1757 Franklin *PR* 7.81: Dally not with other Folks Women or Money. *Oxford* 165; Tilley M1038.

W268 A good old **Woman**
1732 Byrd *Progress* 324: Though she was grown an old woman, yet she was one of those absolute rareties, a very good old woman. **1745** Franklin *Papers* 3.31: And hence there is hardly such a thing to be found as an old Woman who is not a good Woman. *Oxford* 324. See **A39.**

W269 Grasp at a **Woman** and hold a nettle
1817 Barker *How to Try a Lover* 7: This makes good the proverb, sir — Grasp at a woman, and hold a nettle. Cf. Whiting H80.

W270 Hear a **Woman's** counsel
1821 Freneau *Last Poems* 46: *If you will hear, like other men, A woman's counsel now and then.* *Oxford* 909; Whiting W536.

W271 If there were not bad **Women** there would be no bad men
1774 Schaw *Journal* 57-8: She now says if there were not bad women, there would be no bad men. Cf. *Oxford* 326; Whiting W239, *NC* 498(1).

W272 No **Women** indulged like the American
1774 Quincy *London Journal* 434: I could not help realizing the truth of the saying — no women indulged like the American.

W273 The old **Woman** would not have sought her daughter in the oven, *etc.*
1775 JWadsworth in Webb *Correspondence* 1.125: No, no, Sam; I have not been in the oven for nothing. **1769** Davis *Colonial Virginia Satirist* 50: The old Apothegm which says, that the old woman would not have sought her daughter in the Oven if she had not been there herself. **1802** *Port Folio* 2.380: The *Oven*, it must be confest, Was the last place I should have guess'd, And yet 'tis odd the thought struck you, Or any . . . who've not been there too. *Oxford* 571; Whiting F75.

W274 Two **Women** in a house, *etc.*
1793 *Washington *Writings* 33.22: I never again will have two women in my house while I am there myself. Cf. *Oxford* 850; Whiting W500.

W275 When **Women** are on board there is no want of wind
1789 AA in Adams *D and A* 3.165: They [sailors] have an other adage. That there is no want of wind, when they have women on Board.

W276 A **Woman** and a glass are never out of danger
1810 *Port Folio* 2NS 3.313: A woman and a glass are never out of danger. *Oxford* 907-8; Tilley W646.

W277 A **Woman** and an almanac
1737 Franklin *PR* 2.171: Are Women Books? says Hodge, then would mine were An *Almanack*, to change her every Year.

W278 A **Woman** is born in Wiltshire, *etc.*
1738 Franklin *PR* 2.192-3: Jack's Wife was born in Wiltshire, brought up in Cumberland, led much of her life in Bedfordshire, sent her Husband into Huntingtonshire in order to bring him into Buckinghamshire: But he took Courage in Hartfordshire, and carry'd her into Staffordshire, or else he might have liv'd and dy'd in Shrewsbury. *Oxford* 910; Tilley W699.

W279 **Woman** is woe to man
a1700 Saffin *His Book* 191: Are women Woe to men. *Oxford* 908; Whiting W512.

W280 A **Woman** never holds her tongue (*varied*)

c1720 Byrd *Another Secret Diary* 266: A woman never holds her tongue: but when she's contriveing mischief. **1792** Brackenridge *Modern* 33: It is not the nature of the female tongue to be silent. *Oxford* 909, 910; Tilley W675-7; Whiting W513.

W281 A **Woman** will refuse and then accept

1733 Byrd *Journey* 305: She refused the offer at first, but, like a true woman, accepted of it when it was put home to her. *Oxford* 499-500; Whiting N35.

W282 **Woman's** name is curiosity

1775 Fithian *Journal* 123: Pshaw! thought I, Woman thy name is *Curiosity*. Lean 3.445.

W283 **Woman's** work is never done

1722 Franklin *Papers* 1.19: Yet if you go among the Women you will learn . . . that *a Woman's Work is never done*. **1778** Marshall *Diary* 187: She verifies that old saying that "woman's work is never done," 193: My dear wife meets with but little respite all day, that proverb being verified that "woman's work is never done." **a1855** Beecher *Autobiography* 1.25: Flax in winter, wool in summer; woman's work is never done. Barbour 115: Man(14); *Oxford* 909; Tilley W679; Whiting *NC* 499(5).

W284 **Women** and wine are the bane of youth

1742 CCarroll in *MHM* 20(1925) 168: Avoid as Bane of youth Women and Wine, 171: Women & Wine are the Bane of Youth. Cf. Tilley W696; Whiting W358, 359.

W285 **Women** and wine, game and deceit, *etc.*

1746 Franklin *PR* 3.63: Women and Wine, Game and Deceit, Make the Wealth small And the Wants great, **1758** *WW* 345. *Oxford* 910. See **W220**.

W286 **Women** are mutable (*varied*)

1748 Ames *Almanacs* 204: It is a Thing that's indisputable, Women, like winds, are very mutable. **1771** Paterson *Glimpses* 148: For, I think, it is a Maxim, that a woman don't know her own mind half an hour together. **1803** Davis *Travels* 428: Inconstant as a woman's love. **1809** Irving *History* 1.34: [She] with the proverbial fickleness of her sex. **1815** Valpey *Journal* 45: But women loves to Change and so do we. *Oxford* 909, 910; TW 410(20); Tilley W673, 698; Whiting W526.

W287 **Women** are necessary evils

1721 Wise *Word* 192: Women were necessary Evils. *Oxford* 910; Tilley W703.

W288 **Women** have no souls

1638 Winthrop *Journal* 1.284: One Herne taught that women had no souls. **1773** Trumbull *Satiric Poems* 66: And praised *Mahomet's* sense, who holds That Women ne'er were born with souls. **1774** Fithian *Journal and Letters* 111: A conversation was introduced concerning the Souls of Women: Mrs. Carter observed that She had heard they have no Souls. **1789** Brown *Better* 17: These men are all Turks, and think women have no souls. *Oxford* 910; Tilley W709. Cf. Whiting M268. See **N42**.

W289 **Women** have tears at command

?**1712** Byrd *Secret Diary* 285: For fear of being persuaded by her tears which women have always ready at command. Tilley W720; Whiting D120, W537. Cf. Barbour 201(6); *Oxford* 911. See **T29**.

W290 **Women** have their fears

1740 Stephens *Journal(I)* 1.629: For Women will always have their Fears.

W291 **Women** will have the last word

1728 Byrd *Dividing Line* 74: But receiv'd no Answer, unless it was from that prating Nymph Echo, who, like a loquacious Wife, will always have the last Word, 314: A very talkative Echo, that, like a fluent Helpmeet, will return her good Man Seven Words for one, & after all, be Sure to have the Last. **1816** Paulding *Letters(I)* 1.89: Ladies . . . always endeavoured . . . to have the last word, which, like the last blow, is decisive of victory. *Oxford* 911; TW 409(3).

W292 **Women** will have their way (*varied*)

1774 PHutchinson in Hutchinson *Diary* 1.108: We had a little contest, but you know the women always gain their point. **1795** Freneau *Poems* 35: [Eve's] daughters all will have their way, **1816** *Last Poems* 6: *These women will have their own way.* **1821** Knight *Poems* 1.115: And *Eunice,* who, thwart her, will still have her way. *Oxford* 911; TW 409(2); Whiting W519. See **F237.**

W293 **Women's** tongues are made of aspen leaves

1747 Smith(John) *Diary* 97: I drank Tea . . . with some fine women who verified the Antient Remark, Women's Tongues of Aspen Leaves are made. Tilley W677.

W294 A nine days' **Wonder**

1684 WVaughan in Belknap *History* 1.331: Coffin saithe it is a nine dayes wonder and will soon be forgotten. **1741** Belcher *Papers* 2.542: We must all prepare to go thro' the nine days wonder. **1745** Stephens *Journal(II)* 2.185: But probably 'twould Scarcely amount to a Nine days Wonder. **1765** Johnson *Writings* 1.355. **1774** NAppleton in Quincy *Memoir* 174. **1775** Reed *Life* 1.118: The commencement of hostilities was the wonder of a day, and then little thought of. **1776** AA in *Adams FC* 1.352: It has been a nine days marvel and will now cease. **1786** Ledyard *Russian Journey* 95: And only a Nine days Wander remained [a pun of sorts]. **1807** *Port Folio* NS 4.288: Fulton and his nine-days wonder. **1807** *Salmagundi* 212. **1818** Bentley *Diary* 4.512: Things . . . cannot even become in the proverb a nine days wonder. **1834** Longfellow *Letters* 1.430: Every new *notion* takes — is a seven day's wonder — and then no more is heard of it. **1835** *Diary of Millie Gray* (Houston, Texas, 1967) 57: And of course it was a nine days talk — and much excitement in town on the subject. *Oxford* 912; Whiting W555.

W295 Old **Wood** to burn, *etc.*

1702 Mather *Magnalia* 1.497: It was a saying of Alphonsus . . . that "among so many things as are by men possessed or pursued . . . all the rest are baubles, besides old

wood to burn, old wine to drink, old friends to converse with, and old books to read." *Oxford* 593; Tilley W740. See **F303, W222.**

W296 To cut **Wood** with a hammer

1814 Palmer *Diary* 114: O that I was born to cut wood with a hammer.

W297 **Wood** warms a man twice

1819 Kinloch *Letters* 1.460: The proverb of the country is, that wood warms a man twice. Barbour 65: Firewood.

W298 As fat as a **Woodchuck**

1792 Belknap *History* 3.113: The Woodchuck . . . is generally fat to a proverb, and its flesh is palatable food.

W299 As stupid as a **Woodchuck**

1800 Trumbull *Season* 67: I have been as stupid as a woodchuck all day.

W300 Never halloo until you are out of the **Woods**

1770 Franklin *Papers* 17.356: This is Hallowing before you are out of the Wood. **1800** Adams(A) *Letters* 381: It is an old and a just proverb, "Never halloo until you are out of the woods." **1819** Pintard *Letters* 1.210: We made too much schoolboy whooping . . . & forgetting the Indian maxim, *not to halloo till we get thro' the woods,* **1820** 318, **1826** 2.236, **1832** 4.72. *Oxford* 345; TW 411(3).

W301 Not brought up in the **Woods** to be scared at an owl

1815 Humphreys *Yankey* 33: We wan't brought up in the woods, to be scart at an owl in an ivy-bush. *Oxford* 475; TW 411(2).

W302 Not to be out of the **Woods**

1741 Stephens *Journal(II)* 1.11: Mr. Barber . . . preached . . . bringing his hearers into such a Wood, as neither they, nor he himself (I thought) knew the way out of. **1776** Smith *Memoirs(II)* 44: And yet I am not out of the Woods. **1792** Ames *Letters* 1.112: I cannot believe that we are out of the woods. TW 411(5). Cf. *Oxford* 913.

W303 Not to see the **Wood** for trees

1813 JAdams in *Adams-Jefferson Letters*

2.350: I can not see Wood for Trees. Barbour 69: Forest (2); *Oxford* 710; Whiting W561. See **T214.**

W304 To be brought up in the **Woods**

1813 Colby *Life* 1.172: But they acted as if they were brought up in the woods. TW 411(1).

W305 To grow in the **Woods**

1777 HGates in *Trumbull Papers* 3.50: As if the necessary equipment for a soldier grew in the woods. Cf. TW 248: Money (8). See **G107.**

W306 Happy's the **Wooing** that's not long a doing

1734 Franklin *PR* 1.355: Happy's the Wooing, that's not long a doing. *Oxford* 913; Tilley W749.

W307 As white as **Wool**

1826 Royall *Sketches* 69: His head is as white as wool. Whiting W570.

W308 Cool **Words** scald not the tongue

1767 Ames *Almanacs* 387: Cool words scald not the tongue. Cf. *Oxford* 241; Whiting W583.

W309 Few **Words** and many deeds

1776 JMcKesson in *Clinton Papers* 1.420: Can he be recommended as a brave, active, vigilant officer of few words and many Deeds? *Oxford* 254; Tilley W797. See **L181.**

W310 Few **Words** are best

1822 Freneau *Last Poems* 109: Few words are best — the wind blows cold. *Oxford* 254; TW 413(5). Cf. Whiting W586, 587. See **S210.**

W311 Good **Words** cost nothing

1803 GDavis in *Barbary Wars* 3.300: Good words cost you nothing. *Oxford* 327; TW 413(11). See **P275.**

W312 Hard **Words** break no bones

1801 Brackenridge *Gazette* 250: Hard words, and language break nae bane. **1803** Davis *Travels* 92: They [negroes] say, *When Mossa curse, he break no bone.* **1814** Morris *Diary and Letters* 2.570: These . . . are

mere words — hard words, if you please, but they break no bones. *Oxford* 353; Tilley W801; Whiting W634, 644.

W313 Haughty **Words** breed strife

1767 Ames *Almanacs* 387: Haughty words breed strife. Cf. Whiting W630.

W314 In many **Words** there wants not sin

1669 WHubbard in *Saltonstall Papers* 1.157: In many words, and opposition, there cannot want sin. **1696** Mather *Diary* 1.207: And, *in many words, there wants not sin.* Whiting W593. Cf. *Oxford* 510.

W315 Many a true **Word** is spoken in jest (*varied*)

1728 Byrd *Dividing Line* 187: And what he said in Jest wou'd have happen'd true in Earnest, if I had not ordered the Skins of the Deer which we kill'd, to be made use of in covering the Bags. **1803** JJackson in Milledge *Correspondence* 96: As here is many a true word said in jest. **1806** *Emerald* 1.144: Many a true word spoke in jest. **1809** Rush *Letters* 2.993-4: As many true words are spoken in jest, so it was remarked these words of the Governor, though spoken in anger, were strictly true. *Oxford* 841; TW 413(8); Whiting S488. See **J24.**

W316 Many **Words** won't fill a bushel

1758 Franklin *WW* 340: *Many Words won't fill a Bushel.* Barbour 202(9); *Oxford* 916; Tilley W817. See **W332.**

W317 No more **Words** but mum

1714 Hunter *Androboros* 36: No more words, but *Mumm. Oxford* 574; Whiting W602. See **M302.**

W318 Not to get (put) a **Word** in edgeways

1775 Hopkinson *Miscellaneous Essays* 1.2: There is no getting a word or two in, edgeways, amongst them. **1789** Maclay *Journal* 102: And until after three scarce a word could be got in edgewise. **1804** Irving *Journal* 1.64: She could not get in a word edgeways. **1834** Floy *Diary* 71: He spoke so fast that I could not put a word in edgeways. TW 413(10).

W319   One's **Word** is as good as his bond

1777 Carter *Diary* 2.1083: A word that ought to be one's bond between even man and man ought certainly to be so when one's Country was and is the cause of that word. **1778** *New Jersey Gazette* in *Newspaper Extracts(II)* 2.113: Why not take a man's word for his bond? **1810** Rush *Autobiography* 293: He would as soon take John Rush's word as any other man's bond. **1837** Austin *Literary Papers* 64: His word was as good as a promissory note. **1855** Paulding *Letters(II)* 555: No hazard in depending on my word. I would say it is as good as my Bond, were it not that some men's Bonds are no better than their word. Barbour 202(7); *Oxford* 380; TW 413(7); Whiting W609.

W320   One's **Word** is as good as the bank

1765 Adams *D and A* 1.262: He said his Word [was] as good as the Bank.

W321   Sweet **Words** are like honey, *etc.*

1664 Bradstreet *Works* 40: Sweet words are like hony, a little may refresh, but too much gluts the stomach. *Oxford* 381; Whiting H437. See **G5, H266.**

W322   To be as good (not as good) as one's **Word** [The following is a selection from 63 occurrences of the phrase]

1628 *Winthrop Papers(A)* 1.381: Suche . . . doe finde him allwayes as good as his worde. **1634** Wood *New-England* 82: Being as good as his word. **1641** JWinter in *Trelawny Papers* 259: They are never so good as their word. **a1656** Bradford *History* 2.259: He was as good as his word. **1677** JCotton in *Mather Papers* 238: They were as good as their word. **1692** Mather *Wonders* 190: Try, whether I won't be as good as my word. **a1700** Hubbard *New England* 167: The other was as good as his word, and killed him. **1702** Mather *Magnalia* 2.409: He was as bad as his word. **1704** Chalkley *Journal* 47: They . . . were worse than their Word. **1721** Bobin *Letters* 99-100: Harrington . . . has not been so good as his word. **1748** Laurens *Papers* 1.113: I have been as good as my promise. **1756** RDemere in McDowell *Documents* 2.146: He was

determined not to prove worse than his Word. **1774** Boucher *View* 395. **1787** MCarr in Jefferson *Papers* 15.639: She was not as good as her word. **1794** Burr *Correspondence* 28: Is she as good as her word? **1803** Jefferson *Family Letters* 242: [He] was not as good as his word. **1806** Adams *D and A* 4.28: They . . . had been as good as their Words. **1812** JJohnston in Knopf *War of 1812* 6(4) 58. **a1820** Biddle *Autobiography* 189. **1838** Cooper *Letters* 3.327. *Oxford* 317; TW 412-3(4); Tilley M184.

W323   To eat (swallow) one's **Words**

a1656 Bradford *History* 1.362: Others deneyed what they had said, and eate their words. **1728** Byrd *Dividing Line* 129: A precept from so great a Man, three of these worthy Commissioners had not the Spirit to disobey, but meanly swallow's their own Words. **1764** RBland *Colonel* in Bailyn *Pamphlets* 1.346: Will he eat his own words? **1808** M'Nemar *Kentucky* 53: Stone agreed "to eat these dreadful words." **1841** FBlair in Jackson *Correspondence* 6.103: It really was done to give Clay time *to eat and digest his words.* *Oxford* 214; TW 413(9). See **P283.**

W324   To make many **Words** to the bargain

1790 Washington *Writings* 31.2: It is not my intention . . . to higgle, or make many words to the bargain. Cf. *Oxford* 544; Tilley W819.

W325   To speak two **Words** for oneself and one for others

a1700 Hubbard *New England* 80: This gentleman . . . had a design of his own . . . that made him speak two words for himself where he spake one for them. **1702** Mather *Magnalia* 1.59: This man, speaking *one* word for *them,* spake *two* for *himself.* **1721** Wise *Friendly Check* in *Colonial Currency* 2.249: [He] *has spoke two Words for himself and not one for his Country.* **1776** Hodgkins *Letters* 192: Instead of speaking a word for me he spoke two for himself. **1807** *Emerald* NS 1.89: There was one word for you, Sir, and two for himself. Apperson 474: One word.

W326 Two **Words** to a bargain (*varied*)

1806 *Port Folio* NS 2.192: Two Words Make A Bargain. **1812** Melish *Travels* 218: He seemed to forget, that there are always two at a bargain-making. *Oxford* 852; Tilley W827. Cf. TW 389(9). See **S194**.

W327 A **Word** and a blow

1637 Morton *New English Canaan* 62: They find . . . that they abuse the word and are to blame to presume so much, — that they are but a word and a blow to them that are without. **1681** Mather *Diary* 1.12: Well the God of Heaven hath by His Word been calling upon you; expect now to have Him speak unto you by a Blow! **1768** Franklin *Papers* 15.111: It is said of choleric People, that with them there is but *a Word and a Blow*. **1769** WSJohnson in *Trumbull Papers* 1.366. **1800** Cobbett *Letters* 116: With a *thief* it should always be a word and a blow, and the blow *first*. **1803** Paine *To The Citizens* 2.933: To set up the character of a ruffain, that of *word and blow, and the blow first*. **1804** *Port Folio* 4.150: "A word and blow" for ever is his plan. **1812** Knopf *War of 1812* 5(1) 71: A word and a blow will come at the same time. Barbour 202(6); *Oxford* 914; TW 412(2).

W328 A **Word** once uttered cannot be recalled

1792 *Universal Asylum* 7.310: A word once uttered can never be recalled. *Oxford* 914; Whiting W605.

W329 A **Word** to the wise is enough (*varied*) [The following is a selection from 98 occurrences of the saying, 50 of which are Latin, often abbreviated]

1645 Wheelwright *Writings* 208: *Verbum sat sapienti*. **1648** HAtherton in *Winthrop Papers(A)* 5.273: So knowing a word is enugh for a wise man I rest for thet. **1676** Williams *Writings* 5.17: A Word to the Wise is sufficient. **1678** RBlinman in *Mather Papers* 332: Sat verbū sap. **1685** FHooke in Belknap *History* 1.347: A word to the wise is enough. **1685** JStanton in *Trumbull Papers* 1.141: Verbum sapienti satis est. **1694** Makemie *Writings* 102: Ver-

bum est sapienti. **1694** RTreat in *Winthrop Papers(B)* 5.19: A word to yᵉ wise may suffice. **1699** *Wyllys Papers* 355: I do but hint at things, I know verbū sat. &c. **1703** *Penn-Logan Correspondence* 1.209: A word to the wise. **1718** JCustis in Byrd *Another Secret Diary* 291: I shall say no more on this subject, I hope a word to yᵉ wise is sufficient. **1721** *Boston News-Letter* 1.10: I conclude with *Verbum Sapienti*. **1729** Franklin *Papers* 1.136: A Word to the Wise is sufficient, **1732** 238, **1735** 2.86: *Verbum Sapienti satis*, **1758** *WW* 340. **1769** AWard in Ward *Correspondence* 19: Shall content myselfe with Saying a word to the Wise is Enough. **1775** WHDrayton in Gibbes 2.171: I remember the proverb. **1775** EFreeman in *Baxter Manuscripts* 14.245: A hint on this Head is enough. **1776** SAdams in *Warren-Adams Letters* 1.279: *Sat Verbum Sapienti*. **1776** WHDrayton in Gibbes 3.29: And now a word to the wise. **1776** RMorris in Lee *Papers* 1.307: But measures have been taken to obtain such knowledge — *a word to the wise*. **1777** JTrumbull, Jr., in *Trumbull Papers* 3.202: Sat verbum. **1780** TMcKean in Rodney *Letters* 360: Keep this hint to yourself, as you love your Country; *verbum sat sapienti*. **1780** Madison *Papers* 2.18: We return your "word to the wise." **1780** JStark in Sullivan *Letters* 3.240: A hint is enough to the wise. **1783** Freneau *Poems* 2.198: And a word to the wise is, in reason, enough. **1786** Jefferson *Papers* 9.448: Tho' a word is enough to the wise, it is not to the foolish. **1789** Washington *Writings* 30.228: You know they say "a word to the wise is enough," and why not to the witty? **1790** Dennie *Letters* 62: I study *Juvenal*, Verbum sapienti. **1791** S.P.L. *Thoughts* 166: A word to the wise will always suffice. **1792** GMorris in Hamilton *Papers* 12.221: I do not dwell on these Topics because a Word is sufficient to you. **1806** *Port Folio* NS 1.39: The principle of *a word to the wise*. **1819** JAdams in *Adams-Jefferson Letters* 2.542: Sat verbum sapient. **1820** Weems *Letters* 3.280: However we have done our part — *"the word to the wise."* **1826** Audubon *1826 Journal* 48: A word to the wise. **1827** Watterston *Wan-*

derer 189: But a word to the wise, what is it, *verbum fat,* as the Hon. T. N——— says, **1828** Jackson *Correspondence* 3.391: *Verbum sat.* Barbour 202(3); *Oxford* 914-5; Whiting W588.

W330 **Words** are but wind

1650 Bradstreet *Works* 119: Nay what are words which do reveal the mind, Speak who or what they will they are but wind. **1692** Bulkeley *Will* 228: We may talk of law, but our words are wind and not regarded. **1694** NSaltonstall in *Saltonstall Papers* 1.223: Words are but wind. **1754** Johnson *Writings* 4.13: The epigram tells us. **1756** *Johnson Papers* 9.348: Their words are like wind. **1776** Adams(S) *Writings* 3.271: Words however are oftentimes, though spoken in Sincerity, but Wind. **1780** Curwen *Journal* 2.699: Words are but air, light and easily dispensed with. **1781** Oliver *Origin* 56. **1795** Cobbett *Porcupine* 2.30. **1795** *Remarks on the Jacobiniad* 1.34: What's a word, but wind? **1812** Taggart *Letters* 384. *Oxford* 915; Whiting W643. See **W194.**

W331 **Words** are but words

1750 Sherman *Almanacs* 221: Words are but Words, and Words but a mere Joke. Cf. *Oxford* 915; Tilley W832.

W332 **Words** never yet filled a belly

1766 JParker in Franklin *Papers* 13.412: A few good Words, which never yet filled a hungry Man's Belly. Lean 3.462. Cf. *Oxford* 304, 327; Tilley W809, 829. See **P38, W316.**

W333 **Words** not works (*varied*)

1731 *American Weekly Mercury* in *Newspaper Extracts(I)* 1.56: He has a full red Face, full of Words and little Performance. **1746** *Georgia Records* 25.64: It would be seen whether my Love . . . consisted in Words only, or in Deed and in Truth. **1767** *Washington *Writings* 2.476: It is Works and not Words that People will judge from. **1793** Ames *Letters* 1.128: What we fall short in work, we make up in talk. **1797** *Washington *Writings* 36.113: With me, it has always been a maxim, rather to let my designs appear from my works than by my

expressions. *Oxford* 175; Whiting W642. Cf. Barbour 202(15). See **D92.**

W334 All **Work** and no play makes Jack a dull boy

1804 Brackenridge *Modern* 411: All work, and no play, makes Jack a dull boy. **1816** Paulding *Letters(I)* 2.87: "All work and no play makes Jack a dull boy"—so does it make him a dull and stupid man. Barbour 202(1); *Oxford* 916; TW 413(1).

W335 The hardest **Work** is to do nothing

1798 Asbury *Journal* 2.150: The hardest work I have to do is to do nothing. See **M58.**

W336 There is no **Work** in the grave

a1700 Hubbard *New England* 233: For there is no work nor device in the grave. See **S248.**

W337 This is a **Work,** this is a labor

1692 Mather *Letters* 37: This is a work, this is a labor. **1694** Makemie *Writings* 88: *Hic Labor, hoc Opus est.* **1778** Curwen *Journal* 1.450: But it was hic labor, hoc opus.

W338 To do one's dirty **Work**

1789 Jefferson *Papers* 15.97: The Noblesse . . . will always prefer men who will do their dirty work for them. **1797** Freneau *Poems* 3.185: Themselves do their own dirty work. NED Dirty 2b.

W339 A **Work** without foundation falls on the workmen's head

1713 Wise *Churches* 152: That saying, *Debile fundamentum, fallit Opus. A Work, if done, and no Foundation laid, Falls on the Work-Mens head; Thus they are paid.* *Oxford* 318; Tilley F619.

W340 **Works** of darkness hate the light

1692 Bulkeley *Will* 151: Such works of darkness hate the light. Cf. *Oxford* 194; Whiting E184. See **E101.**

W341 He that will not **Work** shall not eat (*varied*)

1719 Chalkley *Journal* 99: *He that will not work, shall not eat.* **1737** Stephens *Journal(I)* 1.57: And my Servants thought it best Working, without which I told them there was no Eating, **1741** (*II*) 1.22: For tis work or Starve there, Ultrum horum. **1747** Stith *History* 94: Every one that would not work, should not eat, 98. **1755** *Johnson Papers* 2.275: No Work no Victuals. **1764** Ames *Almanacs* 350: They who do not work must not eat, **1767** 383. **1772** Copybook in *Wheelock's Indians* opp. 276. **1788** *Columbian Magazine* 2.468: He that won't work shall never drink. **1819** Faux *Memorable Days* 1.214: Nothing industrious generally, except pigs, which are so of necessity. Work or starve is the order of the day with them. *Oxford* 917; Whiting W651.

W342 Not to oversee **Workmen** is to leave one's purse open

1751 Franklin *PR* 4.97: Not to oversee Workmen, is to leave them your Purse open, **1758** *WW* 344.

W343 As good be out of the **World** as out of the fashion

1697 Chalkley *God's Great Love* 346: It is as good to be out of the World, as out of the Fashion. **1796** Barton *Disappointment* 31: A body, (as the saying is) may as well be out of the world as out of the fashion. **1804** Mackay *Letters* 141: Better be out of the World than out of the fashion you know. *Oxford* 602; Tilley W866.

W344 Let (So) the **World** wag(s)

1791 Morris *Diary* 2.134: Let the World wag as it may. **1801** Story *Shop* 118: So let the world wag. **1809** Fessenden *Pills* 103: And look at the world as it wags. **1848** Cooper *Letters* 5.303: So the world wags, **1850** 6.136. *Oxford* 919; Whiting W659.

W345 So (Thus) the **World** goes

1732 Franklin *Papers* 1.243: And cares not how the World goes, so he gets a Game. **1773** CCarroll in *MHM* 14(1919) 368: So goes the World. **1784** MBadger in *Saltonstall Papers* 1.527: Let the World go as it will. **1800** Delano *Narrative* 292: Thus, "thinks I to myself," goes the world! **1819** Wright *Views* 144: Thus goes the world! **1824** Adams *Memoirs* 6.349: And so you see . . . how this world goes. **1827** Cooper *Let-*

ters 1.204: So the world goes here. Whiting W665. See **G15.**

W346 This (is a) wicked **World**

1790 Freneau *Poems* 3.9: This world — this wicked world — will have its way. *Oxford* 887; TW 414(12).

W347 To be out of the **World**

1781 DCobb in *Bingham's Maine* 1.435: At present I am out of the world. NED World 18.

W348 To have the **World** at will

1731 EPrime in Lloyd *Papers* 1.336-7: Many of them . . . have (as it were) the world at will. *Oxford* 918; Whiting W666.

W349 To have the **World** in a string

1705 Ingles *Reply* 155: This is y^t wch Leads ye world in a String. **1766** Lloyd *Papers* 2.705: And finds he has the world in a string. **1783** Freneau *Poems* 2.203: And thought he had got all the world in a string. **1812** Hitchcock *Social* 134: And by possessing *Gaul* and Spain, Nay half of Europe "in a string." *Oxford* 918; Tilley W886.

W350 To set the **World** on fire

1857 JRuffin in *Ruffin Papers* 2.538: I can claim but little originality in its composition and scarcely suppose that it will set the world on fire. Berrey 261.4. Cf. *Oxford* 717. See **R93.**

W351 To take the **World** as it goes

1780 MTucker in *Norton Papers* 438: Do . . . determine to take the World as it goes. **1797** Cabot *Letters* 120: We must take the world as it is. **1807** *Salmagundi* 7: Wisdom, true wisdom . . . takes the world as it goes. **1810** Cleveland *Letters* 146. Whiting W661.

W352 To take the **World** as one finds it

1776 Carter *Diary* 2.1010: I shall advise her to take the world as she finds it. **1792** EHazard in *Belknap Papers* 2.308: We must take the world as we find it. See **T55.**

W353 To (At) the **World's** end

1767 *Johnson Papers* 5.713: Poor me who is at the back of the World [at Michilmackinak]. **1783** Adams *Writings* 1.7: I have been all that time almost at the world's end. **a1806** Jackson *Papers* 39: They would go to the Worlds end with him. **1815** Humphreys *Yankey* 35: I'll go to the world's eend with you. NED World 7d; Whiting W669.

W354   The **World** and his wife

1791 Morris *Diary* 2.303: We have all the World and his Wife here. *Oxford* 918; TW 414(6).

W355   The **World** (goes) upon wheels

1786 *Massachusetts Centinel* in Buckingham *Specimens* 2.41: The world upon wheels shall be all set agog. *Oxford* 918; Whiting W670.

W356   The **World** is a cheat (*varied*)

1808 Hitchcock *Poetical Dictionary* 86: There is another [proverb], which as plainly asserts, that the world is a cheat. **1815** JHewson in *Lincoln Papers* 215: I have tryed the world in adversity & prosperity it promis'd much but perform'd little, and allways deceived me. **1833** Jackson *Correspondence* 5.226: I have said before and now repeat—the world is not to be trusted. Cf. Lean 4.143, 149.

W357   The **World** is full of care, *etc.*

1647 Ward *Simple Cobler* 25: The world is full of care, much like a bubble; Women and care, and care and women, and women and care and trouble. See **W149.**

W358   The **World** is mutable (full of changes)

a1656 Bradford *History* 1.298: So uncertaine are the mutable things of this unstable world. **1720** Carter *Letters* 26: The world is strangely altered, sure, since I was young. **1755** Parkman *Diary* 76.148: It is far from a New Observation that this World is full of Changes. **1779** Allen *Narrative* 70: This is a mutable world. **1812** Randall *Miser* 28: This world is full of changes. Cf. Lean 4.143; *Oxford* 919; Whiting W671. See **T47.**

W359   The **World** is turned upside-down (topsy-turvy)

?1776 TFields in *VHM* 10(1902) 182: I think this Western World is now actually turn'd up side down. **1776** JWarren in *Warren-Adams Letters* 1.217: Here I find the world turned topsy turvy. **1779** Winslow *Broadside* 191: The world is now turn'd up side down. **1815** Humphreys *Yankey* 97. Tilley T165, W903.

W360   A **World** of mischief

1776 MEarle in *Naval Documents* 4.1472: [They] wil otherwise do us a World of mischief. NED World 19a.

W361   A **World** of home news

1800 HJackson in *Bingham's Maine* 2.1048: A world of home news, as the saying is.

W362   The **World** was not made in a day

1814 Wirt *Bachelor* 124: The world was not made in a day. TW 414(11). See **R126.**

W363   The **World** will be the world

1767 JDevotion in Stiles *Itineraries* 462: But the World will be the World after all. Lean 3.408, 4.143.

W364   The **World** will do its own business

c1800 Rush *Autobiography* 156: He had many pertinent common sayings which he applied to the affairs of the world. Two of them I recollect were . . . and The World will do its own business.

W365   To be **Worms'** food, *etc.*

1748 Ames *Almanacs* 201: *To-morrow* he's himself a *Dish for Worms.* **1763** Watts *Letter Book* 169: God grant you and I tho' we must be worm eaten at last, a more civilized exit. **?1785** Barlow *Works* 2.61: The blooming Cheek . . . Is now a Feast for odious worms. **1812** Adams *Writings* 4.421: Ninetenth . . . are either prisoners or food for worms. **1820** Cottle *Life* 382: I view'd myself to be Fit food for worms. Whiting W675.

W366   Tread on a **Worm** and it will turn

1703 Taylor *Christographia* 323.62-3: If you tread upon a worm, it will torn. **1741** Johnson *Writings* 3.128: Tread on a worm and it will turn. **1777** Deane *Papers* 2.10: Go into the Fields and tread on the meanest insect & see if it do not at least try to turn upon you. **1780** AA in *Adams FC* 3.312: He who will not turn when he is trodden upon is deficient in point of spirit. **1798** *Washington *Writings* 37.20: The Directory looked upon us as worms; and not even allowed to turn when tread upon. **1841** Paulding *Letters(II)* 296: It is time for the worm to turn. Barbour 203(3); *Oxford* 837; Whiting W679. See **S270.**

W367   As bitter as **Wormwood**

1814 Adams *Writings* 5.147: The style . . . is bitter as the quintessence of wormwood. TW 415.

W368   To be the **Worse** for wear

1815 Humphreys *Yankey* 78: You look altered; a little the worse for wear [ragged clothes]. **1847** Hone *Diary* 2.798: And not much the worse for wear. *Oxford* 232; TW 415; Whiting T91.

W369   Provide against the **Worst**

1771 Chester *Papers* 50: It is always prudent to provide against the worst. *Oxford* 250; Whiting W683.

W370   An old **Wound** may be healed, but not an ill name

1753 Franklin *PR* 4.405: An ill Wound, but not an ill Name, may be healed. *Oxford* 401; Tilley W928. See **N11, R62.**

W371   To open old **Wounds**

1727 WDummer in *Baxter Manuscripts* 23.219: I Dont Love to open old Wounds.

Cf. Apperson 532: Rip; *Oxford* 678; Whiting W696. See **S334.**

W372   The **Wounds** of a friend are better than the kisses of an enemy (*varied*)

1640 TGostlin in *Winthrop Papers(A)* 4.212: The reproofe of a freind is better then the kisse of an enemie. **1652** Williams *Writings* 4.28: The *wounds* of a *Lover* are better then the *Kisses* of an *Enemy*. **1772** Carter *Diary* 2.727: He was sorry for what had happened because the wounds of a friend sank deep. I made answer very Calmly I was full as sorry because the wounds of ingratitude sank deeper. **1775** Boucher *View* 457: *Deceitful kisses* are given by an enemy, who means to betray; whilst *the wounds of a friend are faithful*. **1804** AAdams in *Adams-Jefferson Letters* 1.274: Faithfull are the wounds of a Friend. **1833** Maria Stewart in Porter *Negro Writing* 132: "Faithful are the wounds of a friend, but the kisses of an enemy are deceitful." Whiting W692.

W373   Two **Wrongs** do not make a right

1783 Rush *Letters* 1.308: Three wrongs will not make one right. **1802** MWillett in Burr *Memoirs* 2.173-4: If two wrongs could make one right, this account might be squared. **1814** Kerr *Barclay* 249: But two wrongs don't make one right. Barbour 204(3); *Oxford* 853; TW 415(3).

X

X1   To scold like **Xantippe**

1782 Freneau *Poems* 2.118: It makes me so wroth, I could scold like Xantippe. Cf. NED Xantippe.

Y

Y1 To catch a **Yankee**

1811 *Niles' Weekly Register* 1.71: In which the former "caught a Yankee." See **T26.**

Y2 To come (the) **Yankee** over one

1779 Allen *Narrative* 39: I found I had come yankee over him. **1813** DMcArthur in Knopf *War of 1812* 3.142: Why my Regt. should be thus yankeed out of their pay I know not. DA Yankee 5. See **T311.**

Y3 To show one **Yankee** play

1776 Letter in *Naval Documents* 4.871: We are determined to shew them Yankee play, as we did on Easter Sunday. Cf. DA Yankee 5.

Y4 A **Yankee** jacket

1816 *Emigrant's Guide* 52: To furnish the d——d English with a *good Yankee Jacket*, which in plain English is a quantity of tar besmeared over the naked body, upon which an abundance of feathers is immediately strewed. DA Yankee 4(10).

Y5 To square the **Yards**

1766 JParker in Franklin *Papers* 13.411: I can hardly Square the Yards [pay my bills]. **1810** Cooper *Letters* 1.18: At the same time dont forget to enclose a handsome sum to square the yards here. TW 416.

Y6 It will be all the same a hundred **Years** hence

1775 Schaw *Journal* 217: He is a vast philosopher and often uses your expression "it will be all one a hundred years hence." **1809** Irving *History* 1.91: He comforted himself with . . . the truly philosophic maxim, that "it will be all the same thing a hundred years hence." **1837** Fletcher *Letters* 155: It all will be the same a hundred years hence. *Oxford* 10; TW 416(1).

Y7 Seven **Years** [The following is a selection from 55 occurrences of the phrase]

1620 RCushman in Bradford *History* 1.115: Ere .7. years be ended. **1637** Morton *New English Canaan* 265: This Country of New Canaan in seven yeares time could show more children livinge . . . then in 27 yeares . . . in Virginia. **1676** Randolph *Letters* 2.208. **1686** Dunton *Letters* 243: Shou'd we have Rambled seven years to find where we were. **c1720** Byrd *Another Secret Diary* 271: I have a constancy that can Follow one & the same scent for seaven years together. **1732** Franklin *Papers* 1.247: I think there has not been one this seven year . . . which I have not had a Hand in. **1753** *Beekman Papers* 1.196: For Seven years past. **1757** Carter *Diary* 1.157: This moon changed on Saturday and I think the old Observation is a good one if it comes in 7 year it is too soon. **1759** Adams *D and A* 1.111. **1770** *Johnson Papers* 7.344: They had not had so fine a Summer there these Seven years. **1774** Adams *Works* 4.56: For seven years together. **1778** Wister *Journal* 161: Had we been acquainted seven years, we could not have been more sociable. **1781** ISmith in *Adams FC* 4.125: We may linger Out the Warr seven Years longer. **1782** Paine *Correspondence* 2.1212: The British have accustomed themselves to think of *seven years* in a manner different to other portions of time. They acquire this partly by habit, by reason, by religion, and by superstition. **1789** Freneau *Poems* 2.324: Till seven long years had round their orbits ran. **1793** Rush *Letters* 2.678: A dull and profligate usurer who has not seen a sick man these seven years. **1794** Drinker *Journal* 246: And she is now lying . . . by the fireside as familiarly as if she had lived with us for seven years. **1809** Pinkney *Travels* 224: Tell a French peasant, that an English rustic never tastes a glass of wine once in seven years, and he will . . . pity the Englishman. **1815** Weems *Letters* 3.128: You have had that dream for 7 years. **1818** Evans *Pedestrious* 177: It has been asserted, that this lake fills once in seven years. As to the time, this must be a whim. *Oxford* 718; Whiting Y1.

Y8 I was not born **Yesterday**

1757 RDemere in McDowell *Documents* 2.398: I was not born yesterday. *Oxford* 76; TW 147.

Y9 **Yesterday** was yours today is mine

1815 Valpey *Journal* 34: Saying Yesterday was your's, my Louse. But now the day is Mine. Cf. *Oxford* 395; Whiting T349.

Y10 A **Yorkshire** bite

1797 Dennie *Letters* 159: That Bully in disguise That noted bite from Yorkshire that magazine of lies. Whiting *Ballad* 35. Cf. *Oxford* 926.

Y11 What's **Yours** is mine and what's mine is my own

1792 WHeth in Hamilton *Papers* 13.216: It puts me in mind of a vulgar saying, which I hope you will pardon me for repeating — "Whats *yours* is mine, & whats *mine* is my own." Barbour 205; *Oxford* 533; TW 245.

Y12 A forward **Youth** is short-lived

1797 Mann *Female* 60: She had often heard —that *a forward and promising youth is short lived.* Cf. *Oxford* 314; TW 155(2).

Y13 He who runs in **Youth** may lie down in age

c1820 Bernard *Retrospections* 81: He who runs in youth may lie down in age [ascribed to Franklin]. Cf. Whiting Y32.

Y14 **Youth** and age (do not agree)

1789 Morris *Diary* 1.313: The old Story: Youth and Age; Liberty on one Side, Jealousy on the other. *Oxford* 929; Whiting Y33.

Z

Z1 The **Zeal** of converts

1797 Boucher *View* 243: Another instance which shews how true the old observation is, that fresh converts always go the greatest lengths. **1824** Pickering *Review* 53: *The zeal of new converts is proverbial. Oxford* 930; Whiting C293.

Z2 As crooked as a **Zigzag**

1812 Luttig *Journal* 44: Sailing the River crooked as a zick zack. DA zigzag. Cf. TW 415: Worm fence.

APPENDIX A

"THOUGHTS ON PROVERBS," BY S.P.L.

[This charming, tongue-in-cheek essay was printed in two parts in *The Universal Asylum and Columbian Magazine* (earlier *The Columbian Magazine*) 7(1791), 76-8, 166-8. Who "S.P.L." was I do not know nor have I thought it worthwhile to search the vital and mortuary records of Philadelphia for the 1790s to attempt an identification. He had a humorous and mildly satiric touch which stands in pleasing contrast to the heavy style and substance of most commentaries on proverbs. Indeed, the only comparable performance is in the salty remarks which James Kelly added to his *A Complete Collection of Scotish Proverbs* (London, 1721), a book too little known even among proverbialists.]

FOR THE UNIVERSAL ASYLUM.

T H O U G H T S *on* P R O V E R B S.

Mr. Editor.

PROVERBS have been defined to be, the experience of ages comprised in a few words. Many a Volume of wise sayings, not to mention those of Sancho Panca, have been written. They often supply the place of extempore wit, by filling up those gaps, which otherwise would obstruct us in our colloquial routes; and he who makes use of them cannot be accused of plagiarism, since by presciptive right, they have long since become public property. They are commons, or open fields, into which every man in the vicinage may lead or drive his cattle, not even his ass excepted; nay, it is affirmed, that the last mentioned animal thrives best on them, and brays their praises, till the responsive neighbourhood seems to partake of the asinine species. This idea reminds me of one proverb *"mocking is catching."* How concisely, how forcibly is this idea expressed in those few words! They inform us, that by imitating the virtuous, we may arrive at virtue, or by following the vicious we may reach the goal of vice.

"Many men of many minds" is at once deep, elegant, and sublime; and, were I to try my hand at making a proverb, I could not invent one equal to it; except, perhaps, "Many men of many faces."

"A fool and his money are soon parted," ought certainly not to be understood according to the letter: otherwise almost every man and woman too must be a fool, since none but misers can pretend to wisdom. Now that which proves too much, is justly said to prove nothing.

"The better day, the better deed," is a vile assertion. Shame on you, ye proverb-mongers! What! are cock-fighting, bull-baiting, horse-racing, &c. sanctified by the Sabbath?

That *"Every dog has his day"* is notoriously false. There are many dogs at forty as blind, in intellects, as puppies, with respect to eye-sight, are, before they are nine days old.

"Joan is as good as my lady in the dark" is very intelligible, and perfectly congenial with the true spirit of republicanism, unless it should be thought too productive of the levelling principle.

"Every Jack has his Gill" has often puzzled me. I at first thought that it alluded to a gill of wine, or any other liquor; but on more mature reflection, I find, that every *Jack* should have his *Gillian*, that is to say, a wife. In this sense, the proverb is unexceptionable.

"Cat after kind" I utterly reject; and so ought every seminary of learning, since it strikes at the very root of education. Is instinct to govern instead of precept and example?

"Promises and pye-crust are made to be broken" includes ideas subversive of decency, morality, and religion, and may unhappily pervade our lives, from the baptismal font to the marriage-vow, and even to the hour of dissolution.

"Home is home, be it never so homely" is highly reprehensible, inasmuch as it may check the spirit of enterprize, and confine us to cottages, when we might be building palaces.

"One fool makes many" never fails to divert us, especially if wittily followed by *"You are the greatest fool of any."*

"Throw your lumps where your love lies" plainly argues that every lover ought to make a beneficial settlement on his beloved. But I will not be positive as to this solution, since another proverb, viz. *"As you like it, you may lump it"* evidently contradicts it.

"Birds of a feather flock together" suits all ranks and conditions, from the predatory hawk, to the lame duck that waddles in the mire of speculation.

"Love me little love me long," although not universally relished, is perfectly conformable to reason and truth, since nothing, that is violent can be lasting. *"Handsome is that handsome does"* is of the same class, and equally praiseworthy; but that *the grey mare should be the better horse* is utterly repugnant to truth and delicacy. It may be said, with equal propriety, that *All cats are grey in the dark.*

508

Having given you this specimen of my abilities, I purpose, should you approve of the attempt, to pursue the task I have undertaken, and am,

Your humble servant

S. P. L.

[Pp. 76-8]

THOUGHTS on PROVERBS.

[Concluded from page 78.]

Mr. Editor,

I have promised to continue my treatise (give me leave to dignify these detached thoughts with that name) on proverbs; and, as a *"Word to the wise will always suffice,"* I hope it will prove beneficial, or at least entertaining, to your readers. I resume my subject with some degree of alacrity; for whether I may *sink* or *swim* in your opinion, and that of the public, I am determined, *through thick and thin,* to fulfil my promise.

"Shall I keep a dog, and bark myself" is natural, energetic, and true. How many official characters may justly have recourse to this apothegm? For, although their dogs may occasionally deserve censure, they are in some degree entitled to pity, for two reasons—firstly, few are inclined to "help a *lame* dog over a stile;" and secondly, "Dogs shew their teeth when they dare not bite."

"To laugh on the wrong side of one's mouth" is, I apprehend, altogether inexplicable, because it is impossible to discriminate betwixt the right side of the mouth, and its opposite. It cannot be supposed, that *right* and *left* are alluded to on this occasion. Therefore, till another Oedipus shall appear, this proverb must remain an unexplained enigma.

"Neck or nothing." What a solemn alternative! Reflect on it, my readers, with the greatest seriousness; and do not pretend to think that a *neck* of mutton, or *nothing,* for dinner, is intended by this wise saying. The imprudent, the indolent, and dissolute should ponder on it with fear and trembling, and ever bear in memory, that he who contributes *nothing* to his own support, by honest bodily or mental exertion, must ultimately endanger his *neck.*

"It is no bread and butter of mine" is uncharitable in the highest degree, and tends to loosen the bands of society. Satan himself could scarcely tempt us to any thing worse than apathy, with respect to the social duties. If *bread* and *butter* are to be undervalued, what is to become of tillage and grazing; and what will be the fate of Philadelphia market? Let me therefore advise my fellow-citizens to advance the public good, by decently *looking at home,* and by moderately *minding their bread and butter.* This leads me to a consideration of

"What is every body's business is no body's business," an idea subversive of

patriotism and freedom. It certainly was first engendered in the brain, and uttered by the tongue, of some degenerate and vile tool of despotism. Be it therefore never expressed by an enlightened American, as its destructive influence may gradually pervade our councils, and fatally subject us to either absolute power or anarchy.

"*Love me, love my dog,*" with respect to *private life,* is a good-natured and sensible saying; but the advice which it affords, ought not to be blindly followed, in matters of public concern, since many a worthy character, in an exalted station, may have at his heels a pack of hungry hounds, and impertinent puppies, who, so far from being entitled to our esteem, ought to be the objects of our contempt.

"*There are none so deaf as those that will not hear*" is one of the greatest satires on the human species, which I have ever read or heard. How deplorable, how detestable must be the wilful ignorance of such men! I do not hesitate to pronounce them more insensible than inanimate nature, since we are informed, by another proverb, that "*Stone walls have ears.*"

I think, Mr. editor, that I have sufficiently extended this essay, and, lest it should be thought tedious, I shall here conclude it, ever mindful of that very common, but sensible proverb, which tells us, that "*Too much of one thing is good for nothing.*"

I am, sir, your very humble servant.

S. P. L.

Philadelphia, 1791.

APPENDIX B

YANKEE PHRASES

[The following poem is taken from the *Port Folio* 3(1803), 87. The practice of editors being what it was, it may well have appeared earlier elsewhere. Certainly it was printed at least twice subsequently; see *Olden Time* 6.59-60. There can be little doubt but that it is an imitation of "A New Song of New Similes" (1727), sometimes attributed to John Gay (see p. xv above), and included among "Doubtful Pieces" in *The Poetical Works of John Gay,* ed. G. C. Faber, Oxford, 1926, pp. 645-6.]

Ever since the era of Dr. Franklin, the love of proverbs has waxed exceedingly fervent, among our countrymen. This debasement of the dignity and elegance of diction, is not less justly than humorously ridiculed, by a Yankee bard, who thus jeers the woeful insipidity of the simple style.

YANKEE PHRASES.

As sound as a nut o'er the plain,
    I of late whistled, chock full of glee:
A stranger to sorrow and pain,
    As happy as happy could be.

As plump as a partridge I grew,
    My heart being lighter than cork:
My slumbers were calmer than dew!
    My body was fatter than pork!

Thus happy I hop'd I should pass,
    Sleek as grease down the current of time;
But pleasures are brittle as glass,
    Although, as a fiddle they're fine.

Jemima, the pride of the vale,
    Like a top, nimbly danc'd o'er our plains:

With envy the lasses were pale —
    With wonder stood gaping the swains.

She smil'd like a basket of chips —
    As tall as a hay pole her size —
As sweet as molasses her lips —
    As bright as a button her eyes.

Admiring, I gaz'd on each charm,
    My peace that would trouble so soon,
And thought not of danger, nor harm,
    Any more than a man in the moon.

But now to my sorrow I find,
    Her heart is as hard as a brick;
To my passion forever unkind,
    Though of love I am full as a tick.

I sought her affection to win,
    In hopes of obtaining relief,
Till I, like a hatchet, grew thin,
    And she, like a haddock, grew deaf.

I late was as fat as a doe,
    And playful and *spry** as a cat:
But now I am dull, as a hoe,
    And lean and as weak, as a rat.

Unless the unpitying fates
    With passion as ardent shall cram her,
As certain as death, or as rates,
    I soon shall be dead, as a hammer.

---

*This is a renowned epithet, in the New-England states. The worthy people who use it mean, very honestly, that such an one is sprightly, jocund, or nimble, and I suppose, with great humility, that an Englishman would say so.

APPENDIX C

PROVERB, PROVERBIAL, PROVERBIALLY

More than forty years ago I published an article solemnly entitled "Some Current Meanings of 'Proverbial'."[1] The content was less solemn than the title, since it consisted of more than three hundred quotations, mainly from what are usually regarded as subliterary works, such as popular fiction and periodicals, in which the word "proverbial" (including "proverb" and "proverbially") appeared. In a majority of cases the word(s) did not refer to a recognizable proverb but had secondary meanings: generally known, commonly repeated, notorious, characteristic, and the like.[2] Often the effect was intended to be humorous, and not infrequently the author's purpose defied interpretation.

The texts on which W is based contain a number of examples of what may be called ad hoc uses of the words in question, passages which can not be fitted into the body of the book, but which seem at the least to deserve recording. They are too few to merit subdivisions other than the words themselves, and indeed any student of proverbial lore is, or should be, wary of other than the simplest classifications. Those who have the patience to compare the examples here with those in the article of 1934 will observe that the earlier uses generally lack the humorous, even tediously playful, nature of the later and that the earlier authors were more apt to apply the words in a denunciatory sense, that is, notoriously bad, rather than commendably good.

1. Proverb

1637 Morton *New English Canaan* 267: And now this Bubbles day is become a common proverbe.

1637 Morton *New English Canaan* 287: Untill an old Souldier, (of the Queenes, as the Proverbe is,) . . . clapt his gunne under the weapons.

1652 Bradford *Dialogue* 19: A such a wicked couple were these tow, that it

---

1. *Harvard Studies and Notes in Philology and Literature* 16(1934), 229-52.
2. Ibid., p. 231, for a probably overrefined breakdown.

grue to be a proverbe, that the pope [Alexander VI] never did that which he said, nor his sone [Cesare Borgia] seldome speake what he ment.

1652 Williams *Writings* 4.209: *Who knows not that the many turnings of Do. Pearne in Cambridge brought it unto a proverb, to wit, to pernifie.* NED Pern *v.*[1]

1653 Keayne *Apologia* 48: So that it is now and was many years ago become a common proverb . . . that my goods and prices were cheap pennyworths in comparison of what hath been taken since.

1702 Mather *Magnalia* 1.260: It was grown almost a proverb, "That Mr. Cotton was Dr. Preston's seasoning vessel."

1702 Mather *Magnalia* 2.645: But, certainly, if the good people of New-England now make it not a proverb for a *liar* of the first magnitude, "He is as very a liar as Tom Maule," they will deprive their language of one significant expression which now offers itself unto them.

1742 *Colden Letters* 2.260-1: The Richest men among the Indian Traders are not in the least ashamed in having the basest cheating of the Indians discover'd & this so far prevails that it has allmost entirely destroy'd the Morals of that part of the Country so that they are become a proverb in other parts of the Country.

1743 *Georgia Records* 23.513: He had then recourse to his Usual Salve, (well known, to all persons at Savannah with whom he converses, even to a proverb) That he was Seventy Years of Age, His Memory decayed, etc.

1758 Caleb Rea *Journal* in *Essex Institute Historical Collections* 18(1881) 93: [They were] march'd thro' the woods by Pontusock, a way so bad that it is become a Proverb.

1772 Hearne *Journey* 307: In fact, it is almost become a proverb in the Northern settlements that whoever wishes to know what is good, must live with the Indians.

1778 Curwen *Journal* 1.427: The streets [of Exeter] are very narrow, ill paved and (I wonder why not to a proverb) dirty.

1778 Paine *American Crisis* 1.122: Till the honor of England becomes a proverb of contempt.

1785 Adams(A) *Letters* 234: The known character, even to a proverb, which is attached to an opera girl.

1785 Asbury *Journal* 1.485: Yet are the inhabitants vain and wicked to a proverb.

1787 Shaw *Journals* 244-5: I found his inattention to the Americans at Canton . . . had proceeded altogether from absence of mind, for which he is remarkable to a proverb.

1787 Shaw *Journals* 246: The united voice of the European residents proclaims them idle to a proverb.

1792 *Universal Asylum* 9.336: But the fireside is not only a friend to the bachelor in solitude; it is noted to a proverb to be always so in company.

1793 *Echo* 85: The French . . . lately have become, 'tis plain, E'en to a proverb, gentle and humane.

1797 Baily *Journal* 242: The uncertainty of titles to Kentucky lands is become quite a proverb.

1799 Carey *Porcupiniad* 2.7: His [W. Cobbett's] name a proverb to express The utmost stretch of wickedness.

1801 AHamilton in McHenry *Letters* 485: [Burr is] in his profession extortoniate to a proverb.

1804 Irving *Corrector* 56: Luscious rendered himself contemptible to a proverb among the professors of the law.

1804 Irving *Corrector* 92: He is hardened in iniquity, and infamous to a proverb.

1806 *Port Folio* NS 1.72: The the eastern people are *bundlers* (I do not say *bunglers*) to a proverb is notorious.

c1810 Randolph *Virginia* 177: The pride of Virginia had so long been a topic of discourse in the other colonies that it had almost grown into a proverb.

1814 Alden *Epitaphs* 3.129: Captain Wormsted was . . . brave to a proverb.

1815 Waterhouse *Journal* 70: It is now the 30th of November, a month celebrated to a proverb in England, for its gloominess.

1819 Faux *Memorable Days* 1.193: They are gay and voluptuous to a proverb, and seem, it is said, better abroad than they are at home.

a1820 Tucker *Essays* 47: The connection between poets and poverty has grown into a proverb.

1824 Flint *Recollections* 266: But the Shakers are industrious and neat to a proverb.

1825 Jones *Sketches* 1.44: I love to think of our nation, as one of the mightiest in the earth; as astonishment and a proverb, for its free, and noble, and happy insitutions: and such, I believe, it is going to be.

1826 Duane *Colombia* 64: Where the women are so numerous . . . and their feet so small, to a proverb small.

1831 Austin *Literary Papers* 47: Natterstrom [a fictitious character] had become a proverb, 48: "As honest as Jow Natterstrom," was in everybody's mouth.

2. Proverbial

1754 Washington *Writings* 1.95: This [few presents for Indians], with the scarcity of Provisions, was proverbial.

1764 Hutchinson *History* 1.97: It became a proverbial expression [in New England], to say of a false man who betrayed his trust, that he was an arrant George Downing.

1775 Boucher *View* 567: The perseverance of bad men, engaged in a bad cause, is almost proverbial.

1776 Izard *Correspondence* 205: The Brussels Gazette, last War, became proverbial, on account of its falsehood.

1776 Lee *Papers* 2.105: It is almost proverbial in War, that we are never in so great danger, as when success makes us confidentially secure.

1777 Smith *MemoirsII* 79: N. England Hypocrisy is as Proverbial as Carthaginian Perfidy or Cretan Falsehood.

1778 Hamilton *Papers* 1.426: It is become proverbial in the mouths of the French officers . . . that they have nothing more to do, to obtain whatever they please, than to assume a high tone.

1779 *Royal Gazette* in *Newspaper Extracts(II)* 3.263: Your [Livingston's] agility in New Jersey is become proverbial, they call you the invisible Governor.

1779 Shaw *Journals* 57: The folly and madness of Britain will become proverbial.

1782 Lee *Papers* 4.28: The first [Nourse] is proverbial for making bad bargains.

1783 Shaw *Journals* 107: Even these they envy us, though attended by a poverty which is almost proverbial.

1784 Shaw *Journals* 183: The knavery of the Chinese . . . has become proverbial.

1786 Smith *Diary* 2.85: He durst say his Name would become proverbial for strange Swearing.

1788 Alden *Epitaphs* 3.79: He [Joseph Hawley] was proverbial for his honesty in his calling.

1788 Barlow *Letters* 81: French cleanliness will never become proverbial except in the language of irony.

1788 Jones *History* 1.162: This fact was so well known in New York, that a light half Joe at length became proverbial, and went by the name of a "Robertson."

1788 Washington *Writings* 29.506: The Augustan age is proverbial for intellectual refinement and elegance in composition.

1791 Long *Voyages* 26: No nation of Savages were ever more true to the British interest, not even the Mohawks, whose fidelity is become almost proverbial.

1793 Barlow *Works* 1.279: [The French's] veneration for King was proverbial through the world.

1793 HKnox in *Bingham's Maine* 1.99: I find it proverbial that he takes things upon trust.

1799 Cobbett *Porcupine* 10.203: Just at the time when Tench [Coxe] was got into vogue, when his *humanity* was grown almost proverbial.

1799 WTudor in *Monthly Anthology* 1(1804) 296: Although there may not at present be any grounds for apprehension that our inhabitants, like those of one of the states of Greece, may be subjected to a nick-name under which history has preserved their records, and which, even at this distant period continues proverbial.

c1800 Dennie *Lay Preacher* 181: England, proverbial for its spirit of inquisitiveness, resembles a bumpkin.

c1800 PPond in Gates *Five Fur Traders* 37: It is Proverbel that fires . . . Stops the Groth of ye Wood and Destroise Small woods.

1801 TPierce in Vanderpoel *Chronicles* 388: Instead of being proverbial for loquacity, the ladies of this state might with propriety become proverbial for taciturnity.

1802 *Port Folio* 2.11: How deplorable will it be, should it ever become proverbial that a President of the United States, like the *Wierd Sisters* in Macbeth, *"Keeps his promise to the ear, but breaks it to the sense!"*

1802 *Port Folio* 2.17: The proverbial patience of a Philadelphia was exhausted.

1803 Austin *Constitutional* 157-8: The cruelty and inhumanity of [Robespierre] has become proverbial.

1804 Brackenridge *Modern* 414: Sir Thomas More's Utopia has become proverbial.

1804 Brackenridge *Modern* 456: The *loquacious Greek* was proverbial.

1805 Bentley *Diary* 3.138: Professor Pearson . . . is proverbial for the severity of his criticisms.

1805 Plumer *Memorandum* 264: He was proverbial for frankness, integrity & correct judgment.

1805 Silliman *Travels* 2.284: The attachment of the Scotch to music is, you know, proverbial.

1805 Silliman *Travels* 2.289: The height of the houses in Edinburgh is proverbial.

1806 Fessenden *Modern Philosopher* 111: Madrid and Edinburgh, it is affirmed, are much more healthy in consequence of a nastiness which is proverbial.

1806 Taggert *Letters* 199: The honour of the real Irish gentleman was proverbial. [Quoted from John Randolph of Roanoke.]

1806 *Weekly* 1.70: A foreigner, whose knavery is proverbial even among his own partisans.

1807 *Salmagundi* 324: The fertility of the Cocklofts is proverbial.

1808 Clay *Papers* 1.334: The Marshal, whose honesty is proverbial.

1809 *Port Folio* 2NS 2.534: Irish Impudence. The phrase is equally proverbial.

c1810 AJFoster *Jeffersonian America* 328: The hospitality of Boston is proverbial.

1810 Adams *Lectures* 2.99: The first of the causes, which has made the sounding emptiness of the bar so proverbial throughout the world, is indolence.

1810 Lee *Diary and Letters* 120: There is a class of women here called *Bédartines* whose honesty is proverbial. "He or she is as honest as a Bédartine." they say.

1811 *Port Folio* 2NS 5.30: The island of Nantucket has been called, "a sand bank," till its sterility has become proverbial.

1812 Hitchcock *Social* 140: Their egregious blunders in the performance of its [the school of politeness] tactics, render them, not only proverbial, but extremely ridiculous.

1812 Melish *Travels* 65: The salubrity of the climate is proverbial.

1813 *Analectic Magazine* in Thornton *Glossary* 2.959: The proverbial shrewdness of that portion of our countrymen vulgarly denominated Yankees.

1813 Bentley *Diary* 4.170: The great wealth of Thomas Emerson was proverbial.

1813 *Port Folio* 3NS 1.425: The extravagance of posthumous panegyric has been for ages proverbial.

1814 Bentley *Diary* 4.226: She married into the family of Skipper W., proverbial for honest simplicity and diligence.

1815 *Reviewers* 5: [The British] whose chastity is proverbial from St. Sebastians in Spain, to Hampton in Virginia.

1816 *Emigrant's Guide* 9: Dutch settlers, whose industry and economy are proverbial.

1816 Lambert *Travels* 2.423: Dr. Dana, proverbial for his pedantry.

1816 *Port Folio* 4NS 1.50: Whence arises this strange instability of a character, in a nation [British] proverbial for its obstinacy.

1816 *Port Folio* 4NS 1.165: But soon — 'tis Love's proverbial crime — Exhaused, he his oars let fall.

1816 *Port Folio* 4NS 1.171: The Port Folio has been so proverbial for its promises and its apologies.

1816 *Port Folio* 4NS 1.302: The Spaniards have become proverbial for their ignorance and imbecility.

1816 *Port Folio* 4NS 2.209: Your . . . zeal in the cause of "man's far better part" is proverbial.

1817 Jackson *Correspondence* 2.288: Major Tatum my Topographical Engineer whose impartiality is proverbial.

1817 SHPerkins in *North Carolina Historical Review* 47(1970) 62: [The slaves'] fidelity to each other is almost proverbial.

1817 Pintard *Letters* 1.56: He was precision itself . . . and proverbial for his systematic life.

1818 Hall *Travels* 35: My travelling contemporaries of both hemispheres, whose courage in this respect [describing a nation after a brief visit], has gained them the proverbial reputation of a race of men, who are never dastardly enough to shrink from the task, on account of a mere want of information.

1818 SHPerkins in *North Carolina Historical Review* 47(1970) 68: [William Gaston's] influence on the verdict Of the jury is almost proverbial.

1818 (JSloan), *Rambles in Italy* (Baltimore, 1818) 28: [The French officers'] passion for personal decoration, for cockades, stars and ribbands, is proverbial.

1818 Weems *Letters* 3.236: My name throughout all the Country is Proverbial for Industry.

1819 Kinloch *Letters* 1.159: Pope Felix the 5th, the same whose life at Ripaille became proverbial.

1819 Noah *Travels* 117: Algeciras is proverbial for containing all the rogues . . . in that quarter of Spain.

1819 Noah *Travels* 166: The superstition of the Spaniards and Italians, who coast along the shores of the Mediterranean is proverbial.

1819 *Port Folio* 4NS 8.165: A reputed American writer in the Newburyport Herald has taken the liberty to advance, that "the *ignorance* of the *reputed* learned men of America is *proverbial* in Europe."

1819 Verplanck *State* 81: William Ross, Esq. of Newburgh . . . His wisdom is quite proverbial.

1819 Waln *Hermit* 64: Demonstrated by a Tea Party, at a house, proverbial for adding, if possible, to its proverbial stupidity.

1820 Adams *Memoirs* 5.203: This rapid . . . change . . . of subjects calling for attention has such an effect upon the memory that the proverbial defect of that quality may be accounted for without supposing it intentional or pretended.

c1820 Bernard *Retrospections* 35: The reserve of an English conveyance is proverbial.

c1820 Bernard *Retrospections* 207: The negroes have always been proverbial for their homage to St. Vitus.

1820 Pintard *Letters* 1.340: Indeed the *Odium Theologicum* is proverbial & for what I see the Odium Medicum also.

1820 Simpson *Journal* 122: Mr. Clarkes fame has got wind, his generosity is proverbial.

1820 Tudor *Letters* 94: The "genteel indifference" for which it [the Episcopal Church] is proverbial is true here as elsewhere.

1820 Tudor *Letters* 165: English insolence became proverbial with those who were often exposed to its observation.

1821 Hodgson *Letters* 2.262: Every thing seems to yield to the proverbial perseverance of New England.

1821 Simpson *Journal* 377: That good management for which they are proverbial.

a1824 Marshall *Kentucky* 2.165: The influence of Colonel Nicholas . . . had . . . become proverbial.

1824 Blane *Excursion* 466: The enterprise of the Yankees is proverbial.

1826 Duane *Colombia* 65: [Women] hold sway over the other sex that is proverbial.

1826 Duane *Colombia* 107: He made us acquainted with Mr. Blandin . . .

proverbial for his hospitality.

1826 Duane *Colombia* 360: A conduct . . . so unlike the proverbial civility and hospitality experienced everywhere else.

1827 Austin *Papers* 2.1704: The morality, industry and agricultural enterprise which characterize the inhabitants of Ohio are well known and proverbial.

1827 Longfellow *Letters* 1.210: Frivolity and lightheartedness are proverbial characteristics of the French.

1829 JHenderson in *Ruffin Papers* 1.483: Mr. Seawell . . . whose unpopularity has been proverbial for years.

1830 Pintard *Letters* 3.179: But as my punctuality is proverbial they never turn out in bad weather.

1832 Ames *Nautical* 38: The proverbial infidelity of sailors's wives, from the spouse of the skipper to the yokefellow of the black cook.

1841 MVan Buren in *Jackson Correspondence* 6.93: I have offended against one whose indulgence to his friends is proverbial.

1843 Paulding *Letters(II)* 330: Such articles will do no credit to your Magazine, and make many deadly enemies, among a race proverbial for their irritability.

1857 UGwynn in *Ruffin Papers* 2.564: The known and almost proverbial integrity of the Judge, insures at least, an unprejudiced decision.

3. Proverbially

1775 Boucher *View* 458: The children of Israel . . . As a people, they were proverbially, *stiff-necked* and *rebellious*.

1789 Anburey *Travels* 2.41: Both sexes [in Boston and vicinity] have universally, and even proverbially, bad teeth.

1792 Bentley *Diary* 1.417: And being intoxicated with his success, he became proverbially a conceited man.

1796 Smith(EH) *Diary* 227: And yet the antedeluvians were proverbially long-lived.

1805 Silliman *Travels* 2.45: *Jeffreys,* now proverbially named the *infamous.*

1807 Janson *Stranger* 36: The month of November, which is proverbially fatal to Englishmen.

1811 EWinslow in *Winslow Papers* 661: The order of men who are usually employed in Lumbering (as it's called) are proverbially licentious.

1818 HBeecher in Beecher *Autobiography* 1.372: Litchfield, though proverbially cold, has not yet felt the severity I have usually experienced in the district of Maine.

1818 HGOtis in Quincy *JQuincy* 376: [Josiah Quincy] is proverbially industrious.

1818 Pintard *Letters* 1.160: Pitt . . . was proverbially a blockhead.

1819 Kinloch *Letters* 1.57: [Montpelier] was almost proverbially the retreat of consumptive people.

1822 MLee in Lee *Diary and Letters* 286: Schooley's Mountain is proverbially healthy.

1823 Thacher *Journal* 491: It was proverbially said [of Israel Putnam] as well by British as Provincial officers, that, in a service of great peril and hardships, from 1755 to 1763, *"he dared to lead where any dared to follow."*

1826 Duane *Colombia* 64: The display of an elegant ankle in a proverbially neat silk stocking.

1826 Duane *Colombia* 574: We had something else to annoy us, besides insects, of which we had heard Villeta was proverbially noisome.

1830 Ames *Mariner's* 73: A nation [the English] proverbially addicted to suicide.

1842 Fletcher *Letters* 181: The winter throughout the U.S. has been so proverbially mild.

1843 Cooper *Letters* 4.407: Insurance officers are proverbially short-sighted.

INDEX OF IMPORTANT WORDS

The purpose of this index is twofold: to make possible the identification of a saying in a form which differs from the lemma, and in some degree to facilitate thematic studies. Experience shows that an index of this kind cannot be altogether satisfactory. The shorter the index the less useful, the longer the index the less usable, and a happy medium between too little and too much is hard to achieve.

The index contains the important words in the lemmas, excluding the alphabetizing words, and a selection of significant words from those quotations which differ markedly in phrasing from the lemmas. It is no doubt superfluous to observe that the same word may be important in one context and unimportant in another. Words from the lemmas and from the first three quotations in any entry are identified by the lemma numbers; for all other words the dates of the quotations are given in parentheses after the lemma numbers. Words from the quotations are listed only for first occurrence within an entry.

If a word appears as more than one part of speech it is broken down grammatically. When nouns occur in both singular and plural, no distinction is made in the index, save in the case of *man* and *woman*. If nouns are found only in the plural they are entered under the plural form, unless the words occur as another part of speech or unless the plural forms throw the words out of alphabetical order. All verb forms, except verbal nouns and verbal adjectives, are entered under the infinitive forms. Adjectives and adverbs appear under their positive forms unless the words appear only in the comparative or superlative, in which cases those forms are used. Expressions of worthlessness or contempt are grouped in the index under Not a jot, Not a straw, Not abate, and so forth, and the few Wellerisms are brought together under that word.

Index of Important Words

Basket: E31, M91
Battalions: H172
Batter: B211
Battle: B224, D43, F94(1809), R6
Bawbee: D183, P191
Bawd: O32
Bawl: C274
Bay: *sb.* B203, S336; *vb.* D231,
 M232
Beam: M255, S519, S528
Bear: *sb.* B81, D244, G195, K25,
 L160, W230; *vb.* B139, C376
 (1798), E122, F210, G142, G176,
 H54, H152, L15, M269(1758),
 P12, T62
Beard: *sb.* H32; *vb.* L163
Beast: E74(1782), F154, M65, N16
Beat: A58, B320, B366-9, D326
 (1770), D335, E12(1775), G17,
 G101, H253, L61, R101, R146,
 R155, S206, S358(1801), S395,
 S430, W108
Beating: P6
Beauteous: R140
Beautiful: A88, E93, G140, M245
Beauty: F50, H264
Becack: H146
Become: J3, M8, N20
Bed: F49, F241, P295, T80
Bedfellow: C186, M193, P226,
 T227, W79
Bed-post: T303
Bee: H123, H268, M123, S367
Beef: A63
Beetle: E4(1809), H117
Before: B252, B374, C14, C48,
 C96, C108, C138, C274, C288,
 D145, E124, F47, F241, G34,
 H148, H154, H331, I26, J12,
 J58, L133, L206-7, M89, M140,
 M248, P42, P306, W193
Beforehand: P39
Befoul: B180
Beg: D277
Beget: F22(1809), K16, L140, P51,
 P296, T54
Beggar: C288, D2, D73, F242,
 H190, M50, P194, P279, R75,
 T168
Begin: B375, C120, C317, F145,
 H333(1778), S67, S322
Beginning: D192, E52, E77, E90,
 F56, M16, N23
Behave: C125
Behind: D112(1809), D130, E10,
 L206, P306
Belie: E106(1799)

Believe: E87, M24, M186, N56,
 T262
Bell: *sb.* C247, F218, M107, S341;
 vb. C82
Bellow: B355
Bell-ropes: C240
Belly: B297, C9, C11, D160, E83,
 E131, M46, R37, S381, W332
Bend: B287, F12(1778), H27, R46
 (1807), T300, W188
Benefit: M87
Benison: B125
Bereave: B73
Beshit: H146
Beside: C383, M102
Best: *sb.* B20, E94, H153, L86
 (1780), R165; *adj.* B166, C238,
 C264, D100, E86, E110, F257,
 F278, H264, H357, M177, P130,
 R14, S197, T74, W64-5, W242,
 W310. *See also* Better, Good
Betimes: D20, R89
Betray: B180, J55
Better: *sb.* L106; *adj.* A141-2, B49,
 B274-5, B303, B383, C66, C102,
 C144, C237, C281, C341, C384,
 D17, D33, D73, D117, D190,
 D214, D240, D251, E36, E51-2,
 E57, E60, E67, E98-9, E108, F49,
 F79, F111, F143, F219, F291,
 F298, F303, G6, G47, H23, H28,
 H61(1760), H143, H166, H232,
 H299, H338, L40, L50, L84-5,
 L117, L175-6, L223, L252, M21,
 M82, M100.3, M108, M180,
 M241, N10, N40, O40, P47,
 P275, R130, S192, S328, T308,
 T313, V20, W85, W222, W237-
 8, W372; *adv.* M20. *See also*
 Best, Good
Between: A130, B103, C122, D179,
 D249, F108, F131, G23, H106,
 H109, L244, P245, S78, S462,
 S542, T99, W185
Betwixt: M6
Beware: A46, B153, D218, H83,
 L156, M134, T113, W22
Bewitch: W146
Bewray: B180(1834)
Beyond: I26-7, S1
Bible: G97, M182
Big: B359, C2, C182, D117, E131,
 F251, J47, M266, N92, O53, S27,
 S54
Big-bellied: S153
Bind: C240, O8, S169(1800),
 W169

Bird: B367, B369(1777), C353,
 D23, E37, F18, F61, H355, N50,
 S29, S36, S279, S537
Birthday: S507
Bitch: D243(1830), G90
Bite: *sb.* B45, Y10; *vb.* B46, B196,
 B327, D241, D325, H55, M1,
 M116, M279, N95, T85, T193
Bitter: *sb.* S541; *adj.* C255, D58,
 G4, H149, P138-9(1815), P140,
 S329, W367
Black: *sb.* B64; *adj.* B17, B163,
 B264, C118, C158, C218, C249,
 C352, D59, D108-9, D126, D321,
 E24, E138, H186, H245, I46,
 J26, L173, M155, M183, N39,
 N70, O23, P56, P87, P183,
 P248, P292, R31, S5, S123, S127,
 S163, S252, S330, S537, T23
Blackamore: E74(1729)-5
Blackbird: S36
Blackness: E74
Bladder: B65
Blame: H154, M250, T269
Blanch: E75(1707)
Blanket: D255, S239
Blare: C10
Blast: R46
Blaze: C226
Bleed: D302, P120
Bless: F31, G72, G90
Blessed: G47, N104
Blessing: G93, L96(1832), M296
 (1830), V5
Blind: *sb.* K33; *vb.* G42; *adj.* B54,
 B57, B122, B194, F272, H353,
 J61, L234, M22, M61, M84,
 M205, N84, P241, S451
Blithe: B169, F194, H156, L31
Blithesome: C116, L31
Block: C165, H325, K50, S439,
 S499
Bloody: H102, Q4, R32
Bloom: G149, P50
Blooming: B219, H156, M90,
 M119, R141, S383-4
Blow: *sb.* D139, H294, S470,
 W327; *vb.* B320, C221, C223,
 G137, G190, H336, M43, N5,
 P236, P268, S245, S480, T258,
 W54, W187-8, W191, W211,
 W214
Blue: B65, D118, I37, S244, W119
Blues: D118(1819)
Blunt: W120
Blush: E10, F6, R147
Board: S152, W275

Index of Important Words

527

C191, C206, C267, C303, C370,
D34, D62, D293, F103, F310,
G155, H328, I3, I8, I10, I61,
L67, M96, N63, P108, P274,
P309, S452, T87, W45

Collar: N31

Collect: S456(1790)

Collegian: M220

Color: H306, M22, T270

Comb: *sb.* H197; *vb.* H132

Combat: W217(1799)

Come: A80, B75, B158, B204,
B257, C1, C10, C44(1788),
C175, C256, C286, C389, D43,
D277, E56, E103, F45, F132,
F141, F151, F167, G67, G111-2,
G170, G173, H259-60, K22,
L134, L199(1815), L205, L249,
M100, M106, M127, M194,
M268, N11, N18(1792), N62
(1814), N108, P161, P163, P265,
R58, R78, R124, S50, S75, S91,
S235, S264, T29, T56, T91-3,
T103, T177, Y2

Comforter: J40

Command: O9, W289

Commendation: P272

Commit: L16

Commodity: T50

Common: A52, B377, C106, D77,
F21

Commotion: I62

Companion: A107, B87, C330,
L231, O31, P258, P317

Company: C245, M45, M192,
R130

Compelled: O8

Compensate: B88

Complain: L219(1753)-20, S310

Compliment: D217, F292, L96
(1809)

Comply: R128(1783)

Compulsion: N21, O8(a1788)

Conceal: B372(1815), H48, S275
(1778)

Concern: L127

Conduct: A42, F275, L255

Conference: C381(1792)

Confirm: E105

Conquer: D207, F293, O9(1813)

Consciences: C302

Consent: *sb.* O8(1793), S209; *vb.*
M284

Considering: C32

Consist: H77, R73

Constant: T296

Constancy: R61(1798)

Constrained: O8(a1811)

Consult: P144

Consume: O18, P50, S253

Consumption: H279(1814)

Contagion: P193

Contempt: F22, I49, P280

Contend: M294

Content: *sb.* L175, M177, W79;
adj. S234

Contented: M177

Contention: B33, B253, L175,
P51, P261

Contentment: L175, W78

Continual: D306

Contrary: *sb.* D298; *adj.* G134
(1726)

Controversy: S547

Convenience: C282, I30

Converse: W295

Converts: Z1

Coo: P132

Cook: G85, M139

Cool: *vb.* B314, C291, H178, S145;
adj. C371, H125, H171, L229,
W308

Co-partner: L231

Copper: F32(1787), K8

Cord: R135

Cordial: F308

Corks: L167

Corn: B371, C244, F87, M122,
O15, O55, R70, S256

Corner: Q1, T272

Cornuted: H289(1789)

Corporation: S100

Correct: T139

Correspond: F1

Corrupt: *vb.* C270; *adj.* T232
(1754), W37

Cost: E109, E129, P7, P225, W311

Cottage: D79, D102, R75

Cough: L233

Counsel: W270

Counsellors: M301

Count: C138, S43(1799), T32,
T307

Countenance: F8, I59

Country: B366, G83, L22, M92,
N15, N63, P301, T223, W23

Courage: D190, D333

Course: M238, Q6

Court: D79, F305, H193, H254

Cover: C121, C226, H251

Covert: E101

Covet: E140

Covetous: S320

Covetousness: L239

Cow: C9-11, G84, M49, S126

Coward: B300, L107

Cowardice: C330

Crabbed: C334

Crack: G57, N126, T192

Cracked: P187

Craft: C318, N56

Cram: L115

Crave: S359

Crawl: B221

Crazy: C287, L212

Cream: C89

Create: N20, W96

Credit: H270, R51

Creditor: B278

Creep: C317, E56, S269

Crime: C121(1744), M192(1815),
P262

Cringe: D256

Crook: H273

Crooked: B286, W15, Z2

Cross: *vb.* I1, R158(1819), S83;
adj. B67, W249

Crouch: T110

Crow: *sb.* C36; *vb.* C241, C243,
H204

Crowd: H216

Crowing: S21

Crown: *sb.* C351, F60(1813); *vb.*
E50

Cruel: A77, C330, D63, G156, S72

Cruelty: C330, M149

Crush: B348(1762)

Crust: P111

Cry: B144, C153, F153, H330,
L249, M166, P61, R100, T43,
W142, W259

Cub: B71

Cuckoldom: H289(1805)

Cuckoldry: H289

Cuckolds: H289

Cudgel: S430

Cuffing: T188

Cunning: *sb.* L255, T270; *adj.*
F279, L61, S47, S102

Cup: S250

Cupboard: B144

Cur: D231, D249-50

Curd: M162(1802)

Cure: *sb.* A12, A50, D191(1739),
O42, P275, R53, S205; *vb.* A24,
E97, K12, T140

Curiosity: W282

Current: S492

Curry: F53, H314

Curse: *sb.* P320; *vb.* B137, O28,
T249, T290, W312

Cursing: B204
Curst: C323, G84
Custody: L16
Custom: H2-3
Cut: *sb.* S146; *adj.* C33, C222, C235, C262, C337, D18, D79 (1801), D167, D174, E25-6, E143, G126, H242, H365, K48, P166, S371, T162, T179, T182, W3, W67, W125, W296
Cute: K34
Cygnet: S538(a1767)

D

Dabble: F106(1812), W41(1799)
Dagger: F9
Daily: S540
Dainty: L237
Dally: W267
Dam: D119, W49
Damage: W19
Dame: S424
Damn: H176
Dance: *sb.* P174(1809); *vb.* A135, C346, F84, G11, H113, P172, P174(1834), P246(1783), T204
Dancing-school: D248
Danger: A74, B353, C331, D87, D101, F289, H83(1809), L2 (1824), L119, M27, N48(1791), N110, R25, W276
Dangerous: D101, D191(1794), E61(1806), E115
Dare: D241, H358
Dark: *sb.* B250, C57, H245, J34, L81; *adj.* C210, D318(1789), E40, E69, G157, H331, M156, M246, N71, P184
Darkness: L131, W340
Dart: *sb.* O25(1764), P26; *vb.* L137, S484
Dash: *sb.* W45(1821); *vb.* S78 (1806)
Daughter: B155, G191, M256 (1764)-8, S318-9, W273
Daughter-in-law: M263
Day: A110, A139, B40, D243, F94, F144, F208, F222, F295-6, H206, H255, L121, M248, P157, R3, R58, S29, S319, S508, S518, T225, W92(1801), W294, W362
Day-light: H331, J34
Dazed: D236
Dead: D86, D251, D282, F201, G6, H35, H87, H214, H322, H325, H349, I22, L129, L185, L195,

M23, M81, N94, Q7, R20, R121, S405, S453, T82, T167, T210, W145
Deaf: A35, E16, H6, P242
Deal: D209(1731), F243, M24, N56
Dear: *adj.* B398, C117, E112, F299, L111, O22; *adv.* E109, F25, G109, R60, W132, W246
Death: A100, D88(1731), D101 (1806), D257, E18(1779), G25, H319, J17, J24, L117, L133, L236, M74(c1820), N114, P100, R54, S538
Debauch: C270(1811)
Debt: B99, D75, D107, E8, I39, K24, L260, S221, V15
Debtor: B278, C341
Decay: *sb.* M114; *vb.* F182(1789), H147
Deceased: D251(1788)
Deceit: W285
Deceitful: F50, W372(1775)
Deceive: T261
Deceiving: A103
Deceptive: A103(1781)
Decide: S547
Decision: O39
Decoration: H289(1735)
Deed: D33, E101, P296(1798), W164, W309, W333
Deep: *adj.* H187, W38; *adv.* M175 (1816), M298, S256
Deer: T224
Defence: S99(1771)
Defend: M242
Defer: A73, H279
Defiance: T194(1797)
Defile: P185
Defy: P101
Degenerate: L110
Delay: L127
Deliver: G73, H190, M25
Delusive: A103(1781)
Delve: A32
Demure: D226, N122
Den: B86
Dependence: A103
Deprivation: V5
Deprive: G99(1819)
Descend: G115, T103
Descry: W137
Deserve: F4, M35, T37, T249, W118
Desirable: N44
Despair: H284, I39
Desperate: D191

Despise: E4(1809), E61, F22, T229 (1780)
Destiny: M106
Destroy: D207(1768), F146(1806), G99, I65, R132
Destruction: F287, P281
Determine: T141(1761)
Detest: T229
Deviate: T226(1804)
Devil: A84, B127, C22, C116, C148, C173, C330, C362, D22, E49, F106, F146, F250, G85, G94, G97, G101, H193, H291, K13, L61, L71(1756), L119, L185, M37, M43, M54, N56, P292, R135(1804), S23, S374, T264, W108
Devotion: I15
Devour: C347(1781), S124(1799)
Diamond: P60, S523, W102(1775)
Die: C9, C144, C313, D73, D76 (1791), D205, D210, D257, D263, E18, F231, F289, F291, G62, G149, H84, H278, H284, I28, K21, K47, L17, L56, L119, M70, M90, P194, S129, S538 (1725), T223, U4(1787)
Diet: D220
Differ: A22, D44, L131, M92, P221, T28
Difference: D79, D202, M153 (1830), S471, T297
Different: C188(1800), E89, M92, T281
Difficult: B129, N107, S254
Difficulties: C282
Dig: G163-4, P182
Dilemma: H293
Diligence: M279
Diligent: B108
Dine: D316, P277, P280, S24, S61
Dinner: C46, D316(1815), G122
Dip: D195
Dirge: S538
Dirt: M298, P64
Dirty: D239, H236, I32, L151, P112, S412, T150, W34, W41 (1804), W338
Disagreeable: A39, R133
Disappear: K11
Disappoint: M56(1763), N104
Discord: A104, C275
Discover: P303, T141
Discretion: A14, O44
Disease: I12(1814), R53
Disguise: D193
Dish: H67, M177, W145, W365

Index of Important Words

End: *sb.* B55, B100, C21, C189, C222, E44, E91, F99-100, H19, T127, T180, T225, W245, W353; *vb.* A76, B130, E55, M100, M146, S262(1780)
Ending: B130-2
Endure: C376, H302
Enemy: B325, G73, L83, M207, W23, W372
Engineer: P91
Enjoy: E1, W80
Enough: A94, C346, D53, D139, D188, D242, F135, F175, G59, G142, G173, H300-1, J39, K55, M28, M181, M296(1822), M309, P23, Q3, R135, S22, W329
Enter: E56, H358, K50
Entering: W97
Enterprising: F271(1816)
Entertain: K31
Entertainment: R97
Equal: B10, H23, J29
Equality: G162
Eradicate: R132
Ermine: S379
Err: M29
Errand: F244
Error: H83(1767), T139
Escape: B78, K55, R26(1812), S78 (1785), S326
Escutcheon: B222
Estate: B238, P239, T217
Eternal: T266
Even: C129, D171
Evening: M246
Event: C189, I29, W25(1773)
Ever: H257
Every: C312, D243, E25, E106, F101, K36(1837), L138, L177, M29, M35, M148, M206, N81, S18, S91
Everybody: B377, M82
Everything: E54, M144, O30, R54, S101, S268, U12
Everywhere: M62, N15
Evidence: M69(1766), P29(1805)
Evil: *sb.* B143, C99, C387, D40, D55(1797), D128, D191, D300, F52, G111-2, H83(1751), I12, L239, R53(1793), S522, T126, T252, W287; *adj.* C270, L51, M30, T232
Exaggerate: T226(1797)
Exalt: R102
Excell: S520
Excellent: L84
Excite: H169(1809)

Excuse: *sb.* I16, W165; *vb.* B300, I16
Exempt: N114
Excercise: T31
Exertions: P298(1781)
Exigency: S388(1786)
Existing: D251
Expect: I36(1764), L182, N104
Expedition: C127(a1788)
Expel: V14
Experience: A48, O40
Experiments: A28(1775)
Expire: F316
Expressions: W333(1797)
Extinct: F316
Extinguish: O21
Extirpate: R132
Extort: O8
Extract: S367
Extreme: D191, R84
Extremity: M59
Extraordinary: D191
Eye: A105, A114, B184-5, C15, D305, D329, F112, G121, H26, J30, L261, M110, M255, R51, S87, S128, S205, T66, T305, W208

F

Fable: F283, G125, G140, H147 (1724), M269, S111(1748), V24 (1773), W152, W264
Face: N91, N95, S283, W186
Fade: F197, L74
Faggot: M42, W169
Fail: F27, F275, H147(1807), H167, S208, T121
Failings: C121
Faint: H157
Fair: A72, B178, C353, D35, D269, F3, F196-7, G50, H157, H247, M129, M243, P11, P198-200, S286, T37, T58, T295, W91
Faith: G171, M63, P313, R65
Faithful: D284, F20(1808), F304, S106, W372(1775)
Faithless: W172
Fall: *sb.* K9, P281; *vb.* B78, B221, B352, C70, E6, F269(1767), G185, L232, L249, M90, M287, N51, N79, P182, R113, R124, S4, S78, S243, S250(1778), S280-1, S290, S407, S412, S462, T231, U4, W339
Fallacious: A103(1794)
Fallen: M80

Fallible: M29(1798)
Falling: R27
False: D297, G69, H188, P233, S68
Falsehood: H24
Fame: T258(1812)
Familiar: A6, F22, G22, H3, H51 (1798)
Family: A17, H204, T234
Famish: I28
Famished: H105(1822)
Far: *adj.* B178, N63, P221; *adv.* C316, M175, N45, P2
Fare: *sb.* D316, N47; *vb.* G65
Far-off: F298
Fart: *sb.* J15; *vb.* H278
Farther: C180, G65, H318, T262
Farthest: W62
Farthing: F188
Fashion: S157, W343
Fast: *sb.* F57; *adj.* B208, B340, L116, Q2, W173; *adv.* B168, D112, F44, H91(1790), H181 (1775), H318, N62, R165
Fasten: L91
Fasting: H278, P202
Fat: *sb.* S490; *adj.* A142, B68, B384, C176, D221, F210, F216, H238, K37, L44, M110, P47 (1787), P113, P234-5, R3, R121, S88, W298
Fatal: D101(1776), T42
Fate: W25(1776)
Father: B363(1768), C148-9, D127, L146, S320, S322, S324, S425, W240
Fathoms: S529
Fatted: C13
Fatten: B371, P216
Faucet: S368
Fault: C121(1786), E62, M68
Faultless: C142
Favor: *sb.* K36; *vb.* F271, H172
Favorable: W204
Fear: *sb.* G96, W290; *vb.* C80, F233, G96
Feast: E52, E65-6, F57, F232, I35, M177, W365
Feather: *sb.* B177-8, D23, E5, J38, N49, P56, S480; *vb.* N49, S291
Fee: G76
Feeble: C140, G153
Feed: A36, C114(1822), C296, H55, H182
Feel: B149, B258, D199, E64
Fell: S496
Fellow: S175, S378

Index of Important Words

Fellowship: M38, M192(1806)
Felon: A67
Female: G57, S29, W280
Fence: H356(1781), V26
Fend: H80
Fetch: F132, M216(1785), S13, T50
Few: *sb.* F284, M95, M149, M241;
  adj. R73, S531, W309-10
Fickle: F273, P233, W174
Fickleness: W286(1809)
Fiddle: *sb.* S69, T282; *vb.* R127
Fiddle-strings: G197
Fidelity: P313
Field: H337, T51
Fierce: G19, G121, H296, L14,
  L154, W20
Fierceness: L8, L162
Fifth: W111
Fifty: F188
Fig: F28, G141
Fight: *sb.* L14; *vb.* A58, B86,
  B360, C87(1815), C243, D140,
  D190, D244, D271, L164, P26,
  P314, S114, T111, W84, W209,
  W217
Fig-tree: G141(1790)
Fill: B297, H337-8, P17, S3, S203,
  W316, W332
Filter: T265
Filth: D234(1652)
Find: F220, H219-20, J7, K52,
  L206, L223, R156, R176, S98,
  S430, T44, T55, T136, W352
Finder: F282
Findfaults: M147
Fine: B294, C209, F61, D121, F80,
  G98, H247(1732), J18, K5,
  L214, M120, S212, T78
Fine-tooth: H197
Finger: B72(1757), C284, S100,
  T179
Fire: *sb.* B230, C97, C145, C224,
  C228, F38, F113, F169, F171,
  F252, F315-7, G108, H336,
  H340, I61, M43, N48, R55,
  R93, S214, S261, S263, S298,
  S308, S360-1, W34-5, W58,
  W151, W158-63, W350; *vb.*
  C161, F163
Fire-drake: T157
Firelight: H335
Fire-side: P258
Firm: A33, A133, P243, R41,
  R107
Firmament: G70 (1789)
First: *sb.* B26, F291, V20; *adj.*
  B224, B233, B344, C146, C170,

D168, F54, H364, I23, L232,
  S99, S423, T284, V15; *adv.*
  C264, G99, H66, K24, W142,
  W327(1800)
Fish: *sb.* D20, K5, L192, S444; *vb.*
  C43, D161, M233, W41
Fisher: W41(1776)
Fisherwoman: E29
Fish-hook: F101
Fishing: W41(1677)
Fishwoman: F153, F160
Fist: C184, P13
Fit: *vb.* B10, C29, E5, G62, P22,
  S164; *adj.* C354, G195
Five: S529, T307
Fixed: F41
Flail: F77
Flame: C226, F200, F317(1771),
  H336, S361
Flash: L135-7(1822)
Flat: D200, F193, M96, P15, T239
Flaws: T152
Flea: C335, D246, T59
Flee: P26, P90, R27, R74, W35,
  W144
Fleet: W175
Fleeting: S109
Flesh: B262, F150, F156, S370,
  T65, W69
Flexible: R46
Flinch: H302(1723), R134(1841),
  S190
Fling: C326
Flint: B218, H169(c1700)
Flitting: M236
Float: C294, O3(1834), S224
Flock: *sb.* S123, S127; *vb.* B116,
  B177
Flood: E23
Floor: H347
Flourish: A51, B59, C16, C128,
  T220
Flow: *sb.* E23; *vb.* L21
Flower: A111, B113-4, S367, W14
Flowing: T103
Fluctuate: W93
Fluke: S440
Flummery: F137
Flutter: F200
Fly: *sb.* S330, E4, G64, L54, M281;
  vb. B171-2, C108, C256, F5,
  F67, F94, F203, F318, H9, J38,
  L137, M123, N62, R74, S131,
  S535, T59, T130, W158, W198
Fly-catcher: F203(1821)
Fly-catching: E4(1702)
Flying: B325

Fly-time: B356
Foe: E60, F301, M134
Foibles: C121(1771)
Foil: D150, W84
Fold: S133
Folks: B280, D138
Follow: C100, D258, M194(1810),
  M246, P203, P281(1776), S112,
  S132, S148(1793)
Folly: B87, F213
Fond: P119
Food: D316, L237, W265
Fool: B300, C67, C310, D279,
  E112, H83(1743), H160, L238,
  M48, M51, M87, W123
Foolish: B132, P79, W329(1786)
Foot: B1, B34, C70, C97, D328,
  G147, H56, H116, H125, H127,
  H209, H305, H315, J60, K39,
  L104, M283, N51, P56, S174,
  T69
Football: F72, H134
Footing: R46
Forbear: B80
Force: P224
Forearm: F265
Forecast: F277
Foreign: S18
Foreigners: D252
Forelock: T147
Foremost: B100, F257-8, T8
Foresee: D17
Foresight: A47, I26(1817)
Forest: F242
Forever: D212(1793)
Forget: F266, P32(1783)
Forgive: I44
Fork: K47
Forked: H289
Forsake: E72
Fortunate: B275, F238
Fortune: F260, M94, M194(1803),
  N41, W25
Forty: K22, M51, M226, T298
Forward: B15, H243, Y12
Foster: H55(1797)
Foul: B180(1834), F3, F17, M129
Foundation: W339
Fountain: T232, W33
Four: C144, E126, P252, T51,
  T307
Four-score: C144
Fowl: F150, F287, H206, L249
  (1782)
Fox: F164, G140, L157
Fractious: W26
Fragile: R47(1828)

Frail: F183
Frame: H147
Fraught: H43
Fray: E52
Free: A53, C244, G44, H319, I62,
L22, M217, R69, S148, T216,
T220, W176
Freedom: B63, S94
Freely: S364
Freeze: B230, E19, M108
Frequent: R41
Fresh: B341, D20, D194, F195,
R142, Z1
Fret: G166, G197
Friend: B263, C222, E60, F18, F20
(1808), F124, F208, G73, I59,
M45, M207, P304, R41, S166,
V6, W82, W248, W295, W372
Friendless: P229
Friendship: A40, C110
Frighten: A44(1822), S110(a1778)
Frost: H228
Frosty: S411
Froth: N69
Frugality: L239(1786)
Fruit: G140, H364, I12(1766),
T232, T237
Fruitful: S347
Fruitless: E71
Fry: F155
Frying-pan: G63
Fuddled: F83
Fuel: C160
Fulfill: P298(1805)
Full: B143, C318, D314, E32, H43,
H66, H123, H192, M46, M288,
P202, S12, T94, T158, V12
Fur: O58
Further: B393

G

G: G58
Gab: G41
Gabble: M5(1815)
Gain: *sb.* H281, L222; *vb.* D37,
F230, L179, M207, P77(1787),
W292
Gainsay: D103
Gale: H79, W168
Gall: D288, H266
Galled: H302
Gallon: F203
Gallop: P195, S266
Gallows: S84, S378
Gallows-tree: R102
Game: B159(1775), C90(1809),

D137, F8, F37(1782), L209,
T309, W285
Gander: S53
Garb: D147
Garden: M54
Garlic: H301, M247
Garment: C29(1777), H251
Garret: C76
Gate: D78
Gather: B113, B117, G141, H56,
L48, S297, S367, S456
Gaudy: P52
Gavelkind: F46
Gay: B170, C343, G168, L34, P56
Gaze: S412
Gear: G3
General: E105-6
Generous: J58
Gentle: D93, D285, G32, L8, M116
Gentleman: D93, J3, J6, M93,
P208
Gentleness: L8, L162
Get: A96, B7, B28(1813), B56,
B100, B193, B218, B270, B367,
C69, C263, D160, D196, E6
(1758), G49, H57-8, H311, J28,
K1, L104, L199(1803), M27,
M239, M288, N83, N104(1812),
O27, P77-8, P130, P278, R49,
S27, S149, S158, S320, S470, T5,
T51, T225, V3, V18, W42, W68,
W199-200, W218, W318
Getting: E72, S57
Giants: D338
Giddy: W10
Gift: G89, I36
Gild: P139
Gilded: B173, H274
Gim: P53
Gingerbread: G45
Girdle: G23, G97
Girl: C156, D161, L150, N41
Give: A42, A59, B12, B27-8, B152,
B164, B392, C5, C289, C308,
C379, D4, D19, D151-2, D180,
D245, E16(1752), F90, F168,
G39, G68, G74-5, G113, H29,
H59, H68, H134-5, H225, H270,
I24, J42, L103, L184, L219,
L256, M131, P152, P309, Q12,
R50, R101, R125, R135, R170,
S147, S162, S209, S251, S278,
S300, S474, V8
Giver: G47(1763), G82
Glad: S324
Glass: *sb.* L210, W276; *adj.* B396,
H333

Glistening: J26(1826)
Glister: G102
Glitter: G102(1702)
Glory: D12
Glossy: S331
Glove: C73, H51
Glow: F319
Glut: W321
Gnaw: B254
Go: A84, B99, B326, B351, B361,
B373, B379, C48(1807), C146,
C148, C197, C205, C239(1723),
C263, C336, C367, C390, D112,
D116, D141-2, D160(1797)-1,
D252, D259, D292, D298, D316,
E6(c1680), F26, F133-4, F166,
F241, G15, G150, H27, H78,
H91(1790), H163, H194,
H248, H259, H277, H304, H315,
H356(1815), J23, K22, K36, L18,
L84, L137, L199, M81, M100
(1760), M197, M214-5, M217,
N3, N12(1805), N79, P2, P188,
P251, R64, R106, R113, S21,
S82, S185, S220, S264, S449, S492
(1789), T29, T64, T71, T108,
T165, T211-2, V4, W11, W69-
70, W77, W125, W135, W154,
W159, W201-2, W208, W218,
W252, W345, W351, W353, Z1
Goats: S134
Gob: G41
God: A26, C180, D124, D136,
D145, E82, F56, L159, L185,
M56, M59, M66, N116, V31
Goddess: A104, F273
Godliness: C193
Gods: F54
Gold: B146, C109, F293, H162,
L150, L239(1786), P322, V16,
W83, W102, W237
Golden: C111, D209, G125, M130
Goldmine: F78(1830)
Good: *sb.* D55(1785), E103, G47,
I19-20, L174, R121, R124, S10
(1721), S148, S522, W191; *adj.*
A43, A71, A119, B39, B131,
B161(1806), B304, B400, C6,
C66, C155, C222, C261, C270,
C324, C341, D41, D180, D189,
E65, F4, F8(1748), F24-5, F74,
F124, F148, F150-1, F201, F210,
F225, F242, F277, F284, G49,
G78, G92, G94, H61(1782), H72,
H75, H89, H93, H145, H164,
H192, H303, H348, H357, H362,
J1, J5, K46, L27, L51, L58, L62,

543

Index of Important Words

Rich: *sb.* D79(1788); *adj.* B7,
B275, C338, F231, H361, J27,
L146, L217, M50, M76, N2,
R121, S306, T58, T168
Riches: C154, C281, H77, H337,
N10, P51, W83(1774)
Ride: B127, B269, C46, C48,
H231, H315, H319-20, L260,
S230, W129
Rider: W16
Ridiculous: M269(1807)
Right: *sb.* L219(1746), M159,
T216, W373; *adj.* H41, H44,
L98, R41, S8; *adv.* T124
Righteousness: D122
Ring: E14(1849)
Rip: G125(1781)
Ripe: F314, G140
Ripen: F308
Rise: B98-9, C317, D36, D246,
F69, F269, L37, P255, R46, S63,
W54
Rising: *sb.* S510; *adj.* S526
Risk: L176, T49
Riverlets: W15
Road: L29
Roar: B357, L165, P126
Roast: H340, R36
Rob: B73, B145, D151(1781),
D278, H313, P92
Robbery: E107
Rock: D306(1811), G43, S456
Rods: B363
Rogue: L54(1732), M24, R135,
T43(1831)
Roil: W41
Roll: B35, L201, S297, T130(1789)
Rolling: S456
Room: C79, E43, S308
Root: A144, D128, H219, I12
(1769), L239, R46
Rope: E55(1780)
Rose: B96, S275(1753), T62
Rosy-posies: R145(1828)
Rot: *sb.* S127, W232; *vb.* W232
Rotten: A107, D104, F242, P166,
R88, S129, S500, T232(1797)
Rough: B69, D169
Round: *adj.* B32, D319-20, P16,
R103; *adv.* D159, F117, W62
Row: B239, W73, W209
Rub: D186, H302, R177, S334
Rubbish: R76
Ruby: W237
Ruddy: R159
Rue: E140
Ruffle: S162

Rug: B350, F171
Ruin: *sb.* P51; *vb.* D101(1777),
G99(1774)
Rule: *sb.* D209, E105-6, E110,
N20, N94, R99, S10; *vb.* D207
(1760), I50, L231, R99, R118,
R131, T138, V16
Rum: K13
Run: A85, C146, C315, C390,
D99, D112, D142(1787), D157,
D271, F94, G27, G60, G144,
H11, H243, H249, H330, L161,
R27, R82, R91-2, S78(1785),
S135, S178, S492, S527, T179-
80, T183, W7, W35, W128,
W161, W208, W250, Y13
Rush: F233
Rust: W85
Rye-dough: I21

S

Sack: B25, C72, S40
Sad: D253
Saddle: *sb.* H324; *vb.* H308, S8
(1782)
Safe: B168, C52, E27, P322, S151-
2, T39
Safety: M198, M301
Sail: *sb.* S153, T209; *vb.* W208-10,
W251
Sailor: A2, D22(1792), T216,
T226(1750)
Saint: N56, S225
Salt: A136, G136, P63, S405
Salve: T132
Same: B204, B285, B338, C165
(1799), G18, H14, K10, L30,
L138, M62, N15, Y6
Sanction: *sb.* S209(1794); *vb.* E51
(1805)
Sand: G60, R137
Satin: T123
Sauce: H357, M177
Savage: *sb.* I33; *adj.* B353
Save: A79, B19, B187, C104, C340,
C360, D301, F30, G73, M63,
P77-9(1782), P81, S10(1821),
S368, S434
Savor: S31, S316, S447
Saws: H86(1865)
Say: A69, B252, D176, D208,
D214, D336, E21, E80, H153,
I43, J12, L86-7, L106, L157,
L180, L183, M82-3, P42
Scabbard: S548, S552
Scabbed: S127
Scabby: S127

Scald: W308
Scalded: C80, H249
Scale: F66, S479
Scalp: E118
Scamper: D157
Scar: W24
Scarce: G13, P84, P99
Scare: A44, O49, W301
Scarlet: S214
Scatter: S262, T64
Scheme: C127(1769)
School: E109(1776), E112, E114
(1811), H83(1798), T13
Schoolmaster: E109(1815), E114
Science: O40
Scissors: B6
Scold: *sb.* F219; *vb.* B389, D265,
X1
Scolding: H341, W153
Scorn: C126
Scornful: D239
Scourge: *sb.* R117; *vb.* R116(1775)
Scramble: A101
Scrape: H203
Scraped: C47
Scratch: A96, R176
Scripture: D120
Scrub: E75(1798)
Sculpture: M148(1808)
Scum: P255
Scurvy: S105
Sea: D304, F26, F151, F276, H30,
R91, S43, W40, W224, W252
Seamen: T216
Sea-shore: S43
Season: E93, R34, T116
Seasoning: H357(1788)
Second: *sb.* V20; *adj.* B158, C152,
H2, T74, V15
Secret: *sb.* T82, T128(1787), W39;
adj. G158
Secure: D45
Security: D203
See: A79, B79, B135, B154, B206,
B393, C83, C156, D85, D158,
E64, E125-6, E135, E137, E140,
F250, F318, G177, H26, H66,
H153, H244, H353, H360, I26,
K29, L26, L166, L209, M175,
M186, M223, M234, M255, P48,
P166, S153, S379, S508, T119,
T214, T262, U1, W4, W107,
W155, W211, W303
Seed: *sb.* B215, W99; *vb.* S352
(1836)
Seek: E101, K52, R75, S525, T272,
W50, W273

Index of Important Words

T

Index of Important Words

C329, D249, D265, E30, F164,
F283, H119, H122, H141, H268,
M223, S36, S159, S260, S348,
S433
Tailors: D131(1803)
Taint: F145
Take: A109, B16, B197, B358,
B371, C32, C101, C373, D79-80,
D130, D152, D266, E81, F44,
F139, F211, F294, G28, G50,
G58, G73, G75-6, G89, G136,
H69, H103, H170, H183, H351,
I24, L78, L163, M79, M127,
M140, M218, N14, N48(c1737),
N51, N82, N97(1747), N120, O2
(1778), O7, P257, R10, R48,
R83, S20, S162, S211, S221,
S238, S240, S281(1802), S303,
S319, S351, S407, S423, S490,
S497, S546, T55-6, T69, T147,
T243, T306, W6, W44, W149-
51, W164, W188, W199, W351-2
Tale: C28, M23, T226(1747),
W152
Talk: *sb.* S309, W333(1793); *vb.*
B210, B266, D144, F160, P298
(1783), R104, R134, S59, S362,
W215
Tall: H112
Tallow: F177
Tame: *vb.* W258; *adj.* S122
Tankard: G164
Tap: P85
Taper: F200(1812)
Tar: *sb.* S125; *vb.* B338
Tar-barrel: B107, B110, T95
Tares: W110
Tarry: T125
Taskmaster: N21
Taste: A18, D201, E89
Tat: T154
Tattle: T13
Taut: B293
Tawny: E75(1749)
Taxes: D61
Tea: E72
Teach: B316, D272, E114, F239,
H307, O45, S350
Teachers: E114(1803)
Tear: *sb.* C347, H169(1702), P136,
W241, W289; *vb.* R46
Tell: B181, C157, C271(1822),
E62, E95-6, G26, H107, H209
(1819), K35, M23, M94, M101,
Q8, S94, S198, S467, T13, T141
(1784), T226(1750), T264, T267
(1798), W211

Tell-tale: T141(1777)
Temper: *sb.* S22; *vb.* G87
Temperance: D220
Temperate: P101
Tempest: C14(1782), M263, R46
Temples: H289(1775)
Temptation: P263
Ten: B58, C19, C360, R56, T152,
T210
Tenant: L28
Tend: I17, L180
Tenderness: A14
Terms: L63
Terrible: F124(1800)
Terrify: A44(1807), S342
Territory: W23
Tether: E55, R135(1806)
Thank: N116, P325
Thee: M126
Theft: R39
Themselves: E97, F13, G77, H199,
L174, M111
There: B66, H211-2, L14
Thick: B112, B214, F102, F199,
G154, H8, H12, H95, H99,
H216, H289, M253, M313,
R168, S44, S410, T80, T233,
W87
Thief: H272, M169, O11, O33,
P294, R39-40, R123, R133
Thieve: M169
Thin: *sb.* T38; *adj.* A60, C122,
H101, H163, K45, L42, P8, P19,
S274, W1
Thing: B133, B159(1786), C275,
C387, D180, E54, F12, G33,
G74, G100, G117, H3, H91
(1809), K36(1837), L123, M144,
M206, M209, M296, M305
(1825), N13, N44, P264, R85,
S61, S153, S254, T102, T116,
T124, T127-8, T137-8, T140,
T144, U14, W18, W243(1769),
Y6
Think: C353, E100, F213, F218,
H73, H308, L183, M89, S57,
T299
Third: D271, G115, T113, T121
Thirsty: N63
Thirty: M51, S193, T298
Thistles: G141
Thong: B346
Thorn: B97, G141, L145, N75,
R145, W76
Though: S62
Thought: H73, P76, W240
Thousand: C19, D95, K22

Thread: E55(1778), S550
Threatened: F212
Three: A110, B65, D26, D220,
F144, F304, G59, G173, P103,
R3, R55, S58-9, S74, S138,
S462, S473(1803), S495, W373
Three-legged: H132
Thrice-told: T16
Thrive: C130, H204, P207, T234
Throat: B259, C349, H242, K48,
L115, R96, T182
Throne: L231, R102
Through: F134, G177, H163,
H356
Throw: *sb.* B186(1821); *vb.* D174,
D187-8, D197, D329, G28, H168,
H276, H333, L167, L257, M115,
M185, M219, N128, O2(1792),
O19(1727), P26, P58, P225
(1804), R156, S35-6, S229, S298,
S382, S446, S461, S489, S552,
T195(1782), T277, W40, W45-6,
W145
Thrust: W53
Thumb: F104, F108, R162
Thumps: K8(1830)
Thunder: D311, L134
Thunder-gust: F242
Thunder-storm: P232
Thyself: K54, P102
Tickle: S76(1813)
Tickling: P13(1816), T255
Tide: T125, W200, W209
Tie: *sb.* G126(1811); *vb.* A113,
G126(1687), K53, L100, S3
Tigers: E74(1720)
Tight: D309, N125
Tile: L249
Till: H337
Timber: M280
Time: A71, D76, D153, D175
(1822), F246, F297, G92, I11,
L230, L252, M21, M30, M83,
N68, P49, P294, S208, S434,
T53, T267
Tines: P189
Tingle: E14
Tip: W229
Tire: H301, V25
Toad: K44
Tobacco: C134, M247, P168
Today: E36, T176, Y9
Toe: B58, F301, H209, T203
Together: B177, B243, B346, E6,
G71, L158, M194(1802), P63,
P119, R122
Toil: L2(1824), T253

Index of Important Words

J33, K14, K22, N12, T169
Upas: T62
Upper: H57, L89, L169
Uppermost: H127
Upright: *adj.* B25, B249, M125;
  adv. S464
Upside-down: W359
Upstairs: K9
Us: E82, G91, H190
Use: *sb.* A47, D120, H2; *vb.* K7,
  N40, P194, V18, W85
Used: E29
Useless: C159
Using: W85
Utmost: E55
Utter: W328

V

Vacuum: N17
Vain: *sb.* L3, M270, N50; *adj.*
  D296-7, F50, P55
Vale: P136
Valet: M67
Valiant: P258
Valid: G129
Valor: D190
Value: *sb.* T50; *vb.* B394, C168,
  F34, G183, L225, P154, R173,
  S476
Vanish: A60, D165, D299, M197,
  S262
Vanity: A75, P280
Vanquish: F207
Variable: W181
Various: M78, W25(1781), W182
Veal: J22
Velvet: S214
Vengeance: J60
Venture: *sb.* B289; *vb.* B238,
  B285, F147, N113
Vessel: T277(1802)
Vice: I12, M34, P303, W99
Victorious: N107, P321
Victory: P326
Victuals: G85(1806), W341(1755)
View: B190
Vigor: T238
Vine: G141(1790)
Vinegar: F203, H266(1795)
Violent: D191(1798), M265, N112
Virgin: S287(1801), S294
Virility: N92
Virtue: M144, N19, P35, P303,
  R72, W99
Visible: S517
Visitors: F144

Voice: A48, M78(1815)
Volatile: E73
Vomit: D234
Voracious: S118
Vows: O8
Voyage: F181, H357(1788)
Vulgar: F160

W

Wag: H32, W344
Wages: L5
Wagon: W111
Wailings: W241
Wait: E98, G173, M81, O3(1824),
  T125
Wake: L117, L168
Walk: *sb.* C245, F159; *vb.* C105,
  E110, H124, K55, M76, T310
Wall: C369, D279, H139, H313
  (1771), H356, W77
Wallet: C84
Wallow: C215(1801), D234, S349,
  S543
Want: *sb.* B88, F235, I12(1787),
  M63, M110, N105, P279, R73,
  W27, W247, W275, W285; *vb.*
  G122, I24(1807), I62, M206,
  M239, P264, W165, W220,
  W314
Wanting: B312, G117, R72, S101
War: C307, G170, L230, M55,
  M213, O25(1761), O30, P47,
  P49-51, W238
Ward: *sb.* W28; *vb.* D17
Ware: H247(1777), R76
Warm: *vb.* W297; *adj.* C119
  (1774), G93, H171, M167
Wash: E75, H46, H65, L151, S349,
  W139
Washer: C283
Wasps: L54(1776), S539
Waste: *sb.* H90; *vb.* C104, I11,
  K23, T136(1783)
Watch: *sb.* S150; *vb.* W48
Water: *sb.* B214, C80, D122, D168,
  D304, D306(1796), F114, F122,
  F124, F134-5, F149, G144, H138,
  H312, L158(1827), L193, M14,
  M115, M164, M217, N63, O16,
  O20, P188(1817), R44, S203,
  S308, S355, S527, S529, V2,
  W103, W177, W185; *vb.* M291
Waterman: W73
Wavering: W183
Way: D243(1812), E88, F237,
  L160, R156, R161, S144, S480,

S499, W211, W292
Wax: H124, M53, N94
Weak: *sb.* R6(1776); *adj.* A56,
  C65, E125, F183, G186, H145,
  I40, L54(1732), M314, R22,
  R44, S370, W30, W77, W169
Weaken: B287
Weaknesses: M68
Weal: H75
Wealth: F230, H148, T168, W148,
  W285
Wealthy: B98, C348, J27
Weapon: D150, W238
Wear: *sb.* D23, W368; *vb.* B139,
  B146, B319, C29, D306, F7,
  F116, H289, P94, S164, S169
  (1766), S253, S389, S502, W167,
  W170
Weary: D26, H63(1747)
Weather: *sb.* C63, D26, D267,
  G123, S466; *vb.* W168
Wedding: W155, W171
Weeds: M54, S306
Week: R3, S50
Weep: C347, H169
Weigh: F66
Weight: F62
Welcome: A65, F290, S288, W31,
  W123
Well: *sb.* P188, T268; *adj.* T163;
  adv. A76, B130, B375, B378,
  D55, D212, D214, D216, F73,
  H337, L247, M35, S406
Wellerism: C265, D330, H353,
  S378, T170
Wench: D26
West: E17
Wet: *vb.* C192, C269, E139, W134;
  adj. D45, D322, E30, F118,
  H202, M122, M283, R9, S13,
  S137, W32
Whale: S381, T277
Wheat: B303, C107, P59, T25
Wheel: B388, D330, F269, S188,
  S373, W355
Whelps: B73, T164
Wherefore: W143
Whet: K48
While: D271, G152, L128, P82
Whim: A18, J19
Whine: C347(1781), G58
Whip: *sb.* C217, H58; *vb.* C92,
  D159, L247, R116(1771)-7(1790)
Whirl: T207, W216
Whisper: P116
Whist: M278
Whistle: *sb.* B225(1816); *vb.* D16,

550

INDEX OF PROPER NOUNS

This index contains all the proper nouns in the lemmas and the important proper nouns from the quotations. Adjectives derived from proper nouns are included. Not all the words are integral parts of sayings. When a proverb is ascribed, correctly or not, to a specific author, be he Solomon or Pope or Franklin, or when it is identified as from a language other than English, be it German, Italian, or French, the designations are entered in the index. In most cases I have added in parentheses the first names of the authors intended.

Index of Proper Nouns